The P.C. Support Handbook

The

Configuration

and

Systems

Guide

By David Dick

Dumbreck Publishing

The P.C. Support Handbook
© 2001 by Dumbreck Publishing
ISBN 0-9521484-7-1

The graphic on the previous page was produced by W H Anderson.
The book cover was designed by Hilary Austin (hilary.austin@virgin.net)

Introduction

This edition of the book reflects the rapidly changing hardware and software specifications of computer technology. Since the last edition, new techniques and products have arrived and these developments are, of course, covered in the book's chapters.

However, we must not lose sight of the book's main objective - to provide students, technicians and hobbyists with a broad understanding of all the computer technology in use today. The new technology is very exciting and is fully explained in this book - but much of it has still to find its way into general use. Organisations still use older computers and older versions of operating systems. The support technician has to work with a broad spread of equipment and the book therefore provides information on XTs through to the Pentium 4 range. It covers DOS use through to Windows 2000/ME use.

The book attempts to accurately reflect the needs of its readers and this edition introduces new material that was specifically asked for by colleges, universities and support departments. The book's contents were again shaped by the wide response to our user survey thus ensuring that it meets the needs of the maximum amount of users. In particular, this edition contains a new chapter on computer peripherals.

The Unix chapter was written by Philip J Irving, Senior Lecturer in Computing at the University of Sunderland. Philip has taught UNIX and Networking for more than seven years. He dedicates the chapter to his wife, Elizabeth and their two children without whose support it would not have been possible. I am also grateful to Chic Thomson for his editorial assistance and additional material.

There are many books on computer architecture, tweaking Windows and on repairing computer components. They are specialised books with a narrow outlook while this book provides a more general approach. The book is updated annually to keep up to date with developments, as a glance through the contents or index pages will show.

The need for skills in both hardware and software installation and maintenance is reflected in the nineteen chapters.

I hope that you will find the book a useful reference.

David Dick

Contents

Computer Basics

Today, computers are used in a wide variety of applications. Almost all aspects of life, work and play are influenced by their use. Sometimes, the computer chip is even embedded inside a piece of equipment such as a video recorder or a washing machine. In these cases, the chip is dedicated to a particular function and the user is only given a small degree of control over its operations.

In industry and commerce, the computer comes in all shapes and sizes, from the hand portable carried round by the busy executive to the giant mainframe that crunches its way through millions of tax bills. The larger machines handle complex operations such as Automatic Banking, Weather Forecasting, Traffic Control, Scientific Modelling, Computer Aided Manufacturing, etc. This book is concerned with the *'microcomputer'*. This is the machine that sits on the office desktop. Despite its relatively small size, it is becoming more powerful every year. It can store larger and larger programs and can run ever faster. Above all, it is programmable - it is not tied to a single program or activity.

Typical uses of microcomputers are:

Budgeting, Payroll Processing, Word Processing, Databases, Stock Control, Project Management, Desk Top Publishing, Graphic Design, Multimedia, Electronic Music, Communication between offices and within the office, World-wide electronic mail, Internet access, etc.

Advantages of computers

- They can carry out repetitive and large volume tasks without fatigue.
- They are much less error prone than humans, providing an output of consistently better quality.
- They are much quicker than humans. Masses of information are always readily available.
- They are more reliable than humans, allowing for better planning and control of output.
- They can work 24 hours a day, in the dark, with minimum heating and little supervision.
- They are immune from human conditions - such as sick leave, maternity leave, strikes, etc.
- They occupy less space than humans; they don't need seats, desks, canteens, toilets, etc.
- Over a period of time, they are cheaper than humans, due to savings in wages, power and accommodation and savings through improved output and quality.

Disadvantages of computers

However, all is not on the plus side.

- Computers can be expensive to install and maintain.
- Trained personnel are required to use the computer applications.
- Trained personnel are required to maintain the machines, the programs and the company data.
- There are problems of compatibility between computers. Programs from a Macintosh system will not run on a PC; PC programs will not run on a Macintosh without special add-ons. There is no *'standard'* computer, although those based around the IBM PC model account for most business and commercial use - providing a common system for exchanging data.
- There are problems of *'concurrency'*. If data (e.g. a price list) is duplicated on several machines and changes are made, which computer holds the most up-to-date version?
- Storing masses of data on computers, particularly when computers are connected together, presents a real security problem. By law, companies have to prevent unauthorised access to their data; this may come from employees or from outsiders *'hacking'* in to the system using modems.
- Any failures in the system threaten the users' activities. Where all a company's activities and data are stored on a single computer, any breakdown in that computer leaves the company unable to function.

Above all, computers are stupid! There is great truth in the phrase - "*Garbage In Garbage Out*". If you enter wrong information into the computer, you get incorrect results! If you place correct information in the computer, but the program is wrong - you still get incorrect results! The computer is merely a machine with no intelligence other than that programmed into it. For example, if the programmer forgets to tell a computer that no employee in the company is likely to be over 70 years old, it will happily accept an employee's age as one million. Consequently, the company's statistics are completely flawed, showing an average employee age of several thousand!

At the end of the day, computers are tools for use by humans and cannot fully replace human common sense and experience.

What is a computer?

There have been *'computers'* for a long proportion of society's history. The abacus and mechanical devices have long been used as an aid to calculation. Today's definition of computers really describes the electronic computing device. A computer is essentially an information processor that is able to perform substantial computation with little or no intervention by human operators.

To function, a computer requires both hardware and software elements. The physical machinery involved in the computer system is called *'hardware'* and consists of components such as the processor unit, monitor, keyboard, disk drives and printer. If it can be touched, it must be hardware. The more efficient the hardware, the quicker the programs will run. Software is the programs that are bought or created for the computer. These carry out specific tasks such as word-processing or accountancy. The better designed the software, the more facilities are offered to the user.

In the microcomputer market, the IBM PC is by far the most common machine, without around 90% of the world share. The *'PC'* stands for *'personal computer'* and the machine first appeared in early 1980's. All subsequent PC machines have been built round this basic architecture. Of course, most machines in everyday use are not manufactured by IBM. They may be Compaq models or Packard Bell, etc. These are termed *'clones'* since they follow the basic architecture of the IBM model. In practice, they perform like an IBM PC in almost all respects (within the limits of copyright).

Microcomputer components

The main components that comprise the typical PC are:

- The main system unit
- Input devices
- Storage devices
- Output devices

The typical process for using a computer is:

1. Load a program into the computer's memory (e.g. a word-processing package). The program is initially held on some storage device such as a floppy disk, CD, or the computer's internal hard disk. A copy of this program is transferred into the memory of the computer; the disk still stores the original copy. The program is then run from the version stored in memory.
2. Input any data (e.g. type in a report).
3. Process the data (e.g. spell check the report).
4. Output the data to screen or printer (e.g. print the report).
5. Save the data (on to a floppy disk or the internal hard disk).

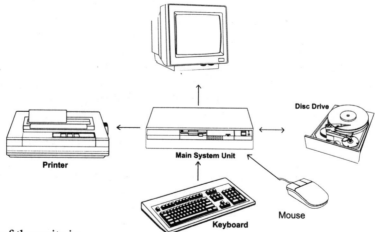

A brief description of the units is:

Main System Unit: This case houses the CPU (Central Processing Unit) chip which carries out all the computer's programming tasks and a range of support chips to communicate with the other hardware devices.

Keyboard: The keyboard allows the user to type in input to the computer (e.g. commands to do things, words for a report, choices from menus, etc.).

Monitor: A screen that allows the facts, pictures, etc. generated by the computer to be viewed by the user.

Disk Drive: Stores the programs and information that the user needs.

Mouse: A pointing device that makes some operations, such as using Windows or drawing packages, easier to use than with the keyboard.

Printer: Produces a permanent copy of the program's output (e.g. a letter or a graph) on to a sheet of paper.

Main System Unit

The main system box comes in a variety of shapes from tiny hand-held plastic cases for portable use to large metal tower cases for network servers and power workstations.   Inside each case, there is a main electronic board, called the *'motherboard'* that houses the CPU, memory, etc.

Motherboard

This comprises a printed circuit board, about the size of an A4 sheet of paper in the case of standard desktop computers.   It has all the computer's processing chips mounted on it, either being soldered directly to the board or being plugged into sockets on the board. All the power, data and addressing information is carried between components on the copper tracks etched on to the printed circuit board. Each motherboard is designed to handle a particular computing processor, since modern processor chips have more sophisticated needs than older processors.   Thus, manufacturers supplied motherboards specially made for use with 386 chips and these are of different design from motherboards intended for use with Pentium chips.   The Pentium II to Pentium 4, in turn, use a different motherboard design than the motherboard for the Xeon chip.

CPU (Central Processing Unit)

The main chip in any computer system is the Central Processing Unit. The speed and design of this chip largely determine the overall speed of the computer.   Early PCs used a chip known as the 8088 and this was followed by the 8086, 80286, 80386SX, 80386DX, 80486SX, 80486DX, the Pentium Pro, the Pentium MMX, the Pentium II and III, Xeon and Pentium 4 chips.   The 8086 machines ran at a speed of 4.77MHz while the current Pentium processors run at speeds of 2000MHz or more.

Apart from their raw speed improvements, modern chips have other in-built advantages over earlier models.   For example, modern computers handle data at a faster rate due to their data bus being 64 bits wide; older models only had a 32 or 16-bit bus and the earliest XT machines had only an 8-bit bus. While the older systems are no longer for sale, machines of all types and speeds are currently in use in commerce, industry and in the home.

The CPU is the heart of the computer system and is a silicon microchip. Its function is to interpret and execute the required instructions (see chapter on Computer Architecture).

Memory

To work, the computer has to temporarily store the program and data in an area where it can be used by the computer's processor.   This area is known as the computer's *'memory'* or sometimes as *'primary storage'.*   Memory consists of computer chips that are capable of storing information. That information may be:

- The program that keeps the computer running (e.g. DOS or Windows).
- The instructions of the program that the user wants to run (e.g. a database or a drawing program).
- The data that is used or created (e.g. letters from word-processing or records from a database).

When the user wishes to run a program (e.g. a game), a copy of the program is loaded from the user's disk and placed in the computer memory. The program is then run from the computer memory.

This makes it possible for the machine to be a word processor, graphics designer, Internet browser, games machine and many other functions. The machine, in fact, will run whatever program is currently in memory. If another program is loaded, that becomes the new function of the machine. This is what makes the computer so versatile - it is not tied to any one activity.

The memory chips consist of a large number of cells, each cell having a fixed capacity for storing data and each has a unique location or address. This type of memory is known as RAM (Random Access Memory) and its contents are *'volatile'.* This means that the program and the data held in the memory is lost when the machine is switched off. This is not a problem for the program as it is only a copy - the original program is still stored on disk.   However, any data created (e.g. a letter or drawing) is only sitting in the memory and will be lost, unless it is saved to disk before the computer is switched off.

Another type of memory is known as ROM (Read Only Memory) and this is non-volatile (i.e. the program code exists even when the machine has been switched off).   This type of chip is used to store chunks of the system's own programs (e.g. to check for the user typing at the keyboard, or to handle disk activities.   When the computer is powered up and running, some of the system programs are run directly from ROM.   Most system programs are loaded into the computer memory from the hard disk when the machine is first switched on.

The operating system takes up a certain amount of the computer's available memory, so not all of the memory is actually available to the user.   Sophisticated software packages such as Microsoft Excel and Microsoft Word take up large amounts of RAM and the user may create large worksheets and documents using these packages that can use up the rest of the available memory.

This means that the more memory in a machine the more efficient the computer runs.   Each year, machines are supplied with more memory and users can usually add extra memory to an existing computer.   For more information, see the chapter on memory.

Measurement of capacity

Memory capacity describes the amount of data a storage device can hold at any one time and is measured in bytes. One byte represents one character. A character can be a letter or a number, or any of the many special characters found on the keyboard including a space. There are many other characters used in the internal workings of the microcomputer that are never seen in print. For example, the *'beep'* for the computer's internal loudspeaker is stored as a single character.

In computing, where operations are often considered in units of 2, the Kilo or K actually means 1,024 characters with similar definitions for the larger numbers.

Kilo is 2 raised to the power of 10, or 2 x 2 x 2 x 2 x 2 x 2 x 2 x 2 x 2 x 2.   Tera is 2 multiplied by itself 40 times, or exactly 1,099,511,627,776.

KB (Kilobyte)	1,024 characters
MB (Megabyte)	1,048,576 characters
GB (Gigabyte)	1,073,741,824 characters
TB (Terabyte)	1,099,511,627,776 characters

A rough measure of memory requirements is:

> 1 byte can store 1 character
> 1 KB can store a few paragraphs of text
> 1 MB can store the text of a reasonably sized book
> 4MB can store a typical MP3 audio clip
> 4GB can store a typical DVD movie

Input devices

Input devices are used to enter or input data into the CPU. The main input device on computers is the keyboard. There is a wide range of other input devices including the mouse, optical scanners, pressure pads and other sensors, graphic tablets, touch screens, communication devices and audio and video capture cards.

Output devices

Output devices convert data from the computer into forms that humans can understand or use. There are two main output devices on the microcomputer system, the monitor screen and the printer. Other output devices include graph plotters, modems, audio boards with speakers, and robot arms.

Backing store

This is also known as external memory or secondary storage and is used for the long-term storage of data. The bulk of information (programs and data) used by computer applications are stored on backing store and must be transferred to main memory before it can be processed by the CPU. Backing store devices include magnetic disks (removable floppy disks and built-in hard disks) and magnetic tape.

The power of the machine

The power of the machine is usually indicated by the speed of the processor; the faster the speed of the chip, the more instructions it can process in any given time.

The following measurements of time are used:

Millisecond	=	1/1,000th of a second
Microsecond	=	1/1,000,000th of a second
Nanosecond	=	1/1,000,000,000th of a second

These measurements are essentially used to describe the time taken for the computer processor to perform one cycle, in which time it may perform a basic operation or part of a more complex operation. In recent years, this method of measurement has been supplemented by an estimate of the number of instructions or operations able to be processed by a computer e.g. a number of MIPS (Millions of Instructions Per Second) or GigaFLOPS (billions of Floating Point Operations Per Second). These are better indications of computing power.

Different models of computer are designed to run at different speeds. Of course, the faster the machine, the greater the purchase price. One measure of speed of a machine is the number of cycles per second at which it can operate (measured in MHz - MegaHertz - millions of cycles per second). The first and slowest PC was just under 5MHz. The fastest speed is always being improved upon and is currently around 2000MHz, with even faster machines on the way.

The choice of machine depends very much upon its expected use. If the machine were used entirely for word processing, a lower speed machine is perfectly satisfactory. Since the slowest part of the process is the typist's thinking and typing time, there is little to be gained by very fast processing in between long pauses at the keyboard. On the other hand, where there is going to be a great deal of machine processing, such as graphics calculations and other number crunching, a faster machine becomes essential.

For even faster processing, the machine can be fitted with an extra chip - called a 'co-processor'. Older CPUs have an optional 'maths co-processor' which takes on most of the mathematical calculations, leaving the main processor free for other tasks. Since the tasks are being shared, the whole program runs much more quickly. This facility is already built into the Pentium chips and many modern motherboards provide a socket for an extra Pentium CPU chip to boost the computer's performance.

Of course, the raw speed of the CPU is not the only factor in determining the machine's overall speed. Other factors, such as the speed of the disk and video card, the amount of RAM available, whether the machine has an efficient caching system, etc., also determine the machine's performance.

Monitors

Most programs send the output from their calculations to a screen (apart from those such as payroll programs that send most of their output to the printer, with only a summary going to the screen). The screen is contained in a unit called the 'monitor' - sometimes also called the VDU ('visual display unit').

Monitor types

Monitors are available in either monochrome (black and white, or perhaps a green or amber screen) or colour. Almost all modern applications are written to provide text and graphics in colour. Sometimes this is used to enhance the use or appeal of the product. On other occasions, such as graphic design, PCB design, etc., the use of colour is essential. A monochrome monitor is still capable of displaying screen output from applications written for colour monitors

Off/On switch at side or on front

Brightness/Contrast controls

but may merge some of the colours into similar shades of grey. A colour monitor comprises more parts and is more difficult to construct and is therefore more expensive. Screen output can vary from user messages and prompts, to displaying complex graphs, pie charts and video.

Screen resolution

The PC supports different degrees of screen resolution. The higher the screen resolution, the better the quality of the picture, allowing graphics to be displayed. The resolution of a screen is measured in 'pixels' (picture elements). Each pixel is an independent dot appearing on the screen. The resolution of a screen is given by the number of pixels in the horizontal and the vertical plane.

The most common screen resolutions are:

VGA	640 x 480
SVGA	800 x 600 up to 1600 x 1200

Other standards, such as the Hercules, CGA and EGA resolutions are extinct as far as new sales are concerned and there are now very few of these monitors in daily use.

The higher resolution models produce a sharper, more detailed picture. The highest resolution becomes a necessity where desktop publishing, CAD or other graphic applications are to be run.   Microsoft Windows and Windows applications are greatly improved with higher resolution monitors; a 1024 x 768 screen will reproduce a greater number of Windows icons on the screen at any one time.   The greater resolution monitors require more demanding construction and these are more expensive to buy.

All monitors have on/off switches and controls for screen brightness and contrast; some models have other, more sophisticated controls.   All monitors have two connecting cables; one to connect power to the monitor and one that connects to the system unit's video output socket.

Keyboard

This is the main input device to the computer that is used to enter data directly into the machine, for processing.   The keyboard has a single cable attached to it and the plug at the end of this cable is attached to the keyboard socket on the computer main system unit. This cable takes the power from the unit to the keyboard and returns information on any keys pressed back to the motherboard.

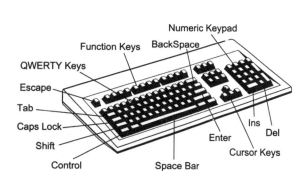

The computer keyboard consists of a normal typewriter layout with some additional keys, a group of function keys, a numeric pad on the right, and a group of direction keys also on the right side.

When you press a key that is engraved with an alphabetic character you will see a lower case letter on the screen, and a key with two engravings will show the character in the lower half of the key top. To get capital letters and the characters on the top half of the key top you must hold down one of the SHIFT keys while you press the other key. If most of your keying requires the use of capital letters, you can press the CAPS LOCK key, which remains ON until you press it again, and this produces the upper case with alphabetic keys only.

The CTRL and ALT keys allow the same key to carry out several functions.   For example, pressing the "L" key, the CTRL and "L" keys together and pressing the ALT and "L" keys together may provide three different results.

The keyboard also provides keys that allow movement across the screen or the insertion or deletion of screen text.

The use of all the keyboard's keys is explained in the chapter on Computer Peripherals.

Disks

A computer needs somewhere to store its programs and data when they are not in the machine's memory. The most common storage medium is the disk system. Programs are loaded from disk to run in the computer memory, as previously mentioned. Additionally, when the program has created its data, it can store it on the disk for later use.

There are two main types of disk storage medium - the hard disk and the floppy disk.

How disks work

The physical characteristics of all magnetic disks are similar.   Thin, non-magnetic plates are coated on both sides with magnetic recording material. A special set of heads is used to both record data on to the disk and to read data from the disk. The method is identical to that used for recording videotapes or audio cassettes. The only real differences are that the medium is a disk instead of a long strip; and the information being transferred is digital data, instead of audio or video information. So, the disk is a direct access device, which means that the reading/writing heads can move directly to the track and sector where the desired information is stored (unlike tape, which is a serial device, where you have to search from one end of the tape to find the information).

Hard disks

A hard disk is supplied with all microcomputers and is mounted inside the machine casing. These disks hold an incredible amount of information, anything from early 10 Megabyte models to current 73 Gbytes and over models. It is known as a *'hard disk'* because it is made from a solid sheet of aluminium. It is then coated with ferric oxide and a number of such disks are stacked on top of each other and placed in an airtight casing. Each disk surface has its own read/write head and they are linked so that they will all move in unison. The disks spin at a constant speed. The slowest models ran at 3600 rpm (12 times faster than a floppy disk) and current models range up to 10,000rpm. Apart from their large capacities, hard disks have a much better access time than a floppy disk. A hard disk's mechanism allows it to read in data, write a file and find files much faster than a floppy disk.

The disks are mounted on a vertical shaft and are slightly separated from each other to provide space for the movement of read/write heads. The shaft revolves, spinning the disks. Data is stored as magnetised spots in concentric circles called *'tracks'* on each surface of the disks. Each disk contains several hundred tracks for the storage of data.

It is possible for the read/write heads of disks to come into contact with debris on the disk surface, such as dust or smoke particles. This might cause the head to *"crash"* into the surface of the disk, damage the disk, and corrupt the data. Special devices have been developed to get over this problem. One such device is the Winchester disk drive. Winchester disks are sealed units containing the disks and the read/write unit. These types of disks are the hard disks used on the microcomputer and are fast and reliable. Hard disks are usually fixed within the microcomputer cabinet and are therefore not very portable. Hard disks are faster to access information and have a higher storage capacity than floppy disks.

Floppy disks

These are flat disks of polyester film with and iron-oxide magnetic coating. The disk is covered with a protective jacket, and reading/writing to the disk is performed through the head access slot. Floppy disks have a capacity of 360KB to almost 3MB, although the most widely used type stores 1.44MB. Floppy disks are very portable and can be used by different microcomputers (provided they are of a similar type).

The construction of hard disks and floppy disks is covered in detail in the chapter on Disks and Drives.

Floppy sizes

The floppy disk comes in two sizes - the current 3.5" size and the older 5.25" type. Each of these disks is capable of being formatted to different capacities, dependent on their quality (i.e. whether they are double/high/quad density). At its basic format, the 5.25" disk stored up to 360 Kilobytes. The later 5.25" disk drives handled quad density disks, each disk having a capacity of 1.2 Megabytes. The 3.5" disk has a basic format of 720 Kilobytes, with the more common high-density version holding 1.4 Megabytes. A 2.88 Megabytes version made a brief appearance but did not last long on the market.

Disk recording terms

Sector	Division of magnetic surface of disk into separate but continuous pie-shaped information zones by either magnetic or physical coding of disk.
Soft Sector	Sectors defined magnetically by software.
Hard Sector	Sectors defined physically by punching holes around inner/outer disk diameter. Now outdated.
Initialisation/Formatting	Magnetically coded pattern recorded on disk to identify each track and sector.
Double-Sided	Disk made for use on drives with two recording heads.
Single-Density	The standard density for floppy disks. No longer used.
Double-Density	Method of recording twice the amount on disk as possible with single-density. This is 360k for 5.25" disks and 720k for 3.5" disks. Now outdated.
High/Quadruple-Density	Method of recording four times the amount on disk as possible with single-density. This is 1.2MB for 5.25" disks and 1.4MB for 3.5" disks.

Care Of Disk Files

- When a 5.25" floppy disk is not in the disk drive, it must be kept in its protective envelope.
- Never touch the recording surface of a floppy disk because a small amount of grease will be deposited, to which dust will stick.
- Never bend a floppy disk.
- Insert a floppy disk into a disk drive carefully to avoid bending or crushing the disk.
- Keep the disks away from excesses of temperature; absolute limits are between 10° C and 50° C.
- Keep the disks away from any form of magnetic field. That includes telephones, printer motors, speakers, power transformers, etc.

Printers

The printer is used to produce a paper copy (often called a *'hard copy'*) of the letters, reports, graphs, etc. produced by the program. They have two connector cables; one for the mains supply and one to take the data from the computer to the printer. The manufacturers produce two different types of connection for printers and these are known as serial and parallel systems. These names describe how the data arrives at the printer from the computer. Serial printers (including USB connections) accept data one bit at a time from the computer; parallel printers have more wires and receive 8 bits, i.e. one byte, at a time. Most printers have only a serial or a parallel connection, while a few have sockets for both types. There are different printers for different jobs. All have different qualities as described next.

Dot Matrix

On a dot matrix printer, characters are formed by striking an inked ribbon with a rectangular array of needles. The dots of ink are transferred to the paper, producing a pattern that can comprise letters,

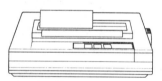

numbers, or even graphics. These types of printers are relatively cheap and fairly fast, printing from 50 to 400 characters per second. The quality of print from a dot matrix printer is much improved if the number of dots that make up a particular character is increased. The earliest machines used a vertical row of seven print needles that printed 5 times for each character. Each character was thus formed from a 7 x 5 array of dots. The latest machines use 18 x 24 arrays of pins or 24 x 24 or 48 x 24 arrays. These printers are commonly in use where quality is less important than cheap and quick copies and are mostly employed for internal use in an organisation.

Ink Jet Printers

An inkjet printer is also a *'non impact'* printer, preferring instead to spray dots of ink on to the paper. The ink is stored in a small plastic case about the size of a matchbox and this case also comprises the printing head. A small printed circuit board takes the signals from the computer right up to tiny holes in the ink reservoir. The ink is attracted through the holes and carries on to strike the paper. This produces an output that approaches the quality of the laser printer, at a fraction of the cost. It typically produces a resolution of about 600 dots per inch and is very quiet in operation. Colour inkjet models use four ink heads and mix their outputs to achieve an even greater range of colours. The inks used are the primary print colours (cyan, magenta and yellow) and black. These are known as CMYK printers.

Laser Printers

A laser printer works on a similar principle to the normal photocopier; in fact, a laser is like the second half of a photocopier. With a photocopier, the image from an inserted master is scanned and turned into a stream of digital information. This digital information is then used to modulate a laser beam on to a drum. The electrostatic charge thus built up attracts the toner powder, which is eventually transferred to

the paper. With a laser printer, the stream of digital information is supplied directly by the computer, via the printer cable. So, the laser printer is like a cut down version of a photocopier.

The resolution of a laser printer is measured in the number of dots in an inch and is normally 600 dpi, with modern versions now at 1200 dpi or higher. They are thus capable of both high quality text and graphics.

The average laser is capable of printing either 8 pages per minute or 12 pages per minute. These speed figures describe the number of pages that the printer can produce once the image is ready to print.   In fact, the normal laser printer makes up a copy of the picture in its own internal memory, prior to starting the printing process.   This time has to be added to the time for printing.   So, for a single copy, the printing speed is fairly slow; if many copies are required, the image is still only built up once and the overall speed becomes closer to the printing speed.

The size of the printer's memory has an influence on the final quality of print that can be handled.   If the printer has only a small internal memory, say 256k or 512k, then it will not be able to store a complete A4 page of graphics.   To reduce retail prices, many manufacturers produce models with small internal memories.   Of course, most printers can have their memory size upgraded by adding extra memory boards, although this is fairly expensive.

Due to their mechanics, laser printers are very quiet in operation.   There is no impact noise, as the paper is not struck; there is only the sound of the motor and its roller mechanisms.

Print quality

Laser printers produce true letter quality print.   Dot matrix printers can produce almost letter quality or NLQ (near letter quality) by increasing the number of dots in the character or by passing over the same line twice.   Dot matrix printers can produce faster output in draft mode.   This produces a readable document fairly quickly.   The printers can be switched from one level of quality to another by a hardware switch on the printer or by sending a signal through the software to the printer.   Inkjet printers produce a quality which somewhat less than a laser but much better than a dot matrix.

All impact printers use ribbons - either ink-impregnated fabric or one-off ribbons.   With fabric ribbons, the quality can be poor at the beginning of the use of the ribbon due to overinking, while the quality also suffers at the end of the ribbon's life due to lack of ink.   Laser printers and inkjet printers, on the other hand, maintain a constant quality of output, with the quality suddenly dropping off as the toner or ink reservoir runs low.

Proportional printing

The standard print size on most machines is 10 characters to an inch.   It is possible to change this using either a hardware switch on the printer or by sending special codes to the printer.   The number of characters printed to an inch can be increased (making the print smaller) to 12, 17 and 20 cpi.   It is also possible to print expanded characters and to produce characters with proportional spacing.   With proportional spacing, a character only occupies as much width of the paper as it actually needs.

This is an example of proportional spacing
This is an example of standard width printing

So, the letter 'm' uses more space than the letter 'i'.   As a result, proportional spacing results in more professional output, similar to typeset documents as seen in books.

However, one problem with proportional spacing is lining up data into columns as seen in this example.   Since each digit occupies a different page width (e.g. an eight is wider than a one), figures do not line up in neat columns.   In this respect, a fixed-width character set produces more readable results.

```
9866   99.55   88
2311   18.11   28

9866 99.55 88
2311 18.11 28
```

The selection of pitch sizes can be achieved by setting the buttons on the printer front panel, for DOS applications.   Windows applications set the pitch using software, through the selection of Windows fonts (see chapter on Windows).

Printer fonts

Dot-matrix printers and all laser printers allow the user to choose the shape or style of the type to be output.   The term 'typeface' describes the shape of the letters and characters.   So, a plain unadorned character would be one typeface, while a fancy Gothic script would be another typeface.   If a

This is a serif typeface
And this is sans serif

typeface has feet and twirls, it is said to be a 'serif' typeface.   If it is a plain typeface, it is described as a 'sans serif' style.   Each typeface comes in a variety of sizes, measured in 'points'; there are 72 points to one inch.   So, a 36-point character is a half-inch character.   The collection of all the sizes of a particular typeface is called the *'fonts'*. A half-inch character would be available in the 36-point font of a particular typestyle.

In addition to the character's outline and size, the user can usually have control over whether the character is printed in normal, bold, italic and underlined.

Printer buffers

Computers send data to the printer at a much faster rate than the printer can print it out; this is because the printer is a slow mechanical device. This would leave the user sitting waiting until the printer had finished the print job before he/she could carry on using the machine. To increase efficiency, all printers have a block of memory built in, called the *'print buffer'*. This is able to read a chunk of data from the computer and, if the block of memory is large enough, the entire file can be transferred to the printer in one operation. This would immediately free the computer for other processing. To keep the retail price down, most printers have a nominal buffer size and additions to this are regarded as extras. Windows can be configured to use some of the computer's memory as an additional printer buffer.

Printer paper

Printers can use different types of paper. A common type of paper is continuous stationery. This is held in place and moved by tractors gripping the sprocket holes at the side of the paper. There are two basic sizes; 13 x 11 inches, which will allow a maximum of 132 standard characters per line and 66 lines on every page and 8 x 11 inches, which gives 80 character lines. This may be plain paper or specially printed paper providing office stationary or commercial facilities such as accounts. This may be single or multi-part stationary (i.e. more than one sheet with carbon backing so that several copies of the data are printed on the different copies of the sheet). Self-adhesive labels are also commonly used on continuous rolls, so that mailing labels are quickly produced.

Many printers also allow the use of single sheets of paper using a friction mechanism as on a typewriter, to hold and move the paper. Cut sheet feeders may also be supplied to guide the paper in the printer. Again, the paper may be plain or pre-printed. Some printers also allow acetate sheets to be inserted so that OHP slides (overhead projector) may be created. These use special acetate sheets that will not melt in the normal heat in a laser printer.

Pointing devices

Windows and many DOS applications now make very good use of a mouse or other pointing device for choosing menu options and drawing activities. Although the activities can be carried out using the keyboard cursor keys, it is much more cumbersome than using a mouse or other pointer.

Mouse

By far the most common pointing device is the mouse, although other devices such as trackerballs, touch screens, pens and joysticks are available. The mouse has won support through its accuracy and ease of use. The most common is the type that houses a large heavy rubber ball, which protrudes from its base. When the mouse is moved over a surface (preferably a *'mouse mat'* - a mat with the correct friction to optimise the ball's movement), the ball rotates inside its case. The ball movement rotates two rollers, one for vertical and one for horizontal movements. Moving the ball diagonally will rotate both rollers. The mouse is designed to convert hand movement into a stream of electrical pulses that is passed via the serial port to the computer. The quicker the mouse is moved, the faster the pulse stream; the further the mouse is moved, the longer is the pulse stream. The incoming signals are used by the program to produce pointer movements on the monitor screen.

The mouse has two, sometimes three, buttons on its casing to allow the user to click on a particular choice or lift/drop the pen while drawing. Some mouse drivers allow the buttons' functions to be transposed, so the mouse can be used more easily with left-handed operators. Finally, some drivers, such as in Windows, allow an option to leave a trail as the cursor moves, so that the cursor position can be easier identified, which is useful on portable computer screens.

Other hardware items

Modem

A modem ('*modulator/demodulator*') allows a computer to communicate with
another computer at great distances over the ordinary telephone network, or
over specially hired lines.   It translates (modulates) the data that is held in the
computer as electronic pulses into audible tones that are capable of being sent down telephone cables.
The modem at the receiving end translates (demodulates) the tones back into electronic pulses for use by
the receiving computer.   For more details, see the chapter on data communications.

CD-ROM

This computer CD player works in a similar way to an ordinary CD player, except that the data that is
read is computer digital data instead of audio data.   The disks used with such players can store around
 650Mbytes of data, which is equivalent to about 500 high-density floppy disks.
The disks are removable and not easily damaged. The only drawback is that the
basic system only reads data from disk to computer.   Read/write systems are
available but are more expensive.   For more information, see the chapter on disks and drives.

Plotter

A plotter is a device to reproduce architectural drawings, road maps and
components designed by CAD (computer aided design) systems.   It uses a
set of pens to draw the lines that comprise the drawings.   It is capable of
producing large size drawings that would not be possible with dot matrix or
laser printers.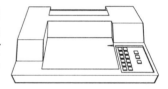

Scanner

 A scanner is a device that analyses a printed piece of work (e.g. picture, drawing or
even text) and converts the image into a file that can be further processed.   A
scanned file of a picture or drawing might be incorporated into desktop publishing
and a scanned piece of text from a book, etc. may be converted back into ASCII text
using a software package called OCR (optical character recognition).

Add-On Cards

When an extra device such as a modem is to be added to a system, the user
can choose to fit external equipment that attaches to the computer's port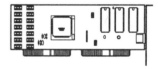
connections or fit an internal board.   Some other devices such as sound-
producing cards are normally only available as internal boards. These boards
contain all the electronics and hardware to carry out their particular function and are plugged into spare
unused slots on the motherboard.   These are known as the computer's '*expansion slots*'.   The add-on
board is fitted and the software to make it function is then installed.

Assembling the system

When a computer is first purchased, it arrives in several boxes.   The monitor is in one box, while the
system unit, keyboard, mouse, manuals and disks are usually packed separately. The monitor has its own
power cable and video cable permanently connected to it in most cases, while the system unit comes as
an independent component with separate cables.

The steps to assembling the system are:
- Choose a suitable location for the computer. Avoid situations of excessive heat, cold, damp,
  dust or vibration. Also avoid locations close to magnetic disturbance such as lift motors,
  power trans-formers, etc. A good location would be one with a flat, stable surface and good
  air circulation.
- Carefully unpack the components from the boxes. The contents of the boxes should then be
  checked against the system checklist, to see that all components have been delivered.

- Read the assembly instructions carefully to ensure that you understand the necessary steps and that any special precautions are understood.
- Gather any tools that you may require. Normally, the only tool is a Philips screwdriver to secure connections to the system unit. Some connections use thumbscrews to make a secure connection and do not require a screwdriver - read the manual.
- Carefully connect the components together, in the order directed by the computer manual. Do not force any connections; if a plug will not easily connect to a socket, it may mean that a connector pin has become bent. It might also mean that the wrong socket is being chosen, or the plug is being inserted upside down!

A typical order of assembly is:
- Place the system unit on the surface to be used.
- Place the monitor on top of the system unit.
- Attach the video cable from the monitor to the video out socket of the system unit.   Ensure that the plug and the socket are of compatible types. An older CGA or EGA monitor cable has a 9-pin plug on the end of its connector cable, while a modern VGA or SVGA monitor has a 15-pin plug. The two are not interchangeable.   A CGA or EGA monitor can only connect to a video outlet of the same type.   Similarly, VGA and SVGA monitors only connect to 15-pin outlets.   Note that the edges of the plugs are shaped so that they only connect one way round.   On some connectors, the plug is secured to the system unit with metal screws and a screwdriver is required to tighten the screws. With other connectors, the plug has plastic thumbscrews that are tightened by hand.

  CGA / EGA   VGA / SVGA

- Connect the mains lead to the system unit.   This cable has a normal 3-pin plug on one end and a connector similar to those used in electric kettles on the other end.   Do not connect the mains plug to the mains at this time; simply plug the other end of the cable into the system unit mains inlet socket.
- Connect the monitor to the mains supply.   Some monitor mains cables have normal 3-pin plugs and these plug directly into a mains supply.   Other monitor power cables have a plug that matches a socket at the rear of the system unit.   These are useful, since switching on the system unit also supplies power to the monitor.   So, if the monitor power switch is left on, both units can be powered up from the system on/off switch
- Connect the keyboard to the system unit.   These are usually 5 or 6-pin plugs and are produced in two sizes.   The larger size plug has a matching socket on the system unit and can only be connected one way since the socket has a key to guide the plug.   With the smaller size keyboard plug, there is also a matching socket.   This smaller socket size is the same type as used for a dedicated mouse socket.   Care should be taken to plug the keyboard into the correct socket. Where the two sockets are of the same size, the system unit should either clearly label them as 'KBD' and 'Mouse', or colour code the sockets and plugs.

  Standard Keyboard   PS/2 Keyboard

- Connect the mouse to the system unit.   The mouse may be of the PS/2 type mentioned above and care should be taken to ensure that the plug is inserted into the correct socket.   Many mouse plugs connect to the system unit's serial port connector. The serial socket usually has nine pins and is marked as 'Serial', 'COM1', or 'RS232'. Sometimes the socket is already used (e.g. for a modem) and the mouse connects to the second serial socket. This often has 25 pins and the mouse connects via a 9-pin to 25-pin adapter.

  9-pin mouse socket   25-pin mouse socket

- Connect the printer to the system unit.   The most common cable is the 'parallel' or 'Centronics' type, which has a 25-pin cable.   The cable at the system unit side terminates in a 25-pin plug that connects to the socket marked 'Parallel' or 'LPT1'.   The other end of the cable connects to the socket on the printer.   Some printers may have a serial connector and   connect to the system unit socket marked as *'COM1'*, *'Serial'* or *'RS232'*. Some system units have two serial sockets, so that the machine can connect a mouse and a printer at the same time. In these cases, the machine is set up to recognise one of the serial outlets as a printer port and the other as a mouse port, and the manual should be checked to determine the use for each port. Finally, connect the printer to the mains supply and ensure that it is supplied with paper and is on-line.

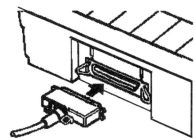

- Check that the monitor is at an angle that affords easy and comfortable viewing and adjust this if necessary; the monitor rests on a plinth that allows the monitor angle to be altered.

Getting up and running

The steps involved are:
- Connect the printer to the mains supply, switch on the printer and run a self-test. The method for doing this will vary from printer to printer and the printer manual should be consulted. With a dot-matrix printer, this usually involves holding a key depressed (such as the LF key) while the unit is switched on; when the key is released, the printer prints out a sample of its output. With a laser printer, this normally involves taking the printer off-line and carrying out a key sequence (e.g. pressing the Shift and Test buttons) or running a test through software.
- Plug in the monitor and system unit mains connectors to the mains supply and switch on the mains at the wall sockets.
- Switch on the monitor and check that the mains indicator light illuminates.
- Switch on the system unit. The computer ON/OFF switch is located on the main body of the machine. It can be a button on the front, or a switch at the side or the rear. Before switching on, ensure that the floppy disk drive is empty. There will often be an additional switch to power the monitor, usually on the front of the monitor casing.

After being switched on, the microcomputer will take about 30 seconds to establish its operating system before it can be used. The computer checks itself to see that its main board, its memory and other key components are working. If the machine passes the self-test and the keyboard and monitor are correctly connected, the monitor screen may show the DOS prompt, which are the C:> characters. More commonly, the microcomputer system is delivered as a *'turnkey system'*. Instead of the operating system prompt of C:> a *'menu'* of operations is displayed, from which a function is selected. For Windows-based machines, the opening Windows options are displayed.

This first level of operation is the point at which you can safely switch the microcomputer system off. It is most important always to return to this level if you have been using another piece of software. Failure to do so can result in either or all of the following circumstances -
- Loss of data through incomplete file update.
- Loss of automatic backup copy of a file.
- Partial update and consequential corruption of database data.

In DOS mode, the connection between the computer and the printer can be tested by pressing the PrtScr key. This should send a copy of whatever is currently appearing on the screen to the printer. If this prints out correctly, then the printer connection is working.

If the system does not work properly, the machine manual on troubleshooting should be consulted. If this is not successful, the chapter on fault detection should be read.

Using the computer

The machine should be used in a way that protects both the operator and the machine. Protection of the user is outlined in the chapters on P.C. Support and Computer Video and covers ergonomics and safety. Protection of the machine is outlined in the chapter on P.C. Support and covers cleaning, maintenance, dust, magnetic fields and static problems.

Software & Data

Software

Software is the program that is bought, or created, for the computer. Without software, a computer is just a black box of electronic equipment that is incapable of any useful function. Software tells the computer exactly what to do and when to do it. Such programs are written in a form of code that only that particular type of computer understands. This machine specific code is called '*machine code*' and code written for an Amiga or an Atari will not run on a PC, for example. The code used by the computer is written using one of the many programming languages. The computer requires step-by-step instructions to reach a solution to a given problem. This series of instructions is known as a program.

The difference between programs and data

- Data is facts or information available for, or the result of, processing. The source of data is usually via the keyboard where an operator types information such as names and addresses, payroll information, measurements, etc.
- Programs are the instructions for processing data. Programs are created by a systems analyst and a programmer. They specify and write a set of instructions that the computer understands and which is able to process the data supplied. Programs can be simple or complex, and can be written by a single programmer or be created by a whole team working for a "*software house*".

Software falls into two main categories - Application software and Systems software.

Application Software

This consists of general-purpose programs and those developed for computer users to solve specific tasks. Typical applications are Word, Excel, Access, PhotoShop and MS Project.

Systems Software

This consists of programs that enable users to make efficient use of the machine. They co-ordinate and maximise the use of the computer's circuitry. Examples of systems software are MSDOS, Windows, Unix and communication utilities.

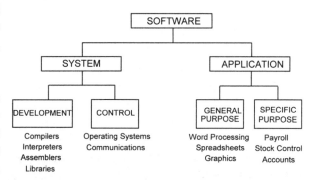

Application and System software act as interfaces between computer users and computer hardware. If this software did not exist, very few computers would be in use. As application and system software become more sophisticated, computers become easier to use.

System Software

System software can be divided into two categories - Control and Development Software.

Development

This software is concerned with the creation of other software; it comprises sets of software tools to allow programs to be written and tested. Knowledge of the appropriate programming language is assumed. JavaScript, for example, is a commonly used language for writing web page programs, while 'C' is commonly used for creating real-time programs.

The writer can choose from the following tools:

- Editors (to enter and modify the program lines)
- Assemblers (to write in machine-specific language)
- Compilers (to turn the writer's program into a form to be saved and run by the machine)
- Interpreters (to convert the written program and run it, one line at a time without being previously compiled)
- Libraries (to store commonly used bits of program, so that the writer can include them in his/her program without having to re-write them from scratch)
- Diagnostic (or '*debugging*') utilities to detect '*bugs*' - errors in the logic of the program.

Control

This software appears on all computers in one form or another. The most common control software is the computer's Operating System. This is the software that controls the machine's disk, screen, keyboard and printing activities, etc. The most commonly used system is Microsoft Windows. This is described in detail in the chapter on Windows Configuration. Other commonly used system software is MSDOS (See the PC Configuration chapter) and various Local Area Networks (LANs) systems.

Application Software

Application software can be further sub-divided into Specific Purpose and General-Purpose categories.

Specific Purpose

These packages are written to carry out a prescribed set of tasks and the user has very little control over the process. Consider the use of a payroll package. The user is prompted to enter details such employee number, number of hours worked, number of night hours, etc. The program then calculates the deductions such as tax and determines the final net wage of the employee; the program then prints the employee's payslip. The role of the user is restricted to feeding the machine with the appropriate answers. A menu may allow different reports to be generated but there is no opportunity to deviate from the pre-programmed activities. Other examples of specific purpose packages are accounting packages, company budgets and stock control software. The advantages of such an approach are:

- Little training, since the program produces a series of simple tasks that is easy to carry out.
- Comprehensive error checking. All likely errors that can be made by users are predicted in advance and the program is written to prevent the user from entering erroneous information (e.g. an age of -17 or entering numbers for a person's name).

The big disadvantage is that programs that are specific to a company's needs are not available off the shelf and have to be specially written as a '*bespoke application*' by a software house, which is a very expensive business.

General Purpose

With general-purpose software, the general routines are included in the package but the user has a great deal of influence over how they are used. With these packages, the user controls the software and not the other way round. Consider a word-processing package. The program will have fixed facilities to enter data, modify it, move it around, check it for correct spelling or grammar, etc. These facilities are available to anyone who uses the package. The difference lies in how each user takes advantage of the facilities. One user's output may be a simple company memo, while another user's output may be a best selling novel or a love poem. The differences are even more striking between different users of graphics packages, where the flair, imagination and artistic abilities of the user are more significant than the packages' abilities.

The normal commercial sector of industry also has great use for general-purpose packages such as spreadsheets (e.g. Excel) and databases (e.g. Access, dBase, FileMaker, etc.). These packages provide basic facilities and these are used to put together a system that can be used by ordinary operators. So, one company might tailor a spreadsheet to provide a budget program while another company might produce a sales forecasting program. Note that these packages are created without the need for a formal programming language. The person tailoring the package need only know the package's internal language. This means that a commercial system can be developed within the company, saving the huge costs involved in ordering a custom designed product from a software house.

Processing systems

The PC can be set up and used in a variety of ways, to meet the organisation's specific needs at any one time. Examples of different processing systems are:

Single-User, Single-Tasking Systems

This is the simplest of systems and the most common one in use. Here, a single computer is used by a single operator at a time (i.e. *'single-user'*), only ever running one program at any one time (i.e. *'single-tasking'*). This only requires a simple operating system and this can be as simple as MSDOS. The single-user machine has to be connected to its own range of input and output devices. If there are two machines in an office and they both need fax facilities, they both require to have fax boards fitted. If both machines require lots of disk space, they both require to have large hard disks fitted.   If both users require a particular package, it has to be installed on both machines.   If they both use the same data, copies of the data have to be placed on the disks of both machines.   The only shared resource might be a printer with an extra switch box that allows the printer to be connected to a number of machines, with only one being actually switched through to the printer at any one time.   This system was predominant in the days of DOS and very old software may still expect to have full, undivided access to resources. Single-user, single-tasking systems are used for such activities as EPOS (Electronic Point-Of-Sale) or data entry stations, where the user is not expected to want to use other software.

In the home, most games also operate in effectively single-tasking mode.   Specialist uses of single-tasking machines include electronic music (using a *'MIDI'* interface to connect the computer to an electronic instrument) and video capture (converting images from camcorders or video players into graphics images or sequences that can be stored on disk).

Multi-Tasking Systems

This system allows a single user to run more than one program at the same time.   So, a user can open a database package and a word-processing package at the same time.   While the word-processor is being used to type a report, the database can be compiling all the facts from the database.   Both programs are functioning at the same time.   The word-processor is the one seen by the user and this is described as being in the *'foreground'*, while the database search is said to be operating in the *'background'*.   Running Windows applications is a good example of a single-user machine being used for multi-tasking.   The user can open up both the Excel spreadsheet and the Word word-processor and data from Excel can be copied over directly into a document being written in Word.   Both packages can be seen on the screen at the same time, with each occupying a different area, or 'window' of the screen.   Other examples of multi-tasking systems are Windows 2000, OS/2 Warp and UNIX.

Multi-User Systems

Each year, more and more PCs are being connected together by special cables and software, to produce *'networked'* systems.   Such systems range from a few PCs wired together using Windows 95/98 software, through to many hundreds of computers linked together with highly complex LAN (local area network) software such as NetWare, NT or Unix systems.   This provides many advantages such as:

- Sharing software resources.   All the application programs can be held on a main computer, known as the *'file server'* and only a single copy is required for each program.   When a computer wishes to run a program, a copy is sent from the server to the computer.   Since there is only one central copy of all programs, additions and upgrades are much easier to perform.
- Sharing data resources. With copies of data being held in separate machines, the information held in each computer soon varies from that held in the other copies. If the data is held centrally, there is no need to have multiple copies in all individual machines. This means that the one central copy is the most current copy available for all users.
- Sharing hardware resources.   If the printers, plotters, modems, etc. are attached to an appropriately configured server or peer station, they are available to all computers connected to the system. This means that even the most expensive piece of equipment can be made available to all computers in the organisation and results in substantial savings over duplicated equipment.
- Communications - since all the machines are interconnected, they are able to send messages to each other via *'E-Mail'* (electronic mail) software.
- Added security.

Real-Time Systems

Large older systems often used *'batch processing'* where a collection of jobs was saved and run in one large batch (usually overnight).   This suited older banking and order-processing systems.   Modern banking involves cash points and Point-Of-Sales outlets where a high-street transaction alters the user's bank balance as soon as transaction is completed.   In real-time systems, the input is immediately accepted and processed very quickly so that further action can be taken using the results of the processing.   Real-time systems use a computer processor to control or monitor activity that is happening in real time. Other examples are robotics, alarm systems, music sequencers and speech recognition.

On-Line Systems

On-line systems use a computer to access a larger system, such as remote banking, or access to central company databases.   It is often used in conjunction with real-time activities.

Licensing Agreements

Software can be obtained in a variety of different ways and in a variety of different pricing structures. The main channels are:

Commercial

This is the most common method of acquiring software. Thousands of products are available with the most common programs being produced by large software houses and corporations such as Microsoft and Lotus. These are copyrighted programs with strictly enforced licences. The various options are:

Single licence

> A single copy is supplied with the installation disks or CDs and user manuals. The software can only be installed on a single machine. Each extra machine is added by purchasing another complete package.

Site licence

> A single copy of the software is bought with permission to install the software on an agreed number of computers; a 20-user licence allows 20 machines to have the software installed. Only one or two copies of the user manual are provided. This is a cheaper method than purchasing a single copy for each machine. An increase in the number of licensed users is achieved by paying for an extension to the existing licensed amount. There is no extra software provided; the increase is purely financial.

Licence by use

> This allows the software to be installed on a large number of computers, but the licence only allows a fixed number of users to be operating the software at any one time. A 20-user licence on these terms would allow the software to reside on 100 machines as long as there was never more than 20 operators using the package at any one time. Increasing the users on this system is identical to the site licence arrangements. This is sometimes called 'per-person' licensing.

Licence by station

> This allows a fixed number of machines to have the software installed. If it's a single-user licence, the software must reside on a single machine; if it's a 10-user licence, then only ten machines can have the software installed. This is sometimes called 'per-seat' licensing.

Network multi-licence

> If an organisation has a local area network, an individual software package for all the computers will reside as a single copy on the file server. Many single-user packages will refuse to work over a network and special network versions have to be bought. In addition, network versions contain facilities to allow many users to read and update the same data without getting in each other's way. If a 20-user network version of a package is bought, then only 20 operators can use the package at any one time. There can be 30, 40 or 100 machines on the network and the package will be available at any one of the computers. When a 21st operator attempts to access the package, the software will not be able to be accessed by that user. Purchasing upgrade disks extends the system. If, for example, a 4-user upgrade were purchased for an existing 20-user system, then the disk would be run to change the maximum allowable from 20 to 24.

Licences may allow the user to make a back-up copy of the installation disks and most allow the user to install the program on a machine or to sell the program provided no copies are kept. Licences usually prohibit the renting/leasing of the program and prohibit additions/alterations to the software. Licences often also attempt to limit the manufacturer's liability for any problems caused by use of the software.

Public domain

Often abbreviated to 'PD'. These programs are not copyrighted by their authors and can be distributed and used free of charge. Users are allowed to alter any program code. This type of software is normally restricted to small programs and utilities. These programs are largely obtained by downloading them from the Internet and from bulletin boards.

Freeware

This is similar to public domain except that the alteration of program code is not permitted. The author retains the copyright over the program and its code. The user is allowed to use and copy the program. It is also sometimes described as 'Bannerware'. A common variation is 'Open Source' software, which encourages users to add their own code and promotes a software sharing community.

Shareware

These are copyrighted and usually full-working versions of programs. The author retains all rights over the program and can alter it or withdraw it from public use if desired. Unlike the normal commercial sector, these are freely distributed on a 'try before you buy' basis. This normally involves allowing the free use of the software for a limited period (typically 30 days) so that a user can evaluate the usefulness of the product for the specified purpose.   If the product is satisfactory, the user has to register the program by sending the author the prescribed fee.   This fee acts as a licence to use the software and may also provide a printed manual, free updates and telephone or mail support. If the product is not found to be satisfactory, the user should stop using it.   These programs are obtained from the Internet, from bulletin boards, CDs supplied with magazines or from shareware distributors.   The user is not allowed to alter the program code.

The quality of shareware programs varies tremendously, from the insultingly bad to entirely professional products.   Some products are *'clones'* of well-known spreadsheet and word-processing packages. Such packages provide broadly similar facilities at a fraction of the normal commercial price.   In other cases, the shareware version is a cut-down equivalent to a well-known product, offering fewer facilities. However, since most users only use a small proportion of a package's facilities, this need not represent a real loss of program functionality for the user. If cost is a factor and compatibility with existing packages is not an issue, then shareware products can be a cost-effective purchase.

In America, the Association of Shareware Professionals provides a standard of writing, support and protection.   In the UK, the equivalent body is the Association of Shareware Professionals (UK) Ltd, Treble Clef House, 64 Welford Road, Wigston Magna, Leicester, LE8 1SL.

Shovelware

This is not an actual licensing category but is included for completeness.   The term has come to describe the habit of supplying large amounts of shareware/PD software on the one CD disk, particularly common as give-aways with computer magazines.   It also covers the cramming of many illegal copies of major application packages on to one CD-ROM for sale as a pirate copy.

Copyright

Software, once written, can be copyrighted and protected by the UK Copyright, Designs and Patents Act of 1988.   The Act was subsequently slightly amended by an EC Directive (which takes precedence) in 1992 and is now referred to as the Copyright (Computer Programs) Regulations.   The Act defines a computer program as a *'literary work'* and the copyright applies to the program for the life of the author, plus fifty years.   In the case of an employee, the copyright is owned by the employer. The Criminal Justice Act makes the Trading Standards Office responsible for copyright law enforcement and breaches of copyright are considered to be criminal offences.

Software Piracy

The copying of software to avoid paying the licence is widespread and is estimated to cost hundreds of millions of pounds in the UK alone; world losses are estimated to be several billion dollars. Huge amounts of money are invested in developing software and potential income is lost through piracy. As a result, the development costs are recouped through increased retail prices to the legal purchasers.   When a user opens a sealed pack of new software, he/she is deemed to have accepted the conditions printed on the envelope. These lay down whether the software is a single user/single computer licence, the restrictions on its use, etc.

It is illegal to:
- Copy copyrighted software without permission from the copyright owner.
- Copy the software's manuals and program notes, without permission from the copyright owner.
- Distribute copyrighted software without permission from the copyright owner.
- Distribute the software's manuals and program notes, without permission from the copyright owner.

Police have search warrant powers to enter premises where there is a suspected breach of the Copyright Act involving computer software and a number of highly publicised fines have been imposed on well-known public and private organisations. Maximum penalties are 6 months/£5000 in the Magistrates Court and 2 years/unlimited fines in the Crown Court.   Six-month jail sentences have already been given in a number of cases of selling counterfeit software.   Successful prosecutions have also been brought against the importation of pirate software, under the Trademarks Act, with sentences up to 4½ years.

There is now some evidence that employers are taking the issue of piracy seriously and many now have policies to prevent unlawful copying of programs or bringing unlicensed software into the workplace.   In some cases, culprits face disciplinary measures up to the level of dismissal.

Anti-Piracy Agencies

One of the major groups is the Federation Against Software Theft which was formed in 1984 to combat computer piracy and is supported by the subscriptions of its around 900 members (mostly corporate users or from the computer industry). It works closely with local police forces and council Trading Standards departments.

Its purpose is twofold:
- To educate and advise computer users against software piracy.
- To support software developers and law enforcement agencies in preventing and detecting computer piracy and to aid the prosecution of offenders.

A group of computer auditors can descend, without warning and at any time, upon a suspected company and serve an 'Anton Piller' court order allowing a search for illegally copied software. An Anton Piller order is a court order that requires a company to allow the inspection team to search the premises and produce a permanent record of all software installed on the premises. The inspection team is usually compiled from computer experts and lawyers and their records may be used in evidence in any legal action against an offending company. The consequences of such an action are severe and include:
- The individual responsible for the installation of the software may lose his/her reputation or even his/her job. Even if that person is not personally responsible, he/she will still be held liable and will pay the price for poor control of staff.
- The offending organisation may have to delete all illegal software and purchase new packages.
- The offending organisation may have to pay for its use of the illegal software.
- The offending organisation will have to pay for all the inspection and legal costs.
- The offending organisation will suffer extremely bad publicity.

To date, FAST has not lost a single court case. They can be contacted at Clivemont House, 54 Clivemont Road, Maidenhead, Berkshire, SL6 7BZ. (Tel 01628 622 121, e-mail fast@fast.org). FAST has concentrated largely on large corporations but has recently declared that it will now also focus on the SoHo (small office/home office) market. This will mainly be an educational drive, with the legal drive directed against those who produce and market illegal copies.

There are a number of other active agencies.

The ELSPA, the European Leisure Software Publishers Association, has its own crime unit. They pay particular attention to pirate games CDs and can be contacted at 01386-830642.

The BSA, Business Software Alliance operates internationally, specialising in combating piracy of business applications. Its members include Microsoft, Novell and Lotus. In the UK it works closely with FAST and can be contacted at 0207-245-0304; its Software Crimeline is 0800-510510.

'Intercept' is a group including major software companies such as Lotus, IBM and Microsoft. It has laid some stress on the detection and elimination of computer pornography.

Although not an enforcing agency, the British Computer Society has a number of specialist working groups in this area - the Law Specialist Group, the Technology of Software Protection Group, the Computer Security Specialist Group and the Data Protection Group. The BCS is at 1 Sanford Street, Swindon, Wiltshire, SN1 1HJ, Tel 01793-417417 (www.bcs.org.uk).

Microsoft provides software to large corporations under its 'Select' scheme and it now intends to invoke a clause in that contract that allows for spot-check audits of software.

Software Audits

In an organisation with many PCs, keeping track of the contents of each machine's hard disk is difficult. A systematic approach has to be adopted to catalogue all the software in use on the machines in an easy form that can be compared with the software licences held by the company. A manual search through all the files on each hard disk and the collation of the results would be very time consuming. Automated systems are available in the form of *'software auditing'* programs such as Lan Auditor, Microsoft's 'LegalWare', EZ-Audit and Dr Solomon's Audit.

Since most PCs are now connected to local networks, most auditing packages are designed to collect information over the network cabling. There is no need to visit individual PCs and the work can be carried out centrally. Of course, auditing programs are available for organisations that do not network their computers. In such cases, visits have to be paid to each machine.

Steps in an audit

- Gather together the entire organisation's licences. In the best organisations, there will already be a responsible person (e.g. MIS manager or Finance Manager) who has these documents catalogued. In most organisations, they are scattered and will have to be tracked down using invoices, manuals, installation disks, local knowledge, etc. This task can be carried out while the other audit tasks are being performed.
- Inform the users about the procedures. This is particularly true for a first audit, as its aim will include educating users on the problems of illegal software, threats from virused games and the organisation's discipline policy on these matters.
- Gather the information. In a non-networked situation, each computer is visited and the auditing procedure is:
    1. Insert the audit floppy disk into the computer and run its program. (After a virus check)
    2. Supply the program with details of the machine being tested (e.g. machine serial number, room number, or other identifying code).
    3. Wait while the program searches the machine's hard disk cataloguing all the known programs in its list. This list includes all the most common applications and can be added to by the user. The program saves the machine's program details to a file on the floppy disk.

In a networked system, the information can be gathered from each remote computer and stored directly to the auditor's hard disk.

- Compile the results. The auditing software can provide a variety of views - i.e. details for each machine as well as totals for particular application packages. It produces a report that combines all the facts from each machine and lists how many copies of each program were found in the company's machines. This is the list that can be compared to the company's licence provision and unlicensed use detected. The reports can be sent to the screen or the printer.
- Decide on action. All experience shows that a mass of unlicensed software will be uncovered. All software not required by the organisation (e.g. games) can rapidly be removed. However, the reports may also highlight any shortages of licences to cover the use of some packages. Waiting for the next financial budget allocation is not a legal option. Either the software has to be immediately removed or extra licences immediately purchased.

Software Installation

Each application has its own differing step-by step routine to install software. In most cases, the installation routine is straightforward. The package contains a CD or a set of disks and an installation guide. The guide may be part of the package's manual or may be a separate booklet. In Windows, software supplied on CD should autostart on inserting the disk, thus beginning the installation procedure automatically. If not, locate the CD drive in Explorer and look for an installation program, probably called 'install.exe' or 'setup.exe'. Floppy disk software is now rare except for device drivers, but if more than one floppy is supplied, the first disk normally contains the setup program.

When an application is set up it may require information to allow it to perform its function properly. For example Microsoft Office products will ask for a user name, so that the author of any file can be identified. Some applications need more detailed information, such as which folder to store created files in. The setup information required varies for each package, and the manual should be consulted.

Further alterations

When the installation program finishes, the new piece of software is stored on the hard disk and is available for use. In nearly all cases the application will set up a program item and a suitable icon to make access to the program easier; these may include an icon on the Start Menu, the Desktop, and/or the Quickstart bar.

In all applications, the settings can be changed later, if for example the user wishes to use the program in a different manner or if the machine is transferred to another department. With Windows, there are a number of additional settings that can be made outwith the installation process, such as altering the keyboard repeat rate timing, changing the sensitivity of the mouse or altering the system's memory usage. These issues are covered later.

Maintaining legality

Before installing software, the support technician should confirm that the software is licensed for installation on the particular machine. A well-run organisation will require documentation on the installation. The technician should fill in a report that states the date of the installation, the person who carried out the installation, the name of the package and any other relevant details.

Computer Data

All organisations store raw data that can be retrieved for later perusal, or can be processed in a way that brings out more generalised information.   Every time a purchase is made at a supermarket checkout, raw data is saved. This records what items were purchased, what day and time, which branch and so on. The Board of Directors, however, are more interested in the organising of these facts and figures in a way that tells them which items are best sellers, which store performs best, which time of day records the highest sales, etc. In most cases, data in both its raw and processed state is valuable. Raw data, for example, can be used to send out mailing lists - while processing the same data can produce information on the total numbers in any one town, etc. Indeed, data and information have become commodities for trading. Lists of affluent purchasers (e.g. those recorded as buying expensive cars, art, conservatories, etc) are sold on to companies for mailshot purposes.

Examples of differing producers of data and information are:

Type of Activity	Type of Data	Type of Information
Weather Centre	Temperatures; barometric readings; wind speeds	Trends in the weather; average sunshine/rainfall for a particular month.
Finance Dept	Invoices paid; income receipts	Balance over a period; main spending areas.
Opinion Polling	Purchasing preferences; voting intentions; public attitudes	Degree of success of an advertising campaign; voting and public opinion snapshots and trends.
College/University	Student details, examination results	Student numbers; proportions by sex, race, etc; total successes in each performance band.

The list could be greatly extended as almost all organisations maintain records for a wide range of purposes. In each case above, information is the result of processing the data in some way. The information is further condensed as it goes further up the organisation's structure. The foreman may require basic daily information for operational reasons, while middle management will want the same information covering a longer term but with less specific detail. Top management will take an even longer view and require even further condensing of the information.

MIS Departments

Large organisations will have their own *'Management Information System'* - a department equipped to gather data and produce useful information for management at all levels.   The department's aim is to improve the quality of management decisions by
* Speeding up the time taken for a significant event to be notified to management.
* Providing all information necessary for the support of planning, control and operational functions.

Usage of information

The three main uses of the stored information are recording, monitoring and planning as shown below:

Historical recording	Used to store for later use (e.g. tax returns, VAT receipts/payments, targeted mailshots, etc).
Monitoring	Used to determine comparisons and trends (e.g. stock control, climatic changes, stock market trends, etc).
Planning	Used to determine future action (e.g. build more schools/roads/houses, extend factories, etc).

The MIS Department would supply information appropriate to the level of management in the organisation as shown below:

Management Level	Responsibilities	Information Required
Top Management	Long-term strategic decisions (e.g. market trends, new products, expansion/ contraction.	Market research, comparisons with competitors.
Middle Management	Tactical decisions on a month-by-month basis.	Future orders, company targets.
Junior Management	Daily operational decisions.	Daily production/staffing/stock figures.

Sources and types of information

Information can be produced from within an organisation - internal sources - or can be gathered from a variety of external sources.

The general classifications of organisational information would include:

Categories	Internal Sources	External Sources
Personal	Personnel records (promotion, discipline, health, etc).	Letters of complaints/praise from the public.
Employment	Training programmes, Company Research & Development results, Production figures	Market Research, Government initiatives (e.g. on training, grants and subsidies.)
Financial	Sales figures, Company accounts, VAT payments, Payroll details	Sales orders, Remittance advice, Purchase Invoices, Returned goods, VAT receipts.
Legal	Data Protection Act procedures, Software audits, Criminal records, rehabilitation records.	Employment legislation, Health & Safety Work legislation, Trade Union laws, Case histories.

The above table outlines the main categories for commercial organisations.

Other information categories can be developed, such as:

Scientific   (e.g. scientific formulae, periodic tables, properties of materials, test results).

Engineering   (e.g. quality controls, tolerances, templates, computer numeric control systems).

Social   (e.g. national census, voters rolls, music charts, club membership lists).

Sources of information

As shown above, sources of organisational information can be viewed as either internal or external with corresponding sub-categories as below:

Internal
- Departments (Accounting, Sales, Purchases, Development, Maintenance, Personnel, Training)
- Individuals (suggestions box, interviews, unofficial *'grapevine'*)

External
- Other organisations (orders, invoices, returns, government agencies e.g. Inland Revenue, Customs & Excise, Health and Safety Executive).
- Individuals (letters from the public).
- Information providers (market research organisations).
- Service providers (on-line databases).
- Product providers (manuals, technical specifications).
- Reference publications (Government pamphlets, tax tables).
- Public records (legal case histories, balance of payments figures, Hansard).

Another categorisation of information is into *'primary'* and *'secondary'* sources.   Primary sources are those recorded at the time of the event, while secondary sources are set down after the event.

Primary sources are frequently more accurate and should be used wherever possible.

Examples of primary information are product specifications, original film footage, authenticated statistics, health and attendance records, and historical records.

Examples of secondary information are product reviews, film reconstructions, politicians' reports, employee appraisements and history books.

Technical sources

In the rapidly changing computer world, computer and I.T. specialists require a constantly updated reference base.   Such a reference base could consist of:
- Bought-in training material.
- Textbooks. These are widely available and often explore beyond the user manuals.
- Manuals. Despite being much maligned, often deservedly, manuals have an important role to play in providing the detail required on any one command or activity.
- Printouts from Internet news groups' on-line help sessions.   There are many news groups where queries can be placed and speedy answers received. Some of these are provided by software houses. This can be a valuable source, since a problem experienced in one workplace has probably also been experienced and solved somewhere else.
- User Group newsletters, magazines and notes from group meetings. For the same reason as above, membership of user groups is advisable.   Most subject areas are covered and there are groups for Microsoft Application users, Windows users, Novell users, PhotoShop users, and many more. These are not hobbyists' clubs (although individual membership is accepted) and are usually composed of representatives from private companies, local authorities, health boards, etc.
- Notes taken during suppliers' on-line help sessions. Many software and hardware suppliers run their own help desks and this issue is covered later.   However, the notes taken when on the telephone to

these 'hot-lines' provide a useful insight into the workings of the particular package system and should be stored for future reference. A standard form can be produced for this purpose.

- Computer magazines. Subscriptions should be arranged for a range of magazines, after careful scrutiny of their general contents. The best magazines provide cover of both hardware and software issues, although some specialise (in Unix, for example). These are mostly monthly productions. Typical contents include:
    - o Product reviews, both of new hardware and new software. Hardware reviews generally provide performance benchmarks, so that different products can be compared. Software reviews provide a roundup of the packages' facilities in comparison to similar products from competitors.
    - o Technological trends. This can prove especially useful in aiding future planning of I.T. provision; planned spending on upgrades and extensions might be delayed awaiting the introduction of better systems.
    - o *'How to'* articles. These cover issues as diverse as *'how to plan your network'* and *'how to create macros in Word'*. These articles tend to present ideas in a popular way and can be either basic or advanced.
    - o *'How things work'* articles. Similar to the above, usually with lots of helpful illustrations and diagrams.
    - o Hints and tips. These sections may be categorised under database, spreadsheet, DTP, etc. headings, or there may be general sections. Many useful small hints are available, some of which are not even documented in the DOS or Windows manual, package manual or other source.

Over a period of time, the shelves will begin to creak with the accumulated volumes of such magazines. Finding a particular article requires a reference system to be built up. Maintaining this system is cumbersome and accessing data is slow. A more useful approach may be to simply cut out the articles and file them in cardboard wallets or boxes under appropriate headings. For example, all articles on computer networking could be stored in a separate wallet, as with material on spreadsheet macros, Windows tips and so on. In that way, all the material on a certain subject is easily accessed. The only overhead is the breakdown of a magazine into the wallets.

- Printouts of all help text files that are supplied with application packages and with hardware driver disks, etc. These might be README.TXT or similarly named ASCII files and they provide up-to-date additions and modifications to the manuals. They often cover known bugs and hardware clashes. There are also a number of Windows files in .WRI format. And, of course, the many help pages in Windows applications are capable of being printed out; this means that the most frequently accessed help pages can be printed out and compiled into a separate booklet or included in wallets with similar information (see paragraph on magazine articles).
- Technical information on CD-ROM as supplied by some software houses.
- Trade papers. These are weekly or monthly publications and are either general in nature or cover specialised areas such as local area networks or data communications.

Problems of data storage

Where large amounts of data are stored in a single computer, a number of potential problems have to be addressed and preventative/corrective measures implemented. The most common problems are:

- **Loss of data** Preventing loss due to system breakdown or data corruption (see Disk Backups)
- **Integrity** Ensuring that data is:
    - Complete (all required facts and figures are entered).
    - Accurate (all entries are correct - perhaps using double entry of data and/or entry validation procedures such as range checking, format checking and the use of check digits).
    - Consistent (e.g. a price list on one computer stores the same data as a price list on another computer).
- **Legality** Storing data in a legal manner (see Data Protection Act).
- **Security** Preventing unauthorised access to data (see Computer Misuse Act).

An organisation's Management Information Systems (MIS) Department would have overall responsibility for the above issues and would institute protective measures in consultation with the P.C. support technicians.

Security

A commercial organisation is greatly concerned about the security of its data since it may contain vital information about company budgets, contract bids, sales projections, business plans, product specifications and a host of other sensitive information. Often, a company's data is more valuable than the installed hardware. Machine breakdown, fire and flood remain the biggest source of data loss and security against these is covered in the section on file backups. The chapter on viruses covers the threat to data security from that source. This section is concerned with the physical security of data from the eyes of unauthorised users. Threats to an organisation's data include fraud, commercial espionage and malicious damage. These are potentially extremely damaging and the problems are now addressed in Government legislation, known as the Computer Misuse Act of 1990.

Computer Misuse Act

It is generally accepted that breaches of data security are still mostly perpetrated by staff within a company, rather the more publicised cases of 'hacking' from external sources. However, due to the increase in networking of PCs and the increase in remote access (i.e. accessing the company computers via a modem) the threat of data loss through hacking is increasing.

The Computer Misuse Act 1990 makes it an offence to:
- Make unauthorised access to computer material.
- Make unauthorised access with intent to commit or facilitate commission of other offences.
- Make unauthorised modification of computer material.

Case law in June 1992 established that the Act applies equally to hacking from a remote machine and to standalone PCs. In December 1993, case law established that the offender need not even touch the keyboard to commit the crime. One party enticed another party to copy confidential information. The court ruled that the party requesting the offence was the major offender. Using a program, erasing a file, altering a file, copying a file and even viewing a file are all offences, if the action is not authorised. The New Scotland Yard Computer Crime Unit (Tel 0207-230-1212) recommends that companies have a warning message displayed at the start-up of a computer, so that the user is left is no doubt about the possible consequences of his/her actions. Any subsequent activity is then being carried out in the full knowledge of the legal position. Penalties extend up to five years imprisonment or a fine, or both. Copies of the Act are available from HMSO suppliers.

Security levels

Some data is more confidential - and more prone to misuse - than other data. The British Computer Society outlines a *"Scale For Sensitivity"* which ranks data on a scale of 0 to 10. Scale Value 0 covers items such as databanks of components, while Scale Value 5 covers bank and medical records. Scale Value 10 covers the most sensitive areas of diplomatic and defence secrets. Organisations can categorise their data and enforce security according to the degree of sensitivity of the data stored.

Achieving security

With a local area network, the access problem is partly solved by a series of passwords and accompanying rights to view, alter and delete data in various sub-directories. These are allocated by the network supervisor in a way that prohibits unauthorised access and use of files.

For a non-networked collection of PCs, consideration should be given to the following measures.

Physical security

A PC that stores valuable programs or data can be physically protected. This can take the simple form of situating the machine in a locked room or room with sign-in, swipe card or clearance badge access. It may also mean purchasing a machine with a removable hard disk, so that the data can be stored in the safe at night. Another option is to install a key system to the computer so that it cannot be accessed without the physical presence of the key in the mechanism. Of course, the technician has to consider that a determined attempt at industrial sabotage will not be prevented by a password or keyed system; the machine may simply be stolen and entry gained at leisure. To prevent this, the machine can be bolted to the desk or can have steel cables connected to go round furniture and be locked. Equipment can also be fitted with an alarm system. The system might include provision to detect the proximity of a person's body or it may detect the physical movement of the computer. It may also be fitted with an anti-tamper device so that the computer alarm cannot be disabled (e.g. the PC Theft Alarm).

Hardware-based security

Hardware-based devices are effective in preventing the casual interference with the system. They are not capable of preventing the professional thief who will steal the machine, disable the security schemes and access the data. Examples of hardware security include:

- Many computers have key switches to disable the keyboard or even disable the power button.
- The use of floppy drive locks. These are blanking plates that can be fitted into the floppy drive and locked into place with a key. This prevents the unauthorised copying of files to floppy disk. If this is used in a network where all printing is to a central location, then the opportunity for removal of data is even further reduced.
- The use of *'dongles'* to prevent illegal use of a piece of software. These were popular for many packages some time ago but most were withdrawn due to user hostility. These were devices that plugged into the serial or parallel port of the computer. The dongle was supplied with a particular application package and the circuitry inside ensured that the application could be run. If the dongle was removed, the application package would not run.
- The use of fingerprint scanners (e.g. the Datawise MT Digit and U.are.U fingerprint readers, or the reader built into the KeyTronic Secure Scanner Keyboard. The recognition software in the computer only allows access to those whose finger scans matched those previously stored in its database. Other biometric systems are being developed using face recognition, iris recognition and voice recognition.
- Pentium III processors have a serial number hardcoded into the circuitry, which could have been used to identify stolen components, but due to wide concern over the use of this information Intel made the facility optional. Users can disable the serial number.

Software-based security

These comprise of two approaches - detection software and prevention software. Detection software does not prevent the breach of security but allows the culprit to be traced, while prevention software stops the security breach from happening. Examples of detection software are:

- Audit/Logging systems, each computer creates a log of all files that were opened, with dates and times; it can also log the use of floppy disks or the serial port. These systems are regarded with some suspicion since they are also capable of monitoring the number of keystrokes entered by a user in a given period and can hence be used for employee performance monitoring.
- Embedding of company information into application logos. When the package is installed for the first time, the user is prompted for the company name, address, etc. and this information is written into the application's .EXE file. Any subsequent installation does not prompt again and uses the previously saved data in the screen logo. This does not prevent illegal copying but makes it more conspicuous.

Examples of prevention software are:

- Password and network security mentioned previously.
- Authentication (the passwords of two users being required before an operation can continue).
- Methods that prevent unauthorised entry to company networks from modems. Authorised entry, via modems and remote access software such as Carbon Copy or PC Anywhere, requires the user to enter the correct password before allowing access to the main computer network. With patience, a hacker will eventually crack the password and be able to enter the network. An improved security system includes a *'callback'* or *'dialback'* facility. In this case, the user phones the main system and provides a valid user name and password as normal. The system software then consults a centrally held database to see what telephone number is associated with that password. It phones back the caller and allows the user's connection. In this way, a hacker will not gain access to the system even if he/she is able to work out the correct password since the call would not be coming from the authorised phone number. This callback facility is offered in Carbon Copy for Windows.
- Using an encryption program to scramble files before they are stored on disk or sent over a communication line. The decryption software to unscramble the file can only be used by those who have the *'key'* code. The most common example of this software is PGP (Pretty Good Privacy). This system, and the government's response to it, has caused some controversy. This is covered in the section on legal problems in the chapter on *'Using the Internet'*.
- The screen blanker, designed to turn off the screen after a pre-set time and requiring a password to restore normal viewing.

Password systems built in to the BIOS

Many computers allow a user password to be allocated to a machine. This is stored in the CMOS memory and a user will not gain access to the computer unless the correct password is given. This prevents the machine from being accessed by unauthorised users but is only a crude system.

Password protection systems

A sophisticated system is often required so that users can share the same machine. Some users will be able to see budget data but be blocked from seeing personnel data. Other users will be able to see personnel data but will be blocked from viewing budget data. In other words, the machine requires selective viewing of sub-directories based on a user's password. This is available in both software implementations and hardware implementations (using add-on cards such as PC Access Control, Sysecure, StopLock, etc.). Beware of systems that encrypt the data on the hard disk. This is intended to thwart the person who gains unauthorised access to data. Check that there is no possibility that the authorised user ends up unable to decipher the data in the event of a hard disk fault or security card fault.

Company policy

The organisation should evolve a security strategy that is well known and accepted by the staff. Staff should understand the need for some of the otherwise niggling procedures, as an educated workforce is the key to data security. It follows that the evolution of the strategy identifies all possible risks. It should cover networks, standalone PCs and remote access systems; it should involve the I.T. professionals and the day-to-day users. The commitment to security has to emanate from the top down and there is evidence of increasing understanding and action from top management.

The strategy should be enshrined in a company policy that details:
- Who is responsible for each level of security (who manages the network security, who carries out the backups, who controls document management, who carries out configuration management, etc.).
- Who will carry out the necessary staff education.
- Who will monitor the efficiency of the policy.
- What are the agreed penalties for breaches of security.
- What are the recovery systems in the event of data loss or corruption.

The policy should outline the main points of the Copyright, Designs and Patents Act, the Computer Misuse Act, the Trademarks Act and the Data Protection Act.

Data Protection Act

The single biggest use of computers is for the creation of databases to store masses of data. This data includes personal information on individuals as employees, clients, patients, etc. The data also includes sensitive financial information on contracts, deadlines, specifications, etc. Since 1984, holders of such data - *'Data Controllers'* - are governed by the Data Protection Act and are legally obliged to register. EU Data Protection Directive (95/46/EC) further tightened UK legislation in this area and became the 1998 Data Protection Act. Despite its name, the Data Protection Act is more concerned with protecting people - protecting them from the effects of wrong information. The central points of the Act are:
- Data should not be available to unauthorised viewers.
- Subjects of the data should have the right to view their own data.

There are, however, a few areas where the Act has exemptions, such as national security and the prevention and detection of crime. Other exemptions include personal, household and recreational use of data and data used for calculating wages and pensions.

The eight principles of the Act are:
1. Data must be processed fairly and legally. The data must not be obtained through subterfuge or impersonation, for example.
2. Data shall only be held for specified purposes. Data users have to tell the Data Protection Commissioner (previously known as 'Registrar') what uses the data is intended for.
3. Data shall not be beyond that required for the specified purposes. A file of customers, for example, should not contain any reference to the religion or political persuasion of the customers.
4. Data shall be kept accurate and up-to-date. Where circumstances change (e.g. medical records), the data must be kept in a current condition.
5. Data shall not be kept longer than is necessary. If data is held on patients for, say, a controlled experiment, the data on individuals should not be kept after the trial is completed; the generalised data, cropped of subject names, may be kept for reference.
6. Personal data must be processed in accordance with the rights of individuals (*'Data Subjects'*).
7. Data shall be protected against unauthorised access.
8. Personal data must not be transferred to non-EU countries unless they have a similar system of data protection.

Rightful access

Wherever personal details are recorded, there is scope for error. These errors could be typing mistakes or the confusion of records (how many John Smiths live in Britain ?). These mistakes have, in the past, resulted in patients being given medical treatment meant for others, for example. Individuals could also find themselves being refused employment, promotion, benefits, credit or other rights, as a result of incorrect data. It is vital that the subjects whose data is being stored have access to their own records to check their accuracy. This could include taking away a copy of the data. Where the information is inaccurate (e.g. wrong age), the user should be able to have it altered. Where the information is incorrect (e.g. wrong person), the user should be able to have the data erased from the file. The Data Protection Commissioner will arbitrate in any disputes between subjects and organisations holding data on them. The subject may also apply to the courts for correction or deletion of incorrect data.

Unauthorised access

It is also important that only those authorised to view the data have access to personal records. Many bodies keep very personal data on individuals, covering areas such as health details, marital details, financial details and promotion and discipline details. It is the responsibility of the body to ensure that there are adequate measures to prevent unauthorised access. A normal procedure would be to ask a subject to complete a request form to view their data. This might incur a search fee of, say, £10. When the form is submitted, the subject should be obliged to provide some proof of identity. In this way, only the actual subject will be able to see his/her own data.

Compensation

Data subjects can receive compensation where incorrect data has caused them harm. Examples of this might be from the loss of data, the use of incorrect data, or the unauthorised disclosure of data. The results might be physical damage (the wrong medicine), financial damage (passed over for promotion) or psychological damage (ridiculed by workmates about an exotic disease, unorthodox religious or political persuasion).

The Data Protection Act requires that users of personal data (ie Data Controllers) be registered with the Data Protection Commissioner. Copies of the notification pack can be obtained from the Office of the Data Protection Commissioner at

> Springfield House, Water Lane, Wilmslow, Cheshire, SK9 5AX Tel: 01625-545745
> or e-mail to mail@dataprotection.gov.uk

Users must instigate procedures whereby the subject can request and gain access to his/her data.

Data Organisation

The chapters on using DOS and Windows explain how to create directories and sub-directories on a disk. This section considers the best method of storing data on a hard disk. A hard disk on a newly supplied computer is often empty apart from the Windows, Program Files and My Documents directories and a few system files. The way that the rest of the disk is organised can affect the efficiency of the disk's later use. The data on the disk should be organised in such a way that it is:

- EASILY IDENTIFIED   • EASILY BACKED UP
- EASILY DELETED   • EASILY PROTECTED

Previous to Windows, most application programs were stored in a directory off the root, and the data files were stored in a sub-directory of that directory. This meant that if a project required work in more than one package, the data files would be scattered around various directories. This poses problems for security and backup purposes.

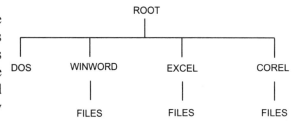

Windows 95 introduced the 'Program Files' folder to store the application programs, and the 'My Documents' folder to store files, although some packages can be set to default to another drive or folder. It is surprisingly common for users to simply put all their data files in 'My Documents'. This would throw all the files into a single folder, thereby mixing together all the data files for different projects.

This is convenient in the sense that all the possible data files for Word are found in the same folder. However, over time, the data will relate to many different projects and it is very easy to lose track of which files belong to which project. Consequently, there is confusion over which files to backup, copy, or delete at the end of a project. This results in many old unused files cluttering the hard disk.

A common solution is to create different sub-directories for each project. For example, the data files for the first project are in C:\My Documents\Project 1, while the documents for Project 2 are in C:\My Documents\Project 2, and so on. If each project contained many files of different types, it could be split up again. So, for example, the word-processed documents for Project 1 are in C:\My Documents\Project 1\Correspondence, while the Excel budget calculations are in C:\My Documents\Project 1\Budget.

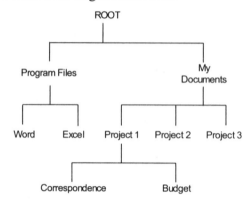

Since the program files are already stored on the installation disks, there should be no need to involve the '*Program Files*' section of the disk structure in any backup strategy. The only exception is for an application that is heavily customised and the backup may be necessary to store the customisation details.

A variation on the above approach is to partition the existing hard disk into two or more distinct areas (see the chapter on Disks and Drives). After partitioning, the original 'C' drive will appear as separate 'C', 'D', etc. drives. The operating system and application programs could be stored on the 'C' drive, while the other partition(s) stores data. For those computers with more than a single hard disk, there is no need for partitioning, since 'C', 'D', etc drives will already exist.

Storage Media Library

Many organisations store a library of frequently used media, as a common resource for use by all authorised staff. Typical library contents would include:

- Computer files on disk or CD-ROM
- Visual aids, such as OHP slides
- Specifications
- Video and audio tape
- Reference books

The material is held centrally and can be booked out for a defined period in the same manner as booking out a publication from a council library.

Computer Library
The type of material that would be found in a library of computer files might include:
Source Code
If a software house has many projects in hand, there is a very good chance that some will use similar or identical routines. Examples might be routines to validate a number or test if a date is valid. Where code is written that is liable to be re-used, the code can be saved in the library. Any writer wishing to incorporate the same facility, can simply copy the code from the library into his/her own project. This saves much development time and testing time, since the code will have been thoroughly tested before being allowed into the library.
Clip Art
Such a collection would include the company logo, copyright-free clip art, digitised pictures and even scanned images of director's signatures. The library may also include copyrighted material as long as permission is sought before using it. Copyright material, for that reason, should be stored separately from copyright-free material.
Sample Applications
Many programs include sample applications written with the package. These are designed to demonstrate what can be achieved with the package and illustrate some of the package's techniques. These tend to be large and would not normally be left on a machine's hard disk. The user would book the sample application out of the library, temporarily install it on his/her computer and delete it again when finished.

Training Packages

Similarly, the company may own a number of computer-based training packages. For reasons of disk space and for licensing reasons, the packages may be stored centrally and only loaned out when required.

Shareware

Some organisations, such as colleges and training institutions, may wish to loan out shareware packages to their students. Some shareware files contain source code in Pascal, C, or Basic and the examination of this code can be a valuable tool for students. Some shareware packages are clones for well-known expensive packages, and poor students may wish to register for a shareware version for home use. This aids the students in their studies and reduces the temptation for them to make pirate copies of the institution's own packages.

Where To Store

The library may reside on a local area network server or on individual floppy disks or CDs held in a central store. If the amount of material is not substantial, the network server's hard disk will be able to accommodate it without any trouble. If, however, the material includes many digitised pictures and other large files, the only solution may be to store the data on floppy disks, ZIP disks or CDs. Also, where there is no local area network, the disk store may be the only solution. Depending upon the scale of the library, a single box of disks up to drawers full of disks may be required.

Librarian Responsibilities

The media library has to be controlled by a responsible person, since there are legal implications to the job (i.e. storing pirate copies, insufficient licence fees, copyrighted material, etc.). The duties of the librarian would include:

Maintaining A Master Set

It is a major job to ensure that backups are kept of all material, since it is almost certain that loaned disks will, at some stage, be lost or returned with damaged, corrupted, deleted or over-written files. The master set should never be loaned out and is only used to generate another clean copy of a disk.

Security

The library, and in particular the master set, must be stored in a lockfast location - preferably a separate location for both sets of disks, to reduce the chances of loss through fire or theft.

Collecting

The librarian must always be on the lookout for new material for the library. This may include freshly written source code procedures or it may include new files from shareware libraries. It may also involve copying files from CD-ROM shareware disks on to floppy disks.

Ordering

The librarian is responsible for the ordering of fresh material and ensuring that the organisation maintains the correct licence fees for the material held in the library. The librarian is also responsible for ensuring that all material held in the library can be legitimately loaned.

Collating

The librarian must group all material of a similar nature together. The files must be collected under defined headings, such as Pascal source code, Basic source code, C source code, disk utilities, etc. Printed catalogues should be drawn up and distributed.

Keeping Paperwork

All records must be kept for inspection by auditors, FAST, etc.

Booking Procedures

Library users should be obliged to sign out and sign in the material, so that a proper track can be kept of the library's stock. The signing-out sheet should incorporate a statement for the borrower to sign. This statement should include the following:

- An acceptance of the organisation's policy on software piracy.
- An agreement to pay for any damaged or lost disks. This will vary between organisations. A college, for example, may demand a non-returnable deposit for loans, while a large corporation may not even have such a clause.

The librarian is also responsible for checking for damages, deletions and overwrites and for pursuing overdue disks.

Operating Systems

and Windows

An operating system is a set of programs to control the hardware and manage the computer's resources. For many years, the only major operating systems for PCs was Microsoft's MSDOS (Microsoft Disk Operating System).   Although it is still in common use, many new users have never seen or used it, since they have been brought up using the Windows family of operating systems.

Why learn DOS

Workers in the IT/computing industry still find machines that only use DOS and DOS-based applications or, like Windows 3.1, are machines that sit on top of DOS.

Even if your machines are Windows based, they still use many of the original DOS concepts such as file extensions, sub-directories and paths. And, when things go wrong and you can't get back into Windows, you revert to DOS commands to restore your system.

MSDOS

The amount of files used for Microsoft DOS depended on the version.   As each version was updated, new facilities were added and the number of files that make up the package increased.   DOS 6.2 comprises almost 150 files.   The main characteristics of an operating system are:

- It conceals the difficulties of handling the hardware.
- It presents the user with a relatively simple interface.
- It communicates with the user, carrying out valid commands and giving error messages when incorrect commands are attempted.
- It relieves users from requiring a detailed knowledge of how the computer hardware works.

With the earliest computers, users had to have a great knowledge of each item of hardware.   When DOS appeared, computers became available to ordinary users.   The user could carry out a range of activities by giving simple commands, in the knowledge that the operating system would translate the simple user command into the set of hardware tasks needed to carry it out.   The operating system could be considered as the foreman of an organisation.   When the manager (i.e. the user) gave an order for work to be carried out, the foreman took on the job of ensuring that the actual physical task was carried out.   The manager need not know where the resources are kept and what activities are involved - that is the job of the foreman.

Using the DOS Operating System

When the computer is powered up, the essential portion of MSDOS is loaded into the computer memory. The system prompt will then be displayed to the user.   This normally shows the drive that the system is currently logged on to (i.e. currently looking at), as below:

       C:\ >

The above prompt tells the user that the current logged drive is the 'C' drive, the machine's internal hard disk. This should be accompanied by a flashing line, known as the *'cursor'* and indicates that the machine is waiting for an instruction.

       Note -   The user cannot run any programs or perform any machine
                    housekeeping tasks until the operating system has been loaded.

To save memory space, only the essential and most-commonly used parts of DOS are loaded into the computer's memory when the computer is switched on.   These essential parts are required to make the computer work and the user has little control over them.   However, some of the more common commands that users require are combined into a single file and loaded into memory.   This means that these commands are quickly available to the user and these are called *'resident'* commands.   The many other utilities remain on the disk until called by the user. If the user requires to use any of these commands (called *'transient'* or *'external'* commands), then DOS loads them into the computer's memory. If all the possible utilities were loaded into the computer on switch on, there would not be enough memory left to do anything else!

Using common DOS commands

The simplest commands comprise a single word instruction, which can be entered in upper or lower case - or even a mixture of upper or lower case.   When all of the command is typed in at the keyboard, the *'Enter'* key should be pressed.   This completes the command, which is then passed to DOS to carry out. DOS will process any command until the Enter key is pressed. The command has to be entered at the keyboard when the DOS prompt is showing. In the following examples, it is assumed that the Enter key will be pressed after entering the command. For example, to see what version of DOS is installed on the machine, the command would simply be VER, followed by pressing the Enter key.   If the machine is logged to look at the 'C' drive, it can be switched to log on to the floppy drive by entering A: followed by the Enter key; logging back to the hard disk would be accomplished by typing C: followed by 'Enter'. Other simple commands are:

CLS   This clears all contents off the monitor screen and moves the prompt and cursor to the top left (i.e. home) position on the screen.

VOL   Every disk, hard disk or floppy disk, can be given an 'electronic' title, to express the general contents it contains.   This title is alterable by the user (see later).   The VOL command displays the disk's current label.

For more complex commands, the command is followed by various options, called *'parameters'*.   For example, to delete a file from a disk, there is no point in simply telling the computer to DELETE - the computer has to be told what file to delete.   Here, the parameter would be the name of the file.   So, to erase a file called REPORT, the command would be

DEL REPORT

Parameters can be a single item or can be more than one item - sometimes separated by spaces, or commas, etc.

The current date and time are held inside the computer and can be viewed or altered by giving the command DATE   followed by the Enter key. This will result in a display such as

Current date is Thu 16-11-99

Enter new date (dd-mm-yy)

To retain the given date, the Enter key is pressed; to alter the date, the new date is entered in the expected format, including the minus sign separators, followed by pressing Enter.

The same technique can be used to view or alter the system time, using the TIME command.

Getting help

From DOS 5 onwards, on-line help has been available to the user.   DOS 6 onwards has particularly useful help pages complete with examples of usage. Simply typing *'HELP'* will produce a list of topics. Typing a command followed by /? will produce assistance.   Typing HELP followed by the command will produce explanations, syntax data and examples.

Using a printer with DOS

All printers can create an exact replica of any text that appears on the screen.

This can be done in a number of ways:

- Wait until a screen of text is displayed and then send a copy of the screen to the printer. This can only display one screenful at any one time.   This is achieved by pressing the PrtScr key or, on some machines, pressing the Shift and PrtScr keys together.
- Echo everything going to the screen to the printer. Everything typed at the keyboard and all other screen output is automatically sent to the printer as well as the screen. This method handles a lot more information than the above method. Pressing the Ctrl and PrtScr keys together sets the printer echo on.   To set the printer echo off again, the same two keys are pressed once again.   So, the two keys toggle the printer echo off and on.   (holding the keys down too long can result in the echo being turned on and then off again, giving the appearance that the action did not work).
- Redirecting output to the printer. This method sends output that was heading towards the screen to the printer instead; no output is displayed on the screen.   This is achieved by placing > PRN at the end of a command.   So, giving the command VER > PRN would send the DOS version number to the printer instead of the screen.   This redirection can be used with many DOS commands.
- Using the PRINT command as explained next.

Using the 'PRINT' command

DOS provides a specific command to print out the contents of any disk file that contains plain text. So, to print out the file called INFO.TXT, the command would be

PRINT INFO.TXT

This command is of no use with program files, since they contain machine code instead of text and therefore display gibberish if printed out.

The full path must be specified if the file is not in the current directory:

PRINT C:\REPORTS\SALES.TXT

Several files can be included in the one PRINT command as in the following example:

PRINT C:\REPORTS\SALES.TXT   INCOME.TXT   COSTS.TXT   C:\SUMMARY.TXT

The command provides for printing in the *'background'*. This means that the user can carry on using other DOS commands while the printing is being done. In fact, if the command is given several times for different files, the files are queued for printing and the system will automatically print them one after the other - while the user is doing something else. If the PRINT command is given without any parameter, it displays a list of files that are in the print queue.

Filenames and Extensions in DOS

All programs and data are held on a storage device until they are ready to be used. The most common storage device is the magnetic disk, although CD disks or memory 'flash cards' are also in use. A file is collection of related data. The data may be instructions to the computer (program files) or database, spreadsheet or similar information (data files). Hard disks are likely to be storing thousands of such files at any one time. Each file has a unique name; no two files are allowed to have exactly the same name in the same disk directory. This unique name is used by the computer to later find and load the file from anywhere on the disk. If a file is saved with the same name as an existing file of that name, the new file's contents replace the existing file contents.

To aid future recognition of files, there are certain conventions followed by DOS and Windows 3.1 for the naming of files. Firstly, all file names may have three parts:

REPORT.DOC

File Name   Dot   File Extension

Filename

The File Name consists of alphanumeric characters and certain other characters up to a maximum of eight characters and with a minimum of 1 character. So, a filename of *'G'* is valid. The filename part is compulsory and DOS will not accept a file without a name. The file name used should express the contents of the file. A file given the name of *'HH'* or *'Z1'* may have significance when it was first saved - but will probably not convey much six months later. More meaningful names such as *'BUDGET99'* or *'APR_MEMO'* should be used. The Excel spreadsheet program, for example, is called EXCEL.EXE, while the DOS help program is called *'HELP.COM'*.

File Extensions

DOS allows a file to have up to a three-letter extension. So files called 'MEMO', 'MEMO.99' and 'MEMO.TXT' are all valid filenames. The extension can be chosen to describe the <u>format</u> of the file's contents. The use of file extensions is optional but is recommended.

Files can have widely differing types of contents:

- The **programs** themselves; i.e. applications such as word-processors, spreadsheets and accounting packages. Most large commercial packages are comprised, not of a single file, but of a collection of linked files.
- The **data** used by applications; i.e. database records, spreadsheet worksheets and graphics files. These are stored in special formats used by the particular package. Data files used in one package cannot be used in another package without converting the file format first. It is therefore important to know the format in which data is stored.
- <u>Text</u> files that are in plain English; i.e. files that can be read via DOS. However, most word-processors allow the text to be underlined, italicised, emboldened, etc. and involves including special codes into these files, thus making them less readable in DOS.

Dot

When a file extension is used, a dot must be used to separate the filename and extension.

Pre-Defined File Extensions

Where the user has a choice, files can be given any file extension that helps convey the file's internal format.   However, a number of file extensions are commonly used and these have to be avoided. Examples of these extensions are:

DOS Extensions

There are a number of extensions that are claimed by DOS itself.   The most important of these are the COM, EXE and BAT extensions, since any file with one of these extensions is regarded by DOS as being a program file.   This means that the program can be run by simply typing the program name, without the dot or extension, and pressing the Enter key.

For example:

      HELP.COM is a command file that is run by typing HELP then Enter.

      MSD.EXE is an executable file that is run by typing MSD then Enter.

      MYPROG.BAT is a batch file that is run by typing MYPROG then Enter.

COM and EXE files are composed of instructions, usually many thousands of instructions, in the special 'machine code' recognisable by the computer's CPU but unreadable by humans.   BAT files are also program files but are in plain English format; they are less versatile than machine code programs but are much easier to write (see chapter on batch files).   DOS also claims a number of other file extensions, such as SYS, CPI and BIN, for its own internal use.

Note that simply giving a file a COM, EXE or BAT extension does not convert that file into a program file.   If a file called REPORT.DOC contained a company report in plain English, changing the file name to REPORT.EXE would have no effect on the file's internal contents.   If the user tried to run the file by typing REPORT followed by Enter, the only result would be an error message.   Each of the three program extensions has a different meaning to DOS, since it has to handle each type differently.

Windows Extensions

Microsoft Windows also claims a number of extensions to itself.   These are in addition to the DOS extensions that it also uses.   Typical Windows extensions are BMP (Bit Mapped Pictures) used for creating background wallpaper effects,   INI (information files) used for storing details of Windows configurations and Windows application details, and GRP (Group) used to store details of what utilities are included in the same Windows group.   Other Windows extensions include DRV, TMP, PIF, FOT and TTF.

Application Extensions

Individual applications claim extensions for their own use.   This makes the use of a program easier, since the housekeeping is then carried out by the program itself.   If the user wishes to open up a file called REPORT, there may be various files with that same file name but different extensions.   There may be REPORT.DOC, REPORT.XLC, REPORT.DBF and so on.   The word-processing application created the text file with the extension .DOC.   The user only had to choose the file name as REPORT, the application automatically added the .DOC extension.   Similarly, the Excel spreadsheet program added the .XLS extension to the worksheet saved by the user as REPORT.   The database package also automatically added the .DBF extension to the file of records that the user saved simply as REPORT. Now, when the user is in a particular application and requests to open the REPORT file, the application will know which file to open by the extension on the end.   The Spreadsheet package will ignore the other files named REPORT and only work with the file called REPORT.XLS.   The same is true of the word-processing and database packages.   The technicalities of this are hidden from the user, who need never even know that the files have been given any extensions.

There is a wide range of application extensions and some are even used by more than one application. This can confuse matters unless files of the same type are kept in their own particular compartments (see later).

Example extensions are:

      ANNUAL.XLS   A worksheet created in Excel

      CLIENTS.DBM   A database file created in dBase

      SCREEN.HLP   A help file (common with many applications)

      ADVERT.CDR   A graphics file created in Corel Draw

      SALES.DOC   A word-processed file created in Word.

Language Extensions

Many programming languages (called high-level languages) create programs by the user initially writing the instructions in an English-like format using a form of word-processor.   This text is then converted into the machine code instructions required by the computer.   This conversion can be a permanent process and the machine code instruction can be saved as a separate, independent EXE file (a process known as *'compiling'*) or the instructions can be simply converted and acted upon immediately, with no second file being created (a process known as *'interpreting'*).   In both cases, the original text is preserved, in case the writer wishes to add to or modify the instructions.   The extensions given to the text files depend upon the programming language in which they run.

Typical examples are:

GAME.BAS	The text of a Basic program. Can be compiled or interpreted.
UTIL.PAS	The text of a Pascal program to be compiled.
PAYROLL.CBL	The text of a Cobol program to be compiled.

Other Extensions

A number of other extensions are commonly in use and are regarded as a standard between packages.   In other words, every package recognises the file as being of the same format.   Examples are:

READ.ME	A text file usually included on the program disk, containing last-minute information about the release.
MEMO.TXT	A file containing plain English text.
JENNIFER.PCX	A graphics file in Paintbrush format, recognised by most word-processing, DTP and graphics packages.
MARGARET.GIF	A graphics file in Graphics Interchange Format, used regularly on the Internet.
STREETS.LST	A list containing related items, such as names or addresses.
NAMES.SRT	A file containing a list of items in a sorted order (e.g. names in ascending order or debts in descending order).

Obtaining A List Of Files

To obtain a list of the current files on a disk, the following command should be entered:

          DIR <Enter>

This command works with both floppy disks and hard disks.   It displays a list of files, giving their names and extensions, file sizes and the dates and times that they were created or last modified as shown:

```
AUTOEXEC BAT       602 02/11/99   18:35
COMMAND  COM     52925 10/03/95    6:00
CONFIG   SYS       350 02/05/99   18:35
MENU     BAT       572 11/10/99    7:44
```

In fact, the command only shows the files in the current directory (see later).

If the user switches to the floppy drive, by typing A: then the DIR command will display the contents of the floppy disk.   If the user switches to the hard disk, by typing C: then the DIR command displays the contents of the hard disk.   It is possible to be logged on to one drive and still see the contents of the other drive.   For example, if the user is currently logged on to the hard disk, then typing DIR A: will display the contents of the floppy disk.   When the command is completed, the user is still logged on to the hard disk and a subsequent DIR command would be of the hard disk.   This is a crucial benefit of DOS; the user can be in one part of a particular drive and still carry out operations in another part of the same disk, or even in another part of another disk.   This is looked at in more detail shortly.

The above command may not prove adequate where there are many files on a disk, since the screen can only show a portion of the files, with the rest scrolling off the top of the screen.   So, DOS provides a couple of refinements to the DIR command.   One of these (DIR/P) displays the contents of the current directory one page at a time and waits until a key is pressed before displaying the next screenful.   The other option (DIR/W) displays the file names in five columns across the screen. This option omits the file sizes, etc. but displays more files on the screen at the same time, as shown:

CALC.EXE	CALC.HLP	CALENDAR.EXE	CALENDAR.HLP	CANYON.MID
CARDFILE.EXE	CARDFILE.HLP	CARS.BMP	CASTLE.BMP	CHARMAP.EXE
CHKLIST.MS	CHORD.WAV	CLIPBRD.EXE	CLIPBRD.HLP	CLOCK.EXE
CLOCK.INI	COMMDLG.DLL	CONTROL.EXE	CONTROL.HLP	CONTROL.INI
GLOSSARY.HLP	GRAPHICS.GRP	GWS.INI	HIMEM.SYS	HONEY.BMP

If it is important to see the dates or file sizes, then the first option must be chosen.   Where the user only wishes to check for the presence of a particular file on a disk, the second option is usually quicker.

Viewing Selected Files

A further refinement to the DIR command is to allow the user to only produce a selected subset of files. This is achieved with the /A switch and results in a listing with files that meet the following attributes:

A	Only list files where the archive bit is set
-A	Only list files where the archive bit is not set
D	Only list directories - ignore all files
-D	Only list files - ignore all directories
H	Only list hidden files
-H	Only list files that are not hidden
R	Only list files that are read-only
-R	Only list files that are not read-only
S	Only list system files
-S	Only list files that are not system files

So, the command DIR/AD would only display the directories in the current directory, while giving the command DIR/AH/S from the hard disk's root directory would display a list of all hidden files on the entire hard disk.   Other switches are /B which is the *'bare'* format; this displays file and directories without any date or size information and the /L switch; this displays text in lower case.

Directories In DOS

A floppy disk can contain hundreds of files; a hard disk can contain tens of thousands of files.   This would make finding and operating on a file very difficult, as each file would be mixed in with the thousands of others.   It is essential, therefore, that files are stored in a logical way, so that they are easy to retrieve and manipulate.   DOS has an electronic disk filing system that is derived from an office manual filing system, where every file is kept in a filing cabinet under a different name or heading. Files could be stored by the office department or function.

Consider, for example, searching for the discipline record of John Smith, the repair worker.   The office may have six filing cabinets but only the one labelled *'Personnel'* will need to be searched, thus removing five-sixths of the data from the search.   The Personnel filing cabinet will have three drawers and only the one labelled *'Discipline'* need be opened - the others are labelled as *'Promotion'* and *'Sick Records'* and are thus ignored in the search.   When the drawer is opened, three wallets are found, labelled as *'Clerical'*, *'Production'* and *'Maintenance'*.   Only the Maintenance wallet need be opened, again narrowing down the search.   Finally, an alphabetical search is made of the files in the Maintenance wallet, until the file of John Smith is found.   The above process provides a very speedy access to any individual file - assuming that files have been stored in a logical order in the first place.

Users of computer systems need to have the same ease of access to their computer data files as they have with their manual paper system.   This is the role of the DOS filing system. DOS provides an electronic equivalent to the manual system. It holds its files in different compartments (called *'directories'* or *'folders'*) on the disk, just as the manual system holds files in

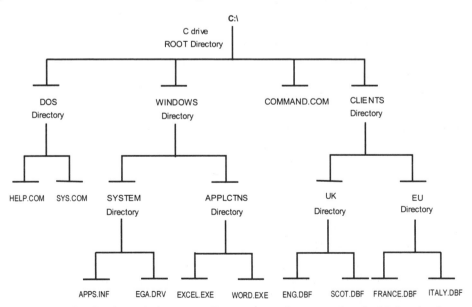

different physical compartments.   If a database is in use, a directory can be created to hold the database files; if a word-processor is being used, then a directory can be created to store all word-processed files, and so on.

The creation of DOS compartments (directories) containing other compartments (sub-directories) results in a structure called the *'tree'*.

The diagram only represents a small fraction of an actual structure; a real hard disk may have hundreds of directories, each containing many different files.

Although the structure is called a tree, it actually drawn as an inverted tree. At the top of the structure is the ROOT directory.   This is the compartment that the user sees when the machine is first switched on (i.e. the root of the whole structure).   When the computer is first booted up and a DIR command is given, the list of files displayed are those in the root directory. In the example in the diagram, there will be only one single file displayed - COMMAND.COM, since all the other files reside inside other compartments.

Spreading from the root directory are branches (directories and sub-directories) and leaves (the data files and program files).   Each branch of the tree (i.e. each directory) may contain leaves (i.e. files) or other branches (i.e. sub-directories).

In the example, the root directory contains one file and three sub-directories called DOS, WINDOWS and CLIENTS.   The directory names can describe the application contained within it (e.g. WINDOWS) or can describe the function or organisational structure of the company (e.g. CLIENTS).

The rules for directory construction are:
- The number of directories and their structure should mirror the needs of the organisation.
- Each directory and sub-directory should be named to clearly label its contents.
- Only the relevant files for a directory should be stored in that directory.
- Do regular housekeeping to ensure that directories are kept up-to-date.   Ensure that only relevant files are being stored in each directory; move files to other directories where appropriate; remove files that are no longer used to prevent the disk becoming clogged up with old unwanted files.

DOS PATHs

To get to any file, a path is taken from the root directory, through any other directories and sub-directories until the file is reached. So, in DOS each file can be fully described in terms of its name and where it is stored.   The full file description is comprised of three parts:
- What disk is it on.
- What directory is it in.
- What the file is called.

Here are a few examples of files included in the example diagram on the preceding page:

```
C:\COMMAND.COM
C:\DOS\HELP.COM
C:\WINDOWS\SYSTEM\APPS.INF
C:\CLIENTS\UK\SCOT.DBF
C:\CLIENTS\EU\ITALY.DBF
```

If the same files resided on a floppy disk, filenames might be

```
A:\COMMAND.COM
A:\DOS\HELP.COM
etc.
```

Since each file can be described in terms of its path as well as its name, files with the same name and extension can now exist on the same disk - as long as they are stored in separate directories.   For example, two files called REPORT.DOC could exist on the same disk in different parts of the directory structure as shown:

```
C:\CLIENTS\UK\REPORT.DOC
C:\CLIENTS\EU\REPORT.DOC
```

Where this happens, the two files can have exactly the same contents or can be completely different files that happen to use the same filename and extension.

Giving the full file specification is a little laborious but can be very useful. For example, the user can be logged on to the floppy drive as the current drive and still print out a file that is sitting down in a sub-directory of the hard disk e.g.

```
PRINT C:\EU\REPORT.DOC
```

When the printing is over, the user is still sitting looking at the floppy drive, as before.

Changing directory

The user can switch between making a hard disk or the floppy disk the one to be currently looked at. The user will also wish to control which sub-directory is the current one for any operations on that drive. This is accomplished with the CD or CHDIR command.

Moving downwards..

The CD command can be used to move the user down into a lower level of the directory structure.

Examples

        CD CLIENTS

would move the user out of the current directory into the CLIENTS directory. If a DIR command were given, only the contents of the CLIENTS directory would be displayed.

        CD UK

would move the user from the current directory, the CLIENTS directory, into the UK sub-directory. If a DIR command were given, only the contents of the UK sub-directory would be displayed.

If the user wished to go directly to the UK sub-directory, this can be achieved with the command

        CD CLIENTS\UK

These examples move the user from the current directory into a lower directory. There are times when the user is neither in the root directory or the CLIENTS directory.

In these cases, the user can give the full path in the command and move straight to the specified directory from anywhere in the structure. Thus:

        CD C:\CLIENTS\UK

makes the UK directory the current directory of the 'C' drive, no matter where the user's current drive is at the time of giving the command.

If the CD command is used without any parameter it will display the drive and directory that the user is currently in.

   NB: Use of this command does <u>not</u> switch the use from one drive to another. For example, a user may be
         on the A: drive and issue the command 'CD C:\CLIENTS'. The user would remain in the A: drive
         but when the command 'C:' was given, the user would be in the CLIENTS directory.

Moving back up the structure..

If the user is in any sub-directory, DOS provides a command to move the user back up the structure.

        CD..

moves the user back up one level of the structure. So, if the user was in the EEC sub-directory, the CD.. command would move the user into the CLIENTS directory. No matter how far down the structure the user happens to be, repeated use of the CD.. command will eventually return the user to the root directory. There are occasions when the user is down several layers of the structure and wishes to immediately return to the root directory, without a whole series of CD.. commands. DOS allows an immediate return to the root directory with the command CD\

Creating new directories

The DOS structure is stored on disk and can be altered at any time by the user. The creation of a new sub-directory is very simple. The user first has to be in the directory where the new sub-directory will branch from. The command is simply MD or MKDIR followed by the name of the new directory. The command can be in upper or lower case, or a mixture of both. The new directory name can be from one to eight characters in length and should describe the contents it is intended to hold.

Some users give the directory an extension of .DIR. This was useful in versions of DOS prior to version 5, since a DIR/W command left the user not knowing whether a particular name that was displayed was a file name or a directory name; a .DIR extension removed any doubt. This is not necessary in DOS 5 onwards, since directories are distinguished from files in a DIR/W command by placing square brackets round directory names.

If a new sub-directory, called 'GERMANY' was to be added to the EEC sub-directory the following commands would achieve it, assuming the user was commencing from the root directory:

        CD C:\CLIENTS\EU
        MD GERMANY

The same effect could also be directly achieved by the single command:

        MD C:\CLIENT\EU\GERMANY

Where many users are sharing an application, sub-directories can be created for each individual user's data. Each subdirectory could be named using the user's initials e.g.:

```
MD \WINDOWS\APPLCTNS\DD
MD \WINDOWS\APPLCTNS\JD
MD \WINDOWS\APPLCTNS\RR
etc.
```

When a DIR command is given, the display for sub-directories is different from that for files:

```
DOS            <DIR>         08/10/95    15:49
EXCEL          <DIR>         20/10/98    19:48
MEDIAPRO       <DIR>         16/07/99    17:37
VIRUS          <DIR>         30/09/99     1:59
WINDOWS        <DIR>         08/10/98    15:50
AUTOEXEC BAT          602    02/05/99    18:35
COMMAND  COM        52925    10/03/95     6:00
CONFIG   SYS          350    02/05/99    18:35
```

A directory has no size displayed and the label <DIR> is displayed instead. When DOS creates a new directory it also creates two new sub-directories within that new directory. These are the *'dot'* and the *'dot-dot'* directories. They are used by DOS to help navigate the system and they are not directly accessed by the user.

e.g.   Directory of C:\DOS

```
.              <DIR>         08/10/98    15:49
..             <DIR>         08/10/98    15:49
DOSSY          <DIR>         30/04/99     2:00
4201     CPI         6404    09/04/97     5:00
4208     CPI          720    09/04/97     5:00
```

Removing a directory

As the organisation's structure changes, so the disk structure will change to reflect it.   This will involve adding new directories, as explained. It will also mean that directories will have to be removed from time to time. For example if an employee leaves, his/her personal directories should be removed and any useful files transferred to another employee's directory.

The RD or RMDIR command will remove a directory from the structure e.g.:

```
RD EEC
```

With all DOS versions, this command only works if the EEC directory contains no files or other sub-directories and the user is currently in the directory above the EEC directory. If the user includes the path in the command - e.g. 'RD C:\EEC' - the directory is removed without the user having to be immediately above the directory in the structure.   Similarly, a user can remove a directory from a different drive from the one currently logged to.   For example, a user can be currently logged to the C: drive and successfully give the command 'RD A:\JOHN'.

DELTREE

From DOS 6 onwards, Microsoft included a utility to delete entire sections of the disk structure with a single command.   The DELTREE command can be given within a particular directory and all the files and sub-directories below that level in the structure will be deleted.   Alternatively, the command can specify a path.   So, the command DELTREE C:\WINDOWS would remove all the Windows directories and subdirectories and all their contents.

The command should be used with extreme caution, as it is very easy to make a mistake and eliminate large sections of the disk contents.   Consider, for example, the consequences of giving the DELTREE command from the root directory of the hard disk!   The user is asked for confirmation before proceeding, unless the /Y switch is added to the command - e.g. DELTREE /Y C:\WINDOWS

Viewing the Structure

DOS provides the TREE command, allowing the user to view the directory structure of a hard disk or a floppy disk.   The example of using the TREE command without any parameters is shown in the left diagram next.   The first vertical line links all the directories that branch off the disk's root directory. The next vertical line is indented and shows the directories that branch off those first-level directories. Any other lower-level directories would be similarly linked with other lines.   In this way, the hierarchy of the disk's structure can be easily seen.   The structure can be saved to a file by giving the command TREE > treefile and the file (*'treefile'* in the example) can be viewed or printed out later.

The structure can be directly printed by sending the output of the command to the printer with the command TREE > PRN.   Since not all printers are capable of printing the graphics necessary to produce the vertical lines, TREE has a switch to display the lines using normal characters in places of graphics characters.   The switch /A is added to the command and the right-hand diagram shows the result of giving the command TREE/A.

```
Directory PATH listing for Volume MS_DOS_6
Volume Serial Number is 1B8F-B11C
C:.
├── DOS
├── WINDOWS
│   ├── SYSTEM
│   └── APPLCTNS
└── CLIENTS
    ├── UK
    └── EU
```

```
Directory PATH listing for Volume MS_DOS_6
Volume Serial Number is 1B8F-B11C
C:.
+---DOS
+---WINDOWS
|   +---SYSTEM
|   +---APPLCTNS
\---CLIENTS
    +---UK
    +---EU
```

The command produces the structure from the current directory downwards; if the user is halfway down a structure, only the remaining lower section is displayed.   If the command is given from the root directory, the entire disk's structure is displayed.   Finally, the command allows the user to view the structure and also see what files are stored inside each sub-directory.   The command is TREE/F but note that it can produce a very long display for a hard disk, due to the thousands of directories and files that are probably on the disk.

Deleting Files

Not all files will remain on a computer's hard disk.   Normally, the programs and data that are regularly required by a user will remain on the hard disk, so that they are readily available.   Other files that are used less often can reside on floppy disk and only be loaded into memory when needed.   Additionally, many files become outdated (e.g. old correspondence, budget figures, etc.).   If they were required for future reference, they would be saved to floppy disk for archiving.   However, if the files are no longer needed, they can be removed from disks, allowing the space to be given to future files.

To delete a file, the DEL or ERASE command is used as:

        DEL REPORT.DOC

This will delete the file, if the file is in the current directory.

The path can be included in the command as:

        DEL C:\CLIENTS\UK\ENG.DBF

This command has a /P switch which prompts the user to confirm that the deletion should be carried out - e.g. DEL *.*/P

Undeleting Files

From DOS 5 onwards, a deleted file can be recovered using the UNDELETE command.   This is only possible if the deleted file is only recently deleted, as after a while the disk space used by the deleted file will be used up by a new file.   If the file is capable of being undeleted, DOS prompts for the first letter of the file to be recovered, as this gets lost after a deletion.   When the first letter is entered, the file is restored back into DOS as if nothing happened.   If a file can not be recovered, the user is informed of this fact.   The command UNDELETE/LIST will display a list of all the files that can be recovered in the current directory.   This is the standard system and a more secure system is available by giving the command UNDELETE/S; this saves all deleted files into a hidden directory (named 'SENTRY').   This occupies valuable disk space but makes recovery simple with the UNDELETE/DS command.

A more user-friendly version of this facility is available from within Windows 95/98 (see later).

Copying Files

There are many occasions when a copy of a file is required:
- To send a copy of a worksheet file from the local office's hard disk to the company's head office.
- To make a copy of a program under development, so that it can be recovered in the event that the latest version fails to be an improvement.
- To make replicas of files in one directory into another directory.

The file is not actually moved to the new destination; the command creates a replica of the file in the new destination and the original file remains where it was.

The syntax of the command is:

COPY source destination

Examples

COPY COMMAND.COM A:

will copy the file COMMAND.COM from the current directory to the floppy disk; the file name on the floppy disk will be the same as that on the source disk.

COPY C:\CLIENT\EEC\ITALY.DBF A:ITALY.BAK

will copy the file ITALY.DBF from hard disk to the floppy disk and also renames the file in the floppy to ITALY.BAK

COPY C:\UTILS\COUNTER.EXE C:\DISKS*.*

will copy the file COUNTER.EXE from one directory on the hard disk to another directory on the same hard disk; the file name will remain unchanged.

COPY C:\UTILS\COUNTER.EXE

will copy the file COUNTER.EXE from the UTILS directory.   Since no destination is given, the file will be copied into whatever directory is the current directory.

With older DOS versions, a file is copied into the target directory, automatically overwriting any file of the same name that happened to already exist in the target directory.   From DOS 6 onwards, users are prompted to decide whether to overwrite or not.   This facility can be disabled by adding the /Y parameter to the command.

Merging Files

Where files contain plain text, they can be merged (usually termed *'concatenation'*) into a single document using a plus sign.   The command

COPY fileA + fileB

will add the file fileB on to the end of fileA.   The file fileB remains unchanged but the fileA is now extended.   The command

COPY fileA + fileB + fileC   fileD

creates a new file called fileD which contains the contents of fileC on to the end of fileB and this added to the contents of fileA.   The three files fileA, fileB and fileC remain unaltered.   If fileD already exists it is overwritten by the new contents.

Moving Files

From DOS 6 onwards, there is a command to move files rather than just copy them.   With the MOVE command, the nominated files are placed in the destination directory and removed from the source directory.

Examples

MOVE C:\UTILS\COUNTER.EXE C:\DISKS

will take the file COUNTER.EXE out of the UTILS directory and place it in the DISKS directory.   The command can also be used to rename an existing directory.

MOVE C:\LETTERS C:\ARCHIVE

will result in a directory called ARCHIVE which contains all the files previously stored in the directory called LETTERS; the LETTERS directory no longer exists.

Where a file of the same name exists in the destination directory, the user is asked whether the file should be overwritten.   This facility can be disabled by adding /Y parameter to the command.

Renaming Files

The DOS command called REN or RENAME can be used to change the name of a file; it cannot change the name of a directory.   For example

REN REPORT.DOC ANNUAL.REP

will take the file called REPORT.DOC and change its name to ANNUAL.REP.   The file's size and contents are unchanged.   The above command assumes that the file is in the current directory.   The full path name can be used, to work with files in a directory other that in the current directory -

REN C:\WORK\REPORT.DOC ANNUAL.REP

Wildcards

Consider having to copy 50 files with the .PAS extension from one directory to another, or having to delete 30 files with the extension .BAK from a directory, or wishing to display a list of all files in a directory with the extension .DOC.   Fifty separate COPY commands or thirty different DEL commands can be given but this is tedious and error-prone since some files might be overlooked.   What is required is a method of handling files in groups - moving a group of files, or deleting a group of files.   Similarly, it is useful to have a DIR command that only displays a desired subset (say all .DOC files) from a directory.

DOS provides this facility with the use of *'wildcards'*.   A wildcard is a character or set of characters incorporated into COPY, DEL, DIR, etc. commands. Wildcards use the question mark (?) and asterisk (*) characters.

The * Wildcard

The * wildcard is used to replace a group of characters in a DOS command.   It can replace anything from zero to 8 characters

Examples

> DIR *.PAS

will display only those files in the current directory that have the .PAS extension.

> DIR BUDGET.*

will display all files with the name BUDGET, regardless of the extension.

> DIR G*.*

will display all files that start with the letter 'G', regardless of the extension.

> DEL A:*.PAS

will delete all files from the floppy disk with the .PAS extension.

> COPY C:\WINWORD\FILES*.DOC A:\ARCHIVE*.BAK

will copy all the .DOC files from the WINWORD\FILES directory of the hard disk in to the ARCHIVE directory of the floppy disk, with each file having its extension changed to .BAK.

Note

There is a potential danger that has to be guarded against when using the * wildcard.   Consider the command

> COPY C:\BUDGET.* A:*.BAK

This command will copy all files with the name BUDGET in the hard disk's root directory into the floppy disk's root directory and give them the extension .BAK.   If the C drive's root directory contained files called BUDGET.XLS, BUDGET.XLC, BUDGET.DOC and BUDGET.DBF, then they will all be copied on to the floppy disk as BUDGET.BAK.   Since only one file can have the name BUDGET.BAK the first three files are lost and only BUDGET.DBF is stored on the floppy disk; all other files will have been overwritten by the next file copy.

The ? Wildcard

The ? character is used in a DOS command to replace any single character in a filename.   Unlike the * character, the ? character does not represent a group of characters. If a number of characters are to be wildcarded, then there will have to be multiple occurrences of the ? character.   The length and structure of files have to be known to use this option.   For example:

> DIR MEM???95.DAT

will find the files MEMJAN95.DAT, MEMFEB95.DAT, MEMAPR95.DAT, etc.   Any memos written in 1993 or 1994 are ignored by this command.   The * wildcard option could not be used here, as DIR MEM*95.DAT would display all files beginning with MEM and using the DAT extension - the 95 part of the command would be ignored, since the * wildcard takes precedence and replaces the last letters of the filename.

Caution

> The user should always use the chosen wildcard with the DIR command before using it with the actual command desired. For example, DEL *.DOC will delete all of a user's .DOC files - but will also delete everyone else's .DOC files !   A quick check with DIR *.DOC would soon reveal the inclusion of any unwanted files.

XCOPY

The COPY command has limitations, in that a copy of multiple files is carried out one file at a time, by copying the first file, then making a separate copy of the second file and so on.   The XCOPY command is a more efficient alternative.   It creates a buffer area using all the available memory of the machine. As many files as possible are then copied from the source into the buffer area before being transferred into the destination.   This is repeated until all the files are copied.   The benefits of the XCOPY command over the COPY command are:

- It is faster with any single file that is larger than 64k.
- It is faster for copying multiple files.
- It can copy an entire section of the source directory structure with the use of the /S switch; a replica of that section of the structure is created on the destination disk.
- It can copy a group of files that are too large for a single floppy; if the files archive bits are set with the ATTRIB command (see later) and the /M switch is used with the command.

Other permissible switches are:

/A	Only copies files with the archive bit set (does not reset the archive bit)
/D : dd-mm-yy	Only copies files that were modified on or after the given date
/E	Creates a replica of any empty sub-directories on the destination
/M	Only copies files with the archive bit set (resets the archive bit)
/Y	Overwrites any existing files without requesting confirmation
/V	Verifies that a file has been written correctly (see later)
/W	Waits for the user to start the copying process
	Produces a *'Press any key to begin copying file(s)'* message
/P	Prompts for confirmation of each file to be copied

Verifying Copying

When copying files, the user may wish to know that the copying process was successful.   To achieve this, MSDOS provides a VERIFY option.   Many books state that this option ensures that the copied file is an exact replica of the original file; this is not the case.   A DOS copy consists of copying the file from disk to memory and then from memory to disk (either a different disk or a different part of the same disk).   DOS verification checks that the newly created file is readable and that its contents are identical to the copy in <u>memory</u>.   If the written version is not identical to the memory version, the user is alerted to the error.   In most cases, this is the same as making a file-to-file check but there may be occasions when the initial copy from disk to memory resulted in a corrupted version being held in memory.   On such occasions, the corrupted version is written to disk and verification will not be aware of any error.

Although verification slows the copying process it is a desirable activity, particularly with the creation of backup copies of files.   Since it slows down copying, the default is not to use verification. Verification can be turned on by using the /V switch with the COPY or XCOPY commands.   Where a series of copies is to be carried out, verification can be enabled before the copies and disabled after the copies.   Typical usage would be:

```
VERIFY ON
copy ....
copy ....
VERIFY OFF
```

Copying an entire floppy

An exact copy of a floppy disk can be made with the DISKCOPY command.   This command has the following characteristics:

- If the source disk is a system disk, the target disk is created as a system disk
- If the target disk is not formatted, the program will format the disk
- If the source disk has clusters marked as bad, the target disk will have the same areas also marked as bad, no matter their actual condition

The syntax is DISKCOPY A: B: if both drives are of the same type.   For a single floppy drive, the command should be DISKCOPY A: A: and the disks should be swapped when requested.

Note   Where a machine has two disks of different types (i.e. 5.25" and 3.5" together or 720k and 1.4MB together) the DISKCOPY command won't work. In this case, use the COMMAND XCOPY A: B: /S /E

File Attributes

Every file on a disk has a set of *'attributes'*. These are flags that indicate the current status of the file (e.g. whether it is a system file or not).

These are normally hidden from users but if the command

ATTRIB *.*

is given, the status of all the files in the current directory is displayed. Each filename is accompanied by up to four possible letters - A, R, S and H.

These attributes can also be set by the user, with the ATTRIB command and the options are:

Read

One of the attributes flags stores whether a file is able to be both read and written to (known as READ/WRITE) or can only be read (known as READ ONLY). If a file is read-only it can still be accessed by users and can appear in directory listings, can have its data extracted and used for calculations, can have its text printed out, etc. However, it cannot be deleted and cannot have its contents altered. Any attempt to delete a read-only file will be disallowed and an error message will result. Similarly, any attempt to alter the contents of a file, such as a word-processed file, would be disallowed. This means that files can be set to prevent accidental erasure, with the command ATTRIB +R *.* The 'R' indicates the read-only flag and the '+' indicates that the read-only is being set on. In the example, all the files in the current directory would be set to read-only. To remove the read-only flag , the plus sign is replaced by a minus sign and the command becomes ATTRIB -R *.* The command can also be used with individual files (e.g. ATTRIB +R REPORT.DOC) or with selective wildcards (e.g. ATTRIB +R *.EXE).

Archive

A file's archive bit can also be set by the user and is mostly used in conjunction with the BACKUP command, to control which files are selectively backed up. The BACKUP command can make a backup copy of all files or can be set to only make a copy of files that have not been previously backed up. The way that the BACKUP command knows whether a file has been previously backed up is via the archive flag. When a file is created or modified, its archive bit is set to on (indicating that it should be backed up). When a file is backed up, its archive bit is automatically set to off (indicating that it has been backed up). A future backup process will only select the files with archive bits set on and will ignore files with archive bits set off. The user can alter the files' archive flags with commands such as ATTRIB +A *.BAK and ATTRIB -A *.BAK

Hidden / System

These flags hide the file from the normal view of the user and so it does not appear in directory listings, cannot be copied and cannot be deleted. The user should not normally adjust these flags. The commands DIR/AS/S and DIR/AH/S will list all files that are set as system and hidden files.

LABEL

The VOL command lets the user see the electronic title attached to a disk. The label also appears at the top of a DIR display. The LABEL command lets the user change the volume label. For example :

LABEL ADMIN

This sets the disk's title to ADMIN. Up to 11 characters are allowed.

To remove a label from a disk, enter the command 'LABEL' with no parameter.

Formatting Disks

Disks, when newly purchased, cannot usually be used for saving users' files (some manufacturers provide disks that are pre-formatted, at an extra cost). Before the computer can read or write disk information, the disks have be formatted. The FORMAT command is used to initialise the recording surface of a disk. This command creates compartments on the disk surface in the form of concentric tracks, each divided into different sectors. These sectors are then able to store the users' files. It also creates information areas to track what is stored on the disk (known as the Directory and File Allocation Table areas). Any faulty surface areas are marked as bad and are not used later. See the chapter on Disk and Drives for greater detail.

The FORMAT command does not check that there is any data already on the disk before formatting. Therefore, any previous contents of the disk are lost forever.

> Caution: Be very careful not to format the hard disk (drive 'C') by mistake.

When the FORMAT command is given for a floppy drive, the machine will attempt to format the disk to the highest capacity possible in that drive.

For example, the command

> FORMAT A:

will try to format a 3.5" disk to 1.4MB if it is a 1.4MB drive, or try to format a 5.25" disk to 1.2MB if it is 1.2MB drive.   This is the simplest form of the command and is all that is required if the disks are at the same quality as the drive's capability.

However, if a 720k floppy is placed in a 1.4MB drive, or a 360k floppy is placed in a 1.2MB drive, then the machine has to be told to format the disk to a lower capacity than the drive is actually capable of. Formatting a 360k disk to 1.2MB will result in the disk being almost useless due to the number of bad sectors; this simply means that the disk could not be set up to handle the higher capacity without many surface errors.   The only solution is to format the disk at the correct capacity.   The 3.5" tends to be a little more sturdy in this regard but still can produce surface errors.

In addition, many drives detect that a 720k disk is in the drive and will not let the user format the disk to 1.4MB capacity.

To format a disk to the correct capacity, the FORMAT command is followed by one of these switches:

Switch	When to use
No switch	5.25" 360k disks in 360k drives
No switch	5.25" 1.2MB disks in 1.2MB drives
/4	5.25" 360k disks in 1.2MB drives
/F:360	5.25" 360k disks in 1.2MB drives
No switch	3.5" 720k disks in 720k drives
No switch	3.5" 1.4MB disks in 1.4MB drives
/F:720	3.5" 720k disks in 1.4MB drives
/N:9/T:80	3.5" 720k disks in 1.4MB drives

So the command

> FORMAT A:/4

will format a 360kB 5.25" disk in a 1.2MB disk drive.

Other switches, available in later DOS versions, are:

> /Q   Provides a 'quick' disk format by omitting to check for faulty disk areas.   This is permissible for cleaning up disks that have already been in use and are known to be in good condition. The switch should not be used with new disks.
>
> /U   Provides an 'unconditional' format of the disk by destroying any information currently on the disk.   This is useful to start afresh with a disk that was giving read and write error messages - although it is probably safer to replace the disk completely.

System Disks

Some floppy disks are required to be *'system disks'*. This means that they contain the special DOS files needed to make the computer boot up from that floppy.   If a floppy disk is made into a system disk (sometimes also described as a *'boot disk'*), it can be placed in the A drive and the computer can be switched on and set up from the floppy disk. If this facility is required the extra switch /S has to be added to the command

> e.g. FORMAT A:/F:720/S

An already-formatted disk can be converted into a system disk by using the SYS command.   For example, the command

> SYS A:

will copy the hidden system files IO.SYS and MSDOS.SYS and COMMAND.COM on to the floppy disk.

Dos Error Messages

A number of errors are possible when typing in DOS commands:
- The user may make a typing error (e.g. 'DIT' instead of 'DIR')
- The user may give an incomplete command (e.g. 'DEL' without naming the file to delete)
- The user may make a logical error (e.g. 'COPY FRED FRED' is trying to copy a file onto itself)
- The user may make an incorrect hardware compatibility choice (e.g. 'FORMAT A:' when a drive is 1.4MB capacity and the disk is only 720k capacity).
- The user may have specified a non-existent file (e.g. 'DEL FRED.DOC' when the file is no longer on the disk).
- The user may omit to specify a file's path (e.g. 'COPY FRED.DOC A:' when the file FRED.DOC exists but is not in the current directory).
- The user may have left a data disk in the A: drive when the machine was switched on (so that the computer is unable to load the operating system from either the hard disk or the floppy disk).
- The user may not have set up the hardware to make the DOS command possible (e.g. issuing a PRINT command when there is no printer attached to the computer; or issuing a 'COPY *.* A:' command when there is no disk in the A: drive)

DOS is not particularly user-friendly when a mistake is made. Part of the job of the COMMAND.COM file is the analysis of commands (called *'parsing'*). While all the above errors are detected, the amount of help given is very limited. DOS does not respond to errors with helpful advice; it produces cryptic messages that the user has to interpret.

The most common DOS error messages are:

Bad command or file name

This message indicates that a command has been given that is not part of COMMAND.COM or is not an external COM, EXE or BAT file in the current directory. This error message is often due to a mistyping of the command and the entered command should be re-checked. If the command is found not to be a spelling error, it is likely that the program is not in the current directory or in a directory specified in the PATH statement; the command should be altered to specify the path where the program file resides.

Invalid parameter

This indicates that either too much or too little information has been specified as parameters after the command. Forgetting to leave spaces between parts of the command (e.g. 'DELFRED.DOC 'instead of' DEL FRED.DOC or breaking up an otherwise legitimate parameter with extra spaces (e.g. 'COPY FRED.DOC M ARY 'instead of' COPY FRED.DOC MARY often causes this error').

File not found

This indicates that the file specified as a parameter is either mistyped or is not in the directory given in the command.

Not ready error reading drive A

This indicates that there is no disk in the floppy drive or, in the case of 5.25" drives, the disk lever is not engaged.

Non-system disk or disk error

This usually indicates that the machine has been started up with a non-boot disk in the A: drive.

Abort, Retry, Ignore, Fail ?

This indicates that a *'critical error'* has occurred. This may indicate a hardware malfunction such as the network going down or there being no disk in the drive. Often it indicates that part of the disk is unreadable. With hard disks, the surface integrity should be checked with a utility; with floppy disks it's often best to recover as many files as possible and replace the disk. Choosing Abort ignores the disk operation and control is passed back to the program or application. Choosing Retry instructs the system to attempt the disk operation for another time. Choosing Ignore ignores that particular cluster read; this may move the program on to a subsequent read operation, resulting in a loss of data. Choosing Fail will inform the program or application that the disk operation failed.

Access Denied

This indicates that the disk is write-protected or that files have their attributes set to read-only.

Environments

Using DOS is not a user-friendly activity, since the user either requires knowledge of the DOS commands or has to continually consult the reference manual.   To overcome this problem, there have been a number of utilities developed under the heading of *'shells'* or *'environments'*.   These utilities seek to protect the user from the need to know DOS commands. They help the user to carry out DOS functions through assistance in the form of menus and pictures.

They can be broadly categorised as menus or *'GUIs'* (graphical user interfaces such as Windows).

Menus

These range from simple menus created by users via batch files (see later) to complex, multi-level, commercial packages such as PowerMenu.   In both cases, the aim is to provide selection for the user from pre-written choices. Thus, for example, formatting a disk is reduced to choosing an option such as *'D'* rather than issuing a DOS command such as FORMAT A:/N:9/T:80.   The menu options are pre-programmed by the user and are then available for all other less experienced users.   Similarly, running a particular program is simply pressing the designated key on the keyboard.   The user sets this up and other users can run the package without knowing the program name or the path in which it resides.

Microsoft Windows

One of the most successful and comprehensive of DOS environments has been Windows 3.1 from Microsoft.   It was as a *'GUI'* - a graphical user interface - and it used a range of icons (miniature pictures) to represent computing functions, so simplifying activities.   For example, if the user was word processing and clicked the printer icon, the document would be sent to the printer.   In this way, it is hoped to reduce the time users spend trying to <u>understand</u> the machine and more time spent actually <u>using</u> the machine. Later versions, such as Windows 95, 98, 2000 and ME, use improved programming to speed operations and provide new facilities - but they all retain the same basic GUI methods.

Microsoft Windows versions use a WIMP environment.   That means they use <u>W</u>indows, <u>I</u>cons, <u>M</u>enus and <u>P</u>ointers (or <u>W</u>indows, <u>I</u>cons, <u>M</u>ouse and <u>P</u>ull-down menus).   In this respect, Windows functions in a very similar way to the earlier DOS shell.   Like the shell, Windows allows files to be clicked on by the mouse and deleted, moved, copied, renamed, printed, etc.   However, Windows is much more than another DOS shell.   It has many additional features, such as:

- Supports multi-tasking - this means that more than one program can be running in memory at the same time.   If desired, one application can be seen on the screen while the other application is working away in the background.   Alternatively, both applications can be seen on the screen at the same time, each application occupying a different portion, or window, of the screen.
- Allows easy copying of data between programs.
- Has its own set of extra utilities, such as Paint (paint program), WordPad (small word processor), Cardfile (small database), Terminal (for connecting the computer to a modem), Calculator, etc.
- Full on-line help system.   This includes a full hypertext system where the user can type in a search entry, find out about that item and be provided options to view items of a similar category. So, for example, if the user is reading help on *'Copying a Help Topic Onto the Clipboard'*, the screen will display a line offering help on *'Annotating a Help Topic'*; if this line is clicked on with the mouse pointer, the user is taken a further page of information on that topic.
- Provides a set of common features and techniques for all Windows applications; this means that every application written to be used under Windows will use the same techniques (e.g. the same way to load and save files, the same way to import a picture, etc.).   This results in users being able to adapt to a new Windows application quickly, since activities learned in a previous package are re-used.   With DOS-based applications, each package would do the same job in a different way; one package would expect a particular function key, another would require a particular key combination using Alt and Ctrl keys, while yet another would expect the operation to be achieved through menu options.

The Windows environment allows for extensive configuration to meet the needs of the user (e.g. screen colours, use of memory, background wallpaper, choice of printers, sensitivity of the mouse, etc.); this is covered in the chapter on Windows configuration.   Windows can be keyboard-operated but it is really designed for mouse operation and is certainly much easier and quicker to use with a mouse.

Using The Mouse

The Windows interface and all applications that work within Windows use the mouse in the same way.

The main mouse activities are listed below.

Point	The mouse is moved so that the screen pointer is positioned over the desired item - e.g. an icon or object.
Click	Click the left mouse button while the pointer is positioned over the desired item. This is most commonly used to select an object.
Double Click	Click the left mouse button twice while the pointer is positioned over the desired icon or object. This is most commonly used to execute an activity - e.g. open an icon or run a program.
Drag	Move the mouse while holding down the left mouse button.
Shift Click	Hold down the *'Shift'* key while clicking on the desired item.
Shift Drag	Hold down the *'Shift'* key while dragging the mouse.

Closing vs Minimising

When the user is finished using an application, that application can be closed by clicking on the *'File'* menu option. This produces a pull-down menu and clicking on the *'Exit'* option closes the program.   The top right-hand corner of applications for Windows 95 and later operating systems has a set of buttons as shown in the diagram. Clicking the *'Close'* button will also close and exit the application.   On the other hand, the user can click on the minimise button that appears on the leftmost button of that set. The application is reduced to an entry on the Task Bar at the bottom of the screen. This is known as *'minimising'* and the application remains active, frozen at the point at which it was minimised.   If the application is later clicked on the Task Bar, it is restored to full-screen, ready to proceed at the same stage it is was at when it was minimised.   The diagram shows Microsoft Word and the Lexmark Printer Utility both

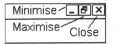

being held in a minimised state.

Using the Clipboard

A big advantage of using Windows is that information in one document can be copied or transferred into another document.   This could involve the copying or transferring of data from within the same application - e.g. copying or transferring a paragraph of text from one Word document to another Word Document. It could also involve the copying of data from one application to a different application - e.g. copying a picture from a Word document into Paint for editing. The stages are:

- Move to the application that contains the desired information.
- Highlight the information to be copied/transferred.
- Use the *'Copy'* or *'Cut'* option to fetch the information from the source application. If the information is <u>cut</u>, it is removed from the source document; if it is <u>copied</u>, a replica of the information is used.   In both cases, the information is placed in a temporary store, known as the *'Clipboard'*.
- Move to the application that is the destination for the data.
- Move the cursor to the spot in the destination document where the information is to be placed.
- Use the *'Paste'* option to place the information into the document at the cursor position.

The contents of the Clipboard can be pasted as many times as required - into different parts of the same document or into different documents. While the machine remains in Windows and no further information cuts are carried out, the Clipboard will store the information.   This is automatic, unless leaving an application results in a particularly large piece of information being left in the Clipboard. In that event, the user is asked to confirm that the information should be left in the Clipboard.

Copying Windows to the Clipboard

It is also possible to copy the entire Windows screen, or any individual window on the screen, to the Clipboard.   The two options are:

- Pressing the *'Print Screen'* key while in Windows results in the entire monitor screen area being saved to the Clipboard.
- Pressing the *'Alt'* and *'PrintScreen'* keys results in the active window area being saved to the Clipboard.

Saving the Clipboard

Windows also contains a Clipboard Viewer. This allows the user to examine the current contents of the Clipboard.   The current contents of the Clipboard can also be given a filename and saved as a file with a .CLP extension.   These files can be recalled to the Clipboard at any time for future pasting into documents.

Windows 95

Windows 3.1 was not a full operating system, as it required DOS to be installed. Most of its activities were directed through DOS drivers and software. It was more correctly described as an *'environment'*. Windows 95 is not really an environment in the sense of simply being an add-on interface to DOS. Indeed, there is no need for DOS to be installed on the machine, unless these facilities are required for running older DOS-only applications.   Windows 95 has its own drivers for memory management, CD handling, etc. This makes it an operating system and graphical user interface in one package.

Windows 95 can run all the old Windows 3.1 and DOS programs.   However, Windows 3.1 is unable to run programs that are specially written for Windows 95.

Benefits of Windows 95

- The *'Documents'* option from the *'Start'* menu stores and display a list of the last 15 files used on the computer, allowing simple recall of commonly used files. Single click on any of the file names and the file is opened inside its appropriate application. So, if a file called 'REPORT.DOC' is clicked, the system loads Microsoft Word and then opens the REPORT.DOC file within it.
- Provides pop-up help windows.   If the user allows the mouse pointer to linger over a command button, a pop-up window displays the function of that button.
- Allows the user to allocate long filenames of up to 255 characters.   It should be understood that Windows 3.1 and DOS programs still use the old eight-dot-three naming system.   So, any files created under Windows 95 that are saved under DOS or Windows 3.1 will have their files names truncated.   A Word file called *'Consumer Report on Beef'* would probably be re-saved as *'CONSUM~1.DOC'*.
- Plays video much more efficiently. The improvement is dramatic and is of the order of two to three times.
- Supports plug-and-play - the system recognise p-n-p components and automatically assigns resources. Newly installed p-n-p compatible cards are automatically recognised by Windows 95.
- Provides a *'Recycle Bin'* as an improvement over Windows 3.1's undelete facility. Files that the user decides to delete appear to be deleted but are, in fact stored in their complete form and can be accessed at any time via the Recycle Bin.   The user can decide to recover a file from the Bin or can permanently empty the Bin's contents.
- Provides more extensive *'Help'* facilities.
- Adds new communications features such as The Microsoft Network, Microsoft Fax, HyperTerminal and Phone Dialler.
- Adds extra diagnostic facilities through the provision of a *'Hardware Wizard'*.
- Easy handling of applications through an *'Add/Remove Programs'* facility.

Problems with Windows 95

- More complex to maintain.
- Not as stable an environment as was hoped for.   Users requiring maximum stability have upgraded from Windows 3.1 directly to NT or Windows 2000, skipping over Windows 95 based operating systems altogether.   Such users expect a more sophisticated and reliable product, while ensuring the benefits of the Windows 95 style interface.
- Retained some 16-bit components along with new 32-bit components.
- More demanding hardware requirements than with Windows 3.1.
  The hardware requirements for Windows 95 are:

	Minimum	Realistic Minimum
CPU	386DX	486/Pentium
Memory	4MB	8MB, preferably 16MB.
Video card	VGA	SVGA
Bus	ISA	PCI or Local Bus
Mouse	Normal	Mouse with right-hand button

Since Windows 95 wants 4MB of memory for its own use, even more RAM is required to provide memory for use by the applications.

Using a local bus or a PCI bus system will result in improved graphics handling.

Windows 98

The basic 32-bit architecture of Windows 98 is largely identical to that of Windows 95. Many of Microsoft's additions to Windows 95 such as Internet Explorer, the OSR2 (Operating System Release 2) update pack, new drivers, etc are now included in Windows 98. In that respect, existing users of Windows 95 who have already added these features will not find Windows 98 to be greatly altered.

Benefits of Windows 98

- Internet Explorer 4 or 5 built in.
- Includes Outlook Express, with e-mail and newsgroup facilities.
- Many more built-in device drivers for modems, printers, etc.
- Supports multiple monitors.   Up to eight video cards can be connected to the machine, each handling its own monitor.   This means that a much larger desktop size can be set, with each monitor displaying a different area of the desktop - or a different application.
- Support for USB and FireWire, and improved Plug and Play.
- Much more comprehensive system diagnostic tools.
- Much larger set of drivers available on the installation CD.
- FAT32 allows single disk partitions greater than 2GB and stores data in smaller clusters, minimising wasted disk space.
- Makes better use of AGP graphics cards and MMX processors.
- More comprehensive *'Help'* facilities including many troubleshooting guides.
- The rewriting of many existing Windows 95 components results in a more stable operating system.

The hardware requirements for Windows 98 are:

	Minimum	**Realistic Minimum**
CPU	486DX	Pentium
Memory	16MB	32MB or more
Video card	VGA	SVGA
Bus	ISA	PCI
Mouse	Normal	Mouse with right-hand button

In addition, since the software is only supplied on CD-ROM, a CD-ROM drive is essential to both initially install the main Windows 98 program and to later install any extra features supplied on the CD.

Windows 2000

Released in February 2000, the interface of this operating system is essentially a slightly upgraded version of the Windows 98 interface. It is, however, designed for use as a corporate desktop platform, and consequently a lot of effort has been put into making it easy to administrate. It shares much in common with its predecessor, Windows NT, such as the ability to use the NTFS file system and restrictions on modifying hardware settings directly.

Benefits of Windows 2000

- Menus now *'fade into view'*.
- Little used menu items disappear behind a slightly raised panel with a chevron on it.
- Users who print to network printers now receive a notification as their print job is done.
- Network Neighbourhood has been replaced by My Network Places.
- Each individual user has a personalised desktop, customised and personalised menus and toolbars.
- Settings for LAN and Dialup integrated into one.
- Enhanced Accessibility for people with disabilities. New *'Narrator'* applet reads your screen back to you, and on screen keyboard available for mouse only use. Apart from being useful for people with disabilities, these can solve problems for able-bodied users in unusual environments.
- Web pages can be stored on the hard disk to make them available offline. This technology was introduced in later editions of Win98, and is now mainstream.
- Built in support for multiple languages, switchable in the task bar.
- Easier upgrades, as long as the machine to be upgraded satisfies the compatibility lists.
- More wizard-based administration, including a wizard to connect to a network.
- Intelligent Mirroring across networks allows a user to sit down at any machine on the network and be presented with their 'own' desktop, menus, and even documents.
- Significant improvements to the Help System, which is now HTML based and improved error messages.
- The safe start-up system, which is used when machines are badly configured, now has the best of Win98's options and the best of NT's options.
- Multiple booting is readily possible.
- Unicode is now used throughout, and the new European currency symbol is fully supported.

- Support for multiple processor motherboards, DVD, infrared and FireWire have been added, while support for colour printers and multiple monitors has been enhanced.
- Windows 2000 uses either Fat32 or NTFS. Fat32 is compatible with prior versions of Windows, but supports large volumes and is less wasteful of partial sector space. NTFS, the NT File system is incompatible with earlier windows versions, but is better suited to multiple access use as it gives users individual rights to read, write, modify and execute files, like UNIX (see chapter on Unix).
- A new file system enhancement called *'Encrypted File System'*, can be used to secure data, in the event of the hard disk or the whole machine being stolen.

System requirements for Windows 2000 are outlined below.

	Minimum	Realistic Minimum
CPU	200MHz Pentium	300MHz Pentium
Memory	32MB	64MB
Hard disk	600MB	1GB
Video Card	VGA	SVGA
Bus	ISA	PCI
Mouse	Normal	Wheelmouse

The operating needs about 600MB of hard disk space for its own files, before any user applications or data are added to the machine.

Windows ME

In 2001 Microsoft introduced the Windows Millennium Edition, or Win ME for short. This is intended to be a personal Operating System and so lacks all of the groupware features of Windows 2000, as well as using the Windows 95 kernel instead of the NT kernel. The interface is very similar to Windows 98, with only a few cosmetic changes. Although it still has a DOS command prompt available, it is more difficult to find, and only operates in protected mode, meaning that very old real mode DOS programs will not work. It is essentially an upgrade of Windows 98, with the added features listed below.

Benefits of Windows ME

- It has a more useable help system, extra wizards and some alterations to icons and colour schemes.
- It has a new *'System Restore'* utility. Over time, with programs alterations, components will have been added, deleted and modified. With Windows ME, these changes are noted and saved. This allows a user to return the system to the state it was in on any previous point, before an alteration was made.
- A new *'System File Protection'* utility guards against any overwriting or deletion of important system files that may occur during the installation of other software.
- A new *'Hibernation'* utility allows the machine to be closed down, with the current active programs and files being noted. When the machine is switched on later, the computer automatically opens these original programs and files.
- A new *'Windows Image Acquisition'* utility builds the downloading images from digital cameras into Windows, rather than requiring the separate utility supplied with the camera.
- A new *'Movie Maker'* utility provides video capture facilities for those with video capture cards. It will automatically create separate clips for each scene in the video. It also provides basic video editing facilities such as cropping, amalgamating clips, and adding fades and voiceovers.
- A new version of the *'Media Player'* includes the playing of CDs and the playing of streamed audio and video. It also includes a 'CD ripper' that converts a track from an audio CD into a compressed WMA file (the Windows alternative to MP3).

Windows XP

The latest version of Windows to arrive has been Windows XP, currently in Beta version. It sports an improved interface with a greater degree of customisation, and improved user management and security. Software supplied with XP includes Internet Explorer 6, which has a built-in firewall, as well as Remote Desktop, Media Player 8 and more wizards such as the digital camera wizard.

With XP, Microsoft is encouraging digital signing of device drivers to ensure compatibility, and has also introduced controversial *'product activation'* measures that allow Microsoft to collect user information in order to install the operating system.

Using Windows 95/98/2000/ME

Since Windows versions from '95 share a great deal of common user interface, the following descriptions cover all systems. Differences are highlighted within the text.

Using the Mouse

The Windows interface and all Windows applications use the mouse in the same way. From version 95 onwards, the Windows operating systems makes extensive use of the right mouse button.

Accessing Programs

With Windows 3.1, programs were accessed by double clicking on their icons within their program groups, accessed via the Program Manager.

An opening screen similar to that shown below replaces this cumbersome method.

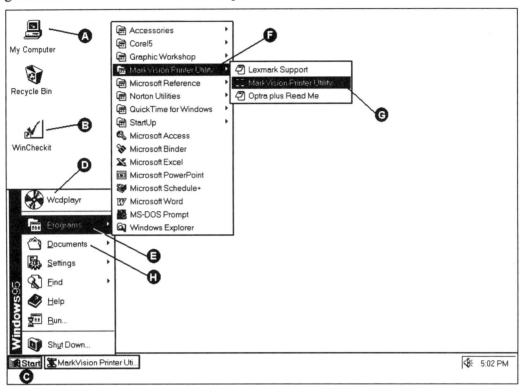

This provides a number of ways to load and run programs.

1. The icon marked **(A)** above opens a window that, like Windows 3.1's File Manager, displays all the files and sub-directories on the computer's disks.   The *'My Computer'* option extends this to provide access to the computer's printers, networking facilities and the Control Panel.

2. Icon **(B)** shows an icon for a user's application that has been placed directly on to the Windows desktop. This is a *'shortcut'* to the application and the program can be run simply by clicking on the icon.   In this way, the user's most commonly used programs can be displayed as soon as Windows 95, 98 or 2000 is loaded.

3. The button **(C)** is labelled *'Start'* and clicking this button displays the menu shown on the left of the screen. The menu option **(D)** displays an application that has been placed on the start menu as an alternative means of accessing often used programs.   Clicking on its menu bar loads and runs the program.

4. One of the *'Start'* menu options is titled *'Programs'* and moving the mouse pointer over the button, marked as **(E)**, displays a menu showing all the programs available on the computer.   Clicking one of the menu options, such as item marked *'Microsoft Excel'* in the example, loads and runs that particular program.

5. In some cases, an entry in the Programs menu is not a single program but a collection of similar programs. For example, the *'Corel 5'* option contains a suite of different drawing, tracing and presentation utilities. Similarly, the menu bar option marked as **(F)** contains three supporting components.   Placing the mouse pointer on that menu option reveals another sub-menu that allows access to the sub-options.   Clicking menu bar **(G)** in the example shown runs the Lexmark printer utility.

6. Clicking option **(H)** on the *'Start'* menu reveals the last 15 documents opened by the user.   Clicking any of these documents opens the corresponding application and then the document.

7. Clicking on the file name when in Windows Explorer, the version of File Manager used in Windows 95 onwards.

8. Clicking on the program name on the bottom Task Bar.

9. Using the *'Run'* option from the *'Start'* menu.   Only useful where the user knows the exact name of the file and the exact sub-directory path in which it is stored, or wishes to run a program that was recently used.

In all cases, when the application is exited the user is returned to menu screens as shown above.

Like Windows 3.1, the environment of Windows 95 onwards allows for extensive configuration to meet the needs of the user (e.g. screen colours, use of memory, background wallpaper, choice of printers, sensitivity of the mouse, etc.).   This is covered in the chapter on Windows configuration.

'Start' Menu Options

Apart from running applications, the *'Start'* menu offers a number of useful facilities.   These are:

Settings	This has at least three sub-options, depending on the version of Windows: Control Panel - Provides similar function to Windows 3.1 for setting keyboard and mouse characteristics, etc. Extra functions include adding new hardware, adding and removing software, and configuring network facilities. Printer - Provides options to add new printers, to set printer ports and to set the configuration of printers. Taskbar - Sets the options for the Taskbar and the Start Menu. Folder Options - In Windows 98, accesses the same dialog as the *'View/Folder Options'* selection from Explorer. Active Desktop - Includes options to customise or update the Windows 98 active desktop. Windows Update - If installed, runs the Windows Update through Microsoft Explorer Dial-Up Networking - In Windows ME, the Settings menu contains a link to the Dial-Up Networking window. In Windows 2000, this is called the *'Network and Dial-Up Connections'* option, and has more functions including network connection management.
Find	Called the *'Search'* menu in Windows 2000, it contains one or more options: Files or Folders - Searches the computer's disk drives (and network drives if on a network) for specific files or folders. Searches can be for specific names, specific contents, specific dates or specific sizes. Computer - If a local area network is installed, this will search for a specific computer by its network name. The Internet - Opens Internet Explorer's *'Search'* facility.
Help	Provides comprehensive help in three ways: Contents - Help is organised in a systematic way providing information in a hierarchical fashion with the user delving deeper if he/she wants more information on a subject. Index - The user can scroll through a long list of help topics or can search by entering a word or phrase. Find - Every word used in every help file can be scrolled through or searched for.
Run	A pull-down menu lists the programs that were recently loaded via the *'Run'* facility. One of these can be selected or the user can click the *'Browse'* option to search for a specific program to be run.
Shut Down	Provides options to close down the computer or restart completely. In windows 95, 98 and 2000 there is also an option to restart in DOS mode; if networking is installed there will be an option to log out. Depending on the power saving settings there may also be a *'hibernation'* option.
Favorites	Provides quick access to commonly used files, folders and webs sites. (Windows 98/2000 only).

Other Accessories

One of the options in the *'Programs'* menu is a collection of utilities under the heading *'Accessories'*. These are supplied as standard with Windows 95 onwards and include:

Available to most Windows 95 users and all Windows 98/2000 users	
Multimedia Utilities	Media Player, CD Player, Sound Recorder and Volume Control.
System Tools	System Monitor, and Disk utilities - Backup, Disk Defragmenter, DriveSpace (not with Windows 2000) and ScanDisk.
Calculator	A calculator providing scientific functions and conversion between different number bases.
Clipboard Viewer	Facilities to view, save and delete the contents of the Clipboard.
Dial-Up Networking	Uses a modem to connect a computer to a network, or to another computer with a modem.
HyperTerminal	An improved version of Terminal, transferring files between two computers over the telephone network. Requires the computers to be connected to modems.
Phone Dialer	A utility allowing users with modems to place telephone calls from the keyboard or from a stored pick list.
Direct Cable Connection	A utility to allow two computers to share their resources. One computer can access the files and printers of the other computer.
Paint	A more basic version of Paintbrush, with facilities to create and edit bitmap pictures. Provides line drawing, box drawing, text overlay, fills, etc.
Imaging	A simple tool to add lines, boxes and text to an existing image. Also provides facilities to scan images and documents, when a scanner is fitted to the computer.
Notepad	A simple word-processing program for small files, less than 64k.
WordPad	An improved version of the Windows 3.1 Write word processing program

Available with Windows 98	
DVD Player	Used to play DVD disks where the computer has a DVD drive.
Disk Cleanup	Detects temporary file, internet cache files, etc that are using up valuable disk space.
System Info	A very powerful utility for testing the computer's system files, Registry, etc.
Maintenance Wizard	A utility to automate checks for disk errors, etc, at times set by the user (e.g. overnight).
Available with Windows 2000	
Fax	Used to send, receive and organise faxes.
Accessibility Options	Improved usability and readability for the visually or physically impaired. See the *Configuring Windows* section for more details.
Synchronise	Used to keep the contents of a desktop machine synchronised with laptops, PDA's etc.

The actual applications appearing on the list will depend upon how the user's machine is configured. This will depend on the version of software installed and the number of items installed onto the hard disk from the installation CD.

Explorer

Windows Explorer allows access to disk operations at file and directory (folder) level.

Explorer has two screen panels. The left panel is the *'folder tree window'* and it displays a graphic representation of the folder structure of the currently chosen disk drive with an icon of a folder for each folder.   It also allows access to the Control Panel and the Printer utilities.   The right panel is the *'folder window'* and it displays icons and names representing the files and folders within a selected

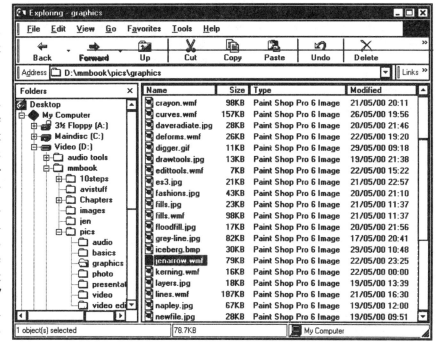

folder. In the folder tree window, the currently chosen folder is highlighted.   To select a new folder to view, the user clicks the mouse pointer on the folder name or its folder icon.   A plus sign on a folder indicates that it contains sub-folders that are not being currently displayed.   The terms *'expanding'* and *'collapsing'* are used to describe the display or non-display of folders.   In the example shown, the *'mmbook'* folder has been expanded and all the sub-folders at the next level are revealed.   In turn, the *'pics'* folder has been expanded and all sub-folders within *'pics'* are listed.   The *'graphics'* sub-folder has been selected and its contents are viewable in the right hand panel.

Windows 98 provides two display options:

View in Classic Mode.
This provides the standard interface as provided with Windows 95 and is shown above.

View as a Web Page.
This is shown on the next page.   The right-hand panel displays the folder's files and highlighting a file provides file details (type, size, date created/modified).   If the file is a graphic file, it is displayed (as with the globe example shown).

The main Explorer activities can be carried out using the mouse and keyboard and these are:
DELETING A FOLDER

Highlight the desired folder icon and press the delete key; when prompted, confirm the transfer of the folder and all its files and sub-folders to the Recycle Bin.   Deleting files and folders, in fact, only sends them to the Recycle Bin area where they can either be recovered or permanently deleted.

EXPANDING A FOLDER

Double click the mouse pointer on the desired folder or single-click on the plus icon to its left; if using the keyboard, highlight the desired sub-folder with the cursor keys then press the plus key.

COLLAPSING A FOLDER

Double click the mouse pointer on the desired folder; if using the keyboard, highlight the desired sub-folder with the cursor keys then press the minus key.

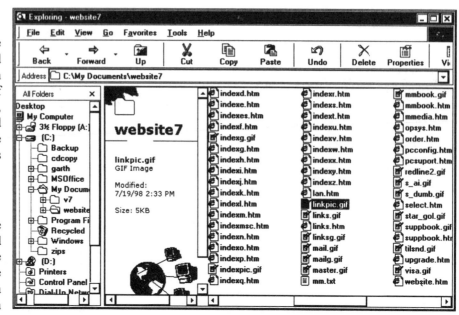

DELETING A FILE

Highlight the desired file in the right panel by clicking the mouse pointer on it; press the Delete key; when prompted, confirm the file's transfer to the Recycle Bin.

UNDELETING

Since files and folders that are *'deleted'* are actually sent to a folder called the *'Recycle Bin'*, they are available for recovery. Double-clicking the Recycle Bin icon on the desktop opens a window that displays all the items available for recovering. The desired files can be selected and the 'Restore' option on the 'File' menu restores them to the folder from where they were deleted. If a file came from a folder that has since been deleted, the folder is also restored. To permanently delete a file or group of files, the file(s) should be selected and the *'Delete'* option chosen from the *'File'* menu. The file(s) are deleted and the disk space is recovered for future use. Choosing the *'Empty Recycle Bin'* option deletes all the files currently in the Bin.

CREATING A FOLDER

Highlight the folder into which the new directory will be added; choose the *'New'* option from the *'File'* menu and the *'Folder'* option from the *'New'* menu. An unnamed sub-directory will be created and it must immediately be given a name.

MOVING A FILE

Click the pointer on the desired file in the right panel so that the file is highlighted. Chose the *'Cut'* option from the *'Edit'* menu. The file is now removed from the source folder. Open the folder that is the intended destination for the file. Go to the *'Edit'* menu and choose the *'Paste'* option. The file is now resident in the destination folder. Another technique involves dragging a file from the right panel to a folder in the left panel. This works for data files that are moved between folders in the same drive. For program files, it will not move the file but will place a *'shortcut'* in the destination folder. In this way, the program can be loaded and run from the destination folder as well as from the source folder where the program file remains. Dragging any file into a folder on another disk drive will copy that file into that folder, whether it is a program or data file.

COPYING A FILE

Click the pointer on the desired file in the right panel so that the file is highlighted. Go to the *'Edit'* menu and choose the *'Copy'* option. The file remains in the source folder. Open the folder that is the intended destination for the file. Go to the *'Edit'* menu and choose the *'Paste'* option. The copy of the file now resides in the destination folder.

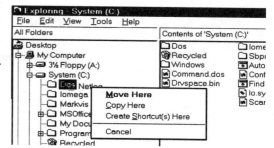

Alternatively, dragging the file with the right mouse button pressed will present the user with a menu of choices as shown. This provides for the copying or moving of a file into the destination folder. It can also create a *'shortcut'* to a program file. A quick way to copy a file to a floppy disk is to highlight the file and click the right mouse button. A menu opens and clicking the *'Send To'* option offers the user the opportunity to copy to the A: drive.

MOVING/COPYING GROUPS OF FILES

Files can be moved or copied as a group in a single operation. If the group of files are contiguous (next to each other) in the file list, click on the first file in the desired group, hold down the 'Shift' key and click on the last file in the group.   This will highlight the entire group of files, which can then be moved or copied.   If the desired files are not contiguous, hold down the Ctrl key while clicking on each desired file.   An addition in Explorer is the ability to click and drag a rectangle around the files to be used.   Any unwanted files within the rectangle can be deselected by holding down the Ctrl key and clicking on them.

COPYING/MOVING A DIRECTORY

The technique is identical to moving/copying files except the folder is highlighted instead of a file.

RENAMING A FILE

Highlight the desired file in the right panel. Choose the *'Rename'* option from the *'File'* menu. When prompted, type in new file name. The file remains in its current directory but is renamed.

RENAMING A FOLDER

Click the pointer on the desired file in the <u>right</u> panel, wait a moment (so that it is not perceived as a double-click) then click again.   A box appears around the folder name and the name can be changed.

PRINTING A FILE

Highlight the desired file in the right panel. Choose the *'Print'* option from the *'File'* menu. The *'Print'* option will only appear on the *'File'* menu if the file is capable of being printed.

FORMATTING A FLOPPY DISK

Insert the floppy disk to be formatted in the drive. Select the floppy disk drive in the left panel and click the right mouse button. This produces a menu from which the *'Format'* option can be selected. A *'Format'* dialog box is opened as shown.   This allows the user to set up the process to match the size of the floppy disk placed in the drive.

The user can choose to give the disk a name by typing an entry in the data entry box provided. The *'Copy system files'* option will, if checked, create a disk that is capable of starting up the computer. These system file use up valuable disk space and the box should only be checked if a boot disk is required.

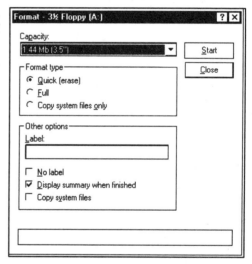

The dialog box provides for three types of formatting:

Type	Purpose
Quick (erase)	Can only be used with disks that were previously formatted. Saves time by not checking for errors on the disk surface.
Full	Checks for surface errors and marks them as bad sectors.
Copy System Files Only	Does not actually format the disk. It turns a working disk into a boot disk.

When the options are chosen, clicking the *'Start'* button begins the formatting.

COPYING A DISK

This utility makes an exact replica of one disk on to another disk; any previous contents on the destination disk are lost. Insert the floppy disk to be copied in the drive. Select the floppy disk drive in the left panel and click the right mouse button. This will produce a menu from which the *'Copy Disk'* option can be selected. A *'Copy Disk'* dialog box is opened. If the machine has a single floppy drive, that drive letter will be highlighted in both windows.   Where a machine has several floppy drives, they will appear in both windows and the user can choose the source and destination drives for the copy.

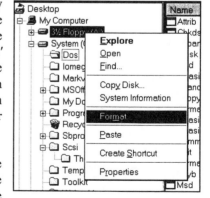

Clicking the *'Start'* button initiates the copying process.

Where two different drives are involved, the user only has to wait until the process is completed.   Where the user nominates the same drive as both the source and destination drives, the program prompts for the switching of the disks when required.

Taskbar

When working in Windows, there will often be a number of applications running at the same time. Some of these may have been automatically loaded at the startup of Windows (see the chapter on Windows Configuration) or they may have been loaded during the Windows session.   Each time an application is loaded, it is added as a button to the Taskbar and when the application is closed the button is removed from the Taskbar.   The Taskbar usually sits along the bottom of the screen and the buttons show every application that is currently open.   Switching between applications only requires the appropriate button on the Taskbar to be clicked.

Windows 95 and later operating systems provide additional access, since pressing the Windows key or the CTRL and ESC keys brings up the *'Start'* menu, superimposed over the current application window.

Leaving Windows 95/98/ME

Choosing the *'Shut Down'* option from the *'Start'* menu displays a dialog box that allows the user to leave Windows 95/98 in one of three ways, as shown.

Option	Function
Shut down the computer	Saves data or changes to applications before closing down.
Restart the computer	Closes down then restarts so that any new settings may take effect.
Restart the computer in MS-DOS mode	Allows the user to have a prolonged DOS session.

Leaving Windows 2000

Choosing the *'Shut Down'* option from the *'Start'* menu displays a slightly different dialog box that allows the user to leave Windows 2000 in one of three ways, as before, only this time the choice is on a pull down combo box. In addition, pressing CTRL+ALT+DELETE brings up the Windows 2000 task manager, which is based on the NT task manager and allows the shutdown options as well as the option to "kill" an individual task.

Using Microsoft Networking

Windows, from 3.11 onwards, includes integrated support for networking. At least three pieces of driver software are required in Windows to use networking capabilities. These are the network card driver, the protocol driver, and the network client. See the LANS chapter for more details on these components.

Once these drivers are properly installed, and the physical cabling is in place, Windows will be able to access the network. The interface, resources and functions that will be available to the user depend on the type of network that is installed, but normally include shared resources such as network printers and file server drives.

Microsoft supplies its own networking client with all versions of Windows from 3.11 onwards. This normally runs through the TCP/IP protocol, and allows the user to logon to Windows NT domains. If additional drivers are installed, peer-to-peer file and printer sharing is possible through Microsoft Networking.

From the user's viewpoint, installation of Microsoft Networking has two major effects. The first is that users will be asked to logon when the PC boots up, and the second is the ability to access the files and printers of peer or server systems. Note that file and printer sharing installation is not required to be able to access the files and printers of other systems – the software is only required when wishing to share the facilities on the current system to others on the network.

The dialog shown on the right is a basic Windows 95/98/ME login box, shown at system startup and when changing users. For those systems that access the network through an NT domain or Novell Netware server, there will be an additional text box where the domain name should be entered. Do not confuse NT domain names with Internet domain names! Ask the network administrator if you are unsure which NT domain to use.

To log in, enter your username and password (the password will be hidden as you type). If this is the first time that username has been used on the system, it will ask the user to confirm the password so that it can store these details in a PWL (PassWord List) file on the local hard disk. Note however that unless you are logging into a server, this is merely the Windows password. If this is the case then hitting the *'Cancel'* button or the *'Esc'* key will bypass the login stage. Additionally, unless logging

into a server, Windows will only attempt to validate the password from its own local list of PWL files. This means any unused username will become a valid login from Windows' point of view. Although the PWL files are stored in an encrypted form, there are programs available that can decrypt these files so network managers should be aware of this as a potential security hole. The easiest way round this is to enter the correct password for the network, and then the '*Set Windows Password*' dialog appears, change both fields to a blank password. This will fool Windows into thinking that the user does not have a password, thus making the issue of PWL viewing irrelevant. This method also avoids problems caused when the network password is changed and the local Windows password remains the same.

Other login methods can be more complex. For example, standard NT and 2000 login boxes contain further options such as dial-up logins, language selection or workstation only logins. Additional client software such as Novell clients may have further capabilities or options.

Accessing Shared Files

If a user is logged in with access to a Microsoft Network, any shared resources are now available to that user. Folders and drives can be accessed through Explorer in the normal way, through selecting '*Network Neighbourhood*' and navigating through workgroups, machine names and resource names.

However, this can be a cumbersome and sometimes confusing method, especially if there are a large number of machines on the network. An alternative is to '*map*' a network drive. This provides a local route to a remote resource for easy access. For example, if a local machine has an A:, C: and D: drive, it could map the (currently unused) E: drive to the network folder \\OFFICE\INVOICES. In this case 'OFFICE' is the name of a machine and 'INVOICES' is the name of a folder or drive on that machine which has been shared. Once the mapping is successful, the user can access that folder or drive as if it were a local drive with the letter E: designated to it.

This mapping can be achieved in one of two ways. If the user knows the UNC (Universal Naming Convention) address of the resource, then it can be mapped by choosing *Tools / Map Network Drive* and entering the UNC path to the resource. If the path is not known, the user can navigate through Network

Neighborhood to find the resource he wishes to map, then right-click on it and select '*Map Network Drive*'. The latter method will fill in the appropriate path automatically, as shown in the example.

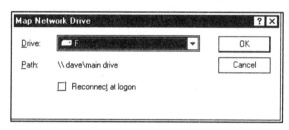

The '*Reconnect at logon*' checkbox will tell Windows to attempt to reinstate the mapping every time it logs on. If it fails it will offer the user to stop mapping this drive at logon.

Accessing Shared Printers

For printers, there is an equivalent to drive mapping, known as '*Capturing*'. This can be done by opening up the '*Properties*' of an existing printer, going to the '*Details*' tab and selecting '*Capture Printer Port*'. However, it is generally easier to navigate to the correct printer on the network, right-click, and select '*Capture Printer Port*'.

The Printer Capture process has a similar effect to mapping a drive: all data sent to the selected local LPT port is redirected to the network printer. For example LPT1 could be redirected to \\OFFICE\LASER. As with the mapping operation it is possible to tell Windows to reconnect the printer at the next logon.

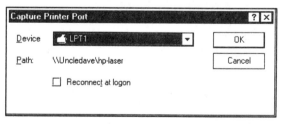

Printer drivers

Sending data straight to a remote printer raises the issue of ensuring that the proper device drivers are in use. If a remote PC shares its printer, then that printer must have appropriate drivers installed on its hard disk. The local user can therefore install the printer driver from the remote machine. This is done by right-clicking on the printer and choosing '*Install*'. This will run through the same installation procedure as if it were a local printer. This install procedure will set up a port redirection just as if the Printer Capture process had been performed. Therefore, the user need only capture a port when printing to another identical model of printer in, for example, another department or floor.

Computer Architecture

The Basic System

A computer consists of various elements - CPU, memory, and a range of Input/Output connections to devices such as discs, keyboard, monitor and mouse. Most of a computer's operations are concerned with the movement of data between these elements (e.g. reading a program from disk into memory, reading spreadsheet data, recalculating results and storing them back to memory). Some of these data transfers are purely internal to the computer (as in the case of spreadsheet updating). Other data transfers are to outside peripherals via cards plugged into expansion slots on the computer motherboard or motherboard sockets (as in the case of printing a spreadsheet).

The diagram shows a simplified view of a computer system. The Address Bus and Data Bus link all the memory and input/output devices to the CPU and the main components are:

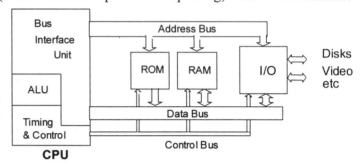

Address Bus

Each memory location has a unique address number. The CPU has to be able to read or write data to any of these addresses. The CPU accesses a memory location by putting the desired address number, in binary format, on to the Address Bus. Devices such as the parallel and serial ports are also part of this addressing system.

Data Bus

When the appropriate memory location is accessed, the CPU can either fetch data from it or write data into it; such data is transferred along the Data Bus.

NOTES:
- Some of the memory is in the form of 'ROM' (Read Only Memory). This is a chip with program coding permanently burned into it. Its contents are not lost if the machine power is switched off. Some, or all, of the system/video/disk BIOS is stored in ROM form.
- Information never flows into the CPU from the Address Bus. The Address Bus is only used to allow the CPU to access various peripheral chips.
- Since ROM cannot be written to, data only flows on to the Data Bus from the ROM chip - and never in the opposite direction.
- Since RAM can either be read or written, there is a need to allow data to flow between memory and the CPU in either direction (only one direction at a time!)
- The I/O expansion bus also has to be capable of both receiving and transmitting data on the Data Bus (e.g. a modem has to transfer data in both directions).

Control Bus

This bus transports several control signals. Many CPUs have two major control lines, one that is brought to a low voltage level to indicate that a read is taking place and one that is brought to a low voltage level to indicate a write taking place. Naturally, only one of these lines can be brought low at any one time. The PC range of processors, the xxx86 range, treats memory and I/O devices differently and therefore has separate control lines for each. The PC's main control lines are:

MEMR	goes low to indicate a read of memory
MEMW	goes low to indicate a write to memory
IOR	goes low to indicate a read of an I/O device
IOW	goes low to indicate a write to an I/O device

The Address Bus and the Data Bus are simply the electrical paths between the CPU and the other chips. They exist as the copper tracks of the computer's printed circuit board and the chips are soldered to these tracks. To allow other peripheral cards to attach to the buses, the buses connect to special sockets called 'expansion slots'. The cards plug in to these slots and pick up the bus connections, as well as power, from the edge connections.

All the bus connections are digital; they can only have two electrical states - either ON or OFF. This is due to the use of digital logic circuits. This means that every piece of information - from an address location number to an alphabetic letter - has to be represented in combinations of these ONs and OFFs. There are various methods of implementing the ONs and OFFs in computer hardware.

Voltage levels	High or Low
Voltage polarity	Positive or Negative
Floppy/Hard Disk, Tape	Orientation of magnetic granules - North/South
CD Disk	Changes in the disk's reflective surface - shallow or deep

CPU

In this diagram, the CPU has been expanded into three parts:

- The ALU - Carries out all the calculations and decision making tasks.
- The Bus Interface Unit - Takes the data to and from the CPU (held inside its internal *'registers'* - i.e. small memory stores) along the external Data Bus to read/write memory and devices. The Data Bus is a two-way bus, as it must carry information in both directions. The Bus Interface Unit also places the required location addresses on to the Address Bus, in order that the required devices can be accessed for reading or writing.
- The Control Unit - Decodes all program instructions and dictates all the CPU's control and timing mechanisms.

Numbering Systems

There are a wide variety of formats for storing data inside a computer. Integer numbers are stored differently from real numbers; text is stored differently in an IBM 370 computer compared to a normal PC. Numbers can be groups into bits, nibbles, bytes and words. Numbers can be described in terms of decimal, binary, octal, hexadecimal and BCD schemes. Before looking more deeply, it is important to have an understanding of most of the numbering systems since numbers are described in different ways in different manuals and different utility programs.

Decimal Numbering

The most common number system in everyday use is the DECIMAL (sometimes called the DENARY) system, which uses the digits from 0 through to 9. The number of different digits used in any numbering system is known as its BASE or RADIX. So, the base of the decimal system is 10. The value of any digit in a number depends on its position within the number. For example, the digit 7 has a higher value in the number 273 than in the number 127.

The number 6,753 is pronounced as *'Six thousand, seven hundred and fifty-three"*

in other words,

$$6 \times 1000$$
$$7 \times 100$$
$$5 \times 10$$
$$3 \times 1$$

In school, some children are taught numbers with column headings thus:

....	10000	1000	100	10	1	1/10	1/100	....
		6	7	5	3			

More mathematically, the column headings are :

....	10^4	10^3	10^2	10^1	10^0	10^{-1}	10^{-2}	....
		6	7	5	3			

It should also be noted that any number raised to the power 0 is always equal to 1.

From this, it follows that any numbering system can employ column headings with base R, as shown:

....	R^4	R^3	R^2	R^1	R^0	R^{-1}	R^{-2}	....

Binary Numbering

Since each line of a bus can only have two states, the whole bus can only carry numbers based on a BINARY numbering system. Numbers are expressed in base 2, with the column headings looking like :

....	2^4	2^3	2^2	2^1	2^0	2^{-1}	2^{-2}	....

Some people prefer to think of the numbering scheme as :

....	16	8	4	2	1	0.5	0.25	....

Every binary number is a collection of 1's and 0's. A binary number can easily be converted to its decimal equivalent.

Consider the binary number 10100:

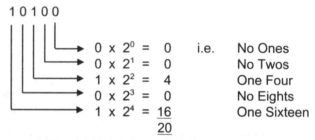

$$0 \times 2^0 = 0 \quad \text{i.e.} \quad \text{No Ones}$$
$$0 \times 2^1 = 0 \quad \text{No Twos}$$
$$1 \times 2^2 = 4 \quad \text{One Four}$$
$$0 \times 2^3 = 0 \quad \text{No Eights}$$
$$1 \times 2^4 = \underline{16} \quad \text{One Sixteen}$$
$$\underline{20}$$

Therefore the binary number 10100 is the same as 20 in decimal.

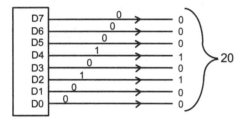

Data lines are numbered from D0 upwards, while address lines are numbered from A0 onwards.   So, an 8-bit wide data bus could carry   numbers between 0 and 255 - a range of 256 different combinations (i.e. the bus has 8 lines giving 2 to the power 8 combinations).   The number 20 on an 8-bit bus would be as in the diagram.

Conversions

The above diagram shows how to convert a binary number into a decimal number.   It is also possible to convert a decimal number into its binary equivalent.   This is done by repeated division, where the decimal number is repeatedly divided by the base (in the case of binary this is 2) until the decimal number is reduced to zero.   The remainder from each division is recorded and these remainders constitute the binary number.

Consider the case of converting the decimal number 11.   Dividing by two gives five with a remainder of 1 (i.e. 11 is made up of 5 groups of 2 and 1 group of 1).   Dividing again by two gives:

```
2 | 11
2 | 5  remainder 1
    2  remainder 1
```

So, 11 = 2 groups of 4, 1 group of 2 and 1 group of 1.

This is repeated thus:

```
2 | 11
2 | 5  remainder 1      ↑       So, 11  =   1 group of   8
2 | 2  remainder 1                          0 groups of  4
2 | 1  remainder 0                          1 group of   2
    0  remainder 1                          1 group of   1
```

So, 11 in decimal is 1011 in binary.   Note that the remainders are read <u>upwards</u>.

Hex Numbering

All data is stored and moved around in binary format - no matter how the program or the user might wish to regard it or organise it.   However, binary numbers can comprise very long strings of 0's and 1's when it is representing a large number.   For example, the binary number 010110011000111100111001 is, in fact, the decimal number 1,468,217.   The binary version is hard to visualise; users find it hard to look at two binary numbers and know which is the largest.   As a result, binary numbers are difficult to handle and are prone to human errors.   When dealing with very large numbers, it is often convenient to express the number in base 16, instead of base 10 or base 2.   This is known as hexadecimal (often shortened to 'hex') and it is simple to convert from binary to hexadecimal.   Also, the data on an 8-bit bus can be represented by just two alphanumeric characters instead of eight binary digits.   The hex system requires symbols to represent from 0 through to 15.   Since 10 to 15 are outwith normal single decimal digits, the letters A to F are used to represent 10 to 15.

Binary	Decimal	Hex
0000	0	00
0001	1	01
0010	2	02
0011	3	03
0100	4	04
0101	5	05
0110	6	06
0111	7	07
1000	8	08
1001	9	09
1010	10	0A
1011	11	0B
1100	12	0C
1101	13	0D
1110	14	0E
1111	15	0F

The table shows the relationship between binary, decimal and hex.

Hex Conversions

These are carried out in the same way as decimal to binary, except that the base used is 16 instead of two.

Examples:
Converting hex number B3 to a decimal number:

```
B3
 |
 |  ----------------->   3 x 1   =       3
 |                                
 └---->  B x 16   =    11 x 16   =     176
                                  =     179
```

So B3 = 179.

Converting 349 to a hex number:

```
16 | 349
16 |  21   remainder 13 ( ie D)  ↑
16 |   1   remainder 5           |
       0   remainder 1           |
```

So, 349 is 15D in hex.

Large numbers can be represented quite compactly in hex. For example, the 640k memory boundary in the computer is A0000. Hex is the preferred way of describing memory addresses and port locations.

Note

Since not every occasion will see a hex number using the A to F characters, there can be confusion. For example, the number at the top of a 4k block of memory is 1000 in hex. This is not the same as the decimal number of one thousand. To prevent confusion, hex numbers are often followed by the letter 'h'. Thus, the number 4096 would be 1000h when given in hex. Similarly, 'd' and 'b' can be used to denote decimal and binary numbers.

ASCII

Not all data stored in memory or carried on the computer buses will represent numbers. Often it will represent alphabetic characters and punctuation symbols. When the data is in alphabetic form, the **ASCII** (American Standard Code for Information Interchange) numbering scheme is employed. Each of the range of alphabetic characters, numeric digits, punctuation symbols, etc. is given a unique number. For example, the letter D is represented by 68, the number 7 is represented by 55, the comma by the number 44 and so on. Upper case letters have a different code from lower case letters and the full set of printable characters uses numbers from 32 to 127. The set of numbers between 0 and 31 is non-printable. They are mainly used to control printers (the number 12, for example, provides a Form Feed control character for a printer). A single byte provides 256 different numbers (0 to 255) but, since no ASCII character number is greater than 127, the codes are contained in a 7-bit sequence. IBM created an extended character set to take advantage of the codes from 128 to 255. Printers using the IBM character set can print out various box drawing and other symbols.

The range of ASCII printable codes is:

Decimal	0	1	2	3	4	5	6	7	8	9
30			space	!	"	#	$	%	&	'
40	(	)	*	+	,	-	.	/	0	1
50	2	3	4	5	6	7	8	9	:	;
60	<	=	>	?	@	A	B	C	D	E
70	F	G	H	I	J	K	L	M	N	O
80	P	Q	R	S	T	U	V	W	X	Y
90	Z	[	\	]	^	_	`	a	b	c
100	d	e	f	g	h	i	j	k	l	m
110	n	o	p	q	r	s	t	u	v	w
120	x	y	z	{	|	}	~	DEL		

Printer control characters include:

12	(0C in hex)	Form Feed
13	(0D in hex)	Carriage Return
10	(0A in hex)	Line Feed

An example showing different ways of representing a string of characters is given below:

ASCII	H	e	l	l	o		!
Decimal	72	101	108	108	111	32	33
Hex	48	65	6C	6C	6F	20	21
Binary	01001000	01100101	01101100	01101100	01101111	00100000	00100001

Note   The number stored in a particular location may be an instruction from a program, it may represent an alphabetic character or it may simply be a number.

Consider the following examples:

"67"	is stored internally as 36h 37h	It is storing two ASCII characters
67	is stored internally as 43h	It is storing an integer number
"C"	is stored internally as 43h	It is storing a single ASCII character

If the computer is asked to print out the contents of a particular location, it has to know whether it is meant to print the number it finds there, or the ASCII character represented by the number.   This is settled by the context in which the print request is made. If the printer is asked to print a string of characters, it will convert the number into its ASCII equivalent before printing it; if the printer is asked to print out the numbers that it finds, the number is printed out without any text conversion.

Other Numbering Schemes
Less common numbering schemes are in use and these include:

EBCDIC
The Extended Binary Coded Decimal Interchange Code (EBCDIC) is an 8-bit code that was introduced by IBM and ICL for their mainframe computers.   It is of little interest to PC users except where data has to be converted between EBCDIC-based machines and ASCII-based PCs.

BAUDOT
This is a five-bit code that was popular for telegraphy, telex and computer-controlled radio communications systems (popular with radio amateurs).   Since it a five-bit system it can only support 32 different combinations.   By using two codes (called *'Letters shift'* and *'Figures shift'*) the system shifts between using the numeric codes to represent alphabetic characters and using the same numbers to represent numbers and punctuation symbols.

BCD
Where the data is only in numeric format, each individual number can be converted into its binary equivalent and handled separately.   Since each individual number will only be between 0 and 9, only four bits are required to store each number.   So, the decimal number 5931 would produce a BCD equivalent of:

5	9	3	1
0101	1001	0011	0001

whereas the normal binary equivalent would be 1011100101011.   This only occupies 13 bits compared to the BCD equivalent.   Since each BCD number has its own collection of four bits it is often used to drive LED meters in instrumentation, monitoring and control computer systems.

OCTAL
Octal numbering works with a base of 8 and therefore uses a 3-bit system.   It is little used today and is only mentioned for completeness.   Conversion between decimal and Octal is similar to that already described for decimal/hex conversion, substituting 8 for 16 in the calculations.

Units of Measurement
As already seen, a stream of data is nothing other than a continuous flow of binary 0's and 1's.   To make sense of the stream of 0's and 1's, the system must break the stream up into manageable groups and process data a group at a time.   The standard ways of organising binary information are given below:

BIT - this is the single binary digit and stores only two conditions (ON or OFF).   This is the basic unit on which the system works.

NIBBLE - this is a group of four bits. It can store 16 different combinations (from 0 through to 15) and is not in common use.   It is used in some parallel printer modes.

BYTE - this is group of eight bits.   It can store 256 different combinations (from 0 through to 255) and is the standard method of representing a single character. The lowest order bit, - the one storing the lowest value is known as the *'Least Significant Bit'* while the largest value is stored in the *'Most Significant Bit'*.

WORD - This is not a fixed amount. A word is a group of bits which is treated by the computer as a single unit for retrieving, processing and storing. So, if a data bus happens to be 8 bits wide, it can process 8 bits at a time; in this case, the computer's word size is a single byte. If the data bus happened to be 16 bits wide, its word size would be 16 bits, or a double-byte. Many books define the word as 16 bits, with a double-word being 32 bits and a quad-word being 64 bits.

When measuring data (either as disk capacity, memory, bus widths or as speed of transfer) it is always referred to in its binary state - e.g. One Bit, One Byte, One Kilobyte, One Megabyte, etc.

	Some important Data Sizes		
2 raised to the power	Bus widths (in bits)	Range of Numbers	Common data sizes (in bytes)
1	A single bit (either 0 or 1)	2	
2		4	
3		8	
4	A nibble (0 to 15)	16	
5		32	
6		64	
7		128	
8	The XT Data Bus (1 byte)	256	
9		512	
10		1,024	A Kilobyte
11		2,048	
12		4,096	
13		8,192	
14		16,384	
15		32,768	
16	The AT Data Bus. (0 to 65,535)	65,536	64Kbytes
17		131,072	
18		262,144	
19		524,288	
20	The XT Address Bus	1,048,576	1Mbyte
21		2,097,152	
22		4,194,304	
23		8,388,608	
24	The AT Address Bus	16,777,216	16Mbytes
25		33,554,432	32Mbytes
26		67,108,864	64Mbytes
27		134,217,728	128Mbytes
28		268,435,456	256Mbytes
29		536,870,912	512Mbytes
30		1,073,741,824	1 GigaByte
31		2,147,483,648	2 Gbytes
32	The 386/486 Address Bus / The 386/486 Data Bus	4,294,967,296	4 Gbytes
64	The Pentium Data Bus	18,446,744,073,709,600,000	

The above table shows the numbers that result from the binary numbering method. Since each number increases by a factor of two, no number can ever be an exact thousand or an exact million. In order to maintain the convenience of expressing size in thousands and millions, sizes have to be rounded to the binary number nearest to the wanted number. This produces the following common expressions of size:

Amount	Calculation (2 raised to the power of n)	Actual Amount
1 kilobyte	2^{10}	1,024 bytes
1 megabyte	2^{20}	1,048,576 bytes
1 gigabyte	2^{30}	1,073,741,824 bytes

Notes This numbering system is not used to measure the speed of a computer's CPU. The CPU clock speed is measured in *MegaHertz* (A MegaHertz, or MHz, being one million cycles per second). The clock speeds quoted are the actual speeds - e.g. 4.77MHz means 4,770,000 pulses per second.

Although memory size and disc capacity are measured in bytes, other devices transmit data serially and are measured in bits per second. Some magazines, books, brochures, web sites, etc. use the terms Mb and MB, or MBps and Mbps as if they were the same measurement. To avoid confusion, this book uses an upper-case 'B' to denote Bytes and a lower-case 'b' to denote bits. So, for example, a card may transfer data in MBps while a modem may transmit data in Mbps.

Computer Arithmetic

The computer constantly carries out arithmetic and comparison operations. These operations may be requested by the user in an application package (eg spreadsheet calculations) or may be used by the computer system (eg for graphics and video).

Binary addition

In denary, adding two numbers might result in a carry over between columns. In the example, adding 7 and 8 produced 15. This is another way of saying one lot of ten and 5 units. This was represented by carrying a one from the units column into the next column.

Tens	Units
	7
	8
1	5

Similarly, adding 1 and 1 in binary produces no lots of 1 and one lot of 2. Again, there was a carry from the units column into the next column. In binary addition, the calculation on any column has to take into account the possibility of a bit being carried over from a calculation on the previous column.

2^1	2^0
	1
	1
1	0

The general rule for binary addition is:
$$0 + 0 = 0$$
$$0 + 1 = 1$$
$$1 + 0 = 1$$
$$1 + 1 = 0 \text{ carry } 1$$

Consider adding 6 and 7 together. Six has a binary pattern of 0110, while seven has a pattern of 0111.

Addition takes place from the lowest value upwards; this means from the right-most column through to the left-most column.

	2^3	2^2	2^1	2^0
6=	0	1	1	0
7=	0	1	1	1
result	1	1	0	1

The example of 6+7 would be processed thus:
- Adding the bits in this column (ie 0+1) produces a 1 without a carry.
- Adding the bits in this column (ie 1+1) produces a 0 with a carry into the next column.
- Adding the bits in this column, plus the carry (ie 1+1+1), produces a result of 1 plus a carry into the next column.
- Adding the bits in this column, plus the carry (ie 0+0+1), produces a result of 1 with no carry.

The final result is 1101 which is the binary pattern for 13.

It is common for arithmetic to take place on full bytes of data. For example, adding 109 and 54 produces:

```
  01101101
  00110110
  10100011
```

However, adding 130 and 140 produces:

```
   10000010
   10001100
  100001110
```

This calculation has produced an answer that cannot be stored in a single byte. The number of bits needed to store the result (i.e. 9 bits) has overflowed the size of the storage area (i.e. 8 bits). This final carry has to be detected and acted upon otherwise the carry is ignored and the computer thinks that 130+140=14!

Binary subtraction

The general rule for binary subtraction is:
$$0 - 0 = 0$$
$$1 - 0 = 1$$
$$1 - 1 = 0$$
$$0 - 1 = 1 \text{ borrow } 1$$

Consider subtracting 3 from 5:

```
        fours twos units
  5=      1    0    1
  3=      0    1    1
          0    1    0
```

In the right-most column, taking 1 unit from 1 unit results in 0 units. In the 'twos' column, there is nothing in the top row to subtract the lower 1 from. So, the 1 is borrowed from the column on its left. However, since each column increments by a factor of 2, borrowing from its left is, in fact, borrowing four - or two lots of 2. Subtracting one lot of two from two lots of two leaves one lot of two which is placed in the middle column of the result.

Negative numbers

The examples on the previous page used simple examples. The example additions only used positive numbers; the subtraction example avoided negative numbers and subtracted the smaller number from the larger number to avoid a negative result. In practice, the computer has to store and calculate negative values.

A byte has eight bits and can store a range of contents varying from all zeros (ie 0) through to all ones (ie 255), storing 256 possible different values. However, this does not allow for negative numbers to be stored. If the most significant bit of the byte was ignored, then the byte would store from 0 to 127 (ie seven ones). The eighth bit can then be used to store an indicator of whether the number was positive or negative.

A zero value in the eighth bit (Most Significant Bit) indicates a positive number, while an eighth bit containing a value of one indicates a negative number.

In the first example, the MSB is 0, so the number is positive; a value of 71 in the example.

MSB   LSB

| 0 | 1 | 0 | 0 | 0 | 1 | 1 | 1 |

The MSB in the second example is 1 indicating a negative number. However, the number stored is not 19 as may be expected. The explanation lies in the way the computer works with negative values.

MSB   LSB

| 1 | 0 | 0 | 1 | 0 | 0 | 1 | 1 |

The computer need not have separate addition and subtraction operations. The calculation of 7-3 can be represented as 7+(-3). Both calculations are identical. The second representation allows the computer to avoid a subtraction; it simply adds together two values - one a positive number and the other a negative number. A subtraction problem has been converted into an addition problem.

Unfortunately, normal binary operations produce the wrong result. The calculation of 7-3 can be represented as:

```
+7       00000111
+(-3)    10000011
result   10001010  = -10
```

This has produced the wrong answer and so other methods are used for storing and manipulating negative numbers. The most common of these is known as *'two's complement'*.

Two's complement

With two's complement, sometimes written as 2's complement, positive numbers are represented in their normal binary conversion.

Negative values are converted using the following rules:

Decimal to 2's Complement Conversion Rules	Worked Example for value of -3
Drop the negative sign	3
Convert to binary	00000011
Invert all bits (convert all 1's to 0's and all 0's to 1's). This stage is known as converting to One's Complement.	11111100
Add 1 to the result	11111101

So, -3 is represented by 11111101. The earlier calculation of 7-3 is now represented by:

```
+7       00000111
+(-3)    11111101
result   100000100= +4
```

The carry resulting from the addition is ignored, producing the correct answer of +4.

Any carry resulting from these calculations is always discarded.

If the MSB (eighth bit) is zero, the number is positive and is converted back to decimal in the normal way.

In some cases, the result of a calculation produces a negative value.

Consider the calculation 4-8.

+4	00000100	2 converted to binary
- 8	11111000	this is 8 in 2's complement
result	11111100	result has MSB set to 1

The resulting value cannot be immediately converted to a decimal number.

If the MSB is set to 1, then the following rules apply:

2's Complement to Decimal Conversion Rules	Worked Example for value of 11111100
Invert all bits (convert all 1's to 0's and all 0's to 1's).	00000011
Add 1 to the result	00000100
Convert to decimal	4
Place a minus sign in front of the number	-4

Hex addition

Hex numbering requires a multiplier of 16 between columns, compared to multipliers of 2 and 10 for binary and decimal respectively.   The carry over methods involved in the earlier examples of decimal and binary addition also apply to hex addition, except that the carry between columns involves a base of 16.   The least significant column stores single units with the column's contents allowed to range from zero (ie 0 lots of 1) to F (ie 15 lots of 1).   The next column stores how many 16s help comprise the number stored; it can range from 0 lots of 16 to 15 lots of 16.   Each subsequent column's contents increase by a factor of 16.   In the table below, the columns represent 1s, 16s, 256s and 4096s - reading from right to left.

The example shows 75 and 211 being added together.   75 converted to hex is 4B while 227 converts to

	16^3	16^2	16^1	16^0
75=	0	0	4	B
211=	0	0	D	3
result	0	1	1	E

E3.   The addition of the first column combines B (ie 11) and 3.   This produces an answer of 14, which is E in hex. The second column adds 4 and D (ie 13).   This produces an answer of 17.   Since the column only stores factors of 16, there is a carry over into the next column and a remainder of 1 placed in second column.

The final result is 11Eh, which is 286 in decimal.

Hex subtraction

Hex notation is the most common way to describe memory locations and address location in computers. For example, the program necessary to drive a SCSI hard disk may be described as sitting in memory between C8000h and D0000h.   To find out how much memory this occupies, the two hex figures should be subtracted; the difference in hex can then be converted to decimal if required.

16^4	16^3	16^2	16^1	16^0
D	0	0	0	0
C	8	0	0	0
0	8	0	0	0

The subtraction would be processed thus:

- The right-most column produces a 0 since 0-0 = 0.
- The second column also produces a 0 since 0-0 = 0.
- The third column also subtracts 0 from 0 producing 0.
- The fourth column subtracts 8 from 0, forcing 1 to be borrowed from last column.   Borrowing one lot of 16^4 effectively means borrowing 16 lots of 16^3.   8 from 16 leaves 8 in the third column.
- Since there was a borrow from the last column, the value of D is reduced to C.   Subtracting C from C leaves 0 in the last column.

This means that the memory requirements were 08000h.

This converts to hex as

0	x	1	=	0
0	x	16	=	0
0	x	256	=	0
8	x	4096	=	32768
		Total	=	32768

The program occupies 32768 bytes of address space - i.e. 32k.

Logic operations

Users constantly use logic operations when carrying out day-to-day activities:

- To make a word bold in Word requires both that the word is highlighted **AND** the Bold option is clicked on the Toolbar.
- DOS **OR** Windows can be used to copy files.

In the first example, both conditions had to be met before the result was met.

This can be shown with the use of a TRUTH TABLE. A Truth Table is a table that shows the results of all possible permutations of conditions.

For the first example, it would be:

Condition A	Condition B	Result (or output)
Word not highlighted	Bold option not clicked	Word not Bold
Word not highlighted	Bold option clicked	Word not Bold
Word highlighted	Bold option not clicked	Word not Bold
Word highlighted	Bold option clicked	Word made Bold

In the second example, either condition being met produced a positive result.

The truth table for the second example is:

Condition A	Condition B	Result (or output)
DOS not used	Windows not used	File not copied
DOS not used	Windows used	File copied
DOS used	Windows not used	File copied

With computer circuitry, the state of particular electrical bus lines or the states of particular bits of data are used to determine the result of an action.

AND

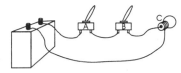 The normal way to demonstrate an electronic AND logic is the use of a battery, a lamp and two switches. The switches are wired in series with each other. This means that both have to be switched to light the lamp. Its truth table is shown below, with the left table describing it fully in words while the right table shows a shortened form:

Condition A	Condition B	Result (or output)
Switch A Off	Switch B Off	Lamp not lit
Switch A Off	Switch B On	Lamp not lit
Switch A On	Switch B Off	Lamp not lit
Switch A On	Switch B On	Lamp lit

Switch A	Switch B	Lamp C
OFF	OFF	OFF
OFF	ON	OFF
ON	OFF	OFF
ON	ON	ON

If a zero is taken as a condition being OFF (or a condition being false) while a one represents a condition being ON (or a condition being true) then the most common method showing a truth table is as shown. The right-most column describes the expected outputs while the other columns described the variety of possible input conditions.

A	B	C
0	0	0
0	1	0
1	0	0
1	1	1

Of course, there may be more than two inputs and this would result in extra input columns.

Example Use

All alphabetic text may require to be converted to upper case. A lower case letter 'a' is ASCII value 97 which is 01100001 in binary, while upper case 'A' is ASCII 65 or 01000001. In fact, the difference between the lower and upper case version of any letter is 32 and this is binary 0010000. Subtracting 32 from the binary pattern would convert from lower to upper case. Since all lower case letters have bit 6 set to 1, a *'mask'* can be used as an AND filter to let all of the binary pattern, apart from the 6th bit (value 32), appear in the output.

```
example input   01100001
AND with 223   11011111
example output 01000001
```

Logic operations are *'bit-wise'* operations; the condition of any output bit is purely the result of the logic operation on the corresponding input bits, independent of the result of any other bit operation. So, for example, bit 3 in the output byte was determined solely by the contents of the third bit in the two inputs - with no carry being used.

OR

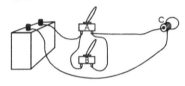

In this example, the switches are wired in parallel and switching on either of the switches will light the lamp. This is known as an OR configuration and its truth table is as shown.

A	B	C
0	0	0
0	1	1
1	0	1
1	1	1

Example Use

All alphabetic text may require to be converted to lower case; this is the reverse of the previous example. Since no upper case alphabet letters have the 6th bit set, 32 has to be added to the input to provide a lower case output.   This is achieved by ORing the input with 32 - a binary mask of 00100000.

$$\begin{array}{r} 01000001 \\ \text{ORing with 32} \quad \underline{00100000} \\ 01100001 \end{array}$$

NOT

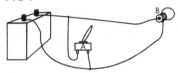

In this case, the lamp is permanently wired to the battery and will normally remain lit.   If the switch is thrown it will place a short circuit across the battery/lamp and the lamp will be extinguished.

A	B
0	1
1	0

Throwing the switch reverses the normal condition (ie the lamp changes from lit to unlit) and this logic is known as a NOT.   It has a simple truth table.

XOR

This is the term for an Exclusive OR, also sometimes known as EOR.   The truth table shows that when there are no input conditions, there is no output; this is identical to a normal OR.   The table also shows that where either of the inputs is on, the output is set to on; this also identical to a normal OR.   However, if both the inputs are set, the output remains off.

A	B	C
0	0	0
0	1	1
1	0	1
1	1	0

Example Uses

Upper case D is ASCII 68 or 01000100 as a byte in binary.   If that pattern is transmitted from one computer to another computer at a distant location, the receiving end can re-transmit what it received. This will be returned (ECHOed) to the sender and the patterns can be compared. using XOR.

Pattern sent	01000100	01000100
Pattern returned	01000100	01100100
Result of XORing	00000000	00100000

In the first example, the pattern returned was identical to the pattern sent and XORing results in a byte full of zeros.   In the second example, the data was corrupted during transmission and XORing produces a value, which is not all zeros.   Therefore, testing for a byte value of zero reports on a successful or an unsuccessful transmission of that character.

Parity Checking

Sending data over distances can result in the corruption of a data byte's contents (see chapter on data communications). Since the ASCII range only requires 7 bits, the eighth bit of the data byte is used to store a check value.   For 'odd parity' systems the total bits set to 1 should be an odd number, while 'even parity' systems maintain the number of bits set to zero as an even number.   Where the receiving computer expects - and receives - the correct parity the output will show no error; any discrepancy will set the output to indicate that an error (ie corruption) occurred.

Expected	Actual	Error
0	0	0
0	1	1
1	0	1
1	1	0

Animations

If any number is XORed with itself, it will produce an output of zero (eg 129 XOR 129 = 0).   This can be used to switch graphics off and on.

It is also a handy way to clear the contents of a CPU register.

How the computer works

The CPU is the intelligence of the machine but it still needs a pre-written program to create, use and modify the user's data. If the computer needs to compare two numbers, or add two numbers, this is carried out <u>inside</u> the CPU and the numbers have to be fetched into the CPU from the computer's memory chips. Similarly, any program instructions have to be fetched into the CPU so that they can be acted upon.

This means that CPUs work with
- programs that are stored in memory
- data that is stored in memory

The memory store can be the machine's main RAM memory or it can be the system ROM (e.g. the BIOS chip). It cannot run programs straight from the disk - it loads the program from the disk into the machine's memory and then runs the program from the memory. Similarly, all data - whether incoming or outgoing - will have to reside in memory at some stage. So, programs and data from disk, tape or CD and data from keyboard, mouse, networks, sensors, etc. are all placed in memory for the CPU to access.

The program, no matter its origin, will end up as a series of instructions stored in the low-level language that the CPU understands. This is the CPU's *'instruction set'* and is different for different CPU variations. Since the CPU can only process numbers, all programs and data are reduced to sequences of numbers. The most complex Windows application is simply stored as a long set of numbers; the most beautiful graphic is similarly reduced to a stored set of numbers. The way that these numbers are interpreted by the CPU gives the program or data its meaning.

Data Handling

The normal process of a computer is a sequence of getting instructions from the program, interpreting them and acting upon them - mostly resulting in the manipulation of data. Therefore, the CPU is constantly reading instructions from the program in memory. It does this by fetching a copy of the instruction from the memory, along the data bus, into the CPU for interpretation. If this instruction requires an alteration of the user's data, this altered data will need to be transmitted from the CPU on to the data bus and used to overwrite the old data held in memory.

Of course, it is imperative that the programs and data are held separately and are not allowed to overwrite each other. To achieve this, the programs and data are stored in different areas of the machine's RAM memory. If the CPU knows where each is stored, it can get at each for reading data from, or writing data to, these specific areas. Every individual memory location has its own unique location number, known as its *'memory address'*. The CPU can only read from, or write to, a particular address by asking specifically for that address - that is the purpose of the address bus. Only one address number can be on the address bus at any one time and only the memory location with the same address number will respond to that address data. So, if the number 7700 is placed on the address bus by the CPU, only location 7700 can be accessed.

Controlling the Flow

There is one final complication. Once a location is accessed, it needs to know whether it is supposed to dump a copy of its contents on to the data bus or whether it is meant to alter its contents to that currently on the data bus. That is the purpose of the Control Bus. When an address is accessed, the lines on the control bus will state whether the location is to be read or written. These control signals are organised by the CPU and are either *'read'* or *'write'* instructions dependent on the task required.

Examples of typical operations may be:
- reading a new instruction from the program.
- reading the contents of the ROM (remember that ROM can't be written to).
- writing to a data memory location (e.g. updating a cell in a spreadsheet).
- writing to a device memory location (e.g. sending a character to the printer).
- reading from a device memory location (e.g. reading a joystick or mouse position).

The process of getting each instruction from memory, interpreting the command and carrying it out is known as the *'fetch-decode-execute cycle'*. The following pages give a simplified version of this process but it should be noted that all computers use variations based on the system outlined. The precise details will vary with the specific architecture of each CPU and the modern techniques used to speed up the process.

Inside the CPU

The diagram shows a simplified layout of a CPU architecture as used in the basic XT PC.   Many improvements are built upon this general framework.

The components are grouped under two headings:

Bus Interface Unit

This comprises the Instruction Queue, Control Unit and Address Segment Registers.   These components move data in and out of the CPU and translate program instructions into CPU tasks.   The BIU also uses the Control Bus to control many of the computer's other components such as memory and peripheral devices.

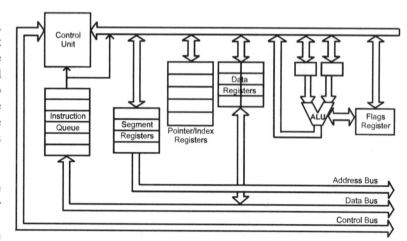

Execution Unit

This comprises the Data Registers, the Pointer Registers, the Flags Register and the Arithmetic Logic Unit. These components carry out the arithmetic and logic calculations and determine program flow using the pointer registers.

Fetching Instructions

The BIU is capable of fetching a number of program instructions in a single procedure. The Instruction Queue shown stores up to six instructions at any one time.   The instructions are individually taken off the top of the queue and sent to the Control Unit where they are decoded.   Since these instructions are already inside the CPU, they are more quickly available than fetching from memory via the Data Bus. This pre-fetching is a simple form of *'pipelining'* and is carried out while the Execution Unit is busy executing internal instructions (eg arithmetical calculations).   In this way, fetching and execution can be overlapped in time.

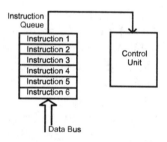

Decoding Instructions

A single machine code instruction will, in practice, require a number of operations to be carried out.   For example, the instruction *'cmp dl, al'* requires that the contents of two registers be compared.   This translates into smaller sub-programs to fetch the contents of register dl and place it in the ALU, fetch the contents of register al and place it in the ALU, initiate the ALU comparison and set the flags register to reflect the results of the comparison.   The Control Unit is responsible for decoding all instructions into sub-programs and transmitting the control signals in the correct sequence, with the required timings.

Storing Data

The CPU has a number of internal short-term memory stores; these are used for storing values that are currently required.   The number of registers used and their size varies with different CPUs.   The simple model has four data registers and these are:

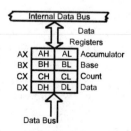

Description	Title	Use
AX	Accumulator	General Purpose. Also used to store values prior to, and resulting from, arithmetic operations.
BX	Base	General Purpose. Also used for forming base-displacement addresses.
CX	Count	General Purpose. Often used for counting.
DX	Data	General Purpose. Also used for accessing machine and system interfaces.

The above registers are 16 bits long and all 16 bits can be read or written to in one operation.   However, to allow more flexibility, each register can be treated as two separate 8-bit registers.   Thus, the AX register is 16-bit, while the lower byte is addressed as AL and the upper byte is addressed as AH.

Other Registers

Another set of registers is designed specifically to locate data held in memory - they *'point'* to the required locations. These registers are:

Description	Title	Use
SP	Stack Pointer	A stack is an area of memory allocated to store data. The stack works in a LIFO manner - Last In First Out. Items are placed in the stack and peeled off later in reverse order. The Stack Pointer is used by the CPU to implement the stack but is not often manipulated by the programmer.
BP	Base Pointer	This is used to access data that has been pushed on to the stack.
SI	Source Index	They can be used to form indexed addresses or to point to strings.
DI	Destination Index	
IP	Instruction Pointer	Other CPUs refer to this as the Program Counter. The register stores the address which holds the <u>next</u> instruction to be fetched. As the program runs, the IP will continually update to reflect the flow of the program code.

A further set of registers, known as Address Segment Registers, combine to store the addresses used for data transfers.   No register in the example system is more than 16 bits wide.   This stores a memory address range of 2^{16}, providing only 65,536 unique address locations.   Since even the oldest PC had 1MB of addressable locations, a 16-bit register is insufficient to store all required locations.   This led to the *'segment + offset'* principle of memory addressing.   One register is used to store the upper part of the memory address (the segment) while another register is used to store the lower part of the address (the offset).   The combined registers form the required address.   A typical address might be DC00:0015. The first four hex characters store the segment address and the last four characters store the offset from that segment address.   The *'effective address'* is calculated by multiplying the segment address by 16 and adding on the offset.   Therefore, the effective address of DC00:0015 is DC015h.

The Address Segment Registers are:

Description	Title	Use
CS	Code Segment	Used with IP to form the address of the next instruction to be fetched
DS	Data Segment	Used with SI to form the address of a particular item in memory.
SS	Stack Segment	Used with SS for stack accesses.
ES	Extra Segment	Similar to DS; used for additional data accesses.

Note The segment address is commonly used (e.g. within the BIOS, DOS commands such as EMM386, memory maps, etc) with the offset <u>assumed</u> to be 0000h. For example, the 640k memory boundary may be quoted as A000h. More correctly, this should be A000:0000.

There are two types of machine code programs. One has the extension .COM (eg FORMAT.COM) and the other uses a .EXE extension (eg ATTRIB.EXE).   With COM files, the entire program including all its data and resources fits within a single 64k segment.   When run, DOS decides which segment to use and only a single 16-bit register is required to address the entire program code.   With EXE files, which are usually of large size, the program occupies several segments and the segment+offset method using two registers is required.

The ALU

The diagram shows the Arithmetic Logic Unit as a V-shaped object being fed by two *'operands'*.   An operand is a value about to be used for arithmetical or logic operations.   Typical activities within an ALU are:

Arithmetic	+ - * /
Logic operations	AND OR NOT XOR
Operand comparisons	Is one operand greater, smaller or equal to another operand
Operand values	Is an operand's value positive, negative or equal to zero

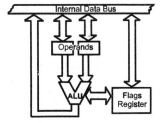

Arithmetic operations typically fetch one operand from the Accumulator and the other operand via a register.   After the arithmetic operation, the result exits the ALU and is placed into the Accumulator.   These data movements take place via the CPU's internal busses.

The CPU also has a Flags Register (known in some other CPUs as the Status Register).   This is a 16-bit register where individual bits are set (ie 1) or cleared (ie 0) to notify specific results from the ALU's operation.

Flags Register

The Least Significant Bit, Bit 0, is set to indicate that an arithmetic operation resulted in a carry. Bit 6 is set when a previous instruction (eg Compare or Subtract) produced a zero result. Bit 11 is set when an overflow occurred (ie the result is too large for the register to store it). The program can test these flags and take appropriate action (if Bit 6 is set then jump to another piece of code; if not carry on).

The program to execute

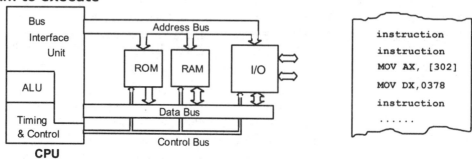

The diagram shows an extract from a program, displaying two instructions from a larger program.

The first instruction is to read the contents of location 302 into register AX. This could be reading the value from an external sensor via an add-on data acquisition card. The next instruction places the value of 0378 into register DX.   This could be setting the system up to write to the parallel printer ports, as 0378 is the normal location of the LPT1 port.   The instructions and their values in hexadecimal are:

MOV AX,[302]   A1 02 03

MOV DX, 0378   BA 78 03

Each of these instructions would be stored in different memory locations and would be in a pure hexadecimal numeric format as shown in the example below:

Location in RAM	Location Contents	Meaning of Contents
1017	??	Part of previous instruction
1018	A1	MOV into register AX the contents of the following address
1019	02	Part of address 302
1020	03	Rest of address 302
1021	BA	MOV into DX the following number
1022	78	Part of 0378
1023	03	Rest of 0378
1024	??	Part of next instruction

The addresses shown for storing the instructions are illustrative only. Each instruction happens to occupy three bytes of memory and addresses are entered in reverse order - 0378 is stored as 78 followed by 03.

The Fetch-Decode-Execute Cycle

The steps in running the example instructions would be:

FIRST INSTRUCTION

1. The CPU's Control Unit places the value of 1018, from the Instruction Pointer, on to the Address Bus. This is the location that stores the beginning of the instruction to be fetched.   Only the RAM byte at location 1018 responds to this action.

2. The Control Unit brings the MEMR control line low.   This signal tells the memory chip that the contents of the location 1018 should be placed on the Data Bus.   The memory chip dumps the current contents of location 1018 - i.e. the value A1 in this example - on to the Data Bus.

3. The CPU reads the value A1 off the Data Bus and restores the MEMR line to high.

4. The CPU reads locations 1019 and 1020 in the same way.   It knows that the instruction consists of three parts by decoding the first value read in.   The Control Unit knows that the value A1 translates to moving a value into the AX register from a port address.   It also knows that the port address is two bytes long.   Therefore it knows that it has to fetch two more bytes of data to make up the entire instruction.

5. The next two reads are used to determine the address for the port read. The CPU now knows that it requires to read the contents of port location 302.

6. The CPU stores the value 1021 into the Instruction Pointer - this is the location to fetch the next instruction when it has finished carrying out the current instruction.

7. The value A1 is converted by the Control Unit into a sequence of control signals, both within and outside the CPU itself, paced by the system clock.

8. The CPU places the value of 302 on to the Address Bus. This is the location that stores the beginning of the instruction to be fetched. Only the data acquisition card will respond to this activity.

9. The CPU brings the IOR control line low, telling the card that the contents of the location 302 should be placed on the Data Bus. The card chip dumps the current contents of the location on to the Data Bus.

10. The CPU reads the value off the Data Bus and restores the IOR line to high.

11. The value read from the Data Bus is placed in the AX register. The instruction has been carried out.

SECOND INSTRUCTION

12. The CPU places the value 1021 from the Instruction Pointer on to the Address Bus. 1021 is the location storing the beginning of the next instruction to be fetched. Only the RAM location 1021 will respond.

13. The Control Unit brings the MEMR control line low. This tells the memory chip that the contents of the location 1021 should be placed on the Data Bus. The memory chip dumps the contents of location 1021 - i.e. the value BA - on to the Data Bus.

14. The CPU reads the BA value off the Data Bus and restores the MEMR line to high.

15. The CPU then proceeds to read locations 1022 and 1023 in the same way. It knows that the instruction consists of three parts by decoding the first value read in. The CPU knows that the value BA translates to moving a fixed value into the DX register. It also knows that this value is two bytes long. Therefore it knows that it has to fetch two more bytes of data to make up the entire instruction.

16. The CPU stores the value 1024 into the Instruction Pointer - this is the location to fetch the <u>next</u> instruction when it has finished carrying out the current instruction.

17. These next two reads are used to determine the value to be placed in register DX. The CPU now knows that it requires to place the number 0378 into the DX register.

18. The DX register has 0378 placed in it. The second instruction is completed.

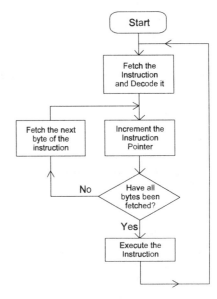

The CPU would then fetch the third instruction by reading the contents of location 1024.   The flow chart shows the sequence of events in processing an instruction.

It should be noted, however, that programs do not continually run in an unbroken sequence.   At certain points in the program, depending upon the result of some test, the CPU may fetch an instruction from another part of the program. Since the instruction does not reside at the address stored in the Instruction Pointer, it has to alter the IP to store the exact address where the new instruction is stored. The process is known as *'branching'*.

Interrupts

The computer runs a program by the repeated use of the fetch-execute-decode cycle, systematically working through the program instructions.   Once a program has started there has to be provision for the user to control the flow of the program (eg by key presses or mouse clicks). The CPU also has to handle external error conditions (eg writing to an unformatted floppy disk or a memory parity error).   If the CPU had to continually test whether the keyboard or mouse had been used, etc, a great deal of machine time would be wasted through this 'polling' of devices.   A more efficient method is to allow the CPU to proceed as normal and only interrupt the program when an event is triggered.

The program sequence can be interrupted at any point by outside events, such as:

- Those generated by the computer's own hardware (such as a user pressing a key or the computer's built-in clock being incremented).
- Those generated inside the CPU in response to an unexpected condition (eg a divide-by-zero error).
- Those generated by add-on cards connected via the expansion slots on the motherboard such as the mouse port, serial port devices, network interface cards, etc.
- Those deliberately embedded inside the software program so that it can gain access to external routines in the ROM (e.g. BIOS routines) or the RAM (e.g. user-created routines).   These are called *'software interrupts'* and examples are sending a character to a parallel printer (one of interrupt 17h routines) or one of the many DOS services provided by interrupt 21h (such as reading and writing to discs, reading the built-in clock, etc.).   Examples of interrupt 21h calls are given in the section on assembly language.

256 different routines are available and each routine has its own interrupt number from interrupt 0 up to interrupt 255.

The first 16 are allocated to hardware interrupts, which means that they are designed to detect activity from hardware elements. The first eight interrupts are allocated for system activities such as detecting mathematical overflow errors or the user pressing the PrtScr key.   The next eight interrupt numbers are mainly for the use of peripheral add-on cards (for the interfacing of modems, mice, etc.). These are called IRQ0 through to IRQ7.

A further eight interrupt lines are available from IRQ8 through to IRQ15.   These are allocated to interrupt 70 onwards as shown in the table.   These IRQs are serviced by an extra controller chip.

Num	Description
00	Divide Error
01	Single Step / Debugging
02	Non-Maskable Interrupt / Parity Error
03	Breakpoint / Debugging
04	Overflow
05	Print Screen
06	Reserved
07	Reserved
08	IRQ0 - Timer
09	IRQ1 - Keyboard
0A	IRQ2 - Cascade to second PIC
0B	IRQ3 - COM2
0C	IRQ4 - COM1
0D	IRQ5 - LPT2
0E	IRQ6 - Floppy Controller
0F	IRQ7 - LPT1

70	IRQ8 - Real-Time Clock
71	IRQ9 - Re-directed IRQ2
72	IRQ10 - Reserved
73	IRQ11 - Reserved
74	IRQ12 - PS/2 Mouse
75	IRQ13 - Maths Processor
76	IRQ14 - Hard Disc
77	IRQ15 - Reserved

There is room for confusion because the IRQ numbers that users see and set within utilities do not equate to the interrupt numbers within the system.   A look at the chart will show that IRQ0 is interrupt 08, IRQ1 is interrupt 09 and so on.

Note that the interrupt numbers are given in hexadecimal notation (i.e. in base 16).   Examples of the first few interrupts and their uses are shown in the table.

When an interrupt occurs, the normal program is suspended and the chosen *'interrupt service routine'* is run instead.   When the interrupt routine is completed, control is passed back to the main program, which carries on from the point where it was interrupted.

MI & NMI

There are two types of interrupt that are external to the CPU:

- Those that prevent the computer program from proceeding any further. Examples of these problems are falling supply voltage in the computer or a memory parity failure. These are so serious that they cannot be disabled via software - i.e. they are interrupts that are unable to be masked.   These are known as NMI (Non Maskable Interrupts) and are not normally altered by the user or technician.
- Those that denote non-fatal errors or are deliberate acts within a program (e.g. BIOS calls).   These interrupts are commonly used by application packages as it makes sense to use the existing routines provided within the BIOS chip.   These are known as MI (Maskable Interrupts) and allow operations that require strict timing - such as disk activities - to carry on unhindered. In these cases, the interrupt request is only carried out when the CPU is ready to handle it.

Since there are two levels of interrupt, there is a separate electrical line for each on the motherboard.

Prioritisation of Interrupts

It is likely that more than one interrupt will occur at any time and the CPU has to be told which ones are the most important to service.   The table shows the priorities for various interrupt conditions. Note that the first column shows system interrupt numbers and not IRQs.   If the CPU is servicing a low priority interrupt and a higher priority interrupt is triggered, the CPU suspends the lower interrupt routine and only returns to it when the higher priority interrupt has been successfully completed.   This practice of interrupts interrupting other interrupts is called the *'nesting of interrupts'*.

Interrupt Type	Priority	Example	Source
Int 0	1	Dividing a number by 0	Inside the CPU
Int 4	1	Overflow - Calculation result is too large to store	Inside the CPU
Software	1	Interrupts calls within program code	Inside the CPU
Int 2	2	NMI - Memory parity error	External to CPU
Hardware	3	MI - Keyboard, I/O, etc	External to CPU
Int 1	4	Single stepping during debugging	Inside the CPU

The hardware interrupts from the slave PIC are serviced first, followed by those generated in the master PIC. IRQs 8, 13 and 14 are pre-allocated to the clock, coprocessor/FPU and disk controller respectively. In addition IRQ 9 is used to cascade to the master PIC.   Similarly, IRQs 0,1,2 and 6 in the master PIC are pre-allocated.   The remaining IRQs are either available (i.e. not yet allocated to any device) or are alterable (e.g. a sound card can use IRQ5 nominally allocated to LPT2).

The IRQs are serviced in the following order: 0, 1, 2, 8, 9, 10, 11, 12, 13, 14, 15, 3, 4, 5, 6, 7

Hardware Interrupt Handling

Program interrupts are handled by dedicated chips called the *'interrupt controllers'* or *'Programmable Interrupt Controllers'* (PICs). These connect to the various hardware lines that require servicing. These can be seen in the expansion slot connector diagrams later in this chapter. One PIC handles the lower eight interrupts while another (Slave PIC) chip handles a further eight interrupts and channels them through the first PIC.

The routines for handling all these interrupts are stored in the computer's memory. This is likely to be within the machine's BIOS chip although a routine could also be stored as a TSR somewhere in the main memory area. When an interrupt occurs, the CPU has to know where the routine for that particular interrupt is stored. This achieved by holding the addresses of all the interrupt routines in the first 1k of the conventional memory - from address 0000h to 0400h. This is known as the *'interrupt vector table'* and each interrupt number has a corresponding 4-byte address that points to where the interrupt handling routine can be found. The diagram shows the relationship between the various components and activities.

Example

Here are the steps that result from the user pressing a key on the keyboard.

- The user presses the key.
- This activates the hardware line from the keyboard to the Programmable Interrupt Controller (PIC).
- The PIC activates the MI line to the CPU.
- The CPU takes a note of where it is in the main program so that it can return to that point again later.
- The PIC places the interrupt number (9 in this case) on the Data Bus.

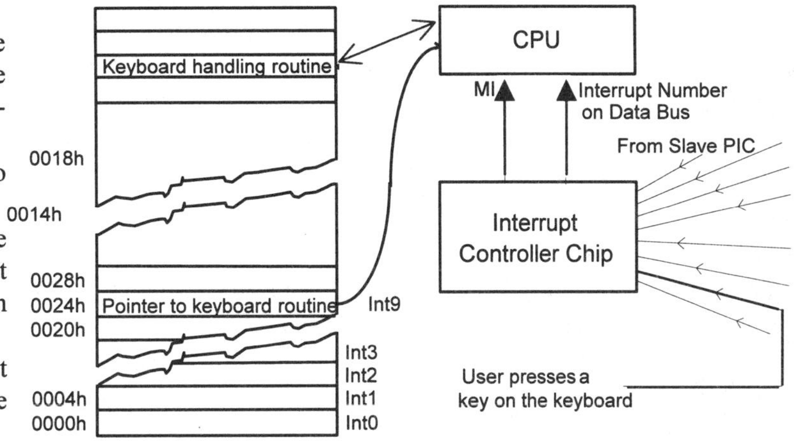

- The CPU uses this number to fetch the address of the keyboard handling routine. Since each interrupt vector is 4 bytes long, the wanted vector is stored at an address given by multiplying the interrupt number by four. So, in this example, the vector is stored at 9x4 = address 36 (which is 24h in hexadecimal).
- The CPU fetches the vector from the interrupt vector table - in this case the four bytes stored from address 24h onwards.
- The CPU runs the routine that is located at this address.
- When the routine is completed, control is passed back to the main program. The CPU remembers where it stopped processing the main program and returns to that point for further processing.

The above sequence will be identical for any add-on cards that are using the IRQ lines.

The NMI (Non Maskable Interrupt) Line is not handled through the PIC and has its own logic chips and its own direct line to the CPU.

Software Interrupt Handling

Interrupt calls that are made within a piece of software are handled in a slightly simpler fashion than that shown above. The CPU is informed of the interrupt number by the software call, the normal operation of the program is suspended and the interrupt number is multiplied by four as in step 6 above. It then carries out steps 7 to 9 as already explained.

Plug-and-Play PCI Interrupts

The older ISA system worked, but because the number of IRQs available was almost always limited to 16, upgrading systems was often a hit-and-miss affair and involved a lot of manual configuration. The PCI system can use Plug-and-Play technology, with several benefits including the ability to share an IRQ between devices. Plug and Play needs three key elements:

- The PC must support it (this is provided in all new computers).
- The adapter cards must support it (almost all new cards and devices have this feature).
- The operating system must support it (Windows 95/98 does; NT, OS/2 and DOS don't).

PCI systems have a PnP-specific BIOS, which extends the normal BIOS POST operations to include device configuration.   This auto-configuring of cards makes alterations and additions to hardware a simpler process. With all other buses, the addition or swapping of cards involves ensuring that there is no clash of memory addresses, IRQs and DMA channels between the existing and the new devices (see the chapter on Upgrading).   These problems are intended to be eliminated with PCI since the BIOS will maintain a list of all memory addresses, IRQs and DMAs in use and provide non-conflicting allocations for new cards.   Each of the new PCI plug-and-play cards has its own *'configuration space'* - usually a set of memory registers that are solely devoted to storing configuration information.   The Plug and Play BIOS chip interrogates these registers to determine the card manufacturer and type and the range of options it can handle. The cards are all capable of working with a range of different memory addresses, IRQs, etc. The BIOS determines the best settings for the cards and sends data to be stored in each card's configuration space detailing what the specific settings for the card are.

With Windows 3.1, the basic plug and play services were supplemented by providing *'BIOS extensions'* (software to link the BIOS facilities and the extra facilities).   Windows, from version 95 onwards, has the additional services designed into the operating system.

Plug and play is fully implemented when users have the required combination of PnP BIOS, PCI motherboard, PnP operating system or BIOS extensions and all add-on cards being of the PnP variety. Additionally, some software still ignores best practice and bypasses some BIOS routines.   True full PnP depends upon all the required features being present - partial benefits can be gained from a lesser specification although this will still involve some manual installation.   PnP still functions when the computer has some older (non PnP) cards installed, as the PnP BIOS assigns the PnP cards' configurations around those of the existing non-PnP cards.

IRQ sharing

The PCI chipset has its own interrupt handling circuitry and does not use the two PICs previously explained.   The conversion from PCI handling to the conventional handling and prioritisation is carried out by circuitry following an agreed standard known as *'Serialised IRQ Support'*. The Plug and Play BIOS will build up a *'PCI IRQ routing table'* that keeps track of IRQs assigned to PnP devices in specified physical slots.   Each PnP device can use up to four interrupts, known as INTA to INTD for each particular device.   The routing table combines this information into *'link values'* that distinguish between devices that share an IRQ.   Sometimes, problems with the information in the Routing Table mean that sometimes simply moving a PnP card into another physical slot can resolve some hardware conflicts.   It is theoretically possible to run a PnP system without IRQs as used on ISA systems; PnP IRQs are used mainly to remain compatible with legacy hardware.   However, an IRQ-free system would require truly *'legacy-free'* hardware with no ISA slots, and also no motherboard ISA devices such as PS/2 mouse and keyboard connectors, serial and parallel ports and so on.

IRQ Steering in Windows

Windows 95 OSR2, Windows 98 and Windows ME support a system called PCI Bus IRQ Steering. This allows the operating system to assign IRQs to devices, overriding the assignments made by the BIOS, although in most cases this is not necessary. If problems arise, the BIOS can be set up to 'set aside' IRQs for older, non-PnP ISA devices to prevent conflicts. PCI Steering systems can change IRQs dynamically, for example if a PCMCIA card is attached to a laptop it can be detected and assigned an IRQ. IRQ Steering is the software interface that allows the Windows operating system to control a computer that shares IRQs between devices. The illustration opposite shows the IRQs allocated on a typical machine, along with the IRQ Steering on the shared IRQs.

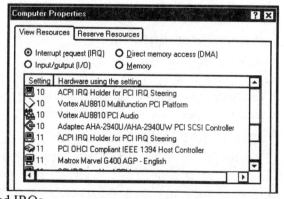

However, PCI Steering is not without its drawbacks. When changing IRQs it can cause the system to hang on occasion, and some devices may conflict with others when PCI Steering forces them to share an IRQ. If this is the case, Windows PCI Steering can be disabled through the Control Panel, and the BIOS usually has a setting called *'PnP Aware OS'* which can be set to *'No'*.

Speeding up the process

It is assumed so far that each new instruction is fetched from the memory <u>after</u> the previous instruction has been fully executed. If this were so, the only way to increase the computer's efficiency would be to increase the rate at which the CPU was clocked through the fetch-decode-execute cycle. Already, clock speeds have been raised from the original 4.77MHz to 2GHz and beyond. However, the laws of physics and the cost of manufacture restrict the ability to continually raise machine clock speeds. Very fast CPUs, for, example, would require very fast address buses and data buses, since these support chips would have to be able to keep up with the demands of the CPU. This would result in a very expensive motherboard. In practice, other methods are used to speed up the CPU's efficiency. These include:

- increasing the data bus width so that a larger data word is handled with each read or write, thus saving on the time required to execute several smaller reads or writes.
- pre-fetching techniques, to read several instructions at a time, saving subsequent reads.
- pipelining techniques, to decode one instruction while carrying out another, saving time.
- using two ALUs, or two or more CPUs, so that several instructions can be processed simultaneously.
- using maths co-processor, or FPUs, to carry out the number crunching while the main CPU carries out other tasks. These are add-on chips to older CPUs, while today's chips have the FPU built in.
- clock multiplying - making the operations inside the CPU chip run faster while maintaining the existing speeds for the main buses and motherboard devices.
- introducing efficient memory caching systems, either built in to the CPU chip and/or as external secondary cache.

Measuring performance

Comparison of performance between different computers requires some standard for measurement. Different systems are in use but they all seek to measure the *'throughput'* of the computer - how much work it can get through in a given time, usually one second.

CPU standards

Since the CPU is stepped by the system clock at speeds ranging from 4MHz to around 2GHz, this could be a starting point for comparison. However, many instructions require more than one clock cycle to complete, so a 900MHz machine will not carry out 900 million instructions per second. In addition, different CPUs may require a different number of clock cycles to carry out the same kind of activity. So, one common measurement is the number of instructions that can be carried out in a second. This is known as the 'MIPS' rating (Millions of Instructions Per Second). Another standard notes that floating point operations (handling real numbers) are the most demanding of a computer's processing time and therefore measures 'MFLOPS' (Millions of Floating Point Operations Per Second) or even Gigaflops. However, these standards do not take into account the word size of the CPU. An instruction that handles a 32-bit number will operate faster than one that only handles 8-bit numbers. This has evolved a definition of *'memory bandwidth'* that looks at the millions of memory bits accessed per second. This standard is dependent on clock speed, the average clock cycles for instructions and the memory word length; it is therefore a more accurate reflection of machine performance. Intel introduced the iCOMP index for comparing 32-bit systems.

Machine standards

The above measurements, though important, do not accurately measure the whole machine's performance. A slow disk system, slow memory chips or a poor graphics card can easily mar a fast CPU performance. For this reason, utilities are available to produce a factor that takes into account all components of the system. Scores are produced for each component (e.g. CPU, maths co-processor, memory, video, and disk) and an overall performance score. Examples of these utilities are PC Bench, PC Tools and Norton Utilities. The figures still have to be interpreted by the user. For example, a machine mostly used for graphics would require the best video and CPU performance while a machine mostly used for databases would benefit greatly from a good disk sub-system; a multimedia workstation would require all components to be top performers.

Application standards

From the user's point of view what matters is the speed in carrying out real-world applications. The time taken to perform normal application tasks is a more useful yardstick of a computer's performance than simple CPU speed or machine speed measurements. A group of CPU chip manufacturers have developed a benchmarking system known as *'P-rating'*. This measures the performance of a particular CPU when carrying out a range of application package activities. This measure is then compared with the performance of an Intel CPU using the same hardware and software, to give a rating. For example, the Cyrix 6x86 processor with a clock speed of 166MHz is given a P200 rating indicating that it performs the range of application tasks as fast as an Intel 200MHz CPU. For machines with Windows-based applications, performance-measuring utilities are WinBench and WinStone.

Von Neumann Model

Computers were, and still largely remain, based around the model developed by Von Neumann in the 1940's. The main points are:

- The same memory is used for storing both input and output.
- The memory holds a 'stored program' of instructions.
- The Program Counter maintains the program flow by pointing to the next instruction.
- The CPU can adopt one of a finite range of states.
- The action taken by the CPU depends upon its current state and current input.
- The instructions are fetched and executed one at a time.

Treating each stage of the fetch-decode-execute cycle as separate sequential activities produces system bottlenecks and other approaches have been developed to increase throughput.

Pre-Fetching & Pipelining

As mentioned, the CPU has its own internal registers that are, in effect, fast access memory stores. These are fast because they are already internal to the CPU and don't suffer the slow fetch times associated with the addressing of external memory chips. Unfortunately, these registers are also used for holding intermediate data for calculations and comparisons. The solution lies in providing other internal stores within the CPU, capable of providing fast access to instructions and/or data. This is called the 'pre-fetch buffer' and Intel's 8086 began with a buffer area capable of storing six pre-fetched instruction bytes. When the wanted instruction was read from memory, the CPU fetched the next instruction(s) at the same time.   The system was designed so that the buffer would be refilled every time it dropped to below five bytes and the CPU was not already accessing memory.

The 80386 attempted a form of 'pipelining' to speed up operations within the CPU. This system realised that while instruction 1 is being executed, instruction 2 and probably instruction 3 are already stored in the CPU.   It is able to apply the decode phase to instruction 2 while concurrently carrying out the execute phase for instruction 1.   This was a sound theory but was never fully exploited in the 386 chip.

The 486 took the pre-fetch a stage further, with its 'burst mode' approach.   The first initial access of a memory address is still relatively slow but reading the subsequent adjacent memory addresses is much faster.   This, coupled to a block of 8k of static cache RAM built into the CPU, resulted in much improved processing times.   The sequence in a 486 was defined as instruction fetch, instruction decode, address generation (described by Intel as 'Decode 2'), execution and write-back (writing its results back to an internal register).   This system allowed instruction 1 to be at the write-back stage, while instruction 2 was at the execute stage and instruction 3 was at the decode stage.   Modern Pentium chips break the pipelining into multiple operations.   This speeds up performance and is known as super-pipelining.

Superscalar Architecture

The Pentium moves the process even further with a 'superscalar architecture', which means that it has two separate ALUs.   Each of these pipelines is capable of processing an instruction and the resultant system is capable of processing two instructions simultaneously. Since not all instructions have to be carried out in a serial fashion, this will speed up some sections of code.   This capability would not be used where an instruction must follow another in time (e.g. the second instruction is dependent upon the output of the first instruction). The Pentium has two internal 8k caches, one for storing instructions and the other for storing data.   Pre-fetch buffers supply the two ALU pipelines, known as the U-Pipe and the V-Pipe.   A new 'Branch Prediction' unit examines the instruction cache, predicts the most likely flow of instructions and feeds the pipelines accordingly.   This moves away from the original principle on which computers were designed.   This was termed the 'Von Neumann' architecture and required that all the program instructions and data be processed by a single CPU using a single data bus.

Parallel Processing

Both pipelining and superscalar systems are elementary forms of parallel processing, in that more than one processing task is taking place at any one time.   Full parallel processing is available with the use of two or more separate CPU chips.   These communicate with each other to share tasks most effectively. This is the basis of the 'transputers' that are being developed at the supercomputer end of the market. However, PCs are already available employing two or four Pentium chips.   These are currently aimed at the network server market, so that server tasks and database engine tasks can be carried out simultaneously. Standalone dual Pentium systems offer around an 80% increase in performance.

Clock-Multiplying

Introduced with Intel's 486 processor, all CPUs are clocked to run faster than the main computer bus speeds. This is termed *'clock multiplying'*. By having extra memory, known as *'cache memory'*, built in to the chip, the CPU can read ahead and pre-fetch both data and program instructions. This way, the amount of traffic between the chip and the bus is reduced by around 50%. As a consequence, the <u>internal</u> speed of the CPU can be doubled or tripled without straining the CPU/bus interface. For example, the overall system can be running at 25MHz while the CPU runs at 50MHz.

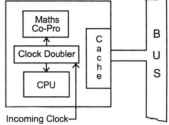

Advantages:

- Around 70% overall system performance improvement, including the built-in maths co-processor.
- It is a cheap system, since it still uses the standard motherboard and standard components;

Disadvantages

- The chip runs very hot, requiring large heat sinks to dissipate the heat.
- There are problems when running some older software packages that use delay loops; the loops may complete sooner than anticipated, causing unexpected results.

The clock-doubled range of chips is known as *'DX2'*. So, a 486DX2/66 is a 486 machine with a 33MHz clock being doubled inside the CPU to 66MHz. Intel's *'clock tripled'* CPUs were designed to treble the internal running of the CPU compared to the normal clock rate of the system. This was the *'DX4'* range and they took a 25MHz machine and ran the CPU at 75MHz. The 100MHz model of the chip could either treble a 33MHz system or double a 50MHz system to produce the 100MHz internal clock rate.

Pentium Settings

The technique continues in the Pentium range and its clones. The *'clock'* frequency (ie number of pulses per second) is divided down and used to supply the timing pulses on the PCI bus. The same clock frequency is also multiplied by a chosen factor and clocks the internal operation of the CPU. The setting of links on jumper blocks determines the clock's working frequency; other jumpers set the multiplication factor. The chart shows a typical range of clock rates and multipliers.

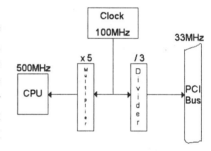

CPU Multiplier	Basic Clock Frequency				
	50MHz	60MHz	66MHz	100MHz	133MHz
x1.5	75	90	99	-	-
x2	100	120	133	-	-
x2.5	-	150	166	-	-
x3	150	180	200	-	-
x3.5	-	-	233	350	-
X4	-	-	266	400	533
X4.5	-	-	300	450	600
X5	-	-	333	500	667
X5.5	-	-	366	550	733
X6	-	-	400	600	800
X6.5	-	-	433	650	866
X7	-	-	466	700	933
X7.5	-	-	500	750	1GHz
X8	-	-	533	800	-
X8.5	-	-	566	850	-
X9	-	-	600	900	1.2GHz
X9.5	-	-	633	950	-
X10	-	-	667	1.0GHz	1.33GHz
X10.5	-	-	700	-	-
X11	-	-	733	1.1GHz	-
X11.5	-	-	766	-	-
X12	-	-	800	-	-
X13	-	-	-	1.3GHz	-
X14	-	-	-	1.4GHz	-
X15	-	-	-	1.5GHz	-
X17	-	-	-	1.7GHz	-
X20	-	-	-	2GHz	-

A Pentium with a 100MHz clock speed and a multiplier of 4 produces a CPU speed of 400MHz. Similarly, a 133Mhz clock speed and a multiplier of 6.5 produces approx 866Mhz CPU clock speed.

Operations via the separate memory bus are processed at the basic clock rate. This is 60MHz for older Pentium and Pentium Pro CPUs, 66MHz for newer Pentiums, Pentium Pros and Pentium IIs, and 100MHz or 133MHz for Pentium II, III or 4 CPUs (running at 350 MHz and above).

Some CPUs have fixed multipliers (see the *'Overclocking'* section in the *'Upgrading'* chapter).

Maths Co-processors

Early PCs allowed the addition of an extra chip to improve the computer's number crunching operations. The 8086 chip had the 8087 companion chip, the 80286 had the 80287, the 80386 had the 80387 and the 486SX had the 80487.   The 486DX and the Pentium range of chips have their own maths co-processors built in to the CPU.   The demand for maths co-processor chips resulted from the design of the 80xxx series of CPU chips. The computer's main CPU is best at handling integer calculations; its speed drops dramatically when confronted with floating point (i.e. fractions) calculations.   The companion chip for the 80xxx series - known as a *'maths co-processor'* - runs in parallel (hence the term *'co-processing''*) with the main CPU.   Mathematical tasks normally undertaken by the CPU are delegated to the co-processor.   The maths co-processor chip, unlike the main CPU, is not designed for a general-purpose role; it is tailored to carrying out its functions in the most efficient way possible.   The co-processor built in to the 486DX chip, for example, has huge 80-bit registers, to manipulate very large numbers with great accuracy.

This provides great potential advantages:

- The co-processor is much quicker at mathematical calculations.
- The main CPU is freed to carry out other tasks.

However, there are a number of other considerations:

- This great improvement only occurs for a <u>proportion</u> of the machine time, since the computer only spends a proportion of its time on mathematical calculations.
- Not all older applications packages can utilise the co-processor. The software has to be able to detect the presence of a maths co-processor and make use of it.
- Some applications benefit much more from the maths co-processor than others.   For example, there is no advantage for word processing, as the number crunching element is almost non-existent.   Besides, by far the slowest link in the chain is the user. The machine spends most of its time waiting for the typist.   There is also little benefit for database operation, as most database activity requires file accesses, which are very slow compared to any processing activity.   The collation of figures for reports would involve some calculations including real numbers expressing currency.   Even here, many reports tend to maintain integer counts and totals. However, dramatic performance increases can normally be expected with computer-aided design packages.   These rely heavily on the calculation of curves, etc. and are all equipped to use a maths co-processor to best advantage.   Similarly, graphics, Desk Top Publishing and other graphic-oriented applications also rely on substantial amounts of number crunching to calculate arcs, vector co-ordinates, etc.

CPU Cache Memory

Standard memory speeds have not progressed at the same rate as processor speeds.   As a result, the CPU can process data faster than the data can be fetched from memory or placed in memory.   The Pentium III front side bus operates at no more than 133MHz while the CPU can run at up to 1.3GHz.   The Pentium 4 system has an effective memory transfer rate of 800MHz, while the CPU can run up to around 2GHz.

Consider that a 1.7GHz CPU cycles every 0.59ns while the fastest access time for main memory is around 1.2ns.   This means that the CPU has to stand idle while the required location in memory is accessed for data to be transferred. This waiting is enforced by *'wait states',* which prolong the CPU's access cycle time.   While this matches the performance of the CPU to that of the computer memory, it slows down the effective CPU operating speed.

This bottleneck could be overcome if the much faster RAM was used as main memory.   However, the cost of using many megabytes of very fast main memory is entirely prohibitive at the present time. It would also be extremely wasteful to have expensive RAM sitting doing little, while most of the computer activity centres round only a small portion of the memory at any one time.

A favoured solution is to use a small block of fast RAM between the CPU and the main memory.   This is known as *'cache memory'.*   Any data held in the cache memory can be transferred to the CPU at greater speeds, due to its faster access time of as little as 0.5ns.   This means that the CPU can access memory without the need for wait states. The result of using cache memory is to dispense with wasted CPU time and to increase computer efficiency. Since the block of fast SRAM is likely to be substantially smaller than the computer's main memory, the cache memory can only hold a portion of the data that is resident in main memory. The aim is to ensure that only the data most likely to be required is stored in cache memory.

This relies on two established facts, collectively known as the *'principle of locality'*.

- The running of applications programs involves jumping and looping through different parts of the long list of program instructions. Despite this, most program activities are sequential - an instruction follows from a previous program instruction, with occasional jumps to other program areas. When arrived at the new program area, the machine then progresses sequentially through the new area. Often, the same few instructions are repeated over and over again as part of some iterative process.
- The data for programs is often grouped together in sequential fashion. For example, a payroll program will process employee 75 after employee 74, and so on. Also, data recently read is likely to be the data to be written. The same payroll program, for example, will read an employee's wage record, calculate new figures and write the new results over the old record data.

If the data is often accessed sequentially, then a group of data is transferred from main memory into cache memory. This one-off transfer will take place at the slowest speed - i.e. that of the main memory, wait states and all. Any subsequent requests for data are transferred to the CPU at the higher cache memory speed. Concentrating the program's main data into the fast memory ensures that the performance is optimised. When another area of data is requested - one not already stored in cache - the data is transferred from main memory into cache memory, along with the contiguous data in main memory. The fetch of the first piece of data, in this case, is actually slower than normal, since an entire block of data was transferred at a wait-state speed. However, since subsequent fetches from that memory block are faster, the overall effect is to speed up processing.

Therein lie the limitations of cache memory:

- If the cache contains data transferred due to a previous CPU request, there is no guarantee that the next CPU request will be for data from the same block. In that circumstance, there is no *'cache hit'*, i.e. the requested data is not to be found in cache memory. The requested data, as part of a new block of data, is transferred from main memory to cache. This means that the time taken to transfer the previous block was largely wasted and the efficiency of the computer has been reduced.
- The benefits of caching vary with the type of application in use. A program that uses a lot of data transfers benefits from a large cache memory. On the other hand, a program that is processor intensive (any number-crunching application) requires less data transfers and does not benefit to the same extent.

Despite these limitations, cache memory greatly improves the computer's overall processing times.

Cache Organisation

Just as any cache memory is better than no cache memory, the way that the cache memory is organised and read/written has a bearing on its performance. The material so far has outlined how data is fetched from main memory to cache, to CPU. Of course, any data that is written to cache memory also has to be reflected in changes to main memory. A number of different methods of reading and writing exist and they affect the performance of the cache. Predictably, the faster the method, the more costly the product. Users have no control over the method of reading and writing cache, other than at the purchasing stage.

Read Methods
LOOK THROUGH
The CPU requests data from the cache. If it is not in the cache, the CPU requests the data from the main memory. This would involve a second read request, which would slow the process.

LOOK ASIDE
The CPU interrogates the cache memory and the main memory at the same time. If the data is in the cache memory, it is transferred at the faster rate; otherwise, it is fetched more slowly via main memory.

Write Methods
WRITE THROUGH
The CPU updates the cache and the data in the cache is used to update the contents of main memory. An improvement on this method is to store all writes to main memory in a queue within the cache and copy from the queue to main memory. This requires an area of cache memory to be set aside to store the data queue but it has

the advantage of allowing the cache to write data to the main memory at a quiet time on the data bus - and without tying up the CPU. This method is used with some 386 CPUs and all 486 CPUs.

WRITE BACK

This is similar to the improved *'write through'* method, except that the main memory is only updated if there is a difference in the contents of the cache and the corresponding section of main memory. This is the method used with all CPUs in the Pentium range.

Cache Architecture

The data transfers are carried out by dedicated *'cache controllers'*.   When the CPU requests access to the data at a particular address, the cache controller checks whether that address appears in the cache memory.   If the address is already in the cache memory - a *'hit'* - then the address contents can be used by the CPU without recourse to the main memory.   If the address is not found in cache memory - a *'cache miss'* - the cache controller has to access the main memory (and update the cache memory).

The hit rate of the cache is determined by:

- The cache size. A large cache stores more address information and increases the likelihood of the required data being in cache. This can be improved by adding increased memory to the cache and is a good way to improve a machine fitted with slow main memory chips of, say, 70ns or 100ns access time.
- The bus size between main memory and cache. A wide bus transfers data between main memory and cache memory at a faster rate, for those occasions when a cache miss is encountered.
- The way the cache is organised. The common methods are 'direct mapped' and 'associative cache'. These control the link between main and cache memory and cannot be altered.

With large caches, a lot of time can be spent searching the cache. If the wanted data is not present, then the extra time has been wasted.   However, if multitasking is required, then a large cache size speeds up processing.   Off-the-shelf computers are supplied with a variety of cache options. Older computers had from zero to 256k of cache. Modern computers have 512k up to 2MB of cache.

Primary/Secondary Cache

Note that the Intel 486 and Pentium chips already have a small area of cache memory built in to the CPU chip. This is known as *'Primary Caching'* or *'Level 1 Caching'*.   This is often considered inadequate and can be supplemented with the addition of extra *'Secondary' or 'Level 2'* caching. The 486 has 8k of primary cache while the Pentium has 8k for instructions and another 8k for data.   The Pentium Pro, like the Pentium, has two 8k caches but it also includes its secondary cache of 256k, 512k or 1MB within the CPU itself rather being an external add-on.   This allows internal cache operations to take place simultaneously with external DRAM operations.   The Pentium II has two 16k L1 caches but reverts to an external cache that runs at half the speed of the CPU.   The Celeron Pentium II has 128KB of cache while the Xeon has a 512KB, 1MB or a 2MB L2 cache, both types running at full CPU speed.

The table shows some common memory speeds:

	486DX	Pentium	Pentium Pro	Pentium II	Xeon	Pentium III	Pentium 4
System	33MHz	66MHz	66MHz	100MHz	100MHz	100MHz	400MHz
CPU	100MHz	233MHz	200MHz	450MHz	400MHz	550MHz	1.7GHz
L1	10ns	4ns	5ns	2-3ns	2ns	2ns	0.6ns
L2	30ns	15ns	5ns	4-6ns	2ns	4ns	0.6ns
Main Memory	60ns	60ns	60ns	10ns	10ns	10ns	1.2ns

Burst Mode

When the CPU accesses a location from main memory, the desired address is sent out and the data from that location is placed into the cache. With burst mode systems, the memory chip's own circuitry calculates the next address locations (usually the next three consecutive

DRAM	6+6+6+6 =	24
SRAM	3+3+3+3 =	12
Pipeline Burst RAM	3+1+1+1 =	6

addresses) and thus minimises the work of the CPU. This speeds up throughput and makes it faster than ordinary EDO memory. Similarly, cache memory can operate in burst mode, speeding up data movements between the second level and first level cache. A typical Pentium 66MHz motherboard system requires 6 clock cycles for each DRAM memory request, while each SRAM request require only 3 clock cycles. Chips that are optimised for *'pipeline burst mode'* achieve subsequent memory requests in only a single clock cycle.

The Range Of Intel CPUs

From the beginning of the PC range of computers, the main CPU has been from the Intel range, supplemented by other manufacturers with *'clones'* or improved versions of each chip in the series. The current series consists of the following chips:

8086   These are no longer manufactured or sold.   Since it only had a 20-bit address bus, it was only capable of addressing 1MB of unique addresses.   This meant that it was unable to support extended memory and was completely incapable of running Windows and most modern DOS applications.   Its speed was much slower than its successors - e.g. the Pentium can be 150 times faster than the XT, when measured in MIPS.

286   Like the 8086, they are no longer sold, and are rarely found in current commercial use.   They are slow, running at speeds from 10MHz to 20 MHz.   With a 24-bit address bus, the AT was able to address up to 16 million different address locations.   To complement this, the AT had two operating modes - *'real mode'*, where it used only 8086 code and acted like a fast XT and *'protected mode'*, where it was able to access beyond the 1MB address limit and employed its added features.   It also ran at about 4 times the MIPS rate of the XT.   Since *'real mode'* is the natural mode for normal DOS operations, the *'protected mode'* was intended for multi-tasking operations, Windows, OS/2, etc.   Unfortunately, the chip was not really powerful enough for these tasks.

386   Also out of production, these chips ran at speeds from 16MHz to 40 MHz and could carry out the effective multi-tasking operations (i.e. run two programs at the same time) that eluded the 286.   It was also the minimum processor for running Windows, with a machine with at least 4MB of RAM.   It introduced substantial improvements in both memory management and an enlarged instruction set.   The chip was available in two varieties - the 386SX and the 386DX.   The SX version had a 32-bit internal data path but had only a 16-bit path between the CPU and the computer's memory.   So, the SX model could only transfer data in 16 bit chunks at a time.   The DX model had a 32-bit data bus between the CPU and the memory chips, allowing larger data transfers and therefore faster throughput.   The ability to use external cache memory, usually about 64k, also improved performance.   The 386SL model was a low power consumption model used in portables.

486 This chip, now obsolete, ran at speeds from 20MHz to 100MHz.   Little change was made to the 386 instruction set, with the emphasis being placed on performance enhancements.   This chip was also available in SX and DX varieties, with the DX having a built-in maths co-processor.   Motherboards using the 486SX chip provided a spare maths co-processor socket to upgrade to a DX.   Apart from the raw CPU clock speed, the 486 was faster than previous chips because it carried out the most common instructions in a single clock cycle (compared to two or three clock cycles for the 386 chip).   This was a move towards the RISC philosophy ('**R**educed **I**nstruction **S**et **C**omputer').   The 486 chip also had a built-in 8k block of cache memory.   This, coupled to a new *'burst mode'*, meant that data was transferred at a far higher rate than the 386 system.   Burst mode allowed memory transfers from consecutive memory locations to be achieved at the rate of one per clock cycle.   The 486DX was also available in clock doubled (DX2) and clock tripled (DX4) models.   The 100MHz DX4 ran faster than the bottom end of the Pentium range - i.e. the 60MHz and 66MHz models.   Since the DX4 range used only a 3.3 volts supply, compared to the normal 5 volts, they consumed less power and created less heat, making them good choices for portables.

Pentium   It was significantly faster than a 486 and was effectively two CPUs in the one chip with a 256-bit internal bus and a 64-bit external data bus.   On most occasions, this allowed two instructions to be executed in parallel, greatly speeding up throughput.   The chip also had the main mathematical operations (i.e. add, divide and multiply) hard-wired into the chip; its maths co-processor was up to 10 times faster than the 486DX maths co-processor.   All Pentium models are *'superscalar'*; the basic Pentium chip had two integer processing pipelines.   It also had a *'branch prediction'* facility that 90% of the time correctly predicted the flow of the program and fetched the instruction from a buffer area.   The Pentium also had a 16k internal cache.   It used CISC technology with some RISC elements.   60MHz and 66MHz chips required a 5 volt supply while models from 75MHz upwards use a 3.3 volt supply for both core operations and input/output operations.

Pentium Pro   This chip used six different pipelines and 40 general-purpose registers.   All the pipelines operated simultaneously, offering greatly improved processing capability.   To fully utilise this architecture, the Pro read the incoming program instructions into an 8k instruction cache.   The instructions were then turned into fixed-length RISC type *'micro-operations'* by three parallel decoders and sent to one of the free pipelines.   In this way <u>parts</u> of the original instructions were being processed independently rather than sequentially.   The CPU had an *'out-of-order'* approach so that instructions that couldn't be immediately executed (eg waiting for data) were not placed in a pipeline where they would prevent other micro-operations from being processed.   In this way, bottlenecks were minimised.   The results of the micro-operations were then assembled in the correct order for use by the external software application.

For even greater speeds, the Pentium Pro had all the necessary logic on board to allow four CPUs to be connected to the same motherboard for parallel running. This is known as *'symmetric multiprocessing'* and example implementations were the IBM PC Server 720 and the Dell XL 5133-4.

The chip used 16k of level 1 cache in a *'unified'* mode. The Pentium used two banks of cache - one for instructions and one for data. If the instruction cache was full the CPU could stall, even if there was spare capacity in the data cache. The Pentium Pro regarded its two 8k caches as a single block of 16k available dynamically for either data or instructions, balancing any changes in load and minimising CPU stalling.

There was also 256k or 512k of second level cache built into the chip. With many CPUs, the cache was a plug-in unit or was soldered to the motherboard. With the Pentium Pro, the cache was internal to the chip and directly connected to the CPU itself. This meant that the cache operated at the full CPU speed while some other external caches operated at only half that speed. This made the Pro's caching much more efficient. The Pro's design is optimised for 32-bit working and actually runs 16-bit code slower than a Pentium. For maximum results, it needs to run 32-bit program code with a 32-bit operating system (eg Windows 98/NT).

Pentium MMX   This is a version of the Pentium with 57 additional instructions in the CPU instruction set. These are multimedia and communications extensions to the CPU giving them the title *'MMX'* - multimedia extensions. The new instructions use a technique known as SIMD - Single Instruction, Multiple Data. One instruction can work on up to 8 bytes of data simultaneously. This provides very fast repetitive processing of data - ideal for video decompression, sound synthesis, multimedia, 3D rendering and other graphics-intensive activities. MMX aware programs - ie those using the new MMX instructions produce speed improvement in these areas. It also runs existing programs faster because of its 32k internal cache (16k for code and 16k for data). It contains a more efficient branch prediction unit. The instruction pipeline also works one level deeper - it can carry out more work in advance than a normal Pentium. MMX chips have 8 enhanced internal registers that are 64 bits wide, comprising virtual registers using the normal registers along with the Floating Point registers). It uses 2.8v for core operations and 3.3v for input/output operations. This reduces power consumption and reduces heat, but means that an MMX chip cannot be used to upgrade a motherboard that does not have a dual voltage supply on Socket 7 CPU holder. Intel has introduced an *'Overdrive'* MMX chip that only runs on 3.3v and is intended for upgrading with older, Socket 5, motherboards. In either case, the motherboard's BIOS chip needs to be MMX compatible.

Pentium II   Previously known as the *'Klamath'*, it is an improved Pentium Pro with MMX additions. Its initial release was a 233MHz CPU with a 100MHz processor/cache interface and a 66MHz system bus. The built in second level cache is taken out of CPU and is mounted, along with CPU on a plug-in card. This card plugs into a special connection slot known as *'Slot One'*, which means that the Pentium II needs a completely re-designed motherboard. It uses a 2.9v supply to reduce heat dissipation. The external second level cache only runs at half the CPU speed, which means that the performance is diminished. However, the 32-bit performance, coupled with MMX capabilities, places Pentium II machines in the lower multimedia and graphics workstations market. The newer Slot 1 Deschutes chip uses the same slot as the standard Pentium II but starts at 300MHz speeds. In conjunction with the new BX chipset, it will also run at system bus speeds of 100MHz (compared to 66MHz). A version aimed at the budget PC market, known as the Celeron, has a 66MHz bus only, as well as reduced cache size.

Pentium II Xeon   The Xeon is intended for high performance workstations and network servers. It requires yet another new motherboard with a *'Slot 2'* connection. It is based on a Pentium II with a lower supply voltage and initial speeds around 400MHz to 450MHz. It requires a higher specification motherboard with faster memory and a new chipset (the 450NX). The Level 2 cache runs at the same speed as the clock and is available in 512KB, 1MB and 2MB sizes.

Pentium III   This chip is the current entry-level standard for computers (the standard at which most people currently buy a new machine, before upgrading). The Pentium III uses the Slot 1 connection for early models, and Socket 370 for later models. It has a bus speed of 100MHz or 133MHz. The internal second level cache is 512k but still runs at only half the CPU clock speed.

The Pentium III introduces KNI, Katmai New Instructions, comprising 70 new machine code instructions aimed at 3D graphics, MPEG2 video encoding/decoding, AC3 audio and image processing. These work on the same principle as the MMX (Single Instruction Multiple Data) moving large amounts of data with a single instruction. The MMX chip's registers were used for both normal storage and MMX operations. The CPU was forced to halt normal register operations to switch into MMX register operations - and vice versa. The switching time overhead reduced overall throughput. The PIII has a new separate set of 128 registers for SIMD operations, thereby speeding up both SIMD and normal register activities.

The Pentium III Xeon is essentially the Pentium II Xeon with the added KNI instructions.

Pentium 4   The Pentium 4 has a 100MHz Front Side Bus, with an internal multiplier of x13 to x20. This gives a processor speed of 1.3 to 2GHz, although even faster speeds are expected in time. However, it is currently only used with the Intel 850 chipset, which requires RAMBUS memory. It uses a technique called 'quad pumping' that quadruples the throughput of the Front Side Bus, essentially giving a 400MHz bus even though it is clocked at 100MHz. The instruction set includes Streaming SIMD Extensions 2 (SSE2) to improve Internet performance as part of Intel's '*NetBurst*' architecture. The Pentium 4's other main features include '*Hyper Pipelining*' based on larger instruction pipelines and deeper prediction techniques, and a '*Rapid Execution engine*' that consists of two clock-doubled Arithmetic and Logic Units.

RISC vs CISC   The main approaches to CPU design are CISC and RISC processors.   CISC (Complex Instruction Set Computer) CPUs provide a comprehensive instruction set and a wide range of address modes. The more complex instructions replace a number of more simple instructions, making programming easier. The subcommands within the instruction may be of different lengths and the processor has to act to provide the required processing space for each subcommand. This takes time and these complex instructions often take more clock cycles to complete compared to a group of simpler instructions, lowering overall throughput. RISC (Reduced Instruction Set Computer) processors perform a more basic set of instructions, each of uniform length. Each instruction is highly optimised, reducing the number of clock cycles for an operation. When combined with caching and pipelining, RISC processors sometimes appear to execute an instruction in zero clock cycles. Hybrid CPUs, combining elements of CISC and RISC are termed CRISC chips.

Alternatives to Intel

With Cyrix being taken over by VIA, the main challenge to the Intel line comes from AMD. The AMD K6-3 is a RISC chip that integrates a 256k cache. Unlike the Pentium II, the K6-3 fits a standard Pentium motherboard Socket 7 CPU connector. The K7 (aka 'Athlon') chip uses its own proprietary slot connector (Slot A), requiring a specially designed motherboard. It has a clock speed of 500MHz to 1.3GHz and a bus speed of 200MHz. Like the K6, it provides its own set of 21 SIMD instructions, known as 3DNow!. However, these are incompatible with KNI instructions. The Athlon MP processor is designed for dual processor systems and aimed at the video editing, graphics rendering and server markets. It uses a Slot A connection and has a 760 MP chipset. The chipset supports a 133/266MHz front side bus, ATA100, AGP4x and PC2100 DDR RAM. In the mobile market the most notable competition comes from Transmeta, whose '*Crusoe*' processor runs from 333MHz to 700MHz.

Summary of Intel P.C. Processors

	8086/88 the 'XT'	80286 the 'AT'	80386	80486	Pentium
Introduced	1978	1982	1985	1989	1993
Number of Pins	40	68	132	168	273
Transistors	29,000	120,000	275,000	1.2m	3.1m
Data Bus Size	8088 8 bit 8086 16 bit	16 bit	32 bit	32 bit	64 bit
Address Bus Size	20 bit	24 bit	SX 24 bit DX 32 bit	32 bit	32 bit
Addressable Memory	1MB	16MB	SX 16MB DX 4GB	4GB	4GB
Clock Speed (MHz)	4.77 / 8	10/20	SX 16/33 DX 33/40	SX 20/25 DX 33/50 DX2 50/66 DX4 100	60/233
Performance (in MIPS)	0.75	2.66	11.4	54	112

	Pentium Pro	Pentium II	Xeon	Pentium III	Pentium 4
Introduced	1995	1997	1998	1999	2001
Number of Pins	387	Slot 1	Slot 2	Slot 1 / Socket 370	423, later 478
Transistors	5.5m	7.5m	7.5m	9.5m	42m
Data Bus Size	64 bit	64 bit	64 bit	64 bit	64 bit
Address Bus Size	36 bit	36 bit	36 bit	36 bit	36 bit
Addressable Memory	64GB	64GB	64GB	64GB	64GB
Clock Speed (MHz)	150/266	166/600	400/450	450/ 1GHz	1.3GHz- 2GHz
Performance (in MIPS)	300	900	n/a	2G flops	2661

Assembly Language

All computer programs are loaded from their backing store (eg disk, tape, CD) and placed in memory. The program instructions are then fetched by the CPU for decoding and execution (see the earlier explanation of the fetch-decode-execution cycle). These could be instructions for an applications package such as Excel or PhotoShop, or could be the instructions for carrying out systems operations under DOS or Windows. Program instructions, of all types, are stored in binary format (eg 1001110001010001). Each binary pattern is unique for a particular CPU instruction and the decoder's job is to turn the incoming binary pattern into the set of control signals required to carry out that instruction. A different instruction would have a different binary number and would be decoded as a different set of control signals. Since these are instructions to run the computer, they are known as 'machine code'. They are in binary but are represented to writers in hex format for easier understanding. This complex process is hidden from the computer user.

From a programmer's point of view, writing programs purely in binary would be both very tedious and error-prone. That is the motive for the development of the range of computing languages that are available. All languages, from ancient old COBOL to modern JAVA, provide the programmer with easier ways to write programs. These programs are later turned into the binary patterns that are stored on file and later used by the computer. Programmers have to learn the particular syntax of a language and get used to the methods used for converting their work into executable programs.

High Level Languages

With high level languages, programmers do not need to know how the CPU works. The program is written as a script file with a line of text for each stage of the application's activity. The script file is saved, usually as ASCII characters, and can be reloaded later and amended just like any other text file.

When the program is ready to test, the language instructions have to be converted into their machine code equivalents and run.

Two methods of conversion are used:

Interpreters

This looks at the script file and takes each line at a time. The instruction in the first line is immediately converted to machine code and run. When the activity is completed, the next line of text is read and similarly converted to machine code and run. The program is run using only the original text file; there is no additional file such as an EXE or COM file.

Examples of interpreted systems are:

BATCH FILES

All batch files, including the AUTOEXEC.BAT that sets up the computer on bootup, have their lines interpreted and acted upon one at a time. Although simple, batch files can be very powerful. The following line in a batch file

        COPY A:*.DOC C\

could produce hundreds of reads from a floppy drive and hundreds of write operations to the hard disk. Each read involves accessing the floppy, reading the file name, checking its extension and perhaps copying the files contents into memory. This one batch file line may result in thousands of CPU activities.

CONFIGURATION FILES

The DOS CONFIG.SYS file and all Windows INI files are used to set up the machine to particular hardware and software requirements. The files are written in English-like commands (eg BUFFERS = 10 or sCurrency = £) and the interpreter converts them into the corresponding memory configuration, etc.

EARLY VERSIONS OF BASIC

The programming language called 'Basic' was very popular in the earlier days of computing, particularly in schools and colleges and among those looking for a gentle introduction into programming. An example line might be:

        INPUT age%

which would result in the CPU waiting for keyboard input, checking that a numeric value was entered and placing the value into a memory storage area.

Later versions of Basic allowed the program to create executable versions (ie compiled versions).

Compilers

With compilers, the entire script file is converted into another separate file containing machine code instructions corresponding to the script commands. The resulting files are usually EXE or COM files, but could be DLL or SYS files. The script is known as the *'source code'* while the compiled output is known as the *'object code'*.

The chart shows that the programmer creates a script file and uses the facilities of the programming environment to convert the script into a binary file equivalent. If the writer has made a syntax error (ie used incorrect syntax) then the conversion stage will report an error. The writer can then edit the script file and try again. If the conversion process was successful, a compiled version of the program will exist and can be run.

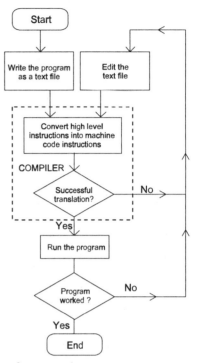

The compiler only tests whether the syntax of the input file is correct (eg the correct order of items, the correct usage of punctuation). The program may still be logically incorrect (eg adding tax to a wage packet instead of deducting it). If the compiled version is run and found to be incorrect, the programmer can recall the text version, edit and re-compile the program.

Languages such as Pascal, Cobol and C use compilers to convert to executable formats. A line in Pascal such as

> Writeln ('Dumbreck');

would instruct the CPU to place the text string on the computer screen and produce a carriage return and line feed (ie place the cursor at the start of the next line). Again, a single line instruction is translated into several differing CPU instructions. This is defined as a *'one to many language'*.

Low Level Languages

High level languages benefit from their ease of use but suffer varying degrees of speed loss, mainly due to their use of general-purpose routines. For example, the Pascal *'Writeln'* routine may be asked to display text as in the above example. It may also be asked to display the contents of a variable (eg Writeln (age) or even a mixture of text and variable values eg 'Writeln ('My name is ',name,' and my age is ', age). This produces a routine that is bulkier and slower than a routine dedicated to a single activity.

Low level languages require that the programmer has a detailed knowledge of the workings of the

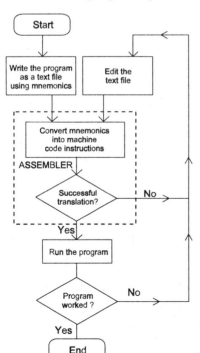

particular CPU that the program is being written for (code for a PC will not run on a Macintosh or an Amiga). The number and size of registers, the methods employed and the available range of machine code instructions can be exploited by the knowledgeable programmer to produce code that runs at the fastest possible rate. This positions low-level programmers in the software markets requiring instant responses. Examples include defence, production lines (eg process control and robotics) and embedded systems (eg modems, Point-of-Sale terminals). Low level programming produces more compact and faster programs.

The text file is written using *'mnemonics'* - small commands giving explicit CPU instructions. For example:

> MOV AL,8

will place the value of 8 into the al register.

This makes the simple assembler a *'one to one language'*, with one CPU instruction per text line. The more developed assemblers are also *'one to many'* since they allow the use of *'macros'* where a single text line substitutes a pre-written collection of instructions. The macro code substitutes for the macro line prior to the assembly process. Some assemblers also support *'many to many'* through the use of IF-THEN-ELSE and DO-WHILE constructs.

The chart below shows the relationship between the source code (the programmer's text), its conversion to object code (ie machine code) and its storage in memory.

High level instruction	Low Level equivalent	Machine Code equivalent	Binary output after conversion
write('A')	MOV DL,41	B2 41	10110010 01000001
	MOV AH,02	B4 02	10110100 00000010
	INT 21	CD 21	11001101 00100001
	INT 20	CD 20	11001101 00100000

The first column shows a single Pascal instruction, which displays the upper case letter A on the screen. The second column shows the equivalent commands in assembler mnemonics. The third column shows the conversion into machine code expressed in hex. The last column shows the actual binary information for the instructions, and this is what is saved to disk as the program file.

A compiler takes the single instruction from the first column and creates the binary output seen in the fourth column. An assembler takes the four instructions shown in the second column and creates the same binary output. The hex shown in the third column is only used where the programmer wishes to view a file or a register's contents.

The second table shows the program as it would be stored in memory, assuming it was placed in address 20000 upwards. The binary for B2 is placed in address 20000, the binary for 41 is placed in address 20001, and so on.

Memory Address	Contents
20007	00100000
20006	11001101
20005	00100001
20004	11001101
20003	00000010
20002	10110100
20001	01000001
20000	10110010

Instruction Sets

Each CPU has a different design, different electronic wiring inside the chip and differing sets of instructions to control the chip's operations. The Intel range of chips for the PC uses the existing core of instructions throughout its range. The commands for the earliest chips such as the 8086 are still to be found in the most modern chips such as the Pentium range. Newer chips provide additional facilities but the basic commands will work with any PC. That explains why so much existing software will run on all machines while new software is written specifically to take advantage of the additional facilities of the Pentium or the MMX.

Instructions are grouped round functions and examples are:

- data transfer
- arithmetic operations
- interrupt instructions

Saving Development Time

Writing in assembly language can be quite a slow and intricate task. Methods have evolved to speed up the development of machine code programs.

These include using:

- LABELS   The program often jumps to particular chunks of coding, depending upon the result of some activity (eg jumping to a piece of code to display an error message if something goes wrong, or returning to an earlier point in a loop). If the programmer can always refer to the start of that coding as a label written in English, then programming becomes faster and less error prone than referring to actual address locations. For example, jumping to a label called hiscore is more understandable than jumping to address 1234h. To indicate that the text is to be regarded as a label, a colon finishes off the word - ie the line would be written as   hiscore:
  When the program is assembled, the assembler places the correct address in place of the label.
- CONSTANTS   The ASCII values for Line Feed and Form Feed are 0Ah and 0Ch. Programming can be simplified by using the letters 'LF' and 'FF' in place of the ASCII codes.
- VARIABLES   Similarly, variables can be set up to store values or text strings such as 'Hello'.
- FUNCTION CALLS   DOS has a wide range of built-in facilities that it uses for its own functions such as reading the keyboard, writing to screen and printer, etc. The programmer can tap into these existing routines and save re-inventing the wheel. These are explained more fully later.
- SCRIPT LIBRARIES   Many activities, such as checking if a date is valid (eg no 30th Feb or no 13th month) are common to many programs. Once the piece of code is written and tested, it can be stored for use with other programs. When another program is being developed, the text can simply be inserted into the new program script at the appropriate point.

- <u>OBJECT LIBRARIES</u>   A collection of similar routines (eg screen handling routines, modem routines, etc) can be combined in a single assembled object file. This produces a set of pre-written routines that are already in machine code format.   This *'library'* of routines is then *'linked'* to the programmer's code to create a stand-alone EXE file.
- <u>MACROS</u>   There are activities that a program might wish to carry out many times in different parts of the program.   Examples might be string handling routines, serial port operations and disk activities.   It is inefficient and error-prone to insert the same code in all of these places; if the code needs altering then every occurrence of the code has to be found and altered.   A better way is define the set of instructions only once, at the beginning of the program.   The set of instructions (known as the *'macro'*) is named by the programmer and every time the code needs to be used only the macro name needs to be inserted in the code.   When the program is assembled, the full code is inserted each time the macro name is found in the program.   If the macro is changed and the program is re-assembled, all the occurrences of the code are automatically updated.

Creating Small Programs

The earlier chart showed the process of turning a single script file into a single-segment COM file. This is adequate for a variety of small utilities that are under 64k in size.   This process, using fully featured assemblers such as MASM or TASM, can handle labels, script libraries, DOS function calls and user-defined macros.   Running the object code through a linker (see below) will convert the program into an EXE file.

Creating Large Programs

Writing a large program in assembler is similar to writing a program in any procedural language such as Pascal.   The stages of program design are:
- Produce a precise specification of the program's needs.
- Break the overall problem down into a set of smaller tasks. If necessary a task can be broken down into smaller sub-tasks.
- Write the program for each task as an independent module.
- Bring the modules together with any external modules from libraries.
- Test and debug the program
- Document the program.

The chart shows a collection of source code modules being converted into their machine code equivalents and then merged with any library code to produce a single EXE file.

If the program is less than 64k in size, the final EXE file can be converted to a COM file using the EXE2BIN program provided with DOS.

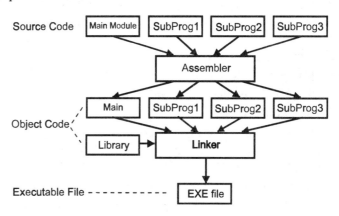

Assembler Tools

The most commonly known assemblers for the Intel range of CPUs are:
- MASM from Microsoft
- TASM, bundled with Turbo Pascal
- A86 (shareware)
- NASM (freeware)
- DEBUG, bundled with MSDOS and Windows

DEBUG is supplied with DOS.   With Windows 95 and later, it is not automatically installed but can be found on the installation CD.   It does not support all the timesaving elements such as labels, macros, constants, variables, etc.   It does, however, support the DOS function calls and is very useful for creating small programs.

Since different tools may be available to different readers, the examples in this chapter use DEBUG since it is available to all DOS users.   It does not provide all the improvements provided by the other assemblers but these are also outlined in the appropriate places.

Script Syntax

With a number of important exceptions, lines in a program script make use of four components, which are shown in the example line of code below:

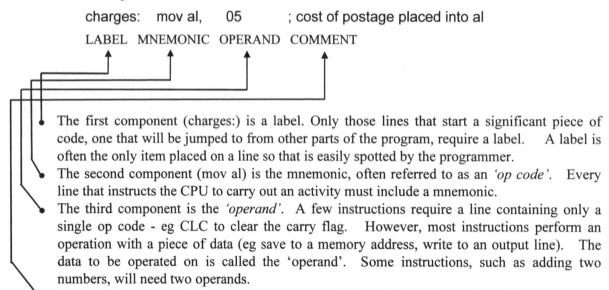

charges: mov al,   05   ; cost of postage placed into al

LABEL MNEMONIC OPERAND COMMENT

- The first component (charges:) is a label. Only those lines that start a significant piece of code, one that will be jumped to from other parts of the program, require a label.   A label is often the only item placed on a line so that is easily spotted by the programmer.
- The second component (mov al) is the mnemonic, often referred to as an *'op code'*.   Every line that instructs the CPU to carry out an activity must include a mnemonic.
- The third component is the *'operand'*. A few instructions require a line containing only a single op code - eg CLC to clear the carry flag.   However, most instructions perform an operation with a piece of data (eg save to a memory address, write to an output line).   The data to be operated on is called the 'operand'.   Some instructions, such as adding two numbers, will need two operands.
- The fourth component is a program comment.   The assembler ignores any information after the semicolon.   The comment is there to document the program so that programmers can explain the purpose of a particular line or group of lines.   Comments can be included in a line along with other components or can be placed on their own in a line.

There are variations on this basic layout, such as defining macros, assembler directives, etc.

Dos Interrupts

Before exploring the instruction set commands, the readily available functions provided by DOS are examined.   These functions are loaded into the system when the computer boots up and can be called from a machine code program. DOS provides 256 interrupt functions - from interrupt 0 (INT 0) through to interrupt 255 (INT FF).   Some of these, like INT 0 (Program Termination) or INT 5 (PrntScr) are single purpose functions.   Other interrupt calls provide a range of other functions; these are chosen by setting registers before initiating the interrupt call.   These are demonstrated in the following examples.

First example

A machine code routine to write all the text from the screen to the printer (ie the DOS PrntScrn command) could be written from scratch - but it already exists in DOS and can be called by a single instruction.   Placing the instruction *'INT 05'* in a program will interrupt the flow of the machine code program, call up the function to print the current screen contents, and then return to continue through the rest of the program.   The code calling PrtScrn can be inserted within an existing program or can be written as a single instruction program for testing. Instructions 6 and 7 demonstrate another DOS function - that of terminating the machine code program and returning control back to COMMAND.COM. Program termination used to be carried out by calling INT 20 but Microsoft's preferred method is to call INT 21 with register AH set to 4C.   This has the added advantages of returning an exit code in AL (handy for batch file programmers) and of closing any open files. Note that values are expressed in hex.

Data to enter	Meaning
RCX	Set the file size to 16 bytes
10	ie (10h)
N SCRNPRT.COM	Name the file
A	Assemble the following code
INT 05	Print the Screen
MOV AH, 4C	Set for program termination
INT 21	Call the DOS INT 21 routine
<Enter>	Signals end of code
W	Write a COM file
Q	Exit DEBUG

Using DEBUG

DEBUG is not as powerful as fully featured assemblers but it has the advantage of coming bundled with DOS.   The script in the left column is entered as a text file using a plain ASCII editor such as EDIT. The heart of the program is only the fifth, sixth and seventh lines. The surrounding code is common to all DEBUG scripts and is used to instruct the compiler how large to make the file, what to name the file and instructions to assemble the code, create a COM file and leave the assembler program.

When completed, the script should be saved with the extension .DBG and fed into the assembler using the following command at the DOS prompt:

DEBUG < FILENAME.DBG

This produces a runnable COM file. The example code would be compiled as SCRNPRT.COM.

Second Example

Many INT calls support multiple functions, depending on the values of their registers prior to initiating the interrupt call.

- INT 10, for example, has over 100 differing video-related functions. Options range from setting video modes to reading light pens.
- INT 13 provides a range of about 50 disk functions with various reading, writing, formatting and verifying functions.

Data to enter	Meaning
RCX	Set the file size to 16 bytes
10	
N PRINTX.COM	Name the file
A	Assemble the following code
MOV DL, 58	Place 88d in register DL
MOV AH, 02	Choose the display option
INT 21	Call the DOS INT 21 routine
MOV AH, 4C	Set for program termination
INT 21	Call the DOS INT 21 routine
<Enter>	Signals end of code
W	Write a COM file
Q	Exit DEBUG

The most widely used of all is the INT 21 which has a huge range of options for handling the keyboard, the screen output, the serial port, disk operations and much more. For example, calling INT 21 with the AH register set to 2 and a numeric value in register DL will display the ASCII equivalent of DL's value on the monitor screen.

The small program shows 88, the ASCII value for an upper case X, being placed in the DL register. Calling INT 21 with AH=2 chooses the 'display a character to the screen' routine and that routine uses the value held in DL for conversion to an ASCII character. An 'X' is displayed.

Third example

Another INT 21 option allows the program to wait for the user to press the keyboard. The ASCII value resulting from the keypress is placed in register AL. This is initiated by placing the value of 8 in register AH prior to calling INT 21.

The script shows instruction 5 through to 11 as the body of the program. Instructions 5 and 6 result in AL holding the keypress result. The character of the key pressed is not displayed (echoed) on the screen. If the fifth line were changed to MOV AH, 01 then the character would be both read into the AL register and displayed on the screen.

Instruction 7 copies the value from AL into DL.

Instructions 8 and 9 display the ASCII value on the screen.

Data to enter	Meaning
RCX	Set the file size to 16 bytes
10	
N PRNKEY.COM	Name the file
A	Assemble the following code
MOV AH, 08	Choose a keyboard read
INT 21	Read keyboard value into AL
MOV DL, AL	Copy ASCII value to DL
MOV AH, 02	Choose the display option
INT 21	Call the DOS INT 21 routine
MOV AH, 4C	Set for program termination
INT 21	Call the DOS INT 21 routine
<Enter>	Signals end of code
W	Write a COM file
Q	Exit DEBUG

Viewing A COM File

DEBUG provides many other useful features in addition to assembling machine code. It can display and alter the contents of the CPU's registers, trace through a program's execution and display a COM file in its original mnemonic form. The DEBUG command is followed by the name of the file to be examined.

DEBUG PRNKEY.COM

A hyphen is displayed; this indicates that DEBUG has loaded the file and is waiting for a command.

Entering the command 'U 100 L 10' means '**U**nassemble the file from location **100** with a **L**ength of **10**h bytes being displayed'. Since the first 256 bytes (i.e. 100h) of a COM file contain the file header, the program always starts at location 100h.

The screen output is as shown with the first column displaying the address location, the second column displaying the hex values and the third column displaying the values as assembler mnemonics. It can be seen that B4 is the hex code for MOV AH, while CD is the hex code for INT. So, B4 is stored in address 100h while 08 is stored in 101h, and so on.

```
-U 100 L 10
220F:100     B4 08     MOV AH, 08
220F:102     CD 21     INT 21
220F:104     88 C2     MOV DL, AL
220F:106     B4 02     MOV AH, 02
220F:108     CD 21     INT 21
220F:10A     B4 4C     MOV AH, 4C
220F:10C     CD 21     INT 21
```

Utilities such as Borland's Turbo Debugger provide much more advanced facilities such as opening windows to keep a watch on the value of expressions and program variables as the program runs.

Data Transfer

The most used command for transferring data is MOV and its syntax is

MOV destination, source

A <u>copy</u> of the data in the source is placed in the destination.   The data in the source remains unaltered and no flags are changed by using this instruction.

The instruction has the following formats:

Format	Examples		Explanation
Register Addressing	mov ax, bx	mov dl, al	The data is copied from one register into another
Immediate Addressing	mov al, 07	mov ax, 0B23	The examples show that the data to be transferred is included in the instruction. Note that these can be both 8-bit or 16-bit operations depending on where the whole register (AX) or just the upper or lower byte (AH or AL) is used.
Direct Addressing	mov al, addloc	mov 553B, al	The first example shows al being given a copy of the contents of the address held in the variable addloc. (ie determine the address held as addloc, go to that memory address, get its contents and copy it into al). The second example shows the contents of al being placed into the memory address 553Bh.
Indirect Addressing	move al,[bx]	mov al,[addloc]	In these examples, bx and addloc are not the addresses where the data is stored. They are *'pointers'* - they store the addresses of the memory locations that hold the actual data. The first example shows al being given a copy of the contents of the address held in the register bx. (ie fetch the address stored in bx, go to that memory address, get its contents and copy it into al). The second example shows al being given a copy of the contents of the memory address held in addloc.
Indexed Addressing	mov dx, bx[si]	mov al, list[si]	The Intel series use a Source Index register to form indexed addresses. This is very useful where a set of values is held in memory and has to be sequentially fetched and processed. The data could be a set of modem commands, a printer control sequence or a series of characters comprising a text message. In each case, the data has to be fetched one byte at a time starting at the first memory address holding the data sequence. After each byte is processed the pointer points to the next piece of data to be processed. The first example shows register dx being fed data stored at the memory location held in bx+si. As si is incremented, the data is sequentially addressed and fed to dx. The second example shows al being supplied with data from list (the label for an address). The contents of al will first contain the contents of list+0, then list+1, list+2 and so on, as the SI register is incremented This addressing method need not be used solely for reading data in a sequential manner. If the fifth byte in the series is required to be accessed, SI is set to 4 (since the first item would be si=0). This allows random access to the data.

The use of labels to replace actual addresses is also known as *'implied addressing'*.

The second example on the last page used immediate addressing (ie MOV DL, 58 and MOV AH, 02).

The third example also used register addressing (ie MOV DL, AL).

Branching

As in high level programming, the flow of code is not entirely sequential. Instructions are not normally carried out in strict order - starting at the beginning and finishing at the end. On some occasions a part of a program may never be called (e.g. code for sounding an alarm) or may be called several times (e.g. code to print three copies of a text). These *'jumps'* to sections of code have two formats:

Unconditional

The jump to a new address is carried out without any reference to the condition of flags in the flags register. For example JMP 1234 or JMP addloc. The sample code is the earlier PRNKEY program with an additional line JMP 100, which passes control back to address 100h (the start of the program code). The program endlessly waits for keyboard input and displays the ASCII value to the screen. The code provides no way to end the program and the user has to press Ctrl-C (the Ctrl and C keys pressed at the same time) to end the program.

Data to enter	Meaning
RCX	Set the file size to 16 bytes
10	
N PRNKEY.COM	Name the file
A	Assemble the following code
MOV AH, 08	Choose a keyboard read
INT 21	Read keyboard value into AL
MOV DL, AL	Copy ASCII value to DL
MOV AH, 02	Choose the display option
INT 21	Call the DOS INT 21 routine
JMP 100	Loop back to start of program
<Enter>	Signals end of code
W	Write a COM file
Q	Exit DEBUG

For those assemblers that support labels, the coding is much easier to understand. Text descriptions are used to replace absolute addresses making reading and debugging much easier. In addition, extra instructions can be added without having to recalculate absolute addresses for jumps (as would be required with DEBUG).

```
Loop:
MOV AH, 08
INT 21
MOV DL, AL
MOV AH, 02
INT 21
JMP loop
```

Conditional

Conditional jumps are performed by:
- testing for a particular condition
- jumping dependent upon the result of the test

The contents of the Flags Register (eg carry flag, zero flag or overflow flag) are set after arithmetic or logical operations are carried out. So, the program flow can be altered by testing the condition of flags. For example, program execution might jump to an error message if an overflow is detected.

The most common conditional jumps are:

Test	Purpose
JZ	Make the jump if the zero flag is set
JNZ	Make the jump if the zero flag is clear
JC	Make the jump if the carry flag is set

The example program shows the CMP instruction being used. Its syntax is

CMP destination, source

It will set the zero flag if both operands are identical and the carry flag is set if the value in the source is greater than the destination value.

The program shown reads and displays all keyboard entries until an upper case A is entered. After reading the keyboard, the ASCII value found is placed in register AL. The value in AL is then compared with 41h, the value of an upper case A. If AL also contains 41h, the zero flag is set; otherwise it remains clear.

Data to enter	Meaning
RCX	Set the file size to 32 bytes
20	
N PRKEY2.COM	Name the file
A	Assemble the following code
MOV AH, 08	Choose a keyboard read
INT 21	Read keyboard value into AL
CMP AL, 41	Is key upper case A?
JZ 110	If 'A' then go to end program
MOV DL, AL	Copy ASCII value to DL
MOV AH, 02	Choose the display option
INT 21	Call the DOS INT 21 routine
JMP 100	Loop back to start of program
MOV AH, 4C	Set for program termination
INT 21	Call the DOS INT 21 routine
<Enter>	Signals end of code
W	Write a COM file
Q	Exit DEBUG

If the zero flag is set, the JZ 110 instruction moves the pointer to address 110h. Since the starting address is 100h, this is 17 bytes into the program and points at the MOV AH, 4C instruction. The program continues its execution from this point and runs the termination code.

If the two operands are not equal (i.e. the keyboard entry was not an upper case A), the zero flag is not set. In this case, the program does not branch to address 110h and execution moves on to the next instruction (MOV DL, AL).

```
Loop:
MOV AH, 08
INT 21
CMP AL, 41
JZ close
MOV DL, AL
MOV AH, 02
INT 21
JMP loop
close:
MOV AH, 4C
INT 21
```

As before, the use of labels would make the program more legible and less error-prone.

Arithmetic

ADD

The syntax for this instruction is

ADD destination, source

The destination and source operands are added together and the result is placed in the destination operand. If the result is too big to fit in the destination, the carry flag is set.

The example program reads in upper case characters, converts them to lower case and displays them; the program terminates when a lower case x is entered.

This is similar to the last example, with the addition of the ADD DL, 20 instruction.   This adds 20h on to the ASCII value read, since the difference between upper and lower case ASCII characters is 32 (e.g. 'A' is 65 while 'a' is 97).

Data to enter	Meaning
RCX	Set the file size to 32 bytes
20	
N ADDON.COM	Name the file
A	Assemble the following code
MOV AH, 08	Choose a keyboard read
INT 21	Read keyboard value into AL
ADD AL, A0	Add 160 to register AL
JC 10C	If carry, jump to end program
MOV DL, AL	Copy new ASCII value to DL
JMP 10E	Jump to display code
MOV DL, 43	Place 'C' in DL
MOV AH, 02	Call the DOS INT 21 routine
INT 21	Loop back to start of program
MOV AH, 4C	Set for program termination
INT 21	Call the DOS INT 21 routine
<Enter>	Signals end of code
W	Write a COM file
Q	Exit DEBUG

Data to enter	Meaning
RCX	Set the file size to 32 bytes
20	
N LOWER.COM	Name the file
A	Assemble the following code
MOV AH, 08	Choose a keyboard read
INT 21	Read keyboard value into AL
CMP AL, 78	Is key lower case 'x'?
JZ 112	If so, jump to end program
ADD AL, 20	Add 32 on to register AL
MOV DL, AL	Copy new ASCII value to DL
MOV AH, 02	Choose the display option
INT 21	Call the DOS INT 21 routine
JMP 100	Loop back to start of program
MOV AH, 4C	Set for program termination
INT 21	Call the DOS INT 21 routine
<Enter>	Signals end of code
W	Write a COM file
Q	Exit DEBUG

The next program demonstrates the JC instruction.   Like the above program, it reads keyboard characters, adds to the ASCII value and displays them.

This program adds 160 (i.e. A0h) on to the ASCII value read.   If the total of the ASCII value and 160 can be contained in AL (i.e. a value no greater than 255), the updated ASCII value is displayed.   This will produce odd characters on the screen since the values are outside the normal alphanumeric range of characters.

If the total is greater than 255, the carry flag is set and the JC 10C instruction will detect this carry situation and display a 'C' on the screen.

SUB

The syntax for this instruction is

SUB destination, source

The source operand is subtracted from the destination operand and the result is placed in the destination operand. If the source operand is a greater value than the destination operand, the carry flag is set.

The example program is the opposite of the earlier LOWER.COM program.   It accepts keyboard input and subtracts 32 from the ASCII value to convert it to its upper case equivalent.   It than displays the character on the screen.   The program is terminated by entering a lower case 'x'.

Data to enter	Meaning
RCX	Set the file size to 32 bytes
20	
N UPCASE.COM	Name the file
A	Assemble the following code
MOV AH, 08	Choose a keyboard read
INT 21	Read keyboard value into AL
CMP AL, 78	Is key lower case 'X'?
JZ 112	If so, jump to end program
SUB AL, 20	Subtract 32 from register AL
MOV DL, AL	Copy new ASCII value to DL
MOV AH, 02	Choose the display option
INT 21	Call the DOS INT 21 routine
JMP 100	Loop back to start of program
MOV AH, 4C	Set for program termination
INT 21	Call the DOS INT 21 routine
<Enter>	Signals end of code
W	Write a COM file
Q	Exit DEBUG

INC/DEC

The INC instruction has a syntax of

INC operand

and adds one to the existing value of the operand. The operand can be the contents of a memory address or can be a register (excluding segment registers).

The DEC instruction has the opposite effect - that of reducing an operand's value by one.

NOTE:

These differ from *'ADD operand, 1'* or *'SUB operand, 1'* in that INC and DEC commands do not alter the carry flag.

MUL

This instruction expects one of the operands to be placed in the AL register prior to being called. Its syntax is

MUL source

where source is the second operand; this could be the contents of a register (e.g. MUL DL) or the contents of a memory address (e.g. MUL addloc).

Data to enter	Meaning
RCX	Set the file size to 16 bytes
10	
N MUL.COM	Name the file
A	Assemble the following code
MOV AL, 08	Place 8 in AL
MUL 09	Multiply AL by 9
MOV DL, AL	Copy value to DL
MOV AH, 02	Choose the display option
INT 21	Call the DOS INT 21 routine
MOV AH, 4C	Set for program termination
INT 21	Call the DOS INT 21 routine
<Enter>	Signals end of code
W	Write a COM file
Q	Exit DEBUG

If the source operand is a byte, (e.g. MUL 2F) then the result is placed in AX.

If the source operand is a double byte (e.g. MUL 14E7) then the lower 16 bits of the result are placed in AX and the 16 most significant bits are placed in the DX register.

The example program shows 8 being multiplied by 9. This produces 72, which is placed into DL for displaying. Since 72 is the ASCII code for an upper case 'H' this letter is displayed to the screen.

Changing the initial value in AL or changing the multiplier will produce different output results.

DIV

First a quick refresher on terminology. Consider the division of 22 by 4 below

22/4

The 22 is the dividend while the 4 is the divisor. It will produce an answer of 5 with a remainder of 2; the 5 is referred to as the quotient.

The DIV assembler instruction can handle single or double-byte operations.

Its syntax is

DIV source

where the source is a single register byte (e.g. DIV DL) or a double memory byte (e.g. DIV addloc).

With single byte divisions, the dividend is placed in AX and the divisor is another single byte register. The quotient is placed in AL while the remainder is placed in AH.

With double byte divisions, the dividend is placed in DX:AX (i.e. LSBs in AX) and the divisor is placed in another double byte register. The quotient is placed in AX while the remainder is placed in DL.

The example program divides 242 by 3. Being byte operations, only the AX and DL registers are involved. The remainder is ignored by the program with the quotient being placed in AL and transferred to DL for display. Since the quotient is 80d it will display an upper case 'P'.

Data to enter	Meaning
RCX	Set the file size to 16 bytes
10	
N DIVR.COM	Name the file
A	Assemble the following code
MOV DL, 3	Place 3 in AL (i.e. divisor)
MOV AX, F2	Place 242 in AX (ie dividend)
DIV DL	Divide AX by DL
MOV DL, AL	Copy quotient to DL
MOV AH, 02	Choose the display option
INT 21	Call the DOS INT 21 routine
MOV AH, 4C	Set for program termination
INT 21	Call the DOS INT 21 routine
<Enter>	Signals end of code
W	Write a COM file
Q	Exit DEBUG

DB

All programs need to produce text for menus, error messages, prompts, etc. This can be achieved using the DB instruction. This stands for 'Define Byte' and allows the programmer to insert variables or strings of characters into the program. The assembler recognises the DB directive, places the text into the program but does not attempt to convert the characters into machine code instructions.

Examples are:

Entry			Meaning
total	DB	3	A numerical variable *total* is created with a value of 3
mark	DB	"Y"	A text variable *mark* has "Y" as its commencing value
msg	DB	"Here is a string of characters"	A string is defined with the label msg

All assemblers support the use of DB but DEBUG does not allow labels and the last entry would be simply entered as

DB   "Here is a long string of characters"

String Writing (1)

This example program demonstrates two techniques - the use of DB and indexed addressing.

The text string "Dumbreck Publishing" is declared at the end of the code using a DB directive.   The string is nineteen characters in length and, when assembled, commences at location 114h. Register CL is used as a counter and is given an initial value of 13h (the length of the string).

The program uses *'indexed addressing'*.   The instruction MOV DX, 114[SI] will, on the first run through the loop, place the contents of location 114 (i.e. 114+0) into DX for displaying.   On the next circuit of the loop, DX is given the contents of location 115 (i.e. 114+1).

In each circuit of the loop, the offset is incremented to point at the next character - while the counter is decremented.   When the counter is zero, the loop is exited and the program is terminated.

Data to enter	Meaning
RCX	Set the file size to 48 bytes
30	
N IDX.COM	Name the file
A	Assemble the following code
MOV CL, 13	Set the counter to 19d
MOV SI, 00	Set offset to zero
MOV DX, 114[SI]	Fetch a text character
MOV AH, 02	Choose the display option
INT 21	Call the DOS INT 21 routine
INC SI	Add 1 to offset
DEC CL	Decrement the counter
JNZ 105	Loop if counter not empty
MOV AH, 4C	Set for program termination
INT 21	Call the DOS INT 21 routine
DB "Dumbreck Publishing"	
<Enter>	Signals end of code
W	Write a COM file
Q	Exit DEBUG

String Writing (2)

Data to enter	Meaning
RCX	Set the file size to 32 bytes
20	
N DBS.COM	Name the file
A	Assemble the following code
MOV AH, 09	Choose 'display string' option
MOV DX, 10B	Point to start of string
INT 21	Call the DOS INT 21 routine
MOV AH, 4C	Set for program termination
INT 21	Call the DOS INT 21 routine
DB "Dumbreck Publishing$"	
<Enter>	Signals end of code
W	Write a COM file
Q	Exit DEBUG

MSDOS provides a function that is dedicated to displaying text strings.   DX is set to point at the start of the string while AH is given the value of 9.

Calling INT 21 will display the string.

Unlike the previous example, the routine has no counter to tell it when the end of the string is reached. Instead, this routine requires that a dollar sign be placed at the end of the text string.   When the routine fetches the dollar character, it does not display it; the character is used to terminate the display routine.

Logic Operations

Earlier pages explained the functions of various logical operations and gave practical uses for each. These can now be re-examined as assembler routines.

AND

The program reads in a keyboard value. If the key read is lower case, then it will not have bit 6 set, whereas all upper case characters have bit 6 set.   This is because the difference between the lower and upper case ASCII value of any letter is 32 and 32 is the equivalent of setting bit 6 in the binary pattern.   So, subtracting 32 from the ASCII value converts it from lower to upper case. This achieved by AND AL, DF since DF is the hex for 223.   This provides a *'mask'* which allows the entire binary pattern, apart from the 6th bit (value 32), to appear in the output.

Data to enter	Meaning
RCX	Set the file size to 32 bytes
20	
N ANDS.COM	Name the file
A	Assemble the following code
MOV AH, 08	Choose a keyboard read
INT 21	Read keyboard value into AL
AND AL, DF	Filter out bit 6 (i.e. subtract 32)
CMP AL, 58	Has 'X' been entered?
JZ 112	If so, jump to end program
MOV DL, AL	Copy ACSII value into DL
MOV AH, 02	Choose the display option
INT 21	Call the DOS INT 21 routine
JMP 100	Loop back to start of program
MOV AH, 4C	Set for program termination
INT 21	Call the DOS INT 21 routine
<Enter>	Signals end of code
W	Write a COM file
Q	Exit DEBUG

$$\begin{array}{ll} \text{example input} & 01100001 \\ \text{AND with 223} & \underline{11011111} \\ \text{example output} & 01000001 \end{array}$$

Since upper case characters have the sixth bit set to zero, the ANDing process leaves their values unaffected. All typing, whether upper or lower case, is displayed in lower case.   This technique is widely used and has many applications.   For example, Novell uses this technique with its Maximum Rights Mask and Inherited Rights Mask to enforce group and user securities on its LAN operating system.

OR

This program performs the opposite function to the previous example. All alphabetic text entered at the keyboard is displayed in lower case, whether the user types in upper or lower case.

Lower case entries are left untouched and upper case entries are converted to lower case.

Since no lower case alphabetic characters have their 6th bit set, 32 has to be added to the input value to provide a lower case output. This is achieved by ORing the input with 32d. With lower case letters, the 6th bit is already set and ORing with 32d has no effect.

Upper case entries do not have the 6th bit set and the ORing with 32d ensures that the bit is set.

Data to enter	Meaning
RCX	Set the file size to 32 bytes
20	
N ORS.COM	Name the file
A	Assemble the following code
MOV AH, 08	Choose a keyboard read
INT 21	Read keyboard value into AL
OR AL, 20	Set bit 6 (i.e. add 32)
CMP AL, 78	Has 'x' been entered?
JZ 112	If so, jump to end program
MOV DL, AL	Copy ACSII value into DL
MOV AH, 02	Choose the display option
INT 21	Call the DOS INT 21 routine
JMP 100	Loop back to start of program
MOV AH, 4C	Set for program termination
INT 21	Call the DOS INT 21 routine
<Enter>	Signals end of code
W	Write a COM file
Q	Exit DEBUG

XOR

This example program continually accepts keyboard input and displays it on the screen, until the space bar is pressed. The coding is identical to earlier examples with the exception of the following lines:

XOR AL, 20
JZ 110

The ASCII value for a space is 32d (20h). The keyboard input value, held in AL, is XORed with 20h.

If the keyboard input is the space bar, then:

Input value	00100000
ASCII for space	00100000
Result of XORing	00000000

Data to enter	Meaning
RCX	Set the file size to 32 bytes
20	
N XORS.COM	Name the file
A	Assemble the following code
MOV AH, 08	Choose a keyboard read
INT 21	Read keyboard value into AL
XOR AL, 20	Was space bar pressed?
JZ 110	If so, jump to end program
MOV DL, AL	Copy ACSII value into DL
MOV AH, 02	Choose the display option
INT 21	Call the DOS INT 21 routine
JMP 100	Loop back to start of program
MOV AH, 4C	Set for program termination
INT 21	Call the DOS INT 21 routine
<Enter>	Signals end of code
W	Write a COM file
Q	Exit DEBUG

Any other input from the keyboard produces a different ACSII code. For example, upper case 'A' produces:

Input value for 'A'	01000101
ASCII for space	00100000
Result of XORing	01100101

In the first case, the output result was zero. In every other case, the output will not be zero. The JZ 100 instruction tests the zero flag. If it is clear, the result of the XOR did not produce a zero and the program can continue to display the character. If the zero flag is set, the XOR produced a zero output. This means that the space bar was pressed and the program jumps to the termination sequence.

Rotate & Shift Instructions

A number of instructions are available to alter the positions of the bits within a register or memory location.

SHL

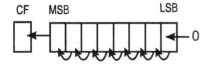

Each data bit in the location, whether a zero or a one, is shifted one bit to the left. The data in bit 0 is moved into bit1, the data in bit 1 is moved into bit 2, and so on. The bit in the most significant bit is moved into the carry flag. A zero is moved into the empty LSB.

So, if the AL register contained 10001010, the instruction

SHL AL, 1

would result in 1 (the MSB) being placed in the carry flag and the AL register's contents would be altered to 00010100. With the same commencing 10001010 in AL, the instruction

SHL AL, 2

would result in a 0 being placed in the carry flag and AL's contents would be altered to 00101000.

The contents of the carry flag after each shift can be tested using the JC test.

The example program reads in a character from the keyboard and displays its output in the following format:

J=01001010

When the keyboard entry is accepted, the binary pattern 01001010 is held in the AL register. It is transferred to BL and each bit is placed into the carry flag in sequence using the

SHL BL, 1

instruction. Since bits shift to the left, the MSB is the first to be placed in the carry flag. This ensures that the bit pattern is displayed on the screen in the correct order (i.e. MSB through to LSB). The carry flag is tested after each shift using the

JC 11B

instruction. If the carry flag is set (i.e. contains a 1), the program jumps to the code that places the ASCII value for one into the display routine. If the carry flag is clear (i.e. contains a 0), the ASCII value for 0 is placed into the display routine.

The instruction DEC CX decrements the counter and will continually loop back for another shift/display until the counter is reduced to zero.

```
RCX                 ;set the file size to 48 bytes
30
N SHL.COM           ;name the file
A                   ;assemble the code
MOV AH,08           ;read the keyboard
INT 21
MOV BL,AL
MOV DL,AL
MOV AH,02           ;print the character
INT 21
MOV DL,3D           ;print an equals symbol
INT 21
MOV CX,8            ;set counter to 8
SHL BL,1            ;move bit into carry flag
JC 11B              ;if bit is 1 jump to display 1
MOV DL,30           ;ready to display 0
JMP 11D             ;jump to display routine
MOV DL,31           ;ready to display 1
MOV AH,02           ;display contents of DL
INT 21
DEC CX              ;decrement the counter
JNZ 113             ;if not yet 0 loop again
MOV AH,4C           terminate program
INT 21
<enter>
W
Q
```

SHR

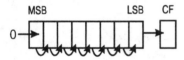

Each data bit in the location, whether a zero or a one, is shifted one bit to the right. The data in the MSB is moved into bit6, the data in bit 6 is moved into bit 5, and so on. The bit in the least significant bit is moved into the carry flag. A zero is moved into the empty MSB.

ROL

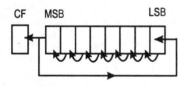

This instruction is similar to the SHL instruction except that the bit coming out of the MSB is placed in the carry flag and is also fed back into the LSB. So, the LSB is not automatically fed with a zero; it is supplied with the data from bit 7. In this way, the data in the location can be constantly rotated around.

ROR

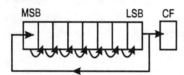

This instruction is identical to ROL except that the bits are rotated round in a rightwards direction.

The bit in bit 0 is placed both in the carry flag and is returned into the MSB, bit 7.

Sub Programs

As in high level programming, sections of program code may require to be used from different parts of the program. Sections of code to validate numbers, check dates, read or write to files, etc may be required at several points in the program. Rather than repeat the code over and over again, the code can be written once and called from those parts in the program requiring these services.

The diagram shows a main program taking a detour from its normal sequential run, to carry out instructions in a sub-routine. When the sub routine code is completed, the program returns to the normal sequential flow.

Routine1 or Routine2 in the diagram could, in practice, be called many times by different parts of the program. The same routine could also be called many times over, if the program call was within a program loop.

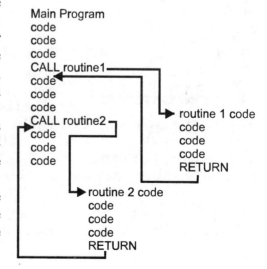

Sub program calls are completely different from the jumps discussed earlier. With jumps, the flow of the program permanently moves to the new area of code jumped to. With sub-programs, the branch to the procedure or function is purely a temporary detour and the program always returns to the point from where the sub-program was called.

```
RCX
40
N CALLS.COM
A
MOV AH,08    ; input a character from the keyboard
INT 21
MOV BL, AL
MOV DL,AL    ; display the keyboard character
MOV AH, 02   ;    "      "      "      "
INT 21       ;    "      "      "      "
MOV DL,3D    ; display an equals symbol
INT 21       ;    "      "      "      "
MOV CX,8     ; set the counter to 8
SHL BL,1     ; move bit into carry flag (this is address 113)
JC 11C       ;
CALL 126     ;   CALL DISPLAY A ZERO
JMP 11F      ;
CALL 12D     ;   CALL DISPLAY A ONE (address 11C)
DEC CX       ; (address 11F)
JNZ 113
MOV AH,4C    ; termination routine
INT 21       ;    "      "
;=======================================
MOV DL,30    ; DISPLAY A ZERO ROUTINE (address 126)
MOV AH,02    ; the display routine
INT 21       ;    "      "      "
RET          ; return to calling code
;=======================================
MOV DL,31    ; DISPLAY A ONE ROUTINE (address 12D)
MOV AH,02    ; the display routine
INT 21       ;    "      "      "
RET          ; return to calling code

W
Q
```

The branch to the sub program is achieved with the CALL instruction. This may be a call to a label or address within the main program, or may be a separate routine from a library that will be linked in at the assembling stage. When a sub-routine finishes, control is passed back to the calling code, using the RET instruction.

In the example, calling the code in Routine1 was achieved by the instruction

CALL routine1

When the program finishes, control is passed back to the program at the point just after the call was made.

So in the example in the previous diagram, after calling Routine1 control would return to the program instruction that immediately follows the CALL instruction.

The example program is that of the previous code to display the binary pattern of a keypress.

It has been altered so that there are separate routines to print out 0 and 1 characters.

Since DEBUG does not support the use of labels, the calls are to absolute addresses. So, CALL 126 calls the routine that starts at address 126. When the routine terminates, the program returns to carry out the instruction JMP 11F.

Stack Operations

In the above program, the processing leaves the program at a particular point in the code, runs one of the sub-routines and returns to the correct position in the original code. The reason it knows where to return is that it stores the return address prior to executing the sub-routine. This address is the one held in the IP (Instruction Pointer). IP always holds the address of the next instruction to be executed. This address is taken from the IP register and placed in a temporary storage area in memory, known as the 'stack'. The IP is then fed with the address of the start of the sub-routine. On termination of the sub-routine, the stored address is fetched back from the stack and placed back in the IP. The program now runs from this address. Consider the table below, which is a fragment from the above program. The

Address	Contents	Meaning
115	JC 11C	
117	CALL 126	Call display a zero
11A	JMP 11F	
11C	CALL 12D	Call display a one
11F	DEC CX	

instruction at address 117 is to call the sub-routine to display a zero. The next sequential instruction is held in address 11A. The address 11A is placed on the stack and the IP is given the address 126 (the start of the sub-routine). When the sub-routine terminates, the value 11A is taken off the stack and placed in the IP.

The program then continues in its normal sequence. Similarly, the value 11F is placed on the stack prior to calling the second sub-routine. 12D is placed in the IP so that the CPU executes the code in the sub-routine. On termination, 11F is taken off the stack and placed in the IP.

In practice, the stack is in regular use and stores a range of values for differing activities such as interrupt handling, procedure and function calls and temporary data storage areas.

The most important fact about the stack is that it is a LIFO (*'Last In, First Out'*) structure. This means that items are placed on the stack in strict order. Items are pulled off the stack in the reverse order that they were stored. So, if items are placed on the stack in the order data1, data2, data3, data4, data5 - they are removed from the stack in the order data5, data4, data3, data2, data1.

The actual addresses used by the stack are at the top of the computer's memory map and are pointed to by the Stack Pointer (SP register). This means that the first item on the stack is placed in the highest part of the stack memory and the stack pointer points at that address. When a second item is placed on the stack, it occupies the second highest position in the stack memory and the stack pointer value is reduced to point to this lower address. As the stack grows up in usage capacity, it grows down in memory and the SP holds lower and lower values.

If a program was badly written and always placed items on the stack without ever removing them, the stack would grow to a point that it would overwrite the program instructions held in memory. To prevent this, the programmer can allocate how much memory to allocate for use as a stack. If this limit were reached, any further attempts to write to the stack would produce *'stack overflow'* errors. It is the responsibility of the programmers to ensure that the program eventually removes all items placed on the stack.

Items are placed on the stack with the instruction

PUSH operand

where the operand can be a segment register, a general-purpose 16-bit register (i.e. AX, BX, CX, DX) or a memory location's contents. The instruction will not place an 8-bit register on the stack (e.g. PUSH AL is not allowed). The instruction

POP operand

has the opposite effect to PUSH, with the item last stored on the stack being placed in the operand. An example of stack operations is shown in the next example program.

NOTE:

Since the stack is a LIFO structure, it is vital that the programmer ensures that POPs from the stack are carried out in the corresponding and opposite sequence to the PUSHes to the stack.

So, a sequence of PUSHes of AX, BX, CX, DX has to be eventually followed by POPs of DX, CX, BX, AX. If items are removed from the stack in the wrong order, the program will almost certainly crash.

Fully Featured Assemblers

DEBUG was capable of handling all the small fragments of code from the previous pages. However, it does not handle labels, macros, variables, etc. For these, the features of more developed products such as TASM are employed.

The minimum outline of a TASM script is as shown.

```
.MODEL SMALL
.STACK 100h
.DATA
    any data goes here
.CODE
    code goes here
    code goes here
END
```

The model can be 'small' or 'large'. The small model expects all jumps and calls to occur within a single addressing segment, usually 64k and executes quickly. The large model is for larger programs and is slower due to its use of the full SEGMENT:OFFSET operand (compared to the small model's OFFSET operand.

The STACK instruction allocates 256 bytes for stack operations.

The DATA section holds any variables and text messages and is treated as data by the assembler (i.e. it does not attempt to translate the data into machine instructions).

The CODE segment holds all the program instructions and numbers are entered in hex notation (i.e. 256 is entered as 100h). If the number is not followed by the letter 'h' it is assumed to be the decimal value one hundred.

The END is a directive, informing the assembler that the program is finished.

TASM example

The example program was written using the Borland's Turbo Assembler (TASM). When run, it informs the user of the version of DOS present on the computer.

It provides a practical example of stack operations and also uses the following new features:

- EQU directive
- Labels
- Data offsets

'Labels' are used in the DATA segment. They define the labels 'MESSAGE1' and 'MESSAGE2' as containing text strings.

The data segment also contains the line

```
BESTVER    EQU    07h
```

This is an *'EQU Assembler Directive'*. The label called BESTVER is defined as a constant with the value 7. The label can now be inserted throughout the program, as many times as is required. When the program is assembled, the assembler replaces every occurrence of the word BESTVER in the script with the value 7. As can be seen, it adds no extra functionality to the program; it just makes the program easier to read.

The instructions

```
MOV AX, @DATA
MOX DS, AX
```

ensure that all data transfer instructions, unless otherwise directed, will refer to the current segment.

The writing of text strings is achieved by referring to the offset where the string is stored. So, the instruction

```
MOV DX, OFFSET MESSAGE1
```

loads DX with the start location for the first text message, prior to calling the *'print string'* DOS routine.

Calling INT 21 with AH=30h, fetches the DOS version number (e.g. v4.0, v6.22, v7.0) and places the major version number in AL; the minor version number (the part after the decimal point) into AH. However, register AH is required later in the program to be set to 2, prior to calling the *'print character'* routine. This would mean that the version number would be overwritten. To prevent this, AX is pushed on to the stack, for later retrieval. In fact, AH is overwritten twice by the program and AX is therefore pushed on to the stack twice.

```
.MODEL SMALL
.STACK 100h
.DATA
    MESSAGE1   DB "Your DOS version is $"
    MESSAGE2   DB 10,13,"Time to upgrade?$"
    BESTVER    EQU  07h
.CODE
Start:
    ;-----------------------------------------
    MOV AX, @DATA
    MOV DS, AX
    ;-----------------------------------------
    MOV AH, 9
    MOV DX, OFFSET MESSAGE1
    INT 21h
    ;-----------------------------------------
    MOV AH,30h    ; get DOS version into AX
    INT 21h       ; major version is in AL
                  ; minor version is in AH
    ;-----------------------------------------
    PUSH AX       ; save AX register
    PUSH AX       ; and again
    ;-----------------------------------------
    ADD AL,30h    ; convert to ASCII number
    MOV DL,AL     ; display the major
    MOV AH,02     ; version number
    INT 21h
    ;-----------------------------------------
    MOV DL,2Eh
    MOV AH,2      ; print a decimal point
    INT 21h
    ;-----------------------------------------
    POP AX        ; recover original AX value
    ;-----------------------------------------
    ADD AH,30h    ; display the minor
    MOV DL,AH     ; version number
    MOV AH,2
    INT 21h
    ;-----------------------------------------
    POP AX        ; recover original AX value
    CMP AL, BESTVER
    JE Done
    MOV AH, 9
    MOV DL, OFFSET MESSAGE2
    INT 21h
    ;-----------------------------------------
    Done:
        MOV AH,4Ch ; terminate program
        INT 21h
END Start
```

The instruction

```
ADD AH,30h
```

takes the decimal value stored in AH and converts it into its ASCII equivalent. For example, a major version number of 5 would have 48 (30h) added to it producing an ASCII value of 53 which is the character '5'.

The instruction

```
CMP AL, BESTVER
```

compares the machine's major version number with the value 7. If the AL value is also 7, the

```
JE Done
```

instruction exits the program. If the AL value is not 7, the user is reminded that the machine's DOS version is not the most up-to-date version.

Macros

With EQU, a piece of data was specified once, at the start of the program. In the previous example program, it was

```
BESTVER  EQU  07h
```

The label was then included in the program in the knowledge that the assembler would replace every occurrence of the label in the script with the value associated with the label.

Macros take the process a stage further with whole segments of code being given a name and the name being included in the program code area.

When the script is being converted to object code, the assembler replaces each occurrence of the macro label with a copy of the code segment contained in the macro. Like the EQU, it adds no extra functionality but allows a faster development of the program, with fewer errors.

The leftmost example shows a program with the CODE section containing the program code and an area that defines all the program's procedures. Each procedure is headed by a label and finishes with a 'RET' instruction.

The rightmost example shows the same program with a number of macros. Each macro has a label followed by the word 'MACRO' and the macro code. The macro finishes with the 'ENDM' instruction.

Each macro is called by placing its label in the code. Thus, where *getdata* appears in the code the code lines of the macro will be substituted at the assembly stage.

Passing Parameters

Macros provide for the passing of parameters. Thus a macro definition of

```
PRINTIT MACRO CHAROUT
    MOV DX, CHAROUT
    MOV AH, 02
    INT 21h
ENDM
```

will assemble the code incorporating the data in the parameter.

Using Procedures

```
.MODEL SMALL
.STACK 100h
.DATA
.CODE
Start:
  code
  code
  CALL getdata
  CALL printit
  code
  code
  CALL printit
  ...
  ...
  code
  CALL getdata
  CALL printit
  code
  code
GETDATA:
  code
  RET
PRINTIT:
  code
  RET
END Start
```

Using Macros

```
.MODEL SMALL
.STACK 100h
.DATA
.CODE
  PRINTIT   MACRO
    macro code here
  ENDM
  GETDATA  MACRO
    macro code here
  ENDM
Start:
  code
  code
  GETDATA
  PRINTIT
  code
  code
  PRINTIT
  ...
  ...
  code
  GETDATA
  PRINTIT
  code
  code
END Start
```

Thus, the following macro calls are valid:

Instruction	Meaning
PRINTIT 68	Assemble as a routine to display the character with ASCII value of 68d
PRINTIT 44h	Assemble as a routine to display the character with hex value of 44h
PRINTIT 'D'	Assemble as a routine to display the character 'D'
PRINTIT 10	Assemble as a routine to produce a line feed
PRINTIT 13	Assemble as a routine to produce a carriage return

Macros vs Procedures

Pros

- Macros are faster than procedures, since there is no time wasted making the CALL and RET operations.
- Procedures don't know what state registers were in before it was called and has to PUSH registers, carry out their code, then POP registers before closing the procedure. Since programmers insert the macro label during programming, the conditions of registers are known and set prior to calling the macro. This eliminates many unnecessary and time-consuming stack operations.

Cons

- Where the macro is called many times, the assembled program can be substantially larger than one using procedures.
- Not as easily debugged, since procedures can be easily *'stepped'* through with most debuggers.

Comparison Of PC Bus Architectures

The following pages examine the performance characteristics of the range of personal microcomputers that have been manufactured, sold and used over the last two decades. All the machines discussed will be around for years to come. Production of XT, AT, 386, 486 and some Pentium ranges has ceased but there are many of these machines still in use. In any case, the support technician has to work with the whole range of machines, from the oldest XT to the newest Pentium or Athlon.

As microcomputers have developed, there has been a race between the improving performance of the CPU, the memory, the peripherals - and the buses that connect them.

When considering various buses, the following questions should be asked:
- How much memory can be accessed?
- How fast can it be accessed?
- Is access to different components at different speeds required?
- How much does it cost?
- How flexible is the machine - (e.g. will cards or CPU modules from one machine still work in the new machine)?

When examining various systems, there is no abstract 'correct answer'. The system for a user is only correct or incorrect for that user's needs. A user requiring a multi-user file server would find an old XT PC absolutely useless; a high-performance machine would be a necessity for such applications. On the other hand, a high-performance (and therefore very expensive) machine is wasted if it is only used for simple word processing since the speed of the system is only relevant for small periods; by far the greatest time sees the machine idling while the user thinks of the next word to type.

The XT

The earliest PCs were the XT range, dating from the early 1980's and designed and manufactured by IBM. Many other companies produced *'clones'* - machines based on the architecture of the IBM XT, with only small differences to avoiding infringing IBM patents. These are often also known, more kindly, as *'PC compatibles'*.

DATA BUS

The XT Data Bus was 8 bits wide (a single byte) and could therefore transfer a number between 0 and 255 at a time.

ADDRESS BUS

The Address Bus was 20 bits wide and so could access up to 1MB of memory (2 raised to the power 20 gives over a million unique address locations)

CLOCK SPEED

Every computer has an oscillator that gives regular timed kicks to the CPU. These pulses are used to move the CPU through the individual activities that comprise each machine code instruction. Each machine code instruction can require one, two, three or four different clock pulses to ensure its completion. The XT was based on the 8088 processor and had a normal clock speed of 4.77MHz (i.e. 4.77 million clock pulses per sec.)

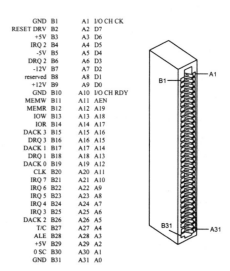

GND B1	A1 I/O CH CK
RESET DRV B2	A2 D7
+5V B3	A3 D6
IRQ 2 B4	A4 D5
-5V B5	A5 D4
DRQ 2 B6	A6 D3
-12V B7	A7 D2
reserved B8	A8 D1
+12V B9	A9 D0
GND B10	A10 I/O CH RDY
MEMW B11	A11 AEN
MEMR B12	A12 A19
IOW B13	A13 A18
IOR B14	A14 A17
DACK 3 B15	A15 A16
DRQ 3 B16	A16 A15
DACK 1 B17	A17 A14
DRQ 1 B18	A18 A13
DACK 0 B19	A19 A12
CLK B20	A20 A11
IRQ 7 B21	A21 A10
IRQ 6 B22	A22 A9
IRQ 5 B23	A23 A8
IRQ 4 B24	A24 A7
IRQ 3 B25	A25 A6
DACK 2 B26	A26 A5
T/C B27	A27 A4
ALE B28	A28 A3
+5V B29	A29 A2
0 SC B30	A30 A1
GND B31	A31 A0

DATA RATE

The 8088 chip took four clock pulses to complete a transfer of data on the data bus. So, the data transfer rate is

$$\text{bus width} * \text{clock speed}/(8 * \text{clock pulses per transfer})$$

The wider the bus width, the more data can be transferred at a time; the greater the clock speed, the faster the transfer activities can be completed. On the other hand, some chips take more clock pulses to complete a transfer than others. In the case of the XT, the data transfer rate is

$$8 * 4.77m/(8 * 4) = 1.2 \text{ million bytes per sec} = 1.14MB/s$$

EXPANSION SLOT LAYOUT

The diagram shows the connector layout of the expansion slot. The slot connections carry not only the address and data lines, but also a range of power and control lines.

The AT

The successor to the XT was the AT PC, which used the 80286 chip with its improved capabilities.

DATA BUS

The width of the data bus was increased to 16 bits; this ensured greater throughput, as it could handle numbers from 0 to 64k at a time.

ADDRESS BUS

This was increased to 24-bit width.   It was now capable of addressing 16MB of memory.   It was now possible to consider add-on memory (see section on extended memory).   With the XT models, there was no point in adding extra memory chips above the 1MB range, since the 8088 chip and the 20-bit address bus was unable to access the additional memory addresses.

CLOCK SPEED

The standard clock speed was increased to 8MHz, although faster machines (10MHz or 12MHz) were also produced.   The 80286 is also able to transfer data in only two clock pulses, compared to the four required by the 8088.

DATA RATE - The data transfer rate was dramatically improved, due to the effect of greater data bus width and the improved chip design.   The data transfer rate for an 8MHz system is

$$16*8m/(8*2) = 7.629MB/s$$

However, there was a problem using the memory chips that were available at that time; their access time (the time required to read/write data to memory locations) was slower than the new improved chip and bus transfer rates.

Since the system can only run at the speed of its slowest element, the effective clock speed was reduced to that which memory could handle.   This introduction of 'wait states' was a reflection of the state of the art of chip development.   The CPU would waste some clock cycles, waiting for the memory to access. With improved chips, the access time is faster and adverts talk of 'zero wait state' systems.   In practice, most AT ISA buses run at around 5MB/s.

It was important that all cards currently in use with XTs would also be able to work in AT machines.   Therefore, the bus layout would have to compatible - and still provide the extra data and address bus connections.   This was achieved by keeping the original XT expansion bus and adding an extension section to the bus for the extra connections.   In that way, XT cards would fit in the expansion slot, while AT cards would also use the slot extension.

This system is termed the 'ISA' system (Industry Standard Architecture) and the 16-bit implementation remained the main system until the introduction of PCI.

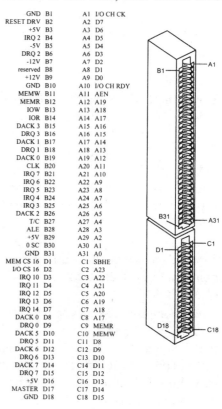

GND	B1	A1 I/O CH CK
RESET DRV	B2	A2 D7
+5V	B3	A3 D6
IRQ 2	B4	A4 D5
-5V	B5	A5 D4
DRQ 2	B6	A6 D3
-12V	B7	A7 D2
reserved	B8	A8 D1
+12V	B9	A9 D0
GND	B10	A10 I/O CH RDY
MEMW	B11	A11 AEN
MEMR	B12	A12 A19
IOW	B13	A13 A18
IOR	B14	A14 A17
DACK 3	B15	A15 A16
DRQ 3	B16	A16 A15
DACK 1	B17	A17 A14
DRQ 1	B18	A18 A13
DACK 0	B19	A19 A12
CLK	B20	A20 A11
IRQ 7	B21	A21 A10
IRQ 6	B22	A22 A9
IRQ 5	B23	A23 A8
IRQ 4	B24	A24 A7
IRQ 3	B25	A25 A6
DACK 2	B26	A26 A5
T/C	B27	A27 A4
ALE	B28	A28 A3
+5V	B29	A29 A2
0 SC	B30	A30 A1
GND	B31	A31 A0
MEM CS 16	D1	C1 SBHE
I/O CS 16	D2	C2 A23
IRQ 10	D3	C3 A22
IRQ 11	D4	C4 A21
IRQ 12	D5	C5 A20
IRQ 13	D6	C6 A19
IRQ 14	D7	C7 A18
DACK 0	D8	C8 A17
DRQ 0	D9	C9 MEMR
DACK 5	D10	C10 MEMW
DRQ 5	D11	C11 D8
DACK 6	D12	C12 D9
DRQ 6	D13	C13 D10
DACK 7	D14	C14 D11
DRQ 7	D15	C15 D12
+5V	D16	C16 D13
MASTER	D17	C17 D14
GND	D18	C18 D15

The 386/486

The range of micros based on the 80386/486 chip brought even better potential performance:

- DATA BUS - 32 bits wide (handling numbers from 0 to 4GB).
- ADDRESS BUS - 32 bits wide (able to address up to 4GB of memory).
- CLOCK SPEED - 20MHz up to 66MHz.
- POTENTIAL DATA RATE = $32*66m/(8*2) = 132MB/s$.
  (i.e. 32-bit bus, 66MHz clock, 2 clock pulses per transfer).

These demands were way beyond the capability of the normal ISA bus and alternative methods had to be found, if computers were to use this progress.   To date, there have been four main responses:

1.   The MCA bus.
2.   The EISA bus.
3.   A separate memory bus.
4.   Local bus systems - VESA, PCI and AGP (see video chapter).

MCA

The IBM response was the introduction of the *MCA* (Micro Channel Architecture) bus with their new PS/2 range of machines in 1987. In fact, IBM introduced both 16-bit (for their 286 machines) and 32-bit versions of the bus. The design broke with tradition, both in construction and method of operation. The XT, ISA and EISA systems all use *'synchronous'* buses. In these systems, the data transfer rate of the bus is tied to the clock speed of the machine's processor. The MCA is *'asynchronous'* and runs as fast as it can in any particular situation.

ADVANTAGES:
- The standard speed for these boards was 20MB/s, which can be specially jacked up to much greater speeds.
- The MCA add-on boards are physically much smaller than all other types of board.
- MCA buses cause less electromagnetic radiation.

DISADVANTAGES:
- Using a 16-bit board brings the machine performance back down nearer to the old ISA boards.
- IBM had strict licensing policies for MCA.
- The technology was largely ignored in the PC market and even IBM eventually dropped it from its range of PCs.

EISA

The licensing demands and conditions of IBM produced a mixed response from other manufacturers. Some, like Olivetti and Research Machines, produced MCA machines under licence. Others, led by Compaq, produced their own improvement to the ISA bus. This is known as *EISA* (Extended Industry Standard Architecture).

DATA BUS - 32 bits wide (0-4GB)

ADDRESS BUS - 32 bits wide (0-4GB)

The bus widths are identical to those of MCA. The big advantage of EISA systems is their *'backward compatibility'*. Any card designed for the ISA system can be used in an EISA bus. This involved a little ingenuity, since the EISA bus has enlarged data and address buses compared to the ISA bus.

BUS LAYOUT

The EISA expansion bus, at first glance, looks identical to an ISA bus. It is the same length and appears to have the same number of connectors on each side of the connector block. The trick in the design of the EISA bus is that it has TWO levels of connectors. The upper level is identical to the ISA bus, allowing normal ISA cards to be plugged in and used. It also has a second set of contacts that are set deeper into the expansion connection. These provide the extra address and data connections for EISA cards.

Plastic keys stop the ISA cards from penetrating to the bottom level of contacts. EISA cards have notches that match the keys. This allows the card to be pushed deeper into the connector and the card's extra connectors make contact with the lower level of bus connections.

	B	A	
ESYNC	B10	A10	VSYNC
GND	B9	A9	HSYNC
P5	B8	A8	BLANC
P4	B7	A7	GND
P3	B6	A6	P6
GND	B5	A5	EDCLK
P2	B4	A4	DCLK
P1	B3	A3	GND
P0	B2	A2	P7
GND	B1	A1	EVIDEO
Audio/GND	B1	A1	CD/SETUP
Audio	B2	A2	MADE 24
GND	B3	A3	GND
oscillator	B4	A4	A11
GND	B5	A5	A10
A23	B6	A6	A9
A22	B7	A7	+5V
A21	B8	A8	A8
GND	B9	A9	A7
A20	B10	A10	A6
A19	B11	A11	+5V
A18	B12	A12	A5
GND	B13	A13	A4
A17	B14	A14	A3
A16	B15	A15	+5V
A15	B16	A16	A2
GND	B17	A17	A1
A14	B18	A18	A0
A13	B19	A19	+12V
A12	B20	A20	ADL
GND	B21	A21	PREEMPT
IRQ 9	B22	A22	BURST
IRQ 3	B23	A23	-12V
IRQ 4	B24	A24	ARB 0
GND	B25	A25	ARB 1
IRQ 5	B26	A26	ARB 2
IRQ 6	B27	A27	-12V
IRQ 7	B28	A28	ARB 3
GND	B29	A29	ARB/GNT
reserved	B30	A30	TC
reserved	B31	A31	+5V
CHCK	B32	A32	S0
GND	B33	A33	S1
CMD	B34	A34	M/IO
CHRDYRTN	B35	A35	+12V
CD SFDBK	B36	A36	CD CHRDY
GND	B37	A37	D0
D1	B38	A38	D2
D3	B39	A39	+5V
D4	B40	A40	D5
GND	B41	A41	D6
CHRESET	B42	A42	D7
reserved	B43	A43	GND
reserved	B44	A44	DS 16 RIN
GND	B45	A45	REFRESH
D8	B48	A48	+5V
D9	B49	A49	D10
GND	B50	A50	D11
D12	B51	A51	D13
D14	B52	A52	+12V
D15	B53	A53	reserved
GND	B54	A54	SBHE
IORQ 10	B55	A55	CD DS 16
IORQ 11	B56	A56	+5V
IORQ 12	B57	A57	IRQ 14
GND	B58	A58	IRQ 15

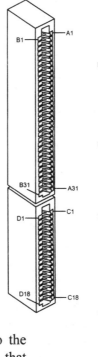

		B	A		
GND	GND	B1	A1	I/O CH CK	CMD
+5V	RESET DRV	B2	A2	D7	START
+5V	+5V	B3	A3	D8	EXRDY
X	IRQ 2	B4	A4	D5	EX32
X	-5V	B5	A5	D4	GND
polarising	DRQ 2	B6	A6	D3	polarising
X	-12V	B7	A7	D2	EX16
X	reserved	B8	A8	D1	SLBURST
+12V	+12V	B9	A9	D0	MSBURST
M-10	GND	B10	A10	I/O CH RDY	W-R
LOCK	MEMW	B11	A11	AEN	GND
reserved	MEMR	B12	A12	A19	reserved
GND	IOW	B13	A13	A18	reserved
reserved	IOR	B14	A14	A17	reserved
BE 3	DACK 3	B15	A15	A16	GND
polarising	DRQ 3	B16	A16	A15	polarising
BE 2	DACK 1	B17	A17	A14	BE 1
BE 0	DRQ 1	B18	A18	A13	LA 31
GND	REFRESH	B19	A19	A12	GND
+5V	CLK	B20	A20	A11	LA30
LA29	IRQ 7	B21	A21	A10	LA28
GND	IRQ 6	B22	A22	A9	LA27
LA26	IRQ 5	B23	A23	A8	LA25
LA24	IRQ 4	B24	A24	A7	GND
polarising	IRQ 3	B25	A25	A6	polarising
LA16	DACK 2	B26	A26	A5	LA15
LA14	T/C	B27	A27	A4	LA13
+5V	ALE	B28	A28	A3	LA12
+5V	+5V	B29	A29	A2	LA11
GND	OSC	B30	A30	A1	GND
LA10	GND	B31	A31	A0	LA9
LA8	MEM CS 16	D1	C1	SBHE	LA7
LA6	I/O CS 16	D2	C2	A23	GND
LA5	IRQ 10	D3	C3	A22	LA4
+5V	IRQ 11	D4	C4	A21	LA3
LA2	IRQ 12	D5	C5	A20	GND
polarising	IRQ 15	D6	C6	A19	polarising
D16	IRQ 14	D7	C7	A18	D17
D18	DACK 0	D8	C8	A17	D19
GND	DRQ 0	D9	C9	MEMR	D20
D21	DACK 5	D10	C10	MEMW	D22
D23	DRQ 5	D11	C11	D8	GND
D24	DACK 6	D12	C12	D9	D25
GND	DRQ 6	D13	C13	D10	D26
D27	DACK 7	D14	C14	D11	D28
polarising	DRQ 7	D15	C15	D12	polarising
D29	+5V	D16	C16	D13	GND
+5V	MASTER	D17	C17	D14	D30
+5V	GND	D18	C18	D15	D31
MACKn		D19	C19		MRE on

DATA RATE

The EISA bus is synchronous and has to run at the slow speed of 8MHz, to allow it to use any slow speed ISA cards.   So, the actual maximum data transfer rate achieved is:

$$32*8m/(8*2) = 15.2MB/s$$

An additional special data rate mode allows data to be transferred in a single clock cycle and this increases the data transfer rate to a maximum of 32MB/s.   Overall then, the bus has to run at the speed of its slowest card.   An EISA bus with an ISA card installed will only run at ISA speeds.

MCA systems, because of the IBM reputation, enjoyed success in sales at the high performance end. EISA systems were common in network file servers but manufacturers produced few other add-on cards. PCI has replaced them both in PCs and in network servers.

Separate Memory Bus

To maximise the computer's efficiency, it is essential that data be transferred between the processor and memory (and vice versa) as quickly as possible.   When a user wishes to use a slow speed card in the computer, this should not be allowed to slow down these CPU/memory transfers.   The solution from the 386 models onwards is to provide a separate high-speed bus linking the processor and memory.   All the communication between CPU and memory is carried over this bus. The normal ISA bus remains to handle disk, video, expansion slots, etc.

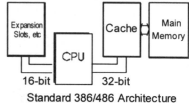

Standard 386/486 Architecture

ADVANTAGES:

- The memory chips runs as fast as the CPU allows, while slower speed cards are catered for on the separate slower bus.   The system runs at its maximum speed.
- Now that the memory has its own separate bus, a block of even faster memory (cache memory) can be introduced between the main memory and the CPU.   The cache memory is used to handle pages of memory data at a time. (see notes on memory)

Local Bus Systems

Technological change left the original PC bus design lacking in terms of bus width and bus speed.

BUS WIDTH

The width of the data bus is a major factor in determining how much data can be transferred over a given period. This data could be memory reads/writes, disk read/writes or graphic card read/writes, along with data connected with a range of peripherals such as printers, modems, scanners, etc.   The original IBM XT model had a data bus that was just 8 bits wide.   The bus was common to the CPU, memory, etc. and the expansion slots that were used to plug in add-ons. This was increased to 16 bits for the AT model and 32 bits for the 386 and 486 machines. The bus architecture was then changed to that shown in the diagram above.   Although the bus between CPU and memory was widened, the data bus to the expansion slots was kept at 16-bit.   This was to allow add-on cards designed for the older architectures, both 8-bit and 16-bit, to still be used on the newer machines.   So graphics cards, although capable of greater throughput, were restricted to slower 16-bit data transfers.   The problem also extended to disk controllers, which were similarly slowed down.

BUS SPEED

The XT data bus was common to local chips and to extension boards and was clocked by the same CPU clock chip.   So all chips and peripherals were clocked to run at 4.7MHz.   Modern architecture may split the local and extension chips into separate buses, but the ISA expansion bus is still separately clocked at a slower speed to allow old add-ons to be used.   Even a 600MHz computer has an ISA slot (i.e. expansion bus) running at between 8MHz and 12MHz.   ISA graphics cards are seriously under driven, slowing video updates.   The fastest Pentium CPU sits on a motherboard that keeps the main bus down to a maximum of between 66MHz and 200MHz.

The Local Bus Solution

All current computers use 'local bus' architectures, where the expansion bus is clocked more slowly than the CPU, for the benefit of slower add-on boards.   However, a 'local bus' connects the memory, video and disk controllers to the CPU on a full 32-bit or 64-bit bus. This bus is clocked at a much higher rate - up to that of the CPU - for maximum data transfer.   Consequently, all cards that run on the local bus outperform their equivalent ISA card versions.   Video performance, in particular, can be spectacularly speeded up but the benefits are available to disk controllers and other local bus cards.   The local bus boards still run ordinary application software and require no special operating system arrangements. Currently, the technology appears both in add-on cards and implemented on the motherboard.   There are two major variations in local bus technology - the older VESA Local Bus and the current Intel PCI bus.

VESA Bus

The first local bus standard was the *'VL Bus'* from VESA (Video Electronic Standards Association). It was used in a wide range of cards. The bus was tied to the speed of the machine's CPU, as the processor had to manage the timing of every card on the bus. The VESA standard provided for clock rates up to 66MHz, although plug-in cards were only used on systems up to 40MHz, as the physical characteristics

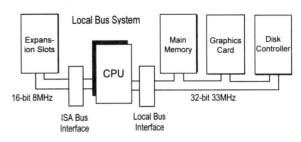

of the electrical connectors and timing problems affect performance beyond 40MHz. With 33MHz systems, there was a three-device limit. Practically, the VL-Bus system was optimised for 386/486 32-bit architecture at 33MHz working. The VESA local bus system did not progress beyond the 486, with the PCI system taking over at Pentium level.

PCI Bus

Current systems use the Intel PCI (*'Peripheral Component Interconnect'*) Bus. Initially designed as a 32-bit connection system for motherboard components, it developed into a full expansion bus system. The diagram shows a typical PCI motherboard configuration for Pentium, Pentium II and a few rare early

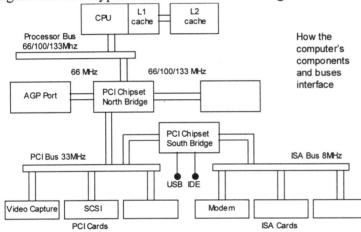

Pentium III chipsets, although the details vary slightly with different CPUs and different memory systems. Furthermore, all Pentium 4 and nearly all Pentium III systems use a hub-based architecture as shown later. The PCI bus exists as a local fast bus, separate from the slower ISA bus. In the example shown, a bridge controller (the *'South Bridge'*) allows the use of older ISA cards on a normal ISA bus. However, it decouples the CPU clock and data path from the bus and interfaces to

them through another chip in the PCI chipset (the *'North Bridge'*). The PCI bus is therefore independent of the machine's CPU. It works equally well with the 486, and the Pentium/Pentium II, and is used with the DEC Alpha workstation and the PowerPC. All that is required is that each CPU has its own CPU-PCI chipset. The chipset comprises two chips. The North Bridge handles the CPU, memory, cache and the PCI bus, while the South Bridge handles USB, IDE drives and the ISA bus. The PCI implementation for Pentium III and Pentium 4 chips is shown later in this chapter.

The system bus was initially designed for a maximum operating speed of 66MHz although this has not been fully implemented. Current PCI buses run mainly at 33MHz, even though motherboards run at up to 200MHz. The PCI bus is synchronised to the system bus but is reduced to a proportion of its speed. Early systems used a 66MHz front side bus, while current Pentium systems use 100MHz or 133MHz. Athlon-based motherboards currently support up to 200MHz. A new standard (PCI-X) is being proposed for fast networking systems, using a 64-bit bus running at 133MHz. Also, the PCI

Comparison of Bus Systems		
Bus Type	**Clock Speed**	**Max Data Rate**
XT	4.77MHz	1.14MB/s
ISA	8MHz	7.629MB/s
MCA	10MHz	20MB/s
PC Card	8MHz	20MB/s
EISA	8MHz	33MB/s
CardBus	33MHz	133MB/s
VESA	50MHz	133MB/s
PCI	33MHz	133MB/s
AGP	66MHz	266MB/s
AGP 2x	66MHz	533MB/s
AGP 4x	66MHz	1066MB/s

Special Interest Group (PCI SIG) is working on what it calls *'Future IO'*, while Intel is developing its own *'Next Generation IO'* standard.

The PCI Bus conforms to the *'Energy Star'* requirements by running at 3.3 volts, although a 5 volt PCI card is detected and still supplied with 5 volts.

Some older computer motherboards had a mix of expansion connectors - e.g. EISA with VESA, ISA with VESA, PCI with VESA, PCI with ISA and some even had ISA, VESA and PCI. For maximum performance, only PCI cards should be used where possible. The exception to this rule is for graphics cards, where AGP should be used if available.

THE PCI SLOT

The PCI standard allows up to 6 PCI connectors for use in personal computing equipment. It comes in several forms. The 5V PCI standard is designed for use in desktop systems, the 3.3 V PCI standard is to be used in portable computers, and the Universal PCI system is for motherboards that are likely to be used in either type of system. Each type is available in 32-bit and 64-bit configurations. The universal PCI connector is essentially a mix of the 5V and 3.3V versions: the voltage on the I/O pins is 5V where there is a 5V bus, and is 3.3V where there is a 3.3V bus. For this reason, the Universal PCI slot is tabulated here. For 32-bit PCI connectors, only pins A1/B1 to A62/B62 are used. 64-bit cards use pins A63/B63 through to A94/B94. 64-bit PCI cards are very rare and so the details of this part of the interface have been omitted.

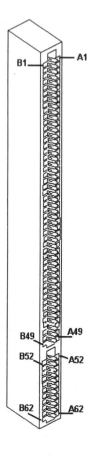

REAR OF PC			
PIN	SIGNAL	PIN	SIGNAL
B1	-12v	A1	Test Reset
B2	Test Clock	A2	+12 V
B3	Ground	A3	Test Mode Select
B4	Test Data Output	A4	Test Data Input
B5	+5V	A5	+5V
B6	+5V	A6	Interrupt A
B7	Interrupt B	A7	Interrupt C
B8	Interrupt D	A8	+5 V
B9	PRSNT1#	A9	Reserved
B10	Reserved	A10	+ V i/o
B11	PRSNT2#	A11	Reserved
B12	Keyway	A12	Keyway
B13	Keyway	A13	Keyway
B14	Reserved	A14	Reserved
B15	Ground	A15	Reset
B16	Clock	A16	+V i/o
B17	Ground	A17	Grant
B18	Request	A18	Ground
B19	+V i/o	A19	Reserved
B20	Address 31	A20	Address 30
B21	Address 29	A21	+3.3V
B22	Ground	A22	Address 28
B23	Address 27	A23	Address 26
B24	Address 25	A24	Ground
B25	+3.3 V	A25	Address 24
B26	C/BE 3	A26	Int device select
B27	Address 23	A27	+3.3 V
B28	Ground	A28	Address 22
B29	Address 21	A29	Address 20
B30	Address 19	A30	Ground
B31	+3.3V	A31	Address 18
B32	Address17	A31	Address 16
B33	C/BE 2	A33	+3.3 V
B34	Ground	A34	Cycle Frame
B35	Initiator Ready	A35	Ground
B36	+3.3V	A36	Target Ready
B37	Device Select	A37	Ground
B38	Ground	A38	Stop
B39	Lock	A39	+3.3 V
B40	Parity Error	A40	Snoop Done
B41	+3.3 V	A41	Snoop Back-off
B42	System Error	A42	Ground
B43	+3.3 V	A43	PAR
B44	C/BE 1	A44	Address 15
B45	Address 14	A45	+3.3 V
B46	Ground	A46	Address 13
B47	Address 12	A47	Address 11
B48	Address 10	A48	Ground
B49	Ground	A49	Address 9
B50	KeyWay	A50	KeyWay
B51	KeyWay	A51	KeyWay
B52	Address 8	A52	C /BE 0
B53	Address 7	A53	+3.3 V
B54	+3.3 V	A54	Address 6
B55	Address 5	A55	Address 4
B56	Address 3	A56	Ground
B57	Ground	A57	Address 2
B58	Address 1	A58	Address 0
B59	+5 V	A59	+V i/o
B60	Acknowledge 64bit	A60	Request 64bit
B61	+5V	A61	+5 V
B62	+ 5V access Key	A62	+ 5V Access Key

INTEL PCI CHIPSETS

The PCI chipset has a crucial role in connecting the CPU and memory with the rest of the computer's resources. It provides the interfaces for the bus, disks, keyboard, memory, I/O ports along with handling interrupts, DMA and timer functions.

All PCI chipsets support the '*Plug-and-Play*' system that is designed to make configuration of device settings an automatic process. See the section on interrupts, earlier in this chapter for more details.

The facilities of different chipsets are as shown in the chart below:

Chipset	Features
FX	The original (i.e. early 1995) PCI Triton chipset of four chips. It introduced support for EDO RAM, pipeline burst cache and bus-mastered EIDE. 128MB is the maximum RAM supported, with 64MB being the maximum memory that can be cached. It has no ECC, USB or SDRAM support and cannot handle Concurrent PCI.
HX	Brought out in early 1996 as a business machine (e.g. network server) chipset of two chips. It is optimised for disk and RAM access. It can address EDO RAM quicker than the FX but can't handle SDRAM or DIMM modules. It provides ECC (error checking & correction) for DRAM. It supports multiple processors, USB and Concurrent PCI (regulates cards that have bus mastering to smooth out the data flow; activity on the PCI bus, CPU bus and ISA bus can be simultaneous). It caches up to 512MB of RAM and supports MMX. It also supports EISA motherboards. No UltraDMA 33.

VX	Introduced along with the HX series, the four-chip VX chipset was aimed at the home user. It is optimised for graphics. It supports EDO, SDRAM, DIMM sockets, USB, Concurrent PCI and MMX. Supports shared memory buffer systems (the motherboard's main memory is also used as graphics memory, to save costs). It can cache up to 64MB of RAM. 128MB is the maximum RAM supported. It has no ECC facility.
TX	Introduced in early 1997, this 2-chip set is the intended replacement for the VX. It supports 72-pin EDO and BEDO SIMMs and 168-pin SDRAM DIMMs, Ultra DMA-33 IDE (providing a 33MB/s burst mode data transfer rate - i.e. twice that of an IDE drive). It supports Concurrent PCI and USB. It caches up to 64MB of RAM. It is also optimised for MMX. It includes DPMA (Dynamic Power Management Architecture) support to reduce power consumption. No ECC or parity support.
LX	Introduced in 1997 for the Pentium II CPUs. It supports up to 1GB of EDO and 512MB of SDRAM, Concurrent PCI, Ultra DMA-33 and USB. It also supports the Advanced Graphics Port (AGP) and dual processors. It only supports a 66MHz memory bus and was commonly used with Pentium Pro systems.
EX	This is a downgraded version of the LX chipset, to produce cheaper systems. It supports a maximum of 256MB of RAM, with no support for ECC or parity RAM. It only supports a single processor on its motherboard and supports AGP and USB. Commonly used with Celeron CPU systems.
BX	Introduced in 1998 for Pentium II CPUs and currently used with Pentium III CPUs. It supports a 100MHz system bus and is therefore too fast for use with FPM and EDO memory. New faster memory DIMMs, called PC100 modules, are required to cope with the shorter 8ns access time. It supports up to 1GB of EDO or SDRAM. It also supports AGP 2x and FireWire (IEEE1394).
GX	Introduced for Pentium II/III and Xeon CPUs. It supports 2GB of SDRAM on a 100MHz bus, USB and AGP2X. Commonly used in high-end workstations and network servers and multiple processor systems.
ZX	A reduced specification chipset for Pentium II/III CPUs. It supports a maximum of 256MB of SDRAM, with no ECC, and only handles a single processor. It handles USB and AGP.
NX	Introduced in 1998 for Xeon CPUs. Targeted for use in high-volume network servers, it can handle up to four multiprocessing CPUs on a 100MHz bus and supports up to 8GB of memory. It has no AGP interface.

The LX and BX chipsets are designed for Slot 1 motherboards. The NX is designed for Slot 2. The GX chipset has both Slot 1 and Slot 2 implementations. All the other chipsets are for Socket 7 motherboards. Full socket details are given in the chapter on upgrading.

810/820/840/850 Chipsets

The 810 series, or Whitney, chipsets were introduced in mid-1999 and were a significant departure for Intel and for mainboard design. No motherboards designed for the 810 chipset and beyond will have any ISA bus slots. As explained earlier, virtually all modern motherboard architectures use a series of three busses, each running at a different speed. These are typically 8MHz for the ISA bus, 33MHz for the PCI bus, and 66/100MHz for the CPU bus. The three busses are interconnected by two so-called bridge chips, the North Bridge connecting the CPU to the PCI bus, and the South Bridge connects the PCI to the ISA (please refer to the discussion of the PCI bus in the previous section).

In the 810 chipset, there are still three busses and two bridges but there is no support for ISA expansion. The slowest bus is the PCI bus. The bridge chip called the I/O Controller Hub (IOCH or ICH) connects from the PCI bus to the new 66MHz Accelerated Hub Architecture (AHA) bus. This hub has built in support for keyboard, mouse, floppy, printer, serial and USB devices as well as audio CODECs.

The bridge chip between the 66MHz AHA bus and the CPU host bus is called the Graphics Memory Controller Hub (GMCH or GCH). This chip has an integrated AGP controller and Hardware Motion Compensation support to improve software reproduction of DVDs.

The same chip supports analogue video out for conventional monitors and digital video out for flat panel displays. It has system management functions which allow the mainboard to be monitored over the network, ACPI compliant switching of power etc. These chipsets will form the basis of a range of machines with integrated sound and video, and eventually separate video cards will become a limited market for specialist applications. The 810 chipset is capable of handling Pentium III chips but is mainly targeted at the budget Celeron-based products.

The 820 Chipset, designed for higher performance Pentium III machines, supports RDRAM memory and AGP4x video systems. It also supports a faster 133 MHz system bus, although this faster speed is only achieved when used with relatively expensive 133MHz FSB (front side bus) memory.

The 840 Chipset is designed for high memory bandwidth applications, and multi-processor Xeon-based systems, as used in servers or very powerful workstations. It can provide up to a theoretical maximum of 3.2GB/s of memory bandwidth with either RDRAM or SDRAM memory.

The 850 Chipset is used exclusively with Pentium 4 processors, and is based on Intel's new 'NetBurst' architecture aimed at improving Internet facilities. It only uses RDRAM memory, but utilises dual channels to retrieve data from two memory modules at a time. Since RDRAM chips transfer 16 bits (2 bytes) of data in each clock cycle, using two channels means 32 bits (4 bytes) are transferred, and with Rambus at 800MHz this adds up to just over 3GB/s of data transferred. The host bus between the GCH and the CPU is running at only 400MHz, but with a bus width of 64 bits (8 bytes), so this matches the speed of the Rambus memory, allowing the full speed of the Rambus to be utilised.

BUS MASTERING

In a normal single-user, single task, system, the bus is under the control of the main processor. The CPU is the *'master'* of the bus. In a local area network server, however, there may be a number of *'intelligent'* cards fitted. Any one of these cards may be capable of being the master of the bus for a while. In this situation, the card's chips carry out the memory data transfers, while the main CPU can carry out any non-bus processing. This would involve multiple *'bus mastering'*. This is not really supported by the ISA bus (both on design and speed grounds). The MCA, EISA and PCI buses are designed to handle multiple bus mastering, where a system of interleaved bus transfer cycles means that a high speed bus can service several slower speed devices (e.g. network interface cards).

Legacy-Free Architectures

Recently, machines have been produced which are advertised as '*legacy-free*'. This concept is based on the theory that eliminating legacy hardware should produce a more elegant solution that is easier to maintain and runs more efficiently. A truly legacy free motherboard will have no ISA, EISA, VESA or MCA slots; neither will it have SIMM memory, or legacy connectors such as serial, parallel, and PS/2 connectors.

This means legacy-free machines must make extensive use of USB devices, for keyboards, mice, and other external attachments (with FireWire coming along later). Current legacy-free machines tend to have little room for internal upgrades, with only a few half-height PCI slots. In fact, some have no PCI slots at all, integrating the sound and video into the motherboard.

A compromise is what is known as '*legacy light*' machines. These take out some but not all legacy components. For example, new Pentium III and 4 motherboards have no ISA slots, removing the need for a South Bridge in the chipset, yet still supporting PS/2 keyboards and mice.

External Interfaces

The preceding pages have covered the <u>internal</u> architecture and the available internal add-ons. Every PC also has a number of <u>external</u> connections (known as *'ports'*), to allow the machine to communicate with the outside world. A range of input and output devices (sometimes a device is both an input and output device) can be connected to these ports.

- Input devices include - keyboard, graphics tablet, scanner, modem, sensors, camcorders
- Output devices include - printer, monitor, plotter, modem, actuators, robots

Peripheral interfaces have a number of common characteristics:

- Data conversion - translating data from the form held inside the computer into the form required by the device (e.g. from computer binary to ACSII for the printer).
- Buffering - the temporary storage of data between the CPU and the peripheral (e.g. holding data until the modem is ready to transmit it).
- Control Signals - the transmission of control information to a device (e.g. moving disk drive heads).
- Status Signals - the reception of information on device readiness (e.g. testing if a printer is on line or out of paper).

Most interfaces are two-way devices. A printer port, for example, has to send control information and data to a printer but it also reads status information back from the printer. Of course, the printable data only goes in one direction (PC to printer). With other devices, the data may flow in both directions; this is the case with a modem that must both transmit and receive data.

INTERFACE METHODS

All connections to the computer and its adapter cards use one of these interface methods:

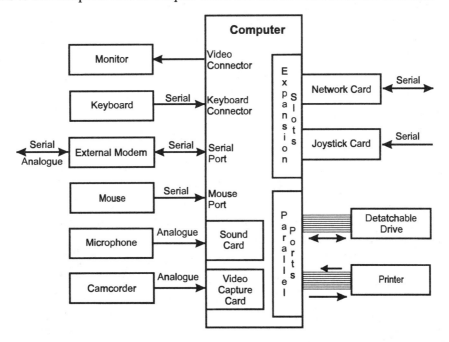

<u>PARALLEL</u>

Data is sent with all the byte's bits being transmitted simultaneously over a set of wires. Used by most printers, disk drives, etc.

<u>SERIAL</u>

The data is transmitted one bit at a time over a single connector wire. This is slower than parallel transmission but is much cheaper (particularly over long distances). Keyboards, monochrome monitors, some printers, the mouse, and LAN cabling use this method.

<u>ANALOGUE</u>

Analogue signals have an infinite number of different states, as would be expected from real-world audio or video sources. They require special adapters to interface to the computer and examples are modems, microphones and video sources such as cameras and VCRs.

Spooling

A spooling system stores print jobs into temporary files.   From there, they can be printed out at the rate that the printer can handle the data.   This saves the user waiting for a print job to finish.   The temporary files are then deleted after the printing if completed.

Buffering

Buffers are memory blocks used to temporarily store data until it is required.   Buffer memory areas are to be found inside printers, modems, video and network interface cards.

The computer itself also creates and uses buffer areas, usually in higher memory areas of the main system memory.   They are used for disk reads and writes and for keyboard buffering.

External Ports

To facilitate the connection of external devices, PCs have a number of external ports at the rear of the machine.   Normally, a PC will have at least a parallel port and a serial port, although some machines may have more.   All machines will have a keyboard interface and an outlet for attaching a monitor. Some motherboards also have joystick ports or USB sockets.

Parallel Port

Also known as the *'Centronics'*, *'LPT'* or *'Printer'* port.   With the advent of improved ports, the conventional port is also now known as the SPP (*'Standard Parallel Port'*).   By convention, the whole cable is described as a Centronics cable.   In fact, the plug that fits the printer socket is a 36-pin Amphenol plug to fit the printer's Centronics socket. The plug at the computer is a normal 25-pin male D-type connector.

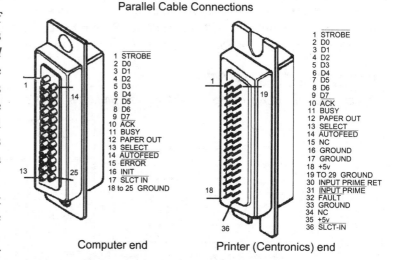

Parallel Cable Connections

Computer end   Printer (Centronics) end

In parallel transmission, the data port has eight separate wires connecting the computer to the external device. There is a separate pin in the socket for

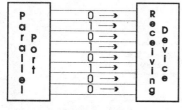

The letter 'T' being sent down a parallel cable

each data wire, plus other pins for the control information.   Five volts on a wire represents logic 1, while zero volts represents logic 0.   In this way, an entire byte of data can be transmitted at a time.

There are problems in sending parallel transmissions over long distances.   Due to the different characteristics of each wire, the time taken for the data to pass down each wire is different.   So, over a long distance, the individual bits that comprise a particular byte may not all arrive at the destination at the same time - even although they were transmitted simultaneously.   This effect is known as *'skew'* and is the reason that parallel transmission, although faster than serial, is restricted to short cables up to two metres in length. Parallel transmission is used for most printer cables (although it is possible to buy serial interface printers).

Port Addresses

IBM defined the first parallel port as LPT1 and the second and third, if fitted, as LPT2 and LPT3.   The system can differentiate between these ports and any other devices because the hardware for LPT1, LPT2 and LPT3 (and the serial ports similarly) only responds to certain defined port address ranges. The three possible ranges for parallel ports are:

Port	Data to Printer (output)	Printer Status (input)	Printer Control (output)
Option 1	3BC	3BD	3BE
Option 2	378	379	37A
Option 3	278	279	27A

When the computer is booted up, one of the address ranges above is allocated to LPT1, LPT2 and LPT3 as the defaults. The system is checked for parallel ports, any devices found are allocated to the ports and the information is stored as part of a device list stored in main memory. Plug and Play systems will dynamically allocate the port addresses. The addresses in use on any particular computer can be found using the MSDOS MSD utility or the *'System/Ports'* option in Device Manager found in Windows Control Panel. If this is not available on the machine, the DEBUG utility can be used. When DEBUG runs, the DOS prompt is replaced by DEBUG's minus sign prompt. When the command

d0040:0008

is entered, a set of hex numbers will appear on the screen. A typical line might be

78 03 BC 03 00 00 00 00

The first two bytes indicate that LPT1 is use and is using address 0378 (note that the bytes are displayed in reverse order) and that LPT2 is in use with address 03BC. To get back to the DOS prompt the letter 'q' has to be entered at the minus prompt. MSD looks up the printer table and displays the findings while DEBUG is used to directly access the table.

Parallel Port Registers

The normal computer parallel port has three registers (memory areas) to store information that will pass between the port and the printer. The three registers are:

The Data Register	Used to send characters <u>OUT</u> to the printer.
	Wired through eight pins (pin 2 to pin 9)
The Printer Control Register	Used to send control information <u>OUT</u> to the printer.
	Wired through four active pins (pins 1,14,16,17)
The Printer Status Register	Used to store printer information coming <u>IN</u> from the printer
	Wired through five active pins (pins 10,11,12,13,15)

The addresses for these registers are as previously described.

The Parallel Port as an Output Port

Whereas the serial port has its own chip to carry out data transmission, the Standard Parallel Port requires these tasks to be carried out by the computer's CPU. The computer can feed data to the printer much faster than the mechanical printing process can deal with it, and so a system of flow control (known as *'handshaking'*) must be used. The process varies slightly but a general description is as follows:

- Place the data in the Data Register to feed the external data lines.
- Pulse the STROBE line (pin 1) low. This should energise the printer end, which should result in the printer reading the data off the data lines and switching its own BUSY line high.
- Check the BUSY line (pin 11). When the printer is ready to receive the next data byte, it will switch its BUSY line low again.
- When the BUSY line goes low, repeat the process.

In other systems, the printer informs the PC that the data is received by bringing the ACKNOWLEDGE line (pin 10) low.

The other port output lines are:

AUTOFEED (pin 14)	Tells the printer to automatically insert a Line Feed after a Carriage Return.
INIT (pin 16)	Initialises the printer on power up.
SELECT (pin 17)	Takes the printer off line. This was often used with daisywheel and golf ball head printers where the document to be printed would have special printer codes embedded in the text. When the text altered (e.g. to an Italics font) the printer would be automatically taken off line to allow the operator to change print heads.

Many modern printers, particularly lasers, ignore all control signals apart from the STROBE signal.

The other port input lines are:

Paper Out (pin 12)	The printer pulls this line high when it runs out of paper. It also pulls the SELECT line (pin 13) high to tell the PC that it is on line and waiting for data.
Error (pin 15)	The printer pulls this line low when it detects an error such as a paper jam.

The easiest way to write to the parallel port is using the existing DOS code accessed by calling up the DOS interrupt routine 21h thus:

```
mov ah, 05h
mov dl, 0Ch
int 21h
```

The Parallel Port as an Input/Output Port

Standard Mode

The Standard Mode, also known as the *'Centronics'* or *'Compatibility'* Mode, is purely an output system and does not expect any input other than status information (e.g. out-of-paper or paper-jam information). No user data enters the computer using this mode.

Nibble Mode

The Standard Centronics interface has four lines that are used to signal problems to the computer (such as shortage of paper).   If the control software is written to examine these lines, then the parallel port offers the possibility of being a two-way device.   Since the data being read <u>into</u> the parallel port is only four bits wide, only half a byte, i.e. a *'nibble'*, can be transferred at a time.   This is described as *'four bit mode'*.   Incoming data is therefore substantially slower than outgoing data and is typically 80Kb per second.   All parallel ports can operate in this mode, since every port has these four input lines.

Byte Mode

Four-bit working is inadequate for fast data transfer and a full bi-directional parallel port was first introduced in 1987, with the IBM PS/2 range of computers.   All computers after about 1993 are likely to have these improved parallel ports.   Here, the eight data lines are capable of both reading and writing data, allowing the port to be an input as well as an output device.   This significantly speeded up data transfers to a maximum of 300Kb per second.   However, the system was still hampered by the CPU having to carry out all the port's handshaking and flow control activities.

EPP

In 1992, the IEEE 1284 standard was brought in.   This has become known as the Enhanced Parallel Port (EPP).   Like the normal bi-directional ports, the EPPs are capable of either sending or receiving data on the data pins.   The main advantage of the EPPs is that they do not require the CPU for flow control as the chips on the cards carry out these tasks.   The EPP performance is a major advance, with typical data transfer rates of 800KB per second (a 2MB/s maximum).

Enhanced Parallel Ports are also *'backward compatible'* with older, non-EPP devices.   This means that a computer with an EPP will have the following characteristics:

- Any device that is EPP compatible device will attach to an Enhanced Port and will detect that the port is of the EPP type.   Subsequent data transfers will be at the maximum rate allowed by the port.   This allows the newer printers and network adapters to operate at their best potential.
- Any device that is not EPP compatible will still attach to an Enhanced Port but the port will operate in standard mode.

If an EPP compatible device is attached to a standard Parallel Port, the device will work in standard mode.   For the user, this should be an automatic process as the device software is able to test the port type and configure itself accordingly.

The EPP was designed for use with hard drives, CD-ROMs, LAN cards, etc.

ECP

The Enhanced Capability Port was promoted by Microsoft and Hewlett Packard and is designed for interfacing to the modern range of printers and scanners. While it is capable of operating in other modes, the ECP mode provides added features such as DMA operation and RLE (Run Length Encoding) compression of data.   Compression ratios of up to about 64:1 are supported, making it an ideal interface for the transferring of scanned bitmaps.

Windows 95/98 has built-in support for ECP ports and the IRQ and DMA can be set up in the *'Device Manager'* menu.   Naturally, the printer must also be ECP capable.

PARALLEL PORT DEVICES

A whole range of storage and other devices exist for connection to the computer's parallel port.   These include 3.5" floppy drives, 5.25" floppy drives, fixed hard disks, removable cartridge drives, optical R/W drives, CD-ROM drives and tape streamers (fast-running tape decks using 1/4" cartridges or DAT tapes, for data backup and restore purposes).   Peripherals other than storage devices include scanners, video cameras, sound cards and LAN adapters.

The advantages of parallel port peripherals are:
- Ease of connection.   There is no need to open machines to fit or configure cards.
- Portability.   The peripheral is a free-standing device that will connect to any computer.
- Can be used to extend laptops and notebooks, which lack internal space for expansion.
- Allows a machine with the IDE card limit of two hard disks to attach a third, external, drive.
- Sharing resources.   A printer, for example, is not tied to a particular computer; it is neither fitted into a machine nor does it require an adapter card to be fitted to a machine.   This allows the peripheral to be easily moved to another location where it can currently be most usefully employed.
- Sharing Data.   Devices such as the ZIP drive allow 100MB of data to stored on a removable disk that can then be inserted into any other ZIP drive for reading.
- Easy recovery from machine failure.   In the event that a machine breaks down, its data is held on a mass-storage device that can be quickly transferred to another working machine.   A set of portable 10GB hard disks or a 24GB DAT streamer would handle most of an organisation's data comfortably.

To ensure that the computer's only parallel port is not lost to the device, parallel port peripherals normally provide an additional parallel port.

Serial Port

A serial transmission system is cheaper to use, since it only requires a single channel between the PC and the external device.

In a serial system, data that arrives in parallel format from the bus is converted into a stream of bits that is sent sequentially along the single cable.   A chip called UART (Universal Asynchronous Receiver Transmitter) carries out this conversion task. The PC uses a standard known as RS232C and is implemented as COM1 and, if fitted, COM2, COM3 and COM4.   An updated version known as RS-232D meets CCITT V.24, V2.28 and ISO IS2110 standards.

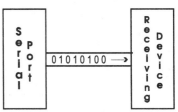

The letter 'T' being sent down a serial cable

Another version, the RS 422 / RS485, is used extensively to control equipment. This allows multi-drop connections from a controller, via a two-wire bus to up to 32 devices at a range of up to 1200m/4000ft.

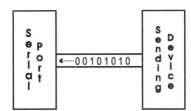

The letter 'T' being received into the serial port

Common devices to be found on a serial port are printers, plotters, modems, remotely controlled instruments and machinery.   Although the above example shows data being transmitted <u>out</u> of the port to a device, it should be stressed that the RS232 port is essentially a bi-directional port.   This means that data can also be passed <u>in</u> to the port from an external device.

A good example of an input device is a serial mouse.   Other examples are bar code readers, electronic tills and remote monitoring equipment.

In the case of a modem, the port will transfer data both <u>in</u> and <u>out</u> of the PC.

The serial port is often used for instrument control.   The computer sends out commands on the RS232 port to the instrument's serial interface.   The commands may set up the instrument for certain purposes and initiate the resultant readings, which are transmitted back to the computer on the same serial cable. This can be used over short distances for activities such as manufacturing test beds and the digital control of electronic or radio equipment.   When used via modems or dedicated telephone lines, longer distances are achieved.   This allows for the remote control of apparatus and remote data logging.

Like the parallel ports, the serial ports are detected at power up and their addresses stored in memory. The normal address for COM1 is 3F8h and the normal address for COM2 is 2F8h.   As with the parallel ports, the serial port addresses in use on any particular computer can be found by using the MSDOS MSD utility or the Windows 95 Control Panel/Ports utility.

Alternatively, the DEBUG utility can be used to interrogate the table with the command:
d0040:0000
The RS232 port and serial communications are covered in detail in the chapter on Data Communications.

PC CARDS (PCMCIA) & CardBus

Announced in 1990, the PCMCIA standard (Personal Computer Memory Card International Association) appeared as a standard interface for portable computer users. All major hardware and software suppliers support the standard. The standard aims to allow the easy connection of a range of add-ons. PCMCIA products are now referred to as *'PC Cards'*. The PCMCIA connection is the portable's equivalent of the ISA expansion slots on a desktop machine. Each add-on card is about the size of a credit card and the original intention was to provide the easy connection of additional memory chips.

Memory Cards

The cards, some of which are also sometimes described as *'Flash memory'*, have a 68-pin plug at one end and connect to sockets inside palmtop/notebook computers and digital cameras. Once inserted, they act like a normal bank of memory configured as a RamDisc. When a card is withdrawn, it retains the data stored in its chips until it is required again. This also provides portability, as the card can be pulled out of one machine and inserted in another machine, just like a floppy disk. The cards mostly use static RAM as the storage medium with a small lithium battery maintaining the data contents. Flash RAM handles larger capacities but has some problems in ensuring that the programming voltages to set the memory contents are the same on all machines using the PCMCIA interface. Memory cards are available in sizes from 128kB to 64MB although they are very expensive at the high capacity sizes.

PCMCIA Interface

PCMCIA is now used mainly as a hardware I/O standard, allowing the connection of a whole range of devices already associated with desktop PCs. These include disk drives, CD-ROMs, sound cards, digital cameras, video capture cards, data acquisition cards, modems, faxes, and LAN interface cards. These connect through the PCMCIA interface and ignore any ISA, MCA or EISA bus that might be on the machine. The system dynamically assigns I/O addresses and IRQs to the cards during the boot-up or when cards are inserted.

Advantages

- Speed. Intel claims that flash RAM has an access time that is 10,000 times faster than a hard disk.
- Software will appear in this credit-card format.
- Easy change of cards, while the computer is still running - known as *'hot plugging'* or *'hot swapping'*. The new card should be automatically detected and recognised by the interface, based on the information stored and supplied by the card.   The functions of some of the pins on the interface are re-mapped according to the device detected. By default, the card is assumed to be a memory card. Since the process is automatic, there is no need to re-boot the computer each time a card is changed.

Disadvantage

- The range of add-ons remains much more expensive then their desktop counterparts.

Physical Versions

- Type 1 of the standard covers the use of the card as a memory storage device. This defines the physical thickness of the card as 3.3mm and size 54mm by 85mm.
- Type 2 announced in 1992, expanded the PCMCIA standard use to cover the connection between card and machine as the basis for designing a range of I/O (input/output) add-on cards for LAN adapters, SCSI controllers, modems, sound cards, video capture cards, etc. This card is 5mm thick and has a size of 48mm by 75mm. This is type most commonly fitted to portable computers and digital cameras.
- Extended versions of Version 1 and Version 2 standards are available. These have the same width and thickness as the normal version but allow for extra long cards to be used.   This allows even more complex circuitry to be mounted on the cards but means that the cards will protrude from the computer's casing by up to 135mm.
- Type 3 is 10.5mm thick to allow for the inclusion of larger peripherals and small hard disk drives such as the 170MB Maxtor drive, the 270MB SyQuest drive and the Hitachi MP-EG1A 260MB digital camcorder's drive.
- Type 4 is 16mm thick to allow for the inclusion of larger capacity hard disk drives. IBM, Western Digital and Hewlett Packard have already produced hard disks to this format, the first two being 1.8" and the HP being only 1.3". Other models are available from Maxtor and Conner.
- Type 5 is 18mm thick and was announced by Toshiba for its wireless network cards.

All types plug into the same 68-pin interface socket, arranged as two rows of 34 pins.   While cards can be inserted upside down, the interface ensures that this will not harm the card or the computer (although it will naturally prevent the card from working).

Standards
- PCMCIA 1.0 stated the minimum specification for early cards.
- PCMCIA 2.1 specified the interfaces used with the 16-bit cards.
- PCMCIA 3.0 is the new CardBus system and supports 32-bit working, DMA and 3.3volt working (older cards require 5 volts while newer portables work on 3.3volts). It has a 32-bit address bus and a 32-bit data bus. It supports bus mastering and runs at 33MHz, providing a throughput of 132MBps. Windows, from version 95 Release 2 onwards, has built-in CardBus card and socket services.

There is still work to be done to finalise file formats so that a card from one machine can be read by another machine. The hardware writing and reading is agreed but the format of the data interchange is still to be agreed. The device driver software has been given the title of *'enablers'*. The low-level *'Socket Services'*, those that read the card data and link to the higher level *'Card Services'*, should ideally be implemented in BIOS. Unsurprisingly, Award and Phoenix (manufacturers of BIOS chips) lead the field in Socket Services. These services configure the card for the machine that is using it. Some cards use their own proprietary enablers, ignoring the Card and Socket Services. In general, software support is lagging the development of this new hardware.

Universal Serial Bus
The Universal Serial Bus (USB) was developed by Intel and it promises to be the new general-purpose PC port. It could eventually replace serial ports, parallel ports and internal interface cards as the means of connecting slow to medium speed external devices such as keyboards, mice, modems, scanners, etc.

Unlike the large 9/25 pin serial connections and the 25/36 pin parallel connections, the USB requires only four wires in a light flex cable. There is one wire for the common ground, two to identify data in each direction and a 5v power supply wire.

It has many distinct advantages:
- The bus is relatively fast with a maximum date transfer rate of 12Mbps and a lower rate of 1.5Mbps for slow devices such as keyboards and mice.
- USB is Plug and Play compliant. So, devices can be *'hot swapped'* - i.e. fitted and removed without rebooting or reconfiguring the machine. The configuration problems previously associated with adding and altering equipment is eliminated. If a new device is fitted while the computer is switched on, it is automatically configured.
- Since one entire USB system requires a single IRQ, problems of running out of machine IRQs will disappear.
- The bus provides its own power supply to any low-power devices that connect to it. There is no longer any need for each external device to have its own power unit. This should make peripherals cheaper and eliminates the tangle of power connections at the rear of machines. However, adding multiple devices may place a strain on the computer's own power supply.
- Devices were once designed to only work their own manufacturer's interface cards (e.g. scanners, some mice). USB devices do not have this restriction. This should make the new USB models of the devices cheaper and easier to connect.

USB allows a single port to connect many devices together is in daisy chain. Up to 127 devices can connect to a single USB port if hubs are used to expand the system. A hub is a star-like connector that connects a group of devices to a single connection point.

The diagram shows a PC with two USB ports. Port 2 connects directly to a hub and this has three outlets connected to USB devices. Typical USB hubs support four, five or seven port outlets.

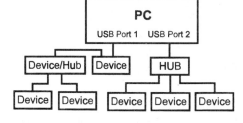

Port 1 connects to two devices that are daisy chained to the port. One of these devices also acts as a hub and has two further devices connected to it.

Hyundai 17B+ and 15G+ monitors are available with three USB ports mounted on the base. So, a PC port may connect to a monitor with the speakers, headphones and microphones connecting directly to the monitor. Or a keyboard could be designed as a hub, with a mouse, joystick and light pen attaching to a connection at the rear of the keyboard.

Many USB devices are now available (e.g. Canon and Kodak digital cameras, Logitech mice, Genius joystick, Samsung, Philips, Sony and Iiyama monitors, Cherry keyboards).

USB is supported by all modern PCI chipsets (i.e. HX, VX, TX, LX, BX, 800 series) but is only supported in Windows 95 Release 2, Windows 98 and Windows 2000. All Windows 3.1 users, and many Windows 95 users cannot currently access USB facilities.

USB2

The current standard for Universal Serial Bus is USB 1.1. This specifies the data rate of up to 12Mb/s, with low speed signalling at 1.5Mb/s, on the same interface as mentioned earlier. The consortium developing USB includes companies such as Intel, Microsoft, Hewlett Packard, Lucent and Philips. It released a new standard (USB 2) at the start of the year 2000. USB 2 is entirely compatible with the existing cables and plugs, but runs at up to 480MHz. This frequency was chosen after calculations showed that it was as high as could be achieved on the existing cabling. Windows XP supports USB2, with the use of additional Microsoft drivers (available from the Microsoft website). The consortium expects USB2 to co-exist with the IEEE 1394 FireWire (see below).

Generally, USB 2 will connect computer peripherals like Ethernet interfaces, printers, and so on, while FireWire connects Audio/Visual and multimedia applications like digital camcorders, digital TV equipment etc. Few USB2 peripherals are available so far, but USB2 hubs and devices are easily integrated with older USB1.1 equipment.

FireWire

Another high-performance serial bus is IEEE-1394, commonly known as *'Firewire'*.   This was developed from the Apple computer range and is also known as the *'Multimedia Connection'* since it allows camcorders, scanners, disk drives, DVD players, CD-ROMs and printers to share a common connecting bus.   The common interface means that it is also suitable for the home networking of PCs.

Like the USB system, it supports up to 63 devices. However, FireWire does not require the use of hubs as each device has a common connection to all other devices - including the PC.   The standard connecting cables are 6-wire; two for the power and four used to connect to consumer audio and video products (TV sets, VCRs, amplifiers, etc).   The four bus wires are configured as two twisted pairs, crossed between ends to provide transmit and receive pairs.   FireWire devices have several sockets and a 1394 cable plugs into the sockets of the devices to be connected.   There are no cable length restrictions (as with LANS) and no need to set device ID numbers (as with SCSI). The only restriction is that the devices must not be cabled in a way that wires the system as a loop.

Sony uses a four-wire variant (known as *'I-link'*) for its products, using the IEEE-1394.1 standard.

Despite its simplicity, FireWire is an extremely fast interface that can move data at 100Mbps, 200Mbps or 400Mbps. Even the slowest speed is capable of simultaneously delivering two full-motion video channels running at the high video rate of 30fps, accompanied by CD quality stereo sound.   It multiplexes data such as compressed video and digitised audio along with device control commands on the common bus.

DVC (Digital Video Cassette) systems made by Sony already use FireWire on their camcorders.   The other major players such as JVC, Hitachi and Philips will also have FireWire systems on their D-VHS (Digital VHS) recorders.   Since DVC requires 3.5Mb per sec (i.e. 28Mbps), it cannot be handled by USB (12Mbps limit) but is well within FireWire's capabilities.   On the other hand, a 90-minute video could require almost 19GB of hard disk space.   This places this aspect of FireWire at the professional end of the video market.

FireWire devices, like USB devices, are hot swappable.

FireWire is fully supported from Windows 98 onwards and as an upgrade to Windows 95.

FireWire 2

Version 2.0 of FireWire has now appeared. Known as IEEE 1394b, it can potentially run up to 1.6Gbps, four times faster than basic FireWire and is easily the fastest external bus that is currently available. It also claims to travel greater distances without degradation, and carries greater power on its cable than the first implementation (allowing more devices to be powered directly by the computer). A 3.2Gbps version for use with optical fibre cables is being developed; this is aimed particularly at multimedia and video distribution

Relative Uses

Both FireWire and USB are competing with Ultra SCSI and Fibre Channel for the high-speed bus market. The likely uses of USB and FireWire are complementary rather than competing.

- USB remains the option for input devices (mouse/keyboard/joystick), audio (sound/music/ telephone), printers, scanners, storage devices (floppy, tape) and slow speed communications (modems, ISDN)
- FireWire offers a higher performance for top-end devices such as DVD drives, DVC cameras, D-VHS recorders and wide-band networking. Some CD-ROM drives and fast hard disk systems also use FireWire interfaces.

Infrared

Sending data by infrared is widespread and is the method used in most TV and video remote control handsets. The beam of light is just below the visible part of the spectrum and data is transmitted by pulsing the light beam on and off. It is a very useful low-power short-range system.

It is now finding its way into the computing field and is being developed by a group of manufacturers known as the Infrared Data Association (IrDA). Uses for IrDA include:

- Wireless keyboards and mice.
- Wireless printers.
- Wireless LAN adapters.
- Wireless peer-to-peer computer networks.

The initial IrDA implementation, introduced in 1994, was seen as a direct replacement for the serial port and had a data rate of 115kbps. It uses RZI (Return-to-Zero Invert) modulation. This means that a light pulse is transmitted for each logic 'zero' in the data stream; a logic 'one' will not produce a light pulse. By 1995, a faster 4Mbps version had been introduced. It uses PPM (Pulse Position Modulation) where a constant stream of light pulses is transmitted. The time between each pulse is not evenly spaced and the exact position in time for the pulse indicates one of four binary values from 00 to 11. The transmission of these 4-bits has named the system 4PPM.

115kbps systems are common in applications such as wireless printer connection whereas the 4Mbps system is commonly implemented in portable computers.

Bluetooth

Bluetooth is an open standard interconnection standard that has been in preparation for a number of years but is yet to make significant impact. Bluetooth capable equipment offers short-range digital voice and data transmission by radio signals, for both point-to-point and multicast applications. Point-to-point transmission is useful for personal applications, where cables and infrared light links are currently used. Multicast will allow the use of networking, email, World Wide Web and no doubt other yet to be developed technologies. The use of radio links presents interesting problems. Higher frequencies only work between antennae that can see each other, so called "line of sight", whilst lower frequencies are subject to fading and interference. The Bluetooth standard overcomes these problems and incorporates encryption technology to ensure privacy where it is needed. Currently there are very few Bluetooth products available, mostly hands-free phone adaptors and notebook PC Cards. These are capable of 720kbps at a range of between 10m and 100m. By the year 2005, the consortium developing Bluetooth technology hopes to see 10Mbps, which is a data rate equivalent to that used in many mainstream office networks. As third generation mobile telephony drives technology development in the area, Bluetooth connections utilising the Wireless Application Protocol (WAP) are expected to become very popular.

Comparison of serial interface performances		
Interface	**Cabling**	**Max Data Rate**
Serial (RS232)	Twisted Pair	115kbps
Infrared (IrDA)	Optical Beam	4Mbps
USB 1	4-wire Cable	12Mbps
USB2	4 wire Cable	480Mbps
FireWire (IEEE 1394)	6 wire Cable	400Mbps
FireWire (IEEE 1394b)	6 wire Cable	1.6Gbps
Bluetooth 1.1	Wireless	720kbps
Bluetooth (full implementation)	Wireless	10Mbps

Display Technology

For many years the term *'Computer Video'* was used to describe the techniques used to transfer computer images to the monitor. These images could be mainly static (as in the case of databases or word processing) or could be animated (as in the case of games, graphic simulations, etc). Now, computer video describes the specific technique of showing real-life video footage for multimedia presentations. This chapter examines the technology of monitors and computer graphics cards and discusses the technical and operational factors to be considered when choosing - and using - such devices.

The visual output of the early mainframe computers was only plain text and numbers.   Usually this output was directed to a line printer.   Even when screens became more common, they were mostly used to *'monitor'* the computing process. The introduction of the personal computers brought the first moves towards a more attractive presentation. IBM machines introduced its *'IBM character set'* for screen and printer and this provided some line and box graphics. There was no need for sophisticated screens and early monitors were crude, low-definition devices.

Two main developments have led to greatly improved monitor design:

- Programs have become increasingly more graphics based (Computer Aided Design, Desktop Publishing, Windows, multimedia, etc.). These programs required monitors that could display ever more detailed output.
- Users were spending much longer periods in front of the monitor, as the computer developed into more of a personal tool.   This raised questions of eyestrain, fatigue and other harmful effects that had to be addressed.

Monitors, and their hardware and software drivers, are becoming increasingly complex devices. There is a wide choice of specifications, techniques, performances and prices. There is no overall *'correct'* choice; there is only an appropriate choice for a particular use. For example, it would be a waste of a company's resources to buy a £2,000 large screen, high performance monitor and graphics accelerator card for a PC that is used only for occasional word processing.   On the other hand, the same expensive monitor and card might be absolute necessities for detailed work in a design office.

Monitor Construction

Monochrome Monitors

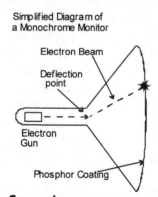

Simplified Diagram of
a Monochrome Monitor

Electron Beam

Deflection
point

Electron
Gun

Phosphor Coating

The construction of computer monitors is identical to that of television screens.   The monitor is based around a CRT (cathode ray tube) that contains the main elements shown in the diagram, plus control and amplifier circuitry. The electron gun, or *'cathode'*, produces an electron cloud that is then drawn as an accelerated stream towards the front screen of the CRT, which is held at a very high voltage.   When the electrons strike the coating on the inside of the tube they cause a temporary phosphorescence of that area of the tube surface. This causes a bright spot to appear in the middle of the monitor screen.

To produce a picture from this system, the two other requirements are:

- The whole of the screen should be covered by the beam.
- The beam should be modulated, to provide a grey scale.

Scanning

The CRT monitor is a serial device.   Each individual area of the screen has to be illuminated to different degrees to provide a picture. It is not practical to have a separate gun for each spot on the screen. The one gun has to handle the whole screen surface.   The process of ensuring that the electron beam systematically covers each part of the monitor screen is known as *'scanning'*.

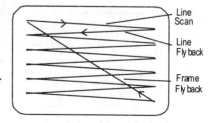

Line
Scan

Line
Fly back

Frame
Fly back

The screen scanning process executes in the same way that a book page is read - from left to right and from top to bottom, one line at a time. The finished picture is, in effect, composed of a set of parallel lines, called a *'raster'*.

To achieve this, electronic circuitry is introduced to deflect the electron beam in both the horizontal and vertical directions. The movement from left to right, and the accompanying rapid *'line flyback'* from right to left is carried out by the *'line scan'* circuitry. The slower movement down the screen and the final rapid *'frame flyback'* is carried out by the *'frame scan'* circuitry. These scans are synchronised by line and frame scan oscillators.

Commencing from the top, left corner of the screen, the beam is moved rightwards at a constant, pre-determined speed. When it reaches the rightmost edge, the electron stream is switched off, while the deflection circuits 'fly back' the position to the left edge of the screen, ready for the next line of scan. The period when the stream is switched off is known as the *'line blanking'* period. This process is repeated hundreds of times, until the entire screen is covered. The exact amount of lines depends on the resolution of the screen standard in use - anywhere between 200 lines and 1000 lines or over. When the last line is traced on the screen, the electron stream is again switched off - the *'frame blanking'* period, while the beam is returned to the top left corner of the screen.

Modulation

In a TV receiver, the intensity of the beam can be varied continuously across the scan of the line, limited only by the quality of the controlling electronics. For computer monitors, each line is considered to have a certain amount of elements along its length. Each element can then be illuminated or not, to produce the picture intelligence. Each of the picture elements is known as a *'pixel'*. The number of picture lines and the number of pixels across each line are a measure of the *'resolution'* of the screen picture. A SVGA screen, for example, has a resolution of 800 x 600 - i.e. is has a matrix of 800 pixels across by 600 pixels down.

If a monitor were to have a modulating input signal that was TTL (transistor-transistor logic) the input voltage would switch between +5 volts and 0 volts. The electron stream would either be completely on or completely off. Such a monitor would not be able to provide shades of grey. If the flow of electrons can be stepped in discrete stages, then a grey scale can be implemented. The input here would be an analogue signal, which is capable of providing degrees of modulation of the electron beam. In an ideal world, the modulating signal would vary in infinitely small steps, to display a huge amount of picture detail. While the monitor can cope with fairly small changes, the memory that would be required to store such variations is currently prohibitive (see later section on memory).

Frame Refresh Speeds

The screen produced by the above process has only a short life, as the glow from the phosphoresced areas will rapidly die away. The whole process has to be repeated regularly enough so that the persistence of vision of the human eye perceives the screen as a continuous display, with no detectable flicker. Where the picture has a dark background, any flicker is less noticeable. Where there is a white background, the constant cycle of lighting a pixel, letting the pixel illumination dull, followed by again fully illuminating the pixel causes the most pronounced flicker. This can be particularly noticeable with Windows, since most backgrounds are light-coloured. Initially, 40 frames per second was considered adequate and a refresh rate of 50Hz (cycles per second) was used. This was discovered to be too slow, as it still produced enough flicker to cause eyestrain and headaches. 40Hz is the rate at which most people can detect flicker. Many people are capable of detecting and being bothered by flicker at up to 70Hz. At 72Hz, flicker ceases to be a factor.

Over the years, the frame refresh speeds - i.e. the vertical scanning frequency - has gradually increased. At the end of 1997, VESA recommended 85Hz as the refresh rate for 14" monitors. VESA has set 70Hz as the lowest acceptable rate for SVGA graphics adapters, with 72Hz as the acceptable standard. With 1024 x 768, VESA has set the rate at 70Hz, although larger screen sizes often use 76Hz. Modern monitors commonly have a top frame refresh speed exceeding 100Hz and some models have a top rate of 160Hz, such as the CTX EX710F. These figures are for non-interlaced systems. The pace of improvement has been tempered by the fact that faster frame speeds increase the system bandwidth and thereby cost more to manufacture.

The frame refresh speed is also commonly known as the *'vertical scan range'*.

Line Refresh Speeds

The frame refresh speeds and screen resolutions have a direct bearing on the required speed from the line scan circuitry. Consider the frame refresh time being kept constant and the resolution being increased. The system has to produce more horizontal lines in the same time, so the line scan time has to be shortened, to get each line drawn faster. This results in a higher line scan frequency. Similarly, if the resolution remains constant but the frame refresh is speeded up, there will still be more lines drawn in the same time - the line frequency has to be increased. A VGA monitor has a line frequency of 31.5KHz. This means that 31,500 screen lines have to be traced out every second. Consider a SVGA screen (i.e. 800 x 600) with an 80Hz refresh rate. 48,000 screen lines would be required to be produced each second (i.e. 600 lines scanned 80 times per second). Monitors have a lower line refresh rate of around 30KHz and maximum refresh rates depend upon the quality of the product. Typical upper rates are around 100KHz for older models and up to 160KHz for top quality models.

The line refresh speed is also commonly known as the *'horizontal scan range'*.

Bandwidth

When a monitor is driven at a high resolution with high frame refresh speeds, much data has to be placed on the screen in a very short time. The ability of a system to achieve high throughput is measured by its *'bandwidth'*. The bandwidth is measured in MegaHertz (millions of cycles per second) and describes how quickly the electronic circuitry can change from the system voltage state to a zero voltage state; this in turn determines how many pixels can be handled per second. A high resolution screen will have more dots along each screen line. This will demand a greater throughput and hence a higher bandwidth. Similarly, a high frame refresh rates involves writing to the screen more often, which also increases the data moved in any one time period - i.e. the bandwidth is increased.

Running in VGA (640x480) mode only requires a bandwidth of 21.5MHz at the commonly used refresh rate of 70Hz.   This bandwidth is determined by multiplying the horizontal resolution, vertical resolution and the frame refresh rate (i.e. 640 x 480 x 70 = 21,504,000)

Higher resolution SVGA modes might require a bandwidth of up to 270MHz (i.e. 2048 x 1536 x 85). The higher the system bandwidth, the more demanding is the monitor circuitry. This partly explains why a high-performance monitor is more expensive than poorer models.

Simply lowering the frame refresh rate would lower bandwidth and reduce monitor costs. This is an unacceptable solution, since it produces severe flicker problems. Incompatible cards and monitors may be easily connected, resulting in driving a monitor with a signal that is changing at a pace beyond its bandwidth capabilities. This would result in the signal not responding fast enough to changes and adjacent unwanted pixels being lit, with the consequent downgrading of clarity.

Interlacing

To provide high-resolution screens at lower cost, a system of *'interlacing'* is contrived. 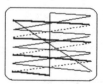 The picture is built up in two halves. Firstly, all the odd lines are built up.   This is immediately followed by filling in all the even lines. If the frame speed is unchanged, then the whole picture takes twice as long to build up as a non-interlaced model. This reduces the required bandwidth and hence cost. The problems of a jerky picture at low refresh speeds are reduced, since each frame refresh manages to update the whole screen, albeit only every other line. This used to be an acceptable compromise, although non-interlaced monitors are the best performers and are now universally sold. Non-interlaced models are also sometimes referred to as *'sequential'* systems. They draw every line, both odd and even, in a straight sequence until the whole screen is painted before returning to the top of the screen.

Synchronisation

The internal circuitry of the monitor contains oscillators to produce the necessary line and field scans. The start of these line and field scans must coincide with that required by the computer's graphics output. The cable between the computer and monitor carries the modulation information.   It also carries line and frame synchronising pulses from the computer.   These pulses are used to keep the oscillators in the monitor running at the correct timing. Without these synchronising pulses, the screen would soon suffer from *'line tear'* and *'frame roll'* as the slight timing differences between the two units became aggregated. The sync signals are usually two different TTL lines varying from 0v and 5v, one each for the line and frame pulses.

Dual Sync / Multi-Sync

Some monitors may only operate on a single line frequency.   When attached to a computer graphics card, it adjusts its running speed to synchronise to that of the video output.   This is a minor automatic adjustment and extends only to very limited frequency boundaries.   Producing this single standard model requires less complex circuitry and is cheaper. *'Dual Sync'* monitors sense the frequency of the incoming signal and lock to it if it is one of its two pre-set line frequencies - normally 31.5Khz and 35.5KHz.

Many modern monitors are capable of automatically locking to a range of different line and frame scan frequencies within the bandwidth it is designed for.   They are said to be *'multi-sync'*, *'multi-scanning'* or *'autosync'*.   If the upper limit of this scanning range is high enough, an element of future proofing is introduced, since the monitor will be able to handle any future specification upgrades (new standards will involve higher refresh rates).   The fact that a monitor's circuitry can synchronise to a range of different refresh speeds, does not necessarily imply that it will perform equally well at all the standards it can cover. Indeed, models that are designed for high-resolution SVGA modes often perform less well when trying to handle lower standards.

Generally, analogue signals will not properly drive an RGB monitor and an RGB signal will not properly drive an analogue monitor. Some monitors are advertised as being both analogue and digital. These monitors have added circuitry to make the conversion.

Typical scan frequencies for the range of screen resolutions are given in the table.

	Line Scan (max)	Frame Scan (typical)
VGA	31.5KHz	60Hz, 70 Hz
640 x 480 VESA	37.5KHz	75Hz
SVGA 800 x 600 VESA standard	35.5KHz	56Hz
	37.8KHz	60Hz
	48KHz	72 Hz
	46.8KHz	75Hz
	53.7KHz	85Hz
1024 x 768 VESA standard	48.3KHz	60Hz
	56.5KHz	70Hz
	60KHz	75Hz
	68.7KHz	85Hz
8514/A	35.5KHz	44Hz interlaced
1280x1024 VESA	80KH	75Hz
	91.2KHz	85Hz

An autosynched monitor is ready, if the facility is provided, to auto- size the screen image.

Auto-Sizing

In basic VGA, 480 lines are used to display a graphics screen, while the VGA text mode uses only 400 lines. An SVGA picture might require 600 or more lines. When the program switches mode, the vertical screen size should adjust to ensure that the picture occupies the entire screen area.   Consider a screen that is adjusted so that a text mode output fills the screen.   If the output is switched to graphic mode - without re-sizing - the graphics screen will be slightly squashed.   Conversely, a monitor adjusted to display a graphics will stretch a text output, unless the screen is re-sized.

Aspect Ratio

This is the ratio of the screen's width to the screen's height.   Monitor CRTs, like conventional TV screens, are built with a ratio of 4:3. To maintain a uniform screen display, the screen must be driven at the same rate - i.e. there should be 4 pixels across the screen for each three pixels down the screen. If this is achieved, then all the pixels on the screen will be square and graphics drawing is simplified. Most VGA and higher modes are in the 4:3 ratio, thus avoiding the need to stretch pixels to fit a 4:3 screen.   Stretching would result in non-square pixels; for example drawing a box whose dimensions were 20 pixels by 20 pixels would not produce a box, but a rectangle.   Similarly, a circle would produce an ellipse.   These problems could be overcome - at the expense of further complexity (i.e. more calculations, more time).

Later standards do not suffer from this problem. The SVGA standard, for example, is 800 x 600, which is exactly a 4:3 ratio.

Whilst a few manufacturers currently produce video monitors to native widescreen video standards, such as 16:9 and 2.23:1, these standards are becoming more popular in games and DVD presentations. They are generally accommodated by "*letterboxing*" the displayed image on a standard 4:3 screen. A band above and below the image is unlit.

Colour Monitors

It is commonly held that a colour monitor must always be better than a monochrome model. This is not true. Indeed, in many cases a monochrome monitor will produce sharper results than a colour version. The techniques required to produce colour screens entail a much more accurate alignment than is necessary with monochrome screens. A colour monitor displaying a monochrome screen may not be as clear as the same display on a monochrome monitor. Certainly, a poorly adjusted colour monitor is much more difficult to use than a poorly adjusted monochrome monitor. For this reason, where colour is not an important factor, such as in certain DTP uses, some users prefer to use a monochrome monitor.

There are many good reasons why users wish, or need, to use colour monitors:

- Art and graphic packages really require colour if they are to be used to the maximum effect. Professional packages allow for 'colour separations'. The various coloured components of the picture create their own separate printouts on a printer. The masters are taken to a commercial printer, where a separate print run is made for each colour. Each run overlays on the same sheet, to reproduce the original artwork.
- Multimedia and video almost always require colour for maximum realism and impact.
- Computer Aided Design packages make use of colour to represent different elements of the design. A street plan, for example, might show water routes in a different colour from electricity supply routes. Also, when technologists design a printed circuit board, each layer of connecting tracks is a different colour, with the silk screen layer being a different colour again. These jobs could be accomplished with a monochrome screen, but the viewing would be much more difficult, therefore less productive.
- Some application programs are written to make use of colour to highlight menus, chosen options, etc. A red message on a blue background is perfectly clear on a colour screen. When viewed on a monochrome screen, it is seen as one shade of dark grey on another shade of dark grey. Colour screens make the reading of such menus easier, with less eyestrain.
- Sales and business presentations are greatly enhanced by colour.

Colour Principles

The human eye processes various light sources that are either:

- reflected from the printed page (known as 'subtractive mixing').
- directly targeted at the eye (known as 'additive mixing').

Subtractive Mixing

Natural daylight reflecting off a non light-absorbent paper (i.e. white) allows the full light spectrum to be reflected. These reflected wavelengths are mixed inside the eye and interpreted as white. Adding ink or paint pigment to the paper surface results in the area affected selectively absorbing some of the wavelengths from the white light source. The viewer sees the resultant colour reflection from the mix. Since the introduction of the pigment have taken away some of the wavelengths, the

Primary Colour Mix	Result
Magenta + Yellow	Red
Cyan + Yellow	Green
Cyan + Magenta	Blue
Cyan + Magenta + Yellow	Black

process is termed 'subtractive mixing'. The primary pigments are Cyan, Magenta and Yellow and the result of mixing them in equal quantities is shown in the table. Other colours and hues are obtained by mixing the primary colours with unequal quantities. In practice, it is easier to introduce a black ink (i.e. one that absorbs all light wavelengths) than to achieve the absolutely equal amounts of Cyan, Magenta and Yellow required for the same effect. Subtractive mixing uses the 'CMY colour model' and CMYK printers use this principle and add a black ink for more consistent blacks and to achieve faster print speeds.

Additive Mixing

The colour monitor exploits the fact that the three main colours, as detected by the eye - are red, green and blue. In this case the light is not reflected but is directly transmitted from the CRT screen to the eye. Any other colour of light can be obtained from mixing the three primary colours of light - red, green and blue - in the appropriate ratios. For example, mixing red and green light produces yellow light, while mixing red, green and blue in the same proportions produces white light. Since the monitor CRT uses three different light sources to produce the colours, the process is termed 'additive mixing'. If no light sources are added to the mix, no wavelengths reach the eye and the screen is perceived as being black.

CRT Construction

The monochrome monitor screen was only concerned with *'luminance'* - i.e. how bright a particular pixel on the screen should be. Screen brightness might vary from being off (i.e. black) through to fully on (i.e. white) and shades of grey (i.e. guns partly on). The colour monitor is concerned with luminance - but it is also concerned with the <u>colour</u> of each pixel - known as the *'chrominance'* information. The colour output from the PC is sent out as three separate signals - one each for the red, green and blue components. Other outputs carry the vertical and horizontal synchronisation signals. These video outputs are produced by the graphics card of the computer. A specially constructed monitor is required to produce the colour display.

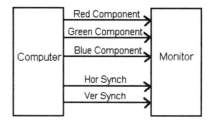

The Shadow Mask Tube

The diagram shows the most commonly used model of colour tube, which is called the *'shadow mask tube'*. The tube was originally invented by the Radio Corporation of America and first demonstrated as early as 1950. Although originally produced for colour TV tubes, the same technology is used in most current computer monitors. More modern, improved, and more expensive alternatives now exist in the *'Trinitron'* tube.

The shadow mask tube is really three tubes in one and has three electron guns, one each for the red, green and blue components of the screen. Each of these guns produces an electron beam that can be either switched off and on (as in the RGB monitors) or have its intensity varied (as in analogue monitors).

The inside of the tube is coated with many thousands of tiny dots of red, green and blue phosphor. These dots are arranged in triangles comprising a dot of each colour. It is this cluster of dots, referred to as *'triads'* or *'dot trios'*, which provides the luminance and chrominance for a single pixel. When a colour phosphor is hit by an electron beam it emits a beam of coloured light and the mixing of the various beams of colour takes place in the viewers' eyes to produce the final perceived colour for each triad.

It is the job of each gun to emit, modulate, focus and accelerate its own electron beam towards its own set of phosphor dots. However, as a single beam scans, it would illuminate dots that were part of another colour set. To prevent this, a metal sheet is placed inside the tube,

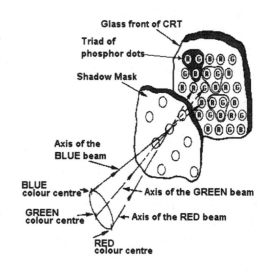

between the guns and the screen, about 1cm from the screen. This screen is perforated with tiny holes and these are aligned so that only the 'red' beam will ever be able to illuminate the red phosphors, the 'green' beam will only ever illuminate the green phosphors and the blue phosphors are only ever illuminated by the electron beam from the 'blue' gun. There is a single hole in the mask for each triangle of dots. The rest of the screen is *'shadowed'* off from the beam by the mask - hence the name *'shadow mask tube'*. Since the holes only occupy a minority of the area of the mask, the mask absorbs the vast majority of the emitted electrons. As a result, colour tubes need much greater beam currents and a higher final anode voltage than a monochrome tube.

SIGNAL			COLOUR
R	G	B	
0	0	0	Black
0	0	1	Blue
0	1	0	Green
0	1	1	Cyan
1	0	0	Red
1	0	1	Magenta
1	1	0	Yellow
1	1	1	White

COLOURS AVAILABLE WITH RGB

To obtain a pure white screen, all the guns are driven at the same amplitude. If any of the guns suffers partial or total failure, the picture will have a *'colour cast'*. A total failure of the red gun, for example, would result in a cyan cast (the complementary colour of green and blue). A partial failure of the blue gun produces a yellowish tinge to the display. Changing characteristics of components might lead to colour casts and these are usually eliminated by altering variable controls on the printed circuit board. Some monitors may provide external controls, to allow the drive of each gun to be altered.

Colour Purity

Colour purity confirms that a pure red (or green or blue) video drive produces a screen that is uniformly red (or green or blue) all over the screen area. Achieving and maintaining the alignment of each beam with its corresponding set of mask holes and phosphor dots is a tricky business. This work is carried out by trained staff, who have to open up the monitor case to carry out the adjustments.

The first adjustment is CENTRE PURITY, which ensures that the beams pass through the colour centres. If centre purity is incorrectly adjusted, then a pure red picture would begin by producing red at the left side of the screen. It would then drift away to other colours. Another adjustment is EDGE PURITY, which tackles the more common problem of obtaining purity in the corners of the monitor screen. Here a red picture would produce pure red at the screen centre, with loss of purity at the extremities. These tests are carried out by using a test screen of solid red, followed by the same tests for the other guns. In practice, loss of colour purity is not normally sufficiently severe to produce other than 'hot spots' - area where the solid colour suffers a change in tone.

NOTE: This effect can also be caused by shadow mask magnetisation (see next section). The purity should only be adjusted if de-gaussing proves ineffective.

Convergence

Any picture on a colour monitor is a mixture of three separate pictures. Even a monochrome display on a colour monitor is only a mixture of the red, green and blue pictures, in equal quantities. It is essential that the three pictures be correctly aligned with each other. This involves ensuring that any one graphics pixel is achieved by illuminating the phosphors in the same triad. Failures to align are normally at their worst away from the screen centre. For example a screen filled with a white grid might display properly

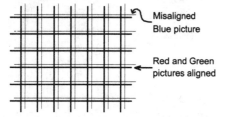

Misaligned
Blue picture

Red and Green
pictures aligned

at the centre while the vertical lines at the edges may be yellow (red + green) with a blue edge (known as 'colour fringing'). Such misconvergence can vary by 0.5mm to 1.5mm across the screen and is a major cause of eyestrain. Static Convergence is concerned with aligning the undeflected beams (i.e. converging the triad in the centre of the screen). Dynamic Convergence is concerned with the total area covered by the beam travel. Note that a tube may have perfect colour purity and still be badly misconverged. Convergence tends to alter with age. At least one model has external controls for convergence - all the others have internal variables for use by trained technicians. Misconvergence is not a problem with Trinitron tubes or monochrome tubes, which only have a single gun.

It is not generally the job of the support technician to fix these problems; the technician only has to detect them and report them for repair.

Degaussing

The electron beams are easily deflected by magnetic fields. The shadow mask is metal and therefore able to be magnetised. If this happens, the unwanted magnetic fields will distort the beam - causing problems with purity. Likely sources of unwanted magnetic fields are loudspeakers and power supplies. In monitors, as in TV sets, a coil surrounds the tube. When the monitor is first switched on, the coil is automatically energised. A high alternating field is produced by the coil, which is gradually reduced over a period of seconds. This removes any residual magnetic field that may have been present on the shadow mask.

In adverse conditions, such as using computers on production lines, near heavy machinery, etc., the excessive local magnetic fields may render the automatic degaussing apparatus only partially effective. In these circumstances, the technician can manually degauss the screen using a degaussing coil or wand. These are plugged in to the mains supply and gradually moved in a circular motion over the face of the shadow mask tube for about a minute. Still maintaining this movement, the coil or wand should be slowly moved away from the face of the screen. At about 6 - 10 feet distance, the degaussing device can be switched off. Do not switch off the device close to the screen; otherwise the device acts as a gaussing device, instead of a degaussing device! All new monitors provide degaussing at switch-on as standard. An extra refinement is to have a degaussing button that will carry out the function at any time during the running of the system.

Trinitron Construction

The Sony Corporation of Japan developed the Trinitron CRT in 1968. Although the tube's construction

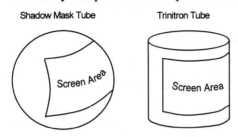

Shadow Mask Tube   Trinitron Tube

follows similar principles to the shadow mask tube, its approach produces a significantly different performance. The screen area (the part seen by the user) of a shadow mask tube resembles part of the surface of a sphere. The screen is curved in both the vertical and horizontal directions. This system provides for easy focusing of the electron beams on to the phosphor inner coating. The screen area of a Trinitron tube looks like part of the rounded surface of a cylinder.

The vertical direction is flat although the horizontal direction remains curved in most models. A few monitors, such as the Sony Multiscan F500, are flat in both planes.

The Trinitron tube has the following advantages over the shadow mask variety:

- Distortion of displayed lines is minimised.
- The screen corners are sharper.
- It suffers less glare from lighting.

Another major departure is in the distribution of the tube's phosphor coating. The Trinitron tube moves away from the triad cluster of coloured phosphors. Instead, the phosphors are arranged in vertical strips in alternating colours. These strips stretch continuously from the top to the bottom of the screen. A set of three colours is called a *'triplet'* instead of a triad. Their construction sometimes covers a greater width than a triad, resulting in a poorer horizontal resolution than a

shadow mask tube. To overcome this, Hitachi introduced an *'Enhanced Dot Pitch'* tube that is more densely coated in the horizontal direction, resulting in more horizontal triplets.

Because the screen is composed of stripes of colour, instead of independent clusters, the quality of the final picture is regarded as being superior - although some have not found it to their tastes. The shadow mask is replaced with an aperture grille that has a vertical slot for each vertical phosphor triad. The aperture grille contains less metal than a shadow mask. However, because the Trinitron tube has larger areas of phosphor to excite, it has to pass more current. This causes the grille to heat up, and distort in extreme cases. For this reason, Trinitron tubes that are run at high brightness levels sometimes exhibit convergence errors due to heat distortion in the aperture grille. This disappears when the tube is run at a lower brightness.

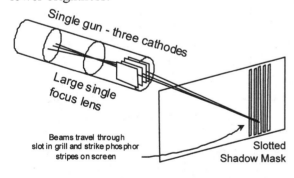

Single gun - three cathodes

Large single focus lens

Beams travel through
slot in grill and strike phosphor
stripes on screen

Slotted
Shadow Mask

The third important difference is in the construction of the guns. Instead of having three separate colour guns, as in the shadow mask, the Trinitron employs a single gun with three cathodes - it produces three beams. The three beams have a common focus plane, which results in a sharper image and better focusing over the entire screen area. The use of a single focusing lens allows a larger gun dimension than the individual guns of the shadow mask tube. This results in higher beam density. This, together with fewer losses in the mask, results in a much brighter picture. Trinitron quality is measured in *'slot pitch'* or *'grill pitch'* instead of dot pitch. A 0.26mm slot pitch is about 0.28mm or 0.29mm dot pitch. The aperture grille is held in place by two fine supporting wires that run across the screen. This results in two fine horizontal lines appearing on the screen when a plain light pattern is displayed, but this generally does not present problems to users.

The Trinitron tube is used in a range of Sony, Taxan, Philips and Eizo monitors.

Energy Saving

The *'green'* machines currently being marketed are ones where positive steps have been taken to protect the environment by reducing the power consumption of the computer, the monitor, or both, during periods of inactivity. A typical 14" monitor consumes between 65 Watts and 100 Watts of power, while a 17" monitor consumes around 150 Watts.

Power-saving efforts centre round:

The Energy Star Programme - this is the voluntary code of practice agreed between the American Environmental Protection Agency and manufacturers. The code stipulates that units should be capable of entering a *'low power'* state of 30W maximum.

The DPMS System - this is the power-saving method recommended by VESA and can be used to meet the Energy Star standard. It is known as the *'Display Power Management Signalling'* system and depends upon the monitor and the graphics card both being DPMS compatible. Spare lines on the monitor connecting lead are used to carry the control signals from the PC to the monitor. The graphics card signals to the monitor how to control its energy-consuming components - i.e. the HOR and VER drive circuitry, the very high CRT voltages and the current to the tube's cathode. Differing power savings can be made, dependent upon the time required to bring the monitor back to full operation. The *'Suspend'* operation lowers power consumption to about 10-20% of its normal level and allows for a fairly fast recovery time. The *'Active Off'* operation lowers power consumption to about 5% but has a slower recovery time.

TCO-92 - this is a more stringent standard from Sweden that requires a 30W maximum on standby and 8W maximum on power down.

Meanwhile, Hitachi has produced its own power saving system that is not VESA compatible. It uses a serial port connection between the monitor and the computer. The provided software allows the serial connection to power down the monitor when it is not in use and controls the normal monitor settings.

Note

Although the main unit consumes less power than the monitor, steps can be taken to save energy by closing down the disk drive power or reducing the disk speed and by running the CPU at a reduced speed. Most computers are now available with the energy-saving techniques implemented either in software or in the BIOS. The facilities range from a single power-down facility to independent power-down times for CPU slow-down, hard disk power-down, monitor power-down and system power-down; intervals can be from one or two minutes up to one or two hours. Major manufacturers such as AMI and Phoenix incorporate these features in their new BIOS chips. In 1994, VESA introduced a standard for implementing power management via the BIOS (known as VBE/PM, the VESA BIOS Extension for Power Management). EIZO monitors already switch themselves off if no incoming signal is detected.

Resolution

The quality of a screen picture, in terms of its detail, can be defined by its *'resolution'*. The screen resolution is measured by the number of pixels across the screen, by the number of pixels that can be displayed in the vertical direction. The number of colours for each resolution in the table shows the most common figures. The colours available for higher resolutions are really limited by production costs, rather than technical considerations.

Mode	Resolution	Colours
Base VGA	640 x 480	16
SVGA	800 x 600	256
8514/A	1024 x 768	256
XGA	1024 x 768	256
EVGA/SVGA	1024 x 768	256
Unnamed	640 x 480	256 – 16M
Unnamed	800 x 600	256 – 16M
Unnamed	1024 x 768	256 – 16M
Unnamed	1280 x 1024	256 – 16M
Unnamed	1600 x 1200	256 – 16M

Even these high resolutions are unable to fully meet modern needs. Advertisers used to talk a lot about WYSIWYG (What You See Is What You Get). This means that the screen displays the image in the exact size and detail as would be expected in the final printed output. The higher resolutions of modern printers place an increasing demand on WYSIWYG DTP and graphics systems.

Consider that an A4 sheet is approximately 97 square inches - say 80 square inches printable area after taking borders into consideration. A typical laser printer or inkjet printer has an output at 600 dpi (dots per inch), or 360,000 dots per square inch. So, to display a full A4 sheet on screen - at printer resolution - would require 80 x 360,000, or a full 28,800,000 dots. Clearly, even the highest screen resolution is incapable of fully displaying detailed DTP and CAD work. With current printers having 1200dpi or higher capability, the problem is greatly worsened.

These limitations are minimised by the *'zoom'* facility offered by many packages; this allows a close up view of a small area of the printed output. While zooming allows the fine detail to be inspected, it is no longer at the correct physical size. Many would argue that this is not a problem since users could not visually resolve 360,000 individual dots on a one inch square in any case.

Dot Pitch

In a shadow mask tube, the holes in the mask are set at pre-defined intervals across its surface.   The triads of colour phosphors are laid on the inner screen at a matching pitch.   The distance between the centre of one triad to the centre of the next nearest triad is known as the *'dot pitch'*.   The dot pitch, therefore, is a measure of the finest quality possible in the picture from that particular monitor.   The dot pitch is measured in fractions of a millimetre.   The lower the dot pitch value, the more closely spaced are the individual illuminated spots - hence the better picture detail.   Since adjacent triangles are offset, the dot pitch value is usually a diagonal measurement.

Users, however, view their monitors in terms of the screen resolution mentioned earlier.   The dot pitch requires to be converted into the maximum horizontal resolution that the particular monitor can support.

The value of the horizontal *'dots per inch'* is a more useful measure when deciding the quality of a monitor.

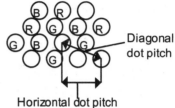

The horizontal dot pitch normally works out at a factor of around .866 times the manufacturers quoted diagonal dot pitch.

The table shows the <u>maximum</u> number of dots that can appear across different screen sizes.

Advertised screen size			14"	15"	17"	19"	21"
Theoretical width of screen			11.2"	12"	13.6"	15.2"	16.8"
Diagonal dot pitch	Horizontal pitch	Dots per inch	Maximum theoretical number of horizontal dots				
0.22mm	0.19mm	133	1492	1599	1812	2025	2238
0.25mm	0.22mm	117	1313	1407	1595	1782	1970
0.26mm	0.23mm	112	1263	1353	1533	1714	1894
0.28mm	0.24mm	104	1172	1256	1424	1591	1759
0.31mm	0.26mm	97	1094	1172	1329	1485	1641

The exact figures will vary by manufacturer and those in the table are working approximations.

Manufacturers tend to err on the side of over-estimating the active image area of their screens.   An inspection of a range of 17" monitors reveals that the actual screen diagonal size varies from 16.34" down to as little as 15.25".   If the actual viewable area is less than the calculated area, then it follows that the actual number of viewable pixels is also likewise reduced.   This means that the above table significantly overestimates the specification of the monitors. The real world performance is less than that shown.   In the case of the 15.25" view from a 17" monitor, it means that the number of viewable pixels is less than 90% of the figure shown in the table.

As can be seen, there is a direct relationship between dot pitch, screen size and the maximum screen resolution.   A .28mm dot pitch monitor has around 1424 dots per line on a 17" screen but has only around 1172 dots per line on a 14" screen.   The 17" monitor in this case is capable of handling 1280 x 1024 mode with ease.   The 14", on the other hand, has fewer dots on the screen than the number of individual pixels required by the 1280 x 1024 picture.   The result is a marked loss of detail and the blurring of small characters.   Since even the table shows idealised figures, the 14" monitor is best run at no more than 800 x 600.

Although the smallest dot pitch is more desirable, they are more costly to manufacture. .21mm and even .2mm dot pitch monitors are available but are expensive.   Typical dot pitch sizes for colour SVGA monitors are 0.25m and 0.27mm. Some manufacturers claim that a .28mm 14" monitor is a 1024 x 768 model and this is only true if an inferior picture is acceptable, since each individual pixel cannot possibly be separately displayed.   For large-screen monitors, the dot pitch can be greater without any loss of detail.   Alternatively, the dot pitch can be reduced; in this case, more detail can be crammed on the screen (e.g. more columns of a worksheet).

Even where a screen's construction quality allows for the reproduction of high resolution, the higher resolution modes may not be able to be used.   A 14" monitor, for example, would display tiny icons and extra small text if it were driven at high resolutions.   The table shows the most likely resolutions to be used with a particular screen size.

Resolution	Best Monitor Size
640 x 480	14"
800 x 600	15"
1024 x 768	17"
1280 x 1024	19"
1600 x1200	21"

Video Standards

VESA

The Video Electronics Standards Association was formed out of a group of independent vendors of graphics controllers, who were unprepared to allow IBM to continue to set the standards.   Members include Intel, Orchid, Taxan, Tseng Labs and Video 7. The slowness of IBM in developing beyond VGA and its eventual production of an IBM-bound product in XGA, led VESA to produce their own advanced 800 x 600 standard in 1989; this became known as the Super VGA Standard (see below).   IBM is now a member of VESA, as are over 200 companies internationally.   VESA has gone on to tackle the problems caused by different manufacturers having different standards, by establishing a set of mode numbers that provide a common reference point for all graphics adapters. (See full VESA table later)

Common Graphics Modes

Below is a brief description of the most popular graphics modes currently to be found in use.   The earlier ranges, such as MDA, Hercules, CGA and EGA, are no longer manufactured but these graphics mode are still supported even in the most modern video card.

MDA

Mono Display Adapter. This was the original screen for the earliest personal computers, as defined by IBM in 1981. It only supported a monochrome text mode of 80 x 25 characters.

HERCULES

This is the earliest high resolution graphics standard. It introduced a graphics mode and could display 720 x 350 pixels, in monochrome only. Support for this mode was always limited.

CGA

Colour Graphics Adapter. This is the original IBM standard for colour monitors.   Although introducing colour, the CGA standard had a poorer resolution than the Hercules model. Its maximum resolution was 640 x 200 pixels in 2-colour mode and 320 x 200 in 4-colour.

EGA

Enhanced Graphics Adapter. Introduced by IBM in 1984 and was a great improvement on the CGA standard.   It was able to display 16 colours from a palette of 64, at the much improved resolution of 640 x 350. Like the MDA, Hercules and CGA systems, the EGA is no longer available.

VGA

Video Graphics Array.   Introduced by IBM in 1987 and remains a popular mode.   It introduced the first screen with square pixels, i.e. a 4:3 aspect ratio. It was also the first standard to dispense with TTL levels of screen drive and introduce varying levels of colour intensity. It handles a palette of 256 colours at 320 x 200, and 16 colours with a resolution up to 640 x 480.   It also supported refresh rates of 60Hz or 70 Hz. The 16-colour version quickly became the industry standard.   Although now overtaken by superior resolutions, it is still useful for troubleshooting, as it is the basic Windows resolution in Safe Mode.

MCGA

Multicolour Graphics Adapter.   This is basically a cut-down version of the VGA system.   To save memory on the video card, it had no 640 x 480 16-colour mode.   Since memory is now relatively cheap, MCGA is ignored in favour of VGA. The 256 colour low-res mode of many VGA cards was often referred to as MCGA mode.

SVGA

Super VGA. The original VESA specification was for a 16-colour 800x600 screen. This produced over 50% more dots than VGA, for the same screen area.   This allowed for example, spreadsheets to display more worksheets columns on the screen, by displaying 132 characters instead of the usual 80 characters. It was also very useful for Windows and its applications, since the user could see more icons on the screen at any one time as well as having improved resolution. This was the most common standard supplied with new models.   Later VESA standards allowed for greater resolutions and colour depth. It covers refresh rates of 56Hz, 60Hz or 72 Hz. Some high-res modes that are not true VESA modes are still referred to as SVGA – see below.

8514/A

An IBM top-end product aimed at the CAD market, which has its own separate processor for graphics activities. Like other graphics cards, the 8514/A had its own onboard screen memory but this screen memory was not organised by the computer's CPU. The 8514/A adapter board contained its own graphics chip - a graphics co-processor - which relieved the main CPU of this task. Because the chips are processing in parallel, the system speed is significantly improved. The inability of the 8514/A card to handle CGA, EGA and VGA software severely limited IBM's flagship product and all manufacturers (including IBM) have moved on to better things. Ultimately, the 8514/A standard proved to be merely the jumping-off point for other improved standards. An example of this card was the Paradise 8514/A.

EVGA

Enhanced VGA. Introduced by VESA in 1991. A non-interlaced, 70 Hz refresh rate 8514/A standard that is only common in large-size screens.

XGA

Extended Graphics Array. Originally an interlaced standard from IBM that is more versatile than the 8514/A. The 8514/A and the XGA systems failed to replace VGA as IBM hoped. Originally, XGA was only compatible with the IBM MCA bus. The 1024 x 768 mode is interlaced but the VESA standard is non-interlaced. XGA cards have three modes:
- a normal, memory-mapped VGA mode
- a 132-column text mode
- a mode where the card's graphics co-processor is used.

The card supports 256 colours at SVGA and 1024 x 768 - and 65,536 colours at VGA.

Notes
- There is a certain amount of uncertainty in dealers' specifications. Not all suppliers subscribe to the VESA coding. Often, the term SVGA simply means *'better than VGA'*. A 1024 x 768 card is sometimes called Ultra VGA. Often, the higher resolution (1280 x 1024 and upwards) models are referred to as *'Workstation'* monitors.
- This confusion also involved VESA members, since they were producing graphics products before they came together to create common standards. As a result, a large range of goods produced by VESA members was outwith their own standards. These lower specification products are 'unofficial' VESA standards and products.
- Some monitors are incapable of working down to 800x600 but are still marketed as *'SVGA'*.
- A display adapter advert that states *'up to 32,767 colours'* or *'16 million colours'* may only apply to a low resolution with higher resolutions only supporting 256 colours. VGA and SVGA monitors, being analogue, are able to support any range of colours, and are limited only by resolution and refresh rate.
- The specification of a monitor should be checked, rather than relying on its title in an advertisement.

Screen Sizes

Higher resolution monitors allow more information to be simultaneously displayed on the screen - more of a worksheet, more of a database record, an entire A4 page of DTP.

Advantages
- Less time is spent on scrolling a window on the output.
- More data visible on screen at the same time means fewer errors.

Disadvantages
- Putting more information on the same size of screen means that text, icons and graphics are all smaller than before - and therefore more difficult to read. A 14" model of SVGA monitor, for example, is only useful to those with gifted eyesight.
- To maintain the required readability requires a bigger, and therefore more expensive, monitor. The user is forced to move from a 15" model to a 19" or even 21" model. Unfortunately, there appears to be a geometric ratio between screen size and cost.
- Bigger screens have problems maintaining an even resolution over the entire screen area. Some extreme areas become slightly fuzzy, due to convergence problems. An even quality can be maintained using *'dynamic beam focusing'*, but this involves extra, costly, construction complexities.

The average monitor is a 15" or 17" model with 19" becoming popular. 20" to 22" models are becoming widespread for DTP and CAD use. For specialist work, multimedia and other presentations, monitors are available up to 50", at staggering prices.

Notes

- When a manufacturer's specification refers to the screen size, it is describing the measurement between any two diagonal corners.
- This measurement usually does not describe the <u>actual</u> screen area. It is common for the phosphor coating to only extend over a proportion of the front screen, resulting in a permanent, unlit border round the screen.

- The unused area of the screen does not result in any loss of resolution; it just means that the graphics detail is compressed into a smaller area than the screen dimension suggests.
- Although a small size monitor is capable of displaying a high-resolution screen, it is often not a practical situation, since the size of the text can be too small to be readable. This is being countered by the introduction of *'anti-aliasing',* a technique in the video card that adds artificial shading to lines and letters, to give an appearance of added sharpness.

Screen Drives

RGB

This is the most straight forward of the colour drive methods and is the method used for the now obsolete CGA and EGA standards. For CGA, four connections are used to convey the picture information from the computer to the monitor (other connections are used for the signal ground and the horizontal and vertical synchronisation signals). The RGB system operated by switching the red, green and blue guns off and on from zero volts to around one volt. Any gun, at any time, is either fully switched on or fully switched off. The fourth connection allows any of the eight colours to be displayed in one of two intensities (i.e. - red appears pinkish, etc.). EGA systems provided two wires for each gun - one for on/off and one for intensity. This resulted in 64 possible colours. These drives were described as '*TTL*' types (<u>T</u>ransistor to <u>T</u>ransistor <u>L</u>ogic).

Analogue

For accurate design work, a monitor with sharp images in a range of colours is perfectly adequate. However, for artwork, a greater degree of diversity of colours is required. After all, a 'real' picture has many shades and hues. With RGB drive, any gun, at any time, was either fully on or fully off. This is unable to meet more sophisticated needs. Ideally, each of the guns should be able to have its intensity varied from fully off to fully on - and <u>every</u> intensity in between. The permutations provided would provide the rich variety encountered in normal life. It is argued that, for art and graphic work, a greater <u>variety</u> of colours on screen has a greater impact on the viewer than increased screen <u>resolution</u>.

If a video card runs the three colour drives at 64 different intensity levels, the possible colours produced are 64 to the power 3, which is 64x64x64 = 262,144 colours. When the drives are 256 different levels, the result is 256x256x256= 16,777,216 different colours.

NOTE The construction of some monitors may not allow the display of much more than about 256,000 different colours. The computer system - its memory, its graphics hardware and its software drivers - can now handle over 16 million colours. The drive variations to provide the 16 million colours will still be sent to the monitor but, mainly due to the characteristics of the phosphors, the full range of colours may not be reproduced.

Composite Video

In this method, the output from the PC is a single signal that combines the three colour components and the synchronisation signals. The monitor has to separate these signals, before applying them to the monitor circuitry. Some PCs have a composite output as well as a RGB output. This allows these models to use some TVs as monitors, which can be useful. However, they suffer from poorer quality, as the extra signal processing circuitry introduces more noise and more signal distortion. For these reasons, this method is common on home games computers and is still relatively unusual for PC video cards.

Display Data Channel

VESA has developed a system, known as DDC, whereby the graphics card and monitor can communicate with each other using one of the unused pins on the video connector cable. This is of special significance when used with the Plug and Play facilities of Windows 95 and later. The monitor holds information on its specification and this 128-bit information block is continually transmitted to the graphics card. The data block is called the *'Extended Display Identification'* - EDID. The graphics card can then adjust to the best drive for that monitor. For example, graphics cards will always automatically use the maximum refresh rates supported by the monitor for a particular resolution. It will also automatically use the best screen mode available. These changes take place without any activity on the part of the user although the user is still free to choose the setup if desired.

The current standard has two levels - DDC1 and DDC2. DDC1 describes the basic operation and DDC2 is further split into B and AB categories. The B specification supports a larger range of video modes DDC1 while the AB specification supports a new bus, termed the ACCESS.BUS to control the monitor/graphic card communication. The ACCESS.BUS is a serial system that hopes to rival USB. Almost all new monitors are both DDC1 and DDC2 compliant.

Health & Safety

EC directive 90/270/EEC was passed in May 1990. It took effect from 1st January 1993, with all new and modified workstations coming under its terms. All workstations, both existing stations and new sales, were covered by 1st January 1996. The directive ensures that workers using VDUs are:

- given full information on the use of office equipment
- provided with monitors to required standards on ergonomics and emissions.

In the UK, the Health and Safety at Work Act, through the Health and Safety (Display Screen Equipment) Regulations, embodies the EC directive and the British Health and Safety Executive will provide guidelines on the directive. The directive sets out minimum requirements in a range of areas such as VDU, keyboard, desk, chair, lighting, noise, heat and humidity, along with employer obligations to train employees, reduce employee VDU time, protect employees' eyesight and enact worker consultation and participation. The standards of the directive are contained in its annexe and this is largely based on the ISO standard 9241 *"Ergonomic requirements for office work with visual display terminals"*. Of course, the HSE and employers' organisations such as the CBI have differences with the trade unions on the interpretation of individual items of the directive. The aim should be the creation of a safe, functional and productive working environment for the benefit of all.

The legislation ensures that employers will provide VDU operators with a free eyesight test when requested by an operator. If necessary, the employer will also provide *"corrective appliances"* (spectacles). The definition of a VDU operator is one who uses a VDU for between 3 and 5 hours per day. The HSE provide a pamphlet entitled *"Display Screen Equipment Work"* that explains definitions for different types of VDU user. Legislation also covers the hardware design. As a result of EC action, from 1st Jan 1997, monitors, like other goods, will carry the *'CE'* mark - an EC safety mark. This covers limits of EMI (electromagnetic interference) and EMS (electromagnetic susceptibility).

Radiation

The harmful effect of electromagnetic radiation from monitors has been an issue that is controversial and still not satisfactorily resolved. Some reports, mainly from Sweden, Finland and Denmark, suggest that monitor radiation can induce leukaemia and brain cancer. Others, including the UK Health and Safety Executive, dispute the reports and there are claims that the reports are under-researched and discredited. Still others accept that there is a cancer danger from monitor radiation - but small in comparison to cancer dangers from smoking and diet. Computer monitors produce high magnetic fields. These are essential to the running of the monitor, as high currents are required for the beam deflection circuitry. They are no different from the magnetic fields that are emanated from all 50Hz mains electrical equipment and wiring. It is the effects of sustained exposure that causes concern. After all, a user would not normally sit in front of an electric kettle for 8 hours a day but a computer user could easily spend 8 hours a day less than two feet from a monitor. In this respect, it is similar to the claims of harmful effects of living under high-voltage power lines.

Radiation from monitors occurs mostly from the rear, although an appreciable amount also occurs from the front. The fields diminish sharply with distance.

For increased safety, the following steps can be taken:

- Use an LCD screen, or other non-CRT display, if this is acceptable.
- Use a monochrome monitor, if possible. These have lower radiation levels.
- Purchase a low radiation monitor (usually tagged as 'LR'). Note that if a monitor has a special screen coating to reduce radiation, this coating also reduces the screen brightness.
- Position the monitor about 30" from the user.
- Ensure that no other workers are seated less than 4' from the rear of the monitor.

The EC Directive 90/270 talks of radiation levels being reduced to *'negligible levels'*. Radiation is categorised as both ELF (Extremely Low Frequency - i.e. 5Hz to 2KHz) and VLF (Very Low Frequency

- i.e. 2KHz to 400KHz).   The Swedish MPR-II standard (also called MPR 1990) has become an international standard, because it specifies actual radiation levels.

However, the Health and Safety (Display Screen Equipment) Regulations exempt the UK from the requirements of MPR-II.   Nevertheless, almost all monitors on the market are at least MPR-II standard. The Swedish regulatory body NTUEK, in contrast to the UK, works on the assumption of a link between radiation and cancer and has mandatory minimum radiation levels.

Another standard that is sometimes quoted (e.g. from Hitachi) is the TUV standard from Germany.   This standard covers both radiation levels and refresh rates.   It is a combination of the MPR standard and ISO 9241, which covers image quality.

The Swedish TCO 1992 standard lays down rules on electromagnetic radiation levels, heat emission, automatic low power switching and electrical safety.   To carry a TCO '92 label, the monitor must have a more stringent set of radiation levels than MPR-II as shown in the table. It must also meet other conditions such as having an automatic power-down function, a declaration of its energy overhead, and compliance with European fire and electrical safety requirements

Frequency Band	Electric Field (in volts per metre)		Magnetic Field (in nano Teslas)	
	MPR-II	TCO	MPR-II	TCO
ELF	25	10	250	200
VLF	2.5	1	25	25

(EN 60950).   The manufacturer must also have concluded a certification agreement with TCO.   TCO '95 has the same radiation and power saving requirements as TCO '92 but includes extra issues such as improved screen ergonomics (e.g. screen linearity, luminance uniformity) and banning the use of CFCs and heavy metals in the monitor manufacturing process. TCO '99 outlines even stricter screen ergonomics (even luminance, contrast levels, flicker), halving the standby power consumption of all devices except the base unit, and restrictions on painting and metallicising plastic components.

Physical Layout

The layout of keyboard, monitor and documents in relation to the user's vision and easy physical reach is of great importance.   Prolonged periods of body inactivity, particularly in bad seating, can itself result in backache and neckache. Add uncomfortable seats and badly laid out desks and the situation is worsened. Bad desk layouts not only contribute to back problems - they are also a source of eye problems, as users strain to read monitors and documents in adverse conditions.   In a normal day, the human eye experiences a variety of muscle movements. The eye normally moves rapidly from one object to another, with the vertical, horizontal and focusing changes that are entailed.   In contrast, prolonged viewing of a VDU involves prolonged muscle tension, to maintain concentration on a relatively small flickering viewing area.   VDU users complain of a range of symptoms from redness, watering and ache through to focusing difficulties, loss of clarity and double vision.

A range of measures to improve user conditions includes:

- Size of desk.   An inadequate desk surface usually results in an unmanageable clutter, loss of productivity and user stress.   Consider placing the CPU unit under the desk, or using mini-tower CPU units. Most desks are about 70cm high, which satisfies the average user.
- Seating position. The seat should be comfortable and be of the swivel type, preferably on castors. The seat height and backrest should be adjustable.   Certain users may require footrests to maintain adequate posture.
- Size and type of monitor screen.   The screen size should be adequate for the job being carried out. Detailed CAD or DTP work on a small screen is a sure way to cause eyestrain and lost working days.
- Position of monitor.   The monitor should be moved to suit the user and not the other way round.   EU regulations require that monitors have positional adjustment (e.g. a tilt and swivel base or adjustable monitor arm).   The VDU user should be able to rotate the display from side to side as well as tilt the screen up and down. Many users prefer to stand the monitor directly on the desk surface, rather than on top of the computer case.   Some desks have glass top so that the VDU can be situated under the glass.   This frees the desk space but may introduce extra reflections from office lighting.   A preferred position would involve the user being stationed about 30" from the monitor and looking down on it from a small angle.   Flickering first affects the edges of a user's vision. If a user sits close to a monitor, the effects of flicker are more pronounced.
- Position of monitor controls.   These should be front-mounted for ease of access. Thumbwheel controls provide greater precision setting than tiny knobs.
- Protection of monitor controls. Ideally, the controls should be covered by a flap, to prevent accidental changes to settings.

- Regular breaks - necks suffer most when forced to maintain a fixed position for long periods; eyes suffer from maintaining a fixed focal distance.   Those employees on permanent screen operations - data entry workers, database operators, program coders, etc. - should have scheduled breaks in their working day.
- Use of document holders - these can be adjusted for the most comfortable reading position. This avoids the continual refocusing involved when reading documents that are left on the desk.

Screen Glare

The aim is to minimise the amount of office light that reflects from the screen surface of the monitor. Screen glare makes reading the screen data extremely difficult and is very tiring to user eyes.   The aim is to have as little contrast as possible between the screen and its surroundings.   Preventative measures include both lighting and environment changes and choice of monitors.

- Avoid fluorescent lighting completely.   The room lighting should be diffused.   Both the Lighting Industry Federation and the Chartered Institute of Building Service Engineers provide booklets that cover the problems of poor lighting and the lighting required for areas where VDUs are in use.
- Don't place a monitor in front of windows or other bright light sources.   If there is no alternative to having a monitor face a window, use blinds or curtains.
- The room walls and furnishings should have matt surfaces with neutral colouring.
- Use monitors with FST tubes, as they suffer less glare than conventional tubes.
- High quality monochrome VGA grey-scale monitors produce high contrast results and are preferable to a higher resolution colour monitors with fuzzy areas.
- Use monitors whose screens have anti-glare silica coatings.   The screen can also be etched to refract the light. A smooth panel can be bonded to the surface of the screen.   This lets light out, but minimises glare by breaking up light that strikes the screen. By preventing light entering the tube, the picture contrast is improved - as in Trinitron tubes.
- Use monitors with fast refresh rates as this minimises flicker effects.   Some monitor tubes use long-persistence phosphors to minimise flicker, but they also tend to blur movement.
- Fit a non-glare filter in front of the monitor screen.   These are mostly made from glass, although some are plastic.   But beware, the Association of Optometrists believe that filters reduce glare - at the expense of making the screen more difficult to read.   Keep the screen clean, with an anti-static cleaning compound.
- Use VDU spectacles when working at screens; these are specially tinted and can include prescription lenses.
- Where the application allows user-defined screen colours, choose screen colours carefully. There is evidence that dark lettering on a light background aids readability. It is more protective to the eyes when handling text, as there is no need for the user to constantly adapt to differing contrasts.   On the other hand, dark backgrounds suffer less from the effects of flicker.

Stress

Employees who spend long periods on VDU suffer greater levels of stress than other employees.   The source of such stress appears to be the high levels of productivity expected of data-entry workers, poor working environment and the low esteem associated with jobs that have been computerised.   This is covered by the EC directive, which states

> *"the employer must plan work activities in such a way that daily work on a display screen is periodically interrupted by breaks or changes of activity, reducing the workload at the display screen".*

This is based on the old adage that *'a change is as good as a rest'*. A balanced load of VDU work and other work will improve working conditions and will probably lead to more productivity in the long run. The Health and Safety Regulations requires that employers carry out risk assessment.   This involves assessing the risk to their employees' health and safety, employing competent safety officers, devising appropriate safety measures, and training staff in these safety measures.

Adjustments/Controls

Many of the reported monitor problems of users are easy to resolve. Often, a monitor is simply badly adjusted, or has gone out of adjustment over time.   A few simple tweaks may be all that is required to restore normal working.   Most monitors provide the basic control over its operations in the form of an On-Screen Display (OSD), with older monitors using adjustable knobs or thumbwheels; a few controls require a screwdriver adjustment.

Most quality monitors allow a fair degree of additional trimming of monitor performance, as follows:

Brightness

This varies the density of the electron beam(s) and hence the amount of screen illumination.   In monitors with poor power regulation, an increase in brightness might lead to a shrinking of the picture size.   This may appear with manual alterations to the brightness control - or may occur when the screen content switches from a mainly black content to a mainly white content. The monitor power supply cannot cope with the increased current demands and the voltage to the screen scanning circuitry drops. The reduced voltage means that the scan drive is reduced and the picture occupies a smaller proportion of the screen area. At the extremes, this cannot be cured by user adjustment and the monitor has to be sent for repair or be replaced.

Contrast

This control increases the amplitude of the drive to the gun(s) and hence increases the ratio between different levels of screen brightness. Too much contrast drives the light grey details into displaying as white, thereby losing detail. Too little contrast makes all colours tend to grey, producing a wishy-washy screen.

Hor/Ver Position

These controls adjust the starting points, and hence the stopping points of both the horizontal scan and vertical scan. The effect of these adjustments is to move the picture vertically or horizontally along the screen and this is used to centre the picture.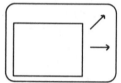

Hor/Ver Size

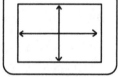 The position controls determine the commencing point of the scans. The size controls vary the <u>amplitude</u> of the beam swing in the horizontal and vertical planes and this determines the actual size of the illuminated portion of the screen. Some monitor models can be adjusted so that the scans fill the entire screen area, eliminating the black border. This increases the effective viewing area and aids readability. However, with shadow mask tubes particularly, this may result in the loss of menu options at the corners (this is particularly a Windows problem, where icons like the minimise/maximise icon sit in the extreme top left-hand corner of the screen).

Pre-Set Controls

Monitors come with the following different approaches to their controls:
- Entirely manual - the user has to make adjustments each time the monitor is used for a different mode. This is thankfully now uncommon.
- Auto-sensing. This works entirely automatically and is the most common approach.
- User choice from either a set of in-built stored settings or from a set of user-entered settings that were digitally set and stored. If none of these options are taken, the system works in auto-sensing mode.

Where digital controls are used, there are usually 8 or 9 settings, although there can be up to 30 predefined modes and user-defined settings. Now, the monitor circuitry automatically sizes and places images as it switches between resolutions. A block of built-in memory is used to store size and positional information for different analogue and digital sources.

Less Common Controls

VER/HOR Convergence Controls

Some monitors, such as the Iiyama Vision Master, allow the user to adjust the convergence of the three colour elements of the picture. In most monitors these are internal controls, as best results are obtained using test equipment. A signal that comprises three colour grids is injected into the monitor, so that the alignment of the colours is achieved more easily. Without a test generator, the adjustment is a more hit-and-miss affair.

Pincushion Control

Like the control above, this control is also concerned about the picture's shape, as opposed to its size or position. It is difficult to maintain linearity at the extremes of the picture area and the result is 'pin*cushion distortion'* as shown in an exaggerated form in the diagram. The Compaq V70 monitor, for example, allows the user some control over the screen's beam linearity.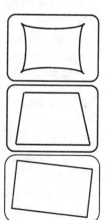

Trapezoidal Distortion

With trapezoidal distortion, the edges of the screen remain straight but the scan length at the top of the screen is progressively lengthened with each successive line scanned. This produces a trapezoidal shape as shown in the diagram. Again, the shape has been exaggerated for clarity.

Available with the Hitachi CM6111ET.

Rotation

This control, if available, is used to rotate the picture. Normally this only ranges a few degrees in either direction, to allow the user to make sure the picture is straight.

Hor/Ver Lock

Also called horizontal and vertical phase. Controls are often marked as HSYNC and VSYNC. These controls vary the locking between the incoming synchronisation signals from the computer video circuits and the monitor's internal oscillators. This adjustment corrects *'roll'* and other problems caused by the two being out of sync.

Other Controls

Many monitors provide additional controls to those listed above. These may include Parallelogram controls (to adjust any vertical 'skew'), moiré controls (to reduce display artefacts), colour purity, and individual RGB controls. The latter controls are used to match on-screen colours to printer colours, and are relatively unusual. They can be found on the Mitsubishi Diamond Pro and Philips Brilliance monitors.

> CAUTION
> Internal pre-sets exist for brightness, convergence, etc. Leave these well alone. These adjustments are intended for trained service staff. And, don't forget that there can be as much as 25Kvolts on the final anode of the cathode ray tube!

Flat Display Panels

In the past couple of years, CRT replacements in the form of flat LCD/TFT panels have started to appear. Other technologies include Gas Plasma displays and IBM's HPA. The technology used in these displays has been perfected in laptop computers over the years and is based on individual pixels being addressed in an array. Such displays may either use a standard video card or may be based on a specialist proprietary digital card (see DVI, below). The differences between flat panel displays and CRTs are:

- As explained earlier, the actual viewing surface of a CRT is less than its quoted screen size. With Flat displays, the entire viewing area is visible and exactly corresponds to the quoted screen size.
- CRT displays have to be constantly refreshed to avoid flicker effects, as explained earlier. Pixels on a flat panel display do not fade between refreshes, such that a frame rate of around 60Hz produces a flicker-free picture. Increasing the frame rate above about 60Hz produces no perceived improvement, while increasing the systems' bandwidth requirements.
- Because flat panels are built from a fixed matrix, they have a native resolution. Driving the display at a different resolution involves scaling (interpolation) of the incoming signal to either shrink it or expand before using it to drive the display. Scaling up may cause pixellation making the image chunky and difficult to read. Alternatively, a signal of smaller resolution can be displayed as a small image in the centre of the screen. Scaling down may result in the loss of some important detail. CRT displays always use the entire screen area for display and cannot scale down.
- Some flat panels need a proprietary adapter card that is not compatible with other displays (CRT or Flat Panel). Some use DVI interfaces, which are expensive and complex. Others are compatible with standard analogue SVGA outputs but require expensive internal electronics to digitise the signal.
- Viewing angles are smaller, and output brightness is usually less than the equivalent CRT display.
- There are only a few manufacturing plants for large LCD "blanks" and the etched glass screens. Because of this, commercially available LCD screens over 19" are extremely expensive.
- Because of the low manufacturing yield and scarcity, flat panels tend to be expensive.

While flat panel displays are a tantalising and interesting technology, they do not currently offer the flexibility of the CRT. However, flat panel technologies are only a few years old, whereas CRT technology is over a century old. There can be little doubt that as flat panel technology matures, they will become cheaper and more common. In the meantime, they are useful in certain areas where space, privacy or subliminal flicker are issues.

DVI Interfaces

Flat panel displays are digital devices, while VGA is an analogue cable. Driving a flat panel display via a VGA cable results in unnecessary loss of detail during the conversion process, and the solution is a new digital cable – DVI. Although DVI interfaces have been around for some time, it is only relatively recently that a standard has been agreed upon. Despite the name, DVI comes in three flavours: DVI-d (digital only), DVI-a (analogue only) and DVI-i (integrated digital and analogue). The connector has three rows of pins for digital only and shared digital/analogue connections, and five pins for analogue only connections. The ATI Radeon cards, for example, provide DVI output connectors.

DVI is also useful with CRT monitors that have DVI inputs, as it means the digital signal can be converted to analogue by the monitor rather than the display card, enabling the monitor to fine-tune the conversion process to suit the characteristics of the particular monitor.

The principle of operation of each of the major types of flat panel displays is explained below:

Liquid Crystal Displays

The Liquid Crystal Display is one of the most popular alternatives to cathode ray tube monitors and is widely used in portable and notebook PCs. It employs the following principles:

Light is only a very high frequency radiated wave. In fact, light is *'unpolarised'* - it is composed of waves in angles of every plane. In an LCD display, the source of this light is usually a fluorescent source behind the screen - such models being described as having a *'backlit'* display. This light is passed through a polarising filter. Only the waves in a single plane will pass through this filter. This single plane is known as the *'plane of polarisation'*. This polarised light is then presented with another polarising filter. If the second filter has the same plane of polarisation as the first filter, then the light is able to pass through and be viewed by the user. If the plane of polarisation is opposed to that of the first filter, then no light wave is able to pass through. It follows, then, that if the second filter can alter its plane of polarisation, it

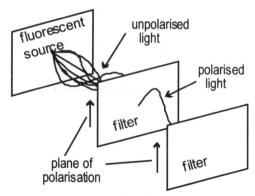

will control the flow of light waves to the user. If the diagram was considered as a single pixel and was repeated thousands of times over, as a matrix, then it would constitute a VDU screen.

In practice, it is not possible to continually alter the plane of polarisation of the second filters. Instead, a cell is composed of a piece of *'nematic'* liquid crystal between the filters. The planes of polarisation of the two filters differ by 90 degrees. Now, the light from the fluorescent source still passes through the first filter in a single plane only. This time, the effect of passing through the liquid crystal is to twist the wave 90 degrees, along the crystal's plane. When the wave reaches the second filter, it is at the correct angle to pass through since they are both aligned. So, the normal state is to pass light. That is why most LCDs have a lit screen as default.

The second diagram shows the effect of applying an electric field to the cell. The molecules of the liquid crystal will line up, its plane will become straight and there is no 90-degree twist to the light wave as it passes through. The light's plane is now different from the second filter and no light will pass through the filter. So, if each pixel area has its electric field switched on or off, pixels are lit or unlit - i.e. a functioning VDU has been created.

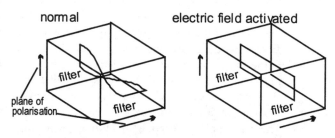

LCD Construction

In practice, the display is not constructed pixel by pixel. Instead, the screen is manufactured as a single entity, with a layer of liquid crystal sandwiched between layers of glass. This, in turn, is sandwiched between polarising sheets. A grid of wires is used to access any particular area of the screen surface. A voltage is applied to the appropriate vertical and horizontal co-ordinates, to activate that particular pixel. This is called *'direct multiplexing'* and although relatively easy to manufacture, it is difficult to control drive to the cells. The main problems are:

- The voltage on the control wires cannot be too high; otherwise there is a likelihood of turning on cells adjacent to the wanted cell.
- The small allowable voltage swings do not provide enough control to achieve satisfactory grey scales and good contrast.
- The scanning arrangements are inadequate. The data on every pixel in a line can be stored and applied to the vertical wires at the same time. However, It is only possible to address a single row at any one time. So, for example, a VGA screen of 480 lines would result in each line only having its pixels set every 1/480th of the time. The greater the vertical resolution the less time is available for holding a particular cell in the 'dark' state. During the rest of the time, the cell is reverting to its 'light' state, with a consequent deterioration of picture contrast.

TFT Displays

To solve these problems, an *'active matrix'* is employed. This uses TFT (thin film transistors) in a matrix, with a single transistor located at the junction of each vertical and horizontal control wire. The voltage at each cell can now be increased, since smaller level signals can be placed on the control wires that are amplified by the transistor. Since this higher voltage now only occurs right at the cell, there is little chance of activating adjacent cells. The result is a sharper picture. Additionally, the higher voltage swings result in faster cell changes and therefore greater contrast. Finally, the higher voltage range available allows much greater control over grey scales. TFT LCDs also improve on scanning difficulties. The short time available for each cell remains unavoidable. However, the construction of the TFT screen results in a capacitance effect on each cell. This maintains the desired charge while the cell is not being addressed and maintains the desired 'dark' state longer, improving screen contrast.

Colour LCDs

LCDs are also available in colour versions. These are expensive, since they have even greater production quality control problems than monochrome versions.

They are available in both passive-matrix and active-matrix versions.

Advantages Of LCDs

- No electron beams, thereby eliminating problems with linearity, misconvergence, pincushion distortion, and sizing/positioning.
- Low power consumption and low voltages.
- Light weight - ideal for portables.
- No radiation or flicker problems, unlike CRTs.
- Flat displays - hang on wall / easy to locate in work area.

Disadvantages

- Restricted viewing angle.
- Poor contrast. Supertwist displays give more contrast but introduce a certain tinge. This is correctable with special film coatings and extra construction complexity. It is called 'triple supertwist'. It is more expensive to manufacture and is used in the best LCD displays.
- Slow speed. When the liquid crystal structure has been pulled into a straight configuration, under the influence of the electric field, it takes a relatively long time to restore to its former state. This explains why LCD screens often 'smear' when scrolling or attempting other fast screen updating.
- Costly to manufacture, due to difficulties of quality control.

Passive Matrix

The cheaper of the versions, this screen is effectively a sandwich of three LCD screens, each screen emitting red, green or blue. All modern systems increase efficiency by using 'dual scan' displays. These split the screen in two vertically and each half is simultaneously scanned and lit. So, a single screen is painted in half the time - i.e. the refresh rate is doubled and flicker is halved.

Active Matrix

Each colour triad comprises the necessary red, green and blue LCD elements and each is activated by its own switching transistor. In this way, the TFT mechanisms described above take place on light waves of pre-determined colour. Since each element is individually switched, the 'ghosting' associated with older screens is eliminated. In addition, TFT elements are less sensitive to heat and brighter backlights can be used. Unfortunately, these screens are expensive to produce, since even a VGA monitor would require almost a million transistors to be assembled on the one screen. A single non-working transistor means that a pixel has lost one of its colour elements. Too many defects mean that the screen has to be scrapped. About a third of all units produced are unable to meet this very demanding quality control.

Plasma Displays

Gas plasma displays are produced by filling the space between two glass plates with neon /xenon gas and then exciting it with a suitable voltage, usually greater than 80V. The exciting electrode is etched onto the glass. The original gas plasma displays were orange and black and had high power consumption. Recently however various companies have resurrected the technology, extended it to full colour and are using it for display panels, High Definition Television (HDTV) displays and desktop monitors. Among the prime movers of this technology in Europe are Philips BV whose FlatTV is plasma based.

Large plasma displays are becoming more common for such locations as airports, hospitals, trains stations, and even domestic television. Many are capable of handling both computer and audio/video input. The NEC 50PD, for example, is a 50" XGA compatible widescreen screen - at the price of a small car!

Developments

A number of alternative technologies have been promised, only to fail to live up to their early promise. Current developments include:

- Improved resolutions from plasma displays.
- Reflective LCDs. There is no backlighting source. Instead, a mirror is placed behind the display and this allows room light to be reflected back or blocked, dependent on the controlling electric field.
- Field Emissive Devices. FEDs promise to be as slim as LCD panels but are cheaper to produce and impose no restrictions in maximum screen size.

Graphics Cards

The rapid development of computer applications such as video, animations, walkthroughs and photorealistic graphics has stretched both the demands on the computer monitor and the video card technology. Graphics cards have undergone significant improvements from the early versions that were designed for text and some crude chunky graphics.

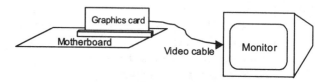

The electronics to drive the monitor is mounted on a separate graphics card that slots into the expansion bus on the computer's motherboard. The monitor cable plugs into a socket on the video card.

Graphic Card Performance

There are a number of factors to be considered when purchasing a graphics card. Such a purchase might be as part of an entire system. It is also possible to buy a matching graphics card and monitor, to upgrade the graphics facilities of an existing system.

The main considerations are:

- RAM size/Resolution/Colour Depth
- RAM type
- Internal bus size
- Chip Set used
- Extra facilities (e.g. video handling, 3D, TV)
- Bandwidth
- External bus type
- Refresh rates
- RAMDAC used

Graphics RAM Size

Screen Memory

The number of colours that a monitor can produce is theoretically endless. Tiny voltage changes to any of the monitor's guns will alter that colour and hence the mix perceived by the viewer. The limitation is in the ability of the computer graphics card to store all the possible colour permutations (in the form of a large range of voltage levels) for each screen pixel. All graphics standards use a 'memory mapped' method of handling screen output. An area of computer memory is reserved for holding the individual pixels that comprise the screen picture. This screen memory is additional to the computer's 640k user area. In all but the lowest resolutions, extra memory for storing the screen's composition is located on the graphics controller card. The data in this memory area is used to regularly update the picture. The computer's CPU (or graphics chipset) has the task of constantly updating the screen memory area. The electronics on the graphics card reads this information and uses it to control the drive to the monitor. For a simple, monochrome system the storage may only require a single bit per pixel. If the bit is 0, the pixel is left unlit; if the bit is 1 then the pixel is illuminated. In colour systems, extra pixels are required, to store the colour and hue of the pixel.

In text modes, the bit pattern for each displayable character (i.e. the alphanumeric set, punctuation and the IBM extended character set) is pre-stored and is copied into the screen memory area. It is a much more complex task in graphics mode. To place a straight line on the screen, the CPU must calculate the position of every pixel in that line and write this information to the appropriate screen memory locations. For an arc, there is the added time required to calculate the curve's co-ordinates. The main memory of the PC was not designed for the current high-resolution screens. The amount of memory put aside to hold the screen information is totally inadequate by today's standards. Out of the 1MB memory area, a maximum of 128KB is laid aside for graphics memory. This would directly address a 640 x 200 screen of 256 colours. To go beyond this specification, the machine has the additional graphics information stored in extra memory with special software routines to access this extra hardware. Consequently, graphics cards have their own memory chips to store graphics information. The RAM size required is determined by the maximum screen resolution and the maximum colour depth (i.e. how many colours to be displayed).

The formula to calculate the amount of memory required for a particular screen standard is:

HORIZONTAL RESOLUTION x VERTICAL RESOLUTION x COLOUR BITS / 8

The number of bits for each pixel depends on the number of colours that the pixel has to display.

For monochrome, only one bit per pixel is required (pixel is either lit or unlit).

For 4 colours, 2 bits per pixel are required, providing 2 to the power of 2 combinations. For 16 colours, 4 bits are required, providing 2 to the power 4 combinations.

For 256 colours, 8 bits are required (i.e. 2 to the power 8 combinations).

A 16-bit system can provide 65,536 different colours for each pixel (called *'high colour'*), while a 24-bit system provides 16.7million colours (often termed *'true colour'*).

Some cards offer 30-bit depth producing 1,073,741,824 colours! Other cards use 32-bits to handle true colour with added effects.

The equation given produces a memory requirement specified in bytes. Dividing the result by 1024 gives a requirement measured in Kilobytes (KB). There are 1024 bytes to a kilobyte. Dividing by a further 1024 produces a measurement in MB (MegaBytes).

EXAMPLES

A 16-colour VGA screen would require

640 x 480 x 4 / 8 = 150 Kbytes

A 16-colour SVGA screen would require

800 x 600 x 4/8 = 234Kbytes (i.e. at least a 256k card)

A 256-colour VGA sized screen would require

640 x 480 x 8 / 8 = 300 Kbytes (i.e. at least a 512k card)

A 256- colour SVGA screen would require

800 x 600 x 8/ 8 = 469 Kbytes (i.e. at least a 512k card)

A 256-colour 1024 x 768 screen would require

1024 x 768 x 8 / 8 = 768 KB (i.e. a full 1MB card)

A 24-bit, true colour 1024 x 768 screen with 16.7 million colours would require

1024 x 768 x 24 / 8 = 2.25MB (i.e. a 4MB card)

Finally, a top of the range system with true colour at 1600 x 1200 would require

1600 x 1200 x 24 / 8 = 5.49MB (i.e. an 8MB card)

SVGA cards used to be supplied in 256KB and 512KB versions; they now come from 8MB to 256MB.

Bits per pixel	Colour Depth
4	16
8	256
16	65,536
24	16.7m

Notes

- If a board's design allows for future expansion, then extra memory can be fitted to the card to allow it to cope with greater resolutions. Many cards allow up to 8MB of memory to be fitted while some cards allow up to 40MB to be fitted.
- Where the fitted RAM size is vastly greater than is currently required for a particular mode, the memory can be divided into *'pages'* - each page containing the data for a full graphics screen. This allows rapid switching between screens, since the second screen can have its pixel pattern built up in memory, while the first screen is being displayed. This is the basis of on-screen animation. An additional use for extra memory is for storing 3D texture maps and other special effects data.
- Most cards can display a number of colours from a larger possible palette (e.g. 16 colours from 64 or 256 from 32,767). A piece of software may wish to use more colours than the card is capable of displaying at any one time. The 'extra' colours are displayed by *'dithering'* using the existing colours, producing a rather coarse hatching effect. This allows cards with poorer specifications to still run the application. This may be acceptable in some applications but photo-realistic graphics, video clips and multimedia applications would demand a wider displayable colour range.

Bandwidth

The term *'bandwidth'* describes both memory and graphics needs and there are important differences. The general description of monitor bandwidth was given earlier. With colour monitors, the graphics data is sent in parallel to three separate guns and the amount of colours being used is not relevant to the bandwidth calculation. The restriction on any one channel's capabilities is measured by the resolution required and the refresh rate. The formula to calculate the required graphics bandwidth is:

HORIZONTAL RESOLUTION x VERTICAL RESOLUTION x REFRESH RATE / 8

So, a 640 x 480 display with a 70Hz refresh rate requires to cope with

640 X 480 X 70 / 8 = 2.56MB /sec, i.e. over 20 million different pixel values per sec

while a 1600 x 1200 display with a 75Hz refresh rate requires to handle

1600 X 1200 x 75 / 8 = 17.17MB /sec, i.e. over 135 million different pixel values per sec

Memory bandwidth is much greater than graphics bandwidth for the same screen because it has to store and transfer the colour details for each pixel.

So, a 640 x 480 display, with a refresh rate of 70Hz and 256 colours requires to transfer

640 X 480 X 70 X 8 / 8 = 20.2MB /sec, i.e. over 160 million different pixel values per sec

while a 1600 x 1200 display with a 75Hz refresh rate and 16m colours requires to transfer

1600 X 1200 x 75 X 24 / 8 = 137.36MB /sec, i.e. over 432 million different pixel values per sec

Where a card is intended for multimedia and video use, the bandwidth capability of both the monitor and the graphics card become crucial factors.

RAM Type

At one stage all graphics cards used standard DRAM (Dynamic RAM) chips as a frame buffer to store the graphics information about that frame. In this *'Single Port'* system, the CPU has to write to the DRAM using the same data and address buses as that used to get data from the DRAM to the VDU driver circuitry. Since these transfers in and out cannot be simultaneous, a bottleneck existed. The logic value on a single pin on the DRAM chips controlled whether the memory was in read or write mode. When toggled to write mode, the CPU updated the screen information. When in read mode, the chips on the graphics card read the information and processed it to drive the monitor.

The last few years saw the introduction of cards using VRAM (video RAM), which overcame the speed limitation imposed by conventional DRAM. With the VRAM *'Dual Port'* system, separate address and data buses were provided for the in an out transfers. Hence, this memory block was capable of being both read and written to simultaneously, with the system preventing attempts to read and write to the exact same memory areas at the same time. Writing was carried out with random access - i.e. only those pixels that need updating were accessed and altered. Since the stream of data to the monitor was in serial format, the read process was always a complete sequential read of the frame buffer. This greatly speeded up the screen handling process and

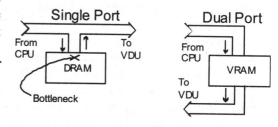

the extra cost was justified where fast screen updates were required. VRAM systems required their own dedicated controller.

A development on VRAM is Windows RAM (WRAM).   This is a modified dual-ported system and is faster then VRAM and up to 50% faster than DRAM.   It carries out some of the tasks (e.g. blitting) normally placed on the graphics controller, thereby speeding up processing. It is manufactured by Samsung and can be found in high performance systems such as the Matrox Millenium II card.

Other memory options are EDO RAM as found in the Orchid Righteous 3DII card and SGRAM as found in the ATI All-In-Wonder Pro and STB Velocity 128 cards.   See the chapter on Memory for details of these memory chips.

DDR SDRAM

An improvement over earlier SDRAM memory is Dual Data Rate or DDR SDRAM. Conventional SDRAM is synchronised with the bus, by carrying out transfers on the rising or falling edge of the bus's clock signal. DDR SDRAM is triggered by both the rising and falling edge of the bus clock. Thus it should optimally perform at twice the speed of conventional SDRAM. In practice, however, such extreme gains are never seen.

External Bus Type

A very wide range of graphics cards is available, using every type of data bus system. Since the fastest data buses have the greatest throughput, the graphics card should be matched to the fastest bus. So, a PCI computer will be able to accommodate a graphics card on either its ISA expansion slot or its PCI expansion slot.   Although an older ISA or PCI graphics card will work in the system, an AGP card would provide a better performance.   Similarly, a VESA card should be used in a VESA local bus machine, although an ISA can be used.   PCI cards and VL cards are not interchangeable, and modern motherboards support the faster AGP rather than VL or PCI.

Bus size is important as well as speed – a 32-bit card can transfer twice as much as a 16-bit card, all other things being equal.   The 8-bit and 16-bit ISA ports are virtually obsolete and are never used for graphics in any recent systems. Graphics cards for PCI Pentium boards use a full external 64-bit data bus, but even these are no longer used in new systems.   AGP cards use their own high-speed 32-bit bus, as well as using techniques similar to DDR memory transfer to achieve x2 or x4 speed.

Internal Bus Size

The bus size in a graphics card's specification refers to its <u>internal</u> architecture, the path between the card's RAM and the card's graphics processor.   The most critical element in graphics performance is not data flow into the graphics board; it is how the board organises and manages the frame buffer held in memory inside the graphics board.   Having a 64-bit internal bus greatly speeds up throughput, enhancing the card's performance.   It also allows some cards to use cheaper DRAM instead of VRAM. The card's memory is organised into interleaved banks, allowing one bank to be written to while the other is being read.   This increases throughput without the expense of VRAM.   However, with increasing resolution, even 64-bit buses can act as a bottleneck and 128-bit versions are now common.   In fact, there are now even 256-bit cards available, such as the GeForce256 Annihilator.   Note that the internal bus size being doubled does not affect the bus connecting the card with the motherboard, and will not result in the card being twice as fast overall.   In fact, in some circumstances the difference will be negligible.

Refresh Rates

Greater resolution and greater colour depth (i.e. bits per pixel) both mean that the card has to move more data for a single frame.   This means that cards commonly have lower refresh rates at higher resolutions and at greater colour depths.   For example, even a high performance card like the ATI Xpert@Work PCI card has a wide variation in refresh rates.   It handles 200Hz at VGA and SVGA, 150Hz at 1024x768, 100Hz at 1280x1024 but is only 85Hz at 1600x1200.   An older S3-based ISA card from 1992 fares much worse with respective rates of 70Hz for VGA, 60Hz for SVGA and 1024x768 and an unacceptable 45Hz interlaced format at 1280x1024.

Chip Set Used

To reduce costs, all SVGA graphics cards are based round a limited range of different VLSI chips, sometimes referred to as the *'graphics engine'*.   These chips are dedicated to the one task and different manufacturers produce a range of chips with different performances.   Example chips are the Matrox range (from the first Millenium to the latest G800), the ATI range (from the Mach8 to the 3D Rage Pro and Radeon) and the nVidia range (from the GeForce to the GeForce3).

All these chips, and others, provide varying performances.   It is best to compare the working speeds of the chipsets as used on various cards. This may use *'Wintach'* readings, measuring how cards cope with actual applications packages or general card tests may be used, measuring the bit manipulation features. Example chip/card features are:

Chip	Graphics Card	Memory Type	Refresh rate at 24-bit SVGA	RAMDAC(s)
Matrox G450	Matrox Millenium G450	DDR	200Hz	360MHz and 200MHz
3dfx VSA-100	3dfx Voodoo5 5500	SDRAM	200Hz	350MHz
ATI Radeon	ATI Radeon VE	DDR	120Hz	300MHz
NVidia GeForce3	Elsa Gladiac 920	460MHz DDR	240Hz	350MHz

Method of Screen Writing

As soon as the PC progressed beyond the CGA standard, the standard machine BIOS (Basic Input/Output System) was inadequate and required extension.   The added graphics functionality is provided by an extra EPROM (Erasable Programmable Read Only Memory) chip on the graphics card.   The efficiency of this BIOS extension affects the screen writing speed.   Some SVGA cards copy the extension software into an area of RAM to speed up screen handling.   This technique is known as *'ROM shadowing'*.

Currently, there are three approaches to screen handling:

- Leave the computer's CPU to do all the screen handling. This is the simplest and cheapest method but it is also the slowest. Watch a screen update in Windows - around 15% of the CPU time is used up in updating the screen cursor alone! The problems worsen if the system is upgraded. Adding a 1600x1200 card, for example, means the CPU has to handle an even bigger amount of screen data - with no extra computing power to process it.
- Use a Co-Processor to take on the graphics work and relieve the CPU. This is fast but expensive and is usually found in CAD environments.
- Use a graphics accelerator card, which is also a quick method and generally found in most modern high performance PCs.

When extra cards take over the graphics, the main machine has to have special software drivers installed, to allow communication to the cards. In Windows, these include the graphics adapter driver, and a graphical language driver such as DirectX or OpenGL.

3D Cards

Games and animations such as walkthroughs and flybys show a quick succession of frames with each frame showing the viewer a different viewpoint on the scene. As the viewpoint is moved, so the shading, shadowing and fine detail will alter. Each scene comprises a range of objects (buildings, people, etc) and each object is made up from many individual graphics polygons, usually triangles. Each triangle has its own colour and surface detail (e.g. grains of sand, bricks, leaves). The scene will have one or more supposed sources of illumination; this could be the sun, streetlights, etc. As the viewpoint is moved the light source will illuminate the triangles differently. To produce a 3D effect, the user is shown perspective (i.e. distant objects are made smaller than close objects) and defocussing (i.e. distant object are not as clear as close objects; they are usually dimmed or 'fogged').

The commonly implemented features in 3D cards are:

Facility	Explanation
Z-Buffering	Since x and y describe the horizontal and vertical co-ordinates, 'z' refers to depth. A Z-buffer stores the depth information of objects (e.g. the dog is behind the tree). This allows 'hidden surface removal' - i.e. time is saved by not drawing parts of an object that are obscured by foreground objects.
Flat shading	The polygons are filled with a uniform colour, which is not as effective but is very quick. Flat shading can be implemented to improve frame rates.
Gouraud shading	Obscures the boundaries between polygons by drawing realistic colour gradients; produces smoother and more natural shapes.
Phong shading	Achieves better results than Gouraud shading but is more demanding of processing power.
Texture mapping	Filling polygons with the same graphics bitmap (e.g. woodgrain or feathers).
Bump mapping	Similar to texture mapping, this technique uses a 'map' of raised or depressed areas that is applied to a surface to produce an irregular 3d shape.
Anti-aliasing	Curved and diagonal edges produce a 'staircase' effect known as 'jaggies'. If the colours of the boundary's surrounding edges are blended, the effect is minimised.
Perspective correction	If an object is receding into the distance, the bit maps used to texture should also gradually diminish. So, a brick wall bitmap would draw smaller and smaller bricks as the wall shrunk towards the horizon.
Mip mapping	Similar to the above, except that new patterns are rendered for distant polygons.
Bilinear/trilinear filtering	Large areas when rendered can appear like a patchwork quilt, with blocks of slightly differing colouring. Filtering determines a pixel's colour on the colour of the surrounding pixels thereby producing a more uniform transition.
Alpha blending	Controls an object's translucency, thereby providing water or glass effects. It is also used to mask out areas of the screen.
Logarithmic fogging	More distant objects are fogged to grey.

The routines to constantly calculate all of these objects and display them on the screen (typically at 20 pictures per second) require a great deal of computational power. This is called 'rendering' and it strains even the most powerful PC. To overcome this problem, many of these computational routines are embedded in graphics card's chipset and called by special software drivers. Initially these drivers, known as APIs (Application Programming Interface), were written by graphics card manufacturers for their own range of cards. The routines for a Matrox card would not work with a VideoLogic card, and so on. As a consequence, games supplied with one card would not work with another graphics card, as the games were specially written to use the card manufacturer's APIs. Games bundled with the Diamond Stealth 3D 200, for example, are specially written for the card's VIRGE chipset.

There was a need for standard interfaces and this has been met by Silicon Graphic's OpenGL and Microsoft's Direct 3D. OpenGL is not designed for the games market but for high-end graphical workstations. With the rise of comparatively cheap PC 3D cards this market is shrinking. Windows 95 Release 2 and later Windows operating systems provide DirectX facilities, which includes Direct3D. Card manufacturers only have to write drivers to interface their cards to the Direct3D API's functions.

Microsoft's DirectX

Microsoft has produced a number of APIs under the title DirectX. These are:

Direct 3D	Provides a standard interface for 3D object display and rendering.
Direct Draw	Reduces CPU time by allowing software direct access to alter video memory.
Direct Sound	Reduces CPU time by allowing software direct access to sound hardware. Also provides synchronisation of video and sound data.
Direct Play	Aids running applications over networks or communications lines.
Direct Input	Speeds up mouse and joystick responses.

RAMDAC Used

The graphics information is stored in memory in digital format and has to be converted into analogue values to drive the gun(s) of the monitor. A chip, known as a RAMDAC (RAM digital/analogue converter) carries out the conversion function. The frame buffer data for each pixel is read in the order that it will be sent to the monitor for display. This data is passed to the RAMDAC for conversion. With 24-bit colour, the numbers stored in memory exactly relate to the intensity of the red, green and blue elements of each pixel. This makes the digital to analogue conversion simple. However, this is not the method with lower colour depths. It is common that a card can only handle a subset of its full range of colours at any one time. For example, a card capable of 65,536 different colours may only be using 256 colours in a particular mode. This subset of colours is known as the *'palette'* and is stored in a look-up table in memory. During normal activities, the screen's pixel colour information is stored as a sequence of logical colour numbers. The colour number for each pixel is read from memory, translated into the values for each gun and these values are given to the RAMDAC to produce the actual colour that will appear on the monitor. Each Windows application package stores information about the palette it uses. When the application is run, Windows sets the RAMDAC to use that palette. When several applications are open at the same time, each application may have different sets of colour numbers in their required palettes. This can result in unexpected colour changes, as the range of colours supported by the card is less than the range of colours requested by the applications. RAMDAC performance is measured both in colour depth (e.g. 24-bit) and conversion speed (up to 250MHz).

Card Connections

The output from the graphics card appears on a socket at the rear of the computer case.
The diagram shows the two types of connector used with PCs.

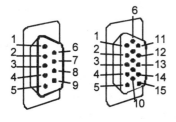

The CGA connector and EGA connector are identical and each has two rows of pins while the VGA/SVGA/XGA connector has three rows of pins. The chart shows the use of the pins.

Pin	Mono	CGA	EGA	VGA/SVGA/XGA
1	Ground	Ground	Ground	Red
2	Ground	Ground	Red Intensity	Green
3	Not Used	Red	Red	Blue
4	Not Used	Green	Green	Not Used
5	Not Used	Blue	Blue	Not Used
6	Intensity	Intensity	Green Intensity	Red Return
7	Video	Not Used	Blue Intensity	Green Return
8	Horizontal Synch	Horizontal Synch	Horizontal Synch	Blue Return
9	Vertical Synch	Vertical Synch	Vertical Synch	No Pin (used as key)
10				Ground
11				Not Used
12				Not Used
13				Horizontal Synch
14				Vertical Synch
15				Not Used

Many cards also offer other connections to extension devices. The range of connections includes:

VESA Feature Connector	This is a set of 26 pins on the graphics board that allows the connection of other video add-on cards e.g. video capture facilities. Unfortunately, the connection only supports VGA and 256 colours.
VAFC	The VESA Advanced Feature Connector is an 80-pin connector that overcomes the limitation of the standard VESA connector. It works up to 1024x768 and has a throughput of 150Mb per second.
VMC	The VESA Media Channel (VMC) is an edge connector on the graphics card. It is designed to handle up to fifteen different audio and video sources on a single channel, allowing a great flexibility in connecting together sound cards, video capture cards, MPEG systems, video conferencing systems and anything that the future may throw at it. Its first appearance is in the Video Logic 928Movie and PCIMovie cards.
Video Input	The ability to display input from live video sources such as VCRs and camcorders, as provided in the Media Vision 1024 card. An extra daughterboard may have to be fitted for this.
TV Aerial Input	A number of graphics cards, such as the ATI Wonder Pro, now have a built-in TV tuner, allowing both viewing of television programmes on the monitor and the capture of television programmes to hard disk.
TV Output	Some graphics cards are capable not only of TV input but output as well. The user may decide whether to output the display to TV or monitor, or possibly both.
RGB output	Used for connecting to high-quality monitors and other video devices that use RGB connectors.

AGP

The Accelerated Graphics Port was developed in response to the huge memory and consequent data transfer overheads required for 3D graphics. A large number of texture maps require to be stored in memory. This allows rapid access to the texture data for the rapid rendering of 3D objects. Fetching directly from disk would be far too slow to maintain the frame refresh rates. However, 3D rendering produces two main problems:

- The memory requirements of these maps can exceed the actual amount of memory in the graphics card.
- Huge amounts of data need to be transferred to produce rendered screens at up to 30 frames per second.

The solution is twofold - use some of the computer's existing memory and access it at far faster data rates. This requires a new motherboard with a new bus system - the Accelerated Graphics Port.

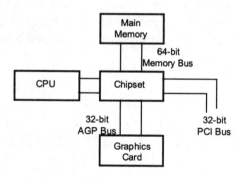

The Accelerated Graphics Port is only available on Pentium systems and these motherboards have their own AGP card slots and use the 440LX chipset onwards. The graphics card no longer sits on the 33Mhz PCI bus.

As the diagram shows, the card is plugged directly into the separate AGP 66MHz bus that connects, via the chipset, to the CPU and memory. This is called 'x1 mode' and provides a maximum throughput of 264MBps - double that of the PCI bus. This data rate is still half of that travelling over the 64-bit connection between the CPU and memory. To compensate, the 440BX chipset provides an 'x2 mode'.

This transfers data on both the rising and falling edge of the clock pulse, which doubles the theoretical throughput to 528MBps. The computer's memory is shared between the application program's usage and the graphics card usage. Systems using the 100MHz bus system push the data rate up to 800MBps and the new AGP4x standard is included in the Intel i8X0 chipsets, where the AGP function is wholly integrated into the chipsets. The AGP 8x standard is in development but currently no system is fast enough to utilise the entire bandwidth it would provide.

Normal 2D graphics do not require this extra performance and normal applications will not particularly benefit from this new technique. Since support for AGP did not appear until a new DirectDraw in Windows 98, the shared memory usage ability of AGP cards were inactive until then. In the short-term, AGP provides a faster data transfer rate. In the long term, it offers a cheap and fast video system.

Other Facilities
The preceding pages outline some of the more important features of graphics cards. However, many more factors may prove important for a particular user or for a particular activity.
These might include:
- Support for DPMS power saving. The ability of the graphics card to control the power usage of the monitor at times when there is no user activity.
- Virtual Screen or virtual desktop. A user may wish to display a great deal of detail on the screen (e.g. many Windows groups or many Windows applications open at the same time). This would normally require a large screen monitor otherwise each window would be too small for comfortable viewing. An alternative is to use a normal monitor screen size and only view a part of the full screen at any one time. Moving the mouse to an edge of the screen scrolls the display in that direction. Thus a 640x480 screen can act as a window on a larger 1280x1024 display held in screen memory.
- Zoom. The virtual desktop provides a scrolling window on a larger screen. The zoom facility allows the user to magnify any portion of the screen, usually to allow detailed editing of graphics or DTP. There is no scrolling in this case. The Number 9 GXE64 Pro card, for example, magnifies the screen up to 5 times normal size.
- Support for the connection of multiple monitors - either through installing multiple graphics cards or fitting the new graphics cards that have twin video outputs. This allows separate multitasking programs to be run on separate monitors.
- Drivers to allow the user to switch resolutions without having to reboot the machine to activate the new screen mode.
- Drivers for a wide range of monitors, applications (particularly AutoCAD and 3D Studio) and operating systems such as Windows 95, Windows 98, Windows 2000, Windows NT and OS/2.
- MPEG-2 players, to handle DVD drives.

Video Handling
Many graphics cards support a range of full motion video options, including MPEG, QuickTime, Video for Windows and Intel Indeo formats. Video playback is often achieved by fitting an extra board or using additional video handling software. Video for Windows (AVI) is the most common PC video format although MPEG systems are becoming very popular. MPEG initially required special hardware to decode the compressed files, although with the advance of CPU power software methods have overtaken more expensive dedicated hardware decoders in many instances. The popularity of DVD players has led to a resurgence of dedicated hardware decoder cards, as these also provide 'theatre quality' audio output.

Co-Processor Cards
Co-processor cards use a second processor to carry out the graphics tasks. The computer CPU passes brief instructions to the CPU on the co-processor graphics board and the co-processor board carries out the graphics calculations and board memory updates. Typical functions given to a co-processor would be text display, line drawing, rectangles, ellipses and area colour fills. The 8514/A boards and the VESA XGA boards initiated this method and other co-processor systems are available, such as the nVidia GeForce range, where the Graphics Processing Unit (GPU) runs at 175MHz to 250MHz. Like main processors, graphics processors can also be overclocked, and this shares the same benefits and risks as main processor overclocking, except that they mainly apply to 3D operations such as computer games.

Accelerator Cards
Like co-processor boards, the accelerator board is designed to relieve the computer's main CPU of valuable graphics processing time. In a co-processor system, a second processor chip is employed for the graphics tasks. In an accelerator system, the main graphics tasks are implemented in hardware. These main tasks are line and box drawing and 'bitblitting' (bit-to-block transfers - i.e. memory flooding). Since these operations are implemented in hardware, there is no need for a processor to determine what needs to be done - the tasks are pre-defined. This results in the graphics functions being carried out more quickly. Most graphics cards on sale currently use some form of graphics acceleration.
A number of hardware-based 3D accelerator cards are produced, based on the 3DFX Voodoo range or the VideoLogic PowerVR PCX2 chipsets. The trend, however, seems to be towards producing combined 2D/3D chipsets such as the 3D Labs Permedia 2.

Note

There can be significant variations in the efficiency of each card's method of handling graphics functions. For example, one particular card may need less information passed to it, in order to carry out a particular graphics function, compared to another card. Some cards will carry out a smaller range of graphics functions, the remaining functions being left for the computer's main CPU to process.

Card Performance

There is no doubt that graphics accelerator cards substantially improve a system's performance. However, manufacturers' claims should be put in perspective:

- The claims only consider the graphics functions being tested in isolation.
- When considered as part of the overall activities of an application program, the performance is nowhere near so spectacular.

VESA GRAPHICS MODES

VESA has established a set of graphics modes and these are given in the table. This provides a common standard for both the manufacturers of graphics cards and the writers of software.

Where a card is described as 'VESA compatible', the manufacturer has ensured that all or a subset of these modes is supported by its card. Similarly, software houses can write software knowing that particular screen resolutions, refresh rates, numbers of colours, etc will be available to run their software. Where graphics cards do not directly support certain modes, software - known as VESA Bios Extensions - can run as TSRs to ensure compatibility.

NOTE: Not all manufacturers stick to this mode numbering scheme.

Mode No (in Hex)	Resolution	Colours	Memory	
0	Text 40 x 25	2	1k	IBM
1	Text 40 x 25	16	4k	
2	Text 80 x 25	2	2k	
3	Text 80 x 25	16	8k	
4	320 x200	4	16k	
5	320 x 200	2	8k	
6	640 x 200	2	16k	
7	Text 80 x 25	2	2k	
8	160 x 200	16	16k	IBM
9	320 x 200	16	31k	IBM
A	640 x 200	4	63k	IBM
B	704 x 519	16	178k	
D	320 x 200	16	31k	
E	640 x 200	16	63k	
F	640 x 350	2	27k	
10	640 x 350	16	109k	
11	640 x 480	2	38k	
12	640 x 480	16	150k	
13	320 x 200	256	63k	
25	640 x 480	16	150k	
26	640 x 480	16	150k	
50	640 x 480	16	150k	
53	800 x 560	16	219k	
58	800 x 600	16	234k	
59	720 x 512	16	180k	
6A/102	800 x 600	16	234k	VESA
70	800 x 600	16	234k	
71	800 x 600	16	234k	
73	640 x 480	16	150k	
77	752 x 410	16	151k	
79	800 x 600	16	234k	
100	640 x 400	256	234k	VESA
101	640 x 480	256	300k	VESA
102/6A	800 x 600	16	234k	VESA
103	800 x 600	256	469k	VESA
104	1024 x 768	16	384k	VESA
105	1024 x 768	256	768k	VESA
106	1280 x 1024	16	640k	VESA
107	1280 x 1024	256	1k	VESA
108	Text80 x 60	16	2k	VESA
109	Text 132 x 25	16	2k	VESA
10A	Text 132 x 43	16	3k	VESA
10B	Text 132 x 50	16	3k	VESA
10C	Text 132 x 60	16	4k	VESA
10D	320 X 200	32K	117k	VESA
10E	320 X 200	64K	125k	VESA
10F	320 X 200	16M	188k	VESA
110	640 x 480	32K	563k	VESA
111	640 x 480	64K	600k	VESA
112	640 x 480	16M	900k	VESA
113	800 x 600	32K	879k	VESA
114	800 x 600	64K	938k	VESA
115	800 x 600	16M	1.37M	VESA
116	1024 x 768	32K	1.41M	VESA
117	1024 x 768	64K	1.5M	VESA
118	1024 x 768	16M	2.25M	VESA
119	1280 x 1024	32K	2.34M	VESA
11A	1280 x 1024	64K	2.5M	VESA
11B	1280 x 1024	16M	3.75M	VESA
11C	1600 x 1200	32K	3.43M	VESA
11D	1600 x 1200	64K	3.66M	VESA
11E	1600 x 1200	16M	5.49M	VESA

Computer Memory

Memory Usage

The memory inside a computer stores a variety of information.

- A computer loads a program into its main memory, from where it can be run. A computer program is a list of instructions for the CPU, each instruction being stored as a numeric code.
- Computer programs exist to manipulate data. The data may be loaded from disk or CD, entered from the keyboard, downloaded via a modem - and a range of other input devices. The data may be in the form of database records, wages data, etc. Whatever its format, the data is always held in the form of numeric values.
- The computer stores some of its own system programs (such as the components of Windows or the MSDOS operating system) and its own system information (such as the nationality of the keyboard in use, screen display information, etc.).

All of these must share the same pool of memory held inside the computer. In addition, the machine stores much of the code it requires to handle its hardware in programs that are permanently blown on to chips. If the computer is to avoid getting into utter confusion, it must allocate these activities to separate areas, each with its own distinct boundaries within the machine's addressable memory.

Memory Access

The machine has to separate one program instruction from the next. This is achieved by storing the machine instructions in different memory locations. This means having each consecutive instruction stored in each consecutive memory address. It is important to differentiate between an address and its contents. The address is a unique location in memory. The contents of this address may be part of an application program or system program, or may be data.

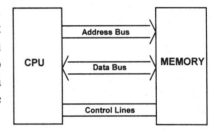

The CPU will fetch an instruction from the memory by placing the instruction's memory address on the Address Bus and a Read signal on one of the Control Lines. The memory chip places the address's contents on to the Data Bus and this is picked up by the CPU. The CPU then carries out the instruction. If the instruction involves writing a piece of data to memory, the appropriate location is placed on the Address Bus, the value to be written is placed on the Data Bus and a Write signal is placed on one of the Control Lines. Once the instruction is completed, the CPU can fetch the next instruction, often stored in the next consecutive program memory address. The simplified diagram uses a single bus for both data and program instructions. This is very common and is called the *'Von Neumann'* architecture.

The PC Memory Map

The IBM XT PC appeared in 1981 with an 8088 processor and only 16k of main memory (with a recommended figure of 64k). These chips had a 20-bit address bus and could only address 1MB of memory. This now seems a ludicrous limitation, in the days of 100MB applications. In 1978, though, when the 8086 was brought out, memory chips were extremely expensive and personal computers would have been lucky to have 100 kilobytes of memory. 1MB was only found on large mainframe computers. The ability of the 8086/8088 chips to address a full megabyte of memory was regarded as a luxury that was unlikely ever to be used. This may have been a reasonable assumption at the time

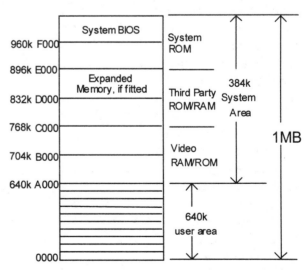

but holds up poorly in the light of the drop in memory prices, the development of more powerful processors and the creation of huge software applications. Overcoming these design shortcomings is dealt with elsewhere.

The diagram that displays the allocation of memory to different parts of the computer system is known as a *'memory map'* and is explained below in terms of a basic configuration, without any memory management. The entire machine memory is divided, for historical reasons, into segments of 64k.   The segments are not shown to scale on the diagram, to aid clarity.

The map shows both decimal numbering and its hexadecimal notation equivalents, since the latter is commonly shown on computer system manuals.

Note

> *Many memory maps use 4 hex characters to describe map addresses. For example, the 640k boundary is often shown as A000h.   The full effective address of 640k is, more correctly, A0000h or A000:0000.*

User Area

Also known as *'Low-DOS'*, the lower 10 segments make up the 640k user area, where DOS and the user applications reside. The bulk of this area is provided for application programs, but some is devoted to system programs and variables.

System Area

The remaining six segments, a total of 384k, are variously called the *'system area'*, the *'upper memory area'* or *'high DOS'* area. This is occupied by the ROM BIOS, various device drivers such as video adapters and disk controllers, and video memory.   These are not all shown on the memory map, since individual configurations can vary greatly. The map, as an example, shows the location of expanded memory.   In fact, the great majority of PCs do not have these expanded memory expansion cards fitted. The exact map locations for scanners, modems, data acquisition equipment, etc. would vary, since their actual addresses might well have to be altered to prevent clashes of addresses. This would be performed by the plug and play system, but in older machines it might be accomplished manually by setting the values of DIP switches mounted on the cards.

The diagram also shows that two 64k sections of memory are set aside for the computer's video needs. The exact amount of video memory that is used depends on the screen standard in use (refer to the chapter on Display Technology for more details on video modes). As can be seen from the diagram, only the most basic of video modes can fit within the RAM allocated, such as the long defunct MDA, Hercules, CGA and EGA modes, as well as the rarely used Mono VGA mode and the VGA text mode used in DOS sessions. The higher resolution modes of EGA and some modes of VGA adapters manage to fit into the High Memory Area by appropriating varying areas of RAM between A0000 and C8000. Full VGA and super VGA modes cannot fit into main memory, even commencing at A0000, and have to use extra memory on graphics boards.

Much of the upper memory space is unused because the designers overestimated the amount of space that would be required by future add-ons and extra system ROMs; the idea that programs would be available as plug-in ROMs never developed.

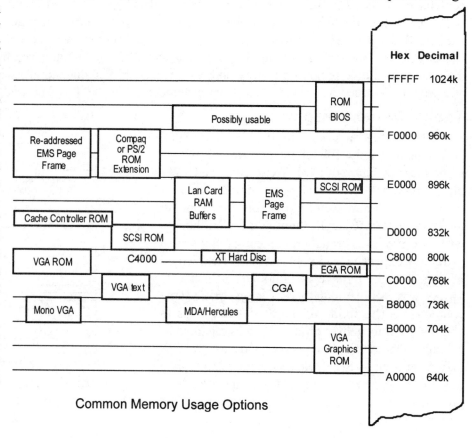

Common Memory Usage Options

This space can be used for other purposes, as described in the section on memory management. The diagram shows the most common memory areas and their uses.

Notes
- Any memory block is exclusive to one use. For example, if the address range D0000h to E0000h is being used for expanded memory, any LAN card or disk controller card would require to be set for operation in another - unused - part of the memory map.
- The ROM BIOS is always located from F0000h to FFFFFh. This is because the PC always looks for an instruction at FFFFFh when the machine is switched on. This instruction starts the bootup process.

DOS and the Memory Map

MSDOS is fundamentally a program loader and file handler and consists of three elements:
- A command processor
- A system kernel
- A hardware-specific BIOS

The separation of the system into parts allows the maximum flexibility when it comes to developing the system and producing improved versions. The first two software components are written to be independent of the physical requirements of the hardware. They are concerned with the functions and interface to the user. The last component has the responsibility of controlling the actual hardware components of the computer system. Since only the BIOS is hardware-dependent, the user interface and system kernel do not have to be revised to accommodate new hardware devices that might be developed.

The DOS distribution disk contains three files:

COMMAND.COM

This provides the standard DOS user interface and prompt, and interprets user commands. DOS has a standard character-oriented user interface but, because it is a separate module, it can be supplemented or replaced with a different one, such as Windows.

MSDOS.SYS

The Microsoft title is MSDOS.SYS, while the IBM version is known as IBMDOS.SYS. This is the DOS kernel, containing many services. It is called by application programs and provides an applications interface that is invisible to the user. It is called by the general interrupt 21h call, much used in DOS programs. The kernel contains the compiled code for the internal services, such as file management and I/O, needed to execute both DOS commands and application program calls. Note that this is the high level control of information flow, concerned with the logic of operations and not their hardware implementation. For example, the kernel contains the file system code (e.g. the sequence of steps and prompts required for a FORMAT command). The kernel is essentially hardware-independent. So, a hardware vendor does not have to rewrite MSDOS.SYS to get it to run on a new machine. Furthermore, the installation of new device drivers requires only that a device driver be written and linked into a list of drivers maintained by the kernel.

IO.SYS

Known in its IBM version as IBMIO.SYS, this component contains the BIOS (Basic Input Output System) software. This should not be confused with the System BIOS, or ROM BIOS, which is burnt onto a chip to control bootup. The IO.SYS file contains hardware-specific code, including a collection of built-in drivers for screen, keyboard, hard and floppy disk, clock and serial and parallel ports. Some, or sometimes all, of the BIOS may be stored in ROM. The BIOS code deals with devices on a low level. For example, it moves the disk's read/write head or writes characters to the video display. It also contains initialisation code that is temporarily brought in to interpret the lines of the CONFIG.SYS file at machine start-up. Because the hardware details are hidden from the rest of the operating system, additions at BIOS level make it possible to add support for new devices without having to make extensive changes to services in the kernel.

Note

All these components have to be present for the machine to function. IO.SYS and MSDOS.SYS are normally hidden files. If any one of three were deleted accidentally, then the machine would fail to operate.

User Allocation

The user allocation is shown in the unscaled memory map. The bottom 256 bytes are always reserved for the machine's interrupt vector table. This is a set of pointers that contains the addresses of particular sets of code to be run, if particular interrupts are triggered. These pointers are held in RAM, so that an expert programmer can alter them to change program functions. For example, a programmer can prevent the PrtScr key from carrying out a screen dump, instead pointing to code that plays a tune! This area should not be touched by the inexperienced. The DOS kernel is the heart of the operating system and has to be permanently present in main memory. The actual amount of space that it occupies depends on the DOS version and whether memory management techniques have been applied. DOS can leave as little as 537k for user use (DOS v4.01) and as much as 617k (DOS 5 with memory management).

Notice that COMMAND.COM is loaded as two separate portions. The lower section is known as the *'resident'* portion and it handles program termination (i.e. pressing Ctrl-Break) or user program errors resulting in program termination. This section provides all the standard DOS error messages. The upper section is known as the *'transient'* portion and provides the user's interface to DOS. It provides the DOS prompt, provides for EXE and COM files to be run and also contains the batch processor (to interpret and execute batch file commands). This portion also processes the *'internal'* DOS commands (DIR, COPY, etc.).

COMMAND.COM (Transient) — 640k
Application Program (Transient Program Area)
COMMAND.COM (Resident)
TSRs
Device Drivers
DOS FILES, Buffers
DOS Kernel
BIOS data
Interrupt Vectors — 0

The memory needs of the DOS buffers, device drivers and TSRs have to be added to the overheads of DOS itself. They occupy a significant proportion of the so-called *'user area'*. The user allocation of 640k can quickly diminish to 500k, or even less.

When the demands on the system are extreme, there can easily be conflicting demands for machine configuration. The setup for one application might slow down another's operations. In some cases, it may prevent another application from loading. At worst, it may allow a program to load, then prevent the work from being saved back to disk. Such difficulties are usually overcome by the re-allocation of programs within the machine memory - a technique called *'memory management'*.

Device Drivers

A device driver is simply a piece of software that is used to provide the correct interface to a particular piece of computer equipment. The equipment might be some external device, such as a printer, plotter or mouse; it might be an internal device, such as a graphics card. It might also be a different way of treating conventional equipment such as a RAM disk or screen writing. DOS, after all, has its own default software for driving the screen, printer, etc.

Consider how a printer and a plotter handle data. The output to a printer is transmitted one character at a time, as a series of ASCII characters. The received ASCII value is used by the printer to select the appropriate sequence of dots, in dot matrix, laser or inkjet printers, or appropriate rotation on a daisy wheel printer. Regardless of the printer type, there is a standard output from the computer's printer port. Plotters, on the other hand, work in an entirely different way. The final print is a result of a series of lines drawn by pen activities. These activities consist of pen up, pen down and pen horizontal movements. Such movements are not the standard output from a printer port. The plotter device driver is the software that translates the data into the corresponding sequence of pen movements. Similar conversion software is required for mice and graphics cards. The software is particular to the piece of equipment in use and therefore the driver would be supplied along with the equipment.

DOS supplies a few of its own device drivers. These are optionally installed by the user and are therefore taking up memory space if the user has a requirement for them. The most used of these is the ANSI.SYS driver, which provides extra facilities for screen handling and keyboard operations. One of the main uses of the ANSI.SYS driver is to intercept output intended for normal video BIOS routines, such as writing a character to the screen. The ANSI driver can provide software to change screen foreground and background colours, alter the cursor position, etc. DOS also provides drivers to create ram disks and handle various other devices. If the extra facilities are not required, the drivers are not installed and memory is not used up.

DOS TSRs

Often, an application cannot provide all the functions that a user might wish. For example, a user may be running a word-processor and wish to enter the client's address, next Wednesday's date or a net price after adding mark-up and taxes. Despite sitting in front of a very expensive database and calculator (i.e. the computer), the user still has to resort to the filofax, calendar or pocket calculator. That is where TSR programs aid productivity. They allow more than one program to be in computer memory at one time. Without leaving the word-processor, the user can temporarily call up an on-screen calculator or other utility, use it, and return to the word-processing program.

DOS supports the use of TSRs (*'Terminate and Stay Resident'* programs), also known as *'memory-resident'* programs. These differ from DOS programs in the way that they use memory and the way that they are called. A DOS program is invoked by executing the appropriate COM or EXE file. This results in the program taking the amount of memory it requires. When the program is exited, the memory is released. A TSR program is also installed by executing a COM or EXE file. This loads the program into the lowest available memory above the device drivers. In some cases, the program is immediately run and is eventually exited by the user. In other cases, it loads itself into memory and immediately returns to the DOS prompt. To the unwary, it may appear that nothing happened. In either case, when the program terminates, it does not release the memory space it occupied. Instead, the program remains in memory and can be called up to be run. A normal DOS program, or even another TSR program, can now also be loaded into memory and loads commencing from the upper address of the first TSR. As the diagram shows, TSRs can be stacked up in memory. Some may be single utility programs, while others may contain a suite of facilities.

| Application Program |
| Productivity Suite TSR |
| Print Utility TSR |
| Calendar TSR |
| DOS Area |

All TSR programs sit inactive in their memory areas, while the main program runs.

At any time, TSRs can be called by the user pressing *'hot key'* combinations; perhaps holding down the ALT key and a particular letter key, or pressing both Shift keys simultaneously. Even while the main application is running, DOS is checking in the background for keyboard operations. As soon as it detects the TSRs hot key combination, control is passed to the TSR program, with the main application being temporarily suspended. Most often the TSR program 'pops up', i.e. the screen of the application is seen as a background with a foreground window displaying the TSR program. The main application is still sitting in main memory and is frozen at the point of TSR invocation. When the user exits the TSR, the main application re-occupies the whole screen and carries on from where it was suspended. The TSR program remains in its own memory area awaiting a future invocation.

Disadvantages

If one or more TSR programs are installed, they may not leave enough space in the memory to allow a large application to be loaded. Some TSRs have an *'uninstall'* parameter; used memory space is recovered by executing it a second time with this parameter. In most cases, however, the only way to reclaim the memory space is to reboot the machine. This initialises the system with a new low marker, indicating the starting point for the loading of applications.

Often, TSRs are included in the AUTOEXEC batch file, so that they are automatically installed in memory at switch on. This is a convenient way to configure a machine to have regularly-used TSRs in place. Of course, in these cases, rebooting the machine will not reclaim the space, since the AUTOEXEC file will always install the TSR. The line invoking the TSR will have to be removed from the batch program script and only installed by the user from the DOS prompt, when required.

TSRs that are always used should be included in the AUTOEXEC.BAT file, while others should be manually invoked. TSRs are available for a wide range of uses, such as spell checkers, thesauruses, calculators, keyboard enhancers, communications programs and small databases and text editors. The most famous of these is the Sidekick program, which has a wide range of facilities and is flexible in its installation options. For example, if memory space is tight, a limited version can be installed which omits the notepad, calendar and dialler. Other files can be run to install other variations. It should be noted that a few TSRs load in at the top of available memory.

The most common TSRs are SHARE.EXE, KEYB.COM and a range of different virus checkers.

Note

Although more than one program is in memory, it is not *'multi-tasking'*. Multi-tasking systems run several programs 'simultaneously'. Usually the CPU time is, in fact, shared between each process, each having a *'time slice'* in a rota. The time slots allocated to each program are small, so the CPU quickly moves from application to application. To the user, each program seems to be running continuously. With TSRs on the other hand, several programs reside in memory, but only one program ever runs at a time. If a TSR is invoked, the CPU time is devoted entirely to that process. When the TSR is exited, the CPU time is devoted solely to the application program.

Overlays

Even at best, the useable area of base memory is around 620k. Very old machines may not have memory over 1MB fitted, but even modern machines are limited by the DOS 640k barrier. How then, does a machine manage to run a large DOS application program? If an application is 10MB, 20MB or 50MB in size, it cannot possibly fit into the user memory area. The solution rests in only loading and running a <u>part</u> of the program at any one time. Accordingly, the program is divided up by the programmer into sections of code that are able to fit into memory; these are called *'overlays'*. These overlays are not independent programs; they are not EXE files that can be executed from the DOS prompt. Instead, they must be loaded into memory by the core program, which will be an executable file. They will usually be identified by the file extension .OVL or similar. Since the overlays cannot be run independently, the application always maintains a core program in memory. This keeps track of all data and decides what overlays should be brought in at any particular time.

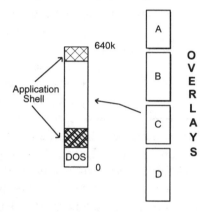

For example, a word processor would not keep its thesaurus or spell-checker in memory at all times, since they are not frequently required. If the user requests a spell-check, then the core program would fetch the spell-checking overlay from disk and place it in the main memory. When spell checking is finished, another overlay can be fetched from disk and its contents can overwrite the spell-checking overlay. This is not the ideal way to run an application, since time is taken in swapping overlays from disk. Alternative methods of handling large programs exist, either accessing the memory more efficiently or accessing memory above the 1MB limit.

Paging

Overlays suffer from two main problems:
- They require the <u>programmer</u> to split the program into manageable chunks.
- They can be inefficient. A 200k overlay may be loaded just to access one of its 2k long routines.

Paging solves the first problem by having its own *'paging unit'* inside the Pentium's memory management unit.   This divides the program into chunks and handles the loading and unloading of these chunks to and from memory. These chunks, known as *'pages'* are normally only 4k in length and this minimises the wasted time involved in handling excessive chunks of program.

Paging also provides a *'virtual memory'* system, where the program can be larger than the physical size of the computer's memory. A 386, 486 or Pentium has a maximum physical address range of 4GB. Thus, a total of one million 4k pages are supported. Since computers have only around 32MB to 256MB of memory installed, any extra pages required for a program can be stored to disk. When a particular page is required, it can be fetched from disk and used to replace another page that is already in memory, using a number of possible *'page replacement policies'*. The continual swapping of pages between memory and disk allows the computer to run a much larger program than would otherwise be supported.

Memory Organisation

As discussed earlier, the computer's memory, both RAM and ROM, is regarded as a contiguous list of locations, and each location is identified by its unique memory address. In the most recent RAMBUS chips, the memory locations are indeed arranged in a contiguous manner along the memory bus. In all other types of RAM, however, the memory is organised as a matrix of storage cells, as in the diagram. For simplicity, the diagram only shows 16 rows and 16 columns, providing 256 addressable locations or cells. Any cell in the matrix can be accessed by specifying its row and column co-ordinates. The memory chip circuitry has to translate any memory address into the corresponding co-ordinates.

In the example, the CPU requests access to address 227 (i.e. 11100011 in binary. This binary pattern is placed on the address bus. The four least significant bits (0011) are used by the column decoder to determine the column co-ordinate, known as the Column Address Select (CAS) line. In the example the CAS value is 3. The four most significant bits (1110) are used by the row decoder to determine the row co-ordinate, known as the Row Address Select (RAS) line - in this case 14. The row and column address lines then access only the single unique cell that corresponds to the address supplied. Note that the convention is to number address bus lines and data bus lines commencing with line 0. So, a 16-bit address bus would number its lines from A0 to A15 and an 8-bit data bus would number from D0 to D7. As can be seen, any cell in the matrix can be individually accessed. Hence the description as a random access device. Also, accessing each cell will incur the same circuit switching time overhead. This is the chip's *'access time'*.

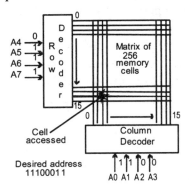

To simplify the diagram, only the address lines are shown. There will also be data lines to transfer data in and out of the cells to the CPU. A data transfer will either be a read operation (the cell's contents are copied on to the data bus) or a write operation (the contents of the data bus are copied into the cells). To instruct the chip on which operation is required, it is fed read/write information on its control lines. If the CPU requires data from memory, it issues a read instruction along with the address to be read. To write data to memory, the CPU places the data on the data bus and issues a write instruction along with the address location.

The diagram shows only a matrix of 256 bits. A practical chip would involve the same architecture, only on a larger scale. The diagram describes a 256 x 1 bit chip, since only one bit at a time can ever be accessed. To read or write a byte, eight of these chips would require to be accessed in parallel. Example commercial DRAMs are 256k x 1 devices, 64k x 4 devices (four 64k devices parallel configured in the same chip) or 1M x 8 devices (a full byte-wide set of 1MB matrix capacity)

Note The cells accessed may contain a program instruction or program data. The circuitry can't distinguish between instructions and data and the programmer has to ensure that the correct addresses are being accessed.

UMA

Unified Memory Architecture is a memory organisation standard set by VESA. Motherboards supporting UMA allow the CPU and video system to share the same pool of main memory. There is no need for video cards to be fitted with 4MB, 8MB or more of their own separate memory, making these cards significantly cheaper. Additionally, chunks of the memory on the current standard video cards are unused when the card is used in low resolution or low colour depths. This may be occurring while there is a real shortage of main memory for user applications and data. With UMA boards, lowering the resolution or colour depth reduces the amount needed by video and the remainder is released for use by programs. Unfortunately, such systems are slower by up to 10% due to the extra processing required to manage the memory and because of the loss of memory from the normal pool available for Windows, applications, etc. UMA provides cheaper but slower computer systems.

AGP

The Accelerated Graphics Port, described in more detail in the *Display Technologies* chapter, is a more modern standard that allows the video card to utilise main memory. Unlike UMA it uses its own high-speed bus to access the RAM, instead of the slower PCI bus. In addition, main memory used by AGP cards is in addition to memory on the video card, not replacing it. Both of these facts make the AGP system much faster than a UMA system. In AGP enabled systems, the BIOS will contain a setting to determine how much RAM the AGP card may use. This is known as the '*Video Memory Aperture*' and is measured in megabytes.

Rom Shadowing

The code inside the system BIOS ROM consists of a set of utilities. The internal POST program checks out the computer hardware on bootup. Thereafter, a set of utilities can be called upon by DOS or by applications. Examples are program code to read a character from the keyboard or write a character to the screen. Similarly, the ROM chip built in to a video card has code to handle the card's screen handling activities. The routines contained in the ROM chips are accessed on a very regular basis but the time required to access code from a ROM is several times longer than accessing data from RAM. If the BIOS code and video code were held and accessed in RAM then their operations would be greatly speeded up and the machine performance would be significantly improved.

Facilities exist to copy the system BIOS and the video ROM code from the ROM chips into normal RAM - a process known as *'ROM Shadowing'*. Shadowing is normally enabled or disabled via the BIOS setup. The BIOS setup normally allows for either only enabling the System BIOS or only enabling the video BIOS code, or enabling both. The chosen ROM code is copied into unused areas in the system area (i.e. 640k to 1MB).

Memory Usage

The main memory of a PC is used for a variety of purposes. The following chart shows the main allocations of RAM; see the memory management section for more details.

Type	Summary
Environment	Part of main memory that is set aside for storing information about the current prompt, search paths and user-defined variables.
User Area	Also known as Base Memory and Conventional Memory. All DOS programs and parts of Windows applications run in this area. Extends from address 0 to 640k.
UMA (Upper Memory Area)	Also known as the System Area and the High DOS area. Extends from 640k to 1MB and is used by the ROM BIOS chip and the ROM chips that are fitted on expansion cards. The parts not used by ROMs are available to provide the window into Expanded Memory, with unused areas being called Upper Memory Blocks (see below).
UMBs (Upper Memory Blocks)	Unused areas of the UMA. Can be used to store device drivers and TSRs if the machine has been memory managed.
EMS (Expanded Memory)	The original way to create extra memory beyond the 1MB limit. A block of memory (often chips on a separate card) can have a part of its contents viewed at any one time through a *'window'* in the UMA. No longer used, but emulated for very old programs.
HMA (High Memory Area)	The first 64k block of memory above the 1MB boundary. Used to store part of DOS when the system is memory managed.
XMS (Extended Memory)	The area of memory above 1MB. Used by Windows and by a wide range of utilities such as disk caches, ram drives, print spooling, etc.

Memory Categories

A summary of the main memory definitions is given below; these are explained in greater detail later.

Type	Summary
DRAM (Dynamic Random Access Memory	Once was the only type used for main memory. It is used for the User Area, System Area and both Extended and Expanded Memory.
SRAM (Static RAM)	Fast access memory normally used for caching inside the CPU (see below).
NVRAM	Non-volatile RAM. A term used to describe any method of retaining memory contents without a power supply, such as EEPROM or battery-powered chips.
EDO	Extended Data Out. A newer, faster alternative to DRAM chips. EDO SIMMs have access times of 50ns, 60ns or 70ns.
BEDO	Burst Mode EDO memory. Sends a group of data bytes to the CPU without involving the CPU in much of the process. Faster than ordinary EDO memory.
SDRAM	Synchronous DRAM. Keeps the CPU and memory timed in step, thereby minimising the control signals between them and greatly increasing data transfer rates compared to both DRAM and EDO.
SGRAM	An even faster version of SDRAM that can operate in burst mode for both write and read operations (SDRAM can only read in burst mode).
VRAM (Video RAM)	A dual-port memory technology used in some video cards to speed up screen updates.
WRAM	Windows RAM. Developed by Samsung for video cards. It is dual-ported like VRAM but supports a block write mode for faster data rates.

Multibank DRAM (MDRAM)	20ns access time memory. A cheaper alternative to SRAM for caching and a faster alternative to DRAM for video cards.
Rambus (RDRAM)	A serial access memory technology able to transfer data at 600 to 800MHz. Synchronised to the bus clock and provides data on both edges of the signal.
DDR (Double Data Rate)	A type of SDRAM that is able to transmit data on both the rising and falling edges of the clock cycle, theoretically doubling data throughput.
PC Modules	A PC Module is a modern memory module that is designed to cope with a specific bus speed and throughput rate, as indicated by the PC number, such as 'PC133'.
Cache RAM (Level 1)	Memory built in to a CPU and sitting between the CPU and external memory to speed up data access. In modern processors the cache RAM runs at the speed of the processor core, and is used to cache machine code micro-operations.
Cache RAM (Level 2)	Initially found on the motherboard, modern PCs have L2 cache on the CPU, also clocked to the processor core, and used to buffer data from memory.
CMOS RAM	Small block of additional memory is used to store information about the computer (e.g. type of drives in use, amount of memory in the machine, etc.).
ROM BIOS	The ROM chip fitted in every PC. When the machine is switched on, it tests the system and loads DOS.
BIOS Extensions	The ROM chips that are fitted to add-on cards to control their operations (e.g. video cards or disk controller cards).

Memory Types

A range of memory products exists, with differing characteristics. However, there are two basic types:

- Those whose contents can only be read, during the running of a program. Some memory's contents may be permanent, while other memory chips may be removed from the computer and re-programmed. Examples of this type are ROM, PROM, EPROM and EEPROM.
- Those whose contents can be read and also written to. Examples are DRAM, SRAM and EDO.

Apart from the above characteristics, memory can be graded in terms of capacity and speed of access. Take, for example, a memory chip that is coded as in the illustration.

The first two digits indicate the product range, the rest of the numbers before the hyphen indicating the chip capacity (in kilobits). The numbers after the hyphen indicate the chip access time, where 60 means 60 nano-seconds and 70 means 70ns. The example is a 256k, 60ns chip, probably one of several located on an old SIMM chip. Note however that there is some variation in labelling (if the chips are even labelled at all).

41256-60

ROM

These are 'Read Only Memory' chips and they are 'non-volatile'; their contents will not be lost if the power is removed. These chips are used in a wide range of electronic control circuits, from industrial machine tools to domestic washing machines. They are also the ideal choice for computer control. A computer's control programs require to be non-volatile.   The computer's basic functions are controlled by system software and there is a potential Catch-22 situation, in that

"the computer needs a program to be loaded, so that the computer can load a program"

By placing part of the operating system software into a ROM chip, the system BIOS, the basic machine control programs are available to be run as soon as the computer is switched on. The programs in the ROM provide the machine's basic input and output functions, to allow application programs to be loaded and run.   Unfortunately, if the system is to be updated, the BIOS chip has to be replaced with a new chip that contains the new program routines. This requires opening the computer case and is a job for experienced support staff or technicians.   As a result ROM BIOS chips have been replaced by EEPROM, or 'Flash ROM' which allow BIOS updates to be carried out in software.

ROM chips are 'mask programmed' devices; the layers of the integrated circuit are manufactured using specifically designed masks. These produce chips that are only capable of performing the required pre-determined programs.   Due to the cost of manufacturing ROMs, they are only used in large quantity runs. This, in turn, means that they are only made when the manufacturer is certain that the programs they contain are debugged.   These chips are also fitted in video, network and disk controller cards.

PROM

This stands for 'Programmable Read Only Memory'.   With ROM, the internal program is dedicated at the production stage; the physical construction of the chip reflects the program that it stores. A cheaper method for small and medium scale use is a ROM-type chip that can be programmed, after the construction stage. Such chips are mass-produced by a chip manufacturer, who has no idea of the use to which they will be put. Once a computer manufacturer purchases the chip, the company's programs can be embedded in it. This is achieved by *'blowing'* fusible links inside the chip, to form the binary codes representing the program's machine code instructions. Every intact link represents a binary 1, with a blown link representing a binary 0. Like the ROM, the PROM chip is also non-volatile.

EPROM

The initials stand for *'Erasable Programmable Read Only Memory'* and it was introduced as a development tool. The problem with ROM and a programmed PROM was that, once produced, they were unalterable. This is perfectly fine for a computer manufacturer - once the program contents are fully debugged. The EPROM is used to test the program. Like PROM, its links are blown to the needs

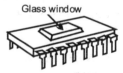

Glass window

of the test program. The EPROM can then be used on the test computer. If the program is satisfactory, it can be used to create mass ROM or PROM versions. If the program needs alteration, the EPROM is subjected to ultra-violet light for a few minutes. This 'heals' the ruptured links, allowing the chip to be blown to the next test program. The blowing and wiping clean process can be repeated many times over, before the chip fabric starts to degenerate. An EPROM chip is easily identified as it has a glass window on top of the chip to allow entry of the ultra-violet light. Due to its more expensive construction, it is only a viable alternative to ROM and EPROM for small-scale use. Example EPROM chips would be the 2764-20 (64k - i.e. 8k x 8 bits) and the 27512-20 (512k - i.e. 64k x 8 bits). The equipment required to program and erase EPROMs can be cheap enough for individual or hobbyist use. For continual development use, the EPROM is often replaced with a *'ROM emulator'*. This is a piece of equipment that plugs into the ROM socket and acts like an EPROM. It contains RAM to avoid the program-erase cycles. Since it is self-powered, it appears to the main computer as a piece of ROM.

EEPROM

A variation on the EPROM is the **EEPROM** - the *'Electrically Erasable and Programmable Read Only Memory'*. Like EPROM, it has holds its contents when the power is removed. However, its contents can be overwritten without resorting to prior cleaning with ultra-violet light. This type of chip is used in many *'flash'* memory devices. The SmartMedia range of cards used in digital cameras and MP3 players, for example, are EEPROM based.

Main Memory

The variations on ROM memory outlined earlier are primarily concerned with the computer's basic control functions, with application programs being loaded from disk into main memory.   However, this is not always the case. Many palmtop computers use ROM to store application programs, to overcome the storage problems associated with such small machines. Due to their tiny physical dimensions, there is no space for a hard disk to store application software. So, the machine stores a word processor, spreadsheet, personal organiser, etc. in ROM. In most computers, however, the application software is loaded into, and run from, main memory.   In addition, there is a need for an area to store program data and video data. These memory areas use RAM, which stands for *'Random Access Memory'*.   Unlike ROM technology, RAM chips are volatile which means that the data stored in the chips only remains there as long as the chips are powered. When the machine is switched off, the chips lose their contents. That is why users are always reminded to save all their data before switching off their machines. In fact, to ensure complete data integrity, the application should be exited, i.e. getting back to the DOS prompt, before switching off. This ensures that any data held in the computer's memory buffers are flushed away to disk. A database, for example, will not save each record as it is entered; it will save a number of records into a buffer area and then save the groups of records.   Although they appear to the user as having been saved, they are still vulnerable to loss, if the power is switched off.   The term *'random access'* is used to distinguish it from serial access devices. With serial access devices, such as tapes, the data is read in with one item following the other. The last item takes longer to fetch than the first item. Random access means that any cell address in the entire memory area can be accessed with a uniform time overhead.

NOTE Confusingly, ROM chips are also random access devices. The difference between ROM and RAM variants is not in their access methods, but in their volatility (or lack of it) and speed.

RAM Types

Computers use two types of RAM. These are termed Dynamic Ram and Static RAM and they have differing constructions and characteristics.   These characteristics include, speed complexity and cost. The speed of the chip is termed its *'Access time'* and is measured in nano-seconds (i.e. 10 to the power minus 9). Both types use arrays of transistor switches to store the binary data. The main difference lies in how the transistors are switched and it is this that affects the chips' characteristics.

Note : Both types use different circuitry and are therefore <u>not</u> interchangeable. Static RAM cannot be plugged into sockets intended for Dynamic RAM and vice versa.

DRAM

Dynamic Ram, or DRAM, is commonly used for the computer's main memory. An incoming data signal with logic level *'on'* (i.e. logic 1) to a cell is used to charge a capacitor, which holds the transistor in its switched state.   The charge in this capacitor quickly leaks away and the transistor would lose its information.   To prevent this, the capacitor has to be constantly *'refreshed'*. The contents of the capacitor have to be read on a regular basis. If it contains a value, the capacitor is fully re-charged to maintain its *'on'* state.   When an incoming logic level wishes to store an *'off'* state (i.e. logic level 0), the capacitor is discharged.

With a main memory of 640k, and 8 cells to every byte, this involves reading and writing to 5,242,880 different cells.   If the machine has a 128MB memory, then over a billion cells have to be refreshed regularly.   For this reason, DRAM - despite technological improvements - is a relatively slow memory system.

120ns or 150ns would be considered as slow access times for modern DRAM, while 70ns or 80ns would be average and 60ns would be considered fast.   Example DRAM chips are:

> 4164-12   with 64k x1 bit organisation and a speed of 120nS
>
> 44256-70 with 256k x 1 bit organisation and 70nS access time
>
> 41256-60 with 256k x 1 bit organisation and 60nS access time

IBM produce a 256MB DRAM and Hitachi produce a 2GB DRAM. On a practical note, modern DRAM uses a simple 5V or 3.3V supply. Earlier DRAM needed both 5V and –5V. The move to single sided DRAM means that a modern motherboard can work with only +5 and +12V supplies, although the RS232 ports will be compromised.

SRAM

Static RAM, or SRAM, does not use the capacitive method. Each cell represents a single bit and the value is held by a more complex set of transistors that are configured as a bistable (commonly called a *'flip-flop'*).   The output of this flip-flop can be 'set' or 'reset', to store either a binary 0 or a binary 1.   In this chip, the cell's state will maintain itself, until it is either altered by a new value, or has its power removed. There is no need to constantly refresh the cells' contents.   The result is that the static RAM chip is significantly faster than dynamic RAM. An access time of 10ns or more would be considered slow, while 5ns would be average and 2ns would be considered fast.

Static RAMs have one major drawback.   They require a more complex structure, with a greater component count for each cell.   As a result, the fastest static RAM is larger and much more expensive than dynamic RAM.   For this reason, it is not used for the main memory chips of the computer.   They are, instead, used for fast cache memory (see later section).   Most SRAM chips are of the DIL (dual in line) or SIL (single in-line) type and are of the SIMM (single in-line memory module) or SIP (single in-line package) variety.

NVRAM

Non-Volatile RAM, as its name suggests, is memory storage that does not lose its contents when the computer (or any other device that uses memory) is switched off. The two main types of NVRAM technology in use are battery-powered SRAM, such as that used in CMOS data storage; and EEPROM chips, such as those used in Flash memory cards. Other NVRAM technologies are in development for commercial use, such as FRAM – Ferromagnetic RAM, which uses magnetic cores to store data.

NVRAM technologies are used in Flash BIOS chips, and as storage for digital cameras, MP3 players and so on. Examples include Sony's Memory Stick, SmartMedia, and CompactFlash.

Speeding Up Access

There are a number of ways that have been developed to improve on the access times produced by the basic method described earlier.

These include:

Fast Page Mode Access

The normal basic access method splits the incoming address value into a Row Address and a Column Address. Where access to the memory is random (i.e. an incoming address is completely different from the previous address accessed) the process already described has to be undertaken. However, there are many times when the access is sequential (i.e. the data to be fetched consists of a block of contiguous addresses). Examples of sequential access would be fetching graphics data or a block of text. With sequential access there is no need to recalculate the Row Address for each cell and a block of data can be accessed by changing the Column Address values alone. The data fetched is known as a *'page'* and is accessed at a faster rate than conventional methods.

Interleaving

This also speeds up sequential accesses and is achieved by splitting the memory up into two or four separate banks. All digital circuits move between high and low states and, after being switched, need a specific time to recover before being switched again. This slows down memory access rates. With interleaved systems, sequential data is stored over the various memory banks. This means that one bank can be accessed while the previous bank is in recovery time. This reduces waiting time and increases sequential data access rates. It also allows banks to perform read/write operations at the same time.

Synchronous Operation

Normal DRAM works asynchronously - the CPU and the memory chips have to use an elaborate set of signals to control data operations. The time to generate these signals and the time for the signals to be recognised impose time delays upon the data transaction. Synchronous operation ties the CPU and the memory in step with the same clock. This eliminates the need for much of the handshaking signals and the generation by the CPU of a wanted address location results in the transfer of a copy of the location's contents without the need of any further CPU to memory communication. Commonly used with Pentium cache RAM (486s used asynchronous cache), it is now appearing for use with main memory.

Fast Access Memory Types

Ranges of memory chips take advantage of the above techniques, and others, to improve memory performance. These memory types currently are:

EDO RAM

This stands for *'Extended Data Out'* memory and is used both for main memory and in video cards as a replacement for VRAM (see below). It is an extended version of page-mode working. With normal page-access memory, the data is removed from the chip's output buffer when the Column Address line is de-activated. With EDO, the data stays available while the chip is getting set up for the next access. Access delays are reduced in this way and a complete memory transaction can take place in a single clock cycle instead of the normal two clock cycles. This will not double the chip's overall speed, since it only improves sequential access times. Overall, typical speed improvements of 5% to 10% are expected. Can't be used in 386s, 486s or older Pentiums. Available as 72-pin SIMMs or 168-pin DIMM versions (at 3.3v or 5v).

BEDO

Burst Mode EDO memory was essentially EDO with the addition of burst mode operation plus some tweaks to the memory access cycle. Only supported by the FX chipset.

VRAM

This is a variation on DRAM chips, where normal data write operations and constant sequential reads occur at the same time. This is especially useful for video memory and is explained in the chapter on Computer Video.

SDRAM

Synchronous DRAM uses synchronous working as outlined earlier. For even faster working, it also uses both interleaving and burst mode techniques. This ensures speeds up to 100MHz, in burst mode, compared to EDO's 50MHz maximum speed and BEDO's 66MHz maximum. Because of its reliance on its clock speed, SDRAM performance is measured in MHz. Current chips are roughly equivalent to 5-15ns access times.

WRAM

Windows RAM was developed by Samsung especially for use in video cards. It is dual-ported like VRAM but supports a block write mode for faster data rates.

MDRAM

Multibank RAM applies the interleaving technique for main memory to second level cache memory to provide a cheaper and faster alternative to SRAM. The chip splits its memory capacity into small blocks of 256k and allows operations to two different banks in a single clock cycle.

SGRAM

The *'Synchronous Graphics Ram'* is an even faster version of SDRAM that can operate in burst mode for both write and read operations (SDRAM can only read in burst mode).   This increased writing speed is very important in graphics applications.   They have 10ns, 12ns and 15ns access times.

RDRAM

Dispenses with the page mode type of interface in favour of a very fast serial interface operating at 800Mbps. This *'Rambus'* interface is a fast local bus between CPUs, graphics controllers and block-oriented memory. Currently adopted for some Nintendo machines and destined to find its way into the PC market.

DDR SDRAM

Originally developed for video cards, DDR is a type of SDRAM that has recently become cost-effective enough for main memory. In the best situations, it can transmit data on both the rising and falling edges of the clock pulse. However in real situations this is rarely achieved.

Chip Connection Types

RAM and ROM chips are available in a variety of different physical constructions as follows.

DIP

Dual in-line packages; sometimes also known as DILs.   These are the traditional outline for industry logic chips and other integrated circuits and were used on early PCs. They are rectangular blocks with connecting pins down two opposite sides. The pins can be soldered directly on to the computer motherboard, or plugged into board-mounted receptacles, called *'I.C. sockets'*.   The diagram shows an example, although there may be more pins, depending on the amount of address lines and data lines required.

SIPs

The SIP (Single In-line Pin package) is found in older models. It is very similar in its construction to the SIMM board, except that its connections are to a row of pins instead of a row of printed circuit pads. These pins are then plugged into a special socket on the motherboard or soldered into place.

SIMMs

The *'Single In-line Memory Module'* is the standard for most machines and consists of a set of memory chips mounted on a small printed circuit board.   There are most commonly eight or nine chips on the board, dependent on whether parity checking is in use. The board has an edge connector similar, although smaller, to that used on add-on cards.   The

memory board plugs into a special set of slots on the motherboard. Since the board is clipped into place, it provides a more secure connection than earlier DIP chips.   The constant heating and cooling of memory chips made them regularly expand and contract until they sometimes popped out of their holders - an effect known as *'chip creep'*. This is avoided with SIMMs making their use more reliable. SIMMs are available in two basic types - 30-pin and 72-pin; this refers to the numbers of pads on the edge connector.

30-Pin SIMM

These are mainly used with now obsolete PCs such as 286's to 486's.   Each SIMM board has an 8-bit data width, with an extra ninth bit if parity is used. SIMM boards are used in sets of four, to connect to a 32-bit data bus.   Chips used on SIMM boards advertised as *'1 x 8'* indicates that it is of 1MB capacity - i.e. 1 mega-bit times 8.   When used in sets of eight, each chip stores a single bit of each data byte. The more common *'1 x 9'* board uses nine chips, with the extra bit included for parity checking. Newer *'composite'* SIMMs use improved chips that replace three conventional memory chips.   Thus, a 3-chip board and a 9-chip board both provide the same amount of memory but with different chips on the board. These boards, despite having the same capacity, are not usually interchangeable.

72-Pin SIMM

These are used with some 386DX's, some 486's and older Pentiums.   They are supplied with 8 or 9 chips on the board.   They have a 32-bit data width and will have four extra bits if parity is being used.

The extra pins to the board carry the address lines and control lines from the motherboard.   It can be thought of as four separate 8-bit chips used to construct a 32-bit wide data path. So, a chip advertised as *'1 x 32 '* indicates that it is of 4MB capacity - i.e. 1 mega-bit

30-pin	72-pin	Parity	Access Time
x8	x32	No	70ns
x9	x36	Yes	70ns
-	EDO	No	60ns

times 32, divided by 8.   Similarly, a *'1 x 36'* is a 4MB chip including parity checking.   An *'8 x 32'* is a 32MB SIMM while an *'8 x36'* is a 32MB SIMM with parity.   72 pin SIMMs are available in 1MB, 2MB, 4MB, 8MB, 16MB, 32MB and 64MB varieties.

SIMM Banks

Motherboards provide slots for inserting SIMMs and these groups of slots are known as *'SIMM banks'*. The motherboard manual should be consulted, as different configurations are possible.
For example:

386/486

The average 386/486 motherboard has eight 30-pin SIMM slots and the slots can be configured to take either 256k, 1MB or 4MB modules. Most motherboards split the eight slots into two banks of four slots. The four slots in the bank must be populated and the four SIMM boards fitted must be of the same type.   It is not possible, for example, to have two 4MB modules and two 1MB modules in the bank.   There would have to be four 4MB modules or four 1MB modules.   This is because a 32-bit data bus width needs to connect to 32 bits of RAM.   Since each 30-pin SIMM provides 8 bits, four boards allow the full 32 bits of data to be accessed at the same time.   If data was accessed a byte at a time, it would require four separate memory accesses to build up a 32-bit data word, resulting in much slower transfer rates.   Some other models, including Pentium motherboards, have only two banks of 2 slots.

Some boards also demand that the configuration of the second bank be identical to that used in the first bank.   So, if the first bank contained four 2MB modules, the second bank would also have to contain four 2MB modules.   Some motherboards provide jumpers so that the second bank can have a different configuration from the first bank.   This allows the first bank to have, for example, four 2MB modules while the second bank has four 1MB modules - giving a total of 12MB.   If this flexibility is not allowed on the motherboard, then upgrading memory can be expensive, as SIMM boards may have to be discarded to allow higher capacity boards to replace them.

It is also important that each SIMM board uses chips with the same access times. If SIMMs have different access speeds, the computer will either operate at the speed of the slowest board or the system may crash if the BIOS has not been configured for the slowest speed.

Since the 486 has a 32-bit data width, it can be fitted with a single 72-pin SIMM.

Pentiums

The Pentium has a 64-bit data bus and requires two 32-bit SIMMs be fitted at a time. The two SIMMs must be of the same capacity - i.e. using two 16MB SIMMs provides 32MB of main memory. Although all Pentiums support 72-pin SIMMs, there are variations in the type of memory supported by particular motherboards.   Try to avoid mixing parity and non-parity SIMMs. Fitting parity SIMMs to non-parity motherboards will probably crash the system; fitting non-parity SIMMs to a parity system will probably disable the parity checking of existing parity SIMMs.   Try to avoid mixing memory speeds as adding a slower SIMM usually brings the whole bank down to its access speeds.   It is usually possible to mix pairs of SIMMs- e.g. one pair of 16MB and a pair of 4MB.   VX and HX chipsets allow each bank to have different memory types (e.g. FPM in one bank and EDO in another bank) and run each bank at its best speed.   FX chipsets allow the mixing of EDO and FPM in the same bank, with all SIMMs being treated as FPM. Some early Pentiums used 30-pin SIMMs.

FPM and EDO SIMMs are identical in appearance. To find out what is currently installed on a computer either check the motherboard manual, use a SIMM tester (this may involve visiting a repair shop) or watch the messages on booting up the computer. Many BIOS chips will produce a message such as *"BANK 0 : EDO"* if EDO installed.

DIMMs

Standard now in most computers is the *'Dual In-line Memory Module'*. It is a 168-pin module that has electrical contacts on both side of the board. It has a greater reliability than SIMMs and is available as a 64-bit non-parity or as a 72-bit parity device. This 64-bit data width directly matches the Pentium's data bus width, allowing a single DIMM to be fitted. Since the system requires fewer memory slots, the motherboard can have a more compact layout. The extra 8 bits on a 72-bit module are used for storing error detection data, such as parity or ECC (see later).

DIMM boards are most commonly fitted with SDRAM chips. Using DIMMs does not in itself lead to any speed improvement, as it is only a connection type. It is the use of SDRAM on DIMMs with interleaving that makes these particular DIMMs faster. DIMMs appear in both rare 5v and common 3.3v versions. They

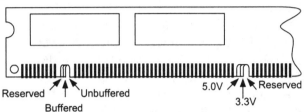

also appear in both the common unbuffered version, or with additional chips that buffer the memory from the data bus. Older DIMMs were available with built-in buffering chips but became out of favour on newer modules as the buffering chips slowed down data access.

Since 3.3v modules must not be used in a 5v system, the modules have different notch spacings. This prevents damage caused by inserting the wrong memory module type. Similarly, the notch spacings prevent buffered and unbuffered modules from being incorrectly inserted.

Older motherboards had both SIMM and DIMM slots but were often incapable of using both at the same time. In these cases, the manual should be consulted, as some or all of the SIMMs may have to be removed to allow the DIMM to function. Modern motherboards come with DIMM slots or RIMM slots only.

As the speed of DRAM and in particular SDRAM increased the manufacturers stopped referring to the speed of memory parts in nanoseconds (nS). A series of standard memory speeds was proposed by Intel and adopted by the industry for SDRAM. Standard DIMMs are therefore available in PC66, PC100 and PC133 varieties, according to the bus speed.

With the adoption of Rambus & RIMMS, and the introduction of DDR memory as system memory, it is unlikely that conventional SDRAM will progress beyond the PC133 specification. Although there are still systems using SDRAM on sale, the most recently produced systems use RDRAM or DDR DIMMS.

DDR DIMMs

Double Data Rate DIMMs are now used in some motherboards. They use DDR SDRAM chips as described earlier. However, this necessitates the use of a DDR capable chipset and motherboard, so it is important to distinguish DDR DIMMs from other types. As a result the DDR DIMM has only one notch, making it physically incompatible with standard DIMM slots, and uses 184 pins.

The names given to DDR chips, as shown in the table below, do not refer to the clock speed as with other 'PC' class memory specifications. Instead they refer to the total bandwidth in kilobytes transferred per second. Thus, a DDR DIMM using an effective bus speed of 200MHz is listed as PC1600 instead of PC200. This was done in order to make DDR DIMMs more attractive in comparison to RIMM memory such as PC800. Note however that this is not measured in Megabytes per second but in millions of bytes per second. With a bus size of 8 bytes and an effective bus speed of 200MHz, the system can transfer up to 1600 million bits per second, but this has to be divided by 1024 to get Kbps, and by 1024 again to get Mbps.

DDR is not generally as fast as RAMBUS memory, but it is considerably cheaper, and is likely to become quite popular as a result.

RIMMs

The *'Rambus'* memory technology is also called RIMM, which according to the Rambus Corporation does <u>not</u> stand for 'Rambus In-line Memory Module' but is simply a name to distinguish the technology. It is very similar to a DIMM connection. It is also a 184-pin module that has electrical contacts on both side of the board. It is specifically designed for RDRAM, and DIMMs and RIMMs are not inter-changeable - a RIMM will not fit in a DIMM slot and vice versa.

RIMMs use RAMBUS technology. This is an extremely fast but essentially serial technology, as opposed to the more usual parallel arrangement. This is because it was originally developed to suit the setup of Nintendo games machines. The typical RIMM system provides four RIMM sockets. Each socket must contain either a RIMM module or a so-called RIMM continuity (or C-RIMM) module. This continuity module is just a short circuit to allow serial memory signals to pass through. New motherboards that have RIMM sockets fitted come with RIMM continuity modules as part of the supplied hardware kit.

Due to the bus structure of a RIMM module, the system has to ensure a consistent memory speed. This is achieved by delaying the response from electrically closer chips to allow further chips to 'catch up'. Thus, a RIMM system will respond slower the more memory that is installed. RIMMs also transfer data in 16-bit chunks instead of 64 bits like DIMMs. However, even with all this in mind, RIMM is generally faster than DIMM. This is in large part due to the high speed of the bus. The types of RIMM that are used in PCs (as opposed to consoles) can reach 800MHz, and RIMMs used with Pentium 4 motherboards utilise dual channels to double throughput again. This is achieved through the Intel i850 chipset – see the Architecture chapter for more details.

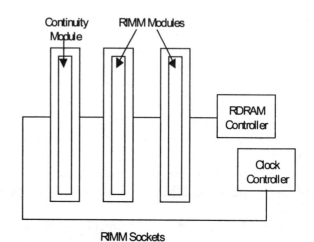

RIMM Sockets

However, with such high speeds, the RIMM chips heat up quite quickly, so they come with metal heat spreaders over the chips. RIMMS therefore look quite different to the previous memory technologies, although they are still using multiple chips inside.

SO-DIMMs and SO-RIMMs

In Notebooks, DIMMs and RIMMs take up too much valuable space. For this reason many notebooks use Small Outline (SO) DIMM and RIMM sockets, which are functionally the same.

Chip Capacity

Memory chips come in a range of capacities, but the following table shows the most common varieties:

Chip type	Typical lower capacity	Typical higher capacity
30-pin SIMM	8 x 64K chips (512KB)	8 x 256K chips (2MB)
72-pin SIMM	8 x 256K chips (2MB)	8 x 4MB chips (32MB)
168-pin DIMM	8 x 2M chips (16MB)	8 x 16M chips (128MB)
184-pin RIMM	8x 4M chips (32MB)	8 x 32M chips (256MB)

Chip Speeds

The table shows the expected performance from the range of memory types:

Standard	Chip Type	Socket type	Physical bus Speed	Effective bus speed	Bus size	Max. Data throughput	Equivalent period
Typical 72-pin SIMM	EDO	SIMM	33MHz	33MHz	32 bits (4 bytes)	63MBps	60ns
PC66	SDR	DIMM	66MHz	66MHz	64 bits (8 bytes)	503MBps	15ns
PC100	SDR	DIMM	100MHz	100MHz	64 bits (8 bytes)	763MBps	10ns
PC133	SDR	DIMM	133MHz	133MHz	64 bits (8 bytes)	1014MBps	7.5ns
PC1600	DDR	DIMM	100 MHz	200MHz	64 bits (8 bytes)	1525MBps	5ns
PC2100	DDR	DIMM	133 MHz	266MHz	64 bits (8 bytes)	2029MBps	3.7ns
PC800	RDRAM	RIMM	800MHz	800MHz	16 bits (2 bytes)	1525MBps	1.2ns
Dual channel PC800	RDRAM	RIMM	800MHz	800MHz	32 bits (4 bytes)	3050MBps	1.2ns

Comparative memory chip sizes

The diagrams below show the outline and size of the common range of memory modules.

These diagrams are full-scale, allowing a chip to be laid on the page to determine its type.

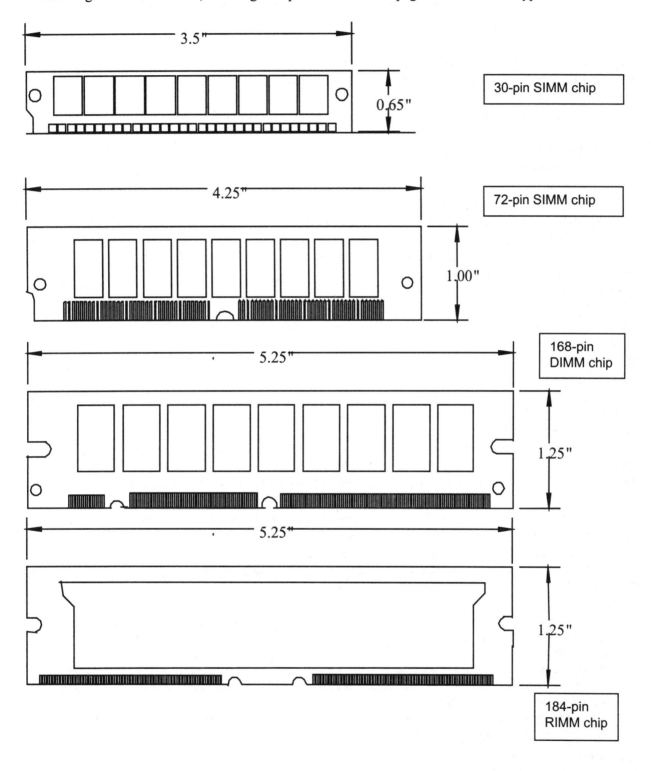

30-pin SIMM chip

72-pin SIMM chip

168-pin DIMM chip

184-pin RIMM chip

Data Integrity

The movement of data in and out of memory is carried out by the 'memory controller'. This circuitry can be configured to check the integrity of the data being held in memory. Lower-end models tend to have no integrity checking, mid-range systems tended to have parity checking, while top-end systems such as network servers have ECC (see later). With the production of ever more reliable memory chips, parity has tended to be dropped, leaving ECC provided on systems requiring the ultimate in reliability (known as *'mission critical'* systems).

Parity

Many machines have built-in parity bit writing and parity checking. This technique attempts to ensure that the data stored in any particular memory location is identical to the original data written and has not been accidentally altered by:

- electrical disturbances (such as transients - i.e. spikes - on the power)
- faulty RAM chips

Faulty memory chips are detected during the POST (Power On Self Test) when the ROM BIOS tests out the system when it is switched on or given a hard reset. Other memory problems, such as power surges, can occur <u>during</u> the user's session and these can cause the alteration of some memory contents. It is these problems that parity checking is designed to detect.

Users see memory as being a byte in width. The eight bits of the byte are used to store the program data. In fact, parity memory attaches a ninth bit to each data byte. This is the *'parity bit'*. When data is written to memory, a count is made of all the binary 'one' bits in the data byte. If the total is odd, then the parity bit is set to one, otherwise it is set to zero. This is an automatic process by the motherboard circuitry. When the data comes to be read, the same calculation on the byte's contents is made prior to sending it to the CPU. If the calculated parity contents are different from the value in the parity bit, then an error is known to have occurred and an error message is given to the user. If

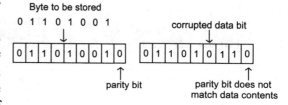

the expected value and the stored value are identical, it is likely that the data is unchanged (this is not guaranteed, since a number of bits in the byte could have been altered and still produce the same parity value as the original data).

In the example illustration, the value 01101001 is being stored in a memory location. It has an even number of binary 1's, so the parity bit is set to 0. If the data is corrupted as shown in the second diagram, there would be five binary 1's, which should result in a 1 in the parity bit. Since the parity bit contains a 0, the error is detected.

A single bit parity is not foolproof, since the corruption of two bits in a byte might render a correct parity check even though the byte is corrupted. As a result, it is not supported by some older motherboards; parity SIMMS can be fitted but the parity bit will be ignored.

Note that if the data were altered due to a permanent fault on the chip, the computer would detect the faulty address when it makes its self-test on being powered up.

Practical Examples

With 72-pin SIMM memory modules, data is organised on 32-bit width and each byte of the 32-bit word would have its own parity bit. A DIMM module with parity uses 64 bits for data storage and a further 8 bits for parity storage. Modules are often quoted as *'x64'* for non-parity versions and *'x72'* for parity versions.

As a consequence of using parity checking, memory modules are often populated with chips in groups of nine. For example, nine 1M x 1 chips would use eight of the chips to produce 1MB of storage (1M x 8 bits) while the ninth chip is used to store the parity for each byte.

A non-parity system can be fitted with parity RAM; the parity bits are simply not used. However, a parity system has to be fitted with parity RAM or it will not work.

Fake Parity

A simple check was used to determine whether a SIMM was parity or non-parity. A two or eight chip SIMM was non-parity while three or nine chip SIMMs were parity types.

However, a few SIMMs have been used on parity motherboards that utilise *'fake parity'* or *'logic parity'*. This reduces the price of the SIMM by not providing the extra memory to store the parity bits. Writes to the SIMM discard the parity calculations since it cannot store them. During memory reads, the SIMM generates the correct parity bit expected by the motherboard.   The motherboard is fooled into thinking that parity checking has been carried out and no memory errors have been found.

ECC

Parity circuits are designed to detect memory errors; they are unable to correct them.   The Error Correction Code (ECC) system, also known as *'Error Checking and Control'*, detects and corrects single bit errors.   A five-bit error checking code is used to provide reliable detection of corruption.   Since there is great detail in the checking code, the information can be used to restore the data byte to its original value.   Any corrections are made without the user even knowing that a problem had occurred; it will not produce error messages.   ECC systems will also detect multiple bit errors. Unlike parity systems, ECC will detect multiple bit errors where two bits appear to self-cancel (i.e. one bit changes from 0 to 1 while another bit changes from 1 to 0).   It does this by using a Cyclic Redundancy Check, (or CRC) which is a special type of mathematical polynomial, implemented in binary. The same CRC system is used to ensure data integrity on Hard Disks, CD-ROMs, Networks and serial communications systems.

Practical Examples

Two SIMMs that are x36 (i.e. 36 width bus) or a single x72 DIMM module provides a total bus width of 72 bits. Of these, 64 bits are used for data transfer and 8 bits are used for ECC information.   However, x36 and x72 chips are also commonly used for parity systems.   In these cases, the way the integrity locations are used depends upon whether the memory controller works on a parity or an ECC system.

CMOS

CMOS (Complementary Metal Oxide Semiconductor) is a low power consumption memory chip.   In PCs, it consists of a small block of additional memory that is used to store information about the computer (e.g. type of drives in use, amount of memory in the machine, etc.).

It is not part of the computer's memory map and is associated with the computer's real-time clock chip. The real-time clock is always supplied with power as it has its own rechargeable battery.   This means that the contents of the CMOS will remain, even when the power is switched off.   The CMOS ensures that the details of the machine's configuration are always available when the machine is first booted up. It is also the reason that the PC knows the time and date when it is first started.

The contents of the CMOS memory can be altered via the BIOS setup procedure offered during bootup. Depending upon the BIOS type, pressing the Delete key or the f1 key during bootup will take the user into the BIOS setup routine.

Breaking the 1MB barrier

As mentioned previously, the early PCs could only address 1MB of main memory due to their 20-bit address bus.   Apart from memory addressability, IBM made a design decision that has affected PC development ever since.   It decided that the top of the map should be given over to system use.   There was no problem with the XT range.   Their processors could address 1MB and their boards allowed for the fitting of up to 1MB of ROM/RAM.   The restrictions became clear when the processor range was upgraded.   The 80286 chip had a 24-bit address bus, capable of accessing 16 million different memory locations; the Pentium chips have 64-bit address buses, capable of accessing 64GB of memory. Memory chips are now comparatively cheap and extra memory can easily be fitted to the motherboard.

This extra memory could have been accessed with relative ease - if only IBM had decided that the system area would be located at the bottom of the memory map.   As it stands, there cannot be a contiguous block of memory, since the 384k system block breaks up the user memory area.   This causes difficulties for programmers and hardware manufacturers alike.

IBM must privately regret the impediment they have inflicted on their own product range.   There is no technical difficulty in producing a PC product with a different memory map.   The system area could be placed at the bottom of the memory map, allowing limitless future expansion above it.   The problem is not one of technology; it is one of compatibility.   No existing software or add-ons would work with this new machine and this has been the deciding factor in maintaining the present architecture - warts and all. All subsequent PC hardware and software developments struggle to get the best from this bad situation.

Note: The following pages explain the operation of a computer system running DOS-based applications and games.   All newer games and all Windows 95 and later applications use a memory management system that automatically handles extended memory, while hiding its operations from the user.

XMS and EMS

The attempts to increase memory addressability, while still living with the current architecture, have revolved around the development of Extended Memory and Expanded Memory.

- With XMS, the extra memory is added to the memory map above the 1MB line.
- With EMS, the memory consists of banks of memory that can slot into the existing DOS memory area.

The 1MB area is commonly known as *'conventional memory'*.

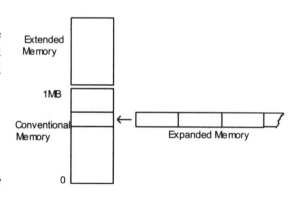

Extended Memory

Extended memory is memory that is mapped to the addresses above 1MB. It is mostly known as *'XMS'*, for Microsoft's e**X**tended **M**emory **S**pecification. XMS cannot be used with 8088 or 8086 machines, since they are only capable of addressing 1MB. For machines from the 80286 on, there is the alternative of the Extended Memory system. These computers make use of extended memory for purposes such as:

Making better use of conventional memory

DOS 5 onwards and utilities such as PC KWIK, Above Disk, QEMM, etc. use extended memory to hold parts of the DOS kernel and the many device drivers that previously occupied normal user memory. This solves the many problems that arise when machines have to connect to networks, use a number of TSRs, etc. These ancillary programs consume considerable amounts of main memory, resulting in users having insufficient remaining memory to run application programs. The memory management utilities are able to re-locate many device drivers, TSRs and even part of the DOS kernel into extended memory, thus allowing the maximum usable space in the conventional memory area. This technique is not restricted to extended memory. Memory managers can also make use of unused UMBs (upper memory blocks) in the upper memory area. This is also beneficial, but there may well not be as much memory to play around with - particularly if the upper memory area is heavily populated with ROMs and adapters, or if there is a lot of drivers, etc. requiring to be moved up.

Providing extra facilities

DOS and commercial packages provide utilities to use the extended memory for new uses, such as print spooler, hard disk cache and RAM disk.

<u>RAM Drive</u>

An area of memory, whose size is set by the user, is allocated to act as a temporary disk drive. Files can be saved to the RAM drive and loaded back from, in exactly the same way as a hard disk. The usual DOS copy and directory commands work with the RAM drive. It provides a very useful fast drive - much faster than fetching from disk. The only storage limit is the amount of memory that is set aside for the system.

<u>Hard Disk Cache - SMARTDRV.EXE</u>

An area of the extended (or expanded) memory can be set aside to store information from the machine's hard disk. This area is termed the *'disk cache'*. It works like memory cache, except that it is even more efficient. Like memory cache, a block of memory is inserted between the CPU and the storage medium. Memory cache is a small block of fast memory interfacing the CPU to slower memory. Disk cache, on the other hand, is a much larger block of memory (between 256k and 8MB) which is inserted between the CPU and a very much slower disk drive. The ability to often fetch information directly from this memory copy rather than from disk can greatly enhance applications that have extensive disk read activities.

<u>Print Spooler</u>

A printer's mechanism works at a very slow rate, in comparison to the speed that print data can be sent to it by a computer. Most printers now have a small in-built block of memory, called the *'print buffer'*. This buffer holds data from the computer, stores it and passes it to the print head control circuitry as and when required. This is fine for small documents, as the entire data can be transferred to the printer leaving the computer free for other operations.   For large documents, the printer buffer is too small and the computer will be tied up while the printing proceeds.   To prevent this, an area of computer memory can be set aside to hold printer document data.   The computer can then be used for other processing, while data is sent to the printer in the background.

Developing More Powerful Applications

The addition of extra memory does not in itself result in its use by DOS applications, since they still work within the 1MB memory range.   From the 80286 onwards, the CPU was capable of addressing larger memory ranges.

To ensure backward compatibility, the chips have two operating modes:

REAL MODE

This simulates normal 1MB DOS running.   It acts like a 'real' 8086 and allows the running of 'older' programs.   In this mode, the chip is only using 20 of its 32 address lines.

PROTECTED MODE

This supports the wider addressing capability, amongst other advantages such as multi-tasking.

Accessing extended memory requires running the CPU in protected mode. Programs used *'DOS extenders'* to allow MSDOS programs access to XMS.   DOS extenders are an interface between a program running in protected mode and the machine's operating system. They automatically switch between real and protected mode.   Programs that take advantage of extended memory include older DOS applications such as Lotus 123 v3.1, AutoCAD and DataEase 4.   DataEase 4, for example, used the XMS memory to store and sort records, which is much faster than sorting to and from disk.   Many DOS extender applications use the base memory (i.e. 640k) for the program and the extended memory area for the data.

Windows uses the now standard Microsoft multi-tasking DOS extender, called DPMI (DOS Protected Mode Interface), to allow applications to be executed entirely within extended memory.   This eliminates time delays introduced with program overlay swapping and EMS page swapping, since the entire program can be fitted into extended memory - and run from there.   This DOS extender is built-in to Windows and is automatically used by all appropriate programs that it runs in protected mode. DPMI can also be used on 286 machines.   The extended memory is accessed via an XMS driver, such as HIMEM.SYS.

Expanded Memory

In 1985, Lotus, Intel and Microsoft co-operated in a system to use extra memory, known as EMS - the Expanded Memory Specification. It is also referred to as LIM memory, after the developers, **L**otus/**I**ntel/**M**icrosoft.   It is used by programs such as Lotus 123 v2.1, dBASE IV, AutoCAD and Supercalc. The expanded memory manager software is called EMM.SYS and the industry standard is version 4, issued in 1987.   It can handle up to 32MB of expanded memory.   Note that the previous version, 3.2, can only store data in the expanded memory. The EMS system carries out its processing in the normal DOS space (within the 1MB range) and can therefore also be used by the humble XT machines.   On the other hand, it is slower, more awkward to use and more expensive than extended memory.   This is due to the way the expanded memory is organised and accessed.

Bank Switching

EMS reserves up to four 16k areas of memory in an unused section of the upper memory area, above 640k.   These new areas are called *'page frames'* and they act as 'windows' on the main EMS memory. The area used starts at address 832k, which is segment D000 expressed in hex notation. The EMS memory is also divided into up to 2000 different 16k areas, dependent on the memory size. These areas are called *'pages'*.   The application is loaded into EMS memory but, at any one time, a portion of this memory (and its contents, either program or data) is electrically switched into a page frame address area. This allows it to be accessed by any normal DOS program that recognises the EMS system.

The EMS expansion card is fitted with memory just of the same type as found in main memory.   These memory chips differ from main memory chips in that they do not connect to the machine's address bus. EMS memory chips have to connect to their own address bus on the expansion card. This is wider than the machine's address bus, as it adds extra bits to identify each page number. Therefore, it follows that a single CPU address would match many different EMS locations.

The program that is using EMS has to give the page number as well as the required address. After all, address 1100 in page 3 is a different location from address 1100 in page 9. The page number is used by the card to ensure that the appropriate page of data is switched in to the page frame in conventional memory. Placing the page frames in the user area is precluded, as there is no way to disable any main memory and two memory chips cannot be simultaneously read. It would also completely confuse existing DOS programs.

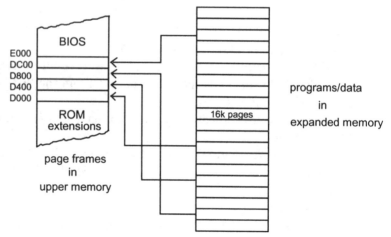

Different card manufacturers will have different physical board designs, but they will all conform to the Expanded Memory Specification. Each card is supplied with its own expanded memory manager. This communicates with the EMS device driver, sometimes called a *'LIM driver'*. This is usually called EMM.SYS for a 286 machine, EMM386.EXE for a 386 machine, or similar. When a software house develops a product to use EMS, they will not be aware of the specific boards on which it will be used. This will not matter, as the boards, in following the same specification, will respond to the same EMS memory call interrupt (67H). When the interrupt is issued, control is passed to the EMS driver. This driver is written to specifically match the design of the board and it converts the standard arguments sent by application into the control sequences required by the particular board.

Paging

If a machine is already fitted with extended memory, the system can be configured so that the CPU sees the XMS as EMS memory. Since there is no specialised EMS circuitry, the bank switching principle cannot be utilised. Instead, a slower system of paging is employed. When the application wishes to address a particular memory address that lies outside the 1MB memory, the EMS manager copies the appropriate page (i.e. the one with the requested address) into one of the 16k windows in upper memory. It is now available for accessing and the EMS manager will make the translation from the requested address to the address where it will actually be found in one of the page frames. Eventually, all the page frames will be occupied. When another address is requested which requires another page to be loaded, there will be no vacant page frame to load it into. In this case, one of the current page frames is written back to EMS memory (since its contents may have been modified) and another page can be loaded by overwriting this frame. In this mode, it acts like an I/O device. In this case, however, the data is being moved in and out of a large pool of EMS memory, rather than disk or external ports.

The software driver (called EMM386.EXE in DOS 5) acts as an EMS emulator and is hence sometimes called a *'Limulator'*. It will switch into protected mode to copy the data from extended memory into the page frame, then revert to real mode to run in DOS mode. Other EMS emulators are part of DRDOS and QEMM. Using extended memory in this way provides EMS activities without the expense of the EMS board. On the other hand, it is much slower since page transfers take milliseconds, compared to microseconds for bank switching. Overall, the EMS system involves complex and time-consuming page swapping or bank switching techniques and is slower than accessing conventional memory, although still faster than disk accesses. For 8088/8086 machines, it is the only available method for running larger applications from memory. For these machines, it allows access to such luxuries as giant spreadsheet worksheets.

All machines wishing to use the EMS system will require:
- to be fitted with a memory board to hold the EMS chips and control circuitry, or have extended memory to configure as expanded memory.
- the application to have the necessary software to automatically detect and control the board's circuitry.

Computer Peripherals

A computer peripheral is a piece of equipment that adds extra power or functionality to the central basic system. Since every computer has to have a motherboard, CPU, and memory, these cannot be classified as peripherals, whereas a scanner or a digital camera is clearly not an essential. There is a grey area in between. For example, a computer can control a robot without the need for a monitor but the monitor is essential for desktop use. In any case, the book cover monitors, graphics cards, sound cards, disk drives, modems, etc. in other chapters.

This chapter looks at:
- The keyboard
- The mouse
- The joystick
- The scanner
- The bar-code reader
- The uninterruptible power supply

Getting data into your computer

Very few computer programs run without any input from the people using the system. Games expect input from joysticks, databases expect input from the keyboard, drawing packages expect input from the mouse, and so on. This chapter looks at some of the devices used to put information into a computer.

The Keyboard

Your keyboard is a piece of hardware that lets you enter alphabetic, numeric, cursor, function key and other information into your computer.

Your keyboard's main features are:

- The computer keyboard consists of a normal typewriter layout with some additional keys incorporated, and a group of function keys (situated on the left with older models and along the top with newer models), a numeric pad on the right, and an optional group of direction keys also on the right side.
- The keys for numeric zero (0) and alphabetic (O), and numeric one (1) and alphabetic '1', the 12th letter of the alphabet, cannot be interchanged.
- Most keys have an automatic repeat function, which means that if you hold a key down for more than a predetermined time (say half a second), the key starts to repeat itself. So, you can enter a whole line of the same character with a single press of a key.
- The normal setting for your keyboard means that when you press a key that is engraved with an alphabetic character you will see a lower case letter on the screen, and a key with two engravings will show the character in the lower half of the key top. To get capital letters and the characters on the top half of the key top you must hold down one of the SHIFT keys while you press the other key. If most of your keying requires the use of capital letters, you can press the CAPS LOCK key, which remains ON until you press it again, and this produces the upper case with alphabetic keys only.
- There are many operations that need to be carried out on a microcomputer that could need a wide range of keys or commands to carry them out. You cannot be given a giant keyboard layout, as this would cause great confusion as well as occupying the entire computer desk area. Manufacturers of modern microcomputers have evolved a standard key-sequence procedure to enable these operations to be achieved while still using a standard-sized keyboard. This involves the use of the CTRL and/or the ALT keys in conjunction with one of the normal keys in the same way as the SHIFT key would be used to give capital letters. This operation is usually indicated in documents as CTRL-B, CTRL-G, etc (or ^G where ^ indicates the use of the control key)
- The keyboard contains an 'Enter' key which is the key with the bent arrow on the right of the centre section of the keyboard. In DOS and in some applications, this key MUST be pressed after a line of text or a command to tell the computer to process that line. It is sometimes also called the RETURN key.
- The keyboard has a single cable attached to it and the plug at the end of this cable is attached to the keyboard socket on the computer main system unit. This cable takes the power from the unit to your keyboard and returns information on any keys pressed back to the motherboard.

- Modern keyboards may have extra keys for special functions such as Windows or Internet operations.
- Some keyboards even include a fingerprint scanner or bar code reader, to prevent unauthorised access to the computer. Only the operator whose fingerprint is recognised is allowed access.

The Control Keys

This set of keys does not produce any printable characters; they are used to control the editing and display activities and are as follows:

Enter ⌨ This key has two functions. One is to move the cursor from one line to the next, as would be expected with a typewriter carriage return key. The second function is to enter a program command. In DOS, the Enter key terminates an entry sequence and lets the machine know that the letters typed in so far constitute a command to be carried out.

Backspace ⌨ This key moves the cursor to the left by one position each time it is pressed. As it travels backwards, it erases any character it passes over.

Shift ⌨ While held down, this activates upper case letters and the top half value of various keys.

Caps Lock This changes the alphabetic keys on the keyboard between shifted (Capital) and unshifted (Lower-case) mode.

Control ⌨ This key accesses the alternate functions of other keys. Hold the Control key down and press the key with the desired function.

Del ⌨ This key removes characters from text at the cursor position, without moving back one character like the backspace key.

Tab ⌨ The Tab key functions similarly to a typewriter tab key. DOS has preset positions on the horizontal line, so that when the Tab key is pressed it moves to these preset positions. The Tab key may also be used in a number of applications such as Microsoft Word.

Ins This key activates an insert mode in which characters can be entered at the cursor position. Characters already on the line are moved to the right to make room for characters entered. If this key is not active, typing a character at the keyboard will result in that key overwriting the character at the current position of the cursor.

Ctrl/Break Control and Break pressed together causes most running DOS programs to halt.

PrtScr When in DOS mode, this key causes the information displayed on the screen to be sent to the printer. Control and PrtScr together will cause the printer to echo everything displayed on the screen.

The **Pause** and **Scroll Lock** keys are rarely used, although some software applications program them for their own particular use.

The QWERTY Group

These are the keys found on a standard typewriter and are used to enter commands or type text. The user can type correspondence, give DOS commands, choose from menus, etc. by pressing these keys.

The Numeric Keypad

The numeric keys along the top of the keyboard are repeated and grouped together at the right-hand side of the keyboard, known as the *'keypad'*. The proximity of the numeric keys is an aid to speedy input for users who are involved in a lot of numeric data entry work. For those not involved in such work, the keypad also doubles up as a cursor movement set of keys. The Num lock key is used to activate and deactivate the number keys on the right-hand keypad. When Num Lock is engaged, key presses in the keypad group are interpreted as the entering of numbers; when Num Lock is not engaged, the same key presses are interpreted as Page Up, Page Down, and other cursor movement key operations. The application package may report that the Num Lock is engaged or the keyboard may have a Num Lock light that lights when in this mode.

Function Keys ⌨

These are marked F1 .. F12 (or up to F10 on some keyboards). They are programmed to perform different functions within different software applications. In DOS they allow the user to retrieve and edit single commands

Cursor Keys

This key moves the cursor up one line each time it is pressed, in certain programs.

This key moves the cursor down one line each time it is pressed, in certain programs.

The cursor-right key moves the cursor one character to the right each time it is pressed. It does not delete any character it passes.

The cursor-left key moves the cursor one character to the left each time it is pressed. It does not delete any character it passes.

End   The End key, inactive in normal DOS activities, is program dependent and moves the cursor to the last character in the current line or screen.

Home   The Home Key, inactive in DOS, is software dependent and moves the cursor to the home position - usually the top left corner of the screen.

PgDn   The Page Down key moves the screen contents up in predetermined increments.

PgUp   The Page Up key moves the screen contents down in predetermined increments.

Windows Keys

Most keyboards have extra keys, allowing some Windows activities to be run by a single key press.

This key brings up the Windows Start menu.

This key brings up the Windows Context menu, whose options depend on the activity at the time. Other options include Sleep, Wake, Power, e-mail, and www buttons.

Keyboards are available in a wide range of designs. Most people use the standard layout, but keyboards are available that split in two, have non-standard key layouts or have improved ergonomic designs. They are also available in cordless and waterproof versions.

How keyboards work

When you press a key on the keyboard, it makes certain connections to a chip inside the keyboard. This chip knows what key has been pressed and sends a code, along the keyboard cable, to the computer. There is another chip inside the computer for handling the keyboard's input.   When it receives the code from the keyboard, it converts it into data that can be used by the computer. This process is explained in more detail in the following pages.

Detecting a key press

A keyboard is a case that contains a set of switches. There are over a hundred different keys on your keyboard and the system has to cope with any of these being pressed. It must even cope with more than one key being pressed at a time (e.g. pressing the shift key and the letter "q" to get an upper-case "Q").

Since your keyboard has over 100 different keys, it is not practical to have a separate wire for each switch back to the computer. Instead, it does this by arranging all the keys on the keyboard into a set of rows and columns.

As a child, you may have played the game of *"Battleships"* where you and your opponent laid out your ships on a grid.   In turn, one player shouted out a row and column and the other player checked if one of his/her ships sat on that location.   So, for example, if one player shouted out "B3", the other player would look along to column B and then look down to the third row.

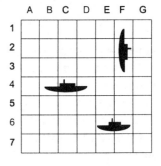

Every box on the grid had a unique location that was identified by its row and column.   In the example, there are seven rows and 7 columns, providing 49 different locations.

The keys on the keyboard are organized in a similar way, this time using a grid of wires as shown in the diagram. Each dot on the diagram represents a switch that connects the horizontal and vertical wires at that location. The grid of wires is connected to a special chip called the *"encoder"*. In this example, there are three columns by three rows, giving nine different places where they join.

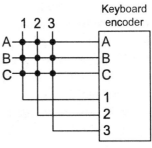

If a switch is wired across each place where the wires cross, there are locations for nine different keys. Although there are nine different keys, it only needs six connections to the keyboard's encoder chip.

If the grid was made up from six rows and six columns, 36 different keys could be connected and only 12 connections would need to be wired to the encoder. Now, if the grid was made up of 10 wires by 10 wires, 100 different keys could be connected with only 20 connections to the encoder.

The keyboard encoder is built so that making a connection between its pin A and pin 1 produces a unique code. Connecting pin A and pin 2 produces a different code, and so on   Since there are nine different permutations in the example, the encoder produces nine different codes.

Now, all that has to be done is to wire a keyboard switch across each junction and make sure that the engraving on the key's top is linked with the unique code that is produced. In other words, if you hit the key marked "G" on the keyboard, the encoder should produce a code that will eventually be understood as being the letter "G".

How the keyboard talks to the computer

The diagram shows how the keyboard connects to the computer.

There is a chip at each end of the keyboard cable:

- one in the keyboard, called the *"keyboard encoder"*.
- one in the computer, called the *"keyboard controller"*

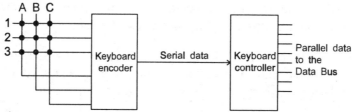

The sequence of events is:

The Keyboard Encoder

- You press a key on the keyboard.
- The key connects two points in the matrix.
- The connection is detected across two pins in the keyboard controller.
- The encoder *"debounces"* the signal (see later).
- The encoder produces a unique *"scan code"* (see later) that corresponds to the changes on its matrix pins.
- The encoder transmits this scan code to the computer, using a serial transmission of data along the keyboard cable (see the wiring of the keyboard cable later in the book).

Keyboard Controller

- The controller receives the data stream from the keyboard.
- The controller generates an interrupt, IRQ1, to let the computer know that it has received data.
- A BIOS routine translates the scan code into an ASCII character for placing on the Data Bus.

How keyboards are constructed

The diagram shows a typical layout of the main key switch circuits inside a keyboard.

For simplicity, the diagram only shows the upper right-hand side of the keyboard - the area where the numeric keypad is to be found.

It shows part of the main board and the matrix of tracks can clearly be seen.

The tracks and contacts may be on a solid board, but they are more likely to sit on a plastic sheet. All the tracks from the main board are plugged in to a small printed circuit board that contains the keyboard encoder and a few other components.

On the left side of the controller there is a socket for plugging in the keyboard cable.

The board also has three LED lights, to show whether the Num Lock, Caps Lock and/or Scroll Lock are active.

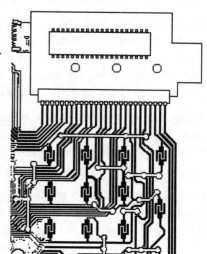

This illustration shows a magnified section of the board layout.   It shows the plates that make up both ends of a switch and tracks from these plates run back to keyboard controller.

If the two plates were shorted together (more on this later), this change is detected by the controller's circuitry.

There are various types of switches that can be used to bridge these plates and these are covered later.

The keyboard connections
The keyboard connects to your computer via a cable that plugs into a socket at the rear of the computer case.   The older keyboards had a 5-pin DIN plug that was about 1/2" in diameter.   They were called *"AT"* plugs.

Modern keyboards use a 6-pin mini DIN plug that is about 3/8" in diameter and these are called *"PS/2"* plugs.

Since many mouse sockets also use PS/2 plugs, there is room for confusion, especially if the two sockets on the computer are not labelled as *"mouse"* and *"keyboard"*.

These diagrams show the types of connectors used on keyboards and the table shows what each pin is used for.

Description	Pins	AT Connector
Keyboard Clock	1	
Keyboard Data	2	
	3	
Ground	4	
Power Supply	5	

Description	Pins	PS/2 Connector
Keyboard Data	1	
	2	
Ground	3	
Power Supply	4	
Keyboard Clock	5	
	6	

Note that not all pins on the plugs are used. Pin 3 is unused on the AT plug and the PS/2 plug does not use pins 2 or 6.

The controller's chips are powered through the *"Power Supply"* and *"Ground"* pins.

The *"Keyboard Clock"* pin is used to ensure that the keyboard encoder and the keyboard controller are properly synchronized.

The output from the keyboard appears on the *"Keyboard Data"* pin and is at *"TTL"* level, which means that it is either at 5v level or zero volts level.

How the key switches work
A range of different types of switch has been used in keyboards.   The most common types are explained below.

Mechanical keys
The simplest form of keyswitch is the mechanical switch, as it acts in the same way as the doorbell switch in any house.

Pushing the switch makes a contact between two plates and releasing the switch breaks the circuit.

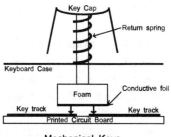

Mechanical Keys

The first diagram shows a key cap (the part you see and press) connected to a small block of foam. A piece of conductive material is attached to the bottom of the block. When you press the key, the foil shorts across the key plates on the main board. As soon as you let go of the key, the return spring pushes the key back up and the contact is broken.

Another type of mechanical switch is the rubber dome type.
A piece of rubber is moulded into a dome shape and the dome is pliable.
Inside the dome is attached a small block of carbon, which is also a conductive material.

Pressing the key on to the dome compresses the dome and the carbon block shorts across the plates in the matrix. When the pressure is lifted, the dome returns to its previous shape.

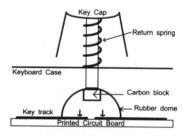

Rubber Dome Keys

Membrane switches

The membrane switch also relies on the electrical contact between two plates going to the controller.
In this case, however, there are two separate sheets, each with their own tracks and plates.

In between these sheets is a thin layer of insulated material that has holes punched in it at the places where the plates are positioned. As a result, there is a small gap between the two plates.

When you push a key, the rod attached to the key pushes the top plate down into the gap, so that it makes contact with the bottom plate. Releasing the key allows the top sheet to flex back to its normal position and the contact is broken.

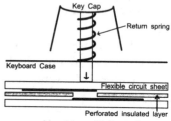

Membrane Keyboard

Capacitive keys

This keys works in a different way from the rest.
The other keys relied on making two plates touch each other.
In this case, the two plates never actually touch.
When you press a key, the top plate is brought closer to the fixed lower plate.
This changes the capacitance between the plates (like tuning a radio) and the change is detected by a special electronic circuit.

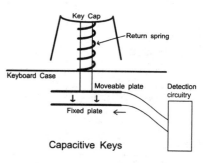

Capacitive Keys

Key bounce

With digital circuits, the electronics can switch a voltage from fully on to fully off, or vice versa, in a very short time indeed. So short, in fact, that it seems to be instantaneous.

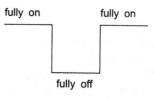

Things are a little different, however, with mechanical switches.
Imagine dropping a ball on to the floor. It eventually goes from a high position to the floor level, but only after bouncing off the floor a few times.
The mechanical switches act in this same way.

This *"bounce"* only takes place for a very short time. But since computers operate extremely fast, this is detected as the key being clicked several times. So, if you hit the 't' key once, it might appear on the screen as "ttttt".

In other cases, pressing a key and releasing it very rapidly can set up a bouncing action producing the same result.

To overcome this, the keyboard controller contains *"debounce"* circuitry.

Once the initial change in voltage is detected, the circuit prevents any further changes from being detected for a short time. This is enough to prevent any bounces from creating false triggering of the controller.

Repeating characters

Each key produces a change when pressed and another change when the key is released. If the keyboard processor detects a 'make' change and does not detect a 'break' change within a certain time, it sends out the key code repeatedly until the key is lifted.   The pace at which it sends out the repeat character is called the *"typematic rate"* and this rate can be set within the BIOS, using DOS or Windows. You can also change how long the key will be depressed before the character starts repeating.

Scan Codes

Every key press produces a change on a pair of pins on the encoder. Each key produces that change on its own unique combination of pins.

The encoder stores a set of codes, one for each pin combination.   When the encoder detects a change between two of its pins, it looks up the code that matches it and sends the code to the computer.

These are called "scan codes" and the set of scan codes vary, depending upon the keyboard in use and the keyboard versions (e.g. UK, US, etc).

The 83-key XT keyboard, the 84-key AT keyboard, the 102-key enhanced keyboard, and the 104-key *"Windows keyboard"* all have differences in scan code output.

The encoder has a small area set aside as a buffer. This means that it can store a list of keypresses for later transmission to the computer.   This is necessary because sometimes keys are pressed in combination.

You will already be familiar with the fact that pressing the Shift key and any letter key produces the capitalised version of that letter.   Using Shift, Alt and Ctrl keys in conjunction with another (e.g. Ctrl-A or Alt-P) produces a set of scan codes.

Here some examples of the scan codes sent from the keyboard to the computer:

Key	Scan Code	Key	Scan Code	Key	Scan Code
a	1E	<	33	Spacebar	39
b	30	>	34	Tab	0F
c	2E	=	0D	Enter	1C
d	20	-	0C	Backspace	0E
e	12	/	35	Caps Lock	3A
f	21	#	2B	Num Lock	45
g	22	0	0B	Scroll Lock	46
h	23	1	02	Left Shift	2A
i	17	2	03	Right Shift	36
j	24	3	04	F1	3B
k	25	4	05	F2	3C
l	26	5	06	F3	3D
m	32	6	07	F4	3E
n	31	7	08	F5	3F

Some keys send more than one scan code.

These include:

Cursor keys		Windows keys	
Up Arrow	E0 48	Left Windows	E0 5B
Down Arrow	E0 50	Right Windows	E0 5C
Left Arrow	E0 4B	Application	E0 5D
Right Arrow	E0 4D		

If you hit one of these keys, the encoder sends the two scan codes, one after the other.

In fact, hitting the Print Screen button sends four codes - E0, 2A, E0, 37.

The encoder's buffer stores the four codes while they are being transmitted to your computer.

You may have noticed that some applications place different meanings to what appears to be the same key.   For example, hitting the Shift key on the left of the keyboard produces a different result from hitting the Shift key on the right of the keyboard.   That is because the scan codes for each key are different (2A and 36 respectively).   Most applications, such as Word, use either key to produce a shift from lower to upper case.

Keyboard lockout

Another chapter looks at handshaking as a way to regulate the flow of data. This technique is also used with keyboards.   Apart from synchronising the keyboard data to the computer, the clock line is used for handshaking.

When the computer pulls the clock line low, the keyboard is placed in a state of *"lockout"* - it is prevented from sending data to the computer. Instead, the characters are stored in the encoder's buffer until the computer is ready to accept them.

The Mouse

While keyboards are the best way to enter textual information, such as names, address, prices, etc - it is very poor at providing positional information.

Although it has keys for up, down, left and right, this is not sufficiently accurate for modern applications such as drawing packages, design software, etc.

In particular, Windows is designed so that menu choices are easily selected with the use of a mouse.

The mouse has become very widespread and very popular because of its accuracy and ease of use.

For these reasons, most computers are supplied with both a keyboard and a mouse.

The main components of a mouse are
- The main case that you move around.
- Buttons (usually two but can be up to five) for clicking selections.
- A cable that connects to the computer.
- Hardware and software at the computer end, to handle the mouse and its data.

Some types also have a small wheel mounted between the keys and this can be rolled with your finger to scroll through the screen content. Alternatively, it can be pressed in and then it acts like a third button. This type is called an *"Intellimouse"* and it provides quicker and more flexible use of applications that can use it.

There are two main types of computer mouse:
- The mechanical mouse
- The optical mouse

In both types, the mouse casing houses a large heavy rubber ball that protrudes from its base. When you move your mouse over a surface, the ball rotates inside its case and this results in a stream of electrical pulses being passed to the computer.   The quicker the mouse is moved, the faster the pulse stream; the further the mouse is moved, the longer is the pulse stream.   The incoming signals are used by the program to produce pointer movements on the monitor screen.

The mechanical mouse

The ball sits inside the case, with only enough protruding from the bottom of the case to allow it to make contact with a mouse mat or other flat surface.

The mouse can be moved in any direction and this means that the ball can be rotated in any direction.

As the diagram shows, the ball rotates two rollers as it moves.

If the ball is moved exactly in a vertical direction, only the bottom roller is rotated, as there is no significant friction on the side roller. Similarly, moving the mouse purely in the horizontal plane means that only the side roller is rotated. If the mouse is moved diagonally, both rollers will be rotated.

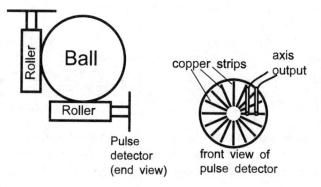

Each roller is connected to a rotating sensor system. With a mechanical mouse, the roller rotates a small insulated disc on which there are etched copper tracks.

Springs rest on the disc and as the disc rotates, the copper tracks will regularly short across these springs.

Each time the springs are shorted, it is detected as a new pulse by the mouse circuitry.

There is one detector for the vertical direction (known as the Y-axis) and one for detecting horizontal movement (known as the X-axis).

This type of mouse is not in common use but is sometimes used in very cheap versions.

The opto-mechanical mouse

The mechanical mouse was in widespread use but was not very efficient and had a short life. The most common mouse today is the opto-mechanical type.

It still uses the same roller system as the mechanical mouse but uses a different pulse detection system.

The rubber ball still rotates the rollers and each roller still has a disc attached to it.

However, this time the disc is plastic and it has slots cut round it as shown in the diagram.

A light source, usually from a LED, sits on one side of the disc. As you move the mouse, the disc rotates and the light shines through the slots when a slot lines up with the light source. When this happens, a light detector, sitting on the other side of the disc, picks up this light and converts it into an electrical pulse. The more you move your mouse, the more the disc is spun and more pulses are generated.

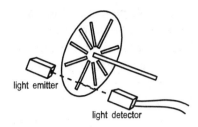

The optical mouse

The biggest problem with the average mouse is that it suffers from the wear and tear of being constantly used - and is open at the bottom, allowing all sorts of dirt to enter the mechanism. To overcome this, a purely optical mouse was developed. It does not use a rubble ball to detect mouse movement. In fact, it has no internal moving parts at all.

Instead, the underside of the mouse is sealed but is transparent. This allows the mouse to shine a light down on to the surface that it is sitting on.   This light is reflected back into a light sensor. As the mouse is moved, the changes detected on the surface are detected and converted into electrical pulses.

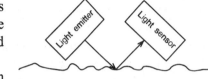

Early models required that a special mouse mat be used with an optical mouse. Modern versions, such as the Microsoft Intellimouse Explorer, work on any surface. You can even roll the mouse up you arm or over your clothes and it will work. This model scans the surface 1,500 times per second and provides greater accuracy than a conventional mouse.

The Trackerball

This is also sometimes known as a *"trackball"* system.   It is really only a mouse turned over on to its back. It works in exactly the same way as the mechanical or opto-mechanical mouse already described. However, in this case the mouse is not moved across your desk or mouse mat. Instead, you use your hand to rotate the ball. This means that the trackerball needs a lot less desk space.

The Joystick

The joystick is the common device used for getting positional information into a computer while playing games.   It is also used for flight simulators and virtual reality systems. Sometimes, the joystick is disguised as steering wheels and pedals or *'joypads'*.   While the layout is different, these devices still work on the joystick principle.

The normal joystick connects to the computer through a game port. This can be a dedicated add-on card or the connection may be provided on a sound card or a multi-function card.

The connection is a 15-pin sub-D socket. This connector can handle four press switches (activated by pressing buttons) and four resistive inputs whose values are altered by moving the joystick lever's position.   This allows two joysticks to be connected to a single socket, with each joystick having two buttons and a lever.

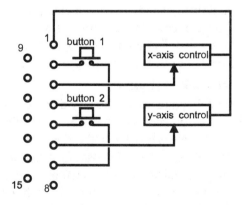

The joystick lever is mechanically linked to two variable resistors that are mounted inside the stick. Moving the joystick in the vertical direction alters the voltage output of one of these resistors, while moving the joystick in the horizontal direction alters the voltage output of the other resistor.   Moving the joystick diagonally alters the output of both resistors.

The diagram shows the wiring of a single basic joystick. Pin 1 takes a five-volt supply to the two variable resistors and the output of these resistors is sent to pins 3 and 6. The voltage level on pin 3 at any one time represents the horizontal position of the joystick (i.e. the x-axis) while the voltage on pin 6 represents the vertical position of the stick (i.e. the y-axis).

The diagram also shows two press buttons.   Pins 4 and 5 are connected to ground and pressing button 1 brings pin 2 down to ground level. Pressing button 2 brings pin 7 down to ground level.

In this example, variable voltages are detected by the game port on pins 3 and 6, while pins 2 and 7 detect voltage drops when buttons are pressed. The game port circuitry converts the altering voltage levels into positional information for the computer program.

To connect a second joystick to the port, the ground level on pin 12 can be taken to a further two buttons that connect to pins 10 and 14. A five-volt supply from pin 9 can connect to two variable resistors and the varying x-axis output is taken to pin 11 and the y-axis output to pin 13.

The port address for the joystick is from 200h to 20Fh, normally 201h. The basic joystick is simple and does not require an IRQ or DMA allocation. There is no interrupt activity and so the program has to specifically ask the game card for a reading of joystick settings. The byte at address 201h uses its 8 bits in the way shown:

Bit 7	Bit 6	Bit 5	Bit 4	Bit 3	Bit 2	Bit 1	Bit 0
Button 4	Button 3	Button 2	Button 1	y-axis stick 2	x-axis stick 2	y-axis stick 1	x-axis stick 1

The status of any push button can be determined at any time by reading the value of the corresponding bit. A value of 1 indicates that the button is not being pressed. The value changes to 0 when the button is held down. The value of any variable resistor is read by sending an OUT command to the port. This starts a timer. When the value of the bit of the particular resistor being read flips from 0 to 1, the timer value is read. The value in the timer is proportional to the stick position.

Apart from the game port, joysticks may also connect to the keyboard. These more elaborate versions have multiple buttons that can be programmed to carry out normal keyboard commands.

Joysticks are now commonly available with USB connectors. A wide range of additional features are now available, including force feedback (to simulate the feeling of a gun recoiling or of going over bumps, striking objects, etc.), programmable buttons, throttle wheels and so on. The concept of variable resistors and push buttons is also used in the manufacture of steering wheels, car pedals and other separate game-playing devices.

Bar-code reader

Everyone has seen a bar-code reader in action. Every time you visit a supermarket or DIY store, the checkout operator runs a reader across the items and the electronic till registers the item name and price.

This is known as EPOS (Electronic Point Of Sale) and bar codes can also be found on goods in bookstores and music stores. It is also widely used on mailing labels, luggage handling and many other applications. In some cases, the goods are passed over a glass plate and in other cases the operator moves a reader gun or wand across the label. Bar code readers can be connected to cash registers, automated handling equipment, and also to ordinary PCs.

The bar code label is printed as a set of vertical stripes. The stripes have various widths and varied spacing. The combinations of stripes widths and gaps are used to represent numeric digits. This is similar to the way that Morse Code uses different lengths of tone to represent characters.

The wand reader

The diagram shows the way that the wand reader works.

A light is shone on the label. If the light shines on a black stripe, the light is absorbed and nothing is detected by the sensor.

However, if the light beam is shone on a white area, the beam is reflected from the label and is detected by a light sensor.

As the label is moved under the light beam, the sensor picks up a series of reflections and converts them into a stream of digital data for use by the computer or other connected equipment.

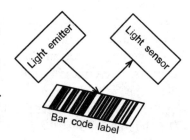

The CCD reader

The wand reader method reads off the data from the label in a serial fashion, with one digit after another being read. Another method is to read the entire label's contents at the one time. The entire label is illuminated and the reflections from the bar code stripes are focused on to a set of sensors, called a CCD (this device is described in the section on scanners).

This system is commonly used and is the type where the operator does not have to swipe the reader across the label. The operator simply points at the label and the data is read off. Although the data is read off in a single operation, the data itself is made up from several numeric characters. So, the electronics inside the reader convert the incoming data into a set of digits for transmitting to the computer in a serial fashion.

Scanners

Many computers are now sold along with a bundle of extras such as speakers, modems and scanners.
The scanner allows you to take a sheet of paper and copy its contents into a file on your computer. The paper may have printed text on it, or it may contain a diagram, a chart or a photograph.
The scanner can be used to bring all kinds of images into your computer. The scanner can be used to capture printed text, line art, logos, hand-written signatures, diagrams, charts and other flat objects such as a driving licence or bus pass.
However, many flatbed scanners are not limited to flat objects and can provide a useable image from objects placed on the glass bed. This allows pages from books and magazines to be scanned, as well as 3-D objects such as a human hand, coins, and so on. Anything that is scanned on a photocopier at the office party is capable of being scanned on a flatbed scanner.

Consider the operation of a photocopier. It has two separate phases.
- The first phase is capturing the image from the document that is placed on the glass.
- The second phase is writing a copy of the image on to a sheet of paper.

These operations can be also be carried out by two of your computer peripherals - your scanner and your printer. Your scanner can capture the image and your printer can print a copy of that image. Indeed, software is available to use them together to act as a photocopier.
So, a scanner is really just the first half of a photocopy machine.

How your scanner works

The most common type of scanner is the flatbed model and the description for this type follows, although the general principles apply to all scanner types.
The photograph (or other object) is placed face down on the scanner glass bed and the capture software is started. This can be a piece of software specially written for the job, or can be any graphics package that has a capture facility built into it.
A bright cold cathode light and a scanning head are mounted on a frame that is able to travel down inside your scanner chassis. It is slowly moved down the document by a stepper motor. The light is shone up on the surface to be scanned and the reflected light from one narrow strip of the document is focussed on to a scanning head. The scanning head contains a single row of light sensors using a CCD.

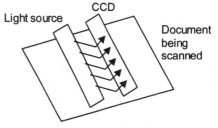

The CCD (charge-coupled device) is a small solid-state chip that contains a set of light sensors. Each sensor is a tiny photodiode that produces a value of electrical charge that varies according to the amount of light that hits it.
When you press the scan button, a microchip reads the amount of charge in each cell. The values from each row are read off and make up the serial image output stream. The scanner's electronics move the image data out of the CCD and convert them from varying light intensity levels into digital values that can be saved as a file to disk.

Since there are a fixed number of sensors in the row, the maximum quality of the picture is decided by the number of sensors. The quality is measured by the number of *"pixels"* that appear in the final picture. A pixel is a *"picture element"* which is smallest dot that will appear on the scanned image. The quality of the scanner's image is given in *"dpi"* which is dots per inch.
The number of pixel sensors has a bearing on the final quality of the scanned image, with greater resolution being achieved by CCDs with a greater number of pixels.

The scanner captures a document's detail one line at a time. Since most flatbed scanners handle an A4 sheet, the width of the scanned area is a minimum of 8.27", with most models having an 8.5" scanning width. If a scanner supports a maximum scanning resolution of 600dpi, the CCD in the scanning head will contain 8.5 x 600 = 5,100 sensors. Even a top-quality 2,400dpi optical resolution requires just over 20,000 sensors.

Either way, the scanner gathers the image data as a series of pixel data and this is sent to the computer via the cable interface.

The quality of the final image depends on the quality of the scanner components - and on the resolution of the scanning mechanism. The scan resolution is measured in dpi (dots per inch). Since many measurements are metric, conversions have to be done into inches to calculate file sizes (see later).

Optical resolution

As explained above, the construction of the CCD determines the maximum scanning resolution. This is called the 'optical resolution' and is usually 300dpi, 600dpi or 1200dpi in the horizontal plane. The stepper motor moves the head in amounts set by the user. If you choose 600dpi for the vertical resolution, the head is moved 1/600th of an inch for each vertical scan. If the scanning head is moved down the bed in movements that are equal to the CCD sensor spacing, the final resolution is equal in both planes (e.g. 300dpi x 300dpi or 600dpi x 600dpi). If the head assembly is moved in smaller steps, the vertical resolution becomes greater than the horizontal resolution (e.g. 600dpi x 1200dpi, 600dpi x 2400dpi or 1200dpi x 2400dpi).

Interpolated resolution

Most manufacturers also quote a figure for their scanner's 'interpolated resolution'. This is a much higher figure, up to 9600dpi, to make the specification appear more impressive. Since the scanner cannot actually detect any more data than its number of CCD sensors, the 'extra' data for the higher resolution is interpolated (i.e. estimated). If, for example, a scanner has an optical resolution of 600dpi and an interpolated scan of 1200dpi is chosen, there is twice as much data to be stored in the file for each line than is being physically scanned. The scanner software looks at the actual readings on adjacent CCD sensors and works out the likely values of colour and contrast that would appear in between. No extra original information has been extracted from the photograph, but the file size is four times larger. In addition, since the process averages out the values at edges, the final scanned image is slightly softened.

File sizes

The size of a scanned image is calculated by taking the area to be scanned and multiplying it by the number of dots per inch. This gives a file size for a monochrome scan (i.e. each screen dot is either completely black or completely white, with a single bit storing the value of each scanned dot). A 256-level grey scale image is achieved by sampling the level of light reflected from each dot and storing it as one of 256 levels. In this way, a single byte stores the dot's value. A 24-bit colour scan is three times the size of a 256 grey-scale scan. A technique, known as 'oversampling', uses 32-bit or even 36-bit colour.

An A4 sheet of paper is the size of this book and many magazines. The dimensions are 210mm x 297mm, or 11.69" x 8.27", when converted to inches. If the entire page were to be scanned in colour, the file size for a range of different scanning resolutions is given in the table.

Take the example of scanning at 600dpi. The page is 8.27" wide, so this requires 8.27 x 600 = 4962 dots of horizontal resolution. The page is 11.69" long, requiring 11.69 x 600 = 7014 dots of vertical resolution. The number of dots to represent the entire A4 sheet is then 4962 x 7014 = 34,803,468 dots. This represents the size for a monochrome image, each dot being either black or white. To store a colour image, each dot is represented by varying amounts of red, green and blue. A byte is required to store each of these colour values. So, the file size is multiplied by three to get the final size in bytes. In the example, a staggering 100MB of storage space is required for an A4 image at a respectable 600dpi.

File sizes for various scanning resolutions (from an A4 sheet at 24-bit colour)	
Scanning resolution	Uncompressed File Size
300dpi	25MB
600dpi	100MB
1200dpi	398MB
2400dpi	1.56GB
4800dpi	6.22GB
9600dpi	24.89GB

Since a photograph in a magazine can expect to be printed at a minimum of 4800dpi, a scanned A4 image would not even fit on an entire DVD disk - unless it was compressed.

Printers

In choosing the printer for a computer system, there are a number of factors that should have an effect on the selection process. For example:

- The quality required. If the printer is for occasional home use (e.g. to print letters to friends etc) or internal business use (for example internal memos or code printouts) then in most cases a low-quality printer will be sufficient. There is no point buying a high-end laser printer if all that will be printed is the occasional leave request form, for example.

- The volume of output. Computers in the home tend to be lightly used, while some office machines can be in almost constant use. The usage requirements will certainly affect which type and model of printer to buy. It is a waste of money to buy a high-end super-fast laser printer if it will only be used on odd occasions, while buying a cheaper printer for high volumes of printing is false economy because the printer will wear out much faster, and printing may be slower.

- Cost considerations. There is more to be considered here than simply the initial outlay of purchasing and installing the system. The idea of '*Total Cost of Ownership*' (TCO) suggests that other factors should be taken into consideration, such as: consumable costs (ink, paper); maintenance costs (for replacement parts as well as the engineer's time); warranties, etc.

- Maintenance requirements. What type of warranty does the printer have, for example? Whenever a printer breaks down in a workplace, there can be a significant reduction in productivity. Also compare the *Mean Time Between Failures* (MTBF) of printers if prolonged downtime will cause serious problems. The higher the mean (average) time between failures, the more reliable the printer is.

- Special requirements. If, say, the user wishes to be able to print on envelopes, opacities or so on, then it should be ensured that the desired printer has that capability. Other factors that may be demanded include duplex printing, colour output, large page sizes such as A3, and so on.

For most cases, the table below shows the general performance of various types of printer in these categories:

	Dot Matrix	Inkjet	Laser
Quality	Moderate	Good	Excellent
Printing speed	Slow to moderate	Moderate	Moderate to Fast
Printer cost	Low	Moderate	High
Consumable cost	Low	Moderate	High
Reliability	Good	Good	Good

Of course, individual printers may vary, and statistics on printer speed (expressed in ppm - pages per minute) reliability (expressed in MTBF - mean time between failures) and similar factors can be found in printer manuals or by checking recent computer magazines.

Once the desired printer has been selected, its purchase should be handled in a similar way to a PC purchase. Check that it comes with the kind of warranty wanted. If the organisation has its own in-house support then a cheaper warranty covering parts may be sufficient, while many small businesses without such support might well require back-to-base or even on-site maintenance warranties.

How printers work

Your printer is used to produce a paper copy (often called a '*hard copy*') of the letters, reports, graphs, etc. produced by your programs. Although there are different types and models of printer, every printer contains at least the following components:

- Power cable connector
- Data cable connector
- Print head
- Printer carriage
- Interface circuitry
- Power supply

These components are explained in more detail below. Depending on the type and model of printer, additional components could be used in the printer.

Power and data connectors

The printer needs two things before it can begin printing. It needs to know what to print, and it needs to have electricity to allow the components to operate. The page information is sent to the printer from the computer via the data cable, while the power is supplied from the mains via a power cable.

The power cable for a printer is a standard "kettle" lead. This is the same type that connects to the PC and the monitor. These leads are interchangeable, even though printer power leads tend to have a distinctive 'L'-shape, and so the power connector on the printer is the same as the power connector on a PC.

The data connector, on the other hand, can be of several types, such as:

- 25-pin D-type parallel connector. This is by far the most common type of connector on the PC end of the cable, but is rarely used as a connector on the printer itself.
- Centronics connector. This is the most widely used connector on parallel printers. (i.e. Printers that receive data via the computer's parallel port). Parallel printers are much more common than serial printers.
- 9-pin D-type Serial connector. This connector is used for serial printers. (i.e. Printers that receive data via the computer's serial port)
- Universal Serial Bus. The more recent USB system is an option on some printers, although older PCs might not have USB ports to take advantage of this connection type.
- Network connector. If the printer is to be used on a computer network, it may have one or more types of network connector to allow it to plug straight in to the network. If this is used, then it should not be connected to any PC through any other of the connectors it may have. However, on stand-alone systems, this connector is not used.

Serial vs. Parallel

As can be seen above, there are two different types of connection for printers and these are known as serial and parallel systems. These names describe how the data arrives at the printer from the computer. A serial printer accepts data in a series of single data bits from the computer; a parallel printer has more wires and so it can receive 8 bits (i.e. one byte) at a time. Most printers have only a serial or a parallel connection, while a few have sockets for both types.

More recently, the USB (Universal Serial Bus) interface has been an option to attach printers. The USB is similar in basic operation to a serial port, though the connectors are very different and the USB is capable of having more than one device attached to a single port.

Standard vs. bi-directional

The standard parallel port on a PC is designed for data output only. This is due to the fact that the main parallel device, the printer, is only used for output.

However, as time went by and technology progressed, printer manufacturers realised that some form of feedback from the printer would be helpful. For example, the user may not realise when the printer runs out of paper. Modern printers often detect such problems and report them immediately to the PC. The user would then be made aware of the problem and be able to rectify it before trying to print anything.

In order for the printer to communicate these problems to the controlling PC, the parallel port on the computer system has to be able to accept data input as well as send data output.

There are two broadly similar methods to allow this input and output to happen on the same cable. They are known respectively as the Enhanced Communications Port, (ECP) and the Enhanced Parallel Port. (EPP) Both of these ports are identical physically to the standard parallel port, only the method of operation of the port is different.

In most cases, a printer that is designed to take advantage of ECP or EPP communications with a computer will still operate on a standard parallel port, but without the feedback information.

Power supply

Although the printer has a mains power connector, the motors and electronics use a much lower voltage than the mains voltage. Like the PC, it has to reduce the voltage supplied to components within the printer. The power supply of a printer is not interchangeable in the way that PC power supplies are interchangeable. If the printer power supply is damaged, the only options are repair or replacement with an identical model of power supply. And as with all power supplies, repair is a safe option only for experienced electrical engineers.

Print head

In many ways, the most important part of the printer is the print head. This component is the one that actually does the work of getting the image placed onto the paper. The way in which it does this varies depending on the type of printer, but the vast majority of printers in use today use a print head that forms an image by creating a pattern of dots on the page.

For example, if the user wished to print out an order form, and the first letter on the document was the letter 'K', then that letter could be represented by the pattern of dots shown in the illustration.

Although it is clear that the letter is indeed the letter 'K', it is not particularly good quality. However, if that pattern of dots was much smaller, say perhaps the size of one of the letters in this paragraph, then the 'dottiness' of the pattern would be considerably less noticeable. In fact, the more dots we can cram into a square inch, the more difficult it is to notice the dots at all – simply use more dots to make up each letter or picture on the page!

This is where the measurement known as '*dots per inch*' (dpi) comes from. The higher the number of dots that a print head can squeeze into an inch square determines just how high quality the output will be. 150dpi (150 dots per inch vertically by 150 dots per inch horizontally) is a reasonable basic resolution for any printer, but high quality laser printers can achieve up to 2,400 x 600dpi or sometimes even higher for professional publications.

High resolution printers that use this method are occasionally referred to as '*near letter quality*' (NLQ) printers. This is to distinguish them from printers that use a set of pre-determined letters etched onto plates, which give '*letter quality*' (LQ). However, these two terms are outmoded since the arrival of extremely high quality laser printers that produce output that is indistinguishable from true letter quality printers while still being able to print graphics and varying fonts.

Printer carriage

The print head does not span the entire page. In fact, in most cases, it does not even span the width of the page. The print head normally only covers a tiny fraction of an inch squared in area. Obviously, this is not enough to cover the entire page, and so the print head has to be moved across the width of the page to print one row of the image. This movement is the job of the printer carriage mechanism. It is simply a mechanical device for moving the print head back and forward across the width of the page.

This allows the print head to create an entire row of dots across the page in one movement. However, a single row is nowhere near an entire page. The solution is to print row after row, while pulling the paper slightly further through the printer so that

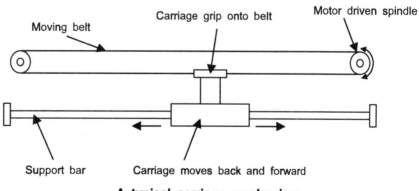

A typical carriage mechanism

each row is printed below the last. This job is performed by the paper transport mechanism. (see later) For ease of understanding the print head is not shown in this diagram – it would attach to the carriage as it moves horizontally.

Paper transport mechanisms

Also known as the *"paper feed mechanism",* there are two methods of moving paper through the printer. These are:

Friction feed

This is the type of feed used in ordinary typewriters.

The paper is held between the main roller and a number of small rollers. As the rollers rotate, the paper is pulled through. This has the advantage that ordinary paper can be fed into the printer; the printer can handle ordinary A4 sheets of paper or pre-printed stationary. It can also handle continuous stationery or fanfold paper but this can cause problems. Since the paper is not of consistent thickness and the rollers do not maintain a constant friction, continuous paper gradually is pulled through unevenly. This effect is known as *'skew'* and becomes a greater and greater problem with the length of the paper being pulled through. With single sheets, the effect of skew should be so slight as to be unnoticeable. Most photocopiers and many fax machines use friction feed systems.

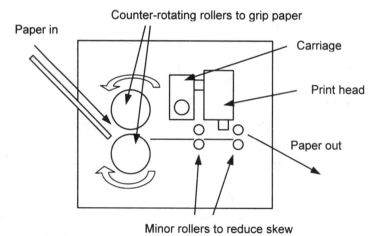

An example of a friction feed mechanism.

Tractor feed

This mechanism uses belt-driven pins on each side of the paper. These pins engage in holes that are punched down both edges of the paper. This ensures that the paper is pulled through evenly. The disadvantage is that it requires the purchase of specially made paper with holes along either side. Fortunately, fanfold paper is in easy supply.

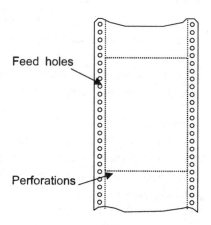

Most fanfold paper comes with tiny perforations, so that the holed edges can be removed. This type of fanfold also has horizontal perforations at intervals so that the final result looks like a normal sheet of A4 paper.

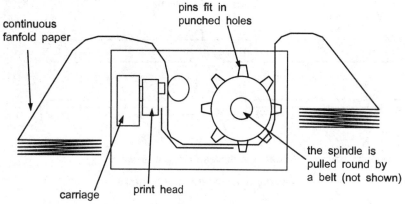

A typical tractor feed system

Interface circuitry

The print head and the printer carriage mechanism are both concerned with physical operations, like moving the print head around and getting it to put ink on the page. However, something has to control the print head and the printer carriage so that this ink is placed in the correct location. In the previous example, where the letter 'K' is being printed, the print head does not know that it is the letter 'K' being printed. It is simply told where to place dots of ink on the page. Likewise, the printer carriage has to be told where to move the head to before it starts printing that letter 'K'. Something has to decide what to print, and where to print it.

Both of these jobs are performed by the interface circuitry. The circuitry is fed digital printer data from the PC via the data cable connector. The interface circuitry has to interpret that information as the correct sequences of dots placed in the correct locations on the page, and then control the paper feed mechanism, the printer carriage and the print head so that they perform their purpose properly according to the desired output.

The Interface Circuitry itself consists of several components, which are listed here roughly in order of use, from PC to final printout:

- Communications circuitry
- Raster Image Processor
- Printer Memory
- Printer Buffers
- Control Circuitry

These components are explained in more detail over the following pages.

Communications Circuitry

As with a PC, the printer requires some control over the flow of data. Printers are generally quite slow devices, especially in comparison with a typical PC. Very few printers indeed can cope with data being churned out of a PC's parallel port at full speed.

The communications circuitry deals with the reception of printer data, and the synchronisation of data transfer from the PC. If the printer is capable of sending information to the PC (such as out of paper warnings) then the communications circuitry deals with the transmission of this data to the PC.

Printer Memory

Not all printers have printer memory. All laser printers, because they print an entire page at a time, require memory to store the page until it is to be printed. Dot Matrix, Inkjet and similar printers print line by line, however, and do not require to build up an entire page image.   The printer memory (which is usually SIMM chips like those inside a PC) store data, usually generated by the Raster Image Processor, until a full page of data is stored. This can then be used by the control circuitry to create the final printout. See the laser printers section for more information on printer memory.

Printer Buffers

As mentioned above, printer memory is not required in a line printer such as an inkjet. However, all printers do have a small area of RAM called a buffer.

Computers are virtually always much faster than printers, and if a computer had to wait every time a single character was printed this would result in significant delays. The printer buffer helps alleviate this problem, by allowing the communications circuitry to fill up the buffer before having to delay the PC from further communications. The control circuitry can then begin printing information from the buffer rather than directly from the PC.   This makes the whole printing process slightly more efficient, sometimes even allowing a small print job to be processed in a single transfer. Like printer memory, many printers allow additional buffer upgrades.

Control Circuitry

The print head (or heads, in a colour printer) need to be told which dots to print and when, and in some printers even how much ink to use. The printer carriage and paper feed, on the other hand, need to be controlled to ensure that the print head is facing the correct part of the page at the correct time. This is the job of the control circuitry.

The control circuitry is given data on the desired page or line data, from printer memory or buffers. This information is then converted into the correct sequence of electrical signals to control the print head and the printer carriage mechanism appropriately.

Raster Image Processor

The part of the circuitry that generates the sequence of dots to be printed is called the Raster Image Processor. (RIP) In order to interpret information from the PC, the interface circuitry is programmed by the manufacturer to accept information in a certain format, and control the printer carriage and print head in order to print out pages accordingly.

There are many printer data formats, but the most common include:
- Plain (ASCII) text
- Epson escape codes
- Binary image data
- Postscript format

These are explained in more detail below.

ASCII text

The American Standard Code for Information Interchange (ASCII) is a data format that is used to represent information consisting purely of text and punctuation marks. It is not possible to print graphics using ASCII.

ASCII is an internationally recognised set of numeric codes that represent upper case letters, lower case letters, numbers, and various punctuation marks and other symbols. For example, ASCII code 67 represents the upper case letter 'C', while ASCII code 32 represents a space. (for example a space between words in a sentence)

Although all printers support standard ASCII codes, the ASCII system is not used purely for printing. Far from it – ASCII codes are used to represent text within the computers themselves, as well as when transmitting text over a modem, storing text on disk, and so on. In fact almost every computer system that deals with plain text uses ASCII.

When a printer receives an ASCII code to print, it has to convert that 8-bit number into a pattern of dots that it uses to output the character represented by the ASCII code. For example, if the ASCII code 75 is to be printed (the upper-case letter 'K'), then the pattern of dots might be as shown earlier. Every other printable ASCII code has a separate pattern of dots, and they all depend on the resolution of the printer and the font styles that printer is able to output.

ASCII control codes

Those ASCII codes from zero to 31 do not represent actual characters, but instead are reserved for 'control codes' that have special uses.

The most important of these are:

- **10**: This is the ASCII code for Line Feed (LF). This code tells the printer to feed the paper up one line. This code is interpreted by the circuitry as a request for the paper feed mechanism to advance the paper one line. It is normally used alongside the ASCII code 13, described below.
- **12**: The ASCII code for a Form Feed (FF). This code will tell the printer to feed the paper an entire page on. How this works depends on the type of printer. For example a dot matrix printer might move the paper on enough to line up the print head with the start of the next page, while a laser printer might not even print anything until a full page of data or a Form Feed is received. Some printers have a 'FF' or 'TOF' (Top Of Form) button to perform the same function.
- **13**: Carriage Return (CR). This code tells the printer circuitry to move the print carriage back to the start of the line to begin printing another series of data. However it does not necessarily mean that the paper should be moved on to the next line of the page. Because of this, the Carriage Return and Line Feed codes are used together in most cases when a new line of output is desired, and are often referred to together as 'CR/LF'. A CR/LF combination will move the print head back to the start of the line and move the paper on to the next line. Together, this makes the printer ready to print the next line of data.

Most software packages and printer drivers, when communicating data to the printer, send both the CR and LF codes. However, some assume that the printer will supply a line feed when a CR code is sent, and so they do not send an accompanying LF code.

To deal with this, most printers have a setting that determines whether the printer automatically inserts line feeds with each carriage return. Sometimes this setting is a switch marked 'CR/LF' or 'ALF' (Automatic Line Feed) while on many laser printers it is an option accessed through a menu.

Setting the automatic line feed option incorrectly can lead to constant reprinting over the same line (if the printer never receives a line feed code and does not automatically generate one), or printing double spaced lines instead of single spaced lines. (if the printer receives a line feed code but also generates another one itself when it receives the carriage return code)

Extended ASCII codes

Standard ASCII is a seven-bit code, in other words it uses seven binary digits to store or represent each ASCII code. Seven binary digits allow a range of 128 possible codes, ranging from zero to 127. This is enough to represent 32 special control codes (such as CR and LF); 52 alphabetic characters (26 each of upper and lower case); 10 numeric characters (zero to nine); and 34 punctuation marks or symbols. (such as the '?' character or the '£' symbol)

However, a standard data byte is 8 bits long, giving a range of 256 codes, from zero to 255. This can represent an additional 128 codes that are not used in standard ASCII.

Rather than let that extra capacity go to waste, most printer manufacturers look to extend the ASCII code set. The first to do this was Epson, who used the upper 128 codes to represent characters that were to be printed in italics.

IBM, on the other hand, used the upper 128 codes to represent foreign characters (such as letters with accents, or foreign currency symbols), and also to represent basic line graphics. (for drawing boxes around text, and so on)

These two systems became widely used in plain text printing, and because of this many printers support both modes. The printers achieve this support by allowing the user to decide whether to use the Epson extended ASCII character set or the IBM extended ASCII character set. How this is set depends on the printer; it may be through DIP switches inside the printer case, or chosen through a menu on the printer interface.

Epson escape codes

Although the Epson extended ASCII set allowed for italic characters, it did not have enough codes to represent other modes of printing, such as bold or underlined. Epson developed a solution to this that still used only an 8-bit byte for each code.

The ASCII code 27 is one of the special ASCII control codes (see above). It represents the 'Escape' character. The escape key is the one on the top left of your keyboard, and it is used to interact with programs. As far as storing or printing text is concerned though, the escape key, and hence the escape code, has no use. Epson realised that this code could be put to use, and developed a system they called 'ESC/P'. In this system, standard ASCII text was sent to the printer as normal. When the 'Escape' code is received by the printer, this informed the printer that the next byte of data was not an ASCII code but an '*escape code*'.

These escape codes could be used to send many kinds of information to the printer. For example the P.C. could tell the printer to start (or stop!) printing in bold, underlined, strikethrough or double-strike typeface. It could change font size or style, change between draft and full quality print, and so on.

For example, the ASCII code 71 represents the letter 'G', while the ASCII code 27 (escape) followed by the escape code 71 tells the printer to begin printing in double-strike mode.

Binary image data

Standard ASCII text is excellent for representing pure text, but it has no graphics capability at all. Even IBM's extended ASCII character set only provides a very basic set of line drawing characters.

In order to output graphics or customised fonts that are not recognised by the printer, the page must be printed as a graphic image. Every page printed by a modern PC printer is composed of dots, usually so small and closely packed together that they are not recognisable as dots to the naked eye.

With ASCII text, the printer simply converts an ASCII code into a particular pattern of dots, and then prints that pattern. With an image file, the pattern of dots is already known. For user-defined fonts, or pages that mix text and graphics, the whole page must be converted into a large image before transmitting to the printer.

This image is not in ASCII text or any other human-readable format. The pattern of black and white dots is transmitted as pure binary information. Unfortunately, the format of the binary information varies between some manufacturers and even sometimes between different models of printer.

For example, a user could print an A4 page with margins set so that the output is 7 inches in width. A 300dpi printer would expect 7x300=2100 binary data bits (263 bytes) to represent each horizontal line, while a 1200dpi printer would expect 7x1200=8400 data bits (1050 bytes) per horizontal line.

Furthermore, there are some printer settings that may be user-adjustable. For example, a modern laser printer will offer the capability to print at different resolutions for different pages. The software will need to inform the printer when it wishes to change resolution. Other printer-specific settings might include setting the page type (e.g. A4 or American Letter size etc.), the tray to use (manual feed, upper paper tray, lower paper tray etc.) and so on.

Printers with special capabilities, such as colour output or duplex (two sides of the paper) printing, will have even more to take into consideration when sending binary data from the PC to the printer.

All of these differences mean that binary output must be customised for the type of printer that is in use; otherwise the output will almost certainly be totally unrecognisable.

Before Windows became widely used, software packages had to be written so that they were capable of sending data in various binary formats to accommodate several printer types. However, the Windows operating system allows a '*printer driver*' to be installed, that is capable of translating the user's document into the correct series of binary digits for that particular printer. In fact, Windows allows several printer drivers to be installed, so that if you have multiple printers attached or available through a network, the user may select any one printer for a particular document.

Printer Emulation

Some printer types are more widely used than others. Among dot-matrix printers, the Epson FX80 was at one time by far the most widely used. The HP DeskJet series are the most common inkjet printers, and the Hewlett Packard LaserJet series are the most common laser printers.

As mentioned earlier, before Windows became common, software had to be written such that they could prepare binary data for various printer types. Any new printer would then in theory require a new add-on to the software. Many manufacturers however realised that they could '*emulate*' the operation of one of these popular printers.

Many laser printers, for example, are able to emulate the operation of a HP LaserJet III. If the software sent binary data that a LaserJet III could recognise, then a printer set to emulate a LaserJet III could understand the data and print as desired.

Setting the emulation of a printer may be achieved by DIP switches inside a dot matrix printer, or by a setting on the control panel of a laser printer, for example.

In Windows, emulation is only required if the printer driver is not readily available – perhaps if the printer is obsolete and no longer supported by the manufacturer.

Postscript

While the user is creating a page in an application such as Microsoft Word, it is not stored as a binary image. The text is stored as ASCII, with images stored as bitmaps or vectors, and control codes throughout to indicate typefaces, font sizes and so on. To print this page as an image to the printer, it is converted to a series of lines of data bits representing black and white dots, as explained earlier

PostScript is a method that allows pages to be regarded as objects instead of binary collections of dots. This can improve print quality as it allows the printer to select certain settings rather than relying on the software which may not know the best way to print on any given printer.

Instead of converting the entire page into a single giant binary file, the page data is transmitted as a text file in a language called '*PostScript*'. This text file contains information that allows the printer to recreate the page. For example it will contain text formatting information, data on objects in object-oriented images, and information that allows the printer to interpret a bitmap image embedded in the PostScript file.

There are other printer languages, such as Hewlett Packard's HPGL, the Printer Control Language (PCL) and so on, which are sometimes grouped together under the heading of Page Description Languages (PDL). They all perform similar functions, but PostScript is the most widely recognised printer language, and is used in high-quality DTP productions. It is not necessary for ordinary household or business use.

Printer types

There are different printers for different jobs. All have different qualities as described next.

Impact printers

This involves an inked ribbon being struck against the paper, impressing ink from the ribbon onto the paper to produce the shape desired. Because of the constant striking of the ribbon, impact printers usually generate a lot of noise when they are in use. There are a variety of forms of impact printer, of which the Dot Matrix is the only variety that is still in use to any real degree.

Dot Matrix

Dot matrix printers operate by using a number of pins on the print head, usually arranged in a rectangular pattern. The printer selects which of these pins it wishes to strike the ribbon to create the final pattern on the paper. This pattern could resemble a letter, a number, or part of a graphic image.

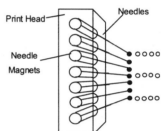

Dot matrix printers are the oldest printers still in use. They are among the cheapest available, and can be reasonably fast, some printing up to 400 characters every second.

The quality of output from a dot matrix printer depends mainly on the number of pins on the print head. Early dot matrix printers involved a vertical row of seven pins that impacted five times along the page to create a matrix of 7x5 dots that each character consisted of.

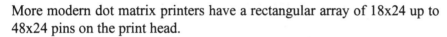

More modern dot matrix printers have a rectangular array of 18x24 up to 48x24 pins on the print head.

Some dot matrix printers increase the quality of output by having two modes – *draft* and *quality*. Draft mode allows the printer to print each line in a single pass, while quality mode means that each line consists of two passes. This two-pass mode is of course slower by a factor of two, but both the resolution and the heaviness of print can be increased when printing in two passes.

The quality of dot matrix printing is also affected by the quality of the ribbon. Often, a new ribbon contains more ink than might be anticipated, resulting in smeared or smudged printouts for a short while. However, as the ribbon nears the end of its useful life it contains less and less ink, which has the opposite effect – resulting in printouts that may not be dark enough.

Dot matrix printers are used for bulk printing, where cost of printing is more important than print quality, for example printouts of inventories, or long sections of program code. Most dot matrix printers can take fanfold paper including specialised stationary, making them better suited to printing off long runs of items such as mailshots, reminder notices or pay slips.

Colour dot matrix printers

Dot matrix printers are able to print in colour, by using a ribbon that has four rows, each with a different ink colour. The ribbon is moved up and down to print each different colour. As a result, each line has to be printed in four different passes to allow all of the colours to be used.
This is obviously much slower, and colour dot matrix printers are no longer widely used.

Other Impact printers

A matrix of dots is not the only way to push ink from a ribbon onto paper. Daisy wheel, thimble, barrel, and chain printers all operate in a similar manner to typewriters. Each character has a typeface permanently located on a daisy wheel, thimble, barrel or chain. The raised character shape is caused to impact against the ribbon, creating a replica of the shape on the paper; similar to the way a rubber stamp leaves ink only where it has raised areas. The use of whole character shapes instead of a number of dots means that every printout has true '*letter quality*', but at the expense of being unable to cope with varying fonts, italics and so on without replacing the impact device, which would involve a significant delay. Also, they are completely unable to deal with graphics at all.

Non-impact printers

Impact printers have a number of disadvantages - they are noisy, relatively slow, and produce limited quality. There are a number of techniques that allow printing without using impact mechanisms, from cheap bubble-jets for home use through to professional wax transfer or dye sublimation printers. Due mainly to cost and speed considerations, the two most widely used non-impact printer types are inkjet and laser printers.

Ink Jet Printers

Ink jet printers avoid using impact to transfer ink, by instead spraying dots of ink onto the paper surface. A small plastic case contains the ink, which is drawn from the reservoir through a pattern of tiny holes on the print head. How said ink reaches the page depends on the technology used - there are a number of inkjet printing methods. The original method was *continuous stream* printing, but the two methods most widely used today are *thermal* (or '*bubble jet*') and *piezoelectric* (or *mechanical*) inkjet printing methods.

Continuous stream inkjets

The first inkjet printers to be developed used conductive ink, in other words ink that could be given an electrical charge. The charged ink was then sprayed in a continuous stream of tiny droplets. Since each droplet was charged, an electromagnetic field could be used to deflect the droplets onto the page, similar to the way a compass needle is moved by the Earth's magnetic field. However, the ink had to be sprayed in a continuous stream, so unused ink had to be deflected away from the page into a container. This could be extremely wasteful.

The continuous stream method was fairly fast at the time it was introduced, being able to print over a hundred characters per second, but is very slow by today's standards.

Another problem with continuous stream inkjets is that it is susceptible to magnetic interference. The charged stream of ink is analogous to the charged stream of electrons in a television set. Just like a television set, if you put a strong magnetic device nearby (like a paperclip holder or a magnetic screwdriver) it will interfere with the final result.

Thermal inkjets

A thermal inkjet printer works by heating the ink every time a dot is required on the page. The print head contains a tiny ink reservoir and a heating element for each dot. The element vaporizes the ink, which consists mostly of water, by rapidly heating it. As anyone who has opened a shaken bottle of fizzy juice can tell you, gas takes up more volume than liquid does, and as a result the expanding gas forces some of the ink out of the reservoir and onto the page. The gas bubble (which gives '*bubble jet printers*' their name) then cools and turns back to liquid, and more ink is sucked into the chamber to fill the empty space left by the ink that was ejected.

This heating and cooling process can occur extremely quickly – it can be repeated thousands of times a second! In addition, inkjet printer heads have rows of several dots, most commonly totalling 16 but which can number up to a hundred, all of which print simultaneously. As a result, thermal inkjet printers are much faster than continuous stream inkjets, some able to print thousands of characters per second. They also do not waste ink by spraying it continuously.

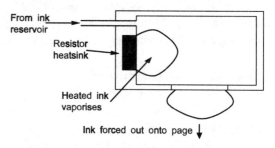

A nozzle in a thermal inkjet print head

However, thermal inkjets are not without their drawbacks.

There is a tiny resistor in the print head that carries out the heating of ink, thousands of times a second, every time a page is printed. Imagine if an electric cooker was turned on and off that much – it would not last as long as it would under normal use. As you might expect, then, thermal inkjet print heads need to be replaced comparatively often. So often, in fact, that thermal inkjet print heads are actually put inside the ink cartridge, which is thrown away when the ink runs out.

The quality of a modern thermal inkjet printer is comparable to mind-range laser printers, at about 600 dots per inch. Inkjet printers are also very quiet in operation – one model of printer was actually named the QuietJet.

Piezo-electric inkjets

The piezo-electric inkjet printing mechanism was actually invented before the bubble jet method, but until relatively recently has been more expensive. In modern systems the quality, speed and cost of piezo-electric inkjets are very similar to those of bubble jet printers.

However, they work on a slightly different principle. A piezo crystal inside the print head reacts to electrical signals by changing shape. This change in shape moves a vibration plate between the crystal and the ink chamber. This in turn causes increased pressure in the chamber, which forces ink out of the chamber. Fortunately, surface tension will prevent excess ink from leaking out.

Since there is no heating element, the print head can be part of the printer instead of part of the ink cartridge, which is more ecologically sound. Furthermore, the ink is not required either to be conductive, or to be able to cope with continual vaporising and condensing. Both of these factors mean that ink cartridges for a piezo-electric inkjet are very slightly cheaper.

Colour inkjet printers

Colour inkjet printers usually use four different ink reservoirs. Normally one cartridge is used for black ink, and another cartridge holds three ink reservoirs – cyan, magenta and yellow. Each colour has its own print head, and combinations of the four inks can theoretically produce any colour.

However, it should be noted that continuous stream inkjets are unable to use multiple print heads because their magnetic fields would interfere with one another.

Laser Printers

Laser printers, or page printers as they are sometimes referred to, are more expensive than dot matrix or inkjet printers, but provide considerably higher quality output. The speed of laser printers vary, with low-end models printing just 2 to 4 pages per minute (ppm) and many lasers printing 10 or even 12 ppm. However these figures usually  assume that the same page is being printed repeatedly; printing out different pages of a document for example would reduce such figures noticeably.

The laser printer operates on the same principles as a photocopier, except that the page image comes from computer data rather than a scanned page. In fact, a photocopier is basically a scanner and laser printer in one, cutting out the computer in the middle! This is the reason why so many photocopier manufacturers also produce laser printers.

Printer memory

Laser printers always build up an image of a page before printing – the time taken to build up a page in the printer's memory is the reason why laser printers rarely achieve their top printing speed in ordinary home or office use. If the same page is printed many times, then the delay caused by collecting data from the PC and building up a page image in memory only happens once at the start of printing, after which time it can be ignored for the following pages. However, in many cases, each page printed will be a different page, and so the delay of building up an image affects every page and slows the printer down considerably.

If a binary page image is sent to a laser printer then building up a page image in printer memory is comparatively simple; however if ASCII text or a Postscript page description is sent to the printer then it has to be able to create a page from that data.

The page image has to be stored somewhere though, and so laser printers require substantial amounts of memory to store the page image until it is printed. The amount of printer memory affects the resolution (in dpi) of page that can be stored. For example, a laser printer with 1MB of memory could store an A4 page at a resolution of 300dpi, but at a resolution of 2400 x 600dpi the amount of memory required would be 16MB. For this reason many laser printers are capable of having their memory upgraded, so that higher resolution pages can be printed.

Once the page image is created in printer memory, it is then printed in exactly the same way a photocopier would print it. However, a laser printer is much more useful to a computer user than a simple photocopier, as the user can print out documents, spreadsheets, computer images etc.

Memory requirements for common laser printer resolutions

Note that these figures are for black and white printing only – colour printing requires more memory by a factor of four.

Resolution	Dots per sq. in.	Dots per A4 page (8 x 11in)	Memory required
75dpi	75 x 75 = 5625 dots	5625 x 8 x 11 = 495,000 dots	64 KB
150dpi	150 x 150 = 22,500 dots	22,500 x 8 x 11 = 1,980,000 dots	256 KB
300dpi	300 x 300 = 90,000 dots	90,000 x 8 x 11 = 7,920,000 dots	1 MB
600dpi	600 x 600 = 360,000 dots	360,000 x 8 x 11 = 31,680,000 dots	4 MB
1200 x 600dpi	1200 x 600 = 720,000 dots	720,000 x 8 x 11 = 63,360,000 dots	8 MB
1200 x 1200dpi	1200 x 1200 = 1,440,000 dots	1,440,000 x 8 x 11 = 126,720,000 dots	16 MB
2400 x 600dpi	2400 x 600 = 1,440,000 dots	1,440,000 x 8 x 11 = 126,720,000 dots	16 MB

How Laser Printers work

Unlike most other types of printer, the laser printer does not have one individual component that can be said to be the print head or the printer carriage. Instead, the laser, which gives 'laser printers' their name, remains stationary as the page moves through the printer. There is a rotating mirror inside the printer that repeatedly reflects the laser beam in a horizontal line.

Some very similar printers use a row of LED's instead of this laser and mirror arrangement. These are usually described as *'page printers'* rather than laser printers. Both versions, however, result in a continuous horizontal line of light as the page passes through the printer.

However, the light is not fired directly at the page, as this would have no effect. Fortunately, the dry toner that is used in laser printers is easily attracted to electrostatic charge in the same way as dust is attracted to the static that builds up on your television screen. So, a laser printer must find a way to create this charge in a pattern that will draw the toner onto the page to form the desired printout.

The laser printer contains a drum which spins round as a page is printed. The drum is coated in a special *Organic PhotoConductive* (OPC) material, enabling it to be electrostatically charged with a high voltage wire, called a *"primary corona wire"*. The primary corona wire uses a grid between the wire and the drum to ensure a regulated charge over the whole drum surface.

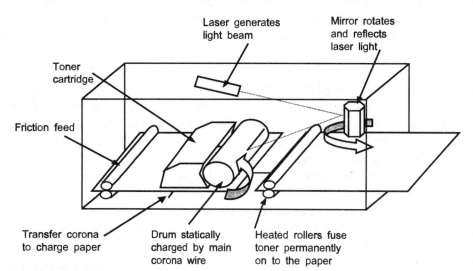

Laser generates light beam

Mirror rotates and reflects laser light

Toner cartridge

Friction feed

Transfer corona to charge paper

Drum statically charged by main corona wire

Heated rollers fuse toner permanently on to the paper

The laser inside the printer then fires a beam of light across the drum as it turns round, usually by bouncing the laser beam off a rotating mirror. The varying light changes the electrostatic charge on parts of the drum. It is this pattern of electrostatically different areas that represent black and white areas on the final printed page.

As the drum rotates past the toner cartridge, the toner is attracted to those areas of the drum that have been struck by the laser beam. This pattern of toner has to be transferred onto the page, and this is achieved by using a stronger static charge than the drum, attracting the toner onto the page. In most laser printers a *'Transfer Corona'* wire charges the page as it feeds into the printer to achieve this effect.

Some laser printers work with a slightly different method, using positive and negative charges instead of strong and weak charges, but the principle is the same.

Before the page leaves the printer though, the toner has to be fused onto the page so that it will not drop back off. So, the page is passed between two heated rollers that melt the toner onto the page. Also, the drum has to be scraped clean in case any excess toner remains, before the next page is printed.

GDI Laser Printers
As mentioned above, laser printers require memory, with which to build up an image of the page before it is printed. However, it is possible for a printer to use the computer's memory to do this, thereby saving on production costs, as the printer does not have to be manufactured with expensive memory chips installed. Windows computers allow this via a system known as the GDI (Graphical Device Interface).

The Uninterruptible Power Supply
An uninterruptible power supply (UPS) runs the computer on its own batteries in the event of a power failure. They are available in a wide range of capacities. Some last for only a few minutes while more expensive models maintain the system for substantially longer periods. The smaller capacity models are adequate for many standalone PCs while the higher capacity models are common on network servers. The aim of UPS is not to maintain normal working for any prolonged period, as the cost of the batteries would be prohibitive. The UPS aims to allow the machine to close down naturally without loss or corruption of files.

The battery pack is kept charged by a regulated mains supply. The diagram shows that the normal computer power supply is still used but is routed through the UPS card.

There are two major types of UPS, these being:

Off-Line Models
The Off-line UPS lets the computer power supply provide the power for the system under normal conditions. If the mains power fails completely or drops below a tolerable level (a *'brownout'*), the UPS card senses the loss and takes control. The backup battery is then used to feed the inverter and the inverter converts the

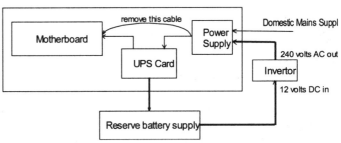

battery's low voltage into the normal mains supply voltage. This provides enough mains power to alert the user and save files. This changeover period lasts a couple of milliseconds and most computers can handle this small loss. In the diagram, the heavy lines indicate the activities that are activated upon mains power loss.

On-Line Models
The On-line UPS is similar to the above diagram. In this case, however, the domestic mains supply is not connected to the PC. The PC is permanently supplied by the inverter. The role of the domestic mains is to keep the batteries topped up. This is a more costly option but it has these extra advantages:
- ○ Since the computer is not directly connected to the domestic mains, it cannot be affected by mains fluctuations, voltage spikes and other line noise.
- ○ There is no switchover delay, as the supply is constantly being fed. This means that there is no possibility of the machine going down during a changeover period. This is a more secure option for servers and machines where there should be no margin of error.

Selecting a UPS
Each UPS has a power rating which is measured in VA (Volt Amperes). This is equivalent to one Watt of power. To determine the VA rating for a particular station:
- • Decide which devices require to be protected; this would include the computer and the monitor, but probably not the printer.
- • Add together the power requirements of each of the protected devices.
- • Since a UPS is usually around 80% efficient, multiply the total by 1.4 to provide the true working rating.

This gives the <u>minimum</u> rating required. For a longer protection time, increase the VA rating. Typical UPS ratings are from 500VA to 2000VA.

P.C. Configuration

Starting up the PC

When a PC is powered up, a procedure known as *'bootstrapping'* occurs. This loads the operating system into the computer memory and sets up the system configuration. Programs cannot be run, or housekeeping tasks performed, until the operating system has been loaded.

The Bootstrapping Process

The normal usage of a PC consists of communication from interface to kernel to BIOS and finally to the machine hardware. When the user initiates an operation, this operation is processed by the command processor before being passed to the BIOS, via the kernel. The boot procedure follows the reverse order. The diagram shows the process simplified:

The main steps are:

1. The computer initiates a POST (Power On Self Test) procedure that is stored in the system ROM (i.e. the BIOS). The POST conducts a self-test of the main board, disks, printer, keyboard, memory, etc. If it finds any fault, it will display an error message and stop. Error messages can range from *"Hard disk failure"* to *"Time of day clock stopped"*. All checks are carried out with a *'hard reboot'* - i.e. switching the power on. A *'warm reboot'* involves either pressing the computer's reset button on pressing the Alt-Ctrl-Del keys. A warm reboot ignores checks such as memory tests.

2. The presence of any *'ROM extensions'* is detected. Apart from the BIOS ROM that is present in all computers, some will have other ROM chips installed for extra control purposes. These are fitted on add-on cards such as video cards and disk controller cards. These extra ROMs contain code to control their own card's activities. If the BIOS finds an adapter card, it runs the code in the extra ROM so that the card's control code can be loaded into memory.

3. If the POST is successful, then control is passed to the bootstrap code resident in the BIOS ROM. This small piece of code triggers the loading process. Modern BIOS systems are configurable, but in general the code will try to read drive A, sector 1, track 0 (the floppy disk's boot sector). If there is no disk in A:, it tries to read the same location on the C: drive. If no boot sector is found on the disks, an error message is given and the system halts. Where the boot sector is found, the code loaded from the boot sector enables the loading process to continue. The code from the boot sector is used to load the kernel and remaining BIOS, with all Microsoft operating systems this consists of the files IO.SYS and MSDOS.SYS. Some old DOS versions load both IO.SYS and MSDOS.SYS at this stage. In other DOS systems, IO.SYS is loaded first and it then loads MSDOS.SYS. In Windows 95 or later, only IO.SYS is loaded and MSDOS.SYS is instead used to store Windows-specific boot information.

4. The system is configured.

IO.SYS, in fact, contains two components- BIOS and SYSINT.

BIOS contain the built-in device drivers that allow standard communications with the computer's keyboard, screen, printer, serial ports, and disk drives.

SYSINT carries out a range of functions, as follows:

    a) determines the configuration of available memory and in DOS the kernel (MSDOS.SYS) is relocated so that it is located at the top of low memory. (It may be located partially in high memory in all but the oldest versions of DOS – see later)

    b) calls code in the kernel to build a table for the devices that the computer is using.

    c) initialises each of the resident device drivers.

    d) reads CONFIG.SYS and adds any other installable device drivers into the list. These software drivers are, in almost all cases, files with the .SYS extension (such as RAMDRIVE.SYS, for installing a RAM drive). These are additions to the operating system, to improve or extend handling of various devices.

The CONFIG.SYS file can be omitted altogether, in which case the computer will work on its own set of default values.   In this case, the system will still work but some of the desired facilities will probably be lost.   If CONFIG.SYS is included, and a system file is mentioned in CONFIG.SYS, the named file must be present in the specified directory.

e) sets up buffer space and file handles in memory, according to the BUFFERS and FILES commands in CONFIG.SYS.

f) loads the command line interpreter (or shell) or Graphical User Interface.   COMMAND.COM is the standard MS-DOS shell.   If there is a SHELL = statement in CONFIG.SYS, the specified shell is loaded instead of COMMAND.COM.   WIN.COM is the standard Windows 95/98/ME Graphical User Interface.

5. AUTOEXEC.BAT is executed.

If the configuration process is achieved satisfactorily, the computer will look for an AUTOEXEC.BAT to run. Again, this file is optional but it is present on virtually all DOS systems and even some Windows systems, since it allows a degree of customisation by the user.   This is a normal batch file, which is used for purposes such as:

- altering the system prompt.
- producing user start-up menus.
- loading the driver for a mouse.

If the batch file is not present, the user is presented with the C: prompt.   If an auto-execute batch file is included, all the commands must be correct to fully set up the system.   If not, an error message is given.

Configuring A Computer System

Configuring a computer system consists of:

- Setting the computer's BIOS as covered below.   There are extensive options that set or optimise the computer's hardware.   It is not recommended that inexperienced users make changes to the BIOS settings, as most settings affect fundamental hardware operation.
- Setting DIP switches and/or jumpers on hardware such as printers, video cards and the like, as prescribed in the products' manuals.   It may also require the selection of specific options from the front panel of printers, monitors, modems, etc.   This applies mostly to older devices, as most add-ons are now plug-and-play.
- Setting up AUTOEXEC.BAT, CONFIG.SYS and any add-on utilities to load the appropriate hardware drivers and balance memory usage to achieve the desired configuration.   This applies particularly to DOS-based or older Windows 3.1 machines.

Machine Configuration

The actual machine configuration needed may vary from user to user as each may have different memory needs, program usage, or requirements to execute certain utilities or application programs. Configuration, then, begins with determining the exact needs of the user.   Of course, these needs might sometimes conflict.   A program with large memory overheads, for example, could not be run in tandem with a large number of background applications or TSRs.   So, the first job of the support technician is to arrive at a working specification for the machine, in conjunction with the user.

Setting a typical BIOS

The illustration shows a typical BIOS Main Menu screen, as presented on a modern PC when the user touches a specific key (most commonly DEL or F2) during startup.

Exact BIOS contents vary widely between manufacturers and even between models and revisions of individual types of BIOS.

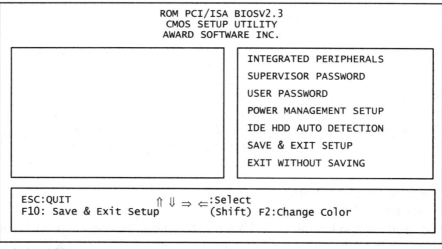

For specific details the manual should be consulted.

The top panel gives information about the BIOS publisher and the BIOS version.

The two panels in the centre of the screen contain options, where changes can be made. The lower panel contains summary instructions on how to use the system.

The options presented on the centre panels are:

Standard CMOS setup	This leads to another screen (see later), where the basic operating parameters of the BIOS, and so the PC is set.
BIOS features setup	This option leads to another screen (see later), where the less fundamental areas of BIOS operation can be modified or examined.
Chipset features setup	Under this option the user can alter aspects of the operation of the machine that are chipset specific. Typical items in this area include memory wait state and caching settings, temperature settings if they are available, etc. Modifications here are not advised, and are machine specific, so this area is not covered in any more depth.
Power Management setup	Modern ATX based PCs will typically have a series of sleep and wakeup modes. The machine is capable of going into low power modes if unattended or unused for periods of time, and of waking up from this sleep based on any of a number of stimuli. For example, LAN activity, Serial Modem activity, USB activity as well as mouse and keyboard activity can all cause the machine to burst into life. The exact detail of which modes it uses, and what delays are set, resides in the Power Management Setup page. Because this information is machine specific, no detail can be entered into beyond this basic outline.
PNP /PCI Configuration	Under this option the user can set whether or not the machine is Plug'N'Play or manually controlled. If the machine is set up not to be Plug'N'Play compatible, then the allocation of IRQs to expansion slots is carried out here.
Load BIOS defaults	This option does not take the user to a separate screen. Instead it loads all the BIOS settings with basic values, i.e. values that are guaranteed to get the machine running. That way, a scrambled CMOS can be quickly and conveniently recovered
Load Performance Defaults	This option is very similar to its immediate predecessor, but where the BIOS defaults turns off the processor's L2 cache and disables any ROM shadowing, this option tries to configure the machine to optimum performance levels.
Integrated Peripherals	Many motherboards have floppy and hard drives controllers, serial, parallel, USB, PS2 mouse and other peripherals integrated on the mainboard. The user might want to configure these, for example to decide which serial port is Com1, Com2, and so on. An Integrated Peripherals BIOS screen allows such adjustments to be made.
Supervisor Password	Selecting this option allows a supervisor password to be set. Such a password will be subsequently needed to access the BIOS. This is designed to stop casual 'passer by' abuse of the CMOS settings. It is not strong security, as most CMOSes can be readily reset.
User Password	This setting is used to add a password for the user. This appears at boot time and a password has to be entered before the machine will start. Like the supervisor password it is not a strong defence mechanism, but can discourage casual abuse of the system.
IDE HDD Auto detection	This option causes the BIOS to interrogate the hard disks in turn for their settings. Since most modern hard drives can operate in various modes (for example in LBA modes and cylinder translation modes), the auto detect will often return a number of options and ask the user to select which he/she wishes to set in the CMOS. A great many modern motherboards use an automatic option in the standard CMOS setup panel (see below) and so force the BIOS to detect the hard disk settings every time the machine is started.
Save & Exit setup	The current values are saved from RAM storage to CMOS, and the machine is rebooted, in order to force the CMOS to be re-read.
Exit Without Saving	This does the same as it's predecessor, but the changes are not saved. This is useful if it is thought that a setting value might have been lost. By abandoning the session, the machine is in the same state as it was at the last boot.

Standard CMOS Settings

The standard CMOS settings are essentially the same on every machine. This is because in order to be fully IBM compatible the basic CMOS values must be compliant. Most machines have considerably more CMOS memory than the IBM standard minimum 42 bytes, and this is used to store the information that appears on other pages of the BIOS setup system.

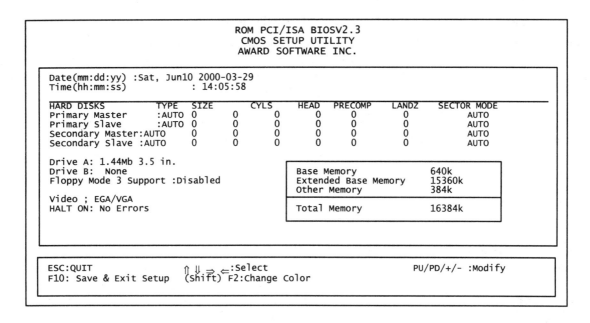

```
                        ROM PCI/ISA BIOSV2.3
                        CMOS SETUP UTILITY
                        AWARD SOFTWARE INC.

  Date(mm:dd:yy) :Sat, Jun10 2000-03-29
  Time(hh:mm:ss)        : 14:05:58

  HARD DISKS        TYPE  SIZE     CYLS    HEAD   PRECOMP   LANDZ    SECTOR MODE
  Primary Master   :AUTO  0       0      0      0        0        0          AUTO
  Primary Slave    :AUTO  0       0      0      0        0        0          AUTO
  Secondary Master:AUTO   0       0      0      0        0        0          AUTO
  Secondary Slave :AUTO   0       0      0      0        0        0          AUTO

  Drive A: 1.44Mb 3.5 in.
  Drive B:  None                   ┌──────────────────────────────────────┐
  Floppy Mode 3 Support :Disabled  │ Base Memory          640k            │
                                   │ Extended Base Memory 15360k          │
  Video ; EGA/VGA                  │ Other Memory         384k            │
  HALT ON: No Errors               ├──────────────────────────────────────┤
                                   │ Total Memory         16384k          │
                                   └──────────────────────────────────────┘

  ESC:QUIT              ⇑ ⇓ ⇒ ⇐:Select              PU/PD/+/- :Modify
  F10: Save & Exit Setup  (Shift) F2:Change Color
```

The contents of the standard CMOS settings page are:

- Amounts of memory detected at POST.
- Date stored in CMOS by Real Time Clock.
- Time stored in CMOS by Real Time Clock.
- Hard Disk type or parameters for type 47 drives or AUTO if the HDD is to be auto detected by the booting BIOS.
- Floppy Disk type. Mode 3 diskette support is sometimes offered. This option is only needed in certain Asian territories and should routinely be disabled.
- Primary Display Adapter type. This is usually simply EGA/VGA. It does not relate to the actual video adapter installed, but to a notional type stored in the CMOS's equipment byte, largely a legacy setting.
- Whether or not a floating-point unit is detected.

Advanced BIOS Settings

The BIOS Features Setup page, or sometimes the Advanced BIOS options page, contains options that are not standard and differ from machine to machine.

```
                        ROM PCI/ISA BIOSV2.3
                        CMOS SETUP UTILITY
                        AWARD SOFTWARE INC.

  Virus Warning          : Disabled      HDD S.M.A.R.T capability :    Disabled
  CPU Internal Cache     : Enabled       Report No FDD for Win95  :    No
  External Cache         : Enabled       Video BIOS Shadow        : Enabled
  CPU L2 Cache ECC Checking    : Disabled
  Processor Number Feature : Enabled
  Quick Power On Self Test : Enabled
  CPU Update Data        : Enabled
  Boot from LAN First    : Enabled
  Boot Sequence          : A,C,SCSI
  Swap Floppy Drive      : Disabled
  VGA Boot from          :        AGP
  Boot up Floppy Seek    : Enabled
  Boot up Numlock Status : On
  Typematic Rate Setting : Disabled
  Typematic Rate(Chars /sec)   : 6
  Typematic Delay(mSec)  : 250
  Security Option        : Setup
  PCI/VGA Pallette Snoop : Disabled
  Assign IRQ for VGA     : Enabled
  OS Select for DRAM > 64MB    : Non OS2
                                    ┌────────────────────────────────────────┐
                                    │ ESC : QUIT           ⇑ ⇓ ⇒ ⇐:Select    │
                                    │ F1  : Help          PU/PD  :Modify      │
                                    │ F5  : Old Values     ShiftF2  :COLOR    │
                                    │ F6  : Load BIOS Defaults                │
                                    │ F7  : Load Performance Defaults         │
                                    └────────────────────────────────────────┘
```

A typical set are shown in the illustration and are detailed below:

Virus Warning
Enabling this makes the BIOS stop the machine and display an error message if any program tries to write to the first sector of the disk, where the Master Boot Record is stored. This can be useful, but is no substitute for a properly configured and updated virus checking program.   It can on occasion interfere with operating system upgrades.

CPU Internal Cache
Disabling this option will cause the onboard cache memory on Pentium or better processors to be disabled. This will drastically slow the performance of the chip but can help to diagnose processor / memory speed problems. If enabling and disabling the onboard cache has no effect on performance then the chip's internal cache is suspect.

External Cache
This is very similar to the previous options, but it disables the L2 cache. Again this option can be used to diagnose processor /memory speed matching or to confirm the operation of the L2 cache circuits.

CPU L2 Cache ECC Checking
Enabling this option will force Cyclic Redundancy Checking to be carried out on the contents of the external cache memory. This will very slightly slow the machine, but can be used in mission critical situations to increase process integrity.

Processor Number Feature
This option enables a specific feature of Pentium III chips. It should be enabled for Intel PIII chips where desired, and disabled for anything else.

Quick Power On Self Test
Setting this to enabled will make the machine carry out only the most basic memory tests. This will cut the startup time to about 20% of the time taken with Full POST. The difference can be significant, especially on machines with lots of memory.

CPU Update Data
This option should be used once when a new CPU has been fitted to tell the bios to interrogate the mask type and stepping number so that the BIOS is always optimally matched to the processor.

Boot from LAN First
If enabled the machine will try to download a boot program from its network card. This is necessary when setting up diskless workstations such as terminal server /winframe machines.

Boot Sequence
This option is used to decide where the machine looks for its system files on startup.

Swap Floppy Drive
On systems with two floppy disks the disk drive at the end of the cable (beyond the twist) is the A: drive. If it is necessary to use the other drive as A: then this option should be enabled.

VGA Boot from
Many modern machines have AGP slots for high speed graphics cards. The same machine will usually also have PCI slots, which can also hold a video card. The setting of this option decides which of the cards is the one that displays the information during bootup.

Boot up Floppy Seek
Used to decide whether the machine waits for its floppy drive to try and locate a system at boot time. If the machine usually boots from hard disk then this should be disabled to increase boot up speed.

Boot up Numlock Status
This option decides whether the keypad keys on the right of the keyboard start as number keys or cursor control keys. Most modern machines have dedicated cursor keys and so this option should be enabled.

Typematic Rate Setting //
Typematic Rate //
Typematic Delay
These options refer to the system built into the keyboard that makes it wait for a short time if a key is held down and then make the key repeat its signal. This typematic behaviour is controlled by these settings.

Security Option
A setting such as this allows the setup of security based options controlled by the BIOS. For instance, whether or not the Passwords setup elsewhere are asked for.

PCI/VGA Palette Snoop
It is possible to have Video Cards on both PCI and ISA busses at the same time. If this is the case then there is likely to be a conflict with regard to palette memory. By enabling this setting such conflicts can be eliminated.

Assign IRQ for VGA
This option will decide whether or not the VGA system uses one of the processors IRQ resources.

OS Select for DRAM > 64MB
IBM's OS2 operating system expects to find a *'hole'* in memory, that is to say an area of memory that cannot be addressed /read from /written to normally. This memory hole is located in a series of consecutive locations above 64MB. If the OS is IBM OS2 then the addressing hole should be installed, otherwise no memory hole setting should be selected.

HDD S.M.A.R.T capability	This option is set if the machine is fitted with Self Monitoring Analysis and Recording Technology. If the hard disk is suitably equipped then it can interrupt the processor to have the BIOS announce that it may need repaired or replaced.
Video BIOS Shadow	DRAM is considerably faster than PROM and so by copying the video BIOS program from its native ROM.

The Operating System

A computer Operating System (or '*OS*') is required for all personal computers, to provide the user with a range of machine and disk utilities. The operating system provides the control software for all the common input/output facilities e.g. getting a keystroke from the keyboard and displaying characters on the screen at the correct position, reading and writing files, and general housekeeping maintenance.

Operating Systems can be broadly classified into two types – *Graphical User Interfaces* or GUIs (such as Windows or Mac systems) and Command Line Interfaces or CLIs (such as DOS or UNIX). This section deals mainly with configuring DOS, but most versions of Windows still support the majority of DOS settings. See the Windows Configuration chapter for further details of setting up a Windows system.

All operating systems have 2 main objectives.

1. To use the resources of the computer efficiently. Some devices in the computer work more quickly than others. Part of the task of the operating system is to ensure that slower peripheral devices do not hold up faster devices.

2. To conceal the difficulties of dealing directly with the hardware of the computer. The operating system takes care of these tasks. So, those who write or use software do not have to have a detailed knowledge of computer hardware. A single command from the user to the operating system, results in many low level commands on the hardware. For example, if the user wishes to save a file, the system software will automatically handle all the complex tasks of checking whether there is free space on the disk, moving the write head to the free area, writing the file information to disk, updating the disk information area, etc.

As can be seen from the diagram, the user never deals directly with the computer hardware. All user commands are handled by the operating system, which passes the appropriate instructions to the hardware. Many application packages allow the user to carry out file handling activities, such as loading and saving tasks. In these cases, the user chooses options from the application menu and these choices are passed on to the OS to then pass on to the hardware. The user talks to the application - the application talks to the OS - and the OS talks to the hardware. However, for the more complex tasks, the user has to directly interface with the OS software. Many of the less common, more complex, OS facilities are not directly available through application packages. These commands have to be entered by the user, either via some OS software in the case of a GUI, or at the keyboard in the case of a CLI. To obtain the maximum use of the operating system requires an understanding of its composition and, in a CLI, its set of commands.

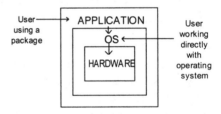

What is MS-DOS

MSDOS stands for '*Microsoft Disk Operating System*' and before Windows 95 it was by far the most common operating system used on PCs. It is still available in some form in all subsequent versions of Windows, though its importance is being reduced. It was created for IBM by the now giant American Microsoft Corporation and was originally known as PCDOS. The roots of MS-DOS are in the CP/M operating system of the 70's. It first appeared in 1981 and had 6 major and many minor revisions. Upgrades have seen additions such as handling hard disks, RAM disks, new display standards, mice, memory-resident programs, expanded memory and networks. Version 4, although it broke through the previous restriction on 32MB disk partitions, never took off. Versions 5 and 6 have been big successes, due to their extra facilities such as memory management and greater flexibility of some of the commands. It is still not the ideal operating system and its many shortcomings created a market for add-on utilities such as Norton Utilities, Xtree, Magellan, etc. In the last few releases, particularly v6 and 6.2, Microsoft added many of the facilities that previously were only gained by purchasing add-ons. These additions include virus protection, file defragmenters and disk surface testers.

MS-DOS acts as a buffer between the user and the computer, and makes difficult tasks like the copying and deletion of programs very easy.   There are other PC operating systems on the market, such as DRDOS and UNIX, but the vast majority of all PC machines in the world use a version of MS-DOS or Windows. Version 7, distributed with Windows 95, is a much-reduced product since most of the facilities are embedded in the Windows environment.

MS-DOS is not a single program - it is a collection of related programs, as a glance at the DOS directory will show. This collection drives the hardware of the computer and manages its resources. Thus, it provides an automatic buffer between the user and the hardware, as shown previously.

CONFIG.SYS

The CONFIG.SYS file allows the user to change the system's default configuration settings.   Typical contents of a CONFIG.SYS file might be as shown:

It is simply a text file, with each text line containing a description of an alteration to the standard system configuration. This means that the file can be created with any standard text editor such as DOS EDIT or any word-processor used in ASCII mode.   It also means that the file can be easily edited to add, delete or modify the commands contained in it.

```
device=c:\WINDOWS\HIMEM.SYS
device=c:\WINDOWS\EMM386.EXE noems
DOS=HIGH,umb
COUNTRY=044,850,C:\DOS\COUNTRY.SYS
DEVICEhigh=C:\DOS\DISPLAY.SYS   CON=(EGA,,1)
devicehigh=c:\dos\ansi.sys
FILES=10
BUFFERS=10
STACKS=9,256
```

Note
- None of the changes to CONFIG.SYS take effect until the system is re-booted.
- To work, the file must be in the root directory.
- A configuration file might only contain a few lines. The size of the file will depend on the system and its intended use.

Commands in CONFIG.SYS

The common commands for inclusion in the configuration file, CONFIG.SYS, are explained next.

BUFFERS

This command is concerned with the transfer of data between the computer and the disk drives. This is a very slow process, compared to transferring data between different parts of the computer memory. Because of the mechanical movements involved in disk activities, it is typically 100 to 1000 times slower than memory transfers. Repeated disk access to read or re-read parts or even individual bytes of a file may incur this delay every time the disk is accessed.

To speed up disk read/write activities, the system can allocate chunks of memory to temporarily store the data that your program most recently read/wrote. These memory blocks are called *'buffers'*, and they constitute a very basic disk caching system. When MS-DOS has to process a disk request, it first looks to see if the required data is already in the buffers.   If the required data is found, it is copied into the main computer memory, by-passing the slower disk access. Each buffer is 512 bytes long, plus 16 bytes for control data, and there may be from 1 to 99 buffers, though in nearly all cases the default is 15. However most machines nowadays either use Windows' VCACHE system or DOS's SMARTDRV system, both of which supersede BUFFERS, and some also have dedicated cache chips on the disk controller (see chapter on disks).

As with all cache systems, there is a trade-off:
1. Although buffers are designed to improve performance, every time the system tries to access data that is not currently in the buffer it results in an additional delay while the buffer is checked. With too many buffers this delay might even slow the system down overall. Unless software requires it, buffers should not be set higher than about 20-30.
2. Since each buffer takes up 528 bytes of main memory, the resource requirements of software used on the machine should be balanced against the performance benefits.

FILES

This command is used to set the maximum number of files that can be in use at the one time.   DOS can assign up to 255 files but the default value sets up 8 file handles, each of which consumes 48 bytes of main memory. MS-DOS uses five of these areas for its own use.   Often, eight will be enough but many DOS and Windows 3.1 applications, including Windows 3.1 itself, require a much higher figure.

Generally, 30 files should be set for use with Windows 3.1, with another 10 added for each application that is expected to be run concurrently.   So, if only Word is in use 40 files are adequate; if the user has Excel and Word open at the same time, then FILES should be set to 50.

As with BUFFERS, the FILES setting should be considered with reference to the amount of main memory the user needs to run their applications.

COUNTRY

Different countries have different keyboard layouts and screen displays, to match the countries' particular language constructions.   Many languages, such as Arabic and Hebrew, require an entirely different character set from the usual 26-character Roman alphabet.   Specially tailored versions of DOS are required in such cases.   However, a large part of the world uses the Roman alphabet with minor variations such as accented or acute letters.   For these a common core system was created, with a single piece of software (COUNTRY.SYS) from which the elements of a particular country could be extracted. Different countries have different methods of displaying the date, time and the separators between numeric values.   For example, countries such as Holland, Sweden and Germany use a comma to separate decimal places and a full stop to separate thousands.   So, the British value of 3,000.99 would appear as 3.000,99.   The date of 1st October 1999 would be displayed on a British machine as 01-10-1999, on an American machine as 10-01-1999 and as 1999-10-01 in Sweden.   The default character set is USA.   To establish the UK display, the CONFIG.SYS should contain the command COUNTRY=044, 044 being the international dialling code for the UK.   This is set up from the COUNTRY.SYS file, perhaps in the DOS folder, and the COUNTRY setting should be told this.

Thus, the full command in CONFIG.SYS should be:

COUNTRY=044,,C:\DOS\COUNTRY.SYS

NOTE   Windows 95 based operating systems can set the keyboard and regional settings through the Control Panel, but most Windows systems contain a COUNTRY setting for DOS sessions.

DEVICE

The bootstrapping process has set up an area in high memory, to hold the details of the default device drivers, as previously mentioned.   A device is typically something that can be read from or written to. A device can be hardware with the mouse being a device that is read while a monitor is a device that is written to.   A device can also be 'virtual', which means that it can act as a device.   An example of this would be a disk file; in this example, the device can both be read and written.   The driver is the software that lets the computer communicate with a device.   A standard set of device drivers is provided and these are:

CON	Short for CONsole. A combined keyboard and monitor device. The way that it is used inside a command determines whether it is a read from the keyboard or a write to the monitor.
AUX	AUXiliary device. A default name for COM1, the first serial port.
PRN	PRiNter. A default name for LPT1, the first parallel port.
LPTs	Line PrinTer. The range of parallel port devices, starting from LPT1.
COMs	COMmunication ports. The range of serial port devices, starting from COM1.
NUL	This is a dummy device; it does not exist as an actual physical device. It is used for testing or disabling screen output. Examples are given in the section on batch files.

These drivers are automatically loaded into a list in memory when the computer is first booted up. DOS and Windows already have these drivers stored within IO.SYS. This list of devices is created even if the hardware devices do not all physically exist in that machine. Where the user wishes to extend the default list, to provide an enhancement to the system, the extra device driver can be added to this list in memory. Examples of extra drivers would be those for mice, network interface cards, RAM drives, file compressors, plotters, etc.   These devices require their own software drivers to interface the computer to the hardware device.   When the list of device drivers is compiled in the machine memory, the extra installed drivers appear in the driver list before the standard drivers.   This means that an installed driver can be used to replace a standard device driver - since any call to a device will find the installed driver first.   For example, ANSI.SYS can be used to replace the standard keyboard driver and the standard screen driver.   Any call routed to the keyboard or screen is intercepted by the ANSI driver, to provide extra facilities beyond those provided in the standard drivers.   This extra functionality has to be paid for by the loss of machine memory occupied by the extra driver software.

Additions are achieved by the use of the command DEVICE=filename in the CONFIG.SYS file. These files also have the .SYS extension and are loaded and given control. The driver then carries out the configuring of itself and the system for the new facility. There are many such extra devices that are supplied by various manufacturers. If an add-on hardware device is purchased, such as a mouse, the package will usually also contain the necessary software driver.

Again, Windows 95 and later systems use the Control Panel to install devices, but older non-Windows compatible device drivers can still be installed using DEVICE=. However, caution should be taken as such drivers can reduce the system efficiency.

Note:

Most drivers are installed as described above but some are installed via AUTOEXEC.BAT instead of CONFIG.SYS. They will not have the .SYS extension but will still be device drivers nevertheless. Examples of such drivers are MOUSE.COM and SMARTDRV.EXE.

DOS and Windows Drivers

The other device drivers supplied with MS-DOS and Windows include:

HIMEM.SYS & EMM386.EXE

These are important memory management drivers and are covered in detail in the later section on memory management.

SMARTDRV.EXE

This driver appeared with DOS version 5 and is used to create a disk cache for the computer, to speed up disk intensive activities. Like BUFFERS, it sets aside an area of memory to store the most regularly used data read from/written to disk. With BUFFERS, the temporary storage occupies part of the 640k memory area, lowering that available for application programs. With SMARTDRIVE, the temporary storage can either occupy extended or expanded memory. If the SMARTDRIVE disk cache system is implemented, there is little need for large BUFFERS, and these can be reduced to 4 or 5 for use with the computer's floppy drives. The minimum syntax is:

DEVICE=SMARTDRV.SYS

and this would create a default disk cache of 256k. The allowable parameters are:

DEVICE=drive\path\SMARTDRV.SYS 1024 512 /a

The parameters in the example are:

- drive\path indicates the drive and directory where the SMARTDRV.SYS file can be found. If no parameter is given, the file is looked for in the hard disk's root directory.
- 1024k (i.e. 1MB) has been set aside for the disk cache. Valid sizes range from 128 to 8192, user values being rounded to the nearest 16 if necessary. If the value given is greater than the memory available, the system sets up the maximum cache that it can. About 2048k is the highest realistic setting as any extra memory allocated after that produces only a minimal extra improvement; the extra memory is best left for Windows use.
- 512k has been designated as the minimum size to which the cache will shrink. Some programs (see section on Windows) will seize the cache allocation if the other extended memory is in use. This can reduce the size of the cache to zero and the second parameter specifies the lower limit to which any program can diminish the cache size.
- The /a parameter creates the disk cache in expanded memory. This would also require that an expanded memory manager be first installed. EMM386.EXE, for example, would appear earlier in the CONFIG.SYS script. If this parameter is omitted, the disk cache is established in extended memory. This would require that HIMEM.SYS appears earlier in the CONFIG.SYS script so that it can handle the extended memory activities requested by SMARTDRV.SYS.

Note:

When determining the maximum size for the disk cache, take into account that application programs probably wish to occupy part of the extended or expanded memory for their own use.

SMARTDRV and Windows 3.1

In a machine running DOS 5 and Windows 3.1, use the Windows SMARTDRV.EXE product instead of the DOS SMARTDRV.SYS file. The Windows version is a special version that is much faster due to its improved caching implementation. It also allows Windows to recover some of the cache space for its own use when required. These maximise the performance of Windows. With DOS 6 onwards, use the DOS version.

To prevent Windows 3.1 from seizing all the cache space, SMARTDRV can be set up to have a minimum as well as maximum size. The maximum size determines the most memory space that is devoted to cache activities. The minimum size determines the lowest point to which the cache will be reduced. So a cache configuration given by SMARTDRV 1024 512 would indicate a 1MB cache which would always have 512k available.

There is a trade off between the amount of extended memory allocated for disk caching and that left for Windows applications. On the one hand, a Windows application requires as much extended memory as it can to store the elements of the program. This avoids the slow process of swapping programs to the hard disk (see the section on virtual memory in the chapter on Windows Configuration). On the other hand, a Windows database will need a large cache area to store as much data as possible. It follows that the second parameter for SMARTDRV, the one that dictates the minimum disk cache size, should be set to a value corresponding to the applications in use on the machine.

Testing SMARTDRV

Asking for a report on cache hits can check the effectiveness of the SMARTDRV caching and cache misses. A cache hit is an occasion when the data was available in cache memory, while a cache miss involved fetching the data from disk. If the cache hits figure is divided by the total data calls (i.e. cache hits plus cache misses) and multiplied by 100, the resultant figure is a measure of the percentage efficiency of the cache system on that particular machine.

With the example given:

$$\frac{27612}{27612+4062} = 87\%$$

```
Microsoft SMARTDrive Disk Cache version 4.0
Copyright 1991,1992 Microsoft Corp.

Room for 256 elements of 8,192 bytes each
There have been 27,612 cache hits
    and 4,062 cache misses

Cache size: 2,097,152 bytes
Cache size while running Windows: 2,097,152 bytes

        Disk Caching Status
drive  read cache  write cache  buffering
-----------------------------------------------
  A:      yes         no          no
  B:      yes         no          no
  C:      yes         yes         no

For help, type "Smartdrv /?".
```

the figure is acceptable. Of course this rating will vary with the amount and type of activity carried out but a figure of 85% upwards would be regarded as an effective caching system while lower figures may require some adjustment in the cache size. The report on cache effectiveness can be invoked by giving the command

SMARTDRV/S

The figure should be calculated over a number of different sessions, so that an average efficiency figure is arrived at. SMARTDRV caches DOS as well as Window operations. If the efficiency of Windows caching alone is to be measured, then tests should be carried out when only Windows has been run since booting up, so that any DOS caching cannot upset the figures.

A likely assignment would be:

Memory Size	SMARTDRV Size	
	Normal	Minimum
2MB	1MB	256KB
4MB	1MB	512KB
8MB	2MB	1MB
>8MB	2MB	1MB

The minimum size set for SMARTDRV should not be below 256k if the system is to have any real effect. Each increase in cache size provides a lesser benefit than the preceding value. A value beyond 2MB would be wasteful except in circumstances where a CD-ROM is being cached. Buffers should be no more than 10 if SMARTDRV is operating; this will save some memory in the conventional memory area.

SMARTDRV and DOS 6 onwards

Microsoft's DOS v 6 provides extra caching facilities from version 4 onwards of SMARTDRV.

DOUBLE BUFFERING

This provides caching support to older SCSI drives, newer SCSI interface cards already being able to interface to Windows without this special help.

The following line is added to CONFIG.SYS:

DEVICE = C:\DOS\SMARTDRV.EXE / DOUBLE_BUFFERING

in addition to the following line

C:\DOS\SMARTDRV

being added to AUTOEXEC.BAT.

The double buffering scheme requires an extra 2.5k from conventional memory and should only be used where necessary.   With these commands in place, the system can be rebooted and the SMARTDRV command given from the DOS prompt.   If any of the entries in the *'buffering'* column on the right hand of the display show *'yes'* then double buffering is required; otherwise double buffering should be removed.

DRIVE CONTROL

Support is provided for *'write caching'* (see chapter on Disks and Drives).   Individual drives can have their read caching and write caching facilities set at bootup time.   If no drives are specifically mentioned in AUTOEXEC.BAT, drives are given default modes of operation.   These can be changed by mentioning the drive and using a + or a - as a switch.

An example assignment might be:

C;\DOS\SMARTDRV C+ D-

The following table shows the variations allowed, using the C: drive as the example.

	Read	Write
C+	ON	ON
C-	OFF	OFF
C	ON	OFF

If no drives are specified, the hard disk(s) is both read and write enabled, while floppies and CD-ROMs are read enable and write disabled.

EXTRA SWITCHES

These include

/X	Disables write caching of all drives
/U	Does not load SMARTDRV's CD-ROM handling code
/L	Will avoid using the UMB area so that it is free for other programs

Entering SMARTDRV/? displays a list of the switches available for the command.

SMARTDRIVE and Windows 95 onwards

SmartDrive was dropped from Windows 95 in favour of an improved caching system called VCACHE. This caching system does not required user assignment as it dynamically allocates itself to make best use of the available memory at any one time.   SmartDrive is still available in Windows 95 and later but only for the purposes of DOS sessions.

ANSI.SYS

This extends DOS' text display capabilities, providing additional character sets, control of colours, effects and so on.   It also allows control of the keyboard.   ANSI.SYS is not required in Windows but may be installed for the purpose of DOS sessions.

RAMDRIVE.SYS

This creates a virtual disk - i.e. RAM disk - in any expanded or extended memory in the computer (see the chapter on memory). These drivers allow a portion of the computer's memory to be used as though it was a disk drive. It has a drive letter allocated to it and the usual DOS commands (e.g. MD, CD, RD, COPY, DEL) apply to the virtual disk in the same way as they do to an actual physical disk.   For example, if the virtual disk is allocated the drive letter 'D', then the command   COPY C:*.*   D: is quite permissible.

Since there is no mechanical movement (as in disk access) involved in retrieving information from memory, the virtual disk acts as a very fast drive.   Its drawback is that its contents are lost when the power is switched off.

Its main uses are:

1. On a boot disk. Windows 98 based systems create a boot disk that uses a RAM drive. This makes the initial boot slower as the entire floppy is essentially copied into RAM, but once booting is complete it minimises floppy disk access, making for more efficient use of the computer.

2. Programs that are so large that it can't all fit into main memory at the one time. Such programs are split into sections called *'overlays'* and the various sections are loaded into the main memory as and when required.

Only parts of the program are in main memory at any one time. If the other overlay sections reside in virtual memory, then they can be called into main memory with great speed. This causes a noticeable improvement in performance with these larger application programs. A batch file could be written to copy the overlay files from the hard disk into the virtual drive prior to running the application and the application could be configured to expect the files to be in that particular drive.

3. The handling of temporary files. Many programs, particularly Windows applications, create many temporary files during their running. These temporary files are then deleted again when the application is exited. When the application crashes, many temporary files are left on the hard disk. These can range from small files to files of 1MB or more. The need to continually write to disk can be eliminated if the temporary files are stored in the virtual drive. These speeds up the running of applications and can be very noticeable when printing from an application. Windows printing results in the creation of temporary print files and the use of a RAM drive will result in control being passed back to the user from a print operation in a much quicker time. With temporary files, the fact that data is lost from the virtual drive on power down is a distinct advantage; any temporary files left after an application crash are removed automatically and do not clog up the hard disk. If this technique is used, the ram drive size has to be set at a figure to handle the largest files that are expected to be used, since the application will crash if there is not enough space on the virtual drive to store the temporary file.

The minimum syntax for creating a virtual disk is

DEVICE=RAMDRIVE.SYS

This would allocate a default virtual RAM disk size of 64k.

The allowable parameters are:

DEVICE=drive\path\RAMDRIVE.SYS 1024 512 64 /e

The parameters in the example are:

-   'drive\path' indicates the drive and directory where the RAMDRIVE.SYS file can be found. If no parameter is given, the file is looked for in the hard disk's root directory.
-   1024k (i.e. 1MB) of memory has been set aside for the virtual disk. The allowable range is from 16k to 4096k. Where no size is given in the command, the default value is 64k. If the disk demanded is greater than the physical memory present, the RAM drive size is automatically scaled down. In older systems the size of the RAM disk and SMARTDRV buffer should both be considered carefully with mind to the requirements of the operating system. For example a Windows 95 PC with 8MB or RAM cannot afford to allocate a 2MB RAM disk and a 2MB SMARTDRV buffer, as this would leave it with the barest minimum 4MB.
-   The virtual disk sector size has been established as 512 bytes. This is also the default value and is normally left unaltered. However, the user can choose between 128, 256 and 512 as permissible values.
-   The number of files and directories that can be created in the RAM drive's root directory has been set at 64. This is the default value and the permissible range is 2 to 1024. In fact, the virtual disk needs four sectors (the boot sector, the FAT, the directory and at least one data sector). If the size demanded differs from that which can be accommodated, the number is adjusted automatically. Consider the case of a sector size of 512 bytes. Each directory entry requires 32 bytes, so a 512 byte sector can contain 16 entries. If the RAM drive parameter in the CONFIG.SYS file only requests 7 as a maximum for files and directories, it is rounded up to 16 entries; if the parameter given is 19, then 16 entries will be allocated.
-   The /e parameter creates the RAM drive in the machine's extended memory. This would require that HIMEM.SYS appears earlier in the CONFIG.SYS script so that it can handle the extended memory activities requested by RAMDRIVE.SYS. If the parameter was specified as /a, the RAM drive would be created in the machine's expanded memory. This would also require that an expanded memory manager be first installed. EMM386.EXE, for example, would appear earlier in the CONFIG.SYS script. If no parameter is given, the RAM drive is created in conventional memory. Using up conventional memory is to be avoided, as it is likely that only the smallest of application programs will be able to fit into the remaining main memory.

If the default sector size and number of entries are acceptable, then these parameters can be omitted.

As an example, a 2MB virtual disk in extended memory would be specified as:

DEVICE=drive\path\RAMDRIVE.SYS 2048 /e

If there is sufficient memory in the machine, more than one virtual disk can be created by the use of more than one 'device=ramdrive.sys' command.

The RAMDRIVE.SYS file is implemented in IBM's PC-DOS as VDISK.SYS and the /a switch to place the driver in expanded memory is replaced with a /x switch.

RAMDRIVE vs SMARTDRV vs BUFFERS

There are a number of ways that the user can speed up processing through saving programs and data in memory for quick access.   These cache methods are compared below.

BUFFERS	RAMDRIVE	SMARTDRV
Useful in a machine with no extended or expanded memory. Consumes vital conventional memory in DOS systems. Little use in modern systems.	Data is lost if the machine is switched off before data is saved to disk. The process is not automatic; the user has to predict what files might be used so that they can be copied into the RAM drive. All other files are accessed in the normal, slow, way. A useful place to store temporary files or Windows swap files. Useful in a machine with no extended or expanded memory, as a small RAM drive can be set up in conventional memory. The memory allocated to RAMDRIVE cannot be used for other purposes.	The process is entirely automatic. There is no need to predict what data will be used. The system is limitless in the number of files and different sets of data it can handle during the machine's run; it is only limited by the number of files and data sets that can be held in the SMARTDRV memory at any one time. Files are opened and closed to best maintain the fastest flow of data for the user. Changes to files are regularly written away, minimising the loss of data from a power cut.

Disk Cache and Memory Cache

Disk caching is used to speed up data transfers between the disk drive and memory.   This should not be confused with memory caching which is a way of speeding up data transfers between main memory and the CPU.   Memory caching is dealt with in the chapter on Memory.

Proprietary Drivers

Any hardware device is normally supplied with drivers for various operating systems. DOS drivers are generally no longer supplied but older peripherals may still have a DOS driver version, and these are installed using the DEVICE= command in CONFIG.SYS

The device driver to handle the SoundBlaster Pro sound card is installed by adding the following command to the CONFIG.SYS file:

DEVICE=C:\SBPRO\DRV\SBPCD.SYS

To run the *'Stacker'* disk compression system, the following commands would be in the CONFIG.SYS:

DEVICE=C:\STACKER\STACKER.COM C:\STACVOL.DSK
DEVICE=C:\STACKER\SSWAP.COM C:\STACVOL.DSK /SYNC

Note that in the above case, the device drivers also have their own parameters passed in when they are being installed.

A common DOS device requirement is for a CD-ROM driver, even if only to access the Windows setup CD. A typical device might be installed like this:

DEVICE=C:\DRIVERS\NECIDE.SYS /D:MSD0001 /P:220

SHELL

The SHELL command is used to specify a different command processor from COMMAND.COM, such as a replacement supplied by a particular software product. The command is:

SHELL=C:\path\filename

This command can also be used where the normal DOS shell, COMMAND.COM, is not to be found in the root directory:

SHELL=C:\path\COMMAND.COM

These commands can include optional parameters:

SHELL=C:\path\COMMAND.COM/P/E:512

The /P ensures that the shell stays permanently, while the E parameter sets up the *'environment'* size in bytes, rounded up to the nearest 16. The environment space is a piece of memory that stores details of PATHs, the PROMPT, DIRCMD details, COMSPEC details, user defined variables and batch file replaceable parameters (see later).   The default size of the environment is 256 bytes (160 bytes for DOS 3.2) but it can be increased as above, if programs produce an *'out of environment space'* message.   The current contents of the environment area can be viewed by entering the SET command with no parameters. If the /F parameter is added to the command, DOS will provide a *'Fail'* response to a critical error. This avoids the *'Abort, Retry, Fail'* choice when a user attempts to read or write to a floppy drive that does not have a disk inserted. This is usually accompanied by long pauses and several attempts to return to the DOS prompt. With the /F parameter, the user is given a *'Current Drive not valid'* message and is instantly returned to the DOS prompt.

BREAK

MS-DOS will stop executing a command when either CTRL-C or CTRL-Break is pressed. This check is only made when the computer is taking input from the keyboard or sending output to the screen or printer. Pressing the key combinations has no effect, for example, when reading or writing to disk. Where it is required to extend the abilities of MS-DOS or programs to interrupt the process by pressing either CTRL-C or CTRL-Break, the command BREAK=ON can be added to CONFIG.SYS.

However, this addition forces extra checks for these key presses - and this slightly slows down the computer operations. If this facility is not required, it can be turned off with BREAK=OFF (this being the default condition). Pressing CTRL-Break during the execution of an application would normally take the user out of the application and return to the DOS prompt. To prevent this happening, most applications trap the pressing of CTRL-Break and take their own appropriate action.

> **Note:** Although the BREAK command is often placed in the CONFIG.SYS file, it can also be placed in a batch file, or the user can even enter it directly from the keyboard.

LASTDRIVE

This command is used to set the maximum drive letter that MS-DOS will accept. The drive letters vary from A to Z. The default is a last drive of E. Where extra channels are to be added (e.g. extra drives, disk partitions, RAM drives, a network, tape backups) the default can be extended by the command LASTDRIVE=x, where x is the last drive letter in use. Since MS-DOS allocates a data structure in memory for each specified drive, only the drives required should be listed in LASTDRIVE.

SUBST

This command provides a shortcut for users who regularly use a particular directory. It makes a particular sub-directory look like a disk drive. Consider the effects of the following command:

    SUBST W: C:\APPS\WSTAR\FILES

Here, the command links the drive letter *'W'* to a specified drive directory.

After this command, any reference to the W: drive is actually concerned with the FILES sub-directory at the end of the given path.

This means that the command COPY *.* C:\APPS\WSTAR\FILES can be shortened to COPY *.* W:

There will be a new logical drive W: and this will have to be taken into account when setting LASTDRIVE, as discussed above. The current list of assignments can be displayed by giving the SUBST command with no parameters. The /D parameter deletes an association between a drive letter and a path. So,

    SUBST W: /D

will delete the association created in the above example.

Another use for the command is to allow the easy switching of floppy drives where a program insists on fetching data from a particular drive. This can be achieved with

    SUBST A: B:

Creation or deletion of SUBST assignments should be carried out while within Windows. Also, disk commands such as CHKDSK, FORMAT, DEFRAG and RESTORE should not be used with SUBST drives; such commands should always be used with actual physical drive names.

STACKS

Every computer has a number of memory areas to store signals from *'multiple interrupt devices'* (e.g. LANs and hard disks). The computer's CPU has only a limited number of internal registers (memory locations built in to the chip at the manufacturing stage). This can be inadequate for the running of the system. When a program runs, there is a constant need to:

- Process hardware activities in the most efficient way.
- Pass parameters (data and control information) from one program sub-routine to another.

- Memorise the return memory address of the calling sub-routine that temporarily calls another sub-routine. This allows control to return to the correct point in the calling program, when the called routine is exited.

An example of stack operations is a user pressing a key on the keyboard during a file save operation. The system wishes to process the keyboard activity but it wouldn't stop the disk write activity. So it places the keyboard interrupt on the stack and processes it as soon as the disk write is complete.

Under DOS, the computer can have from 8 to 64 stacks, the default being nine. The size of each stack can vary from 0 bytes to 512 bytes, the default being 128 bytes. The default sizes should be left, unless changes are demanded by a particular application. Under certain circumstances, the default values may not be enough and this will result in messages such as *"Internal Stack Failure"* or *"Divide Overflow"*. In these cases, the stacks can be increased, bearing in mind that extra stacks devour main memory. Inadequate stack size leads to loss of information or, even worse, loss of program control (known as a *'crash'*).

The command STACKS=10,256 would reserve space for 10 stacks, each capable of holding 256 bytes. The command STACKS=0,0 can be used to eliminate pre-determined memory stacks where each program that will be run provides its own stack arrangements. When Windows is installed it sets up stacks as 9,256 but this can be reset to 0,0 with no ill effects and memory can be recovered, as long as it does not produce any *'parity error'*, *'Internal Stack Overflow'* or *'Exception Error 12'* messages.

SETVER

Some DOS application programs check the version of DOS that they are running under and this can cause difficulties where the DOS version is newer than an application. For example, an application written to run under DOS 6 may refuse to run under DOS 6.22, while a program written for DOS 6.22 might not run under DOS 7 (Windows). Programs that are written to work under a particular DOS version will check to see if that version is in use on the machine. If it not the recognised DOS version, the program will not load - even if the DOS version on the machine is <u>better</u> than the version being tested for.

SETVER is the solution, and maintains a table of names of application files such as EXE, COM, BIN or SYS files, along with the version number that the file will look for. SETVER will then intercept the package's request for version information and 'fool' it into running by giving it the version it requires. The utility has to be loaded via a CONFIG.SYS line:

DEVICE=drive\path\SETVER.EXE

This loads a table into memory that already contains a list of programs and their correct version numbers. To view the list, simply type SETVER. To add to the list, enter

SETVER drive\path\prog.exe n.nn

where *'prog.exe'* is the file to be added to the list and *'n.nn"* is the DOS version to be tagged to the file. To delete from the list, simply add the parameter /d to the end of the command e.g.-

SETVER drive\path\prog.exe /d

Since SETVER and its table consume memory, it should only be used where problems are being experienced in running certain DOS applications. If a machine contains all the latest software, or the existing software runs happily under the current DOS version, SETVER should be not be included in the CONFIG.SYS file and memory can be saved.

NUMLOCK

The Numlock key controls the use of the numeric keypad section of the keyboard. When pressed, the keypad is interpreted as a set of numbers; pressing the same key again interprets the same key presses as cursor control keys. If a computer is to always start up with the keypad producing numerics, the line

NUMLOCK = ON

should be added to CONFIG.SYS. Similarly the command NUMLOCK = OFF will ensure that the computer always starts up with the keypad recognised as a set of cursor controls.

FCBS

In DOS version 1, files were accessed via *'File Control Blocks'* (FCBs). These are memory sections, each 40 bytes, which store file names and other attributes. Software packages dropped this method, preferring the FILES= command. FCBS can be set in the CONFIG.SYS but is only required for the very oldest systems. It is added by specifying the number of blocks, and the default is four. In nearly all cases it can be safely set to zero, saving a small part of lower memory.

Commands in AUTOEXEC.BAT

AUTOEXEC.BAT is a special file that the system looks for, after carrying out the CONFIG.SYS stage of the configuration process. It is an optional file but, if it is present, the instructions contained within it will be executed one after the other. If it is not present when booting to DOS, then the operating system will instead run the commands DATE and TIME in place of the AUTOEXEC.BAT file. AUTOEXEC.BAT is of the *'batch file'* type to be examined later. This is a special type of batch file, in that it runs automatically each time the machine is switched on. For this reason, it is used for further refinements to the machine configuration. The commonly used commands to be found in this file are:

PATH

To run a particular executable program such as an EXE, COM or BAT file, the user normally either:
- moves into the appropriate sub-directory, using CD, and calls up the program by name.
- calls the program using its full description, including the path of sub-directories
  e.g.   C:\BUSINESS\FINANCE\EXCEL

This is cumbersome and also expects that the user knows the path where the file can be found. This task can be made much easier by including a PATH command in the autoexec file. This command tells MS-DOS where to look for programs, by giving a list of drives and directories that should be searched. The syntax is the word PATH, followed by the first sub-directory to be searched. Each new sub-directory to be searched can be added to the existing path, being separated from the earlier part of the path by a semi-colon. Now, as long as the executable file exists in one of the sub-directories contained in the path, it can be called and run from anywhere in the directory structure.

For example, the following PATH command -
    PATH C:\MS-DOS;C:\UTILS;C:\FINANCE\EXCEL

would instruct MS-DOS to search through the MS-DOS, UTILS and EXCEL directories, if the wanted file was not found in the current directory. Note that the FINANCE directory is not searched.

If the wanted file is not in the current directory or in any of the directories named in the path list, it cannot be called without the user knowing where it resides in the directory structure.

Since the search is conducted in the order specified by the path, the most frequently accessed directories should appear earliest in the path statement.

The path can be up to 128 characters in length and is stored in the *'environment variables'* area, a block of memory taken from the main 640k memory area. Although the PATH command is usually embedded in the AUTOEXEC.BAT file, it can be issued as a direct command from the DOS prompt. Any new paths set up directly from the keyboard will replace any set up by AUTOEXEC.BAT and will remain in force until the machine is rebooted.

To view the currently operating path, the PATH command can be given with no parameters; this will result in the current path being displayed. To clear the current path setting use the command with a semi-colon as parameter - i.e.
                    PATH;

Windows 95 and later operating systems still use the path for certain operations, such as *Start / Run*, but it is of greater importance in DOS.

APPEND

The PATH command only allows users access to executable files and does not provide access to data files. However, most applications require not only the EXE files, but also a number of overlay files, help files, data files, etc. To run such applications, the user requires to access both the executable and non-executable files in an application sub-directory. To achieve this, DOS provides an APPEND command. This command functions in exactly the same way as the PATH command, except that it applies to non-executable files, and has a similar syntax:
            APPEND C:\BUSINESS\FINANCE\EXCEL;C:\DATAFILES

The above command lets the user access data files in the two sub-directories named in the APPEND command, from any part of the directory structure. Like PATH, the APPEND command can contain up to 128 characters and occupies part of the main memory allocation.

To view the currently operating APPEND path, the APPEND command can be given with no parameters; this will result in the current append path being displayed. To clear the current APPEND path setting, use the command with a semi-colon as parameter - i.e. APPEND;

If the command has the /x parameter added, then the APPEND command will also search the APPEND paths for executable files. If the command has the /e parameter added, the path is held as an environment variable called 'APPEND', allowing access to its contents via a batch file.

Note:

Any application called via the APPEND path that needs to create new files will create them in the <u>current</u> directory and not in the application's home directory.

KEYB

The KEYB command is used to set up the correct keyboard for a particular country. The default keyboard is an American layout and the diagram shows the different layout of keys on a French keyboard. If the KEYB command is not included in the autoexecute file, it will produce transposed keys (such as the @ symbol, and the double quotes symbol).

To obtain a British keyboard, the command KEYB UK should be given. In older versions of DOS the location of the COUNTRY.SYS file that contains this information had to be specified, like so:

KEYB UK,,C:\DOS\KEYBOARD.SYS.

This loads a device driver to interpret the keystrokes from the keyboard as the expected QWERTY layout. Compare this with the French keyboard layout, which uses the AZERTY layout. To move from the default USA keyboard to a French interpretation, the AUTOEXEC.BAT script would contain a KEYB FR command. Similarly, KEYB GR configures for Germany, KEYB IT for Italy and KEYB NL for the Netherlands, and so on.

PROMPT

The normal on-screen prompt is C>. This can be altered by the PROMPT command followed by the required symbols.

The list of symbols and their uses is:

SYMBOL	MEANING
$p	Current drive and path
$g	> symbol
$l	< symbol
$t	Current time
$d	Current date
$v	DOS version number
$n	Current drive
$q	= symbol
$h	Backspace and delete
$_	Carriage return & line feed
$b	The | (pipe) character
$$	Dollar sign
$e	ESC character for ANSI calls

The most common use is PROMPT pg, which displays the current directory in which the user is sitting - e.g.   C:\WS5>

If the command is PROMPT $t then the on-screen prompt is: The current time is 11:17:35.45

If the command is

PROMPT $p time=$thhhhhh $g

the prompt is altered to something similar to

C:\WS5 time=3:08 >

The details of the current prompt are stored in the environment area.

MOUSE

The way that a mouse is installed in a computer varies from system to system. Generally on Windows PCs the mouse device in Control Panel is used, providing support for mouse in DOS sessions. However, this does not provide mouse support when booting directly to DOS. There may be a file called MOUSE.COM or similar, that installs a resident program to drive a mouse device. The command MOUSE can be added, if this facility is available and is required. If there is no demand for the mouse, the command should be omitted from the AUTOEXEC file, to avoid wasting memory space. Windows has its own built-in mouse driver and, if all the mouse-driven applications operate under Windows, there is no need to install a separate mouse driver. Sometimes a mouse driver is installed as a system file, via the CONFIG.SYS configuration process. Alternatively, the MOUSE.COM file may be called via the AUTOEXEC.BAT file.

MODE

The MODE command fulfils multiple functions, to do with the standard DOS devices. For example, it can set the speed and data format of a serial port, the size and type of display on the console, or redirect printer data to other devices.

When a user presses PrtScr or re-directs text files to a printer (e.g. TYPE MEMO.DOC > PRN or DIR > PRN), the default is to route the data to the first parallel printer port LPT1.

To route data to a serial port, perhaps in order to print to a serial printer, the user has to give the following DOS command:

MODE LPT1:=COM1:

This will direct any printer output to the serial port until the direction is disabled with the DOS command:

MODE LPT1:

Another common use for the MODE command is to set codepages. Many Windows computer systems will contain the following in the CONFIG.SYS:

```
device=C:\WINDOWS\COMMAND\display.sys con=(ega,,1)
Country=044,850,C:\WINDOWS\COMMAND\country.sys
```

and the following in the AUTOEXEC.BAT:

```
mode con codepage prepare=((850) C:\WINDOWS\COMMAND\ega.cpi)
mode con codepage select=850
```

Here, the MODE command is being used to prepare and then select a codepage that has been attached to country 044 (the UK). The file '*ega.cpi*' contains a font set. While KEYB can be used to interpret incoming data from the keyboard, MODE is being used to format text to the screen properly.

Setting Environment Variables

As explained earlier, the environment area is a section of memory dedicated to holding the details of the PROMPT, the PATH and various other variables.   The environment area is allocated 160 bytes on bootup but this can be increased to as much as 32k using the SHELL command.

The contents of the environment are a series of text statements such as:

COMSPEC=\COMMAND.COM

which tells DOS where to find the transient portion of COMMAND.COM, or:

PATH=C:\;C:\DOS;C:\UTILS

which stores the details of the PATH statement given in the AUTOEXEC.BAT file or a PATH statement subsequently entered directly from the keyboard.

DOS 5 onwards also supports a DIRCMD variable that can be used to change the default display of directory listings.   For example, if a wide directory is preferred, then the AUTOEXEC.BAT file could contain the line SET DIRCMD=/W.   If the AUTOEXEC file contained the line SET DIRCMD=/ON then all directory listings are displayed in sorted alphabetical order.   The command is stored in the environment area.   To view the current environment contents, give the command SET without any parameters.   The prompt and path contents are stored as variables with their variable names.   These variables can be accessed for use within batch files. Thus, a batch file can contain a line saying

echo The current path is %PATH%

Often, applications are required to create temporary files during the running of their programs.   This may be achieved by declaring the sub-directory that will hold these temporary files at the point of installing the application.   Other programs store their temporary files in a directory that is pointed to by the variable TEMP in the environment.   Such a declaration might be:

SET TEMP=C:\TEMP

The application interrogates the contents of the TEMP variable to see where it should write its temporary files. If the machine has been configured to have a virtual disk, then the RAM drive can be made the home for the temporary files. This would greatly speed up program execution, since the reads and writes are to memory and not the hard disk. In this case, the CONFIG.SYS would include:

SET TEMP=D:\

This technique has another benefit. Applications often create temporary files during the running of the program and then delete these files on leaving the application. In this way, a user never sees them. There are times, however, when an application is not exited safely (e.g. the machine is switched off before exiting the application or the program hangs and the machine has to be rebooted). In these cases the temporary files are left on the hard disk. The command DIR *.TMP/S will list any unwanted temporary files; do not run this command from within Windows as the temporary files may still be in use. If the TEMP directory is on hard disk, these files will occupy valuable disk space. If the TEMP directory is a virtual directory in memory then all temporary files are automatically lost when the machine is switched off, requiring no extra maintenance to keep the hard disk free of unwanted temporary files.

It is also possible to use the SET command to create and initialise variables that can be used by batch files or applications programs.

For example, a soundcard might use the following:

    SET BLASTER=A220 I7 D1 T4

DOSKEY

The DOSKEY utility is a command line utility of use only in DOS systems or DOS sessions on Windows machines. It made its first appearance with DOS v5 and it provides four extra facilities:

- Command recall
- Command editing
- Multiple commands on a single line
- Creation of user-defined macros

DOSKEY is a TSR of about 3k in size. Using DOSKEY also consumes a default 512 bytes of memory to act as a buffer to store command line commands and macros. To alter the buffer size, the command

    DOSKEY /BUFSIZE = n

can be given where n is the required buffer size (256 bytes being the minimum).

Command Recall

The simplest use of DOSKEY is to include the command, without parameters, in the AUTOEXEC.BAT file. This loads the program as a TSR that stores each command given by the user at the DOS prompt. The number of commands that can be stored depends on the length of the commands and the allocated buffer size. When the buffer becomes full, any new command is stored at the expense of the oldest command. The process can be regarded as a conveyor belt that stores a list of the most recent DOS prompt commands. All of these commands in the buffer are available for re-use. This saves having to repeat the typing of long and complex commands. If they have already been recently entered, they can be recovered from the buffer and run again.

To place the last command in the buffer back into the command line, press the UP arrow key. This is identical to pressing the f3 in other DOS version. However, pressing the UP arrow key again brings the second last command into the command line. Using this, and the DOWN arrow key, all the stored commands can be fetched - one at a time - into the command line. When a desired command is in the command line, the user only has to press the ENTER key to run the command; the command now becomes the last one in the buffer. To jump to the earliest command in the list, the user presses the PgUp key, while pressing the PgDn key fetches the latest command in the list.

Pressing the f7 key displays the entire list of commands currently stored in the buffer. The earliest command is preceded by the number 1, the next by the number 2 and so on. Once displayed, the user can press f9, followed by the number of the desired command. This brings the command into the command line from where it can be run. If the user knows the start of the command, the first few letters of the command can be entered at the DOS prompt, followed by pressing the f8 key. This displays the most recent command in the buffer that matches the search text. Pressing f8 will find the next latest command meeting the search text. If there are no commands that match the search text, pressing f8 produces no results and the user is returned to the DOS prompt.

Multiple Commands

Before DOSKEY, the user had to use several, independently given commands to carry out complex functions. The first command would have to be typed in and run before the second command could be entered. DOSKEY allows the user to type in several commands in the one command line statement (up to a maximum of 128 characters) and have them all carried out when the ENTER key is pressed.

Consider the following set of commands:

    DIR *.BAK/S > BAKLIST
    DIR *.TMP/S > TMPLIST

The commands in the above example produce two text files.   The first command lists all .BAK files that inhabit the disk, while the second creates a list of all existing .TMP files.   The creation of such lists would prove useful in tidying up the disk.   It would be more convenient if the user could combine both commands on to the one command line.   After entering the line, the user could then leave the machine unattended and the two files would be created one after the other.

If DOSKEY is installed the user can enter the command as one line thus:

  DIR *.BAK/S > BAKLIST ¶ DIR *.TMP/S > TMPLIST

The paragraph mark (i.e. the ¶ symbol) is achieved by pressing Ctrl-T.

User-Defined Macros

A DOSKEY macro is a facility to create *'aliases'* - i.e. a list of commands can be called by invoking a single name.   It can be likened to a single line batch file.   The macro name and its associated commands are stored in the buffer area and can be up to 127 characters in length.   Consider the above example of creating lists of backup and temporary files.   If this was to be a regular activity, the user can be saved the trouble of typing in the long command.   The commands can be entered and named thus:

  DOSKEY GETLISTS=DIR *.BAK/S $G BAKLIST $T DIR *.TMP/S $G TMPLIST

The user then need only give the 'GETLISTS' command to run the macro.   The macro definition can be entered directly at the keyboard but regularly used utilities can be set up in the AUTOEXEC.BAT file. When the machine boots up, the AUTOEXEC.BAT commands are carried out and the DOSKEY lines set up the users own defined macros.   Note that macros use the dollar symbol and the letter 't' to separate commands, instead of the ¶ symbol used when entering directly from the keyboard.   The redirection of input and output symbols used in normal DOS commands are similarly replaced as shown.

DOS	DOSKEY
<	$L
>	$G
>>	GG
|	$B

In normal batch files, parameters can be passed in and these *'replaceable parameters'* are designated from %1 to %9 (see section on batch files for full details).   Macros using DOSKEY can also handle replaceable parameters but they are designated from $1 to $9.   An example macro with replaceable parameters is: DOSKEY GETLISTS=DIR *.$1/S $G FILELIST

DOSKEY can also be used to redefine any existing internal DOS command as in this example

  DOSKEY DIR = DIR/W/P

Memory Management

The aim of memory management is to utilise the whole memory of the machine in such a way that the maximum amount of user memory is available for application programs and data, consistent with achieving the maximum functionality and speed.   In Windows 95 and later, since there is no '640k barrier' to speak of, the memory management is more or less automatic and should not need alteration. However, even Windows systems can boot to DOS for troubleshooting or to run older applications.

> ➡ Memory usage is explained in detail in the chapter on memory and should be
>   reviewed before proceeding with memory management.

Until the advent of DOS 5, there was little room for major memory planning.   Earlier versions allowed for user setting of FILES and BUFFERS sizes and allowed users to install TSR programs via batch files (mainly AUTOEXEC.BAT) and device drivers via CONFIG.SYS.   Careless use of these settings (e.g. installing rarely used device drivers, setting FILES or BUFFERS parameters beyond the actual requirements, setting FILES or BUFFERS below the minimum required by an application, installing many TSRs) could seriously affect machine performance, or even prevent an application running.

These problems could exist while part of the machine memory, areas above 640k, was completely unused.   These unused areas - termed *'upper memory blocks'* - were capable of holding device drivers, etc. but DOS was not able to re-allocate into these areas.   The gap was filled by add-ons such as *'PC KWIK'*, and 'QEMM' which allowed the allocation of device drivers into unused UMBs.

Viewing Memory Statistics

MSDOS provides a utility that displays facts about the machine's memory usage. The MEM command provides information about what is occupying the conventional and upper memory areas of the machine and displays the size and memory location of programs, data, drivers, etc.

The MEM command provides three different switch options, as below:

/CLASSIFY or /C

Lists all the programs that are in conventional memory and upper memory including their size in decimal and hexadecimal. It also provides a summary of the machine's memory usage. An example display may be as shown on the chart on the left.

/PROGRAM or /P

Lists all currently loaded programs, including their name, type (i.e. program, data, environment), size and memory location.

/DEBUG or /D

Similar to /P but also includes internal drivers, as shown on the chart on the right.

Address	Name	Size	Type
-------	--------	------	------
000000		000400	Interrupt Vector
000400		000100	ROM Communication Area
000500		000200	DOS Communication Area
000700	IO	000A60	System Data
001160	MSDOS	0013D0	System Data
002530	IO	005300	System Data
	HIMEM	000430	DEVICE=
	EMM386	000CA0	DEVICE=
		000130	FILES=
		000100	FCBS=
		003E60	BUFFERS=
		0001C0	LASTDRIVE=
0078C0	MSDOS	000040	System Program
007910	COMMAND	000940	Program
008260	win386	000040	Data
0082B0	COMMAND	000100	Environment
0083C0	WIN	0000A0	Environment
008470	WIN	000570	Program
0089F0	win386	0000B0	Environment
008AB0	win386	000540	Program
009000	COMMAND	0000B0	Data
0090C0	COMMAND	000940	Program
009A10	COMMAND	000100	Environment
009B20	MEM	0000A0	Environment
009BD0	MEM	0176F0	Program
0212D0	MSDOS	07ED10	-- Free --
09FFF0	SYSTEM	028E40	System Program
0C8E40	IO	003590	System Data
	RAMDRIVE	0004A0	DEVICE=
	ANSI	001060	DEVICE=
	DISPLAY	002060	DEVICE=
0CC3E0	win386	000090	Data
0CC480	SMARTDRV	007A90	Program
0D3F20	KEYB	001840	Program
0D5770	SHARE	001830	Program
0D6FB0	win386	0000A0	Data
0D7060	DOSKEY	001020	Program
0D8090	UMBFILES	000B90	Program
0D8C30	win386	0073C0	Data

```
    655360 bytes total conventional memory
    655360 bytes available to MS-DOS
    615440 largest executable program size

  15990784 bytes total contiguous extended memory
         0 bytes available contiguous extended memory
   1048576 bytes available XMS memory
           MS-DOS resident in High Memory Area
```

```
Conventional Memory :
```

Name	Size in Decimal		Size in Hex
-------------	--------------------		-------------
MSDOS	26576	(26.0K)	67D0
HIMEM	1072	(1.0K)	430
EMM386	3232	(3.2K)	CA0
COMMAND	2624	(2.6K)	A40
win386	1584	(1.5K)	630
WIN	1552	(1.5K)	610
COMMAND	2800	(2.7K)	AF0
FREE	615616	(601.2K)	964C0

```
Total  FREE :    615616    (601.2K)
```

```
Upper Memory :
```

Name	Size in Decimal		Size in Hex
-------------	--------------------		-------------
SYSTEM	167472	(163.5K)	28E30
win386	29936	(29.2K)	74F0
RAMDRIVE	1184	(1.2K)	4A0
ANSI	4192	(4.1K)	1060
DISPLAY	8288	(8.1K)	2060
SMARTDRV	31376	(30.6K)	7A90
KEYB	6208	(6.1K)	1840
SHARE	6192	(6.0K)	1830
DOSKEY	4128	(4.0K)	1020
UMBFILES	2960	(2.9K)	B90

```
Total  FREE :        0    ( 0.0K)

Total bytes available to programs (Conventional+Upper)
    :    615616 (601.2K)
Largest executable program size
    :    615440 (601.0K)
Largest available upper memory block
    :    0 ( 0.0K)

  15990784 bytes total contiguous extended memory
         0 bytes available contiguous extended memory
   1048576 bytes available XMS memory
           MS-DOS resident in High Memory Area
```

Notes:

- The /D and /P options show the addresses and sizes in hexadecimal only, with the summary information in decimal.
- If the machine is fitted with extended memory, then this is included in the display.
- If the machine is fitted with expanded memory, then this will only be included in the display if it conforms to LIM 4.0 specification.
- The *'largest executable program size'* displays the largest possible program that the computer's conventional memory can store.
- *'Available XMS memory'* is the amount of extended memory being managed by HIMEM.SYS or other extended memory manager.

MSDOS Memory Management

MSDOS allows users to maximise the memory available for user programs by placing drivers, etc. into memory above the 640k user area.

Consider the memory map shown in the diagram. This represents a typical machine without any optimisation. The machine's AUTOEXEC.BAT and CONFIG.SYS files will have inserted a range of drivers and utilities into the user memory area, as shown. Also, the entire DOS kernel sits in the user memory area.

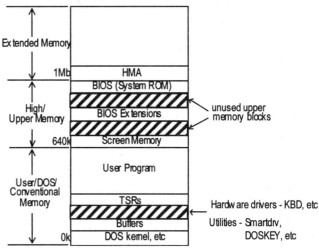

Note:

Most books/manuals define the 640k area as conventional memory and the 1MB area as base memory; others describe base and conventional memory as equivalent terms.

All books accept that the 640k can be described as user memory.

```
Conventional Memory :

    Name          Size in Decimal      Size in Hex
    ----          ---------------      -----------

    MSDOS         63424      (61.9K)      F7C0
    HIMEM          3696     ( 3.6K)        E70
    EMM386         3232     ( 3.2K)        CA0
    RAMDRIVE       1184     ( 1.2K)        4A0
    ANSI           4192     ( 4.1K)       1060
    DISPLAY       18048     (17.6K)       4680
    COMMAND        4704     ( 4.6K)       1260
    SMARTDRV      31376     (30.6K)       7A90
    KEYB           6208     ( 6.1K)       1840
    SHARE          6192     ( 6.0K)       1830
    DOSKEY         4128     ( 4.0K)       1020
    FREE             64     ( 0.1K)         40
    FREE            144     ( 0.1K)         90
    FREE            160     ( 0.2K)         A0
    FREE         508288    (496.4K)      7C180

Total  FREE :    508656    (496.7K)

Total bytes available to programs : 508656   (496.7K)
Largest executable program size :   508288   (496.4K)

15990784 bytes total contiguous extended memory
       0 bytes available contiguous extended memory
 8372224 bytes available XMS memory
       64Kb High Memory Area available
```

Note that while this overcrowding is taking place in the base memory area, it is almost certain that there will be unused areas of memory address in the upper memory area.

Using the DOS MEM/C command would produce a display similar to the display shown.

Note that the total memory available for running application programs is a mere 496KB, which is inadequate for much modern software. DOS itself requires about 62K and the rest of the 640k is eaten up with various drivers and utilities.

The solution lies in moving much of the drivers up into the unused areas of upper memory, while still being able to access them for their normal functions. Even better is moving part of the DOS kernel out of base memory up into extended memory.

Using Extended Memory

All PCs, from the 286 series onwards, which are fitted with extended memory can be manipulated with DOS memory management tools. The first 64k of extended memory (i.e. the first 64k beyond the 1MB conventional memory) is known as the *'HMA'* or *'High Memory Area'*. This should not be confused with the Upper Memory Blocks that reside between 640k and 1MB. The HMA is largely unused by application programs. It is possible, therefore, to use the HMA to store parts of the DOS kernel, instead of placing it in base memory. To achieve this, the CONFIG.SYS should have the following two lines inserted at an early point in the script:

> device = c:\dos\himem.sys
> dos = high

The first line loads the extended memory manager into base memory. HIMEM.SYS acts as an organiser of both the HMA and the rest of extended memory, preventing the simultaneous use of the same area of memory by different programs. This driver is compulsory where Windows is used. Since it manages extended memory and acts as the link between base and extended memory, it follows that this driver must remain in base memory.

However, the addition of this extra driver into base memory frees much more memory than it devours. The HIMEM line should appear before any other line that seeks to use extended memory.

The second line instructs the HIMEM driver to load the DOS hidden files, MSDOS.SYS and IO.SYS into the high memory area.   Since this line appears at an early stage in CONFIG.SYS, it can be assumed that the HMA is unused and so DOS can be safely loaded there.

The MEM/C command would now produce a display similar to that shown.   Note that MSDOS now only occupies just under 26k of base memory.   If this figure is compared with the previous display on the previous page, it can be seen that exactly 36k of DOS has been saved from the base memory.   Yet, it can be seen that just over 50k of extra memory is now available for user applications, since DOS was loaded into the HMA.   The explanation for the difference lies in the added benefits of moving parts of DOS into the High Memory Area.   If BUFFERS is set to 48 or less, then these DOS buffers will also be moved up to the High Memory Area.   If BUFFERS is set to 44 or less, then even a part of COMMAND.COM is moved up into the High Memory Area.   Even with these improvements, device drivers are still using up a substantial part of base memory.

```
Conventional Memory :

    Name              Size in Decimal        Size in Hex
--------------       ---------------------   -------------
    MSDOS              26560     (25.9K)          67C0
    HIMEM               1072     ( 1.0K)           430
    EMM386              3232     ( 3.2K)           CA0
    RAMDRIVE            1184     ( 1.2K)           4A0
    ANSI                4192     ( 4.1K)          1060
    DISPLAY             8288     ( 8.1K)          2060
    COMMAND             2624     ( 2.6K)           A40
    SMARTDRV           31376     (30.6K)          7A90
    KEYB                6208     ( 6.1K)          1840
    SHARE               6192     ( 6.0K)          1830
    DOSKEY              4128     ( 4.0K)          1020
    FREE                  64     ( 0.1K)            40
    FREE                 144     ( 0.1K)            90
    FREE                 160     ( 0.2K)            A0
    FREE              559600     (546.5K)        889F0

Total  FREE :         559968     (546.8K)

  Total bytes available to programs : 559968    (546.8K)
  Largest executable program size :    559600   (546.5K)
  15990784 bytes total contiguous extended memory
         0 bytes available contiguous extended memory
  8372224 bytes available XMS memory
          MS-DOS resident in High Memory Area
```

These can be loaded into the unused Upper Memory Blocks on 386 or better machines.

Using Upper Memory Blocks

Computers, prior to optimisation, will have a number of unused areas of upper memory that are not currently devoted to servicing added hardware such as local area network interface adapters or add-on ROM extensions.   The fitting of cards results in their control chips being mapped in to an area of the upper memory.   So, for instance, a video card usually is placed at segment address C000 (i.e. 768k), an XT disk controller may be at C800 and a SCSI card or cache controller may be at DC00.   This leaves areas of upper memory that are not in use at all. If the CONFIG.SYS file is altered, then these unused blocks can be used for loading the device drivers currently occupying base memory.   From 386 machines onwards, the following lines are required to achieve this:

>   device = c:\dos\himem.sys
>   device = c:\dos\emm386.exe noems
>   dos = high,umb

The first line, as before, loads the interface between base and extended memory.   The second line loads the EMM386 driver.   This driver is dual purpose - it allows access to the Upper Memory Blocks and it can also be used to configure extended memory to act as expanded memory for those programs that use expanded memory.   In the example, we wish to use the first facility and disable the second facility. That is the reason for the *noems* parameter, which stands for *'no expanded memory'*.   The 64k that expanded memory would require for its paging area is now available for storing various drivers. Omitting the *'noems'* parameter, or using the *'ram'* or *'auto'* parameters will result in the system using 64k of UMB space as an EMS page frame.

It should be noted that it is unlikely that all these unused areas of upper memory will actually have memory chips fitted.   Yet DOS expects to find all its TSRs and drivers within the 1MB area.   The EMM386 software solves the problem by storing the drivers, etc. into extended memory and maps (i.e. links) the DOS call to the actual place where the routine is stored.   The third line adds the parameter *umb* to inform the system that a DOS link is established between base memory and the upper memory area.

Now the way is prepared to load devices into any unused UMBs.   In this instance, there is free memory available in the Upper Memory Area.   On other machines, it would be advisable to run MEM/C to check on whether there are any free UMBs - and whether any free block is large enough to store the size of the new driver to be loaded.   There are two methods of loading device drivers into upper memory blocks. This is because device drivers can either be loaded via CONFIG.SYS using 'device= ' commands, or via AUTOEXEC.BAT using COM and EXE files, such as KEYB.COM or SMARTDRV.EXE.

Note: Windows applications do not make use of EMM386, since all their memory management needs are met by HIMEM.SYS.   EMM386 can be used for normal DOS programs, or for DOS programs running under Windows.   The *'noems'* parameter prevents the creation of expanded memory under DOS; Windows can still create expanded memory dynamically - i.e. only when it needs it.

DEVICEHIGH

The normal 'device=' type command in CONFIG.SYS can be replaced with the 'devicehigh=' command in order to load the device driver into the upper memory area. Examples are:

        devicehigh=c:\windows\ramdrive.sys 3076 512 200/e

        devicehigh=c:\dos\ansi.sys

LOADHIGH

Instead of simply entering the filename in the AUTOEXEC.BAT script, the command can be prefaced with the word 'LOADHIGH' to place it in upper memory.   Examples are:

        loadhigh c:\windows\smartdrv.exe 2048 2048

        loadhigh keyb uk,,c:\dos\keyboard.sys

        loadhigh c:\dos\share.exe

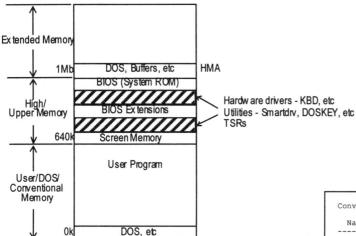

The new, optimised, PC memory map as described in the example now looks similar to that shown on the left.

The MEM/C command would now produce a display similar to that shown below.

The display now provides statistics on both the base memory and the upper memory usage.

Note that although the EMM386 driver occupies some base memory, all the drivers have now been loaded up into the upper memory area.

As before, DOS is reported as being resident in the High Memory Area.

The base memory now available to user application programs has risen to over 607k.

There is still room in the umbs to load another one or two devices, since the display reports that the largest available upper memory block is just under 29k in size.

Note:

The order in which drivers appear in the configuration files can alter performance and this is looked at later.

```
Conventional Memory :

    Name             Size in Decimal         Size in Hex
 -------------      ------------------       -------------
    MSDOS              26576     (26.0K)         67D0
    HIMEM               1072     ( 1.0K)          430
    EMM386              3232     ( 3.2K)          CA0
    COMMAND             2624     ( 2.6K)          A40
    FREE                  64     ( 0.1K)           40
    FREE              621600    (607.0K)         97C20

Total  FREE :         621664    (607.1K)

Upper Memory :

    Name             Size in Decimal         Size in Hex
 -------------      ------------------       -------------
    SYSTEM            167472    (163.5K)        28E30
    RAMDRIVE            1184     ( 1.2K)          4A0
    ANSI               4192     ( 4.1K)         1060
    DISPLAY            8288     ( 8.1K)         2060
    SMARTDRV          31376     (30.6K)         7A90
    KEYB               6208     ( 6.1K)         1840
    SHARE              6192     ( 6.0K)         1830
    DOSKEY             4128     ( 4.0K)         1020
    UMBFILES           2960     ( 2.9K)          B90
    FREE                144     ( 0.1K)           90
    FREE                160     ( 0.2K)           A0
    FREE              29632     (28.9K)         73C0

Total  FREE :         29936     (29.2K)

Total bytes available to programs (Conventional+Upper)
    :       651600    (636.3K)
Largest executable program size
    :       621440    (606.9K)
Largest available upper memory block
    :        29632    (28.9K)

15990784 bytes total contiguous extended memory
       0 bytes available contiguous extended memory
 8372224 bytes available XMS memory
         MS-DOS resident in High Memory Area
```

MEMMAKER

DOS 6 introduced an automated system for PC configuration called *'MemMaker'*.

When this program is run, it boots the PC and monitors how the various drivers and TSRs listed in CONFIG.SYS and AUTOEXEC.BAT are loaded.   It notes the size of each device to be installed. It then compares the available memory blocks with the needs of each TSR and driver.   From this it calculates the optimum usage of the UMBs.

It then alters the LOADHIGH and DEVICEHIGH lines so that each item is loaded into the most appropriate slot to provide maximum usage of the UMB areas.

These alterations make use of the new /L switch that is available in DOS 6.   This switch forces the TSR or driver into the memory block specified in the address given in the switch, regardless of the order of the lines in the CONFIG.SYS or AUTOEXEC.BAT files.

Finally it reboots so that the changes take effect.   If it has inadvertently mapped a device to a memory location in use by an adapter card, this will be detected on the second bootup.   The user is given the choice of undoing the changes or trying again using a less aggressive look at memory.

MemMaker is a handy utility for the inexperienced user or for generating a quick memory management setup.   However, it does not give perfect results and frequently has to be tweaked to provide the best performance.

When MemMaker is first run, it offers the choice of an Express setup which is fully automatic or a Custom setup which lets the knowledgeable user have more choice over the configuration.

Note:

The /L switch does not have to be generated by MemMaker and can be directly entered into CONFIG.SYS and AUTOEXEC.BAT by the user who has sufficient knowledge of the machine's memory map and the size of each module to be installed.

```
DEVICEHIGH /L:1,15792 =C:\DOS\DISPLAY.SYS CON=(EGA,,1)
DEVICEHIGH /L:2,12048 =C:\DOS\SETVER.EXE
DEVICEHIGH /L:1,9072 =C:\DOS\ANSI.SYS
```

Order of Devices

Where a number of TSRs and drivers are to be loaded, the order that they appear in the CONFIG.SYS can have an important influence over the efficiency of the resultant memory management.   In DOS 5 and in DOS 6 without use of the /L switch, TSRs and drivers are installed in the order that they appear in the CONFIG.SYS and AUTOEXEC.BAT files.   When installing a module, it is placed in the largest available UMB slot, whether or not a more suitable slot is available.   So, for example, a 20k module may be installed into a 32k slot, even though a 20k slot is free. A 25k module may therefore find that no slot can store it and the module will have to be loaded into conventional memory. A different order of installation would have placed the 25k module in the 32k slot and the 20k module in the 20k slot, resulting in no wastage of UMB memory and no wastage of conventional memory. MemMaker, or the use of the /L switch can specify the area to store a module and thereby optimise the use of memory.

Some users may be tempted to simply change the order of drivers. However this may have side effects and should be done with care. For example, if a CD-ROM drive is to be cached, then the MSCDEX driver must be loaded <u>before</u> Smartdrive is loaded.

By default, a page frame created by EMM386 is located in a 64k slot commencing at segment address 0D00h, often resulting in a spare memory block above and below the page frame area.   Some larger device drivers are unable to fit in any of these spare slots. If the page frame were located at a different starting address, the smaller memory block areas would be able to form a larger contiguous free area. This would allow larger drivers to be installed.

This can be achieved by adding a 'frame= ' parameter to the EMM386 line as in the following example:

DEVICE=C:\DOS\EMM386.EXE FRAME=C800 HIGHSCAN

This command locates the page frame to commence at segment address C800h, assuming the area is free (check with the MSD Memory utility).   Other possible relocation areas are segment E000h or E800h.

INCLUDE/EXCLUDE

DOS 6 onwards added the *'include'* and *'exclude'* commands to its list of memory management tools, to allow for any imperfections in the optimising process. For example, MemMaker will not include the B000-B7FF (704k to 736k) area in its optimisation, since this is used by SVGA video boards. MemMaker cannot detect the presence of SVGA boards and therefore leaves the area alone. Similarly, EMM386 will not include E000-EFFF (898k to 980k) area in its optimisation, since it is sometimes used for BIOS extensions.

These areas, and others, can be checked to see whether they are occupied by using the *'Memory'* option of Microsoft's MSD utility. This option will display the computer's memory map with information on whether each block of memory is in use or is free. Using the *'Memory Browser'* in the *'Utilities'* option will display a list of the ROMs that are installed in the machine, along with the address at which they are located and their size. From this, it should be possible to appreciate the exact usage of the current machine memory. This examination should also expose any address areas that are being overlooked in the memory management process.

If an unused memory area is to be included in the pool to be used for UMBs, the EMM386 command can be modified with the *'include'* option as shown:

DEVICE=C:\DOS\EMM386.EXE I=E000-EFFF I=C800-DBFF NOEMS

In the above example, two unused areas have been included into the UMB pool. Notice that the addresses are entered in hexadecimal numbering.

It is also possible that an area of addresses could be tested as free when it actually contains a ROM. In this case, the driver would think it was installed to a UMB area when it actually failed to load (since it is impossible to write to a ROM). An attempt to call the driver would instead run the ROM code and this would result in a crash of Windows or the Windows application. DOS 6 also provides an *'exclude'* option to ensure that any such conflicts are avoided. When the clash of address areas is discovered - and this may be a case of trial and error - the area can be excluded from the memory management process as below:

DEVICE=C:\DOS\EMM386.EXE X=DC00-E000 NOEMS

In this example, the area has been found to contain a ROM for a SCSI card.

Using the X= switch followed by the unwanted area has prevented that area from being added to the UMB pool.

Who Does What

Each area of memory is organised and managed by different memory management code as described and these are as shown as a reminder in the following table.

Memory Range	Address Range	Memory Manager
Base	0 - 640k	DOS
Upper	640k - 1024k	EMM386
HMA	1024k - 1088k	HIMEM
Extended (XMS)	1024k upwards	HIMEM
Expanded (EMS)	Page Frame Area	EMM386

Add-On Memory Managers

The techniques outlined above use utilities that are provided free with Microsoft DOS or Windows. More sophisticated utilities are available from third-party suppliers. They replace EMM386, etc. and produce better results. The most widely known example is QEMM from Quarterdeck. Some drivers require more memory during initialisation than they do once they are finally installed. If the early larger requirement is too large for a free UMB, MemMaker will not use that block. This may result in a driver being placed in conventional memory. Programs such as QEMM provide a *'stealth'* facility. This will place part of the code in another memory area during initialisation, knowing that it will be discarded after the driver is installed. In this way, the driver can be fitted into some UMBs that appear to be smaller than the driver's file size.

Multi-Configuration

If a machine is dedicated to the one type of job, then the correct configuration can easily be set up via CONFIG.SYS and AUTOEXEC.BAT.   Where a range of activities has to be carried out then these activities probably have different memory requirements.   One package may require expanded memory while another may wish to use extended memory.   Yet another package may work best with lots of memory configured as a RAM drive. This is overcome by having a range of different configurations saved as CONFIG.1, CONFIG.2, etc.   When a particular setup is required, the required file is copied as CONFIG.SYS.   The same procedure applies to the AUTOEXEC files.   When both required files are copied, the machine can be rebooted so that the wanted configuration will take place.

With DOS 6, a much-improved system was offered where the different configurations all existed inside the same CONFIG and AUTOEXEC files.   On bootup, the user is offered a menu and only the script lines that correspond with the user's choice are implemented.

EXAMPLE   Consider a user with four distinct needs:

1. A spreadsheet package that requires lots of expanded memory.
2. A database package that can make good use of a RAM drive.
3. Access to Windows 3.1.
4. Access to a local area network.

This requires four different configurations as the machine's available memory would not be sufficient to create expanded memory, extended memory, a ram drive and all the necessary drivers and TSRs.

The listing on the next page shows the script of a *'multi-configuration'* system as provided by DOS v6. The heart of the system is the **[menu]** section.   This always commences with the [menu] shown in the first line.   This is then followed by a *'menuitem'* line for each option that is required.

The word after the equals sign is the name of the section of configuration code to be run.   This is followed by name of the option as it will appear on the opening screen.   These are separated by a comma.

```
[menu]
menuitem=Lotus, Run the Spreadsheet
menuitem=DataEase,Run the Database
menuitem=Windows, Run Windows
menuitem=LAN, Enter the Network
menucolor=7,1
menudefault=Windows,10

[common]
device=c:\dos\himem.sys
dos=high
files=40
country=44,,c:\dos\country.sys

[Lotus]
device=c:\dos\emm386.exe 4096
device=c:\dos\smartdrv.exe 2048
buffers=40

[DataEase]
device=c:\dos\emm386.exe noems
dos=umb
device=c:\dos\ramdrive.sys 4096 /e

[Windows]
dos=umb
stacks=0,0
buffers=10
device=c:\dos\smartdrv.exe 2048 2048

[LAN]
stacks=9,256
```

In the example, there are four options.   The *'menudefault'* line specifies which option will be taken if the user does not choose within a certain period of time.   This time is measured in seconds and the example will take the Windows option if the user has not decided within ten seconds.

The *'menucolor'* line sets up the screen colours, with the first number being the foreground colour and the second number being the background colour.   The colour numbers are the standard set shown in the table.

The **[common]** section provides the script lines that are common to all configurations and the lines in this section are implemented no matter which option is chosen.

0	Black
1	Blue
2	Green
3	Cyan
4	Red
5	Violet
6	Yellow or Brown
7	White
8	Black or Grey
9	Bright Blue
10	Bright Green
11	Bright Cyan
12	Bright Red
13	Bright Violet
14	Bright Yellow
15	Bright White

There then follows each of the four different machine configurations, each with a header that corresponds to the menu section.   So, the menu option for spreadsheets is linked to Lotus in the menu.   The menu then looks for the line **[Lotus]** in the script and runs the code within that section.

In this way, the same CONFIG.SYS file can provide user choices at bootup.   To choose a new configuration, the user reboots the machine and takes a new option.

There is only one drawback with multi-configuration systems. They can't be used with MemMaker.   This is because MemMaker uses the /L switch to place drivers in specific addresses and these will probably differ from application to application.

Multi-Configuration AUTOEXEC.BAT

The same technique can be used with AUTOEXEC.BAT as was used with CONFIG.SYS.

It is possible to run different parts of the file dependent upon the choices taken within CONFIG.SYS.

Passing control to different parts of the script is achieved through the line *'goto %config%'*.   When the user chooses an option in CONFIG.SYS - i.e. either Lotus, DataEase, Windows or LAN, that choice was placed in an environment variable called *'config'*. When the CONFIG.SYS file is exited, the variable will still hold the value that was chosen and this can be passed on to the AUTOEXEC.BAT file.   This variable can then be used to decide which section of the script should be enacted.   The environment variable is accessed with the AUTOEXEC.BAT file as %config%.   (see elsewhere for more details of batch files including the 'goto' command and environment variables).

The example listing shows four distinct sections of code, each corresponding to the choices in CONFIG.SYS.   The first section of code carries out the activities that are common to all choices, such as setting a British keyboard, etc.

The Lotus and Windows sections simply run the packages.   The DataEase section loads all the data files to be used into the RAM drive for faster processing, before running the application package itself.   The LAN section loads the various network drivers and places the user at the login stage of entering the network.

```
@echo off
prompt $p$g
keyb uk,,c:\dos\keyboard.sys
path c:\dos\windows
goto %config%

:Lotus
cd 123
Lotus
goto end

:DataEase
copy c:\dease\files\*.* c:\ramdisc\*.*
cd dease
dease
goto end

:Windows
win
goto end

:LAN
ipx
netx
login

:end
```

Debugging the Scripts

If a machine is not configuring itself in the way that was intended, DOS 6 and DOS 6.2 provide facilities for checking out lines in the CONFIG.SYS and AUTOEXEC.BAT files.   With DOS 6, the machine can be booted and the user can wait until the *"Starting MS-DOS..."* message appears.   Pressing the f5 key at this point will by-pass all the commands in the CONFIG.SYS file.   Pressing f8 at the message allows the user to by-pass individual lines of the CONFIG.SYS file.   In this mode, the user is asked whether the line should be carried out and waits for a Y/N reply.   Pressing the Esc key at any stage carries out all the remaining commands in the file while pressing f5 ignores all the remaining commands in the file.   With DOS 6.2, these facilities affect both the CONFIG.SYS and AUTOEXEC.BAT files.   Older DOS versions do not have these facilities and require the files to be amended and the machine rebooted. These options are also available when booting to DOS in a Windows 95 or later operating system.

By a process of removing lines or making lines inactive, the cause of the problem can be located.   A line in AUTOEXEC.BAT can be made inactive by REMming it out.   This means placing the letters REM in front of a command.   It will then be ignored at bootup time.   A line in CONFIG.SYS can only be REMmed out in DOS version 5 onwards; with older DOS versions, the line would have to be temporarily edited out.

Order of Command Calls

The command processor is called COMMAND.COM and this is loaded into memory when the machine is booted up.   Within that file is a range of utilities.   These are known as *'internal commands'* and are listed below:

> CALL, CHCP, CD, CLS, COPY, CTTY, DATE, DEL, DIR, ECHO, ERASE,
> EXIT, FOR, GOTO, IF, LOADHIGH, MD, PATH, PAUSE, PROMPT, RD,
> REN, SET, SHIFT, TIME, TYPE, VOL

This list of utilities is chosen to contain the most basic commands.   To avoid wasting main memory space, not all available MS-DOS commands are included in this file.   The extra commands are available as separate small programs that reside on disk (usually in its own MS-DOS sub-directory).

These commands are only loaded into memory when the program is called. These are called *'external commands'* and some examples are listed below:

CHKDSK, DEBUG, DISKCOMP, DISKCOPY, FDISK, FORMAT, KEYB, LABEL,
MORE, PRINT, RESTORE, SHARE, XCOPY, MSD, CHOICE, MOVE, DELTREE.

When a command is entered by the user at the keyboard, it is analysed by the COMMAND.COM file. It then carries out the search for the appropriate file to run, in the order shown in the diagram. The *'Parser'* is a component of COMMAND.COM and its job is to separate the command itself from any of its parameters.   For example, if a command was 'TYPE WORK.DOC', then the program called 'TYPE' would be searched for and given the parameter 'WORK.DOC'.

- First, a match is sought in the memory resident DOSKEY commands.
- If the program is not found, a match is sought in the internal commands within COMMAND.COM
- If the program is still not found, a match is sought for a file with the .COM extension.
- If this file is not found, a match is sought for a file with the .EXE extension.
- If no EXE file is found, a match is sought for a file with the BAT extension.
- Finally, if no match is found, an error message *'Bad command or file name'* is given.

User command

↓

PARSER

↓

Is it in DOSKEY ? — yes → Execute the DOSKEY TSR program

↓ no

Is it in COMMAND.COM ? — yes → Execute the internal command

↓ no

Is it a .COM file ? — yes → Load and run the COM file

↓ no

Is it a .EXE file ? — yes → Load and run the EXE file

↓ no

Is it a .BAT file ? — yes → Load and interpret the batch file

↓ no

"Bad command or file name"

Installing DOS

Modern versions of DOS cannot boot to a useable OS directly from the manufacturer's floppy disks, since the files are stored in a compressed format. The files have to be decompressed before use but can be used thereafter from either the hard disk or a set of other floppy disks.   In commercial situations, the files would always be held on the machine's hard disk.

Installing DOS on a machine is normally a straightforward process, with little input from the user.

Installation Procedure

The DOS disk marked as disk 1 should be placed in the A: drive and the machine should be booted up. This runs the installation program that begins by checking out the computer's hardware configuration.

First Screen

It presents a first screen of options with default values as shown.   In the United Kingdom, the Country option should be changed to UK and the Keyboard option should be changed to UK English.

Date - date currently stored in the machine's internal clock
Time - time currently stored in the machine's internal clock
Country - United States
Keyboard - US English
Hard Disc or Floppy - Hard Disc installation

Second Screen

The second screen of options presents the options shown. Normally, the default directory should be left as \DOS. This can create a company standard, as the files will always be found in the same directory on every machine in the organisation.   Similarly, few - if any - organisations would

Install to - C:\DOS
Shell on Start-up - Run / Don't Run Shell
Single DOS partition

wish the DOS shell to be invoked on machine start-up, as this invites experimentation from machine users.   The last option is only available on machines that do not already have a DOS partition and have the free space. The setup process works with a single partition as its default.   When all the options are selected, the installation program copies the files from the floppies, decompresses them (using the file EXPAND.EXE) and places them in the chosen directory of the hard disk.   The installer swaps the installation disks when requested by the program. The whole operation takes less than 10 minutes.

Protecting Existing Configuration

The installation process replaces any current versions of AUTOEXEC.BAT and CONFIG.SYS with default files from the floppy disk. The current versions would be over-written and this would mean that important settings and drivers would be lost. So, before carrying out any DOS installation/upgrade, these files should be renamed as AUTOEXEC.OLD and CONFIG.OLD. When the installation process is completed, the new versions of AUTOEXEC.BAT and CONFIG.SYS can be deleted and the .OLD versions renamed back to AUTOEXEC.BAT and CONFIG.SYS. In this way, the carefully tweaked settings are preserved.

System Disks

The support engineer should always carry a floppy system disk, to allow access to a machine where the hard disk fails to operate. This may happen for a number of reasons, such as the accidental deletion of COMMAND.COM or other system files. Where a number of DOS versions exist in an organisation on different machines, a system disk for each DOS version would be advisable.

Multiple Booting

Multiple booting is different from multiple configurations, which is where the machine starts up the same Operating system with different configuration settings. With multiple booting, the machine can start up entirely different operating systems each time it is booted.

As explained elsewhere any hard disk drive's partition table will allow a maximum of four partitions. Each partition can be any one of a variety of partition types, as noted in the table. Only one partition may be *active* at any time, and only the active partition is bootable. In some cases, in order to use a partition of one type, another partition must also be used. For example any creation of a Linux native partition will require the use of a Linux swap partition. This swap partition is one that Linux uses to swap out memory pages for faster access. Thus, a hard disk with a Linux native and a Linux swap partition could also support two further partitions before

Type	OS
00h	Reserved
01h	FAT 12 pri
02h	Xenix
03h	Xenix
04h	FAT 16 pri
05h	Extended DOS
06h	>32MB DOS
80h	Linux Native
81h	Linux Swap
DBh	Concurrent DOS

the four partition limit is reached. It is also worth bearing in mind that a single partition, when allocated as an extended DOS partition (this nomenclature remains, even though DOS as an operating system is obsolete), can hold more than one logical drive. If all of the partitions are to be used with the same operating system then there is no issue, and partitioning can be used simply to keep the individual partitions below the 2GB maximum imposed by some file systems. On the other hand it is perfectly feasible to run different operating systems in different partitions on the same hard drive. Some operating systems can also access data from a partition used by another operating system. Linux, for example, can access a Windows FAT or FAT32 partition and read or write to files therein. In order to Boot with different operating systems, each time the machine is switched on a mechanism must be used for deciding which partition is active. This will in turn decide which OS boots up.

There are various ways of doing this as outlined below:

Boot Manager Partition

A popular and quite easy solution is to dedicate a small partition to a boot loader program. This technique came from other areas of computing and was adopted by DEC for its Alpha Processor systems and IBM for its OS2 operating system. In fact the OS2 boot loader is a well-written example of this type of software and is still extensively used. Programs such as Partition Magic and System Commander use the OS2 loader intact, without modification. How such software works is by occupying a tiny active partition. The partition contains a small program, which on boot-up prompts for the user to choose an OS to load. It usually offers a time-out default choice as well. When an OS is chosen or the time runs out, the boot manager program passes control to the bootstrap loader on the partition selected, which then boots it's operating system normally.

    Advantages: Simple, reliable.

    Disadvantages: Requires software to be purchased. Uses up one of the four partitions allowed.

Boot Loader

Some operating systems supply a boot loader program. For example Linux's boot loader is called LILO, and it does all of the same work as the boot manager outlined above, without needing a separate partition. In this way any partition can be loaded, as with a boot manager partition, but without the disadvantage of taking up one partition.

> **Advantages:** Easy installation (usually installed automatically).
>
> **Disadvantages:** Not always available (e.g. not available for win95).

Program loader

This method of multi-booting uses a program inside one operating system to start another. Again, Linux is an example. A machine with both Win9X and Linux installed can have a directory in the Windows partition, which contains an executable called **loadlin**, and a one-line batch file called linux.bat. The executable is a copy of the Linux kernel, which is the operating system's command line interpretation program. By running the batch file, the user can invoke Loadlin to load linux into memory and use the linux partition table entry for all further work. Thus, Linux is started up from within windows.

> **Advantages:** Quick and simple to use.
>
> **Disadvantages:** Only some OS's have a program loader, Kernel on main partition has to match the target kernel on the other partition.

In addition there are other ways of running multiple Operating Systems that do not involve modifying Partition Tables. Among these are:

Floppy disk boot

This method is acceptable for MS-DOS, DRDOS or any OS that has a small kernel. Simply use a pre-prepared floppy disk with enough of the OS on it to boot the machine and allow further processing. With Linux for example, all of the popular distributions come with boot floppy images (sometimes called root/boot disk images) and a DOS program (rawrite.exe) which allow the images to be copied onto floppy disks using a DOS/Windows system.

CD-ROM boot

Another option is to run the OS directly from a CD-ROM. For example BEOS, a recent OS, uses a tiny kernel and will happily run from a CD-ROM. It must be remembered that in order to use the CD as a boot device, the BIOS must support booting from CD-ROM or ATAPI devices. Many older machines don't allow booting from anything other than the first floppy disk and the first hard disk.

Cohabiting operating systems

There are cases where two operating systems will happily share the same partition. This is of course only possible if the two operating systems use the same file system. NT4 and Windows 2000 can both exist on either NTFS file systems or FAT32 file systems, which are also used by Windows 95/98. Therefore an existing Windows 95 partition can also have Windows 2000 installed, as long as the Windows 2000 installation is FAT32 based, rather than NTFS based. When the machine is started an OS selection screen will appear prompting the user to select which OS to run.

Note:

> Whereas such operating systems as NT, Windows 2000, Linux, Win2k, and BEOS are designed for relatively experienced users, Windows 95/98 is designed for mass market penetration. This means that it is quite robust when it comes to grabbing and keeping the active partition on a hard disk drive. These operating systems do not expect to share their space with another operating system and they are designed to do all they can to ensure that they can always boot. This is so that the mass-market product will generate less service calls. To overcome this, generally it is necessary to install Windows 95/98 before any other OS or boot loader.

Batch Files

Many day-to-day DOS tasks require the user to enter a series of keyboard commands for their completion. Each day, the user had to repeat the same series of commands to produce the same result. To ease this burden, MSDOS has the facility to place these commands in a text file. This file is called a *'batch file'*. The file is given the extension *".BAT"* e.g.:

MOVE.BAT

To execute a batch file, the name of the file is entered, followed by <Enter>, as in other runnable programs. When the file is found, the MSDOS commands within that file are executed one after another without any further keyboard input. In addition to the normal DOS commands, MSDOS provides additional commands for use in batch files. So, the entry of a single command can result in a long sequence of MSDOS commands being implemented.

Common uses for batch files are:

- To automate regularly used DOS sequences, as mentioned above.
- To create customised user menus. For example, the batch file clears the screen, displays the program options, waits for the user's choice of key and runs the appropriate program.
- To automatically load and run a program when the computer is first switched on. This special batch file has to be given the name AUTOEXEC.BAT (or, alternatively, the AUTOEXEC.BAT file can call a specially written batch file for the purpose).
- To provide for automated system checks, which may or may not trigger activities. For example, the detection of the date as a Friday may result in all word-processing files being backed up.

In all cases, the user of batch files need have no knowledge of the workings of the PC or knowledge of the DOS structure, DOS commands, etc. The writer of the batch file can hide all the intricacies of the system from the average user. The skills of the writer are employed once and the batch file is then used many times over - thus creating a productivity aid. Since the instructions are embedded in the batch files, it eliminates the many typing mistakes that hold up operations. If the batch file is written correctly, it should always work correctly.

Creating Batch Files

Batch files are created using a plain ASCII text editor, such as the DOS EDIT utility or a word-processor used in plain ASCII mode. Each DOS command will occupy a separate line of the program. The completed file is then saved onto disk, with the extension ".BAT"

Again, as in other DOS files, the name given to the file should reflect its contents.

The contents of any batch file can be viewed using the DOS TYPE command as below:

TYPE LOOK.BAT   or   TYPE LOOK.BAT | MORE

Example Batch File

Contents of LOOK.BAT

```
echo off
REM This is the first attempt at a batch file !
cls
echo Here is the contents of the DOS Directory ...
cd c:\dos
dir/w
pause
cd \
```

This simple batch file uses a mixture of normal DOS commands and a few commands that only work within batch files. It is explained line by line next:

- Line 1 switches off the screen display of commands. Normally, each command is *'echoed'* to the screen before being carried out. In other words, the text of the command would be displayed on the screen, prior to it being carried out. To present the user with a cleaner screen, the ECHO OFF command is used to prevent the commands from being displayed to the screen. The <u>results</u> of carrying out the command are still displayed to the screen - it is only the text of the command itself that is suppressed. Echoing can be turned on again with ECHO ON. Mostly, ECHO ON is used to assist debugging a batch file, since the progress of the batch file can be viewed as each command is echoed to the screen. The final working version then normally has ECHO OFF added as its first line.

- Line 2 allows REMarks to be added to the program, to explain what is happening to the programmer. The lines will not be sent to the screen, if ECHO is set to off.   Since experienced programmers can create batch files of great length and complexity, comments can be used to document each section of the batch file's code.   These comments can prove extremely useful and timesaving when the batch file is viewed at a later date (perhaps with a view to altering it).   REM statements can also be used to preface the batch file with the details of the purpose of the batch file, any instructions for usage, the name of the writer, the date written, etc.   The REM can be replaced with a semi-colon and this will produce the same result with a slightly cleaner look. (note that the semi-colon can also be used for other purposes, as seen later).
- Line 3 uses a normal DOS command to clear the screen.
- Line 4 displays a message to the screen. Any text after the command ECHO will be displayed to the screen. This command can be used to temporarily overrule the ECHO OFF command.
- Lines 5 and 6 use normal DOS commands to change the current directory to dease.dir and display the directory contents across the width of the screen.
- Line 7 halts execution of the program, displays the message
     Strike any key when ready ...
  and waits for a key to be pressed before executing the remaining lines of the batch program.
- Line 8 changes the current directory to the root directory.

Improving Appearances

- The ECHO OFF command only takes effect <u>after</u> it has been executed. This means that this 'ECHO OFF' line will still appear on the screen, even if it is the first line in the batch script.   This can be overcome if the first line is changed to @ECHO OFF.   Echoing is still switched off but the command does not appear on the screen. This works in DOS from versions 3.3 onwards.

- To produce a more pleasant screen layout, there will be a need to produce blank lines on the monitor screen, usually to space out lines of text.   Entering a blank line in the batch script will not result in a blank line being produced on the screen; the empty script line will simply be ignored.   Also, typing the word ECHO on its own will not work, as this is seen as the same command as ECHO OFF.   A blank line can be produced by using the command followed by a full stop.   Alternatives to the full stop could be one of the following, depending upon the version of DOS being used:
     + " / | : [
  For example,

     ECHO+   or   ECHO[
  will produce a blank line.   Note that there is no space between the ECHO command and the character chosen from the above list.   The user should experiment to find the version for their own DOS version; the full stop is supported by DOS 5 onwards.
- To replace the "S*trike any key when ready ...*" message which automatically results from the use of the PAUSE command, the line
     PAUSE > NUL
  prevents the usual message line from being printed on the screen.   The system will still pause, waiting for keyboard input.   This can be used in conjunction with an ECHO command, to produce the desired message, as in this example:

```
ECHO Press any key to archive the Corel Draw backups
ECHO or press CTRL-Break to exit
PAUSE > NUL
```

Note:
The execution of a batch program can be terminated at any stage, by pressing CTRL-Break.
The execution can be paused by pressing Ctrl-S and can be restarted by pressing any other key.

Other Commands
As shown in the earlier example, the normal MSDOS commands (e.g. MD, CD, etc.) can be used in batch files.   Additional, extended, batch commands such as ECHO and PAUSE are available.
For more sophisticated work, control commands are available.

These include   GOTO
                     IF
                     FOR .. IN .. DO

These commands provide for decision-making within the program and the ability to move around different parts of the batch file script, sometimes implementing one section of the script while implementing other section under different conditions. Batch files using these commands are literally computer programs and their construction is considered as *'batch file programming'*.

Example Batch File

The following batch file is designed to be run at the end of the office day. It will copy all Word files with the extension .DOC to a sub-directory of a floppy disk. The batch file will then delete all backups from the hard disk, to recover disk space.

The batch file program lines should:
- Display a start-up message.   Copying may take some time and it is helpful to produce messages reminding users of the tasks being performed or informing the user of the program's progress.
- Make a directory on the floppy disk called BACKUPS
- Copy the .WBK files from the DUMBRECK\DOCS directory of the hard disk into this new directory.
- Delete all .WBK files from the DUMBRECK\DOCS sub-directory.
- Display the message *"ALL BACKUPS COPIED OVER !"*
- Pause.
- Display the files held on the BACKUPS.WRD directory.

The resultant batch file script would be:

```
REM WDBACK.BAT
@ECHO OFF
REM   This program is designed to save all Word .WBK files
REM    to the BACKUPS of the floppy disk
REM    Written by D. Dick     01/08/00
ECHO Insert a formatted floppy disk in the A: drive and then press any key
ECHO or press CTRL-Break to exit
PAUSE > NUL
MD A:\BACKUPS
COPY C:\DUMBRECK\DOCS\*.WBK A:\BACKUPS\*.*
DEL C:\DUMBRECK\DOCS\*.WBK
ECHO ALL BACKUPS COPIED OVER!
PAUSE
ECHO Here is the contents of the backups directory on the floppy disk:
DIR A:\BACKUPS
```

Notes:
- The four REM lines introduce comments about the batch file and are ignored when the batch file is executed.
- The following three lines provide a message to the user and wait for the user to insert a floppy disk. The program does not check to see whether the user actually inserts a disk; it simply carries on processing the batch files commands as soon as a key is pressed.
- The next line contains a command to create a sub-directory called BACKUPS on the floppy disk. The first time that the batch file is run, this line creates a new BACKUPS directory. When the batch file is run on further occasions, the directory already exists and this line produces an error message. However, the program will not terminate and moves on to the next batch file instruction.

Replaceable Parameters

Up to now, the functions of a batch file have been pre-determined at the time of writing the batch script. All the information required to enable the batch file to be independently executed are included within the batch script. As a result, the finished batch file will always carry out exactly the same set of tasks each time that it is run. This means that where a user carries out a number of similar tasks, separate batch files would have to be written for each task.   Consider the previous example of the batch file called 'WDBACK.BAT'.

This always archives files with the WBK extension. If the user wished to carry out exactly the same tasks with files that had the .DOC extension, then another batch file would have to be written. This new batch file would have the exact same script as the earlier version, except that the letters DOC would replace the letters BAK. If files with the extension .TXT were to be similarly archived, then yet another almost identical batch file would have to be created. This method would result in the creation of a whole range of batch files that contained only slight differences, to allow users to carry out a variety of tasks.

What is required is a single, general-purpose batch file, which is able to accept the required file extension along with the batch file name, e.g.:

WDBACK DOC   or   WDBACK WBK   etc.

Here, WDBACK is the name of a batch file and any file extension can be passed in along with the command. The big advantage with this method is that different file extension names can be passed in each time the batch file is called; the batch file is now general purpose.

A user easily understands this, since this technique is already commonly used with the existing range of DOS commands. For example, the command DEL TEST.DOC uses DEL as the actual program command and in this case TEST.DOC is the file name being passed in with the command. Similar techniques are used with the DIR, TYPE, REN, CHKDSK, FORMAT and other commands.

The part of the command which can be altered each time the user calls the batch file is termed the *'replaceable parameter'* portion and can be a filename, a path, or even a DOS command. The user supplies the actual filename, path or command at the time of executing the batch file.

NOTE: Where required, a batch file can have more than one parameter, e.g.:

WDBACK TXT DOC WBK   or   EXAMINE file1 file2

Normally, a space or comma separates parameters (although semicolons or colons can be used).

Inside the batch file

Since the actual content of the parameter(s) will probably be different every time the batch file is executed, the batch file coding does not know what is going to be passed in. It has to use a general name(s) within its coding. These general names will then take on the values of the parameters that are passed in.

These general names variables inside the batch file are the *'Replaceable Parameters'* and are represented by the percentage character, followed by a digit. These go from %0 to %9. The batch file name is allocated to %0, the first user input parameter is allocated to %1 and so on. Therefore EXAMINE file1 file2 would result in %0 holding EXAMINE, %1 holding file1 and %2 holding file2.

EXAMPLE   A batch file is to be created to send any given file away to any given sub-directory on an archive floppy disk. The batch file will have the following syntax:

STORE filename path

- *STORE* is the name of the batch file.
- *filename* is the file to be archived.
- *path* is the destination directory on the A drive where the file is to be stored.
- A space separates the file name and the directory name.

The program uses two parameters that take the place of the filename and the directory name, being the %1 and %2 parameters. If the batch file was called up using the command line STORE REPORT SALES then the text *'REPORT'* would replace every occurrence of the %1 parameter, while the text *'SALES'* would replace every occurrence of the %2 parameter. The batch lines would then execute as normal. Such a batch file is much more flexible because different file names and directory names can be used each time the batch file is called.

```
REM STORE.BAT
echo file backup in progress
echo changing to the A drive
a:
echo creating the new directory
md %2
echo changing to the new directory
cd %2
echo copying files to the new directory
copy C:\%1
echo file %1 copied to A drive
echo returning to the C drive
c:
```

Now lines 9 and 10 of WDBACK.BAT can be altered to:

COPY C:\DUMBRECK\DOCS*.%1 A:\BACKUPS*.*
DEL C:\DUMBRECK\DOCS*.%1

Allowing the batch file to archive files of any extension given by the user.

Branching & Looping

The example batch files given so far have used *'sequential'* coding; each script line is executed in strict order, from the first line to the last line. This is sufficient for some batch files of limited use. More often, there is a need to control the order of the lines that are executed, dependent on the circumstances in which the batch file is run.

Consider the two examples below:

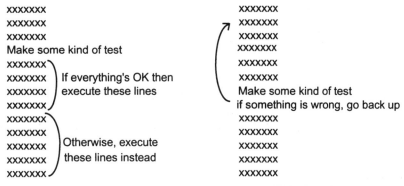

EXAMPLE 'A'   EXAMPLE 'B'

In Example 'A', the first few lines are always executed. There then follows two blocks of coding, only one of which is ever executed each time the batch file is run. If the first block of coding is executed, then the second block is ignored, and vice versa. An example of this might be a block of coding that displays an error message if something goes wrong. In Example 'B', all of the lines are executed. However, some lines might be executed many times over before execution continues in a sequential manner. An example of this is continually checking whether a floppy disk has been inserted before proceeding further.

So, the flow of control may jump down to a lower part of the script, or jump up to previously executed lines. To allow for these jumps in the script execution, MSDOS allows labels to be added to a batch file. A label has a name and is preceded by a colon. The first eight characters of a label are significant, so :labelforhere and :labelforthere would be seen as the same label. At any point in a batch file, the label can be jumped to by the use of the GOTO command.

```
LABEL
DIR A:/W
PAUSE
GOTO LABEL
```

In the above very simple example, the directory of the floppy disk would be displayed, followed by the *"Strike a key when ready..."* message. When a key is pressed, control will be returned to the top of the file and the process will repeat itself again. This would carry on forever. The only way to exit from this particular batch file is to press CTRL-BRK.

NOTES
The GOTO line need not use the colon - i.e. the last line could be either

```
'GOTO :LABEL'  or  'GOTO LABEL'
```

The colon can also be used to place comments into the program, as an alternative to the REM statement, e.g.:

```
REM this is a comment
: this is another comment
```

Decision Making

Batch files only benefit from the GOTO statement when the jumps result from some kind of check. If the result of the particular check is true, then control can be altered. MSDOS allows the use of the IF statement within batch files.

It has three uses:

- to compare two strings (called an *"equality conditional test"*).
- to check for the existence of a file on the disk.
- to test *'errorlevel'* values returned from other programs.

Equality Tests

The command requires the use of two equals symbols (==) to represent equality. Use of the == conditional test allows the creation of batch files which can carry out different parts of the file coding, dependent on the result of the test.

Examples:

        IF %1 == BUDGET GOTO :END

If the input parameter is "BUDGET", pass control to the script following the label entitled "END". Note that the test string is case sensitive - "budget" or "Budget" would not be detected as an input parameter. If all possibilities need to be tested, then more than one equality check will have to be made (or see using the FOR command later).

        IF %1 == %2 GOTO :SAME

If both input parameters are identical, pass control to the script following the label entitled "SAME".

        IF %1 == DATA.NEW   DEL DATA.OLD

If the input parameter is "DATA.NEW", then use the DOS DEL command to erase the file entitled "DATA.OLD".

Improved WDBACK.BAT

In the earlier version of WSBACK.BAT, the user could nominate files of any extension to be archived. If it was considered necessary to prevent users from archiving .COM and .EXE, for example, then the batch file could be altered to:

```
@ECHO OFF
ECHO Insert a formatted floppy disk in the A: drive and then press any key
ECHO or press CTRL-Break to exit
PAUSE > NUL
MD A:\BACKUPS
IF %1 == COM GOTO ERROR
IF %1 == com GOTO ERROR
IF %1 == EXE GOTO ERROR
IF %1 == exe GOTO ERROR
COPY C:\DUMBRECK\DOCS\*.%1 A:\BACKUPS\*.*
DEL C:\DUMBRECK\DOCS\*.%1
ECHO ALL BACKUPS COPIED OVER!
PAUSE
ECHO Here is the contents of the backups directory on the floppy disk:
DIR A:\BACKUPS
GOTO END
:ERROR
ECHO EXE and COM files should not be archived ! Please try again....
:END
```

Note that the 'GOTO :END' line is used to jump over the error message line; if that line were not present, then the batch file would always display an error message - even when the program had no errors.

File Tests

The existence of a file on a disk can be tested with the statement

        IF EXIST %1 ECHO The file is here !

If the file exists, the test is true and the rest of the line is executed.   If the file does not exist, the rest of the line is ignored and control passes to the next line of the batch file.

A more common use of the command is:

        IF NOT EXIST %1 GOTO :END

The NOT is included to reverse the outcome of a test.   So, if the file exists, the test has not proved to be true therefore the rest of the line is ignored and the batch file will continue execution from the next line of the script.   If the file does not exist, the test has proved to be true, the rest of the line is executed and control is passed to the label entitled 'END'.   The code that commences from the label END onwards will probably be used to give an error message to the user and may also terminate the program.

Worked Example

A batch file called MOVE.BAT is required to copy any file from the hard disk's root directory to the hard disk's STORE sub-directory, thereafter deleting that file from the root directory.   This can be easily achieved as follows:

```
COPY C:\%1 C:\STORE
DEL C:\%1
```

However, if the program was expected to allow the transfer of the file to any directory specified in the input parameters, the program could be altered to:

```
COPY C:\%1 C:\%2
DEL C:\%1
```

A typical call would be:

```
MOVE letter.doc backups
```

If the file itself does not exist, then both lines of the batch file will produce an error message upon execution.   The file may not exist, or may exist in a different directory from the one specified in the parameter, or the file name may simply have been misspelled.   In such cases, the lines will not execute properly, but no damage will result.   However, there will be a serious problem if the name of the destination directory is mis-typed or does not exist.   In this case, the COPY will not be successful, but the file will still be deleted from the root directory.

```
REM MOVE.BAT
@ECHO OFF
CLS
IF NOT EXIST C:\%1 GOTO :ERROR1
COPY C:\%1 C:\%2
DEL C:\%1
GOTO :EXIT
:ERROR1
ECHO The file %1 does not exist ...etc
:EXIT
```

The first problem can be dealt with by testing whether the file exists before carrying out the rest of the program.   The program on the right will suffice.   The middle two commands are only executed if the nominated file actually exists.   This batch file could be improved, if an appropriate error message were given to the user, as shown on the left.

```
IF NOT EXIST C:\%1 GOTO :EXIT
COPY C:\%1 C:\%2
DEL C:\%1
:EXIT
```

Directory Tests

The worked example pointed out the dangers of working with directories without first checking that they exist on the disk.

The following three commands can be used to make various directory tests.

IF EXIST %1*.*

This tests whether a directory exists which contains at least one file, in which case the test is true and the command on the rest of the line is executed.   If the test is false, the remainder of the line is ignored and control passes to the next line of the batch script.

IF NOT EXIST %1\NUL

This version of the command tests for a non-existent directory, in which case the test is true and the command on the remainder of the line is executed.

Filenames such as CON, LPT1 and NUL are used to access input/output devices.   These are not true file names but some DOS commands see them as present in every directory.   So, if they are not present in the above test, the directory cannot exist.

IF EXIST %1\NUL IF NOT EXIST %1*.*

This tests for an empty directory, in which case the test is true and the command on the rest of the line is executed.   Note here that one IF statement follows another on the same line.   This is called 'nesting' and allows for more complex tests with a reduced number of script lines.   The second IF statement is only considered if the first IF statement produced a result which was true.   For the overall test to be

```
REM MOVE.BAT
@ECHO OFF
CLS
ECHO Running the %0 program ....
IF NOT EXIST C:\%1 GOTO :ERROR1
IF NOT EXIST C:\%2\NUL GOTO :ERROR2
COPY C:\%1 C:\%2
IF NOT EXIST C:\%2\%1 GOTO :ERROR3
DEL C:\%1
GOTO :EXIT
:ERROR1
ECHO The file %1 does not exist ...
GOTO :ERROR3
:ERROR2
ECHO The directory called %2 does not exist !
:ERROR3
ECHO The copy of %1 to %2 was not successful !
:EXIT
```

true, the directory must exist and must contain no files. If these techniques are used in the example, error checking is introduced, thus making the program more immune to the user typing mistakes or logic errors. An improved version of the program would look similar to that shown.

If the file or destination directory does not exist, then an appropriate error message is given. If both the file name and directory are correct, then the COPY command will be executed. The next line checks whether the file exists in the destination directory. This ensures that the DEL line is only executed if the file copy did take place. Again, an error message can warn the user that the file transfer did not take place. In fact, the ERROR3 message is used with all three error situations. Note that the replaceable parameters can be used in ECHO statements, to inform the user of what program is running, or what files and directories are being processed. This is particularly helpful in batch files that produce a lot of activity, to keep the user informed of progress as the file executes.

Empty Parameters

Most batch files expect one or more parameters to be entered after the batch file name. For a new user, there is no indication of the expected syntax of the command and often users will enter parameters in the wrong order or will fail to enter a sufficient number of parameters. The first case can be detected by equality tests, file tests and directory tests.

Consider a batch file with three input parameters. %0 would be the batch file name and the input parameters would be %1 through to %3. If a user only entered the batch file name followed by one parameter, then %2 and %3 would both have no contents (they would be 'nul' values). Testing for a nul value for %3 would then detect that something was wrong and error messages could be given, etc. Testing of the last parameter works for all circumstances where insufficient parameters are given, since the last parameter will always be nul whether the user has omitted one, two or all parameters.

Testing for a nul parameter value requires a slight alteration to the earlier equality tests. It is not possible to use a simple

                    IF %3 ==   GOTO :NEXT

since this equality test will compare %3 with the word GOTO. Additionally, %3 will itself be replaced by a nul value, leaving the left-hand side of the equation empty. There must be values on both sides of the equality test. This is solved by the use of quotation marks e.g.:

                    IF "%3" == "" GOTO :NEXT

Now, if %3 has a nul value the test is reduced to

                    IF "" == "" GOTO :NEXT

The nul value is now detected and control is passed to the coding commencing after the label 'NEXT'. The same effect could be achieved with variations such as

                    IF %3! == ! GOTO :NEXT

FOR..IN..DO

It is possible to make the same command repeat itself - for example, to operate on a set of different files. The DOS FOR command allows the programmer to specify a group of similar parameters which will be substituted into a command, until each member of the group has been processed. This saves considerable typing time.

It also makes the program more compact and easier to read.

The general format of the command is

                    FOR %%variable IN (parameter list) DO command

The %%variable is similar to variables used in algebraic expressions - e.g. $x = y + z$, where x, y and z are used to represent unknown numbers. These algebraic variables can then have any values substituted in them for evaluating the formula. In the same way, the DOS variables can be used to represent any of the individual parameters within the parameter list.

DOS variables are preceded by two percentage symbols, to distinguish them from replaceable parameters. These variables are case sensitive - %%A is not the same as %%a.

In the next example, a simple batch file is used which will allow the deletion of three files from a floppy disk, with a single command, e.g.:

                    TRASH budget.wbk report.doc memo.doc

The batch file would be called TRASH.BAT and would be as below:

```
@ECHO OFF
CLS
FOR %%A IN (%1 %2 %3) DO del a:\%%A
```

The delete command is executed three times - once for each element in the bracketed parameter list. On each occasion, the variable %%A took on the value of the corresponding element in the parameter list. So, firstly %%A will take on the value of %1 (budget.bak in the example) and will delete that file. On the second run through, %%A will take on the value of %2 (report.doc in the example) and delete that file. On the third and last run through, %%A will take on the value of %3 (memo.doc). If the list held five items, then the process would be run through five time with five files deleted.

The parameter list need not contain replaceable parameters. This example places file extensions into the list. The program will now delete all files with .WBK, .TMP and .A extensions.

```
@ECHO OFF
CLS
FOR %%A IN (WBK TMP $A$) DO del a:*.%%A
```

It is even possible to use wildcards in the parameter list. For example, the following line will list all the files in the current directory:

FOR %%A IN (*.*) DO ECHO %%A

Example using FOR .. IN..DO
Obtaining listings of all text files with a single command

The FOR command allows the user to extend the range of facilities offered by DOS. For example, the TYPE command, when entered directly from the keyboard, can only be used with a single file at one time. Thus TYPE FRED.DOC is permissible but TYPE *.TXT will produce an error message. This can be got round with the FOR command as below:

FOR %%A IN (*.TXT) DO TYPE %%A
FOR %%A IN (*.*) DO TYPE %%A
FOR %%A IN (%1) DO TYPE %%A

The first example selects each text file in the current directory in turn and displays its contents on the screen. The second example will display the contents of all files in the current directory. The last example displays all the files in the directory given in the parameter %1 - for example, passing in C:*.* as the parameter to the batch file.

SHIFT

A batch file to achieve multiple deletions could be:

FOR %%A IN (%1 %2 %3) DO del a:\%%A

This is inflexible because:
- It always expects a fixed number of parameters (three in the above example).
- Since there are only 10 allowable replaceable parameters (%0 to %9) there is a physical limit to the number of files that can be deleted with the one command.

These limitations can be overcome with the use of the SHIFT command. This command simply shifts the contents of all 10 replaceable parameters one place down - what was %6 becomes %5, %9 becomes %8. The contents of %0 are lost. There is no backwards shift command, so the old contents of %0 are irrecoverable.

This program deletes any number of files and is called thus:

SCRUB file1 file2 file3 file4 ... etc

```
REM SCRUB.BAT
:LOOP
IF "%1" == "" GOTO :END
DEL %1
SHIFT
GOTO :LOOP
:END
```

On the first execution, %1 would contain file1 so the equality test on the second line would be false (i.e. - %1 would not contain a nul value). The remainder of that line would be ignored and the program would not be terminated. As a result, the following line would delete file1. The SHIFT command would then place file1 into %0 and file2 into %1, etc.

The GOTO command would take the program back to the top of the coding. Since %1 was still not a nul value, file2 would likewise be deleted. The second execution of the SHIFT command means that the contents of file1 would now be lost, as it was overwritten by file2.   %1 now contains file3 and it would be similarly deleted.

The same process would result in the deletion of file4.   However, after file4 is deleted, the SHIFT command would move file4 into %0 and %1 would now have a nul value.   Control would be passed to the top of the program and this time the equality test would be true, resulting in a GOTO END that would terminate the program.

This type of program is very flexible, since it can successfully run with a large list of file names, limited only by the size of the keyboard buffer. It will also work if the user gives no file name at all.   In that case, help page code lines would be useful and could be added.

CALL

Earlier batch files have shown how ordinary .EXE and .COM files can be called from within a batch file, by entering the program's name as a line of the batch file script.   When the EXE or COM file is finished, control is passed back to the batch file, to the line below the script line that called it.

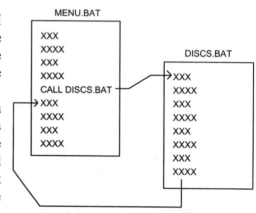

It is also possible to call another <u>batch</u> file from within a batch file, by also simply giving the new batch file's name as a script line.   However, in such a case, the second batch file is then run <u>instead</u> of the calling batch file; when the second batch file is completed, control does not return to the first batch file and all activity stops - the user is returned to the DOS prompt.

MSDOS provides a CALL command to overcome the above problem.   The CALL command allows one batch file to temporarily call another batch file, with the control returning to the first script when the second script is completed.   Control would normally pass to the script line below the line containing the CALL command; in the case of the FOR command, control will return in to the loop.

The example shows a line in MENU.BAT temporarily passing control to DISKS.BAT. As can be seen, when DISKS.BAT is finished, control is automatically passed back to MENU.BAT; there is no need for any special code inside DISKS.BAT to ensure that control is returned to MENU.BAT.

Possible uses for the CALL command include:
- Creating a collection of the organisation's commonly used routines (e.g. giving error messages, file checking, etc.), which can then be called by different batch files when required.   This technique resembles the library of 'procedures' or 'modules' found in programming languages.
- Creating a set of linked routines that together comprise a larger program.   By writing the large program as a collection of smaller units, each batch file can be tested separately, making large batch systems easier to write and debug.

It is common to construct a collection of batch files, which together comprise a user-friendly front end for a non DOS-literate user. Such a collection, for example, may have a main menu that offers the user a choice of activities.   The user responds by pressing the key that corresponds to the desired activity. Each choice would activate a sub-menu with other choices.   The program would then execute another batch file that would carry out the chosen task(s).   At the completion of this activity, control would be returned to the main batch file.

PARAMETER PASSING
The CALL command allows the first batch file to send output to the second batch file, e.g.:
                     CALL C:\MENU\DISPLAY %3
This first batch file is calling a second batch file called 'DISPLAY.BAT' which resides in the 'MENU' directory of the hard disk.   The first batch file is sending its parameter %3 to this new batch file.   This facility allows a number of linked batch files to be used to create a more complex system that would otherwise require to be written in a programming language.

Configuring Windows

Like Windows 3.1, all Windows versions from 95 onwards are multitasking systems, but they perform these tasks much more efficiently. An application in the old 3.1 version loaded in all the DLLs (software components) that it might need during the running of the application. With several applications running, there was soon a shortage of memory. Applications in newer Windows versions only load in components when they are required. This results in less memory overheads and so more applications can effectively multitask. They also support multithreading, which allows different parts of the same application to run at the same time. A user, for example, can carry on using a word processor while it carries out a spell check or a file search.

Installing Windows 95

For Windows 95, the minimum requirements were previously described. The package comes in both CD-ROM and floppy disk versions. It is also available as an upgrade for existing DOS or Windows users and as a full installation version for new machines.

Installation Steps

The steps in the upgrade from Windows 3.1 to '95 are:
1. Insert the installation disk in the floppy disk drive or CD-ROM.
2. Choose the *'File'* option within the Windows Program Manager.
3. Choose the *'Run'* sub-menu option.
4. Type A:\SETUP for floppy install, or D:\SETUP for CD-ROM install, assuming D: is the CD drive letter. Alternatively use the *'Browse'* option to locate the SETUP file. The setup program will load in the files necessary to run *'Windows 95 Setup Wizard'* which will then control the rest of the setup process. If floppy disks are being used, the user is asked to change disks from time to time.
5. The Setup Wizard begins by interrogating the computer system.
6. The Option is given to
    a) install Windows 95 in the existing Windows directory on top of the 3.1 system.
    b) install to another directory to create a *'Dual-Boot System'*. This allows the user to choose during the boot up sequence to run Windows 95 or the existing DOS/Windows operating system software. Pressing f4 during the bootup sequence runs the old software. Since the old settings are maintained, the user has to reinstall all the Windows applications in Windows 95.
8. The option is given to save the DOS and Windows 3.1 system files so that Windows 95 can be uninstalled later and control returned to the previous setup.
9. The Setup program checks the hardware components, enters the results in the Registry (see later) and then offers a selection of Setup Options:
    a) *'Typical'*   Best for most purposes.
    b) *'Portable'*   Also installs software for laptop systems to facilitate file transfers.
    c) *'Compact'*   Installs the minimum set of files; for computers with small hard disks.
    d) *'Custom'*   Allows the expert user to fully customise the system during installation.
10. The *'Typical'* setup option then requests the user's name and company name, and confirmation of some hardware items (e.g. confirming that a CD-ROM drive or video capture card is in use).
11. The option is given to create a start-up disk. This copies all the files required to run the computer in the event that the hard disk develops a problem. Creating the disk is highly recommended.
12. After creating the start-up disk, the Setup Wizard copies the files from the installation floppies or CD on to the computer's hard drive.
13. Restarting Windows boots the computer into Windows 95. The hard disk's boot sector (see chapter on disk drives) has been modified to run Windows 95.
14. Once rebooted, the Wizard performs some final activities such as setting up program icons in the *'Start'* menu.

Installation From DOS

The steps in installing Windows 95 on a machine that does not already have Windows 3.1 are:
1. If installing from floppy, insert the first install disk in drive 'A'. Otherwise insert the Windows 95 boot disk in drive 'A'.

2.   At the DOS prompt, go to the CD-ROM drive if installing from CD, or remain on the 'A' drive if installing from floppy, then type *'setup'*.
3.   The setup program runs ScanDisk to check the integrity of the machine's hard disk.
4.   The remainder of the installation is as described above.

Custom Setup

The *'Typical'* Setup is useful for most purposes but the Custom Setup allows greater flexibility of installation. Custom Setup allows control over the configuration of a range of hardware and software components. The support engineer should have all the required facts at hand before running Custom Setup.   If there is any doubt, the *'Typical'* setup should be used.   A machine that has been installed using the Typical Setup can always be altered later

Uninstalling Windows 95

If the old Windows and DOS configuration was saved during the installation process, Windows 95 can be easily removed. The steps are those described below for removing programs, with Windows 95 being chosen as the component for deletion.   If the automatic uninstall should fail, the alternative is to:
   • Switch off the machine and reboot with a DOS boot disk in the floppy drive.
   • Use the *'SYS C:'* command from the floppy disk.
   • Delete all Windows directories and sub-directories from the hard disk.
   • Look for hidden files in the C: drive root directory. Delete all those that do not match the files on the floppy disk.
   • Remove the floppy disk and reboot the machine.

OSR2

Windows Operating System Release 2 (OSR2) was only supplied with later systems and was not available as an upgrade.   The main improvements over standard Windows 95 were:
   • It handled hard drives that are larger than 2GB without resorting to partitioning.
   • It used disk space more efficiently, producing less waste.
   • It provided better support for playing CD-I movies.
   • It provided added network and Internet features including DirectX.
   • It supported MMX chips.
   • It brought together all the bug fixes, patches and 'service packs' that had been issued over the years.
On the down side, it used a different disk format (known as FAT32) from the original Windows 95 (FAT16).   This meant that many existing low-level utilities would not work with OSR2.   Microsoft's own Scandisk and Disk Defragmenter still worked with OSR2, as did Norton Utilities 2.0.

Installing Windows 98 / ME

For Windows 98 or ME, the minimum requirements were previously described.   The package is supplied on a single CD-ROM with an installation floppy disk. It is available as an upgrade for existing DOS or Windows users and as a full installation version for new machines.

Upgrading From Windows 3.1

The steps in the upgrade from Windows 3.1 to '98 or ME are:
   • Backup the computer's CONFIG.SYS and AUTOEXEC.BAT files.
   • Place the installation CD in the CD-ROM drive.
   • Run the CD's SETUP.EXE file
   • Continue from the section titled *'The Installation Process'*.
   • If the computer has old devices that are not detected by Windows 98, the AUTOEXEC.BAT and CONFIG.SYS should be edited to allow their detection.

Upgrading From Windows 95

The steps in the upgrade from Windows '95 to '98 or ME are:
   • Place the installation CD in the CD-ROM drive.
   • Run the CD's SETUP.EXE file and continue from the section titled *'The Installation Process'*.

Installing on a new hard drive

The steps to install Windows 98 or ME on a newly formatted hard disk are:
   • Insert the installation floppy into the A: drive and switch on the computer.
      Booting up on the floppy disk results in
      • A generic CD-ROM driver (IDE or SCSI as required) being loaded, to allow access to the CD-ROM.
      • A temporary 2MB RAMdrive being created and storing utilities such as FORMAT and CHKDSK.

- Use the FDISK utility on the floppy to partition the hard disk (see the chapter on Disks for more details).
- Format the hard disk using the command *'FORMAT C:/S'* . The FORMAT utility can be found in the RAMdrive and is also stored in the *'Win98'* folder on the Windows 98 CD-ROM.
- Run the CD's SETUP.EXE file and continue from the section titled *'The Installation Process'*.

The Installation Process

For upgrades, the Windows components previously chosen are updated and new Windows 98/ME features are added. Further alterations can be made subsequently using the Add/Remove Programs utility as explained later. For completely new installations the Setup program a selection of Setup Options:

a)   *'Typical'*   Best for most purposes.
b)   *'Portable'*   Also installs software for laptop systems to facilitate file transfers.
c)   *'Compact'*   Installs the minimum set of files; for computers with small hard disks.
d)   *'Custom'*   Allows the expert user to fully customise the system during installation.

In all installations, the Windows 98/ME Setup Wizard is displayed and carries out the following process:

- The Wizard checks if there is sufficient disk space to hold the new installation. If disk space is deficient, the wizard reports on how much space requires to be freed up. The user can abort the installation, clean up the disk and rerun the SETUP program.
- Where old system files exist (i.e. from a previous 3.1 or 95 installation), the user is offered the option to backup these older system files. This allows Windows 98/ME to be deleted and the previous system to be restored.
- The option to create a startup disk is offered. An empty formatted floppy disk can be placed in the A: drive to store a collection of files that allow the computer to be accessed in the event of problems booting up from the hard disk. This option is highly recommended.
- The Wizard checks all hardware devices and may reboot a number of times as it configures the Plug and Play devices and loads their drivers.
- The Welcome screen is displayed, allowing:
  - Registration with Microsoft.
  - A tour of new features.
  - Configuration of the system scheduler to automate fine tune activities.

Uninstalling Windows 98/ME

If the computer's original DOS or Windows operating system have been saved during installation, Windows 98/ME can be removed with the following steps:

- Select the *'Add/Remove Programs'* via the Start/Settings/Control Panel options.
- Select the *'Install/Uninstall'* tab.
- Highlight *'Windows 98'* or *'Windows Millennium Edition'* depending on the Windows system installed.
- Click the *'Remove'* button.

Installing Windows 2000

As explained in the DOS & Environments chapter, Windows 2000 appears to the user to be a slightly upgraded version of windows 98, however the underlying operating system is Windows NT. This means that, like in Windows NT, application programs cannot directly access the hardware, and must use systems and services provided by the systems' Hardware Abstraction Layer (HAL) and or Hardware Emulation Layer (HEL). As a result, the operating system is only guaranteed to work with equipment and peripherals that are on Microsoft approved lists. Drivers for such devices, and there were some 7000 when Win2k was released, are *'digitally signed'* by Microsoft. This means that drivers that are unofficial, or have been tampered with, are flagged. A small utility program called a *'readiness analyser'* is available from the Microsoft website:

(www.microsoft.com/windows2000/upgrade/compat/ready.asp)

This analyses a machine and lists which components, if any, are not guaranteed to be compatible. Having the Readiness Analyser complain about a piece of equipment does not necessarily condemn it. It can often mean that the particular model of video card, scanner, etc has never been formally tested by Microsoft, or proposed as compatible by the manufacturer. More details are available at: www.microsoft.com/windows2000/compatible. The analyser's report includes details on:

Incompatible Hardware

This lists hardware that may not be immediately usable in Windows 2000. This is usually because a Windows 2000 driver has not yet been written for the device. The list might include devices such as graphics tablets, scanners, monitors, sound cards, and video cards.

Incompatible Software

This is a list of applications that will not work under Windows 2000.   The software has to be upgraded to a Windows 2000 version, or removed before any upgrade is carried out.   If they are not removed before upgrading, their uninstall programs may not work.

The Windows 2000 CD is bootable and starts an installation process that has two phases:

- The first, like installing NT, installs any specialist drivers and sets up disk partitions if required.
- The second is very similar to the Windows 95/98 installation routines and last about 30 minutes.

Installing/Deleting Software

During an upgrade, existing applications from the previous operating system may have been added to the *'Programs'* sub-menu of the *'Start'* menu.
Most recent application packages will begin their installation procedures automatically upon insertion of the installation CD in the CD drive.
Windows 95/98/Me applications can also be added via the following steps:

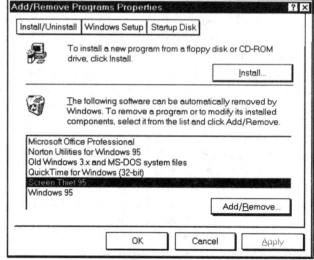

1. Open the *'Start'* menu.
2. Choose the *'Settings'* option.
3. Choose the *'Control Panel'* option.
4. Choose the *'Add/Remove Programs'* option.
5. Choose the *'Install'* option from the *'Install/Uninstall'* option.

The Install Wizard then carries out the required installation activities. Windows 95/98/Me applications provide uninstall facilities and may be removed by highlighting the application name on the pick list and choosing the *'Remove'* option. Older Windows 3.1 applications can also be installed using the Wizard but since they have no built-in uninstall facilities, they cannot be automatically removed later.

An alternative method involves running the application's Setup program via the *'Run'* option on the *'Start'* menu.   Windows 95 onwards intercepts Windows 3.1 applications installed with this method and converts some of the normal installation activities into its own format (e.g. additions to Program Manager are converted into the later version's Start Menu shortcuts and INI entries are entered in the Registry).

Adding/Deleting Windows Components

Since the *'Typical Setup'* only installs a selection of the available Windows components, extra components can be added later, using the *'Windows Setup'* option within the *'Add/Remove Programs'* window.   A list of linked components is displayed by category.

In the example shown, the *'Microsoft Fax'* box is unchecked indicating that it is not currently installed on the computer.

The *'Disk Tools'* box is checked indicating that all these components are installed.

The *'Accessories'* box is checked but is also greyed.   This indicates that only some of this category's components are installed.

Extra components can be installed by making its box active (i.e. a tick will appear in the box) and clicking the *'Apply'* button.   Similarly, components can be removed by making their boxes inactive (the tick is removed from the appropriate boxes) and clicking the *'Apply'* button.   Highlighting a category and clicking

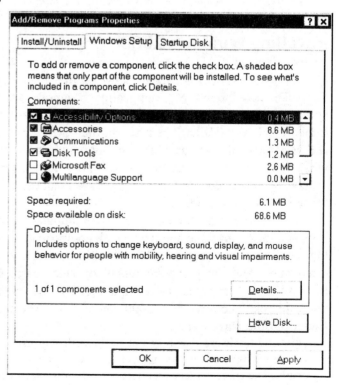

the *'Details'* button displays the list of components within that category.   This allows individual components to be selected or deselected. Windows 95 categories cover:

Accessibility, Accessories, Communications, Disk Tools, Fax, Multilingual Support,
Multimedia, Microsoft Network, Windows Messaging.

In addition, Windows 98 and ME include the following categories:

Desktop Themes, Internet Tools, Online Services, System Tools, WebTV.

A text box explains the meaning of each category and each component as it is selected.

Creating Windows Shortcuts

When applications are installed on a Windows 95 or later system, they appear as an entry in one of the menus displayed from the *'Start'* button.   Windows 3.1 applications and DOS applications will install onto later Windows machines but will probably not appear in these menus.   In addition, it might be useful to allow a particular application to be called up from a variety of places such as several different folders, the Start Menu and even the DeskTop.

These facilities, and others, are achieved with the use of *'shortcuts'* - small files that acts as links to an application file, wherever it is stored.   So, an application program file is stored once on the hard disk but can be pointed to by many different shortcut links in different areas of the menu system.

The steps to create a shortcut for an application are:

- Select the *'Taskbar'* option from the *'Settings'* menu.
- Select the *'Start Menu Programs'* option following by the *'Advanced'* option.
- From the directory structure displayed, highlight the folder where the shortcut is to appear.
- Choose the *'New'* option from the *'File'* menu.
- Select the *'Shortcut'* option and enter the file's name, including the path where it is stored. If this is not known, use the *'Browse'* option to locate the correct folder and filename.
- Select the *'Next'* option and enter the name of the program, as it is to appear on the screen menu.

Document Shortcuts

If a machine regularly uses a few data files (e.g. a database, an accounts main sheet, or a graphics template) these files can also be pointed to by shortcuts.   The steps are identical to those above.   This feature allows a regularly used data file to rest on the StartUp menu and be used by clicking on - without first having to run the application package and search for the file.

The Startup Group

Windows 95 onwards contains a *'StartUp'* folder. Any programs added to this folder are run automatically when Windows is started.   This allows utilities such as virus checkers and printer monitoring software to run in the background. It also allows an application program to be run. For instance, if a computer was used mainly for word processing, the machine could be configured to boot up straight into Microsoft Word. A shortcut that points to Word is placed in the StartUp folder and this will run Word. If the user wishes to run another package, exiting Word takes the machine into the normal Windows interface.

Customising the Start Menu

When the computer boots into Windows 95 or later version, it displays a *'Start'* button on the bottom taskbar. Clicking this button displays a menu similar to that on the right.   The bottom seven entries on the menu are the standard choices.   Where an entry has an arrowhead, clicking the entry produces another menu. The top three entries have been added later by the user so that commonly used applications can be quickly accessed without hunting through sub-menus.   This is achieved by:

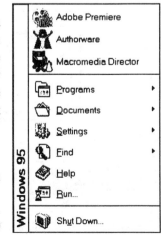

- Choosing the *'Settings'* option from the *'Start'* menu.
- Choosing the *'Taskbar'* option from the *'Settings'* menu.
- Choosing the *'Start Menu Programs'* (*'Advanced'* in Windows ME) option from the *'Taskbar'* menu'.
- Choosing the *'Add'* option from *'Start Menu Programs'* or *'Advanced'* menu.
- Typing in the full name of the application file (i.e. drive, path and filename) or using the *'Browse'* utility to search for the file on the disk.

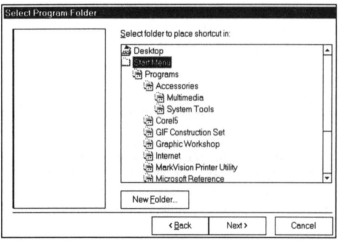

- A screen such as that shown displays the user's disk structure and the wanted folder should be highlighted before clicking the *'Next'* button. If required, a new folder can be created at this stage.
- If the *'Start Menu'* is chosen as the destination option, the application will appear on the Start Menu on bootup. If the *'Programs'* option is chosen, the application will appear in the Programs menu. If a sub-folder is chosen (e.g. *'Internet'* in the example shown) then the application can be run by opening that particular folder.
- When a folder has been selected, the application name as it will appear in the menu, can be entered.

An existing application can be deleted using the *'Remove'* option in the Taskbar properties menu.

Altering The Setup

The main configuration options as determined by the Windows Setup routine can be altered to suit personal choice or to accommodate changing hardware and software demands. This can range from adding and deleting programs as already described, through to altering the configuration of hardware such as keyboard, monitor, modem, printers, mouse and sound cards. It includes the system settings such as date and time, fonts to be used, user passwords, etc. These alterations are made via the *'Control Panel'*, which is accessed as an option from the *'Settings'* option on the *'Start'* menu. The diagram gives an example of the alterations that may be available and some of the most common alterations are described next.

Display

Choosing the *'Display'* option in the *'Control Panel'* offers four or more choices, (depending on operating system, drivers and software) for altering display properties. The *'Settings'* menu, as shown in the diagram, alters the main display characteristics. These are:

- Selecting the number of colours to be used (this depends on the maximum number of colours offered by the video card).
- Setting the screen resolution by clicking on the slider and moving it to the required setting (the maximum resolution depends on that supported by the screen and by the video card). Some systems also provide a second, similar option to select a 'desktop area'. These systems allow the user access to a desktop that is larger than the screen, by scrolling the portion of the desktop that is displayed on-screen at any one time.
- An option only available in Windows 98 onwards is the multiple monitor capability. This tickbox is used to select whether to use this monitor in a multi-screen system.
- Windows 98 onwards has an *'Advanced'* button providing five or more sub-options, again depending on the hardware and software in use.

The five main components are General, Monitor, Adapter, Performance and Color Management.

General	Select large or small fonts for use with text to be displayed on the desktop.
Monitor	Select the driver for the monitor in use (might require the floppy disk that came with the monitor, if Windows does not have the correct one in its stored list).
Adapter	Select the driver for the graphics card in use (might require the floppy disk that came with the card, if Windows does not have the correct one in its stored list). Also allows user selection of the card's refresh rate.
Performance	Select the maximum rate at which the graphics card can handle data. This is also accessed through the *'Advanced Graphics Settings'* feature covered later.
Color Management	Select the colour profile that makes the monitor display colours exactly as they will be when they are used for colour prints.

Display Settings In Windows 95

Windows 95 Display properties does not have the multiple monitor option, and the *'Advanced'* button was instead a *'Change Display Type'* button which was a more basic dialog box with less control over display options. The video card and monitor could be selected from a list of manufacturer models. Where the desired type is not in the list (probably because it has been introduced since Windows 95 was written) the *'Have Disk'* option can be clicked. This allows the appropriate software to be loaded from a disk supplied by the manufacturer of the video card or monitor.

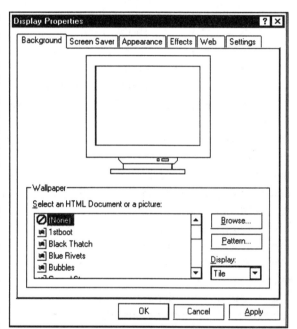

The *'Background'* option allows the setting of:
- a background wallpaper, chosen from a list of wallpapers.
- a background wallpaper using any other graphic on the hard disk, selected via the *'Browse'* option.
- a background pattern, selected via another dialog box in Windows 98 and ME, or via a selection box in 95.

In addition, Windows 98 onwards allows the desktop to display an HTML page, which can be an existing document, or a user-created page.

The *'Appearance'* option allows the screen display to be set to the user's preferences. This includes the colours for Window text, message boxes, etc. Alternatively, the user can choose from a number of default colours schemes.

The *'Screen Saver'* option lists a selection of possible screen savers and these can be previewed before one is selected. A *'Wait'* text box sets the time delay before activating the screen saver. In Windows 98 and ME, the Screen Saver tab also includes monitor energy saving settings.

The *'Display'* configuration within Windows 98 onwards provides two other tabs:

Effects	Selects the size of icons, smoothing of screen fonts, etc. The same functions are available in Windows 95 through the *'Plus Pack'*.
Web	Creates an *'Active Desktop'* where elements of the web are displayed on the desktop. These could be output from web channels, web site tickertapes, etc.

Personalised Backgrounds

The Windows background can use any .BMP as wallpaper, such as those supplied as Windows background images, or those scanned or drawn by the user. To maximise system resources, the wallpaper file used should be as small as possible. A small graphic displayed using the *'Tiled'* option uses the same amount of system memory as one displayed with the *'Centred'* option, but much less than a large graphic displayed using the *'Centred'* option. Windows 98 and ME can use *'active'* desktops, containing HTML, GIF images and JPEG images.

Graphics Acceleration

The graphics card has to be able to keep up with the rate at which graphics data is being sent to it. As of version 95, Windows provides control over the rate of sending data to the graphics card. This is known as the *'Advanced Graphics Settings'* feature and it can be found by clicking on *'Control Panel'* followed by clicking the *'System'*, *'Performance'* and *'Graphics'* buttons. Four settings options are available. The lowest setting, called *'None'*, ignores the graphics card's drawing functions and uses Windows own drawing functions. The highest setting, called *'Full'*, assumes that the system works normally and sends data at the highest rate. The intermediate settings provide more limited card functions.

'95 Mouse Customisation

From the *'Mouse'* option in *'Control Panel'*, the response of the mouse can be altered as shown.
The *'Motion'* sub-menu provides for:

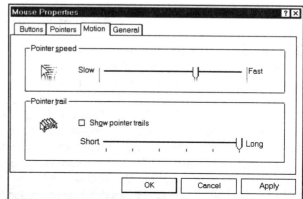

- dragging a slider control to set the speed at which the pointer moves across the screen.
- dragging a slider control to set the length of trails from the moving pointer. A mouse used with an LCD screen or large screen monitor can be made more visible if the movement of the pointer leaves a trail behind it, the trail rapidly fading away. The machine can have mouse trails enabled or disabled by clicking the box to contain a check or be empty respectively.

The *'Buttons'* sub-menu sets up the mouse for left or right-handed use. If the user of a machine is left-handed, the mouse is manipulated by the fingers of that user's left hand. The role of the mouse buttons can be reversed, so that the left button carries out the functions of the right button and vice versa, to make for more natural use of the mouse.

The *'Double Click Speed'* is determined by dragging the slider control to the desired setting. There is a test box below the speed bar.

The *'Pointers'* sub-menu offers choices on the shape of the mouse cursor or pointer during operations such as *'Busy'* or *'Select'*.

The *'General'* sub-menu allows the selection of the mouse type currently in use. Most makes of mouse are Microsoft compatible but other common mouse drivers can be chosen from a pick list.

'98 / ME Mouse Customisation

The basic Windows 98 and ME Mouse Properties dialog offers three categories of settings; Buttons, Pointers and Motion (called 'Pointer Options' in ME). Again, different software and hardware, particularly 'wheel' mice, will have additional options.

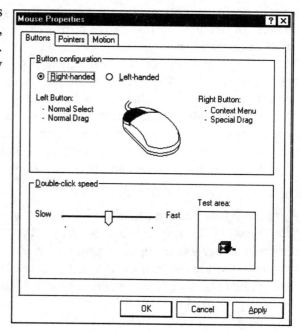

Buttons	Configures the mouse for left or right hand use, sets the double-click speed and, in ME, sets the 'ClickLock' accessibility option.
Pointers	Sets the mouse pointer icons in various situations e.g. busy, selecting, resizing etc.
Motion / Pointer Options	In '98, sets the mouse on-screen movement speed and pointer trails. ME also has options for the mouse to 'SnapTo' dialog buttons, hide the pointer while typing or show a sonar-style circle around the mouse when the CTRL key is pressed.

Keyboard Customisation

If the *'Keyboard'* option is chosen from the *'Control Panel'*, the response of the keyboard can be altered via the options shown.

The *'Language'* sub-menu, as shown, provides for:

- Determining the keyboard layout. Different countries place different characters and symbols on the keycaps. To ensure that key presses correspond to the language of the country in which it used, the keyboard layout has to be configured in Windows. In the United Kingdom, that would mean choosing an English (British) setting as opposed to the English (American) setting, which places certain symbols on the keyboard in a different layout from British users.
- Determining the keyboard variations within certain counties. This does not apply to Britain and the standard *'British'* option would be chosen.
- Setting up hot-key switching between languages, where the same machine is used in a multi-lingual environment. The *'Add'* option allows extra keyboard options to be added to the selection list.

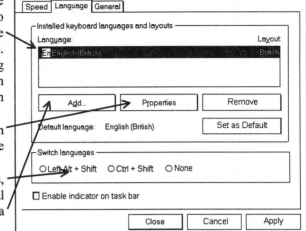

The *'Speed'* sub-menu provides for:

- Setting the *'Repeat Delay'*. A slider control determines how long a key has to be depressed before it begins to auto-repeat the character; dragging the slider to a faster or slower setting along a speed bar sets the value.
- Setting the *'Repeat Rate'*. This determines the speed at which the key will auto-repeat the character. This setting is also achieved by dragging the slider to a faster or slower setting along a bar. Below the speed bar there is a test box to test the settings, before exiting the window by clicking on the *'OK'* button.
- Setting the *'Cursor Blink Rate'*. This determines the cursor's flash speed and is also set by dragging a slider.

The *'General'* sub-menu provides for matching the software to the physical keyboard in use. Most keyboards are covered by the *'Standard 101 or 102 key or Microsoft Natural Keyboard'* category, but the option can be changed by clicking the *'Change'* option and selecting the keyboard type currently in use. Windows 98 and ME do not have this option, the facility being accessed through the Device Manager.

Setting the Date And Time

The computer's real-time clock can be set within Windows. It has exactly the same effect as using the DATE and TIME commands under DOS. The date and time settings within *'Regional Settings'* only control the way they are displayed; they do not alter the computer's internal clock. This facility is called up via the *'Date/Time'* option in *'Control Panel'*.

CD Autoplay

From version 95 onwards, Windows is able to automatically play CDs when they are inserted into the CD-ROM drive. These can be normal audio CDs or the growing number of applications (including the Windows installation CD) that have an *'autorun.inf'* file that commences the running of the application.

This facility can be enabled and disabled through the *'Start/Settings/Control Panel/System/Device Manager'*. The CD should be highlighted from the list of devices and the *'Properties'* and *'Settings'* options selected. Ticking the *'Auto Insert Notification'* box allows CDs to be automatically detected. Unchecking the box means that the CD's contents are viewed and run in the same way as any disk drive.

Audio CDs

The default situation in Windows is that audio CDs are automatically played by the CDPLAYER.EXE program.

This can be altered using the *'View'* option within Explorer. Choose the *'View'* then *'File Types'* options to display a list of file types. Highlight *'Audio CD'* from the list and click the *'Edit'* button. The new panel displayed includes an *'Action'* box that shows a *'play'* option. Highlight the *'play'* option and click the *'Edit'* button. This will display the following command line:

```
cdplayer.exe /play
```

Deleting the '/play' from the line results in the audio CD being detected and the CD player software being called up - but the music will not begin until the user presses the 'play' button on the player.

Deleting the entire line results in audio CDs not being detected. If the shift key is held down while an audio CD or an autoplay CD is inserted into the CD-ROM drive, then the disk will not automatically play.

Windows Fonts

Fonts are collections of alphabetic, numeric, punctuation and symbol characters as seen on the computer monitor or printed to paper. Fonts have three characteristics:

TYPE FACE -   the actual *shape* of the characters, such as Arial (a sans serif face i.e. plain outline with no feet or twirls), Times Roman (a serifed face used in many publications) and Gothic.

TYPE SIZE -   the actual *height* of the characters as measured in points, there being 72 points to an inch. A 36-point headline, then, is half an inch high.

TYPE STYLE -   such as bold, italics or underlined.

In addition, Windows handles fonts in two ways:

Bitmap

A bitmap font holds an actual picture of each character, composed of a collection of pixels. This means that each point size must either have a different bitmap or an existing bitmap has to be scaled up or down. In addition, each type style has to be independently stored. So, there is a bitmap for the normal version, the bold version, the italicised version and the underlined version - not to mention the bold underlined, etc. Bitmap fonts occupy lots of disk space, particularly for the larger point sizes. They are faster than True Type since the image can be dumped to the printer without any translation.

True Type

True Type fonts do not store an exact bitmap picture of every typeface, size and style. Instead, it stores a <u>description</u> of a typeface. This description is stored as geometric mathematical formulae that outline the shape of the various parts of the character in normal, bold, italic and bold italic modes. When an application chooses to use a particular font, the font description is fetched and scaled to the required type size. Windows then generates a bitmap of the font for use with the screen or printer. This process is known as 'rasterising'. A slight manipulation of the factors in the formulae allows the faces to be scaled to any size. This has two distinct advantages:

- The computer need only store the set of four descriptions for each typeface, compared to a set for every font size with bitmaps.

- The mathematical formulae of true type fonts maintain smooth curves even with large type sizes, whereas bitmaps tend to become very 'blocky' and ugly at larger sizes.

Fonts and Printing

The fonts to be selected for use on a particular machine will depend on the type of printer it is connected to.

The common methods for printing text are:

- Using the font resident in the printer. Installing a printer's software may have resulted in fonts being added to the Windows system. If these fonts are used, Windows is compatible with the printer and, after a minimum of setup, the data is sent to the printer as a set of ASCII codes. This is a fast method, since there is no special translation required. However, the printer software may not have installed a matching set of screen fonts and Windows will have to use the closest match. Hence, the user will have lost WYSIWYG (What You See Is What You Get).

- Sending the bitmap straight to the printer. This may be from a bitmap font or may be the bitmap that was created by rasterising a True Type font. A normal A4 page would need around 1MB to store all the page's information. However, it is common for printers to only have an internal memory buffer of 512k or less. That is why a highly complex sheet is often ejected after only printing the top half of the page. The solution lies in adding more buffer memory to the printer or in using some method of compressing the data.

- Describing the fonts to be used to the printer. Once the printer has stored the definition of each font, the computer can send plain ASCII with the consequent saving in time. There are various methods dependent on the printer in use. These include PCL5 (Hewlett Packard's Printer Control Language 5) and Postscript. In each case the printer driver converts each font before sending it to the printer. Printers that support PDL (Microsoft's Page Description Language) have some True

Type fonts already embedded in the printer. Since the fonts don't have to be downloaded, printing is greatly speeded up. They are also able to download True Type fonts at a faster rate than PCL5 or Postscript downloads.

Setting Up Fonts

The management of fonts is carried out from the *'Fonts'* option in the *'Control Panel'*. This displays a list of the fonts that are already installed in Windows. These are the fonts that are available within Windows applications such as Word, Excel, etc. The *'File'* sub-menu allows:

- The addition of new fonts via the *'Install New Font'* option on the *'File'* menu. This opens an *'Add Fonts'* window where the location of the new font can be given and the name of the font highlighted before clicking the *'OK'* button. The location can be a floppy disk and a box can be checked to copy the font(s) from the original location into the Windows fonts directory.
- The deletion of existing fonts from the system. Highlight the font from the pick list and choose the *'Delete'* option from the *'File'* menu.

Font Name	Filename	Size
Aardvark Bold	aardvrkb.ttf	27K
Adelaide	adelaidn.ttf	36K
Alefbet	alefbetn.ttf	20K
Algerian	Alger.ttf	68K
Algiers	algiersn.ttf	83K
Arabia	arabian.ttf	47K
Architecture	architen.ttf	33K
Arial	ARIAL.TTF	65K
Arial Black	Ariblk.ttf	47K
Arial Bold	ARIALBD.TTF	65K
Arial Bold Italic	ARIALBI.TTF	71K
Arial Italic	ARIALI.TTF	61K
Arial Narrow	Arialn.ttf	61K

336 font(s)

Maintaining Fonts

Over a period of time, the number of fonts will grow as many applications add their own fonts into Windows. In many cases, the new fonts look very similar to existing fonts. As a result, no new facilities are added and yet the hard disk - and Windows' fonts menus - becomes rapidly expanded.

The following fonts should always remain on the computer, as they are the standard Windows set and are used by many application packages and by Windows itself:

Font Name	Example
Arial	I am Arial
Courier New	I am Courier New
Symbol	α σ δ φ γ η φ κ λ
Times New Roman	I am Times New Roman
Wingdings	☺ ◆ ♎ ♐ ♑ ♒ ♋ ♌

In addition, Microsoft uses fonts whose names start with MS - e.g. MS San Serif - for screen writing and these should also remain in Windows.

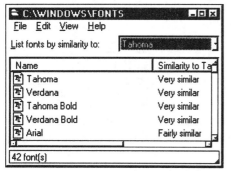

In a very full system, there may be many fonts that are almost identical. This can be checked by choosing the *'List Fonts by Similarity'* option in the *'View'* menu of the *'Fonts'* with *'Control Panel'*.

It will produce a screen similar to that shown. In the example it can be seen that the Verdana and Tahoma fonts are very similar, while the Arial font is only fairly similar to Tahoma.

An inspection of these lists allows decisions to be made on which fonts are almost duplicates and can be removed from the system.

Printers

Printer options can be set up using the *'Printers'* option from the *'Settings'* option found in the *'Start'* menu. This produces the screen shown on the right. Clicking the *'Add Printer'* icon runs the Add Printer Wizard, which steps the user through the installation options.

Double-clicking on a particular printer icon produces a status window for that printer. Clicking the *'Properties'* option in the *'Printer'* menu produces the properties screen, which will be similar to that shown below.

The *'General'* sub-menu allows a test page to be printed to check that the printer is functioning properly.

The *'Details'* sub-menu offers the following:

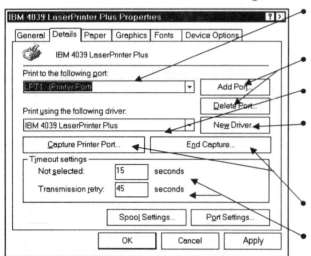

Set the printer port to be used for the printer connection. The pick list displays the possible ports to choose from (e.g. LPT1, LPT2, COM1, and COM2).

This list can be altered by adding extra ports or deleting existing ports.

Set the printer driver to be used with the printer. The pick list displays any drivers that are already installed.

New drivers can be installed by clicking the *'New Driver'* button. This displays a pick list of all available Windows printer drivers. If the required driver is not in the list but is supplied with a printer, then it is installed by choosing the *'Have Disk'* option.

Direct printing to a remote printer on the network or to the local printer attached to the computer.

Set the amounts of time that will expire before a *'Not Selected'* message is displayed or before attempting to re-send a document to the printer.

- The *'Spool Settings'* button opens a sub-menu to configure print spooling arrangements. Windows 95/98 speeds up operations by creating a temporary file for a file that is to be printed. The temporary file provides the source for the printer allowing printing in the *'background'* - the user can carry on with other processing. There are options to commence printing as soon as the first page of a document is spooled or after the entire document is spooled. The first option is faster but the second option provides smoother background printing. The sub-menu also provides selection of two data formats for the spool file. EMF is the normal choice with RAW being used for Postscript printers. A final option allows printers that have bi-directional ports to be configured.

- The *'Port Settings'* button opens a sub-menu that allows for the spooling of MS-DOS print jobs.

The *'Paper'* sub-menu offers:

- Setting the paper size to be used in the printer.
- Setting printing to portrait or landscape mode.
- Setting the way paper is handled (e.g. hand-fed single sheets or automatically from paper trays).
- Setting the number of copies that are to be printed.
- Determining whether to print in duplex mode (i.e. on both sides of the paper); only available if the printer is a duplex machine.

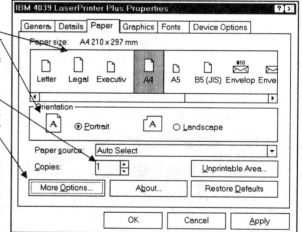

The *'Graphics'* sub-menu sets the printing resolution in dots-per-inch (if the printer supports high resolutions, the graphics are clearer), the method of dithering to print colour graphics as greyscales and the intensity of shading to be used.

The *'Fonts'* sub-menu allows printers that have add-on fonts cartridges to be recognised. It also allows True Type fonts to be downloaded as bitmap soft fonts or to be printed as graphics; the latter option is useful where a document uses many typefaces.

The *'Device Options'* sub-menu allows Windows 95 onwards to recognise extra memory that has been added into a printer. It also allows control over the printer memory usage so that large files do not cause the printer to run out of memory.

Default Printer

The default printer is the one that is used when a job is printed without first specifically mentioning which printer should be used. It follows that the default printer should be the one that is mostly commonly used. If there is only one installed printer then it is automatically the default printer. The default printer choice is set using the *'Set as Default'* option within the *'Printers'* sub-menu of the *'Settings'* option in the *'Start'* menu.

Configuring Serial Ports

If a printer's serial port is to be used then the configuration of that port is achieved by clicking on the *'System'* icon, which appears in *'Control Panel'*. Clicking on the *'Device Manager'* option reveals a list of the machine's resources.   Selecting a Communication Port such as COM1 will bring up a dialog box, from which the user can set the port's baud rate (i.e. speed of transmission) and other settings.   These include the composition of the data (i.e. size of data packet and whether the printer expects parity bits and stop bits), and the transmission protocols. (i.e. whether the usual Xon/Xoff method of flow control is in operation or whether the device carries out its own hardware control of data flow)   The correct settings for these parameters can be found by consulting the manual for the serial printer to be connected.

Volume Control

Windows, from version 95 onwards, provides control over the audio volume from the desktop. The following steps install this facility to the desktop:

- From the *'Start'* button choose the *'Settings'*, *'Control Panel'* and *'Multimedia'* options.
- Check the box marked *'Show volume control in the taskbar'*.

A loudspeaker icon is added to the Windows taskbar.

Clicking on this icon displays a mouse-controlled volume control slider that adjusts the audio volume. Checking the *'Mute'* box completely disables all audio output.

This effectively provides a 'master' volume control and its settings affect the output of all audio devices.   If the volume is set low then the audio outputs of the microphone, line-in (e.g. tape deck) or MIDI device are all reduced.   If the *'Mute'* box is checked, all devices are silenced.

However, there are times when a more detailed control over the audio levels of individual audio sources is required.   For example, it may be necessary to disable a microphone input when the sound card is recording from a tape deck, as the sound from the loudspeaker may be picked up by the microphone causing 'howling'.   Alternatively, if both the microphone and tape deck sources are required, it may be necessary to mute the loudspeaker.

Windows, from 95 onwards, provides a facility for mixing the volume levels of a range of audio input devices. From the *'Start'* button, choose the *'Programs'*, *'Accessories'*, *'Multimedia'* (or the *'Entertainment'* option in Windows 98/2000) and finally *'Volume Control'* options.

Alternatively, double click the loudspeaker icon on the taskbar. This displays the following panel:

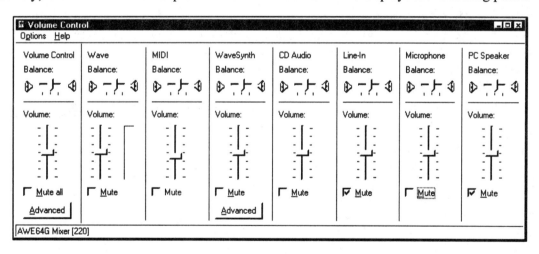

Each device can be individually muted or have its volume level set.   This proves useful when creating multimedia productions and when working with audio recordings.

File Associations

Users can use applications to work on data in three ways:

1. Open the application (e.g. word processor, paint program, etc) and, once in the application, open the file to be worked on (e.g. letter, graphics file, etc).
2. Drag the file to be opened and drop it onto a program icon or link to a program.
3. Find a file within Windows Explorer and double-click on it.   This opens the application, followed by opening the file.

The last method makes use of *'file associations'*.   A file's extension is linked to a corresponding application.

As new applications are added to the computer, the file extensions used by the new application is added to the database of associations.

Where more than one application can process a file with a particular extension, only one application can be the default association - i.e. the one activated when the file is double-clicked in Explorer. Of course, this does not prevent the other application processing the file using method 1 above.

These default associations can be viewed and altered within Windows Explorer by pulling down the *'View'* menu, or in Windows ME the '*Tools*' menu.

In Windows 95, the *'Options'* choice and in Windows 98/ME, the *'Folder Options'* choice both provide a *'File Types'* tab similar to the example shown.

In the example, files with the *'AU'* and *'SND'* extension are played using the *'MPLAYER2'* application.

The *'Edit'* option allows the default application to be altered.

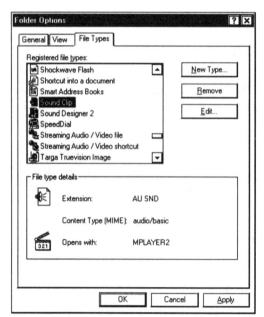

Recycle Bin

The Recycle Bin is a useful addition to Windows 95 and later versions but it can easily clog hard disk space with old files if not controlled. The space allocated to the Recycle Bin can be individually set for each disk drive, or a maximum figure can be specified for all drives. A third option is not to use the Recycle Bin and to lose all files on deletion.

The steps to optimise the Recycle Bin allocations are:
- Right-click on the Recycle Bin icon or folder in the Explorer listing.
- Choose the *'Use one setting for all drives'* option.
- Move the slider to the required allocation (usually around 5%).

Country Specific Settings

Windows can support a range of different languages and these may have different date time formats (i.e. DD/MM/YY or MM/DD/YY), along with numeric and currency formats (i.e. £ symbols or $ symbols, using commas as numerical separators instead of full stops, etc.).

These options can be accessed via the *'Regional Settings'* icon in *'Control Panel'*.

- The *'Regional Settings'* sub-menu offers a range of languages and countries, and the desired country can be chosen from a pick list. This option controls the way applications will handle and present data, taking into account any special or accented characters in a language.
- The *'Number'* sub-menu determines the way numbers are presented in Windows applications such as Excel. The results of any changes are shown in sample windows.
- The *'Currency'* sub-menu alters the symbols that are used for currency and also the symbols to be used for decimal and thousands separators.
- The *'Time'* and *'Date'* sub-menus determine the way that the date is displayed within Windows (e.g. in the UK dates are shown as day-month-

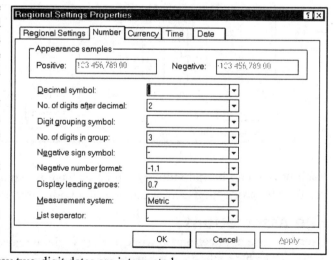

year while the US uses month-day-year) and the way two-digit dates are interpreted.

Managing Memory

The concept and principles of virtual memory and disk caching are explained elsewhere in the book.

Windows 95 based systems automatically grabs all available physical memory in the computer, intending to use it for a range of utilities such as disk cache, fonts, etc. This memory is held by Windows 95/98 even when it is not in use. So, even a newly switched on machine will show that all the available memory is allocated. As the program runs, Windows dynamically shares the memory between the system's resources and the user's applications. This does not always work out very efficiently and can leave a user's application being swapped to the *'virtual memory'* on the disk drive, while the memory set aside for disk caching is not being fully utilised.

Windows automatically detects the amount of memory available for disk caching and sizes the cache to that value. However, as the program tasks and sub-tasks are regularly being switched in and out of memory, the constant resizing of the cache leads to extra processing as everything is moved around in the memory to fit the new size. The wasted processing time can be minimised by setting the maximum and minimum values of the disk cache. The following lines can be added to the SYSTEM.INI file:

```
[vcache]
MinFileCache =2048
MaxFileCache=8192
```

The maximum value depends upon the actual amount of physical memory present. About half the actual memory is a reasonable figure for the setting. These settings speed up normal processing as more of the application is in memory. Where users are carrying out heavy database, video or imaging work, the settings may be increased to reflect the greater reliance on sustained data throughput.

Virtual Memory

Windows, from version 95 onwards, detects how much disk space is available for virtual memory and automatically resizes the virtual memory amount when required. Windows is often left to organise its own management but user configuration can be achieved via the *'System'* icon in *'Control Panel'*. Clicking the *'Performance'* option followed by the *'Virtual Memory'* option reveals dialogue boxes to set the drive to be used along with minimum and maximum sizes.

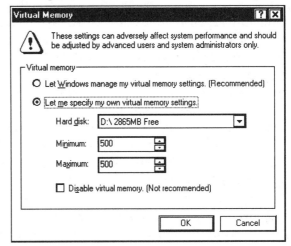

Setting a high value minimises the number of times that the area will have to be resized. If the minimum value is set to the same value as the maximum value, the swap file size remains constant and saves Windows from managing the file.

Before creating a swap file, ensure that the disk is defragmented and the surface is checked with ScanDisk. Even better, create a separate partition for the swap file. Where there is more than one disk drive in the computer, the drive with the fastest access times and the highest data rate should be used for the swap file. This will improve overall performance

Note:

There is a balance between disk cache size, swap file size and performance. If the disk cache minimum size is too large, there is not sufficient physical memory for processing and more is saved to slower virtual memory (increasing thrashing). If the maximum value is too small, handling of large files is slowed down. These problems mainly affect computers with small RAM sizes. The larger the amount of memory installed, the less the problems, and the smaller the size of the swap file needed.

Windows and DOS

Almost all new applications are designed for Windows but there are still some DOS programs in use. It is important that DOS utilities and applications can still be run under Windows.

A DOS program can be run by using the *'Run'* option in the *'File'* menu of Program Manager, or by double clicking on an icon for a DOS package.

If fuller access to the DOS directory system is required, the user can shell out to DOS via the *'Dos Prompt'*. In '95 and '98 this can be accessed by clicking the *'Start'* Button, choosing *'Programs'* from the pick list displayed and selecting the *'MS-DOS Prompt'* option. In WinME it is in the *'Accessories'* group. This opens a window in which the user can carry out all the normal DOS activities (e.g. DIR, FORMAT, COPY, etc.) or run a DOS package.

When first opened, the DOS window does not occupy the whole screen. For a larger viewing area, the window can be maximised by pressing the Alt and Enter keys. Pressing the same key combination a second

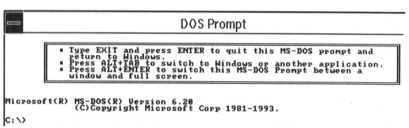

time toggles the window down to the initial partial screen size.

Where a user requires a long DOS session, it can be accessed via the system boot options, thus avoiding any Windows overheads. The *'Shutdown'* option of the *'Start'* menu provides a *'Restart in MS-DOS mode'* facility for this purpose.

Backwards compatibility with Windows 3.1 programs

Software designed to work under Windows 3.1, as well as some early Windows 95 software, operates slightly differently from newer software. Software designed after the changeover to the 32-bit Windows 95 platform utilises the 32-bit method of operation. Older, 16-bit, applications have to be specially catered for by the newer Windows versions, which can cause difficulties. For example, some 16-bit software will not run on Windows NT/2000 at all, and almost all 16-bit applications lead to greater instability in general when used on a 32-bit Windows platform.

Additionally, older 16-bit software differs in the way in which it stores application-specific information. For example, the most recently used (MRU) files in Microsoft Word are stored when the user exits the program, for recall at the next use of the package. With older Windows 3.1 software, .INI files were used to store this information. An INI file (short for INITialisation) contains everything the specific piece of software needs to know, in a human-readable text format. Typically, an INI file consists of several sections, the heading of each section being surrounded by square brackets. Under each section are various settings, each given a name and most being given some kind of data. From Windows 95 onwards, this same information is stored in the registry (see later in this chapter).

Since these older programs were written before the registry was invented, it continues to use INI files. Two INI files of particular note are WIN.INI and SYSTEM.INI, which stored information on the Windows interface setup and the system setup respectively. For example, a typical WIN.INI setting would specify the desktop wallpaper, while a SYSTEM.INI setting might specify the mouse driver to use. Some 16-bit applications, being unaware that such information is now stored in the registry, continue to look in the WIN.INI and SYSTEM.INI for any system information it needs. For that reason, these two INI files are maintained by newer Windows operating systems, to help older software work correctly.

Configuring DOS Applications

Older application packages, and many computer games, are designed to run in DOS mode. Since they were written prior to Windows 95, they do not have the newer Windows installation routines.

In addition, many older games and a few application packages require Expanded Memory, which is not the way that memory is normally configured in Windows. Consequently, DOS programs have to be manually installed and configured in Windows 95 onwards. This is carried out in three stages:

- Installing the software.
- Creating a shortcut.
- Adjusting the configuration.

The installation routine will depend upon the package but usually involves expanding files from the floppy disk(s) and placing them in a sub-directory of the hard disk.

The procedure for creating a shortcut to the program has already been explained.

That leaves the matter of setting how the DOS program will perform under Windows. The steps are:

- Choose the *'Settings'* option from the *'Start'* menu,
- Choose *'Taskbar'* from the menu; this displays a *'Taskbar Properties'* dialog box.
- Choose the *'Start Menu Programs'*, followed by the *'Advanced'* options.
- Find the required DOS program file in the directory structure and highlight it.
- Right-click the file to display the DOS program's *'Properties'* in the dialog box shown.
- Select the memory type required by the DOS program and set the memory amount recommended for its use.

The settings only come into play when the DOS program is run. When the program is exited, control of memory is returned to the Windows memory management system.

System Monitor

Windows 95 and onwards provide comprehensive reporting on the demands of the system and pinpointing system bottlenecks. The *'System Monitor'* and is accessed from the *'System Tools'* menu of

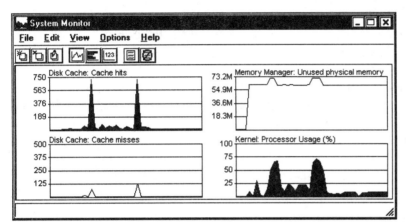

the *'Accessories'* option within the *'Programs'* option. If it is not present in the System Tools menu, then use the Settings/ Control Panel/Add Programs/ Windows Setup/Accessories buttons to install this feature. The Windows installation CD may be required for this.

The Edit pull-down menu offers options to add, delete and modify the items that appear in the report window. The example shows a Pentium III 500MHz computer running a movie file while carrying out various file and other activities. The Pentium III chip can easily handle the video processing, never exceeding 75% CPU usage. The disk caching is working well, with a large amount of cache hits, and the amount of available main memory is large enough to avoid much disk swapping. In addition, a range of other activities, such as swap file, disk cache size and free memory can be monitored. Windows 2000 provides an even wider range of monitoring options.

Startup Options

During the machine's bootup sequence, it displays a *'Starting Windows 98'* or similar message. If the f8 key is hit at this point, a menu is displayed, with between four and eight options, depending on the Windows version and setup. These options may include the following:

- Normal. This boots into Windows normally as if this menu had been skipped.
- Logged (BOOTLOG.TXT). The system boots normally but all bootup operations are recorded in the text file BOOTLOG.TXT for debugging purposes. This includes files and drivers loaded, and whether each loading was successful.
- Safe Mode. The system will boot without loading any but the most basic drivers, (e.g. no CD-ROM, no sound card, basic VGA resolution) so that any problem software or drivers that are preventing a normal bootup can be changed or removed.
- Safe mode with Network Support. As above, but Network drivers will be loaded. This is useful for re-installing software over the network to save time when problems arise. This option will of course only appear if the system has network capabilities.
- Step-by-step confirmation. This option will step one line at a time through CONFIG.SYS and AUTOEXEC.BAT entries if they exist, as well as certain Windows settings, each time asking the user to confirm whether a step should be carried out. This gives the user time to see the effects of each command and any text error messages.
- Command prompt only. This option takes the user directly to the DOS prompt without loading Windows. It will process the AUTOEXEC.BAT and CONFIG.SYS files as normal. This option is not available to Windows ME users.

- Safe mode command prompt only. Similar to the above, except that it does not attempt to use the AUTOEXEC.BAT and CONFIG.SYS files. This option is also no longer available in Windows ME.
- Boot to old operating system. Where Windows has been installed as an upgrade to DOS version 6.22 or earlier, this will allow the user to boot to that version of DOS instead of Windows. This option only appears in systems that have been upgraded and where the user has chosen to keep the existing system at install time. Even then, this option is very rarely used.

The boot options in Windows 2000 are slightly different; there is an additional '*VGA Mode*' and '*Last Known Good Configuration*', both of which are used for troubleshooting purposes. There is also a special '*Debugging mode*' and in Windows 2000 machines used as network domain controllers there is a '*Directory Services Restore mode*'.

Booting into DOS

The startup menu method of obtaining access to DOS is cumbersome, as the user has to wait for long periods while the system boots. Similarly, when the DOS application is finished, typing '*EXIT*' returns the user to Windows before the shutdown option is available.

For regular users of DOS, there are a couple of methods of speeding up DOS access. They both involve amending the MSDOS.SYS file, which is located in the root directory of the boot drive in Windows 95 or 98. Since the file is a hidden file, it will have to be unhidden by highlighting the file name within Explorer, clicking the right mouse to reveal a drop-down menu, and choosing the 'Properties' option and unchecking the 'hidden' and '*read-only*' boxes. The MSDOS.SYS file is a plain ASCII text file and can be edited with any plain text editor such as WordPad or DOS EDIT. The section in the file called [options] can be amended so that the Startup menu is always displayed upon bootup, without the user having to press f8 at exactly the right time. This is achieved by adding the line '*BootMenu=1*' in the [options] section. Adding the line '*BootGUI=0*' in the [options] section ensures that the user is always taken directly into DOS upon bootup. To get into Windows, the user has to type WIN.

Win 2000 Startup

Windows 2000 can be configured as a multiple-boot system. This allows the user to start the computer in Windows 2000 or DOS, Windows 3.1, 95, 98 or ME, depending upon the options installed. Each operating system must be installed on a different disk partition.

Device Manager

The Device Manager provided in Windows 95 onwards, is the most important tool for viewing and altering the configuration of the computer's hardware.

In Windows 95, 98 and ME, Device Manager is a tab that is accessed via the '*System*' icon in the '*Control Panel*', which is an option in the '*Settings*' menu off the Start menu. For Windows 2000 users, follow the same instructions but also select the '*Hardware*' tab and click the '*Device Manager*' button. It offers two views of system devices:

- Listing all hardware in order of their type (e.g. all hard drives are grouped together regardless of EIDE or SCSI interface).
- Listing all hardware in order of their type of connection (e.g. all SCSI devices such as disk drives and CD-ROMs are grouped together, while all the serial devices are listed together).

If an exclamation mark is displayed next to any device, it indicates that a conflict has been detected between the resources allocated to the device and resources required for its proper operation.

Double clicking on a device produces a screen that reports on the configuration and state of that device.

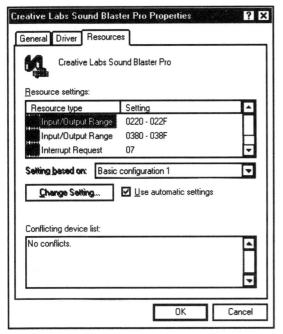

The example shows a report on a sound card and the address space, IRQ and DMA channel used is clearly displayed. The bottom box also reports that the configuration of the device is not conflicting with the usage of other hardware devices in the computer.

Unchecking the *'Use automatic settings'* box allows the values to be altered. The setting to be altered can be double clicked and a new value can be entered.

The *'Driver'* option displays details of the current software driver being used to handle the device. Again, this can be altered if a newer driver is issued.

Similar reports are available for all devices on the system, including disk drives, the mouse, keyboard, monitor, modems, serial and parallel ports and network cards.

Windows 2000's Device Manager has a slightly different interface but operates in a similar manner. For example to view the resources such as IRQ and DMA channels, select *'View'* / *'Resources by type'* instead of double-clicking the Computer icon.

The Windows Registry

The hard disk of Windows 3.1 users soon contained a large collection of files that held all the Windows components and applications together. This was made up of the Windows INI files and usually separate INI files for each application. Added to this was the clutter of duplicated DLL files as different applications installed exactly the same DLL (e.g. Visual Basic DLLs) in various directories across the disk. Maintaining the system caused problems. Users found, for example, that deleting components for

one application often removed a DLL that was shared with another application, thus preventing the second application from running.   With Windows 95 onwards, the collection of INI files and duplicate DLLs is replaced with a single database of all system and application information.   This is the SYSTEM.DAT file and it includes both hardware and software information, although support for separate INI files is present for backward compatibility.

Additionally, users have their own personalised desktop, held in a USER.DAT file.   The *'Passwords'* icon in *'Control Panel'* allows the machine to be set up with different desktop options for different users. Users are then free to set up their own preferences and these are associated with that user's password.

Windows provides a program for editing the Registry, called *'REGEDIT'*; it is stored in the Windows directory.   The left window of the Editor displays the Registry information under six sub-groups.   The right window has two columns, displaying the name of each configuration detail and the data stored.   The utility also has a *'Find'* facility, which can be used to locate a particular device in the Registry.

WARNING   Altering the Registry should only be tackled by experienced users as incorrect changes can prevent Windows from booting up.   Attempt the editing *'tips'* in magazines at your peril.

Registry Backups

If the Registry is corrupted or damaged, some or all of the machine's configuration can be lost.   There are many utilities that create backups of the Registry to provide a clean replacement copy in the event of problems.   Microsoft provides two such programs on the installation CD, inside the *'Misc'* sub-directory of the *'Other'* directory.   These are called *'CFGBACK'* and *'ERU'* and both contain instructions for use. Add-on utilities such as WinRescue are also available to handle Registry backups.

Windows 98 and ME include the option to backup the Registry along with a normal disk backup.

Registry Security

The registry is a very intricate and important part of the Windows system, so ensuring that it runs efficiently will make for a smoother operation of Windows as a whole.   Windows 95, 98 and ME do not offer registry security as standard, although the registry can be made inaccessible through use of the *Policy Editor* on networked machines.   Windows 2000 and NT, however, are designed to be multi-user network systems, and security of such an important part of the system on a network is vital.   Therefore, Windows NT and 2000 have *access rights* to various parts of the registry, which can be set by the administrator.   As standard, the administrator has rights to view and change any part of the registry, while normal users as standard only have read/write access to their own HKEY_LOCAL_USER part of the registry.   This will prevent tampering with system devices and so on.

Additional Windows 98 and ME Facilities

The following facilities are supplied with Windows 98/ME and are not available in Windows 95.

DVD

Windows 98/ME have a built-in DVD software player.   This is reached through the *'Programs'*, *'Entertainment'* and *'DVD Player'* options from the *'Start'* button.   DVD players with hardware decoders will also offer their own interface.

Magnifier

This utility opens an extra screen window where the main screen contents are magnified around the area pointed to by the mouse cursor. This is primarily aimed at visually impaired but is also useful for viewing graphics or fine detail in a large spreadsheet, zooming in during presentations, etc.

This utility can be added by choosing the *'Settings'*, *'Control Panel'*, *'Add/Remove Programs'*, *'Windows Setup'*, *'Accessibility'* and *'Accessibility Tools'* options from the *'Start'* button.

The utility is invoked using *'Programs'*, *'Accessories'*, *'Accessibility'* and *'Magnifier'* options from the *'Start'* button.   The user can control the amount of screen space devoted to the magnified view and can set the degree of magnification.

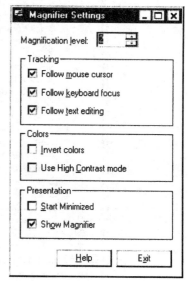

Multiple Monitors

Windows 98/ME can handle up to eight PCI graphics cards and eight monitors. In practice, motherboards will not have that many spare PCI slots. However, setting up a second monitor is an easy task. First, a second graphic card is installed and a monitor attached (see the chapter on Upgrading).

When the computer is switched back on, the *'Settings'*, *'Control Panel'*, *'Display'*, and *'Settings'* options are chosen from the *'Start'* button. This will open a window like the one shown earlier in the chapter (see 'Display'). However, the window will display two monitor icons instead of the normal single icon.

Each icon will have a number, with monitor 1 being the one that will display the right side of the desktop and monitor 2 displaying the left side. The icons can be moved around with the mouse to alter the arrangement. Thus, monitor 2 can be switched to display the right side. If desired, the icons can even be positioned vertically if monitors are to be stacked. When the Monitor 2 icon is positioned, it should be clicked to highlight it, followed by clicking the *'Extend my Windows desktop onto this monitor'* box. Once set up, objects can be dragged from the main screen to the secondary screen.

For example, if Monitor 2 is the one on the right, dragging an object off the right hand side of Monitor 1 places the object into the secondary monitor.

Additional Windows 2000 Facilities

Windows 2000 provides additional facilities to add to those listed above as Windows 98 extras. In particular, it has extensive new tools to configure the interface for users with visual or physical disabilities. The new utilities are:

Accessibility Wizard

This allows the user with particular needs to set up his/her machine. Although the new accessibility enhancements are mentioned here, the old access enhancements, like visual events, sticky keys etc., are still available.

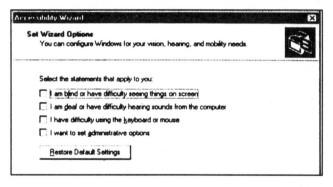

The wizard interface guides the user step by step through a series of choices. Wizards are useful tools for administrators as they can be written, using Windows scripting, to do almost any task. They can however also represent a security hazard, and so "new" wizards should be checked for validity by a suitably experienced support person. Whilst the accessibility options are welcome additions to the operating system, they are no substitute for fully featured professional software for users with special needs. Microsoft recognises this and prompts the user to remind them of it

Magnifier

Included in earlier versions of Windows, it has been enhanced for Windows 2000.

Narrator is a new Windows 2000 utility that is designed to help users with no sight. Its control panel is shown in the illustration. Pressing the "VOICE" button brings up a new panel that allows the user to tweak the way the voice sounds, to suit their individual requirements.

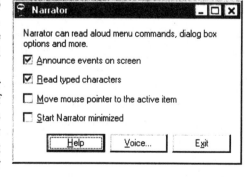

The initial settings are probably useful but the voice does rather drone on a bit, particularly when a "busy" window, with lots of toolbars, is opened. The voice will immediately read out the details of all of the toolbars. Whilst useful on smaller windows with only one or two controls, the narrators output can be utterly confusing when it is presented with a full functioned word processor or spreadsheet.

On-Screen Keyboard

The on-screen keyboard is new in Windows 2000, although a version of it has been available for some time on fully featured terminal emulators. The On Screen Keyboard allows users who cannot use a keyboard but who can use a mouse-like interface (or perhaps a puff switch) to use the PC, albeit slowly. It also has uses for able-bodied users in situations where use of a keyboard is inappropriate, but use of a mouse, trackball, or touch screen is possible. Typical situations would include industrial settings where swarf, dirt or airborne contamination is a problem.

Disks & Drives

Disk Basics

The computer's disk systems are designed for the long-term storage of programs and user data. When the power is removed from a machine, the contents are lost from memory, so the disks (sometimes called *'backing store'*) are used for their preservation. The disk systems used to store data range from large hard disk packs used in large mainframe computers, to tiny 1.5" and smaller hard disks in portable notebook computers. In addition, almost all PCs allow data to be stored on removable disks called *'floppies'*. This allows data to be moved around by carrying disks from machine to machine, or sending a disk through the mail. Hard disks, on the other hand, are permanently built-in to the machine and are not normally accessible by the user. Some new systems employ removable hard disks, to exploit the high capacity of hard disks while retaining the mobility of floppy disks but these are still relatively uncommon.

Despite the wide differences in size and storage capacity, all magnetic disks work on the same basic principles. Even the newer optical disks, while using substantially different technology, adopt the same general approach. Disk drives are *'direct access'* devices, which means that the reading and writing of data can occur at any part of the disk. Tape storage, on the other hand, is a *'serial access'* device - the system has to search in a series from one end of the tape until the wanted data is found.

Tracks

Data is written to a disk magnetically in a similar way to recording on audio tape or videotape. In this case, however, the media used is not a long continuous cassette of tape but the same type of surface material in the shape of a disk. The disk is rotated to allow access to all parts of its surface. So, data is written in circles round this disk. Regardless of the type of disk, the data is organised on the disk in concentric circles known as *'tracks'*. The tracks number from the outside of the disk to the inside, with the outermost track being called track 0. The number of tracks on a disk varies from 40 or 80 on floppy disks to about 1000 on some hard disks. The *'density'* of a disk is the number of tracks that the disk can handle e.g. for 3.5" disks, Double Density means that it can support 80 tracks per side.

The density of a disk is often quoted in TPI - tracks per inch. A typical 3.5" floppy is a 96tpi disk, meaning that each track is 1/96th of an inch wide. So, an 80-track disk format would use up slightly less than one inch of the available disk diameter. A 48tpi disk is usually used for 40 track disks.

Writing/Reading Data

A disk is coated on both sides with a magnetisable material, to allow it to store a magnetic pattern that will represent the computer's data. Iron-oxide coatings were universally used in older drives, with improved cobalt-oxide coatings appearing in newer models. The coating is magnetised under the influence of a coil of wire called the read/write head (the same coil that writes data is also used to read back data when required). The disk is mounted on a vertical shaft that spins it at 300 rpm in the case of floppy drives and from 4000 rpm to over 13,000rpm for hard disk drives. The read/write head can be moved to any track on the disk by an electric actuator and it floats just above the surface of the disk. This movement is organised by electronic circuitry known as the *'disk controller'*.

So, by moving the head to the desired track and waiting until the desired portion of the track rotates under the head, any part of the disk can be accessed for reading or writing. Writing involves energising the coil to create a magnetic field, which in turn creates an altering magnetic pattern on the disk surface. At a later date, when the magnetised area of the disk is passed under the head, the magnetic fields on the disk induce a current in the read coil. These pulses of current are cleaned up and used to convert back to the binary data that was originally recorded.

The dimensions of the read/write head areas are dependent on the number of tracks that are used on that disk. If a 5.25" floppy disk drive only has to cope with 40 tracks, its head is twice as wide as another 5.25" drive that has to cope with 80 tracks on the same disk radius. On a large capacity hard disk with many hundreds of tracks, the head dimensions are even more finely engineered. The heads commence their numbering from head 0.

Sectors

A floppy disk holds from 4.5k to over 18k of data on a single track, with a hard disk storing 30k to 50k. To make the most economical use of tracks, they are divided into compartments known as 'sectors'. Sectors number from 1 upwards and each sector normally holds 512 bytes, i.e. 1/2k, of user data. Therefore, a 9-sector track on a 5.25" DD floppy stores 4.5k of data, while a 36-sector track on a hard disk stores 18k of data. The number of sides and the maximum number of tracks are determined by the hardware of the disk drive and are outwith the control of the user. However, the size and number of sectors are set under software control (hence the description 'soft-sectored')

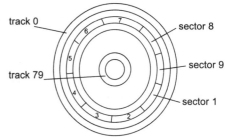

In fact, at the end of each sector there are two bytes that are additional to the 512 of the sector. These do not contain user applications and data; they are used to ensure the integrity of the data in the sector. These are known as 'Cyclic Redundancy Check' bytes. When the data is written to the sector, a formula is applied to the data to produce a check number that is stored in the extra two bytes. When the data is read back again later, the data from the sector is stored in a buffer before being passed on for processing. The same formula is applied to the data in the buffer and it should produce the same answer as that stored in the two check bytes. If the computed CRC figure matches the stored CRC figure, the data in the buffer is fit to be passed on. If there has been any corruption of the data in the sector, or even any corruption of the check bytes, then the formula produces an answer that does not match. When the machine's built-in test routines in the BIOS find this error, they send an error code to the application program that is using the disk reading code. For example, if DOS is using the BIOS code to read a sector, a corrupted sector will produce the familiar *"Sector read error, Abort, Retry, Fail?"* message. The CRC bytes occupy disk space but do not appear in the figures for usable disk space (e.g. a 1.4MB disk is the user's figure after taking into account CRC bytes).

Clusters

In practice, sectors are mostly grouped in a unit called a 'cluster'. The cluster is the smallest area of disk that can be used to store an independent item of data. So, if a particular disk used 4 sectors to a cluster, a batch file of only a few hundred bytes would still consume 2k of disk space. If a program or a piece of data requires more than one cluster's worth of space, it can be stored in subsequent unused clusters. The number of sectors to a cluster is determined by the Filing System (FS) used on the disk.

Formatting

All disks, floppy or hard, have to be formatted - a process sometimes also called 'initialisation'. This lays down data on the disk that is never seen by users; it is solely used to distinguish between one track and another and between one sector and another. The read/write head is moved to the desired track and sector before reading or writing data in that sector. So, every block of data can be uniquely addressed by the read/write head used, the track used and the sector used to store it. Before any read or write operation is started, the system ensures that it has really arrived at the correct track and sector. A mechanical or electronic glitch may position the head over the wrong sector, resulting in either reading the wrong data or overwriting data. To overcome this, the data sections laid down on a disk are preceded by a Sector ID that contains the track number, the sector number and the sector size. If the information in the sector ID matches the desired location, the read or write operation proceeds normally. In the event of an incorrect head movement, the sector ID will not match the wanted location and the head is returned to track zero for another attempt. The Sector ID requires 57 bytes, so a sector size is really 571 bytes (57 for the Sector ID, 512 for the user data and 2 for the CRC).

Preparing a hard disk with sector IDs is known as 'low level formatting'. A complimentary 'high level formatting' process consists of preparing the disk for use by the operating system. A low level format, normally performed by the hard disk manufacturer, is carried out by the disk controller card and results in a disk that has its sectors identified and organised according to the required interleave (see later). A high level format uses some of these sectors to set up the structures needed to store details of the files and their whereabouts. For DOS and most Windows systems, this includes the boot sector area, the File Allocation Tables and the root directory, all of which are dealt with later. Modern hard disks rarely allow a low-level format, and when they do they require a special utility. A high level format is carried out by a software program such as Explorer or the DOS FORMAT command. With floppy disks, this command carries out both low and high level formatting.

See the chapter on *'Operating Systems & Windows'* for instructions on formatting via DOS and Windows.

Floppy vs Hard Disks

Floppy disks comprise a single disk with two sides, while a hard disk will comprise several disks, with more sides and therefore greater storage capacity. This, coupled to the more precise engineering of hard disks, means that hard disk capacities far outpace those of floppies. The largest commonly used floppy disk stores 1.44MB of data while the smallest hard disks currently produced store 8GB of data, with larger models storing up to 70GB of data. Fetching data from a hard disk is much faster than from a floppy disk. This is due to factors such as:

- The increased speed of rotation of a hard disk (this is 50 or more times faster than a floppy disk).
- With the exception of power saving modes, a hard disk is spinning continuously while the computer is switched on. By comparison a floppy drive motor is only energised when data is to be read or written. This means that a hard disk is always ready at the correct speed of rotation while a floppy drive has to get up to the correct operating speed before any disk activity can take place.
- The data is packed more tightly on a hard disk, so more data is read off from the reading of a single track compared to a floppy disk's track.

As programs become more sophisticated, they become ever larger, with some packages needing hundreds of megabytes of disk space. The extra capacity and vastly better speed make hard disks the obvious choice for storing application programs. Where large data files are in use, such as databases and graphical/DTP activities, there is also a speed advantage to storing the data on a hard disk. Floppies have the advantage of being cheap and portable and are a popular choice for storing backup copies of data. Software used to be supplied on a set of floppy disks, but is mostly now supplied on CD-ROMs.

The floppy drive is normally known as the A: drive. If a second floppy is fitted in a machine, it is known as the B: drive, while the first hard disk is called the C: drive. Most machines have a single hard disk, although others can be added as Drive D, Drive E, etc. Some hard disk systems only allow two hard disks per machine, while others allow four or more hard disks.

Floppy Disks

Floppy disks for PCs come in two sizes - the older 5.25" and the current 3.5" size. This refers to the diameter of the disks inside the protective casing. Both disks are made from mylar plastic coated with ferric oxide. A normal PC can have one or two floppy drives, each being of either 3.5" or 5.25" type. A modern floppy disk drive has two heads (one for each surface). The earliest floppy disks were single-sided (i.e. only one read/write head on one side of the disk) but these are almost all gone from use, leaving all floppy drives as double-sided models. The table shows the characteristics of the floppy disk types commonly in use.

	Tracks/ side	Sectors/ track	Formatted Capacity	Unformatted Capacity	Sectors per cluster
5.25" Double Density	40	9	360k	500K	2
5.25" Quad Density	80	15	1.2M	1.6M	1
3.5" Double Density	80	9	720k	1.0M	2
3.5" High Density	80	18	1.4M	2.0M	1
3.5" Extra Density	80	36	2.8M	4.0M	2

5.25" Disks

The disk sits in a vinyl wallet, or *'jacket'*, to protect the magnetised surface from exposure to dust or grease. The disk spins at 300 rpm inside the jacket, so the jacket lining is coated with a soft, non-woven material that is very lightly lubricated to minimise friction. The write-protect notch allows or prevents writing to the disk. A tab can be placed over the notch to disable any writing to the disk. In this way, important data can be written to the disk and then protected against accidental erasure or modification. When the tab is removed, the disk can again be written to. The wallet has a slot in both sides, to expose the surface so that the read/write heads can reach the magnetised coating on the disk. The read/write head is brought close to the disk surface by the action of closing the disk drive lever after the disk is inserted. When not in use, the disk should be kept inside its cardboard sleeve, to protect the exposed area. This disk also has an *'Index Hole'*. This hole is cut both in the jacket and in the disk itself. As the disk rotates inside the jacket, a point is reached when both holes will align. At this point, a light from one side of the disk is able to pass through the hole and be detected by a light sensor on the other side of the disk. The timings of these pulses of light tell the computer exactly how much rotation has taken place. This information, when combined with the head movement, can place the read/write head on any sector on any track with great accuracy.

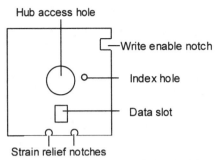

In the centre of the disk, there is a *'Hub Access Hole'*. This hole allows the mechanism's drive hub to hold the disk while it is being rotated. Another feature of 5.25" disks is the set of *'Strain Relief Notches'* on the disk wallet. These are cut in the jacket close to the head access slot, to reduce creasing when the jacket is stretched.

The lower density product - i.e. Double Density - uses 40 tracks and 9 sectors per track. This means that there are 360 sectors on each side, giving a total of 720 sectors on the entire disk. Since each sector is 512 bytes, the disk can store 360k of data. The higher density version - described as Quad Density - increases the number of tracks to 80 and the number of sectors in each track to 15, giving a storage capacity of 80 x 15 x 2 sides x 512 bytes = 1.2MB. A double density disk has a coercivity of 300 Oersteds while a quad density disk has a coercivity of 600 Oersteds (see later).

When data is written to a disk, the level is taken as being 100%. When that same data is read from the disk, its level is lower than the original figure. This reduction is known as the *'clipping level'*. A known-brand disk normally returns a clipping level of around 50%, while bulk disks are around 40%. Disk drives, however, are able to adequately cope with clipping levels down to about 20%.

Problems with 5.25" Disks

Trying to format a 360k to Quad Density usually results in a substantial proportion of the disk being seen as bad sectors. This is due to the coercivity of the disk surface being too low, allowing the magnetised areas to have an undue influence on each other, and resulting in the inability to accurately store data. This means that even those sectors that are initially reported as being usable can often cause problems with time, as one magnetic area starts to influence a neighbouring area. Since the outer tracks are less densely packed than the inner tracks, they are the least affected by these problems. While it is possible to format a Quad Density disk to 360k, there are possible problems inherent in using the higher write head current with the lower coercivity surface. In any case, there would be few occasions when a user would wish to use a high capacity disk in low capacity mode.

Always use disks at their intended capacity, to prevent unwanted side effects. For instance, a disk that a user has written to in both 360k and 1.2M drives will have data laid down in both wide and narrow formats, since the 1.2M drive has a narrower write head. This can lead to occasions when a narrow track of data (i.e. the one written to in a 1.2M drive) is sitting inside a wider track of data (i.e. one written earlier on a 360k drive). When the data is read on a 1.2MB drive the narrow head only reads the narrow track and all is fine. However, when the same disk is read in a 360k drive, the wider head picks up the pattern on the wider track as well as the pattern on the wanted track. The results can be unpredictable.

3.5" Disks

The inner disk of this type of floppy is constructed similarly to the larger floppy, except that it has smaller dimensions and a higher quality coating. It can store more data than the 5.25" despite its smaller proportions. The 3.5" is more robust since it is housed inside a rigid plastic case. The read/write slot is protected by a metal or Teflon slider that covers the slot when the disk is outside the drive. When the disk is placed in the drive, the drive mechanics push the slider back so that the read/write head can gain access to the magnetic surface. 3.5" disks have a write-protect hole that can be covered or uncovered by sliding a plastic cover over it. When the hole is covered, the disk can be written to. This is the opposite of the 5.25" disk that can only be written to when its write-protect notch is uncovered.

Double Density disks have 80 tracks with 9 sectors per track. This gives a capacity of 80 x 9 x 2 sides x 512 bytes = 720kB. High Density disks have 80 tracks and 18 sectors in every track. They have double the capacity of double density disks - giving a capacity of 1.44MB. Some dealers offer *'2MB disks'*. These are just high-density disks, being quoted with their unformatted capacities. When the formatting data is placed on the disk, the disk is left with a usable capacity of 1.44MB. The coercivity of a 720kB disk is 600 Oersteds and a 1.4MB disk's coercivity is 700 Oersteds.

A high-density disk has a permanent extra hole punched in its body; this hole is not designed to be covered and uncovered like the write protect hole. The hole's presence or absence indicates whether the disk is a double density or high density version. The drive decides to use high or low head currents by checking for the presence or absence of this hole.

Problems with 3.5" Disks

Like the case of 5.25" disks, the 3.5" disk increases its storage capacity by increasing the number of sectors in a track - in this case from 9 sectors to 18 sectors per track. A 720kB disk writes 8,718 bits of data for every inch of track, while a 1.4MB disk writes 17,434 bits per inch. Unlike the 5.25" disk, both the DD and HD versions of the 3.5" disk have 80 tracks. This means that the read/write head dimensions in a 720kB drive are identical to those of a 1.4MB drive, eliminating the problem of tracks embedded within tracks.

Again, the reduced sector length results in storage integrity problems that are solved by doubling the coercivity of high-density disks. This requires a particularly thin coating, under one micron, of fine grain oxide, compared to the 720kB disk coating of just under two microns. So, 1.4MB drives can write and read 720kB disks without difficulty. While 720k drives cannot read 1.4MB formatted disks, they can reliably read double density disks that have been formatted to 720k in a 1.4MB drive.

Users should still not attempt to format 720kB disks to beyond their rated capacity. Although 3.5" disks will report less sector errors when formatting, the surface is still less reliable than would be expected. The high-density notch is designed so that 1.4MB drive mechanisms will detect the presence of an HD disk. However, some machines are not equipped to make this detection. It should be noted that the difference between DD and HD disks is not the hole's presence or absence, but the coercivity of the disk surface.

Protecting Floppy Disks

The disk media is easily affected by the environment and users should be encouraged to practise good housekeeping. As the diagram shows, the gap between the head and the oxide coating is tiny compared to commonly found elements in the real world. A smoke particle is around 250 microns, a fingerprint is around 300 microns, a dust particle is around 400 microns, while a human hair is a gigantic 0.03 ins.

If a particle of smoke or dust was to be trapped between the head and the disk surface, the oxide coating would be torn from the disk and the surface would almost certainly be permanently damaged. The data contained in that sector, cluster, or even entire track would be lost forever. In extreme cases, the drive's head itself could

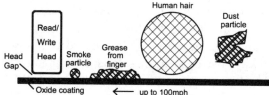

also be damaged. This problem is greatly minimised with hard disks, as the mechanism is contained within a sealed unit. But, with floppy disks, the danger is much greater. That explains why users are recommended not to smoke in the presence of computers. Of course, smoking does not automatically mean that damage will occur. Luckily, smoke and dust particles often bounce off the surface and are not trapped in the head gap.

However, there is an added danger with 5.25" disks. The disk surface is open to outside corruption through the head access slot. If a user holds a 5.25" disk such that a fingerprint or palm print is placed on the disk surface, a layer of grease is deposited on the oxide coating. If this happens, a smoke or dust particle can become embedded in the grease. Now, the particle won't bounce off and is more likely to be dragged into the head gap.

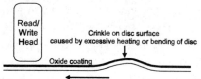

Other problems can be caused by leaving the disk exposed to excessive heat. This may warp the disk surface as shown in the diagram. If a 5.25" disk is forced into a drive, or bent in any other way, the disk is similarly warped or crinkled. This raised portion will hit the read/write head as it rotates and part of the disk surface will be scraped off, with resultant damage to the disk and the loss of data.

Apart from protecting the disks themselves, there is a need to take care of the disk drive mechanisms. From time to time, computers have to be transported from one place to another. The sudden jolts to the machine could cause the read/write heads to bounce around and crash against each other.   A cardboard or plastic insert can be placed in the drive and the drive door closed.   This layer of card prevents the heads from bouncing around and allows the drive to be moved around in safety.   With hard disks, this is not possible as they are housed in sealed cases.   Hard disk heads must be moved to a part of the disk surface where no data is stored.   Here, they can safely rest on the disk surface without scraping the oxide coating.   This is called *'parking'* and is covered later.

Do's & Dont's Of Disk Handling
- Avoid keeping computers in dusty surroundings; enforce smoking bans in computer areas.
- Avoid placing or storing disks in excessive temperatures.
- Don't touch the exposed surface of a 5.25" disk; keep unused disks in their protective envelopes.
- Avoid magnetic fields - don't place disks on top of printers, loudspeakers, telephones, etc.
- Floppy disks should never be folded or bent in any way.
- Always insert floppy disks carefully into drives.

Detecting Disk Changing
A floppy disk drive needs to detect that a disk has been removed from a drive and a new disk has been inserted.   This may take the form of a microswitch inside the drive that is depressed when the disk is inserted.   The switch changes state when a disk is removed and changes state again when a new disk, or even the same disk, is inserted.   The status of this *'media change line'*, line 34, is used by various applications and utility programs.   If a drive is not fitted with this mechanism, or the mechanism becomes faulty, the machine will not know that a disk has been changed.   This can lead to unexpected results.   For example, a user gives a DIR command on a disk, swaps the disk and gives another DIR command.   Instead of displaying the new disk's contents, the files of the original disk are displayed once again.   Since the system does not know that the disk has been changed, it is displaying the old directory contents directly from the copy of the FAT and directory stored in memory rather than reading the new directory information.   Worse still, any new writes would be based on the memory version of the disk's FAT instead of the actual disk FAT - with data being written to the wrong part of the disk.

Hard Disks
Hard disk systems are composed of:
- A sealed drive unit.
- Disk controller electronics, either on a controller card or built in to the drive.
- Connecting cables between the drive and the computer motherboard.

While the floppy is a single plastic disk, hard disk units consist of two or more disks in the one sealed unit.   The extra disks boost the drive's storage capacity and each of these disks is known as a *'platter'*. The term applies to both sides of that particular disk. So, if a drive had three platters, it would contain 6 sides. Like floppies, areas of the hard disk's coating are magnetised and demagnetised to store the data. The disk is aluminium and coated with ferric oxide or cobalt oxide.   In some newer models, the disk is made of glass.

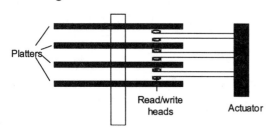

The original XT hard disk was composed of two platters and had a capacity of 10MB.   Modern drives can have many platters, depending on the capacity of the drive. An older 210MB hard disk may have six platters (i.e. twelve sides) while IBM's 32.8GB model, with higher quality surface coating, requires only ten platters.
The older models of hard disk drives were 5.25" and newer models are 3.5" in diameter.   There is no relationship between the size of the disk and its capacity.   The 3.5" models are generally faster and quieter than the 5.25" version.   A full-height drive is about 3.25" high, while a half-height drive is about 1.63" high.   Nearly all 3.5" drives are half-height models.

Cylinders
Many specifications and publications refer to the term *'cylinders'* when describing a disk's construction. Mostly, the term is used freely as the equivalent of *'tracks'*.   With hard disks there are a number of different platters and the heads are mechanically linked and are therefore placed over a <u>set</u> of tracks at any one time.   The collection of tracks covered is known as the drive's *'cylinder'*.   In a hard disk, each

platter has an identical set of cylinder numbers and these number from zero upwards. So, cylinder 2 would be the third track on side 0, the third track on side 1, the third track on side 2 and so on. Since a

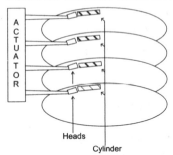

floppy disk has only two sides, the term is never used. The inner tracks are smaller than the outer tracks, so the data is stored more densely in the sectors of these tracks. The density of the innermost track determines the drive's maximum capacity.

When a disk is constructed, it is provided with one or more extra inner tracks. These are used to provide a landing zone for the read/write heads. When machines are powered down, (very old machines may require a 'park' command) the read/write heads are moved to sit in the landing zone so that they will not be able to scratch the surface of any sectors used for storing data. A drive rated as 771 tracks might only format the disk to 770 tracks, using track 771 as the landing zone. Some systems also use spare inner tracks to compensate for bad tracks. This can result in different utilities displaying different results; some are counting the tracks for data while others are counting the total tracks.

With IDE and SCSI systems, the electronics can be used to hide the *real* surface structure from the machine. As far as the machine is concerned, the drive has say 953 tracks, with each track containing 36 sectors. This will indeed be the *'logical'* view given to the machine by the drive. In fact, the drive may well have a completely different physical layout. Since the disk's outer tracks cover a much greater surface than the inner tracks, the outer tracks can be used to store up to three times more sectors per track than the inner tracks. This is known as *'zone bit recording'* and provides greater storage with improved reliability. The exact internal layout need not be known by the machine or by the user, since the electronics on the drive make the drive appear to have the normal regular track and sector layout.

Heads

Each side requires its own read/write head and these number from zero upwards. All the heads are mounted on the same actuator arm, so that they all move in unison as a single unit. When one head is on the sixth track in from the edge, then all the other heads are also on the sixth track of their disk sides. This achieves efficiency and economy of head motion. All the sectors in the same cylinder number (of all platters) are used, before moving the head inward to the next cylinder number.

The maximum read without moving the head to another track is calculated by multiplying the number of sides by the number of sectors in the track; this is then multiplied by the sector size, usually 512 bytes.

So, for the XT machine, 4 x 17 x 0.5 = 34k could be read.

For a 12GB hard disk, 16 x 63 x 0.5 = 504k could be read.

Each platter has a read/write head for each side. Where a drive is reported to have an odd number of heads, it is due to the extra head and side being used for storing positional information instead of data. The smaller the dimensions and tolerances, the more likely that the drive could go out of alignment. To prevent this and the effects of temperature changes (see later), one disk side is given over to *'servo tracks'* that ensures that the head assembly maintains its tracking. As long as the head on the servo track's side is kept in alignment, then the other heads must maintain alignment, since they are mechanically linked.

Elevator Seeking

Modern hard disk electronics use a technique known as *'elevator seeking'*. The requests for disk reads are stored in a queue so that reads located in the same disk area are read while the head is at that location. The reads are not in the same sequence as originally requested and the electronics sorts out the data to compensate. This technique reduces the amount of head movement thereby speeding up disk access.

Calculating Disk Capacities

Like floppy disks, the capacity of a hard disk is found by multiplying the total number of sides by the number of tracks by the number of sectors per track by the number of bytes per sector.

For example, the hard disk issued with the IBM XT machine had 2 platters, 17 sectors and 305 tracks. Since each sector was 512 bytes, it had a capacity of 4 x 17 x 305 x 512 = 10MBytes. The IBM AT machine had the same specification, except that it had 615 cylinders. So, its capacity was 4 x 17 x 615 x 512 = 20MBytes. However, there are a number of other factors that have to be taken into account when attempting to calculate the usable surface of a hard disk.

A Worked Example

Consider the case of a disk advertised as a *"12GB"* disk. This may be based on the following formula

sides	tracks	sectors	
16 x	233611 x	63	= 23547888 sectors at 512 bytes = 12,056,518,656 bytes.

However, this is not a 12GB disk.   The final figure has to be divided by 1024 to arrive at the total expressed in KB (since there are 1024 bytes in a kilobyte).   Dividing the result by a further 1024 gives the answer in MB and dividing by a final 1024 produces an actual disk size of 11.228GB.   This is a full 790MB less than the manufacturer's advertised size.

However, this is not the end of the story.   The disk space that is actually available to the user to store programs and data is smaller still. The hard disk is consuming the following overheads:

	Sectors	Bytes
Partition	36	18432
DBR	1	512
FATs	22996	11773944
Directory	32	16384
Totals	23065	11809272

The Partition, DBR, FAT and Directory are covered later. A further 11.2MB of disk area is used for file management (i.e. 118029272/1024/1024). This leaves a user area of 11.228GB - 790MB - 11.2MB = 11.218GB.   The so-called 12GB hard disk, in fact, provides a user area of just over 11GB.

To compound matters, some manufacturers and suppliers used to quote the <u>unformatted</u> size of a hard disk. The sector numbering which is written during formatting consumes a considerable amount of the disk surface and the *'formatted capacity'* is a more accurate reflection of the true usable size of the disk. The total capacity of a disk is generally around a quarter more than the final formatted disk capacity.

Comparison Of Sector Coding

The BIOS always identifies a particular sector by a three-dimensional co-ordinate - the cylinder number/side number/sector number. On the other hand, DOS (e.g. DEBUG) and many add-on utilities refer to sectors by their ascending sequential number - in the above example going from 1 to 23,547,888. The conversion of DOS logical sector numbering and the actual physical layout of sectors/tracks/heads is carried out by the machine's BIOS.

Increasing Disk Capacity

The capacity of disk surfaces is continually rising as improving technology allows the packing of ever more data on to each square inch of disk surface.   This increased packing density, also known *as 'areal density'* relies upon:

- Improved surface coatings
- Improved head technology

Disk Coating

To achieve higher data density, the number of tracks is increased and the length of a sector is shortened. This means that the area free to be magnetised to store a single bit is diminished in both directions, both in length and in breadth.   If no steps were taken, the magnetised effects on the disk surface would influence each other and upset the data storage. To prevent this, the disk has a surface coating that is difficult to magnetise. This reduces the interference between the adjacent magnetised areas.

The degree of resistance to magnetisation is known as *'coercivity'* and is measured in units called *'Oersteds'*. It measures the amount of magnetic force that is required to change magnetic particles from sitting in a North-South orientation to a South-North orientation. A low coercivity disk will have its magnetic particles in the disk coating more readily affected than those of a high coercivity coating.   A 3.5" floppy disk has a coercivity of 700 Oersteds, while modern drives have ratings of around 2,000 Oersteds. Research is continuing to produce surfaces with higher ratings, allowing more data to be stored on the disk surface.

Disk Heads

The write head uses a magnetic field to alter the flux pattern of the disk coating. The magnetic field from the head spreads out like an umbrella, increasing in width as it approaches the disk surface.   The first diagram shows how a head

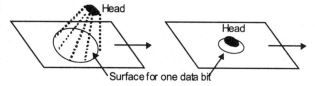

with a large gap requires a large surface to store a single piece of data. In the second diagram, the head is flying much lower, the gap is smaller and the area covered by the magnetic pattern is much reduced. Reduced head gaps result in greater areal density. The original flying height of read/write heads was over 12 microns and now range from 1 to 6 microns. The current tiny high capacity drives are achieved by having the heads fly at less than one micron above the disk surface. With the head being closer to the surface, the head's magnetising effect is also increased.

This technique is currently maximised through *'Proximity Recording'* where the head flies at only 0.8 microns from the disk surface.

Another technique is to make the head of narrower width so that the tracks are closer together and more tracks can be placed on the disk surface. This allows for increased capacities (i.e. more data on the same disk size) or smaller diameter disks (i.e. the same data on a smaller size). Increased packing density also means that manufacturers can make disks cheaper by having less platters and heads.

Magnetoresistive Heads

As the area allowed for each bit is reduced, the signal picked up by the normal inductive read head is weaker, reducing the reliability of the data read. Techniques to improve the signal pickup include:

Technique	Effect	Limitations
Move head closer to disk surface	Increased flux at head increases signal	Head gaps already very small
Place more turns on head coil	More sensitive head increases signal	Increases losses at fast speeds
Move data past head faster	Greater rate change of flux increases signal	Head speeds already very fast

One of the improvements in head technology is the Magnetoresistive (MR) head. MR heads have the following features:

- Separate read and write heads.
- The write head remains an inductive head but with much less windings on the coil. The extra windings were required for adequate data reads but resulted in writing too wide a track. Less windings means the head produces a narrower magnetic pattern and more tracks can be placed on the surface and more bits can be placed on each track.
- The reduced inductance of the write head also means that it can write at faster speeds.
- The read head is made from an alloy whose resistance changes in the presence of a magnetic flux. It is velocity independent - i.e. it is the presence of the flux and not the rate of change of flux that produces the read signal; increasing or decreasing the disk speed has no effect on the signal.
- The read head is tiny and can detect a much reduced data area. Areal density can therefore be increased.
- The read track is smaller than the write track so even slight head misalignment will not produce noise (the read head remains within the written track and does not read data from adjacent tracks).

PRML

Traditional drives translate the incoming signal from the head into digital data using *'peak detection'* - reading a peak value as a binary 1 and lower values as a binary zero. This is an increasingly difficult task for the electronics when the incoming analogue stream is very fast and contains noise. PRML (Partial Response Maximum Likelihood) converts the incoming signal into a digital waveform and runs it through a series of filters. A group of bits is compared at a time, producing a more reliable data translation. The increased reliability allows for a more efficient coding method when writing data; the RLL coding system requires less redundant data. This results in greater capacity from the same disk area.

Maximum Disk Handling

Available disk drives sizes grew at a rate that overtook the computer's handling capacity. Early DOS versions, prior to v3.31, had sixteen bits embedded in the disk boot sector to store the total number of sectors allowed per logical drive. Since the maximum different binary combinations from a 16-bit address is 65,536 and each sector is 0.5k, the maximum disk partition size on early PCs was 32MB.

This restriction was lifted from v3.31 onwards, when a four byte area was put aside in the boot sector area. This is a 32-bit number and can theoretically store a partition size up to 2 Terabytes. However, at first the BIOS for PC compatibles had a design that limited it to handling a maximum of 1024 tracks on any one hard disk, 63 sectors per track and a maximum of 255 read/write heads. The IDE interface, on the other hand, can handle a maximum of 65,536 tracks, 255 sectors per track and 16 heads. A disk system can only work at its lowest common denominator; there is no point in the BIOS supporting 255 heads, for example, if the IDE electronics can only handle a maximum of 16 heads.

This means that a normal IDE disk system can only operate with a maximum disk size of 16 heads covering 1024 tracks with each track holding a maximum of 63 sectors.   With the normal sector size of 512 bytes, the maximum disk size supported is:

	BIOS	IDE	Actual best
Sectors/track	63	255	63
Number of heads	255	16	16
Number of cylinders	1024	65536	1024
Maximum capacity	7.8GB	127.5GB	504MB

$$16 \times 1024 \times 63 \times 512 = 504MB$$

This restriction can be overcome by bypassing the drive mechanism program code in the BIOS.   The normal calls to the BIOS disk routines (i.e. interrupt 13h) are intercepted and sent to a conversion routine which translates between the normal physical CHS (cylinder/head/sector) values and logical CHS values which can have a greater range than those contained in the BIOS.   Ultimately, the logical values, when multiplied together, cannot exceed the product of the BIOS values.

ATA drives address the problem by using LBA (logical block addressing) on the disk controller card along with an LBA-aware BIOS chip. For very old machines whose BIOS code does not support LBA working, a software patch is installed which extends Int 13h working.   Every sector on the drive is numbered in sequence from zero upwards.   The extended BIOS takes the CHS information that is passed to it (via the DOS Int 13h call used for disk reads/writes) and translates it into a 28-bit address specifying the disk sector.   Although the extended 13h functions use 32 bit for addresses, the ATA drives only use 28 bit addresses, limiting the maximum working to 127.5GB ($2^{28}*512/1024/1024/1024$).

Nevertheless, the maximum partition size remained at 2GB for some time.   This limit was imposed by the design of the FAT16 filing system used by DOS, Windows 3.1 and the first release of Windows 95.   The second release of Windows 95, OSR2, and Windows 98 use FAT32 - a 32-bit file system. This takes full advantage of LBA working to handle disks up to 127.5GB as a single partition. Windows NT has its own filing system (NTFS).   This does not use the BIOS for its disk handling and can therefore handle beyond the 8GB limit.   The SCSI interface, due to its disregard for physical disk geometry, has no limitations on the number of heads it can support; SCSI drives have always used a form of LBA working.

Head Actuators

The set of read/write heads in a hard disk assembly is moved in unison, under the influence of a single actuator mechanism.   The head mechanisms come in two varieties:

Stepper Motors

Stepper motors rotate by a small pre-determined amount when the motor coil is energised.   Each step moves the read/write heads in or out exactly one track.   This is a cheap system but is slow and is no longer used.   Stepper motor systems are also more prone to temperature changes than voice coil types.   The physical dimensions of the disk expand and contract with temperature changes.   Since the stepper motor always moves the heads by the same amount with each step, they might not position the head exactly between the track boundaries.   That explains why users are recommended to switch on their computers for some time before using them, if they have been lying in a cold office overnight.   If the heads and tracks are not in exact alignment, then data reads might be inaccurate, as the read head may be reading partly from a neighbouring track.   Even worse problems may result if the user tries to save data under these conditions.   The data may be written partly on the wanted track and partly overwrite data on a neighbouring track.   Stepper systems also require a 'park' utility to move the head away from the active disk surface when the machine is being transported.   When the power is removed from a stepper motor drive, the read/write heads settle on the disk surface at the last track stepped to.

Voice Coils

A voice coil actuator is the more modern method and is given its name from the coil that moves the cone of a hi-fi loudspeaker.   Like the loudspeaker coil, the head coil is within the influence of a permanent magnet.   When the current through the coil is increased, the coil moves.   Since the coil is connected to the head and actuator arm, the arm moves and therefore the heads are moved.   This movement is against the action of a spring. When the current is removed, the spring pulls the heads to an area of the disk surface that does not store data; this is achieved without the user having to run a 'park' utility - in effect, these disks 'auto-park'.   Voice coil systems are faster and more reliable.

The disk in a voice coil drive will shrink and expand with temperature changes, just like any other hard disk. The voice coil mechanism, however, is designed to overcome this particular problem.   Instead of moving the heads by an exact amount, regardless of the prevailing disk temperature, the heads are moved to exactly the correct part of the track. In effect, the heads may move by a slightly different amount for differing temperatures. The heads find out the exact stopping positions for each track by sensing positional information laid down on a special track laid aside for the purpose. As the disk expands, the positional information will also move outwards and the heads will come to rest at the new altered position. This extra track is called the *'servo track'*.

Disk Reliability

Manufacturers usually quote their disks' reliability figures in terms of *'Mean Time Between Failure'* or *'MTBF'*. With older drives MTBFs were of between 20,000 hours and 50,000 hours - i.e. between about 800 days and 2,000 days of continuous use. Modern drives are quoted as having MTBFs of between 300,000 and 500,000 hours. Allowing for manufacturer's optimism this still results in drives that would never become faulty during their useful lives. In this context, 'useful life' would be the functional, rather than mechanical or electrical, life of the drive. Drive technology is moving ahead at a rate that encourages organisations to upgrade their drive systems prior to them becoming faulty beyond repair.

Protecting Hard Disks

Hard disks require most of the safety precautions already mentioned concerning floppy disks to be observed. The need to keep the disk unit away from strong magnetic fields, avoiding smoke and dust, etc. apply as much to hard disks as floppy disks. On the one hand, the hard disk is in a sealed unit and therefore has a better chance of surviving a hostile climate. On the other hand, the repercussions of disk failure are much more serious. If a floppy disk is damaged, it can be thrown in the waste bin at little financial loss. If a hard disk is damaged, it is a very costly item to replace. In addition, a damaged floppy disk should have its backup copy immediately to hand and so productivity is not affected. With a hard disk failure, a new disk has to be ordered up, fitted and have all the backup files restored before the machine is ready for use.

Apart from the above environmental problems, hard disks are particularly vulnerable to knocks and jolts. Unlike the floppy drive, the user is unable to mechanically stabilise the head assembly. If the case of the machine should be jolted while the machine is powered up, the head may make contact with the surface of the disk and scrape off some of the coating from the tracks. If this happens, the data in these sectors is lost and considerable permanent damage can be caused to the disk surface. This is termed a *'head crash'* and it renders sectors unusable. If the head crash happens when the head is positioned over the system areas (see notes on the Master Boot Record and DOS Boot Record) then the entire disk can be rendered unusable. This is because the system files cannot be relocated to any other sector - they must be found in specified tracks and sectors of the disk.

To minimise possible damage, modern drives have auto-park mechanics; that means that the read/write head is positioned out of the way of the data tracks when it is not involved in read or write operations. If this mechanism were not in place, as with very much older drives, then switching off the machine would result in the head dropping onto the disk surface. This would result in damage when the hard disk is powered up and spins with the head lying on the surface. These older drives required the user to run software utilities that placed the head out the way of data tracks before switching off the machine.

Disk Speed

The speed of a disk drive is based on
- The time to get to the required data (known as the *'access time'*)
- The time taken to read that data from the disk (known as the *'data transfer rate'*)

Access Time

The time taken to reach the required data is based on two factors:
1. The time that the head takes to get to the wanted track (seek time) measured in milliseconds. Each track-to-track jump time may be different, since some head movements will wish to move across a larger amount of the disk than other movements. Due to the way that files are written, most track-to-track movements are not very distant. So, the average access time is calculated on the basis of 1/3rd of the tracks, instead of the expected half of the tracks. A poor seek time would be 25ms and a fast seek time would be 8ms. Drives with seek times lower than around 25ms are using voice coil actuators rather than stepper motor actuators.
2. The time taken to get to the wanted sector (latency period). This is the time spent waiting for the wanted sector to rotate to the position directly under the read/write head. On average, this is half a

disk revolution.   At 3600 rpm, this would be 8.33ms, at 4500 rpm this would be 6.67ms and at 10,000 rpm it would be 3ms.

The original PC's 10MB hard disk had an access time of 80ms and the AT was quoted at 40ms.   Modern drives range from about 12ms to under 4ms.

Data Transfer Rate

The rate at which a small amount of data (e.g. a single sector) is transferred is determined by the above factors and is a physical restriction that cannot be adjusted by the user.   When a number of sectors require to be read, the most common case, the way that the disk is low-level formatted plays a large part in achieving the maximum data transfer rate. Low level formatting separates each sector with *'sector IDs'* that determine the sector boundaries.   The maximum data transfer rate is reached when the head reads from a contiguous set of sectors, without having to move the head to another track.   In such a case, the rate would be determined by the sector size, the number of sectors per track and the speed at which the data passes under the read head.

With a floppy drive, the disk rotates at 300 rpm and so the 18 sectors on a 1.44 MB floppy would be read in 0.2 secs.   The transfer rate would be:

$$0.5k \times 18 / 0.2 = 45k \text{ bytes/second or } 360 \text{Kbits/sec}$$

Now, even a slow hard disk spins much faster, at 3600 rpm, giving a track reading time of only 0.01666 secs.   So, for a hard disk with 36 sectors the data transfer rate would be:

$$0.5k \times 36 / 0.01666 = 1.08 \text{MB/second or } 8.6 \text{Mbits/sec}$$

With models rotating at 10,000 rpm the track reading time is 5.99ms and the data transfer rate would be:

$$0.5k \times 36 / 0.00599 = 3.01 \text{MB/second or } 24 \text{Mbits/sec}$$

So, reading a 1MB file from a large hard disk can take third of a second, around sixty times faster than reading from a floppy disk.   Of course, the access time for both drives has to be included and this slightly reduces the dramatic gap in performance between the two drive types. Most controllers also have to decode various timing pulses before sending the data to the computer.   Dependent on the type of card used, this produces various levels of delay and affects the overall data transfer rate.   The above figures are maximums, in that they assume that all the data is read in one contiguous read, with no additional track-to-track movements.

Another major factor in determining data transfer rate is the efficiency of the electronics in the disk controller card.   A very fast disk requires that the controller be able to transfer the data to the motherboard at the same rate.   This is covered later.

Interleave

The floppy controller circuitry can easily cope with the amount of data being transferred. The slow speed of the disk rotation means that data is read off slowly and is easily processed by even the slowest electronic circuits.   With much faster hard disk speeds, there is a potential problem for slow hard disk controllers.   The sectors of a floppy disk are contiguous on the disk surface as shown in the diagram; this is 1:1 interleave factor.

If sectors are contiguous on a hard disk, the controller circuitry may not be able to keep up with the tasks of processing each sector.   The controller has to verify that sector's data integrity and pass on the data to the BIOS, before reading the next sector.   If the sectors are contiguous on the disk, the controller could find that the following sector has already passed under its head when it wishes to read the data.   This would involve waiting until that sector rotated back under the read head again.   The result would be a reduced data transfer rate.

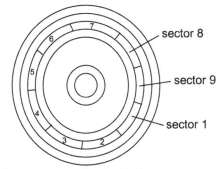

To overcome this, the sectors of a disk can be arranged so that sector 2 will not be placed on the disk directly after sector 1, sector 3 will not follow directly after sector 2 and so on, as is the case with floppy drives. In the diagram, a disk with 17 sectors per track and 1:3 sector interleave is shown. The controller attached to this drive requires time to process the data from the sector 1 before moving on to read sector 2.   Therefore, sector 2 is not contiguous to sector 1 and is placed further along the track. The distance between sector 1 and sector 2 represents the time required for the controller circuitry to cope with the processing. A 1:3 interleave means that the next required sector is always spaced 3 sectors away from the current sector. For a slower controller card, the spacing between sector numbers would be increased. A 1:6 interleave would mean that sector 2 would be spaced 6 sectors away from sector 1. At the time when interleave was an important factor, it was common to have older machines supplied with an incorrect interleave factor. In such cases, a simple interleave adjustment would increase disk performance by as much as 50%.

In many cases, the machines as supplied by manufacturers had a higher interleave setting than was necessary. The disk controller could often cope with a lower interleave setting than the one configured on the disk. It is certainly worth checking the interleave ratio on legacy machines and adjusting them where this can be done. If a disk is checked with a diagnostic utility such as Spinrite, the range of results for different interleave ratios is displayed and the user is informed of the optimum setting for that particular controller.

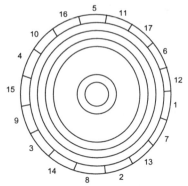

Reducing the interleave ratio can have a dramatic effect on data transfer rates.   For a 26 sectors/track disk, for example, a 1:1 interleave is four times faster than a 1:4 interleave.

Note that any trouble with interleaving is a problem with the controller not the hard disk itself.   If a controller has inefficient circuitry, replacing it with a more modern card will improve disk performance. The effects of the change of card are seen when the disk surface has its interleave altered to match the improved capabilities of the controller.

Note: Modern machines are supplied with a controller that is capable of handling 1:1 interleave arrangements. Virtually all IDE, EIDE, ESDI and SCSI drives are pre-set to 1:1 as standard and should not be altered by the user.

Changing the Interleave Ratio

Disk utilities are available to alter a hard disk's interleave ratio, including Spinrite, Norton Utilities Calibrate and Disk Technician.   These test the controller for the lowest ratio that can be safely used. This is dependent on the controller card, any caching and the size and speed of the bus.   It works by reading the data in the present interleave sequence and timing that read.   It then reads these sectors in different sequences, again carrying out timing of each sequence. The table of interleave timings found is then displayed. The user can then choose to have the disk altered to work with the optimum interleave ratio and the program will then automatically carry out the alteration.   The utilities carry out the process in a *'non-destructive'* fashion, which means that the original data can be left on the disk.

Encoding Methods

Magnetising and demagnetising the disk surface as the head passes along a sector allows the magnetised and demagnetised areas to be written in accordance with the binary 1s and 0s of the data to be written. When the head comes back to read that sector, the magnetised pulses, and their patterns, can be translated back into a stream of 1s and 0s in the same pattern as the original written data.

However, it is not quite that simple. If a long series of 0s were to be written to a sector, this would cause problems when the data was later read.   A long time span without pulses leaves the electronic circuits unsure of the exact number of 0s in that stream.   This may be aggravated by slight speed differences in disk motors.   This synchronisation problem would cause probable data reading errors. Consequently, the pattern written to the sector has to contain synchronisation information along with the actual data. Earlier solutions lay in recording extra synchronisation pulses on the sector along with the actual data, in the ratio of one synchronisation bit to one data bit.   Although this scheme - known as *'Frequency Modulation'* - worked, it was extremely wasteful of disk space.   This technique was employed in the old 100k BBC floppy disk drives.

MFM

The MFM - Modified Frequency Modulation - system is the original PC technique used for floppies and many older hard disks.   This uses a more compact encoding method that produces a reliable disk drive but consumes a rather large amount of the information in each sector for synchronisation purposes.

RLL

The RLL - Run Length Limited - technique has been popular since 1986 when it was patented and introduced by IBM.   Improved hard disk tolerances have meant less surface undulations, allowing the read/write heads to fly closer to the disk surface - as low as 8 microns.   New cobalt coatings have higher coercivity. The combination of lower-flying heads and more coercive materials has meant that more data can be packed on to the same disk area.   RLL uses a more complex encoding algorithm, which means that a smaller proportion of the information written to a sector is synchronisation information - thus allowing more actual data to be placed on a disk of the same physical capacity.   These factors result in storing 50% more user data on the disk.   Also, since more data can be stored in a specific area of disk surface, reading from that area when RLL-encoded will bring in more data than when reading that same area if MFM encoded. Put another way, the data transfer rate of an RLL drive is greater than that of an MFM drive.   Manufacturers use variations of RLL for all current disk drives.

Old, MFM quality drives should not be used with RLL controllers as trying to work the disk at higher densities than they were designed for will cause disk read errors, either immediately or with increasing frequency at a later stage.

INTERFACES

The 'controller' is the electronic circuitry used to control the operations of the drive mechanism and the head read/write activities. In modern machines, this circuitry is built on to the machine's motherboard but older systems implemented this on a separate expansion card.

In early systems, manufacturers produced their own interface arrangements and this meant that users had to always use the manufacturer's specific card and drive components.   Nowadays, one group of manufacturers, including for example Western Digital, produces controllers while other manufacturers, like Seagate and Maxtor, produce the hard drives. Consequently, a number of standard interfaces have been arrived at, to allow the devices to communicate.   While the interface card is mainly for controlling the hard disk, most boards also have built-in electronics to control floppy disks.

The mechanics of drives mostly work in the same way but there are differences in the way that the drive communicates with the motherboard. The most common interfaces are described below.

ST506

The oldest interface is the ST506.   It was produced by Seagate Technology and appeared at the time of the introduction of the IBM PC. It died out around 14 years ago. It was originally used with 5MB drives and had a maximum disk capacity of 140MB.   The stream of data bytes, timing pulses and separators

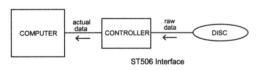

ST506 Interface

read from the disk is translated into data, which is placed on the computer's data bus via the card's connection to the expansion slot. This transfer of data between controller card and expansion slot is shown in the diagram as the flow of 'actual data'. The data from disk to controller card, i.e. the 'raw data', is in serial (therefore slower) format.   ST506 drives are produced in MFM and RLL types with disk to controller transfer rates of 600kB/sec and 900kB/sec, assuming both drives are operated at 1:1 interleave. When 1:1 interleaves are used, no further improvement that can be made between the drive and the card, since all other factors (i.e. speed of rotation, encoding method, sectors/track) are either standard or maximised.   An improved version of the ST506 is the ST412, which meets the IEEE 412 specification and uses voice coils for controlling head movements instead of stepper motors, to speed up disk access times. The ST412 also carries out elevator seeking. Most ST506/412 systems use MFM coding with equal amounts of recorded data being stored on each track.

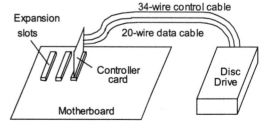

As shown in the diagram, the ST506/412 drive connects to the motherboard via cables to the disk controller card. A 34-wire cable is used to control the drive's choice of head and move the heads to the various tracks, etc. The wires are also used to dictate whether reading or writing is to take place.   Another cable, of 20 wires, is used to carry the data between the controller card and the drive.

The data is in serial format, despite the number of wires in use; the other wires are reserved or earthed.

ESDI

The Enhanced Small Device Interface was produced by a consortium of manufacturers who required better performance than the ST506/ST412 standard. ESDI is also a serial method but the interpretation of the timing pulses is carried out on the drive itself rather than in the controller card. This process is unaffected by any noise on the drive/controller interface and, as a result, the ESDI interface produces a higher data transfer rate. Other improvements include improved disk motor speed tolerance, an improved disk surface (i.e. a higher surface coercivity) and a reduced space between the head and the disk surface (down to 10 microns or less), allowing more sectors per track. In addition, ESDI drives can report their size and layout to the controller, eliminating the need for the user to know and set up the exact disk configuration (numbers of heads, cylinders, sectors, etc.).

Although a device-level system, the ESDI drive possesses a degree of high level communication with the machine. For example, an ST506 controller attempting to format a hard disk would require to given a very long series of commands to move the heads and energise the write heads in the appropriate sequence. With the ESDI system, a single command is passed to the circuitry on the controller and it will carry out the process without any further intervention from the computer. The cables are identical to ST506 cables; it's just that the data they carry is different. So, the physical layout of an ESDI is identical to the diagram already given for the ST506/412 system.

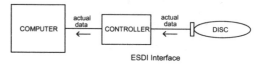

ESDI Interface

The data from disk to controller is, nevertheless, still in the slower serial format. Most ESDI systems produce over 1MB/sec transfer rates with 1.25MB/sec being typical. Both drives and controller are available in different speed formats, so not every drive can be expected to work with every controller. Often produced in high capacity versions and used in higher performance systems, particularly on single-user systems. The ESDI system was most commonly found on the IBM PS/2 range of computers. The ESDI standard is now obsolete, with support moving to SCSI systems at the higher end of the market and to Ultra DMA 66/100 IDE systems at the lower end.

IDE

The system, introduced by Compaq in 1987, stands for Integrated Drive Electronics, sometimes described as Intelligent Drive Electronics, or even Imbedded Drive Electronics. This system is really an ST506/ST412 setup that puts the entire controller circuitry on to the drive itself, to eliminate any losses between drive and controller. With this improved reliability, IDE drives have increased the number of sectors per track, allowing even greater data density on the drive. Most have 34 or more sectors per track and a 63 sector per track drive is not uncommon. They use 1:1 interleave and, also taking into account that the data from the disk is now in faster parallel format, produce fast performances. Theoretical data transfer rates of up to 5MB/sec are possible although around 4MB/sec is more typical.

The fact that the IDE system is designed to appear to the machine as an ST506 system means that the original AT BIOS chip can always accommodate an IDE; there is no need to change the BIOS chip to get it to communicate with the drive system.

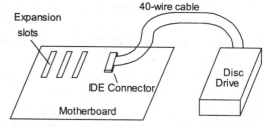

IDE drives connect to the computer via an integrated IDE connector on the motherboard, and avoids using up any expansion slots. The electronics for the drive is already mounted on the computer's motherboard. The drive cable is simply plugged into the motherboard connector. Separate circuitry is provided to handle the floppy drives.

Two IDE disk drives can be connected to an IDE motherboard socket and most motherboards provide two such sockets, allowing a maximum of four IDE devices. These may be a mixture of disk drives, ZIP drives or CD-ROM drives. The motherboard sockets are usually marked as "*Primary*" and "*Secondary*" or as "*IDE1*" and "*IDE2*".

An IDE cable has three plugs - one at either end of the cable and one along the length of the cable. One fits into the motherboard and the other two plug into the disk drives (or other IDE devices).

UDMA66/100 drives need a special low crosstalk cable, which if not supplied with the motherboard can be bought for a few pounds.

An older system, now no longer used, had a *'pass-through'* board that plugged into a spare expansion slot. There were no electronic processing components on this board and it was used solely as a means of making connection to the motherboard (hence the term *'passing through')*.   The board contained only bus buffering chips and some address decoding chips and it had a 40-wire ribbon cable that connected to the IDE drive.   16 of these wires are used as a parallel bus for faster data transfer.

IDE was a popular choice of drive due to its general reliability and its relative cheapness (caused by the reduced circuit complexity as a result of the data interpretation work being done on the drive).   However, it does have the one drawback.   If problems are encountered, the drive cannot be low-level formatted. IDE drives are low-level formatted at the factory and only give the appearance of an ST506 system to the machine. So, if the problems cannot be resolved at a higher level, the design of the IDE drive prohibits using the usual software to carry out low level operations such as low-level formatting and interleave setting.

IDE systems use logical addressing which leaves the job of translating logical sector numbers into actual head, track and sector information to the electronics on the drive. This is an advantage since it simplifies operations, with the drive taking over some housekeeping. For instance, if the drive detects that a track is deteriorating, it can transfer the data to a spare track and mark the original track as bad - all without the knowledge of the main machine.   As far as DOS is concerned, the data is still in the original track - the task of translating what DOS thinks is the wanted sector into the actual new location is the job of the drive circuitry.   That is why the normal utilities that work an absolute sector level have problems with IDE drives.   However, file utilities such as defragmenters operate at a higher level and can therefore still work with IDE drives.

IDE drive controllers are unable to co-exist on the same machine with ST506 controllers or ESDI controllers.   If a machine is to be given a second drive as an IDE drive, the original drive must also be an IDE type.   Most IDE drives are compact 3.5" models.

Setting IDE drives

Where more than one disk drive is connected to a computer system, the computer has to be able to recognize them individually, know which one is the boot drive, etc.   This is achieved by adjusting settings on each drive, so that they are recognised as being unique.

On older drives, these adjustments were provided on the printed circuit board of the drive. On modern drives, they are at the rear of the case on a *"jumper block"*. The block has two rows of pins and various pins can be bridged with small metal connectors with plastic covers.

Motherboards support two IDE connectors (channel 0 and channel 1).   Each connector can support two IDE devices (known as device 0 and device 1).

Device 0 is the *'master'* device and device 1 is the *'slave'* device of each chain.   The master device on channel 0 is usually used as the boot drive (see notes).

Channel 0 is also known as the *'Primary'* channel, with Channel 1 being known as the *'Secondary'* channel.

This means that if a computer has four drives fitted they would be known as:

- The primary master
- The primary slave
- The secondary master
- The secondary slave

Modern systems mount the controller's electronics directly in the drive itself, rather than from a controller card. Where there are two drives on the one cable, only one controller is in operation. This is known as the *'master'* drive. The second drive uses the master's controller for its control instructions. This is known as the *'slave'* drive. This ensures that only one controller is ever active on a single channel.

The drives can be set as *'master'* or *'slave'*.   The *'master'* setting is for a first disk drive and is the one that the system will boot from in a two-drive system. The *'slave'* is the second drive on the same cable. Where there are two drives on the same channel, it is often referred to as a *'chain'*.

Disk drives are usually supplied already configured as master drives and may need to be altered if they are to be used as slave drives.

Notes

- The BIOS can be set to select the boot device. So, even if a drive is jumpered to be the boot device, the BIOS can be set to boot from a floppy drive or from a CD-ROM drive.
- The actual jumper settings vary from manufacturer to manufacturer. The installation notes that come with the drive should be consulted.

DRIVES AND THE BIOS

The early XT machines expected the user to set switches on the controller card to inform the system of the drive number in use with the card. The XT controller card had its own BIOS chip and it stored a table of the most popular types of drive. Each number in the table corresponded to a set of disk parameters. This was satisfactory at the time, since only a limited range of disk types and sizes were available. From the AT onwards, the motherboard BIOS made provision for disk handling and it originally contained a disk table of types 0 to 14.

The machine's BIOS uses an area of CMOS (Complimentary Metal-Oxide Silicone - a type of low-power RAM) that is permanently powered by the machine's internal automatically recharged batteries. This same battery keeps the internal clock operating. The CMOS stores the details of the number of disk drives in use, their type and size. The hard disk details include the number of cylinders, number of sectors per cylinder, number of heads and write pre-compensation tracks. The user runs a setup program and chooses the appropriate description; the type number is used to set up the parameters in the CMOS memory.

Below are extracts from an AMI BIOS:

Drive Number	No of Cylinders	No of Heads	Start of WPC	Landing Zone	Sectors/ track	Disk Capacity
1	306	4	128	305	17	10M
2	615	4	300	615	17	20M
3	615	6	300	615	17	30M
4	940	8	512	940	17	62M
5	940	6	512	940	17	46M
6	615	4	65535	615	17	20M
7	462	8	256	511	17	30M
8	733	5	65535	733	17	30M
9	900	15	65535	901	17	112M
...	...	...	...	...	...	...
42	981	5	981	981	17	41M
43	755	16	65535	755	17	100M
44	887	13	65535	887	34	191M
45	968	10	65535	968	34	161M
46	751	8	0	751	17	50M

Since the original table originated with the XT, the list is not exactly exhaustive or up-to-date. The original table grew to some 47 entries, some of which still describe small disk sizes that will rarely be found in use any longer. To further complicate matters, some manufacturers' tables list their own versions of what characteristics match what table number; fortunately, most lower entries remain identical.

Entries 0 to 14 are identical to the entries in the original AT set. However, a number of entries thereafter have been altered to allow the inclusion of higher-capacity drives than previously specified. This, of course, means that the modified numbers in the table only correspond to that manufacturer's BIOS and will not be available in other BIOS tables. Indeed, the table may well not be the same in future issues of the same manufacturer's BIOS.

Unfortunately, since disk technology is racing ahead, there are many disk types that are not covered by the existing tables held inside most BIOS chips, regardless of manufacturer. A way had to be found to future proof the BIOS, otherwise the chip would have to be updated whenever new drive types became available.

Entry 47

Fortunately, BIOS manufacturer (e.g. IBM, AMI, some Phoenix, etc.) deliberately left the details for table entry 47 left undefined. This allowed a custom configuration to be entered by the user as entry 47. In this way, a BIOS will not age too quickly.

If option 47 is chosen as the drive type, the user is then prompted to enter the following information:

Entry	Meaning
Cylinders	The number of cylinders
Heads	The total number of read/write heads
Write Precompensation - WPC	The starting cylinder for write precompensation to take effect
Landing Zone - LZ	The cylinder to be used as the landing zone for parking the read/write heads
Sectors per track - ST	The number of sectors per track
Size in MBs	The capacity of the disk expressed in Megabytes

The entries listed are the ones to be commonly displayed by a utility. In fact, there are two other entries held in the table.

These are:

- Size in millions of bytes - this holds the disk's capacity in millions of bytes, as opposed to Megabytes.
- Control Byte - the individual bits in this byte are used hold information such as whether the disk has more than eight heads, is a servo drive, etc.

Since the values in the table do not cover new drives, the values that are placed in the CMOS can be any set of values which result in the same, or less, sectors than the actual drive used. As long as the formula

total tracks x number of sectors per track x number of heads

produces a value that is equal or less than the sectors value given in the drive specification, the IDE electronics can handle the logical to physical translations. If the total value of sectors exceeds the actual physical sectors, incorrect clusters are overwritten and data is lost.

EIDE

The rapid development of the other parts of the computer system has left the disk subsystem as the bottleneck for many activities.

Although IDE was very popular, it had a number of disadvantages:

- Its peak data transfer rate, at 4.1MB/sec, was inadequate. The low transfer rate was not a limitation with ordinary 16-bit ISA busses, since they were only capable of working up to a maximum rate of around 3MB/sec. The PCI and VL busses could handle much faster rates, but the IDE controller card was designed to fit into the ISA expansion slots of these machines. Such machines were therefore incapable of handling even the IDE's peak rate and an improved disk interface would be wasted on ISA based computers. A disk interface capable of plugging into the PCI or VL expansion bus could utilise the faster potential on these buses - hence the development of EIDE.
- It is only designed to interface hard disks. Other devices are not easily connected to the interface, although some CD-ROMs now provide IDE connections.
- It can only handle two drives per controller. Many machines do not support more than a single controller, limiting the computer to a maximum of 1GB spread over two drives. At best, a computer will support two controllers, allowing 2GB of disk capacity.

1995 saw the more widespread use of an improved interface known as EIDE or E-IDE (Enhanced IDE) capable of handling four devices. The devices are mostly disk drives but the interface easily handles CD-ROMs and ZIP drives. It is also cheaper than the other alternative fast interface - the SCSI interface.

The EIDE interface offers significant improvement in speed over the standard IDE interface, with a range of possible rates as laid in ANSI specifications. An EIDE disk drive remains compatible with the normal IDE system. Such a drive can be connected to an IDE controller and will work happily, although its transfer rate will slow down to that of the normal IDE performance. It is this compatibility that gives the Enhanced IDE its name.

This originated the current range of improved non-SCSI drive systems that remain backward compatible with older computers. So, for example, a UDMA/66 drive produces a full data transfer rate of 66.6MBps when connected to a motherboard and BIOS that are both ATA/66 compatible. However, its 40-pin plug still connects to an older motherboard IDE connection (the extra 40 wires in the cable are shields for the 40 pins) - although, of course, it runs at the reduced data transfer rate.

ATA INTERFACE

ATA (AT Attachment) is the general standard for connecting disk drives and currently has four flavours:

- ATA-1 describes the original normal IDE working.
- ATA-2 is the foundation of a range of EIDE interfaces. It also incorporates ATAPI (ATA Packet Interface), which describes the ability of the interface to work with other devices beyond disk drives. If a scanner or CD-ROM is described as having an ATAPI standard, it means that it connects to the IDE controller.
- ATA-3 is the upgraded specification that introduced PIO Mode 4 and Multiple Word DMA 2. It also brought in power management - particularly useful for portable computers.
- ATA-4 is the specification that encompasses the newer Ultra DMA drives, also known as Ultra-ATA, Ultra DMA/33, Ultra DMA/66 and Ultra DMA/100.

ATA devices cover a wide range of transfer times, using different data transfer methods.
There are three data transfer methods:

<table>
<tr><td rowspan="2">PIO</td><td colspan="3">The Programmed Input/Output method has the computer's CPU in control. The CPU itself reads the data from the disk interface and writes it to memory (or vice versa for disk writes). Used by the original 80286 PC disk controller and also modern IDE controllers.

PIO has six different working modes:</td></tr>
<tr><td>PIO Mode</td><td>Speed</td><td>Standard</td></tr>
<tr><td></td><td>0</td><td>3.3MBps</td><td>ATA</td></tr>
<tr><td></td><td>1</td><td>5.2MBps</td><td>ATA</td></tr>
<tr><td></td><td>2</td><td>8.3MBps</td><td>ATA</td></tr>
<tr><td></td><td>3</td><td>11.1MBps</td><td>ATA-2</td></tr>
<tr><td></td><td>4</td><td>16.7MBps</td><td>ATA-3</td></tr>
<tr><td></td><td>5</td><td>22MBps</td><td>Not yet implemented</td></tr>
<tr><td rowspan="2">DMA</td><td colspan="3">With the Direct Memory Access method, the circuitry on the disk controller card relieves the CPU of much of its memory read/write activities. The CPU tells the DMA controller which disk to access and what memory area to read/write and the DMA controller handles all the data transfers. This is termed 'Bus Mastering' since the CPU controls all data transfers during this period. During this time, the CPU is freed to carry out other tasks. These tasks cannot involve memory access but can be computer calculations.

There are six variants of DMA transfers:</td></tr>
<tr><td>DMA Mode</td><td>Speed</td><td>Standard</td></tr>
<tr><td></td><td>Single Word 0</td><td>1.04MBps</td><td>ATA</td></tr>
<tr><td></td><td>Single Word 1</td><td>2.08MBps</td><td>ATA</td></tr>
<tr><td></td><td>Single Word 2</td><td>4.17MBps</td><td>ATA</td></tr>
<tr><td></td><td>Multiple Word 0</td><td>4.7MBps</td><td>ATA</td></tr>
<tr><td></td><td>Multiple Word 1</td><td>13.3MBps</td><td>ATA-2</td></tr>
<tr><td></td><td>Multiple Word 2</td><td>16.7MBps</td><td>ATA-3</td></tr>
<tr><td rowspan="2">ULTRA-DMA</td><td colspan="3">Ultra DMA uses techniques such as improved timing and data pipelining to double the maximum data transfer rate achieved by the standard DMA method. It also introduces CRC testing to ensure the integrity of data moving on the bus. This is in addition to the CRC checks discussed earlier, relating to integrity checking when writing to the disk surface.

Ultra-DMA drives will connect to existing IDE motherboards but will not provide the higher transfer rates. Motherboards using LX and TX chipsets onwards support Ultra-DMA drives.

There are several variants of Ultra-DMA transfers:</td></tr>
<tr><td>DMA Mode</td><td>Speed</td><td>Standard</td></tr>
<tr><td></td><td>0</td><td>16MBps</td><td>ATA-4</td></tr>
<tr><td></td><td>1</td><td>24MBps</td><td>ATA-4</td></tr>
<tr><td></td><td>2 (UDMA/33)</td><td>33MBps</td><td>ATA-4</td></tr>
<tr><td></td><td>4 (UDMA/66)</td><td>66MBps</td><td>ATA-4</td></tr>
<tr><td></td><td>5 (UDMA/100)</td><td>100MBps</td><td>ATA-4</td></tr>
</table>

SCSI

The SCSI interface standard is the Small Computer Systems Interface (pronounced *'scuzzy'*). This is an old interface, adopted as an ANSI standard in 1986, which has made a serious impact on the general storage market. The SCSI drive has the controller circuitry built-in and, like the EIDE, it uses logical addressing methods. The drive is connected via a 50-wire or 68-wire cable to an adapter card that connects to one of the computer's expansion slots. Since the controller circuitry is on the drive, the card is described as a *'host adapter'* rather than a controller card. Its only real job is to allow SCSI devices to connect to the computer bus. Since it is a simple device, it is able to connect up to seven or sixteen different devices. The connecting cable can have a number of connector plugs along its length, to connect to a number of internally fitted SCSI devices. External devices, such as DAT drives and external CD-ROMs, can connect to the bus via a D-shell connector on the SCSI adapter card.

When several devices are connected, the system is described as being *'daisy chained'*. The total length of the chain must not exceed 19 feet (reducing to 9 feet for Wide SCSI and only 5 feet for SCSI-3), to minimise transmission errors. Each end of the chain must also be fitted with terminating resistors. These terminate the cable and prevent signals being reflected back down the cable as noise. The terminators may consist of resistors built in to the device and activated by DIP switches, or they may be separate terminating plugs or *'blocks'*. Each external device has two connectors - one for connecting to the existing chain and one for either extending the chain or terminating the chain.

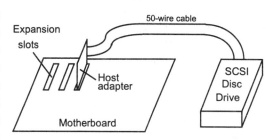

The intelligence built in to the host adapter is designed to relieve the machine's CPU from the tasks of organising the control of the various devices attached to it. The machine CPU can transfer these responsibilities to the circuitry of the host adapter card so that it can carry out other activities.

The IDE drive receives instructions that are both disk-specific and low-level. The SCSI controller, on the other hand, communicates at a higher level and is data-specific, leaving the physical considerations entirely to the device's on-board circuitry. The generalised nature of this interface means that it is able to connect more than just disk drives to the motherboard. A range of devices, such as CD-ROMs, tape drives, scanners, etc. can be connected to the SCSI interface with ease. Each device must be given a different ID number. With SCSI-1 and SCSI-2, these range from 0 to 7 and the host adapter usually defaults to ID 7. Wide SCSI-2 and SCSI-3 support up to 16 devices. The ID number is set in each device with the DIP switches or jumpers on the cards. Adaptec, a major SCSI adapter manufacturer, pioneered the ASPI (Advanced SCSI Programming Interface). This is a single driver that lets DOS communicate with the adapter card and another driver for each device on the chain.

Since each device on the chain may be able to communicate at a different data rate, the adapter card has to alter its data rate to match each device it is working to any particular time. The card can work at the faster rates for faster devices and will slow down to the rates of the slower devices. To achieve this, the card has to set its standard for communicating with each device.

SCSI Versions

A range of different SCSI standards has evolved with the following data transfer rates from the device to the adapter card. These use different data bus widths and different electronic controls.

Bus widths are either 8-bit or 16-bit. This is the bus between the controller and the drive; the controller may well have a 32-bit interface via the PCI connector.

Type	Data Rate	Data Path	Comments
SCSI-1/ SCSI-2	5MB/sec	8-bit	50-pin connector. Asynchronous
SCSI-2 Fast	10MB/sec	8-bit	50-pin connector. Synchronous
SCSI-2 Fast Wide	20MB/sec	16-bit	68-pin connector
SCSI-3 Ultra	20MB/sec	8-bit	50-pin connector. Also called Fast 20.
SCSI-3 Ultra-Wide	40MB/sec	16-bit	68-pin connector
Ultra-2	40MB/sec	8-bit	Also called Fast 40.
Ultra-2 Wide	80MB/sec	16-bit	68-pin connector
Ultra 80	80MB/sec	8-bit	Also called Fast 80
Ultra160 (or U160)	160MB/sec	8-bit	An implementation of Ultra-3
Ultra320	320MB/sec	16-bit	Under development

Fast SCSI doubles the transfer rate by using more stringent electronic parameters that allow timings to be altered and overheads reduced. Ultra SCSI's electronics run at double the normal clock frequency and this produces transfer rates that are double that of Fast SCSI.

Since the data transfer rate between the adapter and an ISA based computer works out at around 2Mb/sec; a SCSI adapter that connects to PCI bus produces far better results.

SCSI systems do not use the machine's BIOS, having placed a device driver in the CONFIG.SYS file to install the necessary control software. This means that a SCSI drive can cohabit with an ST506 or an IDE system in the same machine without any conflicts. In addition, since devices of different transfer rates can work with the same adapter, upgrading to a faster SCSI hard disk will involve no changes to the SCSI adapter. Many CD-ROMs, scanners and Postscript printers now have SCSI-2 interfaces.

Notes:
- The best EIDE performances compete with the middle/top SCSI performance but SCSI systems also have an edge on performance in multitasking environments. The CPU can send an instruction to a SCSI device and carry on with other tasks until the device responds. With EIDE, the CPU has to wait until the device responds before carrying out other tasks thereby slowing down throughput, particularly in situations of multiple I/O requests.
- The performance of the interfaces has outstripped the speed of most current drives, which run at about a 10MB/sec sustained data transfer rate. Even the most modern and fastest drives (such as the 10,000 rpm Seagate Cheetah) can only provide a sustained transfer rate of up to 30MB/sec.
- An ultra-wide controller card, such as the Adaptec 2940UW, has both 68-pin connectors (for ultra-wide devices) and 50-pin connectors (for SCSI-2 devices).

SCA Connectors

The Single Connector Attachment system is not limited to SCSI devices, but SCA usage so far has been almost entirely in SCSI systems. SCA is essentially a method of connecting data and power lines to the attached devices through a single interface. The current specification of SCA is an 80-pin connector.

FireWire Disks

The relatively new FireWire standard (see the Architecture chapter for more details) can be used to connect external hard drives and other storage devices. In theory this means the drives could use the full data transfer speed of the FireWire interface. However, it should be noted that in most cases the hard disks used are simply normal IDE drives with interfaces that allow it to be used through a FireWire bus. Although this gives the advantage of an external, mobile disk, it does not use the full speed capability of the architecture.

Write Precompensation

IDE and SCSI systems use the disk surface to the maximum advantage. They write more data on the more spacious outer tracks and less data on the more compressed inner tracks. To the outside world, however, they present a logical view that represents the disk as having an identical number of sectors in every track. For other systems, this facility is lacking and this can cause problems of reading and writing data evenly over the disk surface. The sectors that are on the inner tracks on a disk (the higher numbered tracks) are smaller in size than the tracks on the outer surface of the disk. Yet, the track has to hold the same amount of data, for say 36 sectors, whether it is on the inner or outer edges of the disk. It follows then, that the data is more compressed on the inner tracks than on the outer tracks. The computer data is written on to the disk surface as a stream of magnetised sections, with each section having its own north and south poles like any other magnet.

A small unmagnetised area separates magnetised sections from the each other. Problems arise when the inner tracks locate these *'magnets'* closer together, with smaller spaces between them. Their proximity results in the magnetised areas affecting each other, with similar poles repelling and opposite poles attracting. The slight alteration of the magnetic pattern may be sufficient to prevent the data being read back correctly. To correct this, the writing process can treat the inner tracks differently from the outer tracks, by taking into account the likely distortions when placing the data on the surface. The writing process is compensating in advance for the problem, so that the final written information will be where it ought. It is this *'compensating in advance'* that gives the process the name *'precompensation'*. When the data is later read, the inner and outer tracks are read and processed in the same way. Since precompensation is concerned with writing data to the correct place on the disk surface, it only affects the writing process and is not used for reading data.

The parameters for each drive include a write precompensation number. This is the number of the first track at which to apply precompensation when writing data. If a 953 cylinder disk has a precompensation value of 150, then write precompensation starts at track 150 onwards. If the value for the same drive is 953, then no precompensation is applied to that particular disk (this might also be stored as -1).

The reduced physical size of disk area for the storage of each data bit can cause another problem. The electric current used to produce the data writing to the outer tracks could result in each data write occupying too large a disk surface area in the inner tracks. The separating non-magnetised areas disappear and the data elements begin to overlap into each other. To prevent this, the current supplied to the write head is reduced on the inner tracks, creating a smaller write area on the disk surface.

Disk Cache

The speed of a computer's throughput is not solely determined by the raw speed of the CPU. Many applications are disk based and large database applications are especially disk-intensive in their operations. So, a large proportion of the time is spent in disk activities rather than processing activities. Windows also makes heavy use of disk operations, particularly if machine memory is small and swap files are in operation. Additionally, Windows uses many DLL (Dynamic Link Library) files. These sub-programs are usable by various applications and function like overlay files. However, this technique also increases the number of disk accesses required to run applications.

There has been continual progress in CPU development from the days of the 8088 processor. Disk development, although making rapid progress of late, has remained the main bottleneck in the system as it is still largely limited by the mechanical nature of its operations.

Cache controller cards have been developed as a highly successful method of improving disk access times. They work on the same principle as memory cache systems explained previously. Memory cache acts as a high-speed buffer between the fast CPU and slower memory. With disk caching, memory chips are used as a high-speed buffer between the fast CPU and very much slower disk devices. It is also argued that the reduced need for disk accesses results in reduced disk wear, prolonging the disk's life

In fact, DOS buffers are an elementary form of caching. Each buffer stores 512 bytes of data - the same size as a disk sector. With buffers set at 20, 10k of memory is set aside for disk caching. With today's giant applications, this is totally inadequate and most modern disk drives use *'track buffering'* instead of sector buffering. This means that an entire track (or more likely several entire tracks) is read at a time into a memory buffer that is located on the drive's own electronics circuit board.

True disk caching can be implemented in two ways:

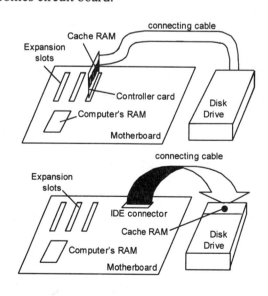

1. Using memory chips that are not part of the PC's normal memory map. In older systems, they were located on a separate disk controller card. The controller card was used to replace the normal IDE or SCSI controller and was plugged into an ordinary ISA expansion bus on the motherboard, as shown in the first diagram.

    This has now been replaced by the system shown in the second diagram. The cache memory chips are now located inside the disk drive case. Modern drives have from 512k up to 16MB of this built-in cache memory. In both cases, they provide extra memory that is dedicated to interfacing slow disk access with fast CPU access.

2. Using a chunk of the computer's memory, usually extended memory, under the control of the DOS or Windows 3.1 SMARTDRV utility, or Windows 95/98 VCACHE utility.

Both caching systems work in the same way. The CPU demands data at a much faster rate than the disk mechanism can fetch it. The cache memory in the disk drive - or in the computer memory - stores copies of the data that was previously read or written. It also reads ahead - it reads in data from sectors beyond that requested. If the machine wishes to read a file, there is a fair chance that the data is already stored in the cache memory. If so, then it can be transferred at a much faster rate than would be the case with reading directly from disk. If the data is found in cache, then it is described as a *'hit'*; if it has to be fetched from disk, then it is a *'miss'*. To improve the *'hit rate'*, the controller predicts the next data to be read (see notes on the principle of locality) and pre-loads this data into cache memory. This is particularly effective with database records and other data that is organised on a sequential basis.

Caching algorithms can deliver around 90% of data requests from the high-speed cache, avoiding interrogating the hard disk. On the other hand, when there is a cache *'miss'*, the system actually operates more slowly than a non-cached system. There is wasted time, while the cache is fruitlessly searched, before the data is fetched from the disk. Of course, if a very large quantity of data is to be handled, a small controller cache, or a small smartdrive cache, will have only a limited effect on efficiency. The larger the cache memory size, the more likely that the data will be found without recourse to disk access. If the user is working with huge database records, or large graphics files or DTP files, then each read required could be larger than the actual cache size and large disk reads would be required on every occasion. This will slow down throughput and give a poor hit rate. (NOTE: This effect should be borne in mind when measuring cache efficiency with SMARTDRV/S; it is possible that the same machine might be perfectly efficient at handling other processing chores).

When fresh data is read in, there are occasions when the cache is already full of older data. The controller decides what data should be overwritten by the new data. This is either based on algorithms called the *'Least Frequently Used'* or the *'Least Recently Used'* methods. As the names imply, either the least popular (the data least requested) or the oldest data is chosen to be overwritten. The LRU (Least Recently Used) algorithm is most commonly used, as it is the fastest. This is the method used by Windows to decide which DLLs should be sent to the swap file when its memory resources become tight. Implementing cache in hardware offers the benefit of greater throughput, since little processor time need be dedicated to cache activity; the controller's built-in CPU decides when data should be read from or written to disk.

Write Caching

Some caching only operates for disk reads. If required, the benefits of caching can be applied to disk writes. With write-behind caching, data to be written to disk is not written immediately, but is held in the cache memory until the machine's CPU is free. In this way, the machine's throughput is not slowed down by forcing the CPU to deviate from other work to carry out the disk writes. Giving the command SMARTDRV/S produces a display that informs whether its write caching is in operation. With a controller card, the writing to disk can be undertaken by the circuitry on the card, fully relieving the CPU.

While write-behind caching improves machine performance, it also leaves data vulnerable. While these systems have a time limit (say four seconds) of holding write data in the cache, this still leaves scope for problems. If there is a power failure, for example, data that is being held temporarily in the controller memory will be lost. Similarly, any batch files that reboot the machine (such as a batch file to choose from different CONFIG files) might reboot while data was still in the cache. In these circumstances, the data should be flushed to disk prior to rebooting - or the write-behind facility itself should be disabled. Disk controllers can have the system set between either write-through or write-behind. This is also possible with SMARTDRV.

Many publications state that SMARTDRV is a read-ahead only cache and does not have write-behind facilities. This is not so. If the command SMARTDRV/C is added to the batch file prior to rebooting, any data in its cache is flushed to disk. If it is vital that there be no opportunity for losing data, then write behind caching can be disabled by the SMARTDRV command followed by the drive letter and the minus symbol e.g. SMARTDRV C: - and restored again by the command SMARTDRV C: +

To have read-only cache on a permanent basis, the Windows SMARTDRV.EXE file in the AUTOEXEC.BAT file (or the SMARTDRV.SYS file in the CONFIG.SYS file, if not using Windows) should only have the SMARTDRV command and the drive letter. If a system does not provide write behind caching, it is said to use the *'write through'* method; in fact, it is simply a normal read-ahead system. Many users prefer to disable write-behind caching since Windows applications are still prone to crashing and this could result in loss of data, corruption of data or even the disk's filing system.

Windows Caching

Windows 3.1 and DOS use SMARTDRV as the cache controlling software. Windows 95 onwards uses a new system called VCACHE. SMARTDRV has minimum and maximum values set during configuration. VCACHE is more intelligent and is able to use the available memory to best advantage. The amount of memory used depends on the demand on the systems resources and the application packages. Depending upon the amount of RAM available at any time, it allocates the amount it needs for cache at that time. If the system demands change, then VCACHE automatically reallocates the amount allocated to caching. Another benefit of VCACHE is that it caches CD-ROMs.

If a user also wishes to run DOS programs in Windows 95 or later, then SMARTDRV can be placed in the AUTOEXEC.BAT file for use with DOS.

DOS Disk Organisation

When a hard disk is formatted, it creates four areas of the disk (like a floppy), plus an additional area for the Master Boot Record (not required for floppies). The actual order on a disk is as follows:
- Master Boot record
- Boot Record
- FAT
- Directory
- Data Area

Each of these areas occupies differing amounts of disk space, dependent upon the disk's overall capacity. Each is described below, with the order changed to ease the explanation.

Data Area

This is by far the largest area of the disk and it contains all the data files and directories (a sub-directory acting in a similar fashion to a data file).

The formatting process sub-divides the data area into many equal sized portions known as *'sectors'*. A sector is the smallest area of the disk that can be independently identified. DOS supports sector sizes of 128, 256, 512 or 1024 bytes but has standardised on a sector size of 512 bytes. Sector size is under software control, hence the description of *'soft-sectored'* disks. Older systems actually punched holes in the disk to define sector boundaries and were described as *'hard sectored'*. These holes were punched in the inner track of the disk and a photoelectric cell detected a light beam as it shone through each passing hole. The number of light pulses detected, when compared to an index hole, determined which sector was being read. This meant that the size and shape of the disk could not be changed but it had the advantage of using the entire surface of each track. Soft sectored systems are more flexible but require to use some of the track area for the synchronising information previously supplied by the punched holes. The ability to control the layout of data on a disk is exploited in some early copy protection schemes. To prevent unlawful copying of disks, manufacturers resorted to non-standard formats such as including a sector that was larger than the rest, or having eight sectors on a particular track instead of nine. Since DOS did not know of their changed layout, the disk could not be read by normal COPY, XCOPY or DISKCOPY commands and the disk could not be duplicated. The disk could still be run, as the program coding would know of the non-standard sections and treated them accordingly.

Note that some utilities report on sectors as *'sector 17551'* while others may refer to *'cylinder 2, head 3, sector 4'*. This is because DOS does not wish to know the exact location of a sector in terms of heads and tracks; it prefers to number sectors in continuous ascending order - sector 0,1,2,3,4....15001, 15002, 15003 and so on.

Disk layouts in PCs can be viewed as having two formats:
1. The physical format that is used by the ROM BIOS. This sees the actual layout in terms of the number of heads, the number tracks, the number of sectors per track and the sector size. These are termed the *'absolute sectors'* and an absolute sector is identified by its cylinder/head/sector.
2. The logical format as used by DEBUG and various other disk utilities. This sees the sectors as continually incrementing from sector one, commencing on the first head and the first track and moving inwards. These are termed the disk's *'relative sectors'* and consist of single numbers. These absolute sectors can be mapped into the actual physical DOS absolute sectors.

Cylinder 0/head 0/ sector 1 contains the hard disk's master partition information and is therefore not included in the DOS sector numbering scheme. Cylinder 0, head 1, sector 1 is the equivalent of DOS sector 0. This sector contains the DOS Boot Record and is normally also ignored in the numbering scheme. The remaining sectors on the disk are then included in the DOS numbering.

Example

> In a typical 36-sector disk with 4 heads, side 0 track 5, sector 3 is an absolute sector.
> To get to that position, four full tracks of 36 sectors must have been scanned by all four heads.
> So, 4x36x4 = 556 sectors. The head, having returned to head 0 is moved to sector 3.
> This means that the relative sector is 556 + 3 = 559.
> Therefore, the absolute sector given by side 0, track 5, sector 3 maps to relative sector number 559.
> Note that this will only be the case with disks with four sides.
> If the disk had six sides, the relative sector would be (6x36x4)+3 = 867.

Clusters

With hard disks, like floppies, space for data is allocated on the basis of 'clusters'. A cluster is the smallest group of sectors that can be utilised as a single unit. A cluster is the smallest disk space that will be allocated to a file, no matter how small the file may be. There can only be one file in any one cluster, although one large file can span many clusters. A cluster is composed of one or more sectors. The cluster size varies with the disk and its formatting. The actual number of sectors in a cluster depends on the type of disk.

A table of typical examples is:

Typical Disk Size	Max Disk Size	Sectors/cluster	Cluster Size
360k 5.25" floppy disk		2	1,024
1.2MB 5.25" floppy disk		2	1,024
720k 3.5" floppy disk		2	1,024
1.44MB 3.5" floppy disk		1	512
32MB hard disk	< 64M	2	1,024
100MB hard disk	< 128M	4	2,048
210MB hard disk	< 256M	8	4,096
500MB hard disk	< 512M	16	8,192
850MB hard disk	< 1GB	32	16,384
1.3GB hard disk	< 2GB	64	32,768
Any disk with OSR2/W'98	< 8GB	8	4,096
Any disk with OSR2/W'98	< 16GB	16	8,192
Any disk with OSR2/W'98	<32GB	32	16,384
Any disk with OSR2/W'98	>=32GB	64	32,768
Any disk with NT	Any size	1	512

There is a compromise between maximising read speeds and getting the maximum use of disk space. Large cluster sizes lead to faster access times and faster transfer times but it does waste disk space for smaller files. However, since many larger applications use large files both for programs and data, it makes sense to use larger cluster sizes in the larger capacity disks. Floppy disks always have very slow access times due to their design. Since speed is not the major factor for floppies, they can concentrate on storage efficiency. The 1.44MB disk, for example, only has a single sector as a cluster.

The clustering of sectors only occurs in the disk's data area - the directories and FATs are organised on an individual sector basis.

The larger the cluster size, the greater potential loss of disk space due to lost capacity in underused clusters. For example, a small batch file of 30 bytes consumes 512 bytes on a 3.5" HD disk - and as much as 32k on a large hard disk. Since a file is never likely to use exact multiples of the cluster size, it follows that there is quite a bit of wasted space on a disk. The DIR command only shows the amount of data stored in a file and does not give the actual amount of disk surface allocated to store the file.

Consider the illustration, which is for a hard disk with 32k clusters. The first two columns display the file names and extensions. The third column shows the file sizes as displayed when a normal DOS DIR command is issued.

According to the DOS report, the 13 files appear to consume 132,929 bytes of hard disk space and they appear to have an average file size of 10.2k.

In fact, they consume 524,288 bytes - a difference of over 291,000 bytes and the average file size is actually 40.3k.

The best case is the COMMAND.COM file, which produces very little waste. The file has been allocated 47,845 bytes and actually consumed 65,536 bytes, with 17,691 bytes being wasted.

The worst case is the WORD.BAT file, which only uses 25 bytes of the 32,768 byte cluster.

It follows that the user should avoid the creation of lots of little batch files for trivial jobs that could be carried out from the command line with little extra effort.

As an alternative, thought could be given to producing DOSKEY macros, since they can be embedded in the AUTOEXEC.BAT file and consume no other disk space.

```
                        Displayed  Actual
                          size      size
AUTOEXEC  BAT               482     32768
BACK      TXT               962     32768
BACKCHK   DAT                28     32768
COMMAND   COM             47845     65536
CONFIG    SYS               224     32768
FILELIST  DOC              4880     32768
GETCHAR   COM                32     32768
HISCORES  3D                275     32768
MENU      BAT               572     32768
PCXLIST                      57     32768
POWERPNT  INI               414     32768
VGA_BIOS  EXE             77133     98304
WORD      BAT                25     32768
                        -------   -------
Totals                  132,929   524,288
                        -------   -------
```

Master Boot Record

The Master Boot Record comprises a single sector - sector 1 (i.e. side 0/track 0/sector 1).

The sector contains a partition table and other information. A partition is a portion of the hard disk that appears, and can be treated as, a separate disk drive. Not only do partitions act like separate hard disks, they are allocated disk drives letters such as 'D', 'E', etc.

A partition is a set of contiguous tracks and a partition has to start on the first sector of a track and end on the last sector of a track.

A disk can have more than one partition and this may be adopted for a number of reasons:
- Through necessity if older DOS and Windows versions are in use (see the earlier section on 'Maximum Disk Handling').
- For operational convenience (e.g. placing all applications in one partition and data in another partition).
- To allow completely different operating systems to reside in different partitions of the disk. Examples of this are:
    - DOS on one partition and UNIX on another partition.
    - Windows 2000 on one partition and Windows 95 on another partition.

The actual disk surface would be configured to logically appear as several separate hard disks - disk drive 'C' would be supplemented by drive 'D', drive 'E' or even drive 'F', etc.

FDISK is the utility that creates disk partitions. After partitioning, each partition can be formatted to the layout for the particular operating system. The partition table stores the location and length of each of the disk partitions. There must always be a partition table, even if the disk contains only a single partition. The number of partitions on a disk and the size of partitions can be later altered with FDISK but, since this process destroys the data in partitions, a full backup would be undertaken before altering disk partitions.

DOS supports up to 24 partitions (i.e. 'C' through to 'Z') but the partition table in the MBR can only store four entries. To overcome this, FDISK allows the disk surface to be divided into a 'primary' partition and a single 'extended' partition. This only uses two of the partition table's entries but the extended partition can then be further divided into many 'logical' partitions, each with their own drive letter. The logical drives do not appear in the MBR partition table.

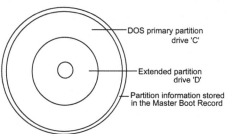

DOS primary partition drive 'C'

Extended partition drive 'D'

Partition information stored in the Master Boot Record

Each DOS partition will contain:
- A DOS boot record, as explained below.
- A FAT for the files in that partition (plus a backup FAT)
- A directory structure for the files in that partition.
- The data area for that partition.

If a disk has more than one partition, then the above is repeated for each partition, although there will still only be one Master Boot Record with the disk's partition table. Where there is more than a single partition, the partition table stores a marker for the active partition. When the machine is booted up, the MBR contains a startup program that passes control to the boot program in the active partition.

Where a disk has more than one partition, the DBR is repeated at the start of each partition. The diagram illustrates the layout of a disk that is partitioned into three logical drives.

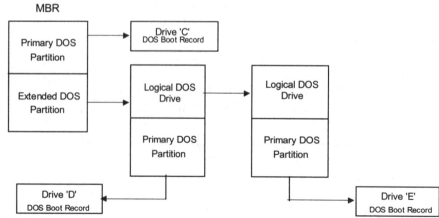

The format of the Master Boot Record can be viewed with any disk editor such as Norton's Utilities:

```
┌ Side 0, Cylinder 0, Sector 1 ════════════════ Partition Table Format ═
│
│                          Partition Table Editor
│
```

System	Boot	Starting location Side	Cylinder	Sector	Ending location Side	Cylinder	Sector	Relative Sectors	Number of Sectors
DOS-16 DM	Yes	1	0	1	5	320	11	17	32719
	No	0	642	1	5	818	17	65484	18054
EXTEND	No	0	321	1	5	641	17	32742	32742
?	No	0	0	0	0	0	0	0	0

If a disk was partitioned into several logical drives, then the master boot record would be displayed in a similar fashion to the one shown on the illustration, the exact locations being dependent on the size of the hard disk and the proportions in which the space was divided.

DOS Boot Record

The first sector of any DOS partition area is the DOS Boot Record, or *'DBR'*. This sector contains disk information and the code that is used along with IO.SYS and MSDOS.SYS to both cold boot and warm boot the machine. It contains a short machine-code program to load the operating system from disk to memory - if the disk is system formatted (i.e. contains COMMAND.COM, IO.SYS and MSDOS.SYS). The boot record is always created, even if the area is not formatted as a system disk. The boot record also stores details of its own formatting - e.g. bytes/sector, sectors/track, etc. For a floppy, there is no master boot record, so the DOS boot record will be in sector 1 of track 0, side 0. If this sector were viewed with Norton Utilities, the first few lines of the screen dump would look like this for a 720k disk: There is a three-byte offset followed by:

- Eight bytes containing the system ID

```
Side 0, Cylinder 0, Sector 1
EB3C9049 424D2020 352E3000 02020100 027000A0 05F90300 ó<ÉIBM  5.0.  etc
09000200 00000000
```

(in this case the hex characters 49 42 4D 20 20 35 2E 30 representing the text 'IBM 5.0').

- Two bytes containing the number of bytes per sector
  (in this case 00 02; since Intel stores numbers in reverse order, this is 0200, which is 512).
- One byte containing the number of sectors per cluster (in this case 02).
- Two bytes containing the number of reserved sectors at the beginning
  (this is 01 00, or 1, for current-sized floppy disks).
- One byte containing the number of copies of the FAT (in this case 02).
- Two bytes containing the maximum number of root directory entries supported
  (in this case 70 00 , or 0070h which is 112).
- Two bytes containing the total number of sectors on the disk
  (in this case A0 05, or 05A0h, which is 1440).
- One byte containing the format ID

(in this case F9 for 720k or 1.2M . A 360k floppy is ID FD,
A 1.44MB disk is ID F0 while hard disks are ID type F8).
- Two bytes containing the number of sectors per FAT (in this case 03 00, or 3).
- Two bytes containing the number of sectors in each track (in this case 09 00, or 9).
- Two bytes containing the number of read/write heads (in this case 02 00, or 2).
- Two bytes containing the number of special reserved sectors (in this case 00 00, or zero).

Note:

The numbers are displayed in hexadecimal, or *'hex'*, a numeric system using the base of 16 rather than the decimal base 10.   Numbers in any column start at 0 and rise to a value of 15.   Since numbers above 9 cannot be shown as a single character, they are replaced by letters of the alphabet.   The number 10 is represented by the letter A, the number 11 by the letter B and so on up to 15 being represented by the letter F.   The right-most column in a hexadecimal number is to the base 1, while the next column is to the base 16, the next to the base 256 and so on, incrementing by a factor of 16 in each column.   To distinguish hexadecimal numbers from decimal numbers, the suffix 'h' is usually added to the number.   So 11h and 11 are different, 11h being 17d.   In the example display above, the total number of sectors on the disk was 05A0.   Starting from the right-most column the number can be calculated thus: 0 lots of 1 + ten lots of 16 + 5 lots of 256 = 0 + 160 + 1280 = 1440.

The comparative figures shown by Norton for a 1.4MB disk are:

```
Side 0, Cylinder 0, Sector 1
EB3C904D 53444F53 352E3000 02010100 02E00040 0BF00900 ó<ÉMSDOS5.0.  etc
12000200 00000000
```

These are similar results to the 720k disk, with the exception of:
- the number of root directory entries allowed which is 00E0 or 15x16 = 240.
- the total sectors on the disk which is 0B40 or 11x256 + 4x16 = 2816+64 = 2880.

The comparative figures shown by Norton for a 210MB hard disk are:

```
Side 1, Cylinder 0, Sector 1
EB3C904D 53444F53 352E3000 02080100 02000200 00F8C900 ó<ÉMSDOS5.0.  etc
24000C00 24000000
```

The main points to note are:
- There are 8 sectors per cluster.
- There are 0200h = 512 entries allowed in the root directory.
- There are 00C9h = 201 sectors storing the data for each FAT.
- There are 0024h = 36 sectors in every track.
- There are 00C0h = 12 read/write heads on the drive.

File Organisation

DOS handles file saves and file reads using a combination of the disk DIRECTORY and the disk FILE ALLOCATION TABLE (known as the *'FAT'*).   The disk Directory stores the list of the files on the disk along with file information such as creation date, etc. (the columns that are viewed when a DIR command is given).   The FAT is a table with an entry for each DOS cluster and is used to map the storage of files. DOS uses buffers to cache copies of the FAT and directory.

Directory

The File Directory is a table of all the files on the disk.   A hard disk can accommodate 512 directories in the root directory and a 1.4MB floppy can store 224 entries.   The DBR stores the number of directory entries that are allowed for a particular disk.   Each directory entry is 32 bytes in length and stores information such as the file name, extension, size, attributes and time and date of creation, as shown in the table.

Purpose	Number of bytes
File Name	8
File Extension	3
File Attributes	1
Unused	10
Date Created/Last Updated	2
Time Created/Last Updated	2
First Cluster	2
File Size	4

The **filename** is allocated 8 bytes and the characters must be in upper case.   The filename must contain at least one character and if the name is less than eight characters, then the entry is padded with space characters (i.e. ASCII character 32).   If the first letter in the entry is a dot (2Eh) then the entry is for a sub-directory.   If the second byte is also a dot, then the entry contains information on the parent directory of the current directory - the cluster number held in the entry points to the parent directory that calls it.

The **extension** is three bytes long and can consist of no characters at all.   Again, any unused bytes are padded with spaces.

The **attributes** byte consists of eight individual bits, each containing separate information about the file. Each bit has the following meaning, if the bit is set to 1:

> Bit 0 : the file is read-only (it cannot be modified or deleted).
> Bit 1 : the file is hidden (it cannot be seen by DIR commands).
> Bit 2 : the file is a system file (same as hidden).
> Bit 3 : the entry is a volume label (it is the disk's volume label and must be in the root directory.   The name and extension data can be combined, allowing a volume label of up to 11 characters.
> Bit 4 : the entry is a sub-directory (it points to the sub-directory chain in the FAT - see later. The entry has no data in the file size field).
> Bit 5 : the file will be used in an archiving program, such as BACKUP.
> Bits 6 and 7 are unused.

So if a file has an attributes value of 23h or 35d, it means that bits 0,1 and 5 are set - so the file is a hidden, read-only file with the archive flag set.

The **time** data is stored in two bytes that record the time that the file was created or was last changed. The system uses a 24-hour clock. The value is valid to the nearest 2 seconds and is calculated thus:

$$\text{Time value} = \text{hours} \times 2048 + \text{mins} \times 32 + \text{secs}/2$$

So, a time of 22:31:12 would result in a value of 22 x 2048 + 31 x 32 + 12/2.

This results in a value of 46,054, which is B3E6h, and would be read in a utility as E6 B3.

The **date** is also stored in two bytes and stores the date that the file was created or was last altered.   The value is calculated thus:

$$\text{Date value} = (\text{current year} - 1980) \times 512 + \text{current month} \times 32 + \text{current day}$$

So, the 15th October 1993 would be stored thus:

$(1993 - 1980) \times 512 + 10 \times 32 + 15 = 6991 = $ 1B4Fh or 4F 1B on a sector editor.

The **first cluster** data points to the beginning of the file's allocation chain, as explained later.

The **file size** data is four bytes long and contains the size of the file.

All entries in a newly formatted disk have the first byte in the name set to 00. When a DEL, COPY, DIR, etc. command is given, DOS stops looking for files when it reaches a 00 first byte - knowing that there are no further files on the disk.

A directory entry for a file also includes the first cluster number on the disk that stores the file - this points to starting point in the FAT so that the rest of the file can be traced should the file require more than a single cluster.

Undeletion

When a file is erased in DOS, the first byte of the filename is set to E5h - all the other Directory information is left undisturbed.   This ensures that the file is ignored in any DOS activities such as DIR and COPY, as files commencing with the E5h character are by-passed.   The contents of the file are not deleted since this would involve needless extra time-consuming disk activity. If a new file to be written needs the space occupied by a deleted file, it can overwrite it at any time. Since the 'deleted' file's data is left intact, it can be easily recovered. If there has been no further file saves that have overwritten the deleted file's directory or FAT areas, a deleted file can be recovered. An *'unerase'* utility, such as the MSDOS UNERASE command or disk tool utilities for users with pre-DOS 5 versions, can be used to search for filenames that begin with the E5h character. The rest of the filename is then presented to the user, who can type in the file's commencing letter.   This letter is written back to the directory entry so that it replaces the E5h value.   The file will again be recognised by DOS commands and is recovered.

Windows provides a *'recycle bin'*, so that files that are supposedly 'deleted' are actually moved to the bin for actual deletion at a later date.   This is a more user-friendly way to restore deleted files, but once the file is actually deleted the UNDELETE program will not work due to Windows' use of long filenames.

File Allocation Table

Commonly called the `FAT`, the table immediately follows the boot record. The disk space required to store the FAT depends on the size of the disk (e.g. a 1.2MB floppy needs 14 sectors to store its FAT, a 20MB AT disk needs 82 sectors and a 201MB disk requires 402 sectors).

Examples of the different disk sector layouts are:

Disk Type	Boot	FAT	Directory	Data	Total
360k	1	4	7	708	720
720k	1	6	7	1426	1440
1.2M	1	14	14	2371	2400
1.4M	1	18	14	2847	2880
32M	1	126	132	63597	63856
201M	1	402	32	411225	411660

The partition table is not included in the hard disk calculations. Since floppy disks and very small hard disks (up to 16MB) only support a maximum of 4096 clusters, the FAT size is set at 12 bits, since 12 raised to the power of 2 is 4096. With larger disks, 16-bit FATs are used, to allow up to 65,636 entries. 16-bit FATs are only supported in DOS from version 3.3 onwards.   12-bit entries are an inheritance from the days when hard disks were small and all disk space was precious. The table contained in the FAT stores an entry for every cluster on the disk.

The value held in the FAT indicates whether that cluster is:

- Already in use (i.e. is storing user data).
- Free for use (i.e. can be used for storing a new file, or part of a new file).
- Marked as Unusable (i.e. there is a faulty sector in that cluster).

The possible values in the FAT are:

Purpose	Contents
In Use (part of a chain)	Another cluster number
In Use (end of a chain - EOF)	FFF8-FFFF
Free/Available	0000
Reserved	FFF0-FFF6
Bad Cluster (marked by FORMAT)	FFF7

With floppy disks, the value for unusable is FF0-FF7, while EOF values are in the range FF8-FFF. Like the directory area, the FAT values are set to 00 when the disk is first formatted. The first entry in the FAT is always the disk ID. This is F9 for a 720k or 1.2M floppy, FD for a 360k floppy, F0 for a 1.44MB floppy and F8 for a hard disk).

Reading a file

If a file is short, under 4k, it will only occupy a single cluster. In such a case, the cluster number stored in the directory entry points to the sole cluster of the program. However, most files are longer than 4k and would therefore occupy several, or many, clusters. The collection of clusters for that file is known as a 'chain' or 'allocation chain'. The start of the chain is the commencing cluster stored in the directory entry.   In the example, this is cluster 77. If entry 77 is examined in the FAT table, it will indicate whether any further clusters are required to be read for that file. For a small file of a single cluster, entry 77 would store the end of file marker - a value between FFF8 and FFFF. No further clusters are read.

For larger files, as in the example, entry 77 stores the location of the next cluster that comprises the file's chain (cluster 78).

Cluster 78, in turn stores the location of the third cluster in the file's chain. Notice that this is cluster 80, since cluster 79 was not written to due to it being a bad cluster.   Cluster 80 then points to the fourth cluster of the chain. In fact, this is the last cluster of the chain, as indicated by end of file marker stored there. The system continues to read data until the end of the chain is reached, or the data read equals the size of the file as stored in the directory.

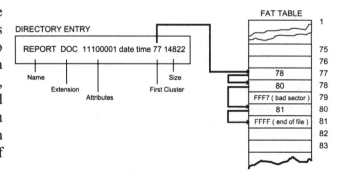

Creating a file

When a <u>new</u> file is written to disk, its details are placed in the Directory, in the first unused entry. This may be a previously unused entry, or it may be overwriting an erased entry. The first FAT entry that is marked as free is used to store the first cluster of the file and two bytes of the directory entry are used to store this initial cluster location. If the file is small enough to fit in the single cluster, the FAT entry is set to FFFF, to indicate end-of-file. For larger files, the next free cluster is found, further user data is stored there and the contents of the initial cluster number in the FAT table are updated to point to this second cluster. This will continue until the entire file is stored - at which point the FAT entry for the last cluster to store that file's data is given the end-of-file value FFFF. When the disk is formatted (or re-tested later with a utility), faulty sectors are isolated by placing the value FFF7 in the corresponding FAT entry. DOS will not attempt to write to these clusters, when allocating new files.

Notes:

- Since the FAT is a central part of the entire disk operation, a second copy is also stored on the disk. Both copies are updated for each file write. The primary FAT is the working version used for DOS reads; the secondary copy is used as a backup in the event of FAT corruption problems. When writing to a file, both FAT copies are updated; when reading files, only the main FAT is used.
- The CHKDSK command does not make good any difference in the two FATs, although add-ons, such as Norton Utilities can detect and repair any FAT damage.
- CHKDSK only reports on the FAT entries that are already marking clusters as bad; it does not detect any newly faulty clusters. Only a special utility program, of which there are many in the commercial and shareware market, will test and mark any faulty clusters that are not currently marked in the FAT as bad. With DOS 6.2 and Windows, SCANDISK will carry out this task.
- To save storage space, 12-bit FATs only occupy the FAT space that they actually require. For floppy disks, early small hard disks under 16MB and small partitions - in fact, any situation where there are fewer than 4096 clusters - the 12-bit code is used and occupies 1½ bytes. So, FAT entries are bunched into pairs with a pair occupying three bytes of the FAT. This improves storage at the expense of a more complex algorithm to extract the chain values from the FAT. This means that a user cannot directly examine a floppy disk's file chain by directly reading the values in the FAT. Fortunately, many utilities allow the FAT to be viewed directly with the conversion being carried out by the utility. With FAT-16 hard disks, the task is more direct, since the FAT entries are 16-bit. This means that each entry in the chain occupies a distinctive pair of bytes in the FAT and tracing of the chain is simplified.

Handling Sub-Directories

The above example was a simple case where all files resided in the root directory of the hard disk. In fact, most files will reside within sub-directories of the disk, to various layers of depth. This means that the sub-directories and their files must fit within the structure outlined above. This is achieved by making a sub-directory an entry within the main root directory, similar to making an entry for a normal file. It will have a directory entry similar to a file directory entry. In this case, however, the *'Directory'* attribute is set to indicate that it is not a file. In this instance, the *'First Cluster'* stored in the directory entry points to a cluster similar to the layout in the diagram. The cluster holds information on the files in its directory in the same way they are stored in the root directory. The cluster stores all the normal date, time and size information.

It also stores the starting clusters of these files which can then have their chains traced in the usual manner, as previously described. The first two entries in the directory cluster are the single dot and double dot that appear whenever a DIR command is issued in a sub-directory. These are compulsory entries. The dot entry refers to the sub-directory itself and the double dot entry points to the parent sub-directory (i.e. the directory that called it).

At the first level down from

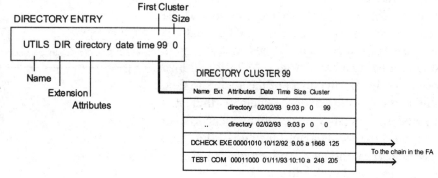

the root, all sub-directories have a double dot entry with a cluster number of zero, to indicate that it was called from the root directory. If the cluster number is not zero, then the sub-directory is more than one level down from the root directory and it stores the cluster number of the sub-directory that is its parent. A large hard disk with a 4096 byte cluster can hold a maximum of 128 entries, since each directory entry is 32 bytes long. The 128 entries may be a mixture of files and other sub-directories. When using smaller disks, or when requiring to store more than 128 files, a second or further directory clusters would be required to store all the additional entries. Where more than a single cluster is devoted to a sub directory, the FAT table is used to point to the next cluster in the sub-directory chain. With a single-cluster sub-directory, the FAT entry will store the end of file marker.

Note:

Since the files and directories in the root directory are created in purely chronological order, many hundreds of files will already be present in the root directory prior to some important directories being created. These directory entries appear well down the list of root directory entries. Should the sub-directory wish to be accessed, the whole directory must be sequentially searched until the sub-directory entry is found. This can slow down file accesses and it would improve matters if directories could appear further up the directory table. Fortunately, Norton has a utility called DS.EXE, which can re-write the directory so that sub-directories appear at the top of the table, prior to single files. The directories and files can be sorted into alphabet order or, if desired, the order of individual directories can be decided to allow the most-frequently accessed directories to appear at the top of the directory table.

Fragmentation

Often, a file is stored as one contiguous block of disk space. However, files can end up occupying several non-contiguous areas of the disk when:
- An existing file is added to. Unless it is the last file in the FAT table (very unlikely), the extra data will have to be placed in the first free clusters.
- A new file is allocated the space of a smaller erased file. Again, the extra data is forced to overflow into a non-contiguous area of the hard disk.

The resultant diffusion of files across the disk can be viewed using the `disk map` facilities of DOS 6 *'DEFRAG'* , Windows *'Disk Defragmenter'*, or Norton Utilities or PC Tools. The continual movement of the head from one area of the disk to another slows data retrieval, by up to 25%.

Fragmentation can be overcome by backing up and restoring the disk, although this is a bit drastic. A better option is to use utilities such as the DOS 6 DEFRAG command, Windows *'Disk Defragmenter'*, Norton's `Speed Disk` or PC Tools' `Compress`. These re-order the allocations to achieve contiguous space for files. The result of defragmenting is to have each file occupying consecutive disk clusters.

Non-Windows versions of defragmentation utilities cannot run under multi-tasking environments, including Windows, since disk accesses might be required to maintain multi-tasking disk swaps. Windows, for example, may wish to use virtual memory to effect multi-tasking and it would be impossible to carry out defragmentation while another program was writing to disk. And, it is always best to carry out a disk defragmentation before attempting to establish permanent swap files in Windows, since these files require a contiguous disk area.

Using DEFRAG

The command can be used with or without switches. When switches are used, these are given at the command line prompt. When used without switches, the user is taken into a user-friendlier front end that provides the same services. The first screen requires the user to choose what disk to work on.

When the drive is selected, a map appears on the screen displaying the used spaces and free spaces on that disk. The user is also given a short report and recommendation similar to that shown. The user can then choose between the *'Optimise'* and *'Configure'* options.

> 98% of drive C: is not fragmented
> Recommended optimisation method:
> Unfragment files only

The Optimise option defragments the disk according to its own recommendation.

The Configure options provide for:

Full Optimisation - All directories are brought to the front, all files are made contiguous and are shuffled to the front of the disk, after the directories. This is the most thorough option but is also the slowest.

Unfragment Files Only - This is the faster option since it only ensures that all files are left contiguous. There is no shuffling of files to the front so gaps are left between files. This speeds up the access of the existing files on the disk but future files are liable to be fragmented due to the gaps left between files.

File Sort - The Directory area stores filenames in random order of chronology - i.e. a new file is added to end of the current Directory entries. Defrag allows for files to be stored in ascending or descending order of file name, file extension, date & time or file size.

If entered at the DOS prompt, the drive letter must be entered and the following possible switches:

/F	Carry out a Full Optimisation	/U	Unfragment Files Only
/SN	Sort files in ascending order of filename	/SN-	Sort files in descending order of filename
/SE	Sort files in ascending order of file extension	/SE-	Sort files in descending order of file extension
/SD	Sort files in ascending order of file date & time	/SD-	Sort files in descending order of file date & time
/SS	Sort files in ascending order of file size	/SS-	Sort files in descending order of file size

EXAMPLE:

DEFRAG C: /F /SS-

carries out a full defragmentation of the C: drive with files sorted in descending order of file sizes.

Windows 95/98 have built-in defragmenters, reached through Programs/ Accessories/ System Tools/ Disk Defragmenter. These offer a choice of disk to defragment, give a report on the current state of fragmentation and can show the details of the defragmenting process.

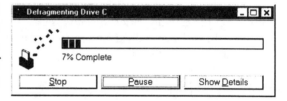

Windows 2000 Disk Defragmenter

The Windows 2000 version is a total rewrite, to accommodate FAT, FAT 32, FAT32X, and NTFS. Defragmentation is, as it has always been, a two-stage process. Firstly, the existing file system is analysed for fragmentation, then the fragmentation is removed by shuffling the contents of disk clusters to put fragments of the same file next to each other. In W2k this two-stage process can be controlled. Analysis can take place without defragmentation and an analysis report can be produced, detailing how much fragmentation has been discovered.

In a new departure, the report gives details of exactly which files are the most fragmented and how. This allows the user to decide whether to undertake the process of defragmentation.

There are good reasons not to defragment, as well as good reason to go ahead. In particular, the time taken to defragment a large drive can be very long. That being the case, the user or support person can schedule a defragment through the night when the machine is idle, where the it is noted that the most fragmented files are ones not currently being used.

Two 'spectrum' style graphs are produced. One is from the analysis phase, which shows the state of the disk. The other is from the defrag-

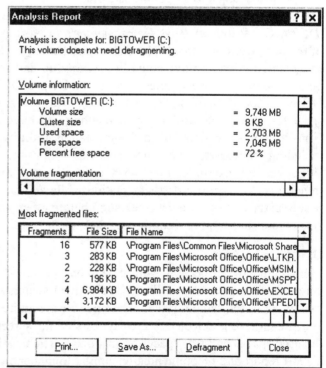

mentation phase, which initially looks just like the analysis display but which gradually changes with the defragmentation process, to show how much of the defragmentation process has been carried out.

FAT Problems

The FAT and directory are the parts of the disk that are continually read and written. Every time a file is created or modified, the directory and FAT entries are updated. Since these areas are the most used on the disk, they are most at risk of corruption through hardware, software or power problems.

Using CHKDSK

The MSDOS CHKDSK command can be a useful utility as long as the user knows what it can and cannot do. It is not a particularly user-friendly repair utility, although it can be a useful diagnostic aid. When run, CHKDSK compares the size of each file as given in the directory entry. It then checks whether there is the correct number of clusters in the file's chain to accommodate the file. In making these checks, a number of problems are detected along the way. These problems are rarely hardware faults. They are usually software glitches that have made rogue writes to the FAT, or users switching off the power before a program has completed its disk housekeeping, or users pressing Alt-Ctrl-Del to escape from a problem they don't understand. Although CHKDSK can be used to effect some disk repairs, it is better to use a more intelligent utility such as Norton's Disk Doctor since it provides a better chance of cleaning up the disk structure without loss of data. Of course, on seriously corrupted disks, even Disk Doctor will report that it cannot successfully recover a disk.

Allocation Errors

The file's size is held in the directory entry. From this can be calculated the number of clusters that it ought to require to be stored. If a file's size indicates that it requires 4 clusters and CHKDSK detects a chain of 3 or 5 clusters it produces an *'allocation'* error message.

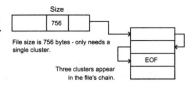

Size

756

File size is 756 bytes - only needs a single cluster.

EOF

Three clusters appear in the file's chain.

Invalid Cluster

Every chain in the FAT table ought to terminate in an end of file marker. If CHKDSK discovers that a

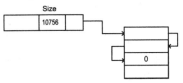

Size

10756

0

chain terminates in a value of zero or a bad file marker, it will produce a *'file has invalid cluster'* message. CHKDSK will tidy up the situation by truncating the file. If the situation remains undetected, then the cluster will be used in a future file allocation. So two file chains will point to the same cluster (see the later section on cross-linked clusters).

Lost Clusters

If the user aborts an application in the middle of a disk write operation, the application should complete the file activity before closing down. If the application is poorly written, or if there is a power glitch or the user has simply turned off the machine prematurely, the file activity may be halted before completion. Since the last act of a file write activity is the

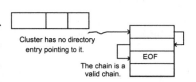

Cluster has no directory entry pointing to it.

EOF

The chain is a valid chain.

updating of the file's directory entry, the chain can end up written to disk without being pointed to by a directory entry. Other causes of *'lost clusters'* messages are applications that only partially delete their temporary files and programs that write directly to the directory and FAT areas. Every time a file is deleted, DOS should mark all the clusters in the chain as being free, thereby putting them back into the general pool for future file allocations. Anything that prevents these clusters being marked as free results in them being ignored in the allocation of future files - even although they are not being used to any good purpose.

Running CHKDSK, dependent on the DOS version, produces one of the following messages:

Errors found, F parameter not specified	Errors found, F parameter not specified.
Corrections will not be written to disk	Corrections will not be written to disk.
1 lost allocation units found in 1 chains.	4 lost clusters found in 3 chains.
1024 bytes disk space would be freed	Convert lost chains to files (Y/N)?

In fact, both messages merely report on the problems found; selecting the *'Y'* option makes no difference whatsoever as the problem is not cleared up. It will produce a report similar to the following:

210546688 bytes total disk space
856064 bytes in 199 directories
16384 bytes would be in 3 recovered files

This option merely reports on the likely effects of cleaning up the disk. To effect a repair, the CHKDSK command should have the /F parameter added at the end. This provides an option to *"Convert lost chains to files?"*. If the user answers *'N'* then the clusters in the chain are marked as free in the FAT table, to return them for further use. If the user answers *'Y'* then the program attaches a directory entry to the chain. Since the original file name is not known, DOS gives it the name FILE0000.CHK, with any subsequent recovered files being titled FILE0001.CHK, FILE0002.CHK, etc. The recovered files can be examined to see if the contents are usable. Often, the recovered file is a valueless temporary file or the file may be in machine code and therefore unreadable without a disassembler utility. However, text files may be examined and the file may be brought back into use and renamed if desired.

Cross-Linked Clusters

If the chains of two different files point to the same cluster, a *'cross-linked clusters'* message results. This is usually the result of clashes of software or disk hardware problems. DOS does not have a utility to repair this situation. However, utilities, such as Norton's Disk Doctor, can carry out an intelligent repair. If there is no utility to hand, the only other method is to save the affected files with new names, delete the original affected files and then rename the files back to their original names. This is not usually fully successful and a file may end up with too much data or data loss. An examination of the recovered file's contents is possible if they happen to be text files; it takes a lot more skill to unscramble files containing machine code instructions. If at all possible, EXE, COM and overlay files that have been cross-linked should be replaced with the original files from the installation disks.

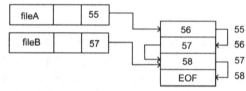

Directory Corruption

If the directory area becomes corrupted, the chains that comprise the files are still intact in the FAT area, but the directory entries no longer point to the start of the chains as they once did. If the user edits the directory with a disk editor such that the first cluster field contains 00, then the CHKDSK/F command will recover the file into a new file called FILE000.CHK and can then be renamed. In this way, the file is recovered without the need to carry out any intensive search of FAT chains. Of course, if many files were corrupted, the above process would produce many files that would have to be interrogated, identified and renamed. This might be an essential, if boring, task where a data file has no backup copy. In the case of application files, it is much quicker to simply re-install the application.

SCANDISK

DOS 6.2 introduced the *'ScanDisk'* utility, as the preferred alternative to CHKDSK and this is also available in Windows. Like CHKDSK, it can carry out tests and repairs on the disk's FAT, directory structure and files. It can also check the disk for faulty clusters, whether or not the cluster currently is being used to store a file. It can check the DOS boot sector and works with hard disks, floppy disks, PCMCIA memory cards and even RAM drives. It is not capable of testing remote drives such as those over a network or over DOS Interlink. It must not be used when other programs are running. It can be called with no parameters and this checks the current drive, or it can be used with a named drive (e.g. *'SCANDISK D:'*), multiple drives (e.g. *'SCANDISK C: D:'*) or can check out all local drives on the computer (e.g. *'SCANDISK/ALL'*).

DOS RECOVER Command

Finally, a word of warning about using the RECOVER command. It has a helpful-sounding name but it can have lethal consequences. The command checks out every cluster in a file or a disk. If a cluster in a chain is found to be defective, the other parts of the chain are saved under a new name and the defective cluster is marked as bad in the FAT. This is not as useful as it may seem, since if a single sector in the cluster is bad, the contents of the entire cluster are ignored in the recovery process. Other disk editors could recover the data from the functioning sectors and thereby recover more information than with the DOS command. The real problem with RECOVER is when it checks an entire disk. If the command RECOVER C: is given, it moves all files into the root directory, deleting all sub-directories. It then renames every single file in the hard disk as FILE0001.REC, FILE0002.REC, etc. - including the system files! And, since the root can only hold 512 entries, all other files are lost! It would be a good idea, therefore, to remove any copies of the RECOVER program from every DOS directory on every machine.

WINDOWS 95/98/ME

Windows 95, 98 and ME reorganise the old file structure to provide the following benefits:

- Supports large partitions (Not in Windows 95 Release 1).
- Minimises disk wastage by using small cluster sizes (Not in Windows 95 Release 1).
- Supports long filenames.

FAT32

With Windows 95 Release 2 (OSR2) onwards, the filing system has become known as FAT32, as distinct from the 16-bit FAT16 that hard disks use with DOS, Windows 3.1 and Windows 95 Release 1.

The earlier chart showed the makeup of a 32-byte directory entry.   Two bytes were allocated to point to the starting cluster of a chain.   16 bits can only store up to 65,536 different numbers making that the maximum number of clusters for a disk of even the biggest size. This means that an 8GB disk would have to use clusters of 128k (i.e. 8GB/65536) and a 32GB disk would require a cluster size of 512k.   This means that a small batch file of 100 bytes would occupy a 0.5M of disk space!   FAT32 future proofs the computer by using two of the ten 'reserved' bytes in the Directory to provide

Max Disk Size	Sectors /cluster	Cluster Size
< 8G	8	4096
< 16G	16	8192
< 32GB	32	16384
> 32GB	64	32768

a four-byte address for clusters.   A 32-bit location can store four thousand million different numbers; this allows the maximum size of a disk to be 4G x 512 bytes - i.e. 2 Terabytes.   It also means that the size of a cluster could be theoretically reduced to a single sector.

To minimise the size of the disk's two FAT areas, a compromise minimum cluster size of 4k is used. FAT16 and FAT32 are incompatible, so if a FAT32 computer were booted with a floppy using FAT16, the FAT32 disk would not be readable.   Fortunately, FAT16 layouts can be converted to FAT32.

Long Filenames

One of the benefits in Windows 95 and later, is having file names up to 255 characters in length, accept spaces and full stops, allow upper and lower case - and still remain backwards compatible with DOS and Windows 3.1.   When upgrading to Windows 95/98/ME, there is no need to re-format the disks as the long filenames can be integrated into the existing Directory and FAT structures.   The older files continue to use the storage methods described earlier, while Windows 95/98/ME files use extensions to the existing system to provide both 8.3 and long file name versions of files that it stores.

The 32 byte Directory entry described earlier remains in use under Windows 95/98/ME.   This only provides for eleven characters for the file name.   This cannot be increased without making the file structure incompatible with DOS and Windows 3.1.   The solution lies in the

attribute byte, shown shaded in the diagram. The purpose of each bit in the byte is explained earlier. There is no occasion when the first four bits are all set at the same time (i.e. the directory entry cannot be both a volume label and a system file).

Microsoft takes advantage for long filenames by setting the first four bits (i.e. the byte stores the value 15 or 0Fh). DOS and older Windows applications do not test for this and therefore only see the traditional 8.3 file format.   Windows 95 applications and utilities check for the attribute byte being set to 0Fh and detect that a long file name is present.   It then uses a chain of LFN (long filename) directory entries, each entry storing another part of the name; this works as an altered version of sub-directories as explained earlier.

Since DOS and older Windows applications require the traditional file naming, the long name is truncated to six letters, a tilde sign and a number as shown in the example.   Traditional 8:3 filenames are unaffected.   Where a file's first six characters are identical to another file, the number at the end of the file name is incremented.

Long File Name	Truncated File Name
REPORT.DOC	REPORT.DOC
Minutes of October	MINUTE~1
Minutes of November	MINUTE~2

Many of the older utilities were designed to run at a low level and do not understand the mechanisms being used by Windows 95/98/ME.   Consequently, they cannot be used and Windows 95/98/ME versions of disk utilities have to be purchased.   Microsoft's Disk Defragmenter and ScanDisk utilities, as supplied with Windows 95/98, understand the new structure and are safe to use. A regular problem experienced with Fat 32 drives is that DOS, Win31 and early Win95 do not recognise FAT32 partitions. It is very easy to forget that a machine has a FAT32 partition and then wonder why the partition cannot be seen when the PC has been booted from a DOS disk for diagnostic purposes.

NTFS

This is the native File System for Windows NT and is also used in Windows 2000, which is NT based. It supports filenames up to a maximum of 256 bytes and partitions up to a maximum of 16 EB or ExaBytes, (i.e. 2^{64} bytes or 17,179,869,184 Gigabytes). It is estimated that all of the words ever spoken by every human being throughout all of history would occupy 5EB of storage. Furthermore, where the performance of FAT and its derivatives degrades as the partition size gets bigger, NTFS's performance is the same on a huge disk as it is on a tiny one. NTFS has also increased security and networking support, and a set of security permissions much more like UNIX's, as befits a system designed for deployment on servers. Other operating systems, including DOS, Windows 3.1, 95 and 98 cannot read NTFS partitions, so a machine with an NTFS partition that is booted from a floppy will look like it has no hard disk. Windows 2000, however, supports both NTFS and FAT 32, NTFS being the recommended file system. It is not possible to make an NTFS floppy disk.

The internals of an NTFS partition are very different from those of a FAT partition. The NTFS partition is listed in the Master Boot Record and Partition Table, as outlined above, and it does have a Volume Boot Record (VBR) just like its FAT cousins. However, the VBR's format is radically different and is principally just a pointer to the first record in the partition's structure (the MFT). The NTFS partition is built around a unit called a *'Master File Table'* or MFT. Where FAT contains a set of pointers or cluster references, an MFT holds much more information about the files and directories that are its concern. Indeed, for smaller files or directories the MFT can even contain the data!

The first record in the partition's MFT is called the *'descriptor'*, and it contains details of the MFT itself. The second is an identical copy of the Descriptor, which (like in FAT) means that faults can be remedied. The third record in the MFT is a log file record. It is an NTFS file that contains a log of file system transactions. This can be used to restore the file in case of mishap. The rest of the MFT contains records for all the files and directories on the partition. NTFS files and directories are *'Objects'* that have both user-defined and system-defined *'attributes'*. The contents of the file are a user-defined attribute. Whereas FAT has directories that contain information like size, date, and RASH attributes these travel inside the MFT record along with the other attributes and the data itself. Directories in NTFS are just sets of pointers to MFT records, nothing more, because all the attributes can be read from the MFT record along with the data. If the data is less than 1500 bytes, it is stored completely in the MFT record. If it exceeds 1500 bytes, the MFT record holds a list of pointers to other clusters that are called *'extents'*. Any record in the MFT, including the descriptors and the log file, can use extents to store extra attributes. Where attributes are stored as part of the MFT record they are referred to as resident attributes, where they are stored on an extent they are called non-resident attributes.

When a data file contains information from another file then that data will be added in an *'extent'* which is entered in the original files MFT record and referred to as a *'stream'*. This can be used to make data move transparently. Thus, a word processor document that contains a spreadsheet will do so in another stream that exists on an extent of the word processor files MFT record. To give a concrete example, a file can be saved as c:\myfile.txt. By then opening c:\myfile.txt:secret, another stream has been opened to put data in. This is stored and carried between NTFS partitions transparently. No indication will exist that the secret part of the file exists.

Initialising a Disk

Disk drives fitted in new computers are supplied pre-formatted. If not, the disk has to be initialised before use. In addition, there are occasions when the best solution to surface problems is to be clean the disk back to scratch. This involves:

- Low level formatting
- Partitioning
- High level formatting

Any files on the hard disk are destroyed by the formatting/partitioning process and must be backed up before the process is started. However, if Partition Magic or the FIPS freeware programs are used, then non-destructive partitioning can be carried out and partition sizes can be re-allocated without loss of existing disk contents. Without these utilities, a floppy disk must be formatted as a system disk and the FDISK and FORMAT files must be placed on this disk.

Low Level Formatting

Low Level Formatting routines create the gaps between the disk's tracks and sector and write the sector IDs. All new IDE and SCSI disks are supplied pre-formatted and only require a low-level format under exceptional circumstances. The manufacturers recommend against this practice. The routines for low-level formatting are usually tucked away and are accessed in one of three ways:

- Via a BIOS routine called via DEBUG. Used in some old systems.
  Run DEBUG and at the minus sign prompt enter G=C800:5 or G=CC00:5 or the address given in the disk controller manual. This displays a menu allowing the low level formatting of the disk.
- Via a hard disk drive utility supplied with the drive or *'Disk Manager'* by Ontrack.
  Used in IDE and IEDE systems.
- Via a BIOS routine called from the setup menu offered during bootup. Used with SCSI drives.

Partitioning

Creating DOS partitions is achieved using the DOS FDISK command on the boot floppy. For non-DOS partitions, the utilities for partitioning would be supplied by the particular manufacturer.

FDISK provides for two different kinds of hard disk DOS partition:

1. The DOS <u>primary</u> partition - this contains the DOS system files and is the 'C' drive.
2. The DOS <u>extended</u> partition - this partition area can be further divided into other logical drives, 'D', 'E', etc. If it remains as a single drive partition then it is logical drive 'D'. Remember that each logical drive is only a proportion of the actual surface area of a single hard disk. From a DOS point of view, it is a completely separate drive, with its own boot record, FATs and directory. As such, it functions as an independent disk drive and can be treated as such when it comes to formatting and ordinary disk read, write and copy activities.

Only one partition can be active at any one time and the primary partition must be the active partition if DOS is to be available at bootup. Running FDISK produces the menu shown.

Option 4 displays current partition information, if the disk has previously been initialised. This can be carried out without any loss of data. However, if the utility is used to change partition sizes, then the data on the hard disk will certainly be destroyed and a backup of all disk contents should be backed up prior to any partition changes. A typical report is:

```
MS-DOS Windows 95
Fixed Disk Setup Program
(c) Copyright Microsoft Corp. 1983-1995

FDISK Options

Current fixed disk drive: 1

Choose one of the following:

1. Create DOS partition or Logical DOS Drive
2. Set active partition
3. Delete partition or Logical DOS Drive
4. Display partition information
5. Change current fixed disk drive

Enter choice: [  ]
```

```
Display Partition Information

Current fixed disk drive: 1

Partition  Status  Type    Volume Label  Mbytes  System  Usage%
C: 1       A       PRI DOS  MS-DOS_5      201     FAT16   100%
```

The 'A' in the second column indicates that it is the active partition.

If a partition was smaller than 16MB, it only needs a 12-bit FAT to store its chain and the second last column would read FAT12. Disks under Windows 95 Release 2 or Windows 98 would display FAT32.

Where the same disk is partitioned into two, the display might show the following:

In this case, since there is more than one partition, the user is offered the opportunity to view the information on the logical drives in the extended partition. A typical display would be:

```
Display Partition Information

Current fixed disk drive: 1

Partition  Status  Type    Volume Label  Mbytes  System  Usage
C: 1       A       PRI DOS  MS-DOS_5      51      FAT16   25%
   2               EXT DOS                150             75%
```

```
Display Logical DOS Drive Information

Drv  Volume Label  Mbytes  System  Usage
D:   GRAPHICS      50      FAT16   33%
E:   APPS          100     FAT16   67%

Total Extended DOS Partition size is 150 Mbytes
```

Partitioning Steps

The steps involved in partitioning a drive are:
- Delete any previous disk partitions, using option 3.
- Create a primary partition, using option 1. This offers options to create a DOS Partition or a Logical DOS Drive. When *'Create Primary DOS Partition'* is chosen, the option is then given to have the

primary partition as the sole partition on the disk. If a single partitioned disk is required, opt to have the primary partition as the maximum possible size. This will be drive C and will be the active partition.

- If a second partition is required, then call option 1 for a second time, followed by choosing the *'Create Extended DOS Partition'* option. The remaining disk space is offered as the size for the extended partition. Since only one extended partition can be attached to each drive, the size entered should be the total amount of remaining disk space.
- If a second partition is created and sized, a new menu appears to offer the creation of Logical Drives in the extended partition. If a single logical drive is required, press the return key. This results in the entire partition being described as drive D and being allocated all of the disk space given to the extended partition. Otherwise, the amount of extended partition space required for the D drive should be typed in (either in Megabytes or as a percentage of the available partition space followed by the percentage symbol) followed by the return key. This will name the logical drive as D and allocate it the nominated amount of extended partition space. Other drive allocations can be similarly made, until the extended partition space is used up.
- If more than one partition is created, option 2 must be used, to make the primary DOS partition the active partition. If this is not done, the machine will not be able to boot up from the hard disk.

Where a machine has more than one hard disk, using FDISK will result in an extra option in the opening menu. This is option 5, which offers *'Choose Current Fixed Disk Drive'*. This allows either disk to be accessed for FDISK operations. The second disk can be either a single partition or can also be partitioned with multiple logical disk drives. Any logical drives on the second disk will commence after the last drive letter used in the first drive. In any case, the machine will always boot to the C drive.

High Level Formatting

When FDISK is exited, the machine displays a message saying *'System will now restart'* and the system disk should remain in the A drive. This returns the system to the prompt. If the machine is switched off at this stage, a later reboot will only result in an *'Invalid media'* message. In this case, the machine should be re-booted from a system floppy disk that contains the DOS FORMAT program. The disk is unable to be used and each partition has to be individually formatted. Use the DOS command FORMAT C:/S to format the primary partition with the DOS system files. Any logical drives can be formatted with the unadorned command e.g. FORMAT D:, FORMAT E:, etc. The high level format generates the boot sector, produces a FAT and directory and checks for defective sectors. Note that using the FORMAT command on a floppy disk carries out both a low-level and a high-level format.

Protecting Files

Computers are susceptible to temperature extremes, power cuts or fluctuations and magnetic fields. This can lead to a sudden machine breakdown and the collapse of the program it is running. Worse still, it can lead to the loss or corruption of important data. In most organisations, the data held in the machine is more important than the machine itself. If a hard disk crashes, it is a simple matter of purchasing and fitting another disk. However, if scores of Megabytes, or even Gigabytes, of data are lost, then countless amounts of person-hours are required to replace this data. In many cases, the data can be reconstituted from paperwork (e.g. customer forms, order forms, etc.). In other cases, the data has no paperwork equivalent (e.g. telephone orders or data that was automatically gathered in real time from remote stations) and this can be lost forever.

Despite all efforts to achieve reliability, these losses remain a distinct possibility. The only defence is to ensure that important data is copied away at regular intervals, thus creating backup copies. In the event of machine failure and data loss, the user can reconstitute the data using the backup version. The user then only has to add the changes that have occurred to the data since the date and time of the backup.

Frequency of backups

The frequency of backups is a matter for the individual organisation and is decided by asking *"how much extra effort would be required to reconstitute lost data if backups were carried out weekly instead of daily?"* or *"is there any data that can afford to be lost at all?"*. If data changes slowly on a particular machine, there is less need to carry out frequent backups. Where the data on a machine regularly changes, the degree of change should be reflected in the frequency of backing up. There are occasions, however, when frequent backups are important even for slowly changing data. Where the data being added contains vital information, a more frequent backup ensures that this information is not lost.

Backup Strategy

Organisations should conduct their backup activities in a way that minimises duplicated effort. When the disk is backed up for the first time, a full backup is carried out requiring much storage space to store the hard disk's data. With large amounts of data, tape streamer backup drives, ZIP drives or writeable CD-ROMs are used. In general, there is little need to back up application programs since they are readily available from the original installation disks or CDs. The only exception may be where an application is heavily customised at installation time and backing up would save these settings.

When the second backup is due, a great deal of time is saved if only new files and those files that have been altered are backed up to disk. This saves wasted time and disks backing up data that has not been changed since the last backup. This second, smaller, set is called an 'incremental' backup. When the third backup is carried out, even fewer files are involved in the backup. The disks are grouped and labelled for an incremental restore, if required. Every so often, say monthly, a complete system backup would be instigated to freshen the set of backup disks, the older sets of disks being recycled.

Using DOS Backup

DOS provides two commands to handle backups

- The BACKUP command creates the backup copies. This can be a copy of the contents of a single directory, with or without its lower subdirectories. This means that the user can start from the root directory and backup the entire disk, if required. As a refinement, the user can decide to only back up selected files, rather than all files in a directory.
- The RESTORE command recreates the copy on the original disk, if required.

Normally, the BACKUP command will be used regularly, say daily, while the RESTORE command will only be used in an emergency. The basic syntax of the command is:

BACKUP C:\TEST.DIR*.* A:

This makes a backup copy of all the files in the TEST.DIR directory of the hard disk on to the floppy drive. It is important to note that this command deletes all the previous contents of the destination disk.

The BACKUP command does not work like the COPY or XCOPY commands, which copy the files in their original format. With these commands, the individual files can still be individually accessed. The BACKUP command copies the files over to the destination disk in a coded form and they cannot be accessed until they have been re-processed with the RESTORE command. The main data files are compacted into a single file, along with a control file that is used to track the files in the backup file. An example of a backup disk is shown. If a backup requires several floppy disks to hold the data, the program will prompt

```
Volume in drive A is BACKUP  001
Directory of A:\

BACKUP  001    166484 14/06/00  18:57
CONTROL 001       889 14/06/00  18:57
   2 file(s)   167373 bytes
                562176 bytes free
```

for the disk to be changed. In that case, DOS numbers each disk label as BACKUP 001, BACKUP 002, etc. and the files on the disk are numbered as BACKUP.001 with CONTROL.001 onwards.

The BACKUP command allows the following parameters to provide added flexibility:

/s	Also backup the files in any sub-directories.
/a	Append the backup files to those already on the floppy disk. The destination disk is not deleted and the new backup data is merely added to the disk.
/m	Back up only those files that have changed since the last backup. This also turns off the 'archive' attribute on the original file, so that it will not be backed up in a future /m backup (unless it has been modified in the meantime, turning on the 'archive' attribute).
/l	Create a log file (BACKUP.LOG) of all the files backed up. This text file lists all the files, along with date and time information, making it easier to trace backup activities.
/d:dd-mm-yy	Only back up files created or modified on, or after, the given date.
/t:hh:mm:ss	Only back up files created or modified on, or after, the given time. If this parameter is used, the /d parameter must also be used.

These options can be entered in upper or lower case and can be used in any sequence or combination.

A typical BACKUP.LOG file might be as shown on the right.

The date and time of the backup are stored, followed by details on the disk number, path, and filename of each file backed up.

```
14/08/2000  18:57:13
001 \WINDOWS\256COLOR.BMP
001 \WINDOWS\ARCADE.BMP
001 \WINDOWS\ARCHES.BMP
001 \WINDOWS\ARGYLE.BMP
```

Restoring Files

This command is used to restore backed up files to their original destination.   As with BACKUP, if the files are stored over several disks, the RESTORE program will prompt for the next disk to be inserted, as appropriate.   An example would be:

RESTORE A: C:\TEST.DIR

The destination directory must be specified as the same one from which the backup was made.   If the files do not exist on the hard disk, then they are created.   If they do exist, they will be over-written.
A range of parameters can be also be used with RESTORE.

/s	Also restores the files in any sub-directories.
/m	Only restores files that have been modified since the last backup. This saves time over-writing files that are unchanged since the backup.
/n	Only restores files that no longer exist on the original drive.
/p	Prompts for confirmation before restoring over newer or read-only files.
/b:dd-mm-yy	Only restores files modified on, or before, the given date.
/a:dd-mm-yy	Only restores files modified on, or after, the given date
/e:hh:mm:ss	Only restores files modified on, or before, the given time.
	If this parameter is used, the /d parameter must also be used.

Examples

RESTORE A: C:*.* /S   Restores all files, including any in any sub-directories from the A drive on to the hard disk root directory.

RESTORE A: C:\WINFILES*.DOC /m   Restores all the files with the .DOC extension that were modified since the last backup, in to the WINFILES directory.

Backup for Windows 95

The Windows 95 version is accessed through the

Start/Programs/Accessories/System Tools/Backup

options and the main screen is as shown. It offers an additional option to compare the files in the backup set with the files on the hard disk.   Entire drives, folders or individual files are selectable.   The example show the entire C: drive being backed up, along with parts of the *'export'* folder of the F: drive.   Components are selected for backup by checking the box of the desired drive, folder or file.   When *'Next Step'* is clicked, the user can choose which device to copy the backup files to.

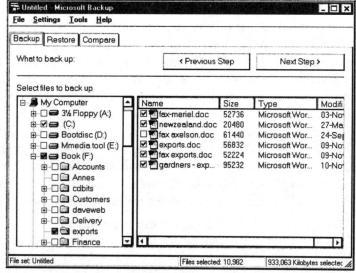

When the *'Start Backup'* option is clicked, the user is asked to enter a name for the backup set of files.   The files are saved with this name and the *'QIC'* file extension (e.g. *'SALES.QIC'*)
If a particular set of files is regularly backed up, the settings for that set of files can be saved.   This saves the trouble of selecting the same set of folders and files every time the backup needs to be carried out. Once the files and the backup destination are selected, the *'SaveAs'* option is selected from the *'File'* menu.   The backup set name is entered and *'Save'* is selected.

Restoring

If the files ever need to be restored, the *'Restore'* tab of the *'Backup'* utility is selected.   From the left windowpane, select the drive that holds the backup file.   From the files displayed in the right pane, select the desired backup set (e.g. *'SALES.QIC'*).   Clicking the *'Next Step'* button provides the option to restore all or selected parts of the backup set.   Clicking the *'Start Restore'* button restores the selected files to the original drives and folders from which they were backed up.   Using the

Settings/Restore/Alternate Location

options allows the user to specify different destination folders for the restore process.

Backup For Windows 98

The Windows 98 version is also accessed through the *'Start'* menu's

Programs/Accessories/System Tools/Backup options and the backup window is as shown. The left panel displays the computer's directory and file structure and the right panel displays the files that have been selected for backup. Entire drives, folders or individual files are selectable.

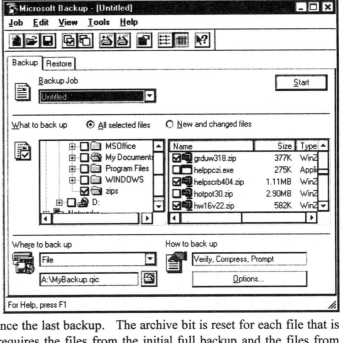

The example shows that certain files in the *'zips'* folder of the C: drive have been selected. Components are selected for backup by checking the box of the desired drive, folder or file.

Clicking the *'Options'* button provides a number of facilities, including:

TYPE

The choices of backup type are:

All selected files

This is a full backup of every file selected.

Incremental backup

Backs up those files that have been modified since the last backup. The archive bit is reset for each file that is backed up. This means that a full restoration requires the files from the initial full backup and the files from every subsequent incremental backup. This requires the storage of the set of all backups and is recommended where different files on a disk tend to be used and altered.

Differential backup

This also backs up of all files that have been modified since the previous full backup. The difference with this method is that backups after the initial full backup do not result in archive bits being reset. This option backs up all files that have been altered since the full backup, even if these files were backed up in a previous differential backup. Thus, the new differential backup supersedes all previous differential backup files. This option only requires the storage of the full backup plus the last differential backup and is recommended where the same files are regularly being modified - e.g. budget files, price lists.

ADVANCED

This automatically backs up the Windows Registry along with files. For this option to work, the user has to previously select the *'Preferences'* option from the *'Tools'* menu and check the *'Backup or Restore System Registry When Backing Up or Restoring the Windows Directory'* box.

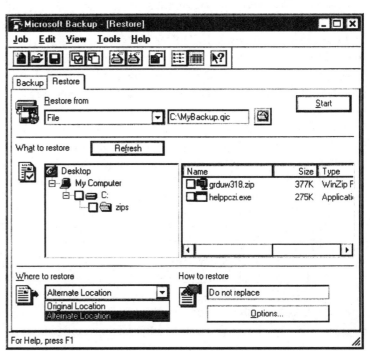

The bottom left of the window displays a *'Where to back up'* dialog allowing the user to choose which device to copy the backup files to. The *'SaveAs'* option from the *'File'* menu allows the user to name the backup set of files. When the *'Start'* option is clicked, the files are saved with this name and the *'QIC'* file extension (e.g. *'LETTERS.QIC'*)

Restoring

If the files ever need to be restored, the *'Restore'* tab of the *'Backup'* utility is selected. The set of files to be restored is chosen from those listed in the *'Restore from'* box. Clicking the *'Refresh'* button displays the folder and files structure of the backup set in the left panel. Clicking any folder in the left panel results in its contents being displayed in the right panel. This way, individual files can be selected for backup, if desired. The bottom left dialog box allows the choice of backing up files to their original folders, or selecting a new drive or folder for the backup. Clicking the *'Options'* button provides extra control such as:

ADVANCED

Restores the saved Registry settings.

GENERAL

The choices allow the restoring of all files, even over existing copies, only restoring over older versions on the computer, and only restoring files where there is no existing version already on the computer.

Clicking the *'Start'* button restores the selected files to the chosen destination drives and folders.

Compression Utilities

There are two main reasons for compressing files:

TO STORE DATA MORE EFFICIENTLY

With the ever-increasing size of application packages, particularly Windows products, there is an inescapable rule of computing that says, *"no matter how big your hard disk is, it's not big enough"*. The 8GB disk that was meant to solve all storage problems rapidly fills up and the previous 1GB system looks decidedly small. The room full of 40MB machines is relegated to running older applications with the hope of a future upgrade. To relieve storage problems, software houses proposed an alternative approach. Instead of making bigger disks, the files could be made smaller! If certain applications or data are used infrequently, they can be stored in a sub-directory in compressed form. When they require to be used, the files can be decompressed. Files storing video, audio and large graphics would be too large to store unless they were compressed.

TO TRANSMIT DATA MORE QUICKLY

The increased use of data communications, including the Internet, has demanded ever-improving methods of compression to reduce download times. If a file is half its original size, it will only take half the time to transmit over the telephone network.

Compression does not create new files. It takes existing files and packages them in a more compact form. The files cannot be used without first being restored to their original form. They are only stored or transmitted in a compressed format; they have to be used in their original format. Some utilities require the user to carry out the decompression before using the file. Other utilities make the process invisible to the user who is completely unaware that compression and decompression are taking place. Compression can work at one of two levels:

- On an individual file, or group of files, basis, such as PKZIP or LHA.
- On an entire disk basis, such as with Stacker, SuperStor or Windows DriveSpace.

File Compression

ARC and ZOO were early compression utilities and are still in use. PKZIP is currently the most-commonly-used file compressor program. These are all shareware programs. Other shareware utilities include LHA (which uses .LZH files), SLIM, PAK and ARJ. Some utilities are optimised for specific files. For example, the ALCHEMY program compresses graphics files by huge amounts. Some use a *'lossy'* algorithm; it sacrifices some tiny details for increased space savings. This is acceptable for graphics or sound files, whereas other data files and program files require being stored with absolute accuracy. Absolutely accurate reproduction requires *'loss-free'* algorithms. Most files, whether programs or data files, contain a large amount of repetitive and redundant information. If the storage of this information is re-organised, vast savings can be made, dependent on the file's format. Some graphics file formats, for example, are already stored in a compressed form and these will produce poorer results than plain ASCII files. The table shows some typical compression results:

File used	Original size	Compressed Size	Program used	Percentage saved
CONTROL.HLP (in Windows)	121672	87028	PKZIP	29%
MONEY.BAS (in DOS)	46225	11081	PKZIP	77%
NEWMACRO.DOC (in Word)	110383	43007	PKZIP	62%
NETWORK.BMP (digitised image)	921656	57992	Alchemy	96%
SONG.WAV (digitised music)	34,178k	3,100k	MP3 encoder	91%

These results are achieved by attacking the file's areas of repetitive data. Consider, for example, a graphics file that has large areas of blue background. Instead of storing every blue pixel separately, the area could be stored as *'5000 pixels of blue'*. This is called *'Run Length Encoding'*, or RLE. When decompressed again, the coded information restores 5000 separate elements of pixel data.

If a file is compressed with a particular utility, it has to be uncompressed by the same utility, since different utilities use different algorithms to achieve compression / decompression.

There are only three or four compression algorithms and utilities use variations on these. The PKZIP and ARC utilities use the LZW (Lempel-Ziv-Welch) algorithm, while ALCHEMY uses a form of Huffman coding to produce JPEG files. The LZW method requires that a table be created, which places different strings from the file in different elements of the table. So, element 400, for example, would represent a particular string in the file being compressed. The code 400 can now replace every other occurrence of the string in the entire file. The string could be an English word within document files, or a run of pixels in graphics files. As the file is compressed, the table is filled up and is used as reference to replace strings with shorter codes in the compressed version. When de-compressing, each occurrence of the code in the compressed file results in the actual string being retrieved from the lookup table and being restored in the decompressed version. In this way, the original file is reconstructed with no losses. The V42bis standard for modem data compression uses BTLZ, a British Telecom variety of the Lempel-Ziv algorithm.

Facilities

- To assist in the management of large groups of compressed files, there have appeared front ends such as SHEZ for DOS and D'Compress for Windows. These essentially provide a friendlier user interface to the basic compression utilities (PKZIP and ARJ respectively).
- To simplify the storage and manipulation of compressed files, most utilities can compile a set of files into one single compressed file.
- To automate file decompression, some utilities create a self-expanding file. The file, or files, is compressed into a single file which then has the decompression utility embedded into the file. This creates a single .EXE file which, when called, runs the decompression code and reconstructs the individual files. It should be noted, however, that the sub-directory would still hold the .EXE file in addition to the decompressed file(s). This can occupy substantial extra disk space if not deleted.
- The compression of a group of files into a single file also simplifies downloading. It is often used in application packages' distribution disks, with the ARC or CAB format (as used by Microsoft).

Disk Compression

Rather than tackling compression at a file level, some techniques address the disk as a whole. They concern themselves with *'disk compression'* rather than *'file compression'*. These utilities are often known as *'disk doublers'*, since they can make the hard disk store up to twice as much data as before. To achieve this, the files on the disk are compressed and decompressed *'on the fly'*. This means that files are compressed before being saved to disk and decompressed when read from disk. This happens in real time, hence the expression *'on the fly'*. With file compressors, the individual files remained as normal DOS files and could be copied in their compressed state. With disk compressors, this is not possible due to the way that the files are stored. Examples of these products are Stacker, SuperStor and XtraDrive. Initially brought out as DOS add-ons, Stacker was temporarily bundled with MSDOS and SuperStor was bundled with DRDOS. Windows 95/98 includes its own utility known as *'DriveSpace'*, although this is not compatible with FAT32 file systems.

The disk is effectively sectioned into two. The smaller section is the normal DOS section on which the machine will boot up; it contains the DOS system files and the CONFIG.SYS and AUTOEXEC.BAT files. A huge hidden file within the DOS partition is used as the store for the compressed files. This much larger section is called the CVF (compressed volume file) by DriveSpace and is named as DRVSPACE.000. To keep the process invisible to the user, Stacker then swaps round the 'C' drive and the 'D' drive. This means that when the machine is booted up, the system is configured from the normal DOS partition (i.e. the <u>actual</u> 'C' drive) and then the compressed section is presented to the user as the logical 'C' drive. The normal section can still be accessed as the 'D' drive.

There is no need to format or partition the disk to achieve this; the task of creating these sections is carried out by the utility's installation program. The installation creates, in effect, an extra drive within a drive complete with its own FAT.

With disk compressors, calls to the disk routines are trapped by the extra software layer sitting between DOS and the disk controller and the data is compressed before being written, or decompressed after being read. Buffers are used to hold the data while it is being processed. As far as DOS is concerned, it is dealing with a perfectly ordinary disk drive; the driver presents the compressed section as an extra logical disk drive, e.g. drive 'D'.

Since the utility is hardware-independent, it can be used with a range of storage devices. It will work with floppy disks, ZIP disks, optical drives and even RAM drives. The drive types used can be MFM, RLL, ESDI, IDE or SCSI.

If an existing disk is to be compressed, the installation will also involve an initial compression of all files already on the disk. If an old machine is fitted with a 500MB or 800MB hard disk, the cost of installing a disk compressor is not economic, given the rapid fall in hard disk prices.

DriveSpace is accessed from the Start/Programs/Accessories/System Tools options. The utility provides the option to compress the entire drive or part of the drive.

Large Capacity Disks

There is a phenomenal growth in mass-storage devices such as CD-ROM and floptical disks. These are now widely available in the commercial and home market and the forecast is for continuing future growth. The read-only versions are used to hold application packages, databases, educational encyclo-paedias, clip art collections and PC support information. Increasingly, programs are being freely distributed in a demonstration format so that users can test the package's abilities. The entire program is already on the CD and a user can call the distributor to purchase the package by credit card. The user is then given a password code to allow them to access the entire package. All the above programs or data are written permanently at the manufacturing stage and cannot be altered by the user.

The WORM drive (write-once read many) is also used for archiving company audit material; the data is written to disk and cannot be altered thereafter. This is usually in CD-R format and provides a secure method of mass storing information than was previously committed to microfiche. There are also two types of device that can be user modified. The new generation of rewriteable CD-ROMs and MO disks (large capacity floppy disks) use magneto-optical systems that allow the data on the disks to be modified.

CD-ROM

The simplified diagram shows the basic layout of a side view of a section of a CD-ROM disk. The plastic disk has an embossed surface consisting of areas of normal thickness ('lands' or 'hills') and sunken areas ('pits'). The disks are stamped out from a master disk. After the high initial costs of creating the

master disk, individual CDs can be stamped out very cheaply as can be seen by the number of computer magazines that include free CDs of shareware and program demonstrations. The changes of height along the track represent the data on the disk, although the coding method is more complex than the simple storage of the data's 1's and 0's. The top surface of the disk is coated with a layer of reflective aluminium (the shaded area of the diagram) and this is covered with a protective plastic layer; the total disk thickness is 1.2mm. Pressed CD-ROMs are known as 'silver disks' due to the colour of the aluminium used.

The disk is read from its underside by firing a laser beam at the revolving surface. The beam reflects from the aluminium coating and is diverted to a photo sensor by a prism.
The normal depth areas - the 'lands' - reflect back most of the laser beam while the 'pitted' areas scatter the beam as shown in the diagram. So, the photo sensor will detect different reflected strengths from the two different surface areas. The laser beam passes through focusing lenses so that the beam is a tiny spot at the point of contact with the disk surface.

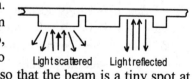

The spot is only 1 micron in size - one millionth of a metre. This means that much more data can be packed on to the disk surface compared to standard magnetising methods. This explains the ability to pack up to 650MB of data on to a single disk. Since the head does not require being close to the disk surface, it does not suffer the risk of head crashes associated with normal floppy and hard disks.

The disk contains only a single track, organised as single spiral similar to a long-playing record, except that the disk is read from the centre outwards. The laser, prism, lenses and photodetector are all enclosed in a single unit that is moved between the inner and outer parts of the spiral. It is the equivalent of the ordinary read/write head of a hard disk. Reaching a wanted sector requires the head to be moved to the approximate location on the spiral track.   The head then follows the track until it reaches a sector header; this header information is then used to locate the wanted sector.

Although CDs use a number of error detection and correction techniques, they should still be handled with care. Grease from a fingerprint diffuses the laser beam while surface scratches deflect the beam.

Disk Organisation

The disk is 120mm in diameter with a 15mm hole is punched in the centre. A 6mm area of the surface, next to the hole, is used by the drive mechanism to clamp the disk while rotating.   The next 4mm area is used to store information regarding the disk's contents; this is known as the VTOC (volume table of contents).   The data area width is 33mm and comprises a single track spiralling outward about 20,000 times and totalling around 3 miles in length.

The outer area of 3mm is used for handling the disk.

Most CDs have a 2352 bytes sector size of which 2k or over is used for data and the remaining bytes for error-detection information.

Hard disks specify a particular disk area in terms of track and sector. CD-ROMs, showing their origins as audio disks, specify areas in terms of minutes, seconds, and sectors within each second.

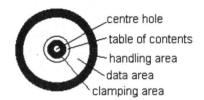

Thus, a 74 minute CD has a capacity of 74 x 60(secs) x 75(sectors) x 2k = 650MB of user data area.

A single-speed drive reads 75 of these sectors per second, giving a transfer rate of 150kB/s.   A double-speed drive reads 150 sectors/sec while a 32x drive reads 2400 sectors/sec, giving transfer rates of 300kB/s and 4800kB/s respectively.   The original single speed model spins at 300rpm and other models are multiples of this - i.e. a quad speed rotates at 1200 rpm and a 48x rotates at 14,400rpm.

There are several methods of organising and accessing data on the disk:

CLV - Constant Linear Velocity.

This was the most common method and is that used with audio CDs and many computer CD disks.   All disk sectors are of identical length. The outer spirals on the surface are longer than inner spirals and can store more sectors per spiral than those closer to the centre.   The disk is consequently spun slower when reading outer tracks compared to inner tracks.   A 4x drive may spin at over 2100 rpm on inner tracks and only 800rpm on outer tracks.   This system achieves the same amount of data read per second, no matter where on the disk the data is stored.   A good quality motor is required to cope with the constantly changing rotational speed.

CAV - Constant Angular Velocity - also known as Full CAV.

It is currently used in hard and floppy drives. The disk motor rotates at a constant speed making it easy to manufacture.   The outer spirals store fewer sectors per inch than inner spirals, resulting in each spiral storing the same number of sectors.   Consequently, CAV drives transfer the same amount of information for every revolution, regardless of the head position.

CAV technology is increasingly adopted by CD drive manufacturers for reading disks.   The writing of CD disks still uses CLV techniques, storing more data on outer spirals.   Since the CAV motor spins at a constant speed, more data per second is read from outer spirals than inner spirals.   This explains why a CAV CD drive may be described as being a '14/32x' model.   The innermost spiral reads at 14x speed while the outermost spiral reads at 32x speed.   The top data transfer rate only occurs at the outermost spirals.   CDs are written from the inner spiral outwards and many CDs do not fill all the available disk capacity. As a result, the average performance of a CAV CD drive is nowhere near the maximum rating.

CAV drives have faster access times than CLV models since they do not suffer delays while the motor speed changes between inner and outer spirals.   Pioneer, for example, claim that their 10x has a 65ms access time in CAV mode compared to around 150ms for CLV models.

PCAV - Partial Constant Angular Velocity.

Many CD drives are now a CLV/CAV hybrid, using CLV (i.e. changing speeds) on the outer tracks and CAV (i.e. constant speeds) on the inner tracks.

CD-ROM Performance

The performance of CD-ROM is determined by the following factors:

- The access time of the drive.
    These times vary from 65ms to 100ms for newer models and 350ms to 900ms for older models.   Compared to hard disk speeds, these are very slow times.   That is because there is one single continuous spiral track.   The read head cannot first go to the exact track and wait for the wanted sector to come

round. It has to make an approximation to the correct distance in, then wait for the first sector header to tell the system where the head is positioned. It then makes a second seek to get to the correct position. This slows down the sector access times.

- The data transfer rate of the drive.
  The most common rates are:

Data Rate	Description	Data Rate	Description
150kBs	single-speed	1500kBs	10x
300kBs	double-speed or 2x	2400kBs	16x
450kBs	triple-speed or 3x	4800kBs	32x
600kBs	quad speed or 4x	7200kBs	48x
1200kBs	8x	7800kBs	52x

These figures do not give a complete picture since a quad speed drive will not provide double the throughput of a double speed, and so on.

This is for a number of reasons:

- The higher transfer rates only apply to long sequential reads. If the head has to make a number of random access seeks, the faster transfers are offset by the substantial individual access times. The result is an average figure somewhat less than the performance suggested by the 8x, 10x, 24x, ratings.
- With CLV models, there is an additional time delay while the motor changes speed when moving between inner and outer tracks.
- For the same reasons above, the sustained data rate shows up better with bigger files.
- AVI video files are often created to run at double speed and drives with faster rates have to work at the slower rate to be compatible with the data being presented.

- The detection and elimination of read errors. Errors occur due to slight imperfections in the boundaries of cells or from fingerprints or scratches obscuring the data read. For small data losses, the error detection system also has an error correction system that alters the read data to the original information. This is an improvement on normal disks and provides a more secure storage medium.

- The size of the drive's buffers. The current drives cache sizes vary from 16k to 1024k, mostly available in 128k or 256k. The cache size can have a significant influence on the smooth flow of multimedia content. SmartDrive can be used to gain a reasonably useful improvement in CD-ROM performance.

PRACTICAL NOTES

- CD drives are available as internal and external models.
- With some models, the disk is placed in a plastic caddy for extra protection from scratching or dust. This case is then placed into the CD drive for use. A slider on the underneath of the caddy is then moved aside, in the same manner as that of a 3.5" disk, to reveal the recorded surface. Other models simply require the disk to be placed in a tray like audio CD players or placed in a top loader.
- Four different interfaces can be used to connect the CD to the computer. Some older models use a connection from a SoundBlaster Card or other sound card; these have the required circuitry to control the CD-ROM. Other older systems connected to a special proprietary interface card. Most modern systems connect to the IDE or the faster EIDE (known as 'ATAPI'- Attach Packet Interface) interface. Faster still is the SCSI interface. This is also a cheap option if a SCSI card is already in use for the hard disk. External models use USB or SCSI connections to the computer.
- For DOS systems, the hardware requires two drivers - the hardware-specific driver supplied with the particular CD and MSCDEX.EXE, the Microsoft CD-ROM Extensions for DOS. The first driver is installed via CONFIG.SYS and the other is installed via AUTOEXEC.BAT. The MSCDEX utility is a TSR that reads the standard ISO 9660 CD disks (i.e. it makes CD files look like normal DOS files); it also provides audio support. The equivalent in Windows 95 onwards is the 32-bit CDFS driver.
- Front panel features include the volume control, headphone socket, activity light and disk eject button.
- Dust protection is improved through double door mechanisms, unit seals and automatic lens cleaning systems.

CD Standards

Many of the standards are named after the colour of cover used to report on the new standard. So, the standard for audio on CD became known as the Red Book standard because it had a red cover.

ISO 9660

Often known as 'High Sierra', since it was first discussed in the High Sierra Hotel in Nevada in 1985. By 1987, a superset of High Sierra, known as ISO 9600, was agreed as the common standard for computer CD-ROMs.

All drives conform to this standard for handling files and directories, with different drivers to allow the standard to work with PCs, Macintosh computer and Unix systems. The PCs version is implemented with the MSCDEX or CDFS driver software.

RED BOOK

Established in 1980, it is also known as CD-DA (Digital Audio). The *'Red Book'* standard was the first of the series and defined the specification for the audio CD currently in use. It specified that the audio would be stored in digital format and be subject to error detection and correction. Each sector stores 1/75th of a second of digitised audio and occupies 2352 bytes. Data is stored as stereo 16-bit audio with a sampling rate of 44.1KHz and a theoretical maximum of 74 minutes of audio per disk. It can handle 99 audio tracks and its TOC stores the starting point of each track (measured in minutes, seconds and sectors).

Standard	Purpose
Red Book	Audio CDs
Yellow Book	Computer data (e.g. application installation CDs)
Green Book	CD-Interactive applications, games and, entertainment
White Book	Video CDs
Blue Book	Music CDs with text
Orange Book	Recordable CDs
Photo CD	Kodak's multi-session picture storage

YELLOW BOOK

The *'Yellow Book'* standard of 1985 defined the computer data CD specification that is now commonly described simply as CD-ROM. This standard is really a storage medium with improved error correction and has three modes:

Mode 1 uses a maximum disk capacity of 650MB to store computer data. It uses the same 2352 byte sector size as Red Book but uses 2k of each sector for data with the remaining bytes being used for synchronisation and error correction codes.

Mode 2 was the original attempt at CD-I and provided for compression of audio and graphic information. It offered a 765MB maximum capacity since it dropped the error correction bytes, allowing each sector to store 2336 bytes of data. Since the disk was spinning at the same speed, its data transfer rate was also greater - 170kB/s instead of the normal 150kB/s. Mode 2, however, was unable to access computer data and audio/visual data at the same time, since they were stored on different tracks of the disk (only one mode is allowed per track). This limited its usefulness and Mode 2 was never developed.

Mode 3 was termed Mixed Mode as it allowed computer data tracks and audio tracks to be placed on the same disk. Usually, the first track contains the computer data with the remaining tracks containing audio data. The audio tracks could be played through a domestic audio CD player in which case the player would be stepped over the data track. A CD-ROM drive would recognise the computer data tracks and would be able to play the audio through its audio output. However, it could not do both at the same time.

Some references to Mixed Mode refer to a drive that can handle both Mode 1 and Mode 2.

CD XA

It is possible for audio and graphic information to be stored in different CD tracks. When each of these data items is used separately there is no problem but multimedia demands that both audio and graphic information be presented in a synchronised manner and this is not easily achieved. The Extended Architecture (XA) specification allows both audio and graphic data to be stored in the same track in an interleaved fashion, thus allowing greatly improved synchronisation. This extends the Yellow Book Mode 2 by having a Form 1 for computer data (2k of data/sector with error detection) and a Form 2 for audio and video data (2324 bytes of data/sector with no error detection). Since Form 1 and Form 2 work under the same XA Mode, they can both be placed on the same track. XA also saved space in the storage of audio by using a method called ADPCM (Adaptive Delta Pulse Code Modulation). This stores the difference between sound samples rather than the values themselves and results in smaller values being produced and saved.

GREEN BOOK

This is also an extension of the Mode 2 of the Yellow Book, designed for playing CD-I interactive applications. It stores files compressed to the MPEG format and interleaves the picture and sound elements. All CD-I tracks are in Mode 2 XA format. Unlike White Book, it does not provide the standard ISO 9660 access and requires a special CD-I player, a PC upgrade such as ReelMagic, or a special device driver, since a normal CD-ROM drive cannot handle the format. Dedicated CD-I players are available with their own CPU and video memory and these connect to a monitor or TV.

CD-BRIDGE

As the name implies, this standard allows a drive to handle CDs that were both XA and CD-I compatible. This special bridge CD disk is really a CD-I disk with extra XA information added to it. The Photo CD disk explained below is an example of a bridge disk. The disk has more than one disk label and this allows the same disk to be played in a CD-I player or an XA CD drive.

WHITE BOOK

Used for Video CD - i.e. the storing of full-motion MPEG-1 video.   The output cannot be taken directly to any ordinary video card. It has to feed a decompression card to restore MPEG files to their original size. MPEG 1 compression results in a CD with up to 74 minutes of VHS-quality video and stereo sound track. Videos that are longer than 74 minutes have to be split up over two disks.   MPEG-1 handling now appears on many video cards, with software or hardware decompression.   Video CD uses XA's Mode2/Form2 working and requires a Mode 2/Form 2 compatible player.

BLUE BOOK

Also known as CD Plus or CD Extra, this is designed to provide multiple sessions on a disk.   The first session contains audio tracks and the second session contains computer data. The main TOC (table of contents) contains information on audio tracks and points to a further TOC storing data tracks.   If the disk is used in a normal hi-fi CD audio player, it will not attempt to play the data tracks as it will not recognise the second TOC.   A blue book drive will recognise and use both TOCs.

The most likely use for Blue Book systems appears to be in the music industry where a CD can be played both in a standard audio CD player and in a computer CD drive. In the latter, photographs and text about the performers can then augment the music.   This, along with White Book covers most manufacturers' approaches to multimedia CDs.

ORANGE BOOK

Also known as CD-R (CD-Recordable), this describes the <u>writing</u> of CD disks.
The three parts to the standard are:
I.   The use of Magneto Optical drives, which allows data to be written to disk, then erased or overwritten.
II. The use of the *'Write Once'* format, where the data is written in a single session or multiple sessions but cannot be altered after it is written.
III. The Rewritable format (CD-RW), which allows the disk to be re-written up to 1000 times. This requires a Multi-Read CD drive or a DVD drive to read disks written by a CD-RW writer.

CD Writers can produce disks in CD-ROM, CD-DA, Mixed Mode, XA and CD-I format and a quad-speed drive will record an entire disk in about 18mins.

Kodak Photo CD

CDs are capable of storing large graphics files and the Kodak Photo CD system allows photographs taken with an ordinary camera to be placed on CD disks.   When the film is taken to the developer, the images can be reproduced in both standard photographic print format and in CD format.   Such photographs can be viewed in the same way as any other graphics file stored on a CD.   A standard CD can store 100 photographs and the full 100 may be built up over a period of time with additional photographs being added at later dates.   This is not a problem as Kodak can add any new photographs to the CD.   However, an older CD is not capable of reading any added data since each new additional group has its own unique storage key and this cannot be accessed by the old technology.   If this extra facility is required, a *'Multi-session'* model must be purchased, as this is capable of reading any subsequent additions.   Almost all models currently on the market are now multi-session.   CD-I players or CD drives that support XA Mode 2/Form 1 are capable of reading these files.

Recordable CD

For large quantity production of CDs, a master copy is laser cut into a glass master copy and this is used to stamp out the lands and pits on the reflective layers of each blank CD.   The master copy costs around £500 to produce but subsequent stamped CDs

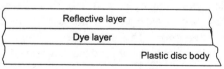

are relatively cheap (which is why they are given away with computer magazines and audio magazines). For small quantities, this is an expensive option. CD-R (CD-Recordable) systems utilise a CD writer that uses disks of a different construction from the standard pressed disks.   Recordable CD blanks have a layer of dye that can be spot heated by a laser beam to fuse the dye with the plastic substrate and create pits.   The blank disks, known as *'gold disks'*, are supplied with a *'pre-groove'* moulded on its surface. The groove provides tracking information for the drive's head servo and provides a cheap way to ensure quality tracking.   The individual blank disk is more expensive than a pressed disk but there is no expensive master to create.

CD-R disks should be able to be read on any normal CD drive.   CD Writers are also capable of reading normal CDs.   The dramatic fall in the price of CD writers has led to their widespread use as a backup device.   Current models record at up to a maximum of twenty-four speed.

Future Technology

A range of techniques is being developed to improve both the capacity and speed of CD-ROMs.
Creating multiple levels of disk.

> IBM is developing a sandwich of ten CD-R disks. By changing the beam's point of focus, different disks in the sandwich are used.

Using higher frequency lasers.

> Blue violet lasers have a higher frequency (i.e. shorter wavelength) than red lasers and so smaller pits can be cut. This results in more data per spiral - up to 10GB per disk.

Spread laser technology.

> CD-ROMs using a spread focus laser beam that reads the track across a broad area, typically seven to nine parallel sets of pits, and then uses a digital signal processor to extract the data. Early production versions quote data rates that are a true 72x.

DVD

The current CDs have the following capacity limitations:

- Most hard disks are now much larger than the 650MB storage of a CD. So, backing up drives involves writing to several CDs per drive.
- A full-length movie stores on two CDs and requires the disk to be changed during viewing.

The response is the high-capacity *'Digital Versatile Disk'*. It is mainly viewed as a mechanism for distributing films and the first DVD disks are of this type. It also provides an ideal medium for a wide variety of applications ranging from training material to encyclopaedias. Their large storage capacity makes the writeable versions a good choice of backup medium.

The disk retains the conventional CD diameter of 120mm but can be double sided and can have two separate layers capable of storing data. The largest capacity types have a sandwich of two layers (i.e. four storage surfaces). With double-sided versions, the disk is flipped over to use the other side.

Single layer disks, both single and double sided, are manufactured in a very similar way to current CD-ROMs. The second layer comprises a resin layer with partially transmissive qualities. The reflections from both layers vary only slightly in intensity requiring a particularly sensitive detection system.

The DVD specifications are known as *'books'* and are shown in the table. Aimed at the production of quality video disks, they support both the original MPEG-1 (i.e. 352x 240 at 30 fields per second) and the current MPEG-2 (i.e. up to 720x480 at 60 fields per second) video standards. DVD disks interleave the video and audio streams.

Book	Specification
A	DVD-ROM
B	DVD-Video
C	DVD-Audio
D	DVD-R (Write Once)
E	DVD-RAM (Erasable)

The planned range of products is shown in the table. A 4.7GB disk stores the equivalent of around 133 minutes of video and three audio streams. DVD5 drives are the models that are currently available.

Product	Capacity	No of layers	No of sides	Mode	Comments
DVD5	4.7GB	1	1	Playback	
DVD9	8.5GB	2	1	Playback	
DVD10	9.4GB	1	2	Playback	
DVD18	17GB	2	2	Playback	
Version 1.0 DVD-R	3.95GB or 7.9GB	2	1 or 2	Record-once	Mostly DVD-ROM compatible
Version 2.0 DVD-R	4.7GB or 9.4GB	2	1 or 2	Record-once	
Type 1 DVD-RAM	2.6GB or 5.4GB	2	1 or 2	Record-many	Cartridge based, not generally DVD-ROM compatible
Type 2 DVD-RAM	4.7GB or 9.4GB	2	1 or 2	Record-many	
DVD-RW	4.7GB or 9.4GB	2	1 or 2	Record-many	In development
DVD+RW	4.7GB or 9.4GB	2	1 or 2	Record-many	In development

Video Standards

The DVD standard supports a range of screen aspect ratios, from 1.33:1 (the 4/3 standard of normal TVs and monitors) to 2.25:1 (wide screen movies).

Most movies are produced at 1.85:1 and domestic wide-screen TV's display at 1.78:1 (usually advertised as 16:9 sets). When movies are played in DVD players, users can control how they are displayed, including *'squeezing'* the image (everyone looks tall and thin) and *'letterbox viewing'* (all the movie is displayed but the upper and lower portions of the screen are black).

Each DVD movie disk has a *'country lock'* - a code specific to a region of the world. DVD disks will only run in players that have the same zone code. Region 1 is USA while Europe is Region 2. This attempts to prevent US disks being played on European DVD drives.

Audio Standards

DVD supports three *'theatre quality'* sound formats - Dolby AC-3 surround sound, MPEG-1 audio and MPEG-2 audio. Europe favours MPEG-2 surround sound, while the USA, Japan and the rest of the world use Dolby AC-3. MPEG-1 is described as *'2.0'* (i.e. two channel stereo) while AC-3 is *'5.1'* and MPEG-2 is either *'5.1'* or *'7.1'*. The number after the dot indicates whether the sound includes support for a low-frequency effects sub-woofer. The numbers before the dot indicate how many main sound channels are supported. So a 5:1 has a centre sound channel, a channel at all four corners of the sound room, and a sub-woofer. MPEG-1 samples at 44.1 kbps while MPEG-2 and AC-3 sample at 48 kbps (see chapter on multimedia for an explanation).

How DVD stores 4.7GB on a single side

A CD's basic capacity is 765MB, although 650MB is left for the user after error correction overheads are deducted. DVD uses a combination of more precise engineering, higher laser frequency, and improved modulation and error correction techniques, to dramatically improve the capacity of a single disk side.

	Standard CD layout	DVD layout	Improvement Factor	New Capacity
Smaller pit length	0.972 microns	0.4 microns	2.4300	1.82 GB
Narrower track pitch	1.6 microns	0.74 microns	2.1622	3.93 GB
More surface used for storing data	86 sq cms	87.6 sq cms	1.0186	4.00 GB
Better error correction	25% of data area	13% of data area	1.1062	4.42 GB
More efficient channel bit modulation	08:14+3	08:16	1.0625	4.70 GB

DVD Data Rates

The table above shows how DVD manages to store much more information on the same surface area than a CD. However, this has other implications, primarily on the data transfer rate of a DVD drive in comparison to a CD-ROM drive. The reduced pit length means that a DVD drive spinning at the same speed as a CD drive will read 2.43 times as much data. However, the base (single speed) velocity of a DVD is almost four times the base (single speed) velocity of a CD-ROM drive. These two factors together mean that a single speed DVD transfers data at the same rate as an 8x CD-ROM drive, and a 6x DVD has a data rate similar to a 48x CD-ROM drive.

Advantages of DVD Drives

- Choice of up to eight language tracks.
- Choice of up to 32 tracks for subtitles and menus.
- Newer DVD drives can read all formats (i.e. all DVD modes and CD-ROM, CD-R and CD-RW disks).

Disadvantages

- Requires an MPEG-2 decoder and a sound card that can handle the disk's audio formats. These cards are available separately as upgrade kits or are available bundled with DVD drives. Software implementations are available (e.g. CompCore's SoftDVD) although their performance is poorer since they use CPU resources rather than dedicated hardware.
- Older DVD drives cannot read CD-R and CD-RW disks.
- Normal CD drives cannot read DVD disks.

DVD Writers

Writeable DVD systems are available in a variety of forms, and there are several other types in development. DVD-R is a write-once system that creates a DVD which many household DVD players will be able to read. However, it is not re-writeable, limiting its usefulness to the PC world.

DVD-RAM is a re-writeable system which can use one of two media types. The DVD-RAM specification version 1.0 allows only 2.6GB per side, while the newer version 2.0 specification allows 4.7GB per side, equal to a mass-produced DVD 5. This makes it useful for creating DVD masters. Some drives, such as Panasonic's LF-D201, are able to read and write to both types of DVD-RAM. The latest systems use removable discs so that DVDs that are created on a DVD-RAM can potentially be used in normal DVD players, but the differences in construction mean that few DVD players currently handle DVD-RAM discs even without their cartridge. Double-sided DVD-RAM disks have to be turned over manually to access both sides.

DVD-RW is a read/write system that is under development and is due to be considered by the DVD Forum. Its development has been delayed many times, and the initial aim of a 2.6GB DVD-RW has now changed to a 4.7GB version. If the final product is fully compatible with all major home DVD players, unlike DVD-RAM, then it is likely to be widely accepted.

DVD+RW is the rival to DVD-RW, being developed by Sony and Panasonic outside of the DVD Forum. Initially both companies believed 2.6GB was too little, and aimed at 3GB rewriteable discs, but this too has been increased to 4.7GB. It has also suffered from many delays in production, but the companies involved have more of a stake in previous CD technologies and as a result DVD+RW is likely to be more backwards compatible than DVD-RW. It should also create discs readable in home DVD players.

There are many other DVD 'standards' in use or in development, such as the 8cm mini-DVDs used in new digital camcorders or the 15GB single-sided discs under development. Even after years of DVDs being on sale, there is still a confusing mass of options, and it is still unknown which will truly become 'standards' in the broadest sense.

Magneto-Optical Drives

Magneto-optical (MO) drives use metal granule coatings on the disk surface. Unlike normal hard disks where the surface area is evenly coated, the MO disk has a raised bump for every data bit on the entire disk. Each data bit occupies an area of just 1 micron in diameter. This surface is then covered by a plastic or glass-based protective coat. The 5.25" types are double-sided disks with two independent sides glued together. The 3.5" type is single sided. The completed disks of both types are enclosed in cartridges similar to the construction used for 3.5" floppies, although larger and about 11mm in thickness. Each disk side has tracks with discrete physical cells capable of storing data.

Each data cell is written to in at least two stages - erase the old data and write the new data, sometimes accompanied by a third stage to verify the write operation. Mostly, these are carried out during separate revolutions of the disk resulting in writing to a disk being substantially slower than reading from a disk. Phase change systems (see later) allow the write operation to be carried out in a single pass.

The coating used has a very high coercivity, which means that it is normally very difficult to change its magnetic polarity. However, the coating is also susceptible to heat. To alter the contents of a cell, a laser beam is directed at it, on a high-power setting. This raises the temperature of the cell to just under 200° C. This greatly reduces the coercivity for a brief period and during this period a magnet is used to set the cell to the desired polarity. When the cell cools again, the magnetic

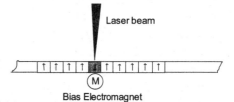

Laser beam

Bias Electromagnet

polarity is effectively locked into the disk. Only the cells that need to have their contents altered require to be subjected to this process. A new system called *'LIMDOW'* (Light Intensity Modulation/Direct Overwrite) carries out the operations in a single pass, greatly speeding up disk writing. The LIMDOW system modulates the light intensity instead of the magnetic field, to write to the surface.

To read the disk, the laser beam reverts to a low-power setting and is reflected off the disk. The magnet is not used in the read process. This method does not rely on the <u>amount</u> of reflection as used in the CD-ROM. Instead, it analyses the <u>polarity</u> of the reflected beam, since the beam is slightly polarised according to whether it is reflected from a '0' or a '1' cell - a phenomenon known as *'The Kerr Effect'*.

The most commonly used disks employ CAV (Constant Angular Velocity), which places data on the tracks using a fixed speed motor. This results in data on the outer track being less densely packed than data on the inner tracks. It is a simple but wasteful system. Other systems use ZCAV (Zoned Constant Angular Velocity), which keeps the motor speed constant within any one track but has a faster speed on outer tracks than inner tracks.

Magneto-optical disks are robust, with life expectancies up to 30 years. Manufacturers claim that the disks have write/rewrite cycles of between 10 million and 1000 million. All these drive systems use SCSI interfaces. Current MO drives are available in a range of capacities.

- 230MB systems (e.g. Olympys PowerMO 230)
- 640MB systems (e.g. the Fujitsu DynaMO 640)
- 1.3GB systems (e.g. some HP drives)
- 2.6GB systems (e.g. the Plasmon DW260)
- 5.2GB systems (e.g. the Sony RMO-S551)

Drives offer only slow access times of between 12ms and 90ms, with most being around 25ms. They perform like slow hard disks. The One Technology One Pro MO has the fastest current seek times of 12ms but this is still slower than modern hard disks. Rotational speeds vary from 1800rpm to 3600rpm and data transfer rates vary from 522kBs to 10MB/sec. Hewlett Packard produce jukeboxes of the larger disks so that storage of between 40GB and 618GB is available.

The hardware is expensive to buy initially but the disks are relatively cheap so it is an economic proposition for large storage needs. The more data that is stored the cheaper it becomes in terms of pence per MB. Some rewriteable optical systems can be configured to also act as a WORM drive, where data security is important.

> **Note** An MO drive uses a motorised ejection of the disk under software control. Although there is an eject button, it is not operational with the power switched off. The drive should not be moved when a disk is in the drive. The head is held in a locked position when there is no disk in the drive, but the head is free to move when a disk is inserted. Moving the drive without the head being locked might cause damage.

Phase-Change Disks

Some systems, such as the Plasmon PD2000 and the Matsushita PD, do not use magnetism to alter the state of the disk surface. These are called *'phase change'* systems and use a disk whose coating can adopt one of two conditions - amorphous or crystalline. The drive mechanism's laser beam can produce two levels of heat at the disk surface. Heating the coating to just below melting point produces a crystalline structure during the rapid cooling down period. Heating to just above melting point destroys the crystalline structure producing the amorphous state at that point on the surface. Unlike conventional MO systems, phase change drives can write the surface in a single pass and this reduces the time for write operations. During read operations, the different surface structures reflect different amount of light from the scanning laser beam and these differences are detected and interpreted in the same way as normal CD drive systems.

Floptical Disks

These are based on ordinary floppy disk technology with the disk surface being magnetised to store the data. The disk is also stored in a normal 3.5" plastic case. The difference lies in the addition of special optical servo tracks to the disk surface to ensure very accurate alignment. These extra tracks appear between magnetic tracks and are used to ensure that the read/write head positions itself exactly in the middle of the desired track. An infrared LED light source reflects off the servo tracks and is picked up by a photodetector. The information indicates the exact position of the read/write head. This increased accuracy allows more tracks to be place on a 3.5" disk size and this results in higher capacity disks. Since the tracks are very narrow, a special narrow head is used to read and write the data.

With drives that are backward compatible - i.e. can also read standard 720k and 1.4M floppies - the drive mechanism also has a second wider head to read these wider tracks.

The most popular floptical drive is the 120MB Panasonic LS-120.

Removable Cartridges

Large capacity disks using conventional magnetised surfaces are available, each with their own particular drive mechanism. This means that disks cannot be exchanged between different cartridge drives. The Iomega *'Zip'* drive has a capacity of 100MB capacity, while their *'Jaz'* model has capacities of 1GB and 2GB. The Zip drive has a seek time of 29ms and the Jaz seek time is 12ms. The Zip has an inferior performance compared to IDE or SCSI hard disks, while the Jaz is almost comparable. Interface types used are the SCSI, IDE or proprietary cards, with the parallel port being used for external models.

IBM Microdrive Disks

IBM has historically always been at the forefront of increasing storage densities for magnetic drives. As well as making huge volumes available on conventional drive sizes, this increased density also manifests itself by making reasonable volumes available on tiny disks. Their recently announced Microdrive Product is a standard magnetic hard-disk which is sufficiently smaller than a PCMCIA card that it can be mounted on a PCMCIA card. The device then becomes a drop-in replacement for proprietary Compact Flash memory, which is used in digital cameras, MP3 players and PDAs and has a typical volume of 8MB. The IBM Compact Flash Microdrive has capacities of 170MB or 340MB, and 1GB devices are promised. This allows huge increases in the storage capacity, and therefore usefulness of the devices that support Compact Flash storage.

Computer Viruses

Viruses in perspective

Computer viruses of various types have gained a great deal of publicity and have diverted a great deal of resources to overcoming their effects. Nevertheless, viruses represent only a small part of an organisation's overall problems of security, integrity and reliability. While a definite area of concern, there are still much more important threats to an organisation. A company might fit virus protection software to all machines, to prevent the corruption of data. At the same time, little or no thought might be given to the physical security of the data; e.g. is it held in a machine in a secure room; is the computer password-protected, etc.

To date, apart from a number of well-publicised cases, virus problems are not yet general; many organisations carry out their daily work without any reported virus infection whatsoever. Nevertheless, computer viruses pose a mounting threat to data and have to be taken seriously. They can range from harmless messages to damage and/or loss of data. They are not the glamorous product of a *'hacker'*, as viewed by wide-eyed schoolboys. They are simply a nuisance that causes much extra work and anxiety to computer departments. As time progresses and systems become ever more complex and more interlinked (via local area networks and national networks), organisations come to rely more and more on the quality of their data as stored on computers. This, in turn, makes virus protection an indispensable part of an efficient computer system or network.

Virus Definitions

It is generally accepted that the first PC computer virus was *'Brain'* which appeared in January 1986 as a floppy disk virus. This changed the disk volume name and used up three extra disk sectors. This was fairly harmless but variations have been developed to infect hard disks, hide themselves from detection and destroy the disk's FAT. This is a good example of the evolution of viruses. Although there are now thousands of listed viruses, many are variants on others and far fewer viruses are commonly to be found. The general *'virus'* categories are:

- VIRUS - a program that attaches other runnable copies of itself to the machine code of other programs and may, or may not, carry out other activities (often described as the *'payload'*).
- WORM - similar to a virus but is aimed at attacking the resources of the computer system, rather than its files. It continually creates copies of itself without requiring user input, thereby clogging up a system. They are most dangerous to network systems.
- TROJAN HORSE - disguises itself as something else, such as a game, a utility or a graphics demonstration. When run, the program will carry out some irritating or harmful activity. A Trojan Horse (or simply '*Trojan*') generally does not replicate and so, when an infected file is deleted, it is gone from the system.
- TIME BOMB - a Trojan that is activated on a certain date or a certain time of day. While Time Bombs can be avoided by simply not using the machine on certain days, this is hardly an ideal solution.
- MACRO VIRUS - a piece of code embedded inside Word document templates or Excel spreadsheets. Opening the document usually initiates the virus code.

Where the activity is initiated by a certain event, the program is also described as a *'Logic Bomb'*. Examples of triggering events are the number of times a program has been executed or the number of times the machine has been rebooted. Some may trigger in combination - i.e. when a certain file is run at a certain date or time. So, the elements of a logic bomb can be found in viruses and in Trojan horses. Virus variants mean that there are an ever-increasing number of viruses to be detected.

Note

This section outlines virus problems and solutions. Since virus numbers increase at an alarming rate, every publication or anti-virus program is out of date as soon as it is produced. The examples, then, are not meant to represent the current state-of-the-art viruses; they are used to illustrate typical strains and their effects. The user is advised to maintain current lists of viruses and maintain the anti-virus software in as current an edition as possible.

The chapter does not dwell on the exact mechanisms that a virus uses. This is intentional; it is not the purpose of this material to point the way for potential virus writers.

The modification or loss of data through a virus is an offence under Section 3 of the Computer Misuse Act of 1990, which states:

> 3.(1) A person is guilty of an offence if -
>   a) he does any act which causes an unauthorised modification of the contents of any computer: and
>   b) at the time when he does the act he has the requisite intent and the requisite knowledge.

Since almost all viruses are imported from overseas, prosecutions under this Act will mostly apply to homegrown virus writers, or those who intentionally introduce an existing virus into a system.

Writing or owning a virus is not an offence but the infection of someone else's computer certainly constitutes an offence under the Act.

Virus Infection Methods

The vast majority of modern viruses are Windows based, due to the platform's popularity. In fact, there are *'virus toolkits'* available to allow those with little or no programming talent to create their own virus. There are two main methods of virus replication:

- File infection. At one time the most common method, this involves executable files being modified by the virus to contain a copy of the virus code. Infected files may come from magazine cover disks, web downloads, or friends' floppies.
- E-mail infection. The majority of viruses now spread via email. The user receives an email with an attachment containing the virus, which either runs automatically due to Windows Scripting or runs when the user tries to read the attachment.

File Infection

Viruses only infect executable code since they need to be able to gain access to computer processing time. Any machine code or script is therefore vulnerable to virus attack including:

- Directly executable files i.e. COM and EXE files.
- Overlay, driver or other transient files such as SYS, DLL, ICO, PIF, FON, CMD, SCR, OCX and VxD files
- Disk boot sector or partition record
- Data files that can contain macros, such as Excel, Word or Access files.
- Email systems that allow scripting, such as Outlook.

When an infected file is executed, the virus code becomes memory resident and is free to carry out its designed disruption. The virus has to ensure that its code is always run before any code of the file to which it is attached, since that is the only time that it can guarantee that it will capture processing time.

Files are infected by one of the following methods:

Appending: The most common method, it involves attaching the virus code to the end of the file. Every COM file has an initial jump instruction, which passes control to the program's main code.   The virus simply alters the jump address to the start of the virus code. The virus code is run and control is finally directed to the actual program code.   Similarly, with EXE files, the code entry point is altered to the start of the virus code before passing control to the actual program.   The virus code will contain a section to replicate itself, plus other possible code sections for activities such as delivering any payload, any triggering routines and any stealth mechanisms. Since the program has extra code added to it, its overall size is increased - a good indication of a virused file.   The *'Cascade'* and *'Jerusalem'* viruses are of this type.

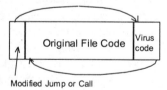

Pre-Pending: Similar to the above, except that the virus code resides at the beginning of the affected program.   Only affects COM files and the overall file length is increased by the infection code.

Over-Writing: The virus code replaces the actual code at the beginning of the file, normally a COM file. In this way, the overall file size is unaffected.   When the program is run, the virus code is executed instead of the expected code.   Since the original code is lost, the program's intended function is lost and the file is irrecoverable.   Rarely used, since it is so easily spotted.   However, some programs will have an unused area at the end of its final sector and the virus code could position itself in this area without affecting the original program code, or altering the original file's size.   The *'Number of the Beast'* virus uses this technique.

Companion: As previously explained, if two files have the same name, the one with the COM extension will take precedence over the one with the EXE extension.   This facility has been used by applications, with the COM file being used to set up any specialist configuration before loading the EXE file of the same name.   The virus writer takes advantage of this order to introduce a companion virus file.   The virus is created as a COM file with the same name as a normal program EXE file, with the COM file's attributes set to hide the file from normal view.   When the user attempts to run the EXE file, the COM file is run first and the virus activity is executed.   Again, this is not a popular virus as it is easily detected.   *'Aids II'* and *'Twin'* are of this type.

Cluster: Here, the file is left uninfected.   However, the Directory entry for the file is altered, so that the starting cluster points to the virus code instead of the wanted file.   The virus runs its own code then runs the file wanted by the user.   Many entries may be affected, each pointing to the same virus.

Email Infection

There are a number of methods used by virus writers to infect systems through email. It is not possible for the email message contents to be infectious; only attached elements may contain viruses. In general terms this means either a file attachment, or a Windows Script.

Virus Attachments: In this case, there is a file attached to the email, which contains a virus. The file itself must be of an executable type, most commonly an EXE or a macro such as VBS or DOC files. The text of the message is commonly designed by virus writers to tempt users into opening and running the infected attachment. These can be prevented either by having virus scanners built into the email reader or the mail server, or by never opening attachments.

Script Attachments: This method only affects those with Microsoft Outlook as their email reader. Messages can contain scripts that automatically execute; virus writers take advantage of this to infect systems, sometimes without users even opening an email message. This can be prevented by setting up Microsoft Outlook not to use the Windows Scripting Host (WSH).

Aims Of Viruses

Replication

The number one aim, sometimes the only aim, of a virus is to replicate itself on to other executable files. This is usually carried out unobtrusively, to avoid bringing itself to the attention of the user.   There are only a few viruses that produce a message during the replication stage.   Some viruses are restricted to this activity; they spend their lives on the machine with the aim to simply infect other programs.   They can be termed *'passive viruses'* from the point of view that, while being a nuisance, they do not threaten the integrity of existing data.   Of course, while many are actual passive types, some may be more lethal - it's just that the correct conditions have not been there for it to activate.   Even those that never do not aim to damage the host system can waste resources and time – email viruses such as *'Melissa'* have been known to cause so much network traffic that servers crash or become unusable.   It makes sense, then, to treat all viruses seriously.

Survival

Once attached to a computer's files or resources, the virus may attempt to escape detection and elimination. This is covered more fully later.

Nuisance

These are sometimes termed *'irritant viruses'*.   They display messages, change round keyboard responses, slow down the system, play a tune or affect the screen display in some way.   They may also result in RAM being occupied while a genuine program is trying to run.   *'Kakworm'* is an email nuisance virus that will cause a PC to shut down after 5pm on the 1st of any month. *'Cascade'* is an older nuisance virus that becomes memory-resident when an infected COM file is executed. The virus then infects other COM files and causes the letters of a piece of text to crumble to the bottom of the screen.   *'Cascade'* began life as a Trojan horse that did not infect other files - another example of the evolution of viruses.

Security Breaches

Some viruses have more sophisticated, but no less damaging, intentions. They try to find a backdoor into systems, and thus have to be as inconspicuous as possible, causing no direct damage or nuisance. However, they are still a serious threat to those with infected PCs. For example, the *'Flcss'* or *'Fun Loving Criminal'* virus infects Windows EXE files, and on Windows NT it patches files to remove security restrictions. The *'Pretty Park'* email virus, once resident on a machine, will try to connect to IRC (Internet chat) lines and pass information on to the virus author, such as dial-up ISP user names and passwords, and ICQ numbers.

Denial Of Service

A few viruses are used for quasi-political aims. Some websites, for whatever reason, have been singled out for attack by virus writers, who use infected home or business PCs as *'zombies'* which are launched against that website in unison. The *'Anna Kournikova'* or *'SST-A'* time-bomb virus spreads via email, and lays dormant until the 26th of the month, at which point it tries to access a Netherlands computing component manufacturer's website. The aim here is to get enough infected zombies to access the site that it will not be able to cope with the demand, thus denying legitimate users of the site access.

Damage

These are viruses that result in damage to files, disks or even hardware. Examples are deleting files, scrambling file contents, changing the disk logical structure, formatting the hard disk or changing security settings. Even irritant viruses can result in problems. Consider the result of losing all screen display when in the middle of a complex set of data entry. Irritant screen messages can also result in a program crashing when the message is written during the execution of the application code.

An example of drive damage is when virus code tells the read/write head of a floppy to move to an inner track that does not exist, causing the head to become jammed in the inner section of the floppy drive. Damage to hardware is, however, rare. A sinister development in the past 12 months has been the arrival of viruses, such as *'CIH'*, which overwrite the PC's flash BIOS, resulting in the effective destruction of the PC. This moves virus protection away from being a matter of eliminating inconvenience and into the realm of truly protecting your PC investment. The AV scanners can all detect and repair infected files, and some motherboard manufacturers have started to address this in various ways, but it may be some time before a truly effective means of overcoming the threat from such programs is found.

Examples of damage to data by viruses are:

- *'Tequila'* is a virus that infects EXE files, increasing their size by 2468 bytes. This is hidden from the user since a DIR command does not display this extra size. This upsets the CHKDSK check of the FAT, producing CHKDSK error messages. The number of entries in the FAT chain may be greater than the size of the file as reported by the virus. If the user runs CHKDSK/F consequently the files are scrambled, as sectors are released from the chain in the belief that they are surplus to the file.

- *'Jerusalem'* is a virus that affects COM and EXE files, adding 1813 extra bytes to the infected file; for that reason, the virus is also known as *'1813'*. COM file sizes are increased once only but EXE files can be repeatedly infected, increasing the file size by 1813 bytes every time. When the date is Friday, 13th, any infected files are deleted; it also produces a black rectangle on the screen. It also slows the machine's performance considerably.

- *'Wazzu'* is a virus that affects *'Microsoft Word'* documents by altering their contents. Each time the document is opened, the virus code embedded in the document's macro often either cut and paste a word from one part of the document to another, or insert the word *'wazzu'* somewhere in the document.

- The *'LoveLetter'* or *'ILUVYOU'* virus has replication as its primary goal, but in pursuit of this goal it will over-write Visual Basic, JPEG or MPEG files with copies of the virus in the hope of spreading by distribution of these files.

- The *'Melissa'* Word macro virus will, at certain times of day, insert the text *'twenty-two, plus triple-word-score, plus fifty points for using all my letters. Game's over. I'm outta here.'* into the opened Word document.

- 'Dodgy' is a virus that infects the hard disk's boot sector. The date it will trigger alters each time the drive is booted, making the activation date vary on different computers. When triggered, it displays the following message:

  "RAVage is wiping data! RP&muRPhy"

  and erases all the files on the hard disk.

Note

If a file is <u>infected</u> by a virus it contains the virus code. If it is an executable file, the virus can be run from that file; if it is solely a data file, the virus is present but is never run. If a data file contains macro code or code applets, these embedded mini-programs can be infected. Additionally, every file is capable of being <u>affected</u> by a virus - i.e. the file is corrupted or lengthened in some way.

Virus Activity

The activities of a virus can be viewed as different stages. Not all stages need be coded in a virus, although some activities are common to all viruses. The main stages of activity are:

Activation - Caused when infected code is invoked

Trigger - Caused by the occurrence by a particular date, time or event. This stage is only included as part of the code in a relatively few viruses.

Infection check - Tests to see if a targeted file is already infected. The virus can do this by examining the directory structure to find a suitable target, or it might lurk in memory waiting for an executable program to be run. The Vienna group of viruses, for example, (648, Austrian, Charlie, etc.) set the file's time stamp to 62 seconds when they infect a file. This time stamp is used when the virus looks to see if a file has already been infected. Times such as 60 or 62 cannot be seen in a directory listing and can only be detected with a disk editor utility.

Infection - If not already infected, the targeted file has the virus code attached to it. This stage would be omitted for simple Trojan Horse and Time Bomb viruses. More recent email viruses may infect by choosing names from the address book instead of file names, and the method of infection is indirect, but the principle is the same.

Activity - A particular action such as displaying a screen message, playing a tune, deleting a file, etc.

Evasion - Another stage, which may be present, is the virus evading detection. This may involve deleting itself from the location where it carried out its particular activity, or some other method. For example, the *'Apology-B'* virus prevents the user from accessing the websites of, or emailing, the most popular anti-virus software producers.

The simplest case is that shown for the Trojan Horse. It is activated when the infected file is invoked and it performs its particular task.

The second diagram shows the stages of a Time Bomb. As can be seen, it is similar to the Trojan Horse, with the addition of a triggering mechanism. It will not always run the virus tasks when the infected file is invoked; it will await the pre-determined circumstances.

The third diagram shows the infection stages of a typical virus. The virus makes an attempt at infecting its target file. The diagram shows that it will carry out a particular activity; this is not always the case, as certain viruses exist with the sole purpose of breeding.

Boot Sector Problems

As explained in the chapter on disks, the Boot Sector is the first sector of any floppy disk, or the first sector in a hard disk partition. The boot sector is a mere 512 bytes long and contains a small program that is loaded into memory by the BIOS when the POST check is completed. This program loads in the operating system components from the disk. This piece of code is the first code that can be modified after bootup, since any previously executed code was of the permanent type burnt into ROM. The virus works by relocating the boot sector code into another sector and placing itself in the vacated position. When the boot sector code is to be executed, the DOS 13h interrupt (for disk read/write operations) is intercepted and the virus code is run before control is passed on to the genuine boot sector code. With a hard disk, this means that both the partition table and the DOS partition are affected. The virus code is loaded into memory when the machine is booted up. In fact, the virus code is loaded before other system and program files. A large piece of virus code will fill the boot sector area and will place the remaining code into another disk sector. It then marks that sector as bad so that it will not be over-written. The most well known example of this type is *'Stoned'*. Although there have been no new boot sector viruses for quite some time, old examples of the type can still infect even the most up-to-date Windows PC. Its varieties include those that produce messages or affect the partition table.

Solutions

With an infected hard disk, a clean boot floppy should be used to boot and run the SYS command to create a new boot sector on the disk. For a bootable floppy disk, formatting the disk but choosing the *'copy system files only'* option will re-write the boot sector. With non-bootable floppy disks, the files should be copied from the disk (Note that only the files should be copied, never the entire disk), the disk should be formatted and the files should be copied back to the disk.

Partition Sector Problems

Some viruses, such as *'Michel-Angelo'* infect the Master Boot Record, or partition table. Again, no new viruses use this approach but modern systems can still be infected. This is the first sector on a hard disk and contains information about the disk (number of sectors in each partition, etc.) and a short piece of executable code to read the boot sector. Every time the machine is booted up, the short program is executed. The MBR virus infects the partition table code so that the virus code is run every time the machine is booted up. When the partition sector is infected, the brute force recovery method is to back up all the disk's files, carry out a low-level format and re-partition the disk.

Solutions

In DOS, a quick solution is to boot the machine from a clean boot disk and give the command FDISK /MBR. This eliminates the virus code from the master boot record on the hard disk but will not repair a damaged partition table. It is useful method to anticipate this problem and create backup copies of the partition table. This can be carried out with the DOS command MIRROR/PARTN. This creates a file called PARTNSAV.FIL on a floppy disk. In the event of partition table corruption, the drive would not be recognised - but the machine can be booted from the floppy and the command UNFORMAT/PARTN can be given. This will restore the partition table to the hard disk. Of course, this only cleans up the partition table. A check will still have to be made of the actual executable files on the hard disk; otherwise an infected file might re-infect the partition table.

File Viruses

File viruses can have the following characteristics:

- **RESIDENT**   Many viruses operate as memory resident programs, either as part of macro space, Windows programs, or DOS TSRs. When an infected file is executed, the virus code in the file is run first. This code places the virus in memory from where it executes. The virus code is then free to infect other files, either immediately, as they are accessed, or at some trigger time. Since the Windows system loads many files into memory at bootup, finding and eliminating a Windows virus can be a troublesome task.
- **NON-RESIDENT**   In these cases, the virus code is run once, before passing control on to the actual file's code. It does not install itself in memory. It only executes the virus code each time that the infected file is run.
- **STEALTH**   Stealth viruses are resident viruses that affect the system in such as way as to hide their existence from the user. Since most infected files have grown in size, reading the file size from the directory would reveal the infection. So, some stealth viruses detect the directory request, subtract the virus code length from the actual directory reading and present the user with the truncated file size. From the user's point of view, the file size has not been altered and it appears unlikely that the file has been infected. The same technique is used to hide any alteration of the disk's boot record or partition table. Such viruses will not be found by anti-virus checksumming systems which simply look for a file's size increasing. This is an old technique that appeared in 'Brain', the first recorded virus. However, using CHKDSK will result in the loss of these files! Additionally, viruses may ensure that when they infect a file, the normal file write update in the directory does not take place. This means that the date and time modified data is left unaltered, so that a change will not betray their presence. Fortunately, stealth viruses cannot hide their presence in memory and anti-virus software can detect memory-resident viruses.

On rare occasions, viruses infect both boot sectors and files. These are known as *'multipartite viruses'* and examples *'Tequila'* and *'Spanish Telecom-2'* (also known as *'Telefonica'*).

Virus Detection/Prevention

Viruses can either be found by inspection of machines or by reported faults. Viruses often become noticeable when several machines exhibit the same characteristics. A problem on one machine could be a hardware or software fault but a number of machines showing the same effect could indicate a virus. Obvious virus problems are those where the effects are easily seen - e.g. unwanted screen messages, music, etc. Other problems may only be noticed after a while. Examples are file sizes being increased, data being corrupted or lost, cross-linked files, a file's date and time being altered, unusual error messages, a shrinking of the available main memory, programs taking longer to load than previously, the hard disk light coming on at unusual moments, etc. Virus protection software works in one of two ways, either through scanning existing files on a disk or memory, or by logging file characteristics and monitoring for any changes. The first method looks for the <u>existence</u> of viruses in a file or memory; the other method looks for the <u>effects</u> of a virus on a file. For added security, both methods should be used. Of course, a detection system is spotting a virus <u>after</u> it has affected the computer system; a prevention system is designed to spot a virus <u>before</u> it has a chance to affect the system.

Scanning Techniques

Anti-virus software detects the presence of a virus by looking for the characteristics that viruses portray. This can mean one of two things:

- A virus will have a distinctive piece of code within it (e.g. writing a message to the screen) that can be detected by the anti-virus software.
- Viruses have to open files, write to files, alter file sizes, write to the boot sector, write to the partition table, etc. Any unusual attempts to carry out these activities can be detected as a possible piece of virus code.

Broadly speaking, the presence of infected files can be detected by looking for the source of the infection or by spotting the telltale signs of effects of the infection. This can be achieved in two ways:

- the user loads and runs detection software as a specific activity.
- the detection software can be pre-loaded as a background program (or TSR in DOS) that tests every executable file for viruses before allowing them to be run. This slows program loading and uses up precious memory but is able to detect viruses before they can spread or cause damage.

These methods are complimentary to each other and both are encouraged.

Signature Scanning

This type of detector scans memory, the boot sector, the partition table and the executable files. It is searching for the occurrence of the string of instruction sequences that are mostly unique to particular viruses. This pattern is usually called its 'signature' and is usually about 16 to 24 bytes in length. Although the virus code can be mostly randomly encrypted each time it infects a file, it still needs a section of unencrypted code to carry out the decryption of the other sections. This code section is its signature. This means that the software is virus-specific; if a new virus appears, a new version of the scanning software is required. The more up-to-date the version of scanning software, the more known signatures are searched for, thereby increasing the chances of detecting viruses. When a known signature is detected, the file or sector is reported to the user as being infected.

To prevent detection, some viruses randomly generate what appears as a completely new encrypted code each time it replicates itself. These are known as 'polymorphic' viruses and the encryption code is often given the glamorous title of 'Mutation Engine'. In these varieties, even the previously unencrypted code is altered. This is achieved in a number of ways - e.g. adding redundant instructions, changing the order of certain instructions, storing values in different registers or using alternative instructions that carry out the same end result as another set of instructions. This produces many possible permutations. When these viruses appear, a huge range of potential signatures would require to be searched for, making their detection almost impossible. An example is the 'Pogue' virus, which plays music and corrupts hard disk data. In response, anti-virus software introduced the 'wildcard' into their virus checking algorithms. This knows where some of the redundant instructions are situated and ignores their specific contents in the signature search. Unfortunately, the added complexity leads to slower operations.

Generic Scanning

A different type of scanning is to ignore signatures that can have many variations. Instead, the scanning software looks for machine code instructions that would result in executable files being written to. These are known as 'generic scanners', 'monitors', or 'heuristic scanners', since they look for points that are common to a range of viruses, rather than any specific virus. To that extent, they are more future-proofed. However, some applications require to re-write their EXE files to reflect a user's configuration and this might be reported as a virus. In development environments, such as software houses and colleges, EXE files are regularly created and modified and this could also lead to many spurious reports of file corruption. Even DOS commands such as FORMAT.COM and SYS.COM might be reported as viruses. This makes a generic scanner an imprecise weapon but it is useful nevertheless.

Some memory-resident versions of generic scanners overcome this by detecting the attempt to write to disk and providing the user with an option to continue with the operation or to abort. This can be used to prevent unauthorised disk formatting, programs going memory-resident, and writing to the disk boot sector. For example, if a memory-resident scanner intercepts a call to write to disk, its program tests whether the boot sector or FAT is being written to and prevents, or gives the user control over, that activity. This is successful unless the virus code writes directly to the hard disk controller via the BIOS, bypassing the DOS calls. This is combated by detecting calls to INT 13, INT 26 and INT 40, which are direct BIOS disk calls. Checks should include spotting attempts to change file attributes from read-only to read-write, renaming COM and EXE files, writing to executable files and writing to the boot sector.

File Fingerprinting (Checksumming)

The other detection method concerns itself with the original characteristics of a file and the effects of an infection. Every new .COM and .EXE file added to a disk can have a CRC check code (sometimes called a 'validation code') calculated and logged. Adding together the values of all the bytes in a file would produce a large number that could act as a simple checksum; using a mathematical formula to the bytes produces a figure that is more unique to that file. These checksums can be attached to the files concerned or they can be held in a separate database. The anti-virus software can then later check these codes for any sign that any file has been altered. This is a more efficient means of detecting virus attacks. Of course, by definition, the viruses are only detected <u>after</u> they have infected the system; this method does not detect the infection process itself. The checking of the existing set of files on the disk can be an automatic process initiated through the Registry or Startup folder, or by a command in AUTOEXEC.BAT. Each file can have its checksum calculated and compared to its previous value. Any difference in values will result in an error report. This can be a time-consuming business with large hard disks but is very effective. However, the calculation of checksums for new files has to be carried out regularly and added to the checksum list, if the system is to be maintained at an efficient level.

Viruses mostly work by changing the first 'jump' or 'call' instruction in a file; the pointer is altered to point to the added virus code rather than the normal program code. So, in many cases, testing the checksum of the first few dozen bytes will detect whether the file is infected. To counteract this, some viruses leave the first pointer untouched and alter the next pointer, which is embedded deeper in the file's code. This evades a simple checksum system and requires a checksum on the entire file to be carried out; this takes longer and occupies more storage space.

Anti-Virus Products

Ever-increasing ranges of anti-virus products are becoming available. Most are software products but a couple of hardware alternatives are around in the shape of cards that fit into the normal expansion bus. These are particularly useful in dealing with boot sector viruses, both on the hard disk and on floppies. Many anti-virus programs are normal commercial products and a few are shareware varieties. Considering the problems, then, a preferred anti-virus product should include the following facilities:

- The ability to run the utilities automatically, e.g. through the Registry, Startup folder or AUTOEXEC.BAT. If a utility has to be actively executed by a user, it will often be forgotten. The experience of creating backups has shown this. The virus checking should be able to run without user-activation, if required.
- The ability to run its utilities as background programs or TSRs. This should be able to scan all files that are executed, modified, copied or unarchived (i.e. restored from compressed form).
- The anti-virus software should be able to test itself for signs of viruses.
- The ability to check memory, disk partition tables, boot sectors, normal files and compressed files.
- The ability to choose between making all tests or making specified checks. A virus can infect an overlay file and although these are commonly given the extensions .OVR or .OVL, they can really be given any extension from a particular application. So, there is no way that a scanner can tell whether a file is a data file or an overlay file containing infected executable code. To be absolutely certain that a machine is virus-free, every file on the disk would have to be checked, not just the .COM and .EXE files. While this is slower, it is a more secure option.
- Few false detections. For example, the virus search strings embedded in one scanner's code should not be detected as a virus by another scanner. This can be avoided by a scanner that encrypts its search strings, which is common in modern anti-virus software. An uninfected machine should produce no false alarms.
- The ability to detect as large a range of viruses as possible.
- A range of protection systems, including specific and generic scanning and checksumming.
- The ability to test all of a file or only selected parts. Most viruses can be detected by checksumming the first or last section of a file. This is a less secure method but operates much more quickly than a full checksumming routine.
- The ability to handle *'stealth'* viruses and macro viruses.
- The ability for users to add known signatures to their check list, including wildcards.
- The ability to prevent viruses writing to the boot sector or partition table.
- The ability to repair infected files.
- The ability to immunise files - fool the virus into believing that the files are already infected.
- A boot sector and partition table restoration facility.
- The ability to create a *'rescue'* disk to store the partition table, boot sector, FAT and CMOS settings.
- A reasonable execution time, although this must in most cases remain subordinate to having the fullest tests carried out. The longer the list of possible signatures, the greater is the scanning time required; background virus monitors require processing time. These are facts of life that have to be lived with.
- A reference book, or dictionary, of all known viruses.
- The availability of regular updates.
- Help line and/or bulletin board service available.

Most up-to-date Anti-Virus software provides multiple functions.

The two main features of any virus checker are the protection software, which runs in the background in order to prevent infected programs from running; (known as '*on-access*' scanning) and the scanner, which searches drives for infected files ('*on-demand*' and '*scheduled*' scanning).

In theory, a combination of the two should prevent any known virus from entering the system, though it may not stop unknown viruses. The most popular anti-virus products perform both of these functions, and include Symantec's Norton Anti-Virus, McAfee VirusScan, Sophos Anti-Virus and F-Prot from Frisk software. Users of DOS and Windows previous to Windows 95 will have a virus checker called VSAFE supplied with the operating system. Windows 95 and onwards do not supply anti-virus products, although most shop-bought PCs have some kind of anti-virus software pre-installed.

Anti-Virus

Viruses And Windows 95/98/2000/ME

Due to the changes to the operating system for Windows 95/98 onwards, long file names, 32-bit file access, etc, software houses produce virus checkers that are specifically designed for Windows 95/98/2000/ME. Earlier versions used TSRs to detect unauthorised disk access. With Windows 95/98/2000/ME, the TSR equivalent is the virtual device driver (VxD) and a virus checking VxD intercepts disk access to 32-bit disk drivers. If the computer is run in DOS mode, the old TSR utilities are still required while DOS programs run in DOS session within Windows 95/98/2000/ME are still protected by the VxD.

Testing your anti -virus product

The European Institute for Computer AntiVirus Research (EICAR) is an organisation that co-ordinates dissemination of information about viruses. As part of their efforts, they have created a non-virus that all virus scanning packages recognise. Thus, an anti-virus package can be confidence checked, without exposing the system to any danger. The steps are:

- Create a text file using NotePad, Edit, or some other ASCII editor.
- Put the following text in the file

  X5O!P%@AP[4\PZX54(P^)7CC)7}$EICAR-STANDARD-ANTIVIRUS-TEST-FILE!$H+H*

  (Note that the first 'O' is the upper-case letter (O) and not the number zero (0). Also, it is advisable to avoid entering any other text in the file, as some virus checkers will no longer recognise the string.
- Save the file as EICAR.TXT.
- Rename the file as EICAR.COM.
- Run your Anti –Virus package to check the directory that contains the file.

Using Anti-Virus Products

Anti-virus capabilities vary from package to package, but the basic steps for ensuring virus protection are similar. The most popular anti-virus product is Norton Anti-Virus. This comes with several programs, including Norton Rescue, Live Update, a Quarantine manager, and more. However, the main package is the one that is used to scan disks and files for viruses.

When loaded, this package gives the user several options.

- System Status. This page gives general information and warnings for the system, such as if the virus definitions file is out of date, or if there are items in Quarantine because they cannot currently be disinfected.
- Scan for Viruses. This is the option that allows the user to manually scan drives, folders or individual files for potential viruses.
- Reports. This section is used to display reports on items in Quarantine, display the anti-virus log, or give information on the list of viruses and their individual threats
- Scheduling. Virus scans can be scheduled to run at any time, allowing time-consuming virus checks to be carried out when the user is not at the machine. Virus list updates and other programs can also be scheduled here.

To perform a manual scan, select the '*Scan for Viruses*' option. The screen will show several options, as shown on the next page. The user should decide what is to be scanned. For example, a technician might use a workstation as a floppy disk scanner, and use that option, while individual user hard disks could be manually scanned if there is a virus alert. Furthermore, unless a separate email scanner is installed, any email attachment should be saved to disk rather than read or executed, and checked for viruses using the '*scan one or more files for viruses*' option.

When the selection is made, another screen will pop up. If you chose to scan all hard disks, all removable drives, or a floppy, then it will immediately begin the scan. Otherwise, the user will be required to select which files or folders to scan.

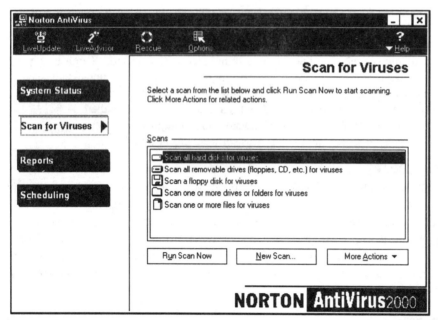

The illustration shows a scan where the entire C: drive is to be scanned, as well as two folders on the D: drive.

Once the package knows where to scan, it will begin the scanning process. After checking memory for resident viruses to ensure a 'clean' uninterrupted scan, it will begin checking the chosen areas. During the scan, a screen will show how many files are scanned, and other details of the process.

If a virus is found, another window will pop up, allowing the user to decide what to do about it. Unless the user is experienced with PCs, the *'Automatic'* handling of viruses should be chosen. Manual handling allows the user to choose whether to repair, delete, or quarantine the file, or exclude it from the virus check if the user is absolutely certain that it is a false alarm.

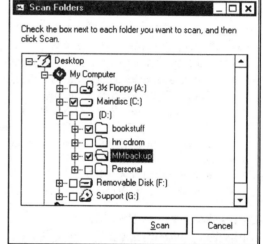

Finally, a window is displayed showing the results of the scan. This gives statistics including the total number of files and boot records scanned, the number of viruses found, and the number of files repaired, quarantined or deleted.

The *'Options'* button on the main screen allows the user to control how Norton Anti-virus works.

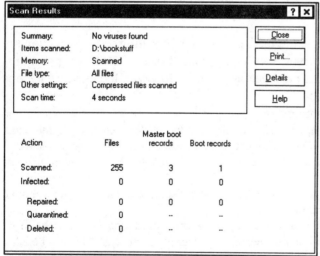

These options include the following:

*   Items to scan in addition to files. The user can disable memory checking if, perhaps, the machine is for floppy disk checking only and therefore should never become infected.
*   How to respond when a virus is found. The default action is as described above, but the reaction to finding a virus can be specified at this point, to avoid the dialog popping up. This is useful when setting up a machine for an inexperienced user.
*   File types to scan. The scanner can be configured to scan program and document files only, or all files - this results in a faster scan and is usually safe because other file types cannot become infected.
*   Other settings. Norton Auto-Protect, the memory resident virus checking part of Norton Anti-Virus, can be enabled or disabled and its settings changed. Email can also be protected for most email clients, and there are various other options including startup scans, alert sounds, exclusions and more.

Virus Elimination

When a virus is detected, swift action should be taken, since delays will result in further potential data loss or corruption. The action required should include:

*   Immediately isolate the machine. Disconnect from any local area network or peer-to-peer system. No further activity should be carried out on the machine until the infection is cleared.

- Inform management and users.
- Collect any disks that were used in the machine.
- Test all machines that used disks taken from the infected machine or that may have been used to access its files in a peer-to-peer LAN.
- Check all machines in the organisation. If an infected game has passed round, employees will be reluctant to admit they used the disk. So, a check should be carried out nevertheless.
- Trace and eliminate the original source of the infection. This is not always an easy task but overcoming the effects of a virus without eliminating the source of the infection only means that the whole process may start over again.
- If the virus is a new strain, report it to the various anti-virus software houses and the police Computer Crime Unit.

The practical steps to eliminate viruses from a hard disk are:

- Boot up the infected machine from a write-protected, virus-checked floppy. This should be a boot disk containing FORMAT, FDISK, UNFORMAT, DEBUG, and copies of the partition table, boot sector, FAT and the CMOS settings. (NB - if the recovery disk contains a CONFIG.SYS or AUTOEXEC.BAT file, ensure that the script lines only refer to files on the floppy disk, since system files on the hard disk may be infected). From DOS 5 onwards, use the /U switch with the FORMAT command; this ensures that the boot sector of the disk is re-written in the case of suspected infected disks.
- Run the virus checking software from a write-protected, virus-checked floppy.
- Identify the infected areas (e.g. memory, boot record, particular files, etc.)
- Use the anti-virus software to disinfect the affected areas, where this is possible and there is no alternative (i.e. there is no backup of the file). This re-writes the files date and time stamps and rewrites the first few bytes of the program code (where the jump to the virus code normally resides). This data is taken from a list in the anti-virus program. This is not always entirely successful.
- For added security, delete all infected files and re-install them or restore them from backup disks. Re-installing from the original disks is preferable, since restoring from backups might restore a virus if it found its way on to the backup disk.
- Re-run the virus checking software on the entire machine.
- Run the virus checking software on all floppy disks that have been used in the machine.

Microsoft Macro Viruses

Until recently, all viruses were contained inside the actual machine code of a program or routine. Data files were exempt from viruses, as they did not contain any executable code. The situation changed when Microsoft brought out Word 6, as it also introduced WordBasic to allow users to create their own 'macros'. Similarly, Excel used Visual Basic for Applications to create spreadsheet macros. Office 97 uses Visual Basic 5 for both Word and Excel macros, while the popular Outlook email program may use Microsoft's scripting language. Macro viruses have now become the most common forms of virus.

Normal Macros

Macros are small, usually single-purpose, routines that are linked to a data document. Examples are macros to alter font characteristics in Word text or to carry out a sort on an Excel table. Macros can be invoked by clicking an icon or entering a particular keyboard combination. They can also be run each time that the Word or Excel document is opened. These legitimate macros are stored in a global template called 'normal.dot'. The 'normal.dot' template describes the document's characteristics such as customised toolbars, shortcut keys, macros, etc. These features, including the macros, are then usable by all documents that are based on the 'Normal' template. Legitimate macros can also be written to replace normal application activities. For example, macros such as *"FileSave"* and *"FileSaveAs"* will replace the normal file saving commands. The calls to the macros are embedded in the data document but the macro code resides in the 'normal.dot' template.

Virus Macros

If a user uses a document that contains a macro virus, the virus code will run when its macro is activated. This may be through an *'AutoOpen'* macro (when the document is opened), an *'AutoNew'* macro (when a new document is created), etc. The virus spreads through copying the virus macros into the user's own 'Normal' template, so that all future documents can be similarly infected from there. All future documents that are created, amended, or sometimes simply opened, are in danger of having the virus macros calls copied into them. These documents are saved as new templates with the extension changed from 'DOT' to 'DOC' to appear like normal documents. There are various types of Word macro virus as listed in the table.

The Excel virus *'Laroux'* does no more than replicate itself and has no destructive payload.

The Access virus, *'A97M/AccessIV'*, also replicates but has no destructive effect.

Virus Name	Virus Effect
DMV	Replicates itself.
Concept	Replicates itself.
Nuclear	Adds the message "STOP ALL NUCLEAR TESTING IN THE PACIFIC!" to all printouts.
Colors	Changes the screen colours.
FormatC	Attempts to format the C: drive.
Hot	Deletes the content of a document then saves the empty version.
Wazzu	Randomly moves words around the document each time it is run. Inserts the word 'wazzu' randomly.
Cap	Deletes all legitimate macros. May remove entries from Word's menus. Only affects Word versions before Office 97.

The *'Mellisa'* virus, which was released 'into the wild' and widely reported in March 99, was the first widespread Macro virus. It was a Word macro virus that used the machine's e-mail facilities to send copies of itself as an attachment. The emails had the subject line *"important message from.."* with the name of someone the recipient knew, so the infected email was likely to be opened. When it was opened, the contents were *"here is that document you asked for"* and an attachment which contained a list of pornographic web sites and the replication code. The replication code then sent the same package to everyone in the original recipients contact list, claiming to be sending it from that person. The furore over the *'mellissa'* virus, which caused no damage other than wasting time and bandwidth, highlighted how susceptible people could be to such threats, and also raised the fact that Microsoft Word documents were fingerprinted with the serial number of the sender, allowing the original sender to be readily traced.

The *'ILUVYOU' virus* that appeared in early summer 2000 took the form of a Microsoft Outlook e-mail with an attachment. The attachment contained a piece of VBSCRIPT code which replaced all .VBS files with copies of itself, overwrote various other files, and then used Outlook to send copies of all of your e-mails, including itself, to everyone in your address book. This macro virus was altogether more destructive, and immediately spawned dozens of similar viruses. Between the release of these two, another virus *'ExploreZip'* was released. This destroys MS Office files, but whereas *meliisa* and *iluvyou* need the MS Outlook client to operate the explorezip will work with any email program that complies with the Mail Application Program Interface (MAPI) standard. It produces obviously automated replies to any email received by an infected machine, the reply including *"some zip file to look through"*.

Detecting Macro Viruses

All known macro viruses can be detected using anti-viral toolkits. Some simple checks can be carried out without the use of virus checkers.

Since the virus code exists only as a macro, the *'normal.dot'* template can be examined using File Templates/ Organizer or Format/ Style/ Organizer. This does not open any document, so the examination can be conducted without the danger of running any virus code. This displays the dialog box shown. The left panel shows the macro calls embedded in a document, while the right panel shows macros stored in templates.

Note that the left panel shows that VIDEO.DOC is being examined and is found to be a normal document. If

that same file were a virused template, it would be displayed in the panel as:

VIDEO.doc (Template)

and would immediately indicate that it was a template given a DOC extension to disguise it. Another good indication of viruses is unusual macro names appearing in a document or in the 'normal.dot' template displayed in the right panel. Macros called *'AAAZA0'* or *'AAAZFS'* are associated with the *'Concept'* virus, while macros such as *'FileOpen'*, *'FileSave'*, *'Payload'*, *'AutoOpen'*, *'AutoExec'*, *'AutoClose'* are commonly used as virus macro names.

Solution

A variety of measures are available for countering macro viruses and these include:

- In Word 97, go to Tools/Options/General and check the *'Macro virus protection'* box. In this mode, it automatically detects some viruses when an infected document is to be opened.
- In Word 97, go to Tools/Options/Save and check the *'Prompt to save Normal template'* box. Since all macro viruses are saved in *'normal.dot'* any attempt to alter the file's contents results in the user being given options to alter the file or to prevent any changes. Of course, the virus macro may include code to turn this facility back off again but it is worth setting.
- For Word 6, go to the Microsoft web site and download a file called mvtool40.exe, which is the Macro Virus Protection Tool. When run, this installs a set of detection macros into *'normal.dot'*. These detect documents that use macros and offer the user the choice of using the macros, opening the file without the macros or abandoning opening the file. It also reports if it finds the common *'Concept'* virus.
- If the template is not often changed, make *'normal.dot'* a read-only file. Find the file in Explorer, highlight the filename, click the right mouse button and choose *'Properties'*. Set the file to read only.
- Use anti-virus software to detect and clean all documents, including the normal template.
- For maximum security, do not use macros. Open existing documents, go to Format/StylesOrganizer or Files/Templates/Organizer and delete all macros. Of course, this loses some of the benefits that legitimate macros can offer the user. Do not use Tools/Macros to delete macros, as this function is commonly intercepted by the virus code.

Web Viruses

With the rapid growth in the use of the Internet, there has been much concern expressed about its ability to spread viruses. The main areas of concern have been:

JAVA   Java Applets are small programs that are downloaded along with web pages. The Java specification describes a 'sandbox' that should keep viruses contained, but specific implementations in various browsers may contain security holes, and these can be exploited by viruses such as *'Strange Brew'*.

E-MAIL   As explained earlier, email viruses have overtaken traditional methods of virus infection.

CHAT   Some chat systems can transmit executable code, or even remotely run programs, and viruses have appeared that exploit these loopholes.

COOKIES   Cookies are small data files that some web sites store on the user's hard disk. Although there are privacy concerns, cookies contain no executable code and cannot be a source of viruses.

Virus Prevention

If a computer system anti-virus strategy is adequately planned and implemented, the risk of virus infection is minimised. The adage *'Prevention is Better than Cure'* emphatically applies to viruses. A rigorous approach to virus prevention can save countless hours repairing the effects of a virus attack. The hours spent in implementing prevention measures will repay themselves many times over in preventing lost production caused by virus attacks. Nevertheless, viruses will still be a threat and it is far better to have a recovery strategy in place before any attack, than running round in a panic when the attack has already occurred.

There is a wide range of activities that can be carried out to provide as virus-free an environment as possible. Remember that a completely virus-free environment is still not a reality, since anti-virus software chases virus development. The degree of enforcement of the activities depends upon the importance of the system in use. Viruses finding themselves on to a home user's machine are less of a problem than viruses finding their way on to a network. Large organisations, with heavy reliance on their computing effort will want to make use of as many safeguards as possible. For these bodies, the data is far more precious than the hardware and the extra time and effort involved is worthwhile. The organisation has to consider the amount of financial loss that would result from a loss of data. The losses could include:

- Repairing or replacing any damaged equipment.
- Lost output while the machines are down.
- Paying for incoming expert help (very expensive).
- Restoring available computer data (from backups).
- Re-entering available data held on paper.
- Re-collecting data not held on paper (e.g. telephone orders which were directly keyed into computers) and re-entering this data.

The strategy for virus prevention and elimination should be adopted as the organisation's policy at as high a management level as possible. This prevents friction at a later date, when machines are declared out of bounds and individual managers are losing precious processing time.

Virus prevention measures can tackle the problem both at the machine end and at the introduction of software into the system. Both activities are complimentary.

A virus-prevention strategy should therefore address both the existing machines and any new software that might be introduced to them. The anti-virus strategy should include

- Naming staff responsible for maintaining current anti-virus software.
- Naming staff responsible for eliminating any virus outbreak.
- Securing outside consultants for anti-virus and data recovery work.
- Compiling detailed procedures for dealing with suspected files, disks, computers or networks.
- Staff training on virus issues.

Protecting the machine

The following practical measures are the responsibility of the whole organisation, although most will be carried out by the technical staff.

- Ensure that access to machines is restricted to only those who require it. This prevents unauthorised access and narrows down the source of any future virus problems. On a standalone machine, special password protection programs can be installed. On local area networks, the system passwords can be rigorously used. Machines should not then be left unattended and switched on, otherwise these passwords are ineffective.
- Where economically practicable, install anti-virus software on each machine. This is usually a cost-effective measure, as the alternative is to have the PC support technician running round all the machines with the single licensed copy. The extra cost of purchasing multiple copies is soon recovered. The purchase of a site licence can make their installation cheaper still.
- Document the existing machine configuration. This should involve noting the size, checksums and date and time of creation/modification of system files and device drivers. This information is vital in future checking for any corruption of the machine. Even better, create a 'rescue' disk. This is a boot disk that is tested as virus-free and contains a copy of the partition table, boot record and machine CMOS settings. This is normally provided as an option with anti-virus software.
- Ensure that the files and sub-directories of the disk are protected as far as possible. For a standalone machine, this involves setting most file attributes to read-only. Many viruses reset the file's attribute while infecting it, but it is successful in preventing infection from some viruses such as 'South African'.
- On a local area network, sub-directory rights should be set to the minimum access rights possible. For example, if a server directory contains only program files, then access to the entire directory should be on a read-only basis. This is not always possible, as some applications need to write their configuration information. Individual files within read/write sub-directories should be set to read-only, where possible. Individual users on the network should be given no more rights than they actually require.
- Ensure that regular backups are carried out, so that the effects of a virus attack can be quickly overcome. Removing the virus may only be part of the recovery process. Deleted and corrupted files have to be replaced and carrying out a restore can be an effective method of replacing these files. Backup copies should not consist solely of a single backup. Copies of previous backups should also be kept, since a virus may not have been detected and the newest backup may itself be infected. From time to time, test that the restore procedures actually work. There is little point in rigorously backing up data if the restore mechanism is flawed (e.g. the tape player may not actually be recording the backup data).
- Enforce strict bans on users bringing in games, or even their own utilities. Although no longer the most common means of spreading viruses, the mobility of floppy disks and CD-ROMs make this a potential risk area. Many organisations, where data integrity is crucial, have policies of dismissal where unofficial use of media is spotted. No disks should be brought into, or taken out of, the computer environment. Where this is impossible, such as with users of portable computers, every disk taken from the laptop or notebook must be virus checked before being placed in a main machine. Note that this restriction should also be enforced with visiting computer service engineers; any diagnostic disks must be virus checked before being used on a machine. Similarly, demonstration disks brought in by salespeople are a likely carrier of infection from company to company and should be rigorously checked before being run.
- Keep users informed about the risks of email viruses. If possible, filter incoming mail through a mail server – this can reduce unwanted 'spam' mail as well as potential virus infections. End-user machines can also install software to warn users before running any scripts received in emails.

- Ensure that only data is kept on users' floppy disks. This minimises viruses spreading since there are no executable code for the virus to attach to. If users are trained to write-protect floppy disks when they only contain readable data, then virus spread via disk boot sectors is also minimised.
- Undertake a training campaign amongst staff, so that the problems from viruses are fully understood. This may well prove a more effective weapon than the big stick and training videos are available.
- Use more than one anti-virus product, since no single piece of software detects all the available viruses.
- Keep the most up-to-date possible versions of anti-virus software, to minimise the prospects of data loss or corruption. The producers of anti-virus software supply monthly or quarterly updates.
- Buy a selection of books on computer security, virus protection and disaster recovery. Evolve the best strategy for the organisation, taking into account the amount of data, its importance, cost, etc.

Installing/Using New Software

Included in the organisation's policy statement on virus prevention should be a section on the introduction of new software into the organisation. This may involve the centralisation of software purchasing and installation so that the policy can be fully implemented. The policy should include:

- Buy only from reputable dealers; avoid the bargains, which may be imitations.
- Don't be tempted to use pirate copies. It is illegal and it carries a high risk of infection.
- Do not use Internet or bulletin board software, postal shareware and public domain disks or 'free' disks supplied by magazines or dealers until they have been fully tested.
- Write protect original disks, whether operating system disks, application disks or even small utility disks, as soon as they are removed from their delivery wrapping.
- Where copyright permits, make a copy of the master disks and write protect the working set of disks.
- Thoroughly test new software before introducing it to the working situation. This should be carried out in a 'clean' environment. Ideally, this should be a standalone computer with no other hardware present except the operating system. Before testing the software, the hard disk contents can be completely erased and fresh system software and anti-virus software installed. Even the NVR (non-volatile RAM) area should be erased and re-written. This ensures that there are no unknown influences on the test. Equally, it ensures that any virused software is unable to affect any other working software.
- Test the software with as many anti-virus packages as possible. Each package tackles the checks in slightly different ways and has different strengths and weaknesses. The range of viruses found by each package is different. So, if several packages are used, the chances of detecting a virus are improved.
- If the tests do not expose any viruses, the software should be documented before being brought into use. This will involve noting, for each file, the file size, file checksum and creation date and time. This can be used to check if files are later affected and altered by viruses.
- Store the master set of disks in a secure place.

Common Viruses

Below is a table outlining the characteristics of some common viruses. The chart concentrates on the damage caused by the virus; nuisance effects such as playing tunes, etc. are not listed.

	Apology-B	CIH-10 (Chernobyl)	ExploreZip	Fun Loving Criminal (Floss)	Happy99 (Ska)	Kakworm	Koumnikova (SST-A)	LoveLetter (ILUVYOU)	Magistr-A	Mawanella (VBSWG-Z)	Melissa	Navidad	Pretty Park	Wazzu
Infects files		X		X	X			X	X		X			X
Drops files	X		X	X	X	X	X	X		X		X	X	
Modifies system	X			X	X									
Windows Resident	X	X	X	X	X							X	X	
Macro resident						X	X				X			X
Email replication	X		X		X	X	X	X	X	X	X	X	X	
File replication		X		X	X				X					X
IRC replication								X						
Stealth		X												
Date trigger		X				X	X				X			
Trigger on activation			X	X				X		X		X	X	X
Wipe Disk		X							X					
Damage files			X					X						
Alter files								X			X			X
Flash BIOS		X							X					
Security loophole				X									X	
Denial of service							X							
Nuisance effects						X	X			X		X		

P.C. Support

The term *'PC Support'* has different meanings in different organisations, dependent upon that organisation's specific needs. However, the functions of PC support staff might include:

Hardware

- Advising on new purchases. Support technicians can provide invaluable information about the reliability of certain brand names and the quality of their after-service. Most technicians are also likely to have a very good appreciation of any shortfalls in the organisation's computing system and are among the staff most likely to be up to date on what equipment is necessary and available.
- Installing and testing new computers; connecting computers to local area networks.
- Installing hardware upgrades, such as adding extra memory modules, modems, fax cards or network interface cards (with any corresponding driver software).
- Carrying out system preventative maintenance such as the periodic examination, cleaning and testing of equipment and running regular diagnostics checks.
- Carrying out first-line repairs such as replacing faulty boards or cables. The extent of the faultfinding and repair activities may vary widely with the organisation and with the capabilities and experience of their support technicians. Some sections may contain staff that are trained service technicians with the ability to repair equipment. Other staff need have no skills with a soldering iron; their role is to find the faulty component and have it replaced or sent for repair. Other organisations have maintenance contracts and PC support is confined to minor hardware and software problems.
- Technicians are often required to undertake more general technical support on their organisation's computing equipment, for example portable appliance testing (PAT test) on IT equipment.

Software

- Installing new software. This involves the installation and testing of the software prior to its use by the organisation. It may also involve creating a training programme for the staff using the software.
- Upgrading existing software - both system software and application software. This may involve upgrading Windows 95 to Windows 2000 or replacing an application package with the latest version number or upgrading available network protocols.
- Updating software. Many packages come with options for regular updates, and these should be installed as soon as they are received. For example, payroll software suppliers might be contracted to supply updates with any changes to Income Tax, National Insurance etc.
- Re-installing individual files that have been corrupted or inadvertently deleted.
- Removing viruses from computers and restoring working applications and data.

Operational

- Carrying out any necessary I.T. staff training. This could be on the use of hardware (e.g. a modem), a new application package, or on carrying out new office procedures using existing equipment.
- Maintaining data security. This may involve the regular backing up of important company data, either on individual standalone machines or on the network server. It may also involve the recovery of data and files from damaged disks.
- Advising and checking on Data Protection Act guidelines.
- Advising and checking on Safety at Work regulations.
- Running a user help desk for users in the organisation.
- Maintaining records of machine configurations, what applications are on each machine, the specific data held on each machine, the detailed fault histories of each piece of equipment, etc.
- Maintaining inventories of IT and computing equipment.

Sources Of User Support

A variety of user support mechanisms are used by organisations and these are:

Manufacturers

Where the goods are supplied directly by a manufacturer, they have the responsibility of ensuring that the product carries out its function correctly. This may take the form of repairing hardware or configuring software. The level of warranty support depends upon the terms of the contract, ranging from same-day, through to next-day, to two-working days and so on. The fast response time is the most expensive but is required where products are used for essential operations (e.g. medical, financial, real-time, etc). Where a manufacturer is remote from an organisation, a local service company is often used to provide a speedier response time. The service staff probably covers a wide range of products and will not necessarily be expert in the product to be serviced. This can be significant, as clear-up time is as important as the response time. After all, the user wants the visit to be effective as well as quick.

In addition to direct maintenance, many hardware and software manufacturers run support lines, bulletin boards and Internet Web sites. These are dedicated to answering specific user problems, publishing FAQs (answer to frequently asked questions) and providing patches, upgrades and updated software drivers. Examples of this are Adaptec (manufacturers of hard disk controllers) and Microsoft (software producers).

Dealers

Where goods are supplied via a dealer, the dealer has the legal responsibility for the warranty, since the contract was with the dealer. Most dealers also offer extended warranties where, for an extra charge, the maintenance of the products is covered for a longer period. Dealers can also be contracted to provide improved response times since, in general, they are located closer to their customers. Many dealers will also provide user training as part of the sales package or for an additional charge.

Third-Party Support

Third party support is independent of the manufacturer and supplier of the products and the services cover a wide range of support levels. These range from supplying a diagnostics software package (where the user requires the knowledge and skills to use it) through to full-scale outsourcing (where all the organisation's problems are covered by an external company). In the first case, a one-off payment is made; with outsourcing, a negotiated annual fee covers the cost of the service. Although third-party charges can be expensive, they are often regarded as an efficient option compared to maintaining an in-house facility with permanent staff, accommodation, training costs, etc. Other third-party services, which are covered later, are:

- Commercial held desks
- Support on CDs
- Training
- Consultancy

In-house Support

For smaller organisations with few computing resources, the cost of a permanent support staff is not justified. For larger organisations, in-house support groups provide the ability to call upon instant services. Additionally, the support staff has intimate knowledge of the organisation's needs and priorities and has local knowledge of the equipment and software in use. The scope of the services can also be much wider as staff can be trained in specialist areas.

Support Methods

External hardware support methods - on-site, back-to-base and swap-out, are covered in the chapter on System Selection. Software support methods are covered later in this chapter.

System Maintenance

Preventative maintenance is preferable to waiting for equipment to fail and then repairing it. It is normally easier to carry out and is also cheaper in the long run. Repairs are often seen as money well spent, as it puts the organisation back into working order, while regular maintenance is often viewed as a tiresome and unproductive task. Any such attitudes - whether among management or support staff - need to be changed, as a defined maintenance programme will both reduce system failures and save money. There is a school of thought that advocates a policy of *'if it ain't broke don't fix it'* and it is certainly true that the over frequent pulling and prodding of equipment can cause problems. As often in life, a balanced approach to maintenance is the correct one. Elements of the computing system should get as much attention as they actually need in practice. This will mean there are different cycles of maintenance for different pieces of equipment. This chapter suggests that three levels of maintenance provide an adequate cover.

Regular Maintenance

The definition of *'regular'* depends on the organisation's structure and policy. For example, a widely dispersed organisation with far-distant local branches would pose problems for a weekly routine. Generally, a regular routine means a fortnightly or monthly cycle, depending on how harsh the computing environment. The elements of regular maintenance are:

- Check all external cables for any mechanical damage (e.g. fraying, crushing, stretching, etc.). Also check that all cables are properly seated in their respective sockets and that none are only partly plugged in. These checks should be of video cables (between unit and monitor), printer cables (between Centronics or RS232 port on computer and the socket on the printer and the power cables (between the units and the mains supply) and any other cables such as mouse, modem or keyboard cables. Any partially connected cables will result in incorrect operation. In the case of power cables, poor connections might result in arcing (i.e. the mains supply jumping the gap between the plug and socket) at the connections and even result in fires in extreme cases.

- Clean the computer's outside case.   This does not directly affect the performance of the machine. It simply keeps the computer looking smart and encourages best practice from its users. In a clean environment, this is a quick operation. If the cleaning removes a lot of dirt, then it indicates a dirtier environment and this may mean that these machines will require a more frequent internal clean (see later). After all, if the outside is getting dirty quickly, this must also apply to the inner machine.

  The rules for cleaning a computer case are:

  o Always use a proprietary case cleaning fluid; this is usually of the foam type. Never use normal domestic cleaning fluids, as these are often abrasive, either physically or chemically.

  o Always use a clean cloth of lint-free material, to avoid introducing lint fragments into the case via the ventilation slots.

  o Never spray or apply the cleaner directly to the case as this may penetrate the case via the ventilation slots. Always apply the cleaning fluid to the cloth, and then apply the cloth to the case.

- Clean the monitor. The monitor screen has a high voltage on its inside coating and this attracts dust very quickly, making the monitor the item most likely to need cleaned first in any system.   Again, use a proprietary cleaning solution. The type purchased should be an anti-static cleaner; this type will avoid aggravating the always-present static problems inherent to monitors of the cathode ray tube type.

- Clean the laser printer. Running through special cleaning papers that are available in laser cleaning kits cleans the internal paper passages. The kits also include swab sticks for cleaning the corona wires. In some cases, the printer's ozone filter may also need to be replaced.

- Clean the keyboard.   This is the hardware component that is subjected to most abuse. Greasy fingers pound it, its users drop biscuit crumbs and cigarette ash over it and even occasionally spill coffee or Coke over it. Not to mention dead skin cells and airborne dust. Like the monitor, it is almost certain to be in need of regular cleaning.   If left untouched, it will produce symptoms such as missing or repeated letters.

  The PC keyboard is a capacitive device. The electronics in the keyboard detect a keystroke by sensing a change in the capacitive potential of a wire matrix mounted behind the keys. The matrix is laid out on a circuit board that contains small 'plates'. The electronic circuits connect to these plates and monitor the capacitive levels.   When a plastic keycap is pressed, it pushes a conductive plate closer to the plates on its parts of the board and thus changes the capacitive potential of the wire matrix. The keyboard electronics then detect this change and send the corresponding scan code to the computer bus. Anything that obstructs the mechanical movement or alters the capacitance of the matrix will affect the keyboard's performance.

  The steps to clean a keyboard depend upon the severity of the problem and could be one of the following:

  ROUTINE CLEANING

  o Hold the keyboard upside down and gently shake it to dislodge loose crumbs, etc.

  o Vacuum between the keys, ideally using a 'mini-vac' designed for the purpose. This produces a sucking action but cleaning is usually most effective with a blowing action this helps to dislodge particles.   If available, use canned air that is available from electronic or office suppliers.   A cheaper alternative is the use of a keyboard 'sweeper' brush or a photographic "puff-brush".

  o Clean the keys with swabs dipped in cleaning solution.

  PROBLEM KEYBOARD

  In extreme cases, such as the spilling of sticky drinks over the keyboard, the keyboard may have to be dismantled for cleaning. In most cases, this will still only involve the removal of the keycaps and the cleaning of the external case beneath the caps. The steps are:

  o Remove the keycaps. These can be gently prised off, always using an upward motion. Some keycaps have small springs under the caps and care must be taken to ensure that none of these are lost. Do not remove the space key cap unless necessary, as they can be very difficult to refit.

  o Remove any sticky material from the keycaps and clean them in warm soapy water. Rinse the keys well to remove all traces of soap and ensure that they are properly dry before fitting again later.

  o Use a low-pressure hose, hair dryer or canned air to blow an airstream down the key tubes, to loosen any internal particles.   Do NOT put your mouth to the tube and blow your own air down the tube as this will introduce moisture into the matrix and possibly upset the capacitance between the plates.

  o Carefully clean the board area under the keys, especially round the plunger mechanisms. Make sure that all debris and sticky substances are removed and that each key's plunger moves freely.

  If the liquid has entered the internal matrix, the matrix will have to be dismantled for cleaning; this is a tricky task.   The keyboard has to be carefully dismantled and even more carefully re-assembled after the cleaning operation.   All the components have to correctly locate and the springs have to be correctly adjusted.   It is a delicate and time-consuming operation. In the commercial environment, it is usually more cost-effective to completely replace a badly contaminated keyboard compared to the man-hours involved in a major strip-down.

- Clean the mouse.   The normal opto-mechanical mouse uses a ball to rub against and rotate a couple of rollers that are housed inside the mouse casing. The mouse ball is designed to be pushed along a flat surface such as a desktop or a specially made mouse mat with the correct surface resistance. As the mouse moves, the ball picks up any dirt or dust on the mat and introduces it into the mouse casing. Eventually, the ball and the rollers both become coated and the result is that the mouse movement becomes jerky and erratic. The ball can be removed by rotating the ring that holds it in place; this is on the underside of the mouse casing. When the ball is removed, the rollers can be seen and these should be cleaned with a swab dipped in cleaning fluid. Make sure that all the perimeter of both rollers is cleaned. The mouse ball should be washed in warm soapy water and properly rinsed and dried before re-insertion into the mouse.

- Check that the user is carrying out backup procedures. Exhortations and office memos to staff urging regular backups are common. It is unclear how well such a policy is implemented. The service check-up is a good time to check whether backup disks are in use.
- Have a word with the users about the machines; this will pick up any training needs of the staff or may identify a problem not detected by the checks (e.g. intermittent problems).

Less Regular

Again, the definition of this time scale is loose but could be quarterly or six-monthly, dependent on the amount of use and the amount of changes that are predicted for the machines. The tests are aimed at picking up any deterioration of the disk surface or disk fragmentation due to prolonged file activities. The tests are also aimed at ensuring that the machine configuration - both the DOS and the Windows configuration, if appropriate - is optimised for the current use of each machine.

The elements of such a programme would be:

- Check the integrity of the surface of the machine's hard disk; this can be done with the DOS CHKDSK or Window's SCANDISK commands or a utility such as Norton's Disk Doctor utility. If any problems are detected, they should be repaired by a utility and the nature of the problems should be recorded. Norton provides for the creation of a text file report on the surface test and this can be printed out and filed. Where surface problems are detected, a more regular visit should be paid to the machine to ensure that the disk is not rapidly deteriorating. If a later visit shows even greater surface problems, it indicates disk deterioration and a replacement should be considered before any precious data is lost. Of course, a problem with the disk surface may be a one off (e.g. jolting of the disk due to moving the machine from office to office or due to the effects of the office Xmas party) and will not repeat itself at a later test. In these cases, the sector corruption was not due to long-term deterioration of the surface but due to physical damage. If future checks show no further sector losses, the test routine can revert to the normal cycle.
- Check the fragmentation of the disk with the DOS 6 DEFRAG command or the Windows Disk Defragmenter utility. Again, if a particularly badly fragmented disk is encountered, this fact should be noted since the machine might be visited more often.
- Tidy the disk. Over a period of time, the hard disk will accumulate unwanted files. These might be files that were created and forgotten, data files left over from an abandoned project, or program files from an unused application. In addition, many programs including Windows create temporary files which are meant to be automatically deleted after their use; such files have extensions such as .A or .TMP. If the program should be unexpectedly halted, then the files are not deleted and still occupy disk space. Some of these temporary files can be quite large - 1MB or more. Temporary files can be identified with a DOS command such as DIR *.TMP/S or a utility such as Wincheckit and deleted. Other unwanted files should be identified, usually in consultation with the user, and then deleted. In some cases, entire sub-directory structures may be deleted. This may result from unwanted applications or directories created for purposes that no longer exist. The technician has to tidy the machine's directory structure and alter the machine's PATH to reflect these changes. In DOS v6, the DELTREE command is used. In Windows, highlight the folder(s), right-click the mouse and choose the 'Delete' option. Be very cautious when using the DELTREE command or Windows folder deletion, as they are very powerful. It not only deletes the files in the nominated directory and removes that directory - it also deletes all files and sub-directories under the directory specified as the parameter. The command does ask the user whether to continue but it is still too easy to delete huge chunks of the hard disk structure in a careless moment.
- Check that the machine's CONFIG.SYS and AUTOEXEC.BAT settings are correct for the current use of machine. If a machine's main use has altered, the existing configuration may no longer be the optimum setting. The number of buffers may need altering or the allocation of the extended memory may require altering. This should be checked and re-set if necessary.
- Check SMARTDRV for optimum operation. As above, if the machine's use was changed - say to more disk-intensive activities - the existing allocation of memory to SMARTDRV may no longer be sufficient to run the system at optimum efficiency. The operation of SMARTDRV should be checked and altered if necessary.

- Check that the Windows configuration is correct for optimum performance with the current applications.   The WIN.INI and SYSTEM.INI can be examined if you understand how they are composed; if not, check the configuration through Windows Control Panel, etc.
- Check that all Windows program are correctly set up, to reflect the applications currently in use.   Programs may have been deleted or moved to other sub-directories and the given paths may no longer point to the programs' actual locations.
- Check that the computer's physical operating environment has not altered.   Check for:
  - Exposure to excesses of temperature or of rapid temperature change.
  - Exposure to dampness, dust or vibration.
  - Exposure to strong magnetic fields such as lifts, machinery, office equipment.
    Strong fields can corrupt disk, taint the monitor purity and produce unpredictable printing.
  - Exposure to strong radio signals such as the office paging system or local taxi transmitter.

Annual Maintenance

These activities address the longer-term problems that arise with PCs and are:

- Clean inside the computer unit's case.   Over a period of time, dust settles on the components on the boards.   This acts as a thermal insulator and reduces the ability of the component to dissipate its heat into the air.   The result is overheating of components and an increase in their failure rate.   Cleaning the board, therefore, increases the working life of the machine.   The cover should be removed from the unit and the boards should be brushed down with a soft-bristled brush.   Even better, use one of the small vacuums to ensure that the dust is completely removed and does not simply settle down on another part of the board.

  NB Before cleaning inside a machine, always make a backup of the hard disk contents as a precaution.

- Check the seating of internal cards and internal cables.   Each time the computer is switched on it warms the components and they expand; when the computer is switched off again, the components contract.   Different components expand and contract at different rates and this tends to make I.C. chips gradually lift out of their socket holders.   Similarly, boards tend to lift out of their expansion slot sockets.
  Re-seat chips by applying a firm but even pressure over the whole surface of the chip; this ensures that none of the chip's pins are accidentally bent.   You may have to support the underside of the board while applying the pressure, to prevent undue strain on the board.   Don't forget to use a wrist earthing strap to prevent any damage to the chips from body static discharge.   Similarly, when re-seating a card, ensure that the edge connector is properly lined up with the expansion socket.   Avoid excessive force.   The use of a rocking motion on the card - from edge to edge - will probably help the insertion process.   Don't forget to tighten the card's securing screw once the card is inserted.
- Clean the edge connectors on expansion cards and cables.   The accumulation of dirt on contacts increases their electrical resistance and can result in data transfer errors; the binary signal is reduced to a level where the next processing stage is unsure whether the signal represents a binary 1 or a binary 0.   Edge connectors can be cleaned with a lint-free cloth or swab dipped in cleaning solution.   Cable connectors can be cleaned by unplugging and re-plugging the connector a number of times; this releases any trapped dirt and the abrasive effect cleans the joint between the connecting areas.
  Don't forget to note the orientation of the cable, to ensure that the plug is re-inserted correctly in its socket.   Some cables will have special markings and these should be noted before removing the connector.   Ribbon cables, for example, usually identify pin 1 with a red stripe on the edge of the ribbon.   Often the printed circuit board or the socket will also be marked with a 1 against pin 1 and this greatly reduces the possibility of errors.   Other connectors only plug in one way round and this solves the problem.   Of course, don't remove all the cables at the one time, in case you have trouble remembering what cable is attached to which connector.
- Clean the machine's floppy disk's read/write heads.   Like an audio cassette player or video player, the disk drive's performance will degenerate if the head is coated in dirt or magnetic oxide   The coating increases the gap between the head and the magnetised surface and causes read and write errors to occur.   The drive's head can be cleaned using a special cleaning disk that is readily available. Always use the *'wet'* cleaner type rather than an abrasive type; this uses a disk that is impregnated with cleaning fluid and has minimal abrasive effect.

   The special disk is placed in the drive and spun like any normal disk.   The cleaning disk can then be removed and should be discarded since it will probably now be holding the dirt particles.   It is not a wise move to re-use the same disk; this may save money but introducing a disk with dirt particles is equivalent to using an abrasive type cleaner.   Hard disks are enclosed in airtight casings and are therefore not prone to the same degree of the ingress of dirt.

- De-gauss the monitor if necessary.   If the screen displays a *'moiré'* pattern then the internal metal screen has become magnetised and requires to be de-magnetised with a de-gaussing coil (see the section on video).   This is usually only a problem with older monitors, since newer models have automatic de-gaussing circuitry.

Printer Maintenance

Even ignoring printer faults, printers are probably the part of the system that requires the greatest amount of maintenance. Any printer that is in regular use will need paper and ink replaced fairly often. Heavy-duty printers in constant use may also need thorough cleaning and replacement drums every few months.

Printer Paper

In most cases, printers will be loaded with A4 paper. The quality of paper purchased is the first concern. An inkjet printer with paper that is too absorbent will produce faded images and text. At the other extreme, paper that is not sufficiently absorbent will smudge. Thickness should also be considered – heavier paper is better quality, but if it is too thick some friction feed printers may not feed it properly. Of course, special requirements such as sticky labels, transparencies or fanfold paper for dot matrix printers might be another factor. Check the printer manual to ensure that the device handles the desired media. This especially applies to transparencies, which can melt if improperly used, jamming the printer.

Adding or replacing paper

The method for adding or replacing paper or other print media can vary depending on the printer. However, most tractor feed mechanisms follow a generally similar method, while most friction feed mechanisms follow another method.

Adding or replacing fanfold paper in a tractor feed mechanism normally involves lifting up flaps to allow access to the feed pins, and placing the paper over these so that the pins slot into the fanfold paper holes. The flaps are then closed and then the *'Line Feed'* button is pressed until the paper reaches the print head. Note that some alteration of the position of the pins may be necessary to ensure the paper is held tight.

Adding or replacing copier paper in a friction feed mechanism normally consists simply of gaining access to the paper tray if necessary, and making sure the paper is stacked neatly and in the correct position. All friction feed printers have a maximum number of pages that can be safely fed into the tray or feeder mechanism. The paper tray can then be replaced if necessary.

Replacing ink

Although less regular than replacing paper, replacing the ink is usually no more difficult. The exact procedure depends on the type of printer and sometimes on the manufacturer - some replacement cartridges even have instructions printed on them. When in doubt, consult the manuals, especially with laser printers that often have high-energy capacitors, but in general the following is applicable to most cases.

Dot Matrix: Replacing an ink ribbon usually means opening the front of the printer. The ribbon cartridge may be held in place by some mechanism or may lift straight out. This can simply be replaced with a new ribbon cartridge and the mechanism put back in place. However, it is usually advisable to make sure the ribbon itself is taut, and that it passes in between the rollers and the print head.

Inkjet: The inkjet will have to be opened to gain access to the ink cartridge. Some may require to be switched on to replace the ink, and a button pressed to move the carriage into the correct position for replacement. Ink cartridges are held in place by a plastic clip that lifts up, usually exposing the cartridge for removal. Before replacing the ink, remove the tape covering the nozzles. The ink can then be replaced, and the clip pulled back down. Close the printer, and if necessary press any buttons required to make the printer initialise the new ink cartridge.

Laser: Replacing toner in a laser is similar to doing so in a photocopier. Turn the printer off, and open it, normally. This is done by pressing in one or more holding flaps and lifting. Take care not to touch the print head (which will be very hot if it has been in use), the electronics (which could result in a nasty electric shock even if switched off), or the mirror if it is exposed. Most cartridge types simply pull out, but before replacing it with a new one there are some steps to be taken. Shake the toner cartridge firmly to dislodge any toner that has clumped together, and remove the toner covering strip that prevents spillage during transit. Now the toner can be replaced, in the same manner as the previous cartridge was removed. Power the printer back on, and if it does not automatically run a self-test then perform one manually to ensure it is operating correctly.

A Maintenance Strategy

The tasks and their timings in the preceding pages are intended to be an indication of the likely elements of a company strategy on system maintenance. The final policy has to take into account any existing maintenance agreements with third parties, the conditions of any equipment guarantees, the current age and condition of the equipment, the severity of the working environment and the abilities of the staff in the support section. While the exact final policy is a matter for each organisation there is one matter which is clear - each organisation must have a clearly defined maintenance strategy, so that the reporting and recording procedures, job descriptions, training needs, backup procedures, equipment stock levels, purchases and maintenance budgeting can all be easily understood and implemented.

Problem Diagnosis

A large part of the PC support technician's life is spent handling *'non-routine conditions'* with hardware and software.   This term describes any situation where the system does not perform as expected.   This can vary from the keyboard *'hanging up'* to smoke belching from the system unit!   From a user point of view, most problems are perceived as hardware faults whether the hardware or the software is at fault. For example, a user report that *'the printer won't work properly'* could be traced to a lost software printer driver or user inexperience with the application package.

The technician has to make a few basic decisions:
- Is the fault really in the hardware?
- Am I competent to deal with the hardware/software fault?
- Is the faulty apparatus worth repairing?

Only those with specialist knowledge should attempt electronic repairs or adjustments.   However, many problems can be tracked down and eliminated with a little thought and a systematic approach.   When the fault is found, it will not always be repaired.   A look at the previous fault history of the machine might reveal a series of similar problems and there are occasions when a complete replacement is cheaper than continual repair.   Examples of this include old computer motherboards that are regularly producing new faults and hard disks that are deteriorating.   In these cases, regular motherboard repairs and hard disk low-level formatting and file restoring is not an economic proposition.   Such decisions are based on a review of the machine's previous fault record, hence the importance of record keeping.

But the support technician's task is not solely about fault diagnosis and elimination.   The technician has to work to a company code, which probably includes the following principles:
- Providing a prompt response to user requests.
- Using a systematic method to diagnose faults.
- Estimating down time of systems.
- Keeping records on hardware and software.
- Being economic with resources.
- Ensuring safe practices.
- Ensuring legal practices.

Providing A Prompt Response

The response to user complaints has to be as prompt as possible for the following reasons:
- To safeguard the health and safety of the workforce or the public.
- To reduce user frustration.
- To reduce machine downtime and maintain user productivity.
- To minimise the possibility of further damage to equipment or data.

The fault report form should include a section for the date and time of receiving the complaint.   It should also contain an entry for the time of the first attendance and an entry for the time the fault was cleared. This is important to maintain a record of the efficiency of the support section.   For office sites that are remote from the head office, an early response might be an initial phone call to identify the symptoms and suggest any simple remedies, with problem faults being attended to by as early a visit as is practical.

Estimating Down Time

Once a fault is diagnosed, the user will require an estimate of the likely downtime of the machine.   All users will be eager to know how long the machine will be out of action and managers may wish to move employees to other jobs where a substantial delay is expected.   In extreme cases, such as waiting for replacement parts, another machine may have to be allocated and the backup disks from the faulty machine used to restore files to the replacement machine, in order to maintain office productivity.   An organisation's maintenance strategy will often contain response time and problem resolution time targets.

Factors in estimating down time
- Does the company have a maintenance contract?
- If so, is it a 24-hour response contract? Bear in mind that the response time is the time elapsing before a visit and not necessarily the time elapsing before a repair.   It is not uncommon for on-site technicians to take the machine back to their workshop for repair. The initial visit may be on site but the repair may still be carried out remotely.   This only happens when the fault is complex and therefore it may well involve waiting for parts, thus further delaying the machine's return to active service. Press the visiting engineer for a realistic estimate of the time the machine will be gone.

- Is the problem affecting occasional, regular or essential users?
- If not maintained externally, is it a hardware or a software problem?

  IF HARDWARE:
  - Is the equipment under guarantee?
  - If guaranteed, is it a return to base guarantee? The time taken to pack the faulty item and the delivery times adds to the delay in getting it back into service.
  - If guarantee is a site visit, what is the response time? Similar factors to those for maintenance contracts apply here (i.e. repair not be within time of first visit).
  - If not maintained externally, are there established sources of supply of replacement components; are the most commonly used replacement components (network cards, cables, etc.) kept in stock?

  Most hardware faults, apart from cables, mice, keyboards, etc., produce longer down times, caused by site visit delays or waiting for parts, etc.

  IF SOFTWARE:
  - Is it a machine configuration problem (e.g. memory management, incorrect CONFIG or AUTOEXEC settings, poor Windows configuration, missing DOS files, damaged Registry, etc.)? For the experienced support technician, these difficulties are generally easily cured and the down time is therefore not significant.
  - Is it an application problem? This could include simple user errors in using the package or tricky interrupt problems between different programs. The latter may take some time to resolve; the former may take even longer, since user training may be required.

Support Level

The level of response and problem resolution for any user depends upon the importance of that user's work and the table shows typical examples:

User category	Type of work	Response Time
Occasional	Any non-essential or irregular user	Next-day or later
Regular	Typist, programmer, graphics designer	Same-day
Essential	Process control, medical, financial	Measured in hours or even minutes

Fault Escalation Procedures

Another factor in the provided support level is the Service Level Agreement or SLA that is in force between the service organisation and the user. This model applies as much for an internal market within an organisation as it does for a 'real' user/vendor arrangement.

A typical SLA works in an increasing severity of a fault.

Firstly, an *'incident'* is reported to the helpdesk, usually by telephone. If the helpdesk cannot get to the root of the 'incident' within a set time, say 30 minutes, then the *'incident'* is escalated to a *'fault'*. At this point a technician is despatched to hopefully cure the *'fault'*.

If the *'fault'* persists beyond the technicians visit then further escalation takes the *'fault'* to a *'problem'*, and so on. The SLA will typically guarantee the user against more than a certain number of faults per annum before service costs are levied, and different customers will negotiate different Service Level Agreements. Service Level Agreements, and how rarely customers incur additional service costs, are often quoted as major selling points by service organisations.

Keeping Records

Every support group has a responsibility to maintain a current database of the organisation's hardware and software, down to individual machine level.   This should include case histories of all problems encountered on each machine. This is important to track recurring or developing problems and thus prevent future difficulties. The data kept by a support group or help desk (see later) should be collected as part of a hardware and software 'audit'.   Items in an audit should include:

- The manufacturer, model, serial number of each computer in use.
- Details of hard disk types (i.e. IDE, UDMA 66, UDMA 100, SCSI or FireWire) and capacity.
- Details of floppy drive quantity, type and capacity (e.g. two 3.5" 1.4MB drives).
- Details of motherboard adaptor slots - number and type (e.g. ISA, PCI, AGP).
- The manufacturer, model, serial number of each piece of ancillary equipment in use (e.g. printers, modems, plotters).
- The location of each item of equipment within the building.

- Any restrictions on access to the equipment (e.g. is computer in security room requiring special permission for access).
- Purchase date of equipment and details of guarantee and any maintenance agreements.
- Copies of the CMOS settings of each machine. Ideally these should be disk copies for easy restoration (using a CMOS saving/restoration utility). As a minimum, there should be manually recorded details, particularly of the hard disk drive parameters).
- Copies of each machine's CONFIG.SYS and AUTOEXEC.BAT. With Windows, the copies of the Registry (or the WIN.INI, SYSTEM.INI and the INI files of applications) should also be stored.
- Details of the cards fitted to each machine, including their purpose (e.g. scanner or fax card), manufacturer, model and serial numbers.
- Copies of the DIP switch positions and jumper settings on each motherboard.
- Copies of the DIP switch positions, jumper settings, address allocation and IRQ settings for each card.
- Copies of all installation guides, hardware manuals and technical notes.
- Master copies of all the installation disks.
- Details of all the software used on the machine.
- Copies of all software master disks.
- Where practical, the original packing and anti-static storage bags, for the easier packing and return of faulty equipment.
- Details of the service history of each item of equipment.

It can be a time-consuming operation to collect data and document the entire existing system in an organisation. Because of this, the process may be best undertaken as part of a rolling programme. Each new purchase may automatically be documented at installation time, while each existing item may only be recorded at the time of a repair or as part of a major equipment service. Although tedious, this system pays dividends in the long run. The software audit ensures that future purchase requirements are more accurately identified. The hardware audit also aids future purchasing decisions and also prevents a whole range of potential difficulties - e.g. highlighting potential address clashes or IRQ clashes between existing and proposed new cards on a motherboard. The storing of copies of configuration information (CMOS settings, CONFIG.SYS, WIN.INI, Registry, etc.) can greatly speed up the restoration of a machine that has had its configuration inadvertently altered or deleted.

Personal Workbooks

It is good practice to keep a personal logbook, over and above any paperwork that is required by the manufacturer. Such a book will usually be hardbound and lined on one side only, with alternate pages left for sketches, diagrams, flowcharts and the like. As work is overtaken, detailed notes are made of equipment, configurations, observations, procedures and so on.

There are various reasons for this.

- A lab-book can save the busy technician time by letting him/her quickly revisit an earlier chain of thought, without having to work through the case again.
- Good records let someone else take over a task if the original technician is on holiday, sick leave, or leaves the organisation for another job.
- Personal record books can also give valuable *'black box'* information if a major incident occurs
- If personal records are well enough kept then the problematic equipment that keeps coming through the section can be identified and weeded.

The Economics Of PC Support Work

Technically minded people have an affinity for the equipment that they are working with, and tend to want to repair equipment "no matter what". However, it is an unfortunate fact of life that all PC support work takes place within an organisation, which must perform economically, in order to survive. As a result, all PC support work must be financially viable. A competent support person must be aware of his/her own costs to his/her organisation, and be prepared to leave a solvable problem unsolved if it would cost his customer or his organisation too much to proceed. In establishing this *economic cut off point* for a repair, the costs of doing the repair must be weighed up against the cost of simply declaring the repair uneconomical and replacing the equipment.

Equipment, whose repair is deemed uneconomic, is said to be "written off". In general, this means that the equipment is removed from the organisation's inventories of assets, and usually its cost is declared to be lost. This accords with the terms of the practice of most organisations, whereby capital equipment like Information Technology is said to be amortised over a period of perhaps 5 years. This means that it is assumed for accounting purposes that the equipment loses 20% of its value each year over the first 5 years, after which it is considered to be worthless. Thus, a piece of equipment that has had light use and is still "as new" after 5 years might be technically entirely worthless. Because of the rapid pace of developments in PC technology, capital equipment on IT budgets is often amortised over 3 year periods or less. PC support personnel must be aware of the amortisation policy of the organisation that owns the equipment they are working on.

Statistics of Equipment Failure

It is a fact of life that all equipment fails eventually. It is part of good practice to understand the ways in which equipment fails and to learn to recognise the so-called *'failure modes'*. Much has been written elsewhere on this subject and many resources are available.

Among the failure modes to be aware of are:

- Wear Failures. These are where equipment is subject to some force or action that causes its gradual erosion. Screen phosphors wear, paper path components and heads on printers wear, and fans and moving parts wear.
- Cycling Failures. Some components will fail after going through a set cycle a large number of times. Switches, for example will happily work hundreds of thousands of cycles before becoming faulty. Note that cycling failures are very like wear failures except that wear is constant, whilst cycling is discrete.
- Catastrophic Failures. Some components fail suddenly, often by design. Fuses are designed to operate in catastrophic failure modes, and some power supplies will fail catastrophically under stress to protect more expensive components elsewhere in the system.
- Out of Spec Failures. Another common failure mode is when a component goes out of its stated specification range. A semiconductor device might be rated to perform for years at a set frequency. If the frequency is increased then the semiconductor overheats and shortens its own life expectancy. The practice of *'overclocking'* CPUs often leads to such failures.
- Misuse Failures. Closely related to Out of Spec Failures are failures induced by abuse of the component. If a computer system box is used on a cushioned surface that blocks ventilation slots, then the temperature rises due to the restricted flow of air and eventually cause a failure. Misuse failures often need to be dealt with very tactfully. Helping a user to understand how they were involved in a fault may need a lot of diplomacy
- Inservice failures. The final and most common failure mode is simple inservice failure. If an item of equipment is used for long enough it will suffer inservice failure, although the definition of 'long enough' may run to hundreds of years.

Studies have shown that most electronic equipment has a 'life' expectancy that can be characterised as follows: Suppose a large number of some device (think light bulbs) was subject to identical conditions. Some would fail almost immediately because they were not very well made.(1) This is referred to as *'infant mortality'* and can be eliminated by *'soak testing'* for a period before being put into service. There then follows a long time when practically no units fail.(2) This is called the working life of the product. Eventually there comes a time when the units will all start to wear out, and gradually the failure rate will increase.(3) This wear out phase ends when all of the units have failed. If the failure rate is plotted against time then the resulting curve looks like the graph illustrated. Such a graph is called a bathtub curve because of its characteristic shape.

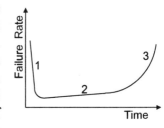

Mean Time Before Failure

For any given component the average life is the time when 50% of a large sample of the components have failed. This is often called the Mean Time Before Failure or MTBF. Because of the shape of the bathtub curve, the mean time before failure is usually on the wearout phase, and so gives an indication of expected component lifetime

Mean Time To Service

Another quoted measure of system reliability is the Mean Time To Service or MTTS. This is weighted average of the MTBFs of all of the individual components in a system and represents the average time expected to elapse before some component or other fails.

Availability

Another oft-quoted statistic is the Availability for a system. This is a measure of what percentage of the time the system is available. For example a server may be guaranteed to offer 99.9% availability, which means the manufacturer hopes it will be unavailable for less than 8 hours per year. 99.99% availability is the promise of less than 50mins per year downtime, or more realistically 8 hours per decade.

Ensuring Safe Practices

There are two separate issues involved:

- Safe practices as applied to users.
- Safe practices as applied to support staff.

Safe User Practices

The organisation should be raising user awareness on issues of safe working practice. Since support staff will spot many user deficiencies in this area, much of the direct input on good practice will come from technicians. The serious issues of staff's physical safety and well-being are covered later in this chapter. This leaves the instilling of good practice on equipment and data handling. Good practice issues include:

- Cold Starts. Never use a computer that has been standing for a long time in a cold environment without first waiting until it has reached a normal room temperature. Writing to cold hard disks, which have been slightly reduced in dimension as a consequence, could result in data loss.
- Moisture. Similarly, a machine which been exposed to a moist atmosphere should be given time to normally dry out before being put into use. Placing voltages on damp circuitry is risking component breakdown as well as data loss.
- Viruses. All staff should appreciate the problems that can be caused by bringing in and using pirate software and be fully aware of any penalty that the company may impose on employees found bringing in or using virused software.
- Disc Handling. All staff should understand and implement rudimentary rules on handling floppy disks to prevent data loss (see section on disks and drives).
- Maintaining the machine's environment. No smoking, eating or drinking at the computer.
- Backups. All staff should fully understand the benefits of carrying out regular backup procedures and have an agreed procedure that they implement.
- Reporting any problems. The first person to detect any problem with a machine is the user. Users should be encouraged to report all problems, even those where there is uncertainty as to whether a fault actually exists. A quick call to the support room or the help desk will soon clear up whether the user is misusing the equipment or whether a problem is developing on the equipment.

Safe Technician Practices

The technician's good practice list is identical to those of the users with the addition of others particular to his/her job. These should include:

- Use proper tools. Using the same screwdriver for all jobs risks personal safety and can damage equipment. Use the proper tool for the job and always carry around a tool set composed of:
  - Box spanners. This is a preferred method of removing the screws that secure the computer's cover, power supply, expansion cards, etc. Using a screwdriver, particularly one of inadequate size, can chew up the head's slot, resulting in the whole screw having to be drilled out to remove it. Additionally, screwdrivers are prone to slip from the head's slot. This can have dire consequences such as scoring the computer's outer case, technicians stabbing themselves with the screwdriver or the screwdriver plunging though another component. With the box spanner, the screw head is held much more tightly and the chance of damaging the screw or other items is negligible.
  - Small and medium sized screwdrivers. If a DIP switch requires having its settings altered, a small screwdriver is ideal. For larger jobs, discard the small screwdriver and use the one up to the size of the task. Using too small a screwdriver can damage both the screw head being worked on as well as damaging the screwdriver itself.
  - Neon screwdriver. This is useful to confirm that there is no mains leakage to the computer casing or to the mains earth. The neon screwdriver is held in the hand and the tip of the screwdriver is placed on the area to be tested. The technician's thumb is placed over the cap at the end of the handle. If the neon bulb glows, then there is an unwanted mains voltage at the spot touched.
  - Phillips head screwdriver. This is often used as an alternative to box spanners where the screw head is of the X-slot Phillips type. This is probably a slightly less safe method than a box spanner but has a lot more grip than a standard slot screwdriver. Where the screw has a rounded Phillips head, this screwdriver has to be used.
  - IC extraction/insertion tools. The pins of ICs (integrated circuit) chips are very fragile and are very easily bent or broken. Always attempt to use the specially designed tools for extracting and inserting chips. These are designed to remove chips in a straight upward motion to avoid pins being bent. Prising the chip's end with a screwdriver removes the chip by bending it in its connector and risks damage to the pins. If a pin becomes bent, an attempt to straighten it with a

pair of fine pliers often results in the pins snapping off. An IC insertion tool is designed to ensure that a chip's pins are all lined up correctly with the chip's holder. It also ensures that an even pressure is applied to the chip when it is being inserted into its holder.

- o A pair of fine pliers. These are useful in changing jumper settings and recovering screws that may fall into the computer case.
- Familiarise yourself with Safety laws, as covered later in the chapter.
- Read the equipment's safety notes, <u>before</u> starting a particular job.
- Avoid Static. The electrostatic charge on the body can rise to several thousand volts and can wreak havoc on any chip that is touched, either directly or by touching part of the card or motherboard. This can be prevented by the wearing of a static earthing band; this attaches to the technician's wrist and has a wire that earths the body to mains earth. The wire must contain a resistor of at least 1MegOhm to limit the current if live mains happens to be touched by the wearer. Some also advocate leaving the computer's mains cable plugged in but switched off at the mains. Since the mains switch does not actually switch the earth connection, the earth is always connected through to the chassis of the computer. This allows the user to touch the chassis and dissipate any static charges prior to handling cards or components.
- Always handle cards by their edges.
- Always leave cards in their anti-static packing until required.
- Never work on a live computer, particularly one that is faulty. A mains supply fault could result in lethal voltages present inside the computer case. With monitors, this is even more important, since around 25,000 volts is present inside the casing.
- Never add or remove a card while a motherboard is powered up. In both cases there is a point when part of the card's edge connector is making contact with the socket on the motherboard, while other parts of the card's connector are unconnected. This could easily result in chips on the card being blown and having to be replaced.
- Never force cards into expansion slots or force connectors together. If there is a particular difficulty, check that the card is free to be slotted in - i.e. there is no debris in the expansion slot and its blanking plate and retaining screw have been removed. With cables, check that they are being aligned properly. Most cables terminate in plugs that have keys to ensure that they are only entered in the correct way round.

PC Faultfinding Specifics

Faultfinding should be carried out with certain principles always in mind. If these are adhered to, then faultfinding changes from being a daunting challenge to being an engaging and entertaining pursuit. These principles include.

- Start with an empty mind. It is very easy to set off down the wrong track altogether because of simple prejudices, i.e. making judgements before starting. Assuming that certain things are usually faulty, or that other things never give any trouble, can waste time energy and effort. Another factor that can cause confusion is the description of faults offered by the user. Although well meaning, system users are liable to assume that their understanding of the system is greater than it is. Start with the premise that anything and everything is possible.
- Concentrate on one fault only. Although you may be presented with a system that appears to have a series of faults, never attempt to fix more than one thing at a time. It may be that perceived multiple faults are all the result of a deeper underlying single problem. In the worst case, when there *are* multiple faults it simply means that by solving them in sequence the system gradually gets better.
- Observe carefully, using all of your senses:

See:	Screen contents, error messages, motion, lights (e.g. on the keyboard, printer, modem and disk drives), thermal footprints (even smoke!).
Hear:	Fans whirring, motors spinning, warning beeps, phone-lines tones, modem negotiations.
Feel:	Fans blowing, vibration from rotating parts, temperature of chips, electrostatic charge on screens.
Smell:	Components burning, dust, odour from spillages, ozone from office machines or from a high-voltage leak in the monitor, printer toner.
Time:	Start-up times, shutdown times, delays in running standard tasks, modem data transfer rates, Internet delays.
Sequences:	Noting the order of events (e.g. does the computer hang before or after a particular device is used).
Test:	Noting the results of physical, electronic or software tests. Could include testing fuses, continuity of cables, results of POST card check, reports from diagnostic software, etc.

Differences: Noting the performance comparisons between two identical computer's running the same application.

Memory: Using your recollections and those of others.

In practice, a number of these factors are used together in forming an opinion. For example, a disk drive may have a LED illuminated, indicating that power is reaching it. However, if no vibration can be felt by lightly touching the drive case, the motor is not spinning and therefore the drive is probably faulty.

- Concentrate on what you really observe, not on what you think that means. It is very easy to say that the whistling you observe could be a faulty hard disk bearing, particularly if there have been hard disk errors reported. However, it could equally well be the PSU fan, processor fan, CD drive, floppy disk or even the monitor's line output stage! Could some of these cause intermittent read faults?

Using A Systematic Method

The process of detecting the fault should not be intuitive, using inspiration or guesswork. Neither should it be a haphazard elimination process, trying out a series of random tests and equipment replacements until the problem is solved. For all but the simplest of faults (i.e. broken cables or other visible effects), a systematic approach should be adopted. This may take the form of a flow chart, a checklist or even a computer expert system. In all these cases, the previous experience of technicians has shaped the best method of diagnosing problems. The experience embodied in the flow of questions and tests in the diagnostic system is then available to others. If the system is followed, the technician should be provided with an answer that accurately diagnoses the problem.

Typical Systematic Methods

Breaking into logically discrete chunks

A good technician understands how the system he/she is working on works at a logical block level, and is able to point to the edges of the logical blocks. In that way, tests can be made at the inputs and outputs of each block - and decisions made based on the presence, absence or state of such signals.

These logical blocks do not need to be physically separate from each other. In the same way that a car contains an engine, clutch, gearbox, suspension etc and these units are often combined with each other, there are interlinked functional blocks within a PC's various subsystems.

A great many of these elements, for example, are on the motherboard.

The illustration shows a simple block diagram of a PC system.

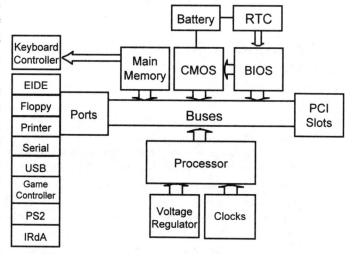

Hardware v Software faults

One of the major decisions to be made when assessing a reported fault is whether the fault is in the hardware or software. The usual way to find this out is to eliminate the software. This involves either:

- Starting the machine with a simple DOS startup floppy, with the minimum drivers needed to operate the device
- Starting windows and stepping through the startup (via f8), to eliminate drivers and handlers for everything except the device under investigation

Iteratively breaking the problem into sub-problems:

Once it has been decided that a fault lies in a certain area, that area can be subdivided into smaller sections that can be independently checked for faults. For example, a fault in a printer might be caused by a faulty interface, faulty paper handling, or faulty imaging, and each of these in turn can be broken down into further sub sections.

Once the problem has been broken down into its logical component parts these should be tested methodically.

There are various ways to do this, among them:

Front to Back.

The first test is done on the input of the first logical block, then the output of that block, which is also the input to the next one, and so on. This methodology has the advantage that inputs are guaranteed to exist and be good on blocks that are working, and to not exist or be bad on blocks that are faulty. When a block can be found which has a good input but a bad output, the fault has been isolated.

    Advantages: Good for tracing signals, intuitive.

    Disadvantages: Signal paths can be tortuous, and can split/join at random.

    Example: In a dialup TCP/IP stack, each software component depending on the previous one. The order is Application - transport layer – MAC layer – Winsock, and the links between each is easily tested.

Back to Front.

In this method, the output is checked. If it is not ok, then the input to the last stage is checked, and if necessary supplied to prove the last stage. Assuming all is well, the tester then moves to the previous stage and tests it, until a fault is found.

    Advantages: Preferable for tracing power faults. The tester is not exposed to power until the fault is found, and is therefore safer.

    Disadvantages: Always working *'beyond the fault'*. This usually means that there is very little output to test.

    Example: Powered speakers don't work, try power at the speaker, then at the plugtop supply box, then at the four-way extension, and then at the mains, until good power is found. The last element that was bypassed is faulty.

Successive Binary Division

In this method, the first test is done in the middle, and depending on the outcome the next test is done either at the 25% or 75% mark. With each test, half of the remaining blocks are eliminated.

    Advantages: Good for systems with a large chain of small blocks. Saves a lot of work.

    Disadvantages: Of limited use on systems that are not linked in a chainwise manner.

    Example: A room in a telesales office contains 60 PCs on a single 10Base2 Ethernet segment, terminated at either end. To find a cable fault, start at machine 30. The termination will be good on one half of the segment but not the other. Lets say the upper half is good. We now check the lower half by dividing into 1-15 and 16-30. If 1-15 is good, we then check 16-30 by dividing into 16-23 and 24-30. Eventually we find the fault in less than 6 tests (compared to an average of 30 tests doing it one machine at a time in order).

Trial by substitution:

One of the most common ways of testing equipment is to deploy an identical replacement and see if the fault *'goes away'* with the new component.

    Advantages: Quick, simple and unambiguous results.

    Disadvantages: A replacement has to be available.

                       The fault that destroyed the original might also destroy the replacement.

    Example: Workstation 13 has no picture on the monitor. Firstly, test the monitor by attaching it to the next workstation, and test the system by attaching it to the monitor at the next system.

Trial by symmetry

It is very easy to compare settings, responses and the like on two identical systems as a means to faultfinding. Indeed some systems have multiple identical channels that can be compared, audio comes in identical stereo pairs and video travels in groups of three, Red, Green, and Blue. Comparing and contrasting can be very enlightening.

    Advantages: Simple informative, easily followed.

    Disadvantages: Not always applicable

    Example: System reports *"hard disk controller error"*. Inspection reveals twin IDE drives, master A and slave B. By swapping jumpers to make B master and A slave, we can compare the IDE controllers on the two drives. If the fault 'disappears' then A's Controller is faulty, if it does not then there is a slight chance that both controllers are faulty, but it is more likely that the IDE port on the motherboard is at fault.

Trial by Isolation

It is sometimes easiest to test components away from their parent system, particularly where the interactions between the component and its parent are complex. This might involve designing a test rig of some sort.

    Advantages: Allows totally unambiguous tests.

    Disadvantages: May involve some extra cost.

Example: NiMH battery for laptop computer appears to be faulty, but it is impossible to test while it is behind its little door powering the laptop. One possible solution is to charge the battery overnight in the computer and then test it outside the PC. Another is to build a dummy battery that makes the proper connections but allows wires to come out to the real battery now situated outside and accessible to test equipment.

Trial by integration

The opposite test strategy also applies. Some situations demand that the equipment under test is integrated in some host system before it can be tested.

Advantages :   Usually go/no go solution.

Disadvantages: Needs an expensive host. Potential damage to host.

Example: PC Power supplies will generally not work without a load; therefore they are best tested by attaching them to a known mainboard or drive. Some workshops keep elderly or redundant equipment for this purpose.

Cascade Faults

Some faults cascade. That is to say a simple fault will cause a condition that causes another fault or faults. This is not a good thing. It is usually discovered when the support person fixes the perceived fault but it immediately recurs. The best advice is to isolate the most obvious suspects and then re-introduce them in a controlled order until the fault is found.

Advantages: The only positive thing that can be said about such a situation is that it is better than an intermittent fault!

Disadvantages: Expensive, difficult to fault-find.

Example: PC blows a fuse. Replacement fuse pops too. This suggests that we are not dealing with a tired fuse, but a condition that is causing the fuse to blow. Suspect power supply and try by replacement. If all is well then the power supply was faulty, if not then something is drawing huge current to cause the supply to blow fuses as a safety measure. Isolate drives, motherboard, etc., and reconnect one at a time until culprit is found.

Intermittent Faults

These are faults that do not always happen, or that happen only occasionally. They will never put in an appearance when you are waiting for them! They can only be found by detective work and intense observation. Sometimes observation by proxy! Get the user to note exactly what error messages occur, and when and what they were doing, and why. Then look for patterns; always first thing in the morning, always on hot days, always just after printing. Try to think laterally. Eventually a factor should emerge that explains the fault.   If it does not then it may be necessary to embark on a program of trial replacements until the fault is isolated

Advantages: Because of their intermittent nature they won't be put at a high priority on the work list. However, they have a way of becoming a bit of an obsession with technicians.

Disadvantages: Can be very frustrating and are a good way of getting the PC support group a bad name.

Example: Laser printer is intermittently blotchy; most days it gives perfect results, some days it is blotchy. Scanning the logs shows that this fault is hardly ever reported in months with an R in the name, but regularly reported May – August. It is also only ever reported in the afternoon. Investigations revealed that the corner where it sits is a suntrap and excess heat from the sun through the window causes the blotchiness.   Such information may have been recovered from a well-documented logbook.

Causes Of Intermittent Faults

There are occasions when there are no error messages displayed and the unit, keyboard, monitor, etc. all seem to be functioning satisfactorily.   The problem seems to be an intermittent one, with the machine hanging up while lying idle, or crashing in the middle of a program.   Either hardware or software can cause these problems.

If the fault develops when there is no software loaded, then the source is easier to determine; the fault must be a hardware one.   While the source of the difficulty may be known, however, tracing the cause of the problem may be more difficult, since the fault cannot be reproduced to order.

Intermittent hardware problems may be:

- Overheating faults.   As manufacturers race to bring ever faster performance machines on to the market, the CPU and other chips are forced to run at alarming clock rates and chip temperatures increase beyond the point of stability.   So much so, that CPU chips have fans built on to their heat sinks, to dissipate the enormous amounts of heat that they generate.
- Design faults. Using memory chips that are not always able to keep up with the speed of the CPU. Try altering the clock speed or the memory timings (through the BIOS settings) and see if the intermittent fault disappears.

- Intermittent connections. These may be dry joints in soldered connections to the motherboard, power supply, disk drive, etc. These may be either component or wiring connections. The application of heat (by a hair dryer or similar) to an area of the board will expand any metal and hopefully expose the intermittent connection. Conversely, if the problem is already present, the application of a freeze spray (available from electronic component suppliers) to selected areas will cool the area and hopefully restore normal operations, thereby showing up the problem connection.
- Software problems are more difficult to detect, as the fault may only occur under specific circumstances. For example, it may require a particular clash of interrupts such as when using a particular function of an application over a local area network. There are so many possible permutations that this may take exhaustive tests to expose. A lot of time can be saved if users are encouraged to note down exactly what they were doing at the time of the fault.
- Lastly, the problem may be due to spikes or fluctuations in the mains supply affecting the data on the buses and causing the machine to crash. This may require the fitting of an uninterruptible power supply (UPS) to the computer. This is particularly important for local area network servers and other important machines in the company.

Breaking Loops

Very often a fault lies within a loop in a system, where the output is dependent on the input, which is dependent on the output. While this loop is intact it is very difficult to find faults. By breaking the loop, the problem is reduced to a straight line problem and the' front to back' or 'back to front' faultfinding techniques can be used.

Advantages: Simplifies a difficult problem.

Disadvantages: finding a place to break the loop and a way of breaking it without upsetting the system can be tricky.

Example: Dot matrix printer suffering head jams. The ribbon is driven by the head motion and if the ribbon is removed, the controller notes the broken ribbon and stops the head to minimise damage. Remove the ribbon and run printer to see what is jamming head, but constantly twiddle the ribbon motion sensor with a screwdriver to simulate ribbon motion and allow system to function.

Environmentally based faults

Thermal

Heat can cause a great many faults. SIMMS were invented because on early PCs, the DIL packaged RAM chips moved a tiny fraction of a millimetre each time the machine heated up and cooled down. Eventually they would 'creep' out of their sockets. Technicians routinely solved memory faults by simply pressing all the RAM chips into place with their thumb. IBM proposed a solution whereby the chips were soldered but still replaceable and held against a spring to stop thermal effects and thus the SIMM was born. Extreme heat warps plastic, causes LCDs to lose their contrast, and causes mayhem with semiconductors. Even moderate heat causes component lifetimes to be shortened. Obstructing ventilation causes heat. Finally, heat sets laser printer toner. Clothes and hands that have become messed with toner should be washed in cold water (as hot water causes the toner to set).

Light

Light is more of an inconvenience than a hazard. Glare, both direct, from a bright window behind the screen, and reflected, say the reflection in the screen of a window across the room, are health and safety hazards. Flashing light at certain frequencies can lead to seizures and illnesses in certain people. Bright light can also erase EPROM bios chips if they are left for a long time with their window uncovered. Bright light will damage the photosensitive drum of a laser printer.

Dust

A coating of dust acts like a blanket and causes items to retain heat and so suffer thermal failure. Dust also wears moving parts that it comes in contact with, causes lightweight switches to stick and obstructs optical sensors and CD/DVD lenses. The contamination of a laser drum with dust can cause repeating patterns on every sheet printed. High voltages attract dust, and so screens and laser printers are particularly vulnerable. Ozone filters in laser printers also clog with dust.

Smoke

Smoke is a lot like dust, and does everything that dust does. In addition, smoke travels in directions other than down, and so tends to get more places. Cigarette smoke leaves a mucky brown tarry residue on the high voltage trays of monitors and can cause arcing. The effects of both smoke and dust can be partially alleviated by using an ioniser. This causes the particles to stick to surfaces close to the ioniser, thus keeping the air elsewhere cleaner.

Magnetic fields

Magnetic fields cause errors in magnetic storage devices. They also cause distortion on picture tubes, and will induce a current in anything that contains a coil of wire. Sources of magnetic fields include loudspeakers, monitors, tools, fridge magnets, and electrical motors of all sorts.   It is also produced by the mains transformers used to power loudspeakers, external modems, external zip drives and even halogen lamps. Audio leads, monitor screens, floppy disks, etc. should all be kept a distance away from such sources.

Electric / Electromagnetic fields

These fields are caused by the mains wiring, and all mains, radio frequency and oscillatory electrical circuits. They can act at a distance and can damage magnetic storage and induce unwanted voltages. Sources include microwave ovens, car ignition circuits, fluorescent lights, CB and amateur radio, mobile phones etc.

Judder /Jar/ Mechanical

Newton's laws of motion explain that there is no force on a moving body. However, starting and stopping causes forces, and the more sudden the jar the greater the force experienced. No system should be exposed to mechanical shocks.

Ingress of liquid

It goes almost without saying that ingress of liquid should be avoided. However should a keyboard have coffee or fizzy drinks spilled upon it then any damage tends to be a result of sugar or fruit acid, not the liquid.   It may well be that washing the component in clean water and then carefully drying it out will restore it to full health.

Special cases

With both power supply systems, which are nearly all switch mode devices, and monitors, which tend also to be switch mode in their construction, there is a huge electronic complexity - and extreme danger from lethal voltages. The time taken to open, examine, fault find and repair such products far exceeds the economic cost of the device.   Additionally, the risks involved are great, even for fully trained personnel.   Both power supplies and monitors are now nearly commodity items and really do not warrant attempts at repair.

Ensuring Legal Practices

Apart from the Health and Safety regulations that technicians will wish to enforce, there are a number of other areas that could lead the organisation into legal difficulty. These are:

- The use of unauthorised software, (e.g. *'pirate'* copies of games or utilities).
- Licensing agreements (e.g. no more than 20 simultaneous users of a package on a network).
- Copyright.
- Data Protection Act.

These issues are covered elsewhere in detail.

Running A Help Desk

Running an organisation's internal help desk tends to require a broader coverage than commercial help desks, which are mostly devoted to a particular product. The help from commercial desks concentrates on support of a particular item of hardware or software, although some general help lines are available.

Aims Of A Help Desk

The aims of the help desk are two-fold:

- To cure the immediate user problems, maintaining productivity and protecting data/equipment.
- To improve the long-term quality of IT in the organisation, through measures such as problem prevention, user training and informed future purchasing.

The task of a help desk is to solve user problems quickly and courteously.   The technicians on the desk cannot possibly know the solution to all problems. Their job is to know where to find the solutions to all problems.   Apart from the most obvious problems (e.g. printer out of paper), the degree of spontaneous help from a support technician will be in direct proportion to the knowledge and experience of that technician.   The remainder of the help must come from an organised system of initial remote diagnosis. The technician has to work from the information supplied by the user to identify solutions.

Scope Of A Help Desk

Some organisations restrict the help desk's activities to that of clearing I.T. problems.   Other organisations expect a wider role from the desk, so that it becomes the clearing house for all company gadgets such as or photocopiers, fax machines, telephones, lifts, coffee machines, shredders, etc.   These pages restrict themselves to the computer role of a help desk.

Record Keeping

A fault report form should be completed for each call.   It includes the date and time of call, the caller's name and telephone number and a number of the details that would already appear in the report form issued to users for their use prior to calling the help desk.   So, by the time the user calls the help desk, he/she will have already formulated a version of the fault.   The form has additional information for the use of the desk technician. This would include:

- Whether cleared by phone. If so, the call duration would be logged.
- Whether passed on to supplier. This would be the result of a diagnosis of a non-trivial fault on a machine that is under guarantee.   If passed on, the time would be recorded and a reference number obtained from the supplier.
- Whether passed to maintenance third party, if an agreement exists and the fault is non-trivial. If passed on, the time would be recorded and a reference number obtained from the supplier.
- Whether the site requires a visit. This report might be passed on to another technician - if so, record the name of the technician and the time of passing on the form.   Also record any equipment or software that might be required to cure the problem.   These may be DOS boot disks, utility disks, spare cables, or whatever is required.

OUTLINE FAULT RECORDING FORM

Help Desk Technician's Name			
		Date of call	
		Time commenced	
Reported by		Time completed	
Tele No.		Location	
Machine No		Inventory Reference	
Make & Model		Processor	
RAM size		Monitor	
Windows version		Hard disk size	
DOS version		Network type	

Problem Description

Diagnosis

Cleared by phone			
Passed to	Supplier	Time	Ref No.
	Third Party	Time	Ref No.
Requires visit	Visiting Technician		Time

Equipment Required

Comments	(e.g. case history)

Identifying Problems

The technician has to determine whether the complaint is of a hardware or software variety. This will often have to be diagnosed through effective questioning techniques, since the user will often blame the hardware for many software or user errors.   There will usually be more hardware than software faults and always more operator errors than any other fault category.   The questions asked allow the technician to determine the likely cause of the problem.   Many problems are of a minor nature. Probably around a third of calls could be saved by training users in the basics of Windows and its applications. Possibly another third are *'printer out of paper'* or *'printer off line'* type of problems - i.e. problems that can be diagnosed and made good without a technician's visit to the actual machine.   Of course, it is difficult to judge whether a user knows the answers to the questions being asked, since user understanding will vary enormously. If the organisation is sufficiently compact, it pays to get to know the users because this provides a basis on which to judge how much to trust their information.   In large organisations, it may pay to have complaints routed through a section contact (the most computer-literate person in the section) so that the help desk becomes familiar with the contact and his/her capabilities.

Aids To Diagnosis

- Use an inventory of the organisation's computing system; know what software and hardware is on the reported machine - just by asking for the machine's identification code.   Apart from diagnosis, this can be an aid to maintaining the office's normal operations.   For example, if a machine has to be withdrawn to await spare parts, it can't be replaced by any other machine - account must be taken of any particular cards that may be inside the problem machine. Replacing the machine might otherwise lose the office its modem link or its fax connection.
- Use a remote access system to the user's computer.   This is extremely useful in a largely dispersed organisation with computer sites remote from the help desk.   Remote control software allows the help desk to link one of its computers to the computer at the remote site via modems.   With this software, the help desk monitor will also display whatever the remote user is seeing.   Even more important, the desk keyboard will act as if it were an additional keyboard on the remote computer.   This way, the help desk technician can take full control of the remote system to examine many of its hardware aspects and all of its software aspects.   Examples of this remote control software are Microcom's Carbon Copy Plus, Telesystems' PCAnywhere and Central Point Software's Commute.
- Consult the machine's previous case history.   Use this information to detect a possible recurring fault or a developing problem.   This also allows the desk to discover the most common faults, both within company and on any particular machine.

Help Desk Resources

As stated earlier, the help desk has to be the source of all knowledge and experience. The resources have to be built up to make this possible and the desk should not rely on the expertise stored in the head of an experienced technician.   Fortunately, a number of different resources are available to build up the desk's reference abilities. These include:

- All hardware and software audit records as previously outlined.
- All software and hardware manuals and technical guides.
- Previous case histories of all equipment.
- Statistical records previously compiled from the above.
- Notes from attendance at training courses.
- Use of suppliers' and dealers' support lines.
- Use of consultants for major difficulties.
- Specially commissioned diagnostic packages as described below.
- Proprietary logging packages as described below.
- Journals and memos from User Groups.   These can include Windows, Lotus, Novell and Independent PC Users. Membership provides reports on others' problems and allows questions to be raised.
- Copies of computer magazines and periodicals.
- Copies of training videos.

CALL LOGGING PACKAGES

This software is created for use on help desks and provides the following facilities:

- Call logging; each call is recorded and saved.
- Call prioritising; the order of the queue of callers can be altered to match the estimated severity of the fault and the seniority of the person complaining.
- Call tracking; used where a fault is not cleared in the one call.

An example is HelpDesk for Windows by Utopia.

SUPPORT ON CD-ROM/DISK

Support On Site is a CD-ROM from Computer Library, a subsidiary of the mighty Ziff-Davis publishing empire.   This comes as an annual subscription service with the following facilities:

- Updated CD sent every month.
- Text retrieval based on a word or a phrase.
- Dozens of software products supported - including dBase, WordPerfect, Wordstar and most of the Lotus and Microsoft range.   A LAN Support version is available.
- Product manuals.
- Product technical notes.
- Drivers, patches and bug fixes.

Other products include:

- Diskbase for Windows with a database of 4,600 different disk drive specifications and 750 disk controller specifications
- Windows Help file creators, such as HDK and SOS Help Info Author, to create pages of user help files in the standard Windows format.
- Laplink for Windows provides remote control facilities such as file transfer, chat mode and the ability of the helpdesk to control the remote PC.
- CheckIt Analyst collects machine data, analyses it and reports on a range of installation and troubleshooting options.

Customised Support Packages

These are packages that are built to order and can cover specific software or hardware, or both.   These packages are expensive but they address the specific needs of a support desk that may not be covered in general-release products such as the Support On Site CD-ROM.   These are based on expert systems and lead the desk technician through the likely symptoms for different faults.   If the organisation has staff with programming skills, then packages such as these can also be developed in-house.

Assisting Users To Access Support

There are times when the aim is to help user to help themselves. This usually depends on the size of the organisation.   If there is an internal support group, then the management will probably wish that all problems would be directed to the group. In a small company, where there is only a small training / PC support force, they may wish to show users how to get their own help. The most common methods are:

Peer Support

This merely entails finding someone who already has the skills in a section, to provide the basic help that is mostly required. Of course, this may involve a process of training of key individuals in departments.

Using On-Line Support

There are now a number of bulletin boards that can provide answers to problems.   Some, like the Microsoft On-Line board, are run by the software house concerned while others, like the Compuserve and CIX boards, are general service boards.   All that is required is a modem connection for the PC to the telephone network. The user can then dial up, log in and either read existing help pages or leave a specific question on the board.   Some areas of bulletin boards are free while others are chargeable; in all cases there are telephone call charges and possibly extra connect charges.

The recent growth of Internet subscribers means that many companies and individuals have access to this international network.   Many Special Interest Groups exist on the Internet and these cover all kinds of hardware and software areas.   Problems that are placed in this arena will receive replies from the best minds throughout the globe.   There are very few queries that go unanswered on the Internet.

Another definition of on-line help is the mass of help information that is now provided within many application packages. Some outstanding examples of this can be seen in Windows applications that even include built-in tutorials. This is not *'on-line'* in the sense of being connected to a telephone line; however, it does provide a high degree of assistance that is always available to the user. The time spent showing users how to access this information can save a great deal of support time in the longer run.

Using A Help Desk

Help desks, unlike bulletin boards, are able to provide immediate support for a problem. Dialling the help desk number and giving a customer number provides the verbal link between the user and, hopefully, the expert in the subject area. Help desks can either be internal (i.e. run by the company itself) or external (i.e. a commercial operation).

External Help Desks

These are normally run by software suppliers (e.g. IBM, WordPerfect), user groups or software maintenance firms. Some are free for the first year; most have annual charges; at least one provides a credit service, where advanced payment covers a specified number of calls to the hot line.

Internal Help Desk

This is run by the company's own PC support team and is dedicated to the company's particular hardware and software needs. In some cases, the support staff can take control of the user's computer in order to analyse and fix the problem; the support technician can see the users screen and can alter the flow and data on the user's machine from the remote help desk console. This is particularly useful where a company has sites that are scattered from the main office.

Fault Reports

In the case of both external and internal help desks, the user has to make some preparations prior to making the call. These are:

- To save any embarrassment, check the problem against manuals. With Windows, check out the hypertext Help menus.
- Make the call when the computer is switched on and the program is running.
- Complete a report form such as the example given.

Outline Support Request Form

		Date of call	Time of call
Make		Model	
Location		On network?	
List of add-ons			
Software including version number			
Outline of Problem State as succinctly and clearly as possible; when does problem arise - what stage in program/process			
Any error messages			

Hardware Diagnostics

Advanced hardware diagnostics are beyond the scope of this volume and beyond the means of most organisations whose business is not the manufacture or repair of computer equipment. However, there are basic hardware and software diagnostic tools available for small and medium organisations, and all PC support personnel should be familiar with them.

The following diagram represents a basic system to aid in diagnosis of a PC fault. It is simply an overview of the general type of steps to take in diagnosing a fault, and is not meant to be a comprehensive fault finding flowchart. It is intended to act as the basis of a systematic approach to locating hardware or device driver faults, and some of the methods involved are discussed in more detail in the following sections. An HTML-based diagnosis system is available on the author's web site at http://www/dumbreck.demon.co.uk.

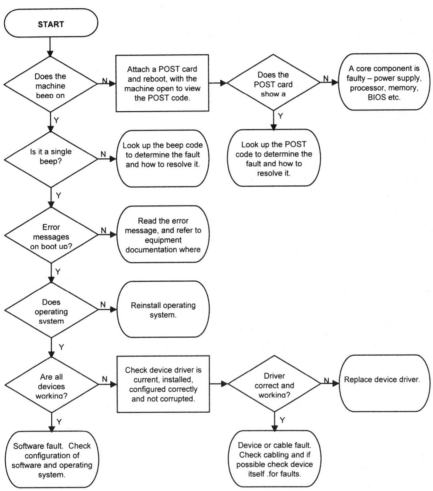

Power On Self Test

When the computer is first switched on, it automatically performs tests on the CPU, ROM, memory, motherboard, hard disk, etc. The machine will not carry on if it finds any fault and will in most cases warn the user by producing a series of warning beeps and/or displaying an error message on the screen.

If there is a single beep, (rarely two short beeps in the case of some very old machines) then the POST check has passed the computer system as operable. Note that the POST test is not nearly as thorough as the checks performed by quality diagnostic software. So, a POST failure definitely means a problem, while a POST pass does not necessarily mean that the machine is fully functional.

If there is more than one beep, or a continuous beep, then a fault has been found. The number and duration of the beeps represent a code that denotes a particular fault. Manufacturers of the various BIOS chips will assign any given beep code to a different error, so in order to ascertain the exact fault the code should be looked up on a list of beep codes for that specific BIOS make and model wherever possible. This may be supplied with the motherboard documentation, or can often be found on the BIOS manufacturer's website.   For example, on some versions of AMI BIOS, two short beeps indicates a memory parity error, while on some versions of AST BIOS, the same code indicates a Keyboard controller failure,

POST Error Messages

If the POST is successful as far as being able to recognise and use a display adapter, then it can use that facility to output more easily recognisable error messages.   Individual error messages for various faults can vary between BIOS manufacturer and version.   Some older machines display a numeric code that should be looked up in a table of error codes like beep codes, while modern BIOS systems generally display a textual error.

Numeric error codes are organised into groups of related errors.   For example, the error codes from 100 to 199 (called the 1xx series) may indicate system board errors, while the 6xx series may cover floppy disk errors.   The errors range from older system problems (e.g. the 5xx series reports on CGA errors) to modern system errors (e.g. the 215xxxx series reports on SCSI CD-ROM errors).

If the computer fails to boot from the hard disk, it may display an error code from the 17xx series for ST506 systems, the 104xxx series for ESDI systems or the 210xxx series for SCSI systems.   If so, the error code indicates the area that requires attention.

Even when a text error message is displayed, there is commonly additional documentation available to help diagnose the exact nature of the fault, and this may well be in the motherboard manual.   The most common messages are:

'KEYBOARD FAILURE'

If the screen displays a keyboard failure message, the following may require to be checked:
- Is the keyboard plugged in, and attached to the correct port on the computer? (e.g. not in the mouse port instead of the keyboard port)
- Is keyboard of the correct type (e.g. an old XT keyboard is accidentally plugged into an AT machine, or perhaps a multi-purpose keyboard has its switch set to the old XT position instead of the AT position)?
- Are any of the keys jammed in the down position?
- Is the correct keyboard driver being used?

A more precise approach is possible if a keyboard error code is displayed.   These are in the 3xx series and cover stuck keys, keyboard cable faults and even displays whether a lockable keyboard has been left locked.   If in doubt, the keyboard can be temporarily replaced by a known working model.

'BOOT FAILURE'

Although technically not POST error messages, boot failure messages are displayed before the operating system or any other software loads up.   If the machine is unable to load the operating system it may produce one of the following messages:

Disk Boot Failure

This indicates corruption of the boot sector.   The disk may still be accessible by booting from floppy (e.g. in order to backup files) but the hard disk itself will not boot.   Depending on whether the boot sector is physically or logically corrupted, a reformat or even SYS command may fix this problem, or at worst the disk may be unsalvageable.   In some cases, a disk repair package such as Norton Disk Doctor or SCANDISK may be able to repair damaged boot sectors.   If a repair or reformat is performed, it will usually be necessary to backup important files before doing so, and restore the files once the disk is back in working order.

In extreme cases, the master boot record may be corrupt, and the only remedy may be to repartition the entire disk using FDISK.

Non-System disk or disk error

This often occurs when a user manages to delete the system hidden files IO.SYS and MSDOS.SYS.   If these are simply copied from another PC onto a floppy and placed in the machine's root directory, they will probably not be recognised by the boot system.   The hidden files must be the first two files in the directory, and their exact location on the hard disk is specified in the boot sector, so simply copying the files will not ensure that they are correctly placed. The SYS command will properly rectify this situation. Sometimes the error message may instead read *'Missing operating system',* and in the worst cases the system may freeze entirely with no error message at the point when it should begin loading the operating system.

Another possible cause is that the device is simply not responding properly, or at all.   This situation is identical to the *'No Boot Device'* error described immediately below.

No Boot Device

The device itself is not being detected. There are a host of possible causes. First, check that the BIOS settings match the drive settings. Most systems have an auto-detect feature and if even this fails to recognise your hard drive then the fault is in the hardware. Check the physical installation of the hard disk. If the disk uses a controller card, check that it is properly seated in the bus slot, and try a replacement card if possible. Ensure that the power and data cables are properly and securely connected to the unit. If necessary, make good any suspect connection and reboot and retest. On rare occasions the disk data cable may be broken; if there is a spare available try substituting it. Finally, if there is more than one drive fitted on an IDE cable then make sure the master/slave settings are compatible. Failing all these tests, the hard drive will need to be replaced.

Even if there is no boot failure message displayed, the problem may still lie in the boot device and the same steps should be taken as per those for the *'Disk Boot Failure'* message.

Failure To Boot From Floppy

Although most computers always boot up from the hard disk, there are occasions when the machine requires to be booted up from a system floppy disk. These might include running diagnostics software or booting from a known virus-free disk before carrying out virus checks on the machine. Also, if the machine fails to boot up from the hard disk, the machine will have to be booted from another device. This is most commonly a system floppy disk, to access the hard disk and diagnose its problem.

If the floppy drive is inoperable, it will be unable to carry out any of the above-mentioned tasks, and in the worst case it may be necessary to repair the floppy drive before the hard drive can be repaired.

The first thing to check is the boot disk itself. Ensure that it is indeed bootable, and that the disk capacity is not too high for the drive (e.g. A 2.8M boot disk will not work in a 1.4M drive). Where possible, use the disk to boot another machine, this will ensure that it is not corrupted and has the correct system files.

Although the BIOS holds floppy drive settings as well as hard drive settings, these are rarely incorrect and easily fixed through the setup procedure.

Check that the drive connections are seated firmly and reseat if necessary. Clean the floppy drive head using a proprietary head cleaner. Finally, check the drive calibration using a diagnostics disk; the drive head or motor speed may require to be re-calibrated.

If all of the above fail, the fault must lie in the drive itself or in the drive controller card. Substitution of the card or drive should indicate which component is to blame.

P.O.S.T. Card

If a fault in a machine is so fundamental that it cannot even produce a beep sound or error message, or if for some other reason beep codes are not of use in locating a hardware fault, then there is a lower level diagnostic method available. This is to insert a POST card into one of the machine's expansion slots.

The Power On Self Test card is a small expansion card that is used to help debug machines that appear to be "dead". During the earliest section of the POST process, the processor must ascertain that the major chips, like interrupt controllers, DMA controllers and the like are functioning. This part of the POST process is <u>before</u> the processor goes looking through address space for external adaptor cards, and so the video card cannot be used to output results. Therefore, another way is needed of letting the processor report on the testing process.

POST Address	Used by
060h	IBM XT
080h	AT/386/486/Pentium
084h	Compaq
090h	ISA PS/2
280h	Clones (Compaq/Dell)
300h	EISA bus systems

Fortunately, since the earliest days, the specification of the IBM PC and all it's derivatives allowed for a single location in I/O space where the status of the POST process should be put by the BIOS as it initialises. The POST card simply monitors the value held at that address, and displays it on a couple of seven-segment LED displays. Most post cards also have LEDS that show the status of the various power lines. Unfortunately the actual POST result address used differs from machine to machine, so before we can use a POST card we have to know what type of machine we are dealing with, and perhaps set the post card to the correct address.

Once this is done, we can insert the card into the machine, switch it on and observe the LEDs on the card. As the machine performs each self-test, the number displayed on the card increments. If it stops, then the BIOS has become stuck at that test and cannot continue. Looking up the result tells us which test was being undertaken, and therefore where the trouble is likely to be. Like beep codes, BIOS error codes vary by manufacturer and version. The results corresponding to each code are published by the BIOS manufacturers on their website, and a booklet of them is often supplied with the POST card.

The table below gives a representative sample of the POST codes generated by AMIBIOS V2.2X.

00	Flag Test	3C	CPU speed calculation	78	Display Configuration Error messages
03	Register Test	3F	Read 8742 hardware switches	7B	Copy system BIOS to shadow memory
06	System Hardware Initialisation	42	Initialise interrupt vector area	7E	8254 Clock test
09	ROM BIOS Checksum	45	Verify CMOS configuration	81	MC146818 Real Time clock test
0C	Page Register Test	48	Test and initialise video system	84	Keyboard test
0F	8245 timer chip test	4B	Unexpected interrupt test	87	Determine keyboard test
12	Memory refresh initialise	4E	Start second protected mode test	8A	Stuck key test
15	8237 DMA controller test	51	Verify LDT instruction	8D	Initialise hardware interrupt vector
18	8237 DMA controller initialise	54	Verify TR instruction	90	Maths coprocessor test
1B	8259 Interrupt controller initialise	57	Verify LSL instruction	93	Determine com ports available
1E	8259 Interrupt controller test	5A	Verify LAR instruction	96	Determine LPT ports available
21	Memory refresh test	5D	Verify VERR instruction	99	Initialise BIOS data area
24	Base 64k address test	60	Address line A20 test	9C	Fixed /floppy controller test
27	Base 64k memory test	63	Unexpected exception test	9F	Floppy disk test
2A	8742 keyboard self test	66	Start third protected mode test	A2	Fixed disk test
2D	MC146818 CMOS test	69	Address line test	A5	External ROM scan
30	Start first protected mode test	6C	System memory test	A8	System keylock test
33	Memory sizing test	6F	Shadow memory test	AE	F1 error message test
36	First Protected mode test	72	Extended memory test	AF	System boot initialisation
39	First Protected mode test failed	75	Verify memory configuration	B1	Interrupt 19 boot loader

Once it has been used diagnostically, the POST card is removed until it is next needed, although it can also be used as a diagnostic tool for programs. Poking values or status bytes into the appropriate location can mean not having to interrupt the flow of a program to see what is going on.

The POST card is usually also the quickest way of diagnosing a PC with a suspect video channel. Inexpensive POST cards are becoming widely available which are preset to the most popular I/O address (080x), however they are arriving at a time where nearly all of the "glue logic" is becoming integrated onto the LSI chipset. Thus if an interrupt controller error or DMA refresh error is thrown up by the POST card, it serves only to tell that motherboard itself must be replaced.

Software Diagnostics

A huge range of utility programs exists to aid the user or technician in maintaining the system in peak performance. Hundreds of commercial products exist with varying strengths and weaknesses. Some, like QEMM and PCKWIK are concerned with maximising the machine's performance. Others, like Sleuth and Checkit, are concerned with analysing and testing the system hardware. Some, like PC Tools and Norton Utilities, have elements of both testing and optimising. Of course, the programs have a large degree of overlap in terms of their functions. When the technician wishes to test out a system, one or more utility packages are probably available to him/her. Since, the commercial products will vary from company to company, only the general utilities can usefully be covered in this section.

Some problems are easily diagnosed; a disconnected cable or a missing system file are quickly spotted and corrected. Other problems are more difficult to diagnose. These include:

- o Not having enough memory to run a program.
- o Reduced or impaired efficiency of components - e.g. the disk caching efficiency, the performance of the disk drive (date transfer rate, fragmentation, corruption of disk surface, etc).
- o Experiencing conflicts between different programs.
- o Experiencing conflicts between the addresses and IRQs (hardware interrupts) of different cards (e.g. a newly-installed sound card refuses to work).
- o Problems with the size and location of video memory.
- o Being unable to adequately test the printer ports, communications ports, mouse, keyboard, etc.

The list of such problems can become large and the use of diagnostic software can save many hours of experimentation. Microsoft supplies some utilities and these are therefore readily available on every machine. Additionally, the support engineer should carry disks with diagnostic software.

DOS Diagnostics

The main disk diagnostic tool in earlier versions of DOS was the CHKDSK command. It is a useful program to highlight errors - as long as its limitations are borne in mind. CHKDSK compares the details in a file's Directory entry against the details for the file's FAT entry (see section on Disks and Drives). This ensures that no two files are using the same disk space, as held in the FAT. It also ensures that the size as recorded in the Directory entry is consistent with the actual amount of clusters devoted to it in the FAT. For example, a file with a size of 15k recorded in the directory entry should occupy 4 clusters (in a 4k cluster disk) or 30 clusters (in a single-sector cluster disk); any allocation that is larger or smaller than this is an error. If a problem is found, CHKDSK responds with a suitable error message such as *'Allocation Error'* or *'Cross-Linked Clusters'*. So, if CHKDSK finds a problem, then there is certainly something wrong with the disk. However, the converse is not true - the fact that CHKDSK may produce no error message cannot be taken as indicating that the disk is in good condition. That is because CHKDSK only concerns itself with files; it does not look at the condition of the rest of the disk surface. So, a damaged sector would not be found until a file had been saved to it. CHKDSK does not attempt to write and read back test data to all sectors of the disk; another utility would be required for that type of test.

DOS 6.2 contains the CHKDSK utility, but also introduced the more powerful program SCANDISK, which performs much the same function but more thoroughly. See the Disks chapter for more information on SCANDISK. DOS 6 and DOS 6.2 also introduced other diagnostic utilities, such as the following:

MSD

The Microsoft Diagnostics utility comprises two files, MSD.EXE and MSD.INI and is a MS-DOS-based program that is also supplied with Windows. It is designed to display diagnostic reports on a wide range of hardware and software items from a user-friendly front end.

The command's syntax is:

msd [/f <filename> or /p <filename> or /s <filename>]

Without any parameters, the user is asked to wait while the system is analysed. Then the diagnostics menu is displayed, providing a choice of various reports and other options. Choosing a button displays a window of information on that particular topic: Memory, Video, Network, Operating System, TSR programs, and so on. Where there is more than one screenful of information, the information can be scrolled through, using the keyboard or the scroll bars. This program can also generate reports to a file or to the printer.

SMARTMON

This utility first appeared in DOS version 6 and is a real-time monitor of the efficiency of the machine's Smartdrv settings. Giving the command SMARTDRV/S from the DOS prompt provides the raw figures on the number of cache hits (data obtained from memory) and cache misses (data obtained from the disk) and the user can calculate the cache efficiency from this information.

Smartmon was also available for Windows 3.1, but as VCACHE is used instead of SMARTDRV in Windows 95 onwards, this program is no longer in use in modern operating systems.

DEFRAG

Also bundled with DOS 6 is a disk defragmentation utility. This is called DEFRAG and is identical to the Speedisk utility from the Norton collection. This produces a report on the degree of fragmentation of files on the disk surface (see the chapter on Disks and Drives). The version used in Windows 95 onwards is called Disk Defragmenter.

Windows Diagnostics

Windows 95 and onwards operate very differently from DOS, demanding a new set of utilities to provide access to the same capabilities.

These include:

System Properties Utility

A number of new diagnostic features appeared with Windows 95. Choosing the *'System'* icon within *'Control Panel'* brings up the *'System Properties'* dialog, with four menu tab options.

The *'General'* option reports on the CPU type and operating system in use.

The *'Device Manager'* option displays a list of the hardware resources. Choosing *'Computer'* from the list and clicking the *'Properties'* button produces the screen shown.

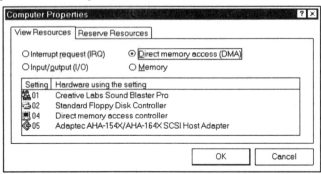

The example shows the DMA assignments in the computer and clicking other buttons will reveal how the IRQs, I/O addresses and memory are allocated.

All hardware devices used by the computer are displayed within Device Manager.

Highlighting an individual device, such as the mouse or monitor, and clicking the *'Properties'* button produces information on that device.

If the device is correctly configured and is functioning correctly, a

'This device is working properly'

message is displayed; otherwise a

'This device is not present, not working properly, or does not have all the drivers installed'

message is displayed.

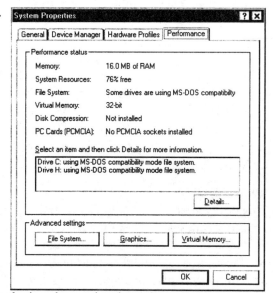

The *'Performance'* option allows the optimising of Graphics (i.e. hardware acceleration features), File System (i.e. CD-ROM speed and cache settings, disk drive read-ahead optimisation) and Virtual Memory (i.e. automatic or user-determined settings). Each of these reports on the current settings and allows them to be adjusted by the user. The example shown above has also detected that the computer disk system is not running at maximum efficiency due to some of the drives having only 16-bit drivers.

Registry Cleaner

Regclean.exe is a program supplied with Windows 95 and 98 that can remove apparently unused registry entries. This can increase the efficiency of the system, by reducing the size of the registry that is loaded at bootup, and also reducing the entries that take up memory.

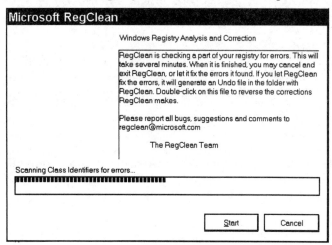

RegClean is not installed along with Windows as standard, although it is on the Windows installation disk.

When RegClean is run, it will remove what it believes to be unused registry entries. However, it can make mistakes and remove important information, so every time it runs it will create a .REG file containing the deleted registry entries. This file will be named according to the machine name and date, and the user may double click on the file to re-enter the registry entries if need be.

Windows 98 Utilities

Windows 98 provides the System Properties utility mentioned earlier. In addition, it introduced a range of very useful diagnostic tools that are available through the Start/Programs/Accessories/System Tools options.

Backup	Saves copies of important files to ensure against disk failure, viruses, etc. See the chapter on Disks.
Disk Cleanup	Recovers disk space by removing unwanted files from the Recycle Bin, Temporary Files folder and Temporary Internet (i.e. web cache) folder. Can be found in the Start/ Programs/Accessories /System Tools options of the Start menu.
Disk Defragmenter	Organises how files are stored on a disk to speed up file access. See the chapter on Disks.
FAT 32 Converter	Reduces the minimum space required to store small files, releasing unused disk space. See the chapter on Disks.
Drive Space	Compresses files so that more can be placed on a disk/drive. See the chapter on Disks.
Scandisk	Tests for any failures of the disk surface. See the chapter on Disks.
Maintenance Wizard	Combines Disk Cleanup, Disk Defragmenter and ScanDisk. See later.
Schedule Tasks	Start an application, or open a file, at a pre-defined interval. See later.
System Monitor	Detects system bottlenecks. See chapter on Windows Configuration.
System Information	Comprehensive reporting utilities. See later.

Maintenance Wizard

This utility allows the user to automate the running of the Disk Defragmenter, ScanDisk and Disk Cleanup tools.

It provides no extra utilities but it does allow the user to set the day and time when the three disk tools will be automatically run. Each tool can be configured to run on a different day or different time from the other tools. The *'Custom'* option also allows the choice of sub-options within ScanDisk and Disk Defragmenter (e.g. which disks to defragment, which drives to ScanDisk, which types of file to delete in Disk Cleanup).

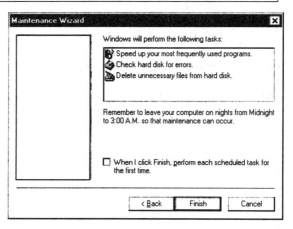

Schedule Tasks

This utility sets up a computer to run a particular application or set of applications at a pre-set day and time.

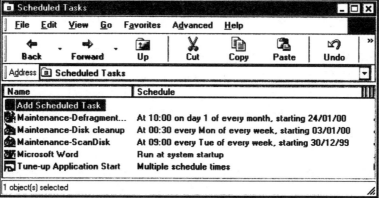

When the *'Add Scheduled Task'* bar is clicked, the utility lists all the applications on the computer and one can be selected.

The user then has comprehensive choices on whether the application is run:

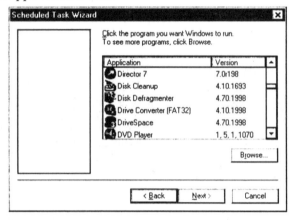

- On a periodic basis. This could be daily, weekly, or monthly. For weekly and monthly options, the user chooses which day of the week/month. All options include the setting the time when the application will run. An example use would be for interrupting the user's activities to run a backup.
- Each time the computer is booted up. This would be useful where a particular computer is used mainly for a single purpose. The computer could be set up to always boot up into a word processor, for example. Since more than one application appears in the list, the computer can be set up to run several applications when switched - e.g. word processor, spreadsheet, fax software, etc.

In the example on the previous page, the computer has been set up for
- A monthly defragmentation.
- A monthly disk cleanup.
- A weekly scan of the disk surface.
- The automatic running of Microsoft Word when the computer is booted up.

System Monitor

This utility was described in the chapter on Windows Configuration. It can also be used as a maintenance tool to check the efficient working of the system components such as swap file, memory, disk caching, etc.

System Information

This utility offers a wide range of system hardware and software testing tools. The opening window is as shown. Choosing *'Hardware Resources'* offers reports on the machine's use of IRQs, DMA channels,

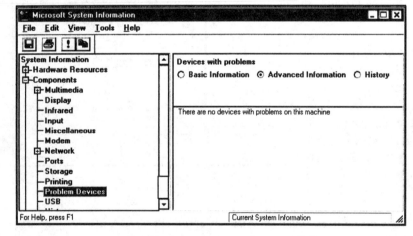

I/O ports, etc. It also reports on any hardware conflicts or any software sharing violations that it detects. These tools are useful for diagnostic purposes and they can also be used when installing new devices.

The example shows the use of *'Problem Devices'* in the *'Components'* category. This shows that the computer being examined has no detected problems with the devices attached to it.

The *'Tools'* drop-down menu provides a further set of utilities, as outlined below.

Registry Checker

The Registry used by Windows 98 is the same as that used by Windows 95. Each time the computer is booted up, the Registry Checker tests for possible corruption to the Registry files and backs up the Registry if it is found to be error-free. If an error is found, the backed up version is restored. The user can also run the utility from the *'Tools'* menu at any time, if a problem is suspected.

System File Checker

The utility scans the computer's system files (i.e. the DLL, COM, VXD, DRV, OCX and other files), checking for any that are corrupted, modified or deleted. If an error is found, the user can re-install the original version from the original installation .CAB files. If the installation of an application program results in a particular system file being overwritten by an older version supplied with the application, this modification is noted and reported during the file checking process.

System Configuration

The System Configuration Utility provides user control over the configuration of the computer when it is booted up. This is very useful when the computer is experiencing setup problems, as it allows user control over which components from the setup script files are installed during bootup.

The utility provides six tabs as shown.

The *'General'* tab offers three bootup options:

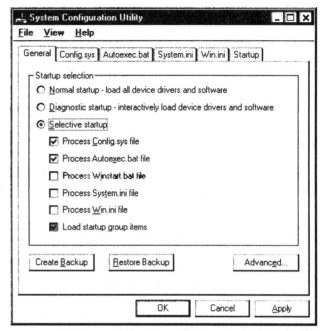

- Normal Startup   this is the normal setup
- Diagnostic Startup   provides a screen offering DOS Mode, Safe Mode, etc.
- Selective Startup   provides control over which files are loaded at startup.

Using Selective Startup

The Config.sys, Autoexec.bat and Winstart.bat (if using real mode networking) files provide real mode drivers while the other files provide protected mode drivers.

If a box is greyed out (as Winstart.bat is in the example), it indicates that the file is empty or is missing.

A likely use of the Selective Startup option for diagnostic purposes is as follows:

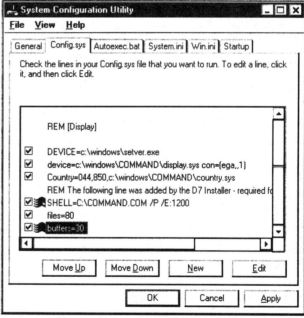

- Check only the *'Process Config.sys'* and *'Process Autoexec.bat'* boxes, as shown in the illustration.
- Click the *'OK'* button and restart the computer.
- If the computer displays any problems during startup, the problem must lie in one of these two script files. See the section on *'Script Line Selection'* for details on the next steps.
- If the computer successfully boots up, the *'Selective Startup'* settings can be altered to include the protected mode drivers (i.e. the System.ini, Win.ini and Startup Group Items files).
- Click the *'OK'* button and restart the computer.
- If the computer displays any problems during startup, the problem must lie in one of these script files. See the section on *'Script Line Selection'* for details on the next steps.

Script Line Selection

When a particular script file is identified as the one producing the error during startup, the individual lines within that file can be selected for, or deselected from, the boot process.

Clicking on a tab (e.g. Config.sys, System.ini, etc) results in a listing of all the lines in that particular script and each line can be chosen by clicking its selection box.

The selection and boot process can continue until the problem device is identified.

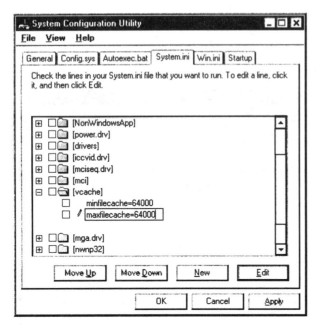

Altering Values

The example on the left shows the *'System.ini'* tab displaying a list of the drivers that are installed on bootup.

Clicking on the left-most box displays the script lines used for that section.

If a line is highlighted and the *'Edit'* button is pressed, the user is able to alter the contents of that line.

In the example, the value of the *'maxfilecache'* component is being altered.   In most cases, the altered values do not come into effect until the computer is rebooted.

Troubleshooters

Windows 95 and 98 provide a range of specialised help guides to aid users with common problems.

These are accessed through the *'Troubleshooting'* option shown when the *'Content'* tab is selected from the *'Help'* facility accessed through the *'Start'* button.

These provide aids to understanding and troubleshooting problems in the following areas:

Dial-up networking	Modem	Startup
Direct Cable Connection	MS-DOS programs	The Microsoft Network
Drive Space	Networking	Direct X *
Hardware conflicts	PC card	Display *
Memory	Printing	Sound *

The last three troubleshooters (those marked with an asterisk) are not available in Windows 95.

Windows Millenium Edition

Windows ME includes some new utilities for system support, probably the most widely reported of which is the *System Restore* function. This enables the user (or the support staff) to save a *'report'* of the current system setup to disk. This is essentially a snapshot of the device drivers, settings, registry entries and so on that are in effect at that time. If changes are made to these settings which result in reduced performance or even PC failure, then the machine can be rolled back to a previous state by restoring the information in one of these reports. While this can take up a non-trivial amount of disk space, and requires some time to maintain, it can be invaluable in a support situation, as it can drastically reduce down time.

Other Support Utilities

Each newer version of Windows provides more comprehensive diagnostic and repair tools. Although these are useful, a whole range of utility software is available, which greatly extends the tools supplied with DOS and Windows.

Uninstallers

In the early days, installing a program involved placing all the files for the program in a single directory. Removing the program was achieved by deleting the directory and its contents.   With Windows applications, the installation process may scatter the application's files over many directories.   Several applications may also share the same program fragments (DLLs, VxDs, etc).   This means that uninstalling is a difficult process.   Windows 95/98/2000 have their own uninstall software, reached through *'Control Panel'* and *'Add/Remove Programs'*.   However, add-on programs do a more thorough uninstall.

Uninstaller software aids the removal of programs and can use two methods.
- When the uninstaller program is installed on the computer, it notes all the disk's current files. When an application is installed, the uninstaller software makes another record of the disk's files and detects the alterations. It knows what extra files were added and where they were stored, simplifying their later removal.
- The uninstaller software may also contain a database describing all the expected components that are associated with a particular application. It can then look for these components and delete them.

Uninstall facilities are provided by Norton Uninstall, CleanSweep, WinDelete and Uninstaller 5.

Disk Housekeeping

The range of utilities designed to manage files and folders include:

PARTITIONING

The chapter on Disks & Drives explained how partitions operate. The creation and modification of partitions under DOS/Windows results in the destruction of existing data on the disk. Tools such as Partition Magic and Partition-It allow the creation and merging of partitions without the loss of data.

DUPLICATE FILES

Over a period, copies of the same file will be stored in different directories of the computer's hard disk(s). This wastes disk space and confuses the user (e.g. which file is the most current). Utilities can detect and delete duplicate files or files that have not been accessed for a long time. Examples of this software are CleanSweep and Norton Utilities.

COMPRESSION

File compression was explained in the chapter on Disks & Drives. Utilities for handling compressed files include PKZip, WinZip, TurboZip, ZipMagic and PKLite. DriveSpace compresses drives.

SOFTWARE UPGRADES

No software is perfect and there are constant issues of upgrades, patches, fixes and new drivers. For large organisations with many different applications, keeping a watch for changes is time-consuming. Oil Change is a piece of software that checks out a machine, noting all its software and version numbers. It also has a large database of all current add-ons, updates, etc, on its own Internet site. The software checks the user's database against its own database and can either update the computer's software automatically or under user control. The *'Versions'* web site at http://www.versions.com offers a cheaper manual update system.

Disk & File Protection

BACKUP TOOLS

The standard backup facilities provided within Windows are often sufficient for everyday needs. Other utilities offer added facilities such as saving files in compressed format, encrypting files as they are backed up, testing each file for viruses before backing up, etc. An example program is NovaBackup.

VIRUS SCANNERS

The problems are outlined in the chapter on viruses. A large range of commercial, shareware and freeware products are available to detect and eliminate viruses. Examples of these products are Dr Solomon's Antivirus, Norton Anti-Virus and McAfee VirusScan.

MACHINE ACCESS

Sophisticated systems for preventing unauthorised access to computers, or allowing different users access to different parts of the disk directory are standard in machines running local area network operating systems. Products such as Bootlock and Winlock, enhance security on standalone computers.

DISK IMAGE

While backup tools are essential for the safety of data files, a serious disk crash could result in Windows and all applications having to be reinstalled and customised again. Software utilities allow the entire image of the disk to be copied to removable media (e.g. CD-R, JAZ drive) or the network server, so that the original drive contents can be reinstalled to a disk in a single operation. Examples of this software are Drive Image, Norton Ghost and Quarterdecks' Diskclone.

APPLICATION REPAIRS

Over time, many pieces of software may be added and deleted from a hard disk. If software is badly written, badly installed or badly uninstalled, fragments may not be added/removed. This may cause programs to run erratically. Additionally, shortcuts to programs may not be installed or shortcuts may be left behind when applications are removed. Cleanup utilities remove abandoned fragments and ensure that all application links are working and relevant. An example utility is First Aid DeLuxe.

DATA ENCRYPTION/DECRYPTION

Many data files store sensitive commercial information that should not be readily readable, particularly if the file is to be transmitted over a network. The solution is encrypting (scrambling) files before storing or transmitting them. The person reading that file has to apply a 'key' to decrypt (unscramble) them. Examples of this software are McAfee PGP, Nuts and Bolts, Stoplock and DataSafe.

System Tools

CRASH PROTECTION

Poor memory sharing between applications, corrupted system files and a range of other problems can cause a computer to hang up. Windows users often have a number of applications or application fragments open at the same time. For example, Word and Excel may both be open, Word processing activities may be carrying on while a file is printing or saving, and so on. When crashes occur, software such as CrashGuard and RealHelp limit the problem to the offending application. This allows files from other applications to be saved.

REGISTRY

The chapter on Windows configuration covered the workings of the Registry and Microsoft's own tools for maintaining and repairing the registry. Registry utilities tend to be in two categories:

- Tools that make backups of the registry for use in restoring corrupted versions. Examples are WinRescue and Rescue Me!.
- Tools that examine the existing registry and make amendments and/or repairs. Examples are First Aid, Norton Utilities and Nuts and Bolts. Windows 98 provides Registry Checker.

EMERGENCY RECOVERY

Crash recovery tools include RealHelp.

DUAL BOOT

Users may wish to have more than one operating system on their computer, with a choice being offered at bootup. System Commander and Upgrade 98 both allow several operating systems to co-exist. For example, a user may wish Windows 95 and Windows 98, or Windows 98 and Unix, etc.

DIAGNOSTIC/REPAIR TOOLS

Many faults on computers can be either hardware problems or software configuration problems. The technician's most important tool is the set of utilities that check and report on the computer's hardware components. Finding faults without such utilities is possible but is much slower. These programs are used for a variety of purposes:

- Hardware testing (e.g. checking memory, printer and serial ports, etc)
- Hardware Performance (checking the working speed of the disk controller, video card, serial port, etc)
- Performance Tweaking (suggesting changes that would improve performance - e.g. swap file size, etc)

The diagram shows the range of hardware and configuration options that can be tested with the WinCheckit utility.

Other very informative packages are First Aid, Nuts & Bolts, Norton Utilities, PC-Check, SiSoft Sandra and WinProbe.

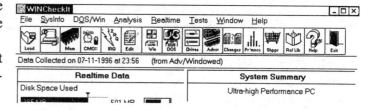

Note:

Often, utility packages carry out many functions. It is common for these products to have virus checking, system checking, disk housekeeping, etc marketed under a single brand name. An examination of their specifications will allow the user to choose the package most appropriate to his/her needs.

Internet Tools

Internet browser add-ons provide a range of filters to prevent unwanted material being downloaded. These may be for reasons of:

- Censorship (e.g. preventing access to porn sites). Users of a computer can be prevented from accessing sites that appear on a database or are user entered. Examples are Net Nanny and Guard Dog.
- Financial saving (e.g. saving connect time downloading junk mail).
- Speed (e.g. saving waiting while adverts and banners are downloaded).

Additional features may include removing Internet 'cookies' and emptying the Internet cache.

Common Faults

Every PC fault is different, and a fully comprehensive list of potential failures in the various components and their resolution could easily fill several volumes. However, there are certain types of faults that occur more frequently than others, and the following is a guide to some of the more typical symptoms found on PCs, and the most common culprits.

User Errors

The great bulk of faults reported to help desks are based on a simple misunderstanding or mistake on the part of the computer user. The user is part of the system, and a poorly trained user will almost certainly report more faults than a well-trained one.

Problems reported as faulty devices might in fact turn out to be devices which are unplugged, not switched on, or unconnected. Software 'bugs' can turn out to be misuse of software or misconceptions about what the software can do.

And of course, users can be the source of most forms of real faults. Many users have spilled coffee or correction fluid over keyboards, some have jammed floppy drives with disks inserted incorrectly, and installation of unauthorised software such as games onto business PCs can result in reduced performance or even virus infection. It may be of use to identify those users who are less 'computer literate' and may require a short training course in how to use their equipment properly.

Power Problems

When the machine is first switched on, the main unit and the monitor should both be powered up. This should result in some form of screen output. This might be the result of the computer self-test or the normal Windows or other operating system screen.

If no video output is apparent, it would be wise to give the machine another hard boot, before carrying out the rest of the checks, since this could be caused by a minor, temporary glitch of some kind.

No Lights/Fan

If there is still no video output, check whether the lights on the front of the computer are lit and whether there is any noise from the computer's disk drive or fan. If there are no lights or motor noises, check that the computer is switched on, attached to a mains supply and that the mains socket is switched on.

If necessary, make good any shortcomings and check whether the computer now shows signs of life. If the computer appears active, restart the system and test again. If the computer remains lifeless, there is a problem with the machine's supply. This might be as simple as a blown fuse or a broken wire inside the mains cable – if so try another as a temporary replacement. Or it may be a blown fuse internal to the machine – if there is no company maintenance engineer, you know what you are doing and you obey all safety precautions, this can be examined. If not then it might indicate that the computer's internal power unit has failed, so the engineer should be called out. It's also worth trying plugging the unit into another mains socket, just in case the wall socket itself is faulty.

Lights And Fan But No Hard Disk Spin Up

In this situation, the problem is that the motherboard is not receiving a *'Power Good'* signal from the power supply. The Power Good line is a wire on the motherboard power connector that is used by the PSU to signal when it is safe for the PC to begin booting. If the Power Good signal is not received, it has the same effect as holding down the reset button permanently – the POST will not begin, and the hard drive will not initialise.

This could be caused by the PSU failing to stabilise the power supply for safe PC operation, or it could simply be a fault in the Power Good line, but either way the PSU should be replaced or sent to a competent electrical engineer.

Monitor Problems

If the PC's lights are on, the fan is working, any hard drives are initialising and there is the single beep that indicates the unit has passed the POST test, then the PC should be functional. If however there is still no display, there remains the possibility of a problem with the monitor, its hardware and software drivers or its connections.

First, check that the mains indicator on the monitor is lit. If the indicator is unlit, then in similar fashion to the computer, check that the monitor is switched on, attached to a mains supply and that the main socket is switched on.   Remember, in some cases, the monitor receives its mains supply from a cable attached to a rear socket on the computer, while other monitors have their own independent mains connections. In addition, check that the computer and monitor units are connected together - i.e. the video cable from the monitor is plugged into the video output socket of the computer. Furthermore, check that the connectors have no bent pins. (This is not technically a power supply problem, but many energy saving monitors will not power up if there is no signal.)   If necessary, make good any shortcomings and check whether the monitor now shows signs of life.

If the monitor remains lifeless, there is a problem with the unit's supply. As with the PC power supply, this might be caused by a blown fuse in the cable, a blown fuse inside the monitor, or an internal power failure. The solutions are also similar.

If the monitor power light is on but the screen does not display any output, it may simply be that the monitor is in need of adjustment.   Ensure that the brightness and contrast controls are at the correct settings; if in doubt, a mid-point setting should provide a viewable screen from which to make the necessary adjustments.

If the monitor fails to respond to adjustments, then the unit ought to be replaced by a known working model.   If the monitor still shows no video, then the computer's video card must be faulty.   If the monitor now displays an output, then the original monitor is faulty and should be repaired.

Video Quality Problems

If a monitor produces a display that is of poor quality, it may be due to a number of problems, either in the monitor itself, in the computer's video card, or in the interface and compatibility between the two.

Display Drivers

These are the pieces of software that are used to ensure the correct interface between the monitor, the video card and even particular application programs.   For instance, Windows provides a set of drivers to match itself to most screen standards and most graphics cards.   Check that the correct driver is in use; a 1024x768 SVGA driver will not display properly on a normal VGA monitor, for example.

In addition to the actual device driver, there may be additional video software, such as Microsoft DirectX, or OpenGL drivers. This particularly applies to video cards optimised for 3D acceleration. Incorrectly configured or out-of-date drivers of these types rarely cause problems with the normal display, but could seriously affect the 3D performance of the card. If this occurs, make sure the device driver and 3D system drivers are installed, up to date, and not corrupted. Failing that, the software may simply be not fully compatible with that type of 3D interface or card – always check the software manual where 3D software is concerned.

Monitor Adjustments

If the computer systems worked previously and there has been no alteration to the driver, the monitor may have gone out of adjustment.   Monitor adjustments are covered in the section on Video but might include adjusting the brightness, contrast, hue, horizontal or vertical position, the horizontal or vertical size, convergence, pincushion or horizontal or vertical locks.   Do not attempt internal adjustments unless you know what you are doing and observe all safety precautions.

> Remember that a monitor has high voltages on some of its components -
> ranging up to around 30,000 volts!

If adjustments do not cure the problem, try temporarily replacing the suspect monitor with a known working model. If the computer now displays properly, the original monitor was obviously faulty.

If the replacement monitor will not work either, the computer's video card is faulty. As a double check, attach the monitor that you removed from the affected machine on to another working computer; the monitor should work happily on the new machine.

If the text characters on the screen flicker or are corrupted then this is probably bad memory chips on the video card; try another video card.

Reinstalling Windows

Sometimes it is necessary to completely replace an existing installation of Windows, whatever version it may be. There may be corruption of essential files, or a fault in a DLL that is too difficult to trace. It may be changing hands and require complete eradication of any data that is potentially sensitive. Or perhaps the system is simply becoming sluggish due to the number of files, registry entries and so on that have been added by software that is no longer in use.

In any case, installation procedures of the various versions of windows may look different, but the basic steps are the same.

1) The very first step is to ensure that all the necessary files are available. This means any drivers that are needed, as well as the Windows CD itself, and a boot disk that can access the Windows CD. Some systems are supplied with such disks, and Windows 98 can create system disks that will access almost all CD-ROM types. However, in some cases it might be necessary to manually create a boot disk with the correct files and settings. Software that is to be installed should also be available.

2) Next, backup any important data. Even if the machine is not to be completely overhauled, this is a good point to backup, as it is possible that data could be changed or deleted during a re-installation. User files are not always the only data that should be backed up; there may be email messages, browser bookmarks, program settings, and so on, all of which could be vital.

3) Now, the technician must decide whether to simply reinstall windows over the existing version, hopefully maintaining existing programs and data, or whether to reformat the hard disk and start over from scratch.

   Reinstallation over an existing copy of Windows (sometimes called an '*overlay*' installation) has the obvious advantage of keeping any user files. However, this type of installation will not always solve the problems of bugs in DLL files, nor will it remove any files or registry entries that are slowing the system down. A full, 'clean' install is the only way to be sure to eradicate all such problems: this will necessitate formatting of the C: drive, perhaps from a boot disk.

4) Next, a way must be found to gain access to the installation procedure. In most modern PCs, this will mean changing the BIOS settings so that the PC will boot from the Windows CD-ROM. However, in some older PCs, or with older versions of Windows, it may be necessary to use a boot disk that includes an appropriate CD-ROM driver in order to access the Setup on the Windows CD. Of course, in an overlay install the machine will still have access to the CD as normal.

5) The actual installation procedure is relatively straightforward. It involves an automatic scan of the hard disk for errors, followed by a series of setup dialogs that will determine how Windows works. These include dialogs to select Windows components for installation, set user information, and select the region the computer is to be used in, amongst others. (See the *Configuring Windows* chapter for more information on the installation sequence) Windows will then begin installing. In the case of an overlay install, Windows may notice system files that have been updated, and will ask the user if these should be restored to the default Windows version. In most cases the newer version that is currently on the disk should be kept, except when it is suspected that these are the files that are causing problems.

6) After installation, the drivers, software and user files should be restored in their previous locations.

Health And Safety

There are many hazards to employees in the workplace; these are not confined to the 'dangerous' jobs such as mining, construction or heavy engineering. Every day, employees suffer accidents at work or slowly impair their health by their work practices.

The Health and Safety at Work Act came into force in 1975 and acts as the basis for safety law in the UK.   It provides a legal framework outlining the responsibilities of both employers and employees, overseen by the Health and Safety Executive.   Any employer with more than five employees is obliged under the Act (Section 2(3)) to maintain a written policy on health and safety, open to view by all employees.   The Act is a complex 117 page document and only the main points are covered in this section.

Other related measures, standards and recommendations are:

- The Office, Shops and Railway Premises Act of 1983.
- BS6266 - Fire Protection for Electronic Data Processing Installations.
- The Illuminating Engineering Society's (IES) recommendations on lighting standards, titled *'Code of Practice for Interior Lighting'.*
- The Fire Precautions Act 1971.
- The IEEE Wiring Regulations.
- The Health and Safety (First Aid) Regulations 1981.
- The Sex Discrimination Act 1986.
- The Race Relations Act.
- HSE pamphlet 23 - *"Hours of employment of women and young persons".*
- HSE pamphlet 36 - *"Working with VDUs".*
- BS7179 and ISO9241 standards on monitor image quality.
- The EEC Directive 90/270 on VDU radiation levels.

Before acting upon any information in this section, the appropriate material should be fully read over. As far as the computing environment is concerned, healthy surroundings are in the interests of all.   A smoky, dusty, damp or cold working environment is against the interests of the people who have to work there and is also damaging to the machines and their data.   In addition, the loss of skilled staff through ill health is not in the interests of anyone; employees lose out physically and the company loses out in loss of output.   Implementing the legislation should not be viewed as a penalty but as an investment to retain and expand productivity with a more contented staff.

PC Support health and safety issues can be roughly divided into two:

- Those that are general to all offices - e.g. heating, lighting, working space, fire hazards, working ergonomics, etc.
- Those more peculiar to computer environments - keyboard injuries, damage from monitors, harmful ozone from laser printers, etc.

Note

It is not the job of the PC support technician to sort out the health and safety problems that he/she encounters.   The law ensures that proper machinery is in place with office safety representatives and probably safety committees.   However, it would be the responsibility of the technician, both legally and morally, to ensure that any situations that break the law - unintentionally or otherwise - are reported to management or safety representatives.

Some of the more common problems to be encountered are:

General

- Are work areas kept clean and tidy? Are waste bins emptied at least once a day?
- Are work areas overcrowded?   Is there the legal minimum of 11 cubic metres of space being provided per employee (with any roof area above 3m in height being excluded from the calculation)?   Are these area allocations compromised by excessive furniture, storage boxes, equipment, etc.?
- Is the working environment satisfactory? Is it properly lit to prevent eyestrain, headaches or accidents?
- Is the workplace properly ventilated to prevent headaches and sinus problems?   (see HSE Guidance Note EH22 on Ventilation of Buildings).
- Are there excesses of temperature (i.e. not less than 60°F after the first hour and not exceeding 72°F)?
- Is the working environment excessively noisy? The 1972 Department of Employment *'Code of Practice for Reducing the Exposure of Employed Persons to Noise'* stipulates 90db(A) as the maximum steady exposure to noise for an eight-hour day or 40 hour week.   For an office environment, a maximum figure of 60db(A) should be aimed for; conversations should be able to be conducted at a normal level.
- Is the furniture laid out to provide the best ergonomic conditions and reduce backache, neckache, etc.?
- Is welfare accommodation satisfactory? Are there sufficient suitable sanitary conveniences, washing facilities (see Section 9 of the Office, Shops and Railway Premises Act) and places for keeping clothes (see the HSE booklet 10 - "Cloakroom Accommodation and Working Facilities 1980)?

- Are there adequate canteen facilities? See the Department of Employment's Health and Safety at Work booklet 2.
- Are the floors, passageways and stairs safe? Are floor coverings well maintained?   Are areas of movement free from obstruction and slippery substances?
- Are all electrical installations in safe condition? Are appliances checked regularly?
- Are the fire precautions adequate? Are all the fire exits in working order and free from obstructions? Are all flammable materials safely stored? Are fire alarms regularly tested? Does the building have a fire certificate? (required where a building houses more than 20 employees or where ten employees work above or below ground floor level)
- Are there adequate first-aid facilities? Are employees trained in first-aid techniques?
- Is there job design to minimise occupational stress?   Has attention been paid to job rotation, job enrichment, staff training, removing job isolation, adjusting supervision levels, improving internal communication, providing adequate rest breaks and workplace creches, having clearly defined standards for employee/client communications?

Computer-Related

All of the earlier questions on general office environments also apply to computer environments and can have a detrimental effect on staff and output.   In addition, there are other hazards that are encountered by computer users compared to other office staff.

VDU Hazards

This issue is fully dealt with in the chapter on display technology.

RSI

The general points on ergonomics are also covered in the chapter on computer video.   However, a serious problem affects workers who are employed on prolonged keyboard work, particularly fast data entry work.   This can cause discomfort, pain or even crippling disability.   These symptoms are caused by the swelling and toughening of the muscles at the base of the wrist.   The muscles eventually become so thick that they press on the nerves that pass through the wrist.   The hand and wrist can become weakened to the point of irreversible damage.   This is known as *'repetitive strain injury'* and it is important that the symptoms are spotted at an early stage.   If diagnosed early enough, the damage can be arrested by means such as job rotation with non-repetitive tasks, reducing the work rate, introducing more work breaks or moving the employee to another job.   Surgery has also proved successful with RSI cases when detected before it has reached an irreversible stage.

Reporting Problems

It is best if a working relationship is established in advance with the organisation's safety representatives and the company employee charged with responsibility for health and safety matters.   If the lines of communication are clearly understood in advance, it will reduce any tensions arising from any deficiencies that are reported.   Since the PC support staff are among the few employees who move around the entire building, they are the most likely to get soundings of employee complaints and problems.   Ideally, a report form should be devised and accepted as the standard method of notifying any potential or actual health and safety problem.

Getting The Full Facts

For a more full account of safety regulations, contact:

> The Health and Safety Executive
> Baynards House
> 1 Chepstow Place
> London W2 4TE
> Tel 0181-243-6000

who can supply the *"Essentials of Health and Safety at Work"* and a range of other such material.   Many titles are free and they supply a twice-yearly list entitled *"Publications in Series"* which can be purchased at HSE centres or at bookshops that stock HMSO titles.   Many of the free pamphlets can be obtained directly from the regional offices of the HSE (see phone book).

Upgrading a computer

Upgrading a computer consists of altering or adding to its component parts, so that the overall system is improved. This improvement may be one of speed or it may be one of added functionality. In some cases, this upgrade can be achieved by external add-ons, or it may result from additions or alterations inside the computer case itself. An example of an external improvement would be the fitting of an external modem or mouse, while an internal upgrade would be adding extra memory or a sound card. The upgrade process would usually consist of the following stages:

- SELECTION
- SAFETY/HANDLING
- COMPATIBILITY
- FITTING
- TESTING
- DOCUMENTING

Selection Issues

The technician has to know the best component to fit for a particular situation. An example would be knowing the required specification for a video output card. There would be no point in buying an AGP card if the machine only had a PCI expansion slot, for example. It is also important to check that the new card can be installed without any interrupt clashes, DMA clashes or I/O address clashes (see later). This would probably involve checking that the add-on card allowed for a range of different settings to be chosen, or is a plug-and-play type. Incorrect selection could lead to poor performance or the failure of the system to operate. These issues should be investigated and settled before the purchase of the item.

Compatibility Issues

The technician has to ensure that the equipment intended for adding to the computer is fully compatible with the existing system. This may involve physical, electronic and software considerations. A technical specification may indicate that a card is satisfactory for a particular purpose but other factors may come into play. For example, the new device may be a full-length card but the computer may only have a half-length expansion slot left unused.

The following guidelines should prove useful:

- Check that the computer will work in the planned operating environment (e.g. is the temperature too high or too low, is the humidity too great, is the computer to be located close to sources of electrical interference such as machinery, does the site suffer from mains noise requiring the fitting of a mains filter, etc). Check the computer's specification for the temperature and humidity tolerances.
- Always read the instructions before carrying out any activity; don't hurry into the upgrade.
- Before installing any equipment, carry out a dry run to ensure that there is adequate space to house the equipment (e.g. a spare expansion slot if fitting a card or a spare bay if fitting a drive).
- The dry run should also check that all the necessary leads have sufficient connectors and will stretch to connect to the new equipment. This may include control/data cables from the disk controller, connector cable from a SCSI card, audio lead to a sound card, etc. It would certainly include making sure that there was a spare power lead on the power supply's cable loom and that the connection would reach to the new equipment. If there is no spare connection, a 'Y' connector can be bought. This involves removing a lead from an existing piece of equipment and inserting it into the Y connector. This connector has two outputs - one to go to the original piece of equipment and one for the new apparatus to be installed.
- Check that the card's IRQs, DMA channels and I/O address locations do not clash with any existing card in the machine. If necessary, consult the manuals of the other cards. If there is any clash, set the jumpers on the new card to avoid any collision. Plug and play cards, along with Window's PCI Bus IRQ Steering, should minimise this problem.
- Always test the new equipment - both its hardware and any software; do not assume that it must be working. Remember that some problems may be immediately obvious while others, such as intermittent clashes of interrupts, may only lead to system crashes on a sporadic basis.

Safety/Handling Procedures

There are a number of general safety, handling and organisational procedures that should be observed when tackling any upgrade. These are designed to both protect the technician and safeguard the equipment. They should become second nature to the support technician and are as follows:

- Always use the correct tools for the job.
- Do not work inside the machine with the power connected.

- Always wear an earthing strap when handling boards and equipment. Use a proper earthing strap with a built-in 1Mohm resistor. Do not make up a simple connection between wrist and earth, as this can prove fatal if a live connection is accidentally touched.
- If any internal connectors are temporarily removed, record which socket they were removed from and note the orientation of the plug in that socket.
- Do not remove the add-on card from its anti-static protection until it is actually required.
- Avoid excessive handling of the card; hold the card by an edge that has little or no etched tracks.
- When installing the card, ensure that the edge connector is properly lined up with the expansion socket.
- Avoid excessive force in installing the card; gently rocking the card from edge to edge with a firm pressure is sufficient. If the card is hard to fit, check that there is no other problem such as an obstruction or a misalignment of the card with the slot.
- Avoid excessive force in plugging in connectors to the card. If the plug is hard to fit, check that there is no other problem such as an obstruction or a reversal of the plug.
- Ensure that the card is securely screwed to the computer chassis. The screw used to secure the blanking plate is used for this purpose.

Practical IRQ Considerations

Early computers only had ISA expansion slots for fitting additional cards. Modern motherboards only provide PCI expansion slots. Each IRQ number corresponds to a physical hardware line - e.g. an activity from a mouse connection or a modem connection. Each IRQ line is allocated to an interrupt number that links to the corresponding routine for handling that device. So, for example, a mouse might be attached to the COM1 port, which is IRQ1. Any mouse movement will trigger the IRQ1 interrupt and this will call the mouse handling routine. When the user installed the mouse driver, the routine was placed in memory and the address of the routine was placed in the interrupt vector table.

Sharing IRQs

It follows that only one routine can be linked to a single IRQ number at any one time. It is possible to have to two or more add-on cards or devices set up with the same IRQ number, as long as they are not used simultaneously. If two devices have the same IRQ setting and both attempt to invoke a call at the same time unpredictable results can be expected, since only one device handler is in memory. Devices, such as a scanner and a modem are unlikely to ever be required at the same time. In this case, the two cards can both have IRQ settings at the same IRQ number. From Windows 95 Release 2 onwards, Windows has the ability to handle multiple PCI devices with the same IRQ - and this is known as *"PCI Bus IRQ Steering"*.

If possible, every card should use a different IRQ setting. This is possible in a computer with few add-ons but conflicts become more likely as more and more adapter cards are added to a system.

Choosing an IRQ

When a new device is to be added to the system, its IRQ requirement must not clash with any existing IRQ requirements of cards already fitted to the system. Add-on cards allow some alteration of their IRQ settings, through the adjustment of jumpers or switches or through software setting. The documentation that accompanies the card will give details of the default IRQ setting and the other settings that it can adopt. Sometimes, there are only a few alternatives while other cards offer a range of 8 alternative IRQ settings to allow the greatest opportunity for fitting the card without interrupt clashes.

The first stage would be to check the usage of the IRQs within the existing system. The *'Properties'* option within Windows 95/98/ME Device Manager can be used for this purpose.

The table shows the result of the IRQ display option of Microsoft's own MSD utility. The display will vary with differing machine hardware configurations but most IRQ assignments will be similar.

```
IRQ   Address      Description       Detected     Handled By
---   ---------    ---------------   ----------   ----------------
 0    0566:00D2    Timer Click       Yes          MOUSE
 1    CF01:1923    Keyboard          Yes              Block Device
 2    F000:EA97    Second 8259A      Yes          BIOS
 3    F000:EA97    COM2: COM4:       COM2:        BIOS
 4    0566:02CD    COM1: COM3:       COM1:        Logitech Serial MOUSE
 5    F000:EA97    LPT2:             No           BIOS
 6    F000:EF57    Floppy Disk       Yes          BIOS
 7    0070:06F4    LPT1:             Yes          System Area
 8    F000:EA42    Real-Time Clock   Yes          BIOS
 9    F000:EECF    Redirected IRQ2   Yes          BIOS
10    F000:EA97    (Reserved)                     BIOS
11    C94C:091F    (Reserved)                     SCSIMGR$
12    F000:EA97    (Reserved)                     BIOS
13    F000:EED8    Math Coprocessor  Yes          BIOS
14    F000:E845    Fixed Disk        Yes          BIOS
15    F000:9272    (Reserved)                     BIOS
```

Notes

- IRQ numbers 0, 1, 4, 5, 6, 7, 8, 9 and 14 are used in almost all machines.
- IRQ numbers 0, 1, 2, 8 and 13 are not wired to the expansions slots.
- **IRQ2**   When an IRQ between 8 and 15 is activated, it is using its own PIC, known as the slave PIC.   This PIC does not have its own connection directly to the MI line of the CPU.   It has to notify the CPU through the master PIC - the one that services IRQ0 to IRQ7.   It does this through the master PIC's IRQ2 line and the Master PIC activates the CPU's MI pin.   This process is known as *'cascading'* and is implemented in hardware - the actual interrupt 0A is not used.   This often means that IRQ2 can be used for another device, being mapped to the IRQ9 line of the slave PIC; any card configured as IRQ2 is really using IRQ9.
- **IRQ3**   This is allocated for a second serial port, COM2.   In the first example, a second port is installed on the machine so the IRQ is in use.   Where a second port is not fitted, the line can be used by another device.   If a second printer port is fitted but not in use, it may be possible to disable the second port's IRQ line, releasing IRQ3 for another device as shown below.
- **IRQ5**   This is allocated for a second parallel port, LPT2.   Since a second port is rarely fitted, the IRQ can be used by another device.   If the second port is fitted but not in use, it may be possible to disable the second port's IRQ line, releasing IRQ5 for another device as in the example below.
- **IRQ7**   This is allocated for the first parallel port, LPT1.   The printer port only needs an IRQ line if it is carrying out bi-directional data transfers.   Disabling the IRQ7 line of the printer port allows all the normal printing operations to be carried out, along with the usual out-of-paper and off-line detection.   In this way, IRQ7 can be released for another device.

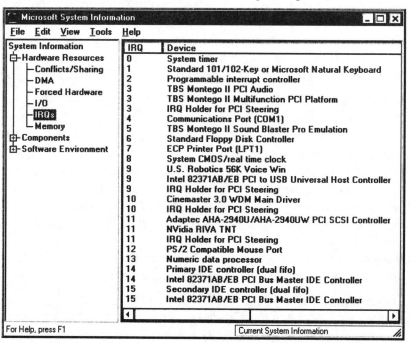

- IRQ10, 11, 12 and 15 are likely to be available for use, despite being displayed as *'Reserved'*.   In the example, IRQ11 is being used for the SCSI controller card.

Windows 98/ME/2000 provides information on IRQ usage, along with other useful information, via its *'System Information'* utility accessed from the *'Start'* button's *'Programs / Accessories / System Tool'* options.

DMA

Some devices require data to be transferred between themselves and the CPU at the fastest possible speed.   These are usually devices handling bulk data such as network cards, scanners, soundboards and hard disks.   Slower devices such as floppy drives and serial/parallel ports do not have as demanding a speed transfer requirement.   The slow devices use the CPU to organise the transfer of data between memory and the devices.   All the data has to pass through the CPU and this ties up a lot of processing time, slowing down the computer's throughput.

To handle the faster devices, the PC uses a special technique known as *'Direct Memory Access'*. An extra chip handles the transfers to and from memory, leaving the CPU to get on with other tasks. This results in a more efficient system and increased throughput.

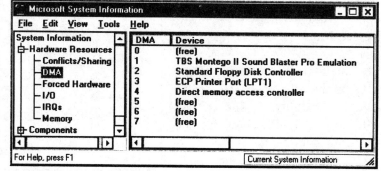

The original XT had four DMA channels, three of which appeared on the expansion bus. The AT onwards has eight DMA slots, with DMA4 being used to cascade to the CPU. DMA Channels 0 through to 3 are used for 8-bit transfers, while Channels 5 to 7 are available for 16-bit transfers only. Windows 98/ME/2000 provides DMA information via its *'System Information'* utility accessed from the *'Start'* button's *'Programs / Accessories / System Tool'* options. The diagram shows typical DMA usage. Some installation routines, such as that for sound cards, carry out their own check of DMA usage and report any possible clashes. Unlike IRQs, no two devices can share the same DMA channel. Older cards did not tend to support DMA.

I/O Address Clashes

The section on buses explained how the data in memory could be accessed for reading and writing. This entailed placing the address of the wanted location on to the Address Bus and enabling the Read or Write lines as required. A Write enable would result in the data on the Data Bus being written into the memory location specified in the Address Bus. A Read enable would result in the data held in the specified address being placed on the Data Bus. In this way, data could be moved round the internal system.

The same technique is used for all the add-on cards such as disk controllers, video cards, sound cards, network interface cards, serial ports, etc. These cards attach to the system via the connections on the expansion slots. Each card has a unique address, or range of addresses, for its own use. The card will ignore any other addresses on the Address Bus and will only respond when an address from its own range appears on the Address Bus. This means that no new card can use the same I/O port address as that already being used by an existing device. The problem only exists

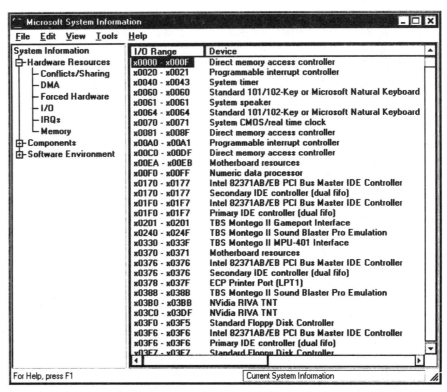

between hardware devices, since the system can differentiate between memory and hardware addresses. The CPU has a number of control lines that tell the system whether memory or a device is to be read/written.

These control signals are:

MEMR	Read from memory
MEMW	Write to memory
IOR	Read from I/O device
IOW	Write to I/O device

The chart shows the lower range of I/O addresses and this will vary slightly dependent upon the machine configuration in use. As can be seen, many of the addresses have their functions allocated, leaving a small range of addresses into which must be fitted additional cards. The range 200h to 20Fh is often used for the fitting of a games port while the 300h to 31Fh range is the common area used for the addition of extra cards (e.g. a Novell network card). Again, Windows 95/98/ME/2000 Device Manager can show some of the current I/O port address usage on the machine.

The First Steps

The first steps in carrying out any internal upgrade are the same and these are:

1. If a major, or particularly tricky, upgrade is planned, the computer's data should be backed up before continuing.
2. Switch off the machine. Ensure that the mains plug is removed from the mains socket. Remove all other cables that connect to the machine.
3. Fit an earthing strap to wrist and earth or computer chassis. This minimises the risk of body static blowing any chips on the card or motherboard.
4. Remove the cover of the computer main unit. There are normally 4 or 5 screws along the rear, which secure the cover to the main chassis. In some models, the screws may be along the side of the casing.   In a very few cases, it is simply a matter of pressing in two side buttons and hinging up the cover. Check the manual, as the some of the rear screws might be used for other purposes such as securing the fan casing or the power supply. In some tower cases, the front panel has to be removed first (read the manual).
5. The screws should be placed in a safe place. If there is much disassembly work involved, the various screws should be placed in labelled envelopes.
6. Where the new add-on interfaces to the outside world (e.g. an internal modem connects to a telephone line, whereas an extra hard disk is entirely internal to the case) remove the blanking plate that blocks off the slot in the external casing.   Do not remove more blanking plates than are required, as these are prevent dust and debris from entering the case.
7. Jot down a sketch of all cables in the existing system, before they are removed or altered. That way, if things go wrong, you can at least get back to where you were before the upgrade. Even better, attach stickers to cables to identify where they came from.

Fitting a CPU Upgrade

The CPU is the *'heart'* of the computer and fitting a faster CPU increases the performance of the computer.

Although the process is simple, consideration should be given to the expected extra performance compared to the extra cost.   Consider the following points:

- Adding more RAM usually has a greater impact on the computer's performance than upgrading the CPU.
- Although the raw speed has been increased, many of the benefits of Pentium systems are still not available (e.g. improved chipsets, improved caching, USB ports, AGP slot, power management).
- Although the CPU is working at a faster pace after the upgrade, the rest of the system has not necessarily speeded up.   For example, the CPU might be clocked at a higher speed, while the main system stills runs at the same speed as prior to the upgrade. The motherboard will still be using slow memory chips.

Since Overdrive chips are relatively expensive, a replacement CPU/motherboard/memory combination might be a more cost-effective alternative to CPU upgrading.

Even where the CPU alone is being upgraded, it is not simply a matter of fitting a new CPU in place of the slower model.   The upgrade must be compatible with the existing motherboard and the main factors are:

Voltage

Older chips ran on 5volts while modern CPUs run on 3.3volts or even 2volts. Fitting a 3.3volt chip into a 5volt socket would destroy the CPU and therefore upgrade chips place an extra small board between the CPU and the motherboard. This contains a voltage regulator, which allows the newer chip to be compatible with older motherboards. Ensure that the upgrade is voltage compatible by checking the motherboard manual.

Overdrive Range		
From	To	Socket
486	Pentium 133MHz	See notes
Pentium 75MHz	AMD K6 300MHz	5 or 7
Pentium 75MHz	Pentium 200MHz MMX	5 or 7
Pentium Pro	Celeron 600MHz	8
Pentium II	Pentium III 600/800	Slot 1

Socket Type

Most older motherboards fit the CPU in a ZIF (zero insertion force) socket that uses a lever to grip and release the CPU pins, preventing possible bent pins caused by forcing the chip into the holder.   A few other motherboards were manufactured with an additional socket for future upgrading. Ensure that the upgrade is pin-compatible (see the ZIF socket table).   Also, ensure that the chip is inserted with the correct orientation (i.e. pin 1 to pin 1).

Almost all 486 motherboards have a P24T socket (consult the manual), and are capable of taking an Intel *'Pentium Overdrive'* upgrade chip.   The 486-to-Pentium version of the chip is designed to match 486 motherboards that only have 32-bit data buses compared to the Pentium's 64-bit data bus.

Socket Number	Number of Pins	Motherboard	Description
1	169	486	Accepts 486 Overdrives only. 5V
2	169/238	486	Accepts 486 and Pentium Overdrives. 5V
3	169/237	486	A 3.3V version of the above
4	235	486	Accepts 486 DX4 CPUs. 5V
5	273	Pentium	Accepts 120MHz and 133MHz Overdrives
6	320	Pentium	Accepts 150MHz Overdrives
7	321	Pentium	The current Pentium standard socket
8	387	Pentium Pro	Accepts Pentium Pro Overdrives

Notes
- Socket 2 uses an inner set of 169 pins for plugging in 486 chips while the outer 238 pins accommodate Pentium Overdrive chips.
- Socket 3 uses the same technique but has a different outer pin layout. The matching 3.3V chips fit happily but cannot be accidentally plugged into 5V Socket 2 motherboards.
- While earlier sockets used in-line arrangements for their pins, Sockets 5, 7 and 8 use a different pin layout called Staggered Pin Grid Array (SPGA).

Alternatives To Overdrive Units
The above upgrades are suitable for improving older systems.

More modern systems have either a Slot A (for AMD chips) or Slot 1 (for Pentium II and Pentium III chips) that is used to connect their CPU modules. This prevents older motherboards from being upgraded to through the simple replacement of the existing chip. The Overdrive units mount the modern CPU on a module that fits an older motherboard socket, thus allowing the connection of faster CPUs. The   most   well   known   supplier   of   Overdrive   modules   is   Evergreen   Technologies (www.evergreenow.co.uk)

Another approach, for motherboards with PCI slots, is the insertion of an Accelera PCI card.   This fits any motherboard that has a PCI slot and contains a 433MHz Celeron CPU (up to 600MHz) and 64MB of SODIMM memory chips. These take over from the existing components.

Hypertec produce a similar unit for fitting into a PC's ISA slot. It can take PC133 SDRAM and a Celeron CPU between 667MHz and 866MHz.

Of course, if the existing motherboard already has a slot connection, there is the likelihood that the CPU can be directly replaced with one that operates at a faster speed. So, for example, a 500MHz Pentium III module can be replaced by a 1GHz module.   Similarly, Slot A CPUs can be upgraded by simple replacement.

Fitting The Upgrade
The steps for fitting an upgrade are:
- Carry out the first steps outlined earlier.
- Locate the CPU, open the ZIF lever and remove the CPU with the tool supplied with the Overdrive CPU.
- Align pin 1 of the overdrive CPU to the motherboard socket pin 1 and press home.
- Close the ZIF lever.
- For a slot-based CPU, remove the CPU module and insert the replacement module.
- If the upgrade uses a different clock speed, set the motherboard jumpers.
- Reassemble the PC.
- If the upgrade kit included new software, install the software.

Overclocking
Most CPUs can run faster than the manufacturer's quoted speed.   This has led to the practice of *'overclocking'* - adjusting the motherboard's jumpers to increase the CPU clock speed.   This is implemented as a free alternative to buying a CPU upgrade.   The principle is simple as there are jumpers for adjusting the bus speed and the multiplier (see the chapter on *'Computer Architecture'*). They set the CPU speed according to the formula

CPU speed = bus speed x CPU multiplier

For example, a bus speed of 100MHz and a 9x multiplier produces a CPU speed of approx. 900MHz. Most motherboards can run at a variety of bus speeds and offer a selection of multiplier values. Therefore, if the multiplier were set to 12x, the CPU would be driven at 1200MHz. Alternatively, setting the bus speed to 133MHz and leaving a 9x multiplier also results in a 1200MHz speed.

The limitations on overclocking are:

- The CPU may not be able to run at the higher rate (this would be noticed at bootup).
- The CPU might run but crash more frequently. Some enthusiasts suggest increasing the chip's supply voltage to overcome any instability but this greatly increases the risk of chip failure.
- The other parts of the system (e.g. memory) might not be able to cope with an increased bus speed.
- Faster CPU rates generate more heat from the CPU and the existing heat dissipation might not be sufficient. Larger heatsinks and additional cooling may be required.
- Slot 1 type processors, Pentium II, Pentium III, Xeons and some AMD Athlons, have speed and multipliers set by the positioning of a series of SMD resistors on the Printed Circuit Board that carries the processor and fits in the slot. Overclocking these is possible by moving these tiny components, but it is a very tricky operation and only for those with lots of experience of surface mount electronics.
- Intel chips are now 'Clock-locked' or 'Overclock Protected'. The chip is manufactured to run at a fixed multiplier rating and increasing the multiplier has no effect, or even decreases the CPU clock rate. In these cases, the bus speed may still be increased to a higher rate (e.g. an old 66MHz motherboard may allow the setting of a non-standard rate of 75MHz or 83MHz).

Since overclocking pushes a CPU and associated components to their limits, the method should not be employed where the computer is used for vital operations.

Motherboard Upgrade

The most dramatic upgrade performance comes from replacing the motherboard /CPU combination. This need not be over expensive, as all or most of the original components (case, disks, video card, etc) may be re-used on the new board. Unfortunately, the memory modules of older boards (e.g. SIMMs) will not fit on modern boards, requiring a memory upgrade at the same time. Generally, an upgrade to last year's performance will cost far less than upgrading to the current top technology, while providing significant performance improvements.

Selection

A large range of options is available and the main considerations are:

CPU	While the current top-speed models command premium prices, last month's 'top-of-the-range' chips are dumped cheaply. This provides a very cost-effective upgrade option, unless you need the very fastest machine that is available.
Chipset	The facilities of the supporting chipsets are explained in the chapter on Architecture
Board type	Most old boards adhered to the 'AT' standard (i.e. 13.8" by 12") and are no longer produced. The Baby-AT boards are smaller (13" x 8.6") but the sockets and slot connectors still match those of the AT boards, allowing them to be fitted as a direct AT replacement. The ATX board is the same size as a Baby-AT (with an alternative 11.2" x 8.2" mini version). The ATX board is not a drop-in replacement for an AT board because: • It has a different socket/slot layout so an ATX upgrade requires an ATX-type case. • It has a different supply voltage. The ATX case also has the required 3.3v power supply (instead of the 5v supply used in AT boards). • ATX boards have different cooling arrangements and require that the case also be upgraded to an ATX type. The Micro-ATX board is a low-cost version using cheaper components.
Memory type	Older motherboards were 72-pin SIMMs but most are now DIMM sockets or RAMBUS. Does upgrading the board require upgrading memory at the same time?
Manual	Never buy a motherboard that is not supplied with a manual - it may become essential.

Removing Old Board

The steps for removing the old motherboard are:

- Carry out a backup of the disk's contents as a precaution.
- Dismantle the system as explained earlier.
- Note the way that the motherboard is mounted; where are the mounting holes?; are plastic stand-offs or mounting posts being used?
- Remove add-on cards from the motherboard's expansion slots (e.g. video card and sound card).

- Unplug the cables from the motherboard, noting their function (e.g. cables to floppy drives, CD-ROMs, power supply, internal speaker, reset button, disk lights, keyboard lock). Note the orientation of cables that are temporarily removed from add-on cards (most cables have a red stripe on one side).
- Unscrew the motherboard and remove it.

Fitting New Board

The steps for fitting the replacement board are:

- Set any jumpers on the motherboard. Check the manual for details. Likely settings would be the clock speed, the CPU multiplication factor and disabling the on-board sound circuitry where an add-on sound card is to be fitted.
- Fit the memory modules.
- Fit the CPU if it has not been supplied pre-installed.
- Hold the board over the case chassis and check that all the mounting holes on the motherboard line up with stand-offs on the chassis. In some cases, fresh holes may require to be drilled in the case to fit mounting posts. Never drill or file the motherboard as this may damage the tracks on the board.
- Fit the motherboard, ensuring that it is clear of the metal casing at all points.
- Fit the add-on cards to the motherboard. If the board layout is different from the old board, the cards may not fit in their original order. If a cable is now found to be too short, the cards will need to be fitted on the board in the best order for all the connecting cables to reach.
- Re-connect the cables to the motherboard. Again, if the motherboard layout is different, cables may have to be re-routed or even extended.
- AT power cables from the power supply are usually wired to two separate plugs, each with six connections. The black leads of each plug should be located together at the middle of the socket and the orange cable should be lined up with pin 1 of the connector. Take care over this - double-check the particular system's connections - as incorrect wiring could damage the motherboard.
- Switch on the computer and run the BIOS setup to configure any alterations to the setup.

Adding Memory

There are a number of very good reasons why a machine should have its memory size increased.

TO HANDLE MODERN APPLICATIONS

Early PCs were supplied with the basic 640k of RAM and most applications did not even use the full memory. With the development of ever-larger operating systems and user applications, 64MB has emerged as an absolute minimum requirement. If large files, multimedia, real time video capture and editing and so on are to be accommodated, main memory should be much greater as shown in the chart below.

Category	Examples of Use	Min Recommended RAM
Light User	Word-processing, e-mail	8MB
Medium User	Database applications	16MB
Heavy User	Large databases, multi-tasking	32MB
Power User	Multimedia authoring, DTP, photo-editing, CAD	64MB
Design User	3D-CAD, CAM solid modelling, video editing	128MB

TO ACHIEVE GREATER SPEED

Extra memory speeds up Windows applications. Windows uses a scheme called 'virtual memory' that utilises the hard disk's unused contiguous space as if it were an area of memory. Since the access time of a disk may be 10ms compared to memory speeds of 60ns (for SIMMs) and as low as 8ns (for DIMMs), Windows will run much faster if it can directly use memory to store applications and parts of the operating system.

TO HANDLE MORE DATA

Most applications can use the extra memory to store and work with their documents. Databases, for example, may sort their records in memory rather than use slow disk operations.

TO ALLOW MULTI-TASKING

Extended memory can be used to run several programs simultaneously.

TO PROVIDE A DISK CACHE

Smartdrv and VCACHE use a section of memory as a disk cache to speed up disk access times.

How To Upgrade

Motherboards may arrive fully populated or partly populated. If a new motherboard is bought, it probably has no memory fitted. The first step is to determine the kind of memory to be fitted.

The most common formats are explained in the chapter on memory and the most likely types to be used in an upgrade are SIMMs, DIMMs or RIMMs as it is uneconomic to upgrade a computer that requires any older memory type.

The different sizes and possible combinations available should be carefully examined before the chips are purchased. For example, a Pentium using SIMM memory must upgrade SIMM memory boards at least two at a time, since chips are 32-bit and the Pentium has a 64-bit bus.

Older DIMM-based motherboards used PC-66 memory module, which used 66MHz SDRAM. Modern motherboards use PC-100 modules or PC-133 modules. Fitting a faster memory module will not improve the computer's performance, as the module will only operate at the switching speed of the system (e.g. a PC-133 module will only switch at 66MHz on a 66MHz motherboard). On the other hand, fitting a slower module in a faster system will reduce the performance of the computer.

If you have an older 5v DIMM socket, ensure that only a 5v module is purchased, as newer 3.3v modules are incompatible. See the chapter on memory for more details.

Fitting SIMM Boards

Find the SIMM banks on the motherboard and note the orientation of the current SIMM boards. These boards have holes to engage with pegs on the slots. Before handling the SIMM, discharge your body static or preferably wear an earthing wristband. Place the SIMM into the socket at an angle of about 30 degrees and engage the SIMM's pegs into the matching holes in the SIMM slot. The board has a notch cut from one of its sides, so that it cannot be inserted the wrong way round. When the board is gently pushed home and rotated vertically, it clicks into place in the bank's retaining side clips. Take care when inserting SIMMs since the pegs break quite easily.

Fitting DIMM/RIMM Modules

Check the motherboard's manual to see whether any SIMM module has to be removed prior to fitting a DIMM. A DIMM bank is inserted vertically into the DIMM socket. The socket has two keys and the DIMM has two matching notches along the bottom of the bank. This ensures that the DIMM is inserted the correct way round. When the DIMM is fully inserted, retaining clips at the side of the socket hold the DIMM in place.

A RIMM module has identical dimensions to a DIMM module and is fitted in the same way. The two modules are not interchangeable and the notches on the DIMM modules are in different positions to those used in SIMM modules (see the chapter on memory) and this prevents the accidental fitting of the wrong type of module.

In the case of both SIMMs and DIMMs, alter any DIP switch settings or jumper settings as necessary, after insertion of the memory bank. This configures the motherboard to recognise the new memory. This is mostly only required by older motherboards, as newer boards automatically detect the amount of memory fitted.

Upgrading Video

Most computers are capable of having their video capabilities improved. The additional hardware involved can be fairly expensive and would normally only be undertaken if there was a good operational reason. The adoption of Windows or DTP software might be reasons for such a move. Indeed, a piece of software may specify that its minimum hardware requirements include, for example, a SVGA screen.

An upgrade is in three stages:
- Obtaining the correct components
- Fitting the graphics card
- Installing the software drivers

Choosing The Correct Components

Before contacting dealers, it is important to know exactly what is required. Detailed descriptions of components are in the previous pages, but the specification has to consider:

RESOLUTION

Should the new highest screen resolution be 800 x 600, 1024 x 768 or higher? The current upgrade may require, say, SVGA resolution. However, new software demands ever-higher screen resolutions. Therefore, consideration should be given to increasing the resolution greater than current needs. Increasing the specification allows the system to cope with possible future demands. Buying for the future may save money in the long term, although it will probably cost more in the short term. A financial compromise might be to purchase graphics boards that are socketed to allow the expansion of the video memory, by plugging in extra memory chips later.

FEATURES

Requirements for handling fast 3-D rendering, DVD or multimedia files demand a card that is optimised for these purposes. Additional facilities such as a built-in TV tuner, or an output for connection to a TV may also be considered.

SCREEN SIZE & TYPE

If the software demands a high resolution, it will also require a larger size monitor screen, which can make a substantial difference to the upgrade price.   Consideration should also be given to the local operating environment and whether FST tubes or anti-glare screens should be purchased.

COLOUR

There is a golden rule about graphics colours; more colour equals more memory and more memory equals higher prices.   In addition, more colours may mean added circuit complexity, such as high performance RAMDACs. This will also increase the price.

SPEED

The upgrade may be to allow the running of an application, such as a spreadsheet, in high-resolution mode. Here, the speed of the CPU or the maths co-processor is more significant than the speed of the screen update. Here, a cheaper board might be sufficient.   In other situations, such as DTP or graphics animation, the speed of the graphics updates demands that the best performance possible is considered.   A graphics accelerator card or a graphics co-processor card is essential.   Factors such as the use of DDR RAM or an AGP bus card should also be considered.

COMPATIBILITY

An upgrade will almost certainly entail the purchase of both a new graphics card and a new monitor.   If the current monitor is a CGA or EGA type, it will have to be upgraded to allow it to meet the new higher specification.   It is vital that the all the components are compatible with each other.

The following questions should be addressed.

- Does the graphics card match the machine?   Does the new graphics card have a PCI or an AGP connection? Is this the same type as that used on the machine's expansion slot?   To get the maximum performance, should consideration be given to changing the computer motherboard to one with an AGP Bus system or a faster processor?
- Does the graphics card match the monitor?   Is the monitor of sufficient resolution for the new task and for any future task? Should extra be paid to ensure future compatibility?   Does the monitor support non-interlaced mode? Does the graphics card support non-interlaced mode?

The above paragraphs are a summary of some of the points to be looked at by the support staff, since they are often consulted about future purchases.   The previous chapters covering video standards, card descriptions, computer bus types, etc. should be consulted for greater detail.   Remember, often purchases are a compromise between users' demands, performance specifications and budgetary constraints.

Fitting The Card

The first steps are the basic ones already outlined.   These should be followed by these next stages:

- Remove any existing graphics board.   A few motherboards have the graphics circuitry mounted directly on to the board.   This is usually disabled by setting a motherboard jumper or by changing the BIOS settings.
- Locate a free expansion slot. Remove the rear blanking plate currently blocking this slot.   Insert the new card carefully into the expansion slot. The card's output socket should protrude from the empty slot.
- Secure the card using the same screw removed with the blanking plate.
- Replace the machine cover.
- Plug the monitor cable into the graphics card socket.
- Re-assemble the case and cabling and switch on.
- Windows should detect the presence of the new hardware and automatically find install its driver. These are specially written software programs, designed to drive the new graphics hardware to the best performance. If the card being fitted does not have a driver stored within the Window's system, the driver from the CD supplied with the video card should be installed.
- Run the Window's Settings/Control Panel/Display Settings to select the required screen resolution, colour depth and refresh rate.

Monitor Connections

The computer's graphics display circuitry may b e mounted directly on the PCB of the motherboard. Alternatively, it may comprise a card plugged into the expansion bus.   In both cases, the display output is taken to the rear of the computer, where it is wired to an output socket.   A cable, or cables, then connects this output to the monitor.

CGA/EGA

Both these old systems have 9-pin D-type sockets at the rear of the PC. The pin layout and numbering is as shown in the diagram and is the view as seen by a user.

VGA/SVGA/XGA

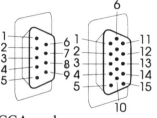

The analogue connectors use a 15-pin D type socket.

In this way, RGB and analogue cards cannot be mistakenly matched with the wrong type of monitors - a VGA monitor lead will simply not plug into a CGA card, for example. The pin layout and connections are shown.

With some high-performance, large-size screens, the red, green and blue signal connections are taken to the monitor on separate coaxial cables with BNC (bayonet) connectors. This minimises interference that may be caused by the colour signal on one lead being induced onto another colour lead.

NOTE: The monitor also needs a mains supply to power its internal circuitry. A direct cable from a 13-amp plug sometimes supplies this power. Sometimes a mains cable connects the monitor to a socket on the rear of the computer - this reduces the number of leads floating around.

Upgrading An IDE Hard Disk

There are many reasons why a new disk drive is fitted to a computer. It may be during the building of a brand new machine. It may be because the existing hard drive has failed. It may be because the existing disk is far too small to store all the user's applications and data. It may even be fitted as an extra disk to work along with the existing disk drive.

There are three main steps involved in fitting a disk drive:

- Set any jumpers (on the drive or drive controller)
- Install the drive into the computer case and connect it to the rest of the system.
- Ensure that the system's software settings allow the PC to recognize the new drive.

This section covers the two possibilities - replacing the old disk with a higher capacity model, and adding an additional hard disk to the system.

Selecting

SIZE - This issue is covered in the chapter on system selection. 10GB has become the minimum requirement for commercial use.

TYPE - Ensure that the model is an UDMA66, UDMA100 or SCSI type; the existing setup can be identified by the cables that connect the drive to the controller card. The possibilities are:

IDE / UDMA	A single, 40-pin strip
SCSI	A single, 50-pin (SCSI-2) or 68-pin (UW) strip
RLL, MFM or ESDI	A 34-pin control strip and a 20-pin data strip

If the controller card is an old MFM or RLL type, then the upgrade will include purchasing a new IDE/UDMA disk controller card to replace the old card, as an IDE drive can not be run from an old RLL or MFM disk controller card. UDMA66 Drives need a special low crosstalk cable, which if not supplied with the motherboard can be bought for a few pounds. The UDMA 66 drive may also need specialist BIOS support, possibly involving a flash upgrade.

SPEED - The speed tends to vary with the disk's size and a 12ms access time was typical of an old IDE 500MB. Modern SCSI and fast UDMA drives often have a high spindle speed, which improves performance (typically under 10ms for a UDMA drive and under 5ms for a SCSI drive).

MEMORY – The amount of cache memory fitted on the disk itself can have a significant effect on the drive's performance. If all else is equal, a drive with more onboard cache is quicker in general use and more reliable than one with less memory.

SMART Self Monitoring And Reporting Technology is built into a great many modern drives. These monitor their own performance and warn the user if there is a danger of imminent failure.

POWER Many new drives have the facility to *"spin down"* after a few minutes of inactivity. This saves power, heat and noise, and increases drive life, but can mean a short delay while the drive spins up again, which some users and some applications dislike.

The rear connectors
The diagram shows the connections that are present at the rear of a typical disk drive.
The disk drive is normally connected to the rest of the system by two cables.

The power socket
This is shown at the right of the diagram. The power cables that feed out of the computer's power supply unit supply 12 volt and 5 volt to power the various peripherals such as hard disks, floppy disks, CD-ROMs and DVD players. One of the spare sockets is connected to the rear socket to power the disk drive. As can be seen in the diagram, the socket on the drive is

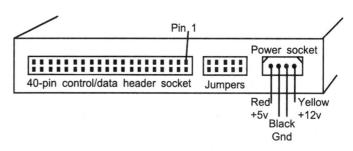

shaped with bevels on two corners, such that the power cable can only be inserted one way. The diagram also shows the colours and voltages of the wires that connect to the power socket.

Control/Data socket
The cable that plugs into this socket has two purposes:
- To allow control signals from the main system to start and stop the drive motor, move the read/write head and other control functions.
- To allow data from the computer to be taken to the write head and to allow data read from the head to be taken back to the computer.

This cable is a grey ribbon, with a red strip along one edge. The red strip indicates that it is the wire for Pin 1 of the socket and this allows the user to fit the cable the correct way round. Pin 1 of the header socket is at the end near the power socket. Some sockets and cables are designed so that they can only be fitted one way round, by engaging a bump on the edge of the plug into a notch in the socket.

In early systems, the control cable was a separate cable from the data cable and the system used three cables to attach the drive to the system.

Setting up an IDE drive
The chapter on disks explained the way that drives are set as 'masters' or 'slaves'. This is achieved by adjusting settings on each drive, so that they are set as being unique. These are found at the rear of the case on a *"jumper block"*. The block has two rows of pins and various pins can be bridged with small metal connectors with plastic covers. The jumper settings on the drive alter the configuration and a common method of setting the jumpers is shown in the diagram.

Single If the jumper block has no jumper links fitted, as shown in the first example, the drive is regarded as being a *'single'* drive. This means that it is the only drive on the IDE cable and is automatically regarded as the master drive.

Master In the second example, a link has been inserted to bridge the middle set of pins (often marked as MASTER or MS), to configure the drive as a master.

Slave The third example shows a link shorting the pins marked as SLAVE or SP (Slave Present), to configure the drive as a slave drive.

Although this is a common method of configuration, other methods are used and the disk's manual should advise. If the manual is missing, the information can usually be found on the manufacturer's web site.

Fitting
The steps for renewing an old hard disk are:
- Ensure that the new disk's parameters are known; this is likely to be printed on a label on the disk. If this is not provided, contact the supplier (by telephone or website) for the information on number of tracks, number of sectors per track, etc. Do not proceed with the remaining steps until these facts are known, as the BIOS will have to be set up to these parameters. This is not required with a modern BIOS, which has an *'IDE HDD Auto Detection'* facility that automatically detects and stores the parameters of each disk detected.
- Ensure that the new disk is configured as a *'master'* disk (see the notes above).
- Make a complete backup of all the existing files on the old hard disk.

- Carry out the initial dismantling steps outlined previously.
- Remove the power cable and ribbon cable from the old hard disk.
- Unscrew and remove the old hard disk from its drive bay.   Place the old drive to one side and retain the screws.
- Carefully remove the new disk drive from its anti-static bag. Avoid touching any exposed electronic components and handle the drive by its casing.
- Fit the new drive into the unused bay and secure with the same screws.
- Fit the power cable and ribbon cable to the new disk drive. Remember, the red end of the ribbon cable aligns to pin 1 - this is true for both ends.
- Refit the computer case and mains cable.
- Reboot the machine and run the BIOS setup program for that machine (see computer's manual)
- Alter the BIOS settings, so that the size and parameters of the new hard drive are saved to the machine's CMOS.   This is through the *'IDE HDD Auto Detection'* facility in a modern BIOS.   In an older system, the user will enter the settings from the keyboard.
- Partition and high-level format the disk, using FDISK and FORMAT utilities from a floppy boot disk (see chapter on hard drives).   Format the active partition as a system disk (i.e. use FORMAT C:/S).
- Install the operating system and applications.
- Restore the data files from the backup files.

Fitting A Second IDE Hard Disk
The following steps outline the addition of an extra IDE drive to a machine with an existing IDE drive.
- Carry out the initial dismantling steps outlined earlier.
- Ensure that the existing setup is an IDE system (the ribbon cable between the controller card and the drive should be a single 40-pin strip).
- Ensure that the machine has:
    - A spare drive bay.
    - A spare power connector (if not, use a 'Y' power adapter).
    - A spare connector on the ribbon cable.
    - A power supply of at least 200W.
- Configure one of the drives as the *'master'*. This is the drive that the machine will boot the system from. IDE hard disks are supplied configured as masters but it may be required to be informed that a slave drive is connected (by setting a *'Slave Present'* jumper).
- Configure the other drive as the *'slave'* (see drive's installation notes). In general the newer drive should be used as master, because it's controller may have extra features that have been developed since the older drive was made.
- Fit the new drive into the unused bay and secure with the screws provided with the installation kit. Where a 3.5" drive has to be fitted into a 5.25" drive bay, a mounting adaptor kit is required.   This uses fixing rails to bridge the gap.   The drive is screwed to the rails and the rails are screwed to the bay.
- Fit the power cable and ribbon cable to the new disk drive.   The drives can be connected to the ribbon cables in any order. There is no requirement for the master disk to be on the first connector.
- Refit the computer case and mains cable.
- Reboot the machine and run the BIOS setup program for that machine (see computer's manual)
- Alter the BIOS settings and save the new hard drive size and parameters to the machine's CMOS. This is through the *'IDE HDD Auto Detection'* facility in a modern BIOS.   In an older system, the user will enter the settings from the keyboard into the entry type 47 of the disk table.
- Partition and high-level format the disk, using FDISK and FORMAT utilities from a floppy boot disk or from the existing drive, if it is the master drive (see chapter on hard drives).

Upgrading To An UDMA Hard Disk
A general description of UDMA drives is given in the chapter on Disks and Drives. The instructions for handling and fitting IDE disks also apply to UDMA drives but there are some important differences.
Ultra-DMA disk drives will connect to existing IDE motherboards but will not provide the higher transfer rates.   Only motherboards using LX and TX chipsets onwards directly support Ultra-DMA drives.   For older motherboards, there is the option to replace the existing IDE controller card with an interface card.   These cards have their own BIOS chips built in and these supplement the existing computer's BIOS. DMA/66 drives only provide top performance if connected to a DMA/66-compatible motherboard/BIOS with a special UDMA66 cable. The UDMA 66 drive may also need specialist BIOS support, possibly involving a flash upgrade. The same conditions apply to UDMA/100 drives.

If the UDMA drive is simply replacing an existing IDE drive, it is a straightforward one-for-one physical replacement, perhaps followed by the installation of the additional driver software. If the IDE controller card is also being replaced, then the old card's cables to the drive and floppy disk should be removed. The power cable should be disconnected and the drive unscrewed and removed. The new drive should be screwed in place and all the cables connected to it. The BIOS configuration, partitioning and high-level formatting are as before.

Upgrading To A SCSI Hard Disk

The IDE interface only allows four devices to be attached. If a computer has a ZIP drive, a DVD player and a CD-writer fitted, there is only support for a single hard disk drive. Where more than four devices are required, a SCSI controller can be fitted. A SCSI drive also has a better sustained data transfer rate than an IDE drive and is commonly used for video editing and other heavy-duty activities.

The basic SCSI system allows 7 devices to be added to the computer, while the higher-performance system allows 15 devices to be added. One end of the cable connects to the controller card and the cable contains multiple plugs along its length to connect to the SCSI devices.

A general description of SCSI drives is given in the chapter on Disks and Drives. After the SCSI type has been decided and the drive purchased, fitting is the easiest of all the drives. SCSI works well alongside existing hard disk systems inside the computer, as it does not use the computer's BIOS chip, relying instead upon additional software that talks to the additional SCSI controller card being fitted. The additional driver software comes with the new drive. If, however, the drive is being used to replace an IDE system, then a SCSI interface card that has a BIOS ROM has to be fitted so that the disk will act as a bootup drive.

Fitting the SCSI system involves the following steps:
- Switch off the power to the computer. Ensure that the mains plug is removed from the computers power socket.
- Fit an earthing strap to your wrist and connect it to the computer casing.
- Carefully remove the disk drive from its anti-static bag. Avoid touching any exposed electronic components and handle the drive by its casing.
- Set the ID value of the SCSI drive. Each SCSI device is given a unique device number (or ID). With most SCSI controllers, the range of ID values is 0-7, with 7 being used by the controller itself. Higher ID numbers are given greater priority when multiple SCSI devices are being accessed. The ID is usually set using miniature rotary switches or jumpers on the drive case.
- If necessary, fit a terminator to the drive. A terminating resistor is fitted to the last device on the cable in a SCSI system. It is not required for IDE drives. A terminator is a bank of resistors placed at the end of the SCSI chain. Their job is to prevent signals that were sent up the cable from reflecting back down the cable, causing interference and losses. A terminator may look like a plug or a solid resistor pack that is inserted into sockets on the drive's circuit board. In some cases the termination is carried out by setting DIP switches and some modern SCSI devices *"auto-terminate"* which means that they work out the termination arrangements by themselves, without any human involvement.
- Fit the controller card in a spare expansion slot. In most cases, the SCSI controller is a card that plugs into a spare expansion slot, although some motherboards are now available with the controller circuitry already built into the motherboard.
- Fit the new drive into an unused bay and secure with the supplied screws.
- Connect the controller cable to the drive.
- Connect a power cable to the drive.
- Refit the computer case and mains cable.
- Install the software driver.
- Configure the SCSI software or the SCSI BIOS.
- Partition and high level format the disk.

Using The New Drive As The Boot Disk

Users may wish to use their new drive as the boot drive for two reasons:
- It is a faster drive than the original.
- They intend to remove the old drive.

The earlier section on replacing a drive involved the re-installation of Windows, all the applications and all the data.

This could be avoided if the following steps were taken:

- Backup everything on the original drive.
- Ensure that a Windows emergency startup disk is to hand.   If not, create one.
- Fit the new drive as second drive.
- Format the new drive's active partition as a system disk (i.e. use FORMAT D:/S).
- Boot the machine back into Windows.
- Enter the DOS box using the *'MS-DOS Prompt'* option.
- Enter the command

      c:\windows\command\xcopy c: d: /s/e/c/r/h/k

and press the *'Enter'* key.

This copies all the files from the old disk to the new disk, including hidden files, system files and the Windows registry.

Windows, all applications and data are now copied to the new drive.   Only the Windows temporary swap file is not copied.

- Close down Windows and switch off.
- Remove the old drive.
- Remove the new drive's *'Slave'* jumper.
- Insert the Windows emergency startup disk into the floppy drive and switch on.
- Use FDISK to make the new drive's partition active.
- Reboot the machine.   This will enter Windows and automatically create a new swap file.

Fitting A 3.5" Floppy Disk Drive

There are a variety of reasons for fitting a 3.5" floppy drive to a computer. These are:

- Replacing a faulty drive.
- Adding a floppy to a new motherboard or new controller.
- Adding a second 3.5" floppy drive.

The first steps in the fitting are the basic ones already outlined.   The remaining steps are:

- If replacing an existing drive, remove the power and data ribbon cables from the old floppy drive. Unscrew and remove the old drive from its bay.   Place the drive to one side and retain the screws.
- Fit the new floppy drive into the unused bay and secure with the same screws.   If the mounting bay is 5.25" wide, the floppy should be fitted with the mounting kit from the old drive. This kit adapts the 3.5" case to a 5.25" bay.
- Fit the power cable to the new disk drive.
- Fit the data ribbon cable to the new disk drive.   Ensure that the red stripe is lined up with Pin 1 on the controller socket.
- Refit the computer case and mains cable.

Adding A Second 3.5" Floppy Drive.

The steps are similar to those above except that the old drive is not removed.   The extra drive is fitted into an unused bay and an additional power lead has to be connected to the drive, via the 3.5" power adaptor.   If the computer does not have a spare power connector, a 'Y' connector should be fitted. The machine's BIOS settings will need to be altered to add a second drive of 1.4MB capacity, while retaining the original drive in the configuration.   Lastly, make sure that the LASTDRIVE setting in CONFIG.SYS allows for the addition of the additional drive.

Fitting A UPS

An uninterruptible power supply (UPS) runs the computer on its own batteries in the event of a power failure.   Their operation is described in the chapter on Computer Peripherals.

The installation steps are:

- Load the UPS software.
- Set the UPS card's I/O port address. With some cards this may happen at a later stage as some setup software autodetects and informs the user what address to select.
- Plug the card into a spare expansion socket and screw into place.
- Unplug the power cable coming from the power supply to connect to the motherboard.
- Connect this cable to the UPS card.

- Connect the additional supplied power cable from the UPS card to the motherboard.
- Connect the external UPS supply into the mains supply.
- Amend the machine's configuration files according to the manual, to load the monitoring routine.   This program may be automatically carried out on running the setup program.

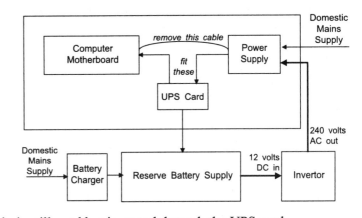

The battery pack is kept charged by a regulated mains supply.   The diagram shows that the normal computer power supply is still used but is routed through the UPS card.

Fitting A Sound Card

The variety of sound cards (e.g. whether wavetables or MIDI facilities are required) is covered in the chapter on multimedia.

The first steps in the fitting are the basic ones already outlined earlier in the chapter.

The additional steps are:

- On an older card, alter the card's base address, DMA and/or IRQ setting if these clash with an address, DMA or IRQ already in use on the computer.   Utilities such as Sleuth, Checkit or Windows 95/98 Device Manager/Properties will list addresses already in use.   Modern cards should be automatically configured through plug-and-play.
- Insert the card into a spare expansion slot and secure with a screw.
- If the computer has a CD-ROM drive fitted, its audio output can be connected to the sound card, so that normal music CDs can be played through the card and its speakers.   The connecting cable can normally only be fitted in one way.
- Re-assemble the case, attach speakers to the card's output socket and switch on.
- Windows should detect the presence of the new hardware and automatically find install its driver. If the card being fitted does not have a driver stored within the Window's system, the driver from the CD supplied with the sound card should be installed.
- Install all the card's applications software.
- Test the card's ability to play music CDs, digitised sounds and synthesised sounds.

Fitting A Scanner

Scanners are used for a variety of purposes, common examples being:

- Converting simple line drawings into graphics files.
- Converting photographic images into high-resolution, multi-coloured graphics files.
- Using OCR (optical character recognition) software to convert scanned printed pages into text files.

Some scanner models are hand-held, where the scanner is rolled over the image to be scanned.   Most models are either flatbed scanners (where the image is placed on a sheet of glass similar to a photocopier) or sheet-fed scanners (where a pile of sheets is automatically fed through the scanner).   Flatbeds are useful for quality photographic work while sheet-fed systems are useful for document management systems where scanning piles of correspondence is productive.   Models are also available in a variety of resolutions and colour depths.   Early models were monochrome whereas current scanners range from 300dpi, 256-grey-scale models through to 2400dpi, 16.8m colour models.

Note:

When choosing a model, consideration has to be given to the capabilities of the rest of the computer. Consider scanning a graphics image that is 3 inches square.   If this is scanned by a 300dpi, 256-colour scanner, its storage capacity can be calculated as -

900 dots horizontally x 900 dots vertically	= 810,000 dots
256 colours, so each dot requires 8 bits; image needs 810,000 x 8	= 6,480,000 bits
divide by 8 to get the answer in bytes; 6,4800,000 /8	= 810,000 bytes
divide by 1024 to get the answer in kilobytes; 810,000 / 1024	= 791k

However, for a full A4 sheet at 2400dpi with 16.8 million colours (i.e. 24-bit), the calculation is

$$11.65" \times 2400dpi \times 8.3" \times 2400dpi \times 24 / 8 / 1024 / 1024 \qquad = 1592MB$$

This single file requires huge storage space and provides huge memory problems in trying to load and manipulate the image in paint and photo-retouch packages. Careful thought has to be given to the use of scanners before choosing the specification.

There are three different ways that your scanner can be connected to your computer:

Parallel

There is a parallel port fitted on nearly every computer and this is usually used for connecting a printer. Where a scanner has a parallel plug connector, the user can unplug the printer from the computer's parallel port and insert the scanner plug, or he/she can fit a parallel *'pass-through'* connector. This connector allows two parallel port devices to be connected at the same time and saves plugging and unplugging each time the scanner is to be used. This parallel interface scanner is easily carried round for use on another computer. The scanner software is installed on the new computer, the scanner is plugged in and the system can be used. There is no internal connection, so the computer does not require to be opened up.

SCSI

This provides faster data transfers than the parallel port system and is useful where lots of photographs need to be scanned. The SCSI interface card usually supplied with the scanner. With the introduction of fast USB scanner interfaces, SCSI scanners have become much less popular.

USB

This is now the most common way to connect a new scanner to a computer. It is easily connected - there is no special adapter card to fit, as with SCSI, or pass-through adapter, as with parallel. The cable from the scanner is simply plugged into the computer's USB socket, the scanner software is installed and the scanner is immediately recognised.

Some scanners provide both SCSI and USB connections while others provide both a parallel and USB connection. However the scanner connects, the scanner's drivers and any software files, such as OCR, need to be installed.

Fitting A CD-ROM

Most applications are now provided on CD-ROM instead of floppy disk format. CD-ROMs also are used to supply shareware, clip art, databases, dictionaries, encyclopaedias, games and a wide range of multi-media files (sound, animations, and graphics).

Selecting

The choice depends on the performance and facilities required. The following decisions are required:

STANDARD

The standards of CD-ROMs are explained in the chapter on Disks and Drives and most modern CD drives provide all options (e.g. playback of normal audio CDs, Green Book, White Book, Blue Book, Kodak Photo-CD, *'multi-session'* working, etc). Consideration may be given to purchasing a combined DVD and CD-ROM drive. When buying budget drives, check the facilities supported.

SPEED

Like a hard disk, the speed of a CD-ROM can be measured in terms of its access time and its data transfer rate. The performances of different models vary greatly, with a seek time of 65ms being the best option, 100ms being acceptable and 200ms or greater being for budget use only. Similarly, different units have varying data transfer rates, from single speed to over 70 times standard speed.

PHYSICAL TYPE

CD-ROMs are available in either internal or external models. If the machine has a spare front 5.25" drive bay (as in, for example, a tower or mini-tower model) then the user has the option of having an internal unit fitted. Otherwise, the external model can be fitted. With both models there is a further choice, as the CD-ROM can be connected to the motherboard in several ways. These are mostly IDE or SCSI interfaces (see the chapter on Disks and Drives). The correct model and interface have to be purchased.

Models come with either top-loading or caddy-holding methods of holding the disk in the drive.

Fitting

Carry out the first five steps described previously. The steps thereafter depend on the type of CD drive.

Internal

- Choose the machine's drive bay and expansion slot that allow the connecting cables to reach both components without undue strain.
- Remove the front blanking plate; this is usually a plastic plate that can be popped out.
- Install the CD-ROM into the guides and firmly press into place.
- When the front of the ROM unit is flush with the front of the computer casing, secure the unit to the casing with the screws provided.
- Connect one of the spare power connectors on the power loom to the CD-ROM. This has a unique shape and can only be connected one way round.
- If the computer has an audio card, connect the audio cable between the CD-ROM and this card. This cable carries audio (i.e. from normal audio CDs) from the CD-ROM to the card and is keyed to only connect one way.
- For an IDE drive connecting to the motherboard's first IDE slot, set the CD drive's jumper to make the unit a 'slave' device and connect the drive on an unused connector on the existing hard disk cable.
- For an IDE connecting to the motherboard's second IDE slot, set the CD drive's jumper to make the unit a 'master' device and connect an IDE interface cable between the drive and the second IDE slot on the motherboard.
- For a SCSI CD-ROM drive, set the drive's SCSI ID to an unused ID and connect the drive to an unused connector on the existing SCSI disk cable.
- Replace the computer cover and re-insert the machine's power cable.
- Windows should detect the presence of the new hardware and automatically find install its driver. If the drive being fitted does not have a driver stored within the Window's system, the driver from the CD supplied with the CD-ROM drive should be installed.
- The CD-ROM is normally be designated as the 'D' drive. If the machine is fitted with other devices (extra hard disks, tape backups, etc.) the CD-ROM is designated the next free unused drive letter.

External

There are five different ways that your CD-ROM can be connected to your computer:

Parallel

There is a parallel port fitted on every computer and this is usually used for connecting a printer. Where a CD-ROM has a parallel plug connector, the user can unplug the printer from the computer's parallel port and insert the CD-ROM. This parallel interface CD-ROM drive is easily carried round for use on another computer. The drive's software is installed on the new computer, the drive is plugged in and the system can be used. However, this is not a popular method, as its only supports relatively low data transfers rates across the interface.

SCSI

This provides faster data transfers than the parallel port system and is useful where the computer already has an external SCSI connector. On bootup, the SCSI's BIOS chip will recognise the new drive's presence.

USB

This is a simple way to connect an external CD-ROM to a computer. The cable from the CD-ROM is simply plugged into the computer's USB socket and the drive is immediately recognised.

FireWire

This is a simple way to connect an external CD-ROM to a computer with a FireWire connection. The cable from the CD-ROM is plugged into the computer's FireWire socket and the drive is immediately recognised.

PC Card

This is a popular way to connect an external CD-ROM to a portable computer. The cable from the CD-ROM has a PC Card on the end and this card is plugged into one of the computer's PCMCIA slots. The drive is immediately recognised.

FITTING A DVD DRIVE

In terms of shape, connectors, power consumption, and so on a DVD drive is identical to the equivalent CD-ROM drive, so fitting a DVD drive is exactly like fitting a CD-ROM. However there are quite stringent hardware requirements that have to be met before a DVD drive can be used to display DVD films etc. As explained in the chapter on disks, the rate that the data is read off a DVD disk is much higher than for a CD running at the same rotational speed. This means that a PC equipped with a DVD needs a certain level of specification (probably a minimum of a 300MHz Pentium) if the user is not to experience occasional disappointment at the DVD performance, particularly if streaming data for multimedia purposes.

DVD Decoding

The data encoded on a DVD is subject to a form of encoding, in order to get large amounts of audio/video information onto the media and recover it intact. This encoding needs to be undone at the player end before the data can be displayed.

There are two ways of doing this:

Software Decoding

This involves the use of specialist drivers supplied with the drive, or included with the player software. Modern versions of Microsoft Windows include media players that can cope with DVD decoding. When a movie is supplied on DVD, the DVD disk will often include a bespoke player to allow software decoding. Specialist software is also available from Cyberlink, Zoran and Xing. The disadvantage of using software to decode the data is that the processor is used much more, and so the overall system is likely to become overstressed and start skipping frames or degrading quality. Modern PC's are capable of handling DVD files.

Hardware Decoding

The alternative is to use specialist hardware to decode the DVD data. Modern Intel Chipsets (810,820,830,850 etc, see architecture section) include the appropriate hardware decoder in their Graphics Memory Controller Hub or GMCH. For motherboards that are not so modern, a PCI card can be bought and fitted which does the same decoding work in hardware and so lessens the load on the processor. The disadvantages of using the hardware solution are firstly the cost involved, which is not great, but might add 50% onto the price of purchase of a typical modern DVD drive, and secondly the fact that another precious PCI resource has been used.

This may be the only solution for a computer with a slow CPU (probably 133MHz upwards).

Although modern graphics cards often provide built-in hardware decoding circuitry, a dedicated decoder card has additional benefits:

- It usually provides composite and S-video outputs, for connection to a TV or video recorder.
- It provides a SPDIF (Sony/Philips Digital Interface) output, for connection to a surround sound system. This provides theatre-quality sound and is a major improvement compared to using the output from the normal audio out socket (which is usually still available).

In both cases, the drive is fitted using the same method as that for fitting a CD-ROM drive.

For software decoding, a third party DVD player (i.e. decoding and control software) needs to be installed, if your computer does not currently have this facility.

The steps for installing a hardware decoder system are:

- Fit the DVD drive into a spare bay.
- Fit the MPEG decoder card into a spare PCI slot.
- Connect the existing VGA output from your video card into the VGA input of the decoder card.
- Connect the monitor's plug to the decoder's VGA output socket.
- Connect the surround sound system to the decoder card's SPDIF socket.
- Replace the computer cover, re-insert the machine's power cable and switch the computer on.
- Install any driver or application software.

Fitting A Network Interface Card

This section covers the fitting of an internal network interface card to a normal computer, so that the machine can be added to an existing Ethernet local area network that uses Unshielded Twisted Pair cable (a common method of wiring a LAN).

Selecting Hardware

The important selection factors are:

Network Type	Ensure that the card is a bus, i.e. Ethernet, card. There are a number of other systems available, notably the IBM token ring network; the cards are not interchangeable, although the connectors may be identical.
Bus Width	Most network cards available today are 32-bit, PCI cards. Older ISA cards may be 16-bit (such as the NE2000 range) or even 8-bit (NE1000 range). The larger bus sizes transfer more data at a time, but are not physically interchangeable.
Card type	The cards are available in three types - DMA, shared memory and I/O mapped. A mixture of these cards is allowed on the same network. Card speeds are 10Mbps or 10/100 Mbps (i.e. it supports both 10Mbps and 100Mbps working).

Fitting

- Carry out the initial steps outlined earlier in this chapter, to safely open the PC. (These steps are not necessary for a PC-Card, as this will attach via an externally accessible slot.)
- Check the card's IRQ and address space allocations to ensure that they do not conflict with the allocations for any existing card. Alter the network card's jumpers if necessary. With modern Plug and Play cards, including PC-Cards, the device should be detected by Windows 95/98.
- Insert the card into a spare expansion slot and secure with a screw. (In the case of PC-Cards, simply push the card into the slot firmly)
- Refit the computer cover.
- Attach a UTP cable via the RJ-45 connector on the card.
- Attach the other end of the UTP cable either to the network hub, or in the case of a simple two-PC network, to the other PC. In the latter case a slightly different cable will be required, known as a cross-over cable.

Note:

In a properly networked building, cable trunking will be used to connect various wall sockets to the hub(s). In this case the UTP '*drop*' cable will attach the PC to the wall socket, and the '*patch*' cable in the network room will attach the wall socket to the hub.

Testing Hardware

The Network Interface Card (NIC) will usually come with a floppy disk containing drivers. As well as the protocol and device drivers needed when installing software, there will often be a small diagnostic program, which can interrogate and configure the card, and be used to send simple packets between two machines fitted with the cards. By using this program, the NIC hardware and network media can be checked out before embarking on the installation of the software

Installing Software

The computer only requires a few small pieces of software in order to function as a network node. These are the driver, protocol and client. See the LANS chapter for a description of these components and how to install them.

Testing - Logging In

- Reboot the computer to install the network software.
- Enter the user login name and password when prompted.
  This should let the user into the network with the security provisions already set up on peer computers and/or network servers.

Fitting A Serial Port

There are a variety of reasons for fitting a new serial port to a computer. These are:

- Upgrading a slower model with a faster model (see the chapter on Data Communications).
- Replacing a faulty serial card.
- Fitting a serial card to a new motherboard.
- Adding extra serial ports to the computer.

Most I/O cards are provided with two serial outputs and one parallel output. The first steps in the fitting are the basic ones already outlined earlier. Each of the fitting options is carried out with slight differences and the remaining steps to be followed are detailed separately.

Upgrading/Replacing A Card

- Unscrew and remove the old card from its slot. Place the card to one side and retain the screws.
- Since this is a replacement card, the IRQ and I/O addresses already allocated to the old card should work with the new card. Check that these have not been changed from the standard addresses as shown in the chart. Windows 95/98/ME Device Manager/Properties will list addresses already in use. If the addresses have been altered for any reason, the new card should be set those addresses (usually by setting jumpers - consult the card's instructions).

Port	I/O Address	IRQ Address
COM1	03F8	IRQ4
COM2	02F8	IRQ3
COM3	03E8	IRQ4
COM4	02E8	IRQ3
LPT1	0378	IRQ7
LPT2	0278	IRQ5

- Insert the new card into the empty expansion slot and secure with a screw.

Fitting A First Card

The fitting instructions are identical to those above except that consideration has to be given to the addresses for the other components being fitted to the motherboard. A computer may wish to work with a number of serial devices (e.g. mouse, modem, scanner, serial printer) and these should not share the same addresses.   If the mouse, for example, is to be set to COM1 with IRQ4 then a modem or scanner card would have its jumpers set for other I/O and IRQ addresses from the list above.

Adding A Second Card

A second serial card would only be required if the computer were to interface to more than the two serial devices supported by a normal card.   The problem with a second serial card is that of avoiding address clashes.   The chart above shows that while COM1 and COM3 have different I/O addresses, they have the same IRQ setting.   This may not be a problem where devices are never used simultaneously (i.e. a scanner on COM2 is never used at the same time as a modem on COM4).   Where devices are to be used simultaneously, (e.g. a mouse and a modem) they cannot share the same IRQ, as the computer would not know which device to service.   Since most computers do not require two parallel devices, one of the COM ports could use its IRQ address if it is not already in use.   So, for example, COM2 could be 02F8/IRQ3 while COM4 could be 02E8/IRQ5.

Connecting A Mouse

The mouse can be connected to the computer in a number of ways, as long as the appropriate driver is used.

The alternative connection methods are:

- Using the computer's existing serial port, either COM1 or COM2, as the connection device.   This is simple to install and use and is a common choice.   The only potential problem is that the existing serial port might be required for another present or future purpose, such as servicing a printer or modem.   Since serial ports come in 9-pin and 25-pin varieties, an adapter might be required to match the mouse to the particular computer.
- Using a dedicated mouse interface on the motherboard.   This has a socket into which the mouse cable is plugged.   Mostly, this is of the PS/2 6-pin outline.   Converters are available to match a non-PS/2 mouse to a PS/2 type port.
- Using an add-on card that plugs into a spare expansion slot.   This is not common but may be the only option, if the existing serial port is occupied.   Unfortunately, a valuable expansion slot is used up this way.   Since a special card has to be bought, the bus mouse is also more expensive.   With an add-on card, check that it does not use IRQs (hardware interrupts) currently in use by other devices in the machine; check with the manual.   Adjust the mouse card's jumpers if necessary; check the card's installation notes for guidance.
- Using a cordless connection between mouse and computer.   A number of these devices use infrared light or radio waves as the transmission medium, rather than a length of cable.   The infrared models need to have the beam of the mouse pointing at the receiver, while the radio model only need be in the general local vicinity to be picked up by the radio receiver.   Radio-linked mice, such as the Logitech MouseMan Cordless, allow for one of 8 channels to be selected.   This is insufficient for a large office and machines sharing the same radio frequency can expect interesting interference problems!   These are not commonly used.
- Using a USB connection.   This allows the user to plug the mouse into any USB socket or hub. Many mouse models now offer both USB and PS/2 connection.

Mouse Drivers

The translation of the incoming data stream into screen activity is carried out by a special piece of software called a 'device driver' that has to be installed before the mouse is used (See the chapter on PC Configuration).   . Windows has its own mouse device driver.   Installation is normally automatic, with the user perhaps being asked whether the mouse is to be used with the COM1 or COM2 port.   When a mouse is purchased, it will include a disk containing the device driver and probably some drawing utilities.   The most significant mouse standards are the Microsoft and the Mouse Systems standards. Virtually all mice conform to the Microsoft standard and many also conform to the Mouse Systems standard.   If the mouse is not Microsoft-compatible, then the driver supplied with the mouse must be used. Using the wrong driver may produce erratic results. Windows allows the sensitivity of the mouse and other details to be set by the user (see the chapter on Windows configuration).

Fitting A ZIP Drive

The Iomega Zip drive is produced with USB, EIDE, SCSI or Parallel Port connections.

PARALLEL PORT

The steps for fitting the parallel port version are:

- Unplug the printer cable from the LPT1 connector at the back of the computer.
- Plug the ZIP cable into the LPT1 connector.
- Plug the other end of the cable into the ZIP drive's rear socket marked *'ZIP'*.
- Plug the printer cable into the ZIP drive's rear socket marked with a printer symbol.
- Plug the drive's power supply into the mains and the supply's output into the drive's power socket.
- Run the Iomega install program supplied on a floppy disk; this can be run through DOS or Windows.
- Install the utilities supplied on the *'ZIP Tools'* cartridge supplied by Iomega.

The above instructions provide a permanent host for the ZIP drive. However, the drive can be carried to another computer. Running the *'guest'* program on the floppy allows the new computer to use the cartridge without having to install the driver or tools.

EIDE CONNECTOR

Another model is an internal drive that fits to an IDE connector.

- Carry out the initial dismantling steps outlined previously.
- Fit the ZIP drive into an unused bay and secure with screws.
- Fit a power cable to the ZIP drive. If there is no spare connection, use a 'Y' connector.
- For a ZIP drive connecting to the motherboard's first IDE slot, set the ZIP drive's jumper to make the unit a 'slave' device and connect the drive on an unused connector on the existing hard disk cable.
- For a ZIP drive connecting to the motherboard's second IDE slot, set the ZIP drive's jumper to make the unit a 'master' device and connect an IDE interface cable between the drive and the second IDE slot on the motherboard.
- Refit the computer case and mains cable.
- Reboot the machine and run the BIOS setup program for that machine (see computer's manual).
- Alter the BIOS settings, so that the size and parameters of the ZIP drive are saved to the machine's CMOS. This is through the *'IDE HDD Auto Detection'* facility in a modern BIOS
- Run the Iomega install program supplied on a floppy disk; this can be run through DOS or Windows.

SCSI CONNECTOR

This is similar to the above except that the drive's SCSI ID is set to an unused ID and the drive is connected to an unused connector on the existing SCSI disk cable.

The USB model is simply connected to a USB outlet and is automatically detected as a device.

Installing a printer

The installation of a printer can be broken down to the following steps:

1. Placing and physically connecting the printer.
2. Installing any relevant drivers and/or software.
3. Testing the printer.

Connecting the printer

A new printer may be supplied with some packaging attached. It is common for manufacturers to put cardboard or other packing inside hollow areas (such as paper trays) to prevent damage during transport, and some even put sticky tape over moving components so that they are not damaged. All of this should be removed - but consult the printer manual to ensure that you do not accidentally remove vital components!

Physically attaching the printer cable to the printer and the PC is the easy part. Simply plug the Centronics (or whatever other cable is used) cable into the printer, and the parallel (or other port) connector into the PC. Then attach the power cable. However, the manual should always be consulted, in case there are any other considerations. (e.g., the attachment of document trays, feeders, etc.).

Many printers are designed for use on a network and some may not even have a connector to a PC, having a network adapter instead. In this case, consult the network administrator as to how it should be connected, as it may affect the network as a whole.

Finding a place to put the printer sometimes causes more problems than actually connecting it up. Printers should not be too near users, especially if they are noisy dot matrix printers. There should be plenty of room to get into the printer to retrieve printouts, add blank paper or replace ink or toner cartridges. Health and safety considerations should be borne in mind when placing the printer in an office.

Installing printer software

All modern printers are capable of producing graphics, and almost all users wish to take advantage of that capability. In order to use this capability, a printer driver must be installed.

The vast majority of home and office PC's use a version of Microsoft Windows as the operating system, and it is Windows itself that handles printer drivers, not the individual software packages. This allows any software package that runs under Windows to access any printer driver Windows has installed.

When purchasing a new printer, it should be supplied with a floppy disk or CD-ROM containing driver software. There may be several ways to install this software.

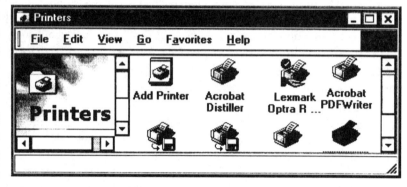

The standard Windows method for installing driver software is through the Control Panel. For example in Windows 98, click on the Start bar, go to Settings, and select Control Panel. The Control Panel window will open up, and the option *'Printers'* is available. Double click on this. (Alternatively, in Windows 98, the Printers panel can be reached directly through Start/Settings/Printers.)

The Printers window will contain all installed printer drivers, as well as an option to add new printer drivers, as shown. The default printer is indicated by a tick next to the icon.

To install a new printer driver, double-click on the *"Add printer"* icon. An on-screen installation wizard will guide you through the process.

Here are the important steps:

The first question the wizard will ask is whether the printer is a network printer or a local printer. Unless you have purchased a network printer and have spoken with the network administrator regarding installation, you should not choose a network installation.

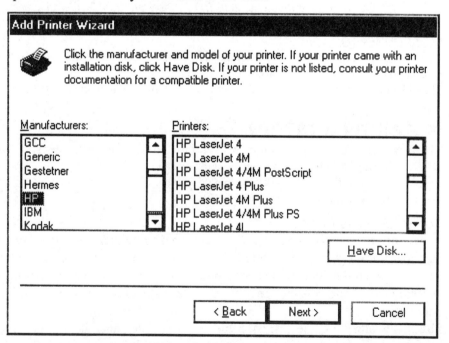

Next, the wizard will ask which type of printer to install a driver for. As shown below, it will offer a range of devices drivers built in to the windows CD-ROM. If the printer is an exact match for any one of these printer models, then that printer driver can be used.

However, even if there is an exact match, it is always a good idea to check that there are no drivers available that are more up to date. These drivers may be more efficient, faster, or use more features of the printer, for example.

These printer drivers will likely be found either on the floppy disk or CD-ROM that was supplied with the printer, or on the printer company's Internet site.

In either case, if the up-to-date drivers can be located, then these should be used instead of the built-in Windows driver. In order to do this, the *"Have Disk"* button should be used instead of selecting one of the existing printer drivers.

Clicking on the *"Have Disk"* button will produce another window, allowing the user to locate the actual driver files, which should be found on the floppy disk or CD-ROM, possibly in a sub-folder. Once the folder is located the user will be presented with a list of printer drivers located in that folder, via a window similar to the one on the previous page.

Once a printer model has been selected, the wizard will ask which port the printer is connected to. (Assuming of course that it is not a network printer) In most cases this will be LPT1, although printers can be set up to print through COM (serial) ports, or to print to a file on disk.

A window is displayed on screen to allow the user to select a port.

The *"Configure Port"* button allows some settings to be changed that alter how the selected port operates. In most cases these settings should not be changed unless the printer manual recommends it.

Finally, the user is asked to enter a display name for the printer driver. This is the name that will be displayed in the *"Printers"* window. So, for example, a user could install a printer driver for the HP LaserJet III printer, but give it a name that is more meaningful to the organisation, such as *"Finance Department Laser Printer"*.

The window also allows the user to set this new printer as the default printer. If there is currently no default printer or the new printer is to be used more often than any existing printer, then it should be set as the default printer. Since most non-networked systems only have access to one printer, they generally have just one printer driver and it is made the default printer.

Finally, the wizard will ask if the user wishes to print a test page, to check that the new printer driver is working correctly. If the printer is working correctly, then the test page will print out various details of the system, and a Windows icon.

Testing the printer

Every time a printer is installed, it should be tested. This applies whether it is a new installation or not – if you move a working printer from one PC to another, it should still be tested!

The Windows printer driver installation wizard ends with a test page being printed. If this test page prints out exactly as it should, then the printer can be used normally under Windows. This test page can also be repeated at a later date if problems occur.

Under some circumstances, it may be necessary to test the printer through DOS rather than Windows - or it may even be necessary to test the printer without any PC attached at all. For example, if printing in Windows is not working, then the user may wish to test printing through DOS to ensure that the printer cable and PC printer port are functional. If even DOS will not print, then it may be necessary to attempt a printer self test to see if the printer is functioning at all.

These three common printer tests are described in more detail below.

Printer self test

The first test that should be carried out once a printer is physically installed, is the printer self test. This does not require that the printer be connected to a PC. Virtually all printers are capable of printing some form of self-test page.

In a laser printer, this is most commonly done through the control panel buttons. For example, the HP LaserJet series has a *'Menu'* button that cycles through various options, one of which enters a sub-menu containing various test and diagnostic printouts.

For a dot matrix or an inkjet printer, the self test is usually accessed by holding down a particular button. Sometimes the printer requires that this be done while the printer is being powered up. Other printers, such as some Apple LaserWriters, print a test page automatically every time they are switched on.

The printer's manual should contain instructions on how to obtain a self test page – this should be consulted for every individual printer, to ensure the correct method is followed.

Self tests are also useful once the printer is installed fully. It can help in troubleshooting errors – a successful printer self test proves that there are no problems with the print head, printer carriage, printer power supply, or certain parts of the interface circuitry. In effect it implies that the fault is either with the PC, or with the communications equipment. (i.e. the ports, cables etc)

DOS test print

One basic test for printers is to use some form of DOS command line that will result in a printout. For example, a plain text file (such as the WIN.INI that should be located in the Windows folder) can be printed in a typical PC setup by using a DOS command such as the following:

TYPE C:\WINDOWS\WIN.INI > LPT1

This command will attempt to print the contents of the file 'WIN.INI'. Because this file is a text file, it is in plain ASCII format and will print on any printer, assuming that the printer is physically working and the communications equipment is correct and working.

The DOS test print is usually not necessary at installation time. It is most useful to diagnose faults. Due to the fact that it is a plain ASCII file, it does not require any drivers, or printer languages. Therefore, if such a command fails to produce a printout, then it implies that the fault is either with the printer itself, or with the communications equipment.

On the other hand, if a DOS test print is successful, then any fault that Windows programs experience with printing must lie with the drivers used by Windows, which are not necessary to print from DOS.

Windows test page

The Windows test page should be generated every time a printer driver is installed, to ensure that the printer is attached and functioning correctly. If problems develop after the installation however, it may be useful to be able to print this test page without having to reinstall the driver.

This can be done through the Printers section of the Control Panel. In the *'Printers'* window, right-click on the desired printer icon, and select the *'Properties'* option.

A window will appear, with various tabs describing various capabilities and settings of the printer. The default tab when the window opens up should be the *'General'* tab. This tab contains a button labelled *'Print Test Page'*. This button will generate the test page and send it to the printer.

The Windows Printer Test Page consists of a Windows logo (which will be printed in colour if it is a colour printer), a title, and some plain text.   The text includes

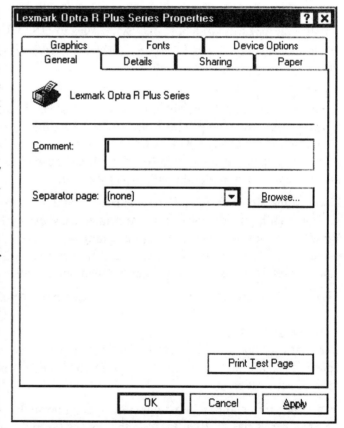

information on the printer driver, such as the printer name and model, driver files in use, and so on.

If the Windows Printer Test Page is created successfully, this shows that the driver is capable of printing to that device, but it does not guarantee that the driver is the most up-to-date version, or that every application will print perfectly. However, if the Windows Printer test page comes out properly, then any faults with printing to the device are probably caused by the software itself. For example, Microsoft Word may be unable to print due to insufficient memory, even though the printer and the Windows driver are quite functional.

Adding Cards Under Windows

The add-on cards fitted to a Windows 95/98/ME/2000 computer can be of two types:

- Plug and Play cards that are automatically detected.
- Cards that need to be set up manually.

Automatic Setup

If the computer's BIOS supports Plug and Play (all modern computers), then the addition of a new PnP card is detected during the bootup stage. If the device exists in the list held in the Window's 'INF' folder, then the driver is automatically installed. Otherwise, the *'Add New Hardware'* Wizard is called up and the user can choose to:

- Let Windows search for an appropriate driver for the card.
- Point to the folder that contains the driver.

The automatic search is through the driver database already installed on the computer. If the driver is found in the database, it is installed. If the driver is not already in the database, the user is prompted to browse through the computer's file system (including floppy disk, CD, etc) to point to the folder containing the driver (a .INF file).

The user is often asked to insert the original Windows installation CD, to access the driver stored there. Often, however, the version on the CD is older than the driver on the floppy disk provided with the add-on card. If this is suspected, then the option for user control of the source folder should be chosen. Alternatively, the latest driver can often be downloaded from the web site of the card manufacturer.

When the driver is installed, the system may prompt for the computer to be restarted.

Sometimes, Windows will detect that a new card has been installed but will not be able to detect what the device is. If the "Unknown Device" message is displayed, then the manual method of device driver installation as outlined below has to be used.

Manual Setup

The *'Control Panel'* has an *'Add New Hardware'* option that invokes an installation wizard to select and configure new hardware. The menu presents a choice of device type - e.g. display adapters, hard disk controllers and network adapters. The example shows the menu displayed when *'Hard disk controllers'* is chosen. The windows list all devices - by manufacturer- that are contained in its database. For newer models, the *'Have Disk'* option allows installation from CD or floppy.

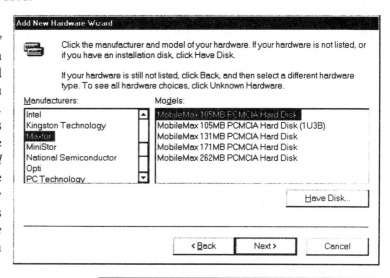

Altering Existing Values

Clicking the *'System'* icon in *'Control Panel'* displays a *'System Properties'* menu from which the *'Device Manager'* option displays a list of existing hardware. Clicking on an item displays the menu shown. The *'Resources'* option displays the current I/O and IRQ settings. Unchecking the *'Use automatic settings'* box allows the values to be altered. In the example shown, Windows reports that no conflict has been detected between this device and others. The *'Driver'* option displays the software drivers that handle the device. The *'General'* option displays information such as the detected manufacturer of the device.

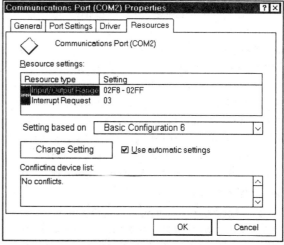

System Selection

Choosing the correct computer system is a difficult decision to be made by home and professional users alike. This is due to the thousands of different products and their ever-changing specifications. Any book, by the time it is published, is out of date in terms of hardware/software specifications and prices. However, the approaches to evaluating, choosing and purchasing hardware/software remain unchanged.

If cost is not a problem, then there are few other problems. The user can simply purchase the most powerful computer incorporating the latest technology, a large screen, high resolution, colour monitor and a high definition colour laser printer. Suitable extras might be a colour flatbed scanner, high-quality video and sound card, modem, rewriteable DVD and CDR drive, digital camera and multimedia editing suite. This setup covers virtually all possible uses and mainly exists as an ideal. For most individuals, and certainly most companies, there are severe financial constraints and expensive equipment is only purchased if it is absolutely essential. Therefore, the selection of computer systems becomes a vital process, as purchasing mistakes might prove costly.

The considerations are not solely technical - there is little point in buying a machine with every conceivable bell and whistle, if it is always breaking down and the technical support from the manufacturer is poor. Questions of warranty and after-sales service can be as important as the technical specifications. When choosing equipment, there is no *'correct'* answer - there is only a correct choice for a particular set of circumstances. For example, a 21" colour monitor is entirely unnecessary for use with a computer used for normal text-based programs such as fleet control, many databases, network servers, etc. On the other hand, for some graphic-based programs - such as CAD (computer aided design), professional DTP, map drawing, etc. - a large-size monitor might be an essential purchase. The needs of different parts of an organisation are different; the accountant may require a wide-carriage dot-matrix printer, while the typing pool requires a high-quality laser printer. This means that the final decisions must be based on knowing what equipment is available and on understanding what is suitable for each situation. The main stages of the selection process can be defined as:

- DEFINITION OF NEEDS
- EVALUATION OF PRODUCTS
- PURCHASING POLICY
- POST-DELIVERY ACTIVITY

Companies may well divide these into further sub-activities. For example, the evaluation process may involve both the technical staff (to evaluate the technical specification) and financial controllers (to evaluate purchasing, running and maintenance costs).

Definition Of Needs

The definition process can be treated as two separate, although linked, stages:
- Define the purpose of the purchase
- Define the equipment to meet that purpose

In many cases, the demand may be for a multi-purpose machine; the users may require to have word-processing, spreadsheet and database facilities on each machine in the office. In other cases, a single machine may be required to only run a single package, such as computer aided design software. The important starting point is that *software needs determine the hardware requirements.*

If the general-purpose computer is based on running Windows products, there are greater demands on the machine; the machine will need more memory than would be required on a computer only running DOS-based applications. If a database is to be used regularly, then a fast hard disk will make the machine more productive. In the CAD case, extensive screen activities are involved in continually re-drawing the intricate designs and especially fast video cards improve that machine's performance. The two examples will probably also have different requirements for add-ons; the first case may only require a simple dot-matrix printer, while the second case may require an expensive plotter.

Rationalisation

The exact number of machines and the exact software requirements has to be determined as the first priority. This may be a matter of negotiation, since users may well wish to have more software on their machines than they will normally use. Since most packages cost hundreds of pounds, over purchasing of software is extremely wasteful.

If a number of machines are in the same room, then perhaps only one computer should be fitted with the software that users rarely use and users can share this machine when required.

Local Area Networks
If many users require access to the same packages, and especially if they require access to the same sets of data, consideration should be given to placing these machines on a local area network. This involves cabling the machines together so that they are all able to share the one version of each package and the one version of the communal data. The licence for multiple users on a network is generally appreciably cheaper than buying multiple copies to place on each individual machine.

Creating A List
A list of equipment requirements should be provisionally agreed as the basis for the preparation of the detailed list of hardware and their specifications. In the light of the evaluation stage results, there may be some amendment to this list, due to financial or other constraints. Indeed, the hardware definition stage might also force a review of needs, due to technical considerations.

Hardware Definition
The next part of this chapter discusses the relative merits of different computer components as an aid to decision making. For more details on a particular topic, the appropriate chapter can be read. To make an informed decision, the full range of facts must be available for comparison. These facts will include product specifications, independent reviews and reports from user groups. Hardware decisions are required on the items listed and guidance is given as to their respective merits for specific purposes.

Case Types
A first consideration is the environment for using the system. The options are:

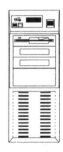

Tower This type of case (also called *'full tower'*) has a large, vertical case with plenty of space inside for the inclusion of extra equipment. The case should have extra drive bays, so that CD-ROMs, extra hard disks, etc. can be easily fitted. The main board used in these models should have plenty of unused expansion slots, so that extra equipment cards can be plugged in. This is the first choice for a system that carries out a lot of the office's extra activities. Examples of this would be using the machine as the server in a local area network or using the machine as the office's main resource for fax cards, modems, scanners, tape backup, etc. The unit normally sits on the floor and the monitor sits on the desktop. New tower units, like most other types of case, now come in ATX form rather than AT form.

Mini-Tower This type has a vertical construction as above but is not so tall. It can store less than a tower but is more expandable than the average desktop machine. It is a good compromise for size and expandability, and as such is now the most common form. It usually sits on the desktop with the monitor close by.

Desktop This was once the most common of all case types and is a horizontal box of varying dimensions, on to which most users place the monitor.

Low-Profile This is a smaller *'slim line'* version of the above, specially miniaturised to occupy less desk space; they are often also of the *'small footprint'* variety, i.e. they have smaller breadth and depth dimensions than ordinary desktop machines and therefore take up less of the desk area. They are neat machines and pleasing to the eye but they have a major drawback with their expandability. Since the case is of a low profile, there is not enough height in the machine to plug any expansion cards straight into the board's expansion slots. A special *'plane'* board has to be fitted vertically into one of the expansion slots. The expansion cards then plug horizontally into one of the expansion slots on the plane board. This normally results in fewer slots being available in low-profile models and, in some cases, the power supply has to be unscrewed to allow the extra cards to be fitted. Unless future expansion of the machines is ruled out, this would not be the first choice for office machines. Low-profile cases are rare nowadays.

Portable These machines are about the size of a portable typewriter and are designed for use with internal batteries, the car's 12 volt lighter socket or a mains adapter. This means that they are very portable and are in regular use by those who require computing facilities away from the office. They have small screens built in to the case lid and these are inferior to standard monitors, particularly for prolonged use.

Notebook   A notebook is an even smaller version of the portable and is around the size of an A4 sheet of paper.   Unlike the portable, they are small enough to carry in a briefcase along with other material and are now more popular than portables.

Handheld   This name covers two types of system: Palmtops, and WAP mobile phones. While a palmtop is a full-fledged computer in its own right (albeit one which is very limited in its capabilities), a WAP device is essentially a mobile phone with a few extra functions added. These include email and limited web browsing.

CPU Options

The type and speed of the computer's CPU have a great bearing on the system's ability to handle tasks. The difference between different chips and chip speeds becomes more noticeable with the increasing complexity of software.   For example, programs designed to take full advantage of Pentium MMX code or Pentium 4 SSE2 code will only give this extra performance to those who own those machines.

Note   The available choices for machine CPU types are covered in the chapter
            on Computer Architecture and should be considered again at this stage.

Other CPU Factors:

Processor Upgrade Options: Some computers allow the CPU to be removed and replaced by a more up-to-date version.   This may involve buying a computer whose motherboard supports such an upgrade option. Often, the upgrade is not as effective as a newly purchased system, since the other components in a new machine (i.e. disk speed, bus type, video cards) will have improved greatly since the older models was phased out.   However, upgrading does provide a degree of *'future proofing'* - i.e. it allows the machine to partially keep up with new technology without the expense of being completely replaced. Recent changes in processor connections and the rapid pace of processor development have made processor upgrades less common, but they are still an option.

Chipsets: The CPU is supported by a *'chipset'* on the motherboard.   The set of supporting chips is designed to handle memory and peripheral interfacing.   The older chipsets are cheaper but support less facilities – for example they may not contain onboard LAN and audio support, or may not support up-to-date RAM types such as DDR or RDRAM. See the chapter on Computer Architecture for more details.

Portables: These machines are mainly battery powered and therefore require low-power version of CPUs.   The older portables only lasted around 3 hours on one charge of the internal batteries but the newer chips are even more low-powered to allow the machine to run for up to a full day on a single charge.

Motherboard Options

Facilities

For those concerned with future-proofing their machine, consideration should be given to purchasing computers that support a 133MHz or 200MHz bus, RIMM sockets and the Universal Serial Bus.

Expansion Slots   Each computer's main board has a number of extra slots into which additional hardware boards can be fitted.   These are known as *'expansion slots'* and the more that are provided, the more expandable the machine becomes.   Typical cards to plug into these slots are modems, hard disk controllers, video capture cards, sound cards and cards for the control of electronic apparatus.   These slots are provided for different card types and a typical computer will offer a single AGP slot, and a number of PCI slots. Modern boards have dropped ISA support entirely though older machines are still in use with ISA. If the machine is likely to have a range of add-ons fitted, the number of expansions slots provided on a motherboard is important. In addition, the points made about low profile cases might further restrict the actual number of cards that can be fitted - even in a machine with several free slots.

External Ports   The machine should be supplied with at least one parallel port, for the printer, and one or more serial ports, for add-ons such as a modem. All but the oldest computers have a dedicated, built-in mouse port in the form of a PS/2 socket.   Some motherboards provide enhanced serial ports for faster data transmission when using modems.   Similarly, most motherboards also provide EPP (Enhanced Parallel Port) bi-directional parallel ports so that parallel port devices such as scanners and external hard disks will provide a faster performance.   USB sockets provide for various add-ons such as scanners and cameras. Finally, the keyboard port may be either PS/2 style, or a larger, older 5-pin socket.

BIOS The BIOS chip is a key component in the system and well-known manufacturers like AMI, Award and Phoenix are safe choices.   These manufacturers ensure that the code in the BIOS chip is compatible with new hardware developments. The main thing to look for in a BIOS is the range of hardware it supports – for example, booting from CD-ROM or ZIP disk.

Memory Options

Size Machines are provided with a wide variety of memory amounts installed. The amount of memory required for a particular machine can be stated at the time of placing the order, or extra memory can be fitted at a later date as an upgrade (see the chapter on upgrades). The memory requirements of a particular application will appear on its specification; this is printed in the application's manual and is usually printed on the box packaging. Assuming the computer uses Windows and Windows-based applications, the machine will need plenty of extended memory. The realistic minimum memory expected by many Windows applications is 8MB and can be as much as 128MB or more. Windows 95 can run on less memory but is too slow for commercial efficiency. Later versions such as Windows 98 or ME are not recommended for use on machines with less than 32MB of RAM. Conversely, the more extended memory that is fitted, the more efficiently Windows applications will run.

Speed The type of memory impacts significantly on its speed. PC133 memory, for example, is theoretically one third faster than PC100 memory. Various extra technologies can be applied to memory chips to improve performance. For example, if your motherboard supports DDR memory, then using DDR SDRAM chips will give better memory throughput.

Format Modern motherboards use DIMMs or RIMMs as a means of holding memory chips, with 72-pin SIMMs being found only in legacy systems. Either system allows easy upgrading of memory, should the need arise. The user simply purchases extra memory modules and inserts them in unused slots, or replaces existing chips with higher-capacity chips.

Cache Memory This is a small block of ultra-fast memory that acts as a buffer between the CPU proper and main memory. It greatly speeds up data transfers, particularly with databases. It is available in 32k, 64k, 128k, 256k and 512k cache sizes. Since cache is now integrated onto the CPU, 256k is fairly standard.

MONITOR OPTIONS

Size The normal supplied size is 15" and this is adequate for general purposes. The supplying of 17" monitors is also common and provides an improved viewing area for the user. For graphics applications such as CAD, artwork, multimedia and DTP, a larger size screen may be necessary. These are normally 19" and 21" models.

Resolution Most machines are now supplied with SVGA (800 x 600 pixels) or better monitors and new software is written to this standard. Any reasonably up-to-date package can use this or even higher resolution modes. Specialist graphics software is capable of working at very high resolutions (1280 x 1024, 1600 x 1200 or higher) and an SVGA monitor will enable the user to take advantage of the improved detail.

Dot Pitch A dot pitch of 0.28 is the basic quality for general uses. If affordable, a 0.25mm pitch or less is preferred for high-resolution work.

Refresh Rate The higher a monitor's screen refresh rate, the less is the flicker and the less is the risk of eyestrain for users spending prolonged periods at the machine. A refresh rate of 70Hz or 72Hz is a satisfactory minimum.

Video Cards If a machine is to be used for Windows applications or extensive graphics work, a high performance video card or Windows accelerator card should be bought. Most cards supplied today have upwards of 8MB of video memory, which is sufficient for most day-to-day work. If high resolution or special 3D effects are required, a higher specification video card should be considered, perhaps with as much as 128MB of RAM. In some circumstances TV-Out, TV Tuner, or MPEG hardware might be wanted.

Other Factors If a machine is to be used for prolonged periods, or placed in an environment with bright light or shiny surfaces, an anti-glare screen should be fitted to the front of the monitor. If a machine is in regular use, or is positioned next to other staff, a low-radiation model should be purchased. If a portable or notebook computer is in regular use, a separate monitor should be purchased, so that the user can connect the machine when appropriate (e.g. a salesperson may use the notebook· with its small screen to collect orders during the day and then connect to the large external monitor for calculating and summarising information back at the hotel or head office). An FST monitor (flatter, squarer tube) provides a screen that maintains its clarity for a longer period than the conventional tube. It has no convergence problems and it is an ideal monitor for intricate design work. Trinitron monitors also provide better quality. For systems in special circumstances, consideration may be given to special display devices such as LCD screens or projectors. (see the Display Technologies chapter)

Hard Disk Options

Size The purchase should be based on the fact that most computers use up more disk space than first predicted. Calculation of the disk's size should not be a simple sum of all the expected software, since each application will generate its own sets of data. A machine used in a typing pool may only generate Word documents, and thus a small 2GB disk may be entirely adequate. A database server or multimedia capture machine might require 40GB, 80GB of storage or even more, while heavy-duty ISP servers will require RAID arrays with huge storage requirements. A single Windows application can require upwards of 250MB of hard disk space just to store its program files. Fortunately, few new systems have less than 10GB of hard disk space, even for budget entry-level PCs. However, if purchasing second hand or using old systems cascaded down within an organisation, hard disk size should be checked.

Type   Hard drives on sale today are generally UltraDMA or SCSI systems, with basic IDE and EIDE drives in use only on legacy systems. Ultra DMA is faster than IDE; SCSI drives are even faster but are significantly more expensive. As a consequence, they are normally only available as an optional extra. SCSI drives are a likely choice for multimedia and video editing activities. FireWire drives currently consist of ordinary UltraDMA drives with a FireWire interface added. This allows for more upgrade options but no real speed increase.

Speed   The speed of a disk is measured in average access time and can range from 4ms to 10ms.   If a disk is rated in excess of 10ms, it is probably old stock.   For applications that are *'disk-bound'*, i.e. use a lot of disk access such as databases, a fast access time can have a significant effect on the machine's overall performance. Additionally, high-volume data applications such as video editing require fast access speeds. Consideration should be given to a large internal cache, which also speeds up operations.

Removable Disk Options

Quantity: Most machines will provide a single 3.5" disk drive as standard. A machine may be ordered with two 3.5" drives where there is likely to be a regular need to make copies of disks.   Using one drive for the source disk (the one to be copied) and another drive for the destination disk (the disk to be copied on to) makes copying a simple process with no need to constantly swap disk in and out of the same drive.   For larger capacity, many computers fit 100MB and 200MB ZIP drives, or LS120 drives that accept both floppy disks and 120MB removable disks.

Miscellaneous Options

Power Supply: A power supply has to be able to handle the current needs of the equipment fitted in the computer case - i.e. the motherboard, hard disk, floppy disks and any cards plugged into the expansion slots such as disk controllers and video cards.   The supply also has to cope with any future add-ons that are plugged into the expansion sockets such as modems, etc.   Additionally, the supply has a wiring loom that provides a few spare power connections.   These are left floating around in the case and can be used to power up add-ons that do not connect directly to the expansion bus, such as the CD-ROM or DVD drive.   A computer power supply of 200W would be needed if the machine is expected to host extra equipment.   For a tower machine used as a network server or power workstation, a 250W or 300W supply would be more appropriate. Another consideration with power supplies is their safety, since they handle mains voltages.   The supply should have a safety kitemark or other seal of approval.   All power supplies in new machines are of the ATX type; unless you have a very old AT power connector motherboard this is the correct option.

Keyboard: A cheap and nasty keyboard of an unknown brand can spoil an otherwise good machine. Where possible the machine should be purchased with a known brand name such as Logitech or Cherry.   Special keyboards are available for one-handed use, or with curved keypads for a more 'natural' feel.

Mouse: A poor mouse, with a sticky and jerky operation, hinders Windows operations and a quality mouse should be purchased with the machine.   Consideration might also be given to *'wheel mice'* that give added functionality.

Printer: Quality of printout must be balanced against cost considerations.   Dot matrix printers are the cheapest, but are only suitable for high-volume, low-quality printouts.   Inkjets give decent quality at a reasonable price, but those who can afford it (such as medium to large size businesses) should consider laser printers, which are expensive but of the best quality.   Laser quality is measured in dots per inch (dpi), and generally speaking higher dpi means higher price. 300dpi is a basic model but is good for most needs.

CD-ROM: Every machine now comes with at least a CD-ROM, with most models offering either CD-R or DVD drives.   These provide additional functions and future proofing.   A currently expensive option that should only be considered for special requirements is a DVD-RAM drive.

Extras: These may include scanners, modems, sound cards, network cards, video capture cards, etc. with the correct mix dependent upon the intended use for the machine.   Most machines on sale include sound cards and modems as standard.

Technical Check List

Case	Tower / Mini-Tower / DeskTop / AT or ATX form Low Profile / Portable / Notebook / Hand-held
CPU	Type: Pentium III/ Celeron/ Athlon / Pentium 4 Speed: < 1GHz/ 1.1GHz / 1.2GHz / 1.4GHz / 1.5GHz / 1.7GHz / 2GHz Cache Size: 32k / 64k / 128k / 256k / 512k
Motherboard	Chipset: 810 / 820 / 840 / 850 / SiS / Via / Ali Memory Slot type: SDR DIMM / DDR DIMM / RIMM Number of free PCI slots: 1 / 2 / 3 / 4 Onboard peripherals: None / Video / Sound / Network
Memory	Size: 64MB / 128MB / 256MB / 384MB / 512MB Speed: 100MHz / 133MHz / 200MHz / 266MHz / 800MHz Type: DRAM / EDO / SDRAM / RDRAM
Hard Disk	Cache Size: 512KB / 1MB / 2MB / 4MB/ 16MB Interface Type: UDMA / UDMA-66 / UDMA-100 / SCSI-2 / SCSI-Ultra / SCSI-UW Access Time: 4ms / 5ms / 7ms / 9ms / 10ms / >10ms
Other Storage	Extra floppy drive / ZIP drive / JAZ drive / DAT tape / CD Writer / DVD- RAM / LS-120
Monitor	Size: 15" / 17" / 18" / 20" / 21" / 22" / 24" Resolution: 800x600 / 1024x768 / 1280x1024 / 1600x1200 / Widescreen Dot Pitch: 0.28mm / 0.27mm / 0.26mm / 0.25mm Refresh Rate: 72Hz / 85Hz / Higher Radiation: Standard / Low radiation Type: CRT / FST / Trinitron / LCD Anti-glare screen: Yes / No Energy saving: Yes / No Plug and Play: Yes / No
Video Card	3D accelerator: Yes / No 3D systems supported: OpenGL / Glide / Direct3D Interface : PCI / AGP / AGP2x / AGP4x Memory: 4MB / 8MB / 16MB / 32MB / 64MB Additional features : TV-Out / TV Tuner / MPEG hardware
CD-ROM	Interface : IDE / SCSI Speed : 32x / 36x / 40x / 44x / 48x / 52x / 56x
Ports	Serial: 1 / 2 Fast Speed Yes/No Parallel: 1 / 2 Enhanced Yes/No PS/2 Mouse: Yes / No Keyboard : PS/2 / AT USB ports: 0 / 1 / 2 Other ports : FireWire / IrDA / Games
Power Supply	Capacity : 200W / 230W / 250W / 300W Safety marked : Yes / No
Mouse	Type: PS/2 / Serial Features: Mouse wheel / Cordless
Printer	Dot-Matrix: 9-pin / 24-pin / 48-pin InkJet: 600x300 / 600x600 / 1200x600 Laser: 300dpi / 600 dpi / 1200dpi Colour: Yes / No LAN compatible: Yes / No
Extras	DVD Player / Network Card / Sound system / Microphone / UPS / Modem / Webcam / Plotter / ISDN card
Warranty	1 year / 3 years / 5 years Back to base / On site / Collect and Deliver / Replacement
Model / Price	Model: Price: £

Evaluation

For a large contract, or a likely repeat contract, a thorough evaluation process would be carried out. This is aimed at pinpointing problems in advance and thereby preventing future difficulties. The evaluation process should include:

- EQUIPMENT TESTING (reliability, compatibility)
- EQUIPMENT COSTING (cost of purchase, installation, training, running, and maintenance)

Equipment Testing

Reliability

The single biggest factor in commercial computing equipment is reliability. This is even more important than the raw speed of a system. If a system breaks down, data may be lost or be temporarily inaccessible. This could have severe consequences for the organisation and must be taken into account during the purchasing of new equipment. Check whether the manufacturer/supplier is running a quality control system to BS 5750 accreditation, or to the ISO 9002 quality assurance standard. In addition, any reputable dealer will be willing to demonstrate equipment. Where a large order is involved, the dealer should be willing to loan equipment so that a thorough test can be carried out. As a minimum, the dealer should offer a 30-day money-back guarantee if the equipment is not suitable. This time should be used to check the machine performance under all possible conditions - running databases, number crunching, graphics, etc.

Many items of equipment are tested by manufacturers who produce figures on the likely running time before there are any problems. This is the MTBF, Mean Time Between Failures, and is measured in thousands of hours. Equipment with a high MTBF rate is likely to run with fewer faults than equipment with a lower rating.

Compatibility

Another important factor in a purchase is its compatibility with current and new hardware and software. Typical questions are:

- Is the current equipment PC compatible? If a company is currently equipped with Apple Macintoshes, purchasing PC equipment will pose problems of using each other's files. This may not be a problem if the Macs are only used for graphics work while the PCs are restricted to clerical or commercial work.
- Is it a UK version? Sometimes bargain hardware and software are non-UK versions being dumped.
- Does new software read old data? Ensure that working data import/export facilities exist.
- Does new software run on intended old machine? Consult the software's minimum requirements. This is particularly true for Windows software.
- Remember that a SCSI bus needs SCSI drives, a PCI card needs a PCI bus, etc.
- Is the machine's CPU Intel-compatible? A CPU chip should act exactly like an Intel chip, since most software assumes that a 100% Intel is in use.

Equipment Costing

The cost of computer hardware and software is not the price paid for their purchase; there are a great many extra factors to be considered.
These include:

Purchase Cost

Many dealers reduce the advertised price of their products by omitting components from the package. Typical 'extras' may be such essential components as monitors and hard disks. So, check the exact items included in any quoted price. Items to confirm include monitor, DOS, Windows, mouse and any bundled software. Ensure that there are no hidden extras.

Installation Costs

For a simple, single computer purchase, there may be no extra cost; the machine might be set up by the dealer as part of the delivery, or it may be installed by company support staff.
For larger or more complex purchases, there are other considerations:

- The time required for installing and testing multiple stations and their software
- The time and material involved in installing a local area network of machines

- The amount of software customisation required. This may be programs specially written by a software house or application packages customised to companies' needs. In both cases, time is required to fully test out the software.
- Duplication of effort when running the old manual system and the computerised system concurrently. This may be required until the robustness of the new system is proven.
- Any extra costs, such as improved seating or desks, or alterations to the office lighting.

Running Costs

The organisation has to budget for the future replacement of faulty or obsolete equipment. This involves estimating the useful life span of the new purchases and the likely costs for replacements at the end of that period. In addition, an estimate has to be made of likely annual consumables such as disks and toner or ribbons for printers. An often overlooked cost for certain systems is the Data Protection Act and the workload it places on systems administrators.

Maintenance Costs

The costs do not end when the systems are bought and installed. Provision has to be made to keep the systems running as smoothly as possible, with as little loss of processing time as possible from breakdowns. The main considerations are:

WARRANTIES

Most warranties last a year, with a few dealers offering two or three year warranties. The first year usually covers all parts and labour and the type of cover thereafter has to be checked. Some, for example, only provide parts cover in the second and third years. Also, the conditions of the warranty vary and the most common arrangements are:

BACK-TO-BASE

This is a cheap option for the supplier and the user. The repair is carried out at the supplier's premises reducing labour costs and delivering a cheaper maintenance contract. However, these policies have negative features:
- Loss of use of the machine for days
- Risk of damage in transit
- Costs in preparing the crate for transporting to the supplier

This option is suitable for computers that are not in regular use or handle low priority work.

ON-SITE

An on-site policy is an expensive option since it includes the payment of the engineer's travelling time. It is a useful option for users as it involves little disruption and the symptoms and operations are more easily explained to the engineer. The guaranteed response time - i.e. the time delay before a visit - should be confirmed. Of course, a fast response time does not guarantee a fast repair and the item remains unusable during that period. This option is suitable for medium to high priority items.

REPLACEMENT POLICIES

For a price, a replacement, or 'swap out' policy can be obtained. The defective item is replaced with a working equivalent while the repair is being carried out (either on-site or at the supplier's premises). This allows the organisation to continue with the minimum disruption. Faster response times to effect the replacement are more expensive than slower responses. This is the best solution for essential items such as printers, peripherals, network servers, etc. In the case of defective computers, replacing the machine usually results in the data on the defective machine being temporarily unavailable - unless the data is transferable to the new machine, or the computer is a network node using centralised data.

MAINTENANCE CONTRACTS

When the normal guarantee period expires, some suppliers provide an extension to their cover and this cost should be confirmed. If there is no policy of extending maintenance cover, terms have to be sought from a separate maintenance company. In both cases, the terms of the service (i.e. on-site, back-to-base or temporary replacement) have to be considered.

Other Support

Some manufacturers provide lifetime telephone support for their machines and the availability and quality of this should be checked (e.g. the times the service is available and whether software, peripherals and network problems are included). Others provide customer support for the first year and charge thereafter. This may be on an annual charge basis or on a per-call basis.

Finally, if a local area network is established, a network supervisor has to be trained and given time to administer the system.

Training Costs

A factor often overlooked in the costing process is the adequate training of the staff expected to use the new hardware and software. The cost of training soon repays itself in increased productivity. The degree of training required for personnel has to be determined (e.g. some staff to a basic level and others to an advanced level) and costed. For large organisations with extensive IT departments in-house training may be available, which is normally substantially cheaper.

Purchasing Policy

The company should have a set of rules on general purchasing and they will mostly apply to computing purchases. These rules may include:

- Dealing directly with the computer manufacturer. This cuts out the middle man and lowers prices - a system known as *'Direct Sales'*.
- Choosing a company with a known track record.
- Placing orders that are conditional on specified delivery times, pricing, or an agreed returns or refunds policy.
- Keeping a copy of all material - adverts, order forms, invoices, receipts, correspondence and records of telephone conversations.

No goods should be charged for until they are despatched.

If personally buying, use a credit card, as buyers are covered by the credit card company's insurance scheme if the supplier ceases trading before the goods are dispatched.

Post Delivery

When the system arrives, the contents of all the boxes should be checked and tested.

Checking

The organisation should have a system for checking and documenting the receipt of all incoming goods. Failure to deliver in time is a breach of the supplier's contract and it may be that the lateness renders the equipment useless. In such a case, the box may be returned to the supplier. If the goods are in time, equipment testing can proceed. At its simplest this may be only a checklist to compare and sign if correct. The first check is to see that the goods have arrived within the required time. Each item is given an initial visual examination to check for obvious damage and to ensure that the item is of the type ordered - e.g. correct model, size, capacity, etc. If the item is present, correct and apparently undamaged, the checklist is ticked against that item.

Testing

Computer equipment should not be placed in a storage cupboard; it should be tested upon arrival. The extent of testing will depend upon the apparatus. The minimum checked should be on basic functionality - i.e. does the printer actually print, do all the keys on the keyboard work, does the monitor display a satisfactory screen. Further checks can be conducted where required - e.g. do all the printer emulations work, does the monitor handle all the required resolutions, etc. All testing must be carried out within the manufacturer's instructions.

If the system is in any way incomplete or non-functional, the supplier should be contacted immediately. Speed and accuracy in reporting any discrepancy or damage is important. Suppliers must deliver the goods as advertised and purchasers are protected by consumer law. In many cases, the initial contact with the supplier is carried out by the technician, so that the technical details can be clearly explained. The technician should also inform the administration of his/her own organisation since they will pursue any legal and financial consequences.

Consumer Law

The main points of the Sale of Goods Act are:

- Goods must be accurately described
- Goods must be of merchantable quality
- Goods must be fit for the purpose for which they have been sold

The main consumer laws are the Consumer Protection Act, the Fair Trading Act, the Sale of Goods Act, the Trades Description Act, the Supply of Goods and Services Act, and the Distance Selling Regulations. For example, if goods are bought unseen, the Mail Order Code of Practice recommends that the user is able to return the goods within 30 days if they are not suitable. In this case, some dealers charge a fee when goods are returned, called a *'re-stocking fee'*, and the consumer may have to pay the transit charges.

Data Communications

There has been a great expansion in demand for communication between computers to allow a variety of data sharing and mailing facilities.   Within an organisation, this is met by creating multi-user systems that connect PCs via a local area network or a Unix system. The demand for communications within an organisation has been matched by the demand for individuals and external organisations to communicate. This communication may remain within a town or may stretch between cities or across the globe.

A wide variety of services have been developed to handle the following facilities:

Speech, file transfer, FAX (including high volume, high-speed Group 4 FAX), voice mail, LAN connection, information and database services, telemarketing (e.g. home/catalogue shopping), image transfer, videoconferencing, e-mail, electronic newspapers, remote surveillance/ security/ monitoring/ diagnostics, telemetry (reading meters from a distance), EPOS/data transfer, home banking, teleworking, teleconferencing, remote training, remote learning, distributed processing and video on demand services.

Basics

Within a computer, most data is moved round in parallel format on the various internal buses. Between the computer and the average printer, the connection is also parallel.   Parallel systems allow the maximum amount of data to be transferred at any given time. However, this is not practical over long distances, as it would require many separate wires for each connection, making the link extremely expensive.   Consequently, most long-distance connections are made using serial transmissions.   The actual link may consist of telephone wires, coaxial cable or even fibre optic links.   Nevertheless, the data is being carried one bit at a time.   The data travelling along the computer bus in parallel format has to be converted into a stream of bits to be sent out of the computer.

This can be carried out in two ways:

- Data is sent to a converter chip mounted on the computer's motherboard. The chip is called a 'UART ' (Universal Asynchronous Receiver Transmitter) and it sends the serial data out of the computer's serial port. Alternatively it may be sent via the USB controller.
- Data is sent to a converter chip that is mounted on a modem card fitted in an expansion slot inside the computer. The serial data is directly used by the rest of the modem card's electronics.

The conversions work in both directions, so that data can be transferred both in and out of the PC.

Interfaces

An interface is the point of connection between two pieces of electronic equipment.   To communicate properly, the devices must both conform to the same specification.   The specification will include the following requirements, with the examples in brackets being for the RS232 interface:

MECHANICAL	Covers the physical elements such as the connection type (e.g. 25-pin, pin layout) and cabling type (e.g. a 15m maximum between devices).
ELECTRICAL	Covers the signal voltage levels passing between devices (eg -5volts to -15volts representing logic 1) and the way that the data is passed (e.g. serially, synchronously, asynchronously).
FUNCTIONAL	Covers the purpose of each signal (e.g. carrying data, sending requests, and detecting the condition of connected devices).
PROCEDURAL	Covers the control and timing of signals between devices (e.g. handshaking procedures).

Practical international standards exist for both analogue and digital transmissions and these issues are covered in the following pages.

Terminology

The following terms are commonly used in describing communication equipment:

DTE   Data Terminal Equipment. A device that can send/receive data. Usually the microcomputer or printer.

DCE   Data Communications Equipment (mostly now called Data Circuit Terminating Equipment).
A device that facilitates serial data communications. From a user point of view, this is usually a modem.

DSE   Data Switching Equipment.   The equipment used to route a call when there is no permanent link between two stations.

Serial Port

The serial ports are detected at power up and their addresses stored in memory.   The normal base address for COM1 is 3F8h, COM2 is 2F8h, COM3 is 3E8h and COM4 is 2E8h.   Prior to DOS v3.3, only two serial ports and 3 parallel ports were supported. Since v3.3, four serial and four parallel ports are supported, although some older BIOS routines only test for two serial ports. The port addresses in

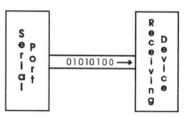

The letter 'T' being sent down a serial cable

use on any particular computer can be found by using Windows Device Manager or the MSD utility.

The PC uses a standard known as RS232C and is implemented as COM1 and, if fitted, COM2.   An updated version known as RS-232D meets CCITT V.24, V2.28 and ISO IS2110 standards.

Physical Characteristics

The serial port is situated at the rear of most PCs. Serial ports are generally 9-pin D-type connectors, although the specification does allow for 25-pin D-type connectors.   If the computer is 9-pin and the device is 25-pin - or vice versa - then a 9-pin to 25-pin adapter or a 9 to 25-way cable can be used to make the connection.   The connector at the rear of the PC is male (i.e. has pins) while the cable end is female (i.e. has sockets).

The RS232 standard was designed to minimise interference on the wires carrying the data signals.

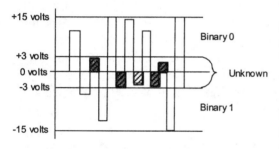

To aid this, the voltages carried are higher than the normal range for digital signals carried inside the PC.   The logic states inside the PC are either zero volts or five volts. With RS232, binary 0 is represented by a voltage of +3 to +15 volts and binary 1 is represented by a voltage of -3 to -15 volts. Ideally, the signals would be +15v and -15v but by specifying a positive and a negative range, allowance is made for signal losses along the line.   Voltages between +3 volts and -3 volts cannot be converted to known values.

These indeterminate values may be caused by interference spikes or may be the result of losses of signal on the line. They are shown shaded in the diagram. The transition from a bit 0 to bit 1 is represented by a change of voltage on the appropriate output pin.

Serial Connectors

The connections for a 25-pin serial port are:

Pin	Purpose	Signal Direction	Signal Name
1	Frame Ground	-	FG
2	Transmit Data	Out	TXD
3	Receive Data	In	RXD
4	Request to Send	Out	RTS
5	Clear to Send	In	CTS
6	Data Set Ready	In	DSR
7	Signal Ground	-	SG
8	Data Carrier Detect	In	DCD
9	+ DC Test Voltage	In	+V
10	- DC Test Voltage	In	- V
11	Equaliser Mode	In	QM
12	Secondary DCD	In	DCD2
13	Secondary CTS	In	CTS2
14	Secondary TXD	Out	TXD2
15	Transmitter Clock	In	TC
16	Secondary RXD	In	RXD2
17	Receiver Clock	In	RC
18	Unused	-	NC
19	Secondary RTS	Out	RTS2
20	Data Terminal Ready	Out	DTR
21	Unused	In	NC
22	Ring Indicator	In	RI
23	Data Rate Selector	Out	DRS
24	Transmit Clock	Out	TC
25	Unused	-	NC

The connections for a 9-pin serial port are:

Pin	Purpose	Signal Direction	Signal Name
1	Carrier Detect	In	DCD
2	Receive Data	In	RXD
3	Transmit Data	Out	TXD
4	Data Terminal Ready	Out	DTR
5	Signal Ground	-	GND
6	Data Set Ready	In	DSR
7	Request to Send	Out	RTS
8	Clear to Send	In	CTS
9	Ring Indicator	In	RI

NOTE
The tables show all the pins for the RS232 standard. In practice, most equipment will use a smaller number of connections, as explained later.

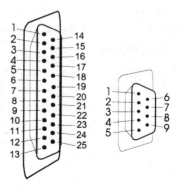

A summary of the signals is:

Voltage	Signal Name	Data Logic	Control Logic
+3 to +15	Space	0	True/High
-3 to -15	Mark	1	False/Low

Note that a positive voltage corresponds to a data bit logic of zero - but oddly also corresponds to a *'true'* logical statement.   Hence, a positive value on *'Transmit Data'* or *'Receive Data'* lines indicates the presence of a zero bit, while a control line such as DTR indicates that it is ready by placing a *'true'* condition (i.e. a positive voltage) on its line.   This is a source of confusion. Some books and manuals refer to the *'enabling'* of a control pin as going high (in the sense of the voltage on the pin) while others describe enabling as going low (in the sense of the logic value).   Diagrams show a bar over a signal to indicate that it is enabled by going low (e.g. $\overline{RD}$)

Modems

All data is held in binary format within the computer.   Ideally, computers would also wish to communicate in binary format.   However, due to the characteristics of long analogue telephone cables, there is too much loss on digital signals for this method to be used.   Telephone lines are designed to carry low frequency signals (from 300Hz to 3500Hz).   To communicate, the binary data has to be converted into a signal in this audio range.   The device that allows these conversions is known as a MODEM, which stands for MODulator/DEModulator.

The diagram shows two computers being connected via a telephone line. There is a modem at each end between the computer and the line.   The computer sending the data feeds the modem with a stream of binary zeros and ones. The modem converts the 'zeros' into one audio tone and the binary 'ones' into a different audio tone.

These audio tones can then be readily sent along a line. At low transmission rates this can easily be a standard telephone line.   At the receiving end, the modem carries out the opposite function, converting one tone back to logic 0 and the other tone back to logic 1.   In this way, the modem reconstitutes the original digital data sent from the first computer. This stream of digital information is then fed to the serial port of the receiving computer.

Essentially, the modem is a two-way device for connecting a computer to a telephone line.

The connection to the computer has to reflect the need to send data from the machine to the modem, and vice versa, including flow control of the data.   Modems differ from printers in that they have a range of error-checking methods and, if an error is detected, a request can be made for the re-transmission of the affected data.   Modems can be supplied as internal or external devices.   The internal modem is a card that plugs into an empty expansion slot on the motherboard. It is generally supplied configured as a COM2 device, to avoid clashes with the existing COM1 port that most computers use as their main serial port at the rear of the computer.   It is likely that the modem will have DIP switches to allow it be configured as COM1 or COM2.   The link between the computer and the modem is via the normal address and data buses.   The communication protocols to the external cable would be set within the communications program, using the Hayes AT command set.

The external modem is supplied as a freestanding unit that sits outside the computer casing. This saves using up an expansion slot on the motherboard, but requires to be fitted to the computer via a serial port. If the computer's serial port is already used for a printer or mouse, then an extra serial port will have to be added, using a serial card in an expansion slot.   The link between computer and modem is via the serial port and protocols between the computer and modem would require to be established.

Modem Wiring

The diagram shows the basic RS232 cable connection between a computer and a modem.   Note that the computer's *'Transmit Data'* pin does not connect to the modem's *'Receive Data'* pin as may have been expected.   This is because all connections are described from the DTE (i.e. the computer) point of view. This means that the pins on the DCE (i.e. the modem) describe their service to the computer rather than the direction of the signals entering or leaving the modem unit.

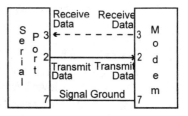

Simplified computer/modem link

This could be expressed thus:

Pin	Computer's point of view	Modem's point of view
Pin 2 (TXD)	Data that I wish to transmit	Data from the computer that I must transmit down the line
Pin 3 (RXD)	Data that I wish to receive	Data received from the line that I must pass on to the computer

Similarly, all other pins, such as RTS, CTS and DTR are wired directly to each other, i.e. pin 4 to pin 4, pin 5 to pin 5 and so on.   The distinction between connecting DTE to other DTEs or to DCEs is important to avoid confusion and to prevent incorrect wiring of connections (see later).

Note

> This approach mainly applies to modems.   With most other devices, the wiring follows expected practice with the computer's *'transmit'* pin being wired to a device's *'receive'* pin and the computer's *'receive'* pin being connected to the device's *'transmit'* pin.

Synchronisation of devices

If two devices are to communicate, the receiving device must run at the same speed as the sending device. To maintain the synchronisation of the two devices, each has a clock.   The clock at the sending end tells the sending device when to transmit a bit of data on to the line.   The clock at the receiving end tells the receiving device when it is time to check whether a 0 or a 1 has arrived.   It is vital that the two clocks be kept at the same speed.   If, for example, the transmitting clock sent 1200 data bits every second and the receiving device checked the line at the rate of 1300 times a second, the result would be the detection of 100 extra spurious bits of data which would completely disrupt the message.

Synchronous Mode

The easiest way to synchronise the two clocks involves the sending clock keeping the receiving clock in step.   This would simplify matters, compared to alternative methods. The big drawbacks are that data has to be sent in a continuous synchronised stream, or in large blocks. This is not always possible or necessary, and it requires another wire between the devices.   It is, however, less prone to distortion than other methods and is therefore usable at higher transmission speeds.   It would not be found as a method for connecting computers to modems.

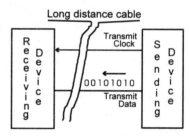

Simplified version of synchronous transmission

Asynchronous Mode

The most common method of connecting PCs is the asynchronous method.   Here, there is no equal spacing between each character transmitted.   A character being sent in real time via a keyboard, for example, could be sent at any unknown moment.   For the system to be able to process a character, the

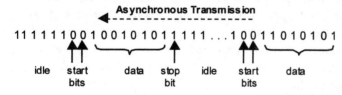

hardware has to be told when a character is about to be received and when the transmission of the character has ceased.   This involves enclosing the bits of the data with extra bits known as the START BITS and STOP BITS. As the names imply, the START BITS take the signal off the idle state, so giving a kick to the clock.   Incoming bits can now be sampled at the clock rate. The STOP BIT returns the system back to the idle state.   Conventionally, the least significant bit of the data (LSB) is transmitted first and the most significant bit (MSB) is transmitted last.   The idle state, also known as the *'mark'* condition, is a logic 1 while the logic 0 is known as a *'space'* condition.

Advantages

- Requires less connection wires.
- Works well with irregular data streams - e.g. keyboard entry transmissions.

Disadvantages

- Start bits can be missed. Data bits are then misread as start bits, producing errors.
- Interference pulses on the line can generate spurious start bits and non-existent bits are decoded.
- The system is slowed down, as a proportion of the data bits transmitted carry no useful information - they are for control purposes only.   For example, a system with 2 start bits and 1 stop bit requires 11 bits to transfer a single byte.

Parity Bit

For the transmission of ASCII files, a 7-bit code is sufficient to cover the ASCII range and the extra bit can be used by the receiving device for error checking.   The eighth bit is known as the parity bit and communication systems can use either even or odd parity - assuming that both devices know that they are checking by the same method. Depending on the system, parity may also be used on 8-bit data packets.

Even Parity

The sending device counts the number of 'one' bits in the character to be transmitted. If the number of these data bits is even, as in the top diagram, the parity bit is set to zero. If the number of 'one' bits is odd, as in the lower diagram, the parity bit is set to one.   Thus the total number of 'ones' in the byte will always be even, no matter how many 'ones' are in the character being transmitted. If any of the data bits or parity bits is accidentally altered during transmission, the receiving device can detect the problem by counting the number of bits. If the total is not an even number, there has been corruption of the data. This provides an elementary check for data errors.

Parity Bit

| | 1 | 0 | 0 | 1 | 1 | 1 | 0 |

Parity Bit

| | 0 | 1 | 0 | 0 | 1 | 0 | 1 |

Odd Parity

Here, the sending device counts the number of 'one' bits in the byte to be transmitted. If the number of these data bits is even, as in the top diagram, the parity bit is set to one. If the number of 'one' bits is already odd, as in the lower diagram, the parity bit is set to zero.   In this way, the total number of 'ones' in the group is always maintained at an odd value.

Note   Parity checking is a useful facility but it is not foolproof. For example, two bits in a byte both being altered from zero to one would produce a correct parity check although the data in the byte had been corrupted. In practice, larger blocks of data are examined for corruption (see section later on Error Detection).

Flow Control

In a half-duplex link, only one of the computers can transmit at any one time. If a modem detects an incoming signal from the remote modem, it must prevent its own computer from transmitting data to ensure that it stays in 'receive' mode. When the incoming signal stops, the modem can then allow the computer to send its data. Traffic on the link is regulated by having the modem control the flow of data out of the computer's serial port.   The process of control is known as *'handshaking'* and can be implemented in hardware or in software (XON/XOFF handshaking)

Hardware Handshaking

In the diagram, the numbers on the side of the computer serial port and the modem port represent the pin numbers to be found in the device connectors.   When the computer and the modem are connected together and switched on, the computer's DTR (Data Terminal Ready) line on pin 4 on its serial port is enabled to inform the modem that it is operational and wishes to establish a connection. The computer DTR pin is wired to the modem's DTR pin.   The modem responds by enabling its DSR (Data Set Ready) line on pin 6 to inform the computer that it is switched on and ready for use. In effect, DSR means *'Modem Ready'*.   At this stage, both devices know that the other is connected and active so data transfer is possible.   This is done using the RTS and CTS lines to control the flow of information between the two

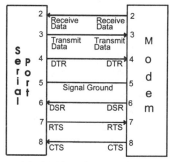

9-pin wiring of Modem Cable

devices.   A typical transmission sequence might be as below:

1. The computer wishes to send data to the modem.
2. The computer enables (i.e. high positive voltage) its RTS (Ready To Send) pin to inform the modem that it wishes to transmit. This signal is conveyed to the modem via its serial port's RTS line.
3. The modem has disabled its CTS (Clear To Send) pin (i.e. there must still be incoming data).
4. This condition is detected by the computer's CTS pin; no data is sent; the machine stays in receive mode.
5. The calling station stops transmitting and this is detected by the modem.
6. The modem enables its CTS line; this is detected by the computer's CTS pin and data is passed to the modem for transmission.
7. The computer sends a stream of text data out of its serial port TxD (Transmitted Data) pin.   This data stream is sent, via the wire, to the TxD pin of the modem.
8. The remote modem detects this incoming carrier and disables its CTS to ensure that the remote computer will read the data and not try to transit.

The CTS line is also used to prevent the computer sending data into the modem when the modem's memory buffer is full.   When the buffer is emptied, the CTS line is used to indicate that the modem is ready to receive more data.   Hardware handshaking is the preferred method for faster modems as there is no unnecessary data being passed around the system, occupying precious processing time.   The hardware handshaking method is also used with a serial printer interface.

Xon/Xoff Handshaking

DTR handshaking uses extra wires to carry the control signals; the handshaking is implemented via hardware.   The other common method is to use a software handshake.   This reduces the amount of connections to only three - one for data in each direction and one common line.   While this simplifies the connections between the computer and the device, it leaves no obvious physical means for passing over handshake signals.   Yet, the computer still needs to know when transmission can and cannot take place.   In this system, specific ASCII numbers, outside the printable range, are used as codes to represent *'stop transmission'* and *'start transmission'*.   This is where the Xon/Xoff method derives its name.

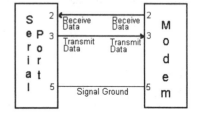

When the modem is switched on, it sends out an ASCII character known as DC1. This is the *'transmit enable'* code and is decimal 17 or 11 hex.   This code is received by the computer, which knows that it is able to commence transmitting data to the modem.   This is the Xon condition.   If there is incoming traffic, the modem sends out an ASCII DC3 character.   This is the Xoff condition and is 19 in decimal (13 in hex).   The computer receives this code and stops transmitting data.

Notes:

- This method is used with a serial printer. It sends out an Xoff code when its internal buffer is full. As it prints, it reduces the amount of characters in its buffer.   When the buffer has sufficient space, it sends out a DC1 code to the computer, which resumes the transmission of data to the printer.
- The ASCII codes DC1 and DC3 stand for Device Control 1 and Device Control 3.
- This method can transmit and receive text files, since the printable ASCII set ranges from 32 to 127. Binary files (i.e. containing machine code) contain a full range of possible numeric values.   This would include the values for the DC1 and DC3 signals, which means that Xon/Xoff is not suitable for transmitting and receiving binary files.

RS232 Pins

A summary of the uses of the main pins on a computer's serial port is shown in the following table.

DTR (Data Terminal Ready)	The computer informs the modem that it is powered up and ready to be active, by switching this pin to an 'ON' state. Most modems require to receive this signal before they will operate.
DSR (Data Set Ready)	The modem informs the computer that it is powered up and ready to be active, by switching this pin to an 'ON' state. Most computer ports require this signal before they will operate.
CTS (Clear to Send)	The modem informs the computer that it able to accept data for transmission, by switching this pin to an 'ON' state. The computer will not send out data while this pin is 'OFF'.
RTS (Ready to Send)	The computer informs the modem that it wishes to give it data for transmission, by switching this pin to an 'ON' state. The modem responds by switching its CTS line 'ON' - unless its memory buffer is full, or it is receiving incoming data.
TXD (Transmit Data)	Carries the data from the computer to the modem's TXD pin, to transmit data. The data goes out the serial port's TXD pin and goes in the modem's TXD pin.
RXD (Receive Data)	Receives the data from the modem's RXD pin, to receive incoming data. The data comes out the modem's RXD pin and goes in the serial port's RXD pin.
DCD (Data Carrier Detect)	Used by the computer to determine whether the modem has an incoming carrier (i.e. whether the line is idle or not). Some communications packages must detect a DCD signal before they will carry on. This signal can be brought from the modem or can be provided locally by a *'wraparound'*. This connects the computer's DTR pin to the computer's DCD pin to simulate an idle condition.
RI (Ring Indicator)	This pin could be used by an auto-answer modem. Its value is raised high when the phone rings. The modem informs the DTE via this change in the RI line and the DTE responds by setting its DTR line high. The modem then answers the call and data is passed from the telephone line to the DTE.
SG (Signal Ground)	This pin is used as the reference for all other signal voltages. So, if a pin swings +15 volts, it means that the pin is 15 volts higher than the voltage on SG. This pin should not be confused with electric earth or Frame Ground (FG).

Modulation

The modem translates digital levels into differing tones on the telephone line. This can be achieved by altering the frequency of the tone according to whether each bit in the incoming data stream is a binary zero or a binary one. This is called FSK (frequency shift keying) modulation. A V21 system uses 1180Hz to represent a binary zero and 980Hz to represent a binary 1, while a V23 system uses 450Hz and 390Hz respectively. Another method is to alter the phase of the tone dependent on the incoming data's binary state. Phase modulation would maintain the same frequency for a 1 and a 0 but would shift the waveform in time between the two states. This is used with V22 systems. It is also possible to combine both the alterations of the tone's phase and its amplitude (Quadrature Amplitude Modulation) so that a single baud can represent four bits. Therefore, a 2400 baud modem can transfer at 9600bps.

Data Compression

Smaller files are transmitted in a shorter time than larger files. This saves both user time and telephone connect time. This has led to the compression of files prior to their transmission. The compressed file is later decompressed at the receiving end. The most common ways to achieve data compression are V42bis and MNP levels, known as 'Classes'. It should be understood that modem compression systems have to achieve this compression at the point of transmission and this limits the degree of compression. It is much better to compress a file using a normal file compression package such as PKZip and then transfer this file over the network. Since packages such as PKZip do not have to analyse the entire file in real time, they can arrive at the highest possible compression ratio.

MNP stands for 'Microcom Networking Protocol' and covers both error detection and data compression. Each higher Class encompasses and expands on the features of the Class below. Class 1 through to Class 4 provides increasingly sophisticated techniques to reduce time delays caused by transmission errors. For example, MNP 3 acts like a synchronous modem, removing the need for start and stop bits and thereby increasing throughput. Microcom's options now extend to MNP 10, which is targeted at noisy systems such as radiophones. Its transmission speed slows down for noisy environments and returns to faster rates when the noise subsides, thus reducing losses. Of the MNP range, MNP 5 is the most commonly used and has become a de facto industry 'standard'. Like other compression systems, it uses a pattern recognition algorithm to replace long or regularly occurring strings of data with shorter tokens that represent those strings. At the receiving end, the communications software reverses the process and rebuilds the original data using the tokens. Although popular, it only compresses in about a 2:1 ratio. Consequently, the CCITT chose a different algorithm for its V42bis compression standard. It uses a more efficient system based a British Telecom version of the famous Lempel-Ziv algorithm, known as BTLV. With a V34 modem, this can produce an effective data transfer rate of 115,200bps.

Breakout Box

Every manufacturer uses the same serial port pins to represent the same functions and all manufacturers work with the same signal voltage levels. However, different devices will use different combinations of these pins. Some devices are wired as DTEs while others are wired as DCEs. While all devices will use the TXD, RXD and GND connections, there is a wide variation in the usage of the other pins. This means that some devices will require the use of a certain pin while other devices ignore that pin. In some cases, pins will require to be connected together before the device will operate. In other cases, that wiring combination will prevent the device from operating. Wherever possible, the device manual should be consulted. The book 'RS-232 Made Easy' by Martin Seyer shows the extent of the problem. It devotes 271 pages to charts and wiring diagrams of different computers, printers, modems, multiplexors, etc.

Often, technicians are working with equipment that has no documentation or with cables whose internal wiring is unknown. In these cases, a device known as a 'breakout box' is invaluable. As the diagram shows, this is inserted in the cable between the computer and the device being connected. If the miniature switches are left in their 'on' setting, every pin is connected straight

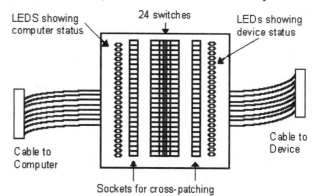

through from computer to device. If all the switches are thrown to their *'off'* setting, the computer is completely disconnected from the device. In this disconnected mode, one row of the LEDs will display the signals that are coming from the computer while the other row of LEDs displays signals from the device. These LEDs are *'tri-state'* the three states being *'off'* along with positive (green) and negative (red) polarities. The breakout box is accompanied by a set of jumper leads that have a plug at each end. When the switches are in their *'off'* state, jumper leads can be inserted into the sockets to connect computer pins to device pins. For example, a lead may be plugged into socket 2 at the computer and socket 3 at the device end. This ability to criss-cross leads allows the technician to quickly test various combinations. When the working combination is determined, a cable can be wired up and soldered as a permanent replacement for the breakout box.

- Care must be taken when buying ready-made cables as some have pins strapped together (i.e. wired together) inside the plug. It is common to find pins 4 and 5 strapped, or even 4,5,6 and 8 strapped.
- Serial printer connections are mostly wired as DTEs.

Reading/Writing with RS232

As mentioned earlier, COM1's base address is 3F8h. This means that the memory location 3F8h is the <u>start</u> of a set of eight bytes that hold information and instructions to control the port's read and write operations. Each byte is known as a *'register'* and these are numbered from 0 through to 7.

The register table for COM1 is:

Register Number	Memory Address	Status	Purpose
0	3F8h	R/W	Data Buffer - stores the byte to be transmitted or the byte received
1	3F9h	R/W	Interrupt Enable - sets what activities will generate a processor interrupt
2	3FAh	Read	Interrupt ID - for 8250 - holds the cause of any particular interrupt. Also a FIFO Register for the 16550 UART
3	3FBh	Write	Line Control - sets the baud rate, stop bits, parity and word length
4	3FCh	R/W	Modem Control - e.g. sets the RTS and DTR lines
5	3FDh	Read	Line Status - stores whether there was a parity error, the user sent a BREAK signal, etc.
6	3FEh	Read	Modem Status - stores the status of the DCD, RI, DSR and CTS lines
7	3FFh	R/W	The 'Scratch-pad' - a general one-byte memory store

Register 6 holds the status of the DCD, RI, DSR and CTS lines as single bits in the 3FEh memory location, in the 8th, 7th, 6th and 5th bits respectively. The following Pascal program reads the Modem Status Register, recovers each required bit value, converts it to a binary value and displays it.

```
PROGRAM read_RS232_port;
USES crt;
VAR
    reading, dcd, ri, dsr, cts : BYTE;
BEGIN
    CLRSCR;    GOTOXY(18,10);
    WRITELN('pin 8    pin 22    pin 6    pin 5');
    WRITELN(' ':18,'DCD       RI       DSR       CTS');
    REPEAT
      reading := PORT[$3FE];
      dcd := (reading AND 128) SHR 7;
      ri  := (reading AND 64)  SHR 6;
      dsr := (reading AND 32)  SHR 5;
      cts := (reading AND 16)  SHR 4;
      GOTOXY(20,12);
      WRITE(dcd,'           ',ri,'          ',dsr,'          ',cts);
    UNTIL DCD = 99;
END.
```

Similarly, the Modem Control Register can be written to by the command   `port[$3FC] := outvalue;`

Transmission Speed

The speed of data transfer is measured in bits per second (bps). The lowest rate of 75bps was used for Prestel connections and the highest current rate is 56kbps. Modem rates used to be measured in *'baud'* and the baud rate and the bps rate were identical. This was only true when one signal on the line represented one single bit of information. Baud really measures the number of frequency changes on the line per second and ignores phase changes, amplitude changes and the fact that the data may be compressed (see later). All of these techniques mean that more data can be passed down a cable while running at a relatively low baud rate. So, when a modem states that it has a certain transfer rate, it need not be actually producing frequency changes at that rate down the cable. The value given may be the <u>effective</u> rate of transfer taking into account the effect of these techniques. These schemes were only introduced on newer machines, above about 3000 bps, and 'baud' and 'bps' should only really be interchangeable terms for older models. All specifications are now usually given in bps.

UART Upgrades

The notes on handshaking addressed the problem of the modem being slower than the serial interface. Increasingly, however, the problem is the reverse situation with serial interfaces being unable to transfer data at the rate required for the new fast breed of modems. Early PCs were fitted with an 8250 or 16450 type UART.   However, the likely top transfer rate of a 16450 is 19,200 bps while current modems are normally 56,000 bps.   To meet these greater demands, the 16550 UART is required. If one of the older UARTs is used in the PC, the computer's serial interface has to be upgraded. The 16550, supplied in any reasonably new machine, is better as it has an internal 16-byte FIFO (first in first out) buffer.   The UART can then handle the bytes in the internal queue while more data is being fetched. This greatly speeds up transfer speeds compared to the earlier UARTs with their one-byte memory.   The type of UART fitted in a machine can be determined by using third-party system information utilities such as SiSoft Sandra. This utility reports on the serial ports in use, the type of chip used and the speed and protocol settings for each port. An upgrade can be achieved in two ways:

- Replacing the current UART chip with a 16550 chip.   This involves removing the old chip from its 40-pin holder and fitting the new chip.   The software has to be 16550 compatible and has to be configured to accept the new chip.   This option is not viable if the UART is embedded in the motherboard or other component such as internal modem card.
- Fitting a new fast serial card that has one or more 16550 chips fitted.   Hayes, the leader in modem technology, has produced an *'Advanced Serial Port'* card where DMA techniques are used to relieve the CPU of many of its data transfer activities thus further speeding up computer throughput.

Error Detection

Modem communication over the normal telephone network is always prone to losses due to poor line conditions. As transmission rates become faster, the losses are increased.   If an interference pulse occurred on a line with a 28800bps system, the transmission would be affected 24 times more badly than a 1200bps system, since 24 times more data will have been transferred during that time.   Serious attention has to be paid to detecting and correcting such errors.   The parity bit system described earlier is only a rudimentary check and only applies to ASCII files.   Since most files are not plain ASCII, they will require to use all eight bits of the byte and there is no parity bit.

CRC Checking

Data is transmitted in *'blocks'* or *'packets'* with a checksum created using the CRC (Cyclic Redundancy Check) method. When the data is compiled into a block prior to transmission, a mathematical formula (using polynomial codes) is applied to the data to produce a check number that is unique to the data stream in the block.   These check digits are then transmitted along with the data. The receiver stores the incoming block of data in a buffer for examination. The same formula is applied to the data in the buffer and it should produce the same answer as that stored in the check bytes. If the computed CRC figure accords with the stored CRC figure, the data in the buffer is fit to be passed on and an 'ACK' signal is returned to the transmitting end to acknowledge the receipt of a block in good condition.   If there has been any corruption of the data in the block, or even any corruption of the check bytes, then the formula will produce answers that do not match. In this case, the device will request that the block of data be re-transmitted.   This is done by returning a 'NAK' signal to the transmitting end.

A number of different block transmission techniques and error detection methods are in common use. Error detection can occur at one or more stages in the transmission process – hardware error detection is covered by the modem V standards (see below).   Software error detection protocols include:

TCP/IP Protocol

The most common protocol in use today, TCP/IP is the de facto protocol of the Internet. Virtually, if not all dial-up ISPs (Internet Service Providers) use TCP/IP to connect a user to the Internet. The *'Transport'* layer of the TCP/IP protocol handles error checking using a two-byte CRC for each TCP packet, and also requires an 'ACK' (acknowledge) reply from the receiving to ensure safe delivery. The TCP/IP protocol is explained fully later.

IPX Protocol

Rarely used for modem connections, IPX is mainly a LAN technology. Even when a LAN is connected to the Internet via a gateway, TCP/IP is usually installed as well as IPX, to handle Internet traffic.

BBS Protocols

There are a variety of protocols that can be used when connecting a PC via modem to a Bulletin Board Service. They all provide error checking, but vary in speed and reliability. This includes XMODEM, YMODEM, ZMODEM, and Kermit protocols. For example, XMODEM uses a one-byte CRC for each 128-byte block, is limited to 9600bps, and can only transfer one file at a time. YMODEM has a two-byte CRC and is able to transfer multiple files at one time. Being older, most of these protocols do not follow OSI standards.

Standards

Created by CCITT, The International Telegraph and Telephone Consultative Committee, working under the ITU (International Telecommunications Union), which is organised by the United Nations.

These standards are divided into a number of groups, including:

- The V-series, dealing with telephone circuits
- The X-series, dealing with data networks
- The G-series, dealing with digital networks (digital exchanges, multiplexing, PCM, etc.)
- The I-series, dealing with ISDN (see later)

V Standards

There is a wide range of definitions and the most common ones are shown in the table. The V standards get their name from the first letter of the word 'vitesse', the French for speed although not all V standards are concerned with transmission rate. V24, for example, specifies the serial port standard and V42 and V42bis cover error correction. The 'bis' added to a V number means that it is the second version of the standard. Dataflex, a large UK modem manufacturer, produces VFC models, also known V.Fast Class models, working at 28,800bps. These were introduced before the ratification of the V34 standard and there are some handshaking differences between their specifications. V.Fast modems can communicate with other VFC models at the top rate but with V35 models, they can only communicate at 14,400bps in about 10% of cases.

V17	Fax 14,400 transmit/receive
V21	300bps transmit/receive. full duplex, dial-up
V22	1200bps transmit/receive. full duplex, dial-up
V22bis	2400bps transmit/receive. full duplex, dial-up
V23	1200bps transmit/75bps transmit, asymmetric duplex, dial-up
V24	The RS232 standard
V27	4800bps transmit/receive. full duplex, leased line
V27ter	4800bps transmit/2400bps receive, half duplex, Group III Fax
V29	9600bps transmit/receive. full duplex, leased line Also 9600bps half duplex Group III Fax
V32	9600bps transmit/receive, full duplex, dial-up
V32bis	14,4000bps transmit/receive, full duplex, dial-up
V34	28,800bps
V34bis	31,200bps or 33,600bps
V42	Error correction using CRC
V42bis	Data compression using Lempel Ziv
V44	Improved compression standard, and storing of phone line performance information to reduce connection times.
V80	Videoconferencing
V90	56,000bps download, 33600bps upload
V92	56,000bps download, 48000bps upload, and also incorporates V.44 and other facilities.

56k Technology

ISDN lines (see later) were once the only mid-band communication links available for those wishing faster data rates, without the huge expense of fast links. ISDN links provide 64k or 128k data rates but the UK pricing policies for ISDN has led to a slow take-up rate. Users are required to have extra telephone lines installed in their premises, buy dedicated ISDN modems and pay expensive line fees. The 56k alternative uses existing rented telephone lines and no extra standing charges beyond the normal telephone charges. ITU v.90 56k modems are now commonplace and supercede the interim x2 and k56flex standards. While v.92 modems are available they require the ISP to support it and these are not yet widely used.

British telephone exchanges work digitally and communications between parts of the telephone network are digital. Likewise, Internet Service Providers (ISPs) now use digital links. Only the cable between the exchange and the subscriber's premises uses analogue techniques. The audio of a normal telephone conversation arrives at the exchange as an analogue signal and is converted into digital information for use in the main network. The audio is converted into 8-bit resolution at an 8KHz sampling rate. This provides a theoretical data rate of 64k but, according to Nyquist's theorem, the reliable bandwidth of a signal is half its sampling rate. So, the conversion supports around 32k, which explains the previous upper 33,600bps limit of analogue modems.

ISDN adaptors, being digital devices in the first place, do not require analogue to digital conversion and vice versa, and can operate at the full 64k per channel.

56k modems use similar techniques of avoiding analogue/digital conversion losses. Since the link from ISP to telecommunications network is often digital, the only analog/digital conversion that is required is from the exchange to the subscriber, instead of having an additional conversion to the ISP. Although theoretically speeds of 64k are attainable, practical concerns limit this to 56k.

Communication stages	Existing technology	56k technology
Data stored at ISP	Digital	Digital
ISP to Network	Digital	Digital
Network to Network	Digital	Digital
Network to local exchange	Digital	Digital
Exchange to subscriber	Analogue (tones)	Analogue (data)
Subscriber conversion	Analogue tones to digital	Analogue data to digital

Such speeds are susceptible to line degradation, and some locations will find it difficult or impossible to achieve the full 56k rate. The modems of Internet Service Providers have to support 56k working before it can be used by subscribers' 56k modems. The 56k transfer rate is only between the ISP and the subscriber, which comprises most Internet traffic. Uploading of data to an ISP is at the lower rate of 33,600bps (or 48,000bps for V.92).

Modem Commands

The computer connects to the modem by a single serial connection. The user will normally interface with the communications package software and will decide on actions by pressing menu options or by clicking on icons or buttons. Basic user choices could include engaging the telephone line, dialling a number, downloading a file and eventually terminating the connection with the remote station. A whole range of other options might be required. For example, some telephone exchanges use the old rotary pulse dialling method while most exchanges use tone dialling. The user might wish to have the modem's inbuilt loudspeaker turned off or a range of other refinements. Although the user makes these choices via the software, the computer has to then inform the modem of these decisions. Since there is only a single serial connection between them, the computer has to send this information in the form of messages along the serial cable. The modem, in turn, will send messages ('result codes') back to the computer to indicate that it cannot get any dial tone, the dialled number is busy, etc.

As long as the modem and the computer understand and use the same set of messages, there is no communications difficulty with the system. The most common way to use these strings is to save them with the communications software's setup information. When the user runs the communications package, the desired command string is automatically associated with the package's corresponding menu and button options. A default set of commands is offered by most packages and the user can alter them for local conditions (e.g. changing the string from a tone dial system to a pulse dial system).

Hayes AT Commands

A popular modem command set is the Hayes AT set developed by Hayes Microcomputer Products. Like other command sets, the Hayes commands are independent of the speed or performance of the modem. An old slow modem and one of the latest models can both use the AT command set. Modems described as 'AT compatibles' refer to their acceptance of this set of commands, or a superset or a subset.

The Command Set

All Hayes commands consist of a string of characters, both alphabetic and numeric, that control modem functions. Each individual command sent to the modem is preceded by the letters 'AT' which stands for ATtention. So, for example, sending the string ATM0 would silence the modem's speaker.

The chart shows the display for the default setting offered in the 'Telix' communications package:

```
═╡ Modem and dialing parameter setup ╞══════════════════════

   A - Init string ............ ATZ^M~~~AT S7=45 S0=0 V1 X4^M~
   B - Dialing prefix 1 ..... ATDT
   C - Dialing prefix 2 ..... ATDT
   D - Dialing prefix 3 ..... ATDT
   E - Dialing suffix ....... ^M
   F - Connect string ....... CONNECT
   G - No connect strings .. NO CARRIER                BUSY
                             VOICE                     NO DIAL TONE
   H - Hang-up string ....... ~~~+++~~~ATH0^M
   I - Auto answer string .. ATS0=1^M
   J - Dial cancel string .. ^M

   K - Dial time ........... 30
   L - Redial pause ........ 1
   M - Auto baud detect .... Off
   N - Drop DTR to hangup .. On

   Change which setting?        (Return or Esc to exit)
```

The initialisation string is the one that is sent to the modem when the package is first run.

The '^M' string is the equivalent of pressing the Enter key if the string was entered at the keyboard and the '~' characters are pauses. A comma is also used as an alternative method of obtaining a pause.

The individual components of the initialisation string are explained in the following chart:

Command	Meaning
Z	Used to reset the modem to the factory default settings.
S7=45	Specifies that the modem will wait for 45 seconds after dialling. If there is no connection to the remote station within that time, the modem hangs up the line and sends a 'No Carrier' message to the computer. The range is 4 to 60 seconds.
S0=0	Used to set the number of rings before the modem auto-answers an incoming call. The permissible range is 0 to 255. A value of zero turns off the auto-answer.
V1	Specifies that result codes will be reported in text format. This is used when the communications session is under manual control. With automated systems, the results codes can be reported in numeric format, using 'V0', so that the numbers can be easier interpreted by the software.
X4	Used to enable the full range of result codes and supports both dial tone and engaged tone detection. Other permissible levels are X0, X1, X2 and X3 and are mainly available for backward compatibility with older models and some non-standard telephone systems.

Dialling Prefix

The dialling prefix in the example is 'ATDT'. The 'D' is an instruction to commence dialling and the 'T' instructs the modem to use tone dialling. If the string had been 'ATDP' it would instruct the modem to use pulse dialling. Pulse dialling is the default and only has to be given as instruction to the modem if the modem had previously been ordered to use tone dialling. The software would add the actual number to be dialled to the end of the string.
So, typical strings might be:

> ATD 0141-775-2889   or   ATD01417752889   or   ATD 9,0141775 2889

The first two strings are directly equivalent since any dashes or spaces between numbers are ignored. The third example is for use in offices where the user has to dial '9' for an outside line. The comma (or '~') is inserted to provide a time delay to allow the office exchange to engage an outside line.

Hang Up String

The hang up string is 'ATH0' which is the 'On Hook' condition, the equivalent of replacing a telephone on its rest. The row of three plus signs switches the modem into 'Local Mode' also known as 'Command Mode'. Generally, the modem wishes to ignore the computer when it is getting on with its communications session. If a long file transfer is underway it will not wish to be disturbed by the computer and will ignore most AT command strings. However, there still has to be a way that the user can interrupt a session and this is achieved with the '+++' string. To prevent accidental triggering (e.g. the data being sent happens to include three plus signs), this escape sequence is only recognised if it is prefaced and followed by a pause. The default pause is 1 second and this is achieved by the '~~~' string that surrounds the three plus signs.

Other common AT commands are:

F	Sets the speed at which the modem will operate. F1 is for V21, F2 is for V23, F3 is for V22, F4 is for V22bis while F5 is for V32/4800bps and F6 is for V32/9600 working. If the command is set at F0, the modem is instructed to make the connection at the fastest rate available.
I	Instructs the modem to return details of its description and version number.
W	Instructs the modem to wait for secondary dial tone before proceeding to dial out. Used for modems connected to office exchanges (PABXs). This is an alternative to use the use of delays as shown earlier.
&K	Instructs the modem to use a specific flow control. AT&K0 inhibits all flow control, AT&K1 enables hardware (RTS/CTS) control and AT&K2 enables software (Xon/Xoff) control.
\C	Determines the level of data compression. \C1 operates in MNP class 1 mode and the range extends up to \C5 for MNP class 5 mode.

The result codes returning from the modem to the computer include:

Number	Text equivalent	Meaning
0	OK	The last command executed without error.
1	CONNECT #	A connection is established at 300/300.
2	RING	An incoming call has been detected.
3	NO CARRIER	Carrier cannot be detected or carrier has been lost.
4	ERROR	An invalid command has been given.
5	CONNECT 1200	A connection is established at 1200/1200.
6	NO DIALTONE	No dial tone has been detected within the specified timeout period.
7	BUSY	An engaged tone or number unobtainable tone has been detected.

Modem Lights

Many modems have external lights to inform the user of their current state and to reassure the user of the success of the various activities.   When a communication session is unsuccessful, the lights can be used to determine the likely

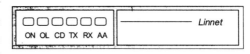

problem.   The diagram shows the layout of a typical modem front panel although there is a wide variety both in the number of lights used and in the titles different manufacturers give to the same light function.
A normal sequence for sending a piece of data by modem would be:

1.   The communications package fetches the data (from memory or from a disk file) to be sent.
2.   The data is sent out the computer's RS232 port.
3.   The data is carried from the computer to the modem via a serial cable.
4.   The data is converted to tones inside the modem.
5.   The tones are sent to the telephone line via a plug connected to a standard telephone socket.

The receiving process is a mirror image of the transmitting process with the data coming in the telephone socket, converted to digital signals and being received by the application via the serial cable and the RS232 port.   The modem's lights can indicate which parts of the process are working allowing the user to determine the source of the problem.

An explanation of the each modem light is:

Light	Meaning	Purpose
ON	Power On	The modem is correctly powered up from its power supply. Also known as 'MR' - Modem Ready or DSR - Data Set Ready.
OL	On Line	The modem is holding the telephone connection. This is the equivalent of a telephone being off its hook. Also known as 'OH' - Off Hook.
CD	Carrier Detect	The modem is in touch with a remote station and is receiving its carrier tones. This means that someone has answered an outgoing call, or the user's modem has answered an incoming call. When this light goes out, the link has been broken. Also known as 'DCD' - Data Carrier Detect.
TX	Transmit Data	This light flickers when data is being transmitted out of the modem. Also known as 'SD' - Send Data.
RX	Receive Data	This light will flicker when it is receiving data in from the telephone line. Also known as 'RD'.
AA	Auto Answer	This lights when the modem has been configured to automatically answer any incoming calls. This is used where a computer has to be left unattended.
HS	High Speed	This light indicates that the modem is working at its highest speed. In some modems, the light flickers for several of the higher speeds.
TR	Terminal Ready	This light indicates that the modem is both powered and in communication with the modem. The computer has sent a DTR signal through the serial port to the modem to inform it that is running a communications package. The modem lights is TR light in response.
RI	Ring Indicate	Indicates the presence of an incoming call. The equivalent of the telephone ringing.
TST	Test	This light indicates that the modem is performing a self-test.
LB	Low Battery	Used with portable modems to indicate that their battery supply is running low.
SQ	Signal Quality	A steady light indicates a good connection; a flickering light indicates a poor quality connection.

Soft Modems

Most computers are now supplied modems already fitted. In a lot of cases these modems are based not on dedicated chips but on simple interface electronics driven by the processor. These don't work without the appropriate software and cause a drain on processor resources while they are in use. They generally are supplied with drivers for only one operating system and so are useless on any other operating system.   They can be identified because very often they are on a simple riser card, which they share with USB ports or network connections that use the same trick. This is known as the AMR (Audio/Modem Riser) slot. Standalone boards are also offered for sale, which use this soft modem technology and are characterised by being noticeably inexpensive. Good retailers will confirm that a proposed purchase is a soft modem, and people with an electronics background can identify telltale signs of the necessary COM port and chipset on non soft modems.

Installing A Modem

Many new home computers come with modems pre-installed. Others may wish to add a modem later, or wish to replace the existing modem. The steps involved in installing a modem are as follows:

-    Physically install the modem or modem card. The fitting of an internal expansion card or PCMCIA card is explained in more detail in the *'Upgrading'* chapter; the only additional fitting involves attaching the modem to the phone line. Most modems come with a telephone cord; the most likely problem is if the modem has a US-style modem jack, requiring an adapter to plug into a UK phone socket. Fitting an external modem involves ensuring the modem has power (this may not be necessary for USB modems), and connecting it to the PC serial or USB port as appropriate. A good external modem will still be automatically detected, however. If not, simply select Add New Hardware from the Control Panel and install manually.

- Install the modem driver. A Plug-and-Play modem should be detected automatically by Windows, as described in the *'Upgrading'* chapter. Generally the modem will come with a driver disk that should be used when prompted by the Windows operating system to select a device driver. If not, the *'generic modem'* driver may suffice for normal use. The *'Dial-Up Adapter'* and *'TCP/IP'* Network components will be automatically installed. TCP/IP is by far the most common Internet protocol and is used by nearly all ISPs; the protocol should only be changed if the manual for the dial-up system specifically says to do so.

- Install and configure the dial-up connection software. Major ISPs such as Demon, AOL and FreeServe supply their own connection software, and the appropriate instructions should be followed to install the software. However, less well established ISPs may not have any connection software, or may simply use a front-end to Windows' connection software, Dial-Up Networking. Even those ISPs with proprietary connection software can usually be accessed through basic DUN if necessary.

Dial-Up Networking

Dial-Up Networking (DUN) is a program supplied with Windows 95 onwards. It can be used to dial in to bulletin boards (BBS) as well as ISPs. Many ISPs supply '*INS*' files, which contain information that will be entered into Dial-Up Networking without involving the user. However, details such as the dial-up phone number, username and password should be noted and kept in a secure place in case of later problems.

If DUN is to be configured manually, select it from the Start menu/Accessories/Communications or open Explorer and select My Computer/Dial-Up Networking. A wizard will pop up, prompting the user to enter details for the system he/she will be dialling into. This includes a name for the connection, and the telephone number to dial. Once a connection is set up, an icon will be added to the DUN screen. At this point the user can add new connections, or double-click on the icon to begin the dial-up process.

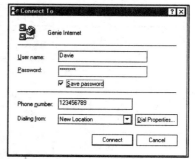

DUN will load up a connection window, as shown. Initially the Username will be taken from the current user's Windows login name, but this should be changed to reflect the username on the ISP. Similarly, the password will be blank at first, and the user should enter the correct password. If this is the first time using this connection, the *'Save Password'* checkbox can be ticked, allowing DUN to store the password so that the user need not enter it every time.

If there are problems connecting to the remote system, right clicking on a connection icon and selecting *'Properties'* gives access to a dialog from which many connection settings can be changed. These include the phone number, modem settings such as start and stop bits, as well as scripting that allows DUN to interact with the remote system on the user's behalf, entering the user name and password automatically. In most cases these properties should not be changed unless the manual states otherwise.

Data Links

A range of possible connection methods between communication stations is possible. These include:

SIMPLEX	Data is sent in one direction only. No longer in common use and is mostly now found as a means of driving older printers where no information is fed back to the computer from the device.
HALF-DUPLEX	The link can carry data in both directions but not simultaneously. It is analogous to a CB radio user who has to be either in talk or listen mode at any one time. A computer sends a packet of information and then switches into receive mode to wait for an acknowledgement from the other end. Once received, the computer can go back into transmit mode for the next packet. Used by Xmodem, Xmodem/CRC, Ymodem and Kermit protocols and common in domestic links to a host (e.g. CompuServe) and small businesses to a main link.
FULL-DUPLEX	The link can carry data in both directions simultaneously. It is analogous to a telephone user who can both talk and listen at the same time. Most modems work in this mode. It permits the use of sliding window protocols, as explained earlier, to speed up transmissions. Used by Zmodem, Sliding Windows Kermit, Sealink and the WXmodem file transfer protocols.

It should be noted that a simplex protocol can be used over a half-duplex channel and a half-duplex protocol can be used over a full-duplex channel. In a half-duplex modem, the entire bandwidth is available for use in the one direction. With a full-duplex system, the available bandwidth is divided into two sub-bands.   The two sub-bands comprise the *'originate carrier'*, which carries data from the DTE to the DCE and the *'answer carrier'*, which carries data from the DCE to the DTE.

Bandwidth

Every communications line is only capable of carrying data over a certain band of frequencies.   The range between the upper and lower limits is known as the *'bandwidth'*.   With audio, radio and television applications, the bandwidth is usually measured in Hertz - with one Hertz being a single cycle per second.   So, the bandwidth for transmitting voice may be less than 4KHz while music and colour TV signals may be 15KHz and 8MHz respectively.   With data communications, users wish to know the maximum data rates that a channel can handle and this is measured in bps - bits per second.

Multiplexors

Many computers or terminals may wish connection to a single computer at a remote location.   If each user were given a separate line to the remote computer, the cost would be unacceptable.   So, one communication channel is shared between different users.   This sharing can be achieved in terms of time or of frequency space.   The device used at each end is known as a *'multiplexor'* or *'mux'*.   Its job is to provide a *'transparent'* connection for the user.   This means that neither the user nor the remote computer need know that a mux is in use; it requires no additional equipment or additional software.   The local end *'multiplexes'* the channels while the remote end *'demultiplexes'* the channels.

TDM

The *'Time Division Multiplexing'* technique is used to transmit multiple digital signals and it gives each terminal a share of the available line time.   Four terminals are shown sharing the same communication line.

The two multiplexors are synchronised so that both connect to point *'A'* at the same time, followed by both connecting to point *'B'* and so on. After *'D'*, connection *'A'* is returned to.   During the connection to each point, a piece of data is transferred over the line.   Each terminal has a series of timeslots when it has exclusive use of the channel.   In the example, each terminal only has one quarter of the line time.   With n terminals, each will have 1/n of the line time.   This needs a communications line with fast transfer rates, with its speed being the total of the combined speeds of the connected slow terminal connections.   With a *'Statistical Multiplexor'*, a low speed channel is only given bandwidth on the high-speed channel if it has data to send.   The sum of the input speeds can now exceed that of the composite channel, since not all low speed channels are normally in use at any one time.   To accommodate occasions of every channel wishing to transmit, buffering is used.   This makes most efficient use of the fast link but it cannot support synchronous data.

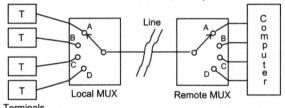

FDM

The other technique, known as *'Frequency Division Mulitplexing'*, also conveys a number of different users' data along a single line.   In this case, all the users' data is transmitted simultaneously, with each terminal being transmitted at a different frequency.   This *'broadband'* approach is further explained in the chapter on Local Area Networks.   The communication line used must have sufficient bandwidth to cope with the bandwidth of each channel, plus a margin between each channel, known as *'guard bands'*.   This is the method used to transmit multiple analogue signals simultaneously.   Fibre optics use the same technique, the difference being that it is referred to as *'wavelength division multiplexing'*.

Attenuation

As a signal moves along a communications wire line its amplitude diminishes with every metre.   These losses are caused by:

- Heat dissipation.   A copper conductor has a finite resistance to the passage of electric current.   Thicker wires reduce line resistance but are very expensive.
- Frequency dependent losses.   The capacitive effect between the elements of a pair of communication wires leaks the signal across the wires, reducing the signal that arrives at the end of the cable.   Higher data rates produce increased changes of signal on the line and increased capacitive losses.

Gain or loss is the ratio of the output voltage from a communications line or device (Vout), compared to the voltage fed into it (Vin).   It is measured in units of *'decibels'* abbreviated to *'dB'*.   This measurement is not linear - it follows a logarithmic scale. It is the ratio $20 \log_{10} (Vout/Vin)$.

Noise

Noise is unwanted electrical signals that exist on the communication channel along with the desired data. As long as the noise stays at a low level there is no serious problem - but when the noise increases to the point where it is treated as a legitimate logic level, it causes false triggering and corrupted messages. The main sources of noise are:

Component Noise - caused by random or unwanted electron fluctuations within both inactive devices (such as resistors) and active devices (such as integrated circuits).

External Interference - caused by everything from natural sources (such as cosmic radiation and electric thunderstorms) to manmade sources (e.g. radiation from electrical appliances).

Crosstalk - caused by signals from one communication line being picked up on another line. This occurs due to the effects of capacitive and inductive coupling between lines that run adjacently.

Practical Links

There are two main options for connecting to remote stations.

Leased Line

Here, BT or another telecommunications company provides a permanent, dedicated cable link between two stations. Since no other person can use the line, there is no waiting; the line is never engaged even at peak times. In addition, the lines are of high quality, providing fewer errors and are usually faster. Of course, they are less flexible as they only connect to a single remote site but are very popular with business to connect different branches. Examples of leased lines are the BT Kilostream, Megastream and Satstream systems. These do not use modems as the connection is digital.

Performances are:

Kilostream	2.4kbs up to 64kbps	Electronic mail, slow scan TV, fax, data, voice
Megastream	2Mbps up to 140Mbps	Often multiplexed (i.e. a group of connections share the bandwidth)
Satstream	2.4kbps up to 1.5Mbps	Satellite system used for short term links, remote site access and video conferencing

Dial-Up Line

Here, the user is sharing a network of cabling and switching apparatus. Lines are not exclusive but are cheaper due to the sharing of physical assets. Unlike a leased line, the user may often find a line is busy. Dial-up lines also suffer from poorer quality, producing a larger amount of errors. Increased errors require repeat transmissions and, since the user pays for the time used, error time costs money. Faster transmissions also usually result in more errors.

Communication Networks

A variety of services are available for data communications over a switched network system.

PSTN

The Public Switched Telephone Network is the normal network used for telephone connections. It is simple and cheap requiring modems to be plugged into the system instead of telephones. It is used by a wide range of both private and company users and is the main medium for information providers such as the Internet, CompuServe and a wide range of commercial and hobby bulletin boards.

The system is *'circuit switched'*. This means that the telephone exchanges set up a link between the calling and called ends. The switching is physical with the older Strowger exchanges or is electronic with modern exchanges. In both cases, once the connection is established, the originating caller has sole use of the cable between both ends. If the caller is in Aberdeen and the called end is in Truro, there will be a connection spanning the entire country that is dedicated to the one call. When the call is terminated, the channel can be used for other connections.

PSDN

The method of switching data traffic in the 1960's and 70's was *'Message Switching'* and this is still used with e-mail systems. It is a *'store and forward'* system, rather than today's real-time transmissions. Traffic is temporarily stored on disk and is sent on when a link is free. If there are three intermediate stations along the transmission route, the storing to disk and forwarding is repeated a further three times. It uses data links inefficiently and allows queues to build up, thus producing bottlenecks. Messages could take minutes or even hours to arrive.

The modern Public Switched Data Network is a parallel network to the telephone system but is dedicated to data communication.   This is a *'packet switched'* system, which means that there is no permanent connection between the two stations during a session.   The data to be transmitted is broken up into smaller chunks called *'packets'* and these are sent to the called end by the best route available at that time.   The cabling between exchanges is used by all connections and the PSE (packet switched exchange)

ISDN

While the main Internet consists of a network of high-speed digital links, the connection between most users and their ISP is analogue.   As the diagram shows, users link to the normal audio telephone network using modems.   The analogue/digital conversion is explained in the chapter on Data Communications. The use of lines that were designed to

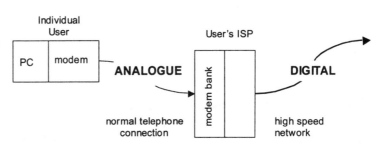

carry low quality audio transmissions has led to innovative modem technology to squeeze the last drop of speed from them.   There are, however, limits to the capacity of ordinary analogue systems.   The ISDN (Integrated Services Digital Network) is a digital carrier network and it has been designed to also be used on the normal telephone line between a subscriber's house and the ISDN connection points at the telephone exchange.   Once connected to the exchange's link, the rest of the link uses the high-speed ISDN data network that currently covers about 97% of the UK market.   Other countries using the ISDN system are Australia, Belgium, Denmark, Finland, France, Germany, Holland, Hong Kong, Italy, Japan, New Zealand, Norway, Singapore, Spain, Sweden, Switzerland and the USA.   The UK currently has a solid commercial base of ISDN30 users but the take up of ISDN2 is slow compared to many other countries.   A survey reported that BT's connection and rental charges were as much as six times higher than in Europe.   The USA, in comparison, has a cheaper pricing policy and has over one million ISDN users.   Overall, ISDN provides high-speed communication over much of the developed world.

Key features of ISDN are:

- High bit-rate - a single ISDN channel has a throughput of 64kbps (i.e. kilobits per second).   This compares very favourably with the average modem used on an analogue telephone system where speeds of up to 56kbps are the norm.
- All-digital interfaces - no need for modems.
- Very fast call setup time (800mS compared to up to 30sec for a dial up connection).
- Reduced noise.
- Supports both circuit switched and packet switched services.
- Supports both digitised voice and digital data.   The human voice is sampled at 8000Hz and quantised to 8 bits giving a 64kbps data rate and getting the maximum quality from the bandwidth of a single channel.

ISDN Services

There are two grades of service offered in the UK:

BTs Basic Rate Service - ISDN2

This service, also called BRI (Basic Rate Interface) is available from British Telecomms and it provides three digital channels into the user's premises.   Two of these, known as the *'B*

Channels', (or Bearer channels) each provide a 64kbps digital data link.   The third channel, the *'D Channel'*, (or Delta channel) provides a 16kbps digital link that is used for signalling purposes. When not in use for signalling, the D channel can also be used to carry digital data traffic.   Hence the maximum data capacity is 2 x 64k + 16k = 144Kbps.   This system is often called the 2B + D system.   The *'BT Home Highway'* service, in general terms, works out about twice the cost of a home telephone line. Usage unit costs are the same as analogue telephone charges.   If both B channels are used at the same time, then each is charged as a separate call.   Most Internet providers support ISDN access and some charge extra for this service.

Primary Rate Service - ISDN30

The Primary Rate Interface (PRI) is currently the other commonly used service and is provided by both BT and Mercury.   It provides thirty B Channels, allowing for a bandwidth of up to about 2Mbps, depending on the number

Signalling Channel
Timing and Synchronisation
30 Customer Channels x 64k

of channels in use at any one time.   As each extra channel is brought into use, the bandwidth - and the usage unit costs - is increased.   ISDN30 is an essential service where the highest data transfer rates are required.

Getting Connected

Connection to the ISDN system is achieved in the ways described below:

ISDN2

This uses the existing copper wire telephone lines into a user's premises. Instead of being connected to a telephone, they are connected to a digital interface as described below.   Of course, alterations are required at exchange end so that the line is connected to the ISDN network instead of the switched telephone network.   The cable comes into a user's premises as a normal twisted pair and is taken into an ISDN wall socket - called an NTE (Network Terminating Equipment). Two connectors come out of the NTE (one pair of wires for the transmitting functions and one pair for the receiving functions). The NTE looks similar to a twin telephone socket and connects to a terminal adapter or ISDN card on a PC.

ISDN Cards

These cards plug into the expansion bus inside the PC and provide various levels of sophistication.   These tend to be *'passive'* adaptors.   This means that they act primarily as an interface between the PC and the NTE.   All the signal processing is carried out by the PC's own CPU.   This makes for a cheaper product.

Card prices start from £70 upwards, dependent upon the facilities offered. Some cards can handle aggregation (see below), some only handle a single B channel, some provide data compression and so on.

Terminal Adaptors

Also known as an ISDN modem, it connects to the serial port of the PC.   It behaves in a similar way to a normal modem and has an extended set of Hayes AT commands. Beware of early models as some of these actually ran slower (at 19.2kbps or 28.4kbps) than the ISDN line.   Since the ISDN line is capable of handling 64kbps, the bandwidth was padded out with the insertion of null data.

External models are usually *'active'* adaptors.   In these models, all the signal processing and protocol handling is carried out by the electronics within the adaptor instead of the CPU.

Modern adaptors run at faster rates than the average serial port on a PC. To use them, the PC needs to have a fast 16550 UART inside, or have a high-speed add-on serial card fitted. Alternatively, terminal adaptors are now available for connection to a USB port.

Extra analogue sockets are often provided for the connection of a normal telephone or fax machine, as modern adaptors allow a normal analogue call to be made. This analogue call can even be made on one channel while the computer is using the other channel for Internet activity. ISDN cards and adaptors are relatively expensive but they are dropping in price with the increased uptake and sales.   In addition, Intel is developing its own set of ISDN chips for its videoconferencing system.

ISDN30

The ISDN2 is not powerful enough for many needs and the ISDN30 system provides for multi-channel use. All 30 channels allow for 1.92Mbps although, in practice, about eight channels are the maximum actually used.

Until recently, direct comparison of throughput on ISDN and modem linkups was muddied by the fact that compression techniques were commonplace on modems.   Comparisons are now more meaningful with the arrival of compression on ISDN systems.

Channel Aggregation

Channels can be grouped in various ways known as *'aggregation'* and *'bonding'* - to increase user bandwidth.   Aggregation allows two or more channels to be used for a single call.   This makes the effective data transfer rate double, triple, and so on.   Bonding (Bandwidth On Demand Interoperability Group) is a dynamic equivalent of Aggregation.   A bandwidth manager monitors the users needs at any one point and maintains the requisite number of ISDN channels open.   These systems require that a channel aggregator be fitted at both ends of the link to maintain synchronisation.

The Future

It is planned to use the ISDN D channel for more than simply call set up and routing. Potential uses are the credit card authorisation and the LAN interconnection markets.

Broadband ISDN (B-ISDN) is expected to be across Europe very soon. It will probably use optical fibre and ATM (Asynchronous Transfer Mode - a data transfer technique specially designed for use with wideband systems such as fibre optics), allowing end users 155Mbps and eventually 622Mbps data rates. Siemens are currently developing a 135Mbps B-ISDN service. Since wideband TV needs 140Mbps uncompressed, this can provide a viable multimedia link as well as high quality videoconferencing and home video-on-demand.

ADSL

Asymmetric Digital Subscriber Line (ADSL) is a relatively recent technology that could eventually become available to over 90% of BT customers if properly adopted. BT trials initially concentrated on video-on-demand services and other interactive services but is now targeted at the Internet and other communication mediums. *'Asymmetric'* refers to the fact that the data rate is different in different directions. In streaming media and Internet traffic this is quite acceptable, as the subscriber sends much less data back to the provider than he receives. The technique of using two line speeds on the same line is not new. V90, a modem standard in common use, can handle 56kbps downstream and 33kbps upstream. ADSL signalling rates are typically 6Mbps in one direction and 0.5Mbps in the other direction. The ANSI working group has approved a standard of 6.1Mbps over standard copper telephone cables, and some systems have a maximum of 9Mbps. BTs rollout of 512Kbps to 2MBps ADSL started in earnest at the start of the new millennium, though high prices and limited availability still present problems. However, BT has now been made to give other companies access to the wires to peoples' houses. This *'unbundling the local loop'* was intended to result in increased competition, bringing prices down and increasing levels of service, but BT's slow opening of exchanges to non-BT ISPs has brought wide criticism.

The ADSL technology uses digital signals from the exchange to the subscriber, with the subscriber's line being split into a data line for ADSL data transfer, and an analogue line for voice communications. The '*splitter*' works by putting the voice data on the digital line at a low frequency channel, and the download and upload streams on higher frequency channels. In the UK, however, ADSL bandwidth is usually shared, with contention ratios ranging from 10:1 to 50:1. While theoretically this could result in speeds actually slower than a 56k modem, in practice it is generally much less drastic.

Symmetric DSL was actually available before ADSL, and has variants known as HDSL (High-Rate DSL), SDSL (Single-line DSL) and VDSL (Very High-Rate DSL). HDSL runs over two or three paired wires and is designed to accommodate T1 and E1 signals, hence the data rates. (see below) Single-Line DSL and VDSL are single wire pair connections, both limited in range in order to achieve higher data rates.

ADSL also has its own variants. Rate Adaptive ADSL (RADSL) is able to adjust transmission speeds dynamically, and thus allows a greater distance between subscriber and exchange at the cost of potentially lower data rates (particularly upstream).

Cable	Range	Speed upstream / downstream
HDSL (US)	Unlimited	1.544Mbps
HDSL (Europe)	Unlimited	2.048Mbps
SDSL	2.5km	1.5Mbps
VDSL	1km	13 to 523Mbps / 2.3Mbps
ADSL	4km	512kbps to 2Mbps / 256Kbps
RADSL	8km	Less than or equal to ADSL

Broadband Cable

A viable alternative to ADSL or ISDN may be broadband cable. Although very different in operation from ADSL, it does share some characteristics. Bandwidth is shared with other cable users and in most cases cable Internet access is asymmetric, with download speeds being higher than upload speeds. Since cable does not rely on the telephone system, each cable provider has its own network. This means each cable network may be slightly different in terms of speed and contention ratios, although in most cases broadband cable is comparable to 512KBps ADSL.

Unfortunately, since new cables need to be in place to provide cable access, provision of the service is limited to those areas that the cable companies decide to invest in, which generally means metropolitan areas. However, cable providers often supply cable television through the same outlet, using a splitter to send TV and data signals to the right appliances.

Physically, broadband cable delivers data to the subscriber via a coaxial or hybrid fibre coaxial (HFC) cable, typically reaching 750MHz in bandwidth. Costs vary depending on the supplier, but again cable is usually broadly similar to ADSL prices.

High-Speed Connections

While UTP may be the most common LAN networking choice, and technologies like Kilostream, Megastream and Satstream are suitable for Metropolitan Area Networks, Wide Area Networks (WANs) are very different. Technologies like ISDN, ADSL and Cable are all involved in getting data from the network (in this case the internet) to the end user. But from the providers' point of view, it needs much higher speed and much longer distance links to provide sufficient bandwidth for all of this data. As can be imagined, the costs for such lines can be astronomical.

The majority of high-speed connections are fibre optical in nature, with the remainder being mainly T1, T3 or E1 wire lines. The table shows some properties of various types of high-speed connections. The European E-rating and the US T-rating systems both use multiple 64Kbps signals, originally over twisted pair cable but now over a variety of media including optical fibre or satellite networks. The OCx system on the other hand, is used solely on optical fibre, and is one type of signalling system used by 155MBps ATM networks.

Cable	Signals	Speed
E1 (Europe)	32 x 64Kbps	2.048Mbps
T1 (US)	24 x 64Kbps	1.544Mbps
T3 (US)	672 x 64Kbps	44.736 Mbps
OC-1	1 x 51.84Mbps	51.84Mbps
OC-3	3 x 51.84Mbps	155.52Mbps
OC-12	12 x 51.84Mbps	622.08Mbps
OC-48	48 x 51.84Mbps	2.43Gbps

Network Routing

Most traffic travels long distances and passes through intermediate stations along the route. These intermediate nodes clean up the signal and pass it on to the next chosen station on the route. Since the data network is a collection of such stations, there are a number of alternative routes that a message could be sent. For example, a message between Inverness and London may travel one of the following paths:

    Inverness → Edinburgh → Newcastle → Leeds → London
    Inverness → Glasgow → Liverpool → Birmingham → London
    Inverness → Glasgow → Newcastle → Birmingham → Leeds → London

or any other permutation. The performance of the network is determined by the way the links are used. One routing strategy, called *'non-adaptive routing'* or *'static switching'*, provides each node on the network with a fixed table of routes. So, for example, all traffic between Inverness and London must pass through Edinburgh, Liverpool and Leeds. The Edinburgh node's table would store the information that all messages for London from Inverness should be passed on to Liverpool, while Liverpool table would know to pass that message on to Leeds. So for every possible source and destination in the system there is a routing table that has been calculated and permanently used by each station. If a station is added, deleted or altered, all the routing tables that are affected have to be manually updated.

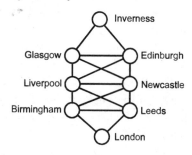

Availability

Non-adaptive routing is an efficient system where traffic demands are relatively light and unchanging. However, its weakness lies in its inability to automatically react to faults in the system. If the Leeds station broke down, then all traffic that was directed through it would be stopped until the fault was repaired. This would introduce unacceptable delays, particularly when the lines between other nodes were working perfectly. The *'availability'* of a station is simply the expected percentage of time that the station will work without problems. So, a station with an availability factor of 0.9 can be expected to work 90% of the time. However, the problem is magnified where a chain of stations is involved. If Inverness, Edinburgh, Liverpool, Leeds and London all had 0.9 availability factors, the overall availability of the system is 0.9 x 0.9 x 0.9 x0.9 x 0.9 = 0.59. Where stations are connected in parallel (e.g. Edinburgh and Liverpool are parallel stations between Glasgow and Newcastle) the availability calculation shows a much more efficient system. If one node completely ceases (egg Edinburgh) the other node (e.g. Liverpool) remains 100% functional. This improvement cannot be utilised by non-adaptive methods, since the routing only directs traffic to a single node whether that node is functional or not.

Congestion Control
Each node is connected to a number of incoming/outgoing connections (the example shows Newcastle connecting to five other nodes while Inverness connects to two). Since each node only handles a defined amount of traffic at any one time, the system stops sending traffic to a busy node until the congestion eases. This routing is a wasteful, since one node may be congested while another is quiet.

Adaptive Routing
Adaptive routing responds to changes in the system (e.g. breakdowns, congestion) by automatically altering the traffic routes. The tables held by each node are no longer fixed; their path information is altered to reflect the current state of the network. There are two ways of implementing adaptive routing:

Centralised Routing
One node on the network constantly collects information on the status of every other network node. Each change in the system results in the centralised management system calculating the best new routes to maximise the efficient use of the system in its new state. The new routing tables are then transmitted to each node for updating their routing activities.

Distributed Routing
With this method, there is no central control and each node carries out its own monitoring, calculation and distribution of routing information. So, for example, if the Newcastle/Leeds link failed or became congested, Leeds would inform Liverpool and Birmingham. Each node responds to its own monitoring and to incoming status information by recalculating its own routing tables.

The calculation for routing tables, known as *'shortest path algorithms'*, would take into account the capacity of the alternate links (throughput in bps), the delays of each link, the cost of using each link and the error rate of each link. The calculation produces the most efficient new route to adopt.

P.C. Links to Large Computers
Data communications allow a P.C. to access the resources of mainframe and other large computer systems. But mainframes were designed to connect to their own brand and design of *'terminals'*. A terminal's main function is to transfer the user's keystrokes to the mainframe and to display the mainframe's output on the user's monitor. The way this is achieved depends upon the design of the terminal and may range from simple ASCII screens to complex graphical screens. Examples are the DEC VT100 ASCII systems and the IBM 3270 series which include colour graphics display stations. Terminals have no computational power other than that required to carry out their input and output functions - all the real program computation takes place inside the mainframe computer.

When a PC wishes to connect to the larger system, it has to communicate in exactly the same way as that expected by a terminal. This is achieved by the communications software, which allows the user to select a particular terminal *'emulation'*. The software ensures that communication between the PC and mainframe works identically to that with a terminal. The mainframe works normally, thinking its communicating with a standard terminal and the software in the PC does all the conversion work.

P.C. to P.C. Links
Users may also wish to link their P.C. to another P.C. so that communication can take place or so that resources can be shared. This link can be either local or remote.

Local Connection
Used where the PCs are in the same room or office. This is commonly used for file transfers between a user's desktop computer in the workplace and the laptop computer that is carried around. Typical users include salespersons downloading current prices and uploading the previous day's orders and civil engineers bringing back information gathered on a site for analysis on the office machine.

In these cases, the PCs can be linked together using:
- A *'null modem'* serial cable connecting the two RS232 ports. The speed of file transfers depends on the maximum data transfer rate of the slowest serial port of the two computers and this speed can be set up using the communications software.
- A parallel cable connecting the two parallel ports. Data is transferred one byte at a time but the maximum transfer rate may be slowed by retransmissions due to transmissions errors.

- A USB or FireWire cable connecting to the USB or FireWire ports on both computers. Although this is another serial method, its transfer rate is far greater than with a serial cable. Special software is required to connect the PCs, however.
- Network cards fitted in each PC and linked together with LAN cabling. This is common with laptops that have PCMCIA card LAN adaptors. It is also reasonably popular as a means of games enthusiasts playing multi-player games. See the LANS chapter for information on how to set up a local Microsoft Network.

Of course, each computer has to run appropriate software to manage the connection.

Examples are:

- *'Direct Cable Connection'* provided with Windows 95/98/ME (see later).
- Laplink, which is a stand-alone product where either PC can access the other's files.
- Peer-to-Peer software such as Windows for Workgroups or Lantastic, which allow the sharing of each other's file and peripheral resources.

Laplink and similar programs are designed for use with either serial or parallel connection between PCs, while network software expects the machines to be fitted with network interface cards and card driver software.

Once connected, all the above systems allow file transfers from one machine's disks to the other's drives. Early communications programs were command driven, but recent packages are more sophisticated and display the other PC's files on screen so that they can be highlighted, either singly or in groups, for copying and other operations.

Null Modem Cable

A modem serial cable has no reversals in the cable wiring. Each pin on a plug is wired to the same plug pin number on the other end of the cable. This approach mainly applies to modems. The diagram shows a basic connection of two PCs without hardware handshaking. The computer's *'transmit'* pin is wired to a device's *'receive'* pin and the computer's *'receive'* pin is connected to the device's *'transmit'* pin. One computer's TXD pin is wired to the other's RXD pin and vice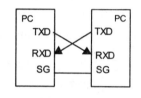

versa. With hardware handshaking, one computer's DTR pin would be wired to the other's DSR pin and vice versa and one computer's RTS line would connect to the other's CTS line. Some communication software refuses to work unless its DCD line is set on. In these case, the RTS and the CTS lines of the first PC should be wired together and taken to the DCD line of the second computer - and vice versa.

These are known as a *'null modem'* cables and they are widely used for transferring files across a serial port with packages such as Laplink.

Remote Connection

Where the PCs are at different sites, connection can be achieved over the public telephone network using modems at each end. Again, each computer requires remote connection software to be installed. The software can provide two separate functions:

Remote Access

Here the incoming PC has access to the remote (known as the *'host'* or *'server'*) PC's resources such as files and peripherals. The user can download from the host system or can place data on the host system. Usually, either user can initiate the connection thereby making the called station the host. Laplink is an example of remote access software that can provide file transfers over a modem, even connecting into a remote Local Area Network. The data rates depend upon the speed of the serial ports, the modems and the quality of the transmission line.

Uses of remote access include:

- Teleworking - This covers a range of work activities such as an employee working from home, working from another branch, working from a customers premises and even group working with other individuals who are similarly located remotely.
- Distance learning - Enrolled students can access lessons, upload their course essays and e-mail enquiries to their tutor. This is an area of much development and the quality of material varies.

Remote Control

Here the incoming PC takes control of the remote PC's activities. The incoming machine's key and mouse activities control the remote machine and the incoming machine can see the same video output as that being displayed on the remote screen. This provides opportunities for remote diagnostics and debugging. The problems at a remote machine can be solved without visiting the remote site.   Usually, one of the systems is permanently set up as the host while the other is used as the *'guest'* or *'client'*.   Examples of this software are pcANYWHERE, Carbon Copy and Reachout.   These products also allow remote control over a network so that any user on the LAN can be directly in communication with, and receive support from, a remote user.

Direct Cable Connection

Windows 95/98/ME has built-in facilities to allow two computers to share files, using a parallel or RS-232 serial cable.   USB and FireWire connections are not supported.   The fastest transfer rates are obtained with computers that have ECP parallel ports.

With all three Windows versions, the first step is installing the Direct Cable Connection software.   If it is not installed, it can be added via the

Start/Settings/Control Panel/Add-Remove Programs/Windows Setup/Communications/Details

menu options; the box beside *'Direct Cable Connection'* should be checked.

With Windows 95, the following additional steps are required:

- Ensure NetBEUI, TCP/IP or IPX is loaded. Check using the
  Start/Settings/Control Panel/Network
  menu options. The Configuration list should show one of these. If not, use the *'Add'* feature to install.
- The *'Client for Microsoft Networks'* must be enabled. The Configuration list should include this feature. If not, use the *'Add'* feature to install.
- File and Printer Sharing must be enabled. If the Configuration list does not show sharing as enabled, click the *'File and Print Sharing'* and *'Add'* buttons.

Running

Start/Programs/Accessories/(Communications)/Direct Cable Connection/Host/Next

sets up the host computer, while

Start/Programs/Accessories/(Communications)/Direct Cable Connection/Guest/Next

sets up the guest computer.   The extra *'Communications'* step is required within Windows '98.

When either the *'Host'* or *'Guest'* option is chosen, a dialogue box allows the selection of the port to be used (serial, parallel or, in Windows '98, infrared).   The same type of port must be used for both computers.   Windows '98 then asks whether file and print sharing with the guest is required.   This option should be enabled for most uses.

Once set up, running

Start/Programs/Accessories/(Communications)/Direct Cable Connection/Listen

at the host computer and

Start/Programs/Accessories/(Communications)/Direct Cable Connection/Connect

at the guest computer connects the two machines for resource sharing.

OSI Standards

Where data has to be transmitted from one location and received at another location, there has to be a set of protocols which ensure that both the transmitting and receiving devices handle data in the same way. These should cover issues such as packet size, the organisation of packet contents, speed of transmission, types of synchronisation and error correction.   It must also cover the lowest level issue of how a single data bit is moved - e.g. voltage levels or current loop detection. As long as both sites use the same protocols, data movement is possible. Where sites are numbered in millions internationally, as in the superhighway, there has to be an international set of standards.   This prompted one description of OSI standards as *"the Esperanto of communications"*.

Application Layer	- - - - - - - - -	Application Layer
Presentation Layer	- - - - - - - - -	Presentation Layer
Session Layer	- - - - - - - - -	Session Layer
Transport Layer	- - - - - - - - -	Transport Layer
Network Layer	- - - - - - - - -	Network Layer
Data Link Layer	- - - - - - - - -	Data Link Layer
Physical Layer	- - - - - - - - -	Physical Layer

Networks, both LANs and WANs, were plagued by differing protocols for different proprietary products and this still inhibits the development of communications.   The International Standards Organisation (*ISO*) addressed the problem and decided to introduce a model for the design of networks.   This was known as the Open Systems Interconnection (*OSI*) model - mostly now known as the ISO/OSI model.

The model seeks to define the functions of the hardware and software involved in networks.   It does this by creating seven levels of communication activity, known as *'layers'*.   The seven layers, when interacting with each other, comprise the total system.   The lowest layer performs the most basic hardware function.   Each succeeding layer adds a greater level of sophistication to the process and the interface between each layer is clearly defined. The ISO/OSI model is not in itself a standard - it is more a set of measures to be used in comparing current and new products. For a long time, few products emerged which used this model. This changed when the US and UK governments made OSI standards mandatory for most large government contracts. X.400 (Electronic messaging), X.500 and X.25 are some of the ISO/OSI standards.

The Seven Layers

The chart shows the differing levels of complexity handled by each layer. Layer 1 only works with single data bits while the upper layers handle entire messages. The highest layer is the layer seen by the user (e.g. e-mail or file transfer) while the rest should be hidden from the user. The *'station'* referred to in the following descriptions could be any communications equipment. At its simplest, it comprises a PC and modem. The *'medium'* is any form of connection between the stations and covers from a telephone line to a vast switched network.

Layer Number	Layer Name	Information Handled
7	Application	Message
6	Presentation	Message
5	Session	Message
4	Transport	Message
3	Network	Packet
2	Data Link	Frame
1	Physical	Bit

LAYER 1 - Physical Layer

The Physical Layer is concerned with moving data between the station and the medium that connects the stations. It sets up, maintains and disconnects the physical link between the stations. The layer defines the electrical (i.e. voltage levels) and mechanical (i.e. pin wiring) requirements for connecting the equipment to the medium. Examples of the Physical Layer are RS-232, X.21 and V35.

LAYER 2 - Data Link Layer

Layer 1 only accepts or sends a stream of data bits without paying any attention to the order or meaning of the bits. So Layer 2 ensures that any corruption of the data stream is detected. The data to be transmitted is fed into the Data Link Layer and it handles a block of data at a time, called a *'frame'*. A checksum is added to the frame and the frame is then passed on to Layer 1 for transmission. The receiving station's Layer 1 detects the incoming data stream and passes it on to Layer 2. If there is no corruption of the data it can be passed on for further processing. Layer 2 is also used for flow control and handles transmissions to and from the nearest DSE (data switching equipment). Examples of the Data Link Layer are Ethernet's CSMA/CD and HDLC (High-Level Data Link Control).

LAYER 3 - Network Layer

Most communication sessions between computers are not directly wired but are routed through a switched network or even a series of network devices. Layer 3 adds unique addressing information to packets so that they are routed to the correct receiving station. The enlarged packet is sent to the Data Link Layer where the error checksum is added and the packet is sent out on to the transmission media (via the Physical Layer). If the address of the receiving station does not match the packet address, the packet is ignored. If it has the matching address, the data is accepted and further processed.

Examples of this layer are X.25 used in wide area packet switched networks, Novell's IPX and the IP of Internet's TCP/IP.

LAYER 4 - Transport Layer

The Transport Layer acts as the interface between the user's activities and the requirements of the data communications network (i.e. the lower three layers). The message to be transmitted arrives at the Transport Layer and is often larger than the maximum size of data packet that can be handled by the lower system. The Transport Layer splits the data into chunks that match the capacity of the network system in use (e.g. 4k blocks) and adds sequence numbers to each block before sending them to the Network Layer. On a switched network, the various blocks may be sent via different routes. The Transport Layer on the receiving end does not care what route the blocks took. It is only concerned with passing on the incoming blocks in the correct sequence. If a block arrives out of sequence (e.g. block 2 is delayed in the network and arrives after block 3) the Transport Layer places the blocks back into sequence. If a duplicate block arrives (e.g. block 2 arrives twice) the Transport Layer detects the duplicate block and ignores it.

The Transport Layer, therefore, provides a pipe between systems to exchange data, operating independently of both higher layer application protocols and lower layer network protocols - effectively the link between user applications and the network.

Examples of the Transport Layer are Novell's SPX and the TCP of Internet's TCP/IP.

LAYER 5 - Session Layer

The first four layers were *'communications oriented'*; they concentrated on the physical network and its rules. Layers 5 to 7 are *'process oriented'* layers. These are high level protocols to allow two OSI-based models to exchange data - regardless of the physical connecting medium. The Session Layer establishes, controls and terminates the dialogue between the two user application processes. It treats the session as a single activity, even although the Transport Layer may have used a number of different connections to complete the data transfer. The layer also controls the flow of information to match the system currently in use (i.e. simplex, duplex, half-duplex). The layer also inserts *'checkpoints'* into the data. This provides points from which to restart if the two ends get out of step (e.g. due to a connection failure).

Examples of this layer are Internet's TELNET and FTP, and Novell's NETBIOS emulator.

LAYER 6 - Presentation Layer

The two computers in the dialogue may use different methods of representing numbers and graphical characters. The Presentation Layer has to ensure that machines with different data representations (e.g. ASCII 7-bit, BCD, etc) can still pass the same meaning from one user to another. The data supplied to the Presentation Layer is converted from its existing format into a universal OSI format (known as ASN.1) before being passed to the Session Layer. When the data arrives at the receiving end's Presentation Layer, it is converted from the universal format into the format used by that particular machine (which may or may not differ from that of the sending machine). The data, in its acceptable format, is then passed up. The layer can also provide facilities such as compression/decompression, encryption/decryption and terminal emulation.

LAYER 7 - Application Layer

The Application Layer is the link between the end user's application package and the communications system. As such, it varies from program to program and from system to system.

Examples of this layer are X-Windows, the X400 standard for e-mail, Novell's DOS redirector and remote job entry functions.

OSI Summary

The chart shows the basic functions of each layer when sending a message - each layer processing data and passing it down one layer. Receiving is the reverse process, with incoming data being processed and passed up one layer.

Layer Number	Layer Name	Purpose
7	Application	Routes data from application packages into the communication system
6	Presentation	Ensures that machines with different data representations can still understand each other
5	Session	Handles simplex/duplex operations over an entire communications session
4	Transport	Divides data into a series of sequenced blocks for transmission
3	Network	Handles the routing of data to the required station
2	Data Link	Carries out flow control and error checking
1	Physical	Handles the physical and electrical characteristics of the communications network

TCP/IP

TCP/IP - *'Transmission Control Protocol over Internet Protocol'* - is the most commonly used set of communication protocols. It is used on the Internet, on Unix systems, on many local area networks, on wide area networks and as a means of connecting dissimilar systems (e.g. between minicomputers and mainframes). Novell provides IP as an alternative to its own IPX in Netware 4.1 and it is supported by Windows 95/98, OS/2 and NT. As long as a system has TCP/IP, it can communicate with any other TCP/IP-equipped system. This means that a PC can talk to a Macintosh while an Amiga can talk to a mainframe. Even better, the software is royalty-free - although many commercial products exist. TCP/IP was introduced in the 1970's as a protocol suite to support ARPAnet, the American defence network that developed into the Internet.

The TCP/IP protocols embody four layers and these broadly compare with the OSI model as shown in the comparison chart.

The TCP component is concerned with maintaining the dialogue between two computers and keeping data packets in order, detecting any corrupted or missing packets and requesting retransmission. The

TCP/IP Layer	Corresponding OSI Layers
Application	5,6,7
Transport	4
Internet	3
Network Interface	1,2

IP component is concerned with the routing of packets to correct locations, from local organisations through to regions and then internationally. The TCP components are a set of communications routines that applications can call upon. The IP component is another set of routines that the TCP layer uses. Some applications do not use the TCP and interface directly with the IP routines.

Application Layer
The 'standard' set of TCP/IP applications include:

Telnet
The PC acts like a terminal to a remote Unix machine and the user can access resources in the same manner as a user who was locally connected to the system. With the growth of the World Wide Web, the use of Telnet has dwindled to use with universities, libraries and some bulletin boards.

FTP
The *'File Transfer Protocol'* allows files to be copied from one computer to another over the Internet. Users can directly use FTP as shown later. In Web sites, the FTP facility may be hidden from the user who clicks on a *'Download File'* icon without realising that this invokes the FTP.

E-Mail
This allows for the transfer of messages between computers even if one of the two machines is switched off. Instead of sending the message directly to the remote computer, it is sent to a *'mail server'* which stores it for future reading by the remote station. The remote station can, at any time and from any location, log in to the mail server and check for any messages that have been left. The two common protocols for e-mail are SMTP and POP (Post Office Protocol).

NFS
The *'Network Filing System'* allows one computer to act as a file server to another remote computer. Since TCP/IP is machine-independent, a PC can use a remote Unix computer to save and recover files.

Remote Execution
A computer in one location initiates an activity on another remote computer.

These applications are under user control and consist of high-level activities (e.g. send this e-mail, fetch a copy of that file). They pass down their needs to the lower layers that work out how the tasks and operations will be achieved.

Transport Layer
With TCP/IP, information is sent in blocks known as *'datagrams'*. For most TCP/IP use, a packet and a datagram are the same size of 500 octets. An octet is 8 bits - i.e. one byte; however, since some systems do not work on an 8-bit word, the octet is the preferred way to describe size. A packet and a datagram are not always the same size. For example, the X.25 interface creates data packets of 128 bytes and so several packets would be required to transport a single datagram. On the Internet, there is no distinction between packets and datagrams and they are often used interchangeably. Messages from the Application Layer are broken into datagrams and transmitted separately. Since packets can get lost in the system or can arrive out of sequence, the task of maintaining the correct data flow rests with the Transport Layer. This layer re-arranges out of order packets and ensures that lost packets are automatically re-sent.

Internet Layer
All datagrams from the TCP are routed through the IP component of the system. This means that datagrams from the Transport Layer are sent down to the Internet Layer for processing and sending on to the Network Interface for transmission. The Internet Layer is concerned with getting the datagram to the correct location, as passed on to it from the Transport Layer along with the datagram. The addressing system for each location is covered later. The Internet Layer adds its own header to the datagram, works out the best route to take for delivering the packet (i.e. directly or via a gateway) and passes it on to the Network Interface.

Network Interface
This layer transmits and receives datagrams over a particular physical network and is specific to the characteristics of that network - e.g. WANs, Ethernet LANs, Token Ring LANs, etc.

SLIP/PPP
IP is designed for routing in a large network. Many home and small business users only own a single modem and dial up into the Internet via a normal telephone line. The server that they dial requires all the sophistication of IP for its connection to the Internet but only requires a simpler system to interface to the dial-up line. The first protocol to allow telephone/modem connections to TCP/IP was SLIP (Serial Line Internet Protocol) and an improved version is PPP (Point to Point Protocol). This consists of a driver to the computer's serial port and out to a SLIP or PPP server.

Port Numbers

A server processes many different stations at any one time.   Each process has to be identified with a particular station to ensure that datagrams do not get hopelessly mixed. Each process is identified by a 16-bit port number and this is generated by the application process initiating the contact.   The more popular server applications are allocated their own port numbers e.g. FTP is port 21 while TELNET is port 23.   A computer wishing to initiate a file transfer would specify its own port number as, say, 2345, while requesting a remote port 21.

Winsock

The combination of address and port number is referred to as a *'socket'*.   The TCP/IP software is known as the *'protocol stack'* and is implemented as either a DOS TSR, a Windows 3.1 DLL or as a VxD in later versions of Windows.   The Trumpet Winsock package and Windows (after v3.1) both provide both SLIP and PPP drivers.   Winsock (Windows Socket Application Programming Interface) is the interface between a Windows version of a client application, such as FTP, and the TCP/IP protocol stack.   The application calls routines from the Winsock DLL and it calls routines from the TCP/IP drivers.   Each commercial implementation of a TCP/IP protocol stack will supply its own WINSOCK.DLL to work with its own proprietary brand of stack.   In this way, writers of applications do not need to know what stack is in use, since it will always communicate with the Winsock DLL and let it carry out the operations to the stack.   Applications that do not make use of Winsock have to write their own interface to the TCP/IP protocol stack.

Datacomms Applications

Worldwide data communications has opened a variety of new applications for industry, commerce and domestic users.   These can be broadly described as:

Remote Control
Remote monitoring, diagnostics, debugging, surveillance, process control.

File Transfer
The copying of files from a remote computer.

E-mail
The sending/receiving/storing/categorising of messages between users.

Information services
The availability of a mass of data, from test reports to train timetables.

Consumer applications
Multi-player games, home shopping, video-on-demand.

Access to these facilities can be provided in four ways.

Internal Organisation
Some of these services, such as remote control, file transfer and e-mail can be contained within an organisation.   All activities are between the people and resources of that organisation.   The equipment used is exclusive to the organisation (e.g. internal networks, external leased private lines) and is not accessible by other users.

Home Bulletin Boards
Hundreds of bulletin board systems (BBS) are set up in a Sysop's (System Operator) home, with a telephone line attached to an auto-answer modem.   These provide a wide range of files for downloading, e-mail, specialist groups and real-time chat.   They are run on a hobby basis with no charge, or charges based on covering the cost of running the service.   Bulletin boards have largely been overtaken by Internet provision.

Internet Providers
These services are run for profit and offer a greater range of facilities than the non-commercial bulletin boards. The company allows access to the resources on the payment of fees, which may include the following elements:

Standing charge	A monthly or quarterly charge, regardless of the amount of usage
Time charges	Charges based on each minute of connect time
Page charges	Charges for particular pages (e.g. financial information)

Free Internet access is provided by some companies, while the running costs may be recovered through advertising, support charges or commission from telephone companies.

426 Using the Internet

Using the Internet

Basics

The Internet is undoubtedly the largest computer resource on the planet. It enjoys a continual massive growth in the numbers using it and the facilities it offers. It is not a single entity; there is no Internet Ltd. At its simplest, it is a communications structure that links a huge number of independent PCs, networks and computer sites.

The main features of Internet use are:

- Many computers systems throughout the world are permanently connected to each other (i.e. *'on-line'*), through an elaborate high-speed worldwide cabling system.
- Between them, these systems store a gigantic collection of information and opinion.
- The network allows the easy movement of information between the permanent sites on the Internet and the users who access the system.
- Individuals usually connect to the system using their own PCs, a modem and their telephone line. Many organisations (colleges, universities, etc) access the Internet through their own LAN.
- Once connected, users have access to the material stored on the Internet. They can also send each other e-mail, download software and conduct commercial activity.

The facilities provided for Internet users include:

User Groups	Consumer reports	Press cuttings
Multi-user chat sessions	Software Fixes, updates	Government statistics
Hardware/Software News	Research papers	Market information
Electronic shopping	Search facilities	Travel information
On-line games	Newswire services	Downloading of programs
Distance learning	Latest drivers	Encyclopaedias
On-line magazines	Databases	Company information
Classified adverts	Web cams	Faxes

These facilities can be broadly categorised as:

Facility	What the user will do	What the user will see
Information Services	Access, read, copy and print material found on the Internet.	Text, graphics, sound, animations, video, forms.
E-Mail	Send/ receive/ store messages between users.	Plain ASCII messages, sometimes with an added non-text *'attachment'*.
File Transfer	Copy files from a remote computer.	Files and directories.
Newsgroups	Exchange views in an open forum of users with similar interests.	Questions, answers and opinions displayed in plain ASCII text.

All of these facilities are covered later.

The Structure

The Internet began in the USA in the 70's as a Government sponsored interconnection of supercomputers for defence purposes and was called *'ARPAnet'* (Advanced Research Projects Agency).   The drive for communication standards in the early years produced the TCP/IP protocol described earlier and the SMTP (Simple Mail Transfer Protocol).   In the 80's, other academic networks joined ARPAnet to produce a large publicly funded university and research network.   The defence areas split away in 1984, leaving ARPAnet to develop into our current Internet.

The original backbone has been extended throughout almost all major industrialised countries of the world, and is organised and run as a group effort by numerous telecommunications companies.   It has been described as *"a network of networks"* and smaller localised clusters of networks are linked by high-speed telephone cables, fibre optic cables, laser links and satellite links.   Each stage of these links is paid for from the subscriptions of those using the local service.   The British network connects main centres, known as POPs *('Points of Presence')* and the entire network is connected to the rest of the world through links from London to America, Stockholm and Paris.

A Point of Presence is a server that remains continually connected to the Internet.   Users connect to the Internet through their own POP, usually by simple dial-up modem or sometimes via digital ISDN links.

The provider of the connection to the Internet is known as an *'ISP'* (Internet Service Provider).   Most ISPs are run by commercial organisations and they may have many POPs throughout a country or region. A UK user may wish to talk to users in Germany or download a file from the USA, so the entire network has to be available to all the world's users.   There is no centralised control of the traffic and data packets can travel a variety of routes between the sending and receiving locations. All packets contain their own source and destination information as well as the data to be sent.

The diagram shows the likely connection of an individual subscriber to the Internet.   The user connects to the ISP using a modem and his/her normal telephone connection.   The ISP is accessed via the normal

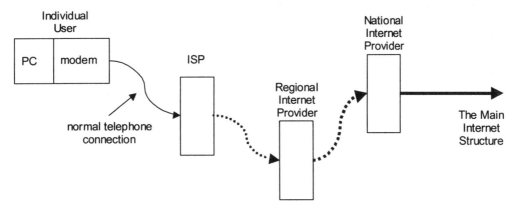

telephone network.   The user pays for any telephone charges and usually pays a standing charge to the ISP.   A smaller ISP pays a larger regional provider for access to the national network.   The regional provider pays a national provider for access to the international network. The national provider, perhaps with government funding, pays for the international connection.   A larger ISP may be sufficiently wealthy to provide its own main links.   This method of funding results in no one actually owning the Internet and explains its title of *'a network of networks'*.

Internet Administration

Although there is little or no control of the Internet's data providers and users, several bodies administer the development of the general structure.   The Internet Society (ISOC) is the overall body that promotes Internet maintenance and evolution.   It approves any new standards and protocols, ensuring that the whole structure remains compatible.   The Society is a non-profit making body and is independent of any government control.

It has a President and a Board of 18 members and is located in Reston, USA.

A main component of the Internet Society is the Internet Engineering Task Force (IETF).   IETF membership is open to any interested individual and the body consists of professionals from the networking industry (e.g. designers, manufacturers and operators).   Its main function is to maintain standards regarding the physical network (i.e. the wiring structure internationally) to ensure the most

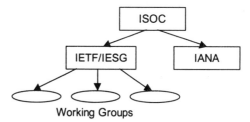

efficient use and expansion of the communications links. Its technical work is carried out in specific topic areas such as Applications, Operations and Management, Routing, Security, etc. Each topic area is covered by a large number of working groups that look in detail at specific aspects.   Each topic area is headed by an AD (Area Director) and each AD sits on the IESG (Internet Engineering Steering Group).

Another main body of the Internet Society is the Internet Architecture board (IAB).   Its functions include reviewing the protocols and procedures used on the Internet and liasing with other national and international bodies that are concerned with communications standards.   It also produces many papers to promote discussion and seek best experience and practice.   These papers are known as RFCs (Request for Comment) and actively seek responses from interested parties.

The Internet Assigned Numbers Authority (IANA) co-ordinates the assignment of unique parameter values for Internet protocols and is chartered by the Internet Society.

The World Wide Web Consortium (W3C) controls the standards for HTML, the web page language.

User Addresses

Each Internet user is allocated a different identification code (their IP address) so that the station can be uniquely identified for routing, e-mail and other purposes.   Each user is registered through the Network Information Centre (NIC), which is run by the USA Department of Defence.   The NIC allocates blocks of IP addresses, to ISPs. These ISPs then allocate them to individual users or groups of users.

All communication on the Internet uses the same protocol (methods of transmission and reception) to allow PCs to communicate with Unix systems, Macintoshes, etc. The Internet protocol is TCP/IP and is explained in the chapter on data Communications.   The IP part of the protocol requires each station on the system to have a unique address. This IP address consists of four bytes and is written with a period separating them.   Therefore, a valid IP address might be

175.73.44.11

The NIC issues blocks of addresses in three ways.

Class A addresses	Class A addresses are issued with the first byte fixed by the NIC. The provider receiving the Class A address can allocate over 16 million unique addresses.
Class B addresses	With Class B, the first two bytes are fixed, allowing the provider to allocate over 64,000 unique addressees.
Class C addresses	This has the first three bytes already allocated, allowing the provider a maximum of 254 unique addresses (the 0 and 255 address being used for other purposes).

Domain Names

Using numbers for the IP address is very confusing and users prefer to be identified by an agreed text substitute.   The text is easier to understand and consists of a hierarchy of allocated *'domain'* and *'sub-domain'* names.   These text equivalents map on to the actual numeric addresses. When a user's account is set up, these details are stored in a DNS (domain name server) and all providers can access these servers to translate text names into the corresponding address for routing purposes.

The *'Top Level Domain'* (TLD) names are allocated by the NIC and the original set of TLDs is shown in the first table. These are specific categories on the Internet and show their organisational status. The list includes allocations for each country. For example, the letters *'uk'* indicate that it is a British TLD, with *'fr'* for France and so on.   America is allocated *'us'* but it is rarely used; if no country is specified in an address, the domain is generally either US or

Top Level Domains	
com	commercial organisation
org	non-profit making organisation
gov	government
mil	military
edu	educational establishment
net	networking organisation
int	international organisation
uk, de, etc	country codes

multinational.   The TLDs that are not specific to any country are called *'generic top level domains'* or *'gTLDs'*.   The *'uk'* top level domain is further allocated into sub-domains.   These include sub-domains such as *'co'* (commercial) and *'ac'* (academic).

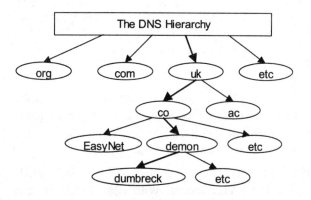

Where a site is stored on an ISP, the ISP name is included as a further sub-domain level name.

The example shows the domain name for the *'dumbreck'* site.   The individual or organisation sponsoring the web site is known as the *'hostname'* or *'nodename'*. Hostnames can be from 3 to 22 characters in length.   Since *'dumbreck'* is located on the Demon ISP, its full address is *'dumbreck.demon.co.uk'*

A larger organisation will own its own web server and will not be a sub-domain of another ISP. Examples are *'tesco.co.uk'* and *'sony.com'*.

Every user has both a unique domain name (e.g. dumbreck) and a unique IP address.

The site address is written with the lowest level first, moving to the highest level.   It is similar to writing an address on an envelope (i.e. name, address, city, and country).

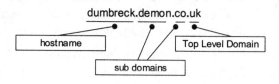

E-Mail Addresses

Internet subscribers with a single address have a potential e-mail problem.   A domestic subscriber may wish e-mail to be sent to different family members.   A company may have many employees who require individual or departmental e-mail addresses.   Setting up separate Internet accounts for each person is far too costly.   Fortunately, most ISPs are prepared to process multiple e-mail accounts for a single Internet account.   Each user has an agreed e-mail name and this is used along with the @ symbol.

So, the following address would be easy to remember:

sales@dumbreck.demon.co.uk

This is the Dumbreck Publishing account and shows the account's host name is *'dumbreck'*; the domain name is called *'Demon'* which is one of the largest commercial Internet service providers based in the UK.   Mail with that address is stored under the *'sales'* mail name.

If a number of computers were based at a site (as in universities), the full address might be:

eddie@science.lumchester.ac.uk

The computer's name is *'science'* and is one computer attached to the *'lumchester'* university in the UK. Eddie is a user of the *'science'* system.

Addressing Shortages

The success of the Internet has caused difficulties in allocating names to all new subscribers.

The Problem

Each IP address contains four bytes.   The first three bytes each store 256 usable combinations and the last byte stores 254 combinations.   In theory, this provides for 256 x 256 x 256 x 254 = 4,264 million unique addresses.   Since there are not 4 billion Internet users, the system would seem to have capacity for some time to come.

However, the way the addresses are allocated limits this.   For example, each of the over 100 Class A addresses consumes well over ten million IP addresses, when very few organisations could hope to use even a tenth of that number.   Even Class B addresses are over specified for the majority of users needs, wasting many more addresses.   To make matters worse, a range of IP addresses are reserved for use on internal networks.   If these problems were not addressed, the Internet would already have run out of allocateable IP numbers, despite having many unused addresses.

Additionally, the requirement to associate a text name to each address (see *'Domain Names'* earlier) has resulted in a severe shortage.   Users want meaningful text names for their address and there are not 4 billion combinations of useable names.   If a set of four numbers was hard to remember, users would have little chance of recalling an address such as *'zzqq2bntr3xa.co.uk'*

This problem is worsened by the now common practice of *'cybersquatting'*.   Cybersquatters are professional Domain Name hoarders, collecting those names that they feel are likely to be in demand in the near future.   When another group or individual wants to register a domain name they could well find that it has already been taken up by an organisation whose only purpose there is to sell the name to them at an inflated price.   Although occasionally court action can evict these groups from their domains, it is still a common practice, with some cybersquatters registering hundreds of names at a time.

The rapid rate of take-up of addresses means that there will soon be no meaningful names left to allocate. The shortage is worsened in certain areas by:

- Americans being reluctant to take up the *'.us'* TLD
- Non-Americans wishing to appear multinational by adopting *'.com'* as a domain, instead of *'.co.uk'*

If some TLDs are fully occupied while others are underused, using up unused names cannot alter the balance.   For example, an unused name in a *'.us'* domain cannot be used by a UK commercial company.

The Solution

The answer lies in the general expansion of the system through:

- Additional addresses
- Additional domain names

Additional Addresses

The original IP system, known as IPv4, has been supplemented by additional techniques such as CIDR (Classless Inter-Domain Routing), DHCP (Dynamic Host Configuration Protocol) and NAT (Network Address Translation) in order to reduce the strain on IP addresses.   Even with these modifications, IPv4 will run out of addresses eventually, and the proposed replacement, IPv6, uses 16 bytes instead of 4.

Even at conservative estimates this allows for over a thousand IP addresses for every square metre of land on Earth.

This vastly exceeds all foreseeable needs and is intended for future uses of the Internet. This would include connecting all domestic appliances to the Internet and communicating with each through their unique addresses. Office workers could switch on their central heating and microwave ovens before leaving the office. Similarly, commercial appliances could be remotely monitored and controlled. Automatic dispensing machines can be checked for low stock without leaving the depot and inhospitable sites can be remotely controlled (e.g. switching on defrosters at remote radio masts).

The new system is known as IPv6 and is being built in to modern software (e.g. the latest browsers) and hardware (e.g. network routers) in anticipation of its implementation. Apart from more addresses, IPv6 also provides faster and more efficient operation, as well as additional features like streaming support.

Additional Domain Names

The ICANN is about to introduce seven new TLDs, as shown in the table. A rival company, New.net has already set up its own group of 20 TLDs (including .ltd, .mp3, .shop and .video). However, these require new browser plug-ins, or co-operating ISPs (not yet including UK ISPs), to allow access to sites with those TLDs. Co-operating ISPs amend their domain name servers to recognise these new TLD suffixes.

Proposed New Top Level Domains	
Info	Open to public
biz	Businesses
name	Individual's names
aero	Aviation groups
museum	Accredited museums
coop	Business cooperatives
pro	Professionals

GETTING ON THE NET

Connection to the Internet requires the following:
- A modem for telephone line access or a terminal adapter for an ISDN link.
- A connection to a service provider. This is usually a dial-up connection or an ISDN link.
- An account with a service provider. All provide basic services such as WWW, e-mail and newsgroups, while some also provide free web site space, technical support, chat rooms, multiple email aliases and additional private services. Costs vary substantially between different suppliers.
- Interface software (e.g. TCP/IP, Winsock) and application software (e.g. Netscape, Explorer).

Dial-up access via the public switched telephone network is available through hundreds of providers such as Demon, PIPEX, etc, although this is a slow system due to the limitations of the medium. ISDN links are faster but more expensive. Larger organisations provide Internet access via internal LAN or other corporate connections routed through a leased line to the Internet. Windows 95, 98 and ME have Internet software built in, making access simple.

The 'Data Communications' chapter explains the major steps in installing a modem and the appropriate software. Some ISP software might require more information than the basic dial-up username and password. For example:
- Host domain name (the name of the computer that the account works to - e.g. dumbreck).
- Your domain name (the name of the provider - e.g. demon).
- Service providers gateway computer IP number (supplied by provider).
- DNS server address (supplied by provider).
- Communications details. These would include dial-up telephone number, transfer speed, timeout period (the amount of time that passes without network activity before the software breaks the connection).

ISPs

An Internet Service provider provides the user with a temporary dial-up connection to the Internet. The ISP has fast permanent links to the Internet and has a bank of modems for use by its subscribers. A subscriber accesses the ISP by dialling the POP telephone number, using the normal telephone line. The telephone exchange connects the subscriber to one of the ISP's

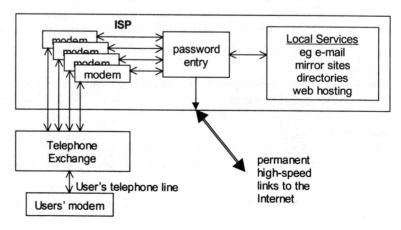

modems and this temporary connection is maintained as long as the user wishes.   The cost of the call is payable to the telephone company.

Once connected to the ISP, the caller has to provide a password to the ISP, to prove that he/she is a valid subscriber.

This process is often embedded in the user's connecting software.   The ISP's dialling code and the user's password are stored on the local computer, to automate the login.   One click of an icon provides the telephone number for the modem and the ISP is provided with the password when requested.

Once into the system, the user can access some of the bandwidth of the high-speed connection for Internet surfing, or can make use of the facilities that are stored locally on the ISP's own server.   Some of these facilities are made available to all Internet users (e.g. subscriber's web sites or mirror sites).   Other on-line providers such as AOL provide facilities that are restricted to their own subscribers.   These subscribers can choose to view the ISP's internal material, or use the ISP as a link to the wider Internet.

World Wide Web

The World Wide Web, usually called the Web or WWW, produces the largest share of all Internet traffic. It combines all existing facilities within a modern graphical environment.   Its documents are read using a browser - a utility to assist the user through the Web.

The Web's features include:

- Hypertext browsing (*'point and click'* on links to other resources).
- Screens displaying graphics and animations.
- Playing video in AVI, MPEG or QuickTime format.
- Running downloaded sub-programs via Java.
- Audio on Demand and Video on Demand.
- 3-d VRML models.
- Real-time voice Telephony.

Typical Uses Of The Www

PERSONAL	Obtaining information on television programs, the weather, etc.
	Requesting product information (e.g. holiday brochures).
PROFESSIONAL	Searching for reference material (e.g. scientists, medical practitioners, journalists).
	Obtaining technical updates (e.g. for computer technicians, engineers).
COMMERCIAL	Conducting e-commerce (electronic commerce).
	Advertising goods and services.
	Taking orders for products; accepting VISA transactions.
	Obtaining the latest information (e.g. financial newspapers, the Stock Market).

The WWW uses special software to package these Internet contents.   This is required at both the ISP end and at the user's end.   This has led to the development of *'Web Servers'* and *'Web Browsers'*.

Web Servers

Web servers are computers permanently attached to the Internet.   A large company or organisation will have its own server to exclusively store its own web site.   Smaller web sites will rent out space on the drives of an ISP or web space may be supplied free as part of the rental agreement.   A single ISP may act as the host to tens of thousands of web sites for small companies, organisations and individuals.

A web site stored on a web server consists of a number of individual web *'pages'*.   Each page is written in HTML (the HyperText Markup Language).   HTML is the language designed to deliver text, graphics, audio, etc to users with the software able to interpret it.   The software that re-creates the web page at the user's end is called a *'Web Browser'*.

Web Browsers

Software that is used on the local computer is known as *'client'* software, while the ISP end uses *'server'* software.   The most used piece of client software is the Web client - known as the *'browser'*.   It translates the HTML files from the server into readable pages at the client end.   It uses the HTML script to build the page's text, graphics, etc in the order written in the script (see chapter on Web Site Creation).   It also makes extensive use of *'hypertext'*.   Hypertext replaced older, text menu-based access systems.

In the Web, the user is presented with an attractive graphical screen document.   The document may contain graphical images and the screen text may have words or phrases that are highlighted.   These highlighted areas point to information in another part of the document - or an entirely different document. The other documents may reside anywhere on the Internet.   So, clicking on a hyperlink area (the highlighted text or icon) downloads the document pointed to by the hyperlink.   This other document may consist of further text with further links, or it may even contain a video clip, an audio clip, a small Java program, etc.   The hypertext features of the Web make it an ideal learning environment, where the user can explore paths that are of particular interest.

By far the two biggest competitors for graphical Web browsing are *'Microsoft Internet Explorer'* and *'Netscape Navigator'*.   Only a very small proportion of users use other browsers.   The two strive to continually add new features (e.g. video, audio, VRML, Java) and many web sites demand that one, or either, of these browsers be used for best results, since their sites are optimised to use the latest Explorer and/or Navigator features.

Inconsistencies

The World Wide Web Consortium (W3C) issues regular updates to the standards for HTML, currently in main version 4.   HTML is intended to be a language that is universally understood by all browsers. However, the following problems exist:

- If the latest HTML innovation or add-ons for animations, audio, video, etc are used, then only browsers equipped with these facilities will be able to make use of all the site's features.
- Various brands of browser, and even different versions of the same brand, may produce different screen results while executing the same HTML command.   In fact, even differently configured installations of the exact same software can produce varying results.
- Due to constant changes/additions, no browser software faithfully implements all available web content.

URLs

Every web site has its own unique domain name and every document on the site has its own reference (given by its file name and the name of any folder that it is stored in).   The combination of the domain name, directory name (if any) and file name

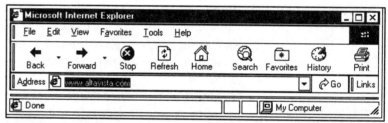

provide a unique description of that document.   This description is known as the URL (Universal Resource Location).   There is a separate URL for every single document on the entire Internet.

Browsers use URLs to fetch documents, either through clicking on hyperlinks or by the user entering the URL from the keyboard.   The diagram shows part of the screen of the Netscape browser.
The URL is a long single item of text without spaces and in the above example is

> http://home.netscape.com/

The part before the colon specifies the type of access.   In the example *'http'* is used; this is the *'Hypertext Transfer Protocol'* and is the method required to read HTML files.   Under HTTP, the browser sends the server requests in text format, and the server returns text files (HTML) that are interpreted and displayed on the screen.   Other possible access options include FTP, Gopher or Archie.   The remainder of the line specifies the server that is being accessed and may optionally include a path and file name at the end.

Valid examples of URLs are:

> ftp://ftp.cdrom.com/pub/cdrom/photo_cd/writeablecd.txt
> http://rohan.sdsu.edu/home/llu/VRML.html

In both examples, file names are being specified along with the sub-directories on which they are stored. The browser's *'bookmarks'* menu manages a user's database of URLs, allowing URLs to be added, deleted and given user-defined titles (e.g. *"stuff about disk specifications"*).   Web sites can then be easily fetched from the pull-down pick list instead of having to be sought and manually entered.

Using Internet Explorer

Every web browser requires that the computer already has a valid IP address, either allocated statically on a network already linked to the Internet, or dynamically such as via a firewall or ISP.   Once an IP address is established, the first thing a user sees in Explorer is the default home page. Explorer can be configured to use any URL to access any resource as a home page.

A typical Microsoft Explorer window might look like the following:

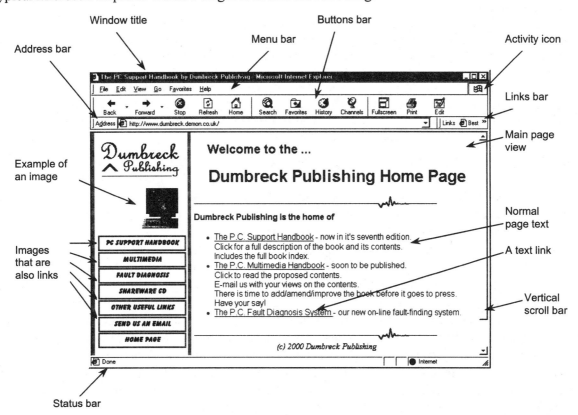

At the top of the window is the title, which all Windows applications normally show. Underneath is the menu bar, also common to most Windows applications. However, users rarely need to access these menus to navigate the web properly. To the right of the menu bar is the activity icon. This icon animates when Explorer is downloading a file for display and is static when downloading is complete. In most cases, Explorer is set up to display the Buttons Bar below the menu bar. This toolbar contains a variety of buttons to aid navigation and usage of the web.

From left to right, those functions are:

- Back: As the web is navigated, Explorer stores a History of the locations that have been visited. The 'Back' button returns the user from the page currently being viewed to the page last viewed. Of course, you can only go back as far as the first page that was displayed when Explorer started up.
- Forward: This is the opposite of the 'Back' button, moving forwards through Explorer's History rather than back.   Of course, if the 'Back' button has not been pressed, the user is at the end of the History and therefore there are no pages to forward of that point and the 'Forward' button is greyed out.
- Stop: If a web page is taking a long time to load (perhaps because of a network fault or a page with a lot of graphics), the 'Stop' button causes Explorer to stop downloading and display as much as it managed to download.
- Refresh: This button forces Explorer to reload the entire page and its contents. This is useful, for example, when the 'Stop' button has halted downloading before a full page is loaded. It is also useful for web pages that update very frequently, such as pages of news or pages that record usage of your website.
- Home: The 'Home' button is a short way to send the browser straight back to the page which has been set as the browser default home page.
- Search: The 'Search' button opens up a special bar called the 'Explorer Bar'. The Explorer bar appears in the left hand side of the main page view, with facilities that allow the user to enter criteria for sending to Microsoft's search engine on the web.

- Favorites: The *'Favorites'* button opens up the Explorer bar, displaying the contents of the user's *'Favorites'* folder. These contents are also accessible via the *'Favorites'* menu on the menu bar, and are also available to other programs.
- History: The 'History' button opens up the Explorer bar, displaying the user's browser history. Explorer not only records the web pages visited in one session, but also the web pages accessed on previous dates.
- Channels: The 'Channels' button opens up the Explorer bar, displaying a listing of web Channels that are available for viewing. A Channel is simply a special web site that transmits web content to the PC in a more dynamic fashion.
- Fullscreen: This button removes almost all of the toolbars from the Explorer window, and maximises the window, so that the web page displays on the entire screen. The F11 key on the keyboard performs the same function.   Full screen display is useful because some web pages are optimised for display on a full 800 x 600 screen, for example.
- Print: This button prints the web page currently being displayed, including graphics.
- Edit: When the 'Edit' button is pressed, Explorer opens up the relevant package for editing the source file of the page currently being displayed. For example, if an HTML file is being viewed, then clicking on 'Edit' calls up a package such as Notepad or FrontPage to edit the current page.

Below the Button Bar lies the address bar, and the links bar. The address bar contains a text box, which contains the URL of the current page being displayed.   If the user wishes to go to a specific URL without having to follow links, he/she types the URL into this text box.   As soon as the 'Enter' key is pressed, Explorer tries to download the contents of the URL.   The links bar is simply a space where the *'Links'* section of the *'Favorites'* folder is displayed for easy access.

The main page view is normally located under all these toolbars and is where the web site contents are displayed.   This will vary depending on the item being viewed, but it generally consists of text and images, some of which may act as hyperlinks to other URLs.   If the web page is larger than the main window size, it may display one or more scroll bars, just like most other Windows applications.

The illustration shows examples of text and images, as well as text links and image links. Note that the bottom image on the left is greyed out. This is commonly used to indicate that the option in grey is the web page that is currently being accessed. Depending on the web page, text links may not necessarily be underlined – they may be bold, specially coloured, or even displayed in normal fonts. You can determine whether a piece of text is a link by moving the mouse to point at it. If the mouse pointer turns into a hand with a pointing finger, then the text that the finger is pointing at is a link.

Finally, at the bottom of the window lies the Status Bar. This toolbar has various functions. Most notable of these is the download status, located next to the Internet Explorer icon.   It may, for example, tell the user that it has downloaded 50% of a 64k file, or it may simply display the message *"Done"* if the download has been completed.

Web Searches

The Web is a vast area to explore and help is required to locate resources.

There are two methods of searching the web:
- Using a *'Search Engine'* (typing in keywords to search for).
- Using a *'Directory'* (a hierarchy of menus).

Hundreds of web sites exist to point the user to their desired area of interest. They may provide little or no content of their own. They do not act primarily as information providers. They exist to organise the user's browsing and searching capability.

Search Engines

Search engines are software tools provided to aid users to locate the material that interests them.   Alta Vista, one of the most popular search engines claims to search through over one million host names, 31 million pages and 4 million newsgroup articles. Other engines include Excite and Lycos, claiming 50 million and 60 million pages respectively.   Most popular sites, such as Yahoo, Lycos, Excite and AltaVista, provide both searching and directory facilities.

In a text search, the user enters the key word or words that describe the item and requests that a search is made of the Internet for items that match the given description.   Searches can be made of the web sites or of the material stored in the user group directories.

There are a few golden rules of searching:

- Be as specific as possible. Asking for a search on *'Computers'* will probably result in an enormous number of matches. Searching through all of these matches would take months. Searching for *"Compaq"*, for example, will narrow the search considerably and produce far fewer useless matches. Searching for a specific model of computer would narrow the search even further.
- If searching for a specific file, use the file extension in the search. A search for *'winzip'* will probably produce many matches that only contain comments such as *"winzip is great!"*. Searching for *"winzip.exe"* will reduce the number of wasted matches.
- Learn and use the differing search syntax available for the search engines used.

Searches allow for more than a single word to be entered and this produces a much more refined search. The common search syntax used by search engines is shown in the following examples:

Search text	Result
car engine car OR engine	Finds any matches on *'car'* (e.g. restaurant car) and any other separate matches on *'engine'* (e.g. steam engine)
"car engine"	Finds matches on car and engine as a single entity; only references to car engines are displayed. *'engine car'* will not be found.
car AND engine car & engine +car +engine	Finds matches only where both the words appear. *'engine'* on its own is not found. *'car'* on its own is not found. *'engine car'* and *'car engine'* will both be found.
car +engine	Finds all matches where *'engine'* appears but not necessarily containing *'car'*. *'racing car'* will not be found, while *'steam engine'* will be found.
car AND NOT engine +car -engine	Finds matches on all car references, except those containing the word *'engine'*

Some search engines allow more complex searches to be built up, by combining various Boolean expressions using parenthesis. For example

car and (engine or steering)

will find all matches to *'car engine'* and *'car steering'* but not *'car sales'* or *'steering rod'*.

Some search engines, such as Bigfoot, WhoWhere and Internet White Pages, specialise in searching for Internet users. This is called X.500 and is based on searching a database that is maintained for the purpose. The database comprises users who have asked to be included or those have become public on the Internet for some reason (e.g. by posting to a newsgroup).

Directories

Search engines are powerful but can have drawbacks. Automated *'robots'* or *'spiders'* roam around the web updating the databases used by search engines. These do not attempt to evaluate the usefulness or relevance of a site's contents. Consequently, a simple search can result in hundreds or thousands of matches - most of which are totally useless.

Web directories (also known as *'portals'*), on the other hand, are compiled and updated by the directory site operators. They select sites and place them into categories that are accessed through user-selected menus. This makes them easy to use and they are ideal for the casual user.

The directory's menu hierarchy system is very popular and most packages use this method. The UK based search engine called Global On-Line Directory (GOD) offers the following list of main topics:

- Arts and Crafts
- Community and Education
- Environment
- Games
- Internet Resources
- Paranormal
- Technology and Computers
- Business
- Entertainment
- Financial Services
- Hot and Sexy
- Leisure and Pleasure
- Sports
- Travel

Clicking on a *'Computing'* option would display a further list of options. Clicking on a *'Multimedia'* sub-option option would display further options, and so on. Eventually there would be no more menus and the user is offered a list of resources (such as reviews, shareware programs, academic papers, etc) that can be downloaded. This is the approach used by the other directory services.

Since directory operators make money from the advertising space they rent out, they tend to maintain their system to cover the most popular material on the web. When a user wants a specific specialised item, it is unlikely to be available via menus and search engines provide the best route.

Browser Enhancements

JAVA

Java, which is essentially similar to the C++ programming language, can be used to create *'applets'*. These are small programs that can be downloaded along with HTML files and graphics files. They are then run within the calling PC. Applets range from simple animated icons and games through to database utilities. They require that the browser support Java as in Netscape 2.0 onwards.

ACTIVE-X

A set of rules developed by Microsoft, it provides around 1000 Windows controls. It is also designed to be downloaded and run within the local computer. Whereas Java is capable of running all platforms (i.e. - on any type of computer) that are Java-enabled, Active-X is solely designed for Windows. Its controls can be written in C, C++, Visual Basic and Java.

REAL AUDIO

Users with sound cards can listen, in real time, to radio programs from around the world. There are already hundreds of stations to choose from and the quality is equivalent to a normal AM radio. AudioNet provides indexing by content, source and theme. Requires the computer to have *'Real Audio'*, *'Streamworks'* or *'TrueSpeech'* installed; these are free add-ons to the user's browser.

REAL TIME TELEPHONY

Users with a sound card and a microphone can talk in real time to other similarly equipped users throughout the world - and at local call rates. Products such as *'Web Talk'* and Intel's *'Internet Phone'* provide the software to call up one of a range of specially created servers. These list all users who are attached to the service and are currently on-line. Both parties in the conversation should use the same software to ensure consistent results, as the technology has not yet evolved fully agreed standards.

VIDEO

The demand for video over the Internet stretches the capabilities of both the communications link and software. RealVideo addresses the problem by optimising video for 28.8kbps and 56kbps transmission and uses streaming (see below) and the dynamic reduction of frame rates (number of pictures shown for each second of video) to overcome inconsistent data rates over the Internet link. Other initiatives are *'CuSeeMe'* which is free video-conferencing software and Intel's *'Video Phone'* software, which provides video windows on a browser. Both require a video or QuickCam camera to capture the user's video.

FLASH ANIMATION

Most up-to-date browsers are supplied with Shockwave Flash plug-ins, while older browsers can be easily updated by downloading the appropriate plug-in. This allows the browser to display Flash animations, which can be anything from a small animated logo, up to multiple screens of web content. Flash 'animations' do not have to be animated in the traditional sense: they can use menus, timing and many other effects. Furthermore, Flash files are quite compact, making Flash a versatile tool for Web productions.

STREAMING

When downloading files over the Internet, the user is only concerned that the total file is fetched successfully. Any delays in the network, due to congestion and re-routing of packets, only influence the downloading time and have no affect on the quality of the file being downloaded. This is not true of audio and video files that have to be presented to the user in <u>real time</u>. Any delays in transmission would result in the break up of the sound or video continuity. To overcome this, *'streaming'* is used. This reads a number of data packets and stores them in a LIFO (Last In First Out) buffer in the computer. The user will have a slight initial delay as the buffer is filled. These data packets are then fed out from the head of the buffer, while incoming packets are fed into the tail of the buffer. During periods of transmission delay, the user is fed information from the buffer, thus maintaining a constant audio or video stream.

VIRTUAL REALITY

VRML (Virtual Reality Modelling Language) is an ASCII description of a 3D scene such as a building, a human heart, a car engine, etc. When VRML viewers are embedded in browsers, clicking an icon takes the user on a screen walk around the objects.

SURROUND VIDEO

Also known as *'panoramic video'*, it provides an environment that completely surrounds the user. Special cameras capture an entire location as a 360^0 photograph and convert it to a graphics image. The left and right edges of the image are aligned and the whole scene can be thought of comprising a cylinder in which the user is located. At any stage, the use can view about one-tenth of the image. Using the mouse or the keyboard moves the user round the image, giving the illusion that the user is situated in the middle of the scene. This is available as Apple's *'QuickTime VR'*, *'Surround Video'* and *'RealVR'*. Developments combining the panoramic background with the 3D objects available in Virtual Reality produce ever more realistic presentations.

Netiquette

Good browsing practice can benefit all Internet users.

- Switch off browser graphics when they are not essential. This reduces download time, saves telephone costs and saves bandwidth for others.
- Access *'mirror'* sites where possible. These are replicas of other busy sites. Congestion is reduced at the main site and overall use of the bandwidth is improved. Since many sites being mirrored are American, European mirror sites reduce the strain on the Trans-Atlantic links.

Mobile Internet

Recently, mobile phones have started to incorporate a form of web browsing. This uses a method called *'Wireless Application Protocol'* (WAP). Due to the slow speed at which mobile phones can reliably transfer data (9,600bps on a GSM mobile), and the limited screen capabilities of the average mobile phone, WAP browsing is necessarily text-heavy.

The much-debated Third Generation (3G) of mobile phones will in theory support up to 2MB/sec transfer rate, but due to the greatly reduced cell size this speed will be limited to very small areas. For true mobile environments speed is quoted as 128Kbps. Interim networks, sometimes called '2.5G' or '2G+' networks, will offer speeds of 28Kbps up to 400Kbps. It should be noted that these speeds are all theoretical maximums, and as with many such systems will rarely be achieved in practice – 14Kbps is a more realistic expectation, rising to 64Kbps in the not too distant future. However, the Fourth Generation (4G) is already in development, with speeds said to reach 100MB/sec.

WAP Browsing

Due to the obvious differences in capabilities between PCs and mobile phones, the HTML language is replaced by Wireless Markup Language (WML) for mobile Internet connections. WML is essentially similar to HTML, but is case sensitive and has stricter tag rules. WML uses 'cards', which are separate mini-pages that can be displayed at different times during browsing of the page. Graphics can be embedded in a WAP page but this is not recommended as it slows download times considerably.

E-Mail

This is one of the most used Internet services. With millions of users connected to the system, it is a cheap way for individuals and companies to exchange information, as there is no extra charge for this service. Many believe that the Internet e-mail service will make the traditional fax services redundant. It is faster than postal services and, unlike fax, does not depend upon the receiving end being switched on and ready.   It is also an improvement on some telephone conversations, as the contents are recorded and exact details (such as numeric values, postcodes, spelling of names, etc) can be reviewed, preventing future errors.

E-Mail Facilities

E-mail can be used in a number of different modes.

- From a user to a provider. The provider is permanently on-line and instantly receives the message.
- From a user to another user. The receiving user is not permanently attached to the Internet and the message is stored on his/her ISP's mail server. The mail is available when he/she next logs in.
- From a user to a group of users. A single e-mail is prepared and sent to multiple e-mail addresses. This is a useful tool for saving time. It is also the method for issuing junk mail.
- Within a groups of users. Subscribers can join *'Mailing Lists'* on a topic of their interest. New contributions on the topic are gathered centrally and a copy of each message is e-mailed to every subscriber on the mailing list.
- Including *'Attachments'*.   An e-mail can have one or more other files sent along with it. The e-mail is sent as a single entity but the receiving user can extract the file(s) for use at the distant end.

Typical Uses Of E-Mail

PERSONAL	Communicating with distant or overseas friends and relatives.
	Requesting product information (e.g. holiday brochures).
	Distance learning students maintaining contact with their lecturers, submitting examination scripts, etc
PROFESSIONAL	Academic exchanges (e.g. between educationalists, scientists, medical practitioners).
	Technical mailing lists (e.g. for computer technicians, engineers).

COMMERCIAL   Press releases to promote a new product or service (sent to editors of newspapers, TV, radio, etc).
Mailshots to potential purchases (sent to existing customers, bought-in mailing lists, etc).
Recipients may have requested regular mailshots, or may be victims of junk mail.
Answering customer queries.

Using E-Mail Software

The most widely used email client, ignoring web-based email providers such as Hotmail or Yahoo!, is Microsoft Outlook. It is by no means the only email package available; the Demon ISP recommends '*Turnpike*' software, and other POP (Post Office Protocol, as opposed to web-based email) clients include Eudora and Pegasus.

Like many Microsoft products, Outlook contains many features that are unnecessary for the majority of users, but its basic features are similar to those provided by other email client software. Outlook can be configured to dial up your ISP automatically if it detects that the computer is not already online. It can then check for new mail at regular intervals, such as every half hour. Alternatively, the user can select *Tools / Check For New Mail* to tell Outlook to retrieve mail. In some versions the '*Send and Retrieve*' button performs this function.

When mail is retrieved, it is stored in the '*Inbox*' folder, unless the user has set up rules to tell Outlook how to deal with mail. For example, if a user receives a lot of junk mail, he /she may set up a rule to automatically delete any mail with the words '*mortgage*' or '*credit*' in the subject line. Or a user who receives a lot of mail from a few clients can separate them into different folders using rules – each folder that contains unread messages will be shown in bold face. The messages are actually physically stored in a file on the hard disk, usually called '*outlook.pst*' in the Windows folder.

Clicking on any folder displays its contents in the right-hand panel, as shown. The user can then double-click on any email to open it in a new window and read it. Messages can also be deleted, replied to, forwarded, printed or saved. Right-clicking on the '*From*' field while reading a message opens a pop-up box including options to add the email name to Outlook's Contact List.

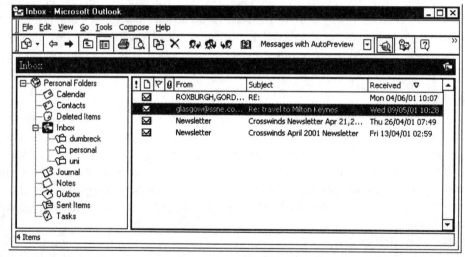

To send an outgoing email, the user should click on *File / New / Mail Message* or click on the '*New*' button in the top left hand corner while browsing any mail folder. This will bring up a new window, which should be used to enter the message details.

The steps for composing a new e-mail message are:

1. Enter the e-mail address of the person(s) receiving the mail in the '*To:*' dialogue box. Clicking on the '*To*' button allows the user to select names from the contact list.
2. If the message is to be Cc'ed (Carbon Copied) to other addresses, enter them in the 'Cc' box. CC'ing an email recipient has the same effect as adding them to the '*To*' field, but is used to indicate that CC'ed recipients are included for information only.
3. Enter a summary of the e-mail in the '*Subject*' dialogue box. This is optional but it is good manners to inform the recipient of the reason for the e-mail.
4. Type the message into the main window. It is normally good netiquette (see later) to discuss only a single subject in each e-mail.
5. Use the '*Insert File*' option to attach any files to the e-mail. This is optional.
6. Click the '*Send*' button.

The message will then go to Outlook's '*Outbox*' folder. From there, it will be sent to your ISP's mail server when '*Send and Receive*' or '*Check for New Mail*' is selected. The ISP will pass the message on to the recipient's ISP within a matter of seconds, and the user will receive the message next time they check their mailbox.

Messages can be composed off-line saving on telephone costs. All recipients will know who received the message. Using *'bcc'* (blind carbon copy), all recipients will receive the e-mail and be unaware that it was also sent to others.

E-mail software also allows messages to be read 'off-line' - i.e. when the computer is not connected to the ISP. Incoming messages are downloaded during a connected session and read later at the user's leisure. It also allows the user to write outgoing messages and mark them for posting. When the user next logs into the Internet, the messages are sent to the ISP. These both save telephone usage costs.

Messages can be saved or printed using the *'File'* menu and can be cut and pasted into other documents using the *'Edit'* menu. As can be seen from the screenshot, Outlook provides many additional features as well as email, such as a Calendar, Journal, Notes, and Task List. Also, new subfolders can be created by the user to store email messages, notes, tasks and other Outlook objects.

MIME and UUENCODE

Note that the main message in the example is in plain ASCII and that another file has been *'attached'* to the message. Where both the sending and receiving e-mail packages support MIME (Multipurpose Internet Mail Extensions) non-ASCII files can be transmitted along with the messages. These can be graphics, executables, spreadsheets - or any other form of binary file. This is because newsgroups were originally designed to carry 7-bit ASCII text. An older but still commonly used variant is UUencode (Unix-to-Unix encode), which converts 8-bit binary files into 7-bit versions for transmission. A UUdecoder at the receiving computer translates the file back into its original binary form.

E-Mail Etiquette

As in verbal or written communication, there are certain rules when using the Internet and its services. These are often referred to *'netiquette'* and the specific advice for those sending e-mail messages is:
- Treat other users with respect. Avoid sexist, racist, culturally insensitive and judgmental language
- Keep sentences short; the recipient is paying the phone time
- Never forward a received e-mail to a third party without permission
- Don't type in upper case
- Use 'smileys' to convey emotions (see below)
- Learn and use e-mail acronyms (see below)

Smileys

Some of the more common smileys are shown below; they have to be viewed with a tilted head.

:-)	smiling	:->	sarcastic	:-x	my lips are sealed
:-(	frowning	I-O	yawning	O:-)	angelic
:-D	Laughing	:-@	screaming	:-I	indifferent
:'-(	Crying	{{{0}}}	hugs	;-)	winking

Acronyms

Acronyms are used to save time (and to show how smart a user is), common ones being:

IMHO	In My Humble Opinion	TYVM	Thank You Very Much
IIRC	If I Recall Correctly	WRT	With Respect To
CMIIW	Correct Me If I'm Wrong	AFAIK	As Far As I Know
BTW	By The Way	IKWYM	I Know What You Mean
OTOH	On The Other Hand	TIA	Thanks In Advance

File Transfer

The Internet supports FTP (*'File Transfer Protocol'*) facilities that allow the user to:

DOWNLOAD: copy files from the remote server to his/her local drive.

UPLOAD: copy files from the local drive to the remote computer (where access is permitted).

Typical uses of FTP

PERSONAL   Collecting clip art, shareware.

Distance learning students downloading tests from a college's server.

PROFESSIONAL   Downloading case histories (e.g. lawyers).

Uploading/Downloading scientific data (e.g. researchers).

COMMERCIAL   Uploading/downloading contracts, prices, specifications.

Updating the contents of the company's web site.

A user, employing *'FTP client'* software, can access a remote *'FTP server'* site.

The FTP server acts as a large remote hard disk.   It is divided into many folders and each folder stores many files.   Each FTP server usually acts a host for a particular area of interest.   It may store academic or scientific files, or it may be a source of shareware programs.

Some servers will request a user name.   By convention, the password *'anonymous'* allows the user to see those files that the remote site will allow public access.   When prompted for a password, the user's e-mail address can be entered. To see non-public files, the user requires a security password.   This can be applied for and may be granted at the discretion of the site organisers.   FTP software often allows the user to set up sessions, with each session having a name and a set of parameters (e.g. ftp site address, user name and password).   Selecting a session automates the logging process.

The client software, under the control of the user, sends commands to change directory or list files.   The server receives these commands and sends back the appropriate information.   This is the *'control'* connection.   Most FTP servers store their non-restricted material within the *'pub'* (i.e. public) directory.

Each directory contains a text file (e.g. 00-INDEX.TXT, README.TXT or INDEX.LST) that provides a brief description of each file in that folder.   Highlighting that file, and clicking the *'View'* or *'Open'* button displays the text on the screen.

When the user clicks on a desired filename, a *'data'* connection is opened and the file can be transferred in either ASCII or binary mode (ASCII for text files, binary for programs, graphics, etc).

When the file is transferred, the data connection is closed and the control connection remains active for further directory navigation and transfers.   Closing the program breaks the control connection and returns the computer to its previous state.

The diagram shows a screen from WS_FTP, a popular Windows FTP client. The left panel shows the drives, directories and files of the computer initiating the transfer. The right panel shows the directories and files of the remote system.   Highlighting a file in the right panel and clicking the leftwards arrow, copies the file to the directory that is active in the left panel

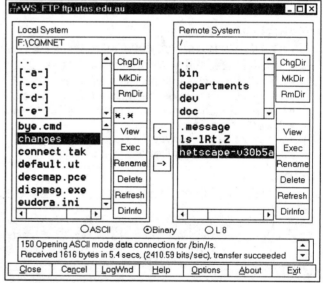

Many Web browsers offer automatic FTP facilities. If a file download hyperlink is clicked the system switches into FTP mode and the only user involvement is in selecting the directory into which the file should be stored. This avoids the user having to learn how FTP operates, as the mechanisms are hidden by the browser's user interface.

Apart from the text files that store descriptions of the files in each directory, there is little more in the way of casual browsing.   FTP users have to already know which FTP sites store particular information and this information can be obtained from publications or by asking within newsgroups.

To save on connect time, many files are stored in a compressed (usually ZIP) format.   A ZIPped file will show as a single file in the FTP site and downloads as a single file.   In practice, the ZIP file may contain a number of separate files that are bound together before compression. The unzipping process converts the single file back into its original parts and uncompresses each file.   A range of utilities such PKZIP, WinZIP and TurboZip are designed for this purpose.   Since some applications have many files, it is best to unzip files into their own directory/folder.   This prevents the files being mixed into other files.   ZIP utilities usually create folders when instructed.

Newsgroups

The Internet has scores of thousands of newsgroups (also known as user groups, special interest groups, conferences or forums) operating on a wide variety of subjects.   A newsgroup is an electronic version of a notice board.   Members contribute to discussions via e-mail and all contributions are stored for a period and are available for all wishing to read them.   Any user can join these groups and read existing messages, contribute to existing discussions or send an e-mail to start a new discussion.

The topics are extremely varied.   Some cover computer topics (programming, hardware, sales); some cover leisure (sports, music, hobbies); some are serious (politics, religion, support groups); some are frivolous (jokes, games); a very small but highly publicised number of topics are unsavoury or illegal (pornography, hacking, pirate software).

There is no central control over newsgroups.   Each newsgroup is organised and run by a volunteer. Newsgroups are all categorised within Usenet's hierarchy as shown in the table.   If a newsgroup is

'*moderated*' the incoming e-mail messages are read and approved before being placed in the newsgroup directory.   This prevents illegal, abusive or irrelevant material from clogging up the newsgroup.   Many groups are not moderated and this often leads to '*flame*' wars, where long, ongoing, abusive exchanges take place between contributors.   Another approach is the '*digest*', where the moderator produces regular summaries of the contributions received.

Hierarchy	Content
comp	computing hardware and software
news	network news
rec	recreations, hobbies, art and sport
sci	science
biz	business
soc	social issues
talk	debate on controversial matters
alt	controversial or unusual contents
misc	subjects that don't fit any of the other hierarchies

User groups are an extremely useful way to gain answers to technical or other queries since the correspondence for the most popular groups may be read by hundreds of thousands of users.   The overall service is called Usenet and newsgroup contents are viewed with a piece of software called a '*newsreader*'.   This software is available in freeware, shareware and commercial versions.

Subscribing

When the user uses the newsreader for the first time, it does not have a built-in list of newsgroups. Since the list regularly alters, the current list has to be fetched from the news server.   Once the list is downloaded, the user can browse through, highlight desired topics and click the '*subscribe*' option.

Off-Line Reading

Once subscribed to a newsgroup, any fresh contributions to the group are downloaded each time the user logs on to the Internet.   The user can read the messages at leisure after logging off the Internet, thus saving on telephone charges.

The example shows a newsreader being used offline to examine a newsgroup's content.   The newsgroup shown is for web page authors, as indicated by the description [alt.html.writers] in the newsreader's title bar.   The dots indicate sub-divisions of the hierarchy - i.e. the '*alt*' hierarchy has a sub-group called '*html*' and it has a further sub-group called '*writers*'.

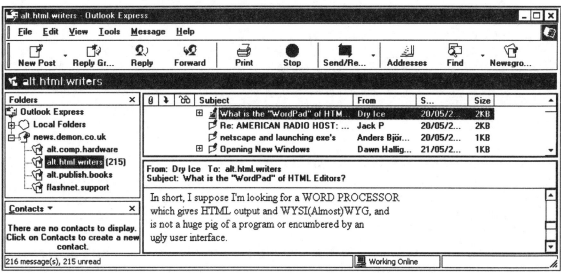

Each subject is a '*thread*' that was begun by a user and added to by other participants. With controversial issues, it is common to have up to several hundred contributions to a thread.

The user is presented with a one-line summary of each thread, allowing the choice to read the messages in the thread.   Message contents can be saved to disk or printed. Users can also opt to send a reply.

Messages are removed after a certain period and some are stored in archives.   Common questions and experiences are regularly summarised and placed in the newsgroups as FAQs (Frequently Asked Questions).

File Sharing Networks

The major file sharing networks, such as the infamous Napster and the longer-established Gnutella networks, are based on a peer-to-peer (or 'p2p') protocol. This is an essentially similar idea to peer-to-peer LANs, except that only files may be shared, not computer resources. The files that are shared are also generally restricted, both by the end user and perhaps by the network.

For example, Napster is a system that allows sharing of MP3 and WMA music files, while Gnutella allows sharing of any file type. However, the end user whose machine is being accessed can determine which specific files are available for transfer.

Peer-to-peer Internet is a powerful and exciting tool, but there are serious copyright concerns. Napster was famously barred by the courts from allowing copyrighted material to be transferred. Gnutella, however, does not use a central server to manage transfers and so may cause more concern. Users should always check the copyright of any content downloaded to ensure they comply with the law.

File sharing is not without its problems. Most home Internet connections are asymmetric – in other words, they download faster than they upload. Since any user downloading from your machine is an upload from your point of view, this affects the maximum download speed of other users.

FACTORS AFFECTING PERFORMANCE

The movement of large files across the Internet places a strain on the system. In particular, the size of programs, sound files and video clips mean long download times.

The diagram shows that there are many hardware components involved in a single connection between a user and a web site.   The link can only run as fast as its slowest component and a problem at any point slows or prevents the successful use of the link.

The factors that contribute to the performance of a connection are:

MODEM SPEED

There are three factors under the direct control of the user - the speed of the modem, the speed of the computer's serial port (if using an external modem) and the computer's software settings.   An old, slow

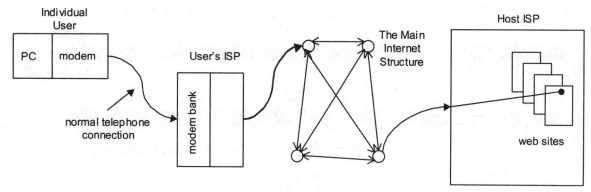

serial port can be upgraded (see the chapter on upgrading) and the modem should be one that runs at the fastest possible speed (currently 56k). The Windows configuration should be set to run the modem at the fastest rate.   Users can also install 'web accelerator' software, which fetches pages in the background while the user views the current page contents.

NOISY TELEPHONE LINE

If the telephone line between the premises and the telephone exchange is noisy, messages are corrupted and have to be re-sent, lowering the effective transmission speed.   Users should insist that telephone operators check out and repair noisy lines. Better still, users should consider upgrading to an ISDN link, as it is both faster and cleaner.

NOT ENOUGH LINES TO ISP

An ISP uses a set of modems (a modem bank) to provide entry points for subscribers.   If an ISP has, say, 500 modems, then only 500 subscribers can access the ISP at any time.   At peak times, all other users will receive a busy tone.   ISPs have to balance the cost of provide extra lines and modems against the losses caused by customers switching to other providers.

INSUFFICIENT BANDWIDTH BETWEEN ISP AND NETWORK

At a certain stage, an ISP may have increased the modem bank to an adequate size but not increased the capacity of the connection between the ISP and the main network.   Although subscribers can all gain access to the ISP, the connections have to share the bandwidth and suffer low data transfer rates.

NETWORK BREAKDOWNS

As the chapter on Data Communications explained, the network will have many connections between its nodes.   If one section of cable should break down or become congested, the traffic can be automatically re-routed around the problem area.   This may result in traffic taking a longer path causing some time delays.

CONGESTION AT SERVER

This is a similar problem to the earlier discussion on the lack of modems at the user's ISP.   If the called ISP has too few modems then the user receives a *'host unavailable'* message.   The user can still access resources on his/her own ISP with adequate speed, since there is no problem on that link.

CONGESTION AT WEB SITE

Even if all other parts of the system are working perfectly, a busy web site can cause delays.   This is particularly true where site space is rented from an ISP.   The ISP only guarantees a specific bandwidth to a site and this slows the site down when it becomes more popular.

Security

Despite the fact that the majority of security breaches are accidental or performed by people working for the affected organisation, deliberate external breaches of security receive disproportionate amounts of publicity. Hacking into systems from outside can be for reasons of industrial espionage, fraud or just to prove a point.   The information held in networks should be protected by the terms of the Data Protection Act and it is the organisation's responsibility to ensure that the Act's terms are met.

Firewalls

The main current solution is to install a *'firewall'* - a hardware and software combination that stands between the organisation's internal network and the Internet.   All communication between internal and external systems is vetted by the firewall.   Its purpose is to prevent unauthorised external access to the network, with minimum effect on the normal legitimate operations of the organisation.   The features of a typical firewall include:

- Monitoring of all incoming and outgoing traffic.
- Disallowing unauthorised access to internal systems from outside systems.
- Disallowing access to unauthorised external systems from internal systems. This could include non-business websites, IRC chat or file sharing networks.
- Suppressing outgoing traffic containing passwords or other confidential information.
- Suppressing incoming traffic containing viruses.
- Logging of all incoming and outgoing access. This can be simply for security reasons or can be used for auditing or billing.
- Traffic flow monitoring, to help prevent Denial Of Service attacks.

Most Firewall systems allow for a *'De-Militarised Zone'* (DMZ).   This is an area internal to the organisation but outside of the firewall.   This should include such systems as web servers or FTP sites. Access to systems in the DMZ must be well regulated.

Firewalls are not foolproof.   For one thing, it only protects against Internet attacks, although some can be configured for dial-up protection as well.   Firewalls can only protect against certain types of viruses, and have to be configured well in order to work well.   Additionally, firewalls are rarely 'transparent' – that is, they rarely perform their function with no effect on the user whatsoever.   However, they are still the single best method of Internet protection for networks.

Encryption

Normal traffic on the Internet is carried in plain ASCII format.   This is too insecure for organisations wishing to transmit confidential information over the Internet.   One answer is to encrypt the message - apply a *'key'* (a mathematical algorithm) to scramble the contents before transmission.   The receiving end can unscramble the message and recover the information, assuming that it also uses the same algorithm.

Incoming traffic security is implemented using *'public'* and *'private'* keys. An organisation can hand out copies of the public key to all parties likely to send them data. The public key allows users to encrypt messages; they cannot be used to decrypt messages. The private key is held by the receiving organisation and this key can successfully decrypt all incoming messages. This is the basis of the popular encryption program called PGP (Pretty Good Privacy).

The use of encryption is a controversial issue between governments and their citizens and organisations. Many governments have tried to enforce *'key escrow'* – a system whereby all private keys have to be given to a third party to allow government access to encrypted messages. This is usually met with wide opposition not only from human rights activists, but also from businessmen who need security for web commerce. The Regulation of Investigatory Powers Act in the UK tried to introduce key escrow but this part of the bill was scrapped. See the section on Privacy, later in this chapter, for more details.

Denial Of Service

A relatively new problem for on-line businesses is Denial of Service (DoS). This is a process whereby malicious hackers deliberately reduce an Internet business system's functionality to the point where that service is effectively denied to all legitimate users. There are a number of ways this can be done, for example:

- Exploiting a flaw in the TCP/IP specification. For example the well-known "Ping of Death" method involves sending IP packets that exceed the maximum length given in the TCP/IP specification. This will cause some systems without appropriate patches to crash, hang or reboot.
- Exploiting a flaw in TCP/IP implementations. An example of this is the so-called "Teardrop" method, whereby fake fragments of IP packets are generated. These fragments appear to overlap each other, creating problems in reconstructing the IP packet at the receiving end. Again, this can cause a crash, a hung system or a reboot, unless an appropriate patch is installed.
- Flooding the system with unwanted data. For example systems may be clogged by sending large numbers of ACK (Acknowledge) requests, preventing or slowing legitimate communications. Software to protect against this kind of attack is also usually available.
- Distributed Denial of Service (DDOS) attacks. This usually involves forcing large numbers of unwitting users into accessing a website at the same time, thus overloading it. This is most commonly accomplished by introducing viruses into user systems worldwide. Firewalls can help prevent this to some degree but are not foolproof.

More mundane DoS attacks could include using up system resources for purposes other than those for which they were designed, or sending many fake requests for goods. Many of these attacks are *'asymmetric'*, meaning that a small, old computer with relatively slow hardware can potentially crash a much more sophisticated system. The best way to counter such attacks is to make sure your operating system and software is up to date with the latest patches, and security software such as router filters are implemented.

Intranets

Companies are developing systems that use Internet facilities <u>within</u> their own network structure. These are called *'Intranets'* and they may have no physical connection to the Internet. An Intranet is a self-contained system of company information, prices, projects, etc for employees to reference via browsers. It may or may not be connected to the Internet but provides similar services such as web pages, e-mail and FTP, although these are all internally organised. An Intranet is not designed to replace the network's file servers for standard file activities. It is likely to use its own internal IP addresses and these will probably not match external Internet assignments. Much freeware, shareware and commercial software is available for creating Web servers. Commercial products offer 'off-the-shelf' solutions that combine easy setup with added facilities such as monitoring, virus detection, encryption and security measures.

Extranets

An organisation with an Intranet often also provides a web site for the public. For security reasons, this web server will not be physically connected to the Intranet. There are certain resources, however, on the Intranet that would be desirable to be shared with an authorised group of users such as customers, clients, partners and mobile employees. These users would access the Extranet via the normal Internet. Extranets require strict security using *'firewalls'* (explained earlier). The username and password of the individual logging in is used to determine which parts of the extranet are available for viewing.

Broader Internet Issues

Apart from the Internet's engineering problems such as bandwidth and the dwindling supply of unallocated user addresses, there are many legal, economic, political and ethical problems facing Internet users. Some of these can be tackled and solved within organisations, while others are of much broader concern and require political will and intervention.

Economic Issues

Although the Internet began as a non-commercial communications link, the balance of net traffic is rapidly switching to commercial uses. Marketing, selling, on-line publishing and commercial databases form the basis of the emerging dominance of financial interests over academic and hobby interests. The arrival of Internet shopping allows subscribers to view goods, specifications and prices and place orders using electronic transactions (i.e. using VISA or other credit cards). Banking and financial dealing is available and the range of Internet pay services will expand.

Information has become one of the most prized commodities in the world. The creation, processing and marketing of financial, commercial and scientific information is a huge industry with enormous power. The possession of information is a driving force in the success of institutions and entire nations. Those without knowledge and current information are destined to lag in the economic race.

This has led to the concept of the *'information rich'* and the *'information poor'*. The rich can afford to buy the information that makes them richer; the poor cannot afford access to the information and remain poor. Even within the developed countries, the majority of the population do not have Internet access. Within the system, premium services (financial newspapers, stock market information, company profiles, etc) are already only available by extra subscription. The Internet is being used by the rich and powerful to maintain and extend their position. The divide is even greater between the developed and developing countries of the world. Many areas do not even have the telephone structure that would support the Internet. Internet access is very restricted in many countries due to financial hardship. This may be worsened if future improvements in the Internet infrastructure are financed by big business, as they may demand priority in use of the bandwidth (possibly on a payment basis).

Globalisation of the world economy

The growth of the Internet has resulted in demands for a legal framework for international co-operation. The increase in teleworking has begun to weaken the traditional work patterns and government control over work. A programmer, for example, may work in Bombay and be paid by a UK software house. Another programmer may work in the UK and be paid through a tax haven country. Teleworking can be a means to avoid national taxes and national labour and health and safety regulations.

The UK government is also actively looking at ways to recover unpaid VAT on software and MP3 files purchased and downloaded over the Internet. Other imported goods pass through Customs and the duty is payable. Software and music files are commonly purchased by credit card and directly downloaded - bypassing the usual excise structure. The government is attempting to establish methods of recovering lost revenue from the software distributors of other countries.

Legal Problems

A range of legal problems shows up the difficulties of obtaining a uniform enforceable framework for Internet use.

Privacy

The Data Protection Act (see chapter on Software) is a UK law guaranteeing individuals rights to privacy regarding information stored about them on computers in the UK. Breaches of this Act within the UK are an offence but breaches committed from another country about a UK citizen would depend on whether that country had similar privacy protection.

On the other hand, there are also concerns amongst some Internet users about government surveillance. The Regulation of Investigatory Powers (RIP) Act was recently passed by the UK parliament. This gives extensive new powers to government agencies to access e-mail and Internet traffic. Patricia Hewitt, the Minister for e-commerce, justifies the move *"because crime has become global and digital and we have to combat this"*.   However, the Bill appears to have political overtones as, for example, it specifically designates *"conduct by a large number of persons in pursuit of a common purpose"* as *"a serious crime"*. In particular, the Bill stipulates that:

- All Internet Service Providers (ISPs) must provide *"interception capabilities"* that permit government monitoring of all Internet access through their systems.   When served with an *"interception warrant"* ISPs will be required to intercept private email and convey the contents to the police or intelligence services. The government has indicated that it will help meet the financial burden of this requirement.
- It will be an offence to fail to comply with an interception warrant, with a maximum two-year prison sentence.
- It will be an offence for an ISP to reveal that an individual is under surveillance or that his/her email is being read, punishable by a maximum five years prison sentence.
- Any private encryption keys must be surrendered to *"properly authorised persons"* on receipt of notice. The order can be served on anyone where *"there are reasonable grounds for believing"* that an encryption key is possessed.
- An individual suspected of having an encryption key is presumed to possess the key, unless he/she can prove otherwise.   It is claimed that this reverses the traditional burden of proof and contravenes the government's own 1998 Human Rights law.
- It will be an offence to fail to reveal a key, with a maximum two-year prison sentence.
- It will be an offence for an individual to reveal that the authorities are making attempts to read his/her mail, with a maximum five-year prison sentence.

While there may be valid arguments for government monitoring in some cases, many people feel that this approach is an infringement of civil liberties and breaks the European Convention on Human Rights.

The Bill includes international collaboration between law enforcement bodies. It would allow the UK interception of *"communications of subjects on the territory of another country according to the law of that country"* at the request of *"the competent authority"* in that country.   In other words, the governments of countries with questionable human rights records can request that the content of e-mails of refugees be sent to them - even when the e-mails are solely within the UK. In many of these countries, opposition to the government or just fighting for democratic rights is regarded as *"serious crime"*.

A committee of Euro-MPs recently reported on the operations of the multi-billion pound *"Echelon"* system.   This system can scan over 2 million electronic communications each minute of the day!   It reports on communications that contain key words that are entered by the operators. It is mainly run by the US National Security Agency, backed by the British spy centre at GCHQ Cheltenham, and supported by the Canadian, Australian and New Zealand governments.   The information that is obtained is not shared with the UK's European partners and the US still denies that the system even exists!   The European Convention on human rights has no control over the situation, as the police, army and secret services are exempt from these laws.

Supporters of the system claim that such interception is necessary to combat terrorism, drug-dealing and the proliferation of weapons of mass destruction.

Opponents of the system claim that there are serious issues of privacy and accountability. They point out that the European Parliament's investigation was instigated after complaints from several EU countries that American and British companies had won very profitable contracts through intercepting the details of rival bids. While interceptions in the UK are meant to require a Home Office Warrant, this would appear to be at odds with the 'blanket' approach adopted by the system. It is also extremely dubious whether the National Security Agency would apply for warrants.

Copyright

The international provisions on copyright apply to Internet material but is as difficult and expensive to pursue as other copyright wrangles.

Libel

The UK Defamation Act of 1996 holds that an ISP is not liable for libel if it acts solely as a transmitter of material that is libellous. It is held to be secondarily responsible as it is not the actual author or editor of the material.   This is in recognition of the instantaneous nature of e-mail and newsgroup postings that make vetting almost impossible.   The mechanics of processing a libel action for an individual from country A against an ISP based in country B that has posted a libellous piece from an individual from country C is complex.

Censorship

With the Internet connecting millions of web sites and tens of thousands of user groups, it is not all surprising that some material causes offence to some users. The Internet, like the Royal Mail, British Telecom, Parcel Force, Group 4, etc, is just a carrier - it distributes what it is given.   The Internet does not cause crimes or outrages any more than crimes or outrages are caused by the existence of the telephone or the mail service.   The public debate has centred on defining offensive material and deciding on the course of action, if any, that should be taken.

Offensive Material

Like all moral debates, there are problems producing a satisfactory definition. Some moral questions, such as murder and rape, have international agreement. Other issues vary with the traditions of that country.   Most Internet information is in English and most newsgroups promote English-speaking Christian culture and morality.   What is regarded as satisfactory conduct in that arena may be disgusting and/or illegal in another part of the world.   Each country has its own laws on a range of issues (e.g. outlawing racial hatred, pornography, political views, etc) but the Internet is <u>international</u> by its nature. If a user in country A is banned from viewing certain material in that country, the material is still available from country B by logging in to that web site.   The material can be sexual or political content. UK government reports that are 'classified' - i.e. banned from publication in the UK - are available freely in other countries that do not operate the same view of what is 'best' for British citizens.

Although Internet pornography generates much press and TV coverage, a survey found:

- 0.002% of newsgroups contained graphics with sexual content.
- Of these, most were of the 'soft' variety to be found in tabloid newspapers.
- The 'hard core' variety was mostly of sex between consenting adults.
- The remainder (i.e. a tiny proportion of the already minuscule 0.002%) displayed *'unlawful sexual practice'*, thereby falling under the UK Obscene Publications Act (see below).
- Many of the sites that fell foul of the OPA are only accessible by credit card - not a commodity possessed by the children claimed to be corrupted by this material.

This is not to condone or condemn such sites, but to place the issue in perspective.

Actions

The Internet remains a great source of knowledge, assistance, commerce and entertainment for the vast majority of its users.   It is one of the few areas that national governments have been unable to control. A large proportion of the Internet community, and the public at large, feel uneasy at some of the Internet's content but are totally against any censorship.   A powerful lobby, representing some religious and political interests, demand sweeping control over the Internet.   In the absence of a consensus, there remain the options of new legislation or accepting that the only laws to be enforced on Internet users and providers are the existing ones prevailing in each individual country.   The relevant UK laws are:

- The Obscene Publications Act of 1959, which makes the publication of an obscene article an offence. The definition of *'obscene'* is its tendency to deprave and corrupt.
- The Criminal Justice and Police Order Act of 1994, which ensured that the OPA's provisions on pornography applied to the Internet in the UK.

Legal restrictions on the Internet have so far proven difficult to formulate and implement. In 1996, the American Communications Decency Act was overturned in their Supreme Court due to the Act's failure to adequately define offensive material.

There is now a trend for governments to pressurise Internet providers into acting as censors for all material that they provide to users.   Since web sites and newsgroups are in permanent flux, the ability of ISPs to constantly monitor millions of pages every day is a totally impractical task.   For the same reason, governments do not expect postal workers to open and read every letter before popping them in letterboxes.   Easier targets are the semi-permanent newsgroups whose titles are suspect and UK providers have evolved their own voluntary code on these.

Some newsgroups are already moderated by their organisers; any offensive or defamatory material received is not placed into the newsgroup.   Another approach is self-regulation by the end-users.   A variety of censoring software is available to prevent children, students or employees from gaining access to material that is deemed unsuitable by the person in control of the PC or local network.   For example, Net Nanny allows a parent to maintain a dictionary of banned words - e.g. URLs and newsgroups, while WinWatch Home also allows children's on-line time to be restricted.   Cyber Sentry and WebTrack are aimed at monitoring and controlling employees' access to the Internet.

Multimedia

The term *'multimedia'* requires some explanation. It is most often spoken of in the same breath as CD-ROM. However the CD-ROM is not always used for multimedia purposes, and multimedia does not necessarily require the use of a CD-ROM. The Novell network operating system, for instance, has a facility to automatically archive files to writeable CD-ROM but no one would describe this as multimedia. On the other hand, a multimedia production can be stored on a large hard disk or fetched from the Internet. Although multimedia can be stored on any storage device, the often huge capacities required are best met by the storage space offered by CD-ROM or DVD. This is the main reason why the two are so often associated. Although it is feasible to store an audio-visual multimedia presentation on a hard disk, high-quality audio or visuals can easily consume most of that hard disk. A 256-colour digitised animation, even in low-resolution MCGA mode on a PC, takes up to 500k of storage space for each second of action. Digitised sound can also consume lots of disk space.

In its simplest definition, multimedia is the use of several types of output to more effectively communicate with the user or viewer. Multimedia elements consist of the following:

- Still graphic images
- Digitised sound/music
- Plain text
- Animated graphics
- Synthesised sound/music
- Digitised photographs
- Moving video images composed of user-recorded material on disk (hard disk or CD)
- Moving video images from pre-recorded material on disk (hard disk or CD)
- Moving video images from normal videotape players

A distinguishing feature of multimedia is the ability of the user to interact with the media. This may be through choosing menu options or clicking the mouse on icons. The vast amounts of data are usually linked through hypertext systems or authoring packages.

Commercial uses of multimedia

There has been a general association of multimedia with computer games and standalone machines. However, there is also wide scope for multimedia in a commercial setting. In the short term this is commonly used for sophisticated training systems and promotional material. This is inevitably going to grow into new areas. Current and future commercial developments of multimedia include:

- Multimedia over local area networks and wide area networks.
- Integration of sound and/or video into application packages.
- Integration of sound and/or video into data produced by applications.

This provides new facilities such as:

- Easy access to centrally stored video training.
- Huge databases of material such as research results, specifications, legal documents, etc. These may include diagrams, personal signatures, scanned documents and voiceprints.
- Electronic publishing - News, books, technical manuals, public information, promotional brochures.
- Applications with greatly enhanced help through video and sound assistance.
- Entertainment such as games, films and music.

Applications for multimedia

New uses are constantly being found for multimedia and these can be generally categorised as:

Training

Training is concerned with the acquisition of specific skills, of the mind or the hand. Examples are learning a foreign language or playing the guitar. Boeing use multimedia material to train their ground personnel.

Education

Education is *'knowledge based'*; specific skills may not flow from the absorption of this knowledge. The theories of evolution, politics, religion, pure science, mathematics, etc may be learned for their own sake rather than to be practised. The Educational Software & CD-ROM Yearbook by REM is jam-packed with details of 1000 different educational CD-ROMs on subjects such as history, science, geography, art and architecture, economics and media studies, etc.

Distance Learning

Distance learning assumes that the student is remote from the educational establishment. This could be for any of a variety of reasons, such as disability, family commitments, working overseas, shift working, etc. Those undertaking study communicate via downloading material, uploading exercises and carrying on e-mail dialogues with support lecturers. Students often use educational CDs where a teacher/lecturer is present to answer specific questions or to clear up any vagueness in the application's presentation. This immediate help is less available with distance learning students and the multimedia material has to reflect this. It must anticipate possible student problems, provide adequate help and guided support. The package should have facilities for student self-assessment, to reinforce students in their learning. Many establishments have, or are preparing, distance learning multimedia-based courses.

Edutainment

Edutainment combines elements of education and entertainment in a manner that imparts knowledge to a user while wrapping the material up as an entertaining experience. Packages featuring the adventures of Peter Rabbit or Barney Bear provide children with animated stories. The text of the story is displayed on screen and each word is highlighted as the story is read out. Children can activate parts of the screen and can control the flow of the story by mouse clicks. Serious learning is taking place in conjunction with the attractive activities. Adult edutainment equivalents are CD with conducted tours of 'The Louvre', investigating 'Great Artists' and exploring 'The Ultimate Human Body'.

Entertainment

These are solely aimed at providing fun with no attempt at any serious education, although in some packages a little general knowledge may be picked up along the way. Applications include the 'Cinemania' and 'Music Central' multimedia databases on films and music, interactive music CDs such as 'Explora' by Peter Gabriel and 'Jump' by David Bowie, and the guide to 'Wines, Spirits and Beers'. Other well-known applications of multimedia are the effects produced in films such as 'Toy Story', 'The Mask' and 'Jurassic Park' and the huge range of games that now exists on CD-ROM.

Simulation

Simulation provides a computer replica of a living or supposed situation and there are applications for use in both entertainment and industry. Leisure applications cover both the real world (e.g. flight simulators) and the imagined world (e.g. fighting the aliens on the planet Zog). Industry has many serious uses for simulations in situations where training staff can be hazardous both to the trainees and to real equipment. Typical applications are training French train drivers using simulations of railway routes and British firefighters learning to handle dangerous situations. Users can learn from their mistakes without any harm being done.

Marketing

Marketing covers the promotion of both opinions and products; it is aimed at altering the views and preferences of those who use the application. After viewing the application, users are hoped to desire certain products, holiday at a particular location, study at a particular university, etc. Example marketing applications are the 'virtual kitchens' demonstrated by Matsushita, unattended public information displays (known as kiosks) promoting clothes or holidays, and CD-ROM travel guides covering from the 'AA Days Out in Britain and Ireland' to 'Travel Mexico' and 'Voyage in Spain'. Multimedia marketing has a large growth potential, both in CD-ROM format and over the Internet.

Home Shopping

This overlaps with marketing activities. While marketing promotes the demand for the product, home shopping provides the convenience to place the order. A growing number of product catalogues are provided on CD or many more are available on the World Wide Web. Users can log into a company's web site and use the search facilities to bring up details of desired products. The user can read the text descriptions and view the images. The product range is huge, from computers to books and clothes. In the case of music CDs, the user is also allowed to hear short clips from albums. The user can instantly place an order and can pay with a credit card.

Reference

Reference material is readily available in book format but multimedia versions provide many extra facilities such as very quick subject searching and cross-referencing, the use of animations to aid explanations and sound and video clips of famous people and events. Examples of reference material are BOOKBANK (British books in print), specifications, dictionaries (e.g. the Oxford Compendium), the Guinness Book of Records and a range of impressive annually updated multimedia encyclopaedias (e.g. Compton's, Grolier, Hutchinson, Microsoft and Britannica).

Electronic Publishing

Electronic publishing is an area with anticipated rapid growth. Its contents can be electronic 'books', sales literature, or information banks. The contents of many daily papers are posted to the Internet and CDs containing a year's contents can be purchased. CD versions involve a single payment, whereas on-line versions may involve paying for connect time compared to hard copy subscription charges. On-line versions provide constantly updated information while CD versions provide archive reference material. As in all publishing, copyright problems presents a legal framework that has to be adopted.

Pioneering Systems
Current multimedia systems have their roots in the development of interactive video, CBT (computer based training) and hypertext systems.

Interactive Video
The system comprised the following components:
- A TV monitor.
- A videodisk player (usually the Philips laservision player which used larger versions of our current CD-ROM disks). The player had a normal TV output.
- A computer or microprocessor built into a special video player.

The disks were larger than modern CD disks and contained previously recorded video sequences that could be viewed by choosing options from the keyboard. Examples of use are Lloyds Bank's training staff in till, cash and cheque transactions and McDonnell Douglas staff training manuals on aircraft maintenance and repair. Some used an actions/consequences approach, where a video displayed an activity and the play was suspended while the user (often in groups) considered and choose from a selection of responses. The chosen response ran another video clip that displayed the consequences resulting from the selection. This method was also adopted for early arcade video games. These were radical applications in the early 1980's and the programmes were very expensive to produce. The user content was mostly video sequences linked together by text and user responses, reflecting the state of technology at that stage. Nevertheless, these elements are in common use in modern multimedia applications.

CBT/CAL
With the growing popularity of desktop PCs, the drive towards interactive systems moved to centre round the computer and its programs. This removed the requirement for specialist apparatus and early CAL/CBT was distributed on ordinary floppy disks. The system provided new levels of user support. Computer Based Training (CBT) developed specific skills (e.g. typing tutors) while Computer Aided Learning (CAL) explored ideas (e.g. science and philosophy). Both applications provided user options and stored user responses in variables. In this way, a user's progress was monitored and appropriate advice given. Users could be given assessments and told their scores. Users could be given a certain number of attempts at a multi-choice question. The support given for a wrong answer could depend on what incorrect choice was entered and the previous experience of the user as judged by previous responses.

CBT/CAL provided an 'intelligent' system which users enjoyed as they had more control over the learning experience. They could work at their own pace, reviewing a page, changing direction and stopping for a break. Early applications tended to have a linear format within each lesson and they lacked the visual impact of interactive video. Again, most of the elements of CBT can be found in current multimedia systems.

Hypertext
Both interactive video and CBT tended to require the user to follow a fixed training pattern with clear end objectives. Options were allowed but they were temporary detours from the main path to be tread by the user. Although this had distinct advantages in certain situations, and is still implemented in some packages today, it did not follow the way humans think and approach issues. Few people learn a subject by systematically working through a linear path of material. Only fiction is read linearly. People learn by association; having grasped a concept it leads them to one or more linked concepts. For example, reading a car repair manual on fixing carburettors may inspire a reader to find out more about how the ignition systems works, what a catalytic converter is, or how to use a double-grommeted nut wrench. Hypertext builds a system that supports that way of thinking. Users can leave a particular subject area and explore something linked - or completely different; they can choose to return to the previous theme or can move onwards or sideways if they wish. Each person will use the system in a different way.

Users move from one subject to another by selecting menu options or by clicking the mouse on a highlighted word (a hypertext link) or on a particular area of the screen (a hotspot). Early systems were solely text based and graphical interfaces followed later.

The best definition of hypertext is that it:

> *"produces large, complex, richly connected*
> *and cross-referenced bodies of information"*

Hypertext is widely implemented in Windows applications' help systems and this *'navigation'* process is one of the cornerstones of multimedia packages. The largest example of hypertext is the World Wide Web.

Hypertext's benefits include good browsing abilities, rapid navigation, the ability to annotate results and the ability to save results and queries for later use. Reported problems with hypertext are disorientation (it is much easier to get lost than when page-hopping with a printed book) and *'cognitive overhead'* (the large variety of options stuns the brain's ability to easily consider alternatives).

Multimedia Hardware

The common aspects of multimedia usually require little or no specialised hardware. It is possible to create a simple multimedia presentation, involving text, graphics and sounds, on a basic computer without any extra add-ons. Of course, the more sophisticated presentations require a high performance machine and special equipment. One range of add-ons is required for the production of multimedia applications, while other hardware is required for the delivery of such applications.

Hardware For Creation

The list below is the minimum for a home-quality production facility. The sound and video hardware would be upgraded for professional quality results.

- Video Capture Card
- Sound Card (with hand microphone, tie-clip microphone or headset system)
- Graphics card with MPEG support
- MIDI interface with Synthesiser/Keyboard
- VCR

- Video Camera (tape or digital)
- Digital Still Camera
- Scanner
- CD-ROM player/writer
- Large, fast hard disks

Hardware For Delivery

Completed multimedia products can either be distributed on CD-ROMs or via the Internet.

CD-ROM

- CD-ROM player
- Graphics card with MPEG support

- Sound Card with speakers
- MIDI interface with Synthesiser/Keyboard

This has the advantage of using a known performance standard and quality is predictable. However, content can become outdated quickly and there is no contact between the manufacturer and the users. As it only offers single-user access and provides the most security, it is the obvious choice when the CD is itself the product designed for sale.

Internet

- Graphics card with MPEG support
- MIDI interface with Synthesiser/Keyboard

- Sound Card with speakers
- Modem or ISDN link

This has the advantage that material can be easily updated and reaches a potentially larger market. Orders and queries can be dealt with on-line. However, the transfer of large graphics and video files is still a major obstacle on the Internet. Since data on the Internet can easily be accessed, it is the obvious choice for general promotional material for a product that can be ordered and supplied outwith the Internet.

Newer CD applications have Internet links to provide the best features of both methods. The core content (text descriptions, pictures, etc) resides on the CD-ROM while constantly changing information (e.g. prices) is downloaded as the application is viewed.

Multimedia Standards

There is a wide range of multimedia products, some requiring greater resources than others if they are to operate efficiently. This has led to the creation of a set of minimum standards by manufacturers and companies such as Microsoft. The Multimedia PC Working Group of the Software Publishers Association has, to date, produced three standards (Levels) of system as shown:

	MPC Level 1	MPC Level 2	MPC Level 3
CPU	386SX, 16MHz	486SX, 25MHz	75MHz Pentium or equivalent
RAM	2MB	4MB	8MB
CD-ROM	150KB/sec data transfer rate (DTR), access time 1second	300KB/sec DTR, multi-session, XA, access time 400ms	600KB/sec DTR, multi-session, XA, access time 250ms
Hard Disk	30MB	160MB	540MB
Audio Card	SoundBlaster compatible with 8-bit sound, synthesiser and MIDI facilities	SoundBlaster compatible with 16-bit sound, synthesiser and MIDI facilities	SoundBlaster compatible with 16-bit sound, wavetable and MIDI facilities
Graphics Card	16-colour VGA	65,536 colour VGA	Scaling capability, direct access to frame buffer for video-enabled graphics
Video Playback	n/a	n/a	MPEG1 capability, 352x240 at 30fps without dropping frames
External ports	MIDI interface, Joystick	MIDI interface, Joystick	MIDI interface, joystick

MPC Standards have not been upgraded for years, as the industry's focus changed to DVD standards.

The elements of multimedia

The following pages consider the main components of a multimedia presentation, outlining how they operate and considering the main factors affecting performance.

Text

The display of multimedia text requires only a standard PC monitor and a main concern is how the text is accessed. The user requires to access specific subjects from a huge range of material. The text-handling software should be capable of detecting and displaying all stored material on the user's chosen subject. The user also requires the ability to explore cross-references in the material, to look at an item in further detail before returning to the main theme. These are the *'hypertext'* elements previously described. These may require the user to type in the data to be searched for or to select from a menu. Another method is to click the mouse on a key word or phrase within the displayed text. These elements can be seen in use in various Windows Help systems.

Text Creation

All multimedia applications employ text and the attributes used should reflect the nature of the application. The attributes to choose from are text face (what the basic face looks like), font (its size), style (normal, bold, italics, underlined), justification (left, right, centred) and colour. A psychedelic or bizarre collection of text faces and colours may fit the mood of some music applications but would be entirely inappropriate for a training package for funeral undertakers. Too much text on the screen repels viewers while text that is too small or too large makes the viewer uncomfortable. The number of words on any one line should be no more than 8 or 10 and each line should make a single point. Text should be presented with a mix of upper and lower case characters. Any one screen should not have text of many different colours. However, colours used to highlight titles or hypertext links are effective. Similarly the choice of words used in the text is important; the grammar should suit the intended audience. Young children should not be bamboozled with complex words and older users should not be patronised. Jargon, abbreviations and acronyms should also be avoided.

The authoring packages that create multimedia projects all have the normal cut, paste and copy facilities to improve the screen layout.

Text Importation

Multimedia authoring packages do not generally have spell-checking or grammar-checking features and the author has to be very careful that misspelled words do not slip through and mar an otherwise professional project. All packages allow text to be imported into the project and this is the safest way to protect against typing or grammatical errors. Text can be entered into a word-processed file, which can be checked before being imported into the authoring package's project. The file types allowed by the authoring package should be checked and the text file should be saved in one of the acceptable formats. In some cases, this may mean converting a Word 7 file, for instance, into an older Word 2 format to be acceptable by the authoring package.

Audio

The nature of audio

Sound from a natural source such as the human voice or a musical instrument is analogue. This means that it alters in a continuous way as shown in the example diagram.

If a number of people were to sing exactly the same musical note, their voices would remain unique and identifiable. This is because of the harmonic content of each person's voice. Apart from sounding the correct frequency of the note, the human voice will introduce an individual collection of other sounds that are mixed with the basic frequency. These other sounds are multiples of the original frequency and it is the quantity and relative volumes of each of these harmonics that makes each person's voice different. In the same way, a piano is very rich in harmonics while a tin flute is devoid of harmonics. The extra components give the piano its 'richness' of tone in comparison to the purer sound of the flute.

A sound that is rich in harmonics contains much more detailed information than a pure sound and this causes problems for their storage on computer, as explained later.

Computer sound is one half of an audio/visual display, and proper sound effects can make a simple, predictable slide show or an animated display much more memorable. The final audio waveform is fed to the loudspeakers, vibrating the internal cones of the speakers in sympathy with the amplitude of the wave.   The vibrating cones vibrate the surrounding air, causing the sound to travel to the human ear.

Pure tone

Same frequency with harmonic content

Digitised Sound

Digitised sound is used in multimedia to accompany animations and graphics, giving a more convincing presentation. It can also be used to link sounds to events. Sound is fed into a sound card in analogue format, from a microphone or other audio source.   As explained, the computer is only capable of storing data in digital format.   So the card has to convert analogue sounds into a digital equivalent.   This is achieved by a chip in the sound card called the *'ADC'* - the *'Analogue-to-Digital-Converter'*.   The ADC converts a sample of sound into a series of numbers that can be stored to disk for later replay. The numbers store the amplitude of the sound waveform at different points during the time of the sound sample.   In most formats, the waveform swings above and below a reference point of zero.   This means that low amplitude levels have a negative integer representing them while high amplitude levels are represented by positive integer numbers. Two factors determine the quality of digitised sound:

- The dynamic range (i.e. the accuracy in terms of absolute amplitudes).
- The sampling rate (i.e. the accuracy of the amplitude at any one instant).

Dynamic Range

The more complex the waveform to be stored, the greater total of different numbers required to store the sound.   The span from the lowest amplitude to the greatest amplitude is known as the *'dynamic range'*. This is sometimes also described as *'resolution'* or *'bit-range'*. In the left diagram, only a small number of bits are allocated to store the waveform so it is incapable of handling the small amplitude variations in the waveform and these details are averaged away.   In that case, the ADC produces a series of numbers that approximate to the overall waveform but the harmonics that make a piano sound different from a guitar are lost as are the harmonics that differentiate between different human voices.   The right-hand diagram shows a greater dynamic range allowing the same analogue signal to be converted into a greater number of digital levels.

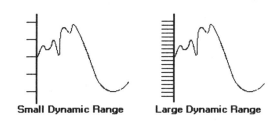

Small Dynamic Range   Large Dynamic Range

This allows for a greater clarity of reproduction, as the replayed sound is closer to the original sound. The early 8-bit sound card had 8 bits to store each sound data sample.   Eight bits allows a range of 256 different levels.   This is sufficient for many purposes but does not provide a high quality sound system. Modern 16-bit sound cards handle a range of 65,536 different sound levels, giving a quality expected from a domestic audio CD system.   This is not a professional quality, since each of the 65,536 levels is a linear step while the human ear responds to amplitude variations in a logarithmic way.   This means that many of the discrete stored levels do not store changes that can be detected by the ear and so are wasted. This is not a problem since only a few professionals use PCs for their audio work. Given these limitations, the 16-bit sound card has obvious quality advantages over an 8-bit card. It does, of course, require twice as much disk storage space as an equivalent 8-bit sound sample.

Sampling Rate

The dynamic range determines the accuracy of the amplitude reading at any one point in time. Of equal importance is the frequency of taking these readings. If the readings are too infrequent, an amplitude change will pass undetected.

If the readings are too frequent, the conversion will produce a giant series of amplitude readings. The timing of the conversions is known as the *'sampling rate'* and is measured in kilohertz (i.e. how many thousand amplitude conversions are carried out each second).

The left diagram shows the effects of a low sampling rate. The sound sample is converted into six samples with varying amplitude levels. When the sample is replayed, the sound card's DAC (Digital-to-Analogue Converter) uses the six levels to reconstruct the sound wave. This sound wave is then amplified and sent to the loudspeakers. As the diagram shows, the final output is an approximation of the original sound with a considerable loss of detail. The inertia in the loudspeaker cones acts to smooth the transitions between different output voltage levels from the DAC. The right-hand diagram shows the same sound sample

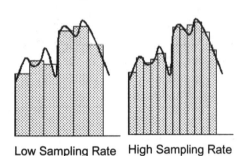

Low Sampling Rate   High Sampling Rate

with twice the sampling rate. The audio is now stored in twelve different samples and this is much more representative of the original sound source. In practice, the sampling rate must be at least double the frequency of the highest frequency to be sampled. Since the average human ear can only hear frequencies up to about 20KHz, a sampling rate of 44KHz is adequate for most uses. Indeed, the human voice itself does not produce sounds above much more than 3KHz.

The original Sound Blaster card was first introduced with a sampling rate of 11KHz. Most cards now usually operate as high as 44.1KHz, the same rate as audio CD and sampling rates are adjustable down to as low as 4KHz.

Storage Overheads

Current sound cards have stereo channels, allowing each channel to process independent contents. This improves the quality of the reproduced sound but requires double the disk space. The table shows the amount of disk space required for even short digitised samples, with the top quality 44.1KHz sampling rate. A four-minute song in stereo requires a staggering 42MB of disk space!

	bytes per sec	bytes per min
8-bit mono	44,100	2,646,000
8-bit stereo	88,200	5,292,000
16-bit mono	88,200	5,292,000
16-bit stereo	176,400	10,584,000

Minimising storage overheads

A number of techniques are employed to minimise the use of disk space and these include:
- Forcing the system down to a 22.05KHz sampling rate when recording in stereo.
- Replacing periods of silence in the audio with a token that describes how long the silence lasted.
- Compressing the file on recording and decompressing again on playback. This can use a CODEC chip (compression/decompression) to carry out these tasks in hardware to speed the process. Software CODECS such as ADPCM (see below) are available as alternatives to hardware implementations. These systems offer a range of possible compression ratios, ranging from low-compression lossless samples to high-compression samples with loss of some detail.

All sound boards use ADCs and DACs. Most cards have a DSP (*'Digital Signal Processing'*) chip to carry out these tasks, combined with handling MIDI and sound file compression /decompression.

Audio File Formats

There is a bewildering array of file formats and acronyms. All elements of multimedia, even simple text, have several different formats, each with its own benefits and restrictions. Dredging through the morass of standards to find the one that is best suited may seem a huge task, but many of the file formats are either very specialised or just too old and inefficient to be of use. For instance, sound samples may come with extensions like VOC, WAV, SND, SOU, AU, IFF, SAM, RAW, ULW; some may even have no extension at all. There are also many samples out there that are *'raw'* samples, and have extensions given completely arbitrarily, such that they may appear to be separate file formats. However, there are only really a few ways to store digitised sound, and the rest is just dressing. All the file formats below may be used to store the same audio content; only the manner of storage would be different.

The most important sound file formats are:

RAW: This extension indicates that the file's contents consist solely of the string of numeric data, with no special processing or headers. Although raw sound samples may be stored with the extension .RAW, more often they have a less obvious name or sometimes no extension at all. SOU and some SND files are raw files with a short header to tell the playback software information on what sampling speed to use for the playback. If the raw sample has no header storing the frequency of the sample, then the user has to calculate, or estimate, the sampling frequency (number of samples per second of digitised sound). It should be obvious when the user hears the sound whether the frequency is correct.

WAV: Introduced along with Windows, the WAV file format is a simple sound sample with a short file header. The benefit of WAV files is that many Windows programs can use them with a single Windows sound driver. Of course, the Windows sound driver is not limited to WAV files, but Windows programs themselves tend to prefer WAV files since they are the native format for Windows sound.

ADPCM: The *'Adaptive Delta Pulse Code Modulation'* system takes standard audio that has been encoded into its normal PCM values and compresses the data so that it requires less space than its .WAV equivalent. By only storing the deltas (i.e. changes between samples) it requires about a quarter of the normal disk space. This method is offered in Windows 95/98 (and is also the technique employed by Sony for its Mini Disc recorder/players).

MP3: MP3 files use the compression standard laid down in MPEG-1 Audio Layer III. Audio MPEG MP3 compression produces file sizes that are up to 12 times smaller than the standard digitised version, with no loss of quality.

MP3 offers new facilities:
- The easy archiving of existing audio files.
- The creation of new audio resources (e.g. local bands, interviews, etc) in a compact format.
- The setting up of online music stores, where music is purchased on the Internet.

This format is now widely support on web sites and in multimedia applications. It is also a popular medium for storing music tracks. MP3 files are played through a computer that has the decompression software installed, or through a dedicated standalone device. A whole industry has grown around portable playing devices that are based on storing audio track in memory cards, miniature hard discs or adapted CD players.

Audio or music tracks stored on audio CDs can also be converted to MP3 files, known as *'ripping'*. Programs such as AudioGrabber and RealJukebox read the digital information straight off the CD tracks and store it on the hard disk as MP3 files. Rippers can also convert CD audio into WAV files. This process also ignores the sound card and provides an identical digital copy. Ripping should only be carried out on copyright free music and sound CDs, as conversion of commercial audio CDs is a breach of copyright law.

Existing WAV files can be converted to MP3 files using applications such as the freeware BladeEnc. MP3 files can also be converted back to WAV files when required, using programs such as WinAmp. Most applications are able to play MP3 files, including Windows 98 onwards.

WMA : Windows Media Audio is Microsoft's response to the MP3 format. The Windows Media Packager can convert MP3 and WAV files into a WMA format, producing a considerably smaller file size.

RA : Real Audio files can be downloaded from the Internet and played later. However, their main advantage is their ability to be *'streamed'*. This requires special player software that downloads an audio track as a set of separate blocks. This allows the audio to be immediately sent to the soundcard for playing, without waiting until the whole file is downloaded. If the blocks arrive faster than they can be played, they are stored in a memory buffer. Of course, if the blocks arrive slower than required, the file cannot be played continuously.

Recording a sound

Although a wide range of digitised sound samples exists, there will be many occasions when a specific message is required. The audio input can come from a microphone or can be from the *'line in'* socket of a sound card to allow the sampling of music or voice from a variety of sources such as CD, cassette tape, video tape, etc. The provisions of copyright will apply to such samples. Sound cards provide their own software to create audio samples and Windows has its own simple utility called *'Sound Recorder'* as shown in the diagram. The right hand button has a

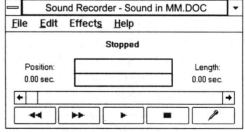

microphone icon and clicking on this icon starts a recording process. The time of the sample is shown on screen as the recording is made. When the recording is finished, the user clicks on the button to the left of the microphone. The final sample length is displayed. Clicking the middle button will cause the sample to be replayed. This system is adequate for day-to-day use but the more sophisticated software of the sound card utilities allows the selection of sampling rates.   With Windows 95, the Sound Recorder is found in the *'Multimedia'* option of the *'Accessories'* menu within the *'Programs'* menu. With Windows 98/ME, it is found in the *'Entertainment'* option of *'Accessories'*.

Editing a sound

A user-created sound sample may not be immediately usable.   It may contain unwanted pauses or require augmenting by special effects before it is used.   The *'Sound Recorder'* utility has some basic tools.   Clicking the arrow key icons moves the sample through different time stages of the waveform and the wave shape can be seen in a window while this is being adjusted.   Facilities include deleting all silences or unwanted sounds before the chosen time point or after the chosen time point.   This allows unwanted sections to be removed and results in a smaller sample file.   Other facilities include introducing echo effects, reversing the sound sample and mixing in other sound samples. The final file can be saved as a WAV file for later use.   The software included with most sound cards, such as Sound Blaster's VOC Editor, provides further facilities.   These include the gradual fading up or down of sounds, the panning of sounds between stereo channels (i.e. the volume of the sound in the left channel is decreased while the volume in the right channel is increased), cut and paste operations and other waveform editing. The DSP - Digital Signal Processing - facility can provide a range of additional effects.   So, for example, the effect of a sound being played in a football stadium or a church can be imposed on any audio being reproduced.

Sound Cards

Early PCs used the internal speaker to provide a limited audio facility. This is still used to *'beep'* for a user's attention but the size of the single internal speaker restricts the quality of the sound generated.

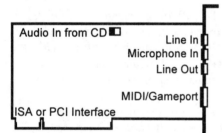

The solution rests in add-on cards that are dedicated to providing high quality stereo sound from a PC. These are now inexpensive and most machines are supplied equipped with a basic sound card. The leader in the field of PC sound is the Sound Blaster card from Creative Labs.   It was neither the first nor, arguably, the best sound card on the market, but it balanced quality and effectiveness with a reasonable price tag. It handles input from many sources, through a variety of physical connections.

The *'Microphone Input'* captures live sounds so that the sound card can store them in a digital fashion.   The *'Line Input'* captures any other audio source such as that from the *'audio out'* sockets of a cassette player, an audio CD player or a domestic video recorder.

The *'Audio In'* internal connector allows the direct entry of an audio source into the card.   This is most commonly connected to the *'Audio Out'* socket on a CD-ROM thus allowing normal audio CDs to be played on the computer's CD player (with the appropriate software). It can also accept to take the audio output from an internal DVD drive.

The *'Games Port'* allows the connection of a joystick or of a MIDI interface.   The MIDI input allows the real-time capture of a musician's work.   This is stored in the MIDI format as explained later.   The MIDI output connects to a MIDI-compatible device such as an electronic music keyboard, synthesiser or drum machine. The MIDI output is used to control synthesizers and drum machines.

Finally, it can receive input via the normal bus connections to the computer.   This allows programs to directly send data to the sound card through the data bus.

Older cards were capable of controlling a CD-ROM and allowed a CD-ROM to be fitted without the need for its own controller card. The cable between the card and the CD-ROM took the control signals to the CD-ROM that carry out the usual drive functions such as moving the head, etc.   The arrival of IDE and SCSI CD-ROM drives resulted in this method being dropped.

The sound card's outputs are the Audio output and the MIDI output. The card has an inbuilt amplifier capable of around 4 Watts of audio output power.   Alternatively, the connection can be taken to the input of another amplifier for greater output.   Connecting to a domestic hi-fi will boost the audio output to the maximum provided by the hi-fi amplifier.   Manufacturers also produce a set of external speakers for sound cards and one of these speakers usually has an in-built amplifier.

The sound card can, therefore, perform the following output functions:

- Playback of audio CD.
- Recording of audio.   An audio source, such a human speech or music is processed into digitised data for later re-processing.
- Playback of digitised audio.   The data is translated from data into audio.
- FM synthesis.   The sound card contains synthesiser chips that are capable of generating a sound that is broadly similar to that produced in the real world.   For example, the chips can produce the sound of a piano or guitar even although no musical instrument was involved in its creation.   The chips can also produce sounds that are intended to have no human equivalent - e.g. the electronic organ.   The most commonly used chips are the OPL2 and OPL3 from Yamaha and they use a frequency modulation technique to produce a sound with the desired harmonic mix.   Each different synthetic sound is known as a 'voice' and most cards have 20 voices, with other models ranging from 11 to 32.
- MIDI equipment interfacing.   The sound card is able to communicate with an external MIDI device, such as a musician's electronic keyboard.   The sound card carries out the processing of the musical score but the MIDI device produces the actual sound from its own synthesiser chips.

The Sound Blaster card also offered compatibility with the older Adlib sound standard.   Other sound cards have appeared since, including new and improved Sound Blaster cards. However, the extra functions generally have less software support than the basic Sound Blaster.   Many sound cards are, or claim to be, Sound Blaster compatible, meaning that software designed for use with the Sound Blaster can be used with these cards.   Some sound cards offer compatibility with many standards.   For example, the Gravis Ultrasound card is Adlib and SoundBlaster compatible, as well as being compatible with the Sound Source card.   These types of sound cards generally offer better performance than the basic Sound Blaster as well as backward compatibility, but quite often little software other than that supplied with the card will use these extra functions.

With the arrival of Windows, it is possible for any Windows application to utilise a sound card's benefits through the use of a single sound driver.   Stereo cards are now standard and produce a sound that the human ear detects on a two-dimensional plane - i.e. between left and right of the listener.   Some current cards now also include 'surround sound' similar to that available on current hi-fi systems.   This simulates a three-dimensional effect where the sound has 'depth' added to the 'width'.

Current Developments
The quality of the output from the budget sound cards is limited and current improvements are:

- Older 8-bit cards had quality limitations and were replaced by 16-bit, 18-bit, 20-bit and 32-bit cards with greater quality output.
- The MIDI interface is now common on sound cards and many are available with MPU-401 compatibility (a music industry standard).
- Synthesised sound output is not comparable with a natural sound.   The richer the sound source is in harmonics, the more difficult it is to reproduce synthetically.   That is why even expensive electronic keyboards have had difficulty in emulating the humble piano.   The solution lay in converting an actual sound into a set of digitised data and storing the sample in ROM on the sound card. This is called Wave Table Synthesis and produces greatly improved sound quality.   The Sound Blaster Live! is able to reproduce up to 192 instruments.
  Wavetable cards normally also provide on-board RAM so that users can use their own captured samples. The Videologic SonicFury, for example, can store up to 1024 software voices.
- Improving on the background noise produced in cards. The Creative SoundBlaster Live! has a signal to noise ratio of 120db compared to the average of 85db for most cards (and only around 60db for older cards).
- Full-duplex working. This allows simultaneous recording and playback.   This is used for multi-track music recording and the provision of Internet telephony.
- SPDIF output (Sony/Philips Digital Interface).   Some cards provide this auxiliary output.   It is a digital output for direct connection to other digital recording devices such as DAT or Mini-Disc machines. Direct digital connections avoid the distortions introduced by digital/analogue/digital conversions.
- Multiple speaker outputs.   These cards have built-in Dolby sound decoders and are used to reproduce the 'surround sound' used in DVD audio. They are designated as '5.1' systems as they feed five speakers and a sub-woofer.
- PCI versions now replace ISA cards.   These cards connect to the 32-bit PCI bus, offering simultaneous audio streams and 3D spatial sound effects. The also reduce the demand on the CPU's time.

Graphic Images

A graphic can be stored as a bitmap, or as a vector image. For multimedia purposes, the majority of uses are filled by bitmap images.

Bitmaps

A bitmapped image is one in which every pixel on the screen or in the image is *mapped* to a *bit* of data. With a monochrome picture there is a direct correlation between the number of screen pixels and the number of bits to store the picture. Each bit only stores whether the pixel is white or black. With colour pictures, each pixel is represented by a group of bits that determine the pixel's colour.

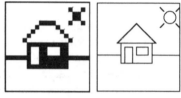

A simple bitmap   A vector image

Vectors

A vector image is one where the data represents not pixels, but *objects*. These objects could be text, circles, squares or such. The two example images display an extremely simplified image, shown in each type of format. Note, however, that the bitmap has been rendered very crudely at small scale to show the basic idea; bitmaps are generally much more complex, and far more graphically impressive. Depending on the image, either form could be more efficient. Bitmapping is far easier to use on complex coloured images such as digitised pictures, whereas a simple piece of computer-drawn clip-art would be much more efficiently stored as a vector oriented image. In the example above, the digitised picture would take up far less disk space. However, if a large bitmapped graphic could be easily converted to a vector image without loss of quality (which is not often the case) then the vector image would most likely be smaller in size. As far as bitmapped images go, the only difference between one file format and another is the way the data is compressed, and how much extra information is needed, such as height and width of the picture, number of colours, etc. This information is normally stored in a portion of the file called a *'header'*.

Picture Scaling

The benefits of vector files lie in their *'scalability'*. The user may wish to expand or shrink a picture so that it fits into a particular space in a document. This should be achieved with no loss of detail or picture distortion. The top diagram shows the result of scaling up a picture that contains a straight line to twice its height and width. Where there was a single pixel there is now a group of four pixels. Scaling the picture to four times its original size results in a group of 16 pixels for every original single pixel. The result is a very *'blocky'* image known as *'pixellation'*. The vector file on the other hand represents the line as *'draw a row of pixels between point A and point B'*. Scaling the picture up still produces a single row of pixels, maintaining the fine detail.

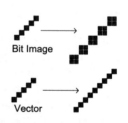

Bit Image

Vector

File Formats

The most common graphic file formats on a PC are:

GIF: The acronym *'GIF'* is meant to be pronounced as *'jiff'*, but is usually pronounced *'giff'*. GIF was designed for fast transfer of graphics data over modems, and stands for <u>G</u>raphics <u>I</u>nterchange <u>F</u>ormat. It uses a technique called LZW or String-table compression to compress graphic images, making them smaller for faster transfer over the CompuServe network. Now a very common file format, GIF files can be found on web sites and graphics packages everywhere. GIF files can have a colour range of any power of 2 - up to 2 to the power of 8. This means it could have 2, 4, 8, 16, etc. up to 256 colours. This doesn't mean that all those colours must be used, however.

PNG: Unisys owns the patent for the LZW compression used in GIF files and this produced a demand for royalties for the use of GIF files. In response, the Portable Network Graphics standard was produced for transferring bitmap graphics files over CompuServe and the Internet. It improves on GIFs by offering 24-bit colour and its own 'zlib' compression system.

PCX: Nobody seems to know what PCX stands for, other than that the first two letters are for *'Personal Computer'*. PCX files use run-length encoding (RLE), which means that simple computer-generated pictures are stored fairly efficiently. It is comparatively inefficient at storing digitised or complicated pictures. Nonetheless, it has been around for some time and is now fairly common. PCX pictures may be found in monochrome (2 colours), 16 colours, 256 colours, 24-bit true colour, or even, rarely, in 4 colours. PCC files are PCX files by another name though they are usually smaller, intended for clipart.

TIFF: The Tagged Image File Format originated on the Mac computer, and was designed for use with desktop publishing. It is a complicated standard, so much so that some alleged TIFF-using packages may not import TIFFs from other packages. It can use a variety of compression schemes, and can have any number of colours, as well as a huge array of options, used by putting *'tags'* in the file header. The more exotic *'tags'* cause TIFF readers to occasionally *'screw up'* on TIFF files. TIFF files tend to be used more for DTP than multimedia.

BMP: BMP stands for Bit-Mapped Picture and is the Windows standard bitmap graphics file. BMP files are used for the background wallpaper in Windows. It is uncompressed, meaning that simple pictures will occupy much more file space than is strictly necessary. It also means that complicated, true colour pictures will not require a sophisticated decoder to display. A damaged BMP file will mean image distortion may occur, while corruption to most compressed files means complete unusability. There is also another format called the RLE format, which is a compressed version of BMP, but this is little used. Finally, a BMP file may be found with the extension DIB, for Device Independent Bitmap, but is basically the same as a BMP file.

JPEG: When the Joint Photographic Experts Group was appointed by the CCITT to design a graphic compression and storage scheme, the JPEG file format was eventually created. It uses *'lossy'* compression, which means that slight detail is lost during compression. The level of detail loss is controllable, and a substantial space saving can be made even with very little detail loss. The JPEG compression standard is a complicated process involving several levels, and at first specialised hardware was needed to perform the process. There is a lossless version of JPEG, but this may require the extra hardware. JPEG files are stored in true 24-bit colour, and the JPEG scheme is much less efficient in storing images of any lower colour range.

WMF: The Windows Meta-File format is a comparatively simple vector oriented format born through the Windows interface. It is very effective for DTP. Like most vector formats, it is little used for multimedia.

Animation

Animation arises from a collection of graphic images being displayed on the screen one after the other in quick succession. The eye possesses a persistence of vision such that, if the images are images are updated quickly enough, the viewer does not detect the sequence as a set of different pictures. In this way, animation creates the illusion of movement. This is the technique used to show movies in the film theatre or on television.

There are two approaches to animation:

Bitmapped

Each frame is comprised of a separate bitmap image. The image can be computer-created or be a photographic image. If all the frames and their full contents were included in the final animation, the file size would be huge. Ideally, an animation should display at 30 frames per second. Even the old MCGA standard common to FLI files used a 320x200 screen resolution and 256 different available colours at any one time. This requires 64Kbits to store a single frame. At 30 frames/sec, this requires 1.875MB for every second of animation - and a staggering 112MB for a single minute's animation. The production of a five-minute computer animation would require around a half of a Gigabyte of storage! If the animation were to improve on the limited 320x200 format to 1024x768 and the 256 colours was to be raised to full 24-bit colour, the requirements would be beyond any feasible storage abilities (67.5MB per second). This explains the use of low-resolution screens and colour range restrictions. It also explains why some systems work at less than the desired 30 frames per second, although anything below 10fps is regarded as too slow to maintain the illusion of continuous movement.

As a result, bitmapped animations tend to use complex frame compression schemes such as delta compression, predictive compression, etc. Delta compression does not store each picture successively after each other in its entirety. Instead, only the changes from each picture to the next are stored. This works well because quite often there is little change between each frame, requiring little data to be stored. This keeps the final file sizes down to a manageable level, to minimise the problem of the amount of data that has to be stored, read and displayed.

Vector

Another approach, useful in cartoon work and web site animation, is the *'Flash'* format. This uses vector drawn images to reduce the file size. It does mean, however, that the format does not handle photographic sequences.

Software

Animation creation software ranges from simple programs such as GIF Animator and Disney's Animation Studio to top-of-the-range professional products such as Autodesk Animator Pro and Macromedia Director.

Graphics Creation

Graphics creation software is available in *'painting'* format (for handling bitmapped images) and *'drawing'* format (for handling line art). The main options when creating graphics are:

FORMAT TYPE Bitmaps can store photographic images while vector graphics consist of many drawn components. Bitmaps provide a range of manipulation options that are not available to vector images but lose much of their quality when scaled (see below). Vector images are scaleable with no loss of quality and would be the likely choice for creating symbols, line drawings and logos.

ELEMENTS Unless the image is from a real-world source (i.e. scanned photograph, picture from a digital camera, or other bit image), it is constructed from a collection of squares, rectangles, circles, polygons, lines, arcs or bezier curves.

CONTENT The elements have certain properties that can be altered for the maximum impact. These are element size (i.e. circle diameter, line width, rectangle dimensions) and appearance (e.g. box or circle colour, line type (plain, dotted).

LOCATION Where the graphics appear on the screen and what proportion of the screen they occupy will depend on the nature of the final application. Large graphics are suitable where they have a crucial role in the presentation (e.g. a car repair program would use large and clear diagrams). Small graphics should be used where they should not distract the viewer from the main presentation. Similarly, graphics backgrounds should not overpower the foreground message.

PERSPECTIVE The monitor screen is two-dimension; all screen content has only width and height. To provide the illusion of depth, images can be made to appear as if they recede into the background. The left box in the diagram has a front panel and rear panel of the same size. The rear panel in the right-hand box is smaller, which is perceived by the viewer as depth.

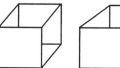

LAYER As in the example shown for text, graphics layering allows one item to partially obscure another. In the boxes above, the front square is layered over the other lines and partially hides them from view.

Graphics Importation

Multimedia authoring packages do not generally provide more than elementary painting features that are sufficient for basic boxes and lines. For all other purposes, images are created in dedicated fully featured graphics packages and the finished item is imported into the authoring project. The file types allowed by the authoring package should be checked, as it is unlikely that every file format is supported by the authoring package. This may require, for example, exporting a Corel Draw image as a BMP file to be acceptable by the authoring package.

Graphics Manipulation

The facilities offered by graphics packages vary and the most common manipulations are:

SCALING The sides of the image can be pulled or squeezed so that it shrinks or expands to fill a given area. While this poses no problems for vector images, bitmaps will lose detail on shrinking and will become *'blocky'* when expanded.

FILLING The diagram shows a number of squares that have been filled with either a plain solid colour, a fountain file (e.g. linear, radial or conical gradations) or a pre-determined pattern (e.g. bricks, curtains, granite).

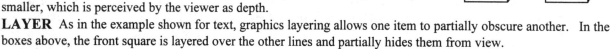

Plain Linear Radial Conical Texture

TRANSITIONS As with text transitions, the graphic can be written to the screen in a pre-defined way such as being drawn from the left or filling in from the centre outwards.

CLIPPING/CROPPING Images often contain more detail than is required. This distracts the viewer from the essential detail and occupies more disk space than is necessary. The image can be clipped or cropped. This brings the picture in from the top or bottom, or left and right borders. The example shows the continent of Africa being taken from a map of the globe.

Cropping

ROTATING The text can be rotated from its normal horizontal axis to any degree and in any direction. This can be used for visual effect or can be used to align the text along the outline of an object.

REFLECTIONS A mirror image of an object can be in either the vertical plane, as in the example, or in the horizontal plane. It is used for visual effect, or to save drawing time by drawing half of a symmetrical shape and creating an identical mirror image of the other half.

Reflections
Reflections

MORPHING This takes two images and creates a set of intermediate images, showing the stages of transformation from one to the other. Morphing can be applied to objects (e.g. swords are turned into ploughshares) or photographs (e.g. Tony Blair turns into Margaret Thatcher).

Full-Motion Video

Where a continuous sequence of movement is to be recorded, a full-motion video card is required. These cards, sometimes called FMV cards, capture complete moving video sequences. The chart shows the number of frames displayed per second in various systems, to maintain the illusion of continual movement.

Typical frame rates and their uses	
0fps	Still frame
15fps	Minimum acceptable for motion
24fps	Motion pictures
25fps	British television
30fps	American television

The capturing of a sequence is done as a single operation and, due to their added complexity, FMV cards are considerably more expensive than simple frame capture cards.

File Formats

There are four main formats for storing video files:

AVI: The Audio Video Interleave format is the Windows standard and is so-called because it stores the audio and video information as a single file, with the video data and audio being divided into blocks and interleaved in the file. Since both streams of data are stored next to each other in time, it aids the synchronisation process. Where video and audio files are held separately, the delays in reading both sets of data from disk and interpreting the separate streams leads to severe problems of keep the sound synchronised to the picture. AVI files can be in compressed or uncompressed format depending whether one of the compression algorithms (see later) has been applied them.

QuickTime: The *'Macintosh'* range of computers made by Apple has long led the field in innovation and is still the most popular system for use with art, design and DTP. The *'Mac'* range was introduced in 1984 and Apple were the first to use a Graphical User Interface (in their 1983 *'Lisa'* computer), colour monitors (in their 1977 Apple II model), built-in sound and eventually video (in their own QuickTime format). The Windows-type environment was embedded in the Mac operating system form its introduction; users never had to struggle with a command-line environment like DOS.

Unfortunately, the Mac computer range is not compatible with PCs as they use a different processor range that uses different machine code instructions. Apple originally produced the QuickTime video format for their range of Macintosh machines. This format also interleaves audio and video information. QuickTime and AVI files can be played on a PC that has a QuickTime driver installed. It is explained more fully later.

MPEG : The Motion Picture Experts Group standard MPEG-1 compression forms the core of VideoCD as used in CD-I players, etc. and can store about 70 minutes of video on a single CD. The later version, MPEG-2, is used with DVD players. MPEG is explained more fully later.

Real Video & WMV : These are two *'streamed'* media formats for use on the Internet, from RealNetworks and Microsoft. They require special player software that downloads a video track as a set of separate blocks. This allows the video to be displayed immediately, without waiting until the whole file is downloaded. If the blocks arrive faster than they can be played, they are stored in a memory buffer. Of course, if the blocks arrive slower than required, the file cannot be played continuously.

Video Storage

Like animations, full-motion video can easily occupy huge amounts of hard disk space.

The chapter on video covered the storage requirements for a single picture frame at different resolutions. Video has to store and play back between 15 and 30 individual screens per second. The highest demand from video on currently available CDs is an 800x600 screen, although this is bound to increase.

The storage capacity per second of video can be calculated thus:

File Size = Bit Depth x Screen Resolution x Frames/Sec

This is divided by 8 to get the answer in bytes and divided again by 1,048,576 to get the answer in MBs. A 256-colour (i.e. 8 bits) VGA (i.e. 640x480) at a 15fps screen update would require

640 x 480 x 8 x 15 / 8 / 1048576 = 4.39MB

The chart shows the amount of storage required for a range of popular displays.

The smallest figure for a full screen image is 4.39MB, while the professional performance figure is around 165MB per second! The two bottom chart entries describe the resolution of MPEG-1 in its uncompressed form. The saving and playing back of live video involves not only the storage but also the transfer of huge

Number of colours	Screen Resolution	Frame Rate	Storage/Sec
256	640 x 480	15	4.39MB
256	800 x 600	15	6.86MB
256	1024 x 768	15	11.25MB
256	640 x 480	25	7.32MB
256	800 x 600	25	11.44MB
256	1024 x 768	25	18.75MB
16.78m	1024 x 768	30	67.5MB
16.78m	1600 x 1200	30	164.79Bb
256	352 x 288	25	2.41MB
16.78m	352 x 288	25	7.25MB

amounts of data; this requires a fast hard disk, a fast CPU and a fast video system.

These storage figures are not practical and a number of methods are introduced to reduce this size:

- Using only a portion of the screen to display the video. If the video occupies a quarter of the screen area, it only needs a quarter of the storage space. This is commonly used on CDs to accommodate the low performance of most disks/CPUs/video cards.
- Reducing the colour palette to 256 colours may mean a barely noticeable loss of colour gradation, but would result in a video clip that is a third of the size of a 16.78m colour clip.
- Lowering the frame rate at which the picture is displayed. This makes savings but the picture is jerkier.
- Compressing the files for storage and decompressing them when they are to be played. Unlike the other three methods, compression need not produce any deterioration in picture quality. The user has the option to make even bigger savings at the expense of some picture quality.

Compression

Data compression schemes are mostly based on the following techniques:

INTRAFRAME This considers each individual frame and discards any trivial data. This is the method used by both JPEG and MJPEG compression systems.

INTERFRAME This considers the differences between successive frames, removes the unchanged parts of the information and applies JPEG type compression on what's left. This is also called *'difference compression'* and is used by the MPEG system.

Other, less well used methods involve converting 24-bit colour down to 16-bit colour and using dithering to represent the lost colours. This reduces file sizes at the expense of introducing a *'grainy'* effect to the clip when played back.

CODECs

The CODEC (compressor/decompressor) is an engine that shrinks the files on saving and expands them again when they are to be used. CODECs can be implemented in either hardware or software. Hardware CODECs are more expensive but, because they use dedicated chips instead of the computer's CPU time, they are significantly more efficient. No CODECs were supplied with Windows 3.1 and these had to be installed by the user.

Windows 95/98 comes with four main CODECs pre-installed:

CINEPAK: Developed by Apple for their SuperMac computers and now licensed to Microsoft, it supports 320x240 at 15fps and both the compression and decompression are implemented in software. Only works for 24-bit colour.

INDEO: This system was developed by Intel and the compression process initially required capture cards that were based on the Intel i750 video processor chip, though this compression can now be implemented in software. This results in an AVI file with Indeo compression. Indeo uses both interframe compression and run length encoding techniques (see below). The playback process can be implemented in software at 320x240 with 15fps and 24-bit colour; this does not require the use of any special hardware. Playback is *'scaleable'* - the faster the CPU, the greater will be the screen size and frame rates used. Where an i750 card is also used for playback, a full-screen at 30fps is supported.

MSVC: The Microsoft Video Compressor, also known as Video 1. Developed to use algorithms that place less pressure on the CPU. Although supported by cards such as the Black Widow Media Master Plus, it has not found a place in general use. This is probably because it only supports 256 or 32k colours.

RLE: Run Length Encoding takes a horizontal area of a colour and stores the length of the band rather than the individual pixels. This is very effective in animations where backgrounds are plain but produces poor results as a video CODEC.

Apart from the four CODECs supplied with Windows 95/98, there are some other very significant drivers that can be installed.
These include:

QuickTime

This is produced in Mac and PC Windows versions and mixes sound and vision into the one file, similar to the AVI format, with added MIDI tracks. It is a software CODEC and therefore needs some of the CPU's time. It also has *'scalable performance'* which means that it automatically adjusts to the capabilities of the machine in use. It handles AVI files and will provide 15fps, 20fps or 30fps depending on the machine speed. Similarly, it will produce from one-tenth screen up to full screen images depending upon the abilities of the system on which it is run. The 3.2 version is intended for use with Pentiums and provides full screen graphics.

MPEG

The <u>M</u>oving <u>P</u>ictures <u>E</u>xperts <u>G</u>roup format uses a complicated set of compression methods including spatial compression, Huffman coding and predictive compression - based on only saving the <u>differences</u> (or 'deltas') between successive frames. It produces a result similar to television's VHS quality. Depending on the quality and speed required, it may sometimes require expensive hardware, but can achieve surprising compression rates. These rates vary depending on the quality of the stored image, because MPEG compression is a type known as *'lossy'* - i.e. the final image has lost small, less noticeable details in order to effect greater compression. Compression ratios up to 50:1 can be achieved before the picture quality deteriorates noticeably.

MPEG-1 Most systems are designed around MPEG-1 with data rates of around 1.4MBps and frame rates up 30fps. It provides the lowest common formats as it can produce 340x240 at 30fps for American NTSC TV (or 352x288 at 25fps for European PAL TV) from a standard CD-ROM player; this is sometimes referred to as SIF - the Standard Interchange Format. Many video clips on CDs are designed for this format and don't therefore take advantage of the significant hardware improvements that modern PCs contain. It is also a common multimedia format.

MPEG-2 MPEG-2 is a standard for higher quality with a resultant increase in data rates. It can deliver a screen resolution of 720x480 at a frame rate of 60fps. This is the basis of DVD products. The increased demands of MPEG-2 have led to further improvements in component specifications.

M-JPEG

Motion-JPEG, called M-JPEG, is similar in basis to the JPEG graphic format. Each individual frame is compressed using JPEG techniques and each frame is stored individually and separately. By concentrating on individual frame compression, it produces less spectacular compression ratios (around 8:1) but provides 24-bit depth, higher quality and easier manipulation. Its increased data rate meant that it could not be supported by the slow speeds of early CD players and is the choice of the professional user. (e.g. video production, video editing).

Since an AVI file may have been encoded using one of a variety of CODECS, Windows 95/98 provides a method to get a report on a file's configuration. If an AVI file is highlighted in *'Explorer'* and the mouse right-hand button is clicked, the *'Properties'* option of the resulting menu produces the screen shown. There are three main options:

- The *'General'* option shows file dates, size, etc.
- The *'Preview'* option runs the clip in miniature.
- The *'Details'* option shows that the file called *'Beatles'* is designed to be run in a quarter of a VGA screen at 15fps using a Cinepak CODEC. Its data rate is only 146kBps, allowing it to be run directly from even the slowest CD-ROM drive. This is a good example of how early AVI files were produced to match the lowest possible hardware performance.

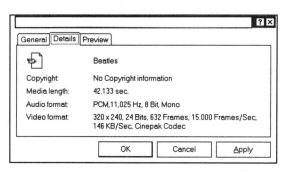

Since even compressed video clips tend to be enormous, most clips found in the public domain are low resolution with a low frame rate. The result is below TV quality, but gets the message across effectively, which is the intention of multimedia in the first place. The clips that are found in many magazines' 'free' CDs are of larger size but they still have to be tailored to the lowest standards, to be compatible with the largest numbers of user machines.

Playback Systems

All video files require to be played back using some type of driver routine. These routines are usually implemented in software although hardware implementations are also available and are more efficient.

Software CODECS

All AVI files compressed by a particular CODEC should be decompressed with that same CODEC. So, an AVI file with Cinepack compression should be run using Cinepack decompression software.

Hardware CODECS

These use dedicated chipsets to produce full screen playback of AVI files and are now universally used. The chipsets play AVI Indeo and Cinepak files full screen. The use of a *'digital movie accelerator chipset'* provides an interpolated algorithm to estimate the extra pixels required to fill the full screen. This prevents *'blockiness'* and *'jagged edges'* on the image but tends to soften the picture. The smaller the original AVI file, the more marked is this loss of contrast.

Playing back MPEG

Clips that were created and saved using MPEG compression require to be decompressed before the video information can be sent to the monitor. The machine showing these clips has to be fitted with an MPEG playback card or have MPEG decoding software routines. The hardware implementation is potentially faster as the card contains chips that are dedicated to MPEG decoding. This saves much of the computer's CPU time and is commonly implemented in graphics cards.

Software CODECs became more popular at one stage. The speed of CPUs and the general data transfer rates of computer systems have increased to a point where software MPEG decoding is possible, dispensing with the need for a dedicated decoder card. This is not a serious option for anything below a 120MHz Pentium, as the added load on the CPU results in dropping of frames. Software CODECs were supplied with some cards and resulted in cheaper card prices. Currently, hardware implementations through dedicated chipsets are more popular.

M-JPEG cards won't handle MPEG files and only play back M-JPEG files. Convertors are available which take the higher specification M-JPEG files and convert them into MPEG files for general use.

Films, concerts, etc are available on DVD disks. They are in MPEG-2 format and require a DVD player and MPEG-2 decompression hardware or software.

Windows 98 supports the MPEG-1 software CODEC while Windows 3.1 and Windows 95 need an extra MPEG-1 driver to be installed. Windows 98/ME can handle MPEG-2, once the DVD card's driver software is installed.

MPEG and CD-I

Dedicated CD-I players were microprocessor-controlled CD playback systems designed to run dedicated interactive video CDs for training, educational and entertainment purposes. They had no keyboard and only used a controller with mouse, joystick or rollerball to control simple on-screen menus. Their output was to a TV set or a colour monitor. They had no hard disk and therefore could not save any information. They had their own internal operating system (RTOS), which was different from any used in PCs. They were produced to the 'Green Book' CD specification (see the chapter on disks and drives). CDs that are made to the *'White Book'* specification use MPEG-1 compression. If a DV (digital video) cartridge is fitted to a CD-I player, the machine can also play back those White Book full-motion video CDs. A range of films, music concerts, etc is now available in CD-I format and these can be viewed on a PC as long as it is fitted with a CD-ROM that reads the CD-I format and an MPEG decoder.

NSP

Digital Signal Processors, DSPs, are used in sound cards, video cards and other devices. These are chips dedicated to tasks such as analogue to digital signal processing and vice versa, along with a range of other data processing functions. These chips are fitted on the boards of sound and video cards. With the introduction of higher performance PCs, there is an attempt to have these specialist processing tasks carried out by the CPU. This is known as *'Native Signal Processing'* and requires fewer add-on cards making the computer system cheaper.

Data Transfer Rates

Users constantly demand improvements in multimedia performance - more colours, higher resolutions, bigger and smoother video clips. The space required to store one minute of video is becoming ever larger. But buying a larger disk drive doesn't solve the problem. The playback system still has only one minute to move around this larger set of data. This places great demands on all components in the system. As the diagram shows, the playback process moves the data from the disk through a chain of components to the monitor. The system is only as powerful as its weakest link.

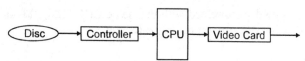

Therefore, the CD player or disk drive must have a fast access time and a fast data transfer rate. For video recording and CD writing the flow in and out of the disk drive must be continuous. Temporary slowdowns in the DTR would result in lost frames while playing and potential loss of the entire disk while CD writing.

One way to guarantee uninterrupted data transfer is to use AV disk drives. The disk controller interface has to be high performance, with IDE being replaced by UDMA-66, UDMA-100, SCSI-2 or even SCSI-UW. The CPU must be at least a Pentium III, with preference to high speed chips.

Finally, the video card specification should include a wide internal bus (e.g. 128-bit), sufficient memory to cope with high screen resolutions and a large colour palette, and a chipset that copes with required demands (e.g. high-speed DAC, 3D playing, MPEG decoding).

Virtual Reality

Virtual reality (VR) has received much publicity and is still in the development stage. Crude versions have appeared in amusement arcades and much work has been carried out in the areas of staff training and work simulation.

VR produces an artificial world that is generated by computer. It uses four elements:

- Database (to store the elements of the scenario - e.g. buildings, trees, roads, etc. These are not stored as graphics images; they are stored in descriptive format).
- Graphics engine (to convert object data in graphics shapes, implementing 3D shading and texture mapping).
- Input (to sense activities in the real world).
- Output (to stimulate human senses).

VR is produced in two ways:

Fully-immersive

The user wears a head-mounted display that contains LCD screens for each eye, along with motion detectors. This is the most realistic method, as the user can only view the scene presented by the computer and there are no outside distractions. The helmet's sensors track head movements, such that turning the head to the left generates a picture that pans to the left. However, it is still expensive, uncomfortable and renders the user prone to motion sickness.

Partially-immersive

The user views the artificial world through a window (i.e. the monitor) as in normal games use. It is less effective than fully-immersive systems, as the surrounding environment distracts from the effect of the simulation.

The main outputs are to the user's sight and hearing. The main inputs are from helmet sensors, joystick, keyboard and foot levers. Future outputs will include smell, touch, heat and taste. Input and output will use data gloves and data suits.

Gathering Data

This chapter does not attempt to discuss the planning and content of a multimedia presentation. This is covered in the author's book *"The PC Multimedia Handbook"*. This chapter concentrates on the practical tasks in multimedia production. Once the presentation's content is formulated, the user has an idea of the material that is required to put across the required concepts. The designer than has to decide on the source of any graphics and animations, special sound effects or musical accompaniment.

There are many varied ways to gather data for a multimedia presentation.

Bulletin Boards/Internet

A very useful source is wide access to bulletin boards and on-line services with a modem. This will ensure access to the latest freely distributable imaging and audio software, as well as plenty of raw data for use in multimedia, and even communication with people who can explain how it can be used. However, this can be an expensive proposition in terms of telephone costs.

CD-ROM Sources

An alternative is CD-ROM. Although CD-ROM at first looks expensive, the amount of data it can store compared with magnetic disks or especially downloading time through modems, means that it will become economical after buying only a few CD-ROM disks. Many CD-ROMs are dedicated to multimedia, as it is well suited to carrying the huge amounts of data needed for multimedia purposes. CD-ROMs are available with clip art, digitised pictures, sound samples, and music clips. Some of these files are public domain and some are copyrighted.

Creating Graphics Files

Many packages are available to view, edit and create graphics and more are appearing all the time.

In addition to the drawing/painting tools described earlier, there are other specialised tools:

Ray Tracing

For the more mathematically inclined, there are many public domain ray-tracing programs, where even a few simple spheres, planes and cubes can be surprisingly effective when used properly. Perhaps the best-known PC raytracer is Persistence Of Vision, which is available from almost any shareware vendor. Professional packages range up to the industry standard 3D Studio package.

Fractals

These programs create images with little or no input from the user. Although a Mandelbrot fractal may be too abstract for use in most multimedia presentations, it can make a very effective background to other graphics, and can also be used in conjunction with a raytracer to produce complex, realistic landscapes.

Fly-Throughs

Programs, such as the shareware program 'Vistapro', create extremely realistic landscapes, and fly-through animations of those landscapes, with little effort on the part of the designer. Walk-throughs and fly-throughs are used extensively in games and are very effective in certain commercial multimedia products such as simulators and marketing promotions.

Screen Capture

Material for multimedia can be culled from almost anywhere, to do almost anything. For example, to create a Computer Aided Learning demonstration to teach people a certain technique in Microsoft Word for Windows, the *Alt+PrtScr* keystrokes can be used to capture the screen in the midst of using the technique. This can be pasted into Paintbrush and saved as a PCX file for later use in a multimedia show.

Scanners

Existing graphic material can be easily be incorporated into presentations with the use of scanners. These capture the graphics contents from any sheet of paper and convert them into a graphics file. Most devices are able to save the data in a variety of formats such as TIFF, BMP, PCX, TGA, or even EPS or JPEG. The scanner is able to handle line drawings, text and full photographs. Models are available to handle monochrome and colour input. Any material that is captured has to be within the laws of copyright. This means that pictures from newspapers and magazines cannot be used without permission. Similarly, the law covers the illegal copying of company logos, company letterheads, £20 notes, etc. Nevertheless, the device is very convenient for converting pen sketches, users' signatures and any authorised photographs.

Flatbed Scanner

The most convenient scanner is the flatbed model. This is usually an A4 size device, where the sheet to be scanned is placed on a glass plate. In this respect, the scanner is similar to a photocopier. However, the data read is saved straight to a disk file rather than being used to directly produce a replica sheet. Some models allow multiple sheets to be scanned. Flatbeds come with either interface cards or with SCSI interfaces.

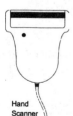

Hand Scanner

Where items to be scanned are small, or there are budget restrictions, handheld models are available. These are smaller and can only scan around 10cm width and users may be forced to scan a document in several strips. The software finds the area of overlap, and aligns the images to create a single larger file. Handheld scanner resolutions are switchable from 100-400dpi, with flatbeds working up to 9600dpi. The specification should be checked as the *'optical scan resolution'* may differ from the *'output resolution'*. The image may be scanned at a lower resolution (say 800dpi) and enhanced in software to produce a file with greater resolution (say 1600dpi). 300dpi is generally considered as minimum standard for DTP work but screen-based multimedia requires much lower scanning rates. Dependent upon the monitor size and the screen mode (VGA or SVGA), only around 60 to 90 pixels are displayed for each screen inch. Any scanning at a higher dpi rate produces no improvement in quality, while consuming much more disk storage space. Monochrome scanners with 256 grey level are now less common as 24-bit colour scanner prices have fallen. Modern scanners are *'Twain'* compatible. This is the Windows interface agreed by major manufacturers such as Hewlett Packard and Logitech.

Still Capture

There are professional imaging centres that can digitise pictures for use on computers, or users can create their own using a video capture card and a video camera. Of course, a digitised picture can rarely be used 'as is'. Generally, a digitised picture has to be manually re-touched, to remove such things as movement artefacts, (generated when a moving image is being digitised) dithering patterns, (visible when a full-colour digitised is reduced to a paletted image for viewing on a PC screen) and so on. Photo retouch packages, such as Photofinish, provide facilities such spot removal, brightness and contrast adjustment, diffusing; it also provides special effects such as motion blur, mosaic and emboss effects, etc. Users may also want to edit the image to include some extra details such as superimposing a logo on a picture, or drawing an arrow pointing out an important feature.

Digital Cameras

An alternative is to use a digital camera. These have all the features of normal cameras (e.g. zoom, focus, shutter speed, etc) but the image is digitised and saved to memory card or to mini-disc inside the camera. The number of pictures that can be stored depends upon the size of the flash memory or mini-disc, the picture resolution and the compression ratio. Older models took 320x240 pictures. Most budget models now take either 640x480 or 1024x768 pictures, while semi-professional models handle around 2048x1536 (i.e. 3.34 megapixels).

The quality from the higher resolution cameras rivals the resolution of a 35mm slide. There remains an argument that it more effective to capture images using a 'real' camera, with the developed photographs being scanned with a high-resolution scanner.

Most digital camcorders are now also able to capture still images. The images are either stored on the videotape or on memory modules such as the Sony Memory Stick.

Similarly, many digital cameras can now capture short video clips. The resolution and clip length are always curtailed, as digital cameras can store much less data than a camcorder's videotape.

Digital cameras use a variety of methods to transfer the stored images to a PC:
- Serial cable.
- Infrared link.
- Floppy disk, as in the Sony Mavica.
- CD-R and CD-RW, as used in the more expensive Sony Mavica range.
- Using a card reader fitted to the PC.

Video Clips

These are available from the Internet but are normally poor quality or of short duration.

Using the video capture cards described earlier, video clips of all types become available. These can range from clips set up by the user (e.g. how to repair a car) to live coverage of events (although the laws of privacy, copyright, etc still apply here). Although the capture card provides the technology, there is still a lot to learn to get the best from a camcorder. Issues such as lighting, sound, placing of subject, developing a storyboard beforehand, etc should be addressed and there are many books and magazines for home moviemakers (including "The PC Support Handbook").

Sound

Sound samples and music files can generally be found in the same places as graphics and animations, but creating sound samples is a relatively inexpensive business. Assuming the use of a sound card such as a Sound Blaster or compatible, a simple microphone can be used to record sounds. Most sound cards capable of sampling come with sample editing software, to allow the addition of special effects such as echo, fade, or mix.

Copyright

While professionals rarely react to their work being adopted for personal use, they will take action when their photographs, film clips, audio tracks, etc are re-used in a commercial product. Great care should be taken to protect against legal action. The Copyright Licensing Agency run a 'Copywatch' scheme to detect illegal copying and advice can be sought from them at 90 Tottenham Court Rd, London W1P 0LP (Tel 0171-436-5931). If in doubt, seek permission or stick to using copyright-free sound, pictures and clip-art collections.

Multimedia Software

The range of software to support the creation of multimedia products includes:

	Typical Example	**Purpose**
Audio Editing	Blaster Master, Software Audio Workshop, Wave for Windows	WAV files can be manipulated in many ways to create the final clip to be included in a production. These include cut and paste, mixing, merging, filtering out frequencies, adding echo effects, looping, muting, reversing, pitch altering, volume altering, panning, fading and waveform editing.
Video Editing and effects	Premiere, Elastic Reality, Morph2, Digital Video Producer	*'Linear editing'* as offered by Video Director copies snatches of recordings from the camcorder directly to the VCR. No capture card is used but it lacks precision and control. Other packages use *'Non-Linear Editing'* where the video clip is digitised and individual frames are easily accessed for editing and the application of effects. Typical facilities are cut and paste, adding filters, transitions between scenes such as fades and wipes, titling, warping and morphing (gradually transforming one object into another object).
Graphic Creation	Paint Shop Pro, Corel Draw, Freehand	To create drawings, charts, cartoons, etc from graphic elements such as lines, boxes, circles and polygons. The line widths, styles (e.g. dotted, arrowed) and colour are alterable and a variety of fill patterns are provided. Text of various sizes, type styles and colours can be added. Packages such as Paint Shop produce bitmap files while others produce vector images (although these can be converted to bitmaps).
Graphic Effects	3D Studio, Visual Reality, Ray Dream Studio	The most common effects are 3D objects using wireframes and rendered fills and animations. Many authoring packages provide animation facilities but these are not as sophisticated as dedicated animation packages.
Image Editing	Photoshop, Picture Publisher, PhotoStudio	Used to manipulate a photographic image. This includes altering the colours, altering contrast and brightness, and zooming, scaling and cropping of the image. It may also include special effects such as quantizing (producing an oil painting effect) and altering the data masks (producing a pop video effect).
Authoring Packages	Director, Authorware, Icon Author, MasterClass, Toolbook	This is the key piece of software that integrates all the sound, video, graphic and text components into a meaningful order to achieve a set purpose.

Software for delivery

The software requirements for the delivery of multimedia are small. Windows 95/98/ME users already have the capability of playing WAV and AVI files. Additional software drivers and CODECs are required to support a full range of playback devices. For example, MPEG and QuickTime playback may require their CODECs to be installed. Sound cards require that their software be configured and if the user is downloading multimedia from the Internet, then communications, browser and specialist software (e.g. RealAudio or RealVideo) is required.

Designing a Multimedia Project

The main steps in designing projects for multimedia are similar to those for any software project, although there are extra considerations. The main phases are:

Analysis

It is vital that a clear understanding of the project is achieved before any other work is undertaken. This prevents many wasted hours and potential disputes with the client commissioning the project. The client will provide a project brief, which is a short summary of the aims of the project. The aim of systems analysis is to convert the project brief into a project plan that can be implemented.

A thorough set of discussions clarifies the detailed aims of the project. This would include issues such as the general content (e.g. education, training, entertainment), the target audience (the likely age, sex, previous knowledge/experience of those using the multimedia) and the mood (serious, light-hearted).

This will lead to the production of a project specification. This is essentially a requirements list covering educational requirements and technical requirements such as the proposed delivery system, screen resolution and colours, screen layout and project navigation).

Prototyping

Prototyping is an excellent, although time-consuming, way to develop an understanding and a client agreement on a project. A prototype is a partial implementation of a project, showing the key structural and layout details. This is shown to the client and used as a means of sharpening up the definition of their needs. Misunderstandings and extra features can be picked up and settled at this stage, before a great deal of expensive and possibly wasted effort has been expended.

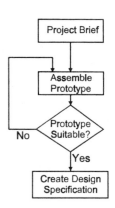

The aim of the analysis phase is to produce precise statements, which can act as a checklist in the later testing phase. Example statements might be that all menus will be in a bottom panel, or that every page should provide help and exit options.

Design

The design phase lays out how the project will work in detail. A number of methods are used by different developers, but a top-down approach (where the main functions are outlined followed by subsidiary functions, continuing to the end of the outline) and flowcharts (showing the links between screen pages) are common development methods. The design phase produces all the content details. This will cover all internal resources (i.e. the company's own talent, hardware and raw material) and requirements for buying in skills (e.g. commissioning photographers, video camera teams, sound studios, graphics artists, animators, voice-over artists, etc). Details of copyright would also be addressed at this stage. The two main guides that are produced from the design phase are:

- STORYBOARD This is a set of sketches and notes that describe each scene, video clip, audio clip, text, navigation icon, and the mood to be set. It provides snapshots of the intended sequence to convey the impression of the final result. Storyboards can be hand-drawn or can be created using storyboard software. They can be finely detailed, listing every sound, colour, etc. This is slower to produce but leaves less margin for error. Storyboards that are more of a rough guide sometimes require more versions to be produced to adequately define the project.
- NAVIGATION MAP This is required for all but the very simplest of projects. It details every connection between one part of the project and another. Users navigate (i.e. move round) the application by choosing menu options, clicking on icons, buttons or hypertext entries, or clicking on 'hotspots' (active areas of the screen - e.g. a county on a map). The map shows where the user is taken on activating one of the navigation tools.

Implementation

The implementation phase is concerned with the production of the components (i.e. creating the graphics and animation, recording the interviews and voiceovers, filming/digitising/editing the video clips, writing the text copy) and integrating them into a project with an authoring package. Large projects would benefit from the use of project management software, to ensure that the most efficient use is made of resources and to achieve a working product in the shortest possible time. A video crew might require a long advance booking, the well-known personality for the presenter/voice-over may only be in the country over a short time period, etc. and the activities have to be planned to prevent hold-ups.

Testing

The testing stage is vital to ensure that the product meets the client's needs and to maintain the reputation of the company. Testing can be of two types:

VALIDATION These tests ensure that the project has been built to the original specification and has not moved away from the client's original intention. These tests are on content, presentation and style, testing whether it addresses the agreed client group, and such issues.

VERIFICATION These tests ensure that the project functions work correctly. This tests that all buttons work correctly, all navigation tools take the user to the intended destination, self-assessed tests provide correct marks, all video and audio clips play correctly, etc.

Maintenance

The maintenance phase looks at making program changes after the completion and distribution of project. This is a potentially costly business if the changes are due to programming. Other changes may be made at the client's request, as an additional chargeable contract. It also involves adding new features for future updates (e.g. Internet linking, client databases).

Authoring Software

All multimedia products can be written using conventional programming languages such as Pascal or C. Alternatively, multimedia authoring packages provide facilities to greatly speed up the development process. Although both methods require analysis and design skill, some authoring packages can produce very useful results with no coding skills whatsoever. Most packages are able to produce run-time versions - executable files that do not require the use of the original package to display them. Packages range from hobbyist products to those with full-blown commercial aspirations. The price generally reflects the facilities provided by the packages and they use a number of different production methods:

Method	Example Packages	Explanation
Icon/Flow Control	AuthorWare, Authority, IconAuthor	A flow chart plots the possible routes between activities; this is the 'navigation map'. An activity is represented by an icon which could be a decision to be made, a user entry to be requested, a new screen of graphics to be shown, a video or sound clip to be run and so on. At the design and implementation stages, groups of icons can be grouped together under a single icon - implementing a top-down design of sub-modules. The example shows the second level of a package that displays a top menu with four choices (e.g. Memory Types, Organisation). Each choice produces a drop-down menu with other choices (e.g. Error Detection, Cache Memory).
Cast/Score/Script	Director	Uses a 'timeline' as in the example, where each vertical frame stores all the objects that will be used during that particular timeslot. Objects can be graphics, video clips, user entry buttons or dialogue boxes, screen effects, etc. Each object can therefore be controlled down to the precision of a single frame (for a 25fps production, this means control down to 1/25th of a second).
Card/Script	Toolbook	Uses a book as its presentation format. Users can flick through the pages of the book and pages can contain text, graphics, video or user input.

Part of a Director score

Part of an Authorware design screen
Level 2

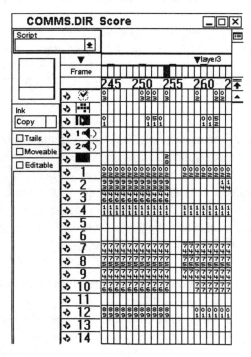

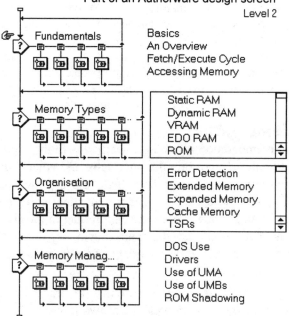

Programming languages such as Delphi, Visual Basic and Visual C are blurring the boundaries between conventional programming and multimedia authoring.

Scripting

Some packages provide very simple navigation links but for greater control of navigation and to support internal logic decisions, the author has to learn the programming language behind the package. The examples show the minimum scripts used by the leading 'Director' and 'Toolbook' packages.

Director's Lingo	Toolbook

on mouseup
    go frame "quiz"
end
	TO HANDLE buttonClick
	    go to next page
	END buttonClick

Multimedia Presentations

Having gathered the graphics, sound and music for the presentation, the author of the presentation will have previously decided the best way to present the information. The presentation type will depend upon the purpose it is intended to achieve. Multimedia presentations are generally of two types:

Linear : The user watches a sequence that has been already determined and has no influence over the presentation. This is best suited to exhibitions, point of sale and other information providing situations. Linear presentations can be achieved with simple software. Although they use multiple forms of media, they are not full multimedia products as there is no real interaction with the user.

Interactive : The user can control the flow of the presentation, to explore particular areas, ignoring others and even returning to a particular area of the presentation. The package may have built-in intelligence to know where a user keeps going wrong and giving targeted advice. This is suited to the learning environment where the user controls the pace and the content of the presentation. Computer Based Training programmes use this method, as each run of the presentation can be different, changing with the needs of the student. CD-ROMs for the domestic market use interactive techniques. Interactive presentations require more sophisticated, and more expensive, software.

Important as the video, sound and other components are, the final presentation is only as good as the skill of the designer - an issue beyond the scope of this chapter.

Presentation Facilities

In all multimedia presentations, the user approaches the application in an interactive way, expecting to be given control over the package. The three most important elements are:

Buttons

The user has to control the flow of information in a package. This will normally be achieved by the user clicking the mouse on on-screen *'buttons'* that represent a particular choice. The choice may be from a selection of menu options (i.e. where to go next) or might be from a selection of possible data entries (e.g. choosing a correct answer or saving or loading a set of data). Buttons can be the default grey variety provided in most authoring packages or can be user-defined such as pictures or shapes.

Alternatives to buttons are using dialogue boxes, where the user is asked to enter data (e.g. user name or age) and *'hot spots'* where areas of the screen act as equivalents of large buttons. Clicking a hot spot has the same effect as clicking a button but a hot spot can be an irregular shape. For example, this allows the user to click anywhere on the Isle of Wight in a screen map of the UK to see more information about that island. Other on-screen system controls are:

- Radio buttons (i.e. only one option can be active at a time).
- Check boxes (i.e. more than option can be active at the same time).
- Scroll bars.
- File/directory selection.

Events

Normal conventional programs are written to be mainly sequential. The program starts at the beginning of the code and finishes at the end of the code. Multimedia products are explored in a different manner. With event-driven systems, code is attached to objects and remains inactive until it is called. Calls can be initiated by the user (e.g. clicking a mouse) or by the system (e.g. a timeout). The clicking of the button or hot spot is tied to a particular action. So clicking the *'Show Interview'* button always plays the same video clip. Clicking a *'More Details'* button may produce an entirely new screen with more information and a further set of buttons. Clicking the *'Quit'* button should exit the user from the package.

Control Structures

For more control, conditional branching can be carried out. So, a user when presented with six buttons representing six levels of difficulty may only be allowed to pursue a higher level if the lower level has been successfully completed. The program has kept the user's previous performance in a set of variables and the branching allowed is a combination of what button the user pressed and what information is already stored. In a multi-choice question, the user may only be allowed three attempts. Control can be passed to internal code using constructs such as:

      IF ..   e.g. if a user score is less than 50% ....
      REPEAT ...   e.g. repeat the question until the user chooses the correct answer.

Local Area Networks

Local Area Networks, usually shortened to *'LANs'*, is a constantly growing area of computing. The major players such as Intel and Xerox only published their specification for the Ethernet system in 1980, with real sales only developing in 1983/4. IBM, the other major contender for the LAN market only appeared in 1985. In the following years, there has been a dramatic growth in their popularity. In 1987, around a tenth of all PCs were connected to a network. Now, the large majority of all non-domestic PCs are attached to LANs. This growth is due to their great contribution to office and industrial automation. The linking of PCs has developed from a *'good idea'* to a powerful aid to industrial and commercial efficiency. PC networks now carry out the tasks previously given to mainframe and mini systems.

The size of networks vary tremendously:

- Six linked computers in a typing pool.
- Hundreds of users in a medium company.
- Thousands of users at a university or large company.

There are many small networks in use and quite a few very large systems. Around 70% of all commercial computers are networked.

What Are LANS

In non-networked organisations, the sharing of information and inter-personal communication is via *people* - in a networked organisation this is achieved via *computers.*   There are a number of definitions of a LAN, some trying to state the likely maximum distance covered, or the maximum speed used.   In the ever-changing technology of computing, a more useful general definition might be:

> *"A local area network is a communication system used to interconnect all of an*
> *organisation's computers, generally within a single building, or a single site".*

In other words, a LAN would normally be owned and run within a single organisation, to link together the computers and peripherals found on a single location. This location could be a single office, or it could cover an entire commercial or production site. In practice, the total distances covered range from a few yards (a typing pool) to over a mile (a shipyard or a university campus). From NetWare 4 onwards, all of the computers across the world owned by a single international company can be used as if they were all in the same building. Although most computers on LANs would be PCs (with or without internal hard disks), the system could encompass minicomputers, mainframes and super computers and even dumb terminals.

Why Link Users

80% of an organisation's communications is from within that organisation. Less than 5% of a company's entire written/verbal communications involves direct interaction with people outside the company.   So, most communication is within the organisation's own boundaries.   Indeed, 90% of all information travels less than half a mile within the organisation - more than three-quarters travelling less than 600 ft. So, much of an organisation's activities is based on the internal sharing of information.   In a normal paper-based company, one whose data is held on cards and stationary files, the files are held centrally. Anyone wishing information can go to the appropriate cabinet and retrieve the desired data. However, in an office with many PCs, the information would be held on many different hard disks. Of course, the user of each PC could print out the machine's information and place it in the central filing area. The problems with this are:

- Wasted storage space.
- Wasted effort.
- The information is never fully up-to-date.
- Only one person can look at the file at a time.

The filing cabinets can be dispensed with, if the information from PCs is transferred to floppy disks. This can solve some of the above problems but can cause new problems - those of data integrity.   For example, if a word-processed file is given to a colleague and both versions are modified, then neither is now complete. What is required is a central store of information, held in electronic form, which can be easily accessed from any PC in the system.   Since most departments are using their own computers, it makes sense that communication between individuals or departments should ignore memos/telephone conversations/central filing cabinets and directly link the computers. The savings that can be made are potentially vast - it is estimated that around 1.4 trillion dollars is spent on staffing of offices in America alone. Even a relatively small saving from the increased productivity is a huge amount of money. The proportion of UK information-related jobs is about 40% and increasing.

How
Each computer in the network has a special card installed, which allows the machines to be connected together with cables.   Each machine has its own software to handle the network's activities. These computer stations are referred to as 'nodes'.

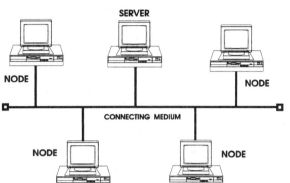

Connected to the cable is a special computer called the 'server' (large installations will use several servers). A server has a set of large hard disks that hold all the application programs and data needed by the stations. The server has particular software to allow it to play its role as the nerve centre of the system.   The nodes send a message to the server, over the cable, requesting a copy of a particular program or item of data.   The server responds by sending a copy of the program or data down the cable. This is then held in the node's memory for use. In fact, the node sees the server disk as if it was the node's own local disk drive.   All the usual COPY commands, etc. work as if the server hard disk was actually inside the node case. In this way, the activities of the network are invisible to the user.

Notes
- To ensure that all users have fair access to the network, the data travelling between machines on the media is split into small 'packets'. These packets are interspersed on the cable with other users' packets.
- Very small LAN systems can use a similar method to the above, except that there is no special server for the system, as all the machines share each other's programs and data via the cable (this is known as a 'peer-to-peer' system e.g. Microsoft Networks).
- For long distance communication within an organisation, or between organisations, wide area networks (WANs) are employed, either using the public network or private rented lines.
- LANs can be connected to WANs, if required. This allows users of a LAN in the Glasgow office to contact LAN users in the London office and exchange messages/data.
- LANs can also connect to other LANs; this is known as 'internetworking'.

LANs and UNIX
LANs are not multi-user systems in the way we understand mainframe and mini computer systems.
- A modern LAN is typically a collection of stand-alone PCs that are all capable of independent processing. They share the same files and resources from the common server. However, each user will run a copy of an application in his/her own node's memory.   A user can load an application from the server and spend all day creating data. Apart from the initial download of the application, there need be no further communication between the node and the server. At the end of the day, the data from the node memory may be sent down the cable to be stored in the server disk.   At its busiest, every user is attempting to move files between the server and the nodes at the same time.   At its quietest, the server is sitting unused, while all the individual nodes are carrying out activities in their own machines.
- A mini computer, in comparison, would connect to a number of terminals and carry out all the processing, for all the users, within the UNIX box. Each station would be given a small share of the mini's CPU time on a 'time sharing' basis. However, since the user's waiting time between bursts of activity is also small, the station activity appears continuous. All the users' data is held and updated centrally; no data is held in the memory of individual stations. This system is ideal for situations where many users are doing essentially the same job (e.g. simultaneous sales producing simultaneous stock-control updates).   Normally, the mini computer is specially built for the job, with extra fast processing power. The normal PC MSDOS operating system would not be up to handling the task and the more powerful (but less friendly) UNIX operating system is the most common operating system for a mini.

Performance tests suggest that LANs outperform UNIX systems in most activities.

It is possible to connect a range of terminals (machines with I/O facilities and no processing power) to a network via a 'Terminal Server' and special extra TCP/IP software.

Advantages of a Local Area Network

The main advantages are listed below (although there is a degree of overlap between them):

Shared Resources

Networks allow individual users to share the organisation's hardware and software resources.

SOFTWARE

Any file on the server hard disk is available to every user.   Thus, only one copy of each program need be stored, rather than, say, 100 copies residing on 100 local hard disks.   When a program is upgraded, there is only a single copy to be tackled - not the 100 versions spread throughout the building.   This also ensures that every user is using the same, most modern, version of the software.

DATA

Similarly, any data in the organisation is available to every station in the entire building. This advantage has led to the development of LAN applications such as multi-user databases, where the input at any computer terminal updates the records for access by any other node on the system. Information is usually the most expensive item in an organisation, including its collection storage and maintenance. It varies regularly and to keep it up-to-date and available is both onerous and expensive. The distribution of the inputting and access to the database over the whole organisation provides the optimum use of the data.

HARDWARE:

Peripherals are often a small part of cost of running a large computer system.   However, specialised devices are often very expensive and are usually located in particular parts of the building.   Such items include:

Plotters	Phototypesetters	Colour lasers
Optical character readers	CD banks	ISDN lines
High capacity disk drives	Tape streamers	Internet links

On a network, access to these devices would be available to all nodes, in any part of the building.   This ensures the maximum use of these resources (e.g. most people only use a printer for less than 5% of the time they use a computer). It also allows connection of devices from different manufacturers.

Finally, the hardware is easily expanded, with little disruption to the existing system.

Cost

Since all the data is stored on the server disk, the organisation need only buy diskless workstations. Money can be saved - or spent on upgrading the rest of the node. There is an increasing demand for node stations with a fast processor and a single floppy drive. The new Macintosh, for example, is sold without any floppy drive.

Efficiency

On a non-networked office, the failure of a machine meant that the programs and data in that machine could not be accessed until the machine was repaired.   This is not a problem on a computer network since, in the event of a node going down, a user can carry on his/her normal work from another node. Of course, if the server was to fail, that it is a very serious matter indeed, since it holds the entire programs/data for the whole company.   This can be overcome by rigorous backup facilities and the use of backup servers that can take over in the event of a main server failure.   This is an expensive solution - but cheap in comparison to potential losses from the lack of computer facilities.   In general then, a network organisation is more efficient than a collection of individual PCs.

On top of the extra hardware efficiencies must be added all the benefits from file sharing and the flexible working possible on a network.   There is now a growing trend to not only sharing resources but also sharing the actual processing power of the system.   The collective computing power of the many individual PCs is awesome, if it can be properly tapped.   If some of the processing tasks can be given to an idle CPU, then the overall processing is speeded up.

Speed

Ordinary telephone connections between computers, using modems, handle data at rates up to 56Kbps. ISDN can increase the rate to 64Kbps or 128Kbps.   In comparison, a LAN can work at 10Mbps, 100Mbps or even 1Gbps. Since a single character requires 8 bits to represent it, a 10Mbps service could transfer the equivalent of the entire contents of a 3½" disk in a single second.

Communication

Most companies have resources that are not connected to the humble desktop PC. These include other networks, the company mainframe, and other branches over public or leased lines (e.g. Kilostream), etc.   Connecting these resources to a network means that they are then all available to every station in the network.

Other communication benefits are:
- Outside resources - via modems, fax machines, ISDN lines, other leased lines and the public packet switched network. This gives access to vast on-line databases containing scientific, commercial, and industrial information.
- Electronic mail - The simplest version sends a message. The sender is informed if the destination station is not connected, otherwise a message appears on the destination screen. Mail servers will store a message if the destination is not connected and will deliver the message when the station does connect.
- FAX gateway - This is a dedicated PC with fax board(s). Cheaper than single-user boards. Most allow faxing via the existing e-mail system. These computer systems use the same standards as normal fax therefore they can communicate with any other fax machine in the world.

Flexible Working

The integration of communications with networks allows for a much more flexible working environment:
- TELEWORKING
  Packages, such as Crosstalk, allow modem access to the computer network over the normal telephone line. Work can now be carried out remotely from the work place - known as *'teleworking'*. This work might be able to be carried out at a time and a place that suits the user, since the network is available 24 hours a day. A salesperson can log in from his/her hotel in the evening and upload the day's orders. A programmer can write software from home and be paid by results. A director can control the business from the comfort of Monte Carlo. Students can download the week's work, write the essays and send them back to their personal directories for marking. Lecturers can stay at home and still mark and tutor students.
- DATA LOGGING
  Data logging (e.g. quantity measurement or salesmen's orders) on portable machines can be transferred via the telephone network to the office server for processing.

Security

Although there is localised processing, control is centralised.   The network supervisor can have a great degree of control over who can enter the network, what directories are available to a particular user and what file activity is allowed.

Currency/Integrity

In non-networked companies, copies of the same data may reside in many different station hard disks. When an item of data is altered, the data on every machine has to be updated.   This is time-consuming and error-prone. If one station is not updated, then the 'facts' depend on the machine interrogated.

Disadvantages

Network systems, while providing distinct advantages, also create possible problems:
- An 'error' in one node may propagate through the network, as in the 1987 Stock Market crash.
- More costly to manage, in terms of time, management rules and technical skills.
- Always costs more than first thought.
- Less secure - there are more access points to the same data.
- More complex software.
- Installation problems; the system takes at least 6 months to set up properly.
- Easy for viruses to propagate through.

It is generally believed that LANs will not replace mainframes/minis for payroll and general ledger applications. Nevertheless, the sales of LANs and mini computer systems will dominate most future applications, apart from the area of super-computers used in defence, national budgeting, etc.

Features Of LANs

When viewing a LAN's characteristics, the following factors are a useful guide:

SIMPLICITY
  The system is relatively simple to configure and use. Working should be transparent to the novice user. Users can employ a large number of facilities with minimal training.

EXPANDABILITY
  New nodes can be added to the system with little hardware and software disruption.

RELIABILITY
  Reliability is of great importance in a network.   For the server it is absolutely vital.   LANs, once the initial settling down problems are overcome, are renowned for their reliability.

INTEGRITY / LOW ERROR RATE
  WAN error rates can be up to 1 in 100,000. In comparison, LANs can be up to 1 in 100,000,000.

CONNECTIVITY

Well over a hundred different LAN systems are currently on sale - with differences in hardware and software. Many hardware and software incompatibilities exist. This causes problems both with connecting together networks and running applications over them. There is a pressing need for agreed standards, to make applications independent of the media and the hardware. LANs often need to be connected to other systems (e.g. to other LANs, to WANs and to mainframes and mini computers).

SPEED

Important, as this is the potential system bottleneck. The measurement of data transfer speeds is difficult, since the actual speeds rarely correspond to the theoretical speeds. The basic measure of data transfer speed is *'bits per second'*, being the number of binary digits that can be transferred between one machine and another in a second. If it takes eight bits to represent each character and a 4Mbps system is in use, data should be transferred at the rate of 500,000 characters per second. So, a 1/2MB file should theoretically be transferred between nodes in a single second. However, the system has to transfer other information - such as the source address, the destination address, etc., with each data packet. Also, the same medium has to be shared with other communicating nodes. Networks can be considered as grouped into four categories of speed:

LOW SPEED-	Less then 1Mbps, used in small groups (less than 6) usually with low-cost systems.
MEDIUM SPEED-	Between 1Mbps and 10Mbps - for larger groups up to 50(as little as 20 if there is heavy traffic on the system).
HIGH SPEED-	Greater than 10Mbps - for large groups or very heavy traffic.
TOP SPEED-	100Mbps up to 1000Mbps - for large organisations or video/multimedia.

LAN Topologies

'Topology' refers to the way in which the nodes are connected to the media, to form the complete network system. Two systems dominate the LAN market - IBM's Token Ring system and the Ethernet system, which uses a *'bus'* topology.

Bus

Half of the world's LANs are this type. Invented by Xerox in the mid-70s, the Ethernet bus system is an international standard. The original configuration was a common data-carrying coaxial cable that wound its way through the different areas of the building and individual stations connected at any point on this cable. Current implementations use twisted pair cable instead of coaxial cable.

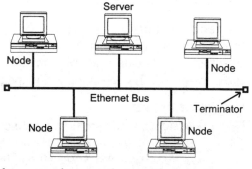

Each station has a *'tap'* on to the bus. Data from a node is transmitted in *'packets'* and each node on the network receives the transmission. Only a packet with the matching address is processed by the receiving node (i.e. station 17 only responds to packets with a destination address of 17). A failure in any one station affects only that station; the rest of the network functions normally.

Each end of an Ethernet coaxial cable had *'terminators'* fitted. These are special connectors that contain 50ohm resistors to absorb the signal thus preventing unwanted reflections of the transmission on the cable. If the signal were allowed to reach the end of a cable and reflect back down to the cable, it would interfere with the fresh signal and cause loss of data integrity. Ethernet runs at 10Mbps on ThinNet, ThickNet or UTP. It can support 30 stations with ThinNet and 100 with ThickNet. The minimum distance between taps is 0.5m. Modern implementations use *'hubs'* to which the stations connect in a star-like layout. Since the cable is not run serially, there is no minimum distance between stations and the each station can be up to 100m distant from the hub. Novell's various versions of NetWare and Windows NT currently dominate the operating system market.

Token-Ring

Ring topologies were slow to develop, until the *'token ring'* system was adopted by IBM. This system has around a third of the market but is threatened by new faster technologies (see later). It is aimed at the larger end of the market, since it covers great distances and allows large amounts of users, through linking of individual rings. The ring is a closed loop, with nodes connected via repeating elements, known as *'ring interface*

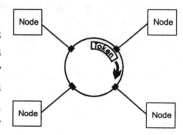

units'. These units boost the signal before passing it on, hence the greater distances covered. There is no central controller. All devices on the ring have equal status. The ring is a one-way system, with all data going clockwise. Data circulates round the loop as a series of point-to-point links between adjacent nodes. The right to send data passes from one node to another in an ordered sequence determined by a token. The token grants permission to send data. A node with a message/data to send waits for an empty token to arrive. It then accepts the token, inserts the message/data into it and sends it on. This token passes the data in the form of a *'packet'*. The packet contains both the source and destination addresses, as well as the data itself. Each node checks the incoming packet, to see whether the destination code is its own. When the data arrives at the destination node, it is copied into a local buffer and the packet is marked to indicate its acceptance. The packet continues round the loop, returning to the sending node with the information that the data was received. Any node that is not the destination node passes the token on unaltered. Token Ring systems use coaxial, twisted pair or optic cable. Older versions operated at 4Mbps; newer versions run at 16Mbps; it can run at 100Mbps on fibre optic cable.

Advantages:
- Copes with heavy traffic better than bus systems (see later).
- Covers greater distances than bus systems, since the signal is re-generated at each node.

Disadvantages:
- If one repeater fails, the entire system goes down.

The network topology does not determine the cabling layout. Although the ring requires that nodes be connected in an electrical loop, the actual wiring need not be run round a building in a physical circle. In fact, it is very common to connect a group of nodes to a network via a *'concentrator'*. The wiring of these nodes is brought to one location and they are then connected together in a ring within the concentrator. As can be seen, the network topology is a ring but the cabling topology is that of a star. Of course, an actual system would have a server in the ring!

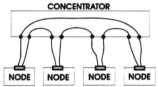

A variation on IBM's system is the *'Cambridge Ring'*, which circulates multiple tokens. This increases the throughput as nodes can use the first free circulating token.

Star

Star networks constitute less than 10% of the market. The wiring to each node radiates from a single point - hence the *'star'* description. All traffic is switched and controlled by a central controller - the *'hub'*. A node wishing to transmit data to another node must make a request to the central controller, which will set up a dedicated path between the respective nodes. Once established, the nodes communicate as if they were on a dedicated point-to-point system.

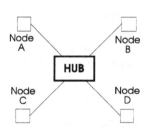

Advantages:
- Protocol may be simple - only the two stations involved in a link need to be involved.
- Because information transmission does not involve all parts of the network, the overall speed of the network may be higher than the maximum transmission rate allowed. For example, station A can transmit to station B, at the same time as station C transmits to station D.
- All data transmitted passes through the Central Hub, so the network can be easily monitored.
- Additional stations are easily and cheaply added, for the cost of the station plus the cabling.

Disadvantages:
- The initial cost of installing the network is high because the expensive Central Hub is required, even if the system only consists of a couple of nodes.
- Problems at the hub close the whole system down.

Note

Most networks using twisted pair cabling connect the computers to the network via hubs. These are different from the hubs mentioned in the star network. In a <u>star</u> network, the hub is the main server processor. Hubs in a <u>bus</u> system are only a means of station connection. The server is wired to the hub and stations connect to one of the hub's 8, 16 or more ports on the basis of one socket per UTP lead. Although wired like a star, it remains a bus system since all stations receive all transmissions. UTP hubs are mains operated, to supply the internal electronics used to balance the signals. A managed hub has more electronics to accept even more PCs and create sub-networks inside the hub. It programs connections between ports and can manage other hubs (e.g. for monitoring and diagnosis purposes).

LANs and Collisions

The benefits of a LAN flow from the fact that many stations share the same transmission medium. However, this is also a potential source of problems. If two or more stations attempt to transmit simultaneously, then the signals interfere with each other. The result is that no useful intelligence is received by any station. This happening is known as a *'collision'*. All LANs, then, have to use a method of preventing or limiting this effect.

Collision Detection

Bus networks, such as Ethernet use this method. It is described as a Carrier Sense Multiple Access-Collision Detection system (CSMA-CD) and uses the principle of *'listen before speaking'*. Here, a station that wishes to send a message will listen on the medium and only start to transmit when the medium is free. It is still possible, however, that two stations could sense the medium as free and begin to transmit simultaneously. An Ethernet station, therefore, listens to its own broadcast, to see whether it is being interfered with. If a collision is detected, the stations immediately cease transmission. The stations then wait for a while before making another attempt at transmission. These are random delays, to prevent the same machines making their second attempt at the same time.

This is improves overall throughput, since it greatly reduces wasted transmission time. However, where many stations are trying to use the medium (during peak spells) there will still be a great deal of wasted time, as the number of collisions will rise. The rise in collisions and the subsequent decline in throughput develop at an alarming rate.

Collision Avoidance

Collision detection is an effective system and is the most common system. However, it has a serious flaw - the very act of detecting a collision means that the collision has already taken place! The node can take measures to overcome the problem, but the damage (in terms of time wastage) has still occurred. An improved method would be to prevent the collision taking place in the first instance. By its design, a token-passing system can only have a single user packet on the system at any one time - therefore the possibility of a collision is nil. This saves wasting time and increases throughput.

Note

As the traffic on a collision-detection system increases, the system performance deteriorates. Useful working is no more than 30-40% of the potential maximum of the system. The traffic on a token-passing system will maintain a steady rate over a wide range of traffic demands. A 4Mbps token ring system can provide as much usable bandwidth as a 10Mpbs Ethernet segment. A 16Mbps system can run at over 80% capacity without problems.

Components of a Network

Computers

At the simplest, the computers attached to a network can be normal run-of-the-mill PCs. The existing PCs in an organisation can have a network interface card fitted in one of the expansion sockets of the machine and a few files added to the hard disk; the result is a network node.

There is a growing market for LAN *'workstations'*. These can be specially built PCs with Ethernet hardware already built on to the board. This opens up a new market for PCs. Since most, or all, of the user's processing will take place at the local node, it would be efficient to have as fast a processor as possible in the local station. However, since all, or most, of the user's data is held centrally, there is no need for a local hard disk. This allows manufacturers to offer high-performance machines for the LAN market, where the cost savings on the disk are spent on faster processors and/or higher resolution monitors.

Manufacturers provide a range of machines that are completely diskless - sometimes called a *'LANstation'*. This offers advantages as far as security is concerned. It greatly reduces the ability of users to purloin copies of data from the organisation, since it is impossible to download data from the network. It also eliminates virus problems on the network, since users cannot bring in and use their favourite games. In such systems, the station is fitted with a remote boot ROM system, which allows the node to be booted directly from the server; the node retrieves the files from the server that it needs to boot. Also available are stations that only have a floppy drive fitted, to allow the transfer of data (where this is required), while retaining major cost benefits.

Network Computers

Network computers, NCs, are computer that have been designed as *'network centric computing'* systems. Earlier workstations were really cut-down PCs that were sold for connection to a network. Network Computers have been specially designed as LAN stations. They are housed in cases about the size of this book and have no disks, no software and not even an operating system. A flash ROM in the NC contains a program that locates the server and downloads all its software from it. The server requires additional software to handle NCs.

Network Interface Cards

The network interface card (NIC) is a device to connect the computer on to the network cabling. In most cases, it is a card that fits into the expansion bus of the computer motherboard. In other cases, it is separate unit that attaches to the computer's serial, parallel or PCMCIA port. External units are particularly useful for portable and notebook computers, where there is no space for internal expansion (these units are often referred to as *'lan adapters'*). Interface units come in a range of types, sizes and speeds. Performance of interface units is a key factor in network performance.

The interface card takes the data from the node computer and puts it into the appropriate format before sending it on the cable to another interface card. When the card receives data it puts into a form that can be recognised by the computer. To achieve this, the card must perform many operations - e.g. buffers must be checked, requests must be acknowledged, sessions must be established, perhaps tokens are sent, collisions may be detected, etc.

The list of activities can be categorised thus:

- Host-card communications
- Packet formation
- Encoding/decoding
- Handshaking
- Buffering
- Parallel-serial conversion
- Cable access
- Transmission/reception

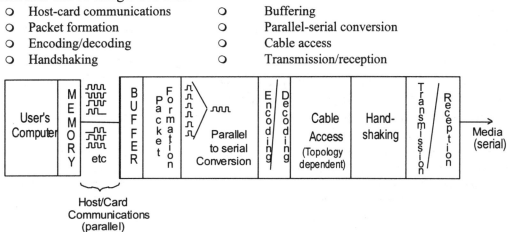

Host-Card Communications

The first need is to move data back and forward between the PC and the interface unit.

This can be achieved in three ways:

Direct Memory Access (DMA)

All Intel-based computers come with a DMA controller that handles the transfer of data from an input/output device to the PC's main memory, thereby relieving the PC's main processor. The controller informs the main CPU that it needs to perform DMA. The CPU then gives up control of the computer bus to the DMA controller. The DMA controller can then take data from the card and place it directly into memory. When all the data is in memory, the DMA controller passes control of the bus back to the computer CPU and informs it of the amount of data placed in memory.

I/O Mapping

A common version is a *'memory-mapped'* system. The computer CPU allocates some of the 640k main memory space to the interface unit (around 12k). Data is read from the card straight into this memory area. There are no extra instructions required to get data from the card, since it is already sitting in the computer memory. All that is required is the movement of data from one part of the memory to another, using standard memory movement instructions. The Western Digital token ring cards use the memory mapped method.

Shared Memory

This is similar to I/O mapping in that the CPU memory is shared with the card's processor. However, both the card and the CPU do their work on the data in the same area, eliminating any subsequent transfers.

Comparisons

○ The shared Memory method is the fastest but is the least used for various cost and execution reasons.

○ The DMA method allows the computer CPU to perform other tasks while it is transferring data (as long as these tasks don't involve memory access).

○ I/O mapping takes up main memory and doesn't relieve the CPU from any work; but it is still usually faster than the DMA method.

Bus Sizes

Interface cards were originally 8-bit but now have 16-bit or 32-bit connections to the computer data bus. The wider the data bus, the more data can be transferred in a single operation - i.e. the wider bus cards have a faster performance. The wider bus cards are, naturally, more expensive than more basic models. The older 8-bit models are generally said to be *'NE1000 compatible'* with 16-bit cards being termed *'NE2000 compatible'* and 32-bit cards being *'NE3000 compatible'*. A 16-bit MCA or ISA card handles around 3Mbps while a 32-bit PCI card handles 7Mbps. This means that ISA cards can only handle up to 10Mbps systems, while the PCI cards can handle the faster 100Mbps systems.

Buffering

The interface units are mostly fitted with buffer chips to store data as it moves between the media and the computer. This temporary storage is provided to compensate for the differing speeds of different parts of the process. Data is received into the interface at a faster rate than it can be processed (e.g. being converted to/from a packet, being converted from serial or parallel). The interface holds the data while it is processed. It is possible to use the PC's RAM as a buffer area, although this takes up main memory and can be slow.

Packet Formation

Part of the responsibility of a network is to give each user a fair proportion of media time. So, if a user wishes to download a giant file from the server, other users do not require to patiently wait until this is transmitted. Instead, all traffic between nodes is composed of subsections of files that can then be interspersed on the media. In this way, a user requiring a small file from the server can have that need served during the time a larger file is being transferred.

A *'packet'* is the smallest independent unit of data that can be sent on the media. The Interface Card has the responsibility of breaking a file into packets before sending them onto the media. Conversely, it will assemble the incoming packets into a coherent file for the computer. The packet's size and layout are dependent on the network's access method. Each packet has three sections:

- The header includes information on the packet's source address and destination address.

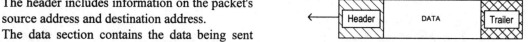

- The data section contains the data being sent (e.g. word-processing or spreadsheet files, or program file). The data section can be as large as 12k but is usually between 1k and 4k (Ethernet, for example has a data section size of 4kbytes).

- The trailer section contains information that is used for checking whether the data has arrived without any corruption. The information is subjected to a mathematical calculation that aims to produce a unique number for each different packet (for the mathematically minded, a constant is derived from a polynomial expression). This is called the *'cyclic redundancy check'* - CRC - and the resultant value is sent in the trailer section. When a node receives the packet, the same calculation is applied to the information. If it produces the same value as in the trailer, then no corruption has taken place - any corrupted data will result in a different calculated CRC value.

Parallel-Serial Conversion

The data that comes from the computer to the interface card is in parallel format. However, the media that carries the transmission is only capable of handling serial transmission. The interface card has the task of converting the data from parallel to serial form. Serial transmission is slower than parallel transmission, hence the need for buffering previously mentioned.

Encoding/Decoding

When data is made up into a packet and converted to serial format, it can be sent down the transmission medium, as a series of offs and ons.

At its simplest, the interface card could transmit a binary 1 as a positive voltage and a binary 0 as a negative voltage. At the other end, the card would translate the series of voltages into a stream of binary 0s and 1s.

However, most interface cards use a less error-prone method known as *'Manchester Coding'*.   This is a *'polar code'* - which means that it does not have positive and negative swings.   A logic high - i.e. a bit 1 - is represented by 0v and a logic low - i.e. bit 0 - is represented by -2.05v.   The serial data uses a *'50% duty cycle'* - which means that the time allocated to each bit of the data stream is divided into two periods.   The first time period holds the actual bit representation.   The second period provides a signal that is always the opposite of the first period.   In this way, a constant change is guaranteed and this is used to ensure that the received signal is accurately synchronised, so that no false decoding occurs.

Media Access
The interface card also has the task of gaining access to the media (e.g. the cable).   This is no simple matter, since only one card can effectively communicate with the media at the one time.   Access is gained to the media in different ways, dependent on the network protocol in use (e.g. Ethernet, etc)

Handshaking
For successful transmission of a packet from one card to another, both cards have to be using the same parameters.   Typical parameters might be maximum packet size, buffer sizes, how many packets before an answer, acknowledge time-outs (how long to wait for an answer), etc.   Before the data packets are sent, the originating card transmits its parameters; the receiving card responds with its parameters.   The most sophisticated card then lowers its specification to match the other.

Transmission/Reception
The lowest level of card activity is to interface all this activity to the media itself.

The transmitting card translates the data stream into a signal of sufficient power to be successfully transmitted down the media.   At the other end, the receiving card has to take the varying signal and convert it back into the data stream for decoding, serial/parallel conversion and depacketing.

Modern network cards are both 10Mbps and 100Mbps compatible.

Node Software
To add a computer to a network, extra software is added to the computer, to allow it to interface with its new network card and to communicate with the network server.

The following software components have to be added:

Device drivers
This software controls input and output to and from the network card. The installation process varies. In Windows 95 and later, installation of the device can be performed through the *'Control Panel'* icon for *'Add/Remove Hardware'*.   With Plug and Play cards, the device is automatically detected and the driver is chosen from Windows' own built-in list or from the NIC's installation disk.   In this respect, installing the device driver is much the same as installing any other device driver.

In DOS, this driver is usually a 'plug-in' TSR such as E2000B.EXE for an NE2000 compatible network card.   These driver files are also called Multiple Link Interface Drivers (MLID's) and can normally be found on a disk supplied with the card.   In Windows, these drivers are listed as Adapters, as can be seen by viewing the Network Neighbourhood Properties.

DOS network clients will often require an additional piece of software called the Link Support Layer (LSL), which serves as an interface between the protocol stacks (below) and the network card driver. This provides functionality that the protocol stack would otherwise need to implement itself.   This functionality in Windows is handled by the device driver itself.   The device drivers cover the OSI Transport layer, providing error recovery and flow control; and the network layer, which handles routing.

Network Protocols
The protocol is the method of communication between network clients and servers. It may be thought of as a language, in that only clients and servers who have the same protocol are able to understand each other.   There are a variety of Protocols available, but by far the most common are TCP/IP that is widely used by Microsoft, and IPX/SPX which was created by Novell.   Other protocols include Appletalk, SDLC or Token-ring.

There are a number of differences between protocols, but from a user's point of view the main difference is the software that uses those protocols. This software is called *'client software'* and is a separate component despite often being closely linked to the protocol. Network protocols cover the presentation layer of the OSI model, which may provide encryption, compression etc; and the session layer, establishing and maintaining connections with other machines. The exact procedure varies between Windows 95/98 and NT, but basically consists of a driver, similar in some respects to the device driver, being added.

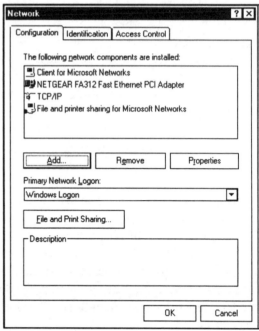

In Windows 95/98, installation of a network protocol is implemented through right-clicking on *'Network Neighborhood'*, then choosing the *'Properties'*, *'Add'* and *'Protocol'* options. The appropriate protocol can then be chosen for installation. When a protocol is installed in Windows, it is usually bound to all existing adapters, so some of these bindings may have to be removed if needed. The Network dialog can also be used to remove or configure any component, although in most cases the standard settings are acceptable. The *'File and Print sharing'* allows the user to select to share either files, or printers, or both. If File and Printer Sharing is not installed then choosing to share files this way will install it automatically.

Each protocol has to be *'bound'* to a particular device driver. In other words the operating system has to be told which protocol(s) are to be used over which network device. In this way, it is possible to have more than one networking device. This is useful in Windows because Dial-Up Networking is considered a network device. For example, you could have an NE2000 network card, with IPX bound to it, in order to operate over a Novell network; and a modem, with Dial-Up Networking drivers, and TCP/IP bound to the DUN driver.

Installation of a network protocol, in DOS, is a matter of executing the appropriate TSR. For example, an IPX network might require the running of the IPXODI.EXE file as well as the LSL.EXE file (although in most cases LSL is loaded before the device driver so that it can interrogate the device driver).

Client software

These are the programs, utilities and services that use the network protocols and the layers underneath. Client software is not necessarily a driver file; anything that directly uses the network protocol is considered client software. For example, a Novell client (for logging in to NetWare networks) will use the IPX protocol, while the Microsoft client (for NT or other Microsoft server products) would use TCP/IP. Internet packages, such as Telnet, FTP or Web Browsers, use TCP/IP. Other packages could use any one or more protocols. This is the *'application layer'* of the OSI model. In Windows 95 and later, the client is considered a *'component'* just like the network adapter driver, and is part of Network Neighborhood properties. It is installed in the same way as network protocols. Internet packages such as those listed above can directly utilise the network protocol without going through the Novell client (or similar client) but they are not considered as components.

However, note that after clicking *'Add'* from the *'Configuration'* tab, there is another option to install *'services'*. A service in Windows is the inverse of client. A client allows the PC access to a server's files or printers, while a service allows other PCs to access its files and printers. See peer-to-peer Networks, later, for more details on file sharing.

In DOS, which generally does not have multi-tasking capabilities, the client software varies, but almost always relies on the client driver. For example, the TSR files NETX.EXE or VLM.EXE can give Novell connectivity and is used by other software to access Novell networks.

Servers

Most networks are based on a *'client/server'* architecture, where one or more computers are at the operational heart of the system.   They handle all the other machines' disk storage requirements and act as a data exchange - routing data to any machine that requires it.   These central machines are called the *'servers'* or *'dedicated servers'*.   A *'non-dedicated server'* is a machine that carries out the functions of a file server, while also being able to be used as normal PC machine. This is often referred to as a *'peer to peer'* network.   It is OK in small systems but would slow things down on a larger system, since the processor would have to share its time between network activities and the activities of the user at the server machine.

There are two types of server -

Utility servers -

These servers carry out the routine roles or the specialist roles in the network, where required (in a small organisation there may be no need of specialist utility servers).

Examples of this type are:

STANDARD :   file servers, print servers.

SPECIALIST :   fax, mail, Internet and CD servers, modem pool servers, micro-to-mainframe gateways.

Application servers -

These servers perform computational tasks for network users (see client/server software later)

Large systems will have a number of servers on the one network system.

Characteristics Of Servers

In the earliest days of networking, manufacturers marketed their LAN servers as specially made machines.   These were overpriced and users realised that a standard PC could be used as a server, if it was powerful and reliable enough.   Consequently, high-performance PCs now capture much of the server sales market.   Dedicated servers are still produced.   They are dedicated boxes of various shapes and sizes, often with no monitor or keyboard.   Since most network activities can be organised from any node, the lack of add-ons is not a disadvantage.   In fact, it is claimed as an advantage, as it provides an extra level of security.   Some of the advertised benefits of dedicated servers over PCs are hype. However, dedicated servers can have distinct advantages.

The following criteria may act as a yardstick for choosing a server:

Speed

The raw processing speed of the server CPU is not as vitally important as it may appear at first glance. Buying the fastest dual Pentium III chip server may not produce a very significant improvement over a machine with a slower, older chip.   This is because the speed of the processor is generally less a bottleneck than the speed of the server's disk drives and NICs.   Consider the following:

- A file server activity does not require much computing time, in comparison to the disk access time.
- If the transmission media (i.e. NICs, cable) is unable to transfer the data quickly, then there is no benefit in having the server process that data at a vastly faster rate.
- Consequently, faster computers do not necessarily produce faster server throughput.

The above is not true in many cases. The CPU speed is important in the following situations:

- Where the server acts as an SQL server.   In this case, the server has to perform considerable computational tasks in addition to a normal server role.
- Where the server runs particular NLMs (Network Loadable Module) that have considerable computational roles.
- Where the server Interface Card is not of the *'bus master'* type.   Here, the NIC circuitry does not relieve the server CPU of data transfer tasks - i.e. biggest part of server's work.
- Some PCs use a Digital Signal processing chip or a virtual peripheral, which means the CPU ends up doing many of the tasks mentioned earlier (like packet formation and parallel to serial conversion).
- If the machine is connected to two networks, (see below) it may be used to provide routing/bridging or packet filtering services between them using software.

The Pentium III is fitted in most new servers.

Multi-Processing

Many servers are fitted with two processors and some include the option to fit further CPUs. This is particularly useful in client/server applications (see later).

Bus Size

The data bus of the node machine is connected to the data bus of the NIC when the card is plugged into the node's expansion slot.   A wide data bus would speed up the transfer of data from the node's memory into the NIC's buffer area (e.g. a 64-bit bus could transfer 64-bit binary data in a single operation, while a 32-bit bus would require to transfer the same 64-bit data as two separate 32-bit operations). In general, a wider data bus speeds up node/NIC communications and reduces bottlenecks.

The AT series, and its clones, used a 16-bit ISA bus and this proved too slow for network I/O tasks. In response, IBM introduced MCA (Micro Channel Architecture). This is a *'bus mastering'* system and it supports 32-bit cards.   However, it hit a number of problems:

- The cards for MCA won't fit ISA slots and MCA slots don't support ISA hardware.
- Users are concerned that they may end up tied in to IBM as a sole supplier.

As a result, other manufacturers have not taken up the MCA system.

To produce a viable alternative, a consortium led by Compaq introduced the EISA system.   This was also a bus mastering system with a 32-bit data transfer rate.   However, it remained AT-bus compatible. Most network systems moved to EISA-based servers but now all current servers use PCI buses.

Memory

The memory of the server is used for a wide range of caching, buffering and other activities.   The minimum RAM for reasonable performance is around 64MB.   The system will run with less memory but the performance will degrade (e.g. a small disk cache allocation means more disk accesses, a small buffer allocation may result in lost packets).   The system may require more memory if it is carrying out heavy processing tasks such as handling databases. Most current servers use PC100 memory modules or RAMBUS modules.

Storage

The server disk drive(s) store all application programs and data for the whole organisation. This demands that the drives are the largest, fastest and most reliable that money can buy.

Disk Speed

The old disk drive technology is being replaced on PCs with the more efficient UDMA system.   On servers, and high specification PCs, the main drive technology is SCSI (Small Computer Systems Interface).   This is the most popular server disk choice and has an access time of between 4ms and 10ms.   Current SCSI card transfer rates are quoted by manufacturers as being 80MB/s.   However, even the fastest SCSI drives currently available cannot deliver a sustained data rate close to the interface's speed.   Huge data rates are delivered, but only for a few thousandths of a second, with the help of the drive's on board memory buffers.

Disk Fault Tolerance

Due to the vital role of data in any organisation, it is not acceptable to have only a single copy on a single server drive.   Although organisations have rigorous and systematic backup procedures, this is insufficient for situations where data is rapidly changing. To ensure that data is always available, networks make use of multiple storage techniques such as disk shadowing and disk mirroring.   The objective is to keep two copies of the data on different drives, in case one copy is corrupted. Of course, there is still a problem if the two drives are in the same server - and that server breaks down! In *'mission critical'* applications (those where it is essential that processing must continue), users employ a system of *'server mirroring'* or *'server clustering'*. Here, if a server goes down, a duplicate server kicks in immediately, with the same applications and data.   So, every update to the current server is also made to the shadow server.

Raid Technology

In large installations with multiple disk drives, access can be speeded up with a process known as *'striping'*.   The data is written/read in parallel fashion over different drives. An extension of this principle is *'RAID'* technology. This is a *'Redundant Array of Inexpensive (or Independent) Disks'* and uses the following features:

- A set of disks is configured to perform like a single large drive.
- Redundancy is built in; extra disks are used, not to store data, but to protect the data.
- Disks are *'hot swappable'*; they can be removed and replaced while the network remains operational; the network carries on without loss of data.

The table shows the levels of protection available.

RAID Level	Method	Advantages	Disadvantages
0	Basic disk striping	Improves performance	No protection. Any disk failing collapses the system.
1	Disks are mirrored	Improves performance. Easily implemented.	Expensive as it requires all data disks to be duplicated (mirrored).
0+1	Data striping on mirrored drives	Improves performance. High level of data protection.	Expense. Slower writes.
2	2 or 3 check disks for every 4 data disks.	Improves performance. High level of data protection.	Expensive. Rarely implemented.
3	One additional disk stores parity bits.	Common, low-cost choice, requiring only one additional disk.	Slows when many disk write requests are implemented.
4	One additional disk stores ECC data.	Improves performance. Can handle multiple read requests.	Only handles one write operation at a time.
5	ECC data spread over all array's disks	Can handle read and write requests simultaneously.	Slow to rebuild after a disk crash.
6	ECC data written to two separate disks.	Good data security, as two disks can fail and data can be rebuilt.	Slower performance than Level 5.

Reliability

Possibly the most important of all factors when purchasing a server is the issue of reliability. A reliable network of average speed is much more productive than a faster system that is always breaking down. Influencing factors are:

- Whether servers have SETUP and diagnostics built in. Some systems are configured to dial a service engineer as soon as a fault occurs.
- The use of an *'Uninterrupted Power Supply'* - (UPS). This smoothes out mains spikes and fluctuations and - in the event of a complete power failure - provides a temporary supply to allow the data to be saved to disk. Some servers have a built-in UPS.
- The use of a standby CPU, in case the main chip fails. This is a bit extreme but might be regarded as important in mission-critical work.
- The replacement of NICs, graphics cards and disk controllers with built-in controllers and interfaces on the server main printed circuit board (PCB). This provides an increased MTBF rate. In other words, this area of the system does not break down so often! It also frees up valuable expansion slots.

Peer-To-Peer LANs

Most medium and large systems use a dedicated server to control the network. There is a trend, in smaller organisation of say less than 10 users, to adopt a network system that has no main server. Instead, all the facilities of a node (i.e. local disk, local printer, etc.) are available to all others on the network. This is known as *'peer-to-peer'* working since there is no master PC. It is simple to implement but provides fewer facilities than a full network operating system. It is also slower, since all PCs also carry out some server activities. It has recently found popularity with hobbyists with several computers at home, for resource sharing or for playing multi-player games. Perhaps the most widely used peer-to-peer system is Microsoft Networking.

Installing Microsoft Networks

The chapter on using DOS and Windows explains how to make use of Microsoft Networking once it is installed. The actual installation procedure is normally quite simple. It can be broken down into the following steps:

Cabling. This is described in more detail elsewhere in this chapter. However, it is worth mentioning that for very simple 10BaseT networks involving just two peer computers, there is no need for a hub. A crossover cable can link the two cables directly – see later in this chapter for a description of a crossover cable.

Attaching. Fitting the network card, and installing the device driver. This is covered in the Upgrading section.

Configuring. This entails the installation and configuration of relevant software. This includes the communication protocol, client software and network services. In the general case, these will be TCP/IP for the protocol, and Client for Microsoft Networks. At the users discretion, the service '*File and Printer sharing for Microsoft Networks*' can be installed for additional functionality.

Windows also has to be configured to attach to a Microsoft Network properly. In *Network Neighborhood / Properties*, the '*Identification*' tab allows the user to change the computer's details on the network. These details are normally entered as the machine is installed, but if installing a new network onto machines or changing the location or user of a machine, this tab allows the PC to be configured on the network. Each Windows installation contains three pieces of network information: Computer name, Workgroup and Computer Description. The name and description are purely for identification purposes on the network, and Windows will give error messages if the Computer Name is the same as another machine's name in the same workgroup.

The Workgroup name tells Windows which Microsoft Workgroup the machine is part of. Machines within the same workgroup will be able to 'see' each other without having to navigate through layers of Network Neighborhood.

The '*Access Control*' tab allows the machine to be set up to share resources in one of two ways. The default is to use share-level access control, as described below. This can be changed to user-level access control, whereby a list of network users and groups is obtained, normally from a server, and access to shared resources can be controlled depending on specific usernames and groups.

File And Printer Sharing

While Microsoft Networking is a widely used method of connecting to NT servers, it is also useful in peer-to-peer networks in allowing file and printer sharing. File sharing through Microsoft Networking is not as flexible or as powerful as using a file server, but it is a relatively inexpensive method of networking.

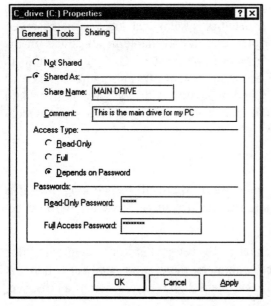

Once Microsoft Networking and File and Printer Sharing drivers are both installed, the user may right-click on any drive, folder, or printer and select the '*Sharing*' option to set up sharing settings for that item. This will bring up a dialog similar to the one shown.

From here the user can control access to his local hard drive, folder or printer. The '*Share Name*' is the name displayed in Explorer on other machines when they view your machine's shared resources. '*Comment*' is just a description that is displayed when these resources are viewed with '*Details*' visible in explorer.

The '*Access Type*' determines how others may access the resource. Read-Only means that only read access is ever allowed, (optionally requiring a password) while '*Full*' means that only full access is ever allowed. (Again with an optional password) The '*Depends on password*' option allows the user to set a password that will allow either type of access. Passwords may be up to 8 characters in length, and may be blank, but if the type of access depends on the password then the Full and Read-Only passwords must be different for obvious reasons.

The Sharing dialog for a printer is similar, but there are no access types, because printers are an output device only. A password may still be set for printer access.

Print Servers

Many users are connected to a particular printer on the network. It is likely that several stations will send text files to the printer over the same period. A printer server will maintain a queue of such files. This appears to be similar to the PRINT command in MS-DOS in that 'spooling' is taking place. In fact, the print server handles the activity differently from MS-DOS. Each incoming print file is copied on to the disk of the print server. The file is then placed in the print queue to wait its turn. When the file is printed, it is deleted from the print server disk. It is also possible, in most networks, to place priorities on a file when it enters the queue, to change the order in which files are printed. A high priority file is allowed to 'jump the queue'.

This system is perfectly acceptable in small, compact systems. The fact that all the documents end up in the one laser printer tray in the one location is not necessarily a problem. However, if the organisation is spread over a wide area, or many floors, then there could be a considerable inconvenience in collecting the printed material. In addition, there could be a problem of security, if sensitive documents are routed to a general pickup point (possibly breaching commercial or personal secrecy, not to mention the Data Protection Act).

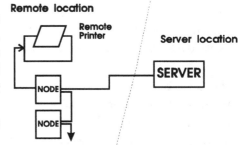

One solution lies in re-directing the de-spooled files from the server to a node on the network. This workstation has a TSR (terminate-and-stay-resident) program in its memory that routes the print file to its local printer. However, ordinary users will use this local node. As such it is liable to be switched off or crashed by the users, making the print process vulnerable.

Note that the term *'remote printing'* means remote from the server, not necessarily remote from the user.

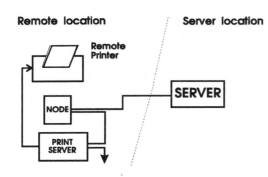

Alternatively, a node on the network could be dedicated to handling an office's printing. The machine will not be used by staff, who will have their own workstations. The file server directs the user requests for printing to this print server which then handles the entire associated file and print activities. This relieves the file server from much of its work and improves the overall efficiency of the system.

Another option for a print server is a printer with its own built-in network card.

LAN Media

The topology of a network describes how one device connects to another. It does not take into account the data transfer speed achievable on the media between the devices. It is analogous to connecting two towns on a map. The route may exist but the pathway could be anything from a country road to a motorway. In other words, the speed of a network is as fast as its slowest link.

There are two main performance factors when considering media:
- Transfer speed (easy to measure)
- Signal reliability

The three most common media types in networks are:
- Coaxial cable
- Twisted pair cable
- Fibre optic cable

Other transmission methods include wireless, infrared, and satellite and microwave techniques. Many systems use coaxial cable but most new installations are using twisted pair cabling.

Wire Systems

By far the most common method of data transmission is to send a simple electrical pulse along a length of wire. This is the basis of both the coaxial cable and twisted-pair systems.

Advantages:

- Cable and its connectors are relatively cheap.
- The cabling is easily installed.
- The ends of the cables are easily connected.

Disadvantages:

- The electrical pulses on the cable are easily upset by electrical and magnetic disturbances.
- The pulses are also upset by temperature and humidity changes.
- The above necessitates careful routing of the network cables (e.g. if cable goes outside to connect to office blocks, it is best to use a pair of modems at either end, rather than use a simple cable link).
- Limited bandwidth compared to fibre optic systems.
- Segment length is short compared to fibre optic systems. Cat3 cable works up to 100m with cat4 and cat5 at 150m.

TWISTED PAIR

This type was initially used in IBM token-rings and Cambridge ring systems. It was also used on StarLan networks (AT&T) and 3Com's Ethernet. The LAN standards of Ethernet, Arcnet and token-ring have been modified to allow them to run on twisted-pair and fibre-optic. Although previously only common in small offices of 10-12 nodes, the faster speeds of the system and the associated electronics has led to a rapid expansion in twisted pair's use as the main medium for larger installations.

Twisted-pair cable is available in both shielded (STP) and unshielded (UTP) varieties.

Unshielded

The basic twisted pair system uses a cable, similar to telephone cable, made up of two insulated copper wires twisted together (usually a total of two pairs). They often use telephone-style jack sockets to connect PCs to the cabling system. The wires are twisted to minimise crosstalk with other cables and to reduce the effects of external interference. It is the cheapest of the media types and, due to its construction, is the easiest to install. Unshielded twisted-pair cabling is used in 4Mbps token-ring systems. Although unshielded pair cable is used for Ethernet systems, additional apparatus such as bridges, equalisers and transceivers can result in the system being significantly more expensive than coaxial cable systems. Nevertheless, unshielded pair is the most common medium for low-cost, short-distance LANs. UTP cables follow the specifications in the chart.

Category	Bandwidth	Typical Data Rate
Cat 1	Up to 20KHz	20Kbps
Cat 2	Up to 4MHz	4Mbps
Cat 3	Up to 16MHz	10Mbps or 16Mbps
Cat 4	Up to 20MHz	16Mbps or 20Mbps
Cat 5	Up to 100MHz	100Mbps or 155Mbps
Cat 6	Up to 250MHz	250Mbps

Note however the differentiation between 'bandwidth' and 'data rate'. Generally speaking a cable can handle one data bit for each Hz. It is of course possible to use less than the maximum data throughput on any given cable. For example Cat3 cable was commonly used in 10Mbps systems despite its maximum bandwidth of 16MHz. On the other hand, it is also possible to exceed the data rate you would expect from such a system, by using data compression. For example ATM can run on Cat5 cable at 155Mbps despite the cable only having a bandwidth of 100MHz.

Shielded

To limit interference problems, the twisted pair can be covered in a metal braid that is grounded. This is known as 'shielded' cable and makes the cable vastly less prone to interference (around 1000 times better). The braid also provides great extra physical strength to the cable. It is this cable that is used for the IBM token-ring (16Mbps) and Cambridge ring system, which runs at 10Mbps. IBM offers both shielded and unshielded versions. The IBM shielded cable is rather more expensive. It consists of two pairs of twisted cable, each wrapped in plastic, then wrapped in aluminium file and copper braid; both pairs being enclosed in a final plastic sheath. The new Cat 7 cable will be shielded UTP.

Plug Wiring

The diagram shows the wiring for the standard RJ-45 plug - the type used with twisted pair.

Token ring systems use pairs 1 and 3.

10Base-T uses pairs 2 and 3.

100Base-T4 uses all four pairs of wires.

100Base-VG uses all four pairs of wires.

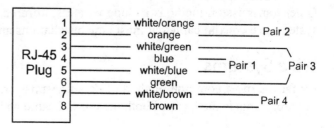

Pin	Function	Data Direction	Function	Pin
1	[TX+]	→	[RX+]	3
2	[TX-]	→	[RX-]	6
3	[RX+]	←	[TX+]	1
6	[RX-]	←	[TX-]	2

Where two nodes require to be connected to each other for PC to PC transfers or game playing, the transmit and receive pins in the cable have to be reversed to create a *'nul modem'* or *'UTP crossover'* cable.

Coaxial Cable

This cable is similar to the type used to connect TV aerials. This was the most popular choice of media, since it offered high speeds, greater bandwidth, fair distances and reasonable costs.

Coaxial cable is designed to minimise the *'skin effect'* problem that affects all wire carriers. As the data transfer rate in a wire is increased, the current in that wire tends to flow along its outer skin. Since there is now less surface to carry the current, there is greater cable resistance, hence greater signal losses. Therefore, twisted pair is less efficient at higher speeds. To help overcome this skin effect, coaxial cable was introduced. Its outer conductor is in the shape of a tube. The copper in its construction is all effectively used. As a result, practically all network operating system software includes drivers for Ethernet cards.

There are two Ethernet standards - thin and thick coaxial cable. Both transmit at 10Mbps. These are called 10Base-2 and 10Base-5. The 10 indicates the maximum system speed in Mbps, the *'Base'* indicates the system runs in baseband mode (see later) and the final number indicates the maximum length allowed for a single cable segment (in hundreds of metres).

Ethernet Thin

Ethernet thin is also known as CheaperNet, ThinNet or 10BASE2. Coaxial cable has two conductors.

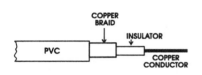

ETHERNET THIN CABLE

The inner conductor is a solid copper core. The outer copper braid acts as the second conductor. The two conductors are held apart by plastic insulation. The cable is enclosed in a PVC casing. The bus cable has to visit every station that is used on the network, where it connects to the node with a BNC connector. ThinNet environments are designed for 30 nodes per segment and a maximum segment length of 185m (extending to 925m with repeaters).   It uses a 50 ohm cable (type RG58) which supports up to 10Mbps baseband working with an error rate of only 1 in 10^7. The coaxial cable has a minimum bending radius of some 15 cm (or six inches).

Ethernet Thick

Also known as Standard, ThickNet or 10BASE5. Its construction is similar to ThinNet, with an added layer of aluminised tape and an extra layer of copper braid.   It is also a 50 ohm baseband cable and uses a coaxial n-type connector.

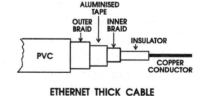

ETHERNET THICK CABLE

Due to its more complex construction, Standard Ethernet is somewhat more expensive than ThinNet. The size of ThickNet (10.3mm thick) also makes it expensive to install, as it is difficult to thread through existing cable runs. However, due its increased conductor size, it suffers fewer losses than ThinNet. Consequently, it covers greater distances (up to 500m, extending to 2500m with repeaters) and handles up to 100 users.   Taps off the cable must be at least 2.5m apart. It is often used as a cabling *'spine'* - i.e. a main backbone from which ThinNet spurs can attach. Minimum bending radius with this type of cable can be 60cm. The use of coaxial cable has declined, in favour of twisted-pair.

Transceivers

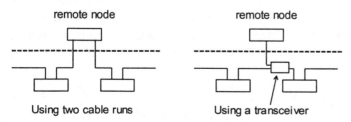

Using two cable runs   Using a transceiver

Notice that, with both thin and thick cable, the station can be situated remotely from the bus cable. To route a cable to the remote site and another cable returning from the site would greatly add to the overall length of the segment.   This in turn limits the remaining distance that can be covered by the cable.

An alternative strategy is to tap a transceiver on to the bus cable.   The node can then be connected to the transceiver by a single cable.   The bus cable is tapped into by connecting a transceiver.   The special cable from the transceiver to the station can be up to 50m in length.   These are expensive cables (costing more than ThickNet cable) and connect to the transceiver with an N series plug.   The other end of the cable connects to the PC card with a 15-pin or 9-pin D connector.   Transceivers have to be at least 2.5m apart and a maximum of 100 transceivers is allowed on a single bus.

Fibre Optic

All electrical conductors suffer from electrical resistance, poor insulation and electrical disturbance, due to unwanted electrical signals.   These effects can be largely overcome by the use of optical fibre cables.   This system uses light as a carrier instead of electrical pulses.   The cable consists of a thin, flexible

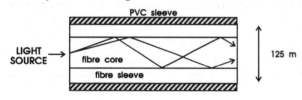

strand of glass, only slightly larger than a human hair.   Plastic-clad silica or all-plastic versions are also available, but they are not as efficient or as easy to use.   Most systems are made from very pure silica, covered with a glass clad.   A light source (either LED or laser) is fed into one end of the cable and the light travels along the cable core, reflecting off the cable's walls (the 'clad').   There is total internal reflection within the cable, occurring at the core/cladding interface.   Total internal reflection occurs because the core has a higher refractive index compared to the cladding.

LED or laser light sources can be used.   LED light sources are much lower powered and are used for shorter distances   (a few kilometres) at speeds of around 200 Mbps.   Laser sources are much more expensive but can handle longer distances and higher transmission speeds (around 1000 Mbps).

Disadvantages:

- Held back by lack of standards.
- Held back by lack of knowledge.
- Most expensive of the media types.
- Difficult to install.

Advantages:

- Handles much greater speeds (10-100 times faster than coax).
- Greater distances than coaxial cable (less attenuation).
- Performs faultlessly at 100Mbps.   It has the lowest error rate, at one faulty bit in every 10,000,000,000.
- It is immune from electromagnetic interference.   Ideal for 'noisy' environments e.g. lift shafts, shop floor production lines.
- Safe in most conditions.   The cable carries only light, so there is no electrical energy to cause a spark in a hazardous or explosive environment (e.g. mines/oil plants/ gas plants).
- Greater security (very hard to tap into; no radiation therefore no unauthorised external monitoring).
- Electrical isolation, therefore no crosstalk.

Most networks do not support fibre optics as standard.   It is available for token-ring and Ethernet systems and is expected to increase its share of use.   Its main use is seen where there is a large volume of traffic or where very large files are used (e.g. video, multimedia, etc)

There are two kinds of optical cable - mono-mode (or single-mode) and multi-mode.

Mono Mode

Mono-mode fibre cable is only about 8 micro-metres in diameter and is used mostly in long-distance communications. Here, the diameter of the core is only a few times greater than the wavelength of the transmitted light and only a single ray is propagated, in almost a straight line.   A large part of the power is propagated in the cladding near the core. The cable is difficult to connect to transmitters and receivers, since precise alignment is required.   It supports a greater data rate than multi-mode, with a bandwidth of 1GHz over 1km being not uncommon.

Multi-Mode

Multi-mode fibre consists of a thicker core, with a surrounding fibre sleeve with different refractive qualities.   Most of the power travels in the core.   The core is many times greater than that used in single-mode. This allows WDM (Wavelength Division Multiplexing) since several different light signals at different frequencies can be transmitted simultaneously. Multi-mode cable is the most common system, since it requires a lower manufacturing tolerance, making it cheaper to produce. They are also easier to attach to hardware.

However, there is no agreement amongst manufacturers as to the dimension of multi-mode cable. All makes use an outer diameter of 125 micro-metres, with the exception of IBM who promote 140 micro-metres. Additionally, different manufacturers promote different inner core diameters (50 to 100 microns).

Light Emitters

The problems of getting the light into the fibre are often the greatest cause of losses in the system. As the surface area of the light emitter and the end of the cable are so small, even a small misalignment can mean that the light does not even enter the cable. Alignment is very critical and needs expertise and the proper equipment. LEDs (Light Emitting Diode) deliver up to 100 microwatts into the cable. They are cheap, have long lives and work up to 100MHz. ILDs (Injection Laser Diodes) deliver a couple of milliwatts into the cable. They are expensive and require complex circuitry (not to mention coolers!) to maintain a stable output. They have bandwidths of over several hundred MegaHertz.

Byte-Wide

Since an individual fibre is so small, it is common to have more than a single fibre in a cable. Normally, they would carry separate data information for different users. In ultra-high performance systems, a single user can use eight separate channels on the cable, one for each bit of a byte. In effect, the user is able to make parallel transmissions at eight times the normal rate.

FDDI

In an attempt at standardisation, ANSI (the American National Standards Institute) has issued the FDDI (Fibre Distributed Data Interface) standard, covering data only. This promotes a 100 Mbps ring topology LAN with 125 micro-metre outer and a range of inner diameters (from 50 to 85 micro-metres) to suit different manufacturers. The system has two rings, the second being a backup (built-in resilience).

Its characteristics are:
- Supports 500 nodes
- Nodes can be up to 2km apart
- Maximum ring circumference of 100km
- Does not require amplifiers or signal conditioning apparatus

A successor, FDDI II, which includes digitised live voice and video, is being developed.

The main uses for FDDI are seen as being:
- Backbone connecting low-speed LAN systems together
- Use for high-performance workstations/image processing
- LANs to mainframes, minis and high-speed devices
- Future need to integrate voice/video on LAN (bandwidth)
- Increase of nodes on networks

Token-ring LANs are more easily supported by fibre-optic cabling than Ethernet.

Wireless Networks

In this system, there is no cable connecting the various nodes. The transmission between the node and the server is carried by either:

Infrared	Line-of-sight only. Cheap to implement. Supported by newer motherboards and by Windows 95/98. No requirement for a licence. IrDA standards are version 1 (115.2Kbps) and version 2 (115.2Kbps and 4Mbps).
Fibreless Laser	Used to connect short distances, typically between buildings. Laser transceivers are fixed in position pointing at each other, limited by atmospheric dispersion effects.
Microwave	Line-of-sight only. Costly but wide bandwidth. Requires a licence. Used by large private and public systems with heavy data throughput requirements.
Radio wave	Implemented as wireless LANs (for small defined areas) or as mobile LANS (see below).

With Wireless LANs, the computer is connected to a radio transmitter/receiver, similar to the kind found in a CB radio. This provides easy communication to the server (e.g. from a remote area of a building). The system requires no cabling and is ideal for setting up temporary networks.

Mobile LANs

Cellular radio has brought mobile phones to a large section of the business community. Many of these users also own small handheld computers. Mobile LANs are ways of integrating the two products so that handhelds, such as the Psion 3C, Apple Newton Message Pad 130 and Hewlett Packard 700LX, can link to the office network system from any location. This technology is still in its infancy and data rates are only 9600bps, which is similar to an older modem. It can handle e-mail, file transfers and slow Internet access.

Mains Wiring

A cheap alternative media is the use of the existing mains cabling, since it already spans every room in a building. To avoid problems with mains fluctuations, a form of frequency modulation is used. These are normally small systems running at relatively slow speeds.

Transmission Methods

There are two main methods of transmitting over a network:

Baseband

This is the most common method for LANs. It is essentially a digital technique, with the node's signal being applied directly to the media, in a similar fashion to TTL or RS232 levels (i.e. +15v represents 0 and -15v represents 1). There is no signal processing and the entire medium bandwidth is used for a single transmission at any one time. Since only one transmission can be handled, high transmission rates are necessary. It is also necessary to share the medium between nodes on a time-sharing basis known as TDM (time division multiplexing).

Digital signals are transmitted as a sequence of 0s and 1s. At its simplest, a negative voltage on the line represents a '0' condition, while a positive signal represents a '1' condition. Changes of signal voltage cannot be used as a means of detecting '0' and '1' states, since a series of 0s or 1s could be sent - producing no voltage change. It is necessary, therefore, to time each pulse to detect whether there are multiple occurrences of the same pulse. This requires that the transmitting and receiving nodes be synchronised. This is achieved by sending the data in a form known as 'Manchester coding', which uses the codes themselves to maintain the necessary synchronisation.

Broadband

Where an organisation has large/complex communication demands, a broadband system will normally be in operation.

The advantages of the broadband system include:
- The ability to carry multiple channels
- The ability to carry analogue signals, e.g. voice and TV
- The ability to cover long distances. Analogue signals do not suffer from degradation to the same extent as digital signals and are easier to boost using analogue amplifiers.
- The ability to interface different baseband systems, using the broadband system as the network 'backbone'.

The disadvantages are:
- High initial cost - planning costs, equipment costs and setup costs.
- Each network adapter needs its own modem.
- Needs regular testing and adjustment (as with a radio, mistuning leads to loss of the information).
- Difficult to insert new stations

A better name for this system would be 'multi-band' since the cable carries more than one data channel, using 'frequency division multiplexing'. The channels are separated by using each data source to modulate a different radio frequency, called the 'carrier' frequency. These carriers are then placed on the media, where they occupy different parts of the radio spectrum. The channels are separated out at the receiving end into the required channels. This is the same technique as used by cable TV firms to place several TV channels on the one TV cable. Each data channel can then effectively be considered as a separate baseband channel, from an access and sharing point of view.

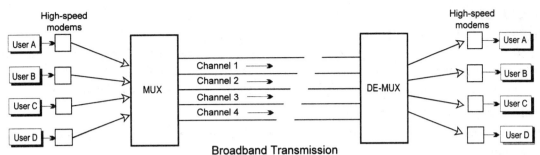

Broadband Transmission

Each channel operates independently of the others and can therefore run at different speeds using different access methods. For example, one channel could be dedicated to networking PCs while another connects IBM 3270 terminals to a mainframe computer. A node will usually be allocated to a particular channel (e.g. a node running AUTOCAD would be attached to the channel allocated to the transfer of the image files). A node could be allowed to choose which channel to connect to.

The width of a broadband channel depends on the data being carried. For data channels, the required bandwidth will increase with increasing data transfer rates. Ethernet, for example, will require 18MHz of bandwidth. LocalNet, on the other hand, opts for 120 slow-speed channels (only 128Kbps) each channel requiring 300KHz of bandwidth. Broadband systems are currently in use to carry multiple data channels and video for LAN applications, although it appears likely that it will be overtaken by fibre-optic systems. The only PC network to use broadband is the IBM token ring system, which transmits on 50.75MHz and receives on 219MHz.

NOTES:

The system uses cable TV equipment - i.e. one way only - and is therefore usually a twin cable system. An alternative is to split the bandwidth into transmit and receive bands.

The system uses expensive, high-speed, modems at each node. Modems can be a single pair of frequencies (1 for transmit, 1 for receive) or can be *'frequency agile'* - can access several channels.

Ethernet and IEEE standards

In the ideal world, all computer devices would easily connect together, using the same electronic methods and the same communication protocols. However, due to the historical development of networks via competing manufacturers, many differences exist between the brand names - even where the products are supposed to conform to the same standard. The chart shows the most common systems in use

Ethernet Specification	IEEE Standard	Band	Usage
1Base5	802.3	Baseband	1Mbps using UTP, STP cable
10Base2	802.3	Baseband	10Mbps using thin coax cable
10Base5	802.3	Baseband	10Mbps using thick coax cable
10BaseF	802.3	Baseband	10Mbps using fibre optic cable
10BaseT	802.3	Baseband	10Mbps using UTP cable
10Broad36	802.3	Broadband	10Mbps using broadband cable
100BaseT	802.3u	Baseband	100Mbps using UTP, fibre optic cable
100VG-AnyLAN	802.12	Baseband	100Mbps using UTP cable
Gigabit Ethernet	802.3z	Baseband	1000Mbps using fibre optic cable

The IEEE Local Networks Standards Committee has developed the series of LAN standards listed below:
- IEEE 802.3 Covers the carrier sense multiple access and collision detection (CSMA/CD) access method and physical layer specification. This is also known as *'Ethernet'* and was mainly developed by Xerox, Intel and DEC. It was introduced in 1980.
- IEEE 802.5 Covers the token passing ring access method and physical layer specification mainly developed by IBM, introduced in 1985.
- 802.1 Covers the system overview, architecture, addressing, internetworking and network management.
- 802.4 Covers the token passing bus access method. Usually found in factory environments, where MAP (Manufacturing Automation Protocol) is its most popular implementation.
- 802.6 Covers the Metropolitan network access method.

Practical Cabling

The simplest network cable configuration is a single segment of cable on which the server and all nodes are located.   This is a perfectly satisfactory layout for a small network but many networks gradually grow both in the number of stations connected and the distance the network has to cover.   Greater usage and greater distances normally leads to additions to the system and these have to be planned.

Effect of segment length on collisions

Consider three nodes on a network, one attached at each extreme end and one in the middle of the segment length.

The left-most node transmits a packet and needs to detect if it has collided with another packet on the cable, say one being sent by the right-most node. A user's packet, being in serial format, takes a finite time to place on the cable. It also takes a finite time to travel to the ends of the cable.   The distance between the two furthest nodes must be short enough for one node's packet to travel to all other nodes (the other end of the cable being the furthest cases) during the lifetime of the other's transmission.   If this is the case, then the packets will corrupt each other and the collision will be detected.   However, if the segment length is too great, the left node's packet will be completely sent before the right node's transmission arrives. A collision has still occurred but has not now been detected. Both packets still collide in the middle of the cable and both are corrupted.

This explains why a limit is placed on the length of a network segment.

Extending A Network

A range of hardware is available to allow a single segment to join with another segment, or several segments, to form a larger network.

Repeaters

Individual segments of a LAN bus can be connected with 'repeaters'.   A repeater receives the transmission from one segment, amplifies and cleans up the signal and re-transmits it to the other segment.   In this way, the maximum cable length and number of stations can be increased from the previous limits.   Repeaters do not have any control over addressing or forwarding and therefore do not ease congestion and collision on the system.   They operate at the OSI physical layer 1.

A multiport repeater has many outlet sockets and copies the transmission over multiple segments.

Bridges

A bridge connects two segments and passes traffic between them. It is used to extend the network size

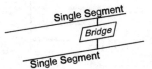

without breaking the limit on any segment size, attached device count, or number of repeaters per segment.   It is very popular with small networks. A bridge can be a standalone piece of equipment but is often a PC with two NICs, one connecting to each segment.

A learning bridge builds up a picture of what addresses are on each side of the bridge and decides whether packets are allowed to cross the bridge.   For this purpose, it operates at the Data Link Layer level 2 and uses the MAC (Media Access Control) sub-layer to check addresses.   The only traffic allowed on a segment is traffic destined for a node on that segment.   Since there is reduced traffic, there are also fewer collisions and less wasted traffic.   However, when a bridge becomes busy, it places traffic in memory buffers and when these buffers become full, users' frames are discarded.

A bridge is also used as a connection between the building's main data backbone and separate segments for each floor.   So, packets addressed

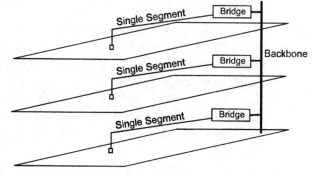

to a node on the ground floor will not be sent on to the segments on the other floors; they will not pass through the first floor and second floor bridges.

Routers

A router is like a bridge except that it works on OSI Network Layer level 3 protocols.   Messages are transmitted to other segments dependent upon their protocol level address (e.g. TCP/IP address) rather than the MAC addresses.   So they can bridge an Ethernet with token ring, translating and passing packets between them.   They are slower than bridges but are used for larger networks, since they are better at handling collisions and bandwidth utilisation.   Routers can communicate with other routers on the network as to which route of the possible options is the most efficient.

Gateways

A gateway is used to connect two networks whose communications protocols are different.   So, a gateway device might connect an Ethernet segment to a Unix system, a mainframe computer or an ISDN or X.25 communications line. Gateways handle a larger range of protocols than a router.   The gateway device carries out the translation of information between the systems.

Design Restrictions

There is a '5-4-3' rule for connecting unbridged systems.

- The system must not have more than 5 repeated segments.
- The system must not have more 4 repeaters/hubs between any 2 stations.
- The system must have no more than 3 of the segments populated.

The layout of the network structure must follow these rules to ensure consistent network operation. In addition, a maximum of 7 bridges is allowed in a system.

Structured Cabling

The above additions can, and often do, develop in a piecemeal way, as the organisation gradually expands.   They keep the network operating but a large collection of such segments and components may eventually not produce the efficient working that is required.   For systems that need reorganised, and particularly for new networks, the principle of structured cabling is important.

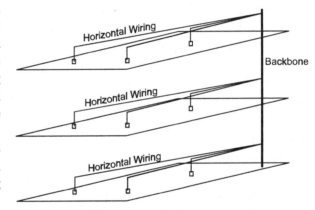

With structured cabling, the total system comprises simple wiring structures that are repeated in various locations, or various floors of the building and then combined.

The diagram shows a 3-floor building with the outline of a structured cabling layout.   The type of cabling and type of hardware components offer a range of options to suit an organisation's operational needs as well as the building layout.

The main features should be:

- A fast cabling type for the building's data backbone. This vertical cabling carries the heavy data needs throughout the building. The backbone could be fibre optic, ThickNet or Cat 5 UTP depending upon the implementation decided upon.
- Floors are 'flood wired'.   Cables are not only routed to where computers currently sit; cables are taken to all places where a computer may be located in the future. This is usually a ratio of connections per square metre of floor space.
- Cabling provides enough spare capacity for future use (e.g. running two cables to each workspace).
- All cables on a particular floor are taken to a 'wiring closet'.   This is a small cupboard or room with a patch panel with connections for each cable.
- All further connections to equipment are carried out in the wiring closet, providing flexibility.
- Fast systems must provide slower speed ports for connecting to printers, routers and bridges that are not designed for fast speeds.
- Data hungry workstations, such as those used for CAD, Multimedia, video and DTP, can be linked to the main system using a fast network card.

Fast Systems

A number of competing technologies exist for fast 100Mbps and above operation.   FDDI has the best performance but is very expensive.

The other options are:
- 100Base-T
- 100Base-VG
- Gigabit Ethernet
- Ethernet switches
- ATM

100Base-T

Also known as Fast Ethernet, this remains a CSMA/CD Ethernet system.   It offers three options:
- 100Base-TX, which uses 2 pairs of the Cat 5 cable.
- 100Base-T4, which uses 4 pairs of Cat 3, Cat 4 or Cat 5 cable.
- 100Base-FX, which uses 2 strands of optical fibre.

100BaseTX and 100BaseT4 have a 100m maximum length between node and hub. The two furthest nodes cannot be greater than 200m apart (including 2 repeaters or hubs which cannot be more than 5m apart in between). Longer distances are achieved using switches or switching hubs.

Fast Ethernet requires new switched hubs and NICs. Existing 10Mbps hubs and NICs can be retained for average users while power users have direct 100Mbps connections as shown in the diagram.

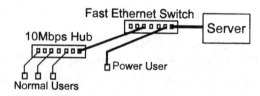

The server has a 100Mbps switched NIC and feeds 100Mbps to the Fast Ethernet switch.   Power users with heavy bandwidth needs are connected directly to this switch to maximise their bandwidth.   The switch also feeds 100Mbps to normal 10Mbps hubs which each feed connecting a number of normally loaded PCs.   The Fast switch could feed 100Mbps to another 100Mbps switch in a 'cascade' of high-speed connections. It is a simpler and cheaper system than 100VG but is less efficient at handling time-dependent data.

100VG-AnyLAN

100VG supports token ring frames but is mainly used with Ethernet.   It doesn't use the standard Ethernet CSMA/CD.   Instead, it uses 'Demand Priority Protocol' which has a normal and high priority level. High priority transmissions are given precedence over lower priority activities to ensure adequate performance for time-critical applications such as process control, multimedia and live video.   It is a high performance system that uses up to 95% of its maximum theoretical capacity.

Like all modern wiring systems, it uses twisted pair connected to hubs and the hubs can be cascaded to three levels of depth as shown in the diagram.

100VG supports the following options
- 4 pairs of Cat 3, Cat 4 - with a 100m limit between node and hub and also between hubs.
- 2 or 4 pairs for Cat 5 - with a 150m limit between node and hub and also between hubs.

Since the system does not have to listen for collisions, the signalling pair used by 10Base-T is no longer used and all four pairs in the UTP can be used to carry data.   So, the multi-core cable designed to carry 10Mbps now carries 40Mbps.   There is also much redundant data sent in a normal Manchester coded packet (see earlier explanation). Two bits of data are transmitted for every bit of actual data.

100Base-VG uses a method called 5B6B NRZ which uses 6 bits to represent every 5 bits instead of the 10 bits required by Manchester encoding.   The system uses round robin access (i.e. token ring access) inside the hub.   The hub checks each node in turn looking for traffic.   So, all ports get a fair share of the bandwidth, apart from any changed priorities imposed by the Demand Priority protocol.

With 100VG, packets are sent to the destination node only, not transmitted to all nodes as in a single bus segment.   It requires new hubs and NICs, since it is no longer based on the collision detection mechanism of layer 2.   The network can retain the existing cabling but a translation bridge is required between the 100VG and 10Base-T components.

Switched Ethernet

While 100Base-T retained CSMA/CD for its high-speed system, Switched Ethernet abandons shared access methods in favour of a point-to-point connection set up by switched components for the duration of the communication.   By eliminating collisions, the existing bandwidth is used much more effectively.

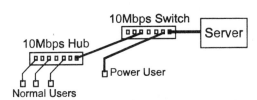

As the diagram shows, the server, power users and normal hubs all connect to the switch.   The users then have *'bandwidth on demand'* - a guaranteed 10Mbps allocation.

Switched Ethernet uses the existing servers, nodes, cabling and NICs but requires changes and additions to the cabling infrastructure (i.e. the addition of an Ethernet Switch and existing nodes reconfigured through extra hubs).   It is a cheap option and is easily set up.   It is a great improvement over standard Ethernet but is not powerful enough for large throughput demands.

ATM

Asynchronous Transfer Mode is available in three options:
- 25Mbps for Cat 5, with a 150m limit between switch and node.
- 155Mbps for multi-mode fibre, with a 2km limit.
- 622Mbps for multi-mode fibre. Probably the upper limit that will be implemented in ATM.

It uses switching hubs and *'cells'* (packets of only 48 data bytes and 5 header bytes).   Cells are transmitted over *'pipes'* (virtual channels) between a node, a switch and another node. The bandwidth for each channel can be set separately, allowing heavy users such as multimedia to run with a guaranteed bandwidth of 155Mbps right up to the node.   At the moment, it is used largely for fast backbones.

Gigabit Ethernet

Used on both mono-mode and multi-mode fibres, it provides fast network backbones with a maximum of up to 3km cable length.   It retains Ethernet's CSMCA/CD method, making it easy to replace or extend an existing network.   UTP and fibre optic in both single mode and multi-mode are the likely carriers of this technology, although there will be a thick copper twin cable standard with a maximum length of 25m.

Software on the network

Most modern software is capable of being run on a stand-alone PC or over a network. An application is loaded from the hard disk of the file server into the memory of the calling node. The program is then run in the machine memory.   This means that the program can be downloaded to as many nodes as require it.   This has encouraged the purchase of single copies of applications, rather than the multi-licence network versions.   The lack of network facilities in the applications could sometimes be overcome by the network utilities of the operating system.

To prevent this, many single-user applications now test to see whether it is being used in a machine with a network operating system.   If it detects such a system, it refuses to run. Some applications operate on a network as standard. Others require that network versions be purchased.

File Problems

The main difference between stand-alone and network use is in the ability to share files. The application program can be easily copied into the memory of several stations.   The problems arise from stations trying to use the same data files.

Consider the case of two station users running Word, which is on the file server in single-user mode. Both users decide to load the same monthly report to make their own amendments/additions.   The first user will successfully load the original file and begin working on it.   While this is happening, the second user can also successfully load the original file and make other changes.

The problem arises when the users save their files, since only a single copy of a unique file-name can exist on the disk.   Both users' amended versions are saved - but whoever saves second overwrites the file the first user saved. In other words, the amendments of the first user are lost - and the user will not even know it has happened.   An even worse situation exists if both users try to save simultaneously.   At best, a new file is created which has elements of both files.   At worst, the disk file organisation may be affected, causing other files to be irretrievable.

There are other occasions when the user would wish an entire file to be used exclusively by a single user. For example, when packing a database (to remove records marked as deleted), no other user should have access to that file.

These problems are overcome by a system of *'file locking'*.

File Locking

This is enacted either by automatic or manual means.

Automatic Locking

When MS-DOS version 3 was issued, it introduced new facilities for 'file locking'. These additions were designed specifically to support multi-user networks and are called the NOS (Network Operating System).   In MS-DOS v3 onwards, when a file is opened (for reading or writing), access to that file is denied to any user. Thus, the file is only available to one user at any one time. This eliminates the file problems previously mentioned.   MS-DOS, from version 3.3 onwards, contains a utility called SHARE.EXE, which maintains a table of all open files. This utility is used by MS-DOS (v3.3 on) compatible network operating systems.   Nowadays the vendors of most Network Operating Systems use file-locking and record-locking techniques, to allow applications to control access to the files. Thus, spreadsheets, databases and word processors can run happily on the network.

The default locking mechanism overcomes the simultaneous update clashes by stopping file sharing completely.   However, most application files are never updated and could therefore be shared by many simultaneous users. To provide this flexibility, the software will not lock a file that is set to be Read Only.   It would seem to make sense, therefore, to set all shareable programs to be Read Only. Unfortunately some applications, usually for reasons of copy protection, write to their own program and overlay files and this makes them effectively unshareable.

In Novell and Windows NT, the supervisor of the network can ensure that certain files are only able to be read but cannot be amended (i.e. written to). This allows multiple users to download and run system files, review product information, etc. from databases and read text files.

When a file is allowed to be written to, it is marked accordingly (by changing a file attribute bit). When one of these files is opened by a user, the file is automatically 'locked' by the network operating system. When another user attempts to open the same file, either a 'file locked' message is presented, or the user may be allowed to open the file on a read-only basis (dependent on the application being used).   If a non-LAN version of an application is in use, other miscellaneous error messages are liable to be generated.

Manual Locking

Automatic locking works well in those situations where the file is kept open (therefore kept locked) during the entire time that the file is being worked on by a user.   However, a number of applications (such as spreadsheets and word processors) only open the file, read the contents into computer memory, then close the file again.   The user works on the data within memory, the file being closed - and therefore free to be opened by other users. When the user is finished working on the data, the file is re-opened to write away the new details. This presents most of the original problems, since the file is only locked during the actual process of reading and writing the data. Apart from the short time needed for disk operations, the file is free to be opened by anyone.

Because of this, many network applications ensure that the file is kept open for the entire period between opening and closing the file.   A more flexible approach is giving the user control over whether the file should be locked. After all, the user may only load in a spreadsheet to view it - with no intention of making any alterations. In that situation, this first user might be quite happy that a second user could load and alter the worksheet file.

Deadly Embrace

Also known as deadlock, this is an ever-present threat for application programmers.
Consider the example shown in the diagram.

Station A requires files A and B to be simultaneously open for its activities.

Station B also requires files A and B to be simultaneously open for its activities.

Station A wishes to use file A followed by file B, then end its program.

Station B wishes to use file B followed by file A, then end its program.

Consider the following sequence:

- Station A accesses file A, locking the file to other users.
- Station B accesses file B, locking it to other users.
- Station A tries to open file B but is locked out.
- Station A cannot continue with its program, so file A is not closed.
- Station B tries to open file A but is similarly locked out.
- Station B cannot continue either, so file B is not closed.

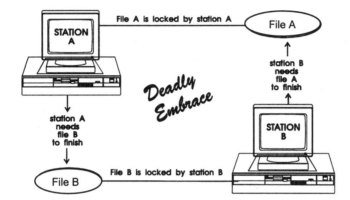

Both stations now wait for the other to release the file they need to complete their program. This is an endless situation called *'deadlock'* or *'deadly embrace'*. The only solution is to terminate one of the programs, with any consequences that may produce.

The simplest way to prevent this problem is to write the software such that an application will acquire all its required resources <u>before</u> continuing with the program. This prevents deadlock but may result in valuable resources lying unused until the application is ready for it.

Record Locking

File locking is the most appropriate method for preventing possible concurrent updates but is unsuitable for databases, particularly large databases. A database is composed of a collection of individual records. A user is often only concerned with viewing/updating a single record in the file. It would be very inefficient if all other users had to wait for consecutive access to the file. A better method would be to lock at a record level, rather than file level. If a user wished access to a particular record, that record would be locked. This would allow the user to modify and save that record; all other users would only have read access to that record during that time. Of course, all the other records could be handled similarly, allowing many users concurrent access to the database - while only one user at a time could have write access to a particular record. In practice, it is usually more practical to lock a portion of the file, rather than individual records.

The above works well for modifying records but causes problems when a user wishes to add a new record to the file. Adding a record changes the file structure and many databases require that the entire file be locked during this alteration. Since the file can only be locked when there is only a single user and since the database is likely to be in continuous use by multiple users, additions to a file could be a time-consuming business.

The general solution is to design the database so that spare blank records are added to a database each time the system is used. This allows users to modify the blank records into new records - without the problems mentioned above.

Other Single-User Problems

Apart from the file-sharing problems already mentioned, there are other difficulties with using single-user software on networks:

Temporary Files:

When running, a number of applications produce temporary files. During this period, a second user is effectively locked out. The solution is to direct the temporary output to different directories, using the applications configuration setups. Creating specific directories for different users overcomes the problem.

Configuration Files:

Configuration files are used to determine the specific hardware, directories, etc. that an application will use. Since different nodes may have different hardware and directory requirements, the same copy of a program may not run on all stations. Dependent on the program, it is usually possible to overcome this by the use of individual batch files for each node.

Word Processing:

Nowadays, word processors have an in-built spell-checker. There is no problem in simultaneous use of this dictionary, when users wish only to read the file. However, there is no control over users wishing to add new words to the dictionary. Since different nodes may well have different needs (e.g. to add financial, scientific or legal words to the dictionary) the file could soon become very large and contain many words never likely to be used by a particular node.

If the network application allows it, users could be granted personal extensions to the main dictionary - which would not be accessed by any other node's search. Of course, this option does not exist on single-user versions.

Copy Protection

Apart from the built-in check that certain applications make for their single-user version being used on a network, many programs have a general copy protection method built in. This prevents unauthorised copying of the program's master disks and often works by the timing of a disk operation or a direct read or write of the disk drive. Since this is impossible over a network, the program is treated as a pirate copy and will not function.

Purchasing Software

Most stand-alone applications are sold on a single-user basis. This requires that the application be used by a single user on a single machine at a single site.

Borland (of Paradox, Turbo C, Turbo Pascal and Delphi fame) have no objection to the user and the site being varied, as long as only a single copy is being used at any one time. From a network point of view, a single copy can be downloaded to any one node at any one time. The responsibility of preventing concurrent use rests with the user. Clearly, using single-user applications on a network can be difficult - not to mention illegal. On the other hand, users don't wish to buy a complete package (disks, manuals, etc.) for every user on the network.

To meet this situation, an organisation can purchase a licence for a set number of concurrent users. For example, a 10-user licence would allow up to 10 users to run the application at the same time, from any of the stations on the network. When an 11th user attempts to use the application, access is denied until of the previous 10 users ceases running the application. Packages such as dBase and SuperCalc provide this method of licensing.

Languages

Networked application packages are very useful but do not meet everyone's needs. Consequently, there is a role for programming languages on a network. This means that the language has to have additional commands to make it operate a network - commands to implement the file locking facilities.

Client/Server Software

Up to recently, networks consisted simply of a collection of PCs which all processed independently. The linking of the stations was only used as a means of resource sharing and communications. As a consequence, many stations could be sitting idle while others were working flat out. The ideal world would have the idle stations carrying out some of the functions of the busy stations. Unfortunately, this is still some way off.   However, there are steps in this direction with the *'client/server'* systems.   In such a system, the user machine (the *'client'* or *'front end'*) concerns itself with the user interface/editing tasks, while the core data remains on the server end (or *'back-end'*).   The backend could, of course, be a mainframe, mini or high-end PC.   Not only does the data to be processed stay in the server, the actual processing of the data can now be done in the server end.

Advantages:

- Improves performance, due to reducing traffic on the network - since part of the processing coding remains on the server and the core data remains on the server. Since this is no longer required to be sent down the network, the normally heavy traffic can thereby be substantially reduced. With applications being ever more complex (thereby ever larger), the traffic reduction savings will become more and more significant.
- Makes savings on hardware upgrades.   With the increasing complexity of applications, came the demand for increased power from workstations. If the main tasks of the workstation are reduced to user interface activities then the node system can be relatively simple (therefore cheaper), while the high performance server `carries out the more demanding activities such as searching, sorting, producing statistics, etc. For example, why have a 600MHz Pentium III processor in each station. If calculations only account for 10% of the workload, then the station is being underused for 90% of the time.

Disadvantages:

- High initial software costs, due to having to buy both server software and client application software.
- The client database software (the software in each node) has to have SQL (Structured Query Language) capability and the database server software is more complex than normal server software.

The most common example of an application server is the SQL database server. Consider an earlier, non client-server type, network database package.   A node would require to carry out all its processing in the node PC. So, to find out a count of all records matching search criteria (e.g. how many Glasgow-based customers in a file), the entire file would have to be copied along the network from the server to the node. The processing of the records would then take place within the node PC. This involves a substantial amount of network traffic.   If the network is a large user of databases, then the system would soon slow down to a snail's pace.

This is where SQL and client/server software comes in.   Structured Query Language provides a common database language, allowing the splitting of functions over different machines (of course, it can also be used on a single-user machine).   It is rapidly gaining acceptance as a standard and will provide some further compatibility between database applications.   Eventually, a single database server using SQL could be used to service requests from stations using different database packages.   The client (sometimes called the *'Front End'*) is the node PC running the database package.   The client's job is to provide the user with the user interface - menus, output screens, query tools.   The database server (sometimes called the *'Back End'*) carries out all the database functions such as storage allocation, indexing, record selection, file statistics, etc.   The user formulates a request in SQL, which is sent to the database server for implementation.   Thus, for a function such as narrowing a search to a subset of records, only the matching records are sent over the network. If the user requests a count of those records matching a set of criteria, then only the final figure is transmitted over the network.

This has the following benefits:

- Substantial reductions in network traffic, greatly enhancing overall network performance.
- More nodes can process the same file simultaneously; database servers are designed to be multi-tasking.

Implementations of the above techniques are now becoming available. Open DataBase Connectivity (ODBC) makes connecting any Client based software, like Access, Excel or user-written programs in Pascal, C or Visual Basic practically trivial, and Back end drivers are readily available for major database packages such as Oracle, Sybase, DB2 and most mainframe systems.

As explained in the chapter on DOS and Windows, an operating system is a set of programs to control the computer hardware and manage the computer's resources. So far, only operating systems for personal computers have been discussed. These are essentially single user operating systems and, whilst they are important, there are a number of other operating systems designed for applications with multiple users. Open operating systems such as UNIX allow multiple users to perform multiple tasks on the same computer at the same time.

This chapter examines the characteristics of multi-user operating systems using the world's most popular operating system, UNIX.

Characteristics of multi-user operating systems

At a most basic level, operating systems act as an interface between the user and the computer system allowing the user to utilise the facilities offered by the hardware. Computers work on electronic representations of binary digits and it is the manipulation of these bits that is at the heart of the computer system. The operating system allows the use of these functions. It provides facilities to utilise the floppy disk drive, the hard disk drive, the keyboard, the screen, etc. It also provides useful utilities such as the ability to save, rename, format, obtain directory listings, etc. In short the operating system makes the hardware usable. Thus the applications talk directly to the Operating system, which then interfaces with the hardware:

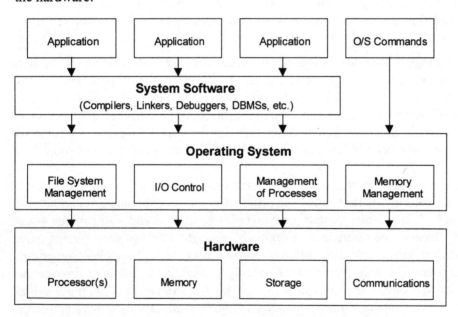

It therefore follows that *"usable"* depends upon the application and therefore the requirements of the operating system. For example, the requirements of a set of traffic lights are substantially different from those of a word processor. Similarly, the facilities required to support word processing would be different from those required to support a multi-user, multi-tasking environment. UNIX is fundamentally a multi-user multi-tasking operating system, which means it is capable of undertaking many tasks for many users simultaneously.

There are essentially 4 types of operating system:

Single User Single Tasking

This type of operating system can only undertake one operation at a time for a single user. DOS is a good example of such an operating system.

Single User Multi tasking

This type of operating system can undertake several jobs (seemingly simultaneously) for a single user. Windows 3.0 or 3.1 is a good example of this - the user can have many windows open, work is carried out on the "background" windows whilst the user uses the foreground window.

Multi User Single Tasking

Such an operating system would be capable of accepting a single job from multiple users. In reality, there would be little call for such an operating system.

Multi User Multitasking

This operating system is capable of executing multiple jobs for multiple users (seemingly concurrently). UNIX is a good example of this.

It is interesting to note that all of the types of operating system detailed above can run on PC hardware.

Multi User Multitasking Operating System Features

Multi-user multi-tasking operating systems are perhaps one of the most complex operating systems and are responsible for such tasks as:

- Scheduling of jobs
- Allocation of resources
- Hardware operations
- User operations
- Protection of the work of each user
- Protecting the working memory of each user
- Providing disk storage and quotas for each user
- Running the multiple jobs of each user

Often several users wish to execute the same program. Consider a class that is studying ORACLE. If there are 25 in the group and ORACLE took up just 2MB, it would require 50MB RAM just to load - a huge waste of resources. Resources can be conserved by loading only one copy of the program, and allowing 50 users access to it. Programs that can be used in such a way need to be compiled as *"re-entrant"*. This means that each user can run a different part of the same program by taking a *"thread"* through the program. The diagram shows a section of computer memory. Users A, B & C are all using the same copy of the compiler. Users C & D are both using the same copy of ORACLE:

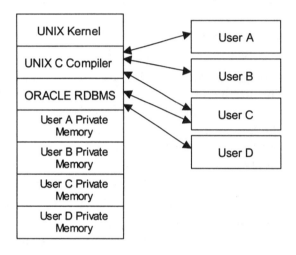

The "Process" Concept

While it is possible for re-entrant programs to exist, it should be remembered that it is still possible for programs not to be re-entrant and therefore have multiple copies of the same program running. Therefore the term *"program"* cannot be used and a new term is needed - the Process.

A process is best described as an *"instance of a program under execution by a user"*. When a user starts a new process, the Operating System needs to keep track of each user and his/her environment. It needs to have a pointer to their position in the program and their own work area. To do this, it creates a data structure called a Process Control Block (PCB). A typical PCB includes:

- An ID number (the Process ID or PID), by which the Operating System and other processes can reference it.
- The ID number of the process's parent (PPID).
- Processor state information (registers and stacks).
- Process Control Information (scheduling and state information, data structures, interprocess communication, process privileges, memory management, resource ownership and location).

Whilst this considerably reduces system resource requirements, it clearly demonstrates how complex operating systems are becoming.

If a user has several processes in execution, it is only humanly possible to be active in one at any one time. This is regarded as the "foreground" process and will normally be given more resources (by the operating system) than the other processes known as "background" processes. In UNIX, a user can cause a job to execute in the background by appending a space followed by an & e.g. runprog & will cause the program runprog to execute in the background. Users can switch between background and foreground tasks using the bg (background) and fg (foreground) commands:

```
$ sleep 10
$
$ sleep 100 &
[2]    5798
$ bg
[2]    sleep 100 &
$ fg %2
sleep 100
^Z[2] + Stopped (SIGTSTP)        sleep 100 &
$ bg %2
[2]    sleep 100 &
[1] - Done              sleep 100 &
$
```

In the above example, the sleep command (which creates a null process, which sleeps for n seconds) is used. With the first command, the sleep command ties the system up for 10 seconds. In the second example because the & is used, the system is available but, the sleep 100 command is executed in the background. The bg command shows that it is in the background with a job no of 2. The fg %2 command brings that job to the foreground (and ties up the screen), ctrl Z interrupts the job and bg %2 is used to send it back into the background.

Process Creation With Unix

The creation of a process in UNIX is transparent to the user - the operating system will simply establish a PCB for each process the user creates, monitor and control the user's process. For instance if the ps -ef|more command is issued, UNIX will automatically create two processes - one to handle the ps -ef command and the other to handle the more command. These processes needed to communicate - the results from the ps -ef command have to be sent to the more command for formatting one screen at a time. Once the processes have completed, then they pass their return code to their parent and terminate.

Sometimes it is easier to think of UNIX as a lazy operating system (or parent!) which never does anything for itself - each time it needs to do something it creates a child (process) to do it. Where necessary it will create two and arrange for them to communicate. Once the child (process) completes, it notifies the parent of this (by its return code) which, once accepted, the parent has no further use for the child and allows it to die. Should an error occur and the parent (process) die before the child (process) completes, the child will have no one to inform of its return code and will wander around the system aimlessly looking for its dead parent (process).

Such processes are known as *"Zombies"* and UNIX has a *"child (process) catcher"* in the form of a process called init. init looks for such children, accepts their return code and then kills them! A Process with a parent PID of 1 is the top of the tree.

The init process is created on startup by the operating system and runs forever and the UNIX term for such processes is a *"daemon"*.

UNIX has a number of daemons for tasks such as:

- Terminal control
- Printer control
- Networks
- User logins
- Telnet
- FTP
- WWW

The Kernel

There is a special process in the UNIX operating system, usually called UNIX. This is the core part of that UNIX installation - the heart of the installation, without which the machine cannot function. It must never be deleted and must be backed up. The kernel is loaded from disk on boot up, thus if the UNIX file is deleted, then the system will not restart. If accidentally deleted, the system should be left running and help sought immediately - normally a problem will not be encountered until the system is taken down.

Unlike other Operating Systems, the Kernel of a UNIX system is not tied to a specific hardware platform - a true UNIX C kernel can be recompiled and used on any machine. Occasionally, installation of new software will require recompilation of the kernel to allow the software to operate properly. It is strongly recommended that a backup of the kernel is taken before installing such software.

In practice, it is unlikely that the kernel would be compiled for use on new hardware. More often the manufacturer's pre-compiled version of UNIX would be purchased. This will be optimised for their hardware, including useful *"additional"* features for their customers, be tried and tested and most importantly well supported.

Memory Allocation

If multiple programs or multiple sets of data are resident in memory at any one time there cannot be a guarantee of where those programs will load. The programs could load in low memory one day and high the next. For instance if Fred loads his program first then it may be in low memory but, if Jo loads hers first, it will be in higher memory. Thus programs on a multi-user multi-tasking operating system like UNIX cannot dictate where they will load. For this reason they must not use specific memory addresses but instead must be relocatable (i.e. operate where the operating system dictates they will load).

To achieve this, relocation registers are used. Such registers require programs to operate on a base and offset principle. With this principle, the program is allocated a "base address" and all addresses in this program must be offsets to that address. Consider a simple program of which line 1 effectively says Jump TO line 10. In a base offset situation the compiler would change this to Jump 10 lines. Thus if the base register was allocated as 40 the program would jump to line 50 and would therefore still work.

It is interesting to note that DOS does not employ such a method fully, and that is why there is the 640K memory problem with DOS.

It is sufficient to understand this principle and that it is achieved using relocation registers.

Associated Problems

Whilst such a technique allows several programs to be resident in memory and to run successfully, there are further complications. The major complication being the division of the computer's memory – how much space should be allocated for each program?

In the first attempts at sharing memory (static partitioning) designers needed to determine how much space should be allocated for each program. If the limit was set too small, then the larger applications would not fit. If it were set too high, then memory would be wasted and other applications would be unable to fit in. Thus allocating fixed space was very quickly considered unacceptable.

It was determined that Operating Systems needed to vary the size of the memory allocation (variable partition memory) allocating just enough space for the programs to operate in. Again, the Operating System is responsible for the control of this. As programs terminate the Operating System must reclaim this space.

Although a vast improvement over static partitioning, this is far from perfect. Firstly, consider size. If the first program to load is large, then there may be insufficient room to load another. Indeed, there may be insufficient room to load the data to work with the program!

Such situations were particularly common when new versions of programs were installed - it is very unlikely that a revised application is smaller than it's predecessor and more memory (if available) may need to be installed.

Further, consider the case where several programs and data are co-residing in memory. When one of the smaller programs terminates, it will leave two *"holes"* in memory (one from the data and one from the program). Together, these may amount to enough memory to run a further application but because they are two separate chunks rather than a whole (contiguous) chunk, a further application cannot run. This leads to uncontrolled memory fragmentation.

It is very difficult to devise algorithms that will deal with uncontrolled memory fragmentation and so a better way had to be found.

Paging

To address these problems, the concept of paging was born. In a paged system (such as UNIX) a process is split into a number of chunks known as pages (typically 4K in length). Memory is divided up into page frames of the same size. The process of program loading then consists of loading a page into a page frame.

Process A Page 1
Process A Page 2
Process A Page 3
Process A Page 4

Process A Page 1
Process A Page 2
Process A Page 3
Process B Page 1
Process B Page 2
Process A Page 4
Process B Page 3

As processes vacate the system, frames will become empty. By allowing parts of a process to be loaded into these vacated frames, maximum use is made of memory:

Relocation of the job is affected by paging because it is possible for programs to be *"split up"* and loaded in a non-linear fashion. In such cases, memory becomes fragmented but, because this is controlled by the Operating System, it is acceptable.

Paging presents further benefits:
- It allows the computer to run a program which is larger than its memory
- It allows the combined size of all programs to be larger than main memory
- Programs can begin execution immediately without waiting until fully loaded into memory

Virtual Memory

Often the size of combined jobs is far greater than available memory, which would normally mean that a program could not run, or a user cannot have access. By careful consideration of the problem, it can be noted that the programs to be loaded and the memory they will be loaded into are divided into pages of equal size. Further, the programs that are to be loaded usually follow a linear chain of execution and so only the initial pages are needed to begin execution of the process. By loading only a fragment of the program, say the first 10 pages, then there is enough of the program to begin execution and enough free memory to load small chunks of all the programs required.

Obviously, care must be taken to load the next pages of the program when they are needed otherwise the program will be prevented from running. Preferably, the pages need to be loaded in advance of being required otherwise unnecessary delay will be caused. Failure to load a required page in advance is termed a *'page fault'*.

By operating in such a fashion, the system can execute a program whose entire size is larger than computer's memory or combined jobs whose size is larger than the computer's memory. The operating system is using the computer's disk storage to create *"virtual memory"* limited only to the size of hard disk storage (which may be several GB). Whilst this is a useful facility, it must not be relied upon. Disc storage is many times slower than memory, which causes significant delay.

Fundamentally, virtual memory operates by swapping pages out of memory that aren't being used, and replacing them with pages that are about to be used. When swapping out a page, the operating system must know (via a flag) whether the page is *"dirty"* (a page that has been modified) or *"clean"* (a page that has not been modified). If the page is clean then there is no need to save it back to the storage media and so write time (and associated disk access time) can be saved.

To further enhance performance, the operating system keeps track of the frequency of use of pages and swaps out the least frequently used ones. For instance if there are 100 people all accessing pages of ORCALE® and one user accessing pages of the C compiler then the used C compiler pages are a prime candidate for being swapped out - there is a greater probability of the ORACLE® ones being re-used.

Thrashing

Although virtual memory sounds like a dream come true it must be remembered that disk access is many thousands of times slower than the CPU. This means that pages retrieved from disk take much longer - hence the Operating System tries to minimise the number of faults. Users must try not to push Virtual Memory systems beyond their limits. If too many programs or too much data is loaded in comparison to the computers real memory then there is a risk of the system *"thrashing"*.

Thrashing is the term given to the situation where the computer spends more time loading and saving pages to and from disk than it does doing useful work. When systems start to thrash it is immediately noticeable - it is not uncommon for a machine's response time to fall from 5 seconds to 5 minutes when it starts to thrash. The solution is usually simple and inexpensive - more real memory!

Computer systems also use virtual memory to save details of processes in execution and may swap out processes that have suspended (blocked) waiting for disk I/O, etc. For this reason the systems need a swap file which is usually limited to 1.5 to 2 times the size of the computer's actual memory.

Memory Protection

It is essential that each process does not interfere with another or its data. However it is desirable (e.g. oracle indexes) that process code and data can be shared. Thus the operating system must undertake to manage the machine's memory and allow only authorised processes to address their parts of memory. It does this by monitoring memory address calls made by the processes and intercepts these if they are not valid for that process. Usually it will report to the process that it has an "invalid address reference". For this reason, UNIX is less susceptible to virus attacks than DOS, which operates no such control. Note that in DOS this error message could mean that there is no more memory however, in UNIX there could be the memory but it isn't allowed to be used.

Resource Sharing

Using the process concept, the computer's memory is shared amongst many processes and users. With such operating systems, other resources are also shared such as the processor, printer, disk storage, etc. Management of this sharing also falls to the operating system.

The type of resource shared determines the sharing mechanism. For instance, a processor can be shared by moving processes on to it in a controlled fashion (see scheduling). However, a printer must be given over to a process until the specified print job is complete – otherwise two processes would print over each other's job and render both unusable.

UNIX has programs known as daemons to handle such situations. Print daemons are also known as *"spoolers"*, which refers to the term given to the way they operate. Basically, when a user issues a command to print in UNIX (lp), a copy of the job to be printed is placed into a queue (known as *"spooling")*. When the printer has finished printing the current job, then it will take the next job out of the queue and begin to print.

Other devices – tape drives, etc. will have their own device handlers which become part of the operating system and extend its abilities to controlling these devices. For instance, a tape drive for backup purposes must not be used by more than one user at a time. Device handlers or *"drivers"* will be shipped with the product and future releases of the operating system to allow the operating system to make use of the device.

Scheduling

As it is possible for more than one process to reside on a UNIX system, each process needs to be executed on the CPU(s). Just as there needs to be management of the memory of the system, there also needs to be a method for organising the execution of these processes.

The simplest of UNIX systems, which involves just one processor, will be considered - there are systems that offer several but even more complex algorithms are required for such control.

If there is only one processor, then each process in the machine (including all the processes and daemons belonging to the operating system itself) need time on the processor. Some processes (especially those belonging to the operating system) need more time than others and so a method of organising the sharing of the CPU (known as scheduling) needs to be established.

First, there is a need to interrupt the processor itself. To achieve this, the computer uses interrupts, which are a normal, every minute occurrence. Basically, an interrupt alerts the processor to an event. Such events may include a successful fetch from a disk (to let the processor know its data is ready), a hardware failure, an interrupt generated by a network card, etc. These interrupts are classified - obviously a hardware fault is more serious than data being ready.

When the computer has <u>finished</u> the current instruction it will deal with the interrupt but, <u>it must finish the current instruction</u> i.e. an instruction in execution on the microprocessor is indivisible. It will then deal with the interrupt with the highest priority.

There are essentially two types of scheduling:

Non Pre-emptive Scheduling
In this type of scheduling, a job holds the CPU until it has completed or voluntarily terminates. All other processes on the system must wait until it voluntarily gives up the CPU or it *"blocks"* while waiting for I/O. This type of scheduling is employed in some network operating systems such as Novell. It can cause a problem if the process *"hangs"* - it will never voluntarily give up the CPU and until it does, no other processes can use it - all jobs are effectively *"dead"*.

Further, such scheduling is unfair as larger jobs may tie up the CPU for considerable amounts of time during which no other process can use it.

Pre-emptive Scheduling
An operating system utilising pre-emptive scheduling will actually take the CPU away from the current job and pass it on to another when certain conditions arise. Such conditions are again interrupts, which may be generated by it blocking awaiting input/output, a hardware problem, or that it has had its time allocation, etc. In the case of time allocation, the interrupt is generated from a hardware timer unit.

Again the current instruction is indivisible. UNIX is a pre-emptive operating system.

One of the major features of such systems is the allocation of a *"time slice"* to each process. The processes each have their turn on the CPU for a given amount of time (the time slice) at the end of that period of time, the process is taken off the processor and another placed on.

This is the so-called *"round robin"* scheduling algorithm where each process is given an equal timeslice and they are cycled on the processor in strict rotation (see below). Also, should one of the processes *"hang"*, then it will eventually be removed from the processor and the others allowed to proceed.

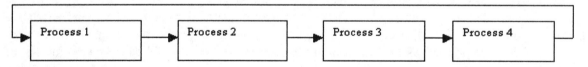

Initially this seems a fair way of allocating time to processes, however, on closer examination jobs fall into two categories:
- Those which are CPU intensive
- Those which are not CPU intensive

CPU intensive jobs are those that require large amounts of time on the CPU (they may be large mathematical problems).   The non-CPU intensive jobs will rarely fill their time slice on the processor, as they will almost always block awaiting input/output. Thus with round robin, the CPU intensive jobs effectively have more time per cycle on the CPU which is unfair on the other applications. Also, it wastes resources because actually switching between jobs (context switching) takes time and it may slow down I/O bound jobs. Often, it is the I/O bound jobs that are required to execute more quickly.

Multilevel Feedback Queues
UNIX operates a method of scheduling known as multi-level feedback queues in an attempt to resolve the contentions of round robin scheduling. With this type of scheduling, a new process enters the queuing system at the top level and is given an appropriately long timeslice for that level, in an attempt to make it complete in one timeslice. Should it fail to complete in one, then after leaving the CPU it is placed in the second level queue where it is given a shorter timeslice (again, equal to all other processes in this queue). Should it still fail to complete upon timing out, then it is placed in the third queue where it is given an even shorter timeslice (equal to all the other processes in that queue). Finally, should it still fail to complete, then it is placed in the fourth and final queue where it is given an even shorter timeslice, and where it will cycle (on a round robin basis) until completed. Thus the CPU intensive jobs very quickly find their way into the fourth queue taking up less resources than the less CPU intensive jobs:

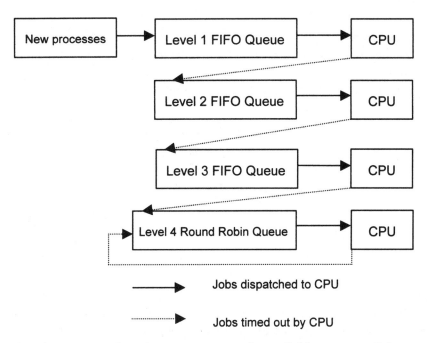

→ Jobs dispatched to CPU

┄┄► Jobs timed out by CPU

The above assumes only one processor is available as part of the computer system. In general, UNIX machines tend to have multiple processors but only one undertakes the *"main"* processing; the others handle communication, etc.

In order to increase the processing power available, UNIX machines are often *"clustered"* around a shared or networked filing system (NFS). This means that a user wishing to use the system could log into a machine of their choice and access files created on another machine. If the user was accessing a database held on the other machine, then it is possible for the machine hosting the database to perform some processing before passing on the requested information. The processing is thus split between two machines (in this case) and is known as *"distributed processing"*.

Processes in UNIX also have a priority between –20 and +20. Operating system daemons have the highest priority – normally towards +20. Users have a priority of 0 and can only alter their priority in the negative direction. Thus, a user can lower the priority of the less important jobs to get the more important one to run quicker. The priocntl command is used for this but should be avoided by all but experienced users.

Deadlock and Prevention

Complex operating systems with several processes running concurrently can save on the amount of resources required by sharing. Thus several users can share one printer for example. As there are fewer devices than there is demand, there can be contention between 2 or more processes for a device or devices. If not carefully controlled, in such positions deadlock becomes a serious threat to system integrity.

Two or more processes are said to be deadlocked (or in a deadly embrace) if each waits on a resource held and not released by the other:

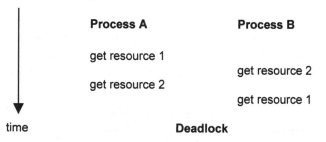

Starvation then occurs as processes wait on future execution sequence before they can proceed. Given time, more and more processes would join the queue waiting for these devices and end in starvation. Effectively, the system would grind to a halt.

Systems cannot be allowed to deadlock and the solution involves forcing processes to release a resource they are holding before requesting another resource. Access to the resources must also be controlled if they are not to conflict. The following solutions to deadlock problems have been devised:

Semaphores

Semaphores are a manual method of controlling access to a piece of code requiring a shared resource. For instance if a user wishes to print, they should check that the printer is available before attempting to use it. If it is not, then they should wait until it is.

Semaphores operate in exactly the same way as early trains used to obtain access to a single (bi-directional) piece of track:

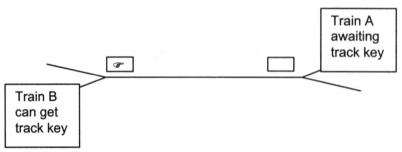

As train B approaches the shared piece of track, the driver takes the key and opens the points allowing access to the track. Train A must wait until the key is in the box - the points cannot be operated without it. When train B reaches the end of the shared track, the driver must place the key in the box. The driver of train A can then retrieve the key and use the track (placing it in the box at the other end of the track).

Systems programmers operate a similar principle by declaring a semaphore. The semaphore is initially set to 1 (available). When a process requires a resource; it executes a wait (on a named semaphore). If the value of the semaphore is 1, then 1 is deducted and it is allowed to proceed. If another process requires access to the same resource, as the semaphore is zero it will have to wait. When the first piece of code finishes with the shared resource, the programmer codes it so that it will SIGNAL the appropriate semaphore (adding 1 to its value). A waiting process will then wake up (subtract 1 from the semaphore) and then proceed.

Just as it is possible for the train driver to forget to replace the key and bring the railway to a halt, it is possible for the systems programmer to forget to SIGNAL the semaphore (or even put the SIGNAL command in the wrong place). In order to work, semaphores must be implemented very well. Thus just as automation has replaced keys on railway tracks, so semaphores in code have been superseded.

Monitors

Monitors have been introduced as a solution to the semaphore problem. Basically, the system programmer simply places the code accessing the resource between the two relevant monitor statements. Working in an almost identical manner, it is the responsibility of the operating system to control access to monitored code.

Multi Processors and Distributive Processing

Historically, computers had a single CPU and processed data entered. As networks have become more common, it has become possible to make systems more efficient by connecting computers together to share data and co-operate in their processing. Advances in technology have also brought multiple CPU machines.

Parallel Processing

If a problem can be divided into separate and unrelated parts, then those parts can be run separately and as such, the problem can be solved faster than if each part were run on a single processor. Known as parallel processing, this technique can be applied to either different computers or different processors inside the same computer.

Many tasks have some sort of relationship (especially in mathematics where most maths is sequentially based), and as such, parallel processing is a very difficult goal to achieve. Object orientation (OO) helps in this respect, as processing for a single object can be separated from that of other objects. To achieve parallel processing (at the user level) can be relatively easy, the user can log onto multiple machines and have them each processing the user's processes (see rsh and rlogin commands later). However, it is a much more challenging task to break up a single application into semi-unrelated parts that can run independently. Even more challenging, is to write a compiler to do this!

Distributed Systems

One way in which separated tasks can be executed at the same time is to execute them on different machines. This is achieved by a centralised machine dividing up the tasks and allocating them to different computers. The centralised machine then needs to collect the results as the processes finish. Obviously, there is an overhead associated with such management however, if the tasks are large enough, the elapsed time will be less.

Often referred to as "shared-nothing" architecture (because each processor does not share any resources with another), each system has its own memory, disk and data path to the network. For two computers to share memory blocks, places a significant overhead on the systems, as the sharing occurs over a network.

Multi-processor Systems

Here, separate processes are run in parallel using different processors inside the same computer. Multiple processes running on the same computer share disk resources and can also share segments of memory (with less overhead) than with distributed systems.

This type of architecture is sometime referred to as "shared-memory" or "shared resource" architecture. Sequent was one of the first UNIX vendors to develop a multi-processor system specifically designed to allow parallel programs to be written and executed on multiple processors. Now, many UNIX platforms are available in multiprocessor architectures.

Operating Systems - Reprise

UNIX is a good example of a multi-user multi-tasking operating system having all of the essential features necessary to support this. Essentially, the hardware required to support such an operating system can be as little as an ordinary PC with some extension to allow multiple users access. Such an extension can be either a networking card or multiple serial ports. Multiple serial ports would allow the serial connection of a dumb terminal, where a networking card would support the connection of a network using the Transmission Control Protocol/Internet Protocol (TCP/IP) protocol suite. The essential physical components are:

- Processor
- Memory
- Disk storage
- Communications (either networking card or multiple serial ports)
- A backup device is highly recommended

The major software components are:

- The kernel
- Device handlers/drivers
- Daemons

Using UNIX

One of the major benefits of using the UNIX operating system is its portability. UNIX will run on almost any machine from a PC to a mainframe. Thus once a user makes a commitment to the UNIX operating system, their investment is protected – they can move from one hardware platform to another. All of the applications they create and data they generate can easily be ported to their next choice of UNIX hardware. This is achieved because the Operating System has a common interface across platforms and that it comes with an *"open"* networking protocol (TCP/IP). It is not only the portability of the applications and data, which are important, but also the portability of skills. Once the UNIX operating system has been learned, the same command set can be used irrespective of machine type.

Unlike other operating systems, UNIX has a number of command sets. Known as *"shells"*, they all provide essentially the same basic functions but have command structures and extensions to suit specific groups of users. As standard, UNIX offers the C shell (which offers C like features), the bourne shell (a general purpose command set), and the Korn shell (which is an extended version of the Bourne shell offering the functionality of the C shell). Because of its relative ease of use, the Korn shell is becoming the industry standard.

The following diagram shows how applications interact with the shells and how the shells interact with the core operating system.

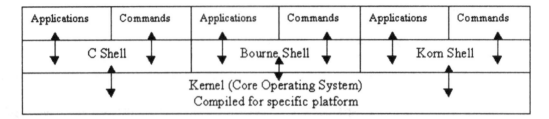

From the above diagram, it can be seen that the applications and user commands do not access the core operating system directly but pass through the shell. Thus if a different hardware platform is selected, the users can still use the same command set.

Whichever shell is used, they all offer similar functions, as shown below. The Korn and C shells however offer full programming support in addition:

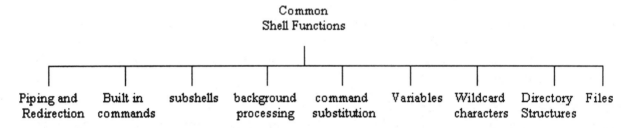

UNIX Commands (Korn Shell)

When learning a new operating system, a command list is a valuable source of reference. The table below gives a comprehensive list of commands, their DOS equivalent (where appropriate) and a brief description of the command. Please note that to specify all of the options for each command would make this a reference book in its own right. Therefore, only popular versions of the commands have been given - the exact syntax and all options supported by the variant of UNIX can be obtained from the UNIX help facility, called man (an abbreviation for manual entry). Unfortunately, in order to use man, the user needs to know the command they require. For instance man ls would give help on the ls command. man entries tend to be very long and cover the command syntax, and its switches (see below), a description of the command and examples of use. The table below should therefore serve as a useful reference.

Variables

Before continuing, it is necessary to understand something about the concept of variables in UNIX. Like a programming language, the shells in UNIX support variables. These variables can be either local to a process or "environmental". When they are local, they are only available in that process and are lost upon termination.

Environmental variables are essentially local variables that have been exported. The export command in UNIX is used to make a variable available to all sub-processes of the parent shell. The concept of a child process has already been discussed - should a parent create a variable and export it, then it is available to all of its children. It should however, be noted that an environmental variable is changed by the child process, then this change is not reflected in any process other than itself and its children (and only then after export). The common way of remembering this rule is to think of it in human terms - someone can inherit physical properties of their parent - hair colour, etc, but cannot pass them back.

UNIX uses variables extensively. PATH is a special variable which is used to hold the given search path of the user. HOME is used to hold the home account reference for the user - thus cd $HOME will take the user immediately back to their home directory - irrespective of their position in the directory structure. Here, the $ instructs UNIX to replace the variable name with its contents before executing the command. The general rule is, that the variable name is used for storing to the variable (read, export, used in arithmetic, assigned a values, etc.) where the variable name prefixed by a $ is used for the contents of a variable. A full list of all environmental variables available to the current shell can be obtained using the env command.

Standard Input/Output (stdio)

UNIX treats everything as a file, and as such output can easily be redirected. UNIX has two special files - standard input and standard output. These are often referred to in UNIX commands and utilities. Normally, standard input is mapped to the keyboard and standard output to the screen.

Please note that UNIX is case sensitive and all commands are lowercase.

UNIX Command (Korn Shell)	DOS equivalent (if applicable)	Description
*	*	Wildcard character
alias [aliasname] command		Allows the command given to be executed by typing the name of the alias. Without any parameters, the alias command displays a list of aliases.
banner text		Produces an on-screen banner using the text provided. Text must be enclosed in " " if there is more than one word.
bg [job ..]		Moves the job into the background. Or resumes stopped jobs.
break n		Used in shell script programming, break exits from the smallest enclosing for, while, until or select loops, or from the nth loop if n is specified.
cal [year]		Gives a calendar for the specified year.
case .... esac		Used for shell script programming, case is used in a similar fashion to most programming languages.
cat filename		Short for concatenate, cat is used to type the contents of the file specified to standard output.
cd	cd	Change directory.
chmod rights filename		Used to change the privileges associated with a file.
continue [n]		The opposite of break. Goes to the top of the smallest enclosing loop, or to the top of the nth loop if n is specified.
cp <filename> <newname>	copy <filename> <newname>	Copy a file.
date		Displays the system date and time.
echo [arg]	Echo	Echos the argument on standard output. Particularly used for displaying the contents of a variable e.g. echo $PATH.
ed		Invokes the line editor ed.
egrep		Extended version of grep (see grep below).
env		Displays a list of all environmental variables currently set in the current shell.
eval [arg...]		Constructs a command by concatenating arg together, and separating each by a space.
exit		Exits the Korn shell (same as Ctrl-D).
export		Exports a variable - once exported, a variable is available to all subshells.
false		Used in shell script programming, false is a conditional value, which is permanently false.
fc		Provides access to the user's history file - to allow commands to be re-executed or edited.
fg [job ..]		Moves background jobs into the foreground.
fgrep		Fast version of grep (see grep below).

find directory expression		Generates a list of pathnames that are in each of the given directories, and applies expression to each of them.
for		Used for shell script programming, for loops operate in a similar way to most programming languages.
function		Used for shell script programming, function allows a function to be declared.
grep [option] pattern [file]		Searches the input files, for lines matching the specified pattern. Each line found is copied to standard output (depending upon switches)
history		Displays a list of commands issued that session - can be recalled using the r command.
if		Used for shell script programming, if statements operate in a similar way to most programming languages.
jobs [-lp] [job]		Used to display information about specified jobs.
kill [-n] pid		Kills processes n is the kill level (discussed later).
let arg		Evaluates one or more arithmetic expressions.
ln file target		Links files to target.
lp *<filename>*	print *<filename>*	Print a file.
lpr*<filename>*	print *<filename>*	Print a file.
ls	dir	Directory listing
mail		Mail utility, discussed later.
mkdir *<dirname>*	md *<dirname>*	Create a directory.
more		A filter, used to page output to the screen one screen at a time. The user advanced by pressing the space bar to advance one screen, or enter to advance one line.
mv *<oldloc> <newloc>*	move *<oldloc> <newloc>*	Move a file.
mv *<oldname> <newname>*	rename <oldname> <newname>	Rename a file.
newgrp [group] [arg..]		Changes the group ID of a process to the group specified.
nohup command		Causes the process created by command to continue to run after the user has exited the system.
pg filename		Displays one or more filenames a screenful at a time.
print arg		Displays output on standard output - similar to echo.
pwd		Print working directory.
r		Recalls commands listed using the history command, use r <command no> where <command no> is the number given in the history listing.
read variablename		Reads the specified variable from standard input.
readonly		Used in shell script programming, sets a variable to read only.
return		Returns from the function to the invoking shell.
rm *<filename>*	del *<filename>*	Remove a file.
rmdir *<dirname>*	rd *<dirname>*	Remove a directory.
select		Used in shell script programming to create a menu - see later.
set		Used to set options.

shift [n]		Used with shell script programming, shift shifts the positional parameters to the left by n. If n is not specified, then 1 is assumed.
sleep -nn	Often used to create a timed pause	Causes the shell to sleep for nn seconds.
sort		A sort utility used o sort files.
stty		Displays terminal settings.
su [userid] [-c command]		Switches user to the userID specified - need to supply password. If userID is omitted, then root is assumed (sometimes known in this context as superuser. If the -c option is used, the command following is immediately executed upon successful switch.
tail		Displays the last part of a file.
tee		Used to pipe the output of one command into two or more others.
test		This command is used to evaluate a condition and is used as a conditional expression to all commands which require a condition (e.g. wile, until, if, etc.) Can be shortened to [ ]. Thus test VAR1 -le 0] will test variable VAR1 to see if it is less than or equal to zero. [VAR1 -le 0] is functionally the same - note the spaces after the first [and before the second] - they are needed.
time		Displays the elapsed time on standard output.
times		Shows how much time the user's current korn shell has consumed.
tr {string1} [string2]		Transliterates characters in a file. For instance tr "[a-z]" "[A-Z]" <filein >fileout will take file in can convert all characters to upper case writing them to fileout.
trap [action] [condition]		Tells ksh the action to take when the specified conditions arise. Often used to trap ctrl-c to stop a user breaking out of a menu system.
true		The opposite to false and used for similar reasons.
ulimit		Sets or displays system resource limits.
umask		Sets or displays a file creation mask - see later.
unalias aliasname		Removes the aliassing of the specified alias.
uniq [input] [output]		Copies lines from input to output, eliminating any adjacent lines that are duplicates.
unset		Used to unset options
until		Used for shell script programming, until loops operate in a similar way to most programming languages.
wait		Instructs ksh to wait until a process has finished.
wc		Word count utility. Counts words, lines and characters in a given file.
what [file ...]		Looks for character strings in the files specified.
whence		
while		Used for shell script programming, while loops operate in a similar way to most programming languages.
who		Displays information about users logged onto the system
whoami		Same as who but only for the user issuing.

Switches

UNIX commands have a format similar to that shown below:

ls   –la   /usr/phil/applications

(a)   (b)   (c)

a is the command – in this case ls for directory listing

b is the switch(es)/flag(s) to extend the command:

      l gives a long listing (including date and time)

      a lists all files (including hidden)

c is the operand – in this case the directory to list

It should be noted that in UNIX, the flags are commonplace and are used with almost all commands to extend the range of the command. Thus the ls command, would simply list the files, ls -l would list the files using the long format. ls -la, would list all the files including hidden files (files in UNIX are hidden by prefixing them with a dot). It is generally accepted that it is better to remember the command and its frequent variants, than all of the options. Thus, whenever the command is required to perform a different function, it can be looked up using the man utility. The two examples below show the ls command in use. The first, ls -lisa, produces a long listing(l) for all files(a) showing the size (s) in blocks and the inode number (i). By default, this listing is given in alphabetical order:

```
$ ls -lisa|more
total 6963
   7324902   2 -rw-------    1 phil     staff     25        Mar 23 11:53 #fred#
   7324800   8 drwx--x--x 46 phil     staff     3584      May 30 12:30 .
   7324817   2 lrwxrwxrwx  1 phil     staff     36        Mar 23 11:52 .#fred ->
phil@isis.sunderland.ac.uk.16165:1
        2   1 dr-xr-xr-x 21 root                root      21        May 30 12:51 ..
   7324877   2 -rw-r--r--  1 phil     staff     446       Jun 27  1997 .ab_library
   7324882   2 -rw-r--r--  1 phil     staff     141       Jun 27  1997 .ab_library.lock
   7328640   2 drwxr-xr-x  2 phil     staff     512       Sep 23  1994 .cetables
   7324804   2 -rw-r--r--  1 phil     staff     747       Mar  8  1996 .cshrc
   7324884   2 -rw-r--r--  1 phil     staff     538       Jun 27  1997 .default.wst
   7324812   2 -rw-r--r--  1 phil     staff     993       Sep 23  1994 .desksetdefaults
   7368960   2 drwxr-xr-x 14 phil     staff     512       Apr 28 20:46 .dt
   7324856   0 -rwxr-xr-x  1 phil     staff     0         Jul  2  1996 .dtprofile
   7324887   2 -rw-rw-rw-  1 phil     staff     29        Jun 27  1997 .eserve-options
   7324819   2 -rw-r--r--  1 phil     staff     28        Apr  8  1997 .forward
   8714894   2 drwxr-xr-x  3 phil     staff     512       Feb 24 15:48 .fullcircl
--More--
```

By using the r option, the order can be reversed:

```
$ ls -lisar|more
total 6963
   7324839   2 -rwx------  1 phil     staff     28        Oct 26  1994 year
   7324900   2 -rwxr-xr-x  1 phil     staff     63        Feb  7  1998 wonder
   7324868   2 -rwx------  1 phil     staff     246       Mar  5  1997 whilex3
   7324866   2 -rwx------  1 phil     staff     68        Mar  5  1997 whilex2
   7324828   2 -rwxrwxrwx  1 phil     staff     69        Mar  5  1997 whilex
   7324857   0 -r--r--r--  1 phil     staff     0         Jul  2  1996 WaterDrops.pm
   7324840  12 -rw-r--r--  1 phil     staff     5572      Jan 27  1998 vmstat.txt
   7324861   6 -rw-r--r--  1 phil     staff     2534      Dec 11  1996 uuencode.txt
   7324933  24 -rw-r--r--  1 phil     staff     11486     May 30 12:30 uucpdos.txt
   7324932  22 -rw-r--r--  1 phil     staff     11156     May 30 12:27 uucp.txt
   7324829   2 -rwxrwxrwx  1 phil     staff     67        Oct  7  1994 untilsp
   9373441   2 drwxr-xr-x  2 phil     staff     512       Apr 27 14:18 unixbook
   7324920   2 -rw-------  1 phil     staff     27        Apr 23 12:14 umask2.txt
   7324803  16 -rw-r--r--  1 phil     staff     7657      Apr 23 12:13 umask.txt
   7324871  52 -rw-r--r--  1 phil     staff     26065     Jun  9  1997 turnnew.gif
   7324821   2 -rwxrwxrwx  1 phil     staff     113       Oct  7  1994 timest
   7324851   2 -rwx------  1 phil     staff     31        Dec  5  1995 testtrap
--More--
```

All UNIX commands behave in a similar manner!

Multi-user extensions

The commands considered thus far could relate equally to a single user operating system. With multi-user Operating Systems, the files of a user need to be protected from other users of the system. In UNIX, this is achieved through file permissions. When using the ls command, a combination of the characters drwx appear on the left hand side similar to that below:

-rwxr--r-x

The first dash denotes that it is either a file (-) or a directory (d). The following 3 characters represent the rights to the owner, in this case rwx indicating that the user has read, write and execute permissions to the file. The 2nd group of 3 characters represent the rights to the group – in this case members of the group that the file belongs to can only read the file. The final 3 characters represent the rights to the rest of the world - in this case read and execute.

To change the permissions of the file, the user needs to own the file or be the systems administrator and would use the chmod command. There are essentially 2 ways of using this command but, the easiest and most common is to use the following table to determine the value of the rights to be added and the command below to add them:

Right required	Value
Read	4
Write	2
Execute (search if the target is a directory)	1

To give more than one right, simply add the values together: for read and execute it is 4+1=5.

chmod abc *<filename>*

where a indicates the rights to the owner, b indicates the rights to the group and c indicates the rights to the rest of the world.

Thus the command to give all rights to all users would be chmod 777 *<filename>*. For web pages, normally chmod 755 * is used. This gives the owner rwx, the group r-x and the rest of the world r-x to all files in that directory.

A file obviously has an owner – the user id that created it. The user can also belong to a group (perhaps the developer group), the file can also belong to a group and it is to this group identity that the group rights apply. For instance if the file belongs to the developer group, then any member of the developer group will have the rights indicated by the group rights. Ownership of the file can usually only be altered by the systems administrator using the chown command, the group can be changed by the systems administrator or the owner using the chgrp command.

Printing

In order to support multi-user access, the printer functions are also extended in UNIX. The basic print command is lp or lpr (an abbreviation for line printer) followed by the filename e.g. lp *<myfile>* would queue the file myfile for later printing.

Often users wish to check the status of printing, perhaps to determine the position of their print job in the queue. This can be achieved using the lpq command. When using the lpq command, notice that each entity in the queue has a unique job number. Should a user wish to remove a job from the queue, then they need to know this job number and use the lprm command as lprm *<jobno>*.

It is usual for a multi-user system to have several printers connected to it and, providing they have permission, the user can select whichever printer they wish to use for a job. This is achieved by using the –P switch in the lp command. Thus lp –P*<printer>* *<filename>* will cause the file named to be printed on the printer named. Status check and job cancellation also support the –P switch.

Editing Files

UNIX provides several editors for the editing of text. Two of the most notable are vi and emacs. Unfortunately, vi is most notable for its user unfriendliness where emacs provides an editing structure that is more suited for C or other program editing. Both editors are essentially basic text editors with many useful functions. Both editors are invoked from the command line by typing their name followed by a filename e.g. vi myfile or emacs myfile (the filename can either be a new file or a file to be edited).

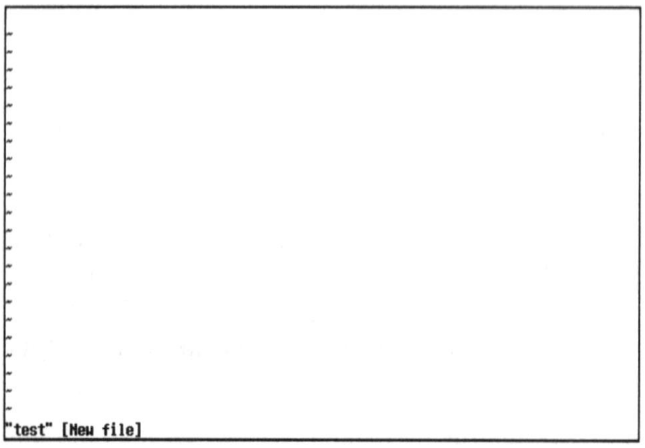

```
                                  "test" [New file]
```

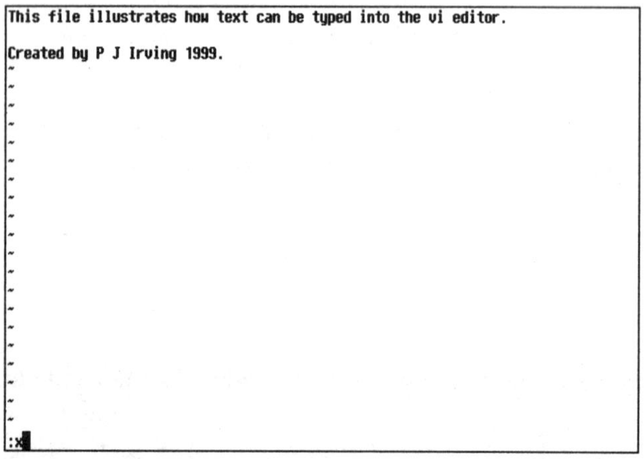

```
This file illustrates how text can be typed into the vi editor.

Created by P J Irving 1999.
~
~
~
~
~
~
~
~
~
~
~
~
~
:x
```

Because the emacs editor is usually only available in the C shell, vi will be considered as it is available in both shells. Many users new to vi, feel it is an acronym for virtually impossible! It is true to say, that vi is very difficult to use but, it is a useful editor to know - as it is available on all versions of UNIX and often one of the only editors available in the event of a systems crash. vi is essentially a full screen editor - when invoked, the editor presents the user with a screen similar to that shown (the filename here is test and it is a new file – as can be seen at the bottom of the screen):

vi has two modes

- Command mode
- Edit mode

In command mode, commands are entered and appear at the bottom of the screen (in the diagram shown the command for save and exit (:x) is being used. A list of commands that can be used in this mode is given in the table below.

The edit mode provides commands and facilities for entering/editing text. To leave edit mode and return to command mode, press the Esc key (most users like to press this twice - to make sure they leave edit mode! When it is pressed twice, a beep should be heard).

Cursor Movement

The cursor can only be moved in command mode (if unsure press Esc twice). Use the cursor keys to move around the screen of text (NB the cursor will not normally move beyond the text). Users should be aware that the cursor cannot be moved around when in text entry mode - this will insert control codes for cursor movement in the document.

Deleting text

Text can be deleted in insert/edit mode by using the backspace key - sometimes this too will insert control codes and the delete key should be used. Unfortunately this depends upon the terminal settings and the user is best advised to try first.

A summary of commands is as follows (please note the colon (:) as it is very important and must precede the commands where indicated). Like UNIX in general, vi is case sensitive:

Command Type	Command	Description
:!command <enter>		Execute command in a subshell and then return to vi.
:r!command <enter>		Execute command in a subshell and read its output into the edit buffer at the current position.
Cursor Movement		Can only be moved in command mode.
		Cursor up or k key moves up one line.
		Cursor down or j key moves down one line.
		Cursor right or the l key moves right one character (will not wrap).
		Cursor left or the h key (will not wrap).
		^ moves to the start to the line.

		$ moves to the end of the line.
		b key - back one word.
		w key - forward on word.
		Ctrl-D down half a screen.
		Ctrl-F forward one screen.
		Ctrl-U up half a screen.
		Ctrl-B back one screen.
		:nn <enter> goes to specified line number.
Cut/Paste	:<range>y<enter>	Cuts (yanks) lines specified in the range e.g.: 1,4y<enter>. Cuts the lines 1-4 (inclusive) and places them in the paste buffer.
	:pu	Pastes (Puts) the text after the current line. To copy the block, it must cut and then pasted immediately back. As the buffer is left unchanged, it can be pasted again.
Deletion	dd	Deletes the current line.
	x	Deletes the character after the cursor.
	dw	Deletes the word the cursor is currently over.
	D	Deletes from the current position to the end of the line.
	:<range>d<enter>	Deletes lines specified in the range e.g.: 1,4d<enter>. Deletes the lines 1-4 (inclusive).
	dw	Deletes the word of which.the cursor is over the first letter.
Exit	:q	quit if the file has been saved.
	:q!	exit and discard changes.
Insertion	i	Inserts text in front of the current cursor position.
	a	Appends text after the current cursor position.
	o	Inserts a line below the current line and enters insert mode.
	O	Inserts a line above the current line and enters insert mode.
	R	Overwrites text.
Joining lines	Ctrl-J	When the cursor is positioned at the end of a line and ctrl-J pressed it appends the line below .
Refresh screen	Ctrl-L	Redraws the screen
Replacing Text (character)		Position the cursor over the character to be replaced, press the r key and type the replacement character.
Replacing Text (word)		Position the cursor at the start of the word, type the two characters cw, type the replacement word followed by the Esc key.
Replacing Text (line)		Position the cursor anywhere on the line, type the two characters cc, type the replacement text followed by the Esc key.
Save	:w <filename>	save file with optional filename (otherwise saves as the name it was opened with).
Search	/sss/<enter>	Searches forward for the current position for string sss.
	?sss?<enter>	Searches backward for the current position for string sss.
	n	Repeat last search.
	N	Repeat last search (in opposite direction).

It should be noted that there are many other commands available in vi however, it is practice that is required to get to grips with this strange editor. What has been provided is the common commands required for a user - further commands and features of this very powerful editor can be obtained using the manual entry for it.

This can be obtained by typing man vi at the prompt:

```
$ man vi

User Commands                           vi(1)

NAME
    vi, view, vedit - screen-oriented (visual) display editor
    based on ex

SYNOPSIS
    /usr/bin/vi [ - | -s ] [-l] [-L] [-R] [ -r [ filename]]
        [ -t tag ] [-v] [-V] [-x] [ -wn ] [-C]
        [ +command | -c command ] filename...

    /usr/bin/view [ - | -s ] [-l] [-L] [-R] [ -r [ filename]]
        [ -t tag ] [-v] [-V] [-x] [ -wn ] [-C]
        [ +command | -c command ] filename...

    /usr/bin/vedit [ - | -s ] [-l] [-L] [-R] [ -r [ filename]]
        [ -t tag ] [-v] [-V] [-x] [ -wn ] [-C]
        [ +command | -c command ] filename...

    /usr/xpg4/bin/vi [ - | -s ] [-l] [-L] [-R] [ -r [ filename]]
        [ -t tag ] [-v] [-V] [-x] [ -wn ]
--More--(4%)
```

Using the facilities of a multi user operating system

There are essentially two ways of accessing the operating system:
- From a terminal (or a PC based telnet session)
- From a UNIX workstation

If accessed from a terminal (or a PC based telnet session), the user will be presented with a login screen similar to that shown below. If a PC with telnet is being used, the multiple telnet sessions can be activated by a user giving the user several virtual screens. The user would simply switch between these screens by selecting them in windows.

```
Welcome to MAINSERV, the University's
main UNIX server.

login:
```

The screen shown from a workstation will vary with the type of workstation.

At the login prompt, the user simply enters their login name followed by return and then their allocated password.

If this is typed correctly, then the user may be presented with several messages and will finally be given a prompt similar to that shown.

```
SunOS 5.6


Welcome to MAINSERV, the University's main UNIX server.

login: phil
Password:
Last login: Fri Apr 16 23:37:06 from phil_pc.sun
Sun Microsystems Inc.   SunOS 5.6     Generic August 2000


$
```

As UNIX is a command driven operating system, then the commands must be typed (and be syntactically correct) at the prompt. The $ prompt indicates that either the Korn or Bourne shell are being used – the easiest way to establish which it is, is to type an unrecognised command e.g. hgjjkjt. UNIX will then respond with an error message – the text preceding the error message indicates the shell: ksh denotes the Korn shell and bsh denotes the Bourne shell. The C shell prompt is a %.

To logout of UNIX the user presses and holds the Ctrl key followed by D. On some systems users are forced to type exit, logout or logoff – depending upon the system administrator. **Please note that if the user changes shells, then they need to logout of each shell.**

UNIX is capable of supporting many different terminal types, some of which may be actual terminals whilst others may be telnet sessions. As each terminal has its own characteristics, then UNIX needs to know which terminal is being used in order to support it correctly. Terminal types in UNIX are identified by the TERM variable. This variable will have a default value set but it may be different to the terminal being used. To determine the value of terminal the user should use the echo command (in the Korn shell) followed by the name of the variable preceded by a $ e.g. echo $TERM. The system will then respond with the current setting e.g. vt420. If the terminal types do not match, then it is usually easiest to change the variable in UNIX and to fall back to a well supported standard e.g. vt100. This can be achieved using:

    TERM=vt100;export TERM

Note that, normally, uppercase characters are used to denote variables in UNIX.

UNIX Commands

There are many commands supported by the UNIX operating system (a full list of Korn shell commands is given later in this chapter). At anytime, the user can obtain help on a command by using the man command. For example, man ls would display the manual entry for the ls command.

One of the unique features of UNIX is that a competent user can actually write a program using the facilities and commands provided by the shell. This is known as Shell Script programming and is in much demand in industry. UNIX also provides the ability for these scripts to become available as commands to other users, and to also be included in shell scripts. This has led to UNIX being described as a "set of tools to build other tools". For this reason, there are a large number of commands available in UNIX, which can be very roughly divided into the following six categories:

- Device Related
- Process Control
- File locate/text processing
- General Commands
- Filing System
- Programming Support

The concept of everything being a file in UNIX is supported by all of the above command categories.

Device related commands refer to commands that in some way interact with devices. For instance, tape streamers, printers, etc. These control the operation of the device (through device drivers) but are seen by the operating systems as merely being files. Thus the standard UNIX command for backing up to tape, tar (short for tape archive), will work with a file as well as a tape streamer. The only difference being the destination of the output:

    tar –cvf /dev/rmt0

c tells tar to create the archive, v is the verbose option, which displays tar's progress, and f indicates that the tar file is being specified. The /dev/rmt0 is a special file – it is the first tape device connected to the system. Hence the /dev/rmt0, the second tape drive will be /dev/rmt1 and so on.

The user could just have simply used the filename myarchive, which would have written the output to this file rather than a tape drive.

Process Control commands refer to the commands that are available to both the user and the system administrator to control processes. For obvious security reasons, a user can only control processes that belong to them, however, the system administrator needs absolute power and therefore can control any process. Users can see processes they have running by using the ps command. This produces a listing similar to that shown.

```
$ ps -ef|more
      UID    PID  PPID  C    STIME TTY        TIME CMD
     root      0     0  0    May 07 ?         0:00 sched
     root      1     0  0    May 07 ?         2:43 /etc/init -
     root      2     0  0    May 07 ?         0:01 pageout
     root      3     0  0    May 07 ?        29:55 fsflush
     root    178     1  0    May 07 ?         0:15 /usr/lib/nfs/statd
     root    431     1  0    May 07 ?         0:00 /usr/lib/saf/sac -t 300
     root     69     1  0    May 07 ?         0:23 /etc/opt/SUNWatm/bin/atmsnmpd -n
     root     71     1  0    May 07 ?         0:10 /etc/opt/SUNWatm/bin/ilmid
     root    173     1  0    May 07 ?         2:06 /usr/sbin/inetd -s
     root    143     1  0    May 07 ?         0:39 /usr/sbin/rpcbind
     root    207     1  0    May 07 ?         1:33 /usr/sbin/syslogd -n -z 14
     root   6284   173  0 11:01:12 ?         0:00 in.telnetd
     root    201     1  0    May 07 ?        43:40 /usr/lib/autofs/automountd
     root    145     1  0    May 07 ?         2:45 /usr/sbin/keyserv
     root    357     1  0    May 07 ?         0:46 /usr/lib/utmpd
     paul  12372 12370  0 11:38:06 pts/49     0:00 -csh
     root    181     1  0    May 07 ?         0:06 /usr/lib/nfs/lockd
     root    306     1  0    May 07 ?         0:03 /usr/sbin/cron
     root    374     1  0    May 07 ?         0:00 /usr/sbin/vold
--More--
```

UID is the user ID of the owner of the process, PID is the process IDentificaiton number, PPID is the PID of the parent process, C is now obsolete but used to be for processor scheduling, STIME is the starting time for the process (including date), TTY is the terminal the process was started from, TIME is cumulative execution time for the process and CMD is the full command name.

Usually processes are left untouched in UNIX and errors are resolved by the operating system. Occasionally, a user may want to intervene – for instance someone could have sent a program away that has gone into an infinite loop – to UNIX it is executing normally and would only be terminated if it demands more resources than it is allowed. In such cases the user may want to terminate the process and can use the kill command to achieve this. The kill command has the following basic syntax:

kill –n PID

Where n is a number denoting the severity of the kill. A kill without a number is equivalent to a kill –15. This is a "soft" kill, which terminates the process and closes all dependent processes. Severity ranges to – 9, which is a "hard" kill. A kill –9 is very severe and instantly terminates the process – dependent processes are left to falter themselves. For this reason kill –9's should be avoided where possible.

File locate and text processing commands are extremely powerful in the UNIX operating system. Such commands allow users to search not only filenames but also actual files for occurrences of strings. Perhaps the best known of these commands is grep. The most basic syntax of grep is:

grep <string> file

string is obviously the search string and file is the file to be searched. For example grep the engsummer would search the engsummer file for occurrences of the word the. Where matches are found the entire line will be output.

grep has two other associated versions. fgrep is a faster (but more limited) version of grep, which can only search for exact characters. egrep is an extended version of grep, which offers more facilities, is usually the fastest and can search for more complex patterns.

UNIX also offers text processing commands such as awk. awk is a programmable text processing utility that scans input lines and processes every line that matches a specified pattern criteria. awk, which got its name from the initial letters of the surnames of its creators (Aho, Weinberger and Kernighan) is an extremely powerful utility – so much so that there are books dedicated to it. It is based upon the C programming constructs and is beyond the scope of this chapter.

The other main text processing command in UNIX is sed, which scans one or more files and performs and editing action on all lines that match a pattern.

Filing system commands, as would be expected, are provided for the manipulation of the filing system. More details can be found on these earlier in the chapter.

Programming support commands provide the constructs necessary to write programs in the shell. The degree of support for programming varies from shell to shell (as does the syntax). The Korn shell provides support for the major programming constructs of sequence, selection and iteration with the following commands:

Construct	Command / Description
Sequence	Placing commands in their logical sequence
Selection	if ... then .... else case
Iteration	for loops until loops while loops

General commands in UNIX form the rest of the command set. Such commands are provided for a variety of purposes such as arithmetic, clearing the screen, production of calendars, testing to see if a file exists, etc. The table below gives a list of the major UNIX commands available in the Korn shell:

Command	Description	Command	Description
alias	Create an alias for a command.	lprm	Remove print requests from the queue.
banner	Produce a primitive banner from text	lpstat	Status of the printer.
bc	Basic calculator.	ls	Directory listing.
cal	Produce a calendar for a given year.	mail	Mail to given users.
cd	Change Directory.	man	Display manual page.
chmod	Change file access privileges.	mesg	Permit or deny messages (from the talk command).
compress	Compress a file – equivalent to zip on a PC.	mkdir	Create directory.
cp	Copy a file.	more	Filter to split up output one screen at a time.
cpio	Copy/send to input/output devices.	mv	Move or rename a file.
cut	Cut a specified column of text from a file.	news	Command to keep user informed of current events – created by administrator.
date	Give current system date/time.	passwd	Change password.
du	Summarise disk usage.	pwd	Print working directory.
echo	Display on screen.	quota	Display disk quota.
ed	Basic line editor.	rm	Remove a file.
egrep	Extended grep.	rmdir	Remove a directory.
emacs	A C shell editor.	sort	Sort a file.
env	Detail the current environmental variables.	talk	Send a message to a user.
exit	Return from a subshell.	tar	Tape archive.
fgrep	Fast grep.	test	Evaluate a condition.
finger	Display information about users.	umask	Default mask for file creation.
ftp	File Transfer Protocol.	unalias	Remove an alias.
grep	File search utility	uncompress	Uncompress the file.

history	Displays command history.	uptime	How long has the system been up.
hostname	Gives name of current host.	users	Display a list of users logged in.
login	Login to a system.	vi	Visual editor.
logout	Logout of a system.	wc	A count of lines or characters in a file.
lp	Print command.	who	Who is currently logged on to the system.
lpq	Detail contents of a print queue.	whoami	What is the current user's ID.
lpr	Submit print requests.		

Input/Output Redirection

UNIX uses the concept of standard input and output to refer to where the commands, parameters, etc. are entered and where the resultant output is sent. Normally these are connected to the keyboard and the screen respectively, however these may be redirected.

Metacharacters are of special importance in UNIX. They are special characters and have specific meaning. The following is a brief list of metacharacters:

$$| \quad > \quad >> \quad < \quad \& \quad \&\& \quad ||$$

The function of these metacharacters is:

Piping (|)

Originally UNIX was built with few utilities as the original designers had fairly strong notions on how utilities should be built. To support their vision, the designers built into UNIX a special mechanism called a pipe.

Basically, a pipe allows the user to specify that the output of one process is to be used as input to another. Two or more processes can be connected together forming a "pipeline" of data flowing from the first to the last process:

Process 1 → Process 2 → Process 3 → Process 4

Pipelines allow many everyday problems to be solved by the simple arrangement of processes. For instance the **who** command allows a user to see who is currently using the system, should there be a number of users, they may prefer the list to be sorted into order. The who command does not have a flag to allow the data to be sorted but this doesn't matter as the user can use a pipeline to pass the output of the who command into the sort command to sort it:

who → sort → (output appears on screen)

Should there prove to be a number of users who quickly scroll off the screen, then the user can add the **more** filter to the pipeline to display only one screen full of information at a time:

who → sort → more → (output appears on screen)

A filter alters the output of a command in some way – more is a filter to break the output up one screen at a time.

The pipeline mechanism is fundamental and extremely powerful, it allows problems to be solved by combining commands and utilities rather than having to write a new one from scratch.

Using the pipeline couldn't be simpler; the vertical bar (|) is simply placed between the commands thus:

who → sort becomes **who | sort**

and,

who → sort → more becomes **who | sort | more**

The screen shot below shows an example of the who command being used:

Pipelines offer still more:

Firstly, as UNIX is a multitasking operating system the second process can begin work before the first process has ended, thus reducing the total time taken.

```
$who|more
john    pts/45    Apr 13  15:00  (123.123.123.123)
bill    pts/44    Apr 26  12:45  (123.123.123.023)
fred    pts/23    Apr 18  09:19  (123.123.123.044)
phil    pts/33    Apr 24  08:15  (123.123.123.099)
root    console   Apr 24  12:02
$
$who|sort|more
bill    pts/44    Apr 26  12:45  (123.123.123.023)
fred    pts/23    Apr 18  09:19  (123.123.123.044)
john    pts/45    Apr 13  15:00  (123.123.123.123)
phil    pts/33    Apr 24  08:15  (123.123.123.099)
root    console   Apr 24  12:02
$
```

Second is flexibility. Should the utility required not be available and can't be constructed by pipelining standard commands, then it can be written in the shell (or even in C) and added into the UNIX repertoire.

Redirection

UNIX provides another useful feature similar to pipelines and that is redirection. Redirection allows the users to either:

- Store the output of a process to a file (output redirection) or
- Use the contents of a file as input to a process (input redirection)

Note the subtle difference between redirection and pipelines (you don't use files in pipelines).

Output Re-direction

Is a very useful feature, as it allows the output of a process into a file so that it may be used in some way later. Perhaps a program is being started and an error message is received but disappears before it can be seen. By redirecting the output to a file it can be viewed at leisure. This is possible in UNIX; the screen is simply another file (remember the file concept!).

The two metacharacters used for output redirection are > and >>.
> creates or overwrites the filename specified where,
>> appends standard output to the end of the file. Should the file not exist, then it will be created.

Examples:
date>dirfile - creates/overwrites a file called dirfile and puts in the system date
ls -l>>dirfile - appends a directory listing to the file created above

```
$ date>datefile.txt
$ cat datefile.txt
Tuesday April 26 21:14:07 BST 1999
$ date>>datefile.txt
$ cat datefile.txt
Tuesday April 27 21:14:07 BST 1999
Tuesday April 27 21:14:29 BST 1999
$
```

Output redirection can also be used to create files by using the cat command. Without parameters, cat simply copies its standard input (which in this case is the keyboard) thus cat>myfile.txt will copy input from the keyboard to the myfile.txt file. To end the cat command use control D.

Input Re-direction

Input redirection allows the user to prepare the data to be input to a process, ahead of it being needed (usually in a file). The file is then used as input to the command and takes the form:
> **command<*filename***

e.g. suppose the user wished to mail themselves a copy of the file created earlier:
> mail phil<myfile.txt

The mail command also accepts multiple recipients and thus could be used to send to several users:
> mail phil caron john mike bill stuart < myfile.txt

It should be noted that this form of mail is from the command line at UNIX, and that there are many other electronic mail packages that provide more functionality.

It is also possible to use the << metacharacters for input redirection. However, this is reserved for special cases where a shell script programmer wishes to supply standard input to other commands as inline text. This is beyond the scope of this chapter.

Input and output redirection can be mixed thus:
> **command<*inputfile*>*outputfile*** is legal.

Here a command will be fed input from the input file and will direct its output to the output file. This would allow a user to provide a text file (perhaps user Ids to be created) to the creation command. The messages from that command will be redirected to the output file. The operation can then be left unattended to create the Ids.

Mail

Briefly touched upon above, the mail command is important and is worthy of further treatment. As standard, UNIX comes with its own email system which includes mail handlers built on the Simple Mail Transfer Protocol (SMTP). mail or mailx (as it is known on some variants of UNIX), are command line commands which allow users to send and receive electronic mail. For the purposes of this discussion, the command mail will be used (this may need to be replaced by mailx on some systems). The use of electronic mail is now widespread and its benefits known. In UNIX, the mail command has many features - not all of which can be described in a chapter. For further information on mail and mailx the man entries should be consulted. The most basic form of the mail command is shown below:

mail -H [-f filename] [userID]

If a list of usernames is supplied, mail reads standard input, mails it to the given users and then terminates. Username can be local login ID's, an internet email address, a filename or a mail group (see below).

If no usernames are specified, then mail assumes that the user wishes to read mail from a mail folder. The default folder used is located in /var/mail/<login ID>, where the login ID is that of the user. The -f option can be used to override this. Such a command will place the user directly in the mail utility's command mode, in which mail prompts with an ampersand (&) and waits. The -H option instructs mail to list the headers from the mail folder without entering command mode. Whilst starting up, mail may be customised by entries in the user's .mailrc file. This is a text file resident in the user's home directory and is quite often used to establish mail groups. The MAILRC variable points at the mail startup file, which is best left as .mailrc. Setting up a group within the .mailrc form is as easy as:

group staff [Caron]+[Phil]+[John]+[Jeremy]

This would create a group called staff, which contains the user Ids Caron, Phil, John and Jeremy. This alias can then be used in place of an email address to email these 4 users.

The table below gives the most useful mail commands:

Command	Description
?	Help.
copy [message list] [filename]	Copies messages into filename (messages are not marked as saved).
delete [Message list]	Deletes the specified messages.
file [filename]	Reads mail from the mailbox specified by the filename. If no filename is specified, then the details of the current mailbox (name, size in bytes and the number of messages contained) are given.
headers [message]	Displays a page of message headers, that include message.
mail [userID]+	Sends the mail to specified users or aliases.
print [messagelist]	Displays specified messages using the more filter.
quit	Exits the email system.
reply [messagelist]	Mails a response back to the senders of messagelist.
save [messagelist] [filename]	Saves messages in messagelist to the filename specified (by default this is mbox, in the users home directory, if none is given).

A messagelist (above) points to one or more mail messages as detailed below:

Syntax	Description
	Means the current message.
nn	The message whose message number is nn.
^	Means the first undeleted message.
$	Means the last message.
*	Means all messages.
nn-pp	Means message numbered from nn to pp (inclusive..
userID	Means all messages from a specified userID.

Administering a Unix system

UNIX machines are very complex and can have several users connected concurrently. As such, the system needs to be administered in a competent and controlled fashion. Such administration is normally the responsibility of the systems administrator. In general, the systems administrator will be responsible for the following tasks:

- Installing and configuring systems software.
- Installing and configuring system nodes.
- Maintaining file system storage.
- Maintaining users and groups.
- Configuring and controlling systems printing.
- Managing the system.

Install & Configure Systems Software

Whilst the UNIX operating system can be compiled and run on virtually any hardware, it is unlikely that this would be the case. Normally, in business, a specialist UNIX machine is purchased and shipped with it is a manufacturer's version of UNIX optimised for the hardware. A good example is IBM who sell a high performance UNIX machine (or "box" as they are termed) called the RS 6000. IBM has developed a version of UNIX called AIX that is optimised and precompiled for this hardware. Such versions of the operating system offer all of the UNIX utilities and commands and boast additional features, which the manufacturer feels useful to its client base.

The price of the entry level version of such computers is fairly low and their performance fairly high. As such it is often worth purchasing such a combination rather than utilising "PC hardware" and a PC version of UNIX, as this is often slower and without the additional facilities. One of the most notably improved facilities is the set of backup/restore routines. Such versions of UNIX also tend to be much easier to install.

Before purchasing a version of UNIX it is essential to catalogue the target hardware. A log should be created which details:

- Type and speed of the processor.
- Amount and type of main memory.
- Type and size of disk storage.
- Type of CD-ROM.
- Type and RAM of graphics card.
- Type of communication (networking card or serial ports).
- Number of connections.
- Size and type of backup device.
- Type and number of printers.
- Details of any other peripherals.
- Previous history of the machine.

This log should then be used in the selection process – especially if the public domain version of UNIX (called LINUX) is being used. Whilst a good operating system, LINUX is largely unsupported meaning that device drivers are not available for a wide range of each type of device. It may then be necessary to adjust the hardware specification to suit the operating system.

If the computer has previously been used for an installation of Microsoft windows (especially later versions of '95), then it is advisable to format the hard drive as a LINUX installation on a disk, which has previously/still, contains windows is very problematic.

Most versions of UNIX and LINUX come with a number of extra utilities such as games, x-windows, etc. which are sometimes not required. Prior to installation, the exact requirements for the installation should be determined and only the required components installed. It is always advisable to install the manual pages and all of the shells. In LINUX, components are sometimes grouped illogically and it is not unknown to have to install the games for X-windows, as X-windows are sometimes part of that installation pack.

As LINUX is the most difficult version of UNIX to install, it is imperative that the instructions supplied with the release are followed closely. A case study of LINUX installation is provided below. An installation log must be maintained when installing the operating system, in general, an installation log should (at minimum) contain:

- Any names assigned to the system or its components - e.g. server name.
- Details of any choices made during the installation (e.g. the installer may have chosen not to install all of the operating system - which parts were installed).
- Target directories specified during the installation.
- Any password(s) set.
- Location of files and directories (even if these were accepted defaults).
- IP address of the system and components.
- Names of printers, queues, terminal, servers, etc.
- Any errors received.

LINUX Installation - A Case Study

This case study covers the most recent release of LINUX (at the time of going to press) - Red hat 5.2 .

Minimum Hardware requirements (Intel base platform) are:

- Intel 386 or greater - through Pentium Pro and Pentium II.
- 40MB hard disk space (if used in character mode), 100MB (if used with X Windows).
- 8MB memory (16MB recommended).
- Supports most common video cards.
- CD-ROM drive (SCSI or IDE).
- 3½" floppy drive.

Installation checklist:

Before beginning the installation of LINUX, the installer should be prepared to supply information regarding the following:

Description	Tips	Completed by the installer
Number, size and type of hard disks installed	Try BIOS settings.	
Which is the hard disk is set as the primary?	Try BIOS settings.	
How much RAM is fitted to the system	Watch the memory check at the POST.	
The interface of the CD-ROM	Try BIOS settings.	
The make and model of the CD-ROM	Try BIOS settings/observe POST	
Type of mouse installed? How many buttons are on the mouse? If it is a serial mouse, which port it is connected to?	Try BIOS settings - most people have a Microsoft equivalent installed.	
Is the BIOS clock set to GMT and what timezone is the computer to be used in?	BIOS settings.	
Does the machine have a SCSI adapter? if so, what is its make, model and interface (EIDE, PCI, etc.)	BIOS/Windows hardware configuration option (from control panel).	
What is the make and model of the video card? How much RAM is fitted on it?	BIOS/Windows hardware configuration option (from control panel).	
What kind of monitor is installed on the system - make and model?	The monitor itself.	
What is the allowable range of horizontal and vertical refresh rates for the monitor?	Monitor handbook.	

If connecting to a network, what are the: • designated IP address • subnet mask • gateway address • Domain Name Server's (DNS) IP address • Domain name • Hostname for the computer (needed anyway) • Type of network card	Network Administrator.	
Which, if any, operating systems will also be running on the machine?	End user - note if using OS/" then disk partitions must be created with OS/" software.	
Will LILO be used?		

The installer will require 3X 3½" floppy disks:
- One for the startup disk (boot.img) and
- One for supplemental disk (supp.img)
- One for a boot disk (created near the end of the process)

The system should be brought up under DOS. The LINUX CD should now be inserted into the CD-ROM drive (D is assumed) and made current (d:). Next, the installer should change to the images directory and use the \dosutils\rawrite.exe command. The rawrite command requests the name of the disk image to write - the command should be used twice - once for boot.img and one for supp.img. These disks should be labelled "LINUX VER Boot disk" and "LINUX VER Supplemental Disk" respectively, where LINUX VER should be replaced by the release and version of LINUX being installed.

The installer should then change to the \dosutils directory and execute the autoboot.bat command. Latest versions of Red Hat LINUX create virtual consoles at this point - these are separate screens that can be selected using the appropriate keystroke:

Screen	Keystroke	Description
1	Alt+F1	Installation dialogue.
2	Alt+F2	Shell prompt.
3	Alt+F3	Install log.
4	Alt+F4	System log (messages from the Kernel.
5	Alt+F5	Other messages.

Although the installer can toggle between screens to see error messages, etc. most of the time will be spent in the installation dialogue screen.

Once the boot: prompt appears, the best way to proceed with later versions of LINUX is simply to press enter. This will cause the system to autodetect the hardware. Once the program starts, the user should see a greeting "Welcome to Red Hat LINUX". First the installer will be requested to enter the required language - English is the default. The installer can make the selection using the arrow keys and pressing enter. The system then requests information on the keyboard installed - the installer should use the tab key to select and press enter. Next the installer is asked to select the installation method - local CD-ROM should be selected. The installer will then be prompted to insert the CD-ROM (which they should do and click OK), and the second phase of installation can begin. LINUX should then autodetect the CD-ROM, if not, then the installer should try repeating the installation typing the word expert after the boot: prompt (this invokes LINUX expert mode which will allow the installer to specify the parameters from the table above (not a recommended option).

LINUX then prompts the installer to select whether it is a new installation or an upgrade - this chapter assumes a new installation and as such, the installer should highlight this (using the cursor keys) and press enter. There are 3 classes of LINUX installation; this chapter assumes a workstation installation (the installer should be very wary of installing a server class as all partitions - including other operating systems - will be overwritten). The system should now begin the installation process, which can take up to 15 minutes depending upon the system and its CD-ROM. It is a good time for the installer to catch up on the installation log!

The installer should then be asked to select a tool to set up the hard disk drives on the system. LINUX offers two - the trusted old fdisk utility and the new Disk Druid (which started shipping with Red Hat version 5). Disk Druid is the easier to use, and as there are countless other references to fdisk, it shall be used in this chapter. Disk Druid has three sections:

Current disk partitions section

Which give a line representing each current partition with 5 fields:

Field	Description
Mount point	Indicates where the partitions will be mounted after red hat is set up and running. At least one partition must have a mount point of \ before the installer can move past the Disk Druid screen in the installation process. NOTE swap space does not get a mount point.
Device	The device name of the partition.
Requested	The minimum sized requested when the partition was defined.
Actual	The actual amount of space allocated to that partition.
Type	The type of partition.

Drive Summaries

In a similar manner to the current partitions section of disk druid, this screen shows information on the hard disks installed on the system. Each line this time has 6 fields:

Field	Description
Drive	The device name of the hard disk.
Geom [C/H/S]	The hard disk's geometry, consisting of three numbers - the number of cylinders, heads and sectors as reported by the hard drive itself.
Total	How much space is on the entire drive.
Used	How much space is currently defined to a partition.
Free	How much space is unallocated (therefore free).
[######]	A text bar graph presenting a visual representation of the space currently used on the hard disk. The # symbols represent utilisation.

Disk Druid's Buttons

The third section of Disk Druid is its buttons. It has 5 across the bottom and six references to function keys:

Button	Purpose
Add	Used to add a new partition - when selected, the appearing dialogue box must be completed.
Edit	Used to modify the attributes of the partition currently highlighted in the Current Discs Partition section. The resulting dialogue box can be edited.
Delete	Deletes the disk highlighted in the Current Discs Partition section.
OK	Writes the changes made to disk and passes the information to the installation process.
Back	Abort button - Disk Druid exists without making the changes.
F2 (keyboard) - Add NFS	Opens a dialogue box to define a read only NFS (Networked Filing System)
F5 (keyboard - Reset	Resets the partitions to the way they were before they were edited (in this session).

Adding a new partition

To add a new partition, the installer should select the add button and press enter. A dialogue box will be presented and will request the following information:

Information Requested	Installer Response
Mount Point	Enter the partitions mount point.
Size	Enter the size in MB of the partition.
Growable?	Space bar checks and unchecks this box. If the size entered above is the exact size of the partition, then the box should be left unchecked, if it is to be allowed to grow then the box should be checked.
Type	The appropriate partition type should be selected.
Allowable drives	The box shows the drives on the system upon which the partition can be created - check the boxes on the ones which the installer will allow the partition can be created.
OK	This button should be selected and the space bar pressed if the installer is ready to create the partition
Cancel	If the installer wishes to cancel the add operation.

It is recommended that the installer create six filing systems:

One for swap space*
One for /
One for /usr
One for /var
One for /home
One for /usr/local

*Determining swap space. To determine the size needed for swap space, the installer should add together the size of all of the applications to be executed at once and add 8MB for the Operating System. The installer should set the swap space to the greater of 32MB or, the actual size.

Selecting the components to install

The next step in the installation cycle is to select the components to install. The complete set of Red Hat 5.2 takes 665MB and some (e.g. all of the languages) are unnecessary. However, as previously mentioned, the location of some of the components is not always obvious and therefore a full installation can be quicker in the long term. To make a full installation select the "everything" option from the bottom of the install list, else select the required options and check the dependencies. This will normally take in excess of 10 minutes.

The system will then autodetect the mouse and ask the installer to confirm. In almost all cases, the autodetect is correct - the installer should check with the list created above before accepting. The installer should also decide whether 2 or 3 button emulation is required (both buttons are depressed to emulate a third).

Configuring X Windows

The next step in the installation process is to configure X-windows (which is a UNIX equivalent of Microsoft Windows). A window appears which asks the installer about the X Window server they wish to create. It should autodetect the graphics card and load the appropriate driver. It will however, ask the installer for details of the monitor. In most cases, the monitor should be shown in the list, if not, then custom should be selected and the details entered from the monitor manual.
CAUTION: using the wrong monitor frequencies can seriously damage the monitor.

Xconfigurator is the utility that configures the monitor and can be executed in the future by typing Xconfigurator when logged in as root (or alternatively by issuing the su -c Xconfigurator command).

Configuring the Network

Next the installer will be asked whether they wish to configure LAN networking for their system. If the system is to be used on a LAN, then they should choose the Yes button and scroll down the list to select the appropriate card. The drivers should be installed automatically.

Setting the Timezone

The installer is next asked to set the system's timezone. The first selection asks whether the computer's BIOS clock is set to GMT and the second asks which timezone the computer is to operate in. These settings can be changed later using the nssysv command.

Printer Configuration

Next, the installer is asked whether they wish to install a printer. If they select Yes, a dialogue box is presented in which 3 selections can be made:

Selection	Description
Local	A printer connected directly to the computer
Remote lpd	A printer connected to the LAN, with which the computer can communicate using lpd.
LAN Manager	To be used if the printer is a networked printer connected via a LAN manager or SMB print server.

Setting Root's password

Being the System Administrator who as absolute powers on the system, this password must be kept secure. The password must be 6 to 8 characters long.

Creating a startup disk

A custom startup disk provides a way of starting LINUX without depending on the normal boot loader. It is recommended that a boot disk be created, as it makes recovery from systems failure much easier.

Selecting Startup Options

The installer needs to tell the system whether it is to start in LINUX by default or boot into the other operating system. This involves either writing the startup loader into the Master Boot Record (if LINUX is to start by default) or into the First Sector of Boot Partitions it the other Operating Systems to load first.

The installer should make the appropriate selection for the screen.

Bootloader

Some systems need to pass special options to the kernel at startup time for LINUX to function properly. If the installer is unsure, then they should omit this. The LINUX bootloader does, however, state that it can load Windows 95 or 98 by giving them a DOS startup label.

The installation should now be complete - the disks (including CD) should now be removed and the system restarted by pressing the return key. Red Hat LINUX should now be ready to use.

Installing an application - A Case Study of Installing Apache Web Server

One of the most powerful features of Red Hat LINUX is a utility called RPM (Red Hat Package Manager). This utility can be used to install, upgrade, uninstall, verify and query applications. The general syntax used for the rpm command is:

        rpm -i [options] [packages]

where options are either - vv to print out all debugging information or -quiet to print out only error messages.

The rpm command has the following options:

Command	Description
rpm -I	Install
rpm -e	Uninstall
rpm -q	Query application
rpm -v	Verify the application

Packages can also be installed using the glint command which will cause the X Windows installer to start, or by using directions for the application itself. The installer will need to be logged on as root or su to root to execute this.

Often, organisations wish to install a web server and as such, an installation of Apache is detailed below:

The Apache web server can be located on either the installation media or on the Red Hat FTP server, and can be installed, as with any application, using the rpm tool or glint (the X Window package management utility). An rpm installation will be considered and can be achieved using:

        rpm - i latest_apache.rpm

where latest_apache.rpm is the name of the latest Apache RPM.

Apache should install files to the following system directories:
- /etc/httpd/conf - Apache configuration files should be stored here which include access.conf, httpd.conf and srm.conf.
- /etc/rc.d/ - A tree under this directory is created which contains the system startup scripts - a complete set is installed for the web server. The scripts are used to automatically start up the server on workstation startup and to halt the system on shutdown or reboot. They can however, be used for the command line.
- /home/httpd - Default icons and CGI (Common Gateway Interface) scripts are stored here.
- /usr/doc and /usr/man - The RPM contains manual pages and readme files. which are placed into these directories. NOTE: readme and other related documentation is placed in a directory under /usr/doc that is named for the server version /usr/sbin - executable files are placed directly in this directory.

Run time Configuration Settings

As previously mentioned, Apache has three configuration files (access.conf, httpd.conf, and srm.conf). These are backward compatible with the NCSA standard, and backups are provided in the RPM file suffixed by -dist.

Runtime configuration of the server is achieved with configuration directives, which are commands, which set some option. They are used to tell the server about various options that the installer wishes to enable, such as file locations, etc. The syntax is given below:

     directive option option

Directives are specified one per line, Some only let values, such as filename, to be specified, others let various options be specified. There are also special directives, called sections, which look like HTML tags. Sections are usually used to enclose a group of directives that apply only to the directory specified in the section:

     <Directory somedir/in/the/tree>
      directive option option
     directive option option
     directive option option
     </Directive>

These constructs can be observed in the conf/access.conf and in conf/httpd.conf files.

Editing httpd.conf

This file contains configuration directives to control how the server runs, where it's logfiles are found, the UserID it runs under, the port it listens to, etc. Most of this file can be left as default. However, at least the following directives should be modified:

Directive	Description
ServerAdmin	This should be a valid Email address or alias, and should be set to the webmaster managing the server (e.g. webmaster@mycomputer.co.uk). This is important, as it will be the address returned to a visitor if there is an error.
User & Group	These should be left as default - nobody and nogroup (which should be present in the /etc/passwd file). These options basically define the security level of the web, which should be limited. If for argument's sake, root was entered here, then a visitor could exploit loopholes in the webpages or CGI scripts, and potentially do lots of damage.
ServerName	This sets the hostname that the server will return. It should be set to a fully qualified domain.
ServerRoot	Sets the absolute path to the server directory. It tells the server where to find all the resources and configuration files. Many configuration files are specified in the configuration files relative to the ServerRoot directory.

Editing srm.conf

srm.conf is the resource configuration file and contains information related to the location of the web document tree, the CGI program directories and other resource configuration files that affect the web site. The two most important directives on the srm.conf file are:

Directive	Description
DocumentRoot	Should be set to the absolute path of the document tree. By default, set to /home/httpd/html, it is the top directory from which Apache will serve files.
UserDir	This directive defines the directory relative to a user's home directory where that user can put HTML files. It must be relative, for each user will end up with their own HTML directory. The default setting is public_html. Thus if a user creates a public_html directory beneath their home directory, it can be accessed using http://servername/~userID.

Editing access.conf

This is the global access control file and configures the type of access users have to the site and the documents made available. It also defines security by detailing the extent to which users can alter the security setting of the Administrator/Installer. The default provides unrestricted access to all files in the DocumentRoot. Normally, this file is left as its default.

Apache is now ready for use - an HTML document is needed and should be placed inside the htdocs directory.

Starting the Server

By default, the server runs in standalone mode - which is best for all but the lightest of traffic. In this mode, the server needs to be started manually using:

/sbin/httpd -f /etc/httpd/conf/httpd.conf

NOTE: this process must be created by root, as only root is allowed to access the required server port (80) and only processes owned by root can change their user and group IDs, as specified in the User and Group directives.

File System Maintenance

Irrespective of the version of UNIX, there are a number of important system files and directories installed that must be protected (by backup) and from unauthorised modification. The main files and directories in question are:

/unix (or the name of system kernel)	This is the kernel of the operating system, without which the system cannot function. Often the system can survive for a short period of time if this file is deleted, however, it is usually only for a short period of time.
init, /etc/inittab, /etc/rc.d and init.d	init is essentially the father of all processes in a UNIX system. Its main role is to create processes from a script stored /etc/initab. Although init starts as the last step of the kernel booting, it is the first command that initialises and configures the system for use. It's basic mode of operation is to parse the entries in /etc/initab and running scripts in /etc/rc.d with reference to a default or desired run level.

Each script in the /etc/rc.d directory can be used to start or stop a service, such as networking, web services, ftp, etc. |

A directory listing of the /etc/rc.d directory reveals some or all of the following files (dependent upon version of UNIX – this is SysV) – note rc0.d – rc6.d which correspond to the system run levels discussed later:

init.d/	rc*	rc.local*	rc.news*
rc.sysinit*	rc0.d/	rc1.d/	rc2.d/
rc3.d/	rc4.d/	rc5.d/	rc6.d/

In the init.d directory a number of scripts should be available which start and stop services. The names should give a clue as to what they do:

amd.init*	cron.init*	functions*	gpm*
halt*	httpd.init*	inet*	keytable*
killall*	lpd.init*	mars_new.init*	named.init*
network*	news*	nfs*	nfsfs*
pcmcia*	portmap.init*	random*	sendmail.init*
single*	skeleton*	smb*	syslog*
yppasswd.init*	ypserv.init*		

/etc/passwd

Discussed later, the /etc/passwd file contains details of the user logins including their home directory, encrypted password (in some cases), their group and indeed some further details which may include full name, office, telephone number, etc.

Whilst the method used to encrypt the password file prevents the users password from being determined, the account can be breached by cutting the password, accessing the account (which will now operate without a password), and pasting it back when finished. Alternatively, another password can be copied and placed over the original, which will allow access to anyone who knew the copied password. For this reason, users should always be advised to validate the last login details displayed by the system, each time they log in. The should report any anomalies to both the system administrator and their line manager. Thus the password file must be protected – it is at the heart of system security.

/etc/group

As discussed in more detail later, this file holds details of all groups on the system and has the following syntax:

group name: password : group ID : users

The password is rarely used in group situation but, like /etc/passwd, if the integrity of this file is breached, the consequences can be serious. It is integral to system security.

Baselining

Immediately following installation is an appropriate stage to "baseline" the system. Baselining consists of taking measurements of the system, which are then filed. These can later be used for comparative purposes. Taking such measurements allows administrators to determine how the system is developing and later, provides a "baseline" against which performance can be measured.

As a minimum, baselines should be taken using the following commands:

- df
- du

df provides information on used and available disk space, in kilobytes, as shown in the example:

```
$ df
Filesystem    kybytes    used   avail  capacity   Mounted on
/dev/staff1    17415     10900   6515     62%      /
/dev/staff2    20300     11000   9300     54%      /usr
```

du provides information on the number of kilobytes that are allocated to each of the specified filenames, as shown in the example.

```
$ du|more
2      ./.wastebasket
16     ./.cetables
2      ./.logs
2      ./.tt
46     ./sql/osaass
236    ./sql
2      ./.netscape/cache
264    ./.netscape
2      ./bupdir
6      ./copydir
6      ./BUPDIR
16     ./mydir
6      ./COPYDIR
130    ./Java
2      ./bin
1026   ./soar6
--More--
```

These commands provide essential information on the filing system. Should the filing system become full, then serious problems will arise. This is particularly true if /tmp becomes full, as all UNIX applications use this as a "scratch" area. Careful monitoring of the system is essential if problems are to be avoided, and can only be taken if you have a baseline to measure from. The /tmp directory normally only contains temporary files and is the only directory from which the administrator can safely delete files – other directories contain essential system files and should not be deleted. Applications will also usually have directories, which grow, for instance an accounting package will have a directory that contains audit trails. The size of this directory will grow as each transaction is made in the accounting package. The system administrator should ensure that these directories have enough space available for their required growth but the administrator of the accounts package should ensure that this directory is maintained and unnecessary files removed.

Measurements should be taken frequently and recorded. The exact frequency depends upon the usage of the machine and the disk quotas imposed on users, but once a week is normally sufficient. Measurements and backups must be taken immediately prior to any software installation or maintenance.

It must be remembered that UNIX is a multi-user operating system and as such, the responsibility for the maintenance of the filing system should be the responsibility of all who use it. The system administrator should not interfere with user accounts unless a problem is encountered. Instead, the users should be made responsible for the maintenance of their own filing system. This requires the users to be trained in the maintenance of filing systems and for them to be encouraged to undertake such maintenance. System administrators can set a disk quota for each user, which limits the storage space they have available. The setting of a "reasonable" quota is essential for it enforces a maintenance discipline within the user and protects the system from large increases in data stored.

Periodically, say once per week, it is prudent to check the integrity of the filing systems. This can be achieved using the file system check (fsck) command, which is available to superusers only. fsck can be used to search for errors or, if the –p option is specified, correct the errors. The types of consistency errors detected by fsck are:

- Invalid block no.
- A used inode is not referenced from any directory.
- An inode's link count is incorrect.
- More than one inode refers to the same block.
- A block is marked as free in the bitmap but is also referenced from an inode.
- A block is marked as used in the bitmap but is never referenced.

fsck is also run from init and is very good at repairing disk errors.

The commands necessary for user filing system maintenance are fairly basic and are covered earlier in this chapter (in the UNIX commands section).

Transferring Data with External Systems

As previously mentioned, UNIX is an "open" operating system, meaning that it is designed to facilitate inter-computer connection. This is perhaps one of the main reasons surrounding UNIX's popularity. The TCP/IP protocol suite (shipped as standard with all variants of UNIX) is at the heart of such communication. Because all UNIX systems run TCP/IP at no cost, then they all share a common protocol suite and can easily communicate. Also shipped free with UNIX are a number of utilities to facilitate inter-computer communication, file transfer and exchange of information. Below, a selection of the most popular of these utilities is discussed:

Telnet

Almost a "household" name, in the computer world, telnet is a piece of software that allows a user to start a remote terminal session on another computer. Originally developed by the National Center for Supercomputer Applications, telnet is now widely shipped with most operating systems including Windows from 95 onwards and all variants of UNIX. Telnet can be invoked from the UNIX command prompt by simply typing telnet <hostname>, where <hostname> is the name of the external computer with which the user wishes to communicate. All processing for such sessions takes place on the host computer.

Machine Equivalence

To aid inter-computer communication, UNIX has a concept of "machine equivalence". This allows a user to execute a command on another machine (on which they have an account) without logging in or supplying a password. This is achieved by use of the .rhosts file.   Suppose that Fred has an account on a machine called UNIX1 and on another machine called UNIX2..   If he creates a file in his home directories on both machines, containing the "official" hostnames (including the internet domain), then the two accounts will be "equivalenced" across both machines. This means that Fred can login into UNIX1 and execute commands on UNIX2 (using selected commands) without having to supply a password. For instance, Fred could run the date command on UNIX2 using the rsh (remote shell command):

        rsh UNIX2 date

System Administrators can also establish global machine equivalence by using the /etc/hosts.equiv file but, for security reasons, this should be treated with great caution.

rcp

Requiring the machines to be set as equivalent, the rcp utility facilitates copying between two UNIX hosts and has the following format:

        rcp [-p] [-r] original file newfile

The -p option attempts to preserve the date and time of modification whilst the -r option copies recursively if the files is a directory. rcp can be used to copy both to and from a remote machine:

rcp UNIX2:originalfile copyoffile   (will copy the file from UNIX2 to UNIX1)
rcp originalfile UNIX2:copyoffile   (will copy file from UNIX1 to UNIX2)

rlogin

rlogin allows a user to remotely log into another UNIX machine. The user's current shell goes to sleep and all commands are executed on the remote machine. Upon logging out (usually ctrl-D) the sleeping shell awakens.

ftp

Again, almost a "household" name in the computing fraternity is the ftp (file transfer protocol) command. ftp allows users to manipulate files and directories on both the local and host computers. Using the .netrc file of the host computer specified, ftp determines if the computer supports anonymous logins (often used on the internet for the downloading of shareware and free files). If it does, then ftp uses this account to log into the remote host - this accounts for the initial time delay when you try to download something from the Internet. If the computer doesn't support an anonymous account or if the user specifies the username on the command line, then ftp will prompt for authentication information.

ftp is a very powerful command and has a number of commands, which are given below. There are many variants of ftp available, and it is now widely available on a number of operating systems including Windows from version 95 onwards.

Command*	Description
!command	The ! causes the command to execute on the local host.
append localfile remotefile	Appends the contents of the file localfile to the remotefile.
bell	Sets the system to send a beep after every file transfer.
bye	Closes the current connection and quits ftp.
cd remotedir	Changes to the specified directory on the remote host.
close	Closes the current connection to the remote host.
delete remotefile	Deletes the file remotefile from the remote host.
get remotefile [localfile]	Gets remotefile from the remote host and places it in the local machine (a local filename may be specified) .
help [command]	Gets help.
lcd localdir	Changes the current local directory to localdir.
ls remotedir	Gives a directory listing of the remotedir.
mkdir remdir	Creates the directory on the remote host.
open hostname	Tries to get a connection with the specified host.
put localfile [remfile]	Copies the localfile to the remote host (remfile may be specified to name the file on the remote computer).
pwd	Displays the present working directory on the current system.
quit	Functionally equivalent of bye.
rename remoteorig remotenew	Renames a file on the host computer from remoteorig to remotenew.
remdir remotedir	Removes the directory remotedir from the remote computer.

*Note: The table above represents the UNIX version of ftp - not all commands may be supported by other versions of ftp

uucp

uucp is very similar to rcp but intended not for regular users but more for email and news transmission over dial-up lines.

NFS

If the site is a large one with several servers, NFS (Networked Filing System) may be installed. NFS allows UNIX hosts to share the same filing structure. Thus if Fred logins in on UNIX his filing structure is common across all machines.

Software Installations/Upgrades

The filing system can be dramatically affected by the installation of new software, and upgrades of existing software. During planning of such installations/upgrades it is essential that:

- The co-residency of software is checked (will all critical software run under the upgrade?- especially if only some of the software is to be upgraded).
- There is adequate space available for the new/upgraded software.
- There are adequate system resources available for the new software (disk capacity, memory, etc.).
- There is adequate system down time planned.

Software installations dramatically affect the systems integrity and must only be attempted if the system has been fully backed up. Usually, the upgrade will be supplied on tape and will be in a specific format (usually either cpio or tar which are the main two formats used for external communication during install/upgrades). The system administrator will need to install using the appropriate command and follow the manufacturer's instructions. The following should be observed during the installation process:

- A full backup is taken.
- The backup is tested.
- System measurements are taken.
- The installation is carried out by competent personnel following manufacturer's guidelines.
- An accurate log is maintained during the installation process.
- The system is verified following the successful installation.
- Measurements are taken following the successful installation.
- A full backup is taken of the upgraded system.
- The backup is tested.

User Maintenance

Like most other multi-user operating systems, UNIX provides for individual user accounts. However, it also provides for groups. A group is a collection of users who are a member of it, and groups form an important part of security and control within UNIX. As well as the user being a member of one or more groups, so are files and directories.

For instance, the file permissions discussed earlier in the chapter, are implemented for owner, group and world. The group permissions determine how the file is to be accessed by members of the group to which it belongs. This facility allows UNIX to support the concept of work groups. If a user is working on two projects (x and y) then they can be made a member of the groups projectx and projecty. Thus from within their own user ID they can access the files and directories belonging to them and the projects (security permissions allowing). Rights of access to such files and directories are controlled by the owner of the files. UNIX groups are also used to control access to devices. Suppose that the finance department has a printer that usually has cheques loaded – fraud would be fairly easy if the printer was available to everyone. The printer should belong to an exclusive group and only be able to be used by members of that group.

When establishing a UNIX system for the first time, careful consideration needs to be given to groups and their members. Usually an organisation will have distinct groups e.g. Personnel, Finance, Manufacturing, etc. which would form natural UNIX groups. The nature of the information stored on the system dictates that groups must be carefully selected. For instance it is probably apparent that not everyone in finance should have access to the printer containing the cheques. However, if everyone has access to the purchase order system, they can create fraudulent purchase orders/invoices. Thus users needs should be carefully discussed with personnel and user IDs should only be created on receipt of a memo from Personnel. This memo should clearly detail the access levels required. System administrators should grant only the minimum access necessary.

Similarly, once employees leave the company, Personnel should notify systems administrators who should then suspend the user account. All memos should be kept by the system administrator, as confirmation for audit purposes. The accounts should be suspended rather than deleted, leaving a trail for subsequent system auditing.

Care must be taken, and the users must be educated, into ensuring that they do not make their files accessible to the group or the world by accident. The umask command can be used to set the default permissions given to newly created files. The first digit defines the rights value to be subtracted from the owner permissions (which cannot be modified). The following two digits define the rights to the group and the world respectively. Thus the command

　　　umask 077

does not alter the rights to the owner but removes all rights to the group and the world. The command

　　　umask 022

removes write access from the group and the world. The screen shot shows an example of the umask command in action:

```
$
$ umask
022
$ date > date.txt
$ ls -l date.txt
-rw-r--r--  1 phil  staff       34 Apr 26 11:34 date.txt
$ umask 077
$ date > date2.txt
$ ls -l dat*.*
-rw-r--r--  1 phil  staff       34 Apr 26 11:34 date.txt
-rw-------  1 phil  staff       34 Apr 26 11:34 date2.txt
$
```

The way in which users, groups and their association are maintained depends upon the variant of UNIX being used. AIX uses a utility called SMIT (System Management Interface Tool) for all maintenance, some UNIX use sysadmsh (system admin shell) and others use adduser, addgroup.

```
$
$ ls -l date.txt
-rw-r--r--  1 phil  staff       34 Apr 26 11:34 date.txt
$
$chgrp student date.txt
$ ls -l date.txt
-rw-r--r--  1 phil  student   34 Apr 26 11:34 date.txt
$
```

Users can change the group of a file (proving they own it) by using the chgrp command:

　　　chgrp financegroup myfile

The screen shot shows an example of chgrp being used.

Similarly, they can change the ownership of the file using the chown command:

chown caron myfile

The screen shot below shows an example of chown being used:

```
$
$ ls -l date.txt
-rw-r--r--   1 phil   staff        34 Apr 26 11:34 date.txt
$
$ chown caron date.txt
$ ls -l date.txt
-rw-r--r--   1 caron student  34 Apr 26 11:34 date.txt
$
```

Facilitating User Access

Once the users have been added to the system using the administration tools provided, the systems administrator and the users themselves (providing they have the knowledge) can automate their login process. In a similar manner to the DOS autoexec.bat file, each UNIX account has a file that runs when the user logs in. Unlike DOS, this file is individual to the user and not the machine. The names of the login files change depending upon the default shell being used. Common shells and their startup files are detailed in the table below:

Shell	Startup file
Korn	.profile, sometimes .prof
C	.cshrc

Notice that they all start with a period (.) which renders them invisible in UNIX – they are only shown by a ls –la, the a option listing all files.

The screen shot below shows an example of a .profile script from the Korn shell:

```
$ cat .profile|more
#       This is the default standard profile provided to a user.
#       They are expected to edit it to meet their own needs.

echo Hello Im running .profile
alias dir="ls -lisa"
PATH=$OPENWINHOME/bin:$OPENWINHOME/lib:$ORACLE_HOME/lib
export PATH
TERM=vt100;export TERM
$
```

The echo statements are similar to DOS and echo out the text that follows them. The alias command (shown) allows the UNIX command ls –lisa to be accessed by dir. The PATH= command sets the path (in a similar way to DOS), the export PATH command makes the PATH accessible to all programs. Finally, the TERM sets the terminal type to be vt100. PATH and TERM are two of many variables set in UNIX that are accessed from applications (such as editors) allowing them to configure themselves accordingly.

As previously mentioned, the shells contain a complete scripting language that can be used to develop applications in the shell and to control a user's access.

The file on the left gives an example of this, with the construction of a simple menu in the korn shell:

This script provides the following simple menu system when executed by the user:

```
$ cat menu
#!/bin/ksh
#Simple menu script written by P J Irving 27/4/99
select REPLY in "System Date" "Current Directory"
"Directory Listing" "Exit"
do
  case $REPLY in
    "System Date")
      date
      ;;
    "Current Directory")
      pwd
      ;;
    "Directory Listing")
      ls -l
      ;;
    "Exit")
      break
      ;;
    *)
      echo "I do not recognise your choice"
      ;;
  esac
done

$
```

```
$ menu
1) System Date
2) Current Directory
3) Directory Listing
4) Exit
#? 1
Tuesday April 27 18:25:31 BST 2000
#? 2
/home/phil/unixbook
#? 3
total 2
-rwx------   1 phil  staff        354 Apr 27 18:20 menu
#? 8
I do not recognise your choice
1) System Date
2) Current Directory
3) Directory Listing
4) Exit
#? 4
$
```

By incorporating this menu system as part of the .profile of the user, the scope of the user on the system can be severely limited. This greatly increases system security.

Whilst on the vast majority of modern UNIX systems, the process of adding a user and maintaining a group is semi-automatic, an understanding of the basic principles is essential in the efficient management of such a system.

Below is the sequence of steps necessary if undertaking these commands manually:

1. Create a home directory for the user.

In general, the home directories for all users on a UNIX System will be located in either /home, /users or /usr depending on the particular variant of UNIX in use. Under SVR4 compliant releases, users' home directories should be placed in /home. However, at the end of the day, it is up the individual System Administrator as to where these directories are to be located, and as long as the Administrator is consistent, there should not be any problems.

2. Choose a login ID for the new user.

Each user on a UNIX system must have a unique login ID. These should be kept fairly short (no more than 8 characters maximum) to cut down on the amount of typing to be done when a user logs in to the system. A list of the login IDs already in use can be obtained by looking at the first field in the /etc/passwd file.

3. Choose a user number.

Each user must also be assigned a unique number. These are kept in the **/etc/passwd** file or **/etc/shadow** files (/etc/shadow if present however can only be read by the System Administrator). In general, the sequence of user numbers given in this file should simply be continued.

4. Assign the new user to a group.

Every user on a UNIX system must also be assigned to a group. On some systems there will simply be one group called users for everyone using the system. On more complex systems, groups may be assigned for the various departments using the system. The groups currently set up on the system can be seen by displaying the /etc/group file.

5. Add an entry to the group file

Groups allow sets of users to be considered collectively, for example, by department. By making alterations to a file's permissions (using the chown command), files can be made accessible to users who are members of the same group as the files' owner. For example, the owner of a file could have read, write and execute permission, members of their group could perhaps be given read and execute permission, and access to the file removed for all other users.

Having decided on which group the new user is to be assigned to, the user's ID should simply be added at the end of the line for that group. If necessary, a new group can be created, with a corresponding (unique) group ID. At this point the number of the group being used should be noted down, as it will be needed in the next step.

A typical group file is shown below:

> **users::20:**
> **staff:*:21:emf,davem,jan**
> **students::22:fk,wlp,sc,wm**

There are three groups, called users, staff and students. There is one line for each group. Each line contains four fields, separated by colons. The first field is the (unique) group name. The second field will either contain an asterisk or nothing. The asterisk indicates that there is a password associated with that group. The third field is the (unique) group number, while the final field is a list of the users belonging to the group. To add user pmm to the staff group, the System Administrator would add the user ID to the end of the line for staff, giving:

> **users::20:**
> **staff:*:21:emf,davem,jan,pmm**
> **students::22:fk,wlp,sc,wm**

6. Add an entry to the password file.

The password file on UNIX Systems is called passwd, and is located in the /etc directory. (as the shadow file under SCO UNIX). When the password file is examined, it will be seen that there is one line for every user on the system. Each line in the password file is comprised of seven fields separated by colons, these being : **User login ID**
> **User password (encrypted)**
> **User number**
> **Group number**
> **User details**
> **User's home directory**
> **Login shell**

A line for the new user must be added to the passwd file. Suppose the passwd file contained the following entries:

pji:x:200:21:Phil Irving,,,:/users/staff/pji:/bin/ksh
caron:x:201:21:Caron MacIntyre,,,:/users/staff/caron:/bin/csh

Note that the x in the second field is used to indicate that there is an encrypted password held in the /etc/shadow - some UNIX systems (including LINUX and HP/UX) actually show the encrypted version of the password, and do not use a /etc/shadow file.

If a new user called Barrie Hardy, with login ID barrieh was to be added to the students group, and a home directory of /users/staff/barrieh had already been set up, the following line could be added to the passwd file:

bh::205:22:Barrie Hardy,,,:/users/staff/barriej:/bin/sh

Note that there is no entry for the user's password. This simply means that the newly set up user can log straight into the system without entering a password, and it would be up to that person to allocate themselves a password at their earliest opportunity.

It should also be noted that the fourth field in the password file contains personal information about the user. This field itself consists of four sub-fields separated by commas. These fields can be used to hold any type of information. Depending on the institution, these could perhaps be allocated to the user's full name, their department, telephone extension, etc.

7. Copy default files to the user's home directory.

Every user on a UNIX System will have a number of files placed in their home directory. Typically, these will consist of .profile, .login, .exrc, .cshrc and .kshrc. Depending on the software being used on the system, additional files may have to be copied into the users' directories. Usually, these default files will be located in a specific location, often /etc/skel. Other systems, notably HP/UX simply copy all files whose name begins with the characters d. from /etc to the user's home directory, removing the d from the filename in the process (from example, d.profile becomes .profile).

8. Setting Permission of Files and Directories

If directories are created manually, by default all three categories (user, group and other) will be given read, write and execute permission. It is most unlikely that the System Administrator would wish to leave the permission set in this way.

Additionally, as the default files are copied from a directory such as /etc/skel, their permissions will also be copied. It may well be that these will also be unsuitable.

Therefore, the chmod command will probably have to be used to make alterations to the permissions on the new user's home directory and their copies of the default files.

9. Giving the newly set up user ownership of their files and directory.

When a System Administrator is setting up a user's home directory and files, these entries will initially belong to the System Administrator, which means that the newly set up user will be unable to make alterations to the various files. Consequently, the System Administrator must give the user ownership of the files and ownership of their home directory. This will normally involve using the chown command to change ownership of the files. In addition, the chgrp command will probably have to be used to change the group ownership of the files concerned.

As an example, if a user with login ID barrieh, belonging to the staff group was being set up, the two commands below would give them ownership of the file .profile :

chgrp staff .profile
chown barrieh .profile

It should be noted at this time that only the System Administrator has permission to make alterations to the group and passwd files stored in /etc. Other users on the system will be allowed to examine (and even copy) these files however.

Most UNIX Systems now provide shell scripts to simplify the procedure for setting up new users on the system. The System Administrator will simply be prompted to enter all the information required (such as username, login ID etc.), and the script will then go on and create a home directory for the user, set file permissions, copy files and alter the group and passwd files as described in the notes. However, in the event of such a program not being available, prospective System Administrators should be familiar with the manual system for setting up users.

Under LINUX, a program called adduser is supplied to simplify this process, and it is described next.

Adduser

This program simply prompts the System Administrator to supply information about the new user, and, having been provided with this information, modifies the group and password files, creates a home directory for the user, copies the default files to this directory and alters the ownership of the files.

The adduser command prompts the user to provide the following information:

Login Name	(maximum 8 characters)
Full Name	(the user's full name which can used later on in printouts, reports etc.)
GID	This is the ID number that the user is a member of. By default, users are placed in the users group (which has an ID of 100).
UID	Every user must have a unique user ID. By default, the adduser program will find an unused user number.
Home Directory	The full path to the user's home directory. By default, home directories are placed inside /home.
Shell	The shell to be executed when the user logs in to the system. Under LINUX, the default is /bin/bash which is similar to the Bourne Shell. More common shells include the Korn Shell (/bin/ksh), the C Shell (/bin/csh) and the Bourne Shell (/bin/sh).

Removing Users

To completely remove a user from the system, it should simply be a matter of reversing the process, which was used to add the user to the system. The main points being:

- Remove user's entry from /etc/passwd file.
- Remove any occurrences of users login name from /etc/group.
- Completely remove the user's home directory.

In most cases, this method is satisfactory. However, there may be occasions where the user has created files outside their own directory, in which case, a suitable shell script would have to be written, to search out and delete any entries belonging to the user in question.

Again, many systems provide a program (generally called userdel) which will remove users from the system, although it should be noted that many programs of this type simply remove the user's entry from the /etc/passwd file, and make no attempt to locate and delete files belonging to the person who is being removed from the system.

Disabling Users

Rather than delete a user, as previously mentioned, it is preferable to suspend or disable their accounts. Some UNIX systems offer utilities to achieve this – some versions of LINUX allow a user's account to be locked. If such utilities are not available, then the accepted means of carrying this out is to edit /etc/passwd, and insert an extra character at the beginning of the password field for that person. This will prevent the user from logging in to the system, but the effects are easily reversed if the user's account is to be restored.

Configure & Control Systems Print

Printers can be attached to UNIX systems in a variety of ways. They can be directly attached to the computer system via serial or parallel ports. They can also be attached via printer server units networked to the UNIX machine and some workstations provide for direct connection to a printer.

In most cases, all printers can be seen and managed by the systems administrator. Usually in UNIX printers need little management, other than "standard" maintenance (toner, ribbons, paper, etc.). Occasionally jobs need to be removed from the print queue. Tasks such as removing a job from a print queue can be undertaken by a user (providing they own the job). System administrator privilege is only necessary when the owner of a job is not available when the job requires attention. The following table provides a summary of printer maintenance commands:

Command	Description	Example
lpstat *printer*	Displays information about the current status of the LP print service.	lpstat –o all
lpq	Displays the status of jobs on the printer specified.	lpq –p stuprinter
lprm	Cancels printing of the specified job.	lprm 123

When installing a print device, the use of that device must be carefully considered. As previously mentioned, if the printer is to print on secure stationary, then it must be secured both physically and logically. The logical security is necessary to remove the threat of someone printing his or her own cheque. Indeed, if the printer contains anything other than blank paper, it will probably need to be controlled. Pre-printed order forms could be open to fraudulent use as could invoices, credit notes, etc. Even letter headed stationary needs to be protected in someway – it is relatively expensive, and can be wasted if used for program listings, etc.

The first step to adding the printer in UNIX is to physically set up and connect the printer – this can either be directly to the machine using serial or parallel ports or can be through the network. Once the printer is physically connected then it must be added to the UNIX operating system. Again, the exact commands used to accomplish this will depend upon the type of UNIX being used.

In general, printers are found in the /dev directory and have the following attributes:

Device Name	Description	Address
/dev/lp0	First parallel printer.	0x3bc
/dev/lp1	Second parallel printer.	0x378
/dev/lp2	Third parallel printer.	0x278

Serial printers are assigned to serial devices for example /dev/ttyS0 for the first serial printer, /dev/ttyS1 for the second and so on.

Almost any printer can be used with UNIX. However, printers using Printing Performance Architecture (PPA) such as HP 720, 820 or 1000-series should be avoided, as drivers are only available for Windows-95. UNIX also supports a software tool known as Ghostscript interpreter. If the printer is supported, then it will allow postscript printing on a non-postscript printer by interpreting the print instructions.

Most variants of UNIX offer utilities for adding printers. LINUX offers the printool command which makes the installation and administration of printers much easier. It is strongly recommended that such tools are used as they will correctly install the printers and configure the appropriate files. This is especially true for networked printers, which are normally quite difficult to establish.

The printool command also allows a printer to be allocated to a group of users. It is important that a log is accurately maintained of the rights of each user to the printing system if possible security conflicts are to be avoided.

Whilst it is preferable to use such tools, it is also prudent to have an understanding of the printing process in UNIX, as it will assist in the management of printers and the processes associated with their management:

In LINUX, the following sequence of events occurs when a job is submitted for printing:
- A print request is issued using lpr.
- lpr generates the output to be sent to the printer.
- The output is copied to the queue in the spool directory for the selected printer. This information is obtained by examining printer definition file (/etc/printcap). During the spooling process, lpr also takes account of any special instructions (such as paper size, fonts etc.).
- Two files are created by lpr in the spool directory. A control file (whose filename will begin with the letters cf) contains information about the job, including the owner ID and information about the job such as line spacing. The second file known as the data file (with a filename beginning df) contains the data to be printed.
- A signal is sent by lpr to the lpd daemon, informing it that a file is waiting in the spool directory.
- The lpd daemon starts another daemon (if one is not already running) to handle the printer's queue (note that a daemon will be present for a particular queue as long as there are files waiting to be printed). The daemon will terminate when the print queue has been emptied.
- lpd checks to printer definition file to determine whether the printer is local or remote.
- If the printer is remote, lpd establishes a connection to the remote machine, passes the control and data files to it, and informs the remote machine's lpd daemon that a request has been passed to its queue.
- If the printer is local, lpd checks that the printer exists and is enabled, then passes the print request to the daemon handling that printer's queue.
- After printing, the control and data files are deleted from the spool directories.

The following table lists the files and commands that are associated with the printing of files:

Filename	Description
/usr/sbin/lpd	This is the line printer daemon that handles print requests.
/etc/printcap	The system's printer definition file, which describes the various printers, the ports they are attached to, and the location of spool directories and log files.
/usr/bin/lpr	Used to submit jobs to the printer, which is done by adding the job to the printer's spool directory.
/usr/bin/lpq	Shows the contents of the queue (i.e. the spool directory) for a given printer.
/usr/bin/lpc	Used to check the status of printers, and can also be used to control them to some extent, for example start and stop the print queue, enable and disable the printer and re-arrange the order of jobs in the queue.
/usr/bin/lprm	Used to remove jobs from the print queue.

In addition, each printer's spool directory contains the following files:

Filename	Description
.seq	Contains the job number counter.
errs	Used for logging by lpd.
lock	Used by lpd to prevent more than one job being sent to the printer at any one time.
status	Contains the message that is reported by lpc's stat command.

Overview of the lpd daemon:
- Printing services are handled by the lpd daemon (lpd standing for line printer daemon). On systems based around AT & T, the services are handled by the lp daemon.
- In general, this daemon will be initialised in one of the systems rc scripts (typically /etc/rc.d/rc.local) as the system moves into multi-user mode, and will remain active while the system is running. Note that the daemon can be terminated by the System Administrator.
- If the daemon has to be re-started, this can be done by the System Administrator by executing /usr/sbin/lpd.
- The daemon reads the printer definition file (/etc/printcap) to establish which printers are connected to the system.
- lpd starts another two daemons called listen and accept to handle incoming print requests.

Managing Printers
Systems control their printers through the lpc utility. It provides its own command line interface at which users can enter lpc commands.
The lpc command allows the following printer management functions to be undertaken, and is the only means of controlling printers and the queues under LINUX:
- Enable the printer's spooler.
- Disable the printer's spooler.
- Display printer status.
- Remove requests from the printer's queue.
- Promote print requests.
- Start the printer.
- Stop the printer.

The table following lists the various commands, which can be entered at the lpc, prompt, together with any parameters, which have to be supplied with them.
It should be noted that lpc can only control local printers. The management of remote printers must be undertaken by logging in to the remote machine (as root), and carrying out the printer management from there.

Table of lpc Commands

Command	Description
start printer_name	Starts the printer queue daemon for the specified printer, which will allow it to print requests. Both this command and the two below alter the printer's lock file.
abort printer_name stop printer_name	Stops the printer, although it will still be possible to spool requests, which can be printed when the printer has been re-started. The only difference between the two commands is that stop allows a job being printed to be completed, whereas abort stops any jobs in the process of being printed. Note that abort cannot stop a job that has already been passed to the printer's memory.
down printer_name message	Should be used when a printer has a fairly serious problem, which means it has to be taken off-line for an extended period of time. If the optional message is supplied, it will be placed in the status file, and will be displayed to users who try to pass jobs to the printer.
up printer_name	Re-activates a printer that has previously been 'downed'.
clean printer_name	Removes all jobs currently in the specified printer's queue, including any active print jobs (which have not already been passed to the printer's memory).
enable printer_name	Enables the spooling of print requests for the printer.
disable printer_name	Disables the spooling of print requests for the specified printer. Any user who attempts to send a job to a 'disabled' printer will receive a message informing them that the printer has been disabled, and the print request will be denied.
restart printer_name	Restarts the printer daemon. This will only be needed if the daemon has died for some reason.
status printer_name	Displays information about the printer, including whether or not the spool queue is enabled, whether printing is allowed, the number of entries in the spool queue and the status of the printer's daemon.
topq printer_name print_id	Promotes the specified job to the front of the print queue.
topq printer_name user_name	Promotes all print jobs requested by the specified user to be moved to the front of the queue.
help ?	Displays a list of the lpc commands.
exit quit	Exits from lpc.

Managing the Print Queue

The lpc command can be used to manage some aspects of the print queue; two commands, lpq and lprm are supplied specifically for this purpose.

The first command, lpq, if used on its own with no parameters, displays information about the default printer's queue. Alternatively, the -P switch allows a particular printer name to be specified. This information will include the following:

- Print job ID.
- The owner of the job.
- The name of the file being printed.
- The size of the files.

The second command, lprm, is used to remove one or more jobs from the print queue. Once again, the default system printer's queue will be accessed unless another printer name is specified.

The lprm command can be used in two ways, one to remove specified jobs from the queue, the other to remove all jobs from the queue.

To remove particular jobs, their ID's (which can be found using lpq) must be supplied on the command line.

Alternatively, **lprm** on its own will cancel all print jobs for the default system printer (usually referred to as lp), while **lprm -Plaser** will remove all jobs from the queue associated with printer laser.

It is worth noting that other variants of UNIX have specific commands for such tasks, for instance, HP/SCO/Solaris, etc. use lpadmin for general administration of printers and cancel for cancelling print jobs.

Manage Systems

Perhaps the single most important task in managing any computer system is providing for its continuity. This involves protecting the organisation's data – most organisations cannot survive without access to it and the following 5 ways of protecting data are frequently recommended:

1. Backup
2. Backup
3. Backup
4. Backup
5. Backup

This is not a misprint – it is intentional. Users and systems administrators must realise that the only way an organisation can retrieve lost data is if it was backed up in the first place. Without a backup, there is little chance of an organisation being able to retrieve its data. When it can, it is often very costly and takes quite a long time. Data is the lifeblood of an organisation and if it is starved of its data, it is unlikely that it will be able to survive uninjured. If the data loss is complete then the organisation probably would never survive. Consider a credit card company who lost all of their customer's balances – they would probably never be able to get the money they are owed. If a bank had major problems and lost the balance of its customer's accounts, how would their customers react?

It should also be understood that most systems change on a frequent basis – especially the data element. As such, regular backups should be taken and the organisation should be prepared to loose any data that isn't backed up. The organisation should ask itself how much data they are prepared to loose – if the answer is very little, then regular backups must be taken. Backups cannot be undertaken piecemeal, they are essential to the well being of the organisation. As such, it should be made someone's responsibility on their job description to take regular backups, and someone else's responsibility to ensure that they are taking place. If not, then backups may not happen which could cause catastrophe to the organisation. Backups must be planned and a set of "idiots" instructions produced to ensure that everyone understands how to take a backup.

Back up now complete, what next?

It is no good simply backing up a computer and trusting the backup has worked. The backup needs to be verified to ensure that the data has actually been copied. The test of the tape needs to be thorough – a backup is only as good as its test. A backup should always be tested.

Occasionally, some conscientious people will take a tape listing from the backup tape to verify that something has been written. On most tapes, the directory of the backup is at the very front of the tape and it may well have written the directory but nothing else. The only way that a backup can be truly verified is to restore all of the files.

Unless the organisation has a separate computer with the same version of the operating system installed, this is usually not possible and an alternative must be found. The files should never be restored onto the same computer – if the backup has failed then the original files will be corrupted.

If the organisation does not have a "spare" computer then it is best to write a script which places a copy of a master text file around the filing system in predetermined locations (usually around mission critical data – before and after). The backup should then be taken and these text files removed from the computer. An attempt should then be made to restore the files from the backup and compare them to the master. If the copies verify OK then there is a high probability that the actual backup will be OK. If they do not, then another backup should immediately be made on another tape.

Little attention should be paid to the success messages generated by the backup device and instead should be thoroughly tested. Unbelievable as it may sound, but some drives do not generate an error message during the backup process but only during the restore. If an attempt were not made to restore the tape, then it would never be known that the backup hadn't worked. If a "real" restore had to be made, then the organisation could be in serious trouble.

Backups can be easily made on UNIX using either tar or cpio commands. The tar command normally has the following syntax:

```
tar –cvf /dev/rmt0    (for backup)
tar –tvf /dev/rmt0    (for tape listing)
tar –xvf /dev/rmt0    (for extraction of files)
```

```
$
$ tar -cvf backdir/bup date*.*
a date.txt 1K
a date2.txt 1K
$
$ tar -tvf backdir/bup
tar: blocksize = 6
-rw-r--r-- 1069/10      34 Apr 26 11:34 1999 date.txt
-rw------- 1069/10      34 Apr 26 11:34 1999 date2.txt
$rm da*.*
$ls –l da*.*
da*.*: No such file or directory
$ tar -xvf backdir/bup date.txt
tar: blocksize = 6
x date.txt, 34 bytes, 1 tape blocks
$ tar -xvf backdir/bup date2.txt
tar: blocksize = 6
x date2.txt, 34 bytes, 1 tape blocks
$
```

The screen shot shows tar being used to create a backup, list the contents of the backup and finally to restore 2 files:

Further details can be obtained from the manual entries of tar. Users should be wary that tar can corrupt certain types of files (only the backup copy is corrupt). These include ORACLE databases that must be either exported (an ORACLE command) prior to backup, or must be backed up using cpio (which does not corrupt).

Types of Backup

Just as selecting the right backup device is important, there are 3 main backup techniques and the selection of the most appropriate technique is just as important.

The different backup techniques are discussed below, together with UNIX examples:

Full

Performing a full backup frequently, is usually the best way of protecting the system. This involves taking a copy of **all** the data, applications, and systems files (including the operating system) and storing it to tape. Literally, everything on the system is copied to tape.

Because of the volume of information being stored, this type of backup takes the longest to perform. Should the organisation need 24-hour access to its data then this kind of backup can be restrictive. However, because all of the information is on one backup set, this type of backup is the quickest to restore the system. Often it is the time taken to rebuild the system that is critical, and as such, this type of backup may be the most appropriate.

Obviously if there is a lot of data and applications on the system, the backup device must be capable of holding all of this information.

Sometimes full backups require a large number of tapes that need to be stored – again little thought should be given to expense.

Because all information is stored on every backup set, it is possible to recover anything from any set. Thus if a change was made to the operating system which drastically affected users, the system could be quickly returned to a stable state on any of the days a full backup was taken. A good organisation could return to a month ago or even further.

Full backups are perhaps the easiest in UNIX, and can be simply achieved using the standard tar command:

> tar –cvf /dev/rmt0

Incremental

Incremental backups are a technique used to cut down on the time taken for a full backup. With an incremental backup, a full backup is taken and then the first incremental backup will copy only the files modified (be they system or data) since the full backup. The 2nd incremental backup will only copy the files modified (system or data) since the first incremental backup and so on.

This drastically cuts down on the time taken to backup but can lead to a complex chain of tapes, as each tape contains only files modified since the last backup. This means that it takes a lot longer to restore and that the backup is dependent upon more tapes, which increases the probability of failure. Should one tape fail in the batch, then they may be unable to continue with the restore or may have lost valuable data. In contrast to a full backup, where an older version of the file could be recovered from another tape.

When using this type of backup, the system administrator should try to keep to a minimum the number of days between a full backup. At most there should be 5 days in between full backups.

To undertake an incremental backup in UNIX is slightly trickier. Firstly, the files that have been modified since the last backup need to be located. The easiest way to achieve this is to use find command using the date of the last backup. In a good installation, this would be the previous day.

The find command finds all the files that have been modified today:

    find / -mtime –1 ! –type d –print

Thus the above command will find all files starting from the root directory (/). The ! means not and the – type d means directory. Thus it will not find directories as not everything in the directory may have changed.

UNIX allows command substitution, which allows a user to use a command in place of a string or a variable. This is achieved using the ` quotes, usually located at the top left of the keyboard. Thus the above command can be incorporated into the tar command:

    tar -cvf /dev/rmt0 ` find / -mtime -1 ! -type d -print`

Differential

Differential is really a compromise between the previous two backup techniques. With differential backup, a full backup is taken and then subsequent differential backups are taken. Each differential backup copies all files modified since the **last full backup**. This affords a higher level of protection than incremental backups but not as high as a full backup. It also takes longer to backup than an incremental backup but less time than a full backup. Finally, it takes longer to restore than a full backup and not as long as an incremental backup.

Differential backups in UNIX require a slightly different version of the find command. When the full backup is taken, the system administrator would create a file (e.g. /tmp/lastbackup) which would have the date and time of the backup associated with it. The above command could then be modified to search for files, which are newer than this:

    tar -cvf /dev/rmt0 ` find . -newer /tmp/lastbackup ! –type d -print`

Thus all of the files which have been modified since the date of the /tmp/lastbackup file will be archived. The date and time of the /tmp/lastbackup file can be easily modified using the touch command:

    touch /tmp/lastbackup

Choosing the Technique

The choice of technique really depends upon the length of time available for the backup process. If the organisation can afford the time for a full backup then they should do this at least nightly. Using either of the other techniques is a compromise.

Backup Cycles

Introduction

Backup devices and techniques to be used in backing up the data have so far been discussed. What must also happen is to ensure that the tapes are used in accordance with the manufacturer's guidelines (in terms of heat, humidity and acclimatisation) and to ensure that backup tapes are cycled.

Firstly the manufacturers issue instructions with tapes detailing constraints on their operating conditions. These include storage temperatures and humidity and usually they will detail a time taken for the tape to acclimatise to the environment of the tape drive. This can often take several hours and the tape should not be used until acclimatised - the use of non-acclimatised tapes can damage the drive and jeopardise the backup.

Simply observing the guidelines is not sufficient; a cycling technique with the tapes must be used. This involves having several tapes. Consider the case where only one backup tape is used - and used successfully for a backup. The next time the system is backed up, the tape will have to be overwritten - the same tape containing the only copy of the data. Should there be a power loss whilst the computer is backing up, then the copy of the data on the hard drive may be lost, and the user will certainly loose the copy on tape as it will have only been partially written. Thus all of the data will have been lost.

Selection and purchase of the tapes should be undertaken with caution. Firstly, only the best quality tapes should be purchased from a reputable manufacturer and supplier. The tapes purchased should be from multiple batches – in case of a batch problem.

Tapes have a finite life and will eventually wear out. The tapes will usually state an expected life or mean time between failure (MTBF) and a tape should never be used beyond these guidelines. Should a tape fail prematurely, then it may be prudent to discontinue use of all tapes from that batch.

Cycling of tapes is of utmost importance – each tape should be used frequently and to a similar extent. Tapes stretch as they are used – especially at first. If they are underused, then reliability may be impaired just as if they are overused. Systems Administrators should ensure that each tape is used a similar amount of times. This cannot be achieved by random selection and presented below are two cycling techniques, which allow for the efficient cycling of tapes, the second affords a high level of protection for the organisation (this assumes a full backup every night):

Grandfather/Father/Son

This is perhaps one of the simpler, yet effective backup cycles. The first tape created becomes the son and is kept. The second tape created becomes the new son, the older one becoming the father. When the third tape is used, it becomes the son, the oldest tape becomes the grandfather and the previous son becomes the father.

Thus there is a whole generation of backup tapes and it is possible to recover back to the third backup. In a daily cycle, this means that files lost up to three days ago can be recovered. As computer systems become larger with more users, often lost files are not noticed in three days. Consider a part time class at University – they may only be in once per week. If they discover a lost file at this point, it is too late to recover it using this method of cycling. Thus organisations have adopted more complex strategies for cycling.

4 Week Cycle

Full backups for 5 days (the last working day's tape is kept - Monday's to Thursdays used again the next week)
Same weeks 2 – 4

Week 5 first of the last working day of the week tapes (week1) comes into use
Assuming all data can be fitted onto one cartridge and 5 working days, this requires 24 cartridges
NEVER ONLY USE THE FRIDAY's TAPES FOR FRIDAY - THEY ARE BEING UNDERUSED AND COULD FAIL

In addition, the organisation should:
- Replace tapes regularly (the purchase date should be written on the tape together with a tally for the number of times used).
- Upon receiving any errors, the tape should be replaced immediately.
- Clean the drive regularly following manufacturers instructions.

Always store tapes offsite in a fireproof safe.

Backup Devices/Media

It is very important to purchase and use the correct hardware for the backup process and there are a number of factors that influence the choice of equipment. In this section some of the current backup devices are detailed with their strengths and weaknesses:

Reel Tapes
These are the old fashioned tapes that are often seen on Science Fiction or Spy movies. They are huge reels mounted in expensive drives. The drives need to be well engineered (and hence expensive), as they need to prevent the tape from being snapped.
Typically these drives hold around 100-140 MB of data and drive costs can be as high as £25,000 (GBP). They are wholly unsuitable for today's requirements. They are also very slow compared to newer devices.

1/4" Cartridges
These represent an advance in tape technology from the reels. The tapes are more technically advanced than their predecessors and the drive mechanism improved. These tapes hold between 100 and 200MB and both the drive and the tape cost significantly less than reel to reel tapes. These drives are still frequently used on UNIX machines as they provide an ideal "common" platform to ship upgrades.

8mm Cartridges
These represented a vast improvement over their predecessors and employed a helical scan mechanism (similar to that used by domestic video recorders) to get a huge increase in storage capacity. With the helical scan method, the heads are mounted onto a cylinder (known as a drum) that revolves at high speed in the opposite direction to the tape travel. This greatly improves the capacity of the tape.

The technology is also much cheaper, tapes being around £20. Indeed, they used a special video 8 cartridge – similar to that used by domestic camcorders. The quality of the tape is somewhat higher than video 8 cartridges and they are known as Data8 cartridges. Storage capacity was from 1.2GB up to around 20GB (using compression techniques). However, they are fast being replaced by DAT systems.

DAT cartridges

All of the devices discussed so far rely upon being restored from the same make and model of device – the tape is format specific. If the drive manufacturer goes out of business and the drive fails then serious problems may be encountered trying to obtain a drive that will read the tape. This is a tie, which is undesirable. Sony introduced the DDS specification with DAT cartridges; DDS (Digital Data Storage) is a unified way of reading and writing to a DAT tape. Thus a DAT tape written in a Sony machine can be read in a HP machine or any other. Also employing helical scan, DDS can achieve high storage capacities of around 25GB per cartridge (using compression). The tapes are relatively cheap (around £10 GBP) as are the drives (around £400 GBP). They are highly reliable and are one of the best backup devices on the market. DDS2 is the current standard.

CD-ROM

CD-ROMs are not really a backup device but are a good archiving device. Their relatively low capacity (650MB) makes them unsuitable for most backup applications and there is little software to support writing to a multiple disk set. As they are WORM (Write Once Read Many times) technology, it would be a rather expensive way of backing up. The same applies to CDRWs. However, they do make an excellent archive medium and can easily be distributed. They are good for archiving as they support random access and are optically based (therefore last longer than magnetic sources).

Digital Linear Tape (DLT)

As servers continue to grow in size, they begin to outstretch the capacity of DAT (even with compression). DAT multi-changers are available which automatically feed in new tapes during the backup process. However, even multi-changers can be pushed to backup large servers. DLT is a relatively new technology with a higher capacity than DAT. DLT can store approximately 80GB per cartridge and multi-changers are available which allow up to 2TB unattended backup capacity.

DLT is currently relatively expensive and is really aimed at the large server market.

Redundant Array of Inexpensive Disks (RAID)

These devices are not really backup devices, but are fault tolerant disk subsystems. There are approximately 8 levels of RAID, each affording differing levels of protection. RAID Level 1 is straightforward disk mirroring. Thus a write to drive 1 is also written to mirror drive 1. If drive 1 fails, then the data can be recovered from mirror 1.

RAID devices are usually separate subsystems and usually contain two power supplies and two interfaces to the outside world. Thus the chances of failure are dramatically reduced.

Whilst RAID systems afford high availability to data, they are not backup devices and **MUST** themselves be backed up at regular intervals.

Choosing the device

There are many factors that influence the choice of backup device. The most important factors are discussed below:

Budget

Often choice is made depending upon the amount of money available for the project. Unfortunately, with backup devices, cost (whilst important) should take a second place to other major factors. What is the point of buying a lower cost backup solution, which doesn't have sufficient capacity for the machine? It may also be found that a few hundred pounds has been saved on the device but that it requires attended operation to backup. This can run into £1000s (GBP) in staff time.

Capacity

The device must offer sufficient capacity (in unattended mode) to backup the system. A heavy contingency must be placed on this figure (of say 50% or more) to allow for future expansion of the system. Ideally purchase a backup device with a capacity, which far exceeds current needs.

Speed of the Device

Speed of the device is also of critical importance – especially the time taken to restore. The critical time for the speed of a backup device is the time it takes to restore. If a restore is required, then it is likely the organisation cannot function until it has taken place – time is then of utmost importance. The time taken to backup should also be as short as possible – especially if the organisation needs to cease trading whilst the backup takes place. In such cases, the backup intrudes upon business time and therefore the backup time becomes very important.

Type of device

The type of device also has a large impact upon choice. Standards such as DDS and DDS2 mean that there is more freedom with respect to devices. Should the old device fail, then it can be replaced with any drive from any manufacturer as long as it is compliant to the same standard.

This can also afford a level of protection – should the device fail when it is needed most, then one can usually be sourced fairly easily. Of course, given the value of the data to the organisation, it may well choose to hold a spare device.

Disaster Recovery

Introduction

One of the most important roles undertaken by a Systems Administrator is that of backup and recovery of backed up information. Another important task is their ability to recover from a disaster.

Unfortunately, backups and recovery only represent a small part of the tasks of the systems administrator with respect to preserving system availability. Another major factor in maintaining the availability of the system is disaster recovery planning.

It should be realised that disasters must be faced, and as such, disaster recovery should be a major part of reducing those risks to an acceptable level.

Disasters

No one can prevent disasters from happening and the type of disaster cannot be controlled – it may simply be a user who has accidentally deleted files through to a fire in the computer room. It is possible to take steps to minimise the risk by installing fire protection equipment, etc. but this will rarely reduce it to an acceptable level. For instance it may reduce the chances of loosing the data to fire but you could still lose the data to theft.

Hardware & Software Maintenance Contracts and Insurance

Most organisations will have a hardware and software maintenance contract in place. Software contracts will cover any new versions of the operating system and bug fixes to the present. Hardware maintenance contracts will cover any failures of the hardware and subsequent new parts. Insurance policies will cover loss or damage to the computer equipment. What none of these will cover is for the use of equipment whilst the organisation's is being repaired or replaced. In some instances repair and replacement of the computer equipment can take a considerable period of time (over a week) – especially in the case of total loss. In such circumstances it is possible for the organisation to go out of business before the equipment has been delivered.

The subject of Disaster Recovery is designed to plug the gap between the provision of such insurance and contracts and the needs of the organisation. However, disaster recovery is only as good as the last backup. Once again, there are 5 recommended ways to protect data:

1.   Backup
2.   Backup
3.   Backup
4.   Backup
5.   Backup

90% of disaster recovery planning involves backups, and that backups are the only way that data can be protected - backups must be taken, and regularly. Bear in mind that backups cannot be undertaken piecemeal - it must be made someone's responsibility (on their job description) or else it just won't happen.

Equally as important as taking backups is to regularly test those backups - a backup is only as good as its test - and a backup should always be tested. Remember it is not sufficient to do a directory of a tape and restore some files from it!   Major files should not be restored in case they fail - a few selected files here and there which don't matter are best.

Disaster Recovery Planning Options

Should access to information on a computer system be lost, then there is a serious risk of going out of business, as such. Auditors now want proof that an organisation has Disaster Recovery plans in place.

Below, the various schemes available for Disaster Recovery together with their advantages and disadvantages are discussed:

Self protection

Under this scheme the organisation provides for its own protection. It can be found that this is a very expensive solution - as another machine may need to be kept as a spare in case anything happens to the one currently in use. Each time the current machine is upgraded, the spare machine will also need to be upgraded. This will provide for the situation of a hardware failure. Should the organisation be burgled or be struck by fire or flood, then the probability is that both machines will be lost. It is best if the spare machine is resident on another site.

The organisation may also need another room in another building to which it can move should disaster strike. It will also need to ensure that it has the technical expertise and resources available to effect such a changeover.

This type of protection is becoming less and less common and is only really common with organisations large enough to protect themselves and with appropriate kit - e.g. a university could take computer equipment from academic use and use a room in another building.

Mutual protection with another organisation

This is not very popular and is probably the least recommended option. It relies upon two organisations being prepared to offer each other mutual protection in terms of accommodation and access to their computer systems. Such mutual protection should be agreed in contract before commencing but, if one of the organisations pulls out at the last minute, the legal wrangling process could see the demise of the other company.

The organisations that choose to team up in this way need to give some thought to their partners - as this could expose trade secrets and intellectual property rights. It is popular between schools, colleges and some universities but is becoming less popular.

This type of protection demands high technical expertise as effectively two organisations have software and data resident on the same machine! The process of establishing such a complicated system could take so much time that the organisation would be out of business anyway!

Commercial plans

With the ever increasing usage of IT and the requirement of auditors that some sort of disaster recovery plan is in place, there has been an increase in the number of companies offering this sort of service. With a commercial plan, a company will provide access to a machine for an agreed annual fee.

Commercial plans with a reputable company who hold kit that can be utilised, represent one of the safest disaster recovery packages. There are many companies offering disaster recovery planning and the following is intended as a guide to selection:

Equipment held and quantity.

If the equipment being held by the Disaster Recovery company is different to that of the organisation, then there will be a period of learning, which needs to take place with the users and systems staff. The time of the disaster is not usually the best time to acquire these skills. If the equipment is different, then it is possible that staff may be unproductive for a few days following the incident. In particular, the organisation should be wary of organisations that insist that they can make different hardware work effectively for them as a temporary measure. Who trains the system manager with the new commands? Who will teach the data entry clerks the new keystrokes & how long will it all take?

The number of machines held by the company should also be ascertained – they may hold 1 machine for every 10 clients – check the number of clients. If they have only 10 then there may be a reduced opportunity of getting a loan machine! Some companies operate this as insurance - with a no claims discount. Be sure the organisation trusts the company. A plan, which doesn't allow for testing should never be bought. Companies offer a number of different plans; the most appropriate one to the organisation should be selected. Measures should be taken to protect some stationary – perhaps some should be left in a bank safety deposit box!

The Levels Available Commercially:

Time on someone else's machine

With this type of cover, a tape is sent to the Disaster Recovery provider and they load the data onto their machine. The organisation then uses their machine to access their data. This type of plan is only really suitable for small to medium sized businesses that have access to reasonably fast telecommunications (a fast modem or ISDN). It is usually the cheapest option available but can be expensive to operate (given the telephone costs). Sometimes this can be claimed under insurance. Printing can be a real issue with such plans.

Machine Delivered - organisation installs

This level of protection means that the disaster recovery contractor will deliver a machine within a given time span. The organisation then needs to install and commission the machine. This amounts to an agreement to "loan" the machine for an agreed period of time, after which it is usually possible to hire it for a longer period.

This is usually the next level in disaster recovery planning and is charged at a higher rate. The price will usually reflect how quickly the contractor will respond and the duration of the loan.

Whilst this is usually better than the first option, simply the loan of a machine may not be sufficient. If the organisation has the technical resources to install and commission the loan machine with their data, they need to ensure they are available (not ill or on holiday) when required. Usually, in the event of a real disaster, the organisation's technical people will be too busy to have time to install and commission the equipment.

Machine delivered and installed - organisation puts on data and applications

This is similar to the option above, except that the disaster recovery contractor will set up the machine (and possibly the network) which will save the organisation's technical people some time, However, the applications and data still need to be installed. Obviously the cost for this will be higher than just for delivery of the machine. However, in the event of a disaster it could be money well spent.

Machine delivered set up and tested

This represents an even more expensive option but is probably worth it because everything is down to the disaster recovery contractor. This means that at the time of a disaster the organisation's technical staff are more free to take a supervisory role and ensure the system is set up and working satisfactorily. With this type of plan, the contractors will turn up within a specified time period, there are fixed times for loan of the system (which can usually be extended on a hire basis).

With this kind of plan, the organisation should ensure that the contractor knows their requirements at the outset.

Full service - including "white room"

This service has nothing to do with the colour of the room, but is a term used by such contractors. Basically, it is a room or a building to which a company can move if their existing building becomes unusable. The room will usually be equipped with computer equipment, terminal and telephone points. This room is usually contracted for a fixed time period - but this could be an unknown length for the organisation and so hiring is again a possibility,

This is obviously much more expensive and only useful for organisations, which don't have another site to which they could move. It does, however, allow them to continue business.

A compromise?

Most contractors will allow an organisation to take out an option and upgrade at the time of the disaster. Although slightly more expensive (in case of a disaster) it could be cheaper if the plan is never used.

Note that the organisation must be careful because the contractor may not have enough machines if everyone does this. In which case, it is likely that the clients who bought the higher level plan will be serviced first.

The organisation should always ensure that the machine will be configured to an appropriate specification.

Organisation's responsibilities

No matter which disaster recovery option is taken, there are certain responsibilities placed upon the organisation. The first and most critically important is backing up – the organisation simply can't recover from a disaster without them. In addition, the backup tapes should be stored in a safe place. If they are in the same building as the computer, then it is likely they will become a victim of the same disaster. The organisation should endeavour to keep them off site in a 2 hour certified fire proof safe.

Fire proof safes

These are specially manufactured safes that are heat shielded and designed to withstand long periods in a fire. They are rated in survival time for diskettes (which are very easily damaged by heat).

Be wary – there are cheap ones available but you only get what you pay for.

The highest level of protection is 2 hour - a safe that isn't at least one hour should not be bought. And a safe certainly should not be bought which isn't certified to the current Swedish standards. The organisation should also ensure that the safe has waterproof seals. Second user safes are also available.

Document backup plans

Backups should also be able to be taken in the absence of the technical staff. The technical staff (systems managers, etc.) should ensure that backup plans are appropriately documented down to a level that can be understood by any user. The organisation should ensure that these are adhered to rigidly.

Prevention is better than cure

Often organisations leave themselves open to disaster – they need to take precautions. Consider the costs of rebuilding:

The Cost of Rebuilding 20MB of data		
Department	**Time**	**Cost**
Sales & Marketing	19 days	$17,000
Accounting	21 days	$19,000
Engineering	42 days	$98,000
Reprinted from National Computer Association of Washington DC. 1990.		

How can organisations protect them themselves?

- Install fire doors with a good lock.
- Ensure the computer room is secure - bars on windows, etc.
- Ensure it has a smoke alarm and adequate fire extinguishers of the appropriate type (CO2).
- Fit an Uninterruptable Power Supply.

Ensure that logical security is good to stop deletion – encourage users to read their last login and ensure it is correct. Discourage users from sharing passwords.

Startup And Shutdown Of The System

Normally, UNIX machines are left up and running as they are multi-user multi-tasking systems and their demands for the system are not easily predicted. The operating system is also highly reliable and very rarely crashes or hangs. The uptime command can be used to see the current status of the system and will reveal how often it is shutdown:

```
$ uptime
 11:12am  up 44 day(s), 16:44,  57 users,  load average: 0.40, 0.36, 0.40
$
```

This shows that this UNIX system has been up for over a month, the number of current connected users and the average number of jobs in the run queue over the last 1, 5 and 15 minutes. However, sometimes it is necessary to close down the system – perhaps there is to be a power cut or an extended period of inactivity (e.g. Christmas vacation), or perhaps new hardware is to be added. The system can be shutdown using the shutdown command as below:

shutdown –g300 "system is closing – Happy Easter"

This will shutdown the system in a grace period of 300 seconds and will display the message *"System is closing – Happy Easter"* to anyone still logged on. After that, the system will kill off all of the daemons and close. NOTE: in LINUX, the –g option is –t.

By using the –i option to the shutdown command, the starting state of the system can be specified from the list below:

State	Description
0	Stop the operating system.
1	State 1 is referred to as the administrative state. In state 1 file systems required for multi-user operations are mounted, and logins requiring access to multi-user file systems can be used. When the system comes up from firmware mode into state 1, only the console is active and other multi-user (state 2) services are unavailable. Note that not all user processes are stopped when transitioning from multi-user state to state 1.
2	Normal multi-user state.
s, S	The single-user state. All user processes are stopped on transitions to this state. In the single-user state, file systems required for multi-user logins are unmounted and the system can only be accessed through the console. Logins requiring access to multi-user file systems cannot be used.
5	Shut the machine down so that it is safe to remove the power. Have the machine remove power, if possible.
6	Stop the operating system and reboot to the state defined by the init default entry in /etc/inittab.

Example:

  shutdown -i S -g 120 "===== disk replacement ====="

will notify users that the system is being shutdown in 120 seconds for a "===== disk replacement =====", the system will next be brought up in single user state.

Once the disk replacement has been made and the system is ready to be brought back to normal, the system administrator will shutdown with:

  shutdown –i 2

which will halt the system in the standard 60 seconds period (i.e. no period of grace). The next time the system is started, it will start in the normal state.

There are other commands that can be used to shutdown UNIX. The reboot command can be used to terminate all processes, perform a sync and load the UNIX kernel from disk. UNIX is then started in multi-user mode.

Whenever possible, shutdown should always be used to shutdown the computer however, with most versions of LINUX, ctrl Alt Del can be used. LINUX essentially treats this as a shutdown –t3 –r now instruction.

Run levels

As previously mentioned, most versions of UNIX support a single user mode as well as a multi-user mode, however some systems support multiple modes that, can be defined by the administrator. Known as "run levels", these modes allow the systems administrator to define specific modes of operation of the computer system. Usually, 8 run levels are allowed levels 0 through 6 and a single user mode. Run levels can be used to support varying requirements of an organisation, each having its own boot script.

Suppose that on Saturdays, XYZ College opens for teaching only. Should their teaching material be resident on the same system as their Management Information System, they can define two run levels – one for everyday use (e.g. no 4) and one for Saturdays (e.g. no 2) which will support teaching material only. Thus on Saturday's the system would be booted using the run level 2. This would mean that all of the MIS software would not be loaded increasing the overall security of the system. On weekdays, the system would be booted using the run level 4. Exactly how this is achieved, is machine and operating system specific – instructions should be available in the system's manual to show how this is achieved and what each run level means.

Run levels can also be used for maintenance purposes – a level can be specified with appropriate boot scripts to start up a system without the database being loaded. This will allow for database maintenance without disrupting the non-database applications.

Reporting and handling faults

As with any system, an accurate log of faults should be kept. Faults are normally reported on a special terminal in UNIX, known as the console. The console is usually directly connected to the UNIX machine, although it can be given to a particular terminal by the systems administrator.

When recording faults, as much detail as possible needs to be kept. Where possible, this detail should also include resolution of the faults.

As a minimum, the fault log should contain:
- Any error numbers or messages.
- Any error numbers displayed in any LED/LCD panels.
- Date & Time (can be very useful).
- The device in question.
- The user in question.
- What the user was doing at the moment the error occurred.
- Number of users connected.
- Any other relevant details (e.g. what a user pressed, fault occurred as 30th user logged on, etc.).

Such detail can help track the problem. Date and time are particularly useful.

Consider the following scenario:

A user works in a flexi-time environment. She starts work at 8:30 everyday and works on a finance package connected to a UNIX machine via a telnet session from a PC. At 8:50, her terminal locks up and has further sporadic errors throughout the day. The systems administrator notes the faults. The second day, the pattern continues and the 8:50 spot seems to be regular each day. The systems administrator then investigates what is happening at 8:50 by physically observing all of the terminals. He discovers that a member of his staff arrives at approximately 8:45 each morning and logins in at 8:50. Upon investigating this person's PC, he determines that it has a conflicting IP address with the finance machine. The offending machine is allocated an IP number and the log closed.

Because such detailed information is kept, future occurrences of a similar event can easily be resolved by using the fault log as a fault reference. Often it is useful to keep an electronic copy of the fault log so it can be copied and distributed as either a fault reference or a training guide. It is particularly useful in database form where search criteria can be applied. At least one copy should always be kept off the UNIX machine; otherwise it may not be able to be accessed when needed most!

Installing & Configuring Nodes
Essentially, there are two types of node known in UNIX:
- Workstation
- Peripheral

A workstation is a user workstation and may be a terminal, a PC or a dedicated UNIX workstation. A peripheral is any other component; it may be a printer, a plotter, a disk subsystem, etc.

Connection of the workstation varies depending upon the workstation itself. Most PCs and dedicated UNIX workstations will connect to the central UNIX machine via a network.

For communication, UNIX is shipped with the Transmission Control Protocol/Internet Protocol (TCP/IP) software as standard. In fact, it is an integral part of UNIX. Dedicated UNIX workstations will have this stack implemented as part of their setup – a PC must be set up to work with TCP/IP.

A dumb terminal is connected to the UNIX machine via a standard serial connection, and is added through the terminal utilities provided with the variant of UNIX being used. Connection through serial lines is quite a rare installation and as such a typical PC installation will be considered.

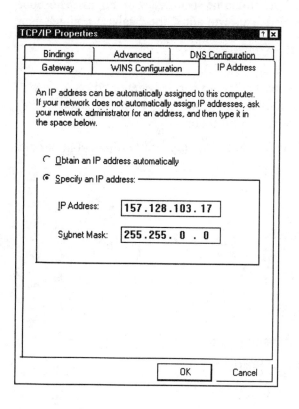

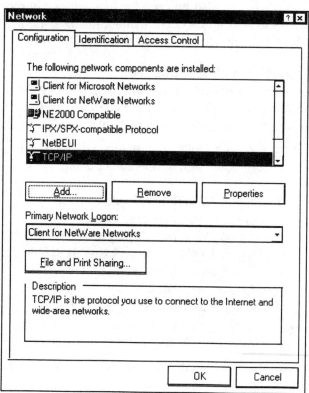

Setting up a PC to work with TCP/IP is usually fairly simple, as standard Windows 95/98 has all the necessary software but the Windows 95/98 CD-ROM is needed. The required settings can be found in the networking section of the control panel.

The option to be selected is the TCP/IP – if the option is not available it can be added using the add button. If it is, the required properties can be set using the *'Properties'* button:

The PC must have an IP address that is:
- Unique to the network (if a LAN only)
- Unique in the world (if given by the Network Info Center – NIC – in the 'States) if the computer is connected to the Internet.

This will normally be the responsibility of the Internet Service Provider (ISP) or the network manager in the organisation.

Once the PC has an IP number and all local settings have been made – the details of which will come from the network manager, the PC should be able to connect with the UNIX system. This is achieved by using the Telnet program supplied with Windows 95/98 and giving it details of the host computer:

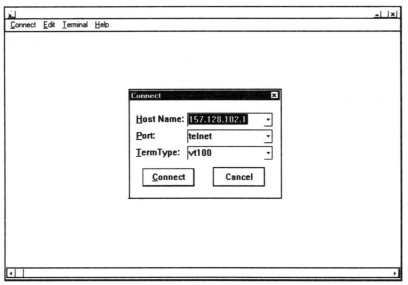

The Host Name is the IP address of the UNIX machine and will be supplied by the Systems Administrator: When the connect button is pressed, connection should be established:

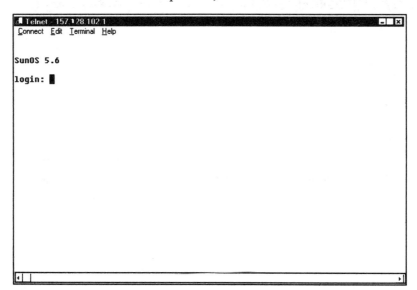

From this point, the PC can interact fully with the UNIX machine.

Note: The IP address may need to be registered with the network and systems administrator before connection to the UNIX machine can be made.

Installing a terminal via a serial port

A serial terminal is usually added to UNIX using the utility provided by the manufacturer of the Operating System. The utility operates by adding (or making changes) to the following files:

File	Description
/etc/termcap or /etc/terminfo	This is an encoded list of every standard terminal's capabilities and control codes. UNIX editors use the value of the environment variable $TERM to index into the file and fetch the terminals capabilities.
/etc/ttys	A list of every terminal on the system, together with the program that should be associated with it when the system is initialised. This is usually getty. If the terminal type is constant and known, this is included. The utility to add terminal will add them into this file.
/etc/gettytab	A list of baud rate information used by getty when deciding how to listen to a terminal.

Before the terminal can be added, the installer needs to determine the terminal type and/or its emulation capabilities, determine the compatibilities with the operating system and set it accordingly.

Unlike a PC running a pseudo terminal, a serial terminal needs direct connection to the computer. The installer must connect the terminal to the computer and determine which serial port it is connected to. Note, the many manufacturers of UNIX equipment provide "fan out" boxes that give many serial ports on a single box, the installer needs to note the box and port address.

Once this information has been gathered, then the installer can commence begin to add the terminal into the system using the utility provided.

Installing new devices

The installation of other peripherals such as tape drives is once again very dependent upon the variant and version of UNIX. Most popular UNIX machines, for example the IBM RS6000, will automatically detect that new hardware has been added to the system. It will then launch, on the console, the appropriate part of the interface tool to configure new hardware. From this point, the user should follow the instructions provided from the manufacturer of the tape drive. The hardware should be fully tested using the routines supplied by the manufacturer, prior to use. In the case of a tape drive, tapes should be verified using the method described earlier.

It is imperative before installing any new hardware that a full backup of the system is taken.

Index

Many page numbers in this index are in bold type. These indicate the major explanations of index entries and may be a good starting point for obtaining information.
The other page references give additional information (e.g. how it is used, comparisons, etc).

Dumbreck ∧ Publishing

Check out our website

www.dumbreck.demon.co.uk

PC Support Handbook

PC Multimedia Handbook

Ordering Information

Glossary

Software Links

Faultfinding System

How to contact us

Useful Links

All pages on this site
©1992-2001
Dumbreck Publishing

● Get familiar with computing terms. Quickly look up the meaning of acronyms (from AGP to ZIF)

● Reviews of the software packages that help you get the best out of our books. All programs are freeware or shareware.

● An expert system that guides you through the steps to identify your computer problem.

● All comments and suggestions are welcomed. Or fill in our short user survey.

● Links to other websites with related content. These sites contain technical information, tutorials, etc.

Our faultfinding section covers problems in the following areas:

Monitor   Base Unit   Keyboard   Mouse   Joystick   Printer
Scanner   Speakers   Network   Modem   Software   Storage

The book on multimedia designed for students

The PC Multimedia Handbook
Technology & Techniques

From the author of *"The PC Support Handbook"*

This book covers the theory and practical activities in following areas:

- **Basics**
- **Multimedia Technology**
- **Screen Technology**
- **Using Windows**
- **Multimedia Design**
- **Computer Graphics**
- **Digital Photography**
- **Digital Audio**
- **Digital Video**
- **Video Editing**
- **Authoring**
- **CD Production**
- **Creating Web Sites**
- **Electronic Presentations**

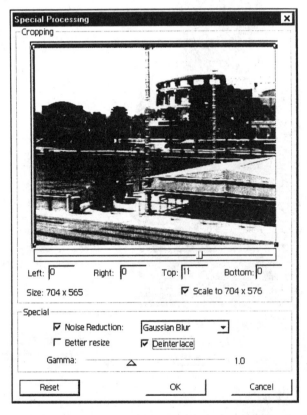

It provides extensive coverage of multimedia hardware and technology, and includes guides in using Windows and applications such as Paint Shop Pro, Adobe Premiere, PowerPoint and Flash.

Further details of the book are available from our web site:
www.dumbreck.demon.co.uk

The book costs £29 per copy.
Where five or more copies are purchased, the price is reduced to £20 per copy.
There is no extra charge for post and packing.

Dumbreck Publishing,
8A Woodland Avenue, Kirkintilloch, G66 1AS
Tel : 0141-775-2889
Fax (orders) ; 0141-775-2889
Fax (editorial) : 0870-0554706
e-mail : sales@dumbreck.demon.co.uk